MODERN
PORTUGUESE-ENGLISH
ENGLISH-PORTUGUESE
DICTIONARY

Edited by

ELBERT L. RICHARDSON

MARIA de LOURDES SÁ PEREIRA
and
MILTON SÁ PEREIRA

GEORGE G. HARRAP & Co. Ltd
LONDON TORONTO WELLINGTON SYDNEY

First published in Great Britain 1944
by GEORGE G. HARRAP & CO. LTD
182 *High Holborn, London, W.C.*1

Reprinted: 1947; 1950; 1953; 1956; 1958; 1961; 1965; 1968

SBN 245 56866 2

Reprinted by lithography and bound in Great Britain
by Jarrold & Sons, Ltd, Norwich

CONTENTS

Part I

PORTUGUESE-ENGLISH
(Reformed Spelling)

Part II

ENGLISH-PORTUGUESE

PART I

PORTUGUESE-ENGLISH
REFORMED SPELLING

Edited by
ELBERT L. RICHARDSON

PORTUGUESE PRONUNCIATION

The pronunciation of Portuguese is very difficult. It can best be learned by listening to a native. The sounds given below are only approximate but it is hoped that they will be found useful and helpful.

Letter	Name	Approximate Sound
a	á	When stressed, like *a* in *father*. When unstressed, like *a* in *about*.
b	bê	Like English *b*.
c	cê	When written with a cedilla, thus ç, or when followed by e or i, like English *s* in *some*. In all other cases, like English *k*.
d	dê	Like English *d*.
e	é	When stressed, e has two sounds, an open sound like *e* in *set* and a close sound like *a* in *fate*. When unstressed, like French mute *e*, except when final, when it has the value of English *e* in *me*.
f	éfe	Like English *f*.
g	gê	When followed by e or i, like English *s* in *measure*. In all other cases, like English *g* in *go*.
h	agá	Always silent. However, see the following combinations below, ch, lh, and nh.
i	i	Like *i* in *machine*.
j	jota	Like *s* in *measure*.
l	éle	Generally like English *l*. At the end of a word or syllable, like English *l* in *old*.
m	éme	Generally like English *m*. At the end of a word, m is not pronounced but indicates that the preceding vowel is nasal.
n	éne	Like English *n*.
o	ó	When stressed, o has two sounds, an open sound like *o* in *north* and a close sound like *o* in *note*. When unstressed, like *oo* in *boot*.
p	pê	Like English *p*.
q	quê	Like English *k*.
r	érre	Pronounced with a trill or roll of the tongue.
s	ésse	When initial, after a consonant, or written double, like *s* in *some*. Between two vowels, like English *z*. When final, like *sh* in *shall*.
t	tê	Like English *t*.
u	u	Like English *oo* in *boot*. Generally silent in gue, gui, que, and qui.
v	vê	Like English *v*.
x	xis	Generally like *sh* in *shall*. In the prefix ex followed by a vowel, like English *z*. In some words it has the sound of English *z* and in some the sound of English *ss*.
z	zê	Like English *z*.

Groups of Letters	Approximate Sound
ch	Like *sh* in *shall*. **ch** is no longer used to represent the sound of *k* but has been replaced by **qu**.
lh	Like *li* in *William*.
nh	Like *ni* in *onion*.
ai	Like English *i* in *ice*.
éi	Like **ei** below but with open *e* sound.
ei	Like *ey* in *they*.
ói	Like *oy* in *boy*.
oi	Like **ói** but with close *o* sound.
au	Like *ou* in *pound*.
éu	Like English *e* in *set* followed by *w*.
eu	Like English *a* in *fate* followed by *w*.
ou	Like English *o* in *note*.
ão	Like *ou* in *pound* nasalized but without the sound of *n*.
ãe	Like *ey* in *they* nasalized.
õe	Like *oy* in *boy* nasalized but with closer *o*.

ACCENTUATION

1. Words ending in a vowel, in **s**, or in **am**, **em**, or **ens** are stressed on the syllable next to the last.

2. Words ending in **l**, **r**, **z**, **im**, **ins**, **um**, or **uns** are stressed on the last syllable.

3. If the stress does not fall in accordance with one or the other of these two rules, it must be indicated by a written accent.

There are two written accents in Portuguese, the acute and the circumflex. The acute is used on **i** and **u**. Either the acute or the circumflex is used on **a**, **e**, or **o**, according as the vowel is open or close. That is, if a written accent must be used on **a**, **e**, or **o** in accordance with rule 3 above, it must be the acute or the circumflex to correspond with the quality of the vowel. Thus the written accents on **a**, **e**, and **o** show that they are pronounced as follows:

> á   has the sound of *a* in *father*.
>
> â   has the sound of *a* in *about*.
>
> é   has the sound of *e* in *set*.
>
> ê   has the sound of *a* in *fate*.
>
> ó   has the sound of *o* in *north*.
>
> ô   has the sound of *o* in *note*.

SYLLABIFICATION

In the Portuguese-English part of this dictionary the syllabification is for the most part based on the vowel as the syllabic unit rather than on the actual syllable, except in the case of falling diphthongs and final diphthongs, which have been kept unbroken. Thus **baixo** is divided as follows: **bai'-xo**, and **anúncio** is divided as follows: **a-nún-cio**.

The written accent is used on the penult of words ending in the diphthongs **io**, **ia**, **uo**, and **ua** (e.g., **anúncio**) because of the convention of counting each vowel of these diphthongs as a separate syllable in applying the rules for written accents.

ABBREVIATIONS

adj.	adjective	**med.**	medical
adv.	adverb	**naut.**	nautical
arch.	architectural	**pers.**	personal
bot.	botanical	**pl.**	plural
conj.	conjunction	**pop.**	popular
demons.	demonstrative	**pref.**	prefix
f.	feminine noun; feminine	**prep.**	preposition
fig.	figurative	**pron.**	pronoun
geol.	geological	**refl.v.**	reflexive verb
hist.	historical	**sing.**	singular
interj.	interjection	**tr.v.**	transitive verb
intr.v.	intransitive verb	**zool.**	zoological
m.	masculine noun; masculine		

GUIDE TO REFORMED SPELLING

As a guide in the use of this dictionary by those who are not familiar with the Reformed Spelling or by beginners who may have to read books printed in the old spelling (still used by some authors), we give below a list with examples of the chief changes brought about by the Reform.

I. Single Letters.

h between two vowels disappears, e.g., **comprehender** becomes **compreender**, **sahida** becomes **saída**.

k becomes qu, e.g., **kioske** becomes **quiosque**.

y becomes i, e.g., **estylo** becomes **estilo**.

z at the end of some words becomes s, e.g., **atraz** becomes **atrás**, **mez** becomes **mês**.

II. Digraphs with h.

ch (= k) becomes qu, e.g., **chimica** becomes **química**, **monarchia** becomes **monarquia**.

ph becomes f, e.g., **philosophia** becomes **filosofia**.

th becomes t, e.g., **theatro** becomes **teatro**.

III. Consonant Groups.

cç becomes ç, e.g., **direcção** becomes **direção**.

ct becomes t, e.g., **actual** becomes **atual**.

gm becomes m, e.g., **augmentar** becomes **aumentar**.

mpt becomes nt, e.g., **assumpto** becomes **assunto**.

pt becomes t, e.g., **adoptar** becomes **adotar**, **escripto** becomes **escrito**.

mn becomes n, e.g., **somno** becomes **sono**.

nct becomes nt, e.g., **instincto** becomes **instinto**.

sc becomes c, e.g., **sciencia** becomes **ciência**.

s after a prefix ending in a vowel becomes ss, e.g., **proseguir** becomes **prosseguir**.

IV. Double Consonants.

bb becomes b, e.g., **abbade** becomes **abade**.

cc becomes c, e.g., **bocca** becomes **bôca**.

dd becomes d, e.g., **addido** becomes **adido**.

ff becomes f, e.g., **effeito** becomes **efeito**.

gg becomes g, e.g., **aggravo** becomes **agravo**.

ll becomes l, e.g., **cavallo** becomes **cavalo**.

mm becomes m, e.g., **commum** becomes **comum**.

nn becomes n, e.g., **anno** becomes **ano**.

pp becomes p, e.g., **apprender** becomes **aprender**.

tt becomes t, e.g., **attentar** becomes **atentar**.

NOTE: In looking for words which contain oi or ou, it should be borne in mind that these diphthongs are interchangeable in many words, e.g., **coisa** and **cousa**, **dois** and **dous**, **oiro** and **ouro**.

PORTUGUESE-ENGLISH

A

See page 12—GUIDE TO REFORMED SPELLING used in this Dictionary

a *m.* first letter of alphabet; *f. pers.pr.; f. demons.pr.; prep.*

à contraction of prep. *a* with feminine article *a.*

äa-tá *m.* bark canoe (used by Indians of Amazon region).

a'-ba *f.* skirt; flap; brim; leaf (of furniture); molding; wing; edge; lower rib; (fig.) protection; (Brazil) coast around a port; **=s** *pl.* outlying districts; *m.* name of prelate in certain oriental churches.

A-ba-bás *m.pl.* Tupi-Guarani tribe inhabiting headwaters of Corumbiava river in Mato-Grosso.

a-ba-cá *m.* Manila hemp.

A-ba-çai' *m.* In Tupi mythology a malevolent character who persecuted Indians, making them insane, possessed of evil spirits.

a-ba-ca'-te *m.* avocado, alligator pear.

a-ba-ca-tei'-ro *m.* avocado tree.

a-ba-ca-tu-aí-a *f.* a fish of Brazil.

a-ba-ca-xí *m.* pineapple; **=s** *m.* tribe of Indians inhabiting banks of river of same name.

á-ba-da *f.* rhinoceros; rhinoceros horn.

a-ba'-da *f.* eaves; large quantity; skirt tucked up to form a receptacle.

a-ba-dá-gio *m.* a meal which members of a parish are obliged to offer to their abbot; income from an abbacy.

a-ba'-de *m.* abbot; (fig.) very fat man.

a-ba-den'-go, **=a** *adj.* belonging to an abbot, or relative to his jurisdiction; **=s** *m.pl.* properties of an abbey.

a-ba-der-nar' *tr.v.* (naut.) to tie securely with small, strong rope.

a-ba-der'-nas *f.pl.* hooks to which ropes and cables are attached for lowering or raising masts.

a-ba-des'-co, **=a** *adj.* characteristic of an abbey.

a-ba-des'-sa *f.* abbess; woman excessively tall and stout; (bot.) variety of mango; (slang) woman who runs or manages a house of prostitution.

a-ba-des-sa'-do *m.* office and jurisdiction of an abbess; ceremonies accompanying the election of an abbess; duration of the office.

a-ba-dí-a *f.* abbotship; abbey.

a-ba-dí'-ta *m.* Abadite.

a-ba'-do, **=a** *adj.* having a brim or edge.

a-ba-e-ta'-do, **=a** *adj.* having a fuzzy surface, similar to woolen fabrics.

a-ba-e-tar' *tr.v.* to cover with fuzz; to wrap in woolen clothing; to clothe; to imitate the fuzziness of woolen fabrics in weaving.

á-ba-e-té *m.* good man; something legitimate or true.

a-ba-fa-ção' *f.* act or effect of smothering.

a-ba-fa-di'-ço, **=a** *adj.* suffocating, stuffy; (fig.) having disagreeable temperament.

a-ba-fa-dor' *m.* mute (on certain musical instruments), felt damper on pianos; *adj.* sultry.

a-ba-fa-du'-ra *f.* closeness, lack of air, act of smothering.

a-ba-fa-men'-to *m.* covering up, suppression, lack of air; (Brazil) unrightful possession of anything.

a-ba-fan'-te *adj.* close, stifling.

a-ba-far' *tr.v.* to swelter, to suffocate; to render mute; to hide, to protect; to cover, to wrap up; to hold back, to delay; (naut.) to flatten out pockets made in sail by wind; — **um negócio** to hush up a deal.

a-ba-fa-re'-te *m.* hindrance, impediment.

a-ba'-fo *m.* stifling heat; protection, caresses; **casa de** — hot-house; sweating-room.

a-ba-gúm *m.* hornbill.

a-bai-o-ne-tar' *tr.v.* to wound with a bayonet.

a-bair-ra-men'-to *m.* act of zoning or dividing into sections.

a-bair-rar' *tr.v.* to divide into zones or districts.

a-bai-xa'-dos *m.pl.* insincere words, adulation.

a-bai-xa=luz' *m.* lamp shade.

a-bai-xa-men'-to *m.* act of lowering or diminishing.

a-bai-xar' *tr.v.* to cause to descend, to lower, to restrain; to bow; to reduce in price; to humble; — **a proa** a to humble a conceited person; — **os ombros** to accept something difficult as a duty or in submission.

a-bai-xa=vóz *m.* sounding-board, canopy which hangs over a pulpit.

a-bai'-xo *adv.* in lower position, down; in a low voice; *interj.* down with !!; **vir** —, to fall down.

a-ba-jou-ja-men'-to *m.* adulation.

a-ba-jou-jar'=se *refl.v.* to adulate, to flatter.

a-ba-la'-da *f.* sudden departure; direction taken by a hunted animal when first disturbed; sudden collapse of wall or structure.

a-ba-la'-do, **=a** *adj.* insecure, shaken, upset.

a-ba-la-dor' *adj.* depressing, causing fear, producing trembling.

a-ba-la-du'-ra *f.* disturbance; shaking.

a-ba-la-men'-to *m.* disturbance; shaking.

a-ba-lar' *tr.v.* to shake, to ruin, to upset; *intr.v.* to march rapidly, to depart suddenly.

13

a-ba-lá-vel *adj.* susceptible of being shaken or ruined.

a-ba-la-us-trar' *tr.v.* to furnish with, or give the form of, balustrades.

a-ba-li-zar' *tr.v.* to outline, or mark out, by stakes or posts, to point out; to distinguish; **-se** *refl.v.* to acquire great skill or competence.

a-ba'-lo *m.* commotion; trembling; tremor, earthquake; fish net used in Baía (Brazil).

a-ba-lo-a'-do, -a *adj.* (Brazil) similar to a balloon in form; like a full sail; enlarged; swollen.

a-ba-lo-ar' *tr.v.* to give the form of a balloon.

a-ba-lo-fa'-do, -a *adj.* swollen, enlarged, vain.

a-ba-lo-far' *tr.v.* to cause to swell or enlarge; **-se** *refl.v.* to become conceited, full of one's self.

a-bal-rôa *f.* grappling hook.

a-bal-roa-ção' *f.* collision.

a-bal-roa-men'-to *m.* collision.

a-bal-ro-ar' *tr.v.* to pull a boat to landing with a grapnel; to collide violently.

a-ba-luar-ta-men'-to *m.* act or work of providing forts.

a-ba-lu-ar-tar' *tr.v.* to fortify; to provide forts; to make similar to a fort.

a-ba-na-ção' *f.* act of fanning; (Brazil) mechanical winnowing of rice.

a-ba-na'-do, -a *adj.* sick, weak, chronically invalid.

a-ba-na-dor' *m.* bellows.

a-ba-na-môs-cas *m.* fly-fan, fly-swatter.

a-ba-não' *m.* act of fanning with great effort; (pop.) a leap or jump from one's mount.

a-ba-nar' *tr.v.* to stir up; to move a fan back and forth; **vir com as mãos —,** to come empty-handed.

a-ban-car'-se *refl.v.* to sit on a bench, to install oneself in a good position.

a-ban-da'-do, -a *adj.* (Brazil) term used for animals which run in droves.

a-ban-dar'-se *refl.v.* to join together in groups, to meet together.

a-ban-de-ja'-do, -a *adj.* in the form of a tray.

a-ban-de-jar' *tr.v.* to give the form of a tray; to winnow grain by throwing it into air from shallow baskets or trays.

a-ban-do-na-men'-to *m.* the act of abandoning.

a-ban-do-nar' *tr.v.* to leave, to abandon; to reject; to renounce.

a-ban-do-na-tá-rio *m.* the person who acquires rights or possessions abandoned by others.

a-ban-do-ná-vel *adj.* that which may or should be abandoned.

a-ban-do'-no *m.* act of abandoning; state of helplessness.

a-ba-ni'-co *m.* a fan.

a-ba'-no *m.* bellows; beach manga (Brazilian tree).

a-ba-ra-tar' *tr.v.* to lower the price.

a-bar-ba'-do, -a *adj.* confused, embarrassed.

a-bar-bar' *tr.v.* to come up to level of; to meet face to face; to swarm; to overburden with difficult problems; to confront, to resist.

a-bar-be-lar' *tr.v.* to restrain with a bit; to make into form of a bit; to cause to appear like a double chin.

a-bar'-ca *f.* rustic sandal; (fig.) a shoe too large and badly made.

a-bar-ca-dor' *m.* monopolizer, one who attempts much.

a-bar-ca-men'-to *m.* act of monopolizing.

a-bar-can'-te *adj.* including, touching upon.

a-bar-car' *tr.v.* to include; to emorace; to reach to; to monopolize; to subbrdinate; to surround; to accomplish; to attempt a great deal.

a-ba-ré *m.* priest, vicar; name given by Indians to a missionary (Brazil).

a-bar-ra-ca-men'-to *m.* cantonment, encampment, temporarily constructed barracks.

a-bar-ra-car' *tr.v.* to set up barracks; to install soldiers in barracks; to construct similar to barracks.

a-bar-ran-car' *tr.v.* to close with obstructions; to make difficult; to impede; **abarrancar-se** *refl.v.* to become hindered or embarrassed.

a-bar-re-tar' *tr.v.* to make in the form of a cap; to put on a cap; **abarretar-se,** to put on one's own cap or hat.

a-bar-ro-tar' *tv.r.* to fill too full; to fill up to the beams (of a ship).

a-bas-ta'-do, -a *adj.* rich, having on hand all supplies needed.

a-bas-ta-men'-to *m.* provisioning on large scale.

a-bas-tan'-ça *f.* abundance, wealth.

a-bas-tan'-ças *f.pl.* pretexts, exaggerated promises.

a-bas-tar' *tr.v.* to provide with the necessary; *intr.v.* to be sufficient.

a-bas-tar-da'-do, -a *adj.* lacking in original qualities, not pure, falsified.

a-bas-tar-dar' *tr.v.* to lose authenticity, to alter; to corrupt, to cause to degenerate.

a-bas-te-ce-dor' *m.* one who, or that which, supplies.

a-bas-te-cer' *tr.v.* see *abastar.*

a-bas-te-ci'-do, -a *adj.* sufficient, well-supplied with.

a-bas-te-ci-men'-to *m.* provisioning on large scale.

a-bas-to'-so, -a *adj.* abundant, well-supplied.

a-ba-ter' *tr.v.* to reduce; to knock down to crush; to kill, to slaughter; to prostrate; to blind with splendor; to humiliate, to belittle; to beat down to the earth (by rain); to lose flesh; **— a bandeira** to lower flag in honor to a superior or in surrender; **— as armas** to surrender; **— as sobrancelhas** to be confused or embarrassed by unexpected shame or fright.

a-ba-ti'-do, -a *adj.* weakened, prostrated, depressed, deeply discouraged.

a-ba-ti-men'-to *m.* weakness (after illness), act of lowering; cutting down (trees); falling (of building structures); lowering of prices.

a-ba-to-car' *tr.v.* to close with stopper (cork).

a-bau-la'-do, -a *adj.* convex.

a-ba-u-lar' *tr.v.* to make convex; to give the form of a rounded trunk top; to make barrel-shaped (road).

a-ba-ú-na *m.* term used for the Brazilian aboriginal Indian of pure race.

ab-a-vós *m.pl.* ancestors.

abc (abecê) *m.* the alphabet; old first reader; elementary notions of any science art.

ab-ces'-so *m.* tumor; abscess.

ab-di-ca-ção' *f.* abdication, document containing the terms of the abdication.
ab-di-ca-dor' *adj.* that which indicates, or brings about, abdication.
ab-di-can'-te *adj.* see *abdicador.*
ab-di-car' *tr.v.* to abdicate, to abandon, to resign, desist from.
ab-dô-men *m.* abdomen.
ab-do-mi-nais' *m.pl.* fish having beard-like fins on lower part of abdomen.
ab-do-mi-no'-so, ⸗a *adj.* abdominous, big-bellied.
a-be-ce-dá-rio *m.* abecedarian; the alphabet; *adj.* in alphabetical order.
a-bei-rar' *tr.v.* to surround; to approach; to touch upon slightly; to go around the edge.
a-be'-lha *f.* honey bee; — de ouro *f.* premium granted by various literary and scientific societies to authors of notable works and to other meritorious persons.
a-be'-lha⸗mes'-tra *f.* queen bee, (pop.) manager of house of ill fame.
a-be-lhão' *m.* bumble-bee.
a-be'-lha⸗ru'-co |*m.* bee-eater (insectivorous bird of bright colors).
a-be-lhei'-ro *m.* bee-keeper.
a-be-lhu-di'-ce *f.* curiosity, indiscretion, inquisitiveness.
a-be-lhu'-do, ⸗a *adj.* daring, in haste, curious, like a busy-body, capable, attentive to work in hand.
a-be-mo-lar' *tr.v.* to lower by a half tone; to put in the key of B flat; to soften; to smooth down.
a-ben-cer-ra'-ge *m.* Abencerrage; último —, one who demonstrates extreme devotion until the very end, last defender of an idea.
a-ben-ço-ar' *tr.v.* to bless.
a-ber-ra-ção' *f.* aberration.
a-ber-rar' *intr.v.* to aberrate; to diverge; to go astray.
a-ber'-ta *f.* place where cultivated land breaking through forests, reaches the river bank; spot with less dense vegetation in a thick forest, permitting the open sky to be seen; small bay, or indentation along the seashore.
a-ber'-to, ⸗a *adj.* not closed, open to view; sincere, frank; vast; dug out; engraved; cut or lacerated; unbuttoned; clear, not cloudy; stretched out, unrolled; available, without limits or restrictions; unprotected.
a-ber-tu'-ra *f.* orifice, aperture; inauguration; the upper part of garments, openings with buttons or other fastenings which facilitate their being put on.
a-bes-pi-nhar'⸗se *refl.v.* to become irritated; to lose one's temper.
a-bes-ta-lha'-do, ⸗a *adj.* (slang) silly, imbecile; stupid; aghast.
a-be'-ta *f.* narrow brim; (diminutive of aba).
a-be-tu-ma'-do, ⸗a *adj.* caulked with tar; sticky, glued together.
a-be-tu-mar' *tr.v.* to caulk with tar; to soil or give appearance of tar.
A-be-xim' *m.* Abyssinian; language of Abyssinia; *adj.* relating to Abyssinia.
ab-gre-gar' *tr.v.* to dismiss; to separate.
a-bi-bli-o-te-car' *tr.v.* to arrange like a library; to compile a bibliography.
a-bi-car' *tr.v.* to approach; to make touch; ⸗se *intr.v.* to make pointed; to touch the wharf, beach, or bank with the prow; to drop anchor.
a-bis-coi-ta'-do, ⸗a *adj.* similar to cook-

ies or crackers; (pop.) robbed, taken away, accomplished.
a-bis-coi-tar' *tr.v.* to give form of, or to cook like, a cracker or cookie; to achieve something unexpectedly; to gain or profit from; to obtain possession of illegally.
a-bi-ei'-ro *m.* sapote tree.
a-bis-mal' *adj.* abysmal.
a-bis-mar' *tr.v.* to fill with fear, wonder, surprise or confusion; to precipitate; ⸗se *refl.v.* to fall into deep thought; to fall into vices, to degrade one's self.
a-bis'-mo *m.* abyss; (heraldry) center of shield.
a-bis-mo'-so, ⸗a *adj.* having or surrounded by abysms.
a-bis-sí-nio *m.* Abyssinian; one who attacks those fallen from power and praises those in power; *adj.* Abyssinian.
á-bi-to *m.* lead carbonate.
a-bi-to-lar' *tr.v.* to measure; to compare with a standard.
a-bi'-u *m.* fruit of sapote tree.
ab-je-ção' *f.* abjection.
ab-je'-to, ⸗a *adj.* abject.
ab-ju-di-car' *tr.v.*, (law) to abjudicate; to take, by order of judge, something from one who holds it illegally.
ab-ju-gar' *tr.v.* to remove the yoke; to place in liberty; to free.
ab-jun-ção' *f.* separation.
ab-ju-ra-ção' *f.* abjuration.
ab-ju-rar' *tr.v.* to abjure.
ab-la-ção' *f.* ablation; apheresis.
a-bla-ti'-vo *m.* ablative case; ⸗a *adj.* ablative.
a-blé-fa-ro, ⸗a *adj.* having no eyelids.
a-blu-ção' *f.* ablution.
a-blu-ir' *tr.v.* to purify by means of water.
a-blu-tor' *m.* that which washes or purifies.
ab-ne-ga-ção' *f.* abnegation.
ab-ne-ga'-do *m.* one who practices or shows abnegation.
ab-ne-gar' *tr.v.* to renounce; to abnegate.
ab-ne-ga-ti'-vo, ⸗a *adj.* involving abnegation.
a-bó-ba-da *f.* vault, arch, construction in domes; ceiling in form of a dome; — celeste heaven; — craniana upper part of head; — de folhagem vault of interlacing branches; — palatina roof of the mouth.
a-bo-ba-da'-do, ⸗a *adj.* dome-shaped.
a-bo-ba-dar' *tr.v.* to cover with a dome, to make in form of a dome.
a-bo-ba-di'-lha *f.* rounded ceiling made of brick, tiling, or plaster.
a-bo-ba'-do, ⸗a *adj.* silly, stupid, mentally weak.
a-bo-bar'⸗se *refl.v.* to pretend to be stupid; to become mentally weak.
a-bó-bo-ra *f.* pumpkin; lazy, cowardly man; — dágua vegetable marrow.
a-bo-bo-ral' *m.* pumpkin garden.
a-bo-bo-rar' *tr.v.* to give form of pumpkin or squash; to cook over a slow fire; to postpone; to put aside to ripen (a plan or an idea); to put in reserve.
a-bo-bo-rei'-ra *f.* vine upon which vegetable is produced, name given to several plants of the *curcurbita* family.
a-bo-ca-nhar' *tr.v.* to bite; to tear with the teeth; to defame, to calumniate.
a-bo-ca-du'-ra *f.* small opening in the wall of a fort through which guns may shoot; act of holding in the mouth.

a-bo-ca-men'-to *m.* touching or holding with the mouth; conversation.

a-bo-ça-men'-to *m.* (naut.) act of holding or securing by means of cables.

a-bo-car' *tr.v.* (naut.) to hold by means of strong ropes or cables.

a-bo-car' *tr.v.* to touch or hold with the mouth; to go up to the entrance of; to carry to the mouth; to call out, to shout loudly; to aim firearms; to play wind instruments; to hold a bull by the nose.

a-boi-ar' *tr.v.* to tie to a buoy; to sing a monotonous, sad song to cattle in order to calm or guide them; to cry out loud, regular shouts to call cattle home.

a-bo-la-char' *tr.v.* to make similar to cookies or crackers; to flatten out, to compress; to cook in the same way as cookies or crackers.

a-bo-lar' *tr.v.* to make round like a cake; to knead; to lower; to humiliate; to crush, to reduce to small pieces; to sharpen cutting utensils.

a-bo-le-tar' *tr.v.* to quarter soldiers in private homes; to install or make comfortable.

a-bo-li-ção' *f.* abolition.

a-bo-li-cio-nis'-mo *m.* doctrine of the abolition of slavery.

a-bo-li-cio-nis'-ta *m.* abolitionist.

a-bo-li-men'-to *m.* abolition.

a-bo-lir' *tr.v.* to abolish, to revoke, to suppress, to do away with.

a-bo-lo-re-cer' *intr.v.* to become molded or musty.

a-bo-lo-re-ci-men'-to *m.* mold.

a-bol-sar' *intr.v.* to have, or take the form of, a pocket; to make pockets, deep pleats, or tucks (in a dress).

a-bo-mi-na-ção' *f.* repulsion, everything which is abominable.

a-bo-mi-na-dor' *m.* one who abominates.

a-bo-mi-nan'-do, -a *adj.* that which ought to be detested.

a-bo-mi-nar' *tr.v.* to abominate, to detest, to hate.

a-bo-mi-ná-rio *m.* register of the anathemas decreed by the Church.

a-bo-mi-ná-vel *adj.* abominable.

a-bo-mi-no'-so, -a *adj.* abominable.

a-bo-nan-çar' *tr., intr.v.* to make calm; to become tranquil.

a-bo-na-ção' *f.* guaranty.

a-bo-na'-do, -a *adj.* rich, worthy of credit.

a-bo-nar' *tr.v.* to declare or present as good or true; to become responsible for some debt, obligation or promise; to advance money; to excuse or justify an employee's absence from work.

a-bo-na-tó-rio, -a *adj.* safe or proper to be financed.

a-bo-ná-vel *adj.* in condition guaranteed for.

a-bo'-no *m.* sum of money paid or advanced for another; a just increase in weight or measure; a defense (of one's opinion).

a-bo-ne-ca'-do, -a *adj.* doll-like; similar to a doll; decorated like a doll; dressed with affectation; wearing articles conspicuous and of no value; hanging heavily (said of mature ears of corn on the stalks).

a-bor-dar' *tr.v.* to approach something or some one; to reach the edge or border of something; to collide intentionally with a ship in order to capture it.

a-bor-dá-vel *adj.* possible to be touched upon or approached.

a-bôr-do *m.* act of going on board, entrance.

a-bor-do-ar' *tr.v.* to spank, to beat, to strike with a cane or stick; to prop up.

a-bo-rí-ge-ne *adj.* aboriginal; -s *m.pl.* aborigines.

a-bor-le-tar' *tr.v.* to supply or trim with tassels.

a-bor-ras-car'-se *refl.v.* to become stormy; to become very angry.

a-bor-re-ce-dor' *adj.* that which annoys or bores, boresome.

a-bor-re-cer' *tr.v.* to annoy, to irritate, to bore; -se *refl.v.* to become wearied or bored.

a-bor-re-ci'-da-men'-te *adv.* in an annoying manner.

a-bor-re-ci'-do, -a *adj.* bored.

a-bor-re-ci-men'-to *m.* weariness, boredom.

a-bor-re-cí-vel *adj.* capable of being annoyed.

a-bor-re-ga'-do, -a *adj.* (geol.) of glaciers having high fronts with smooth, rounded prominences.

a-bor-ta-men'-to *m.* abortion.

a-bor-tar' *intr.v.* to abort; *tr.v.* to produce imperfectly.

a-bor-tí-cio, -a *adj.* born by abortion.

a-bor-tí-fe-ro, -a *adj.* causing abortion.

a-bor-ti'-vo, -a *adj.* not fully developed; causing abortion.

a-bor-ti'-vo *m.* medicine administered to bring about abortion.

a-bôr-to *m.* abortion.

a-bo-ti-ca'-do, -a *adj.* prominent, conspicuous (of eyes which protude abnormally); upholstered.

a-bo-ti-na'-do, -a *adj.* boot-shaped.

a-bo-ti-nar' *tr.v.* to make in form of a boot.

a-bo-to-a-ção' *f.* forming of buds on plants, act of buttoning.

a-bo-to-a-dei'-ra *f.* button-hook, button-hole, seamstress who sews on buttons.

a-bo-to-a'-do, -a *adj.* buttoned up, closed.

a-bo-to-a'-do *m.* kind of fish.

a-bo-to-a-du'-ra *f.* set of buttons.

a-bo-to-ar' *tr.v.* to button; to claim something illicitly; *intr.v.* to rise, or appear, like the sun.

a-bra-â-mi-co, -a *adj.* relating to Abraham.

a-bra-ca-da'-bra *m.* abracadabra.

a-bra-ca-da-bran'-te *adj.* eccentric, extraordinary.

a-bra-ca-dá-bri-co, -a *adj.* singular, eccentric.

a-bra-ça-dei'-ra *f.* iron clamp for stakes or wall.

a-bra-ça-men'-to *m.* act of embracing.

a-bra-çar' *tr.v.* to embrace, to include, to contain, to cover; to admit, to adopt, to follow; to unite, to conform to; to accept, to receive; -se *refl.v.* to hug the shore.

a-bra'-ço *m.* embrace; — de paz welcoming embrace given by Rector and Faculty of Coimbra University to a student when the degree *Doutor em Capelo* is conferred on him.

a-bran-da-men'-to *m.* act of softening; (gram.) voicing.

a-bran-dar' *tr.v.* to tone down; to calm; to soften; to mitigate; to assuage.

a-bran-ger' *tr.v.* to include to take in; to reach to; to achieve; to understand, to comprehend; to contain in a certain area; to catch, to touch.

a-bra-sa'-do, =a *adj.* burning, excited, enthusiastic.

a-bra-sa-dor' *adj.* very hot, burning.

a-bra-sa-men'-to *m.* act or effect of burning.

a-bra-san'-te *adj.* burning.

a-bra-sar' *tr.v.* to turn into live coals, to burn, to heat to a high temperature; to excite, to make enthusiastic.

a-bra-si-lei-ra'-do, =a *adj.* having the manner or features of a Brazilian; imitating Brazilian accent.

a-bra-si-lei-ra-men'-to *m.* act or effect of becoming like a Brazilian.

a-bra-si-lei-rar' *tr.v.* to Brazilianize; to adapt to the Brazilian temperament, manner, or style; =se *refl.v.* to become Brazilianized.

a-bra-si'-vo *m.* an abrasive.

a-bra-so-nar' *tr.v.* to emblazon.

a-bre=bô-ca *m.* gag, spatula.

á-bre-go *m.* wind from the southeast, *i.e.*, from Africa; area to the south in XV and XVI century maps.

a-bre-i-lhós *m.* eyelet punch.

a-bre-jar' *tr.v.* to transform into bogs or swamp; to enter into virgin, quasi-impenetrable, forests; *intr.v.* to abound, to be abundant.

a-bre-la'-tas *m.* can opener.

a-bre-nhar' *tr.v.* to convert into thick forest growth; —=se *refl.v.* to flee to, or hide in, the forest.

ab-re-nún-cio *interj.* Out, Satan !! Flee, Demons !!

a-brep-tí-cio, =a *adj.* in an exalted state of mind; possessed of the devil.

a-bre-vi-a-ção' *f.* abbreviation.

a-bre-vi-a-dor' *m.* that which shortens, etc.

a-bre-vi-a-men'-to *m.* abbreviation.

a-bre-vi-ar' *tr.v.* to shorten, to reduce; to make a résumé or abstract of; to expedite, to conclude in brief time; to represent on a smaller scale; to adjust to; to cut short (a conversation); to give the short sound to a vowel.

a-bre-vi-a-tí'-vo, =a *adj.* serving to shorten, etc.

a-bre-vi-a-tu'-ra *f.* abbreviation.

a-bri-có *m.* apricot.

a-bri-co-tei'-ro *m.* apricot tree.

a-bri-co'-te *m.* Brazilian fruit similar to but larger than the damson; also called abricó do Pará, abricó de São Domingos, abricó selvagem.

a-bri-dei'ra *f.* machine used in the textile industry in Brazil; (slang) alcoholic drink, generally whisky, taken in small quantity before a meal as an aperitif.

a-bri-ga-dor' *m.* that which shelters.

a-bri-gar' *tr.v.* to cover, to shelter, to lodge; to defend; to supply with necessities.

a-bri'-go *m.* covering, protection, shelter.

A-bril' *m.* April; youth; the age of innocence.

a-bri-lhan-tar' *tr.v.* to cut and polish (precious stones, especially the diamond); to ornament; to make radiant; to contribute to the distinction (of an assembly).

a-bri-men'-to *m.* act or effect of opening.

a-brir' *tr.v.* to open, to unfold; to perforate; to remove obstacles; to begin

something, to inaugurate; to engrave, to sculpture; to unveil; to make accessible; — crédito to establish credit; —= se *refl.v.* to speak very frankly and confidentially.

a-bro-ca-da'do, =a *adj.* imitating brocade.

a-bro-cha-dor' *m.* that which closes or fastens.

a-bro-cha-du'-ra *f.* whatever is used as a fastening, act of closing.

a-bro-char' *tr.v.* to tighten; to button; to fasten with a brooch; to decorate with precious stones.

a-bro-ga-ção' *f.* abrogation, revocation, annulment.

a-bro-ga-dor' *adj.* that which annuls, or will cause to be annulled.

a-bro-gar' *tr.v.* to annul; to suppress; to revoke.

a-bro-ga-ti'-vo, =a *adj.* having the quality of annulling.

a-bro-ga-tó-rio, =a *adj.* having the force, or qualities, of an annulment.

a-bro-lhar' *tr.v.*, *intr.v.* to produce, to burst out with buds; to begin to appear (as beard); to break out (skin eruption); to cause, or to originate something undesirable.

a-bro-lho'-so, =a *adj.* full of buds or thorns; containing many difficulties.

a-bro-lho *m.* star cactus; thorn of this plant; difficulties, obstacles, mortification.

a-bron-zar' *tr.v.* to fuse copper, generally with tin, to produce the alloy bronze.

a-bron-ze-ar' *tr.v.* to imitate bronze; to give the color of bronze.

a-bro'-que *m.* kind of cape, blue and white striped, used by Moorish women.

a-bro-que-la'-do, =a *adj.* shield-shaped.

a-bro-que-lar' *tr.v.* to protect or defend with the small ancient shield; *intr.v.* to find solace in.

a-bro-tal' *m.* garden or place for growing daffodils.

a-bru-ma'-do, =a *adj.* characterized by fog; sad.

a-bru-ma-dor' *adj.*, *m.* causing fog or oppression of spirit.

a-bru-mar' *tr.v.* to fill or cover with fog; to darken; (fig.) to become sad, apprehensive.

a-brup'-to, =a *adj.* very steep; sudden; rude.

a-bru-ta-lhar' *tr.v.* to make coarse; —= se *refl.v.* to become coarse, rude, stupid, brutal.

ab-sen-te-ís-mo *m.* absenteeism; (Brazil) the custom or habit of preferring foreign articles to the national; the habit of being absent.

ab-sen-te-ís-ta *m.* one who practices absenteeism.

ab-sín-ti-o *m.* absinthe.

ab-so-lu-tis'-mo *m.* absolutism.

ab-so-lu-tis'-ta *m.* absolutist.

ab-so-lu'-to, =a *adj.* absolute.

ab-sol-ver' *tr.v.* to absolve; (painting) to work together colors already placed on the canvas.

ab-sor-ve-dor' *m.*, *adj.* absorbent.

ab-sor-ve-dou'-ro *m.* absorber.

ab-sor-vên-cia *f.* absorbency.

ab-sor-ver' *tr.v.* to absorb; to consume, to make disappear; to monopolize, to occupy completely; —=se *refl.v.* to meditate, to concentrate one's thoughts.

ab-sor-ví-vel *adj.* absorptive.

ab-stê-mio, =a *adj.* abstemious, frugal, sober; *m., f.* abstainer.
ab-sten-ção' *f.* abstinence.
ab-ster' *tr.v.* to refrain from; —=se *refl.v.* to restrain oneself, to abstain, to be sober and moderate.
ab-sti-nên-cia *f.* abstinence.
ab-sti-nen'-te *adj.* abstinent.
abs-tra-ção' *f.* abstraction.
abs-tra-í-do, =a *adj.* abstracted.
abs-trai-men'-to *m.* abstractedness.
abs-tra-ir' *tr.v.* to abstract, to separate; *intr.v.* to consider separately things which are united generally; —=se *refl.v.* to become absent-minded, to let the attention wander.
abs-tru'-so, =a *adj.* abstruse.|
ab-sur'-do, =a *adj.* absurd.
abs-tra'-to *m.* abstract.
abs-tra'-to, =a *adj.* abstracted.
a-bun-dân-cia *f.* abundance, plentifulness.
a-bun-dan'-te *adj.* abundant.
a-bun-dar' *intr.v.* to abound, to be sufficient; to overflow; to be in agreement with.
a-bun-do'-so, =a *adj.* plentiful.
a-bu-ra-ca'-do, =a *adj.* having holes, full of holes.
a-bu-ra-car' *tr.v.* to make holes in, to fill with holes.
a-bur-gue-sar'=se *refl.v.* to acquire happits and manners of the bourgeois.
a-bu-sa'-do, =a *adj.* annoyed, wearied.
a-bu-sar' *intr.v.* to treat badly, to impose upon; to deceive; to cause damage; to treat lightly; (Brazil) to behave rudely, to annoy, to cause disgust, to be a nuisance.
a-bu-si'-vo, =a *adj.* abusive.
a-bu'-so *m.* abuse, wrong, excessive or unjust use; exorbitant taxation; violation.
a-bu'-tre *m.* vulture; a man with low instincts.
a-bu-zi-nar' *intr.v.* to sound auto horn.
a-ca-ba-ça'-do, =a *adj.* having shape or taste of a gourd.
a-ca-ba-çar' *tr.v.* to make into form of a gourd.
a-ca-ba'-do, =a *adj.* completed, used up, old.
a-ca-ba-men'-to *m.* finishing; end, death.
a-ca-ba-na'-do, =a *adj.* like a cottage; with ears and horns pointing down.
a-ca-ba-nar' *tr.v.* to make in form of a cabin or rustic cottage; to have ears and horns pointing down.
a-ca'-ba-no-ve'-nas *m.* (slang) disorderly person.
a-ca-bar' *tr.v.* to terminate, to finish; to kill; to destroy; to polish off; to consume, to exhaust; to obtain, to achieve; to convince, to persuade; to die, to perish; — de, with infinitive, to express idea of having just (finished or ceased to do something): *e.g.,* Acabo de ler I have just read.
a-ca-bru-nha'-do, =a *adj.* depressed, weakened, melancholic.
a-ca-bru-nha-men'-to *m.* loss of courage, disappointment, affliction.
a-ca-bru-nhar' *tr.v.* to oppress, to afflict; to sadden, to discourage.
a-ça-ca-lar' *tr.v.* to polish, to burnish; to perfect.
a-cá-ci-a *f.* acacia.

a-ca-cia'-no, =a *adj.* ridiculous, pretendedly grave.
a-ca-cia-nis'-mo *m.* something ridiculously trivial made to appear serious.
A-cá-cio *m.* individual like Councilor Acácio, a futile, ridiculous and pretentious character in *O Primo Basílio,* a novel of Eça de Queiroz.
a-ca-fe-ta'-do, =a *adj.* having the color of coffee.
a-ca-fe-tar' *tr.v.* to give the color of coffee to.
a-ça-frô-a' *m.* crocus, flower of this plant, metallic preparation of saffron yellow.
a-ça-frô-a *f.* safflower.
a-ça-fro-a'-do, =a *adj.* saffron-colored.
a-ça-fro-al' *adj.* crocus garden.
a-ça-fro-ar' *tr.v.* to dye with saffron, to give a saffron tint to; —=se *refl.v.* to become pale with fear or anger.
a-cal-ca-nhar' *tr.v.* to step on with the heel; to give the form of a heel to; to belittle, to oppress, to crush; *intr.v.* to wear out or turn over the heel of the shoe in walking.
a-ca-len-tar' *tr.v.* to rock gently, to lull to sleep; to pacify; to mitigate pain; acalento *m.* soothing expression.
a-cal-ma-ção' *f.* calming; quietness, tranquility.
a-cal-ma'-do, =a *adj.* calm.
a-cal-mar' *tr.v.* to calm, to pacify; to moderate, to lessen.
a-cal-mi'-a *f.* period of momentary tranquility.
a-ca-lo-ra'-do, =a *adj.* very animated.
a-ca-lo-rar' *tr.v.* to make hot; to excite; to encourage; to warm.
a-ca-mar' *tr.v.* to place in layers; *intr.v.* to be sick abed; to be bent over to the ground (corn or ripe grain) because of wind or weight of mature heads.
a-ca-ma'-do *m.* forage left on ground to cure.
a-ca-ma'-do, =a *adj.* confined to bed.
a-ca-ma-men'-to *m.* falling of stalks of grain because of wind or heavy heads.
a-cam-pa'-do, =a *adj.* encamped.
a-cam-pa-men'-to *m.* camping; encampment; camp.
a-cam-par' *tr.v.* to camp; —=se *refl.v.* to pitch camp, to encamp.
a-ca-na-lha'-do, =a *adj.* vile.
a-ca-na-lha-dor' *adj.* depraving.
a-ca-na-lhar' *tr.v.* to set a bad example for; —=se *refl.v.* to become low, to degrade oneself.
a-ca-nha'-do, =a *adj.* timid, unpretentious, humble, mentally slow.
a-ca-nha-dor', =a *adj.* causing shyness; intimidating.
a-ca-nha-men'-to *m.* shyness, timidity; small means.
a-ca-nhar' *tr.v.* to limit; —=se *refl.v.* to be timid, to lose courage.
a-ca-nho-ne-ar' *tr.v.* to bombard; to drag a cannon along.
a-ca-nô-ni-co, =a *adj.* anti-canonic.
a-ca-no-nis'-ta *m.* transgressor of canon law.
a-cân-ti-co, =a *adj.* relating to acanthus.
a-can'-to *m.* acanthus (plant, architectural ornament).
a-can-to-a'-do, =a *adj.* hidden; in a corner.
a-can-to-a-men'-to *m.* hiding.
a-can-to-ar' *tr.v.* to place in or adjust a corner; —=se *refl.v.* to retire from social life.

a-can-to-na-men'-to *m.* cantonment.

a-can-to-nar' *tr.v.* to distribute or quarter soldiers.

a-ção' *f.* action.

a-ca-re-a-ção' *f.* confronting, facing.

a-ca-re-a-men'-to *m.* confronting, facing.

a-ca-re-ar' *tr.v.* to face, to confront; —se *intr.v.* to be faced with.

a-ca-ri-cia-dor', ªa *adj. m.f.* demonstrative; demonstrative person.

a-ca-ri-cian'-te *adj.* affectionate, tender.

a-ca-ri-ci-ar' *tr.v.* to caress.

a-car-re-ta-dor' *m.* one who transports baggage or freight; carrier.

a-car-re-tar' *tr.v.* to transfer baggage in small truck or on head; to mount on a carriage (pieces of artillery).

a-car-to-na'-do, ªa *adj.* having the aspect or form of cardboard.

a-car-to-nar' *tr.v.* to make similar to cardboard.

a-ca'-so *m.* hazard, chance, luck, risk, venture, a casual happening, fortune.

a-ca-tó-li-co, ªa *adj.* not Catholic.

a-cau-te-la'-do, ªa *adj.* astute, forewarned, cautious.

a-cau-te-lar' *tr.v.* to take precautions; —se *refl.v.* to become cautious, prudent.

a-ca-va-la'-do, ªa *adj.* grouped in a disorderly fashion.

a-ca-va-lar' *tr.v.* to mate stallion with máre for breeding.

a-ca-va-lei-ra'-do, ªa *adj.* on horseback, in a superior manner.

a-ca-va-lei-rar' *tr.v.* to mount, to ride horse-back.

a-ca-va-le-ta'-do, ªa *adj.* having an easel.

a-ce-da'-res *m.pl.* nets for catching sardines (pilchards).

a-ce-dên-cia *f.* accedence.

a-ce-der' *tr.v.* to be resigned to; to add to; to acquiesce, to join.

a-ce-fa-li'-a *f.* acephalia.

a-cé-fa-lo, ªa *adj.* acephalous, headless.

a-cei'-ro *m.* steel-worker, bar of pig iron; strip of cleared land surrounding forest as fire protection; a-cei'-ro, ªa *adj.* strong, made of steel, having the properties of steel.

a-cei-ta-ção' *f.* acceptance; acceptation.

a-cei-ta-dor' *m.* acceptant.

a-cei-ta-men'-to *m.* acceptance.

a-cei-tar' *tr.v.* to accept.

a-cei-tá-vel *adj.* acceptable.

a-cei'-te *m.* bill of acceptance.

a-cei'-to, ªa *adj.* accepted.

a-ce-le-ra-ção' *f.* acceleration.

a-ce-le-ra-dor' *m.* accelerator.

a-ce-le-ra-men'-to *m.* acceleration.

a-ce-le-rar' *tr.v.* to accelerate.

a-ce-na-men'-to *m.* signal or gesture made by the hands, head, or eyes.

a-ce-nar' *intr.v.* to make affirmative motions or gestures with the head, hands or eyes; to provoke; to call attention.

a-ce'-no *m.* signal.

a-cen-de-dor' *m.* cigar lighter, cigarette lighter.

a-cen-der' *tr.v.* to set on fire, to cause to burn; to light; to stimulate, to enthuse; to increase; — as ventas to entice an animal by allowing it to smell food.

a-cen-dí-vel *adj.* inflammable.

a-cen-tu-a-ção' *f.* accentuation.

a-cen-tu-a'-do, ªa *adj.* marked, accentuated, pronounced.

a-cen-tu-ar' *tr.v.* to accent; (fig.) to emphasize, to make salient.

a-cen'-to *m.* accent.

a-ce-pi'-pe *m.* especially tasty dish; delicacy.

a-ce-ra-ção' *f.* operation of making iron into steel.

a-ce-ra'-do ªa *adj.* sharp, steel-like; having the quality of wounding deeply.

a-ce-ra-dor' *m.* manufacturer of cutlery.

a-ce-ra'-gem *f.* manufacturing of cutlery.

a-ce-ran'-te *adj.* that is used in making steel.

a-ce-rar' *tr.v.* to turn iron into steel; to cover with layer of steel; to strengthen, to make robust.

a-cer-bar' *tr.v.* to acerbate.

a-cer-bi-da'-de *f.* acerbity.

a-cer'-bo, ªa *adj.* acerb, harsh, unripe, cruel.

a-cêr-ca-de *prep.* relative to, concerning, with respect to, about.

a-eer-car'ªse *refl.v.* to touch upon, to approach, to be neighbor to.

a-cer-ta'-do, ªa *adj.* wise, sensible.

a-cer-tar' *tr.v.* to discover, to make correct, to adjust, to make harmonious, to find something being searched for, to be right.

a-cêr-to *m.* prudence, good judgment.

a-cer'-vo *m.* accumulation; disorderly pile of articles.

a-cér-vu-lo *m.* small heap of objects.

a-ce'-so, ªa *adj.* on fire; excited.

a-ces-são' *f.* accession.

a-ces-si-bi-li-da'-de *f.* accessibility.

a-ces-sí-vel *adj.* accessible.

a-ces'-so *m.* access.

a-ces-sí'-vo, ªa *adj.* excessive, not an essential.

a-ces-só-rio, ªa *adj.* accessory; *m.* (gram.) attribute.

a-cé-ti-co, ªa *adj.* acetic.

a-ce-tol' *m.* acetol.

a-ce-ti-le'-ne or a-ce-ti-le'-no *m.* acetylene.

a-ce-tí-me-tro *m.* acetometer.

a-ce-ti-na'-do, ªa *adj.* like satin.

a-ce-ti-nar' *tr.v.* to soften; to satinize.

a-ce-tô-me-tro *m.* acetometer.

a-ce-to'-na *f.* acetone.

a'-cha *f.* fire-wood; — de armas hatchet-shaped ancient weapon.

a-cha-ca-di'-ço, ªa *adj.* sickly; invalid.

a-cha-car' *intr.v.* to fall ill; to have a chronic ailment.

a-cha-co'-so, ªa *adj.* subject to attacks of ill health.

a-cha'-que *m.* chronic suffering; (fig.) vice, moral defect.

a-cha'-da *f.* catching in the act; plateau.

a-cha-dão' *m.* good business deal.

a-cha-di'-ço, ªa *adj.* easily split off or separated.

a-cha'-do *m.* find.

a-cha-dor' *m.* inventor, discoverer.

a-cha-dou'-ro *m.* place where something is found; locale of pre-historic vestiges.

a-cha-men'-to *m.* finding; unexpected profit.

a-char' *tr.v.* to find, to invent, to discover; to suppose, to judge, to note; —se to be.

a-cha-ta-de'-la *f.* winning a discussion.

a-cha-ta'-do, ªa *adj.* flat.

a-cha-ta-du'-ra *f.* flattening.

a-cha-ta-men'-to *m.* flattening.
a-cha-tar' *tr.v.* to flatten, to beat down; (fig.) to come out victor in an argument.
a-cha-vas-ca'-do, ꞏa *adj.* crude, badly finished.
a-cha-vas-car' *tr.v.* to give the natural form.
a-che'-ga *f.* subsidy, advancement; (agr.) drawing earth close around plant.
a-che-ga'-da *f.* sudden attack from close by.
a-che-ga-dei'-ra *f.* female go-between; busybody.
a-che-ga-dor' *m.* gossiper.
a-che-ga-men'-to *m.* proximity, approach.
a-che-gan'-ças *f.pl.* supplementary income, inherited property.
a-che-gar' *tr.v.* to approach, to bring closer.
a-chin-ca-lha-ção *f.* ridiculing in verse or song.
a-chin-ca-lha-dor' *m.* one who ridicules.
a-chin-ca-lha-men'-to *m.* ridiculing in verse or song.
a-chin-ca-lhar' *tr.v.* to ridicule, to make comic verse about.
a-chin-ca'-lhe *m.* ridiculing.
a-chi-ne-sa'-do, ꞏa *adj.* having the manners of a Chinese.
a-chi-ne-sar' *tr.v.* to make similar to a Chinese.
a-chum-bar' *tr.v.* to make similar to lead.
a-ci-a-no-blep-si'-a *f.* visual defect in which blue color cannot be distinguished.
a-ci-ca'-te *m.* the sharp-pointed end of a sting, or thorn; (fig.) incentive, stimulus, irritant.
a-ci-da'-de *f.* acidity.
a-ci-dar' *tr.v.* —se *refl.v.* to acidify.
a-ci-den-ta-ção' *f.* unevenness.
a-ci-den-ta'-do, ꞏa *adj.* uneven, rough.
a-ci-den-tal' *adj.* accidental.
a-ci-den-tar' *tr.v.* to produce irregularities in; to vary; to introduce accidental notes in music.
a-ci-den-tá-vel *adj.* susceptible to accidents.
a-ci-dên-cia *f.* accidence.
a-ci-dez' *f.* acidity.
á-ci-do *m.* acid; **á-ci-do,** ꞏa *adj.* acid, sour.
a-ci-do'-se *f.* (med.) acidosis.
a-ci-ga-nar ꞏse *refl.v.* to take on gypsy manners; to become astute; to cheat.
a-ci'-ma *adv.* in the place above, in the preceding position.
a-cin'-te *m.* something done intentionally to offend; *adv.* purposefully.
a-cin-to'-so, ꞏa *adj.* done to offend.
a-cin-zen-ta'-do, ꞏa *adj.* somewhat greyish.
a-cin-zen-tar' *tr.v.* to give a greyish color to.
a-cir-ra'-do, ꞏa *adj.* intolerant, obstinate, irritated.
a-cir-ra-men'-to *m.* irritation.
a-cir-rar' *tr.v.* to incite, to irritate, to stimulate, to tease, to madden.
a-ci-tri-na'-do, ꞏa *adj.* cider-colored.
a-cla-ma-ção' *f.* acclamation.
a-cla-mar' *tr.v.* to acclaim.
a-cli-ma-ção' *f.* acclimatization.
a-cli-mar' *tr.v.* to acclimate; —se to become acclimated.
a-cli-ma-ti-zar' *tr.v.* to acclimatize.

a-cli'-ve *m.* steep hillside (considered from the bottom); *adj.* hard to climb because of the steepness.
a'-ço *m.* steel; amalgam applied to mirrors; side arms; (fig.) strength, austerity.
a-co-ber-tar' *tr.v.* to cover.
a-coi-tar' *tr.v.* to seek safety in a refuge; to give refuge to; to flee.
a-çoi-ta-men'-to *m.* whipping, lashing.
a-çoi-tar' *tr.v.* to lash, to punish by lashing.
a-çoi'-te *m.* whip.
a-co-lá *adv.* far away; in that place (distant).
a-col-che-tar' *tr.v.* to close with hooks and eyes (garments).
a-col-cho-a'-do *m.* quilted or embroidered bed-spread; **a-col-cho-a'-do,** ꞏa *adj.* upholstered.
a-col-cho-a-dor' *m.* mattress-maker.
a-col-cho-ar' *tr.v.* to upholster, to weave, to embroider, to quilt.
a-co-le-ta'-do, ꞏa *adj.* like a corset.
a-co-lhe-dor' *m.* good host.
a-co-lher' *tr.v.* to welcome, to receive, to admit, to give asylum to, to give credit to, to believe; to take prisoner.
a-co-lhi'-da *f.* welcome, reception.
a-co-lhi-men'-to *m.* welcome, reception, refuge, accommodation.
a-co-me-te-dor' *m.* aggressor, one who stirs up quarrels.
a-co-me-ter' *tr.v.* to assault, to attack; to provoke, to make hostile; to approach in threatening manner.
a-co-me-ti'-da *f.* sudden attack, threat.
a-co-me-ti-men'-to *m.* sudden attack, threat.
a-co-me-tí-vel *adj.* susceptible of attack.
a-co-mo-da-ção *f.* accommodation.
a-co-mo-da'-do, ꞏa *adj.* quiet, calm, comfortable.
a-co-mo-dar' *tr.v.* to accommodate.
a-com-pa-nha-dei'-ra *f.* accompanist.
a-com-pa-nha-dor' *m.* accompanist.
a-com-pa-nha-men'-to *m.* (music) accompaniment; retinue; funeral procession.
a-com-pa-nhar' *tr.v.* to accompany.
a-con-di-ci-o-na-ção' *f.* caution, safeguard; conditioning.
a-con-di-ci-o-na-men'-to *m.* conditioning.
a-con-di-ci-o-nar' *tr.v.* to condition.
a-con-fei-tar' *tr.v.* to make like candy.
a-con-se-lhar' *tr.v.* to counsel; to advise.
a-con-se-lhá-vel *adj.* advisable.
a-con-so-an-ta'-do, ꞏa *adj.* consonant.
a-con-so-an-tar' *tr.v.* to consonantize.
a-con-te-cer' *intr.v.* to come to be a reality; to happen.
a-con-te-ci-men'-to *m.* event, occurrence, happening.
a-cor-da'-do, ꞏa *adj.* awakened, tuned, remembered, settled.
a-cor-da-men'-to *m.* agreement, accord.
a-cor-dan'-te *adj.* harmonious, in accord.
a-cor-dar' *tr.v.* to awaken; to tune; to recover one's faculties; to reconcile; —se *refl.v.* to get awake.
a-cor'-de *m.* chord.
a-côr-do *m.* agreement, accord.
A-ço-re-a'-no *m.* Azorean, of the Azores.
a-cor-ren-tar' *tr.v.* to chain; to put in jail; to enslave.

a-cor-rer' *intr.v.* to respond to call for aid; to give aid promptly; —-se *refl.v.* to take refuge.

a-cor-ri-men'-to *m.* aid, act of lending aid.

a-cor-ti-nar' *tr.v.* to furnish with curtains.

a-cos'-sa *f.* persecution.

a-cos-sar' *tr.v.* to follow close behind some one; to persecute, to annoy; (pop.)

a-cos-tar' *tr.v.* to lean against, to join; *intr.v.* to approach coast, to follow along coast.

a-cos-tá-vel *adj.* said of dock having water deep enough for ship to come alongside, or wharf having docking facilities.

a-cus-to-mar' *tr.v.* to accustom, to make a habit of.

a-çou'-gue *m.* butcher-shop.

a-çou-guei'-ro *m.* butcher.

a'-cre *m.* acre (land measure); *adj.* sour, biting.

A-cre-a'-no *m.* citizen of Acre Territory (Brazil).

a-cre-di-ta'-do, -a *adj.* creditable; accredited.

a-cre-di-ta-dor' *m.* creditor.

a-cre-di-tar' *tr.v.* to believe, to credit.

a-cre-di-tá-vel *adj.* credible, creditable.

a-cres-cen-tar' *tr.v.* to join, to add, to increase.

a-cres-cer' *tr.v.* to accresce, to accrue.

a-cres-ci'-dos *m.pl.* alluvial lands.

a-cres-ci-men'-to *m.* increase.

a-cri-dez' *f.* acridity, bitterness.

a-cri-mô-nia *f.* acrimony.

a-cri-mo-ni-o'-so, -a *adj.* acrimonious.

a-cri-so-la-dor' *m.* purifying agent.

a-cri-so-lar' *tr.v.* to purify (in crucible).

a-cro-ba-ci'-a *f.* acrobacy.

a-cro-ba'-ta *m.* acrobat.

a-cro-bá-ti-co, -a *adj.* acrobatic.

a-cro-ce-fa-li'-a *f.* acrocephaly.

a-cro-ce-fa-lo *m.* individual with an abnormally large head.

a-cro-ma-ni'-a *f.* total and incurable insanity.

a-cro-má-ti-co, -a *adj.* achromatic.

a-cro-ma-tis'-mo *m.* achromatism.

a-cro-ma-ti-za-ção' *f.* achromatization.

a-cro-ma-ti-zar' *tr.v.* to achromatize.

A-cró-po-le *f.* Acropolis.

a-çú-car *m.* sugar.

a-çu-ca-rar' *tr.v.* to sweeten, to sugar.

a-çu-ca-rei'-ro *m.* sugar dealer, sugar manufacturer; sugar-bowl.

a-çu-ce'-na *f.* white lily.

a-çu-da'-gem *f.* artificial irrigation.

a-çu-dar' *tr.v.*, *intr.v.* to provide water in reservoir; to hold water in reservoir.

a-çu'-de *m.* reservoir (in artificial irrigation).

a-cu-dir' *intr.v.* to respond to call for help, to aid.

a-cui-da'-de *f.* acuity; fineness; perspicacity.

a-çu-lar' *tr.v.* to provoke, to incite.

a-cu-mu-lar' *tr.v.* to accumulate.

a-cu-mu-la-dor' *m.* storage battery, accumulator.

a-cu-ra'-do, -a *adj.* done with utmost care.

a-cu-sa-ção' *f.* accusation.

a-cu-sa-do, -a *adj.* accused, defendent.

a-cu-sa-dor' *m.* accuser, plaintif.

a-cu-san'-te *m.* accuser, plaintif.

a-cu-sar' *tr.v.* to accuse; to acknowledge.

a-cu-sa-ti'-vo *m.* accusative case; a-cu-sa-ti'-vo, -a *adj.* accusative.

a-cu-sá-vel *adj.* accusable.

a-cús-ti-ca *f.* acoustics.

a-cús-ti-co, -a *adj.* acoustic.

a-da'-ga *f.* dagger.

a-da-ga'-da *f.* dagger-wound.

a-da-gi-á-rio *m.* book or collection of adages.

a-dá-gio *m.* adage.

a-da-man-ti'-no, -a *adj.* adamantine.

a-dap-ta-ção, *f.* adaptation.

a-dap-tar' *tr.v.* to adapt.

a-dap-tá-vel *adj.* adaptable.

a-dap-ta-bi-li-da'-de *f.* adaptability.

a-de'-ga *f.* wine-cellar.

a-de-gar' *tr.v.* to store in a cellar.

a-del-ga-ça'-do, -a *adj.* narrow, pointed.

a-del-ga-çar' *tr.v.* to make thinner (metal sheet), or stretch longer (wires); to make less dense; to reduce in size, extension or intensity.

a-den'-da *f.* addendum.

a-de-nói-de *m.* adenoid.

a-de-rê-ço *m.* a jeweled ornament, jewelry; —s *m.pl.* stage properties.

a-der-na'-do, -a *adj.* inclined, beaten down, small, almost imperceptible.

a-der-nar' *intr.v.* to lean over so that one side of a boat is almost submerged.

a-de-rên-cia *f.* adherence.

a-de-ren'-te *adj.* adherent; *m.* member, follower.

a-de-rir' *intr.v.* to adhere; to join.

a-de-são' *f.* adhesion; approval, joining.

a-des-ho'-ras *adv.* late, inopportunely.

a-de-sis'-mo *m.* joining new societies; ready acceptance of new ideas.

a-de-si'-vo, -a *adj.* adhesive.

a-des-trar' *tr.v.* to exercise, to make dextrous, or skillful.

a-de'-us *interj.* goodby.

a-di-a'-do, -a *adj.* postponed.

a-di-á-fa-no, -a *adj.* opaque.

a-di-an-ta-men'-to *m.* advancement, progress, improvement; advance payment.

a-di-an-tar' *tr. v.* to move further ahead, to progress.

a-di-an'-te *adv.* ahead, further on.

a-diar' *tr.v.* to postpone.

a-diá-vel *adj.* that may be postponed.

a-di-ção' *f.* addition.

a-di-cio-na-dor' *m.* adder.

a-di-cio-nal' *adj.* additional.

a-di-ci-o-nar' *tr.v.* to add, to increase.

a-dic'-to, -a *adj.* addicted.

a-di'-do *m.* attaché; aid.

a-di-po'-se *f.* obesity.

a-di-po'-so, -a *adj.* fat.

a-di-ta-men'-to *m.* supplement.

a-di-vi'-nha *f.* fortune-teller.

a-di-vi-nha-ção' *f.* divination.

a-di-vi-nhar' *tr.v.* to guess; to divine.

ad-ja-cên-cia *f.* adjacency.

ad-ja-cen'-te *adj.* adjacent.

ad-je-ti-val' *adj.* adjectival.

ad-je-ti-var' *tr.v.* to qualify.

ad-je-ti'-vo, -a *adj.* adjective.

ad-ju-di-ca-ção' *f.* adjudication.

ad-ju-di-car' *tr.v.* to adjudicate.

ad-jun-ção' *f.* adjunction.

ad-jun'-to *m.* adjunct.

ad-ju-rar' *tr.v.* to adjure.

ad-mi-nis-tra-ção' *f.* administration.

ad-mi-nis-trar' *tr.v.* to administer.

ad-mi-ra-ção' *f.* admiration; surprise; ponto de — exclamation point.

ad-mi-rar' *tr.v.* to admire; to surprise; —=**se** *refl.v.* to be surprised.
ad-mi-rá-vel *adj.* admirable.
ad-mis-são' *f.* admission.
ad-mis-si-bi-li-da'-de *f.* admissibility.
ad-mis-sí-vel *adj.* admissible.
ad-mi-tir' *tr.v.* to admit.
ad-mo-es-ta-ção' *f.* admonishment.
ad-mo-es-ta-dor' *m.* admonitor.
ad-mo-es-tar' *tr.v.* to admonish.
ad-mo-es-ta-tó-rio, =a *adj.* admonitory.
ad-mo-ni-tor' *m.* Jesuit novice.
a-do-çan'-te *adj.* that which sweetens.
a-do-çar' to sweeten.
a-do-ci-car' *tr.v.* to sweeten.
a-do-e-cer' *intr.v.* to become ill.
a-do-en-tar' *tr.v.* to become a little sick.
a-do-les-cên-cia *f.* adolescence.
a-do-les-cen'-te *m. adj.* adolescent.
a-do-min-gar'=**se** *refl.v.* to dress in one's Sunday clothes.
a-don'-de *adv.* (pop.) V. *aonde.*
a-do-ra-ção' *f.* adoration, worship.
a-do-ra-dor' *m.* adorer, worshipper.
a-do-rar' *tr.v.* to adore, to worship.
a-do-rá-vel *adj.* adorable.
a-dor-me-cer' *tr.v.* to cause to sleep; *intr.v.* to fall asleep.
a-dor-na-men'-to *m.* adornment.
a-dor-nar' *tr.v.* to adorn.
a-dôr-no *m.* adornment.
a-do-ção' *f.* adoption.
a-do-tar' *tr.v.* to adopt.
ad-qui-ri-ção' *f.* adquisition.
ad-qui-ri'-dos *m.pl.* property acquired during marriage.
ad-qui-rir' *tr.v.* to acquire.
ad-qui-rí-vel *adj.* that may be acquired.
a-dre-na-li'-na *f.* adrenalin.
a'-dro *m.* church-yard.
a-dro-gar' *tr.v.* to adopt a person not a minor.
ad-scre-ver' *tr.v.* to ascribe.
ad-scri-ção' *f.* adscription.
ad-strin-gên-cia *f.* astringency.
ad-strin-gen'-te *adj.* astringent.
ad-strin-gir' *tr.v.* to bind; to oblige.
a-dua'-na *f.* custom house.
a-dua-nar' *tr.v.* to take out of the custom house; to ship out through the custom house.
a-dua-nei'-ro, =a *adj.* relative to the custom house or to duties.
a-du-bar' *tr.v.* to fertilize.
a-du'-bo *m.* fertilizer.
a-du-cir' *tr.v.* to soften metals and render them ductile and malleable.
a-du-e'-la *f.* stave, slightly curved, in a barrel or cask; each of the stones of an arch, or dome; each of the upright boards forming a portal.
a-du-la-ção' *f.* adulation, praise, flattery.
a-du-la-dor' *m.* flatterer, sycophant.
a-du-lar' *tr.v.* to flatter, to fawn on.
a-du-la-tó-rio, =a *adj.* adulatory.
a-dúl-te-ra *f.* adulteress.
a-dul-te-ra-ção' *f.* adulteration.
a-dul-te-ra-dor' *m.* adulteror.
a-dul-te-rar' *tr.v.* to adulterate; *intr.v.* to commit adultery.
a-dul-té-rio *m.* adultery.
a-dul-te-rio'-so, =a *adj.* adulterous.
a-dul'-to *m.* adult.
a-dum-brar' *tr.v.* to adumbrate.
a-dun-ci-da'-de *f.* crookedness.
a-dun'-co, =a *adj.* hooked, crooked.
a-du-rên-cia *f.* burning, causticity.
a-du-ren'-te *m.* caustic treatment.

a-du-rir' *tr.v.* to burn, to cauterize.
a-dus-tão' *f.* cauterization.
a-dus'-to, =a *adj.* burning.
a-du-zir' *tr.v.* to adduce.
ad-ven-tí-cio, =a *adj.* adventitious.
ad-ven'-to *m.* advent; Advent.
ad-ver-bi-al' *adj.* adverbial.
ad-vér-bio *m.* adverb.
ad-ver-sá-rio *m.* adversary.
ad-ver-si-da'-de *f.* adversity.
ad-ver-tên-cia *f.* warning; preface.
ad-ver-ti-men'-to *m.* warning.
ad-ver-tir' *tr.v.* to warn, to give notice, to call attention to.
ad-vin-cu-lar' *adj.* dependent, connected.
ad-vo-ca-ci'-a *f.* advocacy.
ad-vo-ca-tá-rio, =a *adj.* advocatory.
ad-vo-ga'-do *m.* lawyer, advocate.
ad-vo-gar' *tr.v.* to advocate; —=**se** *refl.v.* to follow the profession of law.
a-é-re-o, =a *adj.* aerial.
a-e-ró-dro-mo *m.* airdrome.
a-e-ro-náu-ti-co, =a *adj.* aeronautic.
a-e-ro-pla'-no *m.* airplane.
a-fã' *m.* anxiety, intense work.
a-fa-bi-li-da'-de *f.* affability.
a-fá-vel *adj.* affable.
a-fa-ti-gar' *tr.v.* to cause fatigue to, to tire; to tease, to annoy, to molest; —=**se** *refl.v.* to become tired, to become fatigued.
a-fa-ti-go'-so, =a *adj.* tiring, fatiguing.
a-fa-gar' *tr.v.* to caress; to encourage; to retain in memory with a sense of pleasure; to smooth, to level down hilly places; to touch lightly.
a-fai-mar' *tr.v.* to starve.
a-fa-ma'-do, =a *adj.* notable, well-known.
a-fa-nar' *tr.v.* to seek, to acquire, but feeling tired, weary.
a-fa-no'-so, =a *adj.* causing, or full of, weariness.
a-fa-si'-a *f.* aphasia.
a-fas-ta'-do, =a *adj.* remote, far away.
a-fas-ta-men'-to *m.* distance, remoteness; separation.
a-fas-tar' *tr.v.* to push away, to place at a distance; to prevent; —=**se** *refl.v.* to move away.
a-fa-zer' *tr.v.* to accustom, to create the habit; —=**se** *refl.v.* to feel at home in a foreign country, to become accustomed.
a-fa-ze'-res *m.pl.* occupations, business activities.
a-fe-ar' *tr.v.* to make ugly; to exaggerate the seriousness of.
a-fec-ção' *f.* abnormal body condition, disease.
A-fe-gão', A-fe-ga'-ne or **A-fe-gã'** *m.* native of Afghanistan.
a-fei-ço-ar' *tr.v.* to give feature, form, or figure to, to mold; to adapt, to adjust.
a-fei-ção' *f.* affection, friendship, love.
a-fei-ço-a'-do *m.* friend.
a-fei-ço-ar' *intr.v.* to become affected; *tr.v.* to shape, to form, to fashion.
a-fei'-to, =a *adj.* accustomed, acclimated.
a-fe-ri-ção' *f.* check (to indicate correctness).
a-fe-ri-dor' *m.* person making comparisons, instrument used in checking.
a-fe-rir' *tr.v.* to compare; to check instruments of measure with standard; to check (with a check mark).
a-fer-ra'-do, =a *adj.* insistent, pertinacious, stubborn.

a-fer-rar' *tr.v.* to hold fast; —*se refl.v.* to become obstinate, to harden.

a-fer-re-ta'-do, *=a adj.* marked, blackened, with branding irons.

a-fer-ven-tar' *tr.v.* to parboil, to boil only a short time.

a-fer-vo-rar' *tr.v.* to excite fervor in, to communicate ardor, to stimulate; to place in boiling water and continue cooking at a rapid boil.

a-fes-to-ar' *tr.v.* to decorate with festoons.

a-fe-ta-ção' *f.* affectation.

a-fe-tar' *tr.v.* to pretend, to imitate; to attack some part of the body (a disease); —*se refl.v.* to affect; to present a pose of ridiculous elegance or refinement.

a-fe'-to *m.* affection, friendship.

a-fe-tuo'-so, *=a adj.* affectionate.

a-fi-am-brar' *tr.v.* to cure meat like ham, to cook meat by method similar to that used for ham.

a-fi-an-çar' *tr.v.* to guarantee; —*se refl.v.* to render or give guaranty.

a-fi-a-ção' *f.* sharpening.

a-fi-a-dor' *m.* knife-sharpener, scissors-grinder.

a-fi-ar' *tr.v.* to sharpen (cutting edge); to perfect; to prepare for.

a-fi-ci-o-na'-do *m.* enthusiast, amateur.

a-fi-gu-ra-ção' *f.* imagination, apprehension.

a-fi-gu-rar' *tr.v.* to shape, to fashion; to imagine; —*se* to imagine, to fancy; to picture in one's mind.

a-fi-gu-ra-ti'-vo, *=a adj.* figurative.

a-fi-lar' *tr.v.* to make a check on (weights, measures); to stretch out; to incite dogs against; to make thin, or fine.

a-fi-lha'-da *f.* god-daughter.

a-fi-lha-dis'-mo *m.* (political) patronage.

a-fi-lha'-do *m.* god-son.

a-fi-lha'-gem *f.* favoritism, consideration (to relatives or friends), nepotism.

a-fi-lhar' *intr.v.* to blossom, to bud; to beget offspring.

a-fi-li-ar' *tr.v.* to affiliate.

a-fim' *m.* kinsman.

a-fi-nal' *adv.* finally.

a-fi-na-ção' *f.* tuning, refining.

a-fi-na'-do, *=a adj.* in tune; well-made; expert.

a-fi-na'-gem *f.* refining of metals.

a-fi-nar' *tr.v.* to tune (musical instruments); to refine (metals).

a-fin-ca'-do, *=a adj.* persevering.

a-fin-ca-men'-to *m.* insistence, stubbornness.

a-fin-car' *tr.v.* to place firmly; *intr.v.* to resist, to not give in; —*se* to become obstinate.

a-fi-ni-da'-de *f.* affinity.

a-fi'-o *adv.* in a row, following regularly one after another.

a-fir-mar' *tr.v.* to affirm; —*se refl.v.* to observe carefully in order to make sure.

a-fir-ma-ti'-va *f.* affirmation.

a-fi-ve-lar' *tr.v.* to fasten, to hold together with a buckle.

a-fi-xa-ção' *f.* affixation.

a-fi-xar' *tr.v.* to affix.

a-fi'-xo *m.* affix.

a-flar' *tr.v.* to breathe on, to be moved back and forth by the wind; to inspire.

a-fla'-to *m.* afflatus.

a-fleu-mar' *tr.v.* to make phlegmatic.

a-fli-ção' *f.* affliction.

a-fli-gir' *tr.v.* to afflict.

a-fli'-to, *=a adj.* afflicted, distressed.

a-flo-ra-men'-to *m.* outcrop (vein of mineral ore).

a-flo-rar' *tr.v.* to make level, or flush, with; *intr.v.* to come to the surface, to crop out.

a-flu-ên-cia *f.* convergence; abundance; crowd.

a-flu-en'-te *m.* tributary; *adj.* affluent.

a-flu-ir' *intr.v.* to flow into; to converge; to abound, to be plentiful.

a-flux' *adv.* abundantly.

a-fo-bar'-se *refl.v.* to be greatly upset and hurried; to become confused and wearied.

a-fo-gar' *tr.v.* to drown; to choke; to smother.

a-fô-go *m.* suffocation, affliction, haste, oppression.

a-foi-tar' *tr.v.* to encourage, stimulate, make fearless.

a-foi-te'-za *f.* courage, audacity.

a-foi'-to, *=a adj.* fearless, brave.

a-fo'-ra *adv.* except, outside of; excluding.

a-fo-rar' *tr.v.* to give or receive property in consideration of a yearly rental fee; —*se refl.v.* to be arrogant.

a-fo-ris'-mo *m.* aphorism.

a-for-mo-se-a-men'-to *m.* act of beautifying.

a-for-mo-se-ar' *tr.v.* to beautify.

a-for-qui-lhar' *tr.v.* to prop up with a forked stick; to make forked.

a-for-rar' *tr.v.* to free (slave); to tuck up sleeve or turn back cuff.

a-for-tu-na'-do, *=a adj.* wealthy, lucky, fortunate.

a-for-tu-nar' *tr.v.* to enrich, to make happy.

a-fran-ce-sa'-do, *=a adj.* like French, affecting French manners.

a-fran-ce-sar' *tr.v.* to give French atmosphere.

Á-fri-ça *f.* Africa; meter uma lança em África to succeed in a difficult enterprise.

a-fri-ca'-nas *f.pl.* African women; heavy gold ear-rings; African native jewelry.

a-fri-ca-nis'-mo *m.* Africanism.

a-fri-ca-ni-zar' *tr.v.* to Africanize.

a-fri-ca'-no, *=a adj.* African.

á-fri-co *m.* wind from southeast.

a-fro-di-si'-a *f.* aphrodisia.

a-fro-di-sí-a-co, *=a adj.* aphrodisiac.

a-fro-di'-ta *adj.* cryptogamous.

a-fron'-ta *f.* affront, abuse; suffocation.

a-fron-ta-ção' *f.* suffocation, difficulty in breathing.

a-fron-ta-dor' *m.* insulter.

a-fron-tar' *tr.v.* to affront, to insult.

a-fron-to'-so, *=a adj.* abusive, insulting.

a-frou-xa-men'-to *m.* act of loosening.

a-frou-xar' *tr.v.* to loosen.

a-fu-gen-tar' *tr.v.* to put to flight, to drive away.

a-fun-da-men'-to *m.* sinking.

a-fun-dar' *tr.v.* to sink; to make deep.

a-fu-ni-lar' *tr.v.* to make funnel-shaped, or narrow.

a-fu-são' *f.* affusion.

a-ga-cha'-da *f.* (Brazil) sudden running of startled animals.

a-ga-cha'-dos *m.pl.* adulation, courtesies, salaam.

a-ga-char' *=se refl.v.* to crouch, to stoop; (fig.) to be humiliated.

a-ga'-cho *m.* crouching position.

a-ga-fi'-ta *f.* turquoise.

a-gal-gar' *intr.v.* to acquire proportions, form and nature of greyhound.

a-ga-lha'-do, =a *adj.* having branches.

a-ga-lhar' *intr.v.* to grow branches.

a-gar-rar' *tr.v.* to hold, to grasp, to catch.

a-ga-sa-lhar' *tr.v.* to shelter, to cover against weather; to keep warm.

a-gas-tar'=se *refl.v.* to become irritated, bored, anxious.

a-gas-ta-di'-ço, =a *adj.* easily wearied.

á-ga-ta *f.* agate.

a-gên-cia *f.* agency.

a-gen-cia-dor' *m.* agent.

a-gen-ci-ar' *tr.v.* to negotiate, to manage, to solicit.

a-gen'-te *m.* agent.

a-gi-gan-ta'-do, =a *adj.* having proportions of giant.

á-gil *adj.* agile, nimble, light.

a-gi-li-da'-de *f.* agility.

á-gio *m.* interest, exchange; usury.

a-gio'-ta *m.* stock-jobber; usurer.

a-gio-tar' *intr.v.* to lend money at high rate of exchange.

a-gir' *tr.v.* to act, to work.

a-gi-ta-ção' *f.* agitation.

a-gi-ta'-do, =a *adj.* rough, agitated.

a-gi-ta-dor' *m.* agitator.

a-gi-tar' *tr.v.* to agitate.

a-glo-me-ra-ção' *f.* agglomeration.

a-glo-me-rar' *tr.v.* to agglomerate.

a-glu-ti-na-ção' *f.* agglutination.

a-glu-ti-nar' *tr.v.* to agglutinate.

ag-nos-ti-cis'-mo *m.* agnosticism.

ag-nós-ti-co, =a *adj.* agnostic.

a-go-ni'-a *f.* agony, affliction, nausea.

a-go-nia'-do, =a *adj.* suffering, deeply anxious, tortured in mind.

a-go-nia-dor' *adj.* torturing.

a-go-niar' *tr.v.* to agonize, to cause suffering, to nauseate.

a-go-ni-zan'-te *adj.* dying, in agony.

a-go-ni-zar' *tr.v.* to agonize.

a-go'-ra *adv.* now, at the present time.

a-go-ri'-nha *adv.* a very short time ago, this very time, almost at this very moment.

A-gos-ti'-nho *m.* an Augustinian; *adj.* pertaining to St. Augustine, or any one of the Orders deriving their name from him.

a-gôs-to *m.* August, eighth month of the year.

a-gou-rar' *tr.v.* to augur.

a-gou'-ro *m.* augury, prediction, presage.

a-gou-rei'-ro, =a *adj.* ill-omened; superstitious.

a-gra-ci-ar' *tr.v.* to grant favors or honors.

a-gra-dar' *tr.v.* to please, to satisfy; —=se *refl.v.* to like, to be satisfied with.

a-gra-dá-vel *adj.* pleasing, agreeable.

a-gra-de-cer' *tr.v.* to show gratitude for; to thank; to return favors.

a-gra-de-ci'-do, =a *adj.* thankful, grateful.

a-gra-de-ci-men'-to *m.* thankfulness; acknowledgment; gratitude.

a-gra'-do *m.* pleasure, satisfaction, affability.

a-grar' *tr.v.* to cultivate land, or to prepare the land to be cultivated.

a-grá-rio, =a *adj.* agrarian.

a'-gro *m.* field, cultivated land.

a-gra-va-men'-to *m.* aggravation.

a-gra-van'-te *adj.* aggravating.

a-gra'-vo *m.* offense, damage, injury; judicial proceedings against alleged or real injustice.

a'-gre *adj.* biting, sour.

a-gre-dir' *tr.v.* to attack, to assault, to injure, to insult.

a-gre-ga-ção' *f.* aggregation.

a-gre-ga'-do *m.* aggregate; (Brazil) rentfarmer.

a-gre-gar' *tr.v.* to add, to associate.

a-gres'-te *adj.* agrestal, rural, rough.

a-gres-são' *f.* aggression.

a-gres-si'-vo, =a *adj.* aggressive.

a-gres-sor' *m.* aggressor.

a-gri-ão' *m.* water-cress.

a-grí-co-la *m.* farmer; *adj.* agricultural.

a-gri-cul-tar' *tr.v.* to farm, to cultivate land; *intr.v.* to engage in agriculture as a profession.

a-gri-cul-tor' *m.* farmer, agriculturist.

a-gri-cul-tu'-ra *f.* agriculture.

a-gri-lho-a-men'-to *m.* shackling, chaining.

a-gri-lho-ar' *tr.v.* to shackle the feet, to chain; (fig.) to restrain.

a-gri-men-sar' *tr.v.* to survey agricultural lands.

a-gri-sa-lha'-do, =a *adj.* greyish.

a-gri-sa-lhar' *tr.v.* to make grey in color.

a-gro-no-mi'-a *f.* agronomy.

a-gro-nô-mi-co, =a *adj.* agronomic.

a-grô-no-mo *m.* agronomist.

a-gru-pa-men'-to *m.* group, assembly.

a-gru-par' *tr.v.* to group.

á-gua *f.* water; — arriba *adv.* against the current; — benta *f.* holy water; —=s abaixo *adv.* down stream; — de pé *f.* spring water; — doce *f.* fresh water; — dormente *f.* stagnant water; —=s mortas *f.pl.* neap tide; — potável *f.* drinking water; — furtada *f.* attic; top floor with dormer windows.

a-gua'-ça *f.* puddle.

a-gua-cei'-ro *m.* sudden, heavy shower of short duration.

a-gua-çal' *m.* swamp land.

a-gua'-da *f.* taking on of fresh water by ships; place where fresh water is taken on ships.

a-gua-dor' *m.* watering pot; water carrier.

á-gua=for'-te *f.* nitric acid.

á-gua=for-tis'-ta *m.* engraver.

á-gua=ma-ri'-nha *f.* aqua marine.

á-gua=mor'-na *m.* harmless fellow.

á-gua=rás *f.* spirit of turpentine.

a-guar'-da *f.* waiting.

a-guar-dar' *tr.v.* to await; to guard; to observe.

a-guar-den'-te *f.* whisky, cognac.

a-guar-den-tei'-ro *m.* manufacturer or dealer in whisky; whisky drinker, inebriate, drunk.

a-gua-re'-la *f.* water colors.

a-gua-re-lis'-ta *m.* painter in water colors.

á-gua=su'-ja *f.* questionable business; gossip; disorder; quarrel.

a-gu'-ça *f.* haste, zeal, diligence, activity.

a-gu-çar' *tr.v.* to make pointed; to sharpen (knife); to stimulate, to quicken; to make active, diligent.

a-gu-dez', a-gu-de'-za *f.* sharpness, quick comprehension; subtlety, sagacity.

a-gu'-do, =a *adj.* sharp, acute; sharppointed; fine, subtle.

a-guen-tar' *tr.v.* to sustain, to support, to maintain.

a-guer-ri-lhar' *tr.v.* to make guerrilla warfare.

a-guer-ri'-do, ⸗a *adj.* courageous, unafraid in war.

a-guer-rir' *tr.v.* to accustom to struggles, work or mishaps; to make valorous.

á-guia *f.* eagle; person of great talent and perspicacity.

a-gui-lho-a'-da *f.* goading.

a-gui-lho-a-dor' *m.* goader; (fig.) instigator.

a-gui-lho-ar' *tr.v.* to goad.

a-gui-lho-ei'-ro *m.* goad maker, seller of goads.

a-gu-lha'-da *f.* needle-full of thread; needle-prick.

a-gu-lhar' *tr.v.* to prick with a needle, to torture, to trouble.

a-gu-lhe-a'-do, ⸗a *adj.* needle-shaped.

a-gu-lhei'-ro *m.* needle cushion.

a-gu-lhe'-ta *f.* metal point on shoe lace.

a-gu'-lha *f.* needle, mountain peak; switch (railroad); fermentation point (wine); **— de marear** *m.* mariner's compass.

a-í *adv.* there, in that place; in that respect.

ai'-a *f.* personal maid; children's governess, or companion.

ai'-o *m.* tutor for rich, or noble, children, shield-bearer.

Ai-Je-sús *interj.* indicative of pain, or surprise; *m.* best beloved.

a-in'-da *adv.* still, yet, again, besides, at least, some day, notwithstanding, also; **— bem** fortunately; **— agora** almost at this moment; **— quando** even though; **— que** although; **— uma vez** once more.

ai-pim' *m.* cultivated cassava, table manioc.

ai'-po *m.* celery.

ai-ra'-do, ⸗a *adj.* airy, visionary, vagabond.

ai-ro-si-da'-de *f.* elegance, graciousness, distinction.

ai-ro'-so, ⸗a *adj.* gracious, graceful, elegant.

a-ja-e-za'-do, ⸗a *adj.* caparisoned, bedecked.

a-ja-e-zar' *tr.v.* to adorn, to dress up; to caparison.

a-jan-ta-ra'-do *m.* a heavy lunch at a later hour than usual, *e.g.* Sunday dinner.

a-jar-di-nar' *tr.v.* to make into garden.

a-jei-tar' *tr.v.* to adjust, to arrange, to adapt.

a-jo-a-ne-ta'-do, ⸗a *adj.* having bunions, or enlarged joints of toes.

a-jo-e-lha'-do, ⸗a *adj.* kneeling.

a-jo-e-lhar' *intr.v.* to kneel.

a-jor-na-la'-do, ⸗a *adj.* paid by the day.

a-jor-na-lar' *tr.v.* to work by the day, being paid each day.

a-ju'-da *f.* aid, assistance; **— de custo** allowance, bonus.

a-ju-dan'-te *m.* helper, assistant; adjutant.

a-ju-dar' *tr.v.* to help, to aid.

a-jui-za'-do, ⸗a *adj.* sensible.

a-jui-zar' *tr.v.* to form opinion or judgment; to take question to law.

a-jun-ta-men'-to *m.* crowd, meeting, assembly; addition.

a-jun-tar' *tr.v.* to assemble, to unite, to add, to place close to.

a-ju-ra-men-tar' *tr.v.* to give an oath,

to take an oath; **—⸗se** *refl.v.* to bind oneself by an oath.

a-jus-ta-men'-to *m.* adjustment, agreement.

a-jus-tar' *tr.v.*, *intr.v.* to adjust; to agree.

a-jus'-te *m.* agreement, accord, settlement.

a'-la *f.* isle; wing; row; protecting rail or wall of bridge; flank of army in position for battle.

A-lá, *m.* Allah.

a-lar' *tr.v.* to form in rows, to give wings or handles to, to make fly, to raise (the flag), to lift up.

a-la-bar'-da *f.* halberd.

a-la-bas-tri'-te *f.* variety of gypsum.

a-la-bas'-tro *m.* alabaster.

á-la-cre *adj.* alacritous.

a-la-cri-da'-de *f.* alacrity.

a-la-dro-a'-do, ⸗a *adj.* addicted to thieving; **peso — fraudulent** weight.

a-la-dro-ar' *tr.v.* to rob, to defraud.

a-la-ga-ção' *f.* periodic flooding of a river basin (particularly of the Amazon).

a-la-ga-di'-ço, ⸗a *adj.* wet; subject to floods.

a-la-ga'-do, ⸗a *adj.* full, soaked, running over.

a-la-ga-men'-to *m.* overflow, inundation; ruin.

a-la-gar' *tr.v.* to overflow, to inundate.

a-lam-bi-ca'-do, ⸗a *adj.* affected, presumptuous, ridiculously made up.

a-lam-bi-car' *tr.v.* to distill; to refine to highest degree (speech, manners).

a-lam-bi'-que *m.* alembic.

a-lam-bi-quei'-ro *m.* distiller.

a-la-me'-da *f.* drive-way, or walk, bordered by trees.

á-la-mo *m.* alder (shrub).

a-lan-ce-a'-do, ⸗a *adj.* embittered.

a-lan-ce-ar' *tr.v.* to wound with a lance.

a-la-ran-ja'-do, ⸗a *adj.* orange-colored, orange-shaped.

a-lar'-de *m.* vanity, ostentation, show, parade.

a-lar-de-ar' *tr.v.* to make a great show of, to be ostentatious.

a-lar-gar' *tr.v.* to widen, to amplify, to develop; to let go, to loose; **—⸗se** *refl.v.* to dwell upon at some length; **— o passo** to walk fast.

a-la-ri'-da *f.* clamor of voices; confusion of shouting, or of weeping.

a-lar-man'-te *adj.* alarming.

a-lar-mar' *tr.v.* to alarm, to frighten, to shock.

a-lar'-me *m.* alarm.

a-lar-mis'-ta *m.* alarmist.

a-las-tra-men'-to *m.* spreading.

a-las-trar' *tr.v.* to spread over.

a-la-ti-nar' *tr.v.* to Latinize.

a-la-van'-ca *f.* lever, crowbar; **— de engrenagem** gear lever; **— de câmbio** gear shift; **— de embraiagem** clutch; **— de freio** brake.

a-la-zão' *m.* bay horse; reddish brown color.

al-ba-nês *m.* Albanian; Albanian language; *adj.* Albanian; **al-ba-ne'-sa** *f.* Albanian woman; white anemone.

al-ba-troz' *m.* albatross.

al-ber-ga-dor' *m.* inn-keeper.

al-ber-gar' *tr.v.* to give lodging; to harbor.

al-ber-ga-ri'-a *f.* hotel, hostelry, boarding-house.

al-ber'-gue *m.* shelter; refuge.

al-bi'-no *m.* albino.
al-bú-men *m.* albumen.
al-bu-mi-no'-so, ₌a *adj.* albuminous.
al'-ça *f.* handle; — **de mira** gun-sight.
al-cá-cer *m.* palace, castle, fort, sumptuous habitation.
al-car-ce-re'-no, **al-ca-ce-ren'-se** *m.* one born in a sumptuous home.
al-ca-cho'-fra *f.* artichoke.
al-ca-cho-fra'-do *m.* embroidery in the form of an artichoke.
al-ça'-gem *f.* preparation of printed sheets for binding.
al-cai'-de *m.* alcaide, mayor.
al-ca-les-cên-cia *f.* alkalescence.
al-ca-lí *m.* alkali.
al-ca-li-ci-da'-de *f.* alkalinity.
al-ca-li-nar'-se *refl.v.* to become alkaline.
al-ca-li'-no, ₌a *adj.* alkaline.
al-ca-li-za-ção' *f.* alkalization.
al-ca-li-zar' *tr.v.* to alkalize.
al-ca-lói-de *m.* alkaloid.
al-can-ça-di'-ço, ₌a *adj.* easily reached, easily obtained.
al-can-ça-men'-to *m.* achievement.
al-can-çar' *tr.v.* to reach, to come up to, to achieve, to obtain, to perceive, to understand.
al-can-çá-vel *adj.* attainable; susceptible of accomplishment.
al-can'-ce *m.* range (of a gun), range of vision, reach, achievement, intelligence, value, importance; default (in accounts of a public official).
al-ça₌pão *m.* man-hole, trap-door.
al-çar' *tr.v.* to raise, to elevate, to build.
al-ca-téi-a *f.* pack of wolves; group of any ferocious animals; gang of criminals; **estar de** — to be engaged in the work of a spy (pop.), to watch, to be aware.
al-ca-ti'-fa *f.* large carpet; creeping vine covering the ground.
al-ca-ti-far' *tr.v.* to cover with carpet, to put down carpets; to cover the ground as with a carpet.
al-ca-ti-fei'-ro *m.* carpet manufacturer.
al-ca'-tra *f.* rump cut of beef.
al-ca-trão' *m.* tar, pitch.
al-ca-tro-ar' *tr.v.* to cover with tar, to apply tar or pitch.
al-ca-truz' *m.* bucket on endless chain used to draw water from well.
al-ca-tru-za'-do, ₌a*adj.* concave, curved, bucket-shaped.
al-ci-ão', **al-ci-o'-ne**, **al-ci-on'** *m.* halcyon; one of the polyps.
al-ci-ô-ni-co, ₌a *adj.* halcyon.
al-coi'-ce *m.* brothel, house of prostitution.
al-coi-cei'-ro *m.* owner or frequenter of brothel.
al-co-ol' *m.* alcohol.
al-co-ó-li-co, ₌a *adj.* alcoholic; *m.* alcoholic.
al-co-o-lis'-ta *m.* alcoholist.
al-co-o-li-zar' *tr.v.* to alcoholize.
al-co-rão' *m.* the Koran.
al-co'-va *f.* bed-room; hide-away.
al-co-vis'-ta *m.* effeminate man.
al-co-vi-tar' *tr.v.* to serve as go-between in love affairs, to incite, to gossip.
al-co-vi-tei'-ra *f.* white slave procurer, trouble-maker.
al-cu'-nha *f.* nickname; epithet.
al-cu-nhar' *tr.v.* to give a nickname to.
al-de-ão' *m.* country man, villager.

al-dei'-a *f.* hamlet, rural settlement, (Brazil) in colonial times Indian settlement under supervision of missionary.
al-dra'-bas *f.pl.* leather leggings used by the *sertanejos* (back country people) of Northeast Brazil.
al-dra'-va *f.* door-knocker.
á-le-a or **a-lei'-a** *f.* corridor, alley, garden walk bordered with shrubbery or flowers; luck, good fortune.
a-le-crim' *m.* rosemary.
a-le-ga-ção' *f.* allegation.
a-le-gar' *tr.v.* to allege.
a-le-go-ri'-a *f.* allegory.
a-le-gó-ri-co, ₌a *adj.* allegorical.
a-le-go-ris'-ta *m.* allegorist.
a-le-go-ri-zar' *tr.v.* to allegorize.
a-le-gra-men'-to *m.* pleasure, diversion.
a-le-grar' *tr.v.* to gladden, to beautify, to be slightly tipsy; (arch.) to repoint (building stones).
a-le'-gre *adj.* happy, content, pleased; tipsy.
a-le-gri'-a *f.* joy, contentment.
a-!ei-jão' *m.* deformity; moral defect.
a-lei-ja-men'-to *m.* crippling.
a-lei-jar' *tr.v.* to cripple, to maim.
a-lei-ta-men'-to *m.* suckling.
a-lei-tar' *tr.v.* to suckle, to nurse.
a-lei'-ve *m.* fraud, calumny.
a-lei-ve-si'-a *f.* treachery.
a-lei-vo'-so, ₌a *adj.* disloyal, fraudulent, perfidious.
a-lei-xar' *tr.v.* to place at a distance; —₌se *refl.v.* to go far away.
a-le-lu'-i-a *f.* halleluiah.
a-lém *adv.* beyond, there further ahead, still further on.
A-le-ma'-nha *m.* Germany.
a-le-ma-ni-co, ₌a *adj.* Alemannic; Germanic.
a-le-mão *m.* German; German language.
a-len-ta'-do, ₌a *adj.* energetic, capable, abundant, limitless.
a-len-tar' *tr.v.* to encourage, to animate, to nourish.
a-len-te-cer' *intr.v.* to slow down.
a-len'-to *m.* respiration; food; enthusiasm, effort, courage.
á-le-o, ₌a *adj.* winged; (heraldry) Alerion.
a-ler-gi'-a *f.* allergy.
a-ler'-ta *interj.* attention!; *m.* warning signal to be on the watch; *adv.* vigilantly.
a-le-tri'-a *f.* fine spaghetti, vermicelli.
al'-fa *f.* Greek letter alpha.
al-fa-be-ta-ção' *f.* alphabetization.
al-fa-be-tar' *tr.v.* alphabetize.
al-fa-bé-ti-co, ₌a *adj.* alphabetic.
al-fa-be-ti-zar' *tr.v.* to teach to read.
al-fa-be'-to *m.* alphabet.
al-fa'-ce *f.* lettuce.
al-fa'-fa *f.* lucern, alfalfa.
al-fai-a'-ta *f.* woman tailor.
al-fai-a-tar' *tr.v.* to sew; *intr.v.* to work as a tailor.
al-fai-a-ta-ri'-a *f.* tailor shop.
al-fai-a'-te *m.* tailor.
al-fân-de-ga *f.* custom-house.
al-fan-de-ga'-gem *f.* duty.
al-fan-de-gar' *tr.v.* to store at custom-house, to ship through custom-house, to pay duty for.
al-fan-de-guei'-ro, ₌a *adj.* relative to duty or to custom-house.
al-far-rá-bio *m.* old book of little value.
al-far-ra-bis'-ta *m.* collector and seller of such books.

al-fa-ze'-ma *f.* lavender.
al-fe'-res *m.* second lieutenant, sub-lieutenant.
al-fim' *adv.* finally.
al-fi-ne-tar' *tr.v.* to prick, to satirize, to wound (the feelings of); to pin on.
al-fi-nê-te *m.* pin; al-fi-nê-tes *m.pl.* pin money.
al-fi-ne-tei'-ra *f.* pin cushion.
al-for-jar' *tr.v.* to put in the saddlebag; to put in suit pockets.
al-for'-je *m.* alforja; saddlebag.
al-for-ri'-a *f.* liberty granted to a slave; carta de — to document conferring liberty.
al-for-ri-ar' *tr.v.* to free, to redeem, to grant liberty to.
al-ga-ris'-mo *m.* character by which a number is represented, digit.
al-ga-zar'-ra *f.* noisy conversation, clamor.
ál-ge-bra *f.* algebra.
al-gé-bri-co, ⸗a *adj.* algebraic.
al-ge-bris'-ta *m.* algebraist.
al-ge'-ma *f.* handcuff, manacle; (fig.) oppression.
al-ge-mar' *tr.v.* to handcuff; (fig.) to oppress, to dominate, to shackle.
al-gen'-te *adj.* freezing, glacial.
al-gi-dez' *f.* coldness.
ál-gi-do, ⸗a *adj.* glacial, frigid.
al-gi-bei'-ra *f.* pocket.
al'-go *pro.* something; *adv.* somewhat, to a degree.
al-go-dão' *m.* cotton, cotton cloth; — pólvora or fulminante guncotton.
al-go-do-al' *m.* cotton field.
al-go-do-ei'-ro *m.* cotton plant; al-go-do-ei'-ro, ⸗a *adj.* cotton, relative to cotton.
al-goz' *m.* hangman, executioner; (fig.) cruel man.
al-guém *pro.* someone; person of importance, or distinction.
al-gui-dar' *m.* flat pottery or metal dish, somewhat the shape of an inverted truncated cone.
al-gum' *pro.* some; alguns *pl.* more than one; *adj.* mediocre, average, a little; (placed after noun), none, not any.
al-gu'-res *adv.* somewhere.
a-lha-nar' *tr.v.* to make level; (fig.) to make sincere, frank, affable.
a-lhe-a-ção *f.* alienation.
a-lhe-a'-do, ⸗a *adj.* insane; ecstatic.
a-lhe-ar' *tr.v.* to make alien; to transfer the control of something to another; to alienate.
al-hei'-o *m.* that which does not belong to us; *adj.* strange, foreign, alien, improper, opposed, private, exempt, deprived of; belonging to someone else; insane; — de si absorbed.
a'-lho *m.* garlic.
a-lhu'-res *adv.* in another place.
a-li *adv.* there, in that place.
al-i-a'-do *m.* ally; a-li-a'-do, ⸗a *adj.* allied.
a-li-ar' *tr.v.* to ally.
a-li-an'-ça *f.* alliance; wedding ring; anel de — wedding ring.
a-li-ás *adv.* rather, otherwise.
á-li-bi *m.* alibi.
a-li-ca'-te *m.* pliers.
a-li-cer-ça-dor' *adj.* serving as a foundation, having a foundation.
a-li-cer-çar' *tr.v.* to construct foundation; to build the bases, to cement, to make solid.

a-li-cer'-ce *m.* foundation.
a-li-cia-ção' *f.* seduction, corruption.
a-li-cia-men'-to *m.* deception, seduction.
a-li-ci-ar' *tr.v.* to seduce, to invite, to provoke, to deceive.
a-lie-na-ção' *f.* alienation; insanity.
a-lie-na-bi-li-da'-de *f.* alienability.
a-lie-nar' *tr.v.* to alienate; to madden.
a-i.e-ná-vel *adj.* alienable.
a-lie-ní-ge-na *m.* foreigner.
a-lie-nis'-ta *m.* alienist.
a-li-ja-men'-to *m.* jettisoning, lightening, throwing overboard.
a-li-jar' *tr.v.* to jettison, to lighten.
a-li-má-ria *f.* animal (not man); (fig.) stupid, slow person.
a-li-men-tar' *tr.v.* to aliment, to nourish, to sustain.
a-li-men-tí-cio, ⸗a *adj.* nutritive, edible.
a-li-men'-to *m.* food. —s *m.pl.* alimony; maintenance.
a-li-men-to'-so, ⸗a *adj.* nutritious.
a-lin-dar' *tr.v.* to beautify.
a-li-nea *f.* first line of a paragraph; sub-paragraph.
a-li-nha'-do, ⸗a *adj.* in line, carefully dressed, well-groomed.
a-li-nha-men'-to *m.* alignment.
a-li-nhar' *tr.v.* to align, to aline, to line up.
a-li-nha-var' *tr.v.* (sewing) to baste, to outline.
a-li-nha'-vo or a-li-nha'-ve *m.* basting, outline.
a-li-sar' *tr.v.* to smooth, to level; to soften, to sweeten.
a-lis-ta-men'-to *m.* enlistment, recruiting.
a-lis-tan'-do *m.* man to be recruited.
a-lis-tar' *tr.v.* to list, to enlist, to enroll.
a-lí-vi-ar' *tr.v.* to relieve, to alleviate, to lighten (mourning).
a-lí-vio *m.* relief.
al'-ma *f.* soul, spirit; (fig.) courage, enthusiasm; bore (gun); bridge (violin or similar string instrument).
al-ma-na'-que *m.* almanac.
al-me-jar' *tr.v.* to desire ardently.
al-me-já-vel *adj.* desirable.
al-me'-jo *m.* deep desire.
al-mi-ran-ta'-do *m.* Admiralty, post of admiral.
al-mi-ran'-te *m.* high naval officer.
al-mís-car *m.* musk perfume; styrax.
al-mis-ca-rar' *tr.v.* to perfume with musk.
al-mis-ca-rei'-ro *m.* musk deer.
al-mo-çar' *tr.v.* to lunch.
al-mô-ço *m.* lunch; pequeno — breakfast.
al-mo-cre-va-ri'-a *f.* muleteering; license to muleteer.
al-mo-cre'-ve *m.* muleteer.
al-mo-fa'-da *f.* pillow, cushion; pad.
al-mo-fa-dar' *tr.v.* to cover with cushions, to cushion; to carve in high relief.
al-mo-fa-di'-nha *f.* small cushion; compress, dressing; *m.* dude.
al-mo-fa-dis'-mo *m.* extreme elegance.
al-môn-de-gas *f.* fricasseed meat balls, generally ground beef, highly seasoned.
al-mo-xa-ri-fa'-do *m.* warehouse, stock room.
al-mo-xa-ri'-fe *m.* stock clerk.
a-ló *adv.* on the windy side, in the direction from which the wind comes.
a-lô *interj.* hello.

a-lo-cu-ção' f. allocution.

a-ló-gi-co, ·a adj. alogical, obvious.

a-lo-ja-men'-to m. quarters, lodging, storing away.

a-lo-jar' tr.v. to give lodging to, to quartar soldiers, to deposit in warehouse; — ·se refl.v. to take lodging.

a-lom-ba'-do, ·a adj. lazy, indolent, sleepy.

a-lom-bar' tr.v. to put back on book; to arch, to make slightly rounded.

a-lon-ga'-do, ·a adj. distant, lost (of domestic animals).

a-lon-ga-men'-to m. lengthening, prolongation; lateness.

a-lon-gar' tr.v. to lengthen, to prolong; — ·se refl.v. to separate oneself from something; alongar·se da virtude to forsake virtue.

a-lo-pa'-ta m. allopath.

a-lo-pa-ti'-a f. allopathy.

a-lo-pá-ti-co, ·a adj. allopathic.

a-lo-pé-ci-a f. alopecia; loss of hair.

a-lo-pé-ci-co m. person suffering from loss of hair.

a-lo-pé-cio, ·a adj. causing hair to fall out.

a-lo-tar' tr.v. to allot; (Brazil) to watch over a group of domestic animals, especially horses to keep them from becoming scattered.

a-lou-rar' tr.v. to brown by exposure to heat or fire (roast); to gild; to make golden-colored.

al-pa'-ca f. alpaca; manga de — typist in a government office, secretary.

al-par'-ca f. alpargata; hemp sandal.

al-par-ca-ta-ri'-a f. sandal shop.

al-par-ca-tei'-ro m. sandal maker.

al-pen'-dre m. porch; extension of roof over entrance of building; open terrace, or one having roof supported by posts.

al-pes'-tre adj. alpestrine; rocky, Alpine.

al-pi-nis'-mo m. Alpinism.

al-pi'-no, ·a adj. Alpine.

al-que-brar' tr.v. to bend over, to weaken with age.

al-quei'-re m. alqueire (a measure of volume).

al-qui-mi'-a f. alchemy.

al-qui-mis'-ta m. alchemist.

al-ta-na-ri'-a f. haughtiness, superiority, flight of the imagination, elevated thought; hunting high-flying birds with falcons.

al-ta-nar'·se refl.v. to be haughty or arrogant; to raise oneself up.

al-ta-nei'-ro, ·a adj. high-flying; elevating, superb.

al-tar' m. altar.

al-tar·mor' m. principal altar opposite main entrance.

al-tea-men'-to m. raising, elevating; building.

al-te-ar' tr.v. to raise up, to elevate.

al-te-ra-ção' f. alteration, modification, perturbation, degeneration.

al-te-rar' tr.v. to alter; to decompose; to disturb; to change; to falsify; to excite.

al-te-rá-vel adj. alterable.

al-ter-ca-ção' f. altercation.

al-ter-car' intr.v. to quarrel; al-ter-ca-ção' f. altercation.

al-ter-na-ção' f. alternation.

al-ter-na'-do, ·a adj. alternate.

al-ter-na-dor' m. alternator.

al-ter-nan'-te adj. alternant, alternating.

al-ter-nar' tr.v. to alternate.

al-ter-na-ti'-vo, ·a adj. alternative.

al-ter'-no, ·a adj. alternate.

al-te-ro'-so, ·a adj. of great altitude; majestic; grandiose.

al-te'-za f. height; grandeur; Highness.

al-ti-bai'-xos m.pl. unequal elevations of land; (fig.) mixture of good and bad qualities, vicissitudes.

al-ti-lo-quên-cia f. altiloquence.

al-ti-lo-quo, ·a adj. altiloquent.

al-ti-me-tri'-a f. altimetry.

al-tí-me-tro m. altimeter.

al-ti-po-ten'-te adj. all-powerful.

al-ti-so-nan'-te adj. pompous; thunderous.

al-ti-tu'-de f. altitude.

al-ti'-vo, ·a adj. proud, arrogant; high.

al-ti-ve'-za f. pride, arrogance.

al'-ta f. price increase; discharge; elite; upper part of city.

Al-tís-si-mo m. Most High.

al-tis'-ta m. speculator; player of tenor violin or alto saxhorn.

al'-to m. heaven; seat of government; predominant voice or voices in a chorus; tenor violin, alto saxhorn; al-to, ·a adj. high, elevated; excellent; illustrious; important; excessive; remote; expensive; difficult; al-to adv. loudly, interj. order to stop; — mar high seas; por — superficially, without attention to details; fazer — to stop.

al-to-fa-lan'-te m. loud-speaker.

al-tru-ís'-mo m. altruism.

al-tru-ís'-ta m. altruist; adj. altruistic.

al-tu'-ra f. height; stature; importance; firmament; point, juncture.

a-lu-a'-do, ·a adj. influenced by moon; lunatic; (of animals) in heat.

a-lu-ci-na-ção f. hallucination.

a-lu-ci-na-men'-to m. hallucination.

a-lu-ci-nar' tr.v. to hallucinate; — ·se refl.v. to be mistaken, to be over-zealous to the point of fanaticism.

a-lu-dir' intr.v. to allude.

a-lu-ga-dor' m. renter.

a-lu-ga-men'-to m. rent, renting.

a-lu-gar' tr.v. to rent, to hire, to let.

a-lu-guel' m. rental, rent.

a-lu-ir' tr.v. to ruin, to destroy; intr.v. to waver.

a-lú-men m. alum.

a-lu-mia-ção' f. illumination.

a-lu-mi-ar' tr.v. to illuminate; to light; to instruct or enlighten.

a-lu-mí-na f. alumina.

a-lu-mi-na-ção' f. production of alum.

a-lu-mi-na'-gem f. (photo.) alum bath.

a-lu-mi-nar' tr.v. to mix with alum.

a-lu-mi-na'-to m. aluminate.

a-lu-mí-nio m. aluminum.

a-lu-mi-ni'-te m. aluminite.

a-lu'-no m. a-lu'-na f. pupil, student, apprentice.

a-lu-são' f. allusion.

a-lu-si'-vo, ·a adj. allusive.

a-lu-vi-ão' f. alluvium.

al'-va f. dawn; alb.

al-va-cen'-to, ·a adj. whitish.

al-var' adj. whitish; (fig.) simple, silly, foolish.

al-va-rá m. royal decree.

al-va-raz', al-va-ra'-zo m. leprosy; colorless spots on skin.

al-ve-a-men'-to m. white-washing.

al-ve-ar' tr.v. to white-wash.

al-ve-jar' tr.v. to whiten; to aim at.

al-ve-na-ri'-a f. masonry, brick-work.

al-ve-nel', al-ve-ner' or al-ve-néu *m.* stone-mason, brick-layer.

ál-ve-o *m.* bed (of a river); channel or depression.

al-vé-o-lo *m.* alveolus.

al-ví-ça-ras *f.pl.* reward (for bringing good news or finding something lost).

al-vi-ça-rar' *intr.v.* to reward.

al-vi-ça-rei'-ro *m.* bringer of good news; finder of lost articles.

al-vi-tra-dor' *m.* reminder.

al-vi-tra-men'-to *m.* remembrance.

al-vi-trar' *tr.v.* to remind, to suggest, to propose.

al-ví'-tre *m.* reminder, suggestion.

al-vi-trei'-ro *m.* adviser, projector; news-monger.

al'-vo, *=a adj.* white, pure; al'-vo *m.* target, sight, objective.

al-vor' *m.* whiteness, first light of dawn,

al-vo-ra'-da *f.* gray light of dawn; reveille; early morning singing of birds.

al-vo-re-cer' *intr.v.* to dawn, to become dawn; to begin to be manifested (idea, sentiment, quality).

al-vo-re-jar' *tr.v.* to bleach, to whiten.

al-vo-ro-ça'-do, *=a adj.* overjoyed, restless in spirit.

al-vo-ro-çar' *tr.v.* to put in a state of enthusiasm; to provoke tumults.

al-vo-rô-ço *m.* agitation, joyful surprise, excitement.

al-vu'-ra *f.* whiteness, purity.

a'-ma *f.* children's nurse, wet-nurse; — sêca *f.* nurse for children no longer infants.

a-ma-bi-li-da'-de *f.* amiableness; courtesy.

a-ma-ci-ar' *tr.v.* to soften, to smooth.

a-ma'-do, *=a adj.* beloved; a-ma'-do *m.* a-ma'-da *f.* loved one, beloved.

a-ma-dor' *m.* amateur.

a-ma-do-ris'-mo *m.* amateurism.

â-ma-go *m.* pith (of a plant); essential point; heart of something.

a-mal-di-ço-ar' *tr.v.* to curse; to place curses on.

a-ma-lei-to'-do, *=a adj.* sick with malaria, or intermittent fever.

a-mál-ga-ma *m.* amalgam.

a-mal-ga-ma-ção' *f.* amalgamation.

a-mal-ga-mar' *tr.v.* to amalgamate.

a-ma-lu-ca'-do, *=a adj.* half-crazy, foolish, silly.

a-ma-men-ta-ção' *f.* nursing, feeding from the breast.

a-ma-men-tar' *tr.v.* to breast-feed; to nourish; to feed.

a-man-ce-ba-men'-to *m.* concubinage.

a-man-ce-bar'=se *refl.v.* to commit fornication.

a-ma-nhã' *adv.* tomorrow; *m.* following day, future, period about to be entered.

a-ma-nhar' *tr.v.* to cultivate, to prepare.

a-ma-nhe-cer' *intr.v.* to begin, to dawn, to be at dawn.

a-man-sa-men'-to *m.* taming.

a-man-sar' *tr.v.* to domesticate, to tame, to break.

a-man'-te *m.f.* lover, paramour.

a-man-té-ti-co, *=a adj.* affectionate.

a-mar' *tr.v.* to love, to love dearly, to like very much.

a-má-vel *adj.* pleasant, agreeable, amiable.

a-ma-nu-en-sa'-do *m.* office or function of a secretary.

a-ma-nu-en'=se *m.* amanuensis.

a-ma-ra'-gem *f.* landing a seaplane on water.

a-ma-re-la'-do, *=a adj.* yellowish, pale.

a-ma-re-lão' *m.* hookworm disease.

a-ma-re-le-cer' *intr.v.* to become yellow, to turn pale.

a-ma-re-len'-to, *=a adj.* yellow.

a-ma-re-li-dão' *f.* yellowness.

a-ma-re-li-men'-to *m.* turning yellow.

a-ma-re'-lo, *=a adj.* yellow.

a-mar-ga'-do, *=a adj.* bitter.

a-mar-gar' *tr.v.* to make bitter, to suffer from; *intr.v.* to make a bitter taste.

a-mar'-go, *=a adj.* bitter; (fig.) sad, grievous.

a-mar-gor' *m.* bitterness.

a-mar-gu'-ra *f.* bitterness; (fig.) agony of spirit.

a-mar-gu-rar' *tr.v.* to make bitter, to embitter.

a-mar'-ra *f.* hawser, anchor cable.

a-mar-ra-ção' *f.* anchorage.

a-mar-ra-dou'-ro *m.* anchoring, mooring.

a-mar-ra-du'-ra *f.* fastening.

a-mar-rar' *tr.v.* to fasten, to moor; to marry; to compromise.

a-mar-ro-qui-nar' *tr.v.* to make similar to morocco leather.

a-mar-ro-ta'-do, *=a adj.* bruised.

a-mar-ro-tar' *tr.v.* to crush, to crumple, to come out victor; —=se *refl.v.* to become wrinkled, to lose appearance of newness.

a-mar-te-lar' *tr.v.* to hammer; (fig.) to urge persistently, to annoy with urging.

a-ma-siar'=se *refl.v.* to have illicit relations with.

a-má-sio *m.* a-má-sia *f.* lover.

a-mas-sa-dei'-ra *f.* woman who kneads bread.

a-mas-sa-dou'-ro *m.* kneading-board.

a-mas-sa-dor' *m.* man who kneads bread.

a-mas-sa-men'-to *m.* kneading.

a-mas-sar' *tr.v.* to knead, to make into dough; to flatten out.

a-ma-tro-nar'=se *refl.v.* to assume the airs of a matron, to become fat, to age.

a-ma-zo'-na *f.* Amazon.

a-ma-zo-nen'=se *m.f.* citizen of the state of Amazonas; *adj.* relating to the state of Amazonas.

a-ma-zô-ni-co, *=a adj.* relating to Amazonas.

a-ma-zô-nio, *=a adj.* relating to Amazonas.

âm-bar *m.* amber.

am-bi-ção' *f.* ambition.

am-bi-cio-nar' *tr.v.* to desire ardently.

am-bi-cio'-so, *=a adj.* ambitious.

am-bi-des-tri'-a *f.* ambidexterity.

am-bi-des'-tro, *=a adj.* ambidextrous.

am-biên-cia *f.* ambient.

am-bien-tar' *tr.v.* to adapt to surrounding conditions.

am-bi-en'=te *m.* environment, surrounding conditions; *adj.* that which envelops or surrounds something or some one.

am-bies-quer'-do, *=a adj.* awkward.

am-bi-gui-da'-de *f.* ambiguity.

am-bí-guo, *=a adj.* ambiguous, uncertain, hesitant.

am'-bos *pro.* both, the one and the other, the two.

am-bró-sia *f.* ambrosia.

am-bro-sí-a-co, *=a adj.* delicious.

âm-bu-la *f.* vial, small bottle.

am-bu-lân-cia *f.* ambulance.

am-bu-lan'-te *adj.* ambulant.

am-bu-la-ti'-vo =a *adj.* ambulant, vagabond, having no fixed place.

a-me-a'-ça *f.* threat.

a-me-a-çan'-te *adj.* threatening.

a-me-a-çar' *tr.v.* to threaten; *intr.v.* to be imminent.

a-me-a-lhar' *tr.v.* to accumulate money penny by penny in savings box; to economize.

a-me'-ba *f.* amoeba.

a-me-dron-ta-men'-to *m.* shock, fright.

a-me-dron-tar' *tr.v.* to frighten.

a-mei-gar' *tr.v.* to coax, to fondle.

a-mei'-xa *f.* prune; plum.

a-mei-xal' *m.* grove of plum trees.

a-mei-xei'-ra *v.* plum tree.

a-mém *m.*, *adj.* amen.

a-mên-doa *f.* almond.

a-men-do-a'-da *f.* almond milk.

a-men-do-a'-do, =a *adj.* almond-like; prepared with almonds.

a-men-do-ei'-ra *f.* almond tree.

a-men-do-im' *m.* peanut.

a-me-ni-da'-de *f.* amenity.

a-me-ni-na'-do, =a *adj.* childish, weak, whining.

a-me-ni-nar'=se *refl.v.* to be childish.

a-me-ni-za-dor' *adj.* calming.

a-me-ni-zar' *tr.v.* to make amenable, pleasant, charming.

a-me'-no, =a *adj.* amenable, agreeable.

a-me-nor-réi-a *f.* amenorrhea.

a-mer-ce-a-men'-to *m.* mercy, compassion.

a-mer-ce-ar'=se *refl.v.* to have pity upon, to sympathize with.

A-mé-ri-ca *f.* America; something colossal.

a-me-ri-ca-na'-da *f.* American way of doing things.

a-me-ri-ca'-no, =a *adj.* American.

a-me-ri-ca-nis'-mo *m.* admiration and appreciation for things American, especially of the United States.

a-me-ri-ca-nis'-ta *m.* specialist in American affairs, languages, and customs.

a-me-ri-ca-ni-zar' *tr.v.* to Americanize.

a-me-rín-dio *m.* Amer-Indian.

a-me-ris-sa'-gem *f.* alighting on water.

a-me-ris-sar' *intr.v.* to alight on water.

a-mes-qui-nha'-do, =a *adj.* niggardly; unfortunate.

a-mes-qui-nha-men'-to *m.* act of belittling, humiliating, disparaging.

a-mes-qui-nhar' *tr.v.* to belittle, to humiliate, to disparage.

a-mes-tra-dor' *m.* trainer.

a-mes-tra-men'-to *m.* training.

a-mes-trar' *tr.v.* to teach, to train, to become expert.

a-me-tis'-ta *f.* amethyst.

a-mi'-do or **á-mi-do** *m.* starch.

a-mi-do-a'-do, =a *adj.* starchy.

a-mi-ga-ção' *f.* concubinage.

a-mi-gar'=se *refl.v.* to become friends with, *i.e.* to initiate illicit relations with.

a-mi-gá-vel *adj.* friendly, amiable.

a-míg-da-la *f.* tonsil.

a-míg-da-li'-te *f.* tonsillitis.

a-mi'-go *m.* **a-mi'-ga** *f.* friend.

a-mi-mar' *tr.v.* to pet, to spoil by indulgence.

a-mi-u-da'-do, =a *adj.* minute; frequent, repeated.

a-mi-u-dar' *tr.v.* to repeat, to make frequent.

a-mi-ú-de *adv.* often, repeatedly, frequently.

a-mi-za'-de *f.* friendship.

am-né-si-a *f.* amnesia.

a'-mo *m.* master (of house); employer; husband of woman servant.

a-mo-cam-bar' *tr.v.* to meet together in a hidden spot; to hide; —=se *refl.v.* to become lost in woods (cattle).

a-mo-der-nar' *tr.v.* to modernize.

a-mo-e-dar' *tr.v.* to make into coins; to coin.

a-mo-e-dá-vel *adj.* coinable.

a-mo-fi-na-ção' *f.* fatigue, nuisance.

a-mo-fi-nar' *tr.v.* to annoy, to tire out.

a-moi-tar'=se *refl.v.* to hide.

a-mo-jar' *tr.v.* to milk, to become filled with milk (of a cow's udders).

a-mô-jo *m.* lactation, lactescence.

a-mo-la-dei'-ra *f.* whet-stone.

a-mo-la-dor' *m.* grinder.

a-mo-lan'-te *adj.* persistent, wearying, annoying.

a-mo-lar' *tr.v.* to sharpen on whet-stone or grind-stone; to deceive; to create difficulties.

a-mol-dar' *tr.v.* to mold, to adapt, to accustom; —=se *refl.v.* to adjust to a mold or model.

a-mo-le-ca'-do, =a *adj.* roguish, bad.

a-mo-le-car' *tr.v.* to ridicule, to degrade, to have low practices.

a-mo-le-cer' *tr.v.* to soften, to mollify.

a-mo-le-ci'-do, =a *adj.* soft, tenderhearted.

a-mo-le-ci-men'-to *m.* softening, enervation; effeminacy.

a-mol-gar' *tr.v.* to flatten, to beat down, to bruise, to be victor over.

a-mô-ni-a *f.* ammonia (water solution).

a-mo-nia-ca'-do, =a *adj.* ammoniacal.

a-mo-ní-a-co *m.* ammonia (gas).

a-mon-to-a'-do *m.* mixture, pile.

a-mon-to-a-dor' *m.* plow with large wings.

a-mon-to-a-men'-to *m.* accumulation, pile.

a-mon-to-ar' *tr.v.* to pile up, to accumulate, to bunch.

a-mor' *m.* love; Cupid; **por — de** for love, because of; **—s** *m.pl.* love affair; love-making; beloved.

a-mo'-ra *f.* mulberry (fruit).

a-mo-ra'-do, =a *adj.* mulberry-colored.

a-mo-rei'-ra *f.* mulberry tree.

a-mor-da-ça-men'-to *m.* gagging.

a-mor-da-çar' *tr.v.* to gag, to silence.

a-mo-re-na'-do, =a *adj.* turned brown, almost brown.

a-mor-fi'-a *f.* amorphia.

a-mór-fi-co, =a *adj.* amorphic.

a-mor'-fo, =a *adj.* amorphous.

a-mor-na'-do, =a *adj.* luke-warm, tepid.

a-mor-nar' *tr.v.* to make tepid, lukewarm.

a-mor-ne-cer' *tr.v.* to make tepid; *intr.v.* to cool, to lose enthusiasm.

a-mo-ro-si-da'-de *f.* amorousness.

a-mo-ro'-so, =a *adj.* amorous.

a-mor-per-fei'-to *m.* pansy.

a-mor-ta-lha-dei'-ra *f.* woman embalmer.

a-mor-ta-lha'-do, =a *adj.* wearing mourning; dressed for burial.

a-mor-ta-lha-dor' *m.* embalmer, funeral director.

a-mor-ta-lhar' *tr.v.* to dress corpse for burial; (fig.) to wear coarse clothing indicating person dead to worldliness.

a-mor-te-ce-dor' *m.* shock-absorber; damper.

a-mor-te-cer' *tr.v.* to absorb, to deaden, to weaken; *intr.v.* to appear dead, to faint.

a-mor-te-ci-men'-to *m.* fainting, weakening; thud.

a-mor-ti-za-ção' *f.* amortization.

a-mor-ti-zar' *tr.v.* to amortize.

a-mor-ti-zá-vel *adj.* amortizable.

a-mos-tar-da'-do, =a *adj.* seasoned with mustard.

a-mos'-tra *f.* sample.

a-mo-ti-na-ção' *f.* mutiny, revolt, sedition.

a-mo-ti-na-men'-to *m.* revolt, uprising, mutiny.

a-mo-ti-nar' *tr.v.* to mutiny.

a-mo-ti-ná-vel *adj.* easily incited to mutiny.

a-mou-ris-ca'-do, =a *adj.* in Moorish fashion.

a-mo-ví-vel *adj.* removable, temporary.

am-pa-rar' *tr.v.* to protect, to shelter, to defend.

am-pa'-ro *m.* shelter, sheltering, protection.

am-pe-ra'-gem *f.* amperage, current.

am-pe'-re *m.* ampere.

am-pe-rí-me-tro *m.* ammeter.

am-pé-rio *m.* ampere.

am-pe-rô-me-tro *m.* ammeter.

am-pli-a-ção *f.* enlargement.

am-pli-ar' *tr.v.* to extend, to widen, to enlarge, to dilate.

am-pli-a-ti-for'-me *adj.* having large dimensions.

am-pli-dão' *f.* ampleness, vastness.

am-pli-tu'-de *f.* amplitude; extension, vastness.

am-pli-fi-ca-ção' *f.* amplification.

am-pli-fi-car' *tr.v.* to amplify.

am'-plo, =a *adj.* spacious, ample.

am-pô-la *f.* blister, bubble, ampoule.

am-pu'-la *f.* ampulla.

am-pu-lhe'-ta *f.* hour-glass, sand-glass.

am-pu-ta-ção' *f.* amputation.

am-pu-tar' *tr.v.* to amputate.

a-mu-ar' *tr.v.* to cause or provoke bad humor in some one; *intr.v.* ——se *refl.v.* to pout, to be sulky or surly.

a-mu-la-ta'-do, =a *adj.* mulatto-colored.

a-mu-la-tar'=se *refl.v.* to take color of mulatto.

a-mu-le'-to *m.* amulet.

a-mu-lhe-ra'-do, =a *adj.* effeminate.

a-mu-lhe-rar'=se *refl.v.* to take on the manners of a woman.

a-mun-di-ca'-do, =a *adj.* dirty, unmannerly, without education.

a-mu-ni-cia-men'-to *m.* supplying munitions.

a-mu-ni-ci-ar' *tr.v.* to provide munitions.

a-mu'-o *m.* bad humor.

a-mu-ra'-da *f.* gunwale, bulwark (naut.).

a-mu-ra-lhar' *tr.v.* to fence in, to wall in, to put a wall around.

a-nã' *f.* woman dwarf.

a-na-ba-tis'-mo *m.* Anabaptism.

a-na-co-re'-ta *m.*, *f.* anchorite.

a-na-crô-ni-co, =a *adj.* anachronous.

a-na-cro-nis'-mo *m.* anachronism.

a-na-gra'-ma *m.* anagram.

a-ná-gua *f.* petticoat.

a-nais' *m.pl.* annals.

a-nal' *adj.* anal.

a-nal-fa-be'-to, =a *m.*, *f.* illiterate person.

a-nal-fa-be-tis'-mo *m.* illiteracy.

a-nal-ge-si'-a *f.* analgesia.

a-nal-gé-si-co, =a *adj.* analgesic.

a-na-li-sa-dor' *m.* analyser.

a-na-li-sar' *tr.v.* to analyze.

a-ná-li-se *f.* analysis.

a-na-lí-ti-co, =a *adj.* analytic.

a-na-lo-gí'-a *f.* analogy.

a-ná-lo-go, =a *adj.* analogous.

a-nâm-ne-se *f.* anamnesis.

a-na-nás *m.* pineapple.

a-na-ni-ca'-do, =a *adj.* dwarfish.

a-nâ-ni-co, =a *adj.* dwarf-shaped.

a-na-nis'-mo *m.* dwarfing, dwarfness.

a-não' *m.* dwarf.

a-nar-qui'-a *f.* anarchy.

a-nar-quis'-mo *m.* anarchism.

a-nar-quis'-ta *m.* anarchist.

a-na-ta'-do, =a *adj.* cream-like.

a-na-tar' *tr.v.* to cover with cream.

a-ná-te-ma *m.* anathema.

a-na-te-ma-ti-zar' *tr.v.* to anathematize.

a-na-to-mi'-a *f.* anatomy.

a-na-to-mis'-ta *m.* anatomist.

a-na-va-lha'-do, =a *adj.* razor-shaped; razor-sharp; wounded with a razor.

a-na-va-lhar' *tr.v.* to wound with razor.

an'-ca *f.* hind quarters of an animal, croup (horse); poop (ship).

an-ces-tral' *adj.* ancestral.

an-ces'-tre *m.* ancestor.

an-cia-ni'-a *f.* old age; antiquity.

an-cia-ni-da'-de *f.* antiquity.

an-ci-ão' *m.* an-ci-ã' *f.* very old person.

an-ci'-la *f.* woman slave, or servant; (fig.) aid, subsidy.

an-ci-nhar' *tr.v.* to rake.

an-ci'-nho *m.* rake.

an'-co *m.* elbow.

ân-co-ra *f.* anchor; (fig.) hope.

an-co-ra-dou'-ro *m.* anchorage.

an-co-ra'-gem *f.* anchorage.

an-co-rar' *intr.v.* to drop anchor, to come to port.

an-co-re'-ta *f.* small anchor; small flat wine or whisky cask.

an-da'-ço *m.* small-scale epidemic, restricted to some locality.

an-da'-da *f.* journey, walk.

an-da-dor' *m.* errand-boy.

an-da-du'-ra *f.* gait.

an-da-men'-to *m.* procedure, course, pace, progress; (music) measure.

an-dan'-te *adj.* vagabond, wandering.

an-dar' *intr.v.* to walk, to go, to function.

an-da-re'-co, =a *adj.* slow-moving (of a horse).

an-dai'-me *m.* scaffolding.

An-da-luz' *m.* Andalusian; *adj.* relative to Andalusia.

an'-das *f.pl.* stilts.

an-de-jar' *intr.v.* to wander aimlessly, to ramble.

an-de'-jo, =a *adj.* roving, rambling, fast-walking.

an-dor' *m.* platform (decorated and supported by four persons, one at each corner) on which images are carried in a procession.

an-do-ri'-nha *f.* swallow; (Brazil) push-cart for transporting baggage.

an-dra'-jo *m.* rags, tatters.

an-dra-jo'-so, =a *adj.* ragged, in tatters.

an-dro-fó-bia *f.* androphobia.

an-dró-fo-bo, =a *adj.* having repugnance for male sex.

an-dró-gi-no, =a *adj.* androgynous.

An-rô-me-da *f.* Andromeda.

a-ne-do-tá-rio *m.* collection of anecdotes.
a-ne-dó-ti-co, ⸗a *adj.* anecdotic.
a-ne-do-tis'-ta *m.* anecdotist.
a-ne-do-ti-zar' *intr.v.* to tell anecdotes;
tr.v. to put in the form of anecdotes.
a-ne-do'-ta *f.* anecdote.
a-nel' *m.* ring, each link in chain, curl (of
hair).
a-ne-la'-do, ⸗a *adj.* ring-shaped, curly.
a-ne-lar' *tr.v.* to make into a ring, to
curl.
a-ne-lar' *tr.v.* to desire ardently; *intr.v.* to
breathe with difficulty.
a-ne'-lo *m.* strong desire, aspiration,
anxiety.
a-nê-mo-na *f.* anemone.
a-nes-te-si'-a *f.* anesthesia.
a-nes-te-siar' *tr.v.* to anesthetize.
a-nes-té-si-co, ⸗a *adj.* anesthetic.
a-neu-ris'-ma *m.* aneurism.
a-ne-xa-ção' *f.* annexation.
a-ne-xar' *tr.v.* to annex.
a-ne'-xo, ⸗a *adj.* added, included; *m.*
annex; dependency.
an-fi (amphi) *Greek pref., signifying*
duplicity.
an-fí-bio, ⸗a *adj.* amphibian.
an-fí-bi-os *m.pl.* amphibia.
an-fi-te-a'-tro *m.* amphitheater.
an-frac-tuo-si-da'-de *f.* roughness, unevenness, anfractuosity.
an-frac-tuo'-so, ⸗a *adj.* winding, rough.
an-ga-ri-ar' *tr.v.* to solicit (contribu-
tions), to coax.
an-gé-li-co, ⸗a *adj.* angelic; *m.* birth-
worth, birth-root.
ân-ge-lus *m.* angelus.
an-gi'-na *f.* angina.
an-gli-ca'-no *m.* Anglican.
an-gli-cis'-mo *m.* Anglicism.
an-gló-fi-lo *m.* Anglophile.
an-gló-fo-bo *m.* Anglophobe.
an-glo-ma-ni'-a *f.* Anglomania.
an'-glos *m.pl.* Angles.
an'-glo⸗sa-xão' *m. & adj.* Anglo-Saxon.
ân-go-ra or an-go-rá *adj.* Angora.
an-gú *m.* sort of gruel made with corn
starch, rice flour, or manioc; (fig.)
complication, mixture.
an-gú⸗de⸗ca-ro'-ço *m.* confusion, unexpected result.
an-gu-lar' *adj.* angular.
ân-gu-lo *m.* angle, corner.
an-gu-lo'-so, ⸗a *adj.* angular, having
angles.
an-gús-tia *f.* anguish.
an-gus-tian'-te *adj.* causing anguish.
an-gus-tiar' *tr.v.* to cause anguish to.
A-nhan-gá *m.* evil spirit; (in Tupí
language) devil.
a'-nho *m.* lamb.
a-ni-drí'-do *m.* anhydride.
a⸗ní-drí'-co, ⸗a *adj.* anhydrous.
a-ni-drí'-te *m.* anhydrite.
a-ni'-dro, ⸗a *adj.* anhydrous.
a-nil' *m.* indigo.
a-ni-la'-ado, ⸗a *adj.* bluish.
a-ni-lar' *tr.v.* to put bluing in (laundry).
a-ni-li'-na *f.* aniline.
a-ni-ma-ção' *f.* animation, movement.
a-ni-ma-dor' *adj.* encouraging.
a-ni-man'-te *adj.* encouraging, animat-
ing.
a-ni-mal' *m.* animal; (fig.) ignorant,
crude man; *adj.* carnal.
a-ni-ma-la'-da *f.* large number of animals.
a-ni-mal-cu-le'-jo *m.* stupid person.

a-ni-mál-cu-lo *m.* animalcule.
a-ni-ma-li-da'-de *f.* animality.
a-ni-ma-lis'-ta *m.* painter of animals,
sculptor of animals.
a-ni-ma-li-zar' *tr.v.* to animalize.
an-i-mar' *tr.v.* to encourage, to hearten.
â-ni-mo *m.* courage, morale; animus.
a-ni-mo-si-da'-de *f.* animosity.
a-ni-mo'-so, ⸗a *adj.* spirited, courageous.
a-ni-mar' *tr.v.* to cuddle (child), to rock
to sleep.
a-ni-nhar' *intr.v.* to nest; *tr.v.* to make
a nest for.
a-ni-qui-lar' *tr.v.* to annihilate.
a-nís *m.* anise.
a-ni-sar' *tr.v.* to season with anise.
a-ni-se'-te *m.* anisette.
a-nis-ti'-a *f.* amnesty.
a-nis-ti-ar' *tr.v.* to grant amnesty to.
a-ni-ver-sa-ri-an'-te *adj.* anniversary.
a-ni-ver-sá-rio *m.* birth-day, anniversary.
an-ji'-nho *m.* infant (alive or dead);
—s manacles, hand-fetters.
an'-jo *m.* angel; child dressed as angel
(in religious procession).
a'-no *m.* year; — bissexto leap year; —
civil calendar year; — comercial year
with months of thirty days each; dia
de — bom New Year's Day.
a'-no⸗bom *m.* year with regular rainfall
(in Brazilian northeast).
a-nó-di-no, ⸗a *adj.* anodyne, calming.
a-noi-te-cer' *intr.v.* to become night; to
spend the night.
a-no-ja'-do, ⸗a *adj.* nauseated; in
mourning.
a-no-ja-men'-to *m.* nausea.
a-no-jar' *tr.v.* to nauseate, to disgust.
a-no-jo'-so, ⸗a *adj.* nauseating, disgust-
ing.
a-no-ma-li'-a *f.* anomaly.
a-nô-ma-lo, ⸗a *adj.* anomalous.
a-nô-ni-mo *m.* pseudonym; *adj.* anonymous; (term used for commercial firm
whose name indicates nature of business).
a-nor-mal' *adj.* abnormal.
a-nor-ma-li-da'-de *f.* abnormal.
a-nor-te-ar' *tr.v.* to turn toward the
north (ship).
a-no-ta-ção' *f.* annotation.
a-no-tar' *tr.v.* to annotate.
an-quí'-nhas *f.pl.* buttocks; bustle
(woman's dress).
ân-sia *f.* anxiety; —s *f.pl.* nausea.
an-siar' *tr.v.* to cause anxiety to; to desire ardently.
an-sei'-o *m.* anxiety, state of being
anxious.
an-sie-da'-de *f.* anxiety, anxiousness.
an-sio'-so, ⸗a *adj.* anxious.
an-ta-gô-ni-co, ⸗a *adj.* antagonistic.
an-ta-go-nis'-mo *m.* antagonism.
an-ta-go-nis'-ta *m.* antagonist, adversary.
an-ta'-nho *m.* last year, times gone by.
an-te *prep.* before, in front of; (*Lat. pref.*
signifying antecedence).
an-te-bra'-ço *m.* forearm.
an-te-câ-ma-ra *f.* waiting-room, entrance hall.
an-te-ce-dên-cia *f.* antecedence.
an-te-ce-den'-te *adj.* antecedent; —s
m.pl. antecedents.
an-te-ce-der' *tr.v.* to precede; *intr.v.* to
be previous.
an-te-ces-sor' *m.* predecessor.
an-te-ci-pa-ção' *f.* anticipation.

an-te-ci-pa'-do, =a adj. ahead of time, advance, anticipated.
an-te-ci-par' tr.v. to anticipate, to do in advance.
an-te-da'-ta f. antedate.
an-te-da-tar' tr.v. to antedate.
an-te-di-lu-vi-a'-no, =a adj. antediluvian.
an-te-guar'-da f. vanguard.
an-te-ló-quio m. preface, prologue.
an-te-ma-nhã' adv. just before daybreak; f. beginning dawn.
an-te-mão' adv. previously.
an-te-me-ri-di-a'-no, =a adj. antemeridian.
an-te-mu'-ro m. rampart, external wall.
an-te'-na f. antenna; (ship) sailyard.
an-te-no'-me m. title preceding name.
an-te-nup-ci-al' adj. antenuptial.
an-te-o'-lhos m.pl. blinds (of a bridle).
an-te-on'-tem adv. day before yesterday.
an-te-pa-rar' tr.v. to defend, to guard against.
an-te-pa'-ro m. bulkhead.
an-te-par'-to m. pangs preceding birthpains.
an-te-pas-sa'-do m. ancestor.
an-te-pas'-to m. hors d'oeuvres.
an-te-pe-núl-ti-mo, =a adj. antepenultimate.
an-te-por'-ta f. double-door, screen.
an-te-por-ta-ri'-a f. roof extended over doorway.
an-te-por'-to m. sheltered spot in doorway.
an-te-pro-je'-to m. rough design or estimate.
an-te-ri-or' adj. anterior, previous.
an-ter-ros'-to m. title page (of a book).
an'-tes adv. before; on the contrary; formerly; quanto — as soon as possible.
an-te-ver' tr.v. to foresee.
an-te-vés-pe-ra f. part of day preceding late afternoon.
an-te-vi-dên-cia f. foresightedness.
an-ti Gr. pref. anti.
an-ti-con-cep-ci-o-nal' adj. contraceptive.
an-ti-cris'-to m. anti-christ.
an-tí-do-to m. antidote.
an-ti-fa'-ce or an-ti-faz' m. veil.
an-ti-fra'-se f. antiphrasis.
an-ti-gui-da'-de f. antiquity; length of service.
an-ti'-go, =a adj. old, ancient, antique.
an-ti-hi-gi-ê-ni-co, =a adj. unsanitary.
an-tí-lo-pe m. antelope.
an-ti-mô-ni-o m. antimony.
an-ti-pa-ti'-a f. antipathy.
an-ti-pa-tí-co, =a adj. disagreeable, unpleasant.
an-ti-pa-ti-zar' intr.v. to feel an aversion, to feel repugnance.
an-ti-pi-ré-ti-co, =a adj. antipyretic.
an-ti-pi-ri'-na f. antipyrine.
an-ti-po-da m. antipodes.
an-ti-qua'-do, =a adj. antiquated.
an-ti-quá-rio m. antiquarian.
an-tir-rá-bi-co, =a adj. efficient in treatment for rabies.
an-tis-sêp-sia f. antisepsis.
an-ti-sêp-ti-co, =a adj. antiseptic.
an-tí-te-se f. antithesis.
an-ti-tó-xi-co, =a adj. antitoxic.
an-ti-to-xi'-na f. antitoxin.
an-tô-jo m. capricious appetite; whim.
an-to-lo-gi'-a f. anthology.

an-to-ní-mia f. antonymy.
an-tô-ni-mo m. antonym.
an-to-no-má-sia f. antonomasia.
an-tra-ci'-te f. anthracite.
an-tra-cô-me-tro m. anthracometer.
an-traz' m. anthrax.
an'-tro m. antrum; cave.
an-tro-po-ge-ni'-a f. anthropogenesis.
an-tro-po-lo-gi'-a f. anthropology.
an-tro-pó-lo-go m. anthropologist.
an-tro-po-me-tri'-a f. anthropometry.
an-tro-po-mor'-fos m.pl. monkeys which approach the human in form.
a-nual' adj. annual.
a-nua-li-da'-de f. annuity.
a-nuá-rio m. annual publication.
a-nuên-cia f. consent, approval.
a-nuen'-te m. one who gives permission.
a-nu-i-da'-de f. annuity.
a-nu-ir' intr.v. to nod, to be in agreement.
a-nu-la-ção' f. annulling.
a-nu-la-dor' m. annuller.
a-nu-lar' adj. annular, ring-shaped; m. ring-finger; tr.v. to annul, to repeal.
a-nu-lá-vel adj. annullable.
a-nun-cia-ção' f. Annunciation.
a-nun-ci-ar' tr.v. to announce.
a-nún-cio m. announcement, prophecy, prediction.
a'-nus m. anus.
a-nu-vi-ar' tr.v. to cover with clouds; intr.v. to become cloudy.
an-ver'-so m. face of coin or medal.
an-zol' m. fish hook.
ao contraction of preposition a with masculine article o.
a-on'-de adv. to what place, whither.
ao-pé adv. close by, on the edge of.
a-or'-ta f. aorta.
a-pa-dri-nhar' tr.v. to be god-father for, to defend, to protect.
a-pa-ga'-do, =a adj. extinct, no longer burning.
a-pa-ga-pó m. fine, misty rain.
a-pa-gar' tr.v. to extinguish (light), to weaken, to placate; —se refl.v. to become extinct.
a-pa-ge-ar' tr.v. to serve as page; to flatter.
a-pai-xo-na'-do, =a adj. in love, passionate.
a-pai-xo-nar' tr.v. to arouse passion of; —se refl.v. to fall in love with, to become infatuated with.
a-pa-la-vra-men'-to m. pledge, bargain, agreement.
a-pa-la-vrar' tr.v. to agree upon, to contract (by word of mouth).
a-pal-pa-dei'-ra f. woman aid in custom house who examines women travellers for contraband.
a-pal-pa-de'-la f. examination by feeling or touch; groping.
a-pal-par' tr.v. to touch with hands, to examine by feeling with hands, to feel one's way.
a-pa-ná-gio m. appanage, apanage.
a-pa-nhar' tr.v. to gather, to harvest, to pick up, to catch, to reach, to obtain, to imitate; intr.v. to get a beating.
a-pa-ni-gua'-do m. follower, member, one receiving patronage.
a-pa-ni-guar' tr.v. to dispense patronage to, to favor.
a-pa'-ra f. chips, shavings, peelings.
a-pa-ra-dos m.pl. extra support at regular intervals for perpendicular wall.
a-pa-ra-dor' m. buffet, service table.

a-pa-ra-fu-sar' *tr.v.* to screw, to fasten with screws.

a-pa-rar' *tr.v.* to pare, to shave down roughness of; to sharpen (pencil); to cut (nails).

a-pa-ra-tar' *tr.v.* to ornament, to make sumptuous.

a-pa-ra'-to *m.* apparatus, device, instrument; pomp, ostentation.

a-pa-ra-to'-so, =a *adj.* pretentious, magnificent.

a-pa'-ro *m.* cut in quill pen; metallic tip of pen.

a-par-ce-la'-do, =a *adj.* full of reefs (of sea).

a=par'=de *prep.* near, together with, in view of.

a-pa-re-cer' *intr.v.* to appear, to be present, to happen, to be revealed.

a-pa-re-ci-men'-to *m.* appearance, happening.

a-pa-re-lha'-do, =a *adj.* ready, prepared.

a-pa-re-lha'-gem *f.* apparatus, equipment.

a-pa-re-lha-men'-to *m.* preparation, equipping, setting up.

a-pa-re-lhar' *tr.v.* to equip, to prepare, to set up.

a-pa-re'-lho *m.* apparatus, equipment.

a-pa-rên-cia *f.* appearance, aspect.

a-pa-ren-ta'-do, =a *adj.* having kinship with, having aristocratic or influential relatives.

a-pa-ren-tar' *tr.v.* to make kin or related.

a-pa-ren'-te *adj.* apparent, obvious, seeming.

a-pa-ri-ção' *f.* apparition, ghost, sudden manifestation of.

a-par-ta'-do, =a *adj.* distant, remote, turned from right road.

a-par-ta-men'to *m.* apartment; separation.

a-par-tar' *tr.v.* to separate, to set apart, to turn aside, to dissuade, to wean.

à-par'-te *m.* side remark, aside, interruption; *adv.* separately.

a-par-te-ar' *intr.v.* to interrupt with asides, to heckle.

a-par-tis'-ta *m.* individual who habitually interrupts, heckler.

a-par-va-lha'-do, =a *adj.* idiotic, silly, disoriented.

a-par-va-lhar' *tr.v.* to confuse; to lead astray.

a-par-vo-a'-do, =a *adj.* silly, foolish.

a-par-vo-ar' *tr.v.* to make some one appear simple or foolish.

a-pas-cen-tar' *tr.v.* to pasture, to lead to pasture; to shepherd.

a-pas-si-var' *tr.v.* to put into the passive voice, to use in sense of passive voice.

a-pa-ta-ca'-do, =a *adj.* wealthy, having money.

a-pa-te-ta'-do, =a *adj.* demented, insane.

a-pa-ti'-a *f.* apathy.

a-pá-ti-co, =a *adj.* apathetic.

a-pau-lis-ta'-do, =a *adj.* having air and aspect of Paulista (citizen of São Paulo).

a-pa-vo-ran'-te *adj.* appalling, terrifying.

a-pa-vo-rar' *tr.v.* to appall, to terrify.

a-paz-i-guar' *tr.v.* to pacify, to reconcile.

a-pe-ar' *tr.v.* to dismount; to demolish; *intr.v.* to alight.

a-pe-di'-do *m.* article sent in to a newspaper.

a-pe-dre-ja-men'-to *m.* stoning.

a-pe-dre-jar' *tr.v.* to throw stones at; to offend, to insult.

a-pe-ga-ção' *f.* taking possession, seizing.

a-pe-gar' *tr.v.* to stick to, to like a great deal, to adjoin.

a-pê-go *m.* attachment, affection; plow or wagon beam.

a-pe-la-ção' *f.* appeal.

a-pe-lan'-te *m.* appellant.

a-pe-lar' *tr.v.* to appeal to; *intr.v.* to appeal (law).

a-pe-li-dar' *tr.v.* to give nickname to, to name; to convene.

a-pe-li'-do *m.* surname of family; call to arms.

a-pe'-nas *adv.* only; with difficulty; *conj.* as soon as.

a-pên-di-ce *m.* appendix.

a-pen-di-ci'-te *f.* appendicitis.

a-pe-nho-rar' *tr.v.* to pledge, to pawn.

a-pen-sar' *tr.v.* to append.

a-pen'-so *m.* appendage.

a-pep-si'-a *f.* dyspepsia.

a-per-ce-ber' *tr.v.* to apperceive; to distinguish.

a-per-cep-ção' *f.* apperception.

a-per-fei-ço-a'-do, =a *adj.* perfected, beautifully finished.

a-per-fei-ço-a-men'-to *m.* perfecting; improvement; curso de — advanced course.

a-per-fei-ço-ar' *tr.v.* to perfect; to improve.

a-per-fei-ço-á-vel *adj.* perfectible.

a-per-ga-mi-nha'-do, =a *adj.* like parchment.

a-per-re-ar' *tr.v.* to worry, to make anxious; to annoy.

a-per-ta'-do *m.* narrow gorge; a-perta'-do, =a *adj.* tight, severe; miserly.

a-per-tão' *m.* large crowd, crush, jam.

a-per-tar' *tr.v.* to tighten, to be close upon, to squeeze together; to clasp.

a-pêr-to *m.* crowd; haste; difficulty; dangerous situation; urgency.

a=pe-sar'=de *prep.* in spite of, notwithstanding.

a-pe-sen-tar' *tr.v.* to increase weight; to make heavy.

a-pes-so-a'-do, =a *adj.* (preceded by *bem*) of good stature, of fine appearance.

a-pes-ta-na'-do, =a *adj.* having eyelashes, or especially long eyelashes.

a-pe-te-cer' *tr.v.* to covet, to long for; *intr.v.* to tempt the appetite.

a-pe-tên-cia *f.* appetite.

a-pe-ti'-te *m.* appetite.

a-pe-ti-to'-so, =a *adj.* appetizing.

a-pe-tre-char' *tr.v.* to equip.

a-pe-tre'-cho *m.* equipment.

a-pi-á-rio *m.* apiary.

a-pi-ca'-do, =a *adj.* peaked, having an apex.

á-pi-ce *m.* apex, vortex.

a-pi-e-dar' *tr.v.* to move to pity, to cause compassion; —se *refl.v.* to take pity upon, to sympathize with.

a-pi-cul-tu'-ra, *f.* apiculture.

a-pi-men-tar' *tr.v.* to season with pepper; (fig.) to make malicious.

a-pin-ce-lar' *tr.v.* to brush, to make brush-shaped, to apply (with brush) a coat of whitewash, or tint.

a-pi-nha'do, =a *adj.* heaped up, conglomerate.

a-pi-nhar' *tr.v.* to heap, to heap up; to stick together like scales of pine cone.

a-pi-pa'-do, =a *adj.* cask-shaped.

a-pi-par' *tr.v.* to make cask-shaped.

a-pi'-que *adv.* almost, almost standing on end; **ir — to** be wrecked (of a ship).
a-pi'-ro, =a *adj.* apyrous.
a-pi-tar' *intr.v.* to whistle.
a-pi'-to *m.* whistle.
a-pla-car' *tr.v.* to appease, to pacify.
a-pla-i-nar' *tr.v.* to plane; to make level.
a-pla-nar' *tr.v.* to level (land), to make equal, to remove (difficulties).
a-plás-ti-co, =a *adj.* non-plastic, aplastic.
a-plau-dir' *tr.v.* to praise, to eulogize; to applaud; *intr.v.* to clap hands in applause.
a-plau-sí-vel *adj.* plausible; praiseworthy.
a-plau'-so *m.* applause, applauding.
a-pli-ca-ção' *f.* application; diligence; embroidered lace, appliqué.
a-pli-ca-bi-li-da'-de *f.* applicability.
a-pli-ca'-do, =a *adj.* studious; used.
a-pli-car' *tr.v.* to apply; to use; to devote.
a-pli-cá-vel *adj.* applicable.
a'-plo *m.* beam of plow; bird-of-paradise.
a-po-ca-lip'-se *f.* disclosure, revelation; *m.* book of Revelation.
a-pó-co-pe *f.* apocope.
a-pô-cri-fo, =a *adj.* apocryphal.
a-po-dar' *tr.v.* to make puns, to apply nicknames to.
a-po-de-rar'=se *refl.v.* to take possession of, to make oneself master on.
a-po-dre-cer' *tr.*, *intr.v.* to decompose, to become putrid.
a-po-dre-ci-men'-to *m.* putrefaction, decomposition.
a-pó-fi-se *f.* apophysis.
a-po-ge'-u *m.* apogee.
a-poi-a'-do *m.* support, backing, applause; *interj.* well done!, hear, hear!
a-po-i-ar' *tr.v.* to give support, to applaud, to aid.
a-pôi-o *m.* base, pivot; protection; approval.
a-po-ja-du'-ra *f.* abundance of milk in breast.
a-po-jar' *intr.v.* to become full of milk, or swollen with any liquid.
a-po-le-gar' *tr.v.* to rub between fingers, especially thumb and fore-finger.
a-pó-li-ce *f.* policy, share of stock, accident insurance certificate.
a-po-lo-gé-ti-co, =a *adj.* apologetic.
a-po-lo-gi'-a *f.* apology.
a-po-lo-gi-zar' *intr.v.* to apologize.
a-pon-ta-dor' *m.* time-keeper (for workmen); prompter (in theater).
a-pon-ta-men'-to *m.* reminder, note.
a-pon-tar' *tr.v.* to sharpen, to make pointed, to point out, to note, to mention casually; to take large stitches (sewing); *intr.v.* to begin to appear.
a-po-pléc-ti-co, =a *adj.* apoplectic.
a-po-ple-xi'-a *f.* apoplexy.
a-po-quen-ta'-do, =a *adj.* worried.
a-po-quen-tar' *tr.v.* to reduce; —=se *refl.v.* to humble oneself.
a-por' *tr.v.* to appose; to affix.
a-por-tar' *intr.v.* to come into port, to drop anchor.
a-por-tu-gue-sar' *tr.v.* to give Portuguese form, characteristics or features (especially to language).
a-pós *prep.* after, behind; *adv.* afterwards.
a-po-sen-ta-ção' *f.* retirement.
a-po-sen-tar' *tr.v.* to receive as guest, to provide lodging; to retire on pension.
a-po-sen'-to *m.* room, apartment, residence, house.

a-pos-sar' *tr.v.* to give possession; —=se *refl.v.* to take possession.
a-pos'-ta *f.* bet.
a-pos-tar' *tr.v.* to bet, to risk, to take a chance.
a-pós-ta-se *f.* apostasis.
a-pos-ta-si'-a *f.* apostasy.
a-pós-ta-ta *m.f. adj.* apostate.
a-pos-tà-tar' *intr.v.* to apostatize.
a-pos-ti'-la *f.* apostil, comment, note.
a-pôs-to, =a *adj.* affixed, apposed; elegant.
a-pos-to-la'-do *m.* apostolate.
a-pos-to-lar' *tr.v.* to preach the gospel.
a-pos-tó-li-co, =a *adj.* apostolic.
a-pós-to-lo *m.* apostle.
a-pós-tro-fe *f.* apostrophe (rhet.).
a-pós-tro-fo *m.* apostrophe (to show the omission of a letter).
a-pos-tu'-ra *f.* posture; —s *f.pl.* framework of ship.
a-po-te-o'-se *f.* apotheosis.
a-pó-te-se *f.* apothesis (surg.).
a-pou-ca'-do, =a *adj.* timid, humble, not provided for.
a-pou-ca-men'-to *m.* humility; lack of energy; low intelligence.
a-pou-car' *tr.v.* to disdain, to reduce to small quantity, to diminish.
a-pra-zar' *tr.v.* to determine period of time or certain date; to convoke for given time; to designate, to postpone.
a-pra-zer' *intr.v.* to please, to cause pleasure.
a-pra-zi-bi-li-da'-de *f.* pleasurableness.
a-pra-zí-vel *adj.* pleasant, pleasing.
a-pre-çar' *tr.v.* to determine or mark price.
a-pre-cia-ção' *f.* appreciation.
a-pre-ci-ar' *tr.v.* to appreciate.
a-pre-cia-ti'-vo, =a *adj.* appreciative.
a-pre-ciá-vel *adj.* appreciable.
a-prê-ço *m.* esteem, valuation, consideration.
a-pre-en-der' *tr.v.* to apprehend.
a-pre-en-são' *f.* apprehension, capture, imprisonment.
a-pre-en-sí-vel *adj.* apprehensible.
a-pre-en-si'-vo, =a *adj.* apprehensive.
a-pre-fi-xar' *tr.v.* to put prefixes to (words).
a-pren-der' *tr.v.*, *intr.v.* to learn, to acquire knowledge of, to retain in memory.
a-pren-diz' *m.* apprentice, beginner.
a-pren-di-za'-do *m.* apprenticeship; learning.
a-pre-sar' *tr.v.* to take prisoner; to make fast, to capture.
a-pre-sen-ta-ção' *f.* presentation.
a-pre-sen-tan'-te *m.* one who presents a letter of exchange for payment.
a-pre-sen-tar' *tr.v.* to present, to offer, to recommend.
a-pre-sen-tá-vel *adj.* presentable.
a-pres-sa'-do, =a *adj.* urgent, hurried, in a hurry.
a-pres-sar' *tr.v.* to hurry, to make haste; —=se *refl.v.* to hurry.
a-prês-so *m.* haste, hurry.
a-pres-ta-men'-to *m.* equipment, apparatus.
a-pres-tar' *tr.v.* to equip, to install, to make ready.
a-pres'-te *m.* **a-pres'-to** *m.* equipment; preparation.
a-pri-li'-no, =a *adj.* relating to April.
a-pri-mo-ra'-do, =a *adj.* nice, elegant; made with great care.

a-pri-mo-rar' *tr.v.* to perfect, to excel in.

a-pri-o-ris'-mo *m.* reasoning *a priori.*

a-pri-o-ris'-ta *m.* one who reasons *a priori.*

a-pris'-co *m.* cattle pen, cave, rough hut, sheepfold; (fig.) bosom of the Church.

a-pri-si-o-na'-do, -a *adj.* captive, in prison.

a-pri-si-o-na-men'-to *m.* imprisonment.

a-pri-si-o-nar' *tr.v.* to make prisoner, to imprison.

a-pro-ar' *tr.v.* to tack, to steer.

a-pro-ba-ti'-vo, -a *adj.* approbative; approving.

a-pro-ba-tó-rio, -a *adj.* approbatory.

a-pro'-che *m.* approach, line of approach (siege).

a-pro-fun-dar' *tr.v.* to make profound, to study all ramifications, to treat in detail.

a-pron-tar' *tr.v.* to make ready, to conclude.

a-pro-pó-si-to *adv.* apropos; opportunely.

a-pro-pria-ção' *f.* appropriation.

a-pro-pria'-do, -a *adj.* appropriate, useful, opportune.

a-pro-pri-ar' *tr.v.* to appropriate, to adapt.

a-pro-va-ção' *f.* approval.

a-pro-var' *tr.v.* to approve.

a-pro-vei-tar' *tr.v.* to take advantage of; *intr.v.* to be profitable or of some advantage.

a-pro-vei-tá-vel *adj.* worth using, usable, profitable.

a-pro-vi-si-o-nar' *tr.v.* to provide, to furnish with provisions.

a-pro-vei-ta-men'-to *m.* progress; good use; profit.

a-pro-xi-ma-ção' *f.* approximation, estimate; neighborhood.

a-pro-xi-mar' *tr.v.* to place next, to approach; —-se *refl.v.* to be arriving; to almost attain.

a-pru-ma'-do, -a *adj.* perfectly vertical, plumb.

a-pru-mar' *tr.v.* to plumb.

a-pru'-mo *m.* vertical position; uprightness; haughtiness, aplomb.

ap-ti-dão' *f.* aptness.

ap-ti-tu'-de *f.* aptness.

ap'-to, -a *adj.* apt.

a-pu-nha-lar' *tr.v.* to wound with dagger, to offend deeply.

a-pu-pa'-da *f.* hooting, shouting.

a-pu-par' *tr.v.* to hiss.

a-pu'-po *m.* bantering.

a-pu-ra'-do, -a *adj.* delicate, elegant.

a-pu-ra-men'-to *m.* liquidation, balancing of accounts; counting.

a-pu-rar' *tr.v.* to verify; to liquidate; to remove impurities or foreign substances; —-se *refl.v.* to become clear.

a-pu'-ro *m.* refinement in dress, language; money resulting from liquidation.

a-pur-pu-ra'-do, -a *adj.* purple colored, covered with purple.

a-qua-for'-te *f.* aqua fortis (nitric acid).

a-quá-rio *m.* aquarium.

a-quá-ti-co, -a *adj.* aquatic.

a-quar-te-lar' *tr.v.* to lodge in barracks or quarters (troops).

a-quar-ti-lhar' *tr.v.* to sell by retail.

a'-qua-tin'-ta *f.* aqua-tint.

a-que-ce-dor' *m.* heater (for house, water, etc.).

a-que-cer' *tr.v.* to warm, to heat, to irritate; *intr.v.* to become hot.

a-que-ci-men'-to *m.* heating.

a-que-ci-vel *adj.* that may be heated.

a-que-du'-to *m.* aqueduct.

a-que'-le *m.* a-que'-la *f. demons. pr.* and *adj.* that (thing or person distant from person speaking or spoken to).

à-que-le *m.* à-que-la *f.* contraction of prep. *a* with pro. to that (person or thing).

a-quém *prep., adv.* from this side; less, below.

a-qui-es-cên-cia *f.* acquiescence.

a-qui-es-cen'-te *adj.* acquiescent.

a-qui-es-cer' *intr.v.* to acquiesce.

a-qui *adv.* here, in this place, at this time.

a-qui-la-tar' *tr.v.* to weigh in carats; (fig.) to evaluate merits of.

a-qui-li'-no, -a *adj.* aquiline.

a-qui'-lo *demons. pro.* that (thing or things).

à-qui-lo contraction of prep. *a* with aquilo to that (thing or things).

a-qui-nho-ar' *tr.v.* to divide into shares or lots.

a-qui-si-ção' *f.* acquisition.

a-quó (used with *estar* and *ficar*) fasting; in ignorance.

a-quo-si-da'-de *f.* wateriness.

a-quo'-so, -a *adj.* aqueous.

ar' *m.* air, wind, breeze, climate; **tomar ares** to take a walk; **ao ar livre** in the open; **dar ares** to look like; **beber ares** to be very devout.

a-ra'-gem *f.* breeze, gentle wind.

a'-ra *f.* altar, altar-stone.

Á-ra-be *m.* Arab, Arabian language; *adj.* Arabian.

a-ra-bes'-co *m.* arabesque.

a-rá-bi-co, -a *adj.* Arabic.

a-ra-bis'-ta *m. f.* Arabist.

a-ra'-da *f.* plowed land.

a-ra'-do, -a *adj.* cultivated.

a-ra'-do-ne *m.*

a-ral' *m.* land cleared and ready for cultivation.

a-rar' *tr.v.* to plow, to cultivate.

a-rá-vel *adj.* arable.

a-ra'-me *m.* wire; — **de aço** steel wire; — **farpado** barbed wire; — **multifilar isolado** insulated stranded wire.

a-ra'-nha *f.* spider; arachnid; (fig.) person who works slowly; **teias de —** spider web.

a-ra'-ra *f.* arara (macaw).

a-rau'-to *m.* herald, messenger.

ar-bi-tra'-gem *f.* arbitration.

ar-bi-tra-men'-to *m.* arbitration.

ar-bi-tral' *adj.* settled by arbitration.

ar-bi-trar' *tr.v.* to arbitrate.

ar-bitrá-rio, -a *adj.* arbitrary.

ar-bi-trio *m.* arbitration; will; decision.

ár-bi-tro *m.* arbiter, arbitrator.

ar-bo-res-cer' *intr.v.* to grow like trees, to grow into trees.

ar-bo-re'-to *m.* orchard, arboretum.

ar-bo-ri-za-ção' *f.* arborization.

ar-bo-ri-za'-do, -a *adj.* full of trees.

ar-bo-ri-zar' *tr.v.* to plant with trees.

ar-bus'-to *m.* shrub, bush.

ar'-ca *f.* coffer, strong box; ark; breast, chest.

ar-ca-bou'-ço *m.* skeleton, bony framework of chest, wooden frame of building.

ar-ca-buz' *m.* arquebus, harquebus.

ar-ca'-da *f.* arcade.

ar-ca'-do, -a *adj.* arched.

ar-cá-dia *f.* ancient Roman literary academy, imitated in Portugal; Arcadia.

ar-ca-dis'-mo *m.* literary influence of the arcadias.

ar-cai'-co, *=a adj.* archaic.

ar-ca-ís-mo *m.* archaism.

ar-ca-ís-ta *m.* archaist; antiquary.

ar-can'-jo *m.* archangel.

ar-ca'-no *m.* secret, mystery; *adj.* hidden, concealed.

ar-cão' *m.* pommel (of a saddle).

ar-car' *tr.v.* to arch.

ar'-ce *Greek pref.* signifying superiority.

ar-ce-bis-pa'-do *m.* archbishopric.

ar-ce-bis'-po *m.* archbishop.

ar-ce-dia-ga'-do *m.* archdeaconate, archdeaconship, archdeaconry.

ar-ce-di-a'-go *m.* archdeacon.

ar-chei'-ro *m.* archer.

ar-cho'-te *m.* torch; — **de acetilene** acetylene torch.

ar'-co *m.* arc, bow (for shooting arrows); arch (of bridge); — **iris** rainbow; curvature of dome or vault.

ar-dên-cia *f.* heat, glow; eagerness, zeal.

ar-den'-te *adj.* ardent.

ar-der' *intr.v.* to burn, to be in flame, to glow (of live coals); to feel ardent desire.

ar-di-dez' *f.* courage, boldness.

ar-di-de'-za *f.* courage, boldness.

ar-di'-do, *=a adj.* burned, fermented; courageous, valiant.

ar-dil' *m.* astuteness, subtlety, strategy.

ar-di-lo'-so, *=a adj.* astute, sagacious.

ar-dor' *m.* ardor, courage, zeal; heat.

ar-do-ro'-so, *=a adj.* arduous.

ár-duo, *=a adj.* arduous, difficult, troublesome.

ar-dó-sia *f.* slate.

a'-re *m.* land surface measure equivalent to 100 square meters.

á-re-a *f.* area.

a-re-a'-do, *=a adj.* sandy; scoured with sand.

a-re-ar' *tr.v.* to scour with sand, to cover with sand.

a-re-fa-ção' *f.* drying out of substances to be pulverized.

a-rei'-a *f.* sand; any fine powder.

a-re-ja-men'-to *m.* ventilation.

a-re-jar' *tr.v.* to aerate, to ventilate.

a-re'-jo *m.* airing, ventilating.

a-re'-na *f.* arena; bull-ring.

a-ren'-ga *f.* harangue, gossip, fussing, quarreling.

a-ren-gar' *tr.v.* to fuss, to quarrel, to nag; to harangue.

a-ren'-que *m.* herring (fish).

a-ré-o-la *f.* corner of a garden.

a-re-o-me-tri'-a *f.* aerometry.

a-re-ô-me-tro *m.* aerometer.

a-res'-ta *f.* splinter; edge; (fig.) **pessoa cheia de** *=s* difficult person, person hard to deal with.

a-res'-to *m.* judgment (law); decision.

ar-fa'-da *f.* rolling of a ship, pitching of a ship.

ar-far' *intr.v.* to pant, to breathe hard; to pitch (of a ship).

ar-ga-mas'-sa *f.* cement, mortar.

ar-gen-ta'-do, *=a adj.* silvery.

ar-gen-tá-rio *m.* wealthy man; silver chest, silver cupboard.

ar-gên-teo, *=a adj.* of silver; bright as silver.

ar-gen-ti'-no, *=a adj.* silvery, bright as silver.

Ar-gen-ti'-no *m.* citizen of Argentina.

ar-gi'-la *f.* clay, argil; **ar-gi-lo'-so**, *=a adj.* clayey.

ar-go'-la *f.* ring, pillory; knocker.

ar-go-li'-nha *f.* popular game.

ar-go-nau'-ta *m.* Argonaut.

ar-gô-nio *m.* argon.

ar-gu'-cia *f.* subtlety in argument, intellectual sharpness.

ar-guei'-ro *m.* little straw, splinter, granule; small particle of anything; something insignificant.

ar-gu-ir' *tr.v.* to accuse, to reprehend; *intr.v.* to argue.

ar-gui-ção' *f.* rebuke, arguing, questioning.

ar-gu-men-ta-ção' *f.* argumentation.

ar-gu-men-tar' *intr.v.* to discuss, to argue.

ar-gu-men-ta-ti'-vo, *=a adj.* argumentative.

ar-gu-men'-to *m.* argument.

ar-gu'-to, *=a adj.* acute.

á-ria *f.* (music) aria.

a-ri-dez' *f.* aridity.

á-ri-do, *=a adj.* arid.

a-ris'-co, *=a adj.* sandy; (fig.) peevish, unsocial, intractable.

a-ris-tar'-co *m.* critic; severe but just censor.

a-ris-to-cra-ci'-a *f.* aristocracy.

a-ris-to-cra'-ta *m.* aristocrat.

a-rit-man-ci'-a *f.* supposed art of prophesy by use of numbers.

a-rit-mé-ti-ca *f.* arithmetic.

ar-le-quim' *m.* harlequin.

ar-le-qui-na'-da *f.* harlequinade.

ar'-ma *f.* arm, weapon; (fig.) recourse, expedient; *=s f.pl.* arms, armed forces, military profession.

ar-ma-ção' *f.* arming; setting up; equipment, outfit; armature.

ar-ma'-da *f.* fleet, navy, armada.

ar-ma-di'-lha *f.* trap, snare.

ar-ma-men'-to *m.* armament.

ar-mão' *m.* front wheels of a piece of ordnance.

ar-mar' *tr.v.* to arm; to equip.

ar-ma-ri'-nho *m.* small cupboard; cloth shop.

ar-ma-rio *m.* cupboard.

ar-ma-zém *m.* warehouse; deposit; store; **grandes armazéns** department store.

ar-ma-ze-na'-gem *f.* storage; storage charges.

ar-ma-ze-nar' *tr.v.* to store, to store away; to deposit.

ar-mi'-nho *m.* ermine.

ar-mis-tí-cio *m.* armistice.

ar-mo-ri-al' *m.* armorial.

ar-mo-riar' *tr.v.* (heraldry) to place a symbol of nobility on.

a'-ro *m.* hoop (iron or wood); adjacent area.

a-ro'-ma *f.* aroma.

a-ro-má-ti-co, *=a adj.* aromatic.

ar-pão' *m.* harpoon.

ar-par' *tr.v.* to wound with harpoon.

ar-pe-jar' *intr.v.* to play arpeggios.

ar-pe'-jo *m.* arpeggio.

ar-pe'-u *m.* grappling hook.

ar-po-ar' *tr.v.* to hurl out the harpoon, to strike with harpoon.

ar-que-a-ção' *f.* curvature; ship capacity; volume of rounded containers.

ar-que-a'-do, *=a adj.* arched, curved.

ar-que-ar' *tr.v.* to arch, to curve.

ar-quei'-ro *m.* archer, maker of bows, seller of bows (for bow and arrow).

ar-que-jar' *intr.v.* to pant, to puff and blow.

ar-que'-jo *m.* difficult breathing as in asthma; anxiousness.

ar-que-o-lo-gi'-a *f.* archeology.

ar-que-ó-lo-go *m.* archeologist.

ar-qui-con-fra-ri'-a *f.* principal sisterhood or brotherhood.

ar-qui-di-o-ce'-se *f.* arch-diocesis.

ar-qui-du'-que *m.* arch-duke.

ar-qui-du-que'-sa *f.* arch-duchess.

ar-qui-e-pis-co-pa'-do *m.* arch-episcopate.

ar-qui'-lho *m.* metal or wood ring which holds secure stretched skin of drum head.

ar-qui-mi-li-o-ná-rio *m.* multi-millionaire.

ar-qui-pé-la-go *m.* archipelago.

ar-qui-te'-to *m.* architect.

ar-qui-te-tô-ni-co, *=a adj.* architectonic.

ar-qui-te-tu-ral' *adj.* architectural.

ar-qui-var' *tr.v.* to place in the archives, to file.

ar-qui-vis'-ta *m.* archivist.

ar-qui'-vo *m.* archive.

ar-ra-bal'-de *m.* suburb, outlying district.

ar-ra'-ia *f.* ray fish; populace, mob; frontier.

ar-rai-a'-do, *=a adj.* radiated, streaked.

ar-rai-al' *m.* encampment; small village.

ar-ra-i-ga'-do, *=a adj.* having roots, firmly held.

ar-ra-mar' *intr.v.* to grow branches; —*se refl.v.* to spread out.

ar-ram-pa'-do *m.* ramp, slope.

ar-ran-ca'-da *f.* seed-bed from which plants are to be transplanted; jerk, start, sudden pull.

ar-ran-car' *tr.v.* to pull out, to jerk out.

ar-ran'-co *m.* violent start or pull.

ar-ran-cha-men'-to *m.* group of rough ranch houses.

ar-ran-char' *tr.v.* to unite in groups (settlers); —*se refl.v.* to establish oneself temporarily.

ar-ra-nha-céu *m.* sky scraper, tall building.

ar-ra-nha-du'-ra *f.* scratch.

ar-ra-nhão' *m.* scratch.

ar-ra-nhar' *tr.v.* to scratch; to scrape; to know slightly (a language or other subject); to play badly (musical instrument).

ar-ran-jar' *tr.v.* to arrange; to obtain.

ar-ran'-jo *m.* arrangement; economy.

ar'-ras *f.* pledge; marriage settlement.

ar-ra-sa'-do, *=a adj.* demolished, level, overflowing.

ar-ra-sa-men'-to *m.* ruin, demolition.

ar-ra-sar' *tr.v.* to raze.

ar-ras-ta'-do, *=a adj.* miserable, despised.

ar-ras-ta-dor' *m.* trail, narrow path.

ar-ras-ta-men'-to *m.* pulling, dragging.

ar-ras-tão' *m.* violent pull; effort to pull.

ar-ras-tar' *tr.v.* to pull along, to creep or move with difficulty, to drag, to trail.

ar-ras'-to *m.* trail; dragging.

ar-rá-tel *m.* arratel (measure of weight).

ar-ra-zo-a'-do, *=a adj.* reasonable, just.

ar-ra-zo-ar' *tr.v.* to present reasons for; *intr.v.* to discuss, to talk over; to accompany oneself with guitar, improvising.

ar'-re! *interj.* signifying anger, fatigue; also to urge animals along.

ar-re-a-men'-to *m.* furniture; fittings.

ar-re-ar' *tr.v.* to harness; to furnish, to equip, to decorate; *intr.v.* to bend over, to lose energy, to give up.

ar-re-ba-nhar' *tr.v.* to assemble in flocks, to gather up; to sweep up (last crumbs).

ar-re-ba-ta'-do, *=a adj.* precipitate, inconsiderate, irascible.

ar-re-ba-ta-men'-to *m.* ecstasy, passion, excitement; hastiness.

ar-re-ba-tar' *tr.v.* to snatch, to rob; to irritate.

ar-re-ben-ta-ção' *f.* breakers (surf).

ar-re-ben-ta'-do, *=a adj.* broken, ruined, without resources.

ar-re-ben-ta-men'-to *m.* explosion, blast.

ar-re-ben-tar' *tr.v.* to break, to burst, to explode.

ar-re-bi-ta'-do, *=a adj.* having brim turned up; (fig.) cocky, proud, bad-humored.

ar-re-bi-tar' *tr.v.* to turn up brim (of hat), to cock a hat.

ar-re-bi'-que *m.* cosmetics; ridiculous and exaggerated decoration.

ar-re-bol' *m.* redness of rising or setting sun.

ar-re-bo-lar' *tr.v.* to make ball-shaped, to tinge color of setting sun.

ar-re-ca-da-ção' *f.* collection (of taxes); check-room (for baggage).

ar-re-ca'-do, *=a adj.* placed for safe keeping; careful, economical.

ar-re-ca-dar' *tr.v.* to collect (money), to take possession of, to seize; to keep in safe place.

ar-re-da'-do, *=a adj.* distant, remote, moved away.

ar-re-dar' *tr.* to move away, to retire, to place apart.

ar-re-di'-o, *=a adj.* far away, lonely.

ar-re-don-da'-do, *=a adj.* rounded; round-shaped.

ar-re-don-da-men'-to *m.* rounding, completing.

ar-re-don-dar' *tr.v.* to make round, to complete, to round out.

ar-re-dor' *adv.* about, in the vicinity; *adj.* neighboring; *m.pl.* environment, surrounding area.

ar-re-fe-çar' *tr.v.* to sell for low price; to abase.

ar-re-fe-cer' *intr.v.* to cool, to lose energy; *tr.v.* to moderate (zeal, activity).

ar-re-ga-çar' *tr.v.* to turn up (sleeves, trousers), to tuck up (skirt).

ar-re-ga'-ço *m.* reprehension.

ar-re-ga-la'-do, *=a adj.* wide open.

ar-re-ga-lar' *tr.v.* to stare, to open one's eyes wide.

ar-re-ga-nhar' *tr.v.* to show teeth in grin or snarl.

ar-re-ga'-nho *m.* wild, ferocious aspect.

ar-re-gi-men-ta-ção' *f.* enlistment.

ar-rei'-o *m.* harness; decorations.

ar-re-li'-a *f.* tumult; anger; irritation.

ar-re-liar' *tr.v.* to irritate, to cause a tumult.

ar-re-ma-tar' *tr.v.* to put finishing edge on; to complete; to buy in auction.

ar-re-ma'-te *m.* finishing, completion; finish (hem, embroidery) to an edge.

ar-re-me-dar' *tr.v.* to mimic, to counterfeit, to ape or mock.

ar-re-mê-do *m.* ridiculous, coarse imitation.

ar-re-mes-sar' *tr.v.* to throw away, to

fling away; —₌se *refl.v.* to rush headlong into.

ar-re-mês-so *m.* onset, attack.

ar-re-me-ter' *intr.v.* to rush upon, to advance impetuously.

ar-re-me-ti'-da *f.* heroic action, assault, conflict.

ar-ren-da-men'-to *m.* renting; rent; lease; income from rent.

ar-ren-dar' *tr.v.* to rent, to let, to hire.

ar-ren-da-tá-rio *m.* tenant.

ar-ren-dá-vel *adj.* rentable.

ar-re-pe-lar' *tr.v.* to pull or snatch out (hair, feathers); —₌se *refl.v.* to pull out one's own hair in deep regret.

ar-re-pe-lão' *m.* strong hair-pulling, tug on the hair.

ar-re-ne-ga-ção' *f.* apostasy, renouncement.

ar-re-pen-der'₌se *refl.v.* to repent (for past deeds), to change one's ideas; to retract.

ar-re-pen-di'-do, ₌a *adj.* repentant, contrite.

ar-re-pen-di-men'-to *m.* repentance, contrition; change of opinion.

ar-re-pia'-do, ₌a *adj.* with hair on end; terrified.

ar-re-pi-ar' *tr.v.* to raise, to stand up (of hair), to cause horror.

ar-re-pi'-o *m.* chill; shivering.

ar-res-tar' *tr.v.* to arrest, to confiscate.

ar-res'-to *m.* seizure of goods or possessions by judicial order; embargo.

ar-re-va-sa'-do, ₌a *adj.* complicated, hard to pronounce.

ar-re-ve-sar' *tr.v.* to turn wrong side out; to make meaning obscure or complicated.

ar-ri-ar' *tr.v.* to lower, to pay out gradually (rope, line, fish net); — **bandeira** to lower flag in surrender or to honor.

ar-ri'-ba *adv.* above; up; *interj.* Get on!!; *f.* elevated mountain ridge; high river bank.

ar-ri-ba-ção' *f.* arrival, arriving; **aves de** — migratory birds.

ar-ri-ba'-da *f.* arrival, landing; convalescence.

ar-ri-bar' *intr.v.* to arrive (by water); to take refuge in a harbor; to desert, to flee; to convalesce.

ar-ri-ma-di'-ço, ₌a *adj.* dependent, parasitic.

ar-ri-mar' *tr.v.* to support, to lean against; to put in rhyme.

ar-ri'-mo *m.* support, aid, protection.

ar-ris-ca'-do, ₌a *adj.* dangerous, rash.

ar-ris-car' *tr.v.* to risk, to venture.

ar-rit-mi'-a *f.* arrhythmia.

ar-rit-mí-co, ₌a *adj.* arrhythmic.

ar-ri-vis'-mo *m.* system of succeeding in life at whatever cost.

ar-ri-vis'-ta *m.* unscrupulously ambitious person; opportunist.

ar-ri'-zo, ₌a *adj.* rootless.

ar-ro'-ba *f.* arroba (measure of weight).

ar-rô-cho *m.* short, strong stick on which to twist rope in order to tighten it.

ar-ro-cha-du'-ra *f.* tightening cords on bales, or other heavy bundles, by twisting with short stick.

ar-ro-gân-cia *f.* arrogance.

ar-ro-gan'-te *adj.* arrogant.

ar-ro-gar' *tr.v.* to arrogate.

ar-ro-ja'-do, ₌a *adj.* daring, impetuous, rash.

ar-rô-jo *m.* boldness, audacity, temerity.

ar-ro-la-men'-to *m.* inventory.

ar-ro-lar' *tr.v.* to list, to take inventory; to calm (children).

ar-ro-lhar' *tr.v.* to put in stopper, to cork; to overcome adversary, to flee, to pick herva-mate leaves.

ar-rô-lo *m.* lullaby.

ar-rom'-ba *f.* song for guitar.

ar-rom-ba-men'-to *m.* forcible entry.

ar-rom-bar' *tr.v.* to break open forcibly, to break off relations, to abate.

ar-ros-tar' *tr.v.* to confront, to resist; —₌se *refl.v.* to encounter face to face.

ar-ro-tar' *intr.v.* to eruct; (fig.) to boast, to swagger.

ar-rô-to *m.* belching.

ar-ro-te-ar' *tr.v.* to grub virgin land; (fig.) to educate.

ar-ro-téi-a *f.* virgin land beginning to be cultivated.

ar-rou-ba-men'-to *m.* rapture, ecstasy.

ar-rou-bar' *tr.v.* to enrapture, to put into a state of ecstasy.

ar-ro-xa'-do, ₌a *adj.* violet, purple, tinted.

ar-ro-xe-ar' *tr.v.* to make purple, to make violet, to color.

ar-roz' *m.* rice.

ar-ro-zal' *m.* field planted with rice.

ar-rua-men'-to *m.* arrangement by streets; grouping similar business establishments on same street.

ar-ru-ar' *tr.v.* to lay out streets; *intr.v.* to take walks in streets.

ar-ru-fa-di'-ço, ₌a *adj.* easily irritated.

ar-ru-far' *tr.v.* to exhaust, to irritate; —₌se *refl.v.* to be in bad humor, annoyed.

ar-ru'-fo *m.* pouting; lover's quarrel.

ar-rui-na'-do, ₌a *adj.* bankrupt; lost; ruined.

ar-ru-i-nar' *tr.v.* to ruin, to damage, to destroy; —₌se *refl.v.* to be left without resources, to be lost.

ar-ru-i-va'-do, ₌a *adj.* somewhat reddish in color.

ar-ru-lar' or **ar-ru-lhar'** *intr.v.* to sing crooningly, as doves.

ar-ru'-lho *m.* lullaby.

ar-ru-ma-ção' *f.* putting in order; orderly arrangement.

ar-ru-ma-dei'-ra *f.* chamber-maid.

ar-ru-mar' *tr.v.* to put in order; to fit into; to take a given direction or line of action.

ar-se-nal' *m.* arsenal.

ar-se-ni-a'-to *m.* arsenate.

ar-sê-ni-co *m.* arsenic.

ar-te-fac'-to *m.* workmanship; artifact.

ar'-te *f.* art, craft, skill.

ar-tis'-ta *m.* artist.

ar-tís-ti-co, ₌a *adj.* artistic.

ar-tei-ri'-ce *f.* artfulness, cunningness, astuteness.

ar-tei'-ro, ₌a *adj.* cunning, astute, contrary, artful.

ar-te'-lho *m.* ankle.

ar-te-mão' *m.* main sail of ship.

ar-té-ria *m.* artery.

ar-te-rial' *adj.* arterial.

ar-te-rio-scle-ro'-se *f.* arteriosclerosis.

ar-te'-sa *f.* kneading trough.

ar-te-são' *m.* vaulted roof; decoration in relief on domes or ceilings; skilled workman.

ár-ti-co, ₌a *adj.* Arctic.

ar-ti-cu-la-ção' *f.* articulation.

ar-ti-cu-la'-do *m.* article (of a partnership or covenant); **-s** *m.pl.* (zoöl.) articulata.

ar-ti-cu-lar' *tr.v.* to articulate; to put in the form of articles.

ar-ti-cu-lis'-ta *m.* writer of newspaper articles.

ar-tí-cu-lo *m.* joint, knuckle; articulation; article, item.

ar-tí-fi-ce *m.* artisan, workman.

ar-ti-fi-cial' *adj.* artificial.

ar-ti-fi-cia-li-da'-de *f.* artificiality.

ar-ti-fí-cio *m.* artifice.

ar-ti-fi-ci-ar' *tr.v.* to produce industrially.

ar-ti'-go *m.* article (gram.), article (newspaper), paragraph in documents; *m .pl.* merchandise.

ar-ti-lha-ri'-a *f.* artillery.

ar-ti-lhei'-ro *m.* artilleryman, gunner, canoneer.

ar-ti-ma'-nha. *f.* artifice, astuteness.

ar-trí-ti-ce, **-a** *adj.* arthritic.

ar-tri-tis'-mo *m.* arthritis.

ar-vo-a'-do, **-a** *adj.* faint, light-headed, dizzy.

ar-vo-ar' *tr.v., intr.v.* to make dizzy or giddy.

ar-vo-ra'-do *m.* soldier with the duties of a sergeant; **ar-vo-ra'-do,** **-a** *adj.* raised up, standing upright.

ar-vo-rar' *tr.v.* to hoist, to lift up, to unveil, to appoint to an office.

ár-vo-re *f.* tree; axle; spindle.

ar-vo-re'-do *m.* arboretum; forest.

ar-vo-re-cer' *intr.v.* to grow into a tree.

ar-vo-re-jar' *tr.v.* to plant with trees.

as *fem.def.art.pl.* the; *demons.pro.* signifying those; *pers.pro.* them, they (*fem.*); **às** contraction of *prep. a* with pronoun *as;* **ás** *m.* ace, person expert in some activity, especially aviation.

a'-sa *f.* wing, fin, handle; *pl.* sides of nostrils; rapidity.

a-sa'-do *m.* utensil with handles; **a-sa'-do,** **-a** *adj.* having handles, having wings.

a-sa-ne'-gro *m.* evil-doer.

as-cen-dên-cia *f.* ascendancy, ancestry.

as-cen-den'-te *adj.* ascendant, rising; *m.* ancestor.

as-cen-der' *intr.v.* to rise, to ascend.

as-cen-são' *f.* ascension.

as-cen-sor' *m.* elevator.

as-ce'-ta *m., f.* ascetic, hermit.

as-cé-ti-ca *f.* asceticism.

as-cé-ti-co, **-a** *adj.* ascetic.

as-ce-tis'-mo *m.* asceticism.

as'-co *m.* loathing, aversion, nausea.

as-co-ro'-so, **-a** *adj.* dirty, repellent; infamous.

ás-cua *f.* live coals; bits flying from red-hot metal when hammered.

as-fal'-to *m.* asphalt.

as-fi-xi'-a *f.* asphyxia.

as-fi-xi-ar' *tr.v.* to asphyxiate.

a-si-lar' *tr.v.* to place in asylum, to give refuge to.

a-si'-lo *m.* asylum.

as'-ma *f.* asthma.

as-má-ti-co, **-a** *m., f.* person suffering from asthma; *adj.* asthmatic.

as'-na *f.* female donkey; triangular framework of rafters, beams (generally of wood) upon which the roof is laid.

as-nal' *adj.* bestial, asinine.

as-na-ri'-a *f.* drove of asses.

as-nei'-ra *f.* nonsense, folly; stubbornness.

as-nei'-ro, **-a** *adj.* asinine, foolish.

as-ni'-ce *f.* asinity.

as-'no *m.* ass, donkey.

as'-pa *f.* St. Andrew's cross; *pl.* quotation mark; sail beams of wind mill; horns of animals.

as-pec'-to *f.* aspect.

as-pe-re'-za *f.* asperity; roughness.

as-pe-ro, **-a** *adj.* rough, rugged, disagreeable to the taste.

ás-per'-ges *m.* sprinkling with holy water.

as-per-gi-men'-to *m.* sprinkling; purging.

as-per-gir' *tr.v.* to purge (with hyssop), to sprinkle.

as-per-são' *f.* aspersion; sprinkling.

as-per-sar' *tr.v.* to sprinkle.

ás-pi-de *f.* asp; (fig.) evil tongue.

as-pi-ra-ção' *f.* aspiration.

as-pi-ra'-do, **-a** *adj.* aspirate.

as-pi-ra-dor' *m.* aspirant; aspirator.

as-pi-rar' *tr.v.* to suck into (pump); to aspirate; *intr.v.* to aspire to, to be a candidate.

as-pi-ri'-na *f.* aspirin.

as-que-ro-si-da'-de *f.* indecency, obscenity.

as-que-ro'-so, **-a** *adj.* nauseating, obnoxious, repellent.

as'-sa *f.* thickened or concentrated vegetable juice.

as-sa'-do *m.* roast; —**s** *m.pl.* difficulties; inflammation.

as-sa-dor' *m.* one who roasts; roaster (utensil).

as-sa-du'-ra *f.* roasting, baking.

as-sar' *tr.v.* to roast, to bake.

as-sa-la-ri-ar' *tr.v.* to pay a stipend to.

as-sal-ta'-da *f.* attack, assault.

as-sal-tar' *tr.v.* to assault.

as-sal'-to *m.* assault, charge, attack.

as-sam-bar-car' *tr.v.* to monopolize; to take for one's exclusive use.

as-sa-nha'-do, **-a** *adj.* angry, furious.

as-sa-nhar' *tr.v.* to make angry, to irritate, to aggravate.

as-sas-si-nar' *tr.v.* to assassinate, to murder.

as-sas-sí-nio *m.* assassination.

as-sas-sí-no *m.* assassin.

as-saz' *adv.* enough, sufficiently.

as-sa-zo-na'-do, **-a** *adj.* seasoned, mature, ripened.

as-se-ar' *tr.v.* to clean; to adorn; to spruce up.

as-se'-cla *m.* partisan, member of sect.

as-se-dar' *tr.v.* to clean flax fiber; to make soft like silk.

as-se-di-ar' *tr.v.* to besiege, to molest with persistent questions.

as-sé-dio *m.* siege.

as-se-gu-ra-ção' *f.* assurance, security.

as-se-gu-ra'-do, **-a** *adj.* made secure, established.

as-sei'-o *m.* cleanliness; care in dress.

as-sem-bléi-a *f.* assembly.

as-se-me-lhar' *tr.v.* to assimilate, to imitate.

as-se-nho-re-a-men'-to *m.* mastery, ownership.

as-se-nho-re-ar'-se *refl.v.* to become master, or owner of; to enter into possession of.

as-sen-ta'-da *f.* jury session to examine witnesses.

as-sen-ta'-do, **-a** *adj.* seated, firm, agreed upon.

as-sen-tar' *tr.v.* to enter (in account-book), to lay, to place on seats; to agree to, to fit well (clothing).

as-sen'-te *adj.* firm; agreed upon.

as-sen'-to *m.* seat, chair; entry (in bookkeeping); foundation; enlistment; residence.

as-sen-ti-men'-to *m.* assent, assenting.

as-sen-tir' *intr.v.* to assent.

as-sep-si'-a *f.* asepsis.

as-sép-ti-co, ˗a *adj.* aseptic.

as-ser-ção' *f.* assertion.

as-ses-tar' *tr.v.* to aim at, to point in direction of, to shoot.

as-se-ve-ra-ção' *f.* asseveration.

as-se-ve-rar' *tr.v.* asseverate.

as-se'-xo, ˗a *adj.* asexual.

as-si-du-i-da'-de *f.* assiduity.

as-sí-duo, ˗a *adj.* assiduous.

as-sim' *adv.* thus, so, in this way; *conj.* — que as soon as.

as-si-me-tri'-a *f.* asymmetry.

as-si-mé-tri-co, ˗a *adj.* asymmetric, asymmetrical.

as-si-mi-la-ção' *f.* assimilation.

as-si-mi-lar' *tr.v.* to assimilate; to make similar; to compare.

as-si-mi-lá-vel *adj.* assimilable.

as-si-na-ção' *f.* notification, citation.

as-si-na'-do *m.* signed document.

as-si-nan'-te *m.* subscriber; signer.

as-si-nar' *tr.v.* to sign, to subscribe to; *intr.v.* to write one's name, to become a subscriber (to a publication).

as-si-na-tu'-ra *f.* signature; subscription.

as-sis-tên-cia *f.* audience, attendance; aid, assistance; medical attention, first-aid ambulance.

as-sis-ten'-te *m.* personal physician, obstetrician.

as-sis-tir' *intr.v.* to be present; *tr.v.* to aid, to help; to treat (in illness).

as-so-a-lha'-do, ˗a *adj.* having a floor.

as-so-a-lhar' *tr.v.* to put flooring down; to divulge; to expose to sun.

as-so-ar' *tr.v.* to blow nose, to clean nose of mucus.

as-so-ber-ba'-do, ˗a *adj.* proud, haughty; wealthy; overworked.

as-so-ber-bar' *tr.v.* to insult, to humiliate, to dominate; —˗se *refl.v.* to be haughty.

as-so-bian'-te *adj.* whistling.

as-so-biar' *intr.v.* to whistle; to hiss; to whistle music.

as-so-bi'-o *m.* whistle.

as-so-bra-dar' *tr.v.* to lay planks of flooring; *intr.v.* to make second floor or attic.

as-so-cia-ção' *f.* association, society.

as-so-cia'-do *m.* member.

as-so-ciar' *tr.v.* to associate, to join, to unite.

as-so-la-ção' *f.* devastation.

as-so-ma'-da *f.* summit, highest point.

as-so-ma'-do, ˗a *adj.* irritable, headstrong, tipsy.

as-so-mar' *intr.v.* to appear in distance, to peep out; —˗se *refl.v.* to fly into a passion, to become very animated because of drink.

as-so'-mo *m.* token, sign.

as-som-bra-ção' *f.* (Brazil) terror at the supernatural.

as-som-bra-di'-ço, ˗a *adj.* easily frightened.

as-som-bra'-do, ˗a *adj.* shaded; terrified; dizzy from drinking.

as-som-brar' *tr.v.* to shade; to frighten;

intr.v. to cause astonishment; —˗se *refl.v.* to be covered by shadow; to be surprised.

as-som'-bro *m.* surprise; miracle, wonder; terror.

as-so-nân-cia *f.* assonance.

as-so-pra'-do, ˗a *adj.* proud, puffed up.

as-so-prar' *tr.v.,* *intr.v.* to breathe out in puffs; to whisper in ear; to puff up with vanity.

as-su-a'-da *f.* riot, tumult.

as-su-mir' *tr.v.* to assume.

as-sun-ção' *f.* assumption.

as-sun-gar' *tr.v.* to raise, to push up.

as-sun-tar' *intr.v.* to listen to, to consider, to pay attention.

as-sun'-to *m.* subject, theme, matter.

as-sus-ta'-do, ˗a *adj.* timid, frightened, undecided, vacillating.

as-sus-tar' *tr.v.* to frighten; —˗se *refl.v.* to be frightened.

as-te-ni'-a *f.* asthenia.

as-te-ris'-co *m.* asterisk.

as-te-ris'-mo *m.* constellation; asterism.

as-tig-má-ti-co, ˗a *adj.* astigmatic.

as-tig-ma-tis'-mo *m.* astigmatism.

as-tra-cã' *m.* astrakhan.

as-tral' *adj.* astral.

as'-tro *m.* star; (fig.) eminent person; very beautiful woman.

as-tro-lo-gi'-a *f.* astrology.

as-tró-lo-go *m.* astrologer.

as-tro-no-mi'-a *f.* astronomy.

as-trô-no-mo *m.* astronomer.

as-tú-cia *f.* astuteness.

as-tu-cio'-so, ˗a *adj.* astute, cunning.

as-tu'-to, ˗a *adj.* astute, cunning.

a'-ta *f.* minutes of any meeting; *pl.* resolutions, other determinations made by group.

a'-ta *f.* fruit of the Brazilian *ateiro* (a tree).

a-tei'-ro *m.* Brazilian tree.

a-ta-ba-lho-ar' *tr.v.* to say or do something without reason, to confuse or disturb.

a-ta'-ca *f.* cord, string, lace.

a-ta-ca-dis'-ta *m.* wholesale merchant.

a-ta-ca'-do, ˗a *adj.* attacked, laced up; wholesale.

a-ta-can'-te *adj.* aggressive.

a-ta-car' *tr.v.* to attack, to seize.

a-ta'-do *m.* bundle, package; **a-ta'-do,** ˗a *adj.* shy.

a-ta-du'-ra *f.* bandage, ligature.

a-ta-fu-lhar' *tr.v.* to fill too full, to eat too much.

a-ta-la'-ia *f.* guard, look-out, watchtower, crow's nest.

a-ta-lai-ar' *tr.v.* to place sentinels, to guard.

a-ta-lha'-da *f.* strip cut in timber as fire protection.

a-ta-lhar' *tr.v.* to cut, to shorten route, to interrupt, to narrow.

a-ta'-lho *m.* short cut, by-path.

a-ta-man-car' *tr.v.* to bungle, to do something hastily and badly.

a-ta-men'-to *m.* timidity, self-consciousness.

a-ta'-que *m.* attack, aggression, sudden illness.

a-tar' *tr.v.* to dress (wound), to tie up, to submit, to impede.

a-ta-re-fa'-do, ˗a *adj.* very busy, occupied with many tasks.

a-ta-re-far' *tr.v.* to assign a task.

a-tar-ra-car' *tr.v.* to make horse-shoe ready.

a-tar-ra-xa-dor' m. screw-driver.

a-tar-ra-xar' tr.v. to make secure with screws, to screw.

a-ta-ú-de m. coffin.

a-ta-vi-ar' tr.v. to beautify.

a-ta-vi'-o m. adornment, attire.

a-ta-vis'-mo m. atavism.

a-té prep. until, up to, down to, as far as; adv. still, also, even.

a-te-ar' tr.v. to set fire to, to kindle; to promote.

a-te-ís-mo m. atheism.

a-te-ís-ta m. atheist.

a-te-lhar' tr.v. to cover with tiles.

a-te-mo-ri-zar' tr.v. to intimidate, to frighten.

a-ten-ção' f. attention.

a-ten-cio'-so, =a adj. attentive.

a-ten-der' tr.v. to attend, to pay attention to, to take into consideration.

a-ten-dí-vel adj. deserving attention.

a-te-neu' m. athenæum.

a-ten-ta'-do m. criminal attack.

a-ten-tar' tr.v., intr.v. to observe carefully; to make an attempt upon.

a-ten-ta-tó-rio m. unlawful, outrageous.

a-te-nua-ção' f. attenuation.

a-te-nu-ar' tr.v. to attenuate.

a-ter-ra'-do m. landing terrain.

a-ter-ra-dor', terrifying.

a-ter-ra'-gem f. landing (of an airplane).

a-ter-rar' tr.v. to terrify, to cover with earth; intr.v. to land (of an airplane).

a-ter-ris-sa'-gem f. landing (of an airplane).

a-ter-ris-sar' intr.v. to land.

a-têr-ro m. landing; embankment.

a-ter'-se refl.v. to stand by a decision; to take a stand.

a-te-sar' tr.v. to tighten, to hold taut.

a-tes-ta'-do, =a adj. full, running over.

a-tes-tar' tr.v. to fill up to the top.

a-tes-ta'-do m. certificate, attestation.

a-tes-tan'-te m.f. attestant, witness.

a-tes-tar' tr.v. to attest.

a-teu' m. atheist.

a-ti-cis'-mo m. Atticism.

á-ti-co, =a adj. Attic.

a-ti-jo-lar' tr.v. to cover with brick.

a-ti-la-do, =a adj. scrupulous, discreet, expert, elegant, correct.

a-ti-lar' tr.v. to do something with great care; to place the til on.

á-ti-mo m. very short time, instant.

a-ti-na'-do, =a adj. discreet, tactful, judicious.

a-ti-nar' intr.v. to do something tactfully or prudently, to guess right.

a-ti'-no m. tact, circumspection.

a-tin-gir' tr.v. to reach to, to attain, to include; to achieve.

a-tin-gí-vel adj. attainable.

a-tí-pi-co, =a adj. atypic.

a-ti-ra'-da f. shooting, firing (of guns).

a-ti-ra-di'-ço, =a adj. petulant; bold; adventurous, romantic.

a-ti-ra'-do, =a adj. brave, daring.

a-ti-rar' tr.v. to throw, to fling; intr.v. to shoot, to fire; —=se refl.v. to fling oneself forward.

a-ti-tu'-de f. attitude.

a-ti'-va f. active voice.

a-ti-va-ção' f. activation.

a-ti-var' tr.v. to activate.

a-ti-vi-da'-de f. activity.

a-ti'-vo, =a adj. active.

at'-las m. atlas.

at-le'-ta m. athlete.

at-lé-ti-co, =a adj. athletic.

at-le-tis'-mo m. athletics.

at-mos-fé'-ra f. atmosphere.

at-mos-fé-ri-co, =a adj., atmospheric.

a'-to m. act, action, deed.

a-to-ar' tr.v. to tow (ship); to move along aimlessly; intr.v. to balk (animal).

a-to-ar'-da f. rumor, vague notice.

a-to-a-lha'-do, =a adj. damask.

a-to-a-lhar' tr.v. to cover with table-cloth.

a-to-char' tr.v. to wedge in, to make tight with wedge, to force in.

a-tô-cho m. wedge.

a-to-lar' tr.v. to bury in mud or mire.

a-to-lei-ma'-do, =a adj. crazy, foolish, silly.

a-to-lei-mar'=se refl.v. to assume manners of stupid, foolish person.

a-to-lei'-ro m. mud-hole; disgrace; inescapable difficulty.

a-tô-mi-co, =a adj. atomic.

a-to-mis'-mo m. atomism.

a-to-mis'-ta m. atomist.

a-to-mi-zar' tr.v. to atomize.

á-to-mo m. atom.

a-to-ni'-a f. atony.

a-tô-ni-co, =a adj. atonic.

a-tô-ni-to, =a adj. surprised, astonished, stupified.

á-to-no, =a adj. atonic.

a-ton-tar' tr.v. to make dizzy, to surprise greatly.

a-tor' m. actor; agent, doer.

a-to'-ra f. block, length of wood.

a-to-rar' tr.v. to saw into blocks, to cut in half.

a-tor-do-a-men'-to m. dizziness; unconsciousness.

a-tor-do-ar' tr.v. to stun, to stupify.

a-tor-men-tar' tr.v. to torment, to torture, to afflict.

a-tou-ca'-do, =a adj. wearing a bonnet; having form of bonnet; looking like bonnet.

a-tou-ci-nha'-do, =a adj. fat like bacon, greasy.

a-tra-bi-li-o'-so, =a adj. atrabilious.

a-tra-ca'-do, =a adj. over-burdened, overloaded; embarrassed.

a-tra-ca-dor' m. hawser.

a-tra-ção' f. attraction.

a-tra-car' tr.v. to come along-side; to dock, to moor.

a-tra-en'-te adj. attractive.

a-tra-i-ço-a-dor' m. traitor, betrayer.

a-tra-i-ço-ar' tr.v. to betray.

a-tra-i-men'-to m. attraction.

a-tra-ir' tr.v. to attract.

a-tra-ti-vi-da'-de f. attractiveness.

a-tra-ti'-vo, =a adj. attractive.

a-tra-ti'-vos m.pl. charms, graces, attractions.

a-tra-pa-lha-ção' f. embarrassment, timidity.

a-tra-pa-lhar' tr.v. to confuse, to disturb, to embarrass.

a-trás adv. behind, back of.

a-tra-sa'-do, =a adj. behind, obsolete, ancient, under-developed.

a-tra-sar' tr.v. to put behind, to delay, to hold back; —=se refl.v. to move more slowly (of a watch), to be behind time.

a-tra'-so m. delay, behind the times, act of delaying.

a-tra-van'-co m. obstacle, impediment.

a-tra-vés adv. across, from side to side.

a-tra-ves-sa'-do, =a adj. restless, disloyal, oblique, cross-wise.

a-tra-ves-sa-dei'-ro m. cross-road.

a-tra-ves-sar' *tr.v.* to cross, to lay across, to penetrate.
a-trei'-to, =a *adj.* subject to, inclined to.
a-tre-lar' *tr.v.* to lead on leash; to seduce, to dominate; to hitch, to harness.
a-tre-vi'-do, =a *adj.* daring, insolent, petulant.
a-tri-bu-i-ção' *f.* attribution.
a-tri-bu-ir' *tr.v.* to attribute.
a-tri-bu-í-vel *adj.* attributable.
a-tri-bu-lar' *tr.v.* to worry, to cause tribulation.
a-tri-bu'-to *m.* attribute.
á-trio *m.* atrium.
a-tri'-to *m.* friction; misunderstanding; *pl.* difficulties; **a-tri'-to**, =a *adj.* repentent, sorry for.
a-triz' *f.* actress.
a'-tro, =a *adj.* dismal, mournful, black.
a-tro-a'-da *f.* rumbling; thunder.
a-tro-ar' *tr.v.* to make tremble with thunder or loud noise; *intr.v.* to rumble, to thunder.
a-tro-ci-da'-de *f.* atrocity.
a-tro-fi'-a *f.* atrophy.
a-tro-fi-ar' *tr.v.*, *intr.v.* to atrophy.
a-tró-fi-co, =a *adj.* atrophic.
a-tro-pe-lar' *tr.v.* to trip up, to tread on, to push over.
a-troz' *adj.* atrocious, without pity, inhuman, cruel.
a-tual' *adj.* present, present-day; actual.
a-tua-li-da'-de *f.* "up-to-dateness," actuality.
a-tu-ar' *tr.v.* to actuate.
a-tu-ar' *tr.v.* to use personal pronoun *tu;* to speak familiarly.
a-tu-lhar' *tr.v.* to fill completely.
a-tum' *m.* tuna fish.
a-tu-mul-tu-ar' *tr.v.* to provoke mutiny or tumult.
a-tu-ra'-do, =a *adj.* constant, persistent.
a-tu-rar' *tr.v.* to endure, to tolerate, to prolong; *intr.v.* to persevere, to last a long time.
a-tu-rá-vel *adj.* endurable.
a-tur-di'-do, =a *adj.* greatly surprised, open-eyed, dizzy.
a-tur-dir' *tr.v.* to deafen, to astound.
au-da'-cia *f.* audacity.
au-da-cio'-so, =a *adj.* audacious.
au-daz' *adj.* bold, daring.
au-di-ção' *f.* audition, concert.
au-diên-cia *f.* audience, hearing.
au-di-ti'-vo, =a *adj.* auditory.
au-di-tor' *m.* auditor; magistrate; provost.
au-di-tó-rio *m.* audience; auditorium.
au-dí-vel *adj.* audible.
au-fe-rir' *tr.v.* to obtain, to gain.
au-fe-rí-vel *adj.* obtainable.
au'-ge *m.* summit, to highest degree, apogee.
au-gu-rar' *tr.v.* to augur, to conjecture.
áu-gu-re *m.* augur.
au-gú-rio *m.* augury.
au-gus'-to, =a *adj.* august.
au'-la *f.* class, class-room, lesson.
áu-li-co, =a *adj.* courtly, aulic.
au-li'-do *m.* howling, cry of animals.
au-men-ta-ção' *f.* increase, enlargement, addition.
au-men-tar' *tr.v.* to augment; to increase; *intr.v.* to prosper, to better.
au-men'-to *m.* increase, improvement, progress.
au'-ra *f.* aura.
áu-re-o, =a *adj.* aureate; golden.
au-ré-o-la *f.* aureole, halo.

au-re-o-lar' *tr.v.* to adorn with a halo, to glorify.
au-ri-co-lor' *adj.* golden-hued.
au-rí-cu-la *f.* auricle.
au-rí-fi-ce *m.* goldsmith.
au-ro'-ra *f.* aurora.
aus-cul-ta-ção' *f.* auscultation.
aus-cul-ta-dor' *m.* ear-piece (of telephone); auscultator.
aus-cul-tar' *tr.v.* to auscultate.
au-sên-ci-a *f.* absence.
au-sen-tar'-se *refl.v.* to absent oneself.
au-sen'-te *adj.* absent.
áus-pi-ce *m.* soothsayer.
aus-pí-cio *m.* omen; auspices.
aus-te-re'-za *f.* austerity.
aus-te-ri-da'-de *f.* austerity.
aus-te'-ro, =a *adj.* austere.
aus-tral' *adj.* austral, southern.
au-tên-ti-ca *f.* certificate.
au-ten-ti-ca-ção' *f.* authentication.
au-ten-ti-car' *tr.v.* to authenticate.
au-ten-ti-ci-da'-de *f.* authenticity.
au-tên-ti-co, =a *adj.* authentic.
au'-to *m.* act, deed; farce; ceremony.
au-to-bi-o-gra-fi'-a *f.* autobiography.
au-to-cla'-ve *f.* autoclave.
au-to-cra-ci'-a *f.* autocracy.
au-tó-cra-ta *m.* autocrat.
au-to-crá-ti-co, =a *adj.* autocratic.
au-to=de-fé *m.* auto-de-fe.
au-to-gi'-ro *m.* auto-giro.
au-to-gra-far' *tr.v.* to autograph.
au-tó-gra-fo *m.* autograph.
au-to-má-ti-co, =a *adj.* automatic.
au-tô-ma-to *m.* automaton.
au-to-mó-vel *m.* automobile; *adj.* self-propelling.
au-to-no-mi'-a *f.* autonomy.
au-tô-no-mo, =a *adj.* autonomous.
au-to-ô-ni-bus *m.* bus.
au-tóp-sia *f.* autopsy.
au-top-siar' *tr.v.* to perform an autopsy.
au-tor' *m.* author.
au-to-ri'-a *f.* authorship.
au-to-ri-da'-de *f.* authority.
au-to-ri-tá-rio, =a *adj.* authoritarian.
au-to-ri-za-ção' *f.* authorization.
au-to-ri-zar' *tr.v.* to authorize; —-se *refl.v.* to acquire authority.
au-xi-li-ar' *tr.v.* to aid; *m.* helper, assistant.
au-xi-liá-rio, =a *adj.* auxiliary.
au-xí-lio *m.* help, aid.
a-val' *m.* guarantee, security.
a-va-lan'-che *f.* avalanche.
a-va-li-a-ção' *f.* evaluation.
a-va-li-ar' *tr.v.* to evaluate, to recognize the force of, to have some idea of.
a-va-lis'-ta *m.* underwriter.
a-va-li-zar' *tr.v.* to underwrite bonds issued by banks.
a-van'-ça *f.* onset, attack.
a-van-ça'-da *f.* assault.
a-van-ça-men'-to *m.* projection of part of a building.
a-vançar' *intr.v.*, *tr.v.* to advance, to move forward.
a-van'-ce or **a-van'-ço** *m.* advancement, improvement; advantage.
a-van-ta-jar' *tr.v.* to exceed, to be superior to; *intr.v.* to progress; —-se *refl.v.* to have advantage over.
a-van'-te *adv.* in front; *interj.* to the front!!
a-va-ren'-to, =a *adj.* avaricious.
a-va-re'-za *f.* avarice.
a-va-ri'-a *f.* loss, depreciation; salvage expense.

a-va-ri-a'-do, =a *adj*. damaged, ruined.
a-va-ri-ar' *tr.v.*, *intr.v.* to damage, to injure.
a-vas-sa-lar' *tr.v.* to dominate, to turn into vassals, to oppress.
a'-ve *f.* bird.
a-vei'-a *f.* oats.
a-ve-lã' *f.* hazel nut.
a-ve-lu-dar' *tr.v.* to make like velvet; a-ve-lu-da'-do, =a *adj*. like velvet.
a-ven'-ca *f.* maiden-hair fern.
a-ven'-ça *f.* adjustment, agreement.
a-ve-ni'-da *f.* avenue.
a-ven-tal' *m.* apron.
a-ven-tar' *tr.v.* to ventilate, to expose to air.
a-ven-tu'-ra *f.* adventure; chance.
a-ven-tu-ra'-do, =a *adj*. adventuresome.
a-ven-tu-rei'-ro *m.* adventurer.
a-ven-tu-rar' *tr.v.* to risk, to venture.
a-ver-ba-men'-to *m.* marginal note.
a-ver-bar' *tr.v.* to register, to annotate; to use as verb.
a-ver-go-ar' *tr.v.* to bruise with whip or stick.
a-ve-ri-gua-ção' *f.* investigation, inquiry, check.
a-ve-ri-guar' *tr.v.* to inquire into; to ascertain, to find out; to investigate; to determine the truth of.
a-ver-me-lhar' *tr.v.* to turn red or reddish.
a-ver-são' *f.* aversion.
a-ver'-so, =a *adj*. averse.
a-ves'-sas *f.pl.* opposite things; às=— the wrong way, wrong side out.
a-vês-so *m.* bottom side, reverse, bad side.
a-ves-truz' *m.* ostrich.
a-ves-tru-zei'-ro *m.* person who plucks plumes from ostriches.
a-ve-xa'-do, =a *adj*. impatient, in haste.
a-ve-zar' *tr.v.* to put in habit of; —=se *refl.v.* to become accustomed.
a-vi-a-ção' *f.* aviation.
a-via-dor' *m.* aviator.
a-vi-ão' *m.* air-plane.
a-vi-a-men'-to *m.* preparation; =s *m. pl.* tools, instruments.
a-vi-ar' *tr.v.* to prepare, to hasten, to dispatch; to serve promptly.
a-vi-á-rio *m.* aviary.
a-ví-co-la *f.* bird-fancier.
a-ví-cu-la *f.* little bird.
a-vi-cul-tu'-ra *f.* bird breeding.
a-vi-dez' *f.* avidity.
á-vi-do, =a *adj*. avid.
a-vi-go-rar' *tr.v.* to invigorate.
a-vi-la-na'-do, =a *adj*. rough, coarse, low-mannered.
a-vi-li-nar'=se *refl.v.* to degenerate, to become villainous.
a-vil-tar' *tr.v.* to dishonor, to humiliate, to disrespect.
a-vi-na-grar' *tr.v.* to season with vinegar.
a-vin'-do, =a *adj*. harmonized, agreed.
a-vin-dor' *m.* mediator.
a-vir' *tr.v.* to adjust, to reconcile; —=se *refl.v.* to come to an agreement, to make a bargain.

a-vi-sa'-do, =a *adj*. discreet, prudent.
a-vi-sar' *tr.v.* to advise, to notify.
a-ví'-so *m.* notice; counsel, warning; scout-boat.
a-vis-tar' *tr.v.* to sight, to see far away, to catch a glimpse of.
a-vi-va-men'-to *m.* vivification.
a-vi-var' *tr.v.* to vivify.
a-vi-zi-nha-ção' *f.* approaching.
a-vi-zi-nhar' *tr.v.* to approach, to border upon.
a-vô *m.* grandfather.
a-vó *m.* grandmother.
a-vo-a'-do, =a *adj*. silly, light-headed, crazy.
a-vo-ca-ção' *f.* transfer of suit from one court to another.
a-vo-car' *tr.v.* to appeal (case in court).
a-vo-en'-go, =a *adj*. ancestral; a-vo-en'-gos *m.pl.* ancestors.
a-vo-en-guei'-ro, =a *adj*. ancestral.
a-vul-são' *f.* extraction, pulling.
a-vul'-so, =a *adj*. separate; scattered.
a-vul-ta'-do, =a *adj*. voluminous, considerable.
a-vul-tar' *tr.v.* to enlarge, to increase volume.
a-vul-to'-so, =a *adj*. large, bulky.
a'-xe *f.* axis.
a-xi'-la *f.* armpit.
a-xi-o'-ma *m.* axiom.
a-xio-má-ti-co, =a *adj*. axiomatic.
az' *f.* squadron, wing of army, troops.
a-za'-do, =a *adj*. opportune, lucky.
a-zá-fa-ma *f.* crowd, rush, haste, confusion.
a-za-fa-mar'=se *refl.v.* to hurry, to rush ahead, to work energetically.
a-zá-le-a *f.* azalea.
a-zar' *m.* bad luck, disgrace; Asiatic coin.
a-za-ra'-do, =a *adj*. unlucky, unfortunate.
a-ze-da-men'-to *m.* turning sour, souring.
a-ze-dar' *tr.v.* to turn sour.
a-zei-tar' *tr.v.* to oil, to season with olive oil.
a-zei'-te *m.* oil, olive oil; — doce olive oil.
a-zei-tei'-ra *f.* oil cruet.
a-zei-tei'-ro *m.* oil merchant.
a-zei-to'-na *f.* olive.
a-zi'-a *f.* heart-burn, stomach acidity.
a-zi-ar' *m.* bridle bit.
a-ziu-ma'-do, =a *adj*. sour, irritated.
a-zi-u-mar' *tr.v.* to cause sourness or acidity, to irritate.
a'-zo *m.* wish, pretext, occasion.
a-zo-a'-do, =a *adj*. dizzy, disturbed.
a-zo-ar' *tr.v.* to stun, to stupify, to make angry.
a-zor-ra'-gue *m.* whip, lash.
a-zo'-to *m.* nitrogen.
a-zou-ga'-do, =a *adj*. alive, quick, alert.
a-zou-gar' *tr.v.* to coat with mercury, to silver (a mirror).
a-zou'-gue *m.* mercury; (fig.) alert person.
a-zul' *adj*. blue; *m.* blue color.
a-zu-la'-do, =a *adj*. bluish.
a-zu-lê-jo *m.* glazed tile.

B

See page 12—GUIDE TO REFORMED SPELLING used in this Dictionary

B *m.* B, b; second letter of the alphabet.
ba'-ba *f.* drivel, saliva.
ba-ba'-do *m.* ruffling.
ba-ba-dou'-ro *m.* bib.
ba-bar' *tr.v.* to wet with saliva; —*se refl.v.* to drivel, to slobber; to stutter.
ba-bel' *f.* (fig.) confusion of languages or voices; noisiness.
ba-bé-li-co, -a *adj.* in disorder, confused.
ba-ca-lhau' *m.* cod-fish.
ba-ca-lho-a'-da *f.* cod-fish dish.
ba-ca-lho-ei'-ro *m.* cod-fish dealer; cod-fish vessel.
ba-ca-mar-ta'-da *f.* shot from blunderbuss.
ba-ca-mar'-te *m.* blunderbuss (gun).
ba-ca-nal' *f., adj.* bacchanal.
ba-can'-te *f.* bacchante, priestess of Bacchus.
ba-ca-rá *m.* baccarat (game of chance).
ba-cha-rel' *m.* bachelor; loquacious person.
ba-cha-re-la'-do *m.* bachelor's degree.
ba-cha-re-lan'-do *m.* candidate for bachelor's degree.
ba-cha-re-lar'-se *refl.v.* to receive the bachelor's degree.
ba-ci'-a *f.* basin; bowl.
ba-ci'-o *m.* chamber-pot.
ba-ci-lar' *adj.* bacillary.
ba-ci'-lo *m.* bacillus.
ba'-ço *m.* spleen.
bac-té-ria *f.* bacteria.
bac-te-rio-lo-gí-a *f.* bacteriology.
bac-te-rio-lo-gis'-ta *m.* bacteriologist.
bá-cu-lo *m.* staff, bishop's staff.
ba-da-la'-da *f.* sound of clapper, stroke of clapper.
ba-da-lar' *tr.v.* to ring; to reveal indiscreetly.
ba-da-lei'-ra *f.* hook for bell-clapper.
ba-da'-lo *m.* bell-clapper.
ba-de'-go *m.* kind of fish; **ba-de'-go, -a** *adj.* conspicuous, extraordinary.
ba-e'-ta *f.* flannelette; fleecy woolen cloth; baize.
ba-fe-jar' *tr.v.* to breathe or blow gently; (fig.) to favor, to protect.
ba-fe'-jo *m.* light breeze.
ba'-fo *m.* breath, vapor; favor, protection.
ba'-ga *f.* red berry; drop of perspiration.
ba-ga-cei'-ra *f.* trash heap, trash box; junk.
ba-ga'-ço *m.* husk, peelings, skin (of fruit).
ba-ga-gei'-ra *f.* allowance for baggage transportation.
ba-ga-gei'-ro *m.* baggage-man; baggage-car; horse coming in last in race.
ba-ga'-gem *f.* baggage.
ba-ga-te'-la *f.* bagatelle.
ba'-go *m.* each grape of bunch; each fruit of that which grows in a bunch.
ba-gun'-ça *f.* disorder.
ba-gun-cei'-ro, -a *adj.* disorderly.
ba-í-a *f.* bay; stall (for horses).
bai-lar' *intr.v.* to dance.
bai-la-dei'-ra *f.* danseuse.

bai-la'-do *m.* ballet; dance.
bai-la-ri'-no, -a *m.f.* dancer, ballet dancer.
bai'-le *m.* dance, ball.
ba-í-nha *f.* sheath, scabbard; hem (of a garment).
ba'-io, -a *adj.* bay-colored; *m.* bay horse.
bai-o-ne'-ta *f.* bayonet.
bair'-ro *m.* city zone; suburban section.
bai'-xa *f.* low area; drop (in prices); shallows; demotion, discharge.
bai-xa'-da *f.* valley, lowland.
bai-xar' *tr.v.* to lower, to bring down; *intr.v.* to lower, to come down, to go down; to decrease; to lose prestige.
bai-xe'-la *f.* table service (silver or china).
bai-xe'-za *f.* vileness, indignity, inferiority.
bai-xi'-nho *adv.* in a low voice, in secret.
bai-xi'-o *m.* sand-bank, shoal.
bai'-xo, -a *adj.* low; cheap, vile, coarse, inferior, short; *adv.* in a low voice.
bai-xo'-te *adj.* rather low.
bai-xo-re-lê-vo *m.* bas-relief.
ba-jou-jar' *tr.v.* to flatter, to encourage.
ba-ju-lar' *tr.v.* to flatter in a servile way.
ba'-la *f.* shot, bullet; bale; package of paper equivalent to thirty-two reams.
ba-la'-da *f.* ballad.
ba-lai'-o *m.* straw hamper; knapsack made of straw.
ba-lan'-ça *f.* scales; balance; (fig.) equilibrium, judgment.
ba-lan-çar' *tr.v.* to balance, to weigh; to swing.
ba-lan-cé *m.* dance step; die (to make coins).
ba-lan-cei'-ro *m.* balance beam; weigher.
ba-lan'-ço *m.* balance; swinging; rolling, seesaw; careful examination.
ba-lão' *m.* balloon; (Brazil) cone-shaped dirt kiln (in which wood charcoal is burned); balloon skirt.
ba-lar' *t.-v.* to bleat.
ba-las'-tro *m.* ballast.
ba-la-us-tra'-do, -a *adj.* having a balustrade.
ba-la-ús-tre *m.* baluster.
bal-bu-cia-ção' *f.* stammering, stuttering.
bal-bu-ci-ar' *tr.v.* to stammer, stutter, to lisp.
bal-bú-cie *f.* stutter.
bal-búr-dia *f.* confusion, disorder, noise.
bal-bur-di-ar' *tr.v.* to cause noisy tumult.
bal-cão' *m.* balcony; display counter; box (in theater).
bal-dar' *tr.v.* to frustrate, to make useless; —*se refl.v.* to discard cards not needed in the play.
bal-da-quim' or **bal-da-qui'-no** *m.* baldachin; canopy.
bal-de-a-ção' *f.* transfer (of baggage or passengers).
bal-de-ar' *tr.v.* to transfer; to decant.
bal'-do, -a *adj.* lacking, short; short-suited (in cards).
ba-le-ar' *tr.v.* to shoot a bullet into.
ba-le-ei'-ra *f.* whaler (boat).

ba-le-ei'-ro *m.* whale fisherman.
ba-lei'-a *f.* whale; (fig.) fat woman.
ba-lei'-ro *m.* street vendor of home-made candy carried on large tray.
ba-le'-la *f.* false rumor.
ba-li'-do *m.* bleat.
ba-lís-ti-ca *f.* ballistics.
ba-li'-za *f.* mark, stake to indicate limit; buoy; frame-work (ship).
ba-li-zar' *tr.v.* to mark out the boundaries of.
bal-ne-ar' *adj.* bathing.
bal-ne-á-rio, =a *adj.* bathing.
ba-lo-fo'-fo, =a *adj.* light; without body; airy.
ba-lou-çar' *tr.v.* to balance; to swing.
ba-lou'-ço *m.* swing; hammock.
bal'-sa *f.* thick forest; fermented pulp of grapes; small raft used to cross rivers; raft of crude rubber balls, tied together with wire, which float down Amazon river when low water prevents boat traffic.
bal-sei'-ro *m.* vat in which grapes are trampled in making wine; boatman in rubber raft.
bal-sa-mi-zar' *tr.v.* to perfume, to treat with any aromatic substance.
bál-sa-mo *m.* balsam; (fig.) comfort, consolation.
ba-lu-ar'-te *m.* fort; high building supported by strong walls; (fig.) secure place.
bam-be-ar' *intr.v.* to love deeply; to moderate one's enthusiasm; to work in a less intense manner.
bam'-bo, =a *adj.* lax, hesitant, languid.
bam-bo-le-ar' *intr.v.*, —=se *refl.v.* to reel, to stagger, to waddle, to see-saw.
ba-nal' *adj.* banal; common-place.
ba-na-li-da'-de *f.* banality.
ba-na-li-zar' *tr.v.* to make common-place.
ba-na'-na *f.* banana; *m.* (fig.) listless person.
ba-na-nal' *m.* banana grove.
ba-na-nei'-ra *f.* banana tree.
ban'-ca *f.* desk, table; school desk; lawyer's office; law; game of chance, stake.
ban-ca'-da *f.* long bench; special committee; delegation.
ban-car' *intr.v.* to gamble; to pretend, to imagine.
ban-cá-rio, =a *adj.* banking, financial.
ban-car-ro'-ta *f.* bankruptcy, failure.
ban'-co *m.* bank; bench, work-bench, park bench; display counter.
ban'-da *f.* side, band, bandage; ribbon, shoulder-strap; direction.
ban-da'-da *f.* flock.
ban-dar' *tr.v.* to band; to line, to face.
ban-de-ar' *tr.v.* to gather together in a party (politics).
ban-dei'-ra *f.* banner, flag; reflector, shade; upper part of door or window; expedition, exploration (into Brazilian back-country in sixteenth, seventeenth, and eighteenth centuries); group, party.
ban-dei-ran'-te *m.* explorer (in Brazilian back-country).
ban-dei-ro'-la *f.* little flag, streamer.
ban-de'-ja *f.* tray; large straw fan used to winnow grain.
ban-di'-do *m.* bandit.
ban-di-tis'-mo *m.* banditry.
ban'-do *m.* band, group, gang, faction; ban, proclamation.
ban-do-lei'-ro *m.* robber, bandit; (pop.) untruthful person.

ba'-nha *f.* lard; perfumed hair pomade.
ba-nhar' *tr.v.* to bathe, to dip. to water, to wet, to dampen.
ba-nhei'-ra *f.* bath-tub.
ba-nhei'-ro *m.* bath-room; manager or owner of a bathing establishment.
ba-nhis'-ta *m.* bather.
ba'-nho *m.* bath, bathing; — de chuva shower bath.
ba-nho=ma-ri'-a *m.* double boiler.
ba-nir' *tr.v.* to banish, to expel, to exile.
ban'-jo *m.* banjo.
ban-quei'-ro *m.* banker; (on sugar plantation) person in charge of boiling.
ban-que'-ta *f.* stool; small tunnel opening out from a large one.
ban-que'-te *m.* banquet.
ban-que-te-ar' *tr.v.* *tr.v.* to banquet, to wine and dine; —=se *refl.v.* to revel, to live in great state, to be extravagant, to spend much on food and drink.
ba-que-ar' *intr.v.* to fall, to tumble, to fall with a thud; —=se *refl.v.* to throw oneself to the ground, to prostrate oneself.
ba-ra-fun'-da *f.* disorderly multitude; noise; confusion.
ba-ra-lha-dor' *m.* shuffler, player whose turn it is to shuffle.
ba-ra-lhar' *tr.v.* to shuffle (cards).
ba-ra'-lho *m.* deck, pack of cards.
ba-rão' *m.* baron.
ba-ra'-ta *f.* cockroach; butter-churn racing automobile.
ba-ra-te-a-men'-to *m.* reduction.
ba-ra-te-ar' *tr.v.* to reduce, to lower, to cheapen; to haggle.
ba-ra-tei'-ro, =a *adj.* liberal, cheap.
ba-ra-te'-za *f.* cheapness, moderateness.
ba-ra'-to, =a *adj.* cheap; ba-r '-to *adv.* cheap, cheaply; *m.* rake-off, bonus.
bar'-ba *f.* beard; chin; long hairs around mouth of some animals; fazer a — to shave; — a — face to face.
bar-ba-di'-nho *m.* Franciscan monk.
bar-ba'-do, =a *adj.* bearded.
bar-ban'-te *m.* twine.
bar-ba-res'-co, =a *adj.* of Barbary.
bar-ba-ri'-a *f.* barbary.
bar-ba-ri-da'-de *f.* barbarity, barbarousness.
bar-ba-ris'-mo *m.* barbarism.
bar-ba-ta'-na *f.* fin (of a fish); bony layer in roof of whale's mouth.
bar-be-ar' *tr.v.* to shave; —=se *refl.v.* to shave oneself.
bar-bei'-ro *m.* barber.
bar'-ca *f.* ferry-boat, lighter.
bar-ca'-ça *f.* large ferry-boat, large lighter; Brazilian coastal boat.
bar-ca-ro'-la *f.* barcarole.
bar'-co *m.* row-boat.
bár-di-co, =a *adj.* bardic.
bar'-do *m.* bard; hedge; sheep-fold.
bar-ga'-nha *f.* bargain; fraudulent transaction.
bar-ga-nhar' *tr.v.* to exchange, to barter.
ba-rí-to-no *m.* baritone.
bá-rio *m.* barium.
ba-ro-lo-gi'-a *f.* barology.
ba-ro-mé-tri-co, =a *adj.* barometric.
ba-rô-me-tro *m.* barometer.
ba-ro-na'-to *m.* baronage.
ba-ro-ne'-sa *f.* baroness.
ba-ro-ne'-te *m.* baronet.
ba-ro-ni'-a *f.* barony.
bar-quei'-ro *m.* boatman.
bar-qui'-lha *f.* log-line (of a ship).
bar-qui'-nha *f.* small boat; child's coffin.

bar'-ra *f.* bar (metal or wood); harbor entrance; clay, mud.

bar-ra'-ca *f.* hut, temporary stall in fair or open-air market.

bar-ra-ção' *m.* tool-shed; deck canvas.

bar-ra'-co *m.* wooden shack.

bar-ra-quei'-ro *m.* stall-owner; owner of a shack.

bar-ra-quim' *m.* small stall.

bar-ra-quis'-ta *m.* rubber gatherer.

bar-rar' *tr.v.* to cover with clay or mud; to impede, to exclude.

bar-ra'-gem *f.* dam.

bar-ran'-co *m.* obstacle, hollow, precipice; misfortune.

bar-ran-quei'-ra *f.* high river bank.

bar-rei'-ra *f.* bar, barrier, toll-gate, entrance gate; claypit; custom gate; obstacle.

bar-re'-la *f.* lye.

bar-ren'-to, *-a adj.* clayey, clay-colored.

bar-re-ta'-da *f.* tipping of hat.

bar-re'-te *m.* cap, béret.

bar-re-te-ar' *tr.v.* to melt gold into bars or bricks.

bar-ri'-ca *f.* cask.

bar-ri-ca'-da *f.* barricade.

bar-ri-car' *tr.v.* to barricade.

bar-ri'-ga *f.* abdominal cavity; pregnancy; projection; — **da perna** calf of leg.

bar-ri-ga'-da *f.* abundance (of food), belly-full.

bar-ri-ga'-do, *-a adj.* abnormally large stomach.

bar-ril' *m.* barrel.

bar'-ro *m.* clay; soil proper for pottery work.

bar-ro'-so, *-a adj.* clayey, like clay, full of clay; having face pimples.

ba-ru-lhei'-ra *f.* noise; shouting; confusion.

ba-ru'-lho *m.* noise; confusion.

bas-cu-lhar' *tr.v.* to sweep with long-handled broom; (fig.) to investigate.

bas-cu'-lho *m.* long-handled broom, wall-brush; servant.

bás-cu-lo *m.* scales.

ba'-se *f.* base; **ba-se-a'-do,** *-a adj.* based, founded upon.

ba-se-ar' *tr.v.* to base on, to found upon, to lay the foundations of; to strengthen.

bá-si-co, *-a adj.* basic.

ba-sí-li-ca *f.* basilica; reliquary.

bas'-ta *interj.* Enough! No more!

bas-tan'-te *adj.* enough, sufficient; *adv.* enough, in sufficient quantity.

bas-tão' *m.* baton, staff.

bas-tar' *intr.v.* to be enough, to be sufficient.

bas-tar-di'-a *f.* bastardy, degeneration.

bas-tar-di'-nho *m.* handwriting neither cursive nor round hand.

bas-tar'-do, *-a adj.* spurious, bastard; **bas-tar'-do** *m.* bastard; slanting writing.

bas-ti-dor' *m.* embroidery hoop or frame; movable lateral sections of scenery on stage.

bas'-to, *-a adj.* thick, compact; numerous; many.

bas-to-ne'-te *m.* small baton; rod-shaped bacillus.

ba'-ta *f.* woman's dressing-gown.

ba-ta'-lha *f.* battle; combat; (fig.) struggle, strong effort.

ba-ta-lha-dor' *m.* soldier, fighter; struggler.

ba-ta-lhan'-te *adj.* battling, struggling.

ba-ta-lhão' *m.* battalion; (fig.) crowd.

ba-ta-lhar' *intr.v.* to give battle, to fight, to struggle.

ba-ta'-ta *f.* potato.

ba-ta-ti'-nha *f.* small potato; medicinal plant.

ba-te-dei'-ra *f.* butter churn; disease which attacks pigs.

bá-te-ga *f.* pattering of rain; heavy downpour.

ba-tel' *m.* small boat.

ba-ten'-te *m.* rabbet, door-post; door (of double doors); beach where surf breaks.

ba-ter' *tr.v.* to knock, to beat, to strike; to diminish volume of; to coin (money); to conquer; to flap (wings); to race.

ba-te-ri'-a *f.* battery.

ba-ti'-da *f.* track; reconnoitering; beating.

ba-ti'-do, *-a adj.* trivial, common.

ba-ti'-na *f.* cassock.

ba-trá-quios *m.pl.* batrachia (frogs, toads).

ba-tu'-que *m.* generic name of Negro dances accompanied by percussion instruments; hammering; noise-making.

ba-tu'-ta *f.* baton; (Brazil) champion, notable person; well-informed individual.

ba-ú *m.* trunk.

bau-ni'-lha *f.* vanilla; vanilla extract.

ba-zar' *m.* bazaar.

ba-zó-fia *f.* vanity, ostentation; ragout, stew.

ba-a-bá *m.* abc, elementary notions.

ba-tis'-mo *m.* baptism; (pop.) adulteration of wine or milk by addition of water.

ba-tis-té-rio *m.* baptistry.

ba-ti-za'-do *m.* christening.

ba-ti-zan'-do *m.* person to be baptized.

ba-ti-zar' *tr.v.* to baptize; to bestow a name or epithet on.

be-a'-ta *f.* excessively pious woman; woman who pretends devotion.

be-a-tão' *m.* hypocrite.

be-a-ti'-ce *f.* hypocrisy.

be-a'-to *m.* devout man; **be-a'-to,** *-a adj.* exaggeratedly devout, fanatic.

be-a-ti-fi-ca-ção' *f.* beatification.

be-a-ti-fi-car' *tr.v.* to beatify.

be-a-ti-tu'-de *f.* beatitude, blessedness.

be-be-dei'-ra *f.* drunkenness.

bê-be-do *m.* drunk; **bê-be-do,** *-a adj.* drunk, drunken, intoxicated.

be-be-dou'-ro *m.* drinking trough.

be-ber' *tr.v.* to drink; (fig.) to drink in; *intr.v.* to drink, to be a drinker.

be-ber-rão' *m.* heavy drinker.

be-ber-raz' *m.* heavy drinker.

be-ber-re'-te *m.* heavy drinker.

be-bi'-da *f.* drink.

be-bí-vel *adj.* potable, drinkable.

be-bê *m.* baby.

be-ber-ri-ca-dor' *m.* tippler.

be-ber-ri-car' *tr.v., intr.v.* to sip, to tipple.

be'-ca *f.* academic hood; gown and cap, or other insignia, distinctive of certain public offices (judge, etc.).

be'-co *m.* alley; dead-end street; (fig.) very embarrassing situation; great difficulty.

be-del' *m.* beadle.

bei-ci'-nho *m.* small lip; **fazer** *-s* to pucker the lips about to weep.

bei'-ço *m.* lip; edge; something jutting out; **morder os beiços** to be humiliated; **lamber os beiços** to be pleased.

bei-ja-dor' *m.* kisser.
bei-ja-flor' *m.* humming-bird.
bei-ja-mão' *m.* kissing the hand.
bei-ja-pé *m.* kissing the foot.
bei-jar' *tr.v.* to kiss, to touch lightly.
bei-ji'-nho *m.* light kiss; flower; best part of anything.
bei'-jo *m.* kiss.
bei'-ra *f.* bank, proximity; eaves of house.
bei-ra'-da *f.* margin, surrounding area.
bei-ra-mar' *f.* seashore, beach, coastal region.
be'-la *f.* belle, beautiful woman.
be-la-do'-na *f.* bella-donna.
bel-da'-de *f.* beauty.
be-le'-za *f.* beauty.
bel'-ga *m.*, *f.*, *adj.* Belgian.
be-li'-che *m.* cabin (ship).
bé-li-co, =a *adj.* relative to war.
be-li-co-si-da'-de *f.* bellicosity.
be-li-co'-so, =a *adj.* bellicose.
be-li-ge-rán-cia *f.* belligerence.
be-li-ge-ran'-te *adj.* belligerent.
be-lí-ge-ro, =a *adj.* bellicose.
be-lis-cão' *m.* strong pinch.
be-lis-car' *tr.v.* to pinch, to irritate.
be-liz' *adj.* sprightly, quick; *m.* wide-awake, prudent person.
be-lo, =a *adj.* beautiful, pleasing to ear; be'-lo *m.* perfection.
bel-pra-zer' *m.* wish, will; a — willingly.
bem' *m.* good, virtue, happiness, usefulness; person well-beloved; bens *m.pl.* property, belongings; *adv.* well, much, healthy; *interj.* that's right!!
bem-a-for-tu-na'-do, =a *adj.* happy, prosperous.
bem-a-ma'-do *m.* sweetheart; *adj.* well-beloved.
bem-a-ven-tu-ra'-do *m.* saint, one blessed by heaven; *adj.* very happy.
bem-a-ven-tu-ran'-ça *f.* great happiness, glory, heaven.
bem-cri-a'-do, =a *adj.* well-bred, courteous.
bem-es-tar' *m.* well-being, comfort.
be-mol' *m.* flat (in music).
bem-pa-re-ci'-do, =a *adj.* good-looking, pretty.
bem-pôs'-to, =a *adj.* well-dressed, airy, elegant.
bên-ção *f.* blessing, approval.
ben-di'-to, =a *adj.* blessed.
ben-di-zen'-te *adj.* laudatory.
ben-di-zer' *tr.v.* to bless, to praise, to glorify, to speak well of.
be-ne-fi-cên-cia *f.* beneficence.
be-ne-fi-ci-ar' *tr.v.* to benefit, to improve, to treat, to process.
be-ne-fi-ciá-rio *m.* beneficiary.
be-ne-fí-cio *m.* benefice, benefit.
be-ne-mé-ri-to, =a *adj.* distinguished, worthy of honors or praise.
be-ne-plá-ci-to *m.* approval, permission, consent.
be-ne-vo-lên-cia *f.* benevolence.
be-né-vo-lo, =a *adj.* benevolent.
ben-fa-da'-do, =a *adj.* fortunate, happy.
ben-fa-lan'-te *adj.* eloquent, discreet.
ben-fa-ze'-jo, =a *adj.* charitable.
ben-fa-zer' *intr.v.* to do good; *m.* charity, benevolent disposition.
ben-fei-tor' *m.* benefactor.
ben-fei-to-ri'-a *f.* improvement (on property).
ben-ga'-la *f.* cane; walking stick.
ben-ga-lar' *tr.v.* to strike with a cane.
be-nig-ni-da'-de *f.* benignity.

be-nig'-no, =a *adj.* benign.
ben-jo-im' *m.* benzoin.
ben-que-rer' *tr.v.* to be devoted to, to love.
ben-quis'-to, =a *adj.* loved, generally esteemed.
ben'-to, =a blessed.
ben-zer' *tr.v.* to bless, to be consecrated to some religion in a ceremony; —=se *refl.v.* to make sign of cross on oneself.
ben-zi'-na *f.* benzene.
ben-zo-a'-to *m.* benzoate.
ber'-ço *m.* cradle.
be-ri-be'-ri *m.* beri-beri.
be-ri'-lo *m.* beryl.
be-rin-ge'-la *f.* eggplant.
ber-lin'-da *f.* berline; small shrine in which to keep an image.
ber-lo'-que *m.* watch charm.
ber'-ro *m.* bellow (of animals); loud, sharp shout; bot-fly.
be-si'-gue *m.* bezique (card game).
be-sou'-ro *m.* beetle.
bês-ta *f.* animal; pack animal; stupid person.
bes-tei'-ra *f.* foolishness.
bes-tei'-ro *m.* archer.
bes-ti-al' *adj.* bestial, brutal.
bes-ti-a-li-da'-de *f.* bestiality.
bes-ti-a-li-zar' *tr.v.* to bestialize.
bes-ti-da'-de *f.* bestiality; stupid remark.
bes-tun'-to *m.* cunningness; weak intellect.
be-sun-ta-de'-la *f.* greasing, oiling.
be-sun-tão' *m.* dirty fellow, untidy person.
be-sun-tar' *tr.v.* to grease, to soil with greasy substance.
be'-ta *f.* beta; deep shaft in rock (in gold-mining).
be-ter-ra'-ba *f.* beet.
be-ter-ra-bal' *m.* beet field.
be-tu'-me *m.* bitumen.
be-tu-mi-no'-so, =a *adj.* bituminous.
be-xi'-ga *f.* bladder; chicken-pox; be-xi'-gas *f.pl.* small-pox; pock marks.
be-xi-go'-so, =a *adj.* pitted with pock marks.
be-zer'-ra *f.*, be-zer'-ro *m.* calf, veal.
bi-an-gu-lar' *adj.* biangular.
bi-a-tô-mi-co, =a *adj.* diatomic.
bi-bá-si-co, =a *adj.* dibasic.
bi-be-lô *m.* bibelot, curio.
bi-be-rão' *m.* nursing bottle.
bíb-lia *f.* Bible.
bí-bli-co, =a *adj.* biblical.
bib-li-ó-fi-lo *m.* bibliophile.
bi-bli-o-gra-fi'-a *f.* bibliography.
bi-bli-o-grá-fi-co, =a *adj.* bibliographic.
bi-bli-ó-gra-fo *m.* bibliographer.
bib-li-o-ma-ni'-a *f.* bibliomania.
bib-li-o-te'-ca *f.* library.
bi-bli-o-te-cá-rio *m.* librarian.
bi'-ca *f.* spigot, spout, water-drain; ease in passing examinations.
bi-ca'-da *f.* peck; beak-full.
bi-car-bo-na'-do, =a *adj.* having two portions of carbon.
bi-car-bo-na'-to *m.* bicarbonate.
bi-cé-fa-lo, =a *adj.* bicephalous.
bi-ceps' *m.* biceps.
bi'-cha *f.* worm, reptile; worm (in distillery); insignia (on sleeve of uniform), queue, line of people.
bi-cha'-da *f.* group of animals.
bi-cha-ri'-a *f.* group of animals; vermin; crowd, rabble.
bi-chei'-ra *f.* infected sore.

bi-chen′-te *adj.* having infected toe-nails.
bi′-cho *m.* animal, beast, insect; ugly person; intractable individual; — **do mato** solitary person; **matar o** — to drink brandy or other alcoholic drink before meal; **jôgo do** — lottery; (slang) bed-bug, louse.
bi-cho′-so, ◦a *adj.* wormy, worm-eaten.
bi-ci-cle′-ta *f.* velocipede.
bi-ci′-clo *m.* bicycle.
bi′-co *m.* beak; point; — **blanco** *m.* horse having white mouth.
bi-co-lor′ *adj.* bicolored; having two colors.
bi-côn-ca-vo, ◦a *adj.* biconcave.
bi-con-ju-ga′-do, ◦a *adj.* divided into two branches.
bi-con-ve′-xo, ◦a *adj.* biconvex.
bi-cor′-ne *adj.* having two points, crescent-like.
bi-cús-pi-de *adj.* bicuspid.
bi-dé *m.* bidet (form of sitz bath).
bi-e′-la *f.* connecting rod.
bi-e-nal′ *adj.* biennial.
bi-ê-nio *m.* biennium.
bi′-fe *m.* beef; filet mignon; small grilled steak.
bi-fur-car′ *tr.v.* to bifurcate.
bi-ga-mi′-a *f.* bigamy.
bi-ga-mo *m.* bigamist.
bi′-gle *m.* beagle.
bi-go′-de *m.* mustache.
bi-go-dei′-ra *f.* heavy mustache.
bi-gor′-na *f.* anvil; small bone in ear.
bi-go′-ta *f.* (naut.) deadeye.
bi-go-tis′-mo *m.* bigotry.
bi-ju-te-ri′-a *f.* bijoutry; trinkets.
bi-la-bi-al′ *adj.* bilabial.
bi-la-te-ral′ *adj.* bilateral.
bi′-le *f.* bile.
bi′-lha *f.* earthen-ware bottle for water; porousness of earthen-ware bottle providing evaporation and thus cooling the water.
bi-lhar′ *m.* billiards.
bi-lhar-dei′-ro *m.* billiard player.
bi-lhar-dis′-ta *m.* billiard player; lazy busy-body.
bi-lhe′-te *m.* note; short letter; ticket; — **postal** post card; — **de banco** banknote.
bi-lhe-tei′-ra *f.* card tray; woman ticket-seller.
bi-lhe-te-ri′-a *f.* ticket window.
bi-li-ão′ *m.* billion.
bi-li-á-rio, ◦a *adj.* biliary.
bi-lin′-gue *adj.* bilingual.
bi-li-o′-so, ◦a *adj.* bilious.
bi′-lis *f.* bile.
bil′-ro *m.* bobbin (used in making pillowlace); (fig.) small, well-groomed man.
bil′-tre *m.* vile, infamous man.
bi-ma-no, ◦a *adj.* two-handed; bimanual.
bim-ba-lha′-da *f.* simultaneous ringing of several bells.
bi-men-sal′ *adj.* bi-monthly, twice per month.
bi-mes-tral′ *adj.* every two months.
bi-mes′-tre *m.* two months.
bi-ná-rio, ◦a *adj.* binary.
bi-no-cu-la′-do, ◦a *adj.* two-eyed.
bi-no-cu-lar′ *adj.* binocular.
bi-nô-cu-lo *m.* binocular.
bi-nô-mio *m.* binomial (theorem).
bi-o-gra-fi′-a *f.* biography.
bi-o-grá-fi-co, ◦a *adj.* biographic.
bi-ó-gra-fo *m.* biographer.
bi-o-lo-gi′-a *f.* biology.

bi-o-ló-gi-co, ◦a *adj.* biological.
bi-o-lo-gis′-ta *m.* biologist.
bi-ó-lo-go *m.* biologist.
bi-om′-bo *m.* screen (furniture).
bi-o-qui′-ce *f.* hypocrisy, primness.
bi-ó-xi-do *m.* dioxide.
bi-par-ti′-do, ◦a *adj.* bi-partite.
bi-pe-de *m.* biped.
bi-po-la-ri-da′-de *f.* bi-polarity.
bi-quei′-ra *f.* gutter, water drain.
bi-ri-ce′-ra *f.* small, insignificant thing.
bi-ró *m.* mouthful; small portion of food taken at one time.
bir′-ra *f.* fault-finding; nagging; anger.
bir-ren′-te *adj.* obstinate, crabbed.
bir-re-fra-ção′ *f.* double refraction.
bi-ru′-ta *f.* wind sock (aviation).
bis *adv.* twice; *interj.* encore!!
bi-sar′ *tr.v.* to repeat, to call for encore.
bi-são′ *m.* bison.
bi-sa-vô *m.* great-grandfather.
bi-sa-vó *f.* great-grandmother.
bis-bi-lho-tar′ *intr.v.* to be mixed up in gossip and quarrels.
bis-bi-lho-tei′-ro *m.* gossiper, tale-bearer.
bis-ca′-te *m.* work of little importance.
bis-ca-te-ar′ *intr.v.* to get along from hand to mouth.
bis-coi-tei′-ra *f.* cooky-jar.
bis-coi-tei′-ro *m.* maker of crackers, seller of crackers.
bis-coi′-to *m.* cracker, cookie.
bis-mu′-to *m.* bismuth.
bis-na′-ga *f.* lead tube; tooth paste, vaseline; aromatic liquid squirted from lead tube at Carnival time.
bis-na-ga′-da *f.* squirting.
bis-na-gar′ *tr.v.* to squirt.
bis-ne′-to *m.* great-grandson.
bi-so′-nho *m.* raw recruit; ◦a *adj.* inexperienced, shy, beginner.
bis-pa′-do *m.* bishopric.
bis′-po *m.* bishop.
bis-se-ção′ *f.* bisection.
bis-se-tor′ *adj.* bisecting.
bis-se-triz′ *f.* bisectrix.
bis-sex′-to, ◦a *adj.,* *m.* leap year.
bis-sí-la-bo, ◦a *adj.* dissyllabic.
bis-tra′-do, ◦a *adj.* brownish color of ripe wheat.
bis′-tre *m.* bister.
bis-tu-rí *m.* bistoury.
bi-tá-cu-la *f.* binnacle.
bi-to′-la *f.* pattern, standard, gage, norm.
bi-to-lar′ *tr.v.* to measure, to evaluate, to establish a norm, to make a pattern.
bi-zan-ti′-no, ◦a *adj.* Byzantine.
bi-zar-ri′-a *f.* good manners, gallantry.
bi-zar′-ro, ◦a *adj.* genteel, good-looking, well-groomed; generous, knightly; strange.
blan-di-cia *f.* gentleness, blandishment, cajoling.
blan-di-ci-o′-so, ◦a *adj.* caressing, flattering.
blas-fe-ma-dor′ *m.* blasphemer.
blas-fe-mar′ *tr.v.* to blaspheme.
blas-fe-ma-tó-rio, ◦a *adj.* blasphemous.
blas-fê-mia *f.* blasphemy.
blás-fe-mo, ◦a *adj.* blasphemous.
bla-so-nar′ *tr.v.* to blazon; to boast.
bla-so-na-ri′-a *f.* blazonry.
bla-te-ra-ção′ *f.* blatancy.
bla-te-rar′ *tr.v.* to blurt; *intr.v.* to bleat (of sheep or camel); to speak raucously, noisily.

blau' *m.* blue color; *adj.* blue (shade usually seen on heraldic shields).
blen'-da *f.* blende.
ble-nor-ra-gi'-a *f.* blennorrhea, gonorrhea.
blin-da'-gem *f.* armor-plate.
blin-dar' *tr.v.* to cover with armor plate.
blo'-co *m.* block; (fig.) bloc; **em —** wholesale, as is, without minute examination.
blo-que-ar *tr.v.* to blockade, to lay siege to.
blo-quei'-o *m.* blockade.
blu'-sa *f.* blouse, smock, white cover-all used by surgeons during operations.
bo'-a *f.* boa constrictor.
bo-á *m.* boa, scarf of fur or feathers.
bo-as⹀vin'-das *f.pl.* welcome.
bo-a-tei'-ro *m.* rumor-monger, gossiper.
bo-a'-to *m.* rumor, hearsay.
bo'-bo *m.* court jester (Middle Ages); **bo'-bo,** ⹀**a** *adj.* crazy, foolish, silly.
bo-ba'-gem *f.* nonsense, foolish talk.
bo-béi-a *f.* silliness, joking; leftovers.
bo-bi'-na *f.* bobbin, coil, reel.
bo-bi-ne'-te *m.* bobbinet.
bo-cal' *m.* mouth of vase, bottle, or well; mouth-piece (of wind instruments); socket, nozzle; *adj.* pertaining to mouth.
bo-çal' *adj.* stupid, unrefined, coarse.
bô-ca *f.* mouth, opening, muzzle (gun); entrance.
bo-ca'-ça *f.* large mouth.
bo-ca'-do *m.* bit, mouthful, morsel; mouthpiece of bridle.
bo'-ças *f.pl.* hawser, cable
bo-ce-jar' *intr.v.* to yawn.
bo-ce'-jo *m.* yawn.
bo-cel' *m.* astragal; muzzle-ring of cannon.
bo-ce-lão' *m.* heavy molding at base of column.
bo-ce'-ta *f.* jewel-box.
bo-che'-cha *f.* cheek.
bo-che-cha'-da *f.* slap in cheek.
bo-che'-cho *m.* mouthful of liquid.
bó-cio *m.* parotitis.
bo-có, ⹀**a** *adj.* childish, foolish; *m.* box or small trunk covered with untanned skin having hair on outside.
bo'-da *f.* wedding; wedding feast; celebration of wedding anniversary; **bodas de prata** twenty-fifth wedding anniversary; **bodas de oura** fiftieth wedding anniversary.
bo'-de *m.* male goat; mulatto; (fig.) grown man; **— expiatório** scape-goat; **estar de — amarrado** to be much annoyed or irritated.
bo-de-jar' *intr.v.* to bleat like a goat, to stutter.
bo-de'-jo *m.* bleat of goat.
bo-de'-ga *f.* saloon, low-class restaurant.
bo-de'-lha *f.* sargassum; sea-oak.
bo'-do *m.* distribution of food and money to poor on special occasion.
bo-do'-so, ⹀**a** *adj.* dirty, bad-smelling.
bo-dum' *m.* odor of perspiration; fetid odor of goats.
bo-ê-mia *f.* Bohemia; (fig.) unconventional living.
bo-ê-mio *m.* Bohemian, gipsy.
bo-fé *adv.* truthfully, frankly.
bo-fe-ta'-da *f.* blow by hand in face; slap; (fig.) insult, injury.
bo-fe-tão' *m.* hard blow in the face.
bo-fe'-te *m.* slap in the face.
boi' *m.* ox; **junta de bois** yoke of oxen.
bói-a *f.* buoy; cork on fish nets; cork on

life belts; (Brazil) food included in wages.
boi-a'-da *f.* herd of oxen.
boi-a-dor' *m.* spot along river where turtle float in sun.
boi-an'-te *adj.* floating; buoyant.
boi-ar' *tr.v.* to place a buoy; *intr.v.* to float.
boi-co-ta'-gem *f.* boycott.
boi-co-tar' *tr.v.* to boycott.
boi-co'-te *m.* boycott.
boi-ei'-ro *m.* ox-driver.
bo-i'-na *f.* cap, barret (worn by Basque people).
boi-o'-te *m.* young ox, male calf.
boi-rel' *m.* small cork float.
bo-iz' *f.* bird trap.
bo'-jo *m.* large abdomen; bulge; prominence; capacity.
bo-ju'-do, ⹀**a** *adj.* having a large abdomen.
bo'-la *f.* ball.
bo-la'-da *f.* blow with a ball; chase (of a cannon).
bo-lão' *m.* large ball; rounded mass of any plastic substance, dough ball.
bo-la-pé *m.* ford (in a river).
bo-lar' *tr.v.* to hit with a ball; *intr.v.* to throw a ball.
bo-la'-cha *f.* thin cracker (generally not sweet).
bo-la-chei'-ro *m.* manufacturer or seller of crackers.
bol'-bo *m.* bulb.
bol-bo'-so, ⹀**a** *adj.* bulbous.
bol-che-vis'-mo *m.* Bolshevism.
bol-dri-é *m.* baldric; shoulder-strap.
bo-le-a'-do, ⹀**a** *adj.* rounded by lathe; having rounded surface.
bo-le-ar' *tr.v.* to make ball-shaped, to round; to captivate.
bo-lei'-a *f.* whipple tree, single tree; driver's seat in carriage or automobile.
bo-lei'-ma *f.* coarse cake; (fig.) stupid person.
bo-lei'-o *m.* shaping into a ball.
bo-le'-ro *m.* Spanish dance, with accompanying music; woman's tunic.
bo-le-tim' *m.* bulletin.
bo-le'-to *m.* billeting orders.
bo-léu *m.* fall, shake-up, unexpected sharp turn made by vehicle.
bô-lha *f.* bubble, blister.
bo-lhar' *tr.v.* to boil, to make bubble; *intr.v.* to blister.
bo-lho'-so, ⹀**a** *adj.* full of bubbles, full of blisters.
bo-li'-na *f.* bowline.
bo-li-nar' *intr.v.* to haul sail to windward.
bo-li-ne'-te *m.* capstan; wooden tray for washing sand in gold mining.
bo'-lo *m.* cake.
bo-lor' *m.* mold; (fig.) old age, decadence.
bol'-sa *f.* purse; money; establishment for financial activities, exchange; bourse; treasury; saddle-bag.
bol-sei'-ro *m.* purse manufacturer or seller.
bol-si'-nho *m.* pin money.
bol-sis'-ta *m.* banker, broker.
bôl-so *m.* pocket.
bom' *m.* *adj.* good, satisfactory, favorable, charitable, worthwhile, proper, secure, perfect, large, ample, lucrative; *interj.* signifying approval, surprise.
bom'-ba *f.* bomb; pump, siphon, shock absorber, bumper (between railway cars); failure on examination; **— dágua**

sudden heavy downpour of rain accompanied by thunder.

bom-ba'-cha *f.* baggy trousers worn by Turkish women.

bom-ba'-cho *m.* small water pump.

bom-ba'-da *f.* loss; deception.

bom-bar'-da *f.* bombard.

bom-bar-de-a-men'-to *m.* bombardment.

bom-bar-de-ar' *tr.v.* to bombard.

bom-bar-dei'-o *m.* bombardment.

bom-bás-ti-co, =a *adj.* bombastic.

bom-bei'-ro *m.* fireman; spy.

bom'-bo *m.* bass drum.

bom-bom' *m.* bonbon.

bom-bor'-do *m.* larboard, left side of ship.

bo-na-chão' *m.* kindly, simple, naïve person.

bo-na-chei-ri'-ce *f.* kindliness, good nature.

bo-nan'-ça *f.* good weather at sea; (fig.) tranquility, calmness.

bo-nan-ço'-so, =a *adj.* serene, quiet.

bon-da'-de *f.* goodness, benevolence, gentleness.

bon-do'-so, =a *adj.* kindly, benevolent.

bon'-de *m.* street car.

bo-né *m.* cap.

bo-ne'-ca *f.* doll; (fig.) lovely woman; over-dressed woman.

bo-ne'-co *m.* puppet; show-window figure; preliminary drawing or design.

bo-ni-fi-car' *tr.v.* to benefit, to give bonus to.

bo-ni-fi-ca-ção' *f.* bonus, allowance.

bo-ni-te'-te *adj.* rather pretty, nice.

bo-ni-te'-za *f.* prettiness.

bo-ni'-to, =a *adj.* pretty, pleasing to eye, good; censurable (in irony).

bo-no-mi'-a *f.* bonhomie.

bon-zó *m.* lottery ticket.

bo-quei-rão' *m.* large opening; mouth of river or canal; mountain cut.

bo-que-jar' *tr.v., intr.v.* to touch with mouth; to murmur, to speak in low voice.

bo-qui-a-ber'-to, =a *adj.* open-mouthed, surprised; with look of imbecility.

bo-qui'-nha *f.* kiss; snack.

bo-ra'-to *m.* borate.

bó-rax *m.* borax.

bó-ri-co, =a *adj.* boric.

bor-bo-le'-ta *f.* butterfly; (fig.) inconstant person.

bor-bo-le-te-ar' *intr.v.* to have carefree, irresponsible existence; to be irresponsible.

bor-bo-re-jar' *intr.v.* to make a noise like boiling water.

bor-bo-ri-nhar' *intr.v.* to sound like vague murmuring.

bor-bo-ri'-nho *m.* tumult, disorder; murmur, buzz.

bor-bo-tão' *m.* sudden spurt (water); boiling up.

bor-bo-tar' *tr.v., intr.v.* to spurt out, to expel in jerks; to bud forth.

bor-bu'-lha *m.* skin blister; bubble; bud (plant); boiling of water; spot or defect.

bor-bu-lha'-gem *f.* bubbling; blistering.

bor-bu-lhar' *intr.v.* to blister, to bubble, to boil.

bor-bu-lho'-so, =a *adj.* bubbling; blistered; blooming, full of buds.

bor'-da *f.* edge, extremity, margin, coast; **dar — a** to almost tip over (a boat).

bor-da-dei'-ra *f.* embroiderer.

bor-da'-do *m.* embroidery.

bor-da-du'-ra *f.* embroidering; embroidery; borders (of a garden); trimming.

bor-da-le'-sa *f.* large barrel.

bor-dar' *tr.v.* to embroider; to put a border on.

bor-dão' *m.* staff; lowest tone on certain instruments; (fig.) support, protection.

bor-de-jar' *intr.v.* to navigate, changing direction frequently; to zig-zag; to stagger because of being drunk.

bor-del' *m.* brothel.

bor-de-lei'-ro *m.* brothel habitué.

bor'-do *m.* side of ship; board; direction of ship; **a — on** shipboard; **aos —s** walking in zig-zag fashion (being drunk).

bor'-la *f.* tassel; (fig.) academic cap (doctoral).

bor-nal' *m.* lunch box; feed-bag.

bor-ne-ar' *tr.v.* to aim, to put in line with sight (gun).

bo-ró *m.* chip (in roulette); counterfeit paper money.

bôr-ra *f.* sediment in liquids; excrement; (fig.) lowest social class; **— de seda** coarse outside layer of silk cocoon.

bor-ra=bo'-tas *m.* good-for-nothing.

bor-ra'-cha *f.* rubber; eraser; hot-water bottle.

bor-ra-chão' *m.* drunkard; horn with stopper for alcoholic beverages.

bor-ra-chei'-ra *f.* drunkenness; nonsense, gibberish; work poorly done.

bor-ra-chei'-ro *m.* rubber-gatherer.

bor-ra'-cho *m.* drunk, drunkard; squab.

bor-ra-chu'-do *m.* Brazilian mosquito; **bor-ra-chu'-do**, =a *adj.* swollen.

bor-ra-dor' *m.* day-book; notebook whose handwriting is illegible; rough painter.

bor-ra'-lha *f.* hot ashes.

bor-ra-lhei'-ra *f.* ash-pit.

bor-ra-lhei'-ro, =a *adj.* home-loving.

bor-ra'-lho *m.* banked embers; (fig.) home, household.

bor-rão' *m.* ink blot; preliminary outline; minutes; indecorous action.

bor-rar' *tr.v.* to blot; to soil, to rub out, to scribble over.

bor-ras'-ca *f.* storm, cyclone; (fig.) sudden adversities; attack of temper.

bor-ri'-fo *m.* sprinkle; light shower (rain); spray coming from nozzle.

bor-ze-guim' *m.* buskin.

bos-ca-re'-jo, =a *adj.* wooded, sylvan.

bos'-que *m.* forest, large group of trees.

bos'-sa *f.* swelling from bruise or blow; protuberance.

bos'-ta *f.* manure, animal excrement.

bos-tal' *m.* corral for cattle.

bo'-ta *f.* boot, high shoes.

bo-ta-fo'-ra *f.* ship-launching; gathering to bid bon voyage to visitor, farewell party.

bo-tâ-ni-ca *f.* botany.

bo-tâ-ni-co *m.* botanist; **bo-tâ-ni-co**, =a *adj.* botanical.

bo-tão' *m.* plant bud; blister; button.

bo-tar' *tr.v.* to throw down, to place.

bo'-te *m.* row-boat, small sail boat.

bo-te'-lha *f.* bottle; bottle-full.

bo-te-lhei'-ro *m.* butler; one who looks after wine.

bo-te-quim' *m.* place where coffee and soft drinks are sold.

bo-te-qui-nei'-ro *m.* dealer in soft drinks.

bo-ti'-ja *f.* earthen-ware oil cruet.

bo-ti'-na *f.* low shoe.
bo-to-car' *intr.v.* to jump out.
bou'-ba *f.* small ulcer.
bou-ben'-to, **-a** *adj.* having ulcers.
bou-çar' *tr.v.* to clear virgin land for cultivation.
bo-vi'-no, **-a** *adj.* bovine.
bra-be'-za *f.* ferocity, savagery.
bra'-bo, **-a** *adj.* ferocious, uncultured, rude.
bo-ti'-ca *f.* pharmacy.
bo-ti-ca'-da *f.* pharmaceutical preparation.
bo-ti-cá-rio, **-a** *m.f.* pharmacist, druggist.
bra-ça'-da *f.* armful.
bra-ça-dei'-ra *f.* handle on shield.
bra-çal' *adj.* relative to the arms, done with the arms; **serra — cross-cut saw.**
bra-ça-ri'-a *f.* throwing darts, throwing lances.
bra-ce-a'-gem *f.* minting money, right to mint money.
bra-ce-jar' *tr.v.* to extend from side to side, to stretch out like arms; to diffuse.
bra-ce-le'-te *m.* bracelet; wrist watch.
bra'-ço *m.* arm; part of arm between elbow and shoulder; laborer; branch (tree).
bra-dar' *tr.v.*, *intr.v.* to cry out; to shout out, to say in loud voice; to divulge.
bra'-do *m.* shout, complaint, clamor.
bra-guí-lha *f.* fly (on trousers).
bra-ma-dor', **-a** *adj.* emitting roars or shouts.
Bra-ma-nis'-mo *m.* Brahmanism.
bra-mar' *intr.v.* to roar, to shout; (fig.) to become furious, to become very angry.
bra-mir' *intr.v.* to roar, to shout out in anger.
bra-mi'-do *m.* bluster, roaring (of lions or of the sea).
bra-mo'-so, **-a** *adj.* angry, tempestuous.
bran'-ca *f.* white hair; silver money.
bran-ca-cen'-to, **-a** *adj.* almost white.
bran-ca-gem *f.* colonial retail tax on bread and meat.
bran-ca-ra'-na *f.* light mulatto.
bran-ca-rão' *adj.* light mulatto.
bran'-co *m.* white man; white of egg; space between lines; whiteness; **bran'-co**, **-a** *adj.* white, pale, blank.
bran-dir' *tr.v.* to brandish.
bran'-do, **-a** *adj.* bland.
bran-du'-ra *f.* blandness; fine rain, dew.
bran-que-ar' *tr.v.* to whiten, to bleach (clothes), to whitewash.
bran-que-a-ri'-a *f.* bleaching establishment.
bran-que-jar' *intr.v.* to be white, to look white.
bra'-sa *f.* live coal; ardor; (fig.) anxiety.
bra-sei'-ro *m.* brazier.
bra-si-lei-ris'-mo *m.* Brazilianism.
bra-si-lei'-ro, **-a** *m.f. adj.* Brazilian.
bra-si-lia'-na *f.* publications dealing with Brazil.
bra-zo-nar' *tr.v.* to emblazon.
bra-zu'-me *m.* ardency, vehemence.
bra-va'-ta *f.* arrogant threat; vainglory, bravado.
bra-va-tei'-ro *m.* boaster, threatener.
bra-ve'-za *f.* ferocity; impetuousness.
bra-vi'-o *m.* bad land; **bra-vi'-o**, **-a** *adj.* coarse, savage, rude, rustic.
bra'-vo, **-a** *adj.* brave, courageous, admirable; wild.
bra-vu'-ra *f.* bravery, valor.

bre'-ca *f.* cramp.
bre-car' *tr.v.* to manipulate brakes of vehicle.
bre'-cha *f.* breech; vacant space; (fig.) damage, loss.
bre-jei-rar' *intr.v.* to be vagrant, blackguard.
bre-jei'-ro, **-a** *adj.* vile, malicious, vagabond.
bre-jen'-to, **-a** *adj.* having wild undergrowth.
bre'-jo *m.* unbroken land, virgin land.
bren'-ha *f.* thick bush; confusion; complication.
bre-ta'-nha *f.* kind of linen or cotton cloth.
Bre-tão' *m.* Briton, Britisher; Breton; language of Brittany; *adj.* relative to the British Empire or Brittany.
breu' *m.* pitch.
bre'-ve *adj.* short, brief, rapid; *adv.* soon, in short time; *m.* brief.
bre-vi-á-rio *m.* breviary.
bre-vi-da'-de *f.* brevity.
bri'-ga *f.* quarrel, combat, dispute.
bri-ga'-da *f.* brigade.
bri-ga-dei'-ro *m.* brigadier.
bri-ga-dor' *m.* one who quarrels or struggles.
bri-ga-lhão' *m.* one constantly quarreling or easily provoked to quarrel.
bri-gar' *intr.v.* to quarrel.
bri'-gue *m.* brig (ship).
bri-lhan'-te *adj.* brilliant, resplendent; *m.* cut diamond.
bri-lhan-ti'-na *f.* brilliantine.
bri-lhan-tis'-mo *m.* brilliance, splendor.
bri-lhar' *intr.v.* to shine, to have brilliance; (fig.) to be distinguished.
bri'-lho *m.* bright light; splendor; (fig.) vivacity, scintillation.
brim' *m.* cotton or linen canvas.
brin-ca-dei'-ra *f.* game, play, diversion.
brin-ca-lhão' *m.* person always ready for play.
brin-car' *intr.v.* to play; to joke; to jump for joy (child).
brin'-co *m.* toy; ear-ring.
brin-dar' *tr.v.*, *intr.v.* to toast, to drink to health of; to make a gift to.
brin'-ue *f.* toast; gift, offering.
brin-que'-do *m.* toy.
brí'-o *m.* sense of honor or dignity; mettle.
bri-o'-so, **-a** *adj.* lively, generous, brave.
bri-o'-che *m.* brioche, cake.
bri-ol' *m.* bunt, bunt line.
brí'-sa *f.* breeze, ventilation.
bri-ta-dor' *m.* pulverizer, pulverizing machine.
bri-tar' *tr.v.* to separate; to break into small pieces.
bro'-a *f.* corn pone.
bro-ca'-do *m.* brocade.
bro'-ca *f.* auger.
bro-car' *tr.v.* to drill, to bore.
bro-car'-do *m.* axiom; sentence (law).
bro'-cha *f.* ordinary paint brush; whitewash brush.
bro-cha'-do, **-a** *adj.* having a paper binding.
bro-cha-dor' *m.* book sewer.
bro-cha'-gem *f.* sewing books.
bro-char' *tr.v.* to sew books or pamphlets.
bro-chu'-ra *f.* paper-bound book, pamphlet.
bro'-che *m.* brooch; buckle.
brô-mio *m.* bromine.
bron'-co, **-a** *adj.* coarse; stupid; rough.

brôn-qui-os *m.pl.* bronchi.
bron-qui'-te *f.* bronchitis.
bron'-ze *m.* bronze.
bron-ze-a'-do, =a *adj.* bronzy.
brôn-ze-o, =a *adj.* of bronze, hard like bronze.
bro-tar' *tr.v.* to produce, to create; *intr.v.* to bud, to unfold, to be born.
brô-to *m.* cutting; young shoot.
bru-a'-ca *f.* small suitcase or bag made from untanned skin.
bru'-ços *m.pl.* de — *adv.* prone; on one's face.
bru'-ma *f.* mist, fog; (fig.) mystery, uncertainty.
bru-ma-cei'-ro, =a *adj.* glowering, dark.
bru-mo'-so, =a *adj.* foggy.
bru-ni'-do, =a *adj.* starched, glazed, shiny.
bru-nir' *tr.v.* to burnish; to give a luster to (of starched linen).
brus'-co, =a *adj.* brusque.
brus-qui-dão' *f.* asperity, brusqueness.
bru'-ta: à — *adv.* violently; in large quantity; according to no rule; unfeelingly.
bru-tal' *adj.* brutal, violent.
bru-ta-li-da'-de *f.* brutality.
bru-ta-li-zar' *tr.v.* to brutalize.
bru-ta-mon'-tes *m.* dunce, stupid fellow.
bru'-to *m.* brute; em — in the rough, not finished; bru'-to, =a *adj.* brutal, raw, rough, coarse.
bru'-xa *f.* witch, hag; malicious old woman.
bru-xa-ri'-a *f.* witchcraft; sorcery.
bru'-xo *m.* sorcerer.
bu-bô-ni-ca *f.* bubonic plague.
bu'-cha *f.* wadding; food which fills but gives little nourishment; bushing.
bu'-cho *m.* stomach (of animals but not birds).
bu-chu'-da *adj.* pregnant; full.
bu'-ço *m.* mustache.
bu-có-li-co, =a *adj.* bucolic.
bu-dis'-mo *m.* Buddhism.
bu-dis'-ta *m., f., adj.* Buddhist.
bu-ei'-ro *m.* drain pipe; chimney; vent pipe.
bú-fa-lo *m.* buffalo.
bu-fão' *m.* buffoon.
bu-fe'-te *m.* buffet.
bu'-fo *m.* owl; buffo.
bu-gi'-a *f.* wax candle; small candlestick; female monkey.
bu-gi'-o *m.* kind of monkey; piledriver.
bu-jão' *m.* plug, peg.

bu'-la *f.* bulla; printed instructions accompanying medicine.
bul'-bo *m.* see bolbo.
bul-cão' *m.* black cloud preceding thunder storm; cloud of smoke.
bu'-le *m.* tea-pot; *f.* will, wish.
bu-le-var' *m.* boulevard.
bu'-lha *f.* noise, confusien, disorderly shouting.
bu-lí-cio *m.* murmuring sound, uproar, hubbub; restlessness; bustle.
bu-li-cio'-so, =a *adj.* restless; mischievous.
bu-lir' *intr.v.* to stir, to flutter; to pick a quarrel, to be annoying.
bum-bum' *m.* thunder, explosion, boomboom.
bu'-que *m.* small boat used as aid to fishing galleon.
bu-ra'-co *m.* opening; aperture; hole.
bu-ra-quei'-ro *m.* area full of holes.
bu-rel' *m.* coarse cloth, of kind used for friar's habit; (fig.) mourning.
bur'-go *m.* burg.
bur-go-mes'-tre *m.* burgomaster.
bur-guês *m.* townsman; member of middle class; bourgeois.
bur-gue-si'-a *f.* bourgeoisie.
bu-ril' *m.* burin.
bu-r'-la'-da *f.* stroke or cut with burin.
bu-ri-lar' *tr.v.* to engrave with a burin.
bur'-la *f.* trick, fraud, joke.
bur-lar' *tr.v.* to deceive, to defraud.
bur-les'-co, =a *adj.* burlesque.
bu-ro-cra-ci'-a *f.* bureaucracy.
bu-ro-cra'-ta *m.* bureaucrat, public employee.
bu-ro-crá-ti-co, =a *adj.* bureaucratic.
bur'-ra *f.* female donkey; iron money chest or bank.
bur-ri-ca'-da *f.* large number of donkeys; faux pas.
bur-ri'-ce *f.* folly, stupidity.
bur'-ro *m.* male donkey; saw-horse; pony (translation to aid students).
bu-run-dan'-ga *f.* slang; foreign language badly spoken.
bus'-ca *f.* search, investigation.
bus-ca'-do, =a *adj.* unnatural, affected.
bus-car' *tr.v.* to look for, to search for, to fetch, to go and get.
bus-ca-pé *m.* kind of fireworks which run on ground and end in explosion.
bús-so-la *f.* compass.
bus'-to *m.* bust.
bu-zi'-na *f.* automobile horn.
bu-zi-nar' *intr.v.* to sound automobile horn; to speak with impertinence.
bú-zio *m.* diver; conch shell.

C

See page 12—GUIDE TO REFORMED SPELLING used in this Dictionary

C *m.* C, c, third letter of the alphabet.
cá *adv.* here, in this place; among ourselves.
cã' *f.* white hair; *m.* khan.
ca-ba'-ça *f.* gourd.
ca-bai'-a *f.* Turkish tunic; pekin.
ca-bal' *adj.* complete, full; exact.
ca-ba'-la *f.* cabal, intrigue; conspiracy.
ca-ba-lar' *intr.v.* to intrigue, to plot.
ca-ba-lís-ti-co, =a *adj.* cabalisṭic.
ca-ba'-na *f.* cabin, hut.

ca-ba-nei'-ro *m.* poor man; man living in a cabin; large basket.
ca-ba-ré *m.* cabaret.
ca-be-ça'-da *f.* butt (with the head); headband of bridle.
ca-be-çal' *m.* cotton dressing (around wound); pillow head (of bed).
ca-be-ça'-lho *m.* title, head-line.
ca-be-cão' *m.* yoke (of smock or gown).
ca-be-cei'-ra *f.* head of table or bed.
ca-be'-ça *f.* head.

ca-be'-ço *m.* rounded top of hill or mountain.

ca-be-çu'-do, =a *adj.* having large head; stubborn.

ca-be-dal' *m.* funds, capital; tanned skin used for making shoes.

ca-be-de'-lo *m.* sand bank, little cape (at mouth of river).

ca-be-lei'-ra *f.* hair, head of hair.

ca-be-lei-rei'-ro, =a *m., f.* hair dresser.

ca-be'-lo *m.* hair; hair-spring (of watches).

ca-be-lu'-do, =a *adj.* hairy.

ca-ber' *intr.v.* to be compatible, admissible or opportune; to be contained in.

ca-bi'-da *f.* acceptance; influence.

ca-bi'-de *m.* wardrobe; coat-hanger.

ca-bi-nien'-to *m.* acceptance, opportunity.

ca-bi-nei'-ro *m.* railway signal man.

ca-bis-bai'-xo, =a *adj.* with head bent over; (fig.) ashamed.

ca-blar' *intr.v.* to send cable, to cable.

ca'-bo *m.* cable; extremity; cape, headland; military rank.

ca-bo-chão' *m.* cabochon.

ca-bo-cla'-da *f.* suspicion, perfidy; band of *mestizos.*

ca-bo'-clo, =a *m., f.* mestizo of Indian and white blood; *adj.* copper-colored, bronze-colored; having skin bronzed from sun-burn.

ca-bo-gra'-ma *m.* cablegram.

ca-bo-ré *m.* mestizo of Negro and Indian blood.

ca-bor-tar' *intr.v.* to lie, to be untruthful.

ca-bo-ta'-gem *f.* coastwise navigation or shipping.

ca-bo-tar' *intr.v.* to run ships along coast, from port to port.

ca-bo-ti-na'-gem *f.* life or habit of wandering comedian.

ca-bo-ti'-no *m.* wandering comedian; (fig.) self-advertizer.

ca'-bra *f.* goat.

ca-brei'-ro *m.* goatherd.

ca-bres-tan'-te *f.* capstan.

ca-bres-tão' *m.* re-enforced capstan.

ca-bres-te-ar' *intr.v.* to travel or move along (of a horse) guided only by halter; (fig.) to be easily influenced or led by some one.

ca-bres'-to *m.* halter; lead-ox.

ca-bril' *m.* goat pen, corral.

ca-bri-o'-la *f.* caper, quick turn of body, leap.

ca-bri-o-lé *m.* cabriolet.

ca-bri'-to *m.* kid (term of endearment).

cá-bu-la *m.* poor student; *f.* absence from class; *adj.* astute.

ca'-ça *f.* hunt; investigation; persecution.

ca-ça'-da *f.* hunting party.

ca-ça-dor' *m.* hunter.

ca-ça-po *m.* young rabbit; (fig.) short, stout man.

ca-çar' *tr.v.* to hunt; to seek, to search for.

ca-ça-ro'-la *f.* casserole.

ca-ca'-u *m.* cacao.

ca-ce-ta'-da *f.* blow with club; bore.

ca-ce'-te *m.* cudgel, club; *adj.* fatiguing, boring.

ca-ce-te-ar' *tr.v.* to beat with a club; to urge on with insistence.

ca-cha'-ça *f.* rum made from sugar cane.

ca-cha-chel'-ro *m.* heavy drinker of rum.

ca-cha'-ço *m.* nape of neck.

ca-cha-çu'-do, =a *adj.* thick-necked; (fig.) proud, stiff-necked.

ca-chão' *m.* bubbling, boiling.

ca-che-a'-do, =a *adj.* curly, wavy.

ca-che-ar' *intr.v.* to form a head, (grains), to begin to flower (vegetables).

ca-chei'-ra *f.* rough stick.

ca-chim-ba'-da *f.* pipeful (of tobacco).

ca-chim'-bo *m.* pipe, tobacco-pipe.

ca-chi-nar' *intr.v.* to laugh at sneeringly; to belittle.

ca'-cho *m.* bunch (of fruit or flowers).

ca-cho-ei'-ra *f.* water-fall, small cataract.

ca-chor-ra'-da *f.* group of dogs, pack of hounds; support of ship in dry-dock; shiftless fellow; meanness, vile act.

ca-chor'-ro *m.* dog; young of wolf or lion.

ca-chor-ro=chi-mar-rão' *m.* ownerless dog.

ca-chum'-ba *f.* mumps.

ca-ci'-fe *m.* jack-pot, sum to be won.

ca-ci'-fo *m.* coffer, chest; cache.

ca-cim'-ba *f.* well; water-hole.

ca-cim-bar' *intr.v.* to get full of holes.

ca-ci'-que *m.* cacique, political boss.

ca'-co *m.* piece of broken pottery; snuff.

ca-ço-a'-da *f.* joke, playfulness.

ca-ço-ar' *tr.v., intr.v.* to play jokes, to tease.

ca-co-dí-lio *m.* cacodyl.

ca-co-fo-ni'-a *f.* cacophony.

ca-ço-le'-ta *f.* fire-pan of old-fashioned rifle; small frying-pan; crucible.

ca-çu'-lo *m.* youngest son, youngest child.

ca'-da *adj.* each, every.

ca-da-fal'-so *m.* scaffold, platform.

ca-dar'-ço *m.* tape, bias binding.

ca-das'-te *m.* stern-post (of a ship).

ca-das'-tro *m.* census; survey.

ca-dá-ver *m.* cadaver, corpse.

ca-da-vé-ri-co, =a *adj.* cadaverous.

ca-de-a'-do *m.* padlock.

ca-dei'-a *f.* chain; jail; **ponto de —** chain-stitch.

ca-dei'-ra *f.* chair; subject taught; professorial functions; headquarters; =s *f.pl.* rump.

ca-dei-ri'-nha *f.* kind of litter carried by men; seat formed by hands of two persons on which third person is carried.

ca-de'-la *f.* bitch.

ca-dên-cia *f.* cadence.

ca-den'-te *adj.* cadent; decaying, frail.

ca-der-ne'-ta *f.* memorandum book; notebook; teacher's register; bank book.

ca-der'-no *m.* notebook.

ca-de'-te *m.* cadet.

ca-di'-nho *m.* crucible.

ca-di'-vo, =a *adj.* senile, very mature.

ca-du-car' *intr.v.* to grow old; to have no further value; to lose strength.

ca-du-ceu' *m.* caduceus.

ca-du-ci-da'-de *f.* decadence; old age.

ca-du'-co, =a *adj.* senile, aged; valueless; frail; deciduous.

ca-fé *m.* coffee; café.

ca-fe-ei'-ro *m.* coffee plant.

ca-fe-í-na *f.* caffeine.

ca-fe-tei'-ra *f.* coffee-pot.

ca-fe-zal' *m.* field of coffee plants.

ca-fe-zis'-ta *m., f.* coffee addict, person fond of coffee; coffee planter.

ca-fi'-fe *m.* persistent lack of success; bad luck; discouragement.

cáf-ten *m.* panderer; one who lives on proceeds of commercialized vice; white-slave procurer.

caf-ti'-na *f.* woman engaged in white slave traffic.

ca-fu'-a *f.* cove, hiding-place; poverty-stricken home; (Brazil) dark room in which students are punished.

ca-fu-né *m.* thumping head with fingers.

ca-go-san'-ga *f.* ipecac.

cai-a-dor' *m.* whitewasher.

cai-a-du'-ra *f.* whitewashing; coat of whitewash.

cai-ar' *tr.v.* to whitewash; to make white; (fig.) to pretend.

cai-brar' *tr.v.* to set rafters in place.

cai'-bro *m.* rafter.

cai-ça'-ra *f.* fence or hedge made from branches; sort of stockade made by sticking posts in ground and allowing branches to grow; country-man; uncouth person.

ca-í-da *f.* fall; decline; decadence.

ca-í-do, **=a** *adj.* discouraged; behind in payment.

ca-í-dos *m.pl.* back salary; left-overs; caresses.

ca-im'-bra *f.* cramp.

cai-men'-to *m.* fall, (fig.) prostration, discouragement; (Brazil) inclination toward falling in love with some one.

cai-pi'-ra *m.* country-man; uncouth person.

cai-pi-ris'-mo *m.* customs and manners of country people.

cai-po'-ra *f.* will-o'-the-wisp; *m.*, *f.* unlucky person.

cai-po-ris'-mo *m.* misfortune, bad luck, unhappiness.

ca-í-que *m.* caïque (kind of boat).

ca-ir' *intr.v.* to fall, to fall to the ground; to take place; to incur; to hang.

cai'-ro *m.* fiber of cocoa-nut.

cais' *m.* dock, wharf.

cai'-xa *f.* box, chest, case; *m.* cashier; cash-book.

cai'-xa=dá-gua *f.* water tank.

cai-xei'-ro *m.* cashier; book-keeper; salesman; deliveryman.

cai-xão' *m.* coffin.

cai-xo'-te *m.* small, rough box.

cai-xo-tei'-ro *m.* box-maker.

ca-já *m.* Brazilian yellow plum.

ca-ja'-do *m.* shepherd's crook.

ca-jú *m.* cashew-nut.

ca-ju-a'-da *f.* cashew juice.

ca-ju-ei'-ro *m.* cashew tree.

cal' *f.* lime; **a pedra e — unshakeably, obstinately.

ca'-la *f.* small bay or port; cut in fruit or cheese (to be able to determine its quality).

ca-la-bou'-ço *m.* dungeon.

ca-la-bre *m.* heavy rope, cable.

ca-la-bre-ar' *tr.v.* to fertilize; to adulterate (wines); to prepare; to pervert.

ca-la'-da *f.* silence, quiet.

ca-la'-do *m.* vertical distance from keel of ship to water line; **ca-la'-do**, **=a** *adj.* silent, quiet, taciturn.

ca-la-fe-ta'-gem *f.* caulking; oakum.

ca-la-fe-tar' *tr.v.* to caulk; to close up.

ca-la-fê-to *m.* caulking; oakum; weather-stripping.

ca-la-fri'-o *m.* shivering from cold; goose pimples on skin because of cold.

ca-la-mi-da'-de *f.* calamity.

ca-la-mis'-tro *m.* curling iron.

ca-la-mi-to'-so, **=a** *adj.* calamitous.

ca-lan'-dra *f.* calender.

ca-lan-drar' *tr.v.* to calender.

ca-lão' *m.* low language peculiar to criminals; slang.

ca-lar' *tr.v.* to impose silence, to silence; *intr.v.* to keep silent.

cal'-cas *f.pl.* trousers, pants.

cal-ça'-da *f.* side-walk, paved street.

cal-ça-dei'-ra *f.* shoehorn.

cal-ça'-do *m.* shoe, foot-wear.

cal-çar' *tr.v.* to put on (shoes, boots, slippers, trousers, gloves); to pave; to cover with steel (the cutting edge of tools); *intr.v.* to fit.

cal-ca-nhar' *m.* heel (of foot or shoe); vulnerable point of anything.

cal-car' *tr.v.* to step on, to crush under foot, to disdain; to copy design through transparent paper.

cal-ci-fi-ca-ção' *f.* calcification.

cal-ci-fi-car'=se *refl.v.* to undergo calcification.

cal-ci-na-ção' *f.* calcination.

cal-ci-nar' *tr.v.* to burn.

cal'-ço *m.* wedge.

cal-cu-la-dor' *m.*, *adj.* calculator; one who thinks only of personal interests.

cal-cu-lan'-te *adj.* calculating.

cal-cu-lar' *tr.v.* to calculate, to conjecture.

cál-cu-lo *m.* calculation; calculus, stone, gall-stone.

cal'-da *f.* thin syrup made with sugar and water; syrup made with fruit juice and sugar; incandescence of iron; **=s** *f.pl.* hot springs.

cal-de-ar' *tr.v.* to make incandescent; to temper.

cal-dei'-ra *f.* kettle, boiler.

cal-dei-rão' *m.* large kettle, large boiler; pool, large puddle.

ca-le'-che *m.* calèche.

ca-le-fa-ção' *f.* calefaction; heating.

ca-lei-dos-có-pio *m.* kaleidoscope.

ca-le-jar' *tr.v.* to produce callus; to make callous; to harden or render insensitive.

ca-len'-das *f.pl.* calends.

ca'-lha *f.* chute; rain spout.

ca-lha-ma'-ço *m.* large, old book; (pop.) ugly stout woman.

ca-lham-bé'-que *m.* small vessel.

ca-lhar' *intr.v.* to enter a chute, to run through a chute; to happen; to be opportune.

ca-li-brar' *tr.v.* to calibrate.

ca-li'-bre *m.* caliber.

cá-li-ce *m.* chalice; wine glass.

ca-li-ci'-da *m.* medicine to destroy callus.

cá-li-do, **=a** *adj.* hot, ardent, fiery; astute, sagacious.

ca-li'-fa *m.* caliph.

ca-li-gra-fi'-a *f.* calligraphy.

ca-lí-gra-fo *m.* calligrapher.

ca-lis'-ta *m.* pedicure.

cal'-ma *f.* calm.

cal-mar' *tr.v.* to calm, to quiet.

cal-ma-ri'-a *f.* calm.

cal'-mo, **=a** *adj.* hot, quiet, calm.

ca'-lo *m.* callus; (fig.) insensibility.

ca-lo-me-la'-nos *m.pl.* calomel.

ca-lor' *m.* heat; (fig.) animation, vivacity.

ca-lo-ro'-so, **=a** *adj.* warm, calm, energetic, enthusiastic.

ca-lo-ri'-a *f.* calory.

ca-lo-rí-me-tro *m.* calorimeter.

ca-lo-si-da'-de *f.* callousness.

ca-lo'-te *m.* swindle.

ca-lo-te-ar' *tr.v.* to swindle; *intr.v.* to be a swindler.

ca-lo-tei'-ro *m.* swindler, cheat.

ca-lú-nia *f.* calumny.

ca-lu-ni-ar' *tr.v.* to slander, to calumniate.

cal'-va *f.* baldness.

cal'-vo, =a *adj.* bald, baldheaded.

ca'-ma *f.* bed.

ca-ma'-da *f.* stratum, layer; coat.

ca-ma-feu' *m.* cameo.

ca-ma-le-ão' *m.* chameleon.

câ-ma-ra *f.* room in house; municipal chamber; each house of Congress; inner tube of automobile tire.

ca-ma-ra'-da *m., f.* comrade, colleague.

ca-ma-ra-da'-gem *f.* comradeship.

ca-ma-rão' *m.* shrimp.

ca-ma-rei'-ra *f.* maid of honor.

ca-ma-rei'-ro *m.* valet de chambre.

ca-ma-ri'-lha *f.* court favorites.

ca-ma-ro'-te *m.* state-room (ship); box (theater).

cam-ba'-da *f.* objects strung together (fish, etc.)

cam-ba'-do, =a *adj.* bow-legged; twisted.

cam-ba-la'-cho *m.* barter, exchange, bargaining.

cam-ba-le-ar' *intr.v.* to walk haltingly, to go zigzag, to stagger.

cam-ba-lei'-o *m.* staggering.

cam-ba-lho'-ta *f.* somersault; tumble.

cam-bar' *intr.v.* to bend, to bend the legs; to hobble.

cam-be-te-ar' *intr.v.* to stagger.

cam-bi-ar' *tr.v.* to exchange (money of one country into that of another); *intr.v.* to change (color, opinion, system).

câm-bio *m.* exchange.

cam-bis'-ta *m.* exchange banker; (Brazil) scalper.

cam-brai'-a *f.* cambric.

cam-bu-lha'-da *f.* number of clay sinkers together.

cam-bu'-lho *m.* sinker (of fish net) made of burnt clay.

ca-me-le-ão' *m.* chameleon; (fig.) hypocrite.

ca-me-lei'-ro *m.* camel driver.

ca-mé-lia *f.* camelia.

ca-me'-lo *m.* camel.

ca-mer-len'-go *m.* chamberlain.

ca-mi-nha'-da *f.* journey, walk.

ca-mi-nhan'-te *m.* traveler, transient.

ca-mi-nhão' *m.* truck.

ca-mi-nhar' *tr.v.* to go, to travel, to walk.

ca-mi'-nho *m.* road, way, direction; procedure.

ca-mi'-sa *f.* shirt; corn husk; strait-jacket.

ca-mi-sa-ri'-a *f.* shirt factory; shirt store.

ca-mi-so'-la *f.* undershirt, jacket, smock.

ca-mo-mi'-la *f.* camomile.

cam'-pa *f.* tombstone; small bell.

cam-pa-i'-nha *f.* hand bell; (fig.) person who divulges everything.

cam-pa-ná-rio *m.* bell tower, campanile.

cam-pa'-nha *f.* campaign; extensive fields or plains.

cam-pâ-nu-la *f.* campanula; bell-shaped glass vase.

cam-pe-ão' *m.* champion.

cam-pe-ar' *intr.v.* to camp out, to encamp; to march in conspicuous fashion.

cam-pei'-ro *m.* employee who cares for cattle, cowboy; countryman.

cam-pes'-tre *adj.* rural, rustic; *m.* small cleared area surrounded by forest.

cam-pi'-na *f.* plain, flat open country, pampa.

cam'-po *m.* field; open space; country; plains.

cam-po=de=en-gor'-da *m.* pasture.

cam-po-nês *m.* peasant, farmer, country man.

cam-po=san'-to *m.* cemetery.

ca-mu-fla'-gem *f.* camouflage.

ca-mu-flar' *tr.v.* to camouflage.

ca-mur'-ça *f.* chamois; chamois skin.

ca'-na *f.* cane; sugar cane; long bone (of leg or arm); spoke in steering-wheel; — **de açúcar** sugar cane.

ca-nal' *m.* canal.

ca-na'-lha *f.* vile people; *m.* shameless person; infamous individual.

ca-na-li-zar' *tr.v.* to open canals, in; to lay pipes in, to pipe.

ca-na-pé *m.* couch, settee, sofa.

ca-ná-rio *m.* canary.

ca-nas'-tra *f.* large, shallow basket.

ca-nas'-tro *m.* large, deep basket; human trunk.

can-ção' *f.* song; poem to be sung.

can-ce'-la *f.* latticed gate or door; trellis.

can-ce-la-men'-to *m.* cancellation.

can-ce-lar' *tr.v.* to cancel.

cân-cer *m.* cancer.

can-ce-ro'-so, =a *adj.* cancerous.

can'-cha *f.* race course.

can-ci-o-nei'-ro *m.* collection of songs or poems.

can-cio-nis'-ta *m., f.* songwriter.

can-ço-ne'-ta *f.* short song, canzonet.

can'-cro *m.* cancer; vise; (fig.) something destructive.

can-dei'-a *f.* small oil lamp, generally hanging on wall; candle.

can-dei'-o *m.* torch.

can-de-la'-bro *m.* candelabrum.

can-de-lá-ria *f.* Candlemas (February 2, Purification of the Virgin).

can-den'-te *adj.* candent, glowing.

can-di-da'-to *m.* candidate.

can-di-da-tu'-ra *f.* candidacy.

can-di-dez' *f.* whiteness.

cân-di-do, =a *adj.* white; sincere, pure, innocent, candid.

can-don'-ga *f.* intrigue; gossip; fawning.

can-dor' *m.* whiteness.

can-du'-ra *f.* whiteness; innocence, purity.

ca-ne'-ca *f.* cup, tin-cup.

ca-ne'-co *m.* deep cup.

ca-ne'-la *f.* cinnamon; shin bone; weaver's spool.

ca-ne-lei'-ra *f.* cinnamon tree.

ca-ne-lu'-ra *f.* channeling (half-circle vertical grooves in columns).

ca-ne'-ta *f.* pen holder.

cân-fo-ra *f.* camphor.

can'-ga *f.* ox yoke; porter's pole; outcroppings of mineral ores.

can-ga-cei'-ro *m.* bandit.

can-ga'-ço *m.* refuse; fruit skins and pulp left after extracting juice.

can-ga'-lhas *f.pl.* framework to equalize load on back of cargo animal, one-half on each side.

can-ga-lhei'-ro *m.* driver of cargo animals.

can-gu-rú *m.* kangaroo.

ca-nhão' *m.* cannon.

ca-nho-na'-da *f.* cannonade.

ca-nho-nar' *tr.v.* to equip with cannon.

ca-nho-ne-ar' *tr.v.* to bombard, to cannonade.

ca-nho-nei'-ro *m.* gunner.

ca-nho'-ta *f.* (pop.) left hand.

ca-nho'-to, =a *adj.* left-handed; (fig.)

awkward; unskilful; *m.*, *f.* left-handed person; stub in check-book.

ca-ni-bal' *m.* cannibal.

ca-ni-ba-lis'-mo *m.* cannibalism.

ca-ni'-ço *m.* slender pole; fishing-pole.

ca-ní-cu-la *f.* Canicula; dog-days.

ca-ni-cu-lar' *adj.* canicular.

ca-nil' *m.* kennel.

ca-ni'-no, =a *adj.* canine.

ca-ni-ve'-te *m.* pen knife.

can'-ja *f.* chicken broth with rice; (slang) something easy to do.

can-je-ré *m.* group of persons, generally negroes, to practice conjuring.

can-ji'-ca *f.* big hominy (in some States of Brazil); sort of pudding made from green corn (grated, seasoned with sugar, cooked, cooled in form).

ca'-no *m.* pipe; sewer, water or gas pipe; rifle barrel.

ca-nô-a *f.* canoe.

ca-no-ei'-ro *m.* canoe builder, oarsman.

câ-non or **câ-no-ne** *m.* canon.

ca-no-ni-cal' *adj.* canonical.

ca-no-ni-co, =a *adj.* canonical.

ca-no-ni-za-ção' *f.* canonization.

ca-no-ni-zar' *tr.v.* to canonize.

can-sa'-ço *m.* fatigue; weakness caused by illness.

can-sa'-do, =a *adj.* weary, tired, bored.

can-sar' *tr.v.* to tire, to cause fatigue; to importune, to bore; *intr.v.* to tire, to get tired.

can-ta-lu'-po *m.* cantaloupe.

can-tão' *m.* canton.

can-to-nei'-ro *m.* street cleaner.

can-tar' *tr.v.*, *intr.v.* to sing.

cân-ta-ra *f.* wide-mouthed, big-bellied water pot.

can-ta-ri'-a *f.* masonry; corner stone.

cân-ta-ro *m.* large, big-bellied water-jug of earthen-ware or tin.

can-ta-ro-lar' *tr.v.*, *intr.v.* to hum; to sing out of tune.

can-ta'-ta *f.* cantata.

can-tei'-ro *m.* stone mason; sculptor; flower bed.

cân-ti-co *m.* canticle, hymn.

can-ti'-ga *f.* poem put to music.

can-til' *m.* grooving plane; water bottle.

can-ti'-na *f.* canteen.

can'-to *m.* song; canto; corner, angle; border; corner-stone; remote spot; rough spot (in a board).

can-to-chão' *m.* cantus firmus (Gregorian chant).

can-to-ei'-ra *f.* iron brace to secure corner stone in buildings.

can-to-nei'-ra *f.* corner cupboard; corner brace for furniture.

can-tor' *m.* singer; poet.

can-to-ri'-a *f.* singing in concert.

ca-nu'-do *m.* pipe, tube, reed cut between joints; pleat ironed in garment; curly hair.

cão' *m.* dog; cock (of a gun).

ca-o'-lho, =a *adj.* cross-eyed; one-eyed.

ca'-os *m.* chaos.

ca-ó-ti-co, =a *adj.* chaotic.

ca'-pa *f.* cape, cloak; covering; binding of book.

ca-pa-ce'-te *m.* helmet; ice-cap; cap (of a still); **— de gêlo** ice-cap.

ca-pa'-cho *m.* door mat.

ca-pa-ci-da'-de *f.* capacity.

ca-pa-ci-tar' *tr.v.* to enable.

ca-pan'-ga *f.* safety bag or pocket for money and valuables carried under-

neath clothing when traveling; body-guard.

ca-pan-gar' *tr.v.* to bootleg diamonds.

ca-pa-taz' *m.* foreman, overseer.

ca-pa'-do *m.* castrated sheep or goat.

ca-pão' *m.* capon.

ca-par' *tr.v.* to castrate, to spay.

ca-paz' *adj.* capable, able.

cap-ci-o'-so, =a *adj.* captious.

ca-pe'-la *f.* chapel.

ca-pe-lão' *m.* chaplain.

ca-pe'-lo *m.* monk's hood, cowl; widow's mourning veil; doctorate; cardinalate.

ca-pen'-ga *m.* . cripple; *adj.* crippled.

ca-pen-gar' *intr.v.* to be crippled.

ca-pe'-ta *m.* devil; trouble-maker.

ca-pi-lar' *adj.* capillary.

ca-pi-la-ri-da'-de *f.* capillarity.

ca-pim' *m.* grass.

ca-pi-nar' *tr.v.* to cut; to weed out.

ca-pin-zal' *m.* grazing field, hay-field.

ca-pis-car' *intr.v.* to understand little; to get the sense of.

ca-pi-ta-ção' *f.* capitation, poll tax.

ca-pi-tal' *adj.* capital, essential, chief; *f.* capital (city); capital letter.

ac-pi-ta-lis'-mo *m.* capitalism.

ca-pi-ta-lis'-ta *m.* capitalist.

ca-pi-ta-li-za-ção' *f.* capitalization.

ca-pi-ta-li-zar' *tr.v.* to capitalize.

ca-pi-ta-ne-ar' *tr.v.* to captain, to govern.

ca-pi-ta-ni'-a *f.* captaincy.

ca-pi-tâ-nia *f.* flag-ship.

ca-pi-tão' *m.* captain.

ca-pi-tel' *m.* capital of column; cap of still; ear-drum.

ca-pi-tó-lio *m.* capitol; (fig.) glory, triumph, splendor.

ca-pi-to'-so, =a *adj.* affecting head, causing dizziness, heady.

ca-pí-tu-la *f.* short chapter, lesson.

ca-pi-tu-la-ção' *f.* surrender, capitulation.

ca-pi-tu-lar' *tr.v.* to capitulate; to divide into chapters; *adj.* capitulary.

ca-pí-tu-lo *m.* chapter (of a book).

ca-po-ei'-ra *f.* large coop or pen for domestic fowl; covered passage-way in fortress; *m.* bandit or criminal armed with knife or razor.

ca-po-ral' *m.* corporal.

ca-po'-ta *f.* hood; top (of automobile, victoria, buggy).

ca-po-tar' *intr.v.* to nose down (airplane).

ca-po'-te *m.* cloak, overcoat, rain-coat.

ca-pri-char' *intr.v.* to be capricious, to have whims.

ca-pri'-cho *m.* caprice.

ca-pri-cho'-so, =a *adj.* capricious.

ca-pri-cór-nio *m.* Capricorn.

ca-pri'-no, =a *adj.* similar or pertaining to goats.

cáp-su-la *f.* capsule.

cap-tar' *tr.v.* to captivate, to attract.

cap-tu'-ra *f.* capture, seizure, arrest.

cap-tu-rar' *tr.v.* to capture, to arrest.

ca-pu-chi'-no *m.* Capuchin; man of austere life; small capuche.

ca-pu'-cho, =a *adj.* penitent, austere, solitary; of the Franciscan order.

ca-puz' *m.* hood, cowl.

ca-qué-ti-co, =a *adj.* decrepit, senile.

ca-que-xi'-a *f.* general senile debility.

ca-quí *m.* kaki; Japanese persimmon.

ca'-qui *m.* khaki cloth.

ca'-ra *f.* face, aspect; daring.

ca-rá *m.* kind of yam; kind of **fandango**.

ca-ra-bi'-na *f.* carbine.

ca-ra-bi-na'-da f. carbine shot.
ca-ra-bi-nei'-ro m. carabineer.
ca-ra-col' m. snail; curl; caracol.
ca-rac-te'-res m. printing type.
ca-ra-man-chão' or ca-ra-man-chel' m. garden terrace, generally having trellis with vines.
ca-ram'-ba! interj. signifying surprise or irony.
ca-ram-bo'-la f. red billiard ball; carom.
ca-ram-bo-lar' intr.v. to make a carom.
ca-ra-me'-lo m. caramel; caramel candy; hominy snow.
ca-ra-mu'-jo m. conch; any univalve spiral mollusk.
ca-ran-gue'-jo m. crab.
ca-ran-gue-jo'-la f. large cray-fish; shaky, insecure framework.
ca-rão' m. reprehension; disapproving or frightening facial expression put on purposely.
ca-ra-pu'-ça f. long stocking cap.
ca-rá-ter m. character.
ca-ra-te-rís-ti-ca f. characteristic.
ca-ra-te-rís-ti-co, =a adj. characteristic.
ca-ra-te-ri-za-ção' f. characterization.
ca-ra-te-ri-zar' tr.v. to characterize.
ca-ra-va'-na f. caravan, pilgrimage.
ca-ra-ve'-la f. caravel; ship; ancient silver coin.
car-bo-na'-to m. carbonate.
car-bô-ni-co, =a adj. carbonic.
car-bo'-no m. carbon.
car-bo-ni-za-ção' f. carbonization.
car-bo-ni-zar' tr.v. to carbonize.
car-bún-cu-lo m. carbuncle.
car-bu-ra-ção' f. carburization.
car-bu-ra-dor' m. carburetor.
car-ca'-ça f. carcass.
car-ce-ra'-gem f. imprisonment; jailor's fees.
cár-ce-re m. prison, jail.
car-ce-rei'-ro m. jailor.
car-co-mi'-do, =a adj. worm-eaten, worn out with age.
car-cun'-da see cor-cun-da.
car-dá-pio m. menu.
car-dar' tr.v. to card (wool).
car-de-al' m. cardinal; adj. cardinal, principal, fundamental.
cár-dia f. cardiac end of stomach.
car-dí-a-co, =a adj. m. f. cardiac; sufferer from heart disease.
car-di-al-gi'-a f. pain in the heart; heart-burn.
car-di-nal' adj. principal; relative to hinges; cardinal (number).
car-di-na-lí-cio, =a adj. pertaining to a cardinal.
car-di-o-gra-fí-a f. cardiography.
car-di-o-gra'-ma m. cardiogram.
car-di-o-lo-gi'-a f. cardiology.
car'-do m. thistle.
car'-do, =a adj. bristly, thorny.
car-du'-me m. school (of fish); multitude, large gathering.
ca-re-ar' tr.v. to face, to confront; to entice, to attract.
ca-rei'-o m. lure, enticement.
ca-re'-ca m. bald-headed person; f. baldness.
ca-re'-co, =a adj. bald-headed.
ca-re-cer' intr.v. to need, to be lacking in.
ca-rên-cia f. lack, need, shortage.
ca-res-ti'-a f. high cost of living; scarcity.
ca-re'-ta f. grimace; mask; (fig.) threat.
car'-ga f. cargo, load, burden; charge (of a gun).

car'-go m. public office, official position; responsibility.
car-guei'-ro m. driver of beasts of burden; car-guei'-ro, =a adj. burden-carrying.
ca-ri-a'-do, =a adj. having caries, decayed.
ca-ri-ar' tr.v. to corrupt; intr.v. to form caries; to become decayed.
cá-rie f. caries, decay.
ca-ri-o'-so, =a adj. decayed; relative to caries.
ca-ri-bú m., f. caribou.
ca-ri-ca-tu'-ra f. caricature.
ca-ri-ca-tu-rar' tr.v. to caricature.
ca-ri-ca-tu-ris'-ta m. caricaturist.
ca-rí-cia f. caress, manifestation of affection.
ca-ri-cio'-so, =a adj. caressing, affectionate.
ca-ri-da'-de f. charity.
ca-ri-do'-so, =a adj. charitable.
ca-ril' m. curry powder.
ca-ri'-lho m. silk reel.
ca-rim-bar' tr.v. to mark with stamp, to seal, to cancel.
ca-rim'-bo m. metal stamp; seal.
ca-rim-bó m. primitive drum consisting of hollowed-out tree trunk across one end of which skin is stretched; drum beater sitting astride trunk.
ca-ri'-nho m. affection; care.
ca-ri-nho'-so, =a adj. affectionate, kindly.
ca-ri-o'-ca m., f. native of city of Rio de Janeiro, Brazil.
ca-ris'-ma f. charism.
ca-ri-tel' m. cry for help.
ca-ri-tó m. crab pen; corner cupboard; cabin.
ca-riz' m. countenance; caraway seed.
car-le-quim' m. windlass; jack.
car-me-ar' tr.v. to untangle; to remove knots and tangles from wool before carding.
car-me-li'-na f. inferior quality of vicuña wool.
car-me-li'-ta m., f. Carmelite.
car-me-sim' m. bright carmine.
car-mim' m. carmine.
car-mi-nar' tr.v. to dye carmine color.
car-mi-na-ti'-vo, =a adj. carminative.
car-na-ção' f. carnation (flesh tints in painting); flesh color.
car-na-du'-ra f. fleshy part of body; appearance.
car-na'-gem f. slaughter of animals for food; carnage.
car-nal' adj. carnal.
car-na-li-da'-de f. carnality.
car-nar' intr.v. to cohabit.
car-na-ú-ba f. carnaúba.
car-na-u-bei'-ra f. palm tree which produces wax.
car-na-val' m. carnival.
car'-ne f. flesh; meat; (fig.) animal nature.
car-ne-ar' tr.v., intr.v. to slaughter.
car-nei'-ra f. sheep-skin.
car-nei-ra'-da f. flock of sheep.
car-nei-rei'-ro m. shepherd.
car-nei'-ro m. sheep.
cár-ne-o, =a adj. fleshy; flesh-colored.
car-ni-cei'-ro m. butcher; car-ni-cei'-ro, =a adj. carnivorous; voracious; cruel.
car-ni-fi-car'=se refl.v. to become flesh.
car-ni-vo-ro, =a adj. carnivorous.
car-no'-so, =a adj. fleshy, covered with flesh.

car-nu'-do, =a *adj.* fat, muscular.
ca'-ro, =a *adj.* expensive; dear, held in high esteem; *adv.* dear; at high price, with work and sacrifice.
ca-ro-á-vel *adj.* amiable, friendly.
ca-ro'-cha *f.* dunce cap; tin funnel; *pl.* prevarications.
ca-ro-chi'-nha *f.* legend; fairy story.
ca-ro'-ço *m.* seed.
ca-ro-çu'-do, =a *adj.* having seed.
ca-ro'-la *m.* bigot, sanctimonious person.
ca-ro'-lo *m.* thump on head with knuckles; ear of corn with shuck removed; badly ground meal.
ca-ro-na'-da *f.* carronade (short cannon).
ca-ró-ti-da *f.* carotid.
car'-pa *f.* carp.
car-pe'-lo *m.* carpel.
car-pi-dei'-ra *f.* hired mourner at funerals.
car-pi'-do *m.* plaintive weeping.
car-pi-men'-to *m.* lamentation, weeping.
car-pin-ta-ri'-a *f.* carpentry.
car-pin-tei'-ro *m.* carpenter.
car-pin-te-jar' *intr.v.* to carpenter.
car-pir' *tr.v.* to tear one's hair; to snatch; *intr.v.* to lament, to bemoan.
car'-po *m.* carpus, wrist.
car-qui'-lha *f.* wrinkle; pleat.
car-ra'-ca *f.* carrack, galleon.
car-ran'-ca *f.* frown; grimace; ugly, frightening mask.
car-ran'-ça *m.* individual who lives in past.
car-ran-cu'-do, =a *adj.* sullen, crabbed.
car-ran-que-ar' *intr.v.* to be sullen, to make an ugly face, to grimace.
car-ra-pa'-to *m.* cattle tick; castor oil bean.
car-ra-pa-te-ar' *tr.v.* to apply tick-killing preparation to.
car-ra-pa-ti-ci'-da *m.* tick-killing preparation.
car-ras-cão *m.* strong, green wine; wine to which rum and other adulterants are added to make it strong.
car-re-ga-ção' *f.* load, large quantity; carrying.
car-re-ga-dei'-ra *f.* string from which candles are hung.
car-re-ga'-do, =a *adj.* deep (in color); burdened.
car-re-ga-dor' *m.* porter; packer; loader.
car-re-gar' *tr.v.* to place load on; to load; to charge; to carry; to charge firearm; to charge (with electricity); to impute; —=se *refl.v.* to undertake.
car-rei-ra *f.* road-way; race; career, profession; sphere of activity.
car-rei'-go *m.* ox-cart driver; narrow roadway; path of ants on the march.
car-rê'-ta *f.* small two-wheeled push-cart; cart.
car-re-ta'-gem *f.* cartage.
car-rê-te *m.* small wheel, cylindrical piece (in machinery).
car-re-tel' *m.* spool; pulley; reel of log (ship).
car-re-ti'-lha *f.* small wheel for decorating pastry.
car-rê-to *m.* freight, freight charge.
car-ri-ão' *m.* shuttle race.
car-ri-ça *f.* raft.
car-ril' *m.* track; rail.
car-ri-lhão' *m.* carillon.
car-ri'-nho *m.* toy cart.
car-ri-o'-la *f.* rustic cart with two wheels.

car'-ro *m.* car; vehicle (with wheels); — de mão wheelbarrow.
car'-ta *f.* letter; map; card, playing card; — aberta letter addressed to individual but published in newspaper.
car-ta-bu'-xa *f.* wire brush (of goldsmith).
car-ta'-da *f.* trick (in card games).
car-tão' *m.* pasteboard; visiting card.
car-taz' *m.* poster; safe-conduct.
car-te-ar' *tr.v.* to play cards; *intr.v.* to calculate position of ship on map.
car-tei'-ra *f.* pocket book; brief-case; memorandum book; desk, writing table.
car-tei'-ro *m.* postman; manufacturer of playing cards.
car-tel' *m.* cartel.
car-ti-la'-gem *f.* cartilage.
car-ti-la-gi-no'-so, =a *adj.* cartilaginous.
car-ti'-lha *f.* first reader.
car-to-gra-fi'-a *f.* cartography.
car-to-grá-fi-co, =a *adj.* cartographic.
car-to'-la *f.* high silk hat.
car-to-man'-te *m.*, *f.* fortune-teller who uses cards.
car-to-na'-gem *f.* pasteboard binding (of a book).
car-to-nar' *tr.v.* to bind with pasteboard.
car-tó-rio *m.* document file; archive; office of notary public.
car-tu'-cho *m.* cartouche.
ca-run'-cho *m.* wood termite; rottenness.
ca-rún-cu-la *f.* caruncle.
car-va'-lho *m.* oak tree; oak.
car-vão' *m.* coal; charcoal.
car-vo-a-ri'-a *f.* kiln for making charcoal.
car-vo-ei'-ro *m.* seller of coal or charcoal.
car-vo-e-jar' *intr.v.* to make charcoal.
ca'-sa *f.* house, home; room; buttonhole; column in which numbers stand (units, tens, etc.); space between lines on map or table; — de saúde private hospital.
ca-sa'-ca *f.* full-dress coat; *m.* civilian.
ca-sa-cão' *m.* man's overcoat.
ca-sa'-co *m.* coat.
ca-sa-dou'-ro, =a *adj.* marriageable; thinking of marriage.
ca-sal' *m.* couple, married couple.
ca-sa-le'-jo *m.* rustic shack.
ca-sa-men-tei'-ro, =a *adj.* relative to weddings; *m. f.* match-maker.
ca-sa-men'-to *m.* marriage, wedding.
ca-sar' *tr.v.* to marry.
ca-sa-rão' *m.* large house, large building.
ca-são' *m.* large house.
cas'-ca *f.* peeling, skin, bark; outside covering; (fig.) appearances.
cas-ca-bur-ren'-to *m.* rough bark.
cas-ca'-lho *m.* stone slivers; brittle rock; mixture of pebbles, sand and crustacean fossils; diamond or gold bearing alluvial deposit.
cas-cão' *m.* heavy, thick bark; stratum of pebbles and rock not yet solidly petrified.
cas-car' *tr.v.*, *intr.v.* to remove the bark; to beat; to answer in a sullen manner.
cás-ca-ra *f.* copper ore.
cas-car-rão' *m.* thick bark; anger.
cas-ca'-ta *f.* cascade.
cas-ca-te-ar' *intr.v.* to fall in form of cascade.
cas'-co *m.* skull; helmet; hull of ship.
cas-cu'-do, =a *adj.* having thick shell or hard skin.

ca-se-a-ção' f. transformation of milk into cheese; manufacture of cheese.
ca-se-a-dei'-ra f. woman who works buttonholes.
ca-se-ar' tr.v., intr.v. to work buttonholes.
ca-se'-bre m. shanty, shack.
ca-se-í-na f casein.
ca-sei'-ro, =a adj. pertaining to house; modest.
ca-se-o'-so, =a adj. cheese-like.
ca-si-mi'-ra f. cashmere.
ca-si'-nha f. small house; outdoor privy.
ca-si'-no m. casino.
ca'-so m. case, event; importance; difficulty.
cas'-pa f. dandruff.
cas-pen'-to, =a adj. having dandruff.
cas-po'-so, =a adj. having dandruff.
cas-que-jar' intr.v. to grow new shell or bark; to scar over.
cas-que'-te m. beret; old hat.
cas-qui-nar' intr.v. to give out short, sarcastic laughs.
cas-qui'-nha f. diminutive of casca; thin veneer of fine wood over wood of inferior quality; thin gold leaf used in art work.
cas'-sa f. fine cotton muslin.
cas-sa-ção' f. annulment.
cas-sar' tr.v. to cancel permit already granted.
cás-sia f. cassia.
cas'-so, =a adj. null.
cas'-ta f. caste; breed; quality; nature.
cas-ta'-nha f. nut; chestnut.
cas-ta'-nha=do=Pa-rá f. Brazil nut tree.
cas-ta-nhal' m. grove of nut trees.
cas-ta'-nho m. chestnut /wood; brown color.
cas-ta-nho'-las f.pl. castanets.
cas-tão' m. head (gold, silver, ivory, etc.) of cane.
cas-te-ar' tr.v. to reproduce.
cas-te-lã' f. chatelaine, wife of a feudal lord.
cas-te-lão' m. feudal lord living in a castle.
cas-te-lei'-ro, =a adj. pertaining to a castle.
cas-te-lha'-no m. Castilian.
cas-te'-lo m. castle, fort.
cas-ti-çal' m. candlestick.
cas-ti-çar' tr.v., intr.v. to breed, to mate.
cas-ti'-ço, =a adj. pure-bred, thorough-bred; suitable for breeding.
cas-ti-da'-de f. chastity.
cas-ti-fi-car' tr.v. to make chaste.
cas-ti-gar' tr.v. to chastise; to punish.
cas-ti-gá-vel adj. deserving punishment.
cas-ti'-go m. punishment, discipline; suffering.
cas-tor' m. castor.
cas-to-ri'-na f. soft, heavy cloth, beaver felt.
cas-to-ro'-sa f. machine used in hat industry.
cas-tra-ção' f. castration.
cas-tra-men-ta-ção' f. encamping, fortifying; laying out an encampment.
cas-trar' tr.v. to castrate.
ca-su-al' adj. casual.
ca-su-a-li-da'-de f. casualness; chance.
ca-su'-la f. chasuble.
ca-su'-lo m. cocoon; hull, husk.
ca'-ta f. search; research; (Greek prefix).
ca-tar' tr.v. to look for; to look for parasites on; to examine minutely.

ca-ta-ce'-go, =a adj. short-sighted; half-blind.
ca-ta-clis'-mo m. cataclysm.
ca-ta-cre'-se f. catachresis.
ca-ta-cum'-bas f.pl. catacombs.
ca-ta-dor' m. machine which separates coffee beans according to various types.
ca-ta-du'-ra f. disposition; humor; appearance.
ca-ta-fal'-co m. catafalque.
ca-tá-fo-ra f. cataphora.
ca-ta-lep-si'-a f. catalepsy.
ca-ta-lo-gar' tr.v. to catalogue.
ca-tá-lo-go m. catalogue; detailed report.
ca-ta-lu'-fa f. luster of fabrics caused by interwoven silver or gold threads.
ca-tão' m. (fig.) austere man.
ca-ta-plas'-ma f. cataplasm, poultice.
ca-ta-ple-xi'-a f. cataplexy.
ca-ta-pul'-ta f. catapult.
ca-ta-ra'-ta f. cataract; water-fall.
ca-ta-ri'-na f. balance wheel (of a watch).
ca-tar-rei'-ra f. deep cold.
ca-tar'-ro m. catarrh.
ca-tar-ro'-so, =a adj. catarrhous.
ca-tar'-se f. catharsis, purging.
ca-tár-ti-co, =a adj. cathartic.
ca-tas-sol' m. fabric with changing colors.
ca-tás-tro-fe f. catastrophe.
ca-ta-ven'-to m. weather vane; wind-mill.
ca-te-cis'-mo m. catechism.
ca-te-cú-me-no m. catechumen.
cá-te-dra f. professorship.
ca-te-drá-ti-co m. full professor (in higher institution of learning).
ca-te-dral' f. cathedral.
ca-te-go-ri'-a f. category.
ca-te-gó-ri-co, =a adj. categorical.
ca-te-que'-se f. catechesis.
ca-te-qui-zar' tr.v. to catechize.
ca-te-ré-ti-co, =a adj. slightly caustic.
ca-te-ter' m. catheter.
ca-tin'-ga f. strong, disagreeable body odor; scrubby undergrowth; zone in which vegetation is scrubby and twisted; disagreeable smell.
ca-tin-gal' m. large area of scrubby vegetation.
ca-tin-gar' intr.v. to give off a bad odor, to stink; to haggle; to be stingy.
ca-tin-go'-so, =a adj. odoriferous, stinking.
ca-ti-on'-te m. kation (in electrolysis).
ca-ti-var' tr.v. to captivate.
ca-ti'-vo, =a adj. captive.
ca-tó-di-co, =a adj. cathodic.
ca-tó-dio m. cathode.
ca-to-li-ci-da'-de f. catholicity.
ca-to-li-cis'-mo m. Catholicism.
ca-tó-li-co, =a adj. Catholic.
ca-tor'-ze m. fourteen.
ca'-tre m. folding cot.
ca-tu'-lo m. puppy; young of any animal.
cau-ção' f. deposit; security; pledge; caution.
cau-cio-nan'-te m., f. person giving guarantee.
cau-cio-nar' tr.v. to secure by deposit, to give guarantees.
cau'-cho m. tree of Moraceae family whose latex produces inferior quality of rubber.
cau'-da f. tail; train (of a dress).
cau-dal' adj. capital, large, abundant; m. torrent, water-fall.

cau-da-lo'-so, =a *adj.* abundant, carrying a great amount of water.

cau-da-tó-rio *m.* train bearer (to an ecclesiastic).

cau-di'-lho *m.* military chief; leader.

cau'-le *m.* stem, stalk.

cau-li'-co *m.* small stem.

ca-u-lim' or **cau-li'-no** *m.* kaolin.

cau'-sa *f.* cause; origin.

cau-sa-ção' *f.* causation.

cau-sa-dor', =a *adj.* causative.

cau-sal' *adj.* causal.

cau-sa-li-da'-de *f.* causality.

cau-sar' *tr.v.* to cause.

cau-sa-ti'-vo, =a *adj.* causative.

cáus-ti-co, =a *adj.* caustic; *m.* caustic substance.

cau-te'-la *f.* precaution; receipt.

cau-te-lo'-so, =a *adj.* cautious.

cau-te-ri-zar' *tr.v.* to cauterize.

ca'-va *f.* hole; armhole (of a garment); basement.

ca-va-ção' *f.* digging, excavation.

ca-va'-co *m.* small splinter of wood, sliver; simple, friendly conversation; indication of anger on part of one teased or ridiculed.

ca-va'-do *m.* hole.

ca-va-dor' *m.* laborer, digger; impostor, charlatan.

ca-va-la'-da *f.* asininity, bestial act.

ca-va-lão' *m.* large horse; abnormally tall person.

ca-va-lar' *adj.* concerning horses.

ca-va-la-ri'-a *f.* cavalry; knighthood, chivalry.

ca-va-la-ri'-ça *f.* stable.

ca-va-lei'-ro *m.* horseman, cavalry-man, knight, nobleman; a — de above, overlooking.

ca-va-le'-te *m.* easel.

ca-val-ga'-da *f.* cavalcade.

ca-val-ga-du'-ra *f.* mount.

ca-val-gar' *intr.v.* to ride horse-back.

ca-va-lhei-ris'-mo *m.* nobility, chivalry.

ca-va-lhei'-ro *m.* gentleman, knight; **ca-va-lhei'-ro,** =a *adj.* cultured, noble.

ca-va-lhei-ro'-so, =a *adj.* gentlemanly, distinguished.

ca-va'-lo *m.* horse.

ca-va'-lo=va-por' *m.* horse power.

ca-va-quei'-ra *f.* long, tiresome conversation.

ca-va-qui'-nho *m.* small musical instrument similar to guitar.

ca-var' *tr.v.* to dig; to obtain dishonestly; *intr.v.* to work hard.

ca-vei'-ra *f.* skeleton head; skull; (fig.) very emaciated face.

ca-vei-ro'-so, =a *adj.* of skin and bones, emaciated.

ca-ver'-na *f.* cavern.

ca-ver-nal' *adj.* pertaining to a cavern.

ca-ver-no'-so, =a *adj.* cavernous.

ca-vi-ar' *m.* caviar.

ca-vi-da'-de *f.* cavity.

ca-vi-la-ção' *f.* quibbling, trifling objections.

ca-vi-lar' *intr.v.* to cavil.

ca-vi'-lha *f.* bolt, axle pin.

ca-vi-lhar' *tr.v.* to bolt, to peg, to fasten.

ca'-vo, =a *adj.* deep, hollow, cavernous.

ca-vu-ca-dor' *m.* hard worker.

ca-vu-car' *intr.v.* to work persistently.

ce-ar' *tr.v.* to eat supper, to have supper.

ce-bo'-la *f.* onion.

ce-bo-li'-nha *f.* small onion.

ce-bo-li'-nho *m.* onion seed; onion sprout.

ce-ce-ar' *intr.v.* to lisp.

ce-cei'-o *m.* lisping.

ce-dên-cia *f.* cession, yielding.

ce-der' *tr.v.* to yield, to cede.

ce-di'-lha *f.* cedilla.

ce'-do *adv.* early, soon; prematurely.

ce-di'-nho *adv.* very early, rather early.

ce-dri'-no, =a *adj.* relative to cedar.

ce'-dro *m.* cedar.

cé-du-la *f.* cedula.

ce-gar' *tr.v.* to blind; *intr.v.* to become blind; (fig.) to be fanatic or ignorant.

ce'-go, =a *adj.* blind.

ce-guei'-ra *f.* blindness; infatuation; fanaticism.

cei'-a *f.* supper.

cei-a'-ta *f.* sumptuous supper.

cei'-fa *f.* harvest.

cei-til' *m.* old Portuguese coin valued at one-sixth of a *real;* (fig.) something insignificant.

ce'-la *f.* cell.

ce-le-bra-ção' *f.* celebration.

ce-le-bra'-do, =a *adj.* famous, celebrated.

ce-le-bran'-te *m.* officiating priest.

ce-le-brar' *tr.v.* to celebrate.

cé-le-bre *adj.* famous, noted, well-known; strange, outlandish.

ce-le-bri-da'-de *f.* celebrity.

ce-lei'-ro *m.* granary.

cé-le-re *adj.* swift, quick.

ce-le-ri-da'-de *f.* celerity.

ce-les'-te *adj.* **ce-les-tial'** *adj.* celestial.

ce'-lhas *f.pl.* eye-lashes.

ce-li-ba'-to *m.* celibacy.

ce-li-ba-tá-rio *m.* celibate.

cé-lu-la *f.* cell; seed pod.

ce-lu-lar' *adj.* cellular; having cells.

ce-lu-lói-de *f.* celluloid.

ce-lu-lo'-se *f.* cellulose.

cem' *adj.* one hundred.

ce-men-tar' *tr.v.* to caseharden.

ce-men'-to *m.* dentine.

ce-mi-té-rio *m.* cemetery.

ce-ná-cu-lo *m.* cenaculum.

ce-ná-rio *m.* scenery, properties.

ce'-na *f.* scene.

ce'-nho *m.* hoof disease (of horse and cattle).

ce-no-bi'-ta *m.,* *f.* cenobite.

ce-no-tá-fio *m.* cenotaph.

ce-nou'-ra *f.* carrot.

cen'-so *m.* census.

cen-sor' *m.* censor.

cen-só-rio, =a *adj.* censorious.

cen-su-al' *adj.* relative to the census.

cen-su-á-rio *m.* owner of taxable property.

cen-su'-ra *f.* censure.

cen-su-rar' *tr.v.* to censure.

cen-su-rá-vel *adj.* censurable.

cen-ta'-vo *m.* centavo.

cen-tei'-o *m.* rye.

cen-te'-na *f.* hundred.

cen-te-ná-rio *m.* centenarian.

cen-te-si-mal' *adj.* centesimal.

cen-té-si-mo *m.* hundredth.

cen-tí-gra-do, =a *adj.* centigrade (having one hundred degrees).

cen-ti-gra'-ma *m.* centigram.

cen-ti-li'-tro *m.* centiliter.

cen-tí-me-tro *m.* centimeter.

cên-ti-mo *m.* centime.

cen'-to *m.* hundred; group of a hundred objects.

cen-tral' *adj.* central.

cen-tra-li-za-ção' *f.* centralization.

cen-trar' *tr.v.* to center, to place in center.
cen-trí-fu-go, =a *adj.* centrifugal.
cen-trí-pe-to, =a *adj.* centripetal.
cen'-tro *m.* center; club.
cen-tu-ri-ão' *m.* centurion.
ce-pi'-lho *m.* carpenter's plane.
ce'-po *m.* cutting block consisting of section of tree trunk.
cep-ti-cis'-mo *m.* skepticism.
cép-ti-co *m.* skeptic.
ce'-ra *f.* wax.
ce-rá-ce-o, =a *adj.* wax-like.
ce-râ-mi-ca *f.* ceramics.
ce-râ-mi-co, =a *adj.* ceramic.
cé-ra-mo *m.* pottery vessel.
cêr-ca *f.* fence, wall; — **de** *prep.* about.
cer-ca'-da *f.* fish-trap.
cer-ca-ni'-a *f.* neighborhood, vicinity.
cer-cão' *adj.* neighboring, near-by.
cer-car' *tr.v.* to fence in; to surround; to tighten; to besiege.
cer'-ce *adv.* by the roots.
cer-ci'-lho *m.* tonsure (of priests).
cêr-co *m.* siege; circle.
ce-re-bra-ção' cerebration.
ce-re-bral' *adj.* cerebral.
cé-re-bro *m.* cerebrum; brain.
ce-re-al' *adj.* producing flour or bread; *m.* grain, cereal.
ce-re-be'-lo *m.* cerebellum.
ce-re'-ja *f.* cherry.
ce-re-jal' *m.* cherry orchard.
ce-re-jei'-ra *f.* cherry tree.
cé-re-o, =a *adj.* waxen, wax-colored.
cé-ri-ca *f.* ointment made of wax and olive oil.
ce-ri-mô-nia *f.* ceremony.
ce-ri-mo-ni-al' *adj.* ceremonial.
ce-ri-mo-ni-o'-so, =a *adj.* ceremonious.
cé-rio *m.* cerium.
cer-na'-lha *f.* withers (of a horse).
cer'-ne *m.* heart of tree.
cer-nei'-ra *f.* heart (of a tree).
ce-rol' *m.* shoemaker's wax.
ce-rou'-las *f.pl.* drawers.
cer-ra-ção' *f.* fog, mist; (fig.) hoarseness.
cer'-ta *f.* certainty; something sure.
cer-ta'-me *m.* debate; combat; contest.
cer-tar' *intr.v.* to strive, to strain, to debate, to compete.
cer-te'-za *f.* certainty.
cer-ti-dão' *f.* certainty.
cer-ti-fi-ca'-do *m.* certificate.
cer-ti-fi-car' *tr.v.* to certify.
cer'-to, =a *adj.* true, certain, exact, sure.
ce-ru'-me *m.* ear wax.
ce-ru'-sa *f.* ceruse; white lead.
cer'-va *f.* kind, doe.
cer-ve'-ja *f.* beer.
cer-ve-ja-ri'-a *f.* brewery; beer saloon, pub.
cer-viz' *f.* neck.
cer'-vo *m.* deer.
cer-zir' *tr.v.* to darn.
cer-zi-dei'-ra *f.* darner, mender.
ce-sa-ri-a'-no, =a *adj.* caesarean.
ces-são' *f.* cession.
ces-sar' *intr.v.* to cease, to stop.
ces-sio-ná-rio *m.* assignee, grantee.
ces'-ta *f.* basket.
ces-ta'-da *f.* basket-full.
ces-tão' *m.* large basket.
ces-tei'-ro *m.* basket-maker.
cês-to *m.* small basket (generally without handles but with a top).
ce-tim' *m.* satin.
ce-ti-ne'-ta *f.* sateen.
ce'-to *m.* whale.

ce'-tras *f.pl.* flourishes in hand-writing.
ce'-tro *m.* scepter.
céu *m.* heaven; sky, firmament.
ce'-va *f.* feed; lure, enticement.
ce-va'-da *f.* barley.
ce-va-dei'-ra *f.* feed-bag.
ce-va-dei'-ro *m.* feed-trough.
ce-va-di'-nha *f.* pearl barley.
chá *m.* tea; tea plant.
cha-lei'-ra *f.* tea-kettle.
cha-lei-rar' *tr.v.* to flatter.
chá-ca-ra *f.* country home (generally near city).
cha-cim' *m.* hog.
cha-ci'-na *f.* salt meat, smoked meat.
cha-ci-nar' *tr.v.* to smoke (meat).
cha-fa-riz' *m.* public fountain providing drinking water.
cha'-ga *f.* open wound, running sore; ulcer.
chai'-ra *f.* knife-sharpener (of steel).
cha'-le *m.* shawl.
cha-lé *m.* chalet.
cha'-ma *f.* flame; (fig.) ardor, passion.
cha-ma'-da *f.* signal; roll-call.
cha-ma'-do *m.* call, roll-call.
cha-mar *tr.v.* to call; to call by name; to choose; to name; to convoke.
cham'-bre *m.* dressing-gown.
cha-mi'-ço *m.* dry branches; kindling.
cha-mi-né *f.* chimney.
cham-pa'-nha *m.* champagne.
cha-mus-car' *tr.v.* to brown slightly, to toast.
chan-ce'-la *f.* pendent seal; impression of official seal on documents.
chan-ce-lar' *tr.v.* to stamp with official seal.
chan-ce-la-ri'-a *f.* chancellery.
chan-ce-ler' *m.* chancellor.
chan'-tre *m.* chanter.
chan-tri'-a *f.* chantry.
chão' *m.* earth, soil; floor; plane surface; *adj.* smooth, plane; tranquil; open.
cha'-pa *f.* metal sheet; plate; slate of candidates.
cha-pa'-da *f.* plateau.
cha-pa-dão' *m.* large plateau.
cha-pe-la-ri'-a *f.* milliner's shop.
cha-pe-lei'-ro *m.* milliner.
cha-péu *m.* hat; — **de sol** parasol; — **de chuva** umbrella.
cha-pi-nhar' *intr.v.* to splash.
cha-po-dar' *tr.v.* to prune.
cha-ra'-da *f.* charade.
cha-ra-me'-la *f.* ancient primitive flute or fife.
char'-co *m.* stagnant water; muddy swamp.
char-la-tão' *m.* charlatan.
char-ne'-ca *f.* arid, virgin land, supporting only bushy growth.
char-nei'-ra *f.* hinge, joint; knee-cap.
char'-pa *f.* wide belt; broad bandage; sling for arm.
char'-la *f.* chatter, random talk.
char-lar' *intr.v.* to chat.
char'-que *m.* beef, salted and sun-dried.
char-que-ar' *tr.v., intr.v.* to prepare salted and sun-dried beef.
char-ru'-a *f.* large turn plow, with one wing.
char-ru-a'-da *f.* plowed ground.
char-ru-ar' *tr.v.* to plow.
cha-ru-ta-ri'-a *f.* cigar shop.
cha-ru-tei'-ra *f.* pocket cigar case.
cha-ru'-to *m.* cigar.
cha'-ta *f.* flat-bottom canoe.
cha-te'-za *f.* flatness.

cha-tim' *m.* dishonest business man.
cha-ti-nar' *intr.v.* to do business in unscrupulous manner.
cha'-to, =a *adj.* flat, plane, without elevation.
cha-vão' *m.* very large key; cake mold, model, standard.
cha'-ve *f.* key.
cha-vei'-ro *m.* turnkey.
cha-ve'-lha *f.* plow beam.
cha-ve'-lho *m.* horn; tentacle.
chá-ve-na *f.* tea cup.
cha-vê-ta *f.* axle pin.
cha-ve-tar' *tr.v.* to push axle pin in.
che'-fe *m.* chief; head.
che-fi'-a *f.* leadership.
che-fi-ar' *tr.v.* to lead, to head, to be at the head of.
che-ga'-da *f.* arrival.
che-ga-dei'-ra *f.* tongs.
che-ga'-do, =a *adj.* neighboring, contiguous.
che-ga-dor' *m.* furnace-man; tax collector, rent-collector.
che-ga-men'-to *m.* arrival.
che-gar' *intr.v.* to arrive; to reach certain point or position; to approach; to be sufficient.
chei'-a *f.* flood, inundation.
chei'-o, =a *adj.* full, complete, compact; continuous; content; ample.
chei-ra-dei'-ra *f.* snuff-box.
chei-rar' *tr.v.* to smell; to sniff (snuff, camphor, etc.); to follow or search for by smell; *intr.v.* to give off odor.
chei'-ro *m.* odor; perfume; *pl.* green seasoning (parsley, thyme).
chei-ro'-so, =a *adj.* fragrant.
che'que *m.* check; cheque.
che'-que=cru-za'-do *m.* certified check.
che-vi-o'-te *m.* cheviot (fabric).
chi-a-dei'-ra *f.* shrill, screeching noise; dunning.
chi-ar' *intr.v.* to squeak.
chi-ban'-te *adj.* boastful, proud.
chi-ba'-ta *f.* wicker; slender cane.
chi-ca'-ne *f.* chicanery.
chi-ca-ra *f.* tea cup (larger than chávena).
chi-ca-ra'-da *f.* cupful.
chi'-cha *f.* meat, flesh.
chi-có-ria *f.* chicory.
chi-co-ta'-da *f.* lashing, stroke with a lash.
chi-co-tar' *tr.v.* to lash.
chi-co'-te *m.* leather lash.
chi'-fra *f.* leather scraper.
chi-frar' *tr.v.* to smooth and soften leather with scraper.
chi'-fre *m.* horn, antler.
chi-le'-nas *f.pl.* very large spurs.
chi-li'-que *m.* fainting, unconsciousness; nervous faint.
chil-rão' *m.* shrimp net.
chil'-ro, =a *adj.* insipid, tasteless (of water); insignificant, worthless.
chi-mar-rão' *m.* cattle turned wild from living in woods; unsweetened cambric tea; thin gruel.
chim-bu'-te *m.* short, stout person.
chim-pan-zé *m.* chimpanzee.
chin-chi'-la *f.* chinchilla.
chi-ne'-la *f.* slipper, mule without heel.
chi-ne'-lo *m.* old shoe (with turned-over heel).
chi'-no, =a *adj.* Chinese.
chi-nó *m.* false hair, wig.
chi'-o *m.* screach, creaking noise; squeaky cry.
chi'-que *adj.* chic, smart, fashionable.

chi-quei'-ro *m.* pig pen; extremely untidy home; small pen for any special purpose on farm.
chis'-pa *f.* spark; lightning.
chis-par' *intr.v.* to throw off sparks.
chi'-ta *f.* cheap cotton print fabric.
chi-tão' *m.* cretonne.
cho-ca-dei'-ra *f.* incubator.
cho-ca-lha'-da *f.* ringing of cow-bell.
cho-ca-lhei'-ro, =a *adj.* prattling, gossiping, tell-tale.
cho-ca'-lho *m.* cow-bell.
cho-car' *tr.v.* to hatch, to brood; to breed; *intr.v.* to grow rotten, to ferment; —=se *refl.v.* to become broody (of a hen).
cho-chi'-nha *m.* small, weak individual.
cho'-cho, =a *adj.* dry; empty; brainless; silly; futile; worthless.
chô-co, =a *adj.* hatching, incubating.
chô-co *m.* brooding, hatching; embryo; small cuttlefish.
cho-co-la'-te *m.* chocolate.
cho-co-la-tei'ra *f.* chocolate pot.
cho-fer' *m.* chauffeur; motorist.
cho'-pe *m.* beer on tap.
cho'-que *m.* impact; collision; encounter.
cho-quei'-ro *m.* hen's nest.
cho-ra-dei'-ra *f.* hired mourner; complaint.
cho-ra'-do, =a *adj.* sung or played in a mournful manner.
cho-rar' *tr.v.* to deplore; to weep for; to feel the loss of; to repent of; *intr.v.* to weep; to shed tears.
chô-ro *m.* weeping; complaint, lament.
cho-ro'-so, =a *adj.* weepy, complaining, lamenting.
chou-pa'-na *f.* humble cottage, thatched or covered with palm leaves.
chou'-po *m.* poplar tree.
chou-ri-ça'-da *f.* large portion of smoked sausage.
chou-ri'-ço *m.* smoked sausage.
cho-ver' *intr.v.* to rain; to come in abundance.
cho-ve-di'-ço, =a *adj.* rainy; indicating rain.
cho-vi'-do, =a *adj.* watered by rain.
chu'-cha *f.* food; pacifier (for infants).
chu-cha'-do, =a *adj.* emaciated, lean.
chu-char' *tr.v.* to suck; to nurse.
chu-chú *m.* vegetable similar to vegetable marrow.
chu-cru'-te *m.* sauer kraut.
chu-lé *m.* unpleasant odor of unclean feet.
chu-le-ar' *tr.v.* to whip (sew).
chu-lei'-o *m.* whip stitch.
chu-ma-cei'-ra *f.* bushing, bearing.
chu-ma-ce'-te *m.* small cushion.
chu-ma'-ço *m.* padding (cotton batting, feathers, or other soft material) for garments.
chum-ba'-da *f.* wound made by small shot.
chum-ba'-do, =a *adj.* soldered; filled (of cavity in tooth).
chum-bar' *tr.v.* to solder, to plug (with lead); to fill, to seal (with lead).
chum-bei'-ro *m.* shot bag.
chum'-bo *m.* lead; shot; sinker, weight (on fishing net); (fig.) good judgment.
chu'-pa *f.* orange prepared for sucking.
chu-pa'-do, =a *adj.* lean, emaciated.
chu-pa-dou'-ro *m.* hole through which juice is sucked.
chu-par' *tr.v.* to suck, to absorb; (fig.) to spend, to consume.

chu-pe'-ta *f.* rubber nipple, pacifier.

chur-ras'-co *m.* steak grilled on live coals.

chus' *adv.* more; **não dizer — nem bus**, neither to admit nor deny.

chu-tar' *tr.v.*, *intr.v.* to kick the ball (in football).

chu'-te *m.* kick-off.

chu-tei'-ra *f.* football shoe.

chu-vis-car' *intr.v.* to rain lightly; to drizzle.

chu'-va *f.* rain.

chu-va'-da *f.* heavy rainfall.

chu-vei'-ro *m.* shower-bath; quick shower.

chu-vi'-nha *f.* light, misty rain.

chu-vo'-so, *a adj.* rainy.

ci-ar' *tr.v.* to watch over; *intr.v.* to be jealous; to row backward.

ci-á-ti-ca *f.* sciatica.

ci-bó-rio *m.* ciborium.

ci'-ca *f.* stringent taste of green fruit.

ci-ca-triz' *f.* scar.

ci-ca-tri-zar' *tr.v.* to scar.

ci-ce-ro'-ne *m.* cicerone.

ci-ci-ar' *intr.v.* to lisp; to whisper.

cí-cli-co, *a adj.* cyclic.

ci'-clo *m.* cycle.

ci-clis'-ta *m.*, *f.* cyclist.

ci-clo'-ne *m.* cyclone.

ci-da-dão' *m.*, ci-da-dã' *f.* citizen.

ci-da'-de *f.* city.

ci-da-de'-la *f.* citadel.

ci'-dra *f.* cider.

ci-drei'a *f.* citron.

ci-ên-cia *f.* science; knowledge.

ci-en'-te *adj.* knowing, learned; informed.

ci-en-tí-fi-co, *a adj.* scientific.

ci-en-tis'-ta *m.* scientist.

ci-en-ti-fi-car' *tr.v.* to notify; **—se** *refl.v.* to inform oneself of; to acknowledge.

ci'-fra *f.* cipher, zero; key, explanation.

ci-fra'-do, *a adj.* written in secret characters.

ci-frão' *m.* sign "$", which in writing milreis separates thousand column from hundred.

ci-ga'-no *m.* gypsy.

ci-gar'-ro *m.* cigaret.

ci'-lha *f.* saddle-girth.

ci-lí-cio *m.* cilice; sack-cloth.

ci-lín-dri-co, *a adj.* cylindrical.

ci-lin'-dro *m.* cylinder.

ci'-lio *m.* cilium; eyelash.

ci'-ma *f.* top, highest part.

ci-má-cio *m.* cornice, moulding.

cím-ba-lo *m.* cymbal.

ci-men-tar' *tr.v.* to cement together; to consolidate; to provide foundation.

ci-men'-to *m.* cement; **— armado** reenforced concrete.

ci-mi-tar'-ra *f.* scimitar.

ci'-mo *m.* summit.

ci-na'-bre *m.* cinnabar.

ci-na-bri'-no, *a adj.* cinnabar-colored; prepared with cinnabar.

ci-na'-ra *f.* artichoke.

cin'-cha *f.* saddle-girth.

cin-cho'-na *f.* cinchona.

cin-cho-ni'-na *f.* cinchonidine.

cin'-co *m.* five.

ci-ne'-ma *m.* cinema.

ci-ne-má-ti-ca *f.* kinetics.

ci-ne-ra-ção' *f.* incineration.

ci-ne-ral' *m.* ash heap.

ci-ne-rar' *tr.v.* to incinerate.

ci-ne-rá-ria *f.* cineraria.

ci-ne-rá-rio, *a adj.* containing ashes.

cin-gel' *m.* yoke of oxen.

cin-ge-lei'-ro *m.* owner or driver of yoke of oxen.

cin-gir' *tr.v.* to encircle; to gird; to connect by means of belt.

cín-gu-lo *m.* priest's girdle.

cí-ni-co, *a adj.* cynical.

ci-nis'-mo *m.* cynicism.

cin-quen'-ta *m.* fifty.

cin-quen-tão' *m.* man in the fifties.

cin-quen-te-ná-rio *m.* fiftieth anniversary.

cin-quen-to'-na *f.* woman in the fifties.

cin'-ta *f.* belt; band.

cin-tei'-ro *m.* waistband; hat-band.

cin-tel' *m.* large compass; circular path made by animal hitched to cane-mill grinder.

cin-ti-la-ção' *f.* scintillation.

cin-ti-lar' *intr.v.* to scintillate.

cin'-to *m.* sash; girdle; sword-belt.

cin-tu'-ra *f.* waist; belt.

cin-tu-rão' *m.* belt; sword-belt.

cin'-za *f.* ash; cinder.

cin-zei'-ro *m.* ash-tray; ash-box.

cin-zel' *m.* sculptor's chisel.

cin-zen'-to, *a adj.* gray, ash-colored.

ci-o'-so, *a adj.* jealous.

ci'-po *m.* tombstone; branch of family tree.

ci-pres'-te *m.* cypress; (fig.) death, mourning.

cir'-co *m.* circus.

cir-cui'-to *m.* circuit.

cir-cu-lar' *tr.v.*, *intr.v.* to circulate; *f.* circular letter, circular.

cir-cu-la-tó-rio, *a adj.* circulatory.

cír-cu-lo *m.* circle.

cir-cu-na-ve-gar' *tr.v.* to circumnavigate.

cir-cun-ci-são' *f.* circumcision.

cir-cun-fe-rên-cia *f.* circumference.

cir-cun-fle-xão' *f.* circumflexion.

cir-cun-scre-ver' *tr.v.* to circumscribe.

cir-cun-spe'-to, *a adj.* circumspect.

cir-cun-stân-cia *f.* circumstance.

cir-cun-vi-zi-nhan'-ça *f.* suburb; neighboring area.

ci-rur-gi'-a *f.* surgery.

ci-rur-gi-ão' *m.* surgeon.

ci-rúr-gi-co, *a adj.* surgical.

ci'-sa *f.* excise tax; fraudulent deduction.

ci-sa'-lhas *f.pl.* small metal fragments; chips.

ci-são' *f.* divergence; schism.

cis-ca-dor' *m.* rake.

cis-car' *tr.v.* to rake up, to gather.

cis'-co *m.* trash, rubbish.

ci-sei'-ro *m.* excise tax collector.

cis'-ma *m.* schism; divergence in opinion.

cis-mar' *intr.v.* to be preoccupied, to be absorbed in thought.

cis-má-ti-co, *a adj.* meditative, apprehensive; schismatical.

cis'-ne *m.* swan.

cis-ter'-na *f.* cistern.

cís-ti-co, *a adj.* cystic.

cis-tí'-te *f.* inflammation of bladder.

ci'-ta *f.* reference.

ci-ta-ção' *f.* citation, quotation.

ci-tar' *tr.v.* to cite; to summon.

ci-tá-vel *adj.* quoteworthy, quotable.

ci-tra'-to *m.* citrate.

cí-tre-o, *a adj.* citreous.

cí-tri-co, *a adj.* citric.

ci-tri'-no, *a adj.* lemon-colored.

ci-tro-ne'-la *f.* citronella.

ci-ú-me *m.* jealousy.

ciu-men'to, =a *adj.* jealous.
cí-vel *adj.* civil (law); *m.* jurisdiction of civil court.
cí-vi-co, =a *adj.* civic.
ci-vil' *adj.* courteous, polite, civil.
ci-vi-li-da'-de *f.* civility, courtesy.
ci-vi-li-za-ção' *f.* civilization.
ci-vi-li-za-dor', =a *adj.* civilizing.
ci-vi-li-zar' *tr.v.* to civilize.
ci-vis'-mo *m.* patriotism, good citizenship.
cla-mar' *intr.v.* to shout out; to complain loudly; *tr.v.* to request in loud voice.
cla-mor' *m.* clamor, outcry.
cla-mo-ro'-so, =a *adj.* clamorous.
clan-des-ti'-no, =a *adj.* clandestine.
clan-gor' *m.* clangor, sound of trumpet.
cla'que *f.* claque.
cla'-ra *f.* white of egg; opening.
cla-ra-bói-a *f.* skylight.
cla-rão' *m.* bright light, flash.
cla-re-ar' *intr.v.* to become lighter; to become rare; *tr.v.* to make clear, to explain.
cla-re'-za *f.* clearness, transparency.
cla-ri-da'-de *f.* clarity, brightness.
cla-ri-fi-car' *tr.v.* to clarify; —=se *refl.v.* to repent.
cla-rim' *m.* bugle, clarion.
cla-ri-ne'-ta *f.* clarinet.
cla'-ro, =a *adj.* clear, shining, bright; transparent; of bright color; easily understood; obvious; *m.* blank space.
clas'-se *f.* class; class-room.
clas-si-cis'-mo *m.* classicism.
clás-si-co, =a *adj.* classic, classical.
clas-si-fi-ca-ção' *f.* classification.
clas-si-fi-car' *tr.v.* to classify.
claus-tral' *adj.* claustral.
claus'-tro *m.* cloister.
cláu-su-la *f.* clause.
clau-su'-ra *f.* enclosure; seclusion.
cla'-ve *f.* clef (music).
cla-vi-cór-dio *m.* clavichord.
cla-ví-cu-la *f.* clavicle, collar-bone.
cla-ví-ja *f.* peg; tug pin.
cle-mên-cia *f.* clemency.
cle-men'-te *adj.* indulgent, kindly.
clep-to-ma-ní'-a *f.* cleptomania.
cle-ri-cal' *adj.* clerical.
clé-ri-go *m.* clergyman, priest.
cle'-ro *m.* clergy.
cli-chê *m.* cliché; negative photographic plate.
cli-en'-te *m.* ,*f.* client; customer.
clien-te'-la *f.* clientele.
cli'-ma *m.* climate; environment.
cli-má-ti-co, =a *adj.* climatic.
cli-ma-to-lo-gí'-a *f.* climatology.
cli-max' *m.* climax.
cli'-na *f.* hair of mane and tail of horse.
clí-ni-ca *f.* clinic; practice.
cli-ni-car' *intr.v.* to practice medicine.
clí-ni-co *m.* physician, doctor.
clis-ter' *m.* enema.
cli-var' *tr.v.* to split according to grain or strata.
clo-ral' *m.* chloral.
clo'-ro *m.* chlorine.
clo-ro-fi'-la *f.* chlorophyll.
clo-ro-fór-mio *m.* chloroform.
clo-ro'-se *f.* chlorosis.
clo-ró-ti-co, =a *adj.* pertaining to chlorosis.
clu'-be *m.* club.
clu-bis'-ta *m.* club member.
co-a'-da *f.* filter.
co-ad-ju-tor' *m.* coadjutor.
co-a-dor' *m.* strainer, colander.

co-a-du'-ra *f.* straining.
co-a-gir' *tr.v.* to force, to constrain.
co-a-gu-la-ção' *f.* coagulation.
co-a-gu-lan'-te *adj.* coagulating.
coa-gu-lar' *tr.v.*, *intr.v.* to coagulate.
co-a-les-cên-cia *f.* coalescence.
co-a-lha'-da *f.* clabber.
co-a-lhar' *tr.v.*, *intr.v.* to curdle, to coagulate.
co-a-lhei'-ra *f.* rennet; abomasum (fourth stomach of a ruminant).
co-a-li-são' *f.* coalition.
co-a-ti'-vo, =a *adj.* coactive.
co-a-tor' *m.* collaborator.
co-bal'-to *m.* cobalt.
co-bar'-de *m.* *adj.* coward; cowardly.
co-bar-di'-a *f.* cowardice.
co-ber'-ta *f.* covering; bed-spread; couvert; lid; shelter; protection.
co-ber'-to, =a *adj.* covered.
co-ber-tor' *m.* coverlet, blanket, counterpane.
co-bi'-ça *f.* covetousness, greed.
co-bi-çar' *tr.v.* to covet; to have strong desire for.
co'-bra *f.* snake.
co-bra-dor' *m.* collector.
co-bran'-ça *f.* collecting, receiving.
co-brar' *tr.v.* to receive payment of debt; to cash, to collect.
co'-bre *m.* copper; (fig.) copper coin.
co-brir' *tr.v.* to cover; to hide; to put away; to protect; to lessen or lower sound.
co-ca'-da *f.* coconut candy.
co-ça'-do, =a *adj.* frayed, worn.
co-çar' *tr.v.* to scratch; to beat.
co-ca-í-na *f.* cocaine.
có-ce-gas *f.pl.* tickling.
co-cei'-ra *f.* strong itching.
cô-che *m.* coach.
co-chei'-ra *f.* coach-house.
co-chei'-ro *m.* coachman.
co-chi-char' *intr.v.* to whisper.
co-chi-lar' *intr.v.* to nod; to be half asleep.
cô-cho *m.* hod (for brick or mortar).
co-cho-ni'-lha *f.* cochineal.
có-cle-a *f.* cochlea.
cô-co *m.* coco-nut; water dipper.
co-có *m.* coiffure.
co'-da *f.* coda.
co-de-í-na *f.* codeine.
có-di-ce *m.* codex.
co-di-ci'-lo *m.* codicil.
co-di-fi-car' *tr.v.* to codify.
có-di-go *m.* code.
co-ed-u-ca-ção' *f.* co-education.
co-e-fi-ci-en'-te *m.* coefficient.
co-e'-lho *m.* rabbit.
co-en'-tro *m.* coriander.
co-er-ção' *f.* coercion.
co-er-ci'-vo, =a *adj.* coercive.
co-e-rên-cia *f.* coherence.
co-e-ren'-te *adj.* coherent.
co-e-rir' *intr.v.* to cohere.
co-e-são' *f.* cohesion.
co-e-si'-vo, =a *adj.* cohesive.
co-e-tâ-ne-o, =a *adj.* contemporary.
co-e-xis-ten'-te *adj.* co-existent.
co'-fre *m.* coffer.
co-gi-tar' *tr.v.*, *intr.v.* to cogitate.
cog-na'-to, =a *adj.* cognate.
cog-ni-ção' *f.* cognition.
cog-no'-me *m.* cognomen.
co-gu-me'-lo *m.* mushroom.
co-i-bir' *tr.v.* to curb, to repress.
coi'-ce *m.* kick; butt-end of gun; kick of gun; (fig.) brutality, ingratitude.

coi′-ma f. penalty, fine.
coi-má-vel adj. subject to penalty.
co-in-ci-dên-cia f. coincidence.
co-in-ci-den′-te adj. coincidental.
co-in-ci-dir intr.v. to coincide.
coi-o′-te m. coyote.
coi′-ra f. leather jerkin.
co-ir-mão′ m. first cousins who are sons of brothers.
coi′-sa f. thing.
coi-ta′-do, ₌a adj. poor, miserable; (interjection of commiseration).
coi-va′-ra f. brush not destroyed in first burning of new ground, piled to be burned.
co′-la f. glue, mucilage; material used dishonestly as an aid in an examination.
co-la-bo-ra-ção′ f. collaboration.
co-la-bo-rar′ intr.v. to collaborate.
co-la-ção′ f. collation.
co-la-cio-nar′ tr.v. to compare, to confront.
co-lap′-so m. collapse.
co-lar′ tr.v. to paste, to glue, to stick, to clarify (wines); to confer an ecclesiastic benefice on; to confer a degree on.
co-lar′ m. necklace.
co-la-ri′-nho m. collar.
co-la-te-ral′ adj. parallel; collateral.
col′-cha f. bed-spread.
col-chão′ m. mattress.
col-che′-ta f. eye.
col-che′-te m. hook (of hook-and-eye); dress fastenings.
co-le-a′-do, ₌a adj. flexible, sinuous.
co-le-ar′ intr.v. to shake one's head; to move from side to side.
co-le-ção′ f. collection.
co-le-ci-o-nar′ tr.v. to collect.
co-le′-ga m., f. colleague.
co-lé-gio m. private elementary or secondary school; college (electoral, of cardinals).
co-le-gial′ m. student, pupil.
có-le-ra f. cholera; ire, anger.
co-lé-ri-co, ₌a adj. choleric; suffering from cholera.
co-le′-ta f. collection (in church or for charity), collect (prayer); tax.
co-le-tar′ tr.v. to take up contribution; to designate quota.
co-le-tâ-ne-a f. collectanea; collection.
co-lê-te m. vest; corset.
co-le-ti-vi-da′-de f. collectivity.
co-le-ti-vis′-mo m. collectivism.
co-le-ti′-vo, ₌a adj. collective.
co-le-tor′ m. collector.
co-le-to-ri′-a f. tax office.
co-lhei′-ta f. harvest, crop.
co-lhei-tei′-ro m. harvester.
co-lhêr tr.v. to pick or cut flowers; to gather fruit; to acquire; to achieve; to receive.
co-lher f. spoon; — de chá teaspoon; — de sopa soup spoon.
co-lhe-ra′-da f. spoonful.
co-lhi-men′-to m. plucking; gathering.
có-li-ca f. colic; pl. difficulties.
có-li-co, ₌a adj. colonic.
co-li-dir′ tr.v., intr.v. to collide.
co-li-ga-ção′ f. union, confederation.
co-li-gar′ tr.v. to tie, to bind; to plot.
co-li-gir′ tr.v. to collect, to gather; to conclude.
co-li′-na f. knoll; small hill.
co-li-são′ f. collision.
co-li-seu′ m. colosseum.
co-li′-te f. colitis.
col-mar′ tr.v. to cover with thatch.

côl-mo m. straw of grain plants; thatch.
col-me-ei′-ro m. bee-keeper.
col-mei′-a f. bee-hive; swarm of bees.
co′-lo m. neck; lap.
co-lo-ca-ção′ f. placement, use, position, employment.
co-lo-car′ tr.v. to place; to employ, to use.
co-ló-dio m. collodion.
có-lon m. colon.
co-lô-nia f. colony.
co-lo-ni-al′ adj. colonial.
co-lo-ni-zar′ tr.v. to colonize.
co-lo′-no m. colonist.
co-lo-qui-al′ adj. colloquial.
co-ló-quio m. colloquy.
co-los-sal′ adj. colossal.
co-los′-so m. colossus.
col-tar′ m. coal tar.
co-lum-bi′-no, ₌a adj. columbine.
co-lu′-na f. column.
co-lu-nar′ adj. columnar.
co-lo-ra-ção′ f. coloring, coloration.
co-lo-ran′-te adj. coloring.
co-lo-rar′ tr.v. to color, to disguise, to misrepresent; —se refl.v. to blush.
co-lo-ri′-do, ₌a adj. colorful; **co-lo-ri′-do** m. color.
co-lo-rí-me-tro m. colorimeter.
co-lo-rir′ tr.v. to color, to paint brilliant, to describe brilliantly, to disguise.
co-lo-ris′-ta m. colorist.
co-lo-ri-za-ção′ f. coloring, change of color.
co′-ma f. coma; comma; half tone (music).
co-ma-to′-so, ₌a adj. comatose.
co-ma′-dre f. god-mother.
co-man-dan′-te m. commandant.
co-man-dar′ tr.v. to command.
co-man-di-tá-rio m. silent partner.
co-man′-do m. command, control.
co-mar′-ca f. district, boundary, judicial division of a state.
com-ba′-te m. combat, battle.
com-ba-ten′-te m., adj. combatant.
com-ba-ter′ tr.v. to fight; to combat.
com-ba-ti′-vo, ₌a adj. combative.
com-bi-na-ção′ f. combination, agreement.
com-bi-nar′ tr.v. to combine; to make a plan; to agree.
com-bói-o m. convoy; train of railway cars; caravan of cargo animals.
com-bu-rir′ intr.v. to burn.
com-bus-tão′ f. combustion.
com-bus-tí-vel m. fuel; adj. combustible.
co-me-çar′ tr.v., intr.v. to have beginning; to begin; to initiate.
co-mê-ço m. beginning, origin.
co-mé-dia f. comedy.
co-me-dian′-te m.f. actor, actress.
co-me-di′-do, ₌a adj. moderate, prudent, measured.
co-me-do-ri′-as f.pl. board, maintenance; ration.
co-me-dou′-ro m. feed trough.
co-me-mo-rar′ tr.v. to commemorate.
co-me-mo-ra-ti′-vo, ₌a adj. commemorative.
co-men-su-rar′ tr.v. to measure together, to proportion.
co-men-su-rá-vel adj. commensurable.
co-men-ta-dor′ m. commentator.
co-men-tar′ tr.v. to comment.
co-men-tá-rio m. commentary.
co-mer′ tr.v., intr.v. to eat; (fig.) to dissipate, to consume; to gnaw.
co-mer-cial′ adj. commercial.

co-mer-cian'-te *m., f.,* adj. merchant, business man, trader.
co-mer-ci-ar' *intr.v.* to do business, to engage in commerce.
co-mér-cio *m.* commerce.
co-mes-tí-vel adj. comestible; *m.* food.
co-me'-ta *m.* comet.
co-me-ter' *tr.v.* to commit.
co-me-ti'-da *f.* attack.
co-me-ti-men'-to *m.* daring enterprise.
co-mi-chão' *f.* itching; strong desire.
co-mí-cio *m.* comitia; conference, meeting.
cô-mi-co *m.* comedian; cô-mi-co, ₌a adj. comic.
co-mí'-da *f.* food; what is eaten.
co-mi'-go *pro.* with me.
co-mi-se-ra-ção' *f.* commiseration.
co-mis-são' *f.* commission.
co-mis-sa-ri-a'-do *m.* commissariat.
co-mis-sá-rio *m.* commissary.
co-mis-sio-nar' *tr.v.* to commission.
co-mi-tê *m.* committee.
co-mi-ti'-va *f.* retinue, accompanying group.
co'-mo *conj.* as, like, when; *adv.* how, in what manner.
co-mo-ção' *f.* commotion.
cô-mo-da *f.* chest of drawers.
co-mo-di-da'-de *f.* comfort, well-being, convenience.
co-mo-dis'-mo *m.* selfishness.
cô-mo-do, ₌a adj. comfortable, suitable.
co-mo-do'-ro *m.* commodore.
co-mo-ven'-te adj. moving, stirring, exciting.
co-mo-ver' *tr.v.* to affect with emotion; to move.
com-pac'-to, ₌a adj. compact.
com-pa-de-cer' *tr.v.* to pity, to sympathize with.
com-pa-de-ci-men'-to *m.* compassion.
com-pa'-dre *m.* god-father.
com-pai-xão' *f.* compassion.
com-pa-nhei'-ro, ₌a *m., f.* companion.
com-pa-nhi'-a *f.* company.
com-pa-ra-ção' *f.* comparison.
com-pa-rar' *tr.v.* to compare.
com-pa-ra-ti'-vo, ₌a adj. comparative.
com-pa-rá-vel adj. comparable.
com-pa-re-cer' *intr.v.* to appear personally, to appear by proxy (law).
com-par-ti-lhar' *tr.v.* to participate in, to share in.
com-par-ti-men'-to *m.* compartment.
com-pas-sa'-do, ₌a adj. measured, slow, in rhythm.
com-pas-sar' *tr.v.* to measure with a compass; to slow up.
com-pas'-so *m.* compass.
com-pa-ti-bi-li-da'-de *f.* compatibility.
com-pa-tí-vel adj. compatible.
com-pe-lir' *tr.v.* to compel, to oblige, to force.
com-pên-dio *m.* textbook.
com-pen-sa-ção' *f.* compensation.
com-pen-sa-dor', ₌a adj. compensating.
com-pen-sar' *tr.v.* to compensate.
com-pe-tên-cia *f.* competence.
com-pe-ten'-te adj. competent.
com-pe-ti-ção' *f.* competition.
com-pe-ti-dor' *m.* competitor.
com-pe-tir' *intr.v.* to compete.
com-pla-cên-cia *f.* complacency.
com-pla-cen'-te adj. complacent.
com-ple-men'-to *m.* complement.
com-ple-tar' *tr.v.* to complete.
com-ple'-to, ₌a adj. complete.
com-ple-xi-da'-de *f.* complexity.

com-ple'-xo, ₌a adj. complex; com-ple'-xo *m.* complex.
com-pli-ca-ção' *f.* complication.
com-pli-car' *tr.v.* to complicate.
com-po-nen'-te adj. component.
com-por' *tr.v.* to compose.
com-por-ta-men'-to *m.* deportment, behavior.
com-por-tar' *tr.v.* to bear, to allow of, to involve; *intr.v.* to behave.
com-por-tá-vel adj. bearable, endurable.
com-po-si-ção' *f.* composition.
com-po-si-tor' *m.* composer.
com-pos'-to *m.* compound.
com-pos-tu'-ra *f.* structure, modesty, composure; counter-point; *pl.* cosmetics.
com-po-ta *f.* compote; stewed fruit, preserves.
com-po-tel'-ra *f.* compote dish.
com'-pra *f.* purchase.
com-prar' *tr.v.* to buy, to purchase.
com-pre-en-der' *tr.v.* to undertsand, to comprehend, to contain, to include, to cover.
com-pre-en-são' *f.* comprehension, understanding.
com-pres'-sa *f.* compress.
com-pres-são' *f.* compression.
com-pres-sí-vel adj. compressible.
com-pres-sor' *m.* compressor.
com-pri-dez' *f.* length.
com-pri'-do, ₌a adj. long.
com-pri-men'-to *m.* length.
com-pri-mi'-do *m.* tablet, pill.
com-pri-mir' *tr.v.* to compress; to reduce in volume.
com-pro-me-ter' *tr.v.* to compromise;
—₌se *refl.v.* to assume responsibility for.
com-pro-mis'-so *m.* compromise; obligation; agreement between bankrupt person and creditors.
com-pul-são' *f.* compulsion.
com-pul-só-ria *f.* forced retirement.
com-pul-só-rio, ₌a adj. compulsory.
com-pun-ção' *f.* compunction.
com-pu-ta-ção' *f.* computation, calculation.
com-pu-tar' *tr.v.* to compute.
com-pu-tá-vel adj. computable.
com-pu-tis'-ta *m.* calculator.
côm-pu-to *m.* reckoning; calculation for the purpose of keeping the calendar regular.
co-mu'-a *f.* toilet, latrine.
co-mum' adj. common; *m.* people, community.
co-mu-nal' adj. communal.
co-mun-gan'-te *m.* communicant.
co-mun-gar' *tr.v.* to administer communion to; *intr.v.* to take communion.
co-mu-nhão' *f.* communion.
co-mu-ni-ca-ti'-vo, ₌a adj. communicative.
co-mu-ni-cá-vel adj. communicable.
co-mu-ni-ca-ção' *f.* communication.
co-mu-ni-car' *tr.v., intr.v.* to communicate.
co-mu-ni-da'-de *f.* community.
co-mu-nis'-mo *m.* communism.
con'-ca *f.* ear lobe; water dipper.
côn-ca-vo, ₌a adj. concave.
con-ce-ber' *tr.v., intr.v.* to conceive; to understand.
con-ce-bi-men'-to *m.* act or effect of conceiving.
con-ce-der' *tr.v., intr.v.* to concede, to yield.

con-cei-ção' f. immaculate conception.
con-cei'-to m. concept.
con-cei-tu-a'-do, =a adj. highly regarded, esteemed.
con-ce'-lho m. administrative division or district; municipality.
con-cen-tra-ção' f. concentration.
con-cen-trar' tr.v. to concentrate, to absorb.
con-cên-tri-co, =a adj. concentric.
con-cep-ção' f. conception.
con-cer-nen'-te adj. concerning, respecting, pertaining to.
con-cer-tar' tr.v. to compare, to agree, to reconcile; intr.v. to be in harmony.
con-cer-ti'-na f. concertina.
con-cer-tis'-ta m. f. soloist; player, singer.
con-cêr-to m. concert.
con-ces-são' f. concession.
con-ces-sio-ná-rio m. concessionary, concessionaire.
con'-cha f. conch, shell.
con-ci-da-dão' m. fellow townsman, fellow citizen.
con-ci-ên-cia f. conscience; consciousness.
con-cien-cio'-so, =a adj. conscientious.
con-cien'-te adj. conscious.
con-ci-li-a-ção' f. conciliation.
con-ci-li-ar' tr.v. to conciliate.
con-ci-liá-rio, =a adj. of a council.
con-ci-lia-tó-rio, =a adj. conciliatory.
con-ci-lio m. council.
côn-cio, =a adj. conscious.
con-ci'-so, =a adj. concise.
con-cla'-ve m. conclave.
con-clu-ir' tr.v. to conclude.
con-clu-são' f. conclusion.
con-coc-ção' f. digestion.
con-co-mi-tan'-te adj. concomitant.
con-cor-dân-cia f. concordance.
con-cor-dar' tr.v. to conciliate; intr.v. to be in agreement.
con-cor-da'-ta f. concordat.
con-cor-rên-cia f. competition, rivalry; concurrence.
con-cor-ren'-te m. f. candidate, contestant; adj. competing.
con-cor-rer' intr.v. to cooperate, to vie, to converge, to exist side by side.
con-cre-ção' f. concretion, solidification.
con-cre-ti-zar' tr.v. to make concrete.
con-cre'-to, =a adj. concrete.
con-cu-bi'-na f. concubine.
con-cu-nha'-do m. double brother-in-law (a relationship of two men whose wives are sisters).
con-cu-pis-cên-cia f. concupiscence.
con-cur'-so m. concourse; competitive examination.
con-cus-são' f. concussion.
con'-de m. count.
con-de-co-ra-ção' f. honorary insignia; badge; bestowal of medal.
con-de-na-ção' f. condemnation.
con-de-nar' tr.v. to condemn.
con-de-ná-vel adj. condemnable.
con-den-sa-ção' f. condensation.
con-den-sa-dor' m. condenser.
con-den-sar' tr.v. to condense.
con-des-cen-den'-te adj. condescending.
con-des-cen-der' intr.v. to condescend.
con-des'-sa f. countess.
con-di-ção' f. condition.
con-di-cio-nal' adj. conditional.
con-di-cio-nar' tr.v. to condition, to make conditional.

con-dig'-no, =a adj. due; merited; proportional to merit.
con-di-men'-to m. spices; seasoning of food.
con-dis-cí-pu-lo m. class-mate.
con-do-í-do, =a adj. sympathetic; compassionate.
con-do-lên-cia f. condolence.
con-do-len'-te adj. sympathizing, consoling.
con-dor' m. condor (ornith.).
con-du-ção' f. conduction; transportation.
con-du-cen'-te adj. conducive, tending.
con-du'-ta f. conduct; escort, guard; exhaust pipe.
con-du-ti-bi-li-da'-de f. conductivity.
con-du-tor' m. conductor; driver; transmission (mech.).
con-du-zir' tr.v. to lead, to drive, to conduct.
co'-ne m. cone.
co-nec-ti'-vo, =a adj. connective.
cô-ne-go, =a m., f. canon, canoness.
co-ne-xão' f. connection.
co-ne'-xo, =a adj. connected.
con-fec-cio-nar' tr.v. to make, to prepare, to execute.
con-fe-de-ra-ção' f. confederation.
con-fei-ta-ri'-a f. confectioner's shop.
con-fei-tei'-ro m. candy manufacturer, candy merchant.
con-fei'-to m. candy, sweets.
con-fe-rên-cia f. conference; public discourse; lecture; consultation (of physicians).
con-fe-rir' to confer, to check, to bestow; intr.v. to be in agreement.
con-fes-sar' tr.v. to confess; —=se refl.v. to go to confession.
con-fes-sio-ná-rio m. confessional.
con-fes-sor' m. confessor.
con-fe'-ti m. confetti.
con-fian'-ça f. confidence.
con-fi-ar' tr.v. to confide; intr.v. to have confidence in.
con-fi-dên-cia f. secret; confidence.
con-fi-den-cial' adj. confidential.
con-fi-den-ciar' tr.v. to tell in secret, to say in confidence.
con-fi-den'-te adj. confident.
con-fi-gu-ra-ção' f. configuration.
con-fim' adj. limiting.
con-fins' m.pl. frontiers.
con-fir-ma-ção' f. confirmation.
con-fir-mar' tr.v. to confirm.
con-fir-ma-ti'-vo, =a adj. confirming.
con-fir-ma-tó-rio, =a adj. confirmatory.
con-fis-ca-ção' f. confiscation.
con-fis-car' tr.v. to confiscate.
con-fis-são' f. confession; Christian sect.
con-fla-gra-ção' f. conflagration.
con-fli'-to m. conflict.
con-flu-ên-cia f. confluence.
con-for-ma-ção' f. conformation; acquiescence.
con-for-mar' tr.v., intr.v. to conform, to harmonize; —=se refl.v. to be resigned to, to accept.
con-for'-me adj. similar, identical; agreed; adv. in conformity; conj. as, according as.
con-for-mi-da'-de f. conformity; resignation.
con-for-ta-dor', =a adj. comforting, consoling.
con-for-tar' tr.v. to comfort, to console, to strengthen.

con-for-tá-vel *adj.* comforting, comfortable.
con-fôr-to *m.* comfort, consolation.
con-fra-ri'-a *f.* brotherhood.
con-fron-tar' *tr.v.* to confront.
con-fron'-te *prep.* in front of.
con-fun-dir' *tr.v.* to confuse.
con-fu-são' *f.* confusion.
con-fu'-so, =a *adj.* confused.
con-ge-lar' *tr.v.* to freeze.
con-ge-mi-na-ção' *f.* twinning; doubling.
con-gê-ne-re *adj.* identical.
con-ge-ni-al' *adj.* congenial.
con-ge-ni-a-li-da'-de *f.* congeniality.
con-gê-ni-to, =a *adj.* congenital.
con-glo-me-ra'-do *m.* conglomerate.
con-gra-tu-lar' *tr.v.* to congratulate;
—=se *refl.v.* to be happy because of happiness of others.
con-grat-u-la-tó-rio, =a *adj.* congratulatory.
con-gre-ga-ção' *f.* congregation.
con-gres-sio-nal' *adj.* congressional.
con-gres-sis'-ta *m.* delegate, member.
con-gres'-so *m.* congress; meeting.
con-gru-en'-te *adj.* congruent.
co-nha'-que *m.* cognac.
co-nhe-ce-dor' *m.* expert, specialist, connoisseur.
co-nhe-cer' *tr.v.* to know, to recognize.
co-nhe-ci-men'-to *m.* knowledge, recognition; receipt; acquaintance; bill of lading.
cô-ni-co, =a *adj.* conic.
co-ní-fe-ras *f.pl.* conifers.
co-ní-fe-ro, =a *adj.* coniferous.
co-ni-ven'-te *adj.* conniving.
con-je-tu'-ra *f.* conjecture.
con-je-tu-ral' *adj.* conjectural.
con-jun-ção' *f.* conjunction.
con-ju-ga-ção' *f.* conjugation.
con-ju-gal' *adj.* conjugal.
con-ju-gar' *tr.v.* to conjugate.
côn-ju-ge *m.* married person, spouse.
con-jun-ti'-va *f.* conjunctiva.
con-jun-ti-vi'-te *f.* conjunctivitis.
con-ju-rar' *tr.v.* to conjure, to exorcise;
intr.v. to conspire.
con-ju'-ro *m.* conjuration, conspiracy.
co-nos'-co *pro.* with us.
co-no-ta-ção' *f.* connotation.
con-quan'-to *conj.* notwithstanding.
con-quis'-ta *f.* conquest.
con-quis-tar' *tr.v.* to conquer; to gain, to acquire.
con-sa-grar' *tr.v.* to consecrate.
con-san-guí-ne-o, =a *adj.* consanguineous.
con-scri-ção' *f.* conscription.
con-se-cu-ti'-vo, =a *adj.* consecutive.
con-se-guin'-te *adj.* consequent; por —
adv. therefore.
con-se-guir' *tr.v.* to get, to obtain, to succeed in.
con-se-lhei'-ro *m.* counsellor, adviser.
con-se'-lho *m.* advice, counsel.
con-sen-ti-men'-to *m.* consent, permission.
con-sen-tir' *tr.v.* to consent, to permit.
con-se-quên-cia *f.* consequence.
con-se-quen'-te *adj.* consequent.
con-ser-tar' *tr.v.* to mend, to repair.
con-sêr-to *m.* mending, repairing.
con-ser'-va *f.* preserves.
con-ser-va-ção' *f.* preservation.
con-ser-var' *tr.v.* to preserve, to keep.
con-ser-va-ti'-vo, =a *adj.* preservative.
con-ser-va-tó-rio *m.* conservatoire.

con-si-de-ra-ção' *f.* consideration.
con-si-de-ran'-do *m.* clause; *conj.* whereas.
con-si-de-rar' *tr.v.* to consider.
con-si-de-rá-vel *adj.* considerable.
con-sig-na-dor' *m.* consignor.
con-sig-nar' *tr.v.* to consign.
con-sig-na-tá-rio *m.* consignee.
con-si'-go *pro.* with you, in your company.
con-sis-tên-cia *f.* consistency.
con-sis-ten'-te *adj.* consistent; solid, firm.
con-sis-tir' *intr.v.* to consist.
con-sis-tó-rio *m.* consistory.
con-so-la-ção' *f.* consolation; comfort.
con-so-la-dor' *m.* pacifier, rubber nipple; con-so-la-dor', =a *adj.* consoling.
con-so-lar' *tr.v.* to console, to comfort.
con-so-lá-vel *adj.* consolable.
con-so-li-dar' *tr.v.* to consolidate, to make secure.
con-sô-lo *m.* consolation.
con-sór-cio *m.* marriage.
con-sor'-te *m.*, *f.* husband, wife, spouse.
cons-pí-cuo, =a *adj.* conspicuous.
cons-pi-ra-ção' *f.* conspiracy.
cons-tân-cia *f.* constancy.
cons-tan'-te *adj.* constant.
cons-tar' *intr.v.* to be known, to be said, to be written, to be evident; to consist.
cons-ta-tar *tr.v.* to establish, to ascertain, to find out, to prove.
cons-te-la-ção' *f.* constellation.
cons-ter-na-ção' *f.* consternation.
cons-ti-pa-ção' *f.* deep cold; constipation.
cons-ti-par'-se *refl.v.* to catch cold.
cons-ti-tu-i-ção' *f.* constitution.
cons-ti-tuin'-te *adj.* constituent.
cons-ti-tuir' *tr.v.* to constitute; to establish.
cons-tran-ger' *tr.v.* to constrain.
cons-tran-gi-men'-to *m.* constraint.
cons-tri-ção' *f.* constriction.
cons-trin-gen'-te *adj.* constringent.
cons-trin-gir' *tr.v.* constrict; to constringe.
cons-tru-ção' *f.* construction.
cons-tru-ir' *tr.v.* to construct.
cons-tru-ti'-vo, =a *adj.* constructive.
côn-sul *m.* consul.
con-su-la'-do *m.* consulate.
con-su-lar' *adj.* consular.
con-sul'-ta *f.* consultation, appointment.
con-sul-tar' *tr.v.* to consult.
con-sul-tó-rio *m.* office (of a doctor).
con-su-mar' *tr.v.* to consummate.
con-su-mi-dor' *m.* consumer.
con-su-mir' *tr.v.* to consume; *intr.v.* to waste away.
con-su'-mo *m.* consumption; octroi, tax on commodities brought into town or city.
con'-ta *f.* account, bill; reckoning; story; bead; fazer — que to suppose; tomar
— to take charge; dar — to finish; to carry to successful end.
con-ta-bi-li-da'-de *f.* accounting, bookkeeping.
con-tac'-to *m.* contact.
con-ta-dor' *m.* accountant; meter (for water, gas, and electricity); story-teller; cabinet.
con-ta-do-ri'-a *f.* accounting department.
con-ta-gi-ar' *tr.v.* to transmit something contagious.
con-tá-gio *m.* contagion.
con-ta-gio'-so, =a *adj.* contagious.

con-ta=go'-tas *m.* medicine dropper.
con-ta-mi-nar' *tr.v.* to contaminate.
con=tan'-to=que *conj.* if; provided that.
con-ta=pas'-sos *m.* pedometer.
con-tar' *tr.v.* to tell, to relate; to count; to intend, to expect; *intr.v.* to rely, to depend.
con-tem-pla-ção' *f.* contemplation.
con-tem-plar' *tr.v.*, *intr.v.* to contemplate.
con-tem-po-râ-ne-o, =a *adj.* contemporaneous.
con-temp-tí-vel *adj.* contemptible.
con-temp'-to *m.* contempt.
con-ten-ção' *f.* contention.
con-ten-cio'-so, =a *adj.* contentious.
con-ten'-da *f.* altercation, quarrel.
con-ten-der' *intr.v.* to contend, to quarrel.
con-ten-ta-men'-to *m.* contentment.
con-ten-tar' *tr.v.* to content.
con-ten'-te *adj.* content, contented.
con-ter' *tr.v.* to contain; —=se *refl.v.* to contain oneself, to repress oneself.
con-tes-tar' *tr.v.*, *intr.v.* to contest.
con-te-ú-do *m.* contents, content.
con-tex'-to *m.* context.
con-ti-gui-da'-de *f.* contiguity.
con-tí-guo, =a *adj.* contiguous.
con-ti-nên-cia *f.* continence; military salute.
con-ti-nen-tal' *adj.* continental.
con-ti-nen-te *m.* continent.
con-tin-gên-cia *f.* contingency.
con-ti-nua-ção' *f.* continuation.
con-ti-nu-ar' *tr.v.*, *intr.v.* to continue.
con-ti-nui-da'-de *f.* continuity.
con-tí-nuo *m.* messenger boy; con-tí-nuo, =a *adj.* continuous.
con-to *m.* one thousand milreis (1:000$-000); tale, fable; narrative.
con-tis'-ta *m.* story-teller, short-story writer.
con-tor-ção' *f.* contortion.
con'-tra *adj.*, *adv.* counter; *pref.* counter; *prep.* in front of, in opposite direction to, in contradiction of, against.
con-tra=a-ta'-que *m.* counter-attack.
con-tra-bai'-xo *m.* male singer having voice lower than regular bass; violoncello.
con-tra-ba-lan-çar' *tr.v.* to counterbalance.
con-tra-ban'-do *m.* contraband.
con-tra-ção' *f.* contraction.
con-tra-di-ção' *f.* contradiction.
con-tra-fa-ção' *f.* counterfeiting.
con-tra-fa-zer' *tr.v.* to counterfeit, to forge.
con-tra-fé *f.* summons.
con-tra-for'-te *m.* reenforcement, buttress.
con-tra-gôs-to *m.* aversion, dislike.
con-tra-ir' *tr.v.* to contract.
con-tral'-to *m.* contralto.
con-tra-luz' *f.* false light, reflected light.
con-tra-man-dar' *tr.v.* to countermand, to cancel.
con-tra-mar-char' *intr.v.* to countermarch.
con-tra=mes'-tre, =a *m.*, *f.* foreman, forewoman.
con-tra-mi-nar' *tr.v.* to countermine.
con-tra=pas'-so *m.* short step (to recover when out of step).
con-tra-pé *m.* partner.
con-tra-pê-so *m.* counter-weight.
con-tra-pon'-to *m.* counterpoint.
con-tra-por' *tr.v.* to confront, to refute.

con-tra-pro-du-cen'-te *adj.* proving the contrary.
con-tra-pro-pa-gan'-da *f.* counter-propaganda.
con-tra=re-vo-lu-ção' *f.* counter-revolution.
con-tra-ri-ar' *tr.v.* to oppose, to put obstacles in the way of.
con-trá-rio, =a *adj.* contrary.
con-tra-sen'-so *m.* absurdity, something contrary to good sense, wrong interpretation.
con-tras-tar' *tr.v.* to contrast.
con-tras'-te *m.* contrast; assay, assaying office, assayer.
con-tra-tem'-po *m.* unexpected difficulty; a — *adv.* inopportunely.
con-tra'-ta *f.* contract, engagement.
con-tra-tar' *intr.v.* to contract, to make a bargain.
con-tra'-to *m.* contract, agreement, covenant.
con-tra-tor-pe-dei'-ro *m.* destroyer.
con-tra-ve-ne'-no *m.* poison antidote.
con-tra-ven'-to *m.* head-wind; window shutter.
con-tra-vir' *tr.v.*, *intr.v.* to transgress, to infringe; to reply.
con-tri-bui-ção' *f.* contribution.
con-tri-buin'-te *m.*, *f.* contributor.
con-tri-bu-ir' *intr.v.* to contribute.
con-tri-ção' *f.* contrition.
con-tri'-to, =a *adj.* contrite.
con-tro-lar' *tr.v.* to control.
con-trô-le *m.* control.
con-tro-vér-sia *f.* controversy.
con-tu'-do *conj.* notwithstanding.
con-tu-má-cia *f.* contumacy.
con-tu-mé-lia *f.* contumely.
con-tu-são' *f.* contusion.
co-nu-bial' *adj.* connubial.
co-nú-bio *m.* matrimony, marriage.
con-va-les-cen'-ça *f.* convalescence.
con-va-les-cer' *intr.v.* to convalesce.
con-ven-ção' *f.* convention.
con-ven-cer' *tr.v.* to convince.
con-ven-cio-nal' *adj.* conventional.
con-ven-cio-nar' *tr.v.* to establish by pact or convention.
con-ve-niên-cia *f.* convenience; propriety.
con-ve-nien'-te *adj.* convenient, proper, suitable, near at hand.
con-vê-nio *m.* international pact, covenant.
con-ven-tual' *m.* person residing in a convent; *adj.* conventual, pertaining to a convent.
con-ven'-to *m.* convent.
con-ver-gên-cia *f.* convergence.
con-ver-gen'-te *adj.* convergent.
con-ver-gir' *intr.v.* to converge.
con-ver'-sa *f.* conversation.
con-ver-sa-dei'-ra *f.* tête-à-tête chair or settee.
con-ver-sa-fi-a'-da *f.* proposal lacking in seriousness.
con-ver-são' *f.* conversion.
con-ver-sar' *intr.v.* to converse; (pop.) to flirt.
con-ver-sí-vel *adj.* convertible.
con-ver'-so *m.* lay-brother; convert.
con-ver-ter' *tr.v.* to convert.
con-vés *m.* deck.
con-ves-co'-te *m.* picnic.
con-ve-xi-da'-de *f.* convexity.
con-ve'-xo, =a *adj.* convex.
con-vic-ção' *f.* conviction.

con-vi-da'-do m. guest.
con-vi-dar' tr.v. to invite.
con-vir' intr.v. to be suitable, to be proper.
con-vi'-te m. invitation.
con-vi'-va m. banqueter.
con-vi-val' adj. convivial; concerning entertainment.
con-vi-vên-cia f. familiarity, close association.
con-vi-ven'-te adj. sociable, affable, intimate.
con-vi-ver' intr.v. to associate with, to frequent society of.
con-ví-vio m. banquet.
con-vo-ca-ção' f. convocation.
con-vo-car' tr.v. to convoke.
con-vo-lu-ção' f. convolution.
con-vul-são' f. convulsion.
con-vul-si'-vo, =a adj. convulsive.
con-vul'-so, =a adj. tremulous, convulsive.
co-o-pe-ra-ção' f. cooperation.
co-o-pe-rar' intr.v. to cooperate.
co-o-pe-ra-ti'-vo, =a adj. cooperative.
co-or-de-na-ção' f. coordination.
co-or-de-nar' tr.v. to coordinate.
co'-pa f. cupboard, pantry; hat crown; leafy branches; spread of tree; china, silver necessary for one place at table.
co-pei'-ra f. china cupboard, china pantry.
co-pei'-ro m. butler.
co-pe'-la f. crucible for refining silver.
co-pe-la-ção' f. silver refining.
co-pe'-que m. kopeck.
có-pia f. copy; abundance.
co-pi-ar' tr.v. to copy.
co-pi-o-si-da'-de f. copiousness.
co-pi-o'-so, =a adj. copious, abundant.
co-pi-rai'-te m. copyright.
co'-po m. tumbler, glass, deep cup or container; handguard on sword.
co'-pra f. dried coconut meat.
co-pra-ol' m. dried coconut extraction.
có-pu-la f. sexual intercourse.
co'-que m. coke.
co-quei-ral' m. coconut palm grove.
co-quei'-ro m. coconut palm.
co-que-lu'-che f. whooping cough.
cor-co'-va f. hump.
cor-co-va'-do, =a adj. hump-backed; hunch-backed.
côr f. color; colorant; blush; flag.
cor' m. heart; de — by heart, by memory.
co'-ra f. bleaching.
co-ra-ção' m. heart; (fig.) sentiment, affection, generosity; center.
co-ra-dou'-ro m. bleaching; bleaching ground.
co-ra'-gem f. courage.
co-ra-jo'-so, =a adj. courageous.
co-ral' m. coral.
co-ra-li'-na f. coralline.
co-rar' tr.v. to color, to tint, to bleach; (fig.) to cloak, to disguise; intr.v. to blush.
cor-cun'-da f. hump, hunch; m. hunchback.
cor'-da f. cord; watch spring; dar — ao relógio to wind watch or clock; — dorsal spinal cord.
cor-da'-me m. cordage.
cor-dão' m. string.
cor-dei'-ro, =a m., f. young lamb.
cor-dial' adj. cordial.
cor-dia-li-da'-de f. cordiality.
cor-do-vão' m. cordovan leather.
co-rei'-a f. chorea.

co-re-op'-sis m. coreopsis.
co-ri-á-ce-o, =a adj. coriaceous.
co-riá-ria f. sumach; plant yielding tanning extract.
co-ri-fe'-u m. coryphaeus.
có-ri-on m. chorion.
co-ris-car' intr.v. to flash like lightning.
co-ris'-co m. electric flash; lightning without thunder.
cor-na-li'-na f. carnelian, kind of agate.
cor'-ne m. trumpet.
cor'-no m. horn; antenna similar to horn; horny substance.
cor-ne'-ta f. cornet.
cor-ne-tei'-ro m. bugler.
cor-ne-tim' m. bugle.
cor-ni'-cho m. small horn; soft horny growth.
cor-ni-cur'-to, =a adj. short-horned.
cor-ni'-ja f. cornice.
cor-nim-bo'-que m. small end of horn made into a tobacco-box.
cor-nu'-do, =a adj. horned.
co-ris'-ta m. member of chorus.
cô-ro m. chorus; choir loft; em — in unison.
co-rô'-a f. crown; tonsure (ecclesiastic); royalty; upper facet of diamond; corona; climax.
co-ro-a-ção' f. coronation.
co-ro-a-men'-to m. finishing on top of a building.
co-ro-ar' tr.v. to crown; to climax, to complete, to put finishing touch on.
co-ro-gra-fi'-a f. chorography.
co-ró-gra-fo m. chorographer.
co-ro'-la f. corolla.
co-ró-lu-la f. small corolla.
co-ro-lá-rio m. corollary.
co-ro-nal' adj. coronal; m. coronal suture.
co-ro-ná-ria f. coronary artery.
co-ro-ná-rio, =a adj. having the curvature of crown.
co-ro-nel' m. colonel; (slang) goat, individual left to pay bill.
cor-pi'-nho m. corset cover, camisole.
cor'-po m. corps; body; staff; consistency; principal part of building.
cor-po-ra-ção' f. corporation.
cor-po-ral' m. communion cloth; adj. corporal, corporeal.
cor-po-ra-li-da'-de f. corporeality.
cor-po-ra-li-zar' tr.v. to materialize, to endow with a body.
cor-pu-lên-cia f. corpulence.
cor-pu-len'-to, =a adj. corpulent.
cor-pús-cu-lo m. corpuscle; particle.
cor-rão' adj. swift.
cor-re-ção' f. correction, correctness; reformatory.
cor-re-cio-nal' m. jurisdiction of juvenile court; adj. concerning juvenile court.
cor-re-dei'-ra f. rapids in short section of river.
cor-re-di'-ço, =a adj. slippery, smooth; easy.
cor-re-dor' m. corridor; gallery; covered walk; garden walk; adj. running.
cor-re-dou'-ro m. place suitable for racing.
cor-re-du'-ra f. race; liquid which sticks to side of measure.
cór-re-go m. small stream; new stream opened in flood time.
cór-re-go=sê-co m. dry river, stream resulting from torrential rains.
cor-rei'-a f. rein, leash (of leather).

cor-rei'-o *m.* post-office; postman; mail.

cor-re-la-ção' *f.* correlation.

cor-re-li-gi-o-ná-rio *m.* fellow member of a religion or party.

cor-ren-tão' *adj.* easy-going, affable, smooth, fast-working.

cor-ren'-te *adj.* current, fluent, running, expeditious; *m.* stream, river, current.

cor-ren-to'-so, ᵃ *adj.* having a strong current.

cor-rer' *intr.v.* to run, to move quickly, to hurry.

cor-res-pon-dên-cia *f.* correspondence.

cor-res-pon-der' *intr.v.* to correspond.

cor-re-ti'-vo, ᵃ *adj.,* *m.* corrective.

cor-re'-to, ᵃ *adj.* correct, honest, elegant.

cor-re-tor' *m.* commercial agent.

cor-ri'-da *f.* race; bull-fight; run on bank.

cor-ri'-do, ᵃ *adj.* worried, exhausted.

cor-ri-gen'-da *f.* corrigenda.

cor-ri-gir' *tr.v.* to correct.

cor-ri-mão' *m.* hand-rail, railing.

cor-ri-men'-to *m.* unnatural discharge from some organ of body.

cor-ro-bo-ra-ção' *f.* corroboration.

cor-ro-bo-rar' *tr.v.* to corroborate.

cor-ro-er' *tr.v.* to corrode.

cor-rom-per' *tr.v.* to corrupt.

cor-ro-são' *f.* corrosion.

cor-ro-si'-vo, ᵃ *adj.* corrosive.

cor-rup-ção' *f.* corruption, bribery.

cor-rup-tí-vel *adj.* corruptible.

cor-sá-rio *m.* corsair.

cor-se-le'-te *m.* corselet.

cor'-ta *f.* cut, section.

cor-ta-dor' *m.* cutting utensil; **cor-ta-dor',** ᵃ *adj.* sharp, cutting.

cor-tar' *tr.v.* to cut, to interrupt; to stop; to prune.

cor-ta᠎ven'-to *m.* wind-mill.

cor'-te *m.* cut, gash; dress length of material.

côr-te *f.* court; monarch's residence.

cor-te-jar' *tr.v.* to treat with courtesy; to fawn upon.

cor-te'-jo *m.* ceremonious and solemn salutation; procession; retinue; fawning, flattering.

cor-tês *adj.* courteous, polite.

cor-te-si'-a *f.* courtesy.

cor-te-sã' *f.* courtesan.

cor-te-são' *m.* courtier.

cór-tex *m.* bark.

cor-ti'-ça *f.* cork.

cor-ti-cen'-to, ᵃ *adj.* cork-like.

cor-ti-ce-o, ᵃ *adj.* made of cork.

cor-ti-ço'-so, ᵃ *adj.* having thick bark.

cor-ti'-lha *f.* roulette (for decorating pastry).

cor-ti'-na *f.* curtain.

co-ru'-ja *f.* raven.

co-rum-bás *m.pl.* forgotten or distant places.

cor-ve'-ta *f.* corvette (small warship).

cós *m.* waistband.

co-ser' *tr.v.* to sew.

cos-mé-ti-co *m.* cosmetics.

cós-mi-co, ᵃ *adj.* cosmic.

cos-mo-lo-gi'-a *f.* cosmology.

cos-mo-po-li'-ta *m.,* *f.* cosmopolite, cosmopolitan.

cos'-mos *m.* cosmos.

cos'-ta *f.* coast; bank; ridge; ᵃˢ *f.pl.* back; reverse side; — **abaixo** *adv.* downward; — **acima** *adv.* upward, with difficulty, reluctantly.

cos-tal' *adj.* coastal.

cos-te-ar' *tr.v.* to go along the side of; to navigate along the shore of.

cos-tei'-ro, ᵃ *adj.* coast-wise.

cos-te'-la *f.* rib.

cos-te-lar' *tr.v.* to fold (tobacco leaf) along the central rib.

cos-te-le'-ta *f.* rib, sparerib.

cos-tu-ma'-do, ᵃ *adj.* habitual, usual.

cos-tu-mar' *tr.v.* to have as habit; to be accustomed.

cos-tu'-me *m.* custom, practice; fashion; costume, suit of clothes.

cos-tu'-ra *f.* sewing; seam.

cos-tu-rar' *tr.v.* to sew; *intr.v.* to work at sewing.

cos-tu-rei'-ra *f.* seamstress, dress-maker.

co-ta-ção' *f.* quotation.

co-tar' *tr.v.* to quote.

co-ti-dia'-no, ᵃ *adj.* daily.

co-ti-lé-do-ne *m.* cotyledon.

cô-to *m.* stump, butt (left over parts of cigar or candle; amputated arm or leg); ᵃˢ *m.pl.* enlarged joints of fingers.

co-to-vê-lo *m.* elbow.

cou-ra'-ça *f.* armor plate.

cou'-ro *m.* hide, leather.

cou'-sa *f.* thing; ᵃˢ *f.pl.* property, belongings.

cou'-ve *f.* colewort.

co'-va *f.* cave; small hole, depression; grave; hole made for planting seed.

cô-va-do *m.* old measure of length, two palms, corresponding to sixty-six centimeters.

co-va'-gem *f.* grave digging; cost of grave digging.

co-val' *m.* section of cemetery in which new graves may be dug; cost of burial.

co-vão' *m.* large ditch; grave; coop.

co-va'-to *m.* job of grave-digger.

co-vei'-ro *m.* grave-digger.

co-vil' *m.* den.

co'-vo *m.* fish basket (made of reeds); **co'-vo,** ᵃ *adj.* hollow, concave, deep.

co'-xa *f.* thigh.

co-xal-gi'-a *f.* tuberculosis of hip.

co-xé *adj.* having one leg shorter than other.

co-xim' *m.* pillow, cushion, seat of saddle.

co'-xo, ᵃ *adj.* lame, limping.

co-ze-du'-ra *f.* cooking, boiling, baking.

co-zer' *tr.v.* to cook.

co-zi'-do *m.* stew.

co-zi'-nha *f.* kitchen; cooking, cuisine.

co-zi-nhar' *tr.v.,* *intr.v.* to cook.

co-zi-nhei'-ro, ᵃ *m.,* *f.* cook.

cra-nia'-no, ᵃ *adj.* cranial.

crâ-nio *m.* cranium.

cra-nio-lo-gi'-a *f.* craniology.

cra'-se *f.* crasis.

cras'-so, ᵃ *adj.* crass.

cra-te'-ra *f.* crater.

cra-va-ção' *f.* decoration with nail-head or ornamental tacks; studding; setting (of stones).

cra-va-dor' *m.* jeweler, goldsmith.

cra-var' *tr.v.* to nail; to set, to fasten, to fix.

cra-vei'-ra *f.* standard, size; catch, door-catch.

cra-vei'-ro *m.* carnation plant; nail manufacturer.

cra-ve'-lha *f.* tuning pin of musical instruments.

cra-ve'-te *m.* tongue of buckle.

cra-vi'-na *f.* garden pink.

cra-vi'-nho *m.* bud of clove plant.

cra'-vo *m.* nail, spike; carnation; clove; harpsichord.
cra-vo-a-ri'-a *f.* clove-tree.
cra-yon' *m.* crayon.
cré *f.* slaked lime; fuller's earth, chalk.
cre'-che *f.* nursery school.
cre-dên-cia *f.* altar-table; side-board.
cre-di-bi-li-da'-de *f.* credibility.
cre-di-tar' *tr.v.* to credit.
cré-di-to *m.* credit.
cre'-do *m.* creed.
cre-dor' *m.* creditor.
cre-du-li-da'-de *f.* credulity.
cré-du-lo, =a *adj.* credulous.
cre-ma-ção' *f.* cremation.
cre-mar' *tr.v.* to cremate.
cre-ma-tó-rio, =a *adj.* relative to cremation.
cre'-me *m.* cream; soft custard.
cren'-ça *f.* belief, faith.
cren-dei'-ro *m.* one holding a ridiculous belief; credulous person.
cren-di'-ce *f.* ridiculous belief.
cren'-te *m., f.* believer.
cre-o-li'-na *f.* creolin (antiseptic).
cre-o-so'-to *m.* creosote.
cre'-pe *m.* crepe (fabric); mourning crape.
cre-pi-tan'-te *adj.* crackling.
cre-pi-tar' *intr.v.* to crackle.
cre-pom' *m.* crepon.
cre-pús-cu-lo *m.* twilight.
crer' *tr.v.* to believe; *intr.v.* to have faith.
cres-cen'-te *m.* crescent; *f.* flood, high water, rising tide.
cres-cer' *intr.v.* to grow, to increase; to improve.
cres-ci-men'-to *m.* growth; *pl.* intermittent fever.
crés-ci-mo *m.* excess.
cre-sol' *m.* cresol.
cres-par' *tr.v.* to curl, to make wavy.
crês-po, =a *adj.* curly, wavy.
cres-ta-men'-to *m.* sun-tan; toasting.
cres-tar' *tr.v.* to toast; to make color of toast.
cres-to-ma-ti'-a *f.* chrestomathy.
cre-ti-nis'-mo *m.* cretinism.
cre-ti'-no *m.* cretin, imbecile.
cre-to'-ne *m.* cretonne.
cri'-a *f.* young horse, colt, foal; suckling.
cri-a-ção' *f.* creation; rearing, raising.
cri-a'-da *f.* maid, servant.
cri-a-dei'-ra *f.* wet nurse; brooder.
cri-a-da'-gem *f.* servants, group of servants.
cri-a'-do *m.* waiter, servant.
cri-an-ci'-ce *f.* childish manner, voice, or sayings.
cri-an-ço'-la *m.* grown person who acts like a child.
cri-ar' *tr.v.* to create; to raise, to invent, to cultivate.
cri-a-dor' *m.* cattle raiser, cattle breeder.
cri-an'-ça *f.* child, infant.
cri-an-ça'-da *f.* children, group of children.
cri-crí *m.* or cri-cri'-dos *m.pl.* cry of crickets.
cri'-me *m.* crime.
cri-mi-na-ção' *f.* incrimination, accusation.
cri-mi-nal' *adj.* criminal.
cri-mi-na-lo-gi'-a *f.* criminology.
cri'-na *f.* hair on tail and neck of horse and other animals.
cri-no-li'-na *f.* crinoline.
cri-nu'-do, =a *adj.* hairy, having hairy tail or neck.
cri-ó-li-ta *f.* cryolite.

cri-ou'-lo *m.* (originally) Negro born in America; (any) colored man; white man born in America; native.
crip'-ta *f.* crypt.
críp-ti-co, =a *adj.* cryptic.
cri-sá-li-da or cri-sá-li-de *f.* chrysalid.
cri-san-te'-mo *m.* chrysanthemum.
crí'-se *f.* crisis.
cris'-ma *f., m.* chrism.
cri-sol' *m.* crucible; (fig.) severe trial or test.
cri-só-li-ta *f.* chrysolite.
cri-só-pra-so *m.* chrysoprase.
cris-par' *tr.v., intr.v.* to make or become crisp.
cris'-ta *f.* crest; rooster's comb.
cris-tal' *m.* crystal.
cris-tal'-de-ro'-cha *m.* quartz, rock crystal.
cris-ta-lei'-ra *f.* crystal cabinet.
cris-ta-lei'-ro *m.* crystal collector.
cris-ta-li'-no, =a *adj.* crystalline.
cris-ta-li-za-ção' *f.* crystallization.
cris-ta-li-zar' *tr.v., intr.v.* to crystallize.
cris-tan-da'-de *f.* Christianity.
cris-tão' *m.* Christian.
cris-tia-nis'-mo *m.* Christendom.
cris-tia-ni-zar' *tr.v.* to Christianize.
Cris'-to *m.* Christ.
cri-té-rio *m.* criterion.
crí-ti-ca *f.* critique, criticism.
cri-ti-car' *tr.v.* to criticize.
crí-ti-co *m.* critic.
cri-var' *tr.v.* to riddle; to sift.
crí-vel *adj.* credible.
cri'-vo *m.* sieve, colander; sprinkler; needlework.
cro'-ca *f.* sow that mistreats her pigs; irresponsible mother.
cro-ché *m.* crochet.
cro-co-di'-lo *m.* crocodile.
cro-co-í-ta *f.* crocoite.
cro-má-ti-co, =a *adj.* chromatic.
cro-ma-tis'-mo *m.* chromatism.
crô-mi-co, =a *adj.* chromic.
cro'-mo *m.* chromium.
crô-ni-ca *f.* chronicle.
crô-ni-co, =a *adj.* chronic, inveterate.
cro-ni-quei'-ro *m.* newspaper reporter, chronicler.
cro-nis'-ta *m.* historian.
cro-nô-me-tro *m.* chronometer; stop watch.
cro-que'-te *f.* croquette.
cro-quis' *m.* sketch, rough design.
cros'-ta *f.* crust; scab; hard coating.
cru', cru'-a *adj.* uncooked, raw; shocking (of language); green; blunt; cruel.
cru-bi-xá *m.* black coral found at several places along Brazilian coast.
cru-ci-al' *adj.* crucial.
cru-ci-fi-car' *tr.v.* to crucify.
cru-ci-fi-xão' *f.* crucifixion.
cru-ci-fi'-xo *m.* crucifix.
cru-el' *adj.* cruel.
cru-el-da'-de *f.* cruelty.
crû-e'-za *f.* rawness, cruelty.
cruz' *f.* cross.
cru-za'-da *f.* crusade.
cru-za'-do *m.* old Portuguese gold coin; Brazilian coin worth four hundred *reis.*
cru-za-dor' *m.* cruiser.
cru-zar' *tr.v., intr.v.* to cross; to put in form of cross; to cross-breed.
cu'-ba *f.* vat, hogshead (generally used in making wine).
cu-ba'-gem *f.* cubing (math.); volume.
cu-bar' *tr.v.* to cube.

cu-ba-tu'-ra *f.* reduction of volume to cubic units.

cú-bi-co, *=a adj.* cubic.

cu-bis'-mo *m.* cubism.

cu-bis'-ta *m.* cubist.

cú-bi-to *m.* cubitus, forearm.

cu'-bo *m.* cube.

cu'-co *m.* cuckoo; cuckoo clock.

cu-cúr-bi-ta *f.* coil in still.

cu-e'-cas *f.pl.* short under pants; "B.V.D."

cu-ei'-ro *m.* diaper.

cu-gar' *m.* cougar.

cuí *m.* soot.

cu'-ia *f.* cured and decorated gourd used in making the beverage *mate.*

cu-iei'-ra *f.* calabash.

cui-da'-do *m.* care, precaution; worry, anxiety; *interj.* attention! be careful!

cui-da-do'-so, *=a adj.* careful, zealous, prudent.

cu-li-ná-ria *f.* art of cooking.

cu-li-ná-rio, *=a adj.* culinary.

cul-mi-nân-cia *f.* culmination.

cul-mi-nân'-te *adj.* culminating.

cul-mi-nar' *intr.v.* to culminate.

cul'-pa *f.* fault, sin; guilt.

cul-pa'-do, *=a adj.* faulty; guilty.

cul-pá-vel *adj.* culpable, guilty.

cul-ti-va-ção' *f.* cultivation.

cul-ti-var' *tr.v.* to cultivate.

cul-ti-vá-vel *adj.* cultivatable, tillable.

cul-ti'-vo *m.* cultivation; plowing, preparation of land for planting.

cul'-to *m.* worship; cul'-to, *=a adj.* cultured, educated.

cul-tu'-ra *f.* culture.

cúm-pli-ce *m., f.* accomplice.

cump-li-ci-da'-de *f.* complicity.

cum-pri-dor' *m.* one who fulfils his promises, one who does his duty.

cum-prir' *tr.v.* to execute, to fulfil.

cú-mu-lo *m.* cumulus; highest point; heap.

cu'-nha *f.* wedge.

cu-nha'-da *f.* sister-in-law.

cu-nha'-do *m.* brother-in-law.

cu-nha'-gem *f.* coining.

cu-nhar' *tr.v.* to coin; to stamp.

cu'-nho *m.* stamp (for coining money).

cu-pé *m.* coupé.

cu-pi-dez' *f.* cupidity, greed.

Cu-pi'-do *m.* Cupid.

cú-pi-do, *=a adj.* avaricious.

cu-pim' *m.* termite.

cu-pom' *m.* coupon.

cu-prí-fe-ro, *=a adj.* copper-bearing.

cu-pri'-ta *f.* cuprite.

cú-pu-la *f.* cupola.

cu'-ra *f.* cure, treatment; *m.* curate.

cu-ra-bí *m.* small poisoned arrow.

cu-ra-dor' *m.* guardian, trustee; medicine-man.

cu-ra-do-ri'-a *f.* guardianship.

cu-ran-dei'-ro *m.* quack.

cu-rar' *tr.v.* to cure, to restore to health; to cure (meat), to bleach.

cu-ra'-re *m.* curare.

cu-ra-ri-zar' *tr.v.* to poison with curare.

cu-ra-ti'-vo *m.* cure, treatment, dressing.

cu-ra'-to *m.* work of a curate, parish of a curate.

cu-rá-vel *adj.* curable.

cu-re'-ta *f.* curette.

cú-ria *f.* curia.

cu-ri-ão' *m.* chief of Roman curia.

cu-ri-o-si-da'-de *f.* curiosity.

cu-ri-o'-so, *=a adj.* curious; cu-ri-o'-so *m.* (Brazil) amateur, dilettante.

cur-ral' *m.* corral.

cur-sar' *tr.v.* to take course in, to study; to traverse; *intr.v.* to travel, to cruise.

cur-si'-vo, *=a adj.* cursive.

cur'-so *m.* course.

cur-te'-za *f.* shortness, curtness.

cur-ti-men'-to *m.* tanning.

cur-tir' *tr.v.* to tan, to prepare as leather.

cur'-to, *=a adj.* short; curt.

cur-tu'-me *m.* tanning; tanning material; tannery.

cur'-va *f.* curve.

cur-var' *tr.v.*, *intr.v.* to curve; —*=se refl.v.* to submit, to bow.

cur-va-tu'-ra *f.* curvature.

cur-vi-lí-ne-o, *=a adj.* curvilinear.

cur'-vo, *=a adj.* curved.

cús-pi-de *f.* cusp; bee-sting.

cus-pi-dei'-ra *f.* cuspidor, spittoon.

cus-pi-dor' *m.* spitter; drooling infant.

cus-pi-du'-ra *f.* spit, spittle; spitting.

cus-pir' *intr.v.* to spit.

cus'-po *m.* spit, saliva.

cus-tar' *tr.v.*, *intr.v.* to cost; to be hard.

cus'-to *m.* cost, price.

cus-to'-so, *=a adj.* costly, expensive; hard, difficult.

cus-tó-dia *f.* custody; pyx, tabernacle.

cu-tâ-ne-o, *=a adj.* cutaneous.

cu-te'-la *f.* large meat knife.

cu-te-la-ri'-a *f.* cutlery.

cu-te-lei'-ro *m.* cutler.

cu-te'-lo *m.* chopper, chopping knife; cutlass.

cu-tí-cu-la *f.* cuticle.

cu'-tis *f.* epidermis, skin.

cu-tu-car' *tr.v.* to nudge with elbow or finger.

D

See page 12—GUIDE TO REFORMED SPELLING used in this Dictionary

D, d *m.* D, d, third letter of the alphabet; abbrev. for Dom, Dona; DD. abbrev. for digníssimo in titles.

da contraction of *prep.* de with *fem.art.* a; contraction of *prep.* de with *dem.fem.pro.* a.

dac-ti-lo-gra-far' *tr.v.* to typewrite.

dac-ti-ló-gra-fo *m.* typewriter, typist.

dac-ti-los-co-pi'-a *f.* finger-printing.

da-dei'-ra *f.* hysterical woman.

dá-di-va *f.* gift, donation.

da-di-vo'-so, *=a adj.* generous, liberal.

da'-do *m.* dice cube; known element, known quantity; da'-do, *=a adj.* affable, pleasant, free; da'-dos *m.pl.* data.

da-guer-re-ó-ti-po *m.* daguerreotype.

da-í (contraction of *prep.* de with *adv.* aí) from there; therefore.

da'-la *f.* discharge spout or tube; marble-topped kitchen table.

da-lém *adv.* from far away (contraction of *prep.* de with *adv.* além).

da-lí *adv.* from there (near by) (contraction of *prep.* **de** with *adv.* **alí**).

dá-lia *f.* dahlia.

dal-to-nis'-mo *m.* daltonism.

da'-ma *f.* dame, lady.

da-mas-qui-na-ri'-a *f.* inlaid gold or silver design; parquetry.

da-mas'-co *m.* damask (fabric); damson.

da-na-ção' *f.* damnation; anger; rabies.

da-nar' *tr.v.* to injure, to hurt, to spoil; to anger; to give rabies to.

da-ni-fi-ca-ção' *f.* harm, injury, damage.

da-ni-fi-car' *tr.v.* to damage, to cause damage.

da'-no *m.* damage, hurt, harm; loss.

dan'-sa *f.* dance.

dan-sa-dei'-ra *f.* dancer.

dan-sa-dor' *m.* dancer.

dan-san'-te *adj.* dancing; with dancing.

dan-sar' *tr.v.*, *intr.v.* to dance.

dan-sa-ri'-no, =a *m.*, *f.* dancer, professional dancer.

dan'-tes *adv.* formerly (contraction of *prep.* **de** with *adv.* **antes**).

da-quí *adv.* from here (contraction of *prep.* **de** with *adv.* **aquí**).

dar' *tr.v.* to give, to donate, to present with, to bestow, to yield; *intr.v.* to beat, to strike, to collide, to encounter.

dar-dar' *tr.v.* to injure with dart.

dar-de-jar' *tr.v.* to shoot darts at.

dar'-do *m.* dart; (fig.) insect sting, serpent's tongue.

da'-ta *f.* date.

da-tar' *tr.v.* to date; *intr.v.* to date (from), to count (from).

da-til' *m.* tamarind.

da-ti-la'-do, =a *adj.* tamarind-colored.

da-ti-lei'-ra *f.* tamarind palm tree.

da-tis'-mo *m.* tautology; tedious repetition of synonyms.

da-ti'-vo *m.* dative case.

de *prep.* from, =of, with, by.

de-a'-do *m.* deanship; deaconry.

de-ão' *m.* dean; deacon.

de-ar-ti-cu-la-ção' *f.* dearticulation.

de-ba'-cle *f.* debacle, financial ruin.

de-bai'-xo *adv.* below, beneath; subordinately; — **de** under.

de-bal'-de *adv.* in vain, uselessly.

de-ban-da'-da *f.* disorderly flight.

de-ban-dar' *tr.v.*, *intr.v.* to scatter in flight, to be dispersed.

de-ba'-te *m.* debate, discussion.

de-bi-car' *intr.v.* to peck; (fig.) to eat little.

dé-bil *adj.* weak, infirm.

de-bi-li-da'-de *f.* debility, weakness.

de-bi'-que *m.* snack, bit.

de-bi-tar' *tr.v.* to debit.

dé-bi-to *m.* debt.

de-bo-char' *tr.v.* to debauch.

de-bo'-che *m.* licentiousness, debauchery.

de-bre-ar' *tr.v.* to put brake on (auto).

de-bru-a-dei'-ra *f.* hemming machine.

de-bru-ar' *tr.v.* to hem; to ornament.

de-bru-çar'=**se** *refl.v.* to drop head over breast; to lean over.

de-brum' *m.* hem.

de-bu-lha-do'-ra *f.* husking machine.

de-bu-lhar' *tr.v.* to peel, to remove the shell or husk of grain; to thrash.

de-bu'-lho *m.* shell, husk, chaff.

de-bu'-xo *m.* sketch, first draft, outline.

dé-ca-da *f.* decade.

de-ca-dên-cia *f.* decadence.

de-ca-e'-dro *m.* decahedron.

de-ca-gra'-ma *m.* decagram.

de-ca-í-do, =a *adj.* decadent, decrepit; impoverished.

de-ca-ir' *intr.v.* to decay, to sink into decay, to decline.

de-cal-co-ma-ni'-a *f.* decalcomania.

de-ca-li'-tro *m.* decaliter.

de-cá-lo-go *m.* decalogue.

de-câ-me-tro *m.* decameter.

de-ca-na'-do *m.* deanship.

de-ca'-no *m.* dean (of diplomatic corps, class or corporation).

de-can-tar' *tr.v.* to decant.

de-ca-pi-tar' *tr.v.* to decapitate, to behead.

de-ce-ná-rio, =a *adj.* decenary.

de-cên-cia *f.* decency.

de-cen'-te *adj.* decent, seemly, honest.

de-cên-dio *m.* space of ten days.

de-cê-nio *m.* decennium.

de-ce-par' *tr.v.* to behead, to amputate, to mutilate.

de-cep-ção' *f.* deception, disillusionment, disappointment, surprise.

de-cep-cio-nar' *tr.v.* to deceive, to disappoint.

de-ci-dir' *tr.v.* to decide.

de-cí-duo, =a *adj.* deciduous.

de-ci-frar' *tr.v.* to decipher.

de-ci-frá-vel *adj.* decipherable.

de-ci-gra'-ma *m.* decigram.

de-ci-lí'-tro *m.* deciliter.

dé-ci-ma *f.* tithe; tenth part.

de-ci-mal' *adj.* decimal.

de-ci-mar' *tr.v.* to decimate.

de-cí-me-tro *m.* decimeter.

dé-ci-mo, =a *adj.* tenth.

de-ci-são' *f.* decision.

de-ci-si'-vo, =a *adj.* decisive.

de-cla-ma-ção' *f.* declamation.

de-cla-ma-dor' *m.* declaimer, reciter, pleader.

de-cla-mar' *tr.v.* to declaim.

de-cla-rar' *tr.v.* to declare.

de-cla-ra-ti'-vo, =a *adj.* declarative.

de-cli-na-ção' *f.* declination; decline; declension.

de-cli-nar' *tr.v.*, *intr.v.* to decline, to refuse politely; to inflect noun or adjective; to deviate, to stray.

de-cli-ná-vel *adj.* declinable.

de-clí-nio *m.* decline, decay, decadence.

de-clí'-ve *m.*, *adj.* declining, slanting.

de-cli-vi-da-de *f.* declivity.

de-coc-ção' *f.* decoction.

de-co-la'-gem *f.* take-off.

de-co-lar' *intr.v.* to take off.

de-com-por' *tr.v.* to decompose.

de-com-po-si-ção' *f.* decomposition.

de-co-rar' *tr.v.* to memorize, to learn by heart; to decorate, to ornament.

de-co-ra-ti'-vo, =a *adj.* decorative.

de-co'-ro *m.* decorum.

de-co-ro'-so, =a *adj.* decorous.

de-co-tar' *tr.v.* to cut a dress low; to prune trees; —**se** *refl.v.* to dress leaving neck and shoulders bare.

de-cre-pi-dez' *f.* decrepitude.

de-cré-pi-to, =a *adj.* decrepit.

de-cres-cer' *intr.v.* to decrease, to diminish.

de-cres-ci-men'-to *m.* decrease, diminution.

de-cre-tal' *f.* decretal.

de-cre-ta-lis'-ta *m.* decretist.

de-cre-tar' *tr.v.* to decree.

de-cre'-to *m.* decree.

de-cru'-a *f.* first plowing or cultivation of newly cleared ground.

de-cú-ma-no, =a *adj.* decuman; huge; tenth.

de-cum-ben'-te *adj.* decumbent.
dé-cu-plo, *=a adj.* decuple; ten-fold; ten times as large.
de-cur'-so *m.* course.
de-da'-da *f.* stain or mark made by finger.
de-dal' *m.* thimble.
de-dal=de=re-pu'-xo *m.* sailor's palm thimble.
dé-da-lo *m.* maze, labyrinth.
de-dei'-ra *f.* glove tip; dressing for end of finger.
de-di-ca-ção' *f.* dedication, devotion.
de-di-car' *tr.v.* to dedicate; —=se *refl.v.* to devote oneself to.
de-di-ca-tó-ria *f.* dedication, dedicatory note.
de'-do *m.* finger.
de-du-ção' *f.* deduction.
de-du-ti'-vo, *=a adj.* deductive.
de-du-zir' *tr.v.* to deduce.
de-fe-ca-ção' *f.* defecation.
de-fe-car' *intr.v.* to defecate.
de-fe-ti'-vo, *=a adj.* defective.
de-fei'-to *m.* defect.
de-fei-tu-o'-so, *=a adj.* defective.
de-fen-den'-te *m., f.* defendant.
de-fen-der' *tr.v.* to defend; —=se *refl.v.* to justify oneself, to repel attack.
de-fen-dí-vel *adj.* defensible.
de-fen'-sa *f.* defense, protection.
de-fen-si'-va *f.* defensive.
de-fen-sí-vel *adj.* defensible.
de-fen-si'-vo, *=a adj.* defensive.
de-fen-sor' *m.* defender.
de-fe-rên-cia *f.* deference, compliance.
de-fe-ri-men'-to *m.* condescension, approval.
de-fe-rir' *tr.v.* to yield, to approve, to condescend.
de-fe-rí-vel *adj.* that may be granted.
de-fe'-sa *f.* prohibition; defense; =s *f.pl.* tusks (of an elephant).
de-fi-ci-ên-cia *f.* deficiency.
de-fi-cien'-te *adj.* deficient.
dé-fi-cit *m.* deficit.
de-fi-nha'-do, *=a adj.* thin, debilitated.
de-fi-nhar' *tr.v.* to cause to lose flesh; *intr.v.* to weaken gradually, to grow thin; to pine away.
de-fi-ni-ção' *f.* definition.
de-fi-nir' *tr.v.* to define.
de-fi-ni-ti'-vo, *=a adj.* definitive.
de-fi-ni'-to, *=a adj.* definite.
de-fi-ní-vel *adj.* definable.
de-fla-ção' *f.* deflation.
de-fla-grar' *intr.v.* to flash.
de-flex-ão' *f.* deflection.
de-flo-ra-ção' *f.* withering, deflowering.
de-flo-ra-men'-to *m.* deflowering.
de-flo-rar' *tr.v.* to deflower.
de-flu'-xo *m.* cold, catarrh.
de-fo-re'-te *m.* short rest during work; breathing spell.
de-for-mar' *tr.v.* to deform.
de-for'-me *adj.* deformed.
de-for-mi-da'-de *f.* deformity.
de-frau-dar' *tr.v.* to defraud.
de-fron'-te *adv.* face to face, in front.
de-fu-ma-ção' *f.* smoking, smoke-drying.
de-fu-ma-dou'-ro *m.* smoke-room, smoke-house.
de-fu-mar' *tr.v.* to smoke (as curing process for meat).
de-fun'-to *m.* dead person; *adj.* deceased, defunct.
de-ge-ne-rar' *intr.v.* to degenerate.

de-go-lar' *tr.v.* to behead, to cut one's throat.
de-gra-da-ção' *f.* degradation.
de-gra-dar' *tr.v.* to degrade, to demote.
de-grau' *m.* step (of stairway); degree.
de-gre-da'-do *m.* exile.
de-gre-dar' *tr.v.* to exile.
de-grê-do *m.* banishment, exile.
déi-a *f.* goddess.
dei-da'-de *f.* deity, divinity; (fig.) goddess.
dei-fi-ca-ção' *f.* deification.
dei-fi-car' *tr.v.* to deify.
de-is-cên-cia *f.* dehiscence.
de-ís-mo *m.* deism.
de-ís-ta *m.* deist.
dei-ta'-do, *=a adj.* in bed; lying full length.
dei-tar' *tr.v.* to place on floor; to extend horizontally; to put in, to place; —=se *refl.v.* to go to bed; to lie full length on floor or bed.
dei-xar' *tr.v.* to leave behind; to put aside, to abandon; to leave as inheritance; to permit; to cease; to postpone; to omit; to cede.
de-je-ção' *f.* defecation; substances ejected by volcanoes.
de-je-tar' *tr.v.* to defecate.
de-je-tó-rio *m.* privy, latrine.
de-la-tar' *tr.v.* to denounce.
de-la-tor' *m.* informer, accuser.
de-le-ga-ção' *f.* delegation.
de-le-ga-cí-a *f.* public office.
de-le-ga'-do *m.* delegate; public official.
de-le-gar' *tr.v.* to delegate, to assign; to appoint.
de-lei-ta-ção' *f.* delight, enjoyment.
de-lei-tan'-te *adj.* pleasing, delightful.
de-lei-tar' *tr.v.* to please, to delight.
de-lei'-te *m.* delight.
de-lei-to'-so, *=a adj.* delightful, pleasing.
de-le-té-rio, *=a adj.* deleterious.
de-lé-vel *adj.* easily erased or destroyed.
del-ga'-do, *=a adj.* slim, slender; fine; *m.* slender part.
de-li-be-rar' *tr.v., intr.v.* to deliberate.
de-li-ca-de'-za *f.* delicateness, delicacy; courtesy.
de-li-ca'-do, *=a adj.* delicate; attentive, courteous.
de-lí-cia *f.* delight.
de-li-cio'-so, *=a adj.* delicious.
de-li-mi-tar' *tr.v.* to delimit.
de-li-ne-ar' *tr.v.* to delineate, to outline.
de-lin-quên-cia *f.* offense, guilt.
de-lin-quen'-te *m., f.* transgressor, guilty person; *adj.* guilty, criminal.
de-lir' *tr.v.* to undo, to erase, to desolve.
de-li-rar' *intr.v.* to be delirious, to rave.
de-lí-rio *m.* delirium; exhaltation, enthusiasm.
de-li-rio'-so, *=a adj.* delirious, raving, wild with enthusiasm.
de-li'-to *m.* offense, crime.
de-li-vrar' *tr.v.* to deliver.
del'-ta *m.* delta.
de-lu-dir' *tr.v.* to delude.
de-lu-são' *f.* delusion.
de-lu-só-rio, *=a adj.* deceptive, deluding.
de-ma-go'-go *m.* demagogue.
de-mais' *adv.* too, too much; *indef.pro.* rest, others.
de-man'-da *f.* law-suit, plea; inquest.
de-man-dar' *tr.v.* to seek, to claim, to ask, to demand; to need, to sue.
de-man-dis'-ta *m.* litigious person, caviller.

de-mão' *f.* coat of paint, coat of white-wash; retouch, revision; try; aid, help.

de-mar-ca-ção' *f.* demarcation.

de-mar-car' *tr.v.* to demarcate.

de-ma-si'-a *f.* excess, over-supply; intemperance; temerity, abuse.

de-ma-si-a'-do, =a *adj.* too, too much, excessive, superfluous, abusive.

de-ma-si-ar'-=se *refl.v.* to go beyond reasonable limits.

de-mên-cia *f.* dementia.

de-men-ta'-do, =a *adj.* demented.

de-men'-te *adj.* demented.

de-mé-ri-to *m.* demerit.

de-mi-nu-ir' *tr.v.* to reduce, to diminish.

de-mis-são' *f.* resignation, dismissal, discharge.

de-mi-tir' *tr.v.* to dismiss; to exonerate; —=se *refl.v.* to offer one's resignation.

de-mo-cra-ci'-a *f.* democracy.

de-mo-cra'-ta *m., f.* democrat.

de-mo-cra-ti-zar' *tr.v.* to democratize.

de-mo-gra-fi'-a *f.* demography.

de-mo-lir' *tr.v.* to demolish.

de-mo-ne-ti-zar' *tr.v.* to demonetize.

de-mô-nio *m.* demon.

de-mons-tra-ção' *f.* demonstration.

de-mons-trar' *tr.v.* to demonstrate.

de-mons-tra-ti'-vo, =a *adj.* demonstrative.

de-mons-trá-vel *adj.* demonstrable.

de-mo-ra' -do, =a *adj.* slow, lingering.

de-mo-ra' *f.* delay, detention.

de-mo-rar' *tr.v.* to retard, to delay; *intr.v.* to be long, to take time; to be situated, to live; —=se *refl.v.* to linger, to loiter.

den-dê *m.* palm tree producing nuts from which oil is extracted.

den-dri'-te *f.* den-dri'-to *m.* dendrite.

den'-gue *m.* coyness; *adj.* coy, affected.

den-gui'-ce *f.* coyness, affectation.

de-no-da'-do, =a *adj.* intrepid, impetuous.

de-no-dar' *tr.v.* to untangle, to untie.

de-nô-do *m.* daring, courage, dauntlessness.

de-no-mi-na-ção' *f.* denomination.

de-no-mi-na-dor' *m.* denominator.

de-no-mi-nar' *tr.v.* to name, to entitle, to give a name to.

de-no-tar' *tr.v.* to denote.

den-si-da'-de *f.* density.

den-si-dão' *f.* denseness, density.

den-sí-me-tro *m.* densimeter.

den'-so, =a *adj.* dense.

den-ta-du'-ra *f.* set of teeth, denture.

den-tar' *tr.v.* to bite, to bite into; *intr.v.* to teethe.

den-tal' *adj.* dental.

den'-te *m.* tooth.

den-te-ar' *tr.v.* to indent, to notch.

den-ti-ção' *f.* dentition.

den-ti-frí-cio *m.* dentifrice.

den-ti-lhão' *m.* large tooth.

den-ti'-na *f.* dentine.

den-tis'-ta *m.* dentist.

den'-tro *adv.* within, on the inside.

de-nu-dar' *tr.v.* to denude.

de-nún-cia *f.* denunciation, accusation.

de-nun-ci-ar' *tr.v.* to denunciate.

de-nun-cia-tó-rio, =a *adj.* denunciatory.

de-pa-rar' *tr.v.* to send; to cause to appear; —=se *refl.v.* to appear suddenly or unexpectedly.

de-par-ta-men'-to *m.* department.

de-par-tir' *tr.v.* to divide, to distribute, to narrate in great detail.

de-pas-cen'-te *adj.* feeding, consuming.

de-pe-nar' *tr.v.* to pick or pull out feathers; (fig.) to fleece.

de-pen-dên-cia *f.* dependency.

de-pen-den'-te *adj.* dependent.

de-pen-der' *intr.v.* to depend, to be dependent.

de-pe-ni-car' *tr.v.* to pull out feathers one by one.

de-pi-la-tó-rio *m.* depilatory.

de-ple-ção' *f.* (med.) depletion.

de-cla-ra-ção' *f.* declaration.

de-cla-ran'-te *m.* deponent.

de-plo-rar' *tr.v.* to deplore, to lament.

de-plo-rá-vel *adj.* deplorable.

de-po-en'-te *m., f.* deponent, witness.

de-poi-men'-to *m.* testimony, deposition.

de-pois' *adv.* after, afterward.

de-po-la-ri-zar' *tr.v.* to depolarize.

de-por' *tr.v.* to put down, to deposit, to deliver, to depose; *intr.v.* to bear witness.

de-por-tar' *tr.v.* to deport, to exile.

de-po-si-ção' *f.* testimony, deposition.

de-po-si-tan'-te *m., f.* depositor.

de-po-si-tar' *tr.v.* to deposit.

de-po-si-tá-rio *m.* depositary.

de-pó-si-to *m.* deposit.

de-pra-var' *tr.v.* to deprave.

de-pre-ci-a-ção' *f.* depreciation.

de-pre-ci-ar' *tr.v.* to depreciate.

de-pre-ci-á-vel *adj.* depreciable.

de-pre-da-ção' *f.* depredation.

de-pre-dar' *tr.v.* to depredate, to spoil, to plunder.

de-pres'-sa *adv.* rapidly, in a short time, quickly, fast.

de-pres-são' *f.* depression, dejection; small hole.

de-pri-men'-te *adj.* depressing.

de-pri-mir' *tr.v.* to depress, to lower, to humiliate.

de-pu-ta-ção' *f.* deputation.

de-pu-ta'-do *m.* deputy; congressman, legislator.

de-ra-par' *intr.v.* to skid.

de-ri'-va *f.* drift.

de-ri-va-ção' *f.* derivation.

de-ri-va'-do *m.* derivative.

de-ri-var' *tr.v.* to derive, to be derived; to turn aside the course of stream; *intr.v.* to run (of streams), to rise or originate in.

der'-ma *m.* derma, skin.

der-ma-to-lo-gi'-a *f.* dermatology.

de-ro-ga-ção' *f.* disparagement, derogation.

de-ro-gar' *tr.v.* to repeal, to disparage.

de-ro-ga-tó-rio, =a *adj.* derogatory, disparaging.

der-ra-dei'-ro, =a *adj.* last, final.

der-ra'-ma *f.* per capita local tax; pruning.

der-ra-ma-men'-to *m.* shedding, scattering.

der-ra-mar' *tr.v.* to shed; to scatter; to prune (trees).

der-re-ter' *tr.v.* to melt; to dissolve; to fuse; (fig.) to be greatly moved; —=se *refl.v.* to] be exceedingly attentive and loving.

der-ri-bar' *tr.v.* to demolish, to tear down.

der-ri-são' *f.* derision.

der-ro'-ta *f.* course, path; defeat, rout, destruction.

der-ro-tar' *tr.v.* to rout, to destroy; *intr.v.* to stray from course, to get lost.

de-sa-ba-far' *tr.v.* to uncover; to say frankly; *intr.v.* to breathe freely; to speak openly and freely.

de-sa-ba'-fo *m.* ease, relief.

de-sa'-be *m.* damaged or broken part of wall.

de-sa-bo-nar' *tr.v.* to discredit, to hurt (reputation), to speak ill of.

de-sa-bo-to-ar' *tr.v.* to unbutton, to unfasten; *intr.v.* to bud forth (of plants).

de-sa-bri'-do, ₌a *adj.* rude, insolent, abrupt.

de-sa-bri-gar' *tr.v.* to leave without shelter, to abandon.

de-sa-bri'-go *m.* forlornness, abandonment, lack of shelter.

de-sa-ca-tar' *tr.v.* to annoy, to worry, to be disrespectful to, to profane.

de-sa-ca'-to *m.* disrespect; profanation.

de-sa-cau-di-lha'-do, ₌a *adj.* without a chief or leader.

de-sa-cau-te-la'-do, ₌a *adj.* imprudent, careless, improvident.

de-sa-col-che-tar' *tr.v.* to unhook hook-and-eye fastenings.

de-sa-com-pa-nha'-do, ₌a *adj.* alone, isolated, solitary.

de-sa-côr-do *m.* discord, lack of harmony.

de-sa-cor-ren-tar' *tr.v.* to free, to unchain.

de-sa-cre-di-ta'-do, ₌a *adj.* discredited.

de-sa-fer-rar' *tr.v.* to loose, to free; *intr.v.* to lift anchor (ship).

de-a-fi-ar' *tr.v.* to remove lacing or ribbon; to dare, to challenge.

de-sa-fi-nar' *intr.v.* to get out of tune; *tr.v.* to put out of tune.

de-sa-fi'-o *m.* challenge, provocation; (pop.) dialogue sung extemporaneously in verse.

de-sa-fô-ro *m.* insult; shame; impudence.

de-sa-jei-ta'-do, ₌a *adj.* awkward.

de-sa-li-nha-var' *tr.v.* to remove basting thread.

de-sa-li'-nho *m.* carelessness in dress; slovenliness; disorder; disalignment.

de-sa-lo-jar' *tr.v.* to dislodge; *intr.v.* to change camp.

de-sa-mor' *m.* dislike; cruelty.

de-sa-mor-ti-zar' *tr.v.* to subject property of a deceased person to taxation.

de-sam-pa-ra'-do, ₌a *adj.* deserted, helpless.

de-sam-pa'-ro *m.* abandonment, helplessness.

de-san-dar' *tr.v., intr.v.* to walk or move backwards; to go over the same way again.

de-san'-do *m.* decadence; walking backward.

de-sa-ni-ma-ção' *f.* discouragement.

de-sa-ni-mar' *tr.v., intr.v.* to discourage; to lose courage or hope.

de-sâ-ni-mo *m.* discouragement.

de-sa-pa-ra-fu-sar' *tr.v.* to unscrew.

de-sa-pa-re-cer' *intr.v.* to disappear, to die.

de-sa-pi-e-da'-do, ₌a *adj.* cruel, inhuman, unmerciful.

de-sa-pon-ta-men'-to *m.* disappointment.

de-sa-pon-tar' *tr.v.* to disappoint.

de-sa-pro-va-ção' *f.* disapproval, reprehension.

de-sa-pru-ma'-do, ₌a *adj.* not vertical, out of plumb.

de-sar-mar' *tr.v.* to disarm.

de-sar-ran-jar' *tr.v.* to disarrange; to disconcert.

de-sar-ran'-jo *m.* confusion, disorder.

de-sas-tra'-do, ₌a *adj.* disastrous.

de-as'-tre *m.* disaster.

de-sas-tro'-so, ₌a *adj.* disastrous.

de-sa-tar' *tr.v.* to untie; to solve; to let go.

de-sa-ver-go-nha'-do, ₌a *adj.* shameless, brazen.

des-ba-ra-tar' *tr.v.* to squander, to waste.

des-bo-ta'-do, ₌a *adj.* faded, lifeless.

des-bo-tar' *tr.v., intr.v.* to fade, to become less bright in color.

des-bo'-te *m.* discoloration, fadedness.

des-bra-var' *tr.v.* to tame; to prepare virgin land for cultivation.

des-ca-bi'-do, ₌a *adj.* improper, out of place.

des-cal-ça-dei'-ra *f.* bootjack.

des-cal-ça-dor' *m.* bootjack.

des-cal-çar' *tr.v.* to take off, to pull off.

des-cal'-ço, ₌a *adj.* barefoot, shoeless.

des-can-sa'-do, ₌a *adj.* rested, tranquil, unworried.

des-can-sar' *tr.v., intr.v.* to rest, to repose.

des-can'-so *m.* repose, quiet, rest; delay, pause.

des-car'-ga *f.* discharge (of firearms), discharge.

des-car'-go *m.* discharge, unloading, relief.

des-ca-ro-ça-dor' *m.* seeding machine.

des-car-re-ga-dou'-ro *m.* unloading dock.

des-car-re-gar' *tr.v.* to discharge, to unload.

des-car-ri-lar' *tr.v., intr.v.* to derail; to jump the track.

des-car'-te *m.* discard (in cards).

des-cas-car' *tr.v.* to peel, to remove shell.

des-cen-dên-cia *f.* descent, lineage, extraction.

des-cen-den'-te *adj.* descendent; *m.* descendant.

des-cen-der' *intr.v.* to descend, to be derived from.

des-cen-tra-li-za-ção' *f.* decentralization.

des-cen-trar' *tr.v.* to decenter.

des-cer' *tr.v.* to lower, to place below or lower; *intr.v.* to go below, to go down, to descend; to get off.

des-ci'-da *f.* descent, drop.

des-clas-si-fi-car' *tr.v.* to disqualify; to discredit.

des-co-ber'-ta *f.* discovery; invention.

des-co-ber'-to, ₌a *adj.* discovered, uncovered, nude; divulged.

des-co-brir' *tr.v.* to discover, to invent, to find; ₌se *r.j.v.* to remove one's hat.

des-co-lo-ra-ção' *f.* discoloration, loss of color.

des-co-lo-rar' *tr.v.* to bleach, to discolor.

des-co-lo-rir' *tr.v.* to discolor; *intr.v.* to lose color.

des-com-po-si-ção' *f.* decomposition.

des-com-pos-tu'-ra *f.* insult, censure; careless dress.

des-con-cer-ta'-do, ₌a *adj.* disorderly, negligent.

des-con-cêr-to *m.* confusion, misunderstanding.

des-co-ne-xão' *f.* disconnection.

des-co-ne'-xo, ₌a *adj.* disconnected.

des-con-fi-a'-do, ₌a *adj.* suspicious.

des-con-fi-ar' *tr.v.*, *intr.v.* to suspect, to mistrust, to doubt.

des-con-fôr-to *m.* discomfort.

des-co-nhe-ci'-do, *=a adj.* unknown, not recognized; *m.*, *f.* unknown person.

des-con-so-la'-do, *=a adj.* disconsolate.

des-con-tar' *tr.v.* to discount; to lower price; not to take into account.

des-con'-to *m.* discount; reduction; discounting.

des-con-ten-ta-men'-to *m.* discontent.

des-con-ten'-te *adj.* discontented.

des-con-ti-nu-ar' *tr.v.* to discontinue.

des-co-ra-men'-to *m.* paleness.

des-co-ran'-te *adj.* bleaching.

des-co-rar' *tr.v.* to remove color, to modify color; *intr.v.* to turn pale.

des-cor'-do *m.* troubadour love poem in which poet laments unrequited love.

des-cor-tês *adj.* discourteous.

des-cor-te-si'-a *f.* discourtesy.

des-co-ser' *tr.v.* to rip out; to tear.

des-co-si'-do, *=a adj.* without connection; torn apart; desultory.

des-cré-di-to *m.* discredit; lack or loss of credit.

des-cre-mar' *tr.v.* to separate cream from milk.

des-cren'-ça *f.* disbelief.

des-cren'-te *adj.* incredulous, disbelieving.

des-crer' *tr.v.* to disbelieve.

des-cre-ver' *tr.v.* to describe, to trace.

des-cri-ção' *f.* description.

des-cri-mi-nar' *tr.v.* to absolve from guilt; to free from accusation of guilt.

des-cui-da'-do, *=a adj.* careless, indolent, lazy.

des-cui-dar' *tr.v.* to neglect; to be careless about; —*se refl.v.* to forget; to be negligent.

des-cui'-do *m.* carelessness, mistake.

des-cui-do'-so, *=a adj.* negligent, careless.

des-cul'-pa *f.* pardon, indulgence; absence of guilt.

des-cul-par' *tr.v.* to excuse; to pardon; —*se refl.v.* to ask to be excused, to present reasons why excuse be granted.

des-cul-pá-vel *adj.* excusable.

des'-de *prep.* from beginning of; since; *conj.* since.

des-dém *m.* disdain.

des-de-nhar' *tr.v.* to disdain.

des-de-nho'-so, *=a adj.* disdainful.

des-di'-ta *f.* bad luck, misfortune, infelicity.

des-di-to'-so, *=a adj.* unfortunate, unhappy.

des-do-brar' *tr.v.* to unfold; to develop.

des-do'-bre *m.* unfolding; development.

de-se-jar' *tr.v.* to desire, to want, to wish, to wish for.

de-se-já-vel *adj.* desirable.

de-se'-jo *m.* wish, desire.

de-se-jo'-so, *=a adj.* desirous.

de-sem-bar-ga-dor' *m.* judge of court of appeals.

de-sem-bar-car' *tr.v.* to unload, to remove from ship or train; *intr.v.* to land, to disembark.

de-sem-bar'-que *m.* disembarkment, landing.

de-sem-pe-nhar' *tr.v.* to redeem something in pawn; to free from debt.

de-sem-po-la-dei'-ra *f.* plasterer's trowel.

de-sem-pre-ga'-do, *=a adj.* unemployed.

de-sen-con-trar' *tr.v.* to cause not to

meet; —*se refl.v.* to not meet, to make no contact.

de-sen-cor-po-rar' *tr.v.* to diminish volume.

de-sen-fer-ru-jar' *tr.v.* to remove rust; (fig.) to limber up tongue by speaking.

de-se-nhar' *tr.v.* to draw, to design, to sketch.

de-se'-nho *m.* drawing; design; sketch; general outline of painting.

de-sen-la'-ce *m.* ending; solution; final event; unraveling, denouement.

de-se-no-do-ar' *tr.v.* to remove stains or spots.

de-sen-ro-lar' *tr.v.* to unroll, to open up, to extend.

de-sen-ten-der' *tr.v.* to misunderstand; to pretend misunderstanding.

de-sen-ten-di-men'-to *m.* misunderstanding.

de-sen-ter-rar' *tr.v.* to exhume.

de-sen-to-a'-do, *=a adj.* out of tune, off key.

de-sen-tu-pir' *tr.v.* to remove obstruction.

de-sen-vol-ver' *tr.v.* to unwrap; to clarify; to develop; to present in detail.

de-sen-vol-vi-men'-to *m.* development.

de-ser-ção' *f.* desertion.

de-ser-tar' *tr.v.*, *intr.v.* to desert.

de-ser'-to *m.* desert; **de-ser'-to**, *=a adj.* deserted, uninhabited.

de-ser-tor' *m.* deserter.

de-ses-pe-ra'-do, *=a adj.* desperate.

de-ses-pe-rar' *tr.v.* to remove hope, to cause desperation; to be greatly irritated; —*se refl.v.* to rave; to be furious; to be desperate.

des-fal-car' *tr.v.* to default, to defraud.

des-fa-le-cer' *intr.v.* to faint, to lose strength.

des-fa-le-ci'-do, *=a adj.* fainted, unconscious.

des-fa-le-ci-men'-to *m.* weakness; unconsciousness.

des-fal'-que *m.* default, diminution, shortage, deduction.

des-fa-vo-rá-vel *adj.* unfavorable.

des-fa-zer' *tr.v.* to undo, to destroy; —*se refl.v.* to sell, to dispose of; to get rid of.

des-fe-char' *tr.v.* to remove seal or fastening; to shoot or discharge arms; to set free.

des-fê-cho *m.* outcome, result, conclusion, denouement.

des-fi-gu-rar' *tr.v.* to disfigure; to adulterate.

des-fi-la-dei'-ro *m.* defile, cut in mountains.

des-fi-lar' *intr.v.* to march in ranks, to parade.

des-fi'-le *m.* parade, march.

des-fi-lhar' *tr.v.* to remove superfluous shoots or young plants; to separate part of bees from hive.

des-flo-ra-ção' *f.* defloration.

des-flo-rar' *tr.v.* to remove blossoms; to deflower.

des-flo-res-ci-men'-to *m.* fall of blossoms, fall of flowers; lack of flowers.

des-flo-ri'-do, *=a adj.* having no flowers, having shed flowers.

des-fo'-lha *f.* fall of leaves, removal of leaves.

des-fo-lhar' *tr.v.* to remove leaves.

des-fru-tar' *tr.v.* to enjoy, to make use of.

des-gas-tar' *tr.v.* to use or spend little by little; (pop.) to digest.

des-gos-tar' *tr.v.* to cause disgust; to cause to lose taste for something; *intr.v.* not to like.

des-gôs-to *m.* dislike; discontent; repugnance.

des-gos-to'-so, *=a adj.* discontented; displeasing; insipid.

des-gra'-ça *f.* misfortune, poverty, affliction; disgrace.

des-gra-ça'-do, *=a adj.* unhappy, miserable, poverty-stricken.

des-gra-çar' *tr.v.* to make miserable, to ruin.

des-ho-nes-ti-da'-de *f.* dishonesty.

des-ho-nes'-to, *=a adj.* dishonest.

des-hon'-ra *f.* dishonor.

des-hon-rar' *tr.v.* to dishonor.

des-hon-ro'-so, *=a adj.* dishonorable.

des-hu-ma'-no, *=a adj.* inhuman.

de-si-de-ra'-to *m.* desideratum.

de-sig-na-ção' *f.* designation.

de-sig-nar' *tr.v.* to designate.

de-síg-nio *m.* purpose, plan, design.

de-si-gual' *adj.* unequal.

de-si-gual-da'-de *f.* inequality.

de-si-lu-dir' *tr.v.* to disillusion.

de-si-lu-são' *f.* disillusionment.

de-sin-char' *tr.v.* to remove or decrease swelling; to deflate, to let the air out.

de-sin-fe-ção' *f.* disinfection.

de-sin-fe-cio-nar' *tr.v.* to disinfect.

de-sin-fe-tan'-te *m.* disinfectant.

de-sin-fe-tar' *tr.v.* to disinfect.

de-sin-te-gra-ção' *f.* disintegration.

de-sin-te-res-sa'-do, *=a adj.* disinterested, impartial.

de-sin-te-res-san'-te *adj.* uninteresting.

de-sin-te-res-sar' *tr.v.* to deprive of interest, to deprive of profit; —*se refl.v.* to lose interest.

de-sis-tên-cia *f.* desistance, ceasing.

de-sis-tir' *intr.v.* to desist.

des-le-al' *adj.* disloyal.

des-le-al-da'-de *f.* disloyalty.

des-lei'-xo *m.* negligence, carelessness, neglect.

des-li-gar' *tr.v.* to disconnect, to untie.

des-li-sar' *intr.v.* to glide, to slip along smoothly; to skid.

des-li'-se *m.* skidding; false step.

des-lo-ca-ção' *f.* dislocation.

des-lo-car' *tr.v.* to dislocate; to transfer, to change from one place to another.

des-lum-bran'-te *adj.* dazzling, sparkling.

des-lum-brar' *tr.v.* to dazzle; to beguile, to seduce; to confuse.

de-mag-ne-ti-zar' *tr.v.* to demagnetize.

des-mai-a'-do, *=a adj.* unconscious, colorless; faint.

des-mai-ar' *intr.v.* to faint, to lose consciousness; to turn pale.

des-mai'-o *m.* fainting, unconsciousness; paleness, dullness; discouragement.

des-ma-mar' *tr.v.* to wean.

des-man-char' *tr.v.* to undo, to take apart; to dissolve.

des-man'-cha=pra=ze'-res *m., f.* spoil-sport; troublesome guest; kill-joy.

des-man'-cho *m.* disorder; abortion.

des-man-te-lar' *tr.v.* to dismantle; to raze; to take apart.

des-me-di'-do, *=a adj.* unmeasured, measureless, vast.

des-mem-brar' *tr.v.* to dismember.

des-men-ti'-do *m.* contradiction.

des-men-tir' *tr.v.* to belie, to contradict; (Brazil) to dislocate.

des-mo-bi-li-zar' *tr.v.* to demobilize.

des-mo-ne-ti-zar' *tr.v.* to demonetize.

des-mon-ta'-da *f.* dismounting.

des-mon-tar' *tr.v., intr.v.* to dismount, to demount, to disassemble.

des-mon-tá-vel *adj.* demountable.

des-mon'-te *m.* dismounting; extraction (of ores).

des-mo-ra-li-zar' *tr.v.* to demoralize.

des-na-ci-o-na-li-zar' *tr.v.* to denationalize.

des-na-ta-dei'-ra *f.* cream separator.

des-na-tar' *tr.v.* to remove cream from milk.

des-na-tu-ral' *adj.* unnatural.

des-ne-ces-sá-rio, *=a adj.* unnecessary.

des-nor-te-a'-do, *=a adj.* lost; confused; astray; dizzy.

de-so-be-de-cer' *intr.v.* to disobey.

de-so-be-diên-cia *f.* disobedience.

de-so-be-dien'-te *adj.* disobedient.

de-so-la-ção' *f.* desolation.

de-so-la'-do, *=a adj.* desolate; inconsolable.

de-so-lar' *tr.v.* to desolate; to lay waste.

de-sor-dei'-ro *m.* disorderly, noisy person.

de-sor'-dem *f.* disorder.

de-sor-ga-ni-zar' *tr.v.* to disorganize.

de-so-ri-en-tar' *tr.v.* to disorientate.

des-pa-cha'-do, *=a adj.* prompt, quick.

des-pa-chan'-te *m.* shipping clerk; customhouse official.

des-pa-char' *tr.v.* to dispatch, to hasten.

des-pa'-cho *m.* dispatch; decision, sentence.

des-pe-da-ça-men'-to *m.* tearing to pieces, breaking to pieces; downfall.

des-pe-da-çar' *tr.v.* to break into pieces, to tear apart.

des-pe-di'-da *f.* leave-taking, farewell.

des-pe-dir' *tr.v.* to dismiss; *intr.v.* to bid farewell, to take leave; —*se refl.v.* to say goodby.

des-pe-ga'-do, *=a adj.* free, loose; indifferent.

des-pe-gar' *tr.v.* to unfasten, to loosen, to let go.

des-pei-tar' *tr.v.* to disrespect.

des-pei'-to *m.* disrespect, contempt, ange.

des-pei-to'-so, *=a adj.* disrespectful, malicious.

des-pe-jar' *tr.v.* to empty; to throw out, to clear.

des-pe'-jo *m.* act of emptying; rubbish.

des-pen-der' *tr.v.* to expend, to use, to spend.

des-pen'-sa *f.* pantry; store-room.

des-per-di-çar' *tr.v.* to waste, to squander.

des-per-ta-dor' *m.* alarm-clock.

des-per-tar' *tr.v.* to awaken, to stimulate, to provoke.

des-per'-to, *=a adj.* awake; vivacious.

des-pe'-sa *f.* expense, cost.

des-pi'-do, *=a adj.* unclothed, nude, naked; (fig.) free, exempt.

des-pir' *tr.v.* to undress; to remove covering.

des-po-jar' *tr.v.* to dispossess.

des-pô-jo *m.* robbing, plundering; *pl.* spoils, remains, leftovers, fragments, scraps.

des-pon-tar' *tr.v.* to break point off; *intr.v.* to begin to appear.

des-pon'-te *m.* cutting corn stalk off above the ear.

des-por'-te *m.* sport; recreation.

des-por-ti'-vo, *=a adj.* sporting, sport.

des-po-sa'-do, =a adj. married; engaged to be married.
des-po-sar' tr.v. to marry; to become engaged.
dés-po-ta m. despot.
des-pó-ti-co, =a adj. despotic.
des-po-tis'-mo m. despotism, tyranny.
des-po-vo-ar' tr.v. to depopulate.
des-pra-zer' intr.v. to displease; m. displeasure.
des-pre-gar' tr.v. to draw out (nails); to smooth out (pleats); to spread out (sails).
des-pre-zar' tr.v. to scorn, to despise, to reject.
des-pre-zí-vel adj. despicable.
des-prê-zo m. scorn, disdain; inconsiderateness.
des-pro-por-ção' f. disproportion.
des-pro-por-cio-na'-do, =a adj. disproportionate.
des-qua-li-fi-car' tr.v. to disqualify.
des-qui-ta-ção' f. divorce.
des-qui-tar' tr.v.; —=se refl.v. to divorce.
des-qui'-te m. divorce.
des-sa-bor' m. tastelessness.
des-sal-ga'-do, =a adj. lacking salt.
des-se-car' tr.v. to desiccate, to dry out.
des-si-me-tri'-a f. dissymmetry.
des-ta-ca-men'-to m. detachment.
des-ta-car' tr.v. to detach; to exceed, to stand out, to project.
des-ter-rar' tr.v. to banish, to exile.
des-têr-ro m. exile, banishment, deportation; place of exile.
des-te-mi'-do, =a adj. fearless, courageous, intrepid.
des-ti-la-ção' f. distillation.
des-ti-lar' tr.v. to distill.
des-ti-la-ri'-a f. distillery.
des-ti-na-ção' f. destination, purpose.
des-ti-nar' tr.v. to destine; to appoint.
des-ti-na-tá-rio m. consignee, person to whom something is destined or sent.
des-ti'-no m. destiny; destination.
des-ti-tui-ção' f. destitution; dismissal; poverty.
des-ti-tu-í-do,= a adj. dismissed; needy.
des-to-ca-dor' m. stump-puller.
des-to-ca-men'-to m. clearing stumps.
des-to-car' tr.v. to clear of stumps.
des'-tra f. right hand.
des-tre'-za f. dexterity.
des'-tro, =a adj. dexterous.
des-tro-na-men'-to m. dethronement.
des-tru-i-ção' f. destruction.
des-tru-ir' tr.v. to destroy.
des-tru-ti-bi-li-da'-de f. destructibility.
des-tru-tí-vel adj. destructible.
des-tru-tí'-vo, =a adj. destructive.
de-su-ni-ão' f. disunion.
de-su'-so m. disuse.
des-va-lo-ri-zar' tr.v. to devalue, to depreciate.
des-va-ne-ci'-do, =a adj. dispelled, dispersed, faded; vain, presumptuous.
des-va-ne-ci-men'-to m. fainting; vanity, pride.
des-van-ta'-gem f. disadvantage.
des-van-ta-jo'-so, =a adj. disadvantageous.
des-vão' m. attic; top floor of house; hiding-place.
des-vê-lo m. affectionate care; devotion; vigilance.
des-ven-dar' tr.v. to remove blindfold.
des-ven-to'-so, =a adj. serene; not windy.
des-ven-tu'-ra f. unhappiness; bad luck.

des-vi-ar' tr.v. to turn aside, to change position, to deflect, to switch; to detour.
des-ví'-o m. detour, siding; deviation.
de-ta-lhar' tr.v. to detail; to narrate with full particulars.
de-ta'-lhe m. detail.
de-ten-ção' f. detention.
de-ter' tr.v., intr.v. to detain; to cause to cease; to retain in possession; to halt; to stop.
de-te-rio-ra-ção' f. deterioration.
de-ter-mi-na-ção' f. determination.
de-ter-mi-nar' tr.v. to determine.
de-tes-tar' tr.v. to detest.
de-tes-tá-vel adj. detestable.
de-to-na-ção' f. detonation.
de-to-nar' intr.v. to explode.
de-tra-ção' f. detraction.
de-tra-ir' tr.v. to detract.
de-trás adv. behind; afterward.
de-tri-men'-to m. detriment.
de-tri'-to m. detritus; residual deposit.
Deus' m. God.
deu'-sa f. goddess.
de-va-gar' adv. slowly; without haste.
de-vas-sa'-do, =a adj. accessible, open to view.
de-vas-sar' tr.v. to trespass upon; to divulge, to spread abroad; to penetrate.
de-vas'-so, =a adj. dissolute, licentious.
de-vas-ta-ção' f. devastation.
de-vas-tar' tr.v. to devastate.
de-ven'-tre m. intestines of animals.
de-ve-dor' m. debtor.
de-ver' tr.v. to owe; must, should, ought to, to have to, to be obliged to, to be expected to; m. duty.
de-ví'-do, =a adj. due, just; de-ví'-do m. debt.
de-ve'-ras adv. in high degree; truly, really.
de-vo-ção' f. devotion.
de-vo-lu-ção' f. restoration, return.
de-vo-lu'-to, =a adj. unoccupied; restored.
de-vol-ver' tr.v. to return, to give back.
de-vo-rar' tr.v. to devour.
de-vo-ta-ção' f. dedication, devotion.
de-vo-ta'-do, =a adj. devoted, devout.
de-vo-tar' tr.v. to devote, to dedicate.
de-vo'-to, =a adj. devout, consecrated; de-vo'-to m. devotee.
dex-tri'-na f. dextrin.
dez' m. ten.
de-zem'-bro m. December.
de-ze'-na f. group of ten.
di'-a m. day, day-light; day-time; twenty-four hours, time from sun-rise to sun-rise; — de semena week-day; — útil work-day; — santo holy day; — de anos birth-day; — de juizo Judgment Day; — feriado holiday; — a — day by day, every day; hoje em — now-adays.
di-a-bé'-tes f. diabetes.
di-a'-bo m. devil.
di-a-bó-li-co, =a adj. diabolic.
di-a-cáus-ti-co m. diacaustic curve or surface.
di-a-co-na'-to m. deaconship.
di-a-co-ni'-a f. deaconry, deaconship.
di-a-co-ni'-sa f. deaconess.
di-á-co-no m. deacon.
di-a-crí-ti-co, =a adj. diacritical.
di-a-de'-ma m. diadem.
di-á-fa-no, =a adj. diaphanous.
di-a-fil'-me m. positive film.
di-a-frag'-ma m. diaphragm.

di-ag-no'-se *f.* di-ag-nós-ti-co *m.* diagnosis.
di-a-go-nal' *m.*, *adj.* diagonal.
di-a-gra'-ma *m.* diagram.
di-a-le'-to *m.* dialect.
di-al' *adj.* daily.
di-a-lo-gar' *tr.v.*, *intr.v.* to write, converse, or take part in dialogue.
di-á-lo-go *m.* dialogue.
di-a-mag-né-ti-co, =a *adj.* diamagnetic.
di-a-man'-te *m.* diamond.
di-a-man-tí-fe-ro, =a *adj.* diamond-bearing.
di-â-me-tro *m.* diameter.
di-an'-te *adv.* in front; firstly; ir por — to continue.
di-an-tei'-ra *f.* front, vanguard.
di-an-tei'-ro, =a *adj.* front, in front, first.
di-á-ria *f.* daily receipts or expenses; wage per day.
di-á-rio, =a *adj.* daily; *m.* daily newspaper.
di-a-ris'-ta *m.* editor of daily paper; day worker.
di-ar-réi-a *f.* diarrhea.
di-ás-to-le *m.* diastole.
di-as-tó-li-co, =a *adj.* diastolic.
di-a-ter-mi'-a *f.* diathermy.
di-a-tri'-be *f.* diatribe.
di-ção' *f.* diction.
di-cé-fa-lo, =a *adj.* two-headed.
di-ci-o-ná-rio *m.* dictionary.
di-dá-ti-ca *f.* didactics.
di-e'-dro *m.*, *adj.* dihedral.
di-e-lé-tri-co *m.* dielectric.
di-e'-ta *f.* diet.
di-e-té-ti-ca *f.* dietetics.
di-e-té-ti-co, =a *adj.* dietetic.
di-fa-ma-ção' *f.* defamation.
di-fa-mar' *tr.v.* to defame.
di-fa-ma-tó-rio, =a *adj.* defamatory.
di-fe-ren'-ça *f.* difference.
di-fe-ren'-te *adj.* different.
di-fe-ren-cia-ção' *f.* differentiation.
di-fe-ren-ci-al' *adj.*, *f.* differential.
di-fe-ren-ci-ar' *tr.v.* to differentiate.
di-fe-rir' *tr.v.* to defer; *intr.v.* to be different; to disagree.
di-fí-cil *adj.* difficult, hard.
di-fi-cí-li-mo, =a *adj.* very difficult.
di-fi-cul-da'-de *f.* difficulty.
di-fi-cul-tar' *tr.v.* to make difficult.
di-fi-dên-cia *f.* diffidence.
di-fi-den'-te *adj.* diffident.
di-fra-ção' *f.* diffraction.
dif-te-ri'-a *f.* diphtheria.
di-fun-dir' *tr.v.* to diffuse; to spread, to scatter, to divulge.
di-fu-são' *f.* diffusion.
di-fu'-so, =a *adj.* diffuse, scattered.
di-ge-rir' *tr.v.*, *intr.v.* to digest.
di-ge-rí-vel *adj.* digestible.
di-ges-tão' *f.* digestion.
di-ges'-to *m.* digest, abstract.
di-gi-tal' *adj.* digital; *f.* digitalis.
di-gi-ta-li'-na *f.* digitalin.
di-gi-to *m.* digit.
dig-nar'=se *refl.v.* to have the kindness to; to condescend to; to do the favor of.
dig-ni-fi-car' *tr.v.* to dignify.
dig-ni-da'-de *f.* dignity.
dig-ni-tá-rio *m.* dignitary.
dig'-no, =a *adj.* worthy.
di-gres-são' *f.* digression.
di-la-ta-ção' *f.* dilatation, expansion.
di-la-tar' *tr.v.* to dilate, to expand; to delay, to postpone.

di-la-tá-vel *adj.* dilatable.
di-la-ção' *f.* dilation; delay; postponement.
di-la-tó-rio, =a *adj.* dilatory.
di-le'-ma *m.* dilemma.
di-le-tan'-te *m.*, *adj.* dilettante.
di-le-ção' *f.* special affection; choice.
di-le'-to, =a *adj.* beloved, favorite.
di-li-gên-cia *f.* diligence; stage-coach.
di-lu-en'-te *adj.* diluting.
di-lu-i-ção' *f.* dilution.
di-lu-ir' *tr.v.* to dilute, to dissolve.
di-lu-vial' *adj.* diluvial.
di-lú-vio *m.* deluge; flood.
di-men-são' *f.* dimension.
di-mi-nui-ção' *f.* diminution, decrease.
di-mi-nu-ir' *tr.v.*, *intr.v.* to diminish; to decrease.
di-mi-nu-ti'-vo, =a *adj.* diminutive.
di-mi-nu'-to, =a *adj.* diminutive.
di-nâ-mi-ca *f.* dynamics.
di-na-mi-tar' *tr.v.* to dynamite.
di-na-mi'-te *f.* dynamite.
di-na-mo *m.* dynamo.
di-na-mô-me-tro *m.* dynamometer.
di'-no *m.* dyne.
di-nas-ti'-a *f.* dynasty.
di-nás-ti-co, =a *adj.* dynastic.
di-nhei-ra'-ma *f.* large amount of money.
di-nhei'-ro *m.* money; — de São Paulo Peter's pence.
di-nhei-ro'-so, =a *adj.* moneyed, wealthy.
di-no-sau'-ro *m.* dinosaur.
din-tel' *m.* lintel.
di-o-ce-sa'-no, =a *adj.* diocesan.
di-o-ce'-se *f.* diocese.
di-plo'-ma *m.* diploma.
di-plo-ma-ci'-a *f.* diplomacy.
di-plo-ma'-do, =a *adj.* graduated, possessing diploma.
di-plo-ma'-ta *m.* diplomat.
di-plo-má-ti-co, =a *adj.* diplomatic.
dip-so-ma-ni'-a *f.* dipsomania.
di'-que *m.* dike; (fig.) obstacle.
di-re-ção' *f.* direction; administration; superintendency; steering.
di-rei'-ta *f.* right hand, right side.
di-rei'-to, =a *adj.* right, honest, upright, just, straight; di-rei'-to *m.* law, jurisprudence; right side; *adv.* straight ahead.
di-re'-to, =a *adj.* straight, direct.
di-re-tor' *m.* director.
di-re-to-ri'-a *f.* board of directors.
di-ri-gen'-te *adj.* directing, supervising.
di-ri-gir' *tr.v.* to direct, to administer, to guide, to steer; —=se to go, to betake oneself.
di-ri-gí-vel *m.* dirigible.
di-ri-mir' *tr.v.* to annul, to redeem.
di-rup-ção' *f.* disruption.
di-rup-ti'-vo, =a *adj.* disruptive.
dis-cen'-te *adj.* relative to students; learning or being taught.
dis-cer-ni-men'-to *m.* discernment.
dis-cer-nir' *tr.v.* to discern.
dis-ci-pli'-na *f.* discipline.
dis-ci-pli-nar' *tr.v.* to discipline.
dis-cí-pu-la *f.*=o *m.* student body.
dis-cí-pu-lo *m.* pupil, student; disciple.
dis'-co *m.* discus, disk; record; dial on automatic telephones.
dis-có-bu-lo *m.* discobolus.
dis-cor-dân-cia *f.* discordance, disagreement; being out of tune.
dis-cor-dan'-te *adj.* discordant, out of tune.

dis-cor-dar' *intr.v.* to disagree; to be out of tune.
dis-cór-dia *f.* discord, strife.
dis-cre-pân-cia *f.* discrepancy.
dis-cre-pan'-te *adj.* disagreeing.
dis-cre'-to, *=a adj.* discreet.
dis-cri-ção' *f.* discretion, reserve.
dis-cri-cio-ná-rio, *=a adj.* discretionary.
dis-cri-mi-na-ção' *f.* discrimination.
dis-cri-mi-nar' *tr.v.* to discriminate.
dis-cur-sar' *tr.v.* to expound; *intr.v.* to discourse.
dis-cur'-so *m.* discourse, speech.
dis-cus-são' *f.* discussion.
dis-cu-tir' *tr.v.* to discuss.
di-sen-te-ri'-a *f.* dysentery.
dis-far-çar' *tr.v.* to disguise, to camouflage.
dis-far'-ce *m.* disguise.
dis-jun-ção' *f.* disjunction.
dis-jun-ti'-vo, *=a adj.* disjunctive.
dís-par *adj.* unequal, uneven, unlike.
dis-pa-ra'-da *f.* stampede, running away.
dis-pa-rar' *tr.v.* to shoot, to discharge, to let go.
dis-pa-ri-da'-de *f.* disparity.
dis-pên-dio *m.* consumption; cost; expense.
dis-pen-di-o'-so, *=a adj.* costly, expensive.
dis-pen'-sa *f.* exemption.
dis-pen-sar' *tr.v.* to exempt, to excuse.
dis-pen-sa-tá-rio *m.* one who grants exemption.
dis-pen-sa-tó-rio *m.* pharmaceutical laboratory.
dis-pen-sá-rio *m.* dispensary, clinic.
dis-pep-si'-a *f.* dyspepsia.
dis-pép-ti-co, *=a adj.* dyspeptic.
dis-per-são' *f.* dispersal, dispersion.
dis-per-sar' *tr.v.* to disperse.
dis-per-si'-vo, *=a adj.* dispersive.
dis-po-ni-bi-li-da'-de *f.* availability.
dis-po-ní-vel *adj.* available.
dis-por' *tr.v.* to arrange, to plan, to prepare, to place, to provide; *intr.v.* to dispose, to have authority, to have power to; —*=se refl.v.* to be ready, to be disposed.
dis-po-si-ção' *f.* disposition, preparation, provision.
dis-pu'-te *f.* dispute.
dis-pu-tan'-te *m.* disputant.
dis-pu-tar' *tr.v.* to contest, to dispute.
dis-pu-ta-ti'-vo, *=a adj.* disputatious.
dis-se-ca-ção' *f.* dissection.
dis-se-car' *tr.v.* to dissect.
dis-se-me-lhan'-ça *f.* dissimilarity.
dis-se-mi-nar' *tr.v.* to disseminate.
dis-ser-ta-ção' *f.* dissertation.
dis-sen-ção' *f.* dissention.
dis-sen-tir' *intr.v.* to dissent.
dis-si-dên-cia *f.* dissidence.
dis-si-den'-te *adj.* dissident.
dis-si-mu-lar' *tr.v.* to dissemble; to hide.
dis-si-pa-ção' *f.* dissipation.
dis-si-par' *tr.v., intr.v.* to dissipate.
dis-so-ci-ar' *tr.v.* to dissociate.
dis-so-lu-ção' *f.* dissolution.
dis-so-lu'-to, *=a adj.* dissolute.
dis-sol-ven'-te *adj., m.* dissolvent.
dis-sol-ver' *tr.v.* to dissolve.
dis-so-nân-cia *f.* dissonance.
dis-sua-dir' *tr.v.* to dissuade.
dis-tân-cia *f.* distance.
dis-tan'-te *adj.* distant.
dis-tar' *intr.v.* to be distant, to be away.
dis-ten-der' *tr.v.* to distend.
dis-ten-são' *f.* distension.

dis-tin-guir' *tr.v.* to distinguish; —*=se refl.v.* to stand out, to distinguish oneself.
dis-tin-ção' *f.* distinction.
dis-tin-ti'-vo, *=a adj.* distinctive.
dis-tin'-to, *=a adj.* distinct, marked; different; distinguished, eminent.
dis-tra-ção' *f.* distraction.
dis-tra-i-men'-to *m.* distraction.
dis-tra-ir' *tr.v.* to distract.
dis-tri-bui-ção' *f.* distribution.
dis-tri-bu-ir' *tr.v.* to distribute.
dis-tri-tal' *adj.* relative to a district.
dis-tri'-to *m.* district.
di-ta-dor' *m.* dictator.
di-ta'-me *m.* saying, proverb; dictate.
di-tar' *tr.v.* to dictate; to suggest, to inspire.
di-ta-to-ri-al' *adj.* dictatorial.
di'-to *m.* quotation, dictum, saying.
di-ton'-go *m.* diphthong.
di-to'-so, *=a adj.* fortunate, happy, prosperous.
di-ur-nal' *adj.* diurnal, day (as opposed to night).
dí'-va *f.* diva.
di-vã *f.* couch, divan.
di-ver-gên-cia *f.* divergence.
di-ver-gen'-te *adj.* divergent.
di-ver-gir' *intr.v.* to diverge.
di-ver-si-da'-de *f.* diversity.
di-ver'-so, *=a adj.* different, several, diverse.
di-ver-ti'-do, *=a adj.* gay, amusing; distracted; restful.
di-ver-ti-men'-to *m.* entertainment, diversion, amusement.
di-ver-tir' *tr.v.* to divert, to amuse; —*=se refl.v.* to enjoy oneself.
dí-vi-da *f.* debt.
di-vi-den'-do *m.* dividend.
di-vi-dir' *tr.v.* to divide.
di-vi-na-ção' *f.* divination.
di-vin-da'-de *f.* divinity.
di-vi'-no, *=a adj.* divine.
di-vi'-sa *f.* mark; dividing sign; emblem; motto.
di-vi-são' *f.* division; room.
di-vi-sí-vel *adj.* divisible.
di-vi-sor' *m.* divisor.
di-vór-cio *m.* divorce.
di-vul-gar' *tr.v.* to divulge, to make public.
di-vul-são' *f.* tearing away, tearing apart.
di-zer' *tr.v.* to say, to tell, to speak; to say prayer; to recite; to read; to indicate; to affirm; *m.* style of expression; style.
dí-zi-ma *f.* tithe.
di-zi-mar' *tr.v.* to decimate.
di-zi-mei'-ro *m.* tithe collector.
dí-zi-mo *m.* tenth, tenth part.
dó *m.* do (music); compassion, lament, pity; sadness; mourning.
do-a-ção' *f.* donation; document legalizing gift.
do-ar' *tr.v.* to donate.
do-ba-dou'-ra *f.* reel; (fig.) person busy coming and going.
do-bar' *tr.v.* to reel, to wind into skein.
do'-bra *f.* fold, tuck.
do-bra-dei'-ra *f.* machine to fold books, machine to fold newspapers.
do-bra-di'-ça *f.* hinge.
do-bra-di'-ço, *=a adj.* easily bent, easily folded; collapsible.
do-bra'-do, *=a adj.* duplicated; folded over.

do-brar' *tr.v.* to duplicate; to fold over; to toll.

dô-bro *m.* double.

do'-ca *f.* dock, wharf.

do'-ce *adj.* sweet taste; gentle, affable; benign; *m.* candy; dessert; preserves; jam, jelly.

do-cei'-ro, *=a m., f.* person who makes or sells sweets.

do-çu'-ra *f.* sweetness, gentleness.

do-cên-cia *f.* teaching.

do-cen'-te *adj.* professorial, teaching.

dó-cil *adj.* docile.

do-ci-li-da'-de *f.* docility.

do-cu-men-tar' *tr.v.* to document.

do-cu-men'-to *m.* document.

do-en'-ça *f.* illness.

do-en'-te *adj.* sick, weak, sickly; *m., f.* sick person, patient.

do-en-ti'-o, *=a adj.* sickly.

do-er' *intr.v.* to feel pain; to be sick

dog'-ma *m.* dogma.

dog-má-ti-co, *=a adj.* dogmatic.

do'-gue *m.* pug-dog.

doi-di'-ce *f.* foolishness; insanity.

doi'-do, *=a adj.* foolish; insane, demented, crazy; enthusiastic.

do-í-do, *=a adj.* painful, suffering pain.

dois' *adj.* two; — a — two by two.

dól-man *m.* dolman.

do-lo-mi'-ta *f.* dolomite.

do-lo-ri'-do, *=a adj.* painful, sorrowful, dolorous.

do-lo-ro'-so, *=a adj.* painful, sorrowful.

dom' *m.* natural gift, talent; privilege; sir (honorary title).

do-mes-ti-car' *tr.v.* to domesticate, to tame.

do-més-ti-co, *=a adj.* domestic.

do-mi-ci-li-ar' *tr.v.* to provide with domicile; —=se *refl.v.* to establish one's residence.

do-mi-cí-lio *m.* domicile, residence.

do-mi-na-ção' *f.* domination.

do-mi-nan'-te *adj.* dominant.

do-mi-nar' *tr.v.* to dominate.

do-min'-go *m.* Sunday; — gordo Sunday preceding Ash Wednesday.

do-min-guei'-ro, *=a adj.* relative to Sunday.

do-mi-ni-cal' *adj.* pertaining to Sunday.

Do-mi-ni-ca'-no *m.* Dominican.

do-mí-nio *m.* dominion, domain.

do'-mo *m.* dome; (fig.) church, cathedral.

do'-na *f.* owner; Madam, Miss (title, preceding proper name, used in addressing women).

do-na-tá-rio *m.* donee.

do-na-ti'-vo *m.* donation; dole.

do-na'-to *m.* lay-brother.

don'-de *adv.* from where, from what place (contraction of *prep.* de with *adv.* onde).

do'-no *m.* owner; head of house.

dor' *f.* pain; suffering; affliction; remorse.

do-ri'-do, *=a adj.* hurt, sore; grieved.

dor-men'-te *adj.* dormant; sleeping; *m.* sleeper, railroad tie.

dor-mi'-da *f.* sleep; sleeping place.

dor-mir' *intr.v.* to sleep; to be dead, to be latent.

dor-mi-ti'-vo, *=a adj.* sleep-provoking, narcotic.

dor-mi-tó-rio *m.* dormitory.

dor'-na *f.* large open hogshead or vat in which to trample grapes for wine.

dor-nei'-ra *f.* stationary stone in a grist mill.

dor-sal' *adj.* dorsal.

dor'-so *m.* back.

do-sa'-gem *f.* dosage, proportioning.

do-sar' *tr.v.* to dose, to mix in the proper proportion.

do'-se *f.* dose, amount.

do-ta-ção' *f.* endowment.

do-tar' *tr.v.* to give as a dowry, to give as a donation; to endow.

do'-te *m.* dowry; endowment; property given a convent when a nun takes the veil; natural gift, talent.

dou-ra'-do, *=a adj.* gilded; covered with gold leaf; golden-colored.

dou-ra-du'-ra *f.* gilding, applying gold leaf; gold leaf; object ornamented with gold leaf.

dou-rar' *tr.v.* to cover with gold leaf; to gild; (fig.) to paint in glowing colors.

dous' *adj.* two.

dou'-to, *=a adj.* scholarly, erudite, learned.

dou-tor', *=a m., f.* doctor.

dou-to-ra'-ço *m.* (pop.) man who poses as a person of great learning.

dou-to-ra'-do *m.* holder of doctor's degree; doctorate.

dou-to-ral' *adj.* doctoral.

dou-to-ra-men'-to *m.* conferring of doctor's degree.

dou-to-ran'-do *m.* candidate for doctor's degree.

dou-to-rar' *tr.v.* to confer the doctor's degree on; —=se *refl.v.* to receive the doctor's degree.

dou-tri'-na *f.* doctrine.

dou-tri-nal' *adj.* doctrinal.

dou-tri-nar' *tr.v.* to teach, to indoctrinate.

do'-ze *m.* twelve.

dra'-ga *f.* dredge.

dra-ga'-gem *f.* dredging.

dra-gão' *m.* dragon.

dra-gar' *tr.v.* to deepen, to dredge, to clear with a dredge.

dra-go'-na *f.* epaulet.

drai-na'-gem *f.* drainage.

drai-nar' *tr.v.* to drain.

drai'-no *m.* drain pipe; culvert.

dra'-ma *m.* drama.

dra-ma-lhão' *m.* poor drama, melodrama.

dra-má-ti-co, *=a adj.* dramatic.

dra-ma-ti-zar' *tr.v.* to dramatize.

dro'-ga *f.* drug.

dro-ga-ri'-a *f.* drug-store, pharmacy.

dro-gue'-te *m.* drugget.

dro-guis'-ta *m.* druggist, pharmacist.

dro-me-dá-rio *m.* dromedary.

dru-í-da *m.* druid.

dru-í-di-co, *=a adj.* druidic.

dru'-pa *f.* drupe.

du-al' *adj.* dual.

du-a-li-da'-de *f.* duality.

du-a-lis'-mo *m.* dualism.

du-a-lís-ti-co, *=a adj.* dualistic.

du'-as feminine form of dois two.

dú-bio, *=a adj.* dubious.

du-bi-tá-vel *adj.* dubious, questionable.

du-ca'-do *m.* duchy, dukedom; ducat (coin).

du-cal' *adj.* ducal.

du-cen-té-si-mo, *=a adj.* two hundredth.

du'-cha *f.* shower-bath, douche.

dúc-til *adj.* ductile.

duc-ti-li-da'-de *f.* ductility.

duc'-to *m.* duct.

du-e-lis'-ta *m.* duelist.

du-e'-lo *m.* duel.

du-e'-to m. duet.
dul-ci-fi-ca-ção' f. dulcification, sweetening.
dul-ci-fi-car' tr.v. to dulcify, to sweeten.
dul-ço-ro'-so, =a adj. dulcet.
du'-na f. dune.
du'-o m. duet.
du-o-de-ci-mal' adj. duodecimal, twelfth.
du-o-de-nal' adj. duodenal.
du-o-de-ni'-te f. duodenitis.
du-o-de'-no m. duodenum.
du-pli-ca-ção' f. duplication.
du-pli-ca'-do, =a adj. duplicate, doubled; m. duplicate, copy.
du-pli-ca'-ta f. carbon copy.
dú-pli-ce adj. duplex.
du-pli-ci-da'-de f. duplicity, double dealing.
du'-plo, =a adj. double.

du'-que m. duke.
du-que'-sa f. duchess.
du-ra-bi-li-da'-de f. durability.
du-ra-ção' f. duration.
du-ra-dou'-ro, =a adj. durable, enduring, lasting.
du-ra-má-ter f. dura mater.
du-ran'-te prep. during.
du-rar' intr.v. to last; to endure, to not wear out; to live.
du-rá-vel adj. durable, enduring.
du-re'-za f. hardness; cruelty.
du'-ro, =a adj. hard; arduous; harsh; implacable.
dú-vi-da f. doubt.
du-vi-dar' tr.v., intr.v. to doubt.
du-vi-do'-so, =a adj. doubtful.
du-zen'-tos, =as adj. two hundred.
dú-zi-a f. dozen.

E

See page 12—GUIDE TO REFORMED SPELLING used in this Dictionary

E, e m. E, e; fifth letter of the alphabet; conj. and.
é-ba-no m. ebony.
e-bo-ni'-te f. ebonite.
e-bo-rá-rio m. ivory worker.
e-bó-reo, =a adj. made of ivory; ivory-colored.
e-bri-á-ti-co, =a adj. intoxicating.
e-bri-e-da'-de f. intoxication, drunkenness; exaltation.
é-brio m. drunk.
e-bu-li-ção' f. boiling, ebulition; effervescence; excitement.
e-búr-ne-o, =a adj. of ivory; white and smooth like ivory.
e-cle-siás-ti-co m. ecclesiastic; adj. ecclesiastical.
e-clip-sar' tr.v. to eclipse; —se refl.v. to disappear.
e-clip'-se m. eclipse.
e-clíp-ti-ca f. ecliptic.
e-clíp-ti-co, =a adj. ecliptic.
é-clo-ga f. eclogue.
e'-co m. echo.
e-co-an'-te adj. echoing.
e-co-ar' tr.v., intr.v. to echo.
e-co-no-mi'-a f. economy, economics.
e-co-nô-mi-co, =a adj. economic, economical.
e-co-no-mis'-ta m. economist.
e-co-no-mi-zar' tr.v. to save, to economize.
ec-ti-po-gra-fi'-a f. Braille printing.
ec-to-plas'-ma m. ectoplasm.
e-cu-mê-ni-co, =a adj. ecumenical.
ec-ze'-ma m. eczema.
ec-ze-ma-to'-so, =a adj. eczematous.
e-da-ci-da'-de f. voracity, appetite.
e-daz' adj. voracious.
é-den m. Eden.
e-dê-ni-co, =a adj. relative to Eden.
e-di-ção' f. edition; — prin'-ceps first edition.
e-di-fi-ca-ção' f. edification; building.
e-di-fi-can'-te adj. edifying.
e-di-fi-car' tr.v. to build, to construct, to set up, to edify.
e-di-fí-cio m. building, edifice.
e-di-tal' m. public notice.
e-di-tar' tr.v. to edit, to publish.
é-di-to m. judicial order.

e-di'-to m. edict.
e-di-tor' m. editor, publisher.
e-di-to-ri-al' m. editorial.
e-dre-dão' m. eiderdown coverlet.
e-du-ca-ção' f. rearing, breeding, education, training.
e-du-ca-cio-nal' adj. educational.
e-du-ca-dor', =a m., f. educator.
e-du-can-dá-rio m. educational institution.
e-du-can'-do m. student.
e-du-car' tr.v. to rear, to bring up, to train, to educate.
e-du-ca-ti'-vo, =a adj. educational.
e-du-cá-vel adj. educable, docile.
é-du-lo, =a adj. edible.
e-fei'-to m. effect.
e-fe-me-ri-da'-de f. quality of being short-lived.
e-fê-me-ro, =a adj. ephemeral.
e-fe-mi-na-ção' f. effeminacy.
e-fe-mi-na'-do, =a adj. effeminate.
e-fe-mi-nar' tr.v. to effeminate; to weaken, to degenerate.
e-fer-ves-cên-cia f. effervescence.
e-fer-ves-cen'-te adj. effervescent.
e-fe-ti-var' tr.v. to bring about, to realize.
e-fe-ti-vi-da'-de f. effectiveness, reality.
e-fe-ti'-vo, =a adj. effective, true, real.
e-fe-tu-a-ção' f. accomplishment, realization.
e-fe-tu-ar' tr.v. to carry out, to accomplish.
e-fe-tu-o'-so, =a adj. effectual, efficacious.
e-fi-cá-cia f. efficacy.
e-fi-caz' adj. efficacious.
e-fi-ci-ên-cia f. efficiency.
e-fi-ci-en'-te adj. efficient.
e-fí-gie f. effigy.
e-flu-ên-cia f. irradiation, emanation.
e-flu-en'-te adj. emanating.
e-flú-vio m. effluvium.
e-fun-dir' tr.v. to effuse.
e-fu-são' f. effusion.
e'-go m. ego.
e-go-cên-tri-co, =a adj. egocentric.
e-go-ís-mo m. egoism.
e-go-ís-ta m. egoist.

e-go-tis'-mo m. egotism.
e-go-tis'-ta m. egotist.
e-gré-gio, ₌a adj. illustrious, distinguished.
e-gres-são' f. departure.
e-gres'-so m. former monk.
e-gre'-ta f. egrẹt, aigrette.
eis' adv. here is, here are.
é-gua f. mare.
ei'-ra f. smooth, hard ground used as threshing-floor.
ei-ra'-da f. grain handled at one threshing.
ei-ra'-do m. terrace, open porch.
ei'-va f. flaw; crack; rotten spot (fruit).
ei-var' tr.v. to contaminate, to infect; —₌se to begin to deteriorate, to become rotten.
ei'-xo m. axis; axle; rivet; diameter; Ei'-xo m. (polit.) Axis.
e-ja-cu-la-ção' f. ejaculation.
e-ja-cu-lar' tr.v. to ejaculate.
e-ja-cu-la-tó-rio, ₌a adj. ejaculatory.
e-je-ção' f. ejection.
e'-la she, it (pers.pron. fem. third person, sing.); ê-le he, it (pers.pron. masc. third person, sing.).
e-la-bo-ra-ção' f. elaboration.
e-la-bo-rar' tr.v. to elaborate.
e-las-ti-ci-da'-de f. elasticity.
e-lás-ti-co, ₌a adj. elastic; e-lás-ti-co m. elastic.
ê-le see e'-la.
e-le-fan'-te m. elephant.
e-le-fan-ti'-a f. elephantiasis.
e-le-gân-cia f. elegance.
e-le-gan'-te adj. elegant.
e-le-gen'-do m. candidate.
e-le-ger' tr.v. to elect, to choose.
e-le-gi-bi-li-da'-de f. eligibility.
e-le-gí-vel adj. eligible.
e-lei-ção' f. election.
e-lei'-to, ₌a adj. elected, chosen.
e-lei-tor' m. elector.
e-lei-to-ra'-do m. electorate.
e-lei-to-ral' adj. electoral.
e-le-men-tal' adj. elementary, elemental.
e-le-men-tar' adj. elementary, simple, rudimentary.
e-le-men-tá-rio, ₌a adj. elementary, elemental.
e-le-men'-to m. element.
e-lei'tv-o, ₌a adj. elective.
e-le-tri-ci-da'-de f. electricity.
e-le-tri-cis'-ta m. electrician.
e-lé-tri-co, ₌a adj. electric.
e-le-tri-fi-ca-ção' f. electrification.
e-le-tri-fi-car' tr.v. to electrify.
e-le-triz' f. woman elector.
e-le-tro-cu-tar' tr.v. to electrocute.
e-le-tro-di-nâ-mi-ca f. electro-dynamics.
e-le-tró-dio m. electrode.
e-le-tro'-do m. electrode.
e-le-tro₌i-mã' m. electro-magnet.
e-le-tró-li-se f. electrolysis.
e-le-tró-li-to m. electrolyte.
e-lé-tron m. electron.
e-le-tro-stá-ti-ca f. electrostatics.
e-le-tro-te-ra-pi'-a f. electro-therapy.
e-le-tro-ti-pi'-a f. electrotype.
e-le-va-ção' f. elevation.
e-le-var' tr.v. to elevate.
e-le-va-dor' m., elevator; adj. elevating.
e-li-ci-ar' tr.v. to elicit.
e-li-dir' tr.v. to elide.
e-li-mi-nar' tr.v. to eliminate.
e-li-mi-na-tó-rio, ₌a adj. eliminating.

e-lip'-se f. ellipse.
e-líp-ti-co, ₌a adj. elliptic.
e-li-são' f. elision.
e-li'-te f. elite.
e-li-xir' m. elixir.
e'-lo m. link in chain; tendril.
e-lo-cu-ção' f. elocution.
e-lo-gi-ar' tr.v. eulogize.
e-lo-gi'-o m. eulogy.
e-lon-ga-ção' f. elongation.
e-lo-quên-cia f. eloquence.
e-lo-quen'-te adj. eloquent.
e-lu-ci-dar' tr.v. to elucidate.
e-lu-ci-dá-rio m. commentary, compendium, dictionary.
e-lu-dir' tr.v. to elude.
em prep. in, on, at, into.
e-ma-cia-ção' f. emaciation.
e-ma-ci-ar' tr.v., intr.v. to emaciate.
e-ma-gre-cer' tr.v. to make thin; intr.v. to become thin, to lose flesh; to decrease in value; —₌se refl.v. to become thin, to lose flesh.
e-ma-na-ção' f. emanation.
e-ma-nar' intr.v. to emanate.
e-man-ci-par' tr.v. to emancipate; to free from parental ties; —₌se refl.v. to become free.
e-mas-cu-lar' tr.v. to emasculate.
em-bai-xa'-da f. embassy.
em-bai-xa-dor' m. ambassador.
em-bai-xa-triz' f. ambassadress.
em-ba-la-dei'-ra f. rocker (of chair or cradle).
em-ba-la'-gem f. crating, boxing, packing.
em-ba-lar' tr.v. to rock, to sing to sleep; to wrap up, to pack, to crate, to tie in bundles.
em-ba'-lo m. rocking, swinging.
em-bal-sa-mar' tr.v. to embalm; to perfume.
em-ba-ra-çar' tr.v. to embarrass; to disturb.
em-ba-ra'-ço m. embarrassment; difficulty; pregnancy.
em-ba-ra-ço'-so, ₌a adj. embarrassing.
em-bar-be-cer' intr.v. to grow a beard.
em-bar-car' intr.v. to embark, to board.
em-bar-ca-ção' f. embarkation; ship.
em-bar-ca-dou'-ro m. dock, wharf.
em-bar-ca-men'-to m. embarkment.
em-bar-gar' tr.v. to disturb, to hinder, to put an embargo on.
em-bar'-go m. obstacle, disturbance; embargo; sem — nevertheless.
em-bar'-que m. embarkment.
em-bar-ra-men'-to m. clay daubed between sticks and poles of mud hut.
em-ba'-te m. collision; blow; resistance, brunt.
em-be-ber' tr.v. to imbibe; to soak in; to absorb.
em-be-bi'-do, ₌a adj. imbued with; soaked.
em-be-le-cer' tr.v. to beautify, to embellish.
em-bi-ca'-do, ₌a adj. beak-shaped; ending in a beak.
em-bir-rar' intr.v. to be stubborn, obstinate; to have aversion.
em-ble'-ma m. emblem.
em-ble-má-ti-co, ₌a adj. emblematic.
em-bo-ca-du'-ra f. mouthpiece, mouth of river.
em-bo-car' tr.v. to blow; to drink down, to empty; intr.v. to enter the mouth of a river; to put on the brakes.

em-bô-co *m.* first coat of plaster or lime on wall.

em-bo-li'-a *f.* embolism.

em-bo-lis'-mo *m.* embolism (hist.).

em-bol-sar' *tr.v.* to pocket; to put in one's pocket; to pay debt to.

em-bo'-ra *adv.* fortunately; *conj.* in spite of, although, notwithstanding.

em-bor-ca-ção' *f.* emptying.

em-bor-car' *tr.v.* to empty.

em-bor-nal' *m.* feed bag, nose bag.

em-bos-ca'-da *f.* ambush, ambuscade.

em-bra'-ce *m.* tie-back for curtain.

em-bri-a-gar' *tr.v.* to intoxicate, to cause drunkenness.

em-bri-a-guez' *f.* drunkenness, intoxication.

em-bri-ão' *m.* embryo.

em-brio-ná-rio, =a *adj.* embryonic.

em-bru-lha'-da *f.* confusion, disorder, embarrassment.

em-bru-lhar' *tr.v.* to make into bundle, to wrap in paper; to package.

em-bru'-lho *m.* package, bundle; intentional misunderstanding.

em-bus'-te *m.* deception, lie.

em-bu-ti'-do *m.* inlaid work, marquetry.

em-bu-ti-dor' *m.* inlayer.

em-bu-tir' *tr.v.* to inlay.

em-ci'-ma *adv.* above; — **de** on top of.

e-men'-da *f.* correction; mend.

e-men-dar' *tr.v.* to emend, to correct, to mend; —**se** *refl.v.* to repent, to correct one's faults.

e-men-dá-vel *adj.* reparable.

e-mer-gên-cia *f.* emergence, emergency.

e-mer-gen'-te *adj.* emerging, emergent.

e-mé-ri-to, =a *adj.* emeritus.

e-mé-ti-co, =a *adj.* emetic.

e-mer-gir' *intr.v.* to emerge.

e-mer-são' *f.* emersion.

e-mer'-so, =a *adj.* emersed.

e-mi-gra-ção' *f.* emigration.

e-mi-gran'-te *m., f.* emigrant.

e-mi-grar' *intr.v.* to emigrate.

e-mi-nên-cia *f.* eminence.

e-mi-nen'-te *adj.* eminent.

e-mi-nen-tís-si-mo, =a *adj.* most eminent.

e-mis-são' *f.* emission; broadcast.

e-mis-sá-rio *m.* emissary.

e-mi-tir' *tr.v.* to emit; to utter; to send forth.

e-mo-ção' *f.* emotion.

e-mo-cio-nal' *adj.* emotional.

e-mo-cio-nan'-te *adj.* stirring, causing emotion.

e-mo-lien'-te *adj.* emollient.

e-mo-lir' *tr.v.* to mollify; to soften.

e-mo-lu-men'-to *m.* profit; bonus; emolument.

em'-pa *f.* stake, stick.

em-par' *tr.v.* to provide stakes and supports for vines, etc.

em-pa-car' *intr.v.* to balk, to refuse to go ahead.

em-pa-co-tar' *tr.v.* to make into bundle; to box; to wrap in paper, to pack up.

em-pa'-da *f.* small meat or vegetable pie.

em-pa-dro-ar' *tr.v.* to list as contributor or patron.

em-pa-lhar' *tr.v.* to cover or surround with straw as protection.

em-pa-lhei-rar' *tr.v.* to put cane seats in chairs.

em-pal-mar' *tr.v.* to conceal in the palm of the hand; to steal.

em-pas-ta-men'-to *m.* pasting.

em-pas-tar' *tr.v.* to paste; to bind.

em-pa-tar' *tr.v.* to check; to tie; to tie up money.

em-pa'-te *m.* delay; obstruction; indecision.

em-pe'-nha *f.* shoe leather; uppers (of shoes or boots).

em-pe-nhar' *tr.v.* to pawn, to mortgage, to pledge, to stake; —**se** *refl.v.* to assume obligation, to be greatly interested in obtaining.

em-pe'-nho *m.* promise, pledge; interest, protection.

em-pí-ri-co, =a *adj.* empirical.

em-pi-ris'-mo *m.* empiricism.

em-plas-ma'-do, =a *adj.* full of sores or wounds; covered with plasters.

em-plas'-tro *m.* plaster (healing application).

em-po-bre-cer' *tr.v.* to impoverish.

em-po-bre-ci-men'-to *m.* impoverishment.

em-pô-la *f.* blister.

em-po-lei-rar'=se *refl.v.* to perch.

em-pol-ga-du'-ras *f.pl.* holes through which cord is run (in sling-shot).

em-pol-gan'-te *adj.* gripping.

em-pol-gar' *tr.v.* to seize by hand; to grasp; to hold the attention or interest.

em-po-lhar' *tr.v., intr.v.* to incubate, to brood.

em-pó-rio *m.* emporium.

em-pos'-se *f.* installation (in office), induction.

em-pos'-ta *f.* impost (arch.).

em-pra-zar' *tr.v.* to summon, to appear.

em-pre-en-der' *tr.v.* to undertake, to attempt.

em-pre-en-di-men'-to *m.* enterprise, undertaking.

em-pre-ga'-do *m.* employee, clerk; functionary.

em-pre-gar' *tr.v.* to use, to employ.

em-prê-go *m.* employment, occupation.

em-prei-ta'-da *f.* contract work.

em-prei-tei'-ro *m.* contractor; jobber.

em-prê-sa *f.* enterprise; undertaking; industrial or merchandising company.

em-pres-tar' *tr.v.* to lend.

em-prés-ti-mo *m.* loan.

em-pur-rar' *tr.v.* to push.

e-mu-la-ção' *f.* emulation.

e-mu-lar' *intr.v.* to emulate.

ê-mu-lo *m.* emulator; rival; **ê-mu-lo, =a** *adj.* rivalling, emulous.

e-mul-são' *f.* emulsion.

e-mul-si-o-nar' *tr.v.* to emulsify.

e-nal-te-cer' *tr.v.* to exalt, to elevate, to enhance.

e-na-mo-rar' *tr.v.* to inspire love; —**se** *refl.v.* to fall in love.

en-ca-be-la'-do, =a *adj.* hairy.

en-ca-be-lar' *intr.v.* to grow hair, to become hairy.

en-ca-bri-tar'=se *refl.v.* to climb up, to scale peaks.

en-ca-bu-la'-do, =a *adj.* embarrassed, ashamed.

en-ca-bu-lar' *tr.v., intr.v.* to make ashamed and confused, to be much embarrassed.

en-ca-de-a-men'-to *m.* concatenation, connection, link, interlocking.

en-ca-de-ar' *tr.v.* to chain, to link together; to put in prison; to hold, to capture.

en-ca-der-na-ção' *f.* binding.

en-ca-der-nar' *tr.v.* to bind (books).

en-cai-xa-men'-to *m.* crating, boxing.

en-cai-xar' *tr.v.* to box, to crate.
en-cai'-xe *m.* socket, coupling.
en-cai-xo-tar' *tr.v.* to box, to put in a box.
en-cal-çar' *tr.v.* to trail, to track.
en-cal'-ço *m.* trail, track; trailing.
en-ca-lhar' *tr.v., intr.v.* to run aground, to be stranded.
en-ca'-lhe *m.* obstruction, obstacle; (Brazil) copies of newspapers or magazines not sold and returned to publisher.
en-ca'-lho *m.* sand-bank; *m.pl.* part of horse-shoe on which hoof rests.
en-ca-na-men'-to *m.* network of pipes or canals.
en-can-ta-dor' *m.* enchanter; **en-can-ta-dor'**, **-a** *adj.* enchanting.
en-can-ta-men'-to *m.* enchantment.
en-can-tar' *tr.v.* to enchant.
en-can'-to *m.* delight, enchantment.
en-ca-rar' *tr.v.* to fix eyes on, to look fixedly at.
en-car-ce-rar' *tr.v.* to put in prison, to incarcerate.
en-car-di'-do, -a *adj.* dirty; filthy.
en-car-dir' *tr.v., intr.v.* to soil, to make dirty.
en-ca-re-cer' *tr.v.* to make expensive; to exaggerate.
en-car'-go *m.* incumbency; obligation.
en-car-na-ção' *f.* incarnation; imitation of flesh.
en-car-na'-do, -a *adj.* red, flesh-colored, incarnate; **en-car-na'-do** *m.* bright red color.
en-car-nar' *tr.v.* to give flesh color to; to feed with meat; to incarnate.
en-ca-ro-ça'-da *f.* lumpiness of red soil in South Brazil.
en-car-re-ga'-do *m.* agent; — **de negócios** chargé d'affaires.
en-car-re-gar' *tr.v.* to put in charge, to commission, to entrust, to charge; —**se** *refl.v.* to take on an obligation, to take charge.
en-cáus-ti-ca *f.* floor-wax; encaustic painting.
en-cáus-ti-co, -a *adj.* encaustic.
en-ce-rar' *tr.v.* to wax, to make wax-colored.
en-cer-rar' *tr.v.* to put in safe place; to close or lock up.
en-che-dei'-ra *f.* meat funnel for making sausage.
en-chen'-te *f.* flood, inundation; superabundance.
en-cher' *tr.v.* to fill, to occupy; to satiate.
en-chi-men'-to *m.* filling, stuffing; abundance.
en-cho'-va *f.* anchovy.
en-ci-clo-pé-dia *f.* encyclopedia.
en-ci-clo-pé-di-co, -a *adj.* encyclopedic.
en-ci-mar' *tr.v.* to put an end to, to place on top.
en-cla-vi-nhar' *tr.v.* to interlock fingers of one hand with those of the other.
en-co-lher' *tr.v.* to shorten, to restrict; *intr.v.* to shrink; to be resigned; to be parsimonious; — **os ombros** to shrug one's shoulders.
en-co-lhi'-do, -a *adj.* timid, shrinking.
en-co-lhi-men'-to *m.* shrinking, contraction, shortening.
en-co-men'-da *f.* order.
en-co-men-dar' *tr.v.* to order; to recommend; to commission; to say prayers for; —**se** *refl.v.* to resign oneself to the mercy of.
en-cô-mio *m.* encomium.

en-con-trão' *m.* collision.
en-con-trar' *tr.v.* to meet; to find, to encounter; to come in contact with, to touch.
en-con'-tro *m.* meeting, encounter; quarrel.
en-co-ra-jar' *tr.v.* to encourage, to stimulate.
en-cor-pa'-do, -a *adj.* heavy, thick.
en-cor-par' *tr.v.* to thicken, to give greater consistency.
en-cor-ren-ta-men'-to *m.* enslavement, jailing.
en-cós-pias *f.pl.* wooden mold or form used by shoemakers to stretch shoes.
en-cos-ta'-do *m.* extra employee, extra hand.
en-cos-tar' *tr.v.* to support; to place against; —**se** *refl.v.* to lean against.
en-cos'-tes *m.pl.* buttress, arch-support (wall).
en-côs'-to *m.* back (of chair, sofa); (fig.) support, protection.
en-cren'-ca *f.* complicated situation.
en-cren-car' *tr.v.* to make difficult, to make complicated.
en-cres-par' *tr.v.* to make curly, to ruffle; —**se** *refl.v.* to become rough (of sea).
en-cros-tar' *intr.v.* to form a crust or scale.
en-cru-za-men'-to *m.* cross-roads, crossing.
en-cru-zar' *tr.v.* to cross; to make in form of cross.
en-cru-zi-lha'-da *f.* cross-roads.
en-den-tar' *tr.v.* to match or provide cogs in one wheel with indentations of another.
en-den-te-cer' *intr.v.* to teethe, to cut teeth.
en-de-re-çar' *tr.v.* to address.
en-de-rê-ço *m.* address.
ên-dez *m.* nest-egg.
en-di-a-bra'-do, -a *adj.* furious; possessed with the devil; terrible.
en-di-nhei-ra'-do, -a *adj.* wealthy, opulent.
en-di-rei-tar' *tr.v.* to correct, to put right; —**se** *refl.v.* to stand upright; to recover.
en-di'-via *f.* endive.
en-di-vi-dar' *tr.v.* to put in debt; —**se** *refl.v.* to contract debts.
en-do-cár-dia *f.* or **en-do-cár-dio** *m.* endocardium.
en-do-car'-po *m.* endocarp.
en-do-cri-no-lo-gi'-a *f.* endocrinology.
en-do-en'-ças *f.pl.* pains, sufferings; religious services during Holy Week.
en-doi-de-cer' *tr.v.* to make insane; *intr.v.* to go insane.
en-do-min-ga'-do, -a *adj.* dressed in best clothes.
en-dos-per'-ma *m.* endosperm.
en-dos-sa'-do *m.* indorsee.
en-dos-san'-te *m.* indorser.
en-dos-sar' *tr.v.* to indorse.
en-dôs-so *m.* indorsement.
en-du-re-cer' *tr.v., intr.v.,* —**se** *refl.v.* to harden, to become hard; to accustom oneself to hardships or physical endurance; to become cruel, insensitive.
en-du-re-ci-men'-to *m.* hardening; callus; hard tumor.
e-ner-gi'-a *f.* energy.
e-nér-gi-co, -a *adj.* energetic.
e-ner-va-ção' *f.* enervation, weakening.
e-ner-van'-te *adj.* enervating.

e-ner-var' *tr.v.* to enervate.
en-fa-dar' *tr.v.* to cause fatigue; to bore; to annoy.
en-fa-di'-ço, =a *adj.* easily wearied, easily bored.
en-fa'-do *m.* boredom, tediousness, fatigue.
en-fa-do'-nho, =a *adj.* tiresome, troublesome.
en-far-dar' *tr.v.* to bale; to tie in bundles or shocks.
ên-fa-se *f.* pompousness; emphasis.
en-fá-ti-co, =a *adj.* emphatic.
en-fa-tua-ção' *f.* infatuation.
en-fa-tu-ar' *tr.v.* to infatuate.
en-fei-tar' *tr.v.* to trim, to beautify, to adorn.
en-fei'-te *m.* ornament, adornment, trimming.
en-fei-ti-çar' *tr.v.* to bewitch, to charm.
en-fer-ru-jar' *tr.v.* to form rust, to oxidize.
en-fes-tar' *tr.v.* to fold in middle lengthwise; (Brazil) to cheat at cards.
en-fês-to, =a *adj.* thievish.
en-fer-ma'-gem *f.* nursing, treatment of the sick.
en-fer-mar' *intr.v.* to become sick.
en-fer-ma-ri'-a *f.* infirmary.
en-fer-mei'-ro, =a *m.*, *f.* nurse.
en-fer-mi-da'-de *f.* infirmity; sickness.
en-fêr-mo, =a *adj.* ill, infirm.
en-fi-a'-da *f.* string; several objects strung together, or placed in line; series.
en-fi-a-du'-ra *f.* eye of a needle; hole in bead or pearl.
en-fi-ar' *tr.v.* to thread, to string, to place in a row; to put on.
en-fim' *adv.* at last, finally.
en-for-car' *tr.v.* to hang, to strangle; to sell very cheap; —=se *refl.v.* to commit suicide by hanging.
en-fra-que-cer' *tr.v.*, *intr.v.*, —=se *refl.v.* to weaken, to lose strength.
en-fra-que-ci-men'-to *m.* weakness, debility, weakening.
en-fren-tar' *tr.v.* to confront.
en-fu-re-cer' *tr.v.*, *intr.v.*, —=se *refl.v.* to infuriate; to become furious.
en-ga-lar' *tr.v.* to arch the neck (of a horse); —=se *refl.v.* to assume superior airs.
en-ga-na-di'-ço, =a *adj.* gullible, easily deceived.
en-ga-na'-do, =a *adj.* mistaken, betrayed.
en-ga-nar' *tr.v.* to deceive, to seduce; —=se *refl.v.* to be wrong, to make a mistake, to fall into error.
en-ga'-no *m.* mistake, error.
en-ga-no'-so, =a *adj.* deceptive, causing error.
en-gen-drar' *tr.v.* to engender, to beget.
en-ge-nha-ri'-a *f.* engineering; corps of engineers.
en-ge-nhei-ran'-do *m.* engineering student.
en-ge-nhei'-ro *m.* engineer.
en-ge'-nho *m.* sugar mill and plantation; ingenuity.
en-ge-nho'-so, =a *adj.* ingenious.
en-gol-far' *tr.v.* to engulf.
en-go-ma-dei'-ra *f.* laundress.
en-go-ma'-gem *f.* starching and ironing.
en-go-mar' *tr.v.* to starch; to starch and iron.
en-gor-dar' *tr.v.*, *intr.v.* to gain flesh, to fatten.
en-gra-ça'-do, =a *adj.* comic, laughable.

en-gran-de-cer' *tr.v.* to enlarge; to aggrandize; to elevate in dignity or wealth; —=se *refl.v.* to become more important or illustrious.
en-gra-xa-dor' *m.* boot-black.
en-gra-xar' *tr.v.* to shine (shoes).
en-gra-xa'-te *m.* boot-black.
en-gre-nar' *tr.v.* to gear, to put in gear.
en-gros-sa-men'-to *m.* enlarging; flattery.
en-gros-sar' *tr.v.*, *intr.v.* to make thick, to make heavy; to increase the number or size.
en-gu-lir' *tr.v.* to swallow; to absorb; to consume; to believe.
e-nig'-ma *m.* enigma; puzzle.
e-nig-má-ti-co, =a *adj.* enigmatic.
en-jei-ta'-do *m.* foundling.
en-jei-tar' *tr.v.* to reject, to abandon; to slight.
en-jo-ar' *tr.v.*, *intr.v.* to suffer nausea; to nauseate.
en-jô-o *m.* nausea, sea-sickness.
en-la'-ce *m.* union; marriage.
en-lei-la'-do, =a *adj.* well settled (said of foundation stones, etc.).
en-lou-que-cer' *tr.v.*, *intr.v.* to lose one's reason, to become insane.
e-nor'-me *adj.* enormous.
e-nor-mi-da'-de *f.* enormity.
en-ra-bar' *tr.v.* to follow close behind; to accompany persistently; to lead animals with tail of one tied to head of other.
en-ra-i-zar' *intr.v.* to form roots, to take root.
en-ra-ma'-da *f.* system of branches constituting head of tree.
en-re-dar' *tr.v.* to catch, to plot, to tattle.
en-rê-do *m.* plot; confusion; tattling.
en-ri-que-cer' *tr.v.* to enrich; *intr.v.*, —=se *refl.v.* to become rich or wealthy.
en-ro-ca-men'-to *m.* breakwater.
en-rou-que-cer' *tr.v.*, *intr.v.* to become hoarse, to make hoarse.
en-rou-que-ci-men'-to *m.* hoarseness.
en-sa-bo-ar' *tr.v.* to apply soap, to wash with soap; (fig.) to reprehend.
en-sai-ar' *tr.v.* to try, to attempt; to rehearse.
en-sa-ís-ta *m.* essayist.
en-sai'-o *m.* trial, rehearsal; essay.
en-sal'-mo *m.* method of curing by conjuring, powwow.
en-san'-cha *f.* wide seam.
en-san-char' *tr.v.* to enlarge by letting out seams.
en-san-guen-tar' *tr.v.* to fill with blood; to spot or soil with blood.
en-se-jar' *tr.v.* to await opportunity.
en-se'-jo *m.* opportunity, occasion, chance.
en-si-lar' *tr.v.* to stow in silo.
en-si-na-de'-la *f.* punishment, lesson learned at one's expense.
en-si-na-men'-to *m.* teaching.
en-si-nar' *tr.v.* to teach, to instruct, to indoctrinate, to educate.
en-si'-no *m.* instruction, education, teaching.
en-so-pa'-do *m.* stew.
en-so-par' *tr.v.* to stew; to soak up liquid.
en-sos'-so, =a *adj.* insipid, needing salt.
en-ta'-lha *f.* wood carving, groove.
en-ta-lha-dor' *m.* wood-carver.
en-ta-lha-du'-ra *f.* wood-carving, wood sculpture.
en-ta-lhar' *tr.v.* to carve in wood.

en-ta'-lho *m.* engraved or sculptured figure in wood.

en-tan'-to *adv.* however, nevertheless.

en-tão' *adv.* then, at that time, on that occasion; *interj.* signifying surprise.

en'-te *m.* something existing; being.

en-te-a'-do, *=a m., f.* stepson, stepdaughter.

en-ten-der' *tr.v.* to understand, to recognize.

en-ten-di'-do, *=a adj.* expert, wise; agreed upon.

en-ten-di-men'-to *m.* comprehension, intelligence, talent.

en-te-ri'-te *f.* inflammation of intestines.

en-ter-ra-men'-to *m.* **en-têr-ro** *m.* burial, funeral.

en-'er-rar' *tr.v.* to bury.

en- ti-da'-de *f.* entity.

en to-a-ção' *f.* intonation.

en-to-ar' *tr.v.* to intone.

en-to-mo-lo-gi'-a *f.* entomology.

en-to-mó-lo-go *m.* entomologist.

en-tor-nar' *tr.v.* to turn over, to pour out, to spill out.

en-tra'-da *f.* entrance, entry, door, gate; beginning.

en-tra'-nha *f.* entrails; (fig.) character, nature.

en-trar' *tr.v.* to enter, to penetrate, to invade; *intr.v.* to participate, to begin.

en'-tre *prep.* between, in the midst of; among.

en-tre-a'-to *m.* intermission, interval.

en-tre-cos'-to *m.* rib roast.

en-tre-di-zer' *tr.v.* to talk to oneself.

en-tre'-ga *f.* delivery, surrender.

en-tre-gar' *tr.v.* to give over, to deliver; —*=se refl.v.* to devote oneself; to submit.

en-tre'-gue *adj.* delivered, handed over; occupied.

en-tre-la-çar' *tr.v.* to interlace.

en-tre-li'-nha *f.* space between two lines; interlineation.

en-tre-li-nhar' *tr.v.* to comment, to interline.

en-tre-mei'-o *m.* intermedium, interval.

en-tre-pa'-no *m.* vertical division in cupboard or bookcase.

en-tre-pre'-sa *f.* enterprise.

en-tres-so'*la *f.* inner sole.

en-tre-tan'-to *adv.* however, nevertheless; *m.* meantime.

en-tre-ter' *tr.v.* to entertain, to amuse.

en-tre-te'-la *f.* inter-lining.

en-tre-ver' *tr.v.* to glimpse, to descry; to anticipate.

en-tre-vis'-ta *f.* interview.

en-trin-chei-rar' *tr.v.* to entrench; —*=se refl.v.* to fortify, to strengthen one's position or situation.

en-tris-te-cer' *tr.v., intr.v.* to sadden, to become sad.

en-tro-nar' *tr.v.* to enthrone.

en-tron-ca-men'-to *m.* junction.

en-tu'-lho *m.* debris, broken stones.

en-tu-mes-cer' *intr.v.* to tumify, to swell.

en-tu-pir' *tr.v.* to stop up, to obstruct.

en-tu-si-as-mar' *tr.v.* to enthuse, to encourage.

en-tu-si-ás-ti-co, *=a adj.* enthusiastic.

en-tu-si-as'-mo *m.* enthusiasm.

e-nu-me-ra-ção' *f.* enumeration.

e-nu-me-rar' *tr.v.* to enumerate.

e-nu-me-rá-vel *adj.* that may be counted or rehearsed.

e-nun-cia-ção' *f.* enunciation.

e-nun-ci-a'-do *m.* proposition.

e-nun-ci-ar' *tr.v.* to express, to declare; to enunciate.

en-ve-lhe-cer' *tr.v., intr.v.* to age, to appear aged; to last a long time; to become useless, weakened.

en-ve-lo'-pe *m.* envelope.

en-ve-ne-nar' *tr.v.* to poison.

en-ver-go-nhar' *tr.v.* to make ashamed, to cause shame; to humiliate.

en-ver-ni-zar' *tr.v.* to varnish, to polish.

en-vés *m.* wrong side.

en-ve-sar' *tr.v.* to turn wrong side out.

en-vi-a'-do *m.* envoy, minister.

en-vi-ar' *tr.v.* to send, to dispatch.

en-vi-e-sar' *tr.v.* to twist; to cut on bias.

en-vol-ver' *tr.v.* to involve.

en-xa'-da *f.* hoe.

en-xa-drão' *m.* mattock.

en-xa-gu-ar' *tr.v.* to wash clothing in second water to remove soap.

en-xa'-me *m.* swarm (of bees).

en-xa-me-ar' *tr.v.* to gather into a beehive; *intr.v.* to swarm, to be in great numbers.

en-xa-mel' *m.* light framework of poles and sticks on which clay is daubed in constructing hut.

en-xa-que'-ca *f.* headache.

en-xer'-ga *f.* straw bed; saddle pad.

en-xer-gão' *m.* bed spring; straw mattress.

en-xer-gar' *tr.v.* to see, to descry, to get a glimpse of.

en-xer-ta-dei'-ra *f.* grafting knife.

en-xer-tar' *tr.v.* to graft, to insert, to introduce.

en-xêr-to *m.* graft (on a plant).

en-xô-fre *m.* sulphur.

en-xo-val' *m.* trousseau; outfit; swaddling clothes.

en-xu-ga-dor' *m.* dryer; drying machine; wringer; drying platform.

en-xu-gar' *tr.v.* to dry out moisture; to squeeze dry.

en-xu'-go *m.* drying.

en-xu'-to, *=a adj.* dry, free of humidity.

e-o-li'-na *f.* eolian.

é-pi-co, *=a adj.* epic.

e-pi-cu-reu' *m.* epicure, epicurean.

e-pi-cu-ris'-ta *m., f.* epicure.

e-pi-de-mi'-a *f.* epidemic.

e-pi-dê-mi-co, *=a adj.* epidemic.

e-pi-der'-me *f.* epidermis.

e-pi-fa-ni'-a *f.* Epiphany.

e-pi-gas'-tro *m.* epigastrium.

e-pi-glo'-te *f.* epiglottis.

e-pi-glo-ti'-te *f.* inflammation of epiglottis.

e-pi-gra-fe *f.* epigraph.

e-pi-gra'-ma *m.* epigram.

e-pi-lep-si'-a *f.* epilepsy.

e-pi-lép-ti-co *m.* epileptic; *adj.* epileptic.

e-pí-lo-go *m.* epilogue.

e-pis-co-pa'-do *m.* episcopacy; bishopric.

e-pis-co-pal' *adj.* episcopal.

e-pi-só-dio *m.* episode.

e-pís-to-la *f.* epistle.

e-pi-tá-fio *m.* epitaph.

e-pí-to-me *m.* epitome.

é-po-ca *f.* epoch.

e-qua-ção' *f.* equation.

e-qua-dor' *m.* equator.

e-qua-to-ri-al' *adj.* equatorial.

e-qua-ni-mi-da'-de *f.* equanimity.

e-ques'-tre *adj.* equestrian.

e-que'-vo, *=a adj.* contemporary.

e-qui-da'-de *f.* equitableness; equity.

e-quí-de-o, =a adj. equine.
e-qui-dis-tan'-te adj. equidistant.
e-qui-la-te-ral', e-qui-la'-te-ro adj. equilateral.
e-quí'-no, =a equine.
e-qui-ta-ti'-vo, =a adj. equitable.
e-qui-ân-gu-lo, =a adj. equiangular.
e-qui-lí-brio m. equilibrium.
e-qui-no-cial' adj. equinoctial.
e-qui-nó-cio m. equinox.
e-qui-pa'-gem f. crew.
e-qui-pa-men'-to m. equipment, accouterment.
e-qui-par' tr.v. to provision; to man; to outfit.
e-qui-pa-rar' tr.v. to compare, to match; to accredit (schools).
e-qui-pa-rá-vel adj. satisfying conditions for accreditation.
e-quí'-po m. team.
e-qui-ta-ção' f. horse-back riding.
e-qui-va-lên-cia f. equivalence.
e-qui-va-len'-te m., adj. equivalent.
e-qui-vo-car' tr.v., — =se refl.v. to mistake.
e-qui-vo-co m. mistake; ambiguous interpretation.
e'-ra f. era, epoch.
e-rá-rio m. exchequer, treasury.
e-re-mi'-ta m., f. hermit.
e-re-mi-té-rio m. hermitage.
erg' m. erg.
e-re-ção' f. erection; building; founding.
e-re'-to, =a adj. erect; haughty.
er'-go conj. therefore, consequently.
er-go-ti'-na f. ergot.
er-guer' tr.v. to raise up, to lift up, to elevate.
er'-mo m. desert, solitary place; adj. solitary.
e-ro-são' f. erosion.
e-ro-si'-vo, =a adj. erosive.
er-ra-di-car' tr.v. to eradicate.
er-ra-di'-o, =a adj. lost, wandering.
er-ra'-do, =a adj. wrong, mistaken.
er-ran'-te adj. wandering, uncertain, nomadic.
er-rar' tr.v., intr.v. to make mistake; to wander aimlessly; to sin; to err.
er-ra'-ta f. errata.
êr-ro m. error, mistake.
er-rô-ne-o, =a adj. erroneous.
er-ro-ni'-a f. erroneousness.
e-ru-di-ção' f. erudition.
e-ru-di'-to, =a adj. erudite.
e-rup-ção' f. eruption.
e-rup-ti'-vo, =a adj. eruptive.
er'-va f. grass, herb.
er'-va=ma'-te f. Paraguay tea plant, mate.
er-vi'-lha f. pea; — de cheiro sweet pea.
es-bel'-to, =a adj. slender, graceful.
es-bo-çar' tr.v. to sketch, to outline.
es-ca-bi-o'-so, =a adj. scabby, scaly.
es-ca'-da f. ladder; stairway.
es-ca-da-ri'-a f. series of stairs.
es-ca'-la f. scale.
es-ca-lar' tr.v. to scale, to assault; to graduate by scale; to schedule.
es-cal-dar' tr.v. to scald.
es-cal'-do m. premature ripening due to heat.
es-cal-par' tr.v. to scalp.
es-ca'-po m. scalp.
es-ca'-ma f. fish scale.
es-ca-mar' tr.v. to scale.
es-cân-da-lo m. scandal; shocking situation or event.
es-can-da-lo'-so, =a adj. shameful, indecorous, scandalous.

es-can-ga-lhar' tr.v. to break up, to destroy; to ruin.
es-ca-pa-de'-la f. escape, flight, evasion.
es-ca-par' intr.v. to escape.
es-ca-pa-tó-ria f. subterfuge, excuse.
es-ca'-po m. escapement (of a watch).
es-ca'-ques m.pl. squares on checker board.
es-ca-ri-a-dor' m. screwdriver.
es-=a-ri-ar' tr.v. to countersink.
es-car-la'-te adj., m. bright red color, scarlet.
es-car-la-ti'-na f. scarlet fever.
es-car-ra-dei'-ra f. cuspidor, spittoon.
es-car-rar' tr.v., intr.v. to spit, to expectorate.
es-car'-ro m. spit, spittle, saliva.
es-cas-sez' f. scarcity.
es-cas'-so, =a adj. scarce; rare; avaricious.
es-ca-var' tr.v. to dig out, to make a cavity in.
es-cla-re-cer' tr.v., intr.v. to clarify, to enlighten.
es-cla-re-ci'-do, =a adj. distinguished, gifted.
es-cla-re-ci-men'-to m. enlightenment, elucidation, explanation.
es-cle-ro'-se f. sclerosis.
es-co-a-dou'-ro m. gutter, drain.
es-co-a-men'-to m. running off; drain, drain-board.
es-co-ar' tr.v. to run out slowly (of a liquid), to leak out.
es-co'-la' f. school; (fig.) experience, example.
es-co-lar' adj. school, relative to school; m., f. scholar, student.
es-co-lás-ti-co, =a adj. scholastic.
es-co'-lha f. choice, preference.
es-co-lher' tr.v. to choose, to elect.
es-col'-ta f. escort (troops or ships).
es-col-tar' tr.v. to escort, to accompany.
es-con-der' tr.v. to conceal, to hide.
es-con-di'-do m. hiding-place; es-con-di'-do, =a adj. hidden; às escondidas secretly, in secret, underhand.
es-co'-po m. target, bull's-eye; goal, aim.
es-co'-pro m. carpenter's gouge, chisel.
es-cor-bu'-to m. scurvy.
es-có-ria f. scoria.
es-cor-pi-ão' m. scorpion.
es-cor-re-ga-di'-o, =a adj. slippery, slick.
es-cor-re-gar' intr.v. to slip, to slide; to prevaricate.
es-co-tei'-ro m. boy scout.
es-cô-va f. brush.
es-co-var' tr.v. to clean with a brush.
es-co-vi'-lha f. goldsmith's sweepings.
es-cra-va-tu'-ra f. slavery.
es-cra-vi-dão' f. slavery.
es-cra-vi-zar' tr.v. to enslave.
es-cra'-vo m. slave.
es-cre-ver' tr.v. to write.
es-cri'-ba m. scribe.
es-cri-tó-rio m. office.
es-cri-tu'-ra f. document, deed; Scripture.
es-cri-tu-ra-ção' f. book-keeping.
es-cri-tu-rar' tr.v. to keep commercial books, to write up or execute legal documents.
es-cri-tu-rá-rio m. book-keeper.
es-cri-vã' f. nun who serves as book-keeper in convent.
es-cri-vão' m. notary public, court clerk.
es-cró-fu-la f. scrofula.
es-cró-pu-lo m. scruple (equivalent to six carats).

es-crú-pu-lo *m.* hesitation, scruple.
es-cru-pu-lo'-so, =a *adj.* scrupulous.
es-cru-ti-nar' *tr.v.* to scrutinize; to verify election returns.
es-cru-tí-nio *m.* scrutiny; ballot box; counting of ballots.
es-cu-de'-te *m.* small shield; small metal plate on the outside of key-hole.
es-cu-dei'-ro *m.* shield-bearer.
es-cu'-do *m.* shield, escutcheon; escudo (coin).
es-cul-pir' *tr.v.* to sculpture.
es-cul-tor' *m.* sculptor.
es-cul-tu'-ra *f.* sculpture, statuary.
es-cu'-ma *f.* scum; froth, foam.
es-cu-ma-dei'-ra *f.* skimmer (spoon).
es-cu-man'-te *adj.* foaming; scumforming.
es-cu-mar' *intr.v.* to skim; to remove foam.
es-cu'-na *f.* schooner.
es-cu-rão' *m.* twilight.
es-cu-re-cer' *tr.v.*, *intr.v.* to darken, to grow dark.
es-cu-ri-dão' *f.* darkness; ignorance, blindness.
es-cu'-ro, =a *adj.* dark, shaded; (fig.) mysterious, difficult.
es-cu'-sa *f.* excuse.
es-cu-sa'-do, =a *adj.* useless, unnecessary.
es-cu-sar' *tr.v.*, *intr.v.* to excuse, to dispense with; to become exempt.
es-cu-sá-vel *adj.* excusable.
es-cu-tar' *tr.v.* to listen, to give attention to.
es-fe'-ra *f.* sphere.
es-fé-ri-co, =a *adj.* spherical.
es-fin'-ge *f.* sphinx.
es-for-ça'-do, =a *adj.* valiant, courageous.
es-for-çar' *tr.v.* to strengthen; —=se *refl.v.* to try, to endeavor, to take courage.
es-fôr-ço *m.* effort, strength, energy, zeal.
es-fre-gão' *m.* scouring brush.
es-fre-gar' *tr.v.* to rub together; to scour, to clean.
es-fri-ar' *tr.v.* to cool, to lower the temperature.
es-ga-ze-ar' *tr.v.* to stare at.
es-go-ta'-do, =a *adj.* exhausted, sold out.
es-go-ta-men'-to *m.* exhaustion, draining.
es-go-tar' *tr.v.* to exhaust, to consume, to use up; —=se *refl.v.* to be used up, to be sold out, to lose one's strength.
es-go'-te *m.* es-go'-to *m.* drain, drainpipe; gutter.
es-gri'-ma *f.* fencing.
es-gri-mis'-ta *m.* expert fencer.
es-ma-gar' *tr.v.* to crush, to mash, to macerate.
es-mal'-te *m.* enamel.
es-me-ral'-da *f.* emerald.
es-me-ral-di'-no, =a *adj.* emeraldcolored.
es-mê-ro *m.* great care, accuracy.
es-mo'-la *f.* alms.
es-mo-lar' *tr.v.*, *intr.v.* to give alms, to ask for alms, to beg.
es-mo-len'-to, =a *adj.* charitable.
e-sô-fa-go *m.* esophagus.
es-pa-çar' *tr.v.* to space.
es-pa-cial' *adj.* spatial.
es-pa'-ço *m.* space.
es-pa-ço'-so, =a *adj.* spacious.
es-pa'-da *f.* sword.
es-pa-dão' *m.* large sword.

es-pa-de'-la *f.* flax or hemp brake.
es-pa-de-lar' *tr.v.* to beat (hemp or flax).
es-pá-dua *f.* shoulder-blade.
es-pa'-lha *m.* talkative, expansive man.
es-pa-lha'-do, =a *adj.* free of straw; scattered.
es-pa-lha-fa'-to *m.* noisiness, disorder, confusion.
es-pa-lha-fa-to'-so, =a *adj.* exaggerated, conspicuous, showy.
es-pa-lhar' *tr.v.* to scatter about; to remove straw from grains; to make public.
es-pa-na-dor' *m.* dust cloth, dust brush.
es-pa-nar' *tr.v.* to dust, to remove dust.
es-pan-car' *tr.v.* to spank; to strike.
es-pan-ta'-lho *m.* scare-crow; bug-bear; useless person.
es-pan-tar' *tr.v.* to surprise, to frighten; —=se *refl.v.* to be surprised.
es-pan'-to *m.* surprise, fright.
es-pan-to'-so, =a *adj.* extraordinary, surprising, frightening.
es-par'-go *m.* asparagus.
es-par'-so, =a *adj.* sparse, scattered, loose.
es-par-ti'-lho *m.* corset.
es-par'-to *m.* broom sage, broom grass.
es-pa-te'-la *f.* spatula (wood, used to lower tongue).
es-pá-tu-la *f.* spatula (flexible knifelike utensil).
es-pe-ci-al' *adj.* special.
es-pe-cia-li-da'-de *f.* specialty.
es-pe-cia-lis'-ta *m.* specialist.
es-pe-ci-a-li-zar' *tr.v.* to designate, to give special attention to; —=se *refl.v.* to specialize.
es-pe-ci-a-ri'-a *f.* spices, seasonings.
es-pé-cie *f.* kind; species.
es-pe-ci-fi-car' *tr.v.* to specify; to detail.
es-pe-cí-fi-co, =a *adj.* specific.
es-pé-ci-me *m.* specimen, sample, model.
es-pe-ci-o'-so, =a *adj.* specious.
es-pec-ta-dor' *m.* spectator.
es-pe-cu-la-ção' *f.* speculation.
es-pe-cu-la-dor' *m.* speculator.
es-pe-cu-la-ti'-vo, =a *adj.* speculative.
es-pê-lho *m.* mirror.
es-pe'-ra *f.* waiting, hope, delay, respite, ambush.
es-pe-ra'-do, =a *adj.* hoped for, wished for, expected, anticipated, probable.
es-pe-re=ma-ri'-do *m.* dessert made with eggs and caramel.
es-pe-ran'-ça *f.* hope.
es-pe-ran-çar' *tr.v.* to give hope to, to encourage.
es-pe-ran-ço'-so, =a *adj.* hopeful; promising.
es-pe-rar' *tr.v.* to hope, to expect, to await, to wait for; to lie in wait for.
es-per'-ma *m.* sperm, semen.
es-per-ma-ce'-te *m.* spermaceti.
es-per-tar' *tr.v.* to awaken; to stimulate.
es-per-te'-za *f.* skill; liveliness, courage; sharp business practice.
es-per'-to, =a *adj.* intelligent, active, sharp, smart, expert.
es-pês-so, =a *adj.* thick, dense, opaque.
es-pes-su'-ra *f.* thickness, denseness.
es-pec-ta-cu-lar' *adj.* spectacular.
es-pe-tá-cu-lo *m.* spectacle.
es-pe-tar' *tr.v.* to prick, to penetrate with skewer.
es-pê-to *m.* skewer.
es-pe-tral' *adj.* spectral.
es-pe'-tro *m.* spectrum; ghost, spectre.
es-pe-vi-ta-dei'-ra *f.* candle snuffer.

es-pe-vi-tar' *tr.v.* to snuff (candle).
es-pi'-a *f.* spy.
es-pi-ão' *m.* spy, secret agent.
es-pi-ar' *tr.v.* to spy, to spy on, to observe secretly.
es-pi-char' *tr.v.* to pierce, to perforate.
es-pi'-ga *f.* ear of corn, grain head; spike of flowers; hangnail.
es-pi-gar' *intr.v.* to form ears or heads.
es-pi-gue'-to *m.* sharp, high tone (of musical instrument).
es-pi-na'-fre *m.* spinach.
es-pi-ne'-ta *f.* spinet.
es-pin-gar'-da *f.* rifle.
es-pi'-nha *f.* spine; fish bone; thorn.
es-pi-nha'-ço *m.* spinal column.
es-pi-nhal' *adj.* spinal.
es-pi-nhar' *tr.v.* to prick; to anger.
es-pi-nhei'-ro *m.* thornbush.
es-pi'-nho *m.* thorn.
es-pi-o-na'-gem *f.* espionage.
es-pi-o-nar' *tr.v.* to spy out, to investigate.
es-pi'-ra *f.* turn, round of a spiral.
es-pi-ral' *f.* spiral.
es-pi-ran'-te *adj.* breathing, alive.
es-pi-rar' *tr.v.* to breathe, to exhale; *intr.v.* to be alive.
es-pi-ri-tis'-mo *m.* spiritualism, spiritism.
es-pí-ri-to *m.* spirit; ghost; mind.
es-pi-ri-tual' *adj.* spiritual.
es-pi-ri-tua-li-da'-de *f.* spirituality.
es-pi-ri-tuo'-so, **=a** *adj.* spirited; spiritous.
es-pir-rar' *intr.v.* to sneeze.
es-pla-na'-da *f.* esplanade (open, elevated area providing broad view).
es-plên-di-do, **=a** *adj.* splendid.
es-plen-dor' *m.* splendor.
es-po-li-ar' *tr.v.* to spoil, to plunder; to deprive of; to extort.
es-pó-lio *m.* plunder, spoils; property left at death, estate.
es-pon'-ja *f.* sponge.
es-pon-jo'-so, **=a** *adj.* spongy.
es-pon-ta-ne-i-da'-de *f.* spontaneity.
es-pon-tâ-ne-o, **=a** *adj.* spontaneous.
es-po'-ra *f.* spur.
es-po-rá-di-co, **=a** *adj.* sporadic.
es-po-re-ar' *tr.v.* to spur, to stimulate, to awaken.
es-po'-ro *m.* spore.
es-por'-te *m.* sport.
es-por-tis'-mo *m.* fondness for sports.
es-por-tis'-ta *m.* sportsman.
es-pô-sa *f.* wife.
es-po-sar' *tr.v.* to marry.
es-pô-so *m.* husband.
es-pre-gui-ça-dei'-ra *f.* couch, sofa.
es-pre-gui-çar' *tr.v.* to rouse from sleep; —**=se** *refl.v.* to stretch and yawn.
es-prei-tar' *tr.v.* to spy on, to waylay, to observe secretly.
es-pre-mer' *tr.v.* to squeeze out; to press.
es-pu'-ma *f.* froth, foam.
es-pu-ma-dei'-ra *f.* utensil for removing froth, skimmer.
es-pu-man'-te *adj.* foaming; raving.
es-pu-mar' *tr.v.* to remove froth or foam; *intr.v.* to froth, to foam.
es-pu-mo'-so, **=a** *adj.* foamy, frothy, sparkling.
es-pu'-to *m.* sputum, spittle.
es-qua'-dra *f.* **es-qua-drão'** *m.* squadron.
es-qua-drar' *tr.v.* to form into squadrons; to square.
es-qua-dri'-a *f.* right angle.

es-qua'-dro *m.* square; quadrant.
es-quá-li-do, **=a** *adj.* squalid.
es-quar-te-jar' *tr.v.* to quarter, to cut into quarters; to distribute.
es-quar-te-lar' *tr.v.* to divide into four parts.
es-que-ce-di'-ço, **=a** *adj.* forgetful.
es-que-cer' *tr.v.* to forget, to omit, to neglect; —**=se** *refl.v.* to forget.
es-que-ci'-do, **=a** *adj.* forgotten; forgetful; endless.
es-que-ci-men'-to *m.* forgetfulness.
es-que-le'-to *m.* skeleton.
es-que'-ma *m.* sketch, outline, diagram.
es-quen-ta-dor' *m.* heater, foot-warmer.
es-quen-ta-men'-to *m.* heating, warming.
es-quen-tar' *tr.v.* to heat; (fig.) to irritate.
es-quer'-da *f.* left hand, left side.
es-quer'-do, **=a** *adj.* left; awkward, crooked.
es-qui'-fe *m.* bier; skiff.
es-qui'-na *f.* corner.
es-qui'-va *f.* dodging, ducking.
es-qui-van'-ça *f.* disdain, repugnance, cold reception.
es-qui-var' *tr.v.* to shun, to avoid; to repel; —**=se** *refl.v.* to dodge, to steal away, to escape.
es-qui'-vo, **=a** *adj.* intractable, rude, crude.
es-qui-zo-fre-ni'-a *f.* schizophrenia.
es'-sa *f.* bier.
ês-se *m.* **es'-sa** *f. demons.pron.* that (near the person spoken to).
es-sên-ci-a *f.* essence.
es-sen-cial' *adj., m.* essential.
es-ta-be-le-cer' *tr.v.* to establish; —**=se** *refl.v.* to settle.
es-ta-be-le-ci-men'-to *m.* establishment; settlement.
es-ta-bi-li-da'-de *f.* stability.
es-ta-bi-li-za-ção' *f.* stabilization.
es-ta-bi-li-zar' *tr.v.* to stabilize.
es-tá-bu-lo *m.* stable, cattle shed.
es-ta'-ca *f.* stake, post; prop; picket.
es-ta-ca'-da *f.* stockade, hurdle; corral.
es-ta-car' *tr.v.* to make secure with stakes and supports.
es-ta-ção' *f.* station; telephone exchange; season.
es-ta-cio-nar' *intr.v.* to stop, to delay; to park.
es-ta-cio-ná-rio, **=a** *adj.* stationary.
es-tá-dio *m.* stadium; epoch, period, phase, stage.
es-ta-dis'-ta *m.* statesman.
es-ta'-do *m.* state; situation; condition, status, standing.
es-ta-du-al' *adj.* state.
es-ta-gi-á-rio *m.* one receiving in-service training.
es-tá-gio *m.* apprenticeship; office or shop practice.
es-tag-nar' *tr.v., intr.v.* to stagnate, to paralyze; to become inert or stagnant.
es-ta-lac-ti'-te *f.* stalactite.
es-ta-lag-mi'-te *f.* stalagmite.
es-ta-la'-da *f.* crack, boom, bursting sound.
es-ta-lar' *tr.v., intr.v.* to burst, to crack open, to break apart.
es-ta-la'-gem *f.* inn, hotel.
es-ta-lei'-ro *m.* shipyard.
es-ta'-me *m.* stamen.
es-tam'-pa *f.* stamp, print, cut.
es-tam-pa'-gem *f.* printing, stamping.

es-tam-par' *tr.v.* to print, to stamp.
es-tam-pi'-do *m.* clap, report, explosion.
es-tam-pi'-lha *f.* postage stamp.
es-tan-dar'-te *m.* standard; battle flag; emblem.
es-ta'-nho *m.* tin.
es-tan'-te *f.* bookcase.
es-tar' *intr.v.* to be, to stand.
es-tá-ti-ca *f.* statics.
es-tá-ti-co, -a *adj.* static.
es-ta-tís-ti-ca *f.* statistics.
es-tá-tua *f.* statue.
es-ta-tu-e'-ta *f.* statuette.
es-ta-tu'-ra *f.* stature.
es-ta-tu'-to *m.* statute.
es-tá-vel *adj.* stable.
ês-te *m.* **es'-ta** *f. demons. pron.* this.
es'-te *m.* east.
es-te-a-ri'-na *f.* stearin.
es-tei'-ra *f.* coarse grass mat.
es-ten-der' *tr.v., intr.v.,* **—-se** *refl.v.* to extend; to stretch out.
es-te-no-gra-fi'-a *f.* stenography.
es-te-nó-gra-fo *m.* stenographer.
es-ten-tó-re-o, -a *adj.* stentorian.
es-têr-co *m.* animal excrement, manure; rubbish; filth.
es-te'-re *m.* stere.
es-te-re-ó-ti-po *m.* stereopticon.
es-té-ril *adj.* sterile.
es-te-ri-li-da'-de *f.* sterility.
es-te-ri-li-zar' *tr.v.* to sterilize.
es-ter-li'-no *m.* pound sterling; *adj.* relative to English money.
es-té-ti-co, -a *adj.* esthetic.
es-te-tos-có-pio *m.* stethoscope.
es-ti-a'-da *f.* clear, bright weather after storm; lack of rain; scarcity of water.
es-ti-a'-gem *f. same as* estiada.
es-ti-ar' *intr.v.* to stop raining.
es-tí-bio *m.* stibium, antimony.
es-tig'-ma *m.* stigma.
es-tig-ma-ti-zar' *tr.v.* to stigmatize.
es-ti-le'-te *m.* stiletto.
es-ti'-lha *f.* **es-ti-lha'-ço** *m.* splinter, fragment.
es-ti-lis'-mo *m.* affectation (in writing).
es-ti-lis'-ta *m.* stylist.
es-ti-li-zar' *tr.v.* to style, to polish (writing).
es-ti'-lo *m.* style.
es-ti'-ma *f.* esteem, appreciation; estimate.
es-ti-ma-ção' *f.* esteem; affection; estimate.
es-ti-mar' *tr.v.* to esteem; to estimate.
es-ti-má-vel *adj.* estimable.
es-ti-mu-la-ção' *f.* stimulation.
es-ti-mu-lan'-te *m.* stimulant; *adj.* stimulating.
es-ti-mu-lar' *tr.v.* to stimulate.
es-tí-mu-lo *m.* stimulus.
es-ti-pên-dio *m.* stipend.
es-ti-pu-lar' *tr.v.* to stipulate.
es-ti-rar' *tr.v.* to pull out lengthwise; to stretch, to pull back; to elongate; to place lengthwise; **—-se** *refl.v.* to humble oneself, to prostrate oneself.
es-ti'-va *f.* hold (of a ship).
es-ti-va-dor' *tr.v.* stevedore.
es-ti-va'-gem *f.* work of a stevedore.
es-ti-var' *tr.v.* to stow, to load.
es-to-fa-dor' *m.* upholster.
es-to-far' *tr.v.* to upholster.
es-tô-fo *m.* stuffing (of hair, etc.) for upholstered furniture.
es-tói-co, -a *adj.* stoic.
es-tô-jo *m.* jewelry box or case.
es-to'-la *f.* stole.

es-tó-li-do, -a *adj.* stolid.
es-tô-ma-go *m.* stomach.
es-tô-pa *f.* tow (flax, hemp, etc.).
es-to-par' *tr.v.* to calk with tow.
es-to'-re *m.* window shade, awning.
es-tor-var' *tr.v.* to hinder, to obstruct.
es-tor'-vo *m.* hindrance, obstruction.
es-tou-rar' *tr.v.* to burst open; *intr.v.* to burst, to explode.
es-tou'-ro *m.* crash, explosion, detonation.
es-tra'-da *f.* highway, road; **— de ferro** railroad.
es-tra'-do *m.* low platform, raised (section of) floor; wire bed-spring.
es-tra-gar' *tr.v.* to cause to deteriorate; to corrupt; to destroy.
es-tra'-go *m.* destruction, deterioration, damage, ruin.
es-tran-gei-ra'-do, -a *adj.* outlandish, foreign in manners and speech.
es-tran-gei'-ro *m., f.* foreigner; **es-tran-gei'-ro, -a** *adj.* foreign.
es-tran-gu-la-ção' *f.* strangulation.
es-tran-gu-lar' *tr.v.* to strangle.
es-tra-nhar' *tr.v.* to find something strange, odd, or queer; to be surprised.
es-tra-nhá-vel *adj.* reprehensible; surprising.
es-tra-nhe'-za *f.* strangeness, surprise.
es-tra'-nho, -a *adj.* foreign, uncommon, curious, strange.
es-tra-ta-ge'-ma *m.* stratagem, trick.
es-tra-té-gia *f.* strategy.
es-tra-té-gi-co, -a *adj.* strategic.
es-tra-ti-fi-ca-ção' *f.* stratification.
es-tra-ti-fi-car' *tr.v.* to stratify.
es-tra'-to *m.* stratum.
es-tra-tos-fe'-ra *f.* stratosphere.
es-tréi-a *f.* beginning, initiation, first appearance, first performance.
es-tre-ar' *tr.v.;* **—-se** *refl.v.* to inaugurate, to use or do for the first time.
es-trei-ta-men'-to *m.* union; tightening.
es-trei-tar' *tr.v.* to unite more closely, to bring more closely together, to tighten.
es-trei-te'-za *f.* straightness, smallness; tightness; narrowness.
es-trei'-to *m.* strait; **es-trei'-to, -a** *adj.* tight, narrow.
es-trê-la *f.* star.
es-tre-lar' to fill with stars; to fry (eggs).
es-tre-li'-nha *f.* asterisk.
es-trê-lo *m.* white spot on head of animals.
es-tre'-ma *f.* extremity; frontier.
es-tre-mar' *tr.v.* to delimit, to mark off; to separate; to distinguish.
es-tre'-me *adj.* pure, genuine, real.
es-tre-me-cer' *tr.v.* to shake, to frighten, to cause to tremble, to love deeply; *intr.v.* to shake, to tremble with fright.
es-tre-mu-nhar' *intr.v.* to awaken suddenly.
es-trep-to-co'-co *m.* streptococcus.
es-tri'-a *f.* stria, flute, reed; witch.
es-tri-a-men'-to *m.* striation.
es-tri-ar' *tr.v.* to flute, to channel.
es-tri-bi'-lho *m.* chorus, refrain, burden.
es-tri'-bo *m.* stirrup; platform to facilitate passengers alighting from train.
es-tric-ni'-na *f.* strychnine.
es-tri-den'-te *adj.* strident.
es-tri'-to, -a *adj.* strict; exacting.
es-tri-tu'-ra *f.* stricture, squeezing.
es-tro'-fe *f.* strophe, stanza.
es-tron'-do *m.* thunderous noise.
es-tron-do'-so, -a *adj.* tumultuous, roaring; eminent, famous.

es-tro-pi-ar' *tr.v.* to cripple, to maim.
es-tru-mar' *tr.v.* to fertilize (with manure).
es-tru'-me *m.* fertilizer, manure, dung.
es-tru-mei'-ra *f.* dung-heap; filthy place.
es-tru-tu'-ra *f.* structure.
es-tru-tu-ral' *adj.* structural.
es-tu-á-rio *m.* estuary.
es-tu-car' *tr.v.*, *intr.v.* to cover with stucco, to work in stucco, to apply stucco.
es-tu-dan'-te *m.*, *f.* student.
es-tu-dan-ta'-da *f.* group of students; student's prank.
es-tu-dar' *tr.v.* to study.
es-tu-di-o'-so, =a *adj.* studious; es-tu-di-o'-so *m.* scholar, savant.
es-tu'-do *m.* study.
es-tu'-fa *f.* hot-house, green-house; heater.
es-tu-fa-dei'-ra *f.* roaster.
es-tu-far' *tr.v.* to heat; to roast.
es-tul-ti-fi-car' *tr.v.* to stultify.
es-tul'-to, =a *adj.* stupid, silly, inept.
es-tu-pe-fa-ção' *f.* stupefaction; numbness.
es-tu-pe-fa-cien'-te *adj.* stupefying.
es-tu-pe-fa-zer' *tr.v.* to stupefy.
es-tu-pe-fi-car' *tr.v.* to stupefy.
es-tu-pi-dez' *f.* stupidity.
es-tú-pi-do, =a *adj.* stupid.
es-tu-por' *m.* stupor.
es-tu'-pro *m.* rape.
es-tu'-que *m.* stucco.
es-vai-cer' *tr.v.* to dissipate; to make proud, to puff up; *intr.v.* to faint, to lose heart; — =se *refl.v.* to disappear, to fade away; to weaken.
es-va-ziar' *tr.v.* to empty.
es-ver-de-a'-do, =a *adj.* greenish.
es-ver-di-nha'-do, =a *adj.* greenish, green-tinted.
es-vo-a-çar' *intr.v.* to flutter, to hover.
é-ter *m.* ether.
e-té-re-o, =a *adj.* ethereal.
e-te-ri-zar' *tr.v.* to etherize.
e-ter-ni-da'-de *f.* eternity.
e-ter'-no, =a *adj.* eternal.
é-ti-ca *f.* ethics.
é-ti-co, =a *adj.* ethical.
e-ti'-lo *m.* ethyl.
e-ti-mo-lo-gi'-a *f.* etymology.
e-ti-mo-lo-gis'-ta *m.* etymologist.
e-ti-que'-ta *f.* etiquette; label.
ét-ni-co, =a *adj.* ethnic.
et-no-lo-gi'-a *f.* ethnology.
et-no-lo-gis'-ta *m.* ethnologist.
et-nó-lo-go *m.* ethnologist.
eu' *pers.pron.* I; *m.* ego.
eu-ca-lip'-to *m.* eucalyptus.
eu-ca-ris-ti'-a *f.* eucharist.
eu-ca-rís-ti-co, =a *adj.* eucharistic.
eu-fe-mis'-mo *m.* euphemism.
eu-fo-ni'-a *f.* euphony.
eu-fô-ni-co, =a *adj.* euphonic.
eu-fo'-no *m.* euphonium, harmonica.
eu-ge-ni'-a *f.* eugenics.
eu-gê-ni-co, =a *adj.* eugenic.
eu-nu'-co *m.* eunuch.
e-va-cu-a-ção' *f.* evacuation.
e-va-cu-ar' *tr.v.* to evacuate.
e-va-dir' *tr.v.* to avoid, to evade; — =se *refl.v.* to flee, to escape, to slip away.
e-va-são' *f.* evasion; escape, flight.
e-va-si'-va *f.* subterfuge.
e-va-si'-vo, =a *adj.* evasive.
e-van-gé-li-co, =a *adj.* evangelical, evangelic.
e-van-ge-lis'-mo *m.* evangelism.

e-van-ge-lis'-ta *m.* evangelist.
e-van-ge-li-zar' *tr.v.* to evangelize.
e-van-ge'-lho *m.* gospel.
e-va-po-ra-ção' *f.* evaporation.
e-va-po-rar' *tr.v.* to evaporate.
e-ven-tual' *adj.* eventual.
e-ven-tua-li-da'-de *f.* eventuality.
e-vic-ção' *f.* eviction.
e-vi-dên-cia *f.* evidence.
e-vi-den'-te *adj.* evident.
e-vi-tar' *tr.v.* to avoid, to shun.
e-vo-car' *tr.v.* to evoke; to invoke, to conjure.
e-vo-ca-ti'-vo, =a *adj.* evocative.
e-vo-lu-ção' *f.* evolution.
e-vo-lu-ci-o-nar' *intr.v.* to evolve.
e-vo-lu-cio-ná-rio, =a *adj.* evolutionary.
e-vol-ver'-se *refl.v.* to evolve.
e-vul-são' *f.* extraction.
e-xa-brup'-to *adv.* abruptly, without preparation, violently.
e-xa-bun-dan'-te *adj.* very abundant.
e-xa-ção' *f.* care, exactness, punctuality; collection of taxes.
e-xa-cer-bar' *tr.v.* to exacerbate, to aggravate.
e-xa-ge-ra-ção' *f.* exaggeration.
e-xa-ge-rar' *tr.v.* to exaggerate.
e-xa-gê-ro *m.* exaggeration.
e-xa-lar' *tr.v.* to exhale.
e-xal-ta-ção' *f.* exaltation.
e-xal-ta'-do, =a *adj.* exalted.
e-xal-tar' *tr.v.* to exalt.
e-xa'-me *m.* examination.
e-xa-mi-na-dor' *m.* examiner.
e-xa-mi-nan'-do *m.* person being examined.
e-xa-mi-nar' *tr.v.* to examine, to give an examination to, to interrogate.
ex-ân-i-me *adj.* lifeless.
e-xa-ti-dão' *f.* exactness; punctuality; precision.
e-xa'-to, =a *adj.* exact; punctual.
e-xa-tor' *m.* tax collector.
e-xas-pe-ra-ção' *f.* exasperation.
e-xas-pe-rar' *tr.v.* to exasperate.
ex-ce-ção' *f.* exception.
ex-ce-den'-te *m.* excess; *adj.* exceding.
ex-ce-der' *tr.v.* to exceed; — =se *refl.v.* to outdo oneself; to become unduly angry.
ex-ce-lên-cia *f.* excellence, excellency.
ex-ce-len'-te *adj.* excellent.
ex-ce-len-tís-si-mo, =a *adj.* most excellent.
ex-cel'-so, =a *adj.* very high, sublime.
ex-cep-cio-nal' *adj.* exceptional.
ex-cer'-to *m.* excerpt.
ex-ces-si'-vo, =a *adj.* excessive.
ex-ces'-so *m.* excess.
ex-ce-tu-ar' *tr.v.* to except, to exempt.
ex-ci-ta-bi-li-da'-de *f.* excitability.
ex-ci-tar' *tr.v.* to excite.
ex-ci-tá-vel *adj.* excitable.
ex-cla-ma-ção' *f.* exclamation.
ex-cla-mar' *tr.v.* to exclaim; *intr.v.* to shout.
ex-cla-ma-tó-rio, =a *adj.* exclamatory.
ex-clu-ir' *tr.v.* to exclude.
ex-clu-são' *f.* exclusion.
ex-clu-si'-ve *adv.* exclusively.
ex-clu-si'-vo, =a *adj.* exclusive.
ex-clu'-so, =a *adj.* excluded, omitted.
ex-co-mun-gar' *tr.v.* to excommunicate.
ex-co-mu-nhão' *f.* excommunication.
ex-cre-ção' *f.* excretion.
ex-cre-men'-to *m.* excrement.
ex-cre-tar' *tr.v.* to excrete.
ex-cre'-to, =a *adj.* excreted.
ex-cres-cên-cia *f.* excrescence.

ex-cru-ci-an'-te *adj.* excruciating.
ex-cur-são' *f.* excursion; trip.
ex-cur-sio-nis'-ta *m.* excursionist.
e-xe-cra-ção' *f.* execration.
e-xe-crar' *tr.v.* to execrate.
e-xe-crá-vel *adj.* execrable.
e-xe-cu-ção' *f.* execution.
e-xe-cu-ta'-do *m.* executed criminal.
e-xe-cu-tar' *tr.v.* to execute, to perform.
e-xe-cu-ti'-vo, =a *adj.* executive; *m.* executive.
e-xe-cu-tor' *m.* executor.
e-xe-ge'-se *f.* exegesis.
e-xem-plar' *adj.* exemplary; *m.* copy.
e-xem-plá-rio *m.* book of examples, collection of samples.
e-xem-pli-fi-ca-ção' *f.* exemplification.
e-xem-pli-fi-car' *tr.v.* to exemplify.
e-xem'-plo *m.* example.
e-xé-quias *f.* funeral service, funeral.
e-xe-quí-vel *adj.* executable.
e-xer-cer' *tr.v.* to exercise.
e-xer-ci-tar' *tr.v.* to practice, to exercise.
e-xér-ci-to *m.* army.
ex-hau-rir' *tr.v.* to exhaust.
ex-haus-tão' *f.* exhaustion.
ex-haus-ti'-vo, =a *adj.* exhaustive.
ex-haus'-to, =a *adj.* exhausted.
e-xi-gir' *tr.v.* to require, to insist upon; to exact.
e-xi-bi-ção' *f.* exhibition.
e-xi-bir' *tr.v.* to exhibit.
e-xi-bi-cio-nis'-mo *m.* exhibitionism.
e-xi-gên-cia *f.* exigency, requirement.
e-xi-gen'-te *adj.* exigent, exacting.
e-xi-la'-do, =a *adj., m., f.* exiled; exile.
e-xi-lar' *tr.v.* to exile, to ostracize.
e-xí-lio *m.* exile, banishment.
e-xí-mio, =a *adj.* eminent, distinguished.
e-xi-mir' *tr.v.* to exempt.
e-xis-tên-cia *f.* existence; stock.
e-xis-ten'-te *adj.* existent, extant.
e-xis-tir' *intr.v.* to exist.
ê-xi-to *m.* result, consequence; success.
ê-xo-do *m.* exodus.
e-xo-ne-ra-ção' *f.* exoneration.
e-xo-ne-rar' *tr.v.* to exonerate.
ex-or-bi-tan'-te *adj.* exorbitant.
e-xor-cis-mar' *tr.v.* to exorcise.
e-xór-dio *m.* exordium.
e-xor-ta-ção' *f.* exhortation.
e-xor-tar' *tr.v.* to exhort.
e-xó-ti-co, =a *adj.* exotic.
ex-pan-dir' *tr.v.* to expand.
ex-pan-são' *f.* expansion.
ex-pan-sí-vel *adj.* expansible.
ex-pan-si'-vo, =a *adj.* expansive.
ex-pa-tri-a-ção' *f.* expatriation.
ex-pa-tri-ar' *tr.v.* to expatriate; —se *refl.v.* to withdraw from one's own country.
ex-pec-ta-ti'-va *f.* expectation, probability.
ex-pec-to-rar' *tr.v.* to expectorate.
ex-pe-di-ção' *f.* expedition.
ex-pe-di-cio-ná-rio, =a *adj.* expeditionary.
ex-pe-dir' *tr.v.* to dispatch, to send out.
ex-pe-di-ên-cia *f.* expediency.
ex-pe-di-en'-te *adj.* expedient.
ex-pe-di'-to, =a *adj.* expeditious.
ex-pe-lir' *tr.v.* to expel.
ex-pe-ri-ên-cia *f.* experience; experiment.
ex-pe-ri-men-tal' *adj.* experimental.
ex-pe-ri-men-tar' *tr.v.* to experiment; to test.
ex-pe-ri-men'-to *m.* experiment.

ex-per'-to, =a *adj., m., f.* expert.
ex-pi-a-ção' *f.* expiation.
ex-pi-ar' *tr.v.* to expiate.
ex-pi-a-tó-rio, =a *adj.* expiatory.
ex-pi-ra-ção' *f.* expiration, exhalation.
ex-pi-rar' *tr.v., intr.v.* to expel air from lungs, to expire.
ex-ple-ti'-va *f.* expletive.
ex-ple-ti'-vo, =a *adj.* expletive.
ex-pli-ca-ção' *f.* explanation.
ex-pli-car' *tr.v.* to explain.
ex-pli-cá-vel *adj.* explicable.
ex-plí-ci-to, =a *adj.* explicit.
ex-plo-dir' *tr.v.* to explode.
ex-plo-ra-ção' *f.* exploration; scouting.
ex-plo-ra-dor' *m.* scout.
ex-plo-rar' *tr.v.* to explore.
ex-plo-ra-tó-rio, =a *adj.* exploratory.
ex-plo-são' *f.* explosion.
ex-plo-si'-vo *m.* explosive; *adj.* explosive.
ex-po-en'-te *m.* exponent.
ex-por' *tr.v.* to expose, to expound, to explain.
ex-por-ta-ção' *f.* exportation.
ex-por-ta-dor' *m.* exporter.
ex-por-tar' *tr.v.* to export.
ex-por-tá-vel *adj.* exportable.
ex-po-si-ção' *f.* exposition; exposure.
ex-po-si-tor' *m.* expositor.
ex-pos'-to *m.* abandoned child, foundling; ex-pos'-to, =a *adj.* exposed.
ex-pos-tu-la-ção' *f.* expostulation.
ex-pres-são' *f.* expression.
ex-pres'-so *m.* express train; ex-pres'-so, =a *adj.* express, expressed.
ex-pres-si'-vo, =a *adj.* expressive.
ex-pri-mir' *tr.v.* to express, to make manifest.
ex-pro-pria-ção' *f.* expropriation.
ex-pro-pri-ar' *tr.v.* to expropriate.
ex-pug-nar' *tr.v.* to take by storm, to conquer by force of arms.
ex-pul-são' *f.* expulsion.
ex-pul-sar' *tr.v.* to expel; to drive out violently.
ex-pul'-so, =a *adj.* expelled.
ex-pun-gir' *tr.v.* to expunge.
ex-pur-gar' *tr.v.* to expurgate.
ex-pur'-go *m.* expurgation.
ex-qui-si-ti'-ce *f.* strangeness, eccentricity.
ex-qui-si'-to, =a *adj.* uncommon, elegant; eccentric, strange, odd.
ex-su-dar' *tr.v., intr.v.* to exude, to perspire.
êx-ta-se *m.* ecstasy.
ex-tá-ti-co, =a *adj.* ecstatic.
ex-tem-po-ra-ne-i-da'-de *f.* extemporaneousness.
ex-tem-po-râ-neo, =a *adj.* extemporaneous.
ex-ten-são' *f.* extension.
ex-ten-si'-vo, =a *adj.* extensive.
ex-ten'-so, =a *adj.* extended.
ex-te-nu-a-ção' *f.* extenuation.
ex-te-nu-an'-te *adj.* extenuating.
ex-te-nu-ar' *tr.v.* to extenuate.
ex-te-ri-or' *m., adj.* exterior.
ex-ter-mi-na-ção' *f.* extermination.
ex-ter-mi-nar' *tr.v.* to exterminate.
ex-ter-mí-nio *m.* extermination.
ex-ter-na'-to *m.* day school.
ex-ter'-no, =a *m., f.* day pupil; *adj.* external.
ex-tin-ção' *f.* extinction.
ex-tin-guir' *tr.v.* to extinguish.
ex-tin'-to, =a *adj.* extinct.
ex-tin-tor' *m.* extinguisher.
ex-tir-pa-ção' *f.* extirpation.

ex-tir-par' *tr.v.* to extirpate.
ex-tor-ção' *f.* extortion.
ex-tor-quir' *tr.v.* to extort.
ex-tra-di-ção' *f.* extradition.
ex-tra-hu-ma'-no, ₌a *adj.* superhuman.
ex-tra-ção' *f.* extraction.
ex-tra-ir' *tr.v.* to extract.
ex-tra-mu-ral' *adj.* extra-mural.
ex-tra-or-di-ná-rio *m.* expense outside budget; *adj.* extraordinary.
ex-tra-tar' *tr.v.* to abstract; to select excerpts from.
ex-tra'-to *m.* extract, essence.
ex-tra-va-gân-cia *f.* extravagance.
ex-tra-va-gan'-te *adj.* extravagant.
ex-tra-vi-a'-do, ₌a *adj.* lost, lead astray, perverted.

ex-tra-vi-ar' *tr.v.* to lead astray, to ruin, tc seduce, to pervert; —₌se *refl.v.* to go astray, to get lost.
ex-tra-vi'-o *m.* robbery, corruption; losing one's way.
ex-tre-ma₌un-ção' *f.* extreme unction.
ex-tre-mi-da'-de *f.* extremity.
ex-tre'-mo, ₌a *adj.* extreme, last.
ex-trín-se-co, ₌a *adj.* extrinsic.
e-xu-be-rân-cia *f.* exuberance.
e-xu-be-ran'-te *adj.* exuberant.
e-xul-ta-ção' *f.* exultation.
e-xul-tan'-te *adj.* exulting.
e-xul-tar' *intr.v.* to exult.
e-xu-ma-ção' *f.* exhumation.
e-xu-mar' *tr.v.* to exhume.
e-xú-via *f.* slough, cast-off skin.

F

See page 12—GUIDE TO REFORMED SPELLING used in this Dictionary

F, f *m.* F, f, sixth letter of the alphabet.
fá *m.* fa (music).
fá-bri-ca *f.* factory, mill.
fa-bri-can'-te *m.* manufacturer.
fa-bri-car' *tr.v.* to manufacture, to fabricate.
fa-bri'-co *m.* manufacture, work, repairs; make.
fá-bu-la *f.* fable, story, lie.
fa-bu-la-ção' *f.* narration in the form of a fable; lie; moral (to a fable).
fa-bu-lar' *tr.v.* to narrate in the form of a fable; to lie.
fa-bu-lis'-ta *m.* fabulist.
fa-bu-lo'-so, ₌a *adj.* fabulous.
fa'-ca *f.* knife.
fa-ca'-da *f.* cut or blow with a knife.
fa-ca-dis'-ta *m.* borrower.
fa-ca-lhão' *m.* large knife.
fa-ça'-nha *f.* deed, exploit.
fa-cão' *m.* large knife, butcher-knife.
fa-ção' *f.* faction; political party.
fa'-ce *f.* face, cheek.
fa-cé-cia *f.* facetiousness.
fa-ce-ci-o'-so, ₌a *adj.* facetious.
fa-cei'-ra *f.* flesh over cheek bones of an ox.
fa-ci-al' *adj.* facial.
fa-cê-ta *f.* facet.
fa-ce-tar' *tr.v.* to cut facets on.
fa-cha *f.* torch, taper; hatchet.
fa-cha'-da *f.* façade; frontispiece.
fá-cil *adj.* easy.
fa-ci-li-da'-de *f.* ease, facility.
fa-ci-li-tar' *tr.v.* to facilitate.
fa-ci-o-ná-rio *m.* member of a faction.
fa-ci-o'-so, ₌a *adj.* factious, seditious.
fa-cí-no-ra *m.* criminal.
fa-ci-no-ro'-so, ₌a *adj.* criminal.
fac₌sí-mi-le *m.* facsimile.
fa-cul-da'-de *f.* faculty.
fa-cul-tar' *tr.v.* to concede; to facilitate.
fa-cul-ta-ti'-vo, ₌a *adj.* optional, elective.
fa-cul-to'-so, ₌a *adj.* wealthy, rich.
fa'-da *f.* fairy; (fig.) lovely lady.
fa-di'-ga *f.* fatigue, weariness.
fa-di-gar' *tr.v.* to fatigue, to weary.
fa-di-go'-so, ₌a *adj.* fatiguing, hard.
fa-dis'-ta *m.*, *f.* one who sings or plays a *fado*.
fa'-do *m.* luck, destiny; doleful Portuguese folk song.

fa-go'-te *m.* bassoon.
fa-go-tis'-ta *m.*, *f.* bassoon player.
fai-an'-ça *f.* pottery, porcelain.
fa-ís-ca *f.* flash, flash of lightning.
fa-is-ca-dor' *m.* gold miner.
fa-is-car' *tr.v.*, *intr.v.* to emit, to emit flashes, to scintillate, to shoot forth; to mine gold by sifting the earth.
fai'-xa *f.* band; belt; strip, strap.
fa-lá-cia *f.* fallacy.
fa-la-cio'-so, ₌a *adj.* fallacious.
fa-lan'-ge *f.* phalanx.
fa'-la *f.* voice, speech, style.
fa-la'-da *f.* rumor, talk.
fa-la'-do, ₌a *adj.* talked about, notable.
fa-lan'-te *adj.* speaking, eloquent.
fa-lar' *intr.v.* to speak, to talk; — em to talk about.
fa-la-tó-rio *m.* buzz, murmur.
fal-cão' *m.* falcon.
fal-co-a-ri'-a *f.* falconry.
fa-le-cer' *intr.v.* to die.
fa-le-ci'-do, ₌a *adj.* deceased.
fa-le-ci-men'-to *m.* death.
fa-lên-cia *f.* bankruptcy, failure.
fa'-lha *f.* flaw, crack, blemish, lack.
fa-lhar' *tr.v.*, *intr.v.* to break, to crack, to short-weigh, to short-change, to misfire.
fa'-lho, ₌a *adj.* lacking.
fa-li'-do *m.* bankrupt person.
fa-li-bi-li-da'-de *f.* fallibility.
fa-li-men'-to *m.* crime, error, bankruptcy.
fa-lir' *intr.v.* to fail, to go bankrupt.
fa-lí-vel *adj.* fallible.
fal-sá-rio *m.* falsifier, perjurer.
fal-se'-te *m.* falsetto.
fal-si-da'-de *f.* falsity, falseness.
fal-si-fi-car' *tr.v.* to falsify, to adulterate.
fal'-so, ₌a *adj.* false.
fal'-ta *f.* lack; absence; guilt.
fal-tar' *intr.v.* to be absent; to be lacking; not to aid; not to fulfil promise.
fal'-to, ₌a *adj.* needy, in want, lacking.
fa'-ma *f.* fame, reputation.
fa-mí-lia *f.* family.
fa-mi-liar' *adj.* familiar; pertaining to the family.
fa-mi-lia-ri-da'-de *f.* familiarity.
fa-mil-ia-ri-zar' *tr.v.* to familiarize; —₌se *refl.v.* to become familiar, to become accustomed.

fa-min'-to, =a *adj.* hungry, famished.
fa-mo'-so, =a *adj.* famous; excellent; big.
fa-na-ti-cis'-mo *m.* fanaticism.
fa-ná-ti-co, =a *adj.* fanatic.
fan-dan'-go *m.* fandango.
fan-far'-ra *f.* brass band; fanfare, flourish of trumpets.
fan-far-rão' *m.* braggart, bully.
fa-nho-se-ar' *intr.v.* to nasalize; to speak through the nose.
fa-nho'-so, =a *adj.* nasal.
fan-ta-si'-a *f.* fancy, imaginative; fantasia.
fan-tas'-ma *m.* phantasm.
fan-tás-ti-co, =a *adj.* fantastic.
fan-to'-che *m.* person easily influenced by another; puppet.
fa-quei'-ro *m.* knife-case; silver chest.
fa-quir' *m.* fakir.
fa-rá-di-co, =a *adj.* faradic.
fa-rá-dio *m.* faraday.
far'-da *f.* uniform; livery.
far-dar' *tr.v.* to clothe, to provide with a uniform.
far'-do *m.* baggage; load; burden.
fa-re-jar' *tr.v.* to scent, to smell; to get an inkling of.
fa-re'-lo *m.* coarse bran, stock feed; (fig.) thing of little value.
fa-re-ló-rio *m.* chatter, rambling talk; trifle, insignificance.
fa-ri-ná-ce-o, =a *adj.* farinaceous.
fa-rin'-ge *f.* pharynx.
fa-rin-gi'-te *f.* pharyngitis.
fa-ri'-nha *f.* flour, meal.
fa-ri'-nha=do=rei'-no *f.* wheat flour.
far-ma-cêu-ti-co *m.* druggist; *adj.* pharmaceutic.
far-má-cia *f.* pharmacy.
fa'-ro *m.* scent, smell, flair, track, guide.
fa-ro'-fa *f.* toasted or scalded manioc flour.
fa-rol' *m.* light-house; lantern, head-light.
fa-ro-lei'-ro *m.* light-house keeper.
far'-pa *f.* barb; splinter.
far-pe'-la *f.* hook on end of crochet needle.
far-fa'-po *m.* rag; rags, ragged clothing.
far-rus'-co, =a *adj.* black, soiled with coal or soot.
far'-sa *f.* farce.
far-san'-te *m.*, *f.* farceur, buffoon, jester.
far-sis'-ta *m.* buffoon, jester.
far-tar' *tr.v.* to satisfy, to satiate; to tire out, to bore.
far'-to. =a *adj.* abundant; satiated, satisfied; bored.
far-tu'-ra *f.* abundance; satiety.
fas-cí-cu-lo *m.* leaflet, folder, fasciculus.
fas-ci-na-ção' *f.* fascination.
fas-ci-nar' *tr.v.* to fascinate.
fas-cis'-mo *m* fascism.
fas-cis'-ta *m.*, *f.* fascist.
fa'-se *f.* phase.
fas-ti'-o *m.* lack of appetite; aversion; tediousness.
fas-ti-di-o'-so, =a *adj.* boresome, tiring, dull.
fas-tí-gio *m.* top; highest branch of tree.
fa-tal' *adj.* fatal, ominous.
fa-ta-li-da'-de *f.* fatality.
fa-ta-lis'-mo *m.* fatalism.
fa-ta-lis'-ta *m.*, *f.* fatalist.
fa-ti'-a *f.* slice.
fa-tí-cio, =a *adj.* artificial, factitious.
fa-tí-di-co, =a *adj.* fateful.
fa-ti-gan'-te *adj.* wearying, fatiguing.
fa-ti-gar' *tr.v.* to fatigue, to importune.

fa-ti-go'-so, =a *adj.* wearisome.
fa'-to *m.* suit (of clothes); clothing.
fa'-to *m.* fact; event.
fa-tor' *m.* factor.
fa-tu-i-da'-de *f.* fatuity.
fá-tuo, =a *adj.* fatuous.
fa-tu'-ra *f.* bill.
fa-tu-rar' *tr.v.* to bill.
fau'-no *m.* faun.
fa'-va *f.* bean.
fa-ve'-la *f.* section, suburb, primitive village.
fa'-vo *m.* honey-comb; something sweet, pleasant.
fa-vo'-so, =a *adj.* having small surface depressions; pock-marked.
fa-vor' *m.* favor.
fa-vo-rá-vel *adj.* favorable.
fa-vo-re-cer' *tr.v.* to favor, to promote, to protect, to back.
fa-vo-ri-tis'-mo *m.* favoritism.
fa-vo-ri'-to, =a *m.*, *f.* favorite.
fa-zen'-da *f.* farm.
fa-zen-dei'-ro *m.* proprietor of large farm.
fa-zer' *tr.v.* to do, to make; — **cruzes na bôca** to have nothing to eat; — **conta que to suppose;** — **arte to act in provocative manner;** — **gazeta to be absent from school;** — **por onde to find a way of doing something.**
faz=tu'-do *m.* jack-of-all-trades; factotum.
fé *f.* faith; **dar** — to note; to observe; **fazer** — to merit credit.
fe-al-da'-de *f.* ugliness.
fe'-bre *f.* fever.
fe-bri-cu-lo'-so, =a *adj.* susceptible to fever.
fe-bril' *adj.* feverish.
fe-cha-du'-ra *f.* lock; closing.
fe-char' *tr.v.* to close, to lock, to secure; to conclude; *intr.v.* to come to an end; to heal.
fê-cho *m.* bolt, bar, latch.
fé-cu-la *f.* starch; sediment.
fe-cu-la-ri'-a *f.* starch factory.
fe-cu-lên-cia *f.* feculence; dregs.
fe-cu-len'-te *adj.* feculent.
fe-cun-dar' *tr.v.* to fecundate, to fertilize; *intr.v.* to become fecund, to conceive.
fe-cun-di-da'-de *f.* fecundity.
fe-cun'-do, =a *adj.* fecund, fertile.
fe-der' *intr.v.* to stink.
fe-dor' *m.* offensive odor, stink.
fe-do-ren'-to, =a *adj.* bad-smelling, stinking.
fe-de-ra-ção' *f.* federation.
fe-de-ra'-do *m.* confederate.
fe-de-ral' *adj.* federal.
fe-de-rar' *tr.v.* to federate.
fe-é-ri-co, =a *adj.* pertaining to fairies; magic.
fei-ção' *f.* form, aspect, character; **fei-ções'** *f.pl.* features, countenance.
fei-jão' *m.* French bean.
fei-jo-a'-da *f.* dish made of black beans, dried beef, and vegetables.
fei'-o, =a *adj.* ugly, disagreeable, unpleasant.
fei-o'-so, =a *adj.* very ugly or disagreeable.
fei'-ra *f.* market; fair.
fei'-ra=li'-vre *f.* open-air market exempt from usual taxes.
fei-ti-cei'-ro, =a *m.*, *f.* sorcerer, sorceress.
fei-ti'-o *m.* actual work of making some-

thing; shape, make, workmanship; style, mode.

fei'-to *m.* fact, deed, exploit; **fei'-to**, =a *adj.* done, completed, accomplished.

fei-tor' *m.* superintendent, manager, administrator.

fei-to-rar' *tr.v.* to administer, to manage.

fei'-xe *m.* sheaf; bundle of twigs.

fel' *m.* bile; gall bladder; (fig.) hate. bitterness.

feld-spa'-to *m.* feldspar.

fe-li-ci-da'-de *f.* felicity.

fe-li-ci-ta-çã°' *f.* congratulation, felicitation.

fe-li-ci-tar' *tr.v.* to congratulate.

fe-li'-no, =a *adj.* feline.

fe-liz' *adj.* happy.

fe-lo-ni'-a *f.* treason; rebellion, perfidy.

fel'-pa *f.* nap (of cloth), fuzz.

fel-pu'-do, =a *adj.* downy, fuzzy, having nap.

fêl'-tro *m.* felt.

fê-me-a *f.* female.

fê-me-o, =a *adj.* female.

fe-mi-ni-da'-de *f.* femininity.

fe-mi-ni'-no, =a *adj.* feminine.

fe-mi-nis'-mo *m.* feminism.

fe-mi-nis'-ta *m.*, *f.* feminist.

fe-men-ti'-do, =a *adj.* perjured, perfidious, faithless.

fê-mur *m.* femur, thigh bone.

fe-na-ção' *f.* hay harvest.

fe'-no *m.* hay, fodder.

fen'-da *f.* break; fissure; crack, crevice.

fen-der' *tr.v.* to split, to cleave, to tear open.

fe-nes-tra'-do, =a *adj.* full of holes or openings.

fe-nol' *m.* phenol.

fe-no-me-nal' *adj.* phenomenal.

fe-nô-me-no *m.* phenomenon.

fe'-ra *f.* wild animal; (fig.) cruel person.

fe-ra-ci-da'-de *f.* fertility.

fe-ral' *adj.* cruel.

fe-raz' *adj.* fertile.

fé-re-tro *m.* bier, coffin.

fe-re'-za *f.* ferocity.

fé-ria *f.* week-day; weekly pay-roll; =s *f.pl.* vacation.

fe-ri-a'-do *adj.* holiday.

fe-ri'-da *f.* wound.

fe-ri-men'-to *m.* wounding.

fe-ri'-no, =a *adj.* fierce, cruel.

fe-rir' *tr.v.* to wound, to hurt, to strike.

fer-men-ta-ção' *f.* fermentation.

fer-men-tar' *tr.v.*, *intr.v.* to ferment.

fer-men'-to *m.* ferment.

fe-ro-ci-da'-de *f.* ferocity.

fe-roz' *adj.* ferocious.

fer'-ra *f.* fire-shovel; shovel; branding.

fer-ra-du'-ra *f.* horseshoe.

fer-ra-gis'-ta *m.* hardware merchant.

fer-ra-men'-ta *f.* tools.

fer-rão' *m.* sting, prick.

fer-ra-ri'-a *f.* iron works.

fer-rei'-ro *m.* iron worker; blacksmith.

fer-re'-ta *f.* sharp metal point of spinning top.

fer-re'-te *m.* branding iron.

fer-re-te-ar' *tr.v.* to brand; (fig.) to afflict; to defame, to slander.

fer'-ro *m.* iron.

fer-rô-lho *m.* bolt.

fer-ro-vi-á-rio, =a *adj.* relative to railway.

fer-ru'-gem *f.* rust.

fer-ru-gen'-to, =a *adj.* rusty.

fér-til *adj.* fertile.

fer-ti-li-da'-de *f.* fertility.

fer-ti-li-zar' *tr.v.* to fertilize, to fecundate.

fé-ru-la *f.* ferule; fennel.

fer-ve-dou'-ro *m.* boiling; bubbling, excitement.

fer-ven'-te *adj.* boiling, fervent.

fer-ver' *tr.v.* to boil; *intr.v.* to boil, to bubble.

fér-vi-do, =a *adj.* fervid.

fer-vor' *m.* fervor.

fer-vo-ro'-so, =a *adj.* ardent, fervid.

fer-vu'-ra *f.* ebullition, effervescence.

fes-ta *f.* feast, festival, saint's day; solemnity, commemoration; =s *f.pl.* caresses; **boas** =s good wishes for Christmas or New Year.

fes-te-jar' *tr.v.* to feast, to honor with a celebration.

fes-te'-jo *m.* celebration.

fes-ti-val' *m.* festival.

fes-ti-vi-da'-de *f.* festivity.

fes-ti'-vo, =a *adj.* festive.

fes-tão' *m.* festoon.

fes-to-na'-das *f.pl.* large festoons in painting or sculpture.

fe-ti'-che *m.* fetish.

fe-ti-chis'-mo *m.* fetishism.

fe-tal' *adj.* foetal.

fé-ti-do, =a *adj.* fetid.

fe'-to *m.* foetus.

feu'-do *m.* fief, feudal tenure.

feu-dal' *adj.* feudal.

feu-da-lis'-mo *m.* feudalism.

fe-ve-rei'-ro *m.* February.

fez *m.* fez.

fé-zes *f.pl.* faeces.

fi-a-dei'-ro, =a *m.*, *f.* spinner.

fi-a-di'-lho *m.* woven tape, floss silk.

fi-a'-do *m.* thread, filament; **fi-a'-do**, =a *adj.* trusting; sold on credit.

fi-a-dor' *m.* bondsman; endorser.

fi-an'-ça *f.* bail, surety, guarantee.

fi-an-dei'-ro, =a *m.*, *f.* spinner.

fi-ar' *tr.v.* to reduce to filament or thread; to saw board in half lengthwise; to spin; *intr.v.* to trust, to have confidence in; to sell on credit.

fi-as'-co *m.* failure.

fí-bu-la *f.* buckle.

fi-car' *intr.v.* to remain; to assume; to become; to subsist; — **bem** to look well; — **de fora** to be excluded; to be left out.

fic-ção' *f.* fiction.

fi'-cha *f.* chip (in roulette and other games); filing card.

fi-chá-rio *m.* filing cabinet.

fi'-bra *f.* fiber.

fi-bri'-la *f.* fibril, small fiber.

fi-bri'-na *f.* fibrin.

fi-bro'-so, =a *adj.* fibrous.

fi-dal'-go, =a *m.*, *f.* nobleman, noble woman.

fi-dal-go'-te *m.* ostentatious person; impoverished aristocrat, fake aristocrat.

fi-dal-gui'-a *f.* nobility.

fi-de-dig'-no, =a *adj.* meriting credit; trustworthy.

fi-el' *adj.* faithful; loyal; honest; *m.* inspector, guard, overseer.

fi'-ga *f.* good luck charm (in the form of clenched hand with thumb between forefinger and middle finger).

fí-ga-do *m.* liver.

fi'-go *m.* fig.

fi-guei'-ra *f.* fig tree.

fi-gu-ra-ção' *f.* figuration, representation.

fi-gu-ra'-do, =a *adj.* figurative.

fi-gu-ran'-te *m.*, *f.* stand-in, super-numerary; wall-flower.
fi-gu-rão' *m.* important personage.
fi-gu-rar' *tr.v.*, *intr.v.* to figure, to represent.
fi-gu-ra-ti'-vo, =a *adj.* figurative.
fi-gu-ri'-no *m.* fashion plate, model.
fi'-la *f.* file, row.
fi-la-men'-to *m.* filament.
fi-lan-tro-pi'-a *f.* philanthropy.
fi-lan-tro'-po *m.* philanthropist.
fi-lar-mô-ni-co, =a *adj.* philharmonic.
fi-la-te-li'-a *f.* philately; stamp collecting.
fi-lé *m.* fillet.
fi-lei'-ra *f.* series, line, queue, file.
fi'-lha *f.* daughter.
fi-lha-ra'-da *f.* many children.
fi-lhei'-ro, =a *adj.* prolific.
fi-lhen'-to, =a *adj.* prolific.
fi'-lho *m.* son; descendent; — de leite child whom wet nurse has nourished.
fi-lho'-te *m.* native; young (of animals); favorite.
fi-lho-tis'-mo *m.* favoritism.
fi-li-a-ção' *f.* filiation; adoption, parentage.
fi-li-al' *adj.* filial.
fi-li-ar' *tr.v.* to adopt as child; —=se *refl.v.* to join in a group or corporation; to become affiliated with.
fi-li-gra'-na *f.* filigree.
fil'-me *m.* film.
fi-ló *m.* lace net.
fi-lo-lo-gi'-a *f.* philology.
fi-lo-lo-gis'-ta *m.* philologist.
fi-ló-lo-go *m.* philologist.
fi-lo-so-fi'-a *f.* philosophy.
fi-lo-só-fi-co, =a *adj.* philosophical, philosophic.
fi-ló-so-fo *m.* philosopher.
fil-tra-ção' *f.* filtration.
fil-trar' *tr.v.* to filter.
fil-trá-vel *adj.* filtrable.
fil'-tro *m.* filter.
fim' *m.* end, goal, purpose.
fi-na'-do *m.* deceased.
fi-nal' *adj.* final.
fi-na-li-da'-de *f.* finality, teleology.
fi-na-men'-to *m.* death.
fi-nan'-ças *f.pl.* money, treasury, finances.
fi-nan-cei'-ro *m.* financier.
fi-nan-cis'-ta *m.* financier.
fi-nar' *intr.v.* to come to an end, to die; —=se *refl.v.* to die; to lose flesh.
fin-dar' *tr.v.*, *intr.v.* to put an end to, to end, to finish.
fin-dá-vel *adj.* capable of completion.
fin'-do, =a *adj.* ended, finished, disappeared.
fi-nês *m.* Finn; *adj.* Finnish.
fi-ne'-za *f.* fineness; courtesy; amiability, kindness.
fin-gi-men'-to *m.* hypocrisy, dissimulation, pretense.
fin-gir' *tr.v.*, *intr.v.* to feign, to pretend, to invent.
fi-ni'-to, =a *adj.* finite, transitory.
fi'-no, =a *adj.* fine, thin, subtle, delicate, polite.
fi-nó-rio, =a *m.*, *f.* sly, cunning person; *adj.* sly.
fi-nu'-ra *f.* finesse, subtleness.
fi'-o *m.* fiber, thread; wire; edge (of cutting utensil).
fir'-ma *f.* business company, corporation; signature.
fir-mar' *tr.v.* to affirm; to make firm; to

sign; —=se *refl.v.* to be settled, to be fixed.
fir'-me *adj.* firm.
fir-me'-za *f.* firmness.
fir-ma-men'-to *m.* firmament.
fis-cal' *m.* custom house officer, notary; *adj.* fiscal.
fis-ca-li-zar' *tr.v.* to supervise, to check, to examine, to audit.
fis'-co *m.* public treasury; tax collecting department.
fí-si-ca *f.* physics.
fi-si-o-lo-gi'-a *f.* physiology.
fis-su'-ra *f.* fissure.
fís-tu-la *f.* flageolet; fistula.
fi'-ta *f.* ribbon, band, decoration; ostentation, deception; film.
fi-tar' *tr.v.* to stare at, to listen attentively, to prick up the ears, to think intently about.
fi-ti'-nha *f.* honorary decoration.
fi'-to *m.* goal; target; objective; fi'-to, =a *adj.* fixed.
fi-ve'-la *f.* buckle.
fi-ve-lão' *m.* large buckle.
fi-ve-le'-te *f.* small buckle.
fi-xa-ção' *f.* fixation.
fi-xa-dor' *m.* fixing bath (photo.).
fi-xar' *tr.v.* to fix.
fla-ci-dez' *f.* flaccidity, laxity.
flá-ci-do, =a *adj.* weak, relaxed, flaccid.
fla-ge-la-ção' *f.* flagellation, whipping.
fla-ge-lar' *tr.v.* to flagellate; to whip.
fla-ge'-lo *m.* flagellum; lash; (fig.) calamity.
fla-gran'-te *adj.* flagrant; em — delito in the act.
fla-jo-lé *m.* flageolet.
fla-me-jan'-te *adj.* flamboyant (arch.).
fla-me-jar' *intr.v.* to flame, to breathe out flames.
fla-men'-go *m.* flamingo.
flan'-co *m.* flank.
fla-ne'-la *f.* flannel, flannelette.
flan-que-ar' *tr.v.* to flank.
fla-tu-lên-cia *f.* flatulence.
fla-tu-len'-to, =a *adj.* flatulent.
flau'-ta *f.* flute.
flau-tis'-ta *m.* flutist.
fle'-cha *f.* arrow.
fle-xão' *f.* flection, bending.
fle-xi-bi-li-da'-de *f.* flexibility.
fle-xí-vel *adj.* flexible.
flo'-co *m.* snow flake.
flor' *f.* flower.
flo-ra-ção' *f.* flowering.
flo-res-cer' *intr.v.* to bloom, to blossom, to flower.
flo-res'-ta *f.* forest.
flo-re'-te *m.* foil, rapier.
fló-ri-do, =a *adj.* florid, blossoming, gay.
flo-ri-cul-tu'-ra *f.* floriculture.
flo-ri-lé-gio *m.* anthology.
flo-ris'-ta *m.* florist.
flu-ên-cia *f.* fluency.
flu-en'-te *adj.* fluent.
flui-dez' *f.* fluidity.
flui'-do *m.* flui'-do, =a *adj.* fluid.
flu-ir' *intr.v.* to flow, to run, to move or run in fluid state; to be derived from.
flú-or *m.* fluorine.
fluo-ros-có-pio *m.* fluoroscope.
flu-tu-a-ção' *f.* fluctuation.
flu-tu-ar' *intr.v.* to fluctuate.
flu-vi-al' *adj.* fluvial, river.
flu-xão' *f.* congestion.
flux' *m.* abundance.
flu'-xo *m.* flood, flux.
fo-ca-li-zar' *tr.v.* to focus.

fo-car' *tr.v.* to focus.
fo'-co *m.* focus.
fo-ci'-nho *m.* snout.
fô-fo, **=a** *adj.* light, fluffy; soft.
fo-gal' *m.* old tax on each home.
fo-gão' *m.* stove.
fo-ga-rei'-ro *m.* small portable stove.
fo'-go *m.* fire; hearth, home.
fo-gue'-te *m.* fireworks, rocket.
fo-guis'-ta *m.* fireman, stoker.
foi'-ce *f.* scythe.
fol-clo'-re *f.* folk-lore.
fo'-le *m.* bellows.
fô-le-go *m.* breath; repose, leisure.
fol'-ga *g.* idleness, recreation, rest; width.
fol-ga'-do, **=a** *adj.* ample; easy-going.
fol-gar' *tr.v.* to loosen, to give width; *intr.v.* to recess, to rest.
fol-gue'-do *m.* joke, jest.
fô-lha *f.* leaf, blade, sheet, folio; novo em — new, unused.
fo-lha'-do *m.* rolled out pastry or dough;
fo-lha'-do, **=a** *adj.* leafy.
fo-lha'-gem *f.* foliage.
fo-lhe-a'-do *m.* veneer.
fo-lhe-ar' *tr.v.* to page through, to turn (the leaves of a book), to read hurriedly, to peruse; to veneer, to trim with [gold leaf.
fo-lhen'-to, **=a** *adj.* full of leaves.
fo-lhe'-ta *f.* pamphlet.
fo-lhe-tim' *m.* serial story; literary section.
fo-lhi'-nha *f.* calendar pad (each sheet representing one day).
fó-li-o *m.* folio.
fo'-me *f.* hunger.
fo-men-ta-ção' *f.* promoting; (med.) fomentation.
fo-men-tar' *tr.v.* to promote, to foster.
fo-men'-to *m.* fomentation; (fig.) aid, encouragement.
fo-né-ti-ca *f.* phonetics.
fo-né-ti-co, **=a** *adj.* phonetic.
fo-nó-gra-fo *m.* phonograph.
fon-ta-ne'-la *f.* fontanelle.
fon'-te *f.* font; source; fountain, spring.
fo'-ra *adv.* outside, in a foreign land; *prep.* except; *interj.* Get out!!; — de horas at inopportune time, very late; — de si exalted; beside oneself.
fo-ra-gi'-do, **=a** *adj.*, *m.*, *f.* emigrated; emigrant.
fo-ra-gir'=se *refl.v.* to emigrate.
fo-ras-tei'-ro, **=a** *adj.*, *f.*, *m.* foreigₙ, foreigner, stranger.
fôr-ca *f.* gallows.
fôr-ça *f.* force, strength.
for-ca'-da *f.* bifurcation.
for-ca'-do *m.* pitch-fork.
for-çar' *tr.v.* to force, to oblige.
fór-ceps or **fór-ci-pe** *m.* forceps.
for-ço'-so, **=a** *adj.* necessary, inevitable.
for'-ja *f.* forge; smithy, blacksmith shop.
for-ja-dor' *m.* forger, blacksmith.
for-jar' *tr.v.* to forge, to fabricate; to falsify, to counterfeit.
for-ma-ção' *f.* formation.
for-mal' *adj.* formal, plain, explicit, genuine, textual.
for-ma-li-da'-de *f.* formality.
for-mar' *tr.v.*, *intr.v.* to form; —=se *refl.v.* to be formed; to be trained; to get one's degree.
for-ma-ti'-vo, **=a** *adj.* formative.
for-ma-tu'-ra *f.* graduation; battle-array.
for-mão' *m.* carpenter's chisel.

for-mi-ci'-da *m.* ant-killer (chemical).
fór-mi-co, **=a** *adj.* formic.
for-mi-dá-vel *adj.* formidable.
for-mi'-ga *f.* ant.
for-mi-gão' *m.* large ant.
for-mi-guei'-ro *m.* ant-hill.
for-mo'-so, **=a** *adj.* beautiful.
for-mo-su'-ra *f.* beauty.
fór-mu-la *f.* formula.
for-mu-lar' *tr.v.* to formulate.
for-na'-lha *f.* fire-box.
for-ne-ce-dor' *m.* *adj.* furnisher, supplying.
for-ne-cer' *tr.v.* to supply.
for-ne-ci-men'-to *m.* furnishing, supplying, provision.
for-ni-ca-ção' *f.* fornication.
for-ni-ca-dor' *m.* fornicator.
for-ni'-lho *m.* small oven.
for'-no *m.* oven, kiln, furnace; alto — blast furnace.
fo'-ro *m.* forum; court; rent.
for-ra'-gem *f.* forage.
for-rar' *tr.v.* to line, to put lining in; to cover; to paper; —=se *refl.v.* to steal; to provide for oneself.
fôr-ro *m.* ceiling; wall-paper; upholstering; lining.
for-ta-le-cer' *tr.v.* to strengthen; to encourage.
for-ta-le-ci-men'-to *m.* strengthening.
for-ta-le'-za *f.* fortitude, strength; fortification.
for'-te *m.* fort, fortification; *adj.* strong, solid, intense, hard.
for-ti-fi-ca-ção' *f.* fortification.
for-ti-fi-can'-te *adj.* fortifying, tonic.
for-ti-fi-car' *tr.v.* to fortify.
for-tu'-na *f.* fortune; luck, destiny.
fos-fo-res-cen'-te *adj.* phosphorescent.
fós-fo-ro *m.* phosphorus; match.
fos'-sa *f.* ditch; fossa.
fós-sil *m.* fossil.
fos-si-li-zar' *tr.v.* to fossilize.
fos'-so *m.* moat, canal.
fo-to-gra-fi'-a *f.* photography; photograph.
fo-tó-gra-fo *m.* photographer.
fo-to-gê-ni-co, **=a** *adj.* photogenic.
foz' *f.* mouth of a river.
fra-ção' *f.* fraction.
fra-cas-sar' *intr.v.*, *tr.v.* to fail, to be unsuccessful; to ruin, to break.
fra-cas'-so *m.* failure; ruin, disaster.
fra'-co, **=a** *adj.* weak, not solid.
fra'-de *m.* monk, friar.
fra-des'-co, **=a** *adj.* monkish, monastic.
fra-di'-ce *f.* manner of a monk, saying of a monk.
fra-di-ci'-da *m.* monk-killer.
fra-ga'-ta *f.* frigate.
frá-gil *adj.* fragile.
fra-gi-li-da'-de *f.* fragility.
frag-men-tá-rio, **=a** *adj.* fragmentary.
frag-men'-to *m.* fragment.
fra-grân-cia *f.* fragrance.
fra-gran'-te *adj.* fragrant.
fral'-da *f.* flap; skirt.
fral-di'-lha *f.* leather apron used by blacksmiths.
fram-bo-e'-sa *f.* raspberry.
fran-ga'-lho *m.* rags, tatters.
fran'-go *m.* capon; pullet.
fran'-ja *f.* fringe.
fran-jar' *tr.v.* to trim with fringe.
fran-que-ar' *tr.v.* to frank, to post.
fran'-co *m.* franc.
fran'-co, **=a** *adj.* frank, sincere, earnest.
fran-có-fi-lo *m.* Francophile.

fran-có-fo-bo *m.* Francophobe.
fran-que'-za *f.* frankness, sincerity.
fran-zi'-do *m.* ruffle.
fran-zir' *tr.v.* to ruffle, to gather; — as **sobrancelhas** to frown, to knit one's brow.
fra'-que *m.* cutaway coat.
fra-que'-za *f.* weakness, fragility.
fras'-co *m.* bottle; flask.
fra'-se *f.* sentence (gram.).
fra-se-a'-do *m.* style; manner of speaking.
fra-ter-nal' *adj.* brotherly, fraternal.
fra-ter-ni-da'-de *f.* brotherhood, fraternity.
fra-ter-ni-zar' *intr.v.* to fraternize; *tr.v.* to make friendly.
fra-tri-cí-dio *m.* fratricide.
fra-tu'-ra *f.* fracture.
fra-tu-rar' *tr.v.* to fracture.
frau'-de *f.* fraud.
frau-du-len'-to, =a *adj.* fraudulent.
fre'-cha *f.* arrow.
fre-guês *m.* customer.
fre-gue-si'-a *f.* parish; clientele.
frei' *m.* friar, brother (used before proper names).
frei'-o *m.* bit; brake (machinery).
frei'-re *m.* monk, brother, friar.
fren'-te *f.* front; **em** — **a** in front of.
fre-quên-cia *f.* frequency.
fre-quen-tar' *tr.v.* to frequent.
fre-quen'-te *adj.* frequent.
fres'-co, =a *adj.* fresh; cool, vigorous.
fres-cu'-ra *f.* freshness, coolness.
fre-ta'-gem *f.* freight, shipping by freight.
fre-tar' *tr.v.* to freight, to rent, to charter.
fre'-te *m.* freight, freight charges.
fric-ção' *f.* friction.
fric-cio-nar' *tr.v.* to rub, to massage.
fri-a'-gem *f.* coldness.
fri-al-da'-de *f.* cold, coldness.
fri-e'-za *f.* cold, chill, coldness.
fri-gi-dei'-ra *f.* frying-pan.
fri-gi-dez' *f.* frigidity.
frí-gi-do, =a *adj.* frigid, icy.
fri-gir' *tr.v.* to fry.
fri'-o, =a *adj.* cold.
fri-o-ren'-to, =a *adj.* sensitive to cold.
fri'-sa *f.* frieze (cloth); theatre boxes almost on level with auditorium or orchestra seats.
fri-sa'-do *m.* artificially curled hair.
fri-san'-te *adj.* appropriate; significant; convincing.
fri-sar' *tr.v.* to curl, to point up; to approach, to border on.
fri'-so *m.* frieze (arch.).
fri-ta'-da *f.* fry.
fri-tar' *tr.v.* to fry.
fri'-to, =a *adj.* fried.
fri-tu'-ra *f.* frying; fry.
fri-vo-li-da'-de *f.* frivolity.
frí-vo-lo, =a *adj.* frivolous.
fron'-de *f.* foliage.
fro'-nha *f.* pillow case.
fron'-te *f.* forehead; front.
fron-tei'-ra *f.* frontier.
fron-tei'-ro, =a *adj.* in front, at the front, frontier.
fron-tis-pí-cio *m.* frontispiece.
fro'-ta *f.* fleet.
frou'-xo, =a *adj.* loose, soft, bland, indolent.
fru-frú *m.* rustling of leaves; rustle of silken clothing.
fru-gal' *adj.* frugal.
fru-ga-li-da'-de *f.* frugality.

fru-i-ção' *f.* enjoyment, possession, fruition.
fru-ir' *tr.v.* to enjoy.
frus-tra-ção' *f.* frustration.
frus-trar' *tr.v.* to frustrate, to baffle.
fru'-ta *f.* fruit.
fu-bá *m.* corn meal.
fu'-ga *f.* flight; fugue.
fu-ga-ci-da'-de *f.* fleetness; inconstancy.
fu-gaz' *adj.* fugitive, transitory.
fu-gir' *intr.v.* to flee, to escape.
fu-gi-ti'-vo *m.* fugitive, deserter; **fu-gi-ti'-vo, =a** *adj.* fugitive, transitory.
fu-la'-no *m.* so-and-so (vague designation of person whose name cannot be given or is not known).
ful'-cro *m.* fulcrum.
ful-gen'-te *adj.* shining, brilliant, sparkling.
fúl-gi-do, =a *adj.* brilliant.
ful-gir' *intr.v.* to shine out, to shine forth; to stand out.
ful-gu-ran'-te *adj.* shining, sparkling.
ful-gu-rar' *intr.v.* to flash, to sparkle, to lighten.
fu-li'-gem *f.* soot.
fu-li-gi-no'-so, =a *adj.* sooty.
ful-mi-nan'-te *adj.* stunning, striking (with lightning).
ful-mi-nar' *tr.v.* to blast, to strike down; *intr.v.* to flash.
fu-ma'-ça *f.* smoke, puff.
fu-ma'-da *f.* signal smoke.
fu-ma-dor' *m.* smoker.
fu-man'-te *m.* smoker.
fu-mar' *tr.v., intr.v.* to smoke.
fu'-mo *m.* smoke.
fu-mi-gar' *tr.v.* to fumigate.
fun-ção' *f.* function, entertainment, performance.
fun-cio-nal' *adj.* functional.
fun-cio-na-men'-to *m.* working, functioning.
fun-cio-nar' *intr.v.* to work, to go, to function.
fun-cio-ná-rio *m.* official, civil service employee.
fun'-da *f.* slingshot.
fun-da-ção' *f.* foundation.
fun-da-dor' *m.* founder; **fun-da-dor', =a** *adj.* founding.
fun-dar' *tr.v.* to build, to construct; to found, to institute.
fun-da'-gem *f.* sediment, dregs, residue.
fun-da-men-tal' *adj.* fundamental, basic.
fun-da-men'-to *m.* basis; foundation.
fun-de-ar' *intr.v.* to drop anchor, to come into port.
fun-di-ção' *f.* foundry; melting, smelting.
fun-dí-bu-lo, *m.* ancient sling used in war.
fun-di'-lho *m.* seat of trousers; gore to widen seat of trousers.
fun-dir' *tr.v.* to melt; to cast.
fun-dí-vel *adj.* fusible.
fun'-do *m.* bottom, depth; background (of stage); public funds, capital; **fun'-do, =a** *adj.* deep.
fun-du'-ra *f.* depth, profundity.
fú-ne-bre *adj.* funereal.
fu-ne-rá-rio *m.* funeral urn.
fu-né-re-o, =a *adj.* funereal.
fu-nes'-to, =a *adj.* fatal, disastrous.
fun-ga-dei'-ra *f.* snuff box, tobacco box.
fun-gar' *tr.v.* to sniff, to snuff, to absorb through the nose; *intr.v.* to take snuff; to sniffle; to whistle.
fun'-go *m.* fungus; mushroom.

fun-go′-so, ‗a *adj.* fungous.
fu-ni-cu-lar′ *adj.* funicular.
fu-ní-cu-lo *m.* small stock.
fu-nil′ *m.* funnel.
fu-ni-lei′-ro *m.* tinsmith.
fu-ra‗bo′-lo *m.* busybody.
fu-ra‗bo′-los *m.pl.* forefinger, index finger.
fu-ra-ção′ *f.* cyclone, hurricane, whirlwind.
fu-ra′-do *m.* canal, channel.
fu-ra-dor′ *m.* punching machine.
fu-rar′ *tr.v.* to bore into, to pierce; to riddle.
fu-ren′-te *adj.* furious.
fur-gão′ *m.* van, baggage car.
fú-ria *f.* fury.
fu-ri-o′-so, ‗a *adj.* furious.
fur′-na *f.* cave, cavern.
fu′-ro *m.* hole, orifice.
fu-ror′ *m.* furor, furore.
fur-ta-de′-la *f.* stealing; hiding.
fur-ta‗fo′-go *m.* dark lantern.
fur-tar′ *tr.v.* to steal, to rob.
fur-ti′-vo, ‗a *adj.* furtive, secret.

fur′-to *m.* theft, robbery.
fu-são′ *f.* fusion, fusing, melting.
fus′-co, ‗a *adj.* dark, dusky; fus′-co *m.* twilight.
fu-si-bi-li-da′-de *f.* fusibility.
fu-sí-vel *adj.* fusible.
fu′-so *m.* spindle; fusee (of a watch).
fus-tão′ *m.* fustian.
fú-til *adj.* futile; trifling.
fu-ti-li-da′-de *f.* futility.
fu-tu′-ra *f.* fiancée.
fu-tu-ri-da′-de *f.* futurity, future.
fu-tu-ris′-mo *m.* futurism.
fu-tu′-ro *m.* future; fu-tu′-ro, ‗a *adj.* future.
fu-to-ro′-so, ‗a *adj.* promising, auspicious.
fu-zil′ *m.* rifle.
fu-zi-la′-da *f.* shooting, rifle shots.
fu-zi-la-dor′ *m.* rifleman.
fu-zi-lar′ *tr.v.* to shoot, to execute (by firing squad).
fu-zi-la-rí-a *f.* musketry, firing, shooting.
fu-zi-lhão′ *m.* pin (of a buckle).

G

See page 12—GUIDE TO REFORMER SPELLING used in this Dictionary

G, g *m.* G, g, seventh letter of the alphabet.
ga-ba-ção′ *f.* praise, eulogy, flattery.
ga-bar′ *tr.v.* to praise, to flatter; —‗se to boast.
ga-bar-di′-na *f.* gabardine.
ga-ba-rí *m.* ga-ba-ri′-to *m.* full-size model; templet; gauge (of railway).
ga-bi-ão′ *m.* large basket, hurdle.
ga-da′-nha *f.* scythe; soup ladle.
ga-da′-nho *m.* talon, claw (of bird of prey); long-toothed rake.
ga-da-ri′-a *f.* cattle.
ga′-do *m.* cattle.
ga-do‗de‗cur-ral′ *m.* milch cows with their calves.
ga-do‗de‗sôl-ta *m.* cattle in pasture.
ga-fa-nho′-to *m.* grasshopper.
ga′-go *m.* stutterer.
ga-guei′-ra *f.* stuttering, stammering.
ga-gue-jar′ *tr.v., intr.v.* to stammer, to stutter.
ga-guez′ *f.* stuttering, stammering.
gai-o′-la *f.* bird cage; furniture crate.
gai-o′-lo *m.* bird trap.
gai′-ta *f.* shepherd's pipe.
ga′-la *f.* national holiday; solemnity; gala; dress for festive occasion.
ga-lã′ *m.* gallant; lover (on stage).
ga-lac-tô-me-tro *m.* galactometer.
ga-lan-ta-ri′-a *f.* gallantry.
ga-lan′-te *adj.* gallant.
ga-lan-te-ar′ *tr.v.* to court; *intr.v.* to flirt.
ga-lan-tei′-o *m.* love-making, flirting, gallantry.
ga-lan-ti′-na *f.* chopped meat in aspic.
ga-lão′ *m.* galloon; gallon (liquid measure).
ga-lar-dão′ *m.* premium; glory; recompense, reward.
ga-lé *f.* galley.
ga-le-ão′ *m.* galleon.
ga-le′-na *f.* galena.
ga-le-ri′-a *f.* gallery.

gal-gar′ *tr.v.* to jump over; *intr.v.* to leap, to climb up.
gal′-go *m.* greyhound.
ga-lhar-de′-te *m.* flag, signal flag, pennant.
ga-lhar′-do, ‗a *adj.* gracious; generous.
ga-lhe′-ta *f.* cruet.
ga-lhe-tei′-ro *m.* cruet-stand.
ga′-lho *m.* branch of tree; shoot (plant); horn, antler.
ga-li-cis′-mo *m.* Gallicism.
ga-li′-nha *f.* hen.
ga-li-nhei′-ro *m.* hen house, chicken coop.
ga-li-pó-dio *m.* gallipot.
ga-lis′-ta *m.* game-cock trainer.
ga′-lo *m.* rooster.
ga-lo′-cha *f.* galosh, overshoe.
ga-lo-pa′-da *f.* race, galloping.
ga-lo-pan′-te *adj.* galloping.
ga-lo-par′ *intr.v.* to gallop.
ga-lo′-pe *m.* gallop.
gal-va-ni-zar′ *tr.v.* to galvanize.
gal-va-nô-me-tro *m.* galvanometer.
gal-va-no-plas-ti′-a *f.* electroplating.
ga′-ma *f.* gamut (music).
gam-bér-ria *f.* trip, tripping.
gam-be′-ta *f.* turning, twisting movement; duck, dodge; irregular, reprehensible conduct.
gâm-bia *f.* leg.
gam-bi′-to *m.* gambit; trick or play to beat adversary.
ga-me′-la *f.* small, wild goat; slop bucket.
ga-me′-lo *m.* feed-trough.
ga-me′-ta *f.* gamete.
ga-mo′-te *m.* wooden water scoop.
ga′-na *f.* wish, desire; hunger, appetite.
ga-nân-cia *f.* gain, earnings; usury, illicit profit.
ga-na-cio′-so, ‗a *adj.* lucrative.
gan′-cho *m.* hook, bracket; hairpin.
gan-chor′-ra *f.* boat hook.
gan-cho′-so, ‗a *adj.* curved, hooked.

gâng-lio *m.* ganglion.
gan-gre'-na *f.* gangrene.
gan-gre-no'-so, =a *adj.* gangrenous.
ga-nha-dor' *m.* worker, laborer; bread-earner.
ga-nhan'-ça *f.* profit.
ga-nhão' *m.* day-laborer; winner; one who will do any work to make a living.
ga'-nha=pão' *m.* livelihood, means of support; wage-earner.
ga-nhar' *tr.v.* to earn, to gain, to win, to attain, to acquire possession of; *intr.v.* to profit, to improve, to excel.
ga'-nho *m.* profit.
ga-nho'-so, =a *adj.* ambitious, greedy for gain; self-interested.
gan'-so *m.* gander.
ga-ran'-te *m.* guarantor.
ga-ran-ti'-a *f.* guaranty.
ga-ran-tir' *tr.v.* to guarantee.
ga-ra'-pa *f.* fruit juice beverage.
gar'-ça *f.* heron.
gar-ça=a-zul' *f.* blue heron.
gar-ça=bran'-ca *f.* egret.
gar-çon' *m.* waiter.
gar-dê-nia *f.* gardenia.
gar-fa'-da *f.* fork-full.
gar-fei'-ra *f.* fork-box, fork-case.
gar'-fo *m.* fork, pitch-fork; graft (on plants).
gar-ga-lei'-ra *f.* bung-hole in hogshead or barrel.
gar-ga-lha'-da *f.* loud laughter.
gar-ga-lhar' *intr.v.* to laugh loudly or boisterously.
gar-ga'-lo *m.* neck of bottle.
gar-gan'-ta *f.* neck, throat.
gar-ga-re-jar' *tr.v.*, *intr.v.* to gargle.
gar-ga-re'-jo *m.* gargling; flirtation between young man in street and lady in window.
gár-gu-la *f.* gargoyle.
ga-rim-pei'-ro *m.* prospector; bootleg prospector.
ga-rim'-po *m.* diamond mine, gold mine.
gar-lo'-pa *f.* large plane.
gar-na'-cha *f.* robe or vestment worn by magistrates or priests.
ga-ro-ti'-ce *f.* conduct or chatter of street urchins.
ga-rô-to *m.* street urchin.
gar'-ra *f.* claw, talon, nail, finger, toe; (fig.) tyranny.
gar-ra'-fa *f.* bottle.
gar-ra-fal' *adj.* bottle-shaped.
gar-ra-fão' *m.* large bottle.
gar-ro'-ta *f.* two-year old yearling or heifer.
gar-ro'-te *m.* screw by which collar is tightened until strangulation results; garrote.
gar-ro-ti'-lho *m.* croup, quinsy.
gar-ru-li'-ce *f.* garrulousness.
gár-ru-lo, =a *m.*, *f.*, *adj.* garrulous person; garrulous.
ga-ru'-pa *f.* rump of horse; saddle-bag.
gás *m.* gas.
ga-so'-sa *f.* soda water.
ga-so'-so, =a *adj.* gaseous.
gas-o-li'-na *f.* gasoline.
ga-sô-me-tro *m.* gasometer, gas reservoir.
gás-pe-a *f.* vamp, upper (of shoe).
gas-ta'-lho *m.* clamp; vise.
gas-tar' *tr.v.* to spend, to use, to consume, to wear out.
gas'-to *m.* expense, deterioration, consumption.
gas-tri'-te *f.* gastritis.

gas-tro-nô-mi-co, =a *adj.* gastronomic.
ga'-to, =a *m.*, *f.* cat.
ga-tar-rão' *m.* large cat.
ga-te-a'-do, =a *adj.* having greenish-yellow eyes, having yellowish-red color.
ga-tei'-ra *f.* cat-hole (in door or gate); ventilating openings in basement or foundation walls.
ga-ti'-lho *m.* trigger.
ga-ti'-nha *f.* kitten.
ga-tu-na'-gem *f.* band of ruffians, tramps.
ga-tu-ni'-ce *f.* cheating, trickery.
ga-tu'-no *m.* rogue.
ga-ú-cho *m.* citizen of Rio Grande do Sul, cowboy.
gáu-dio *m.* leisure; enjoyment.
ga-ve'-ta *f.* drawer (in furniture).
ga-ve-tão' *m.* large drawer.
ga-vi-ão' *m.* hawk.
ga-vi'-nha *f.* tendril.
ga-vo'-ta *f.* gavotte.
ga'-za or **ga'-ze** *f.* chiffon (fabric)
ga-ze-tei'-ro *m.* journalist; truant; newsboy.
ga-ze-ti'-lha *f.* news section of periodical.
ga-ze'-ta *f.* newspaper, gazette; truancy.
ga-zu'-a *f.* master key; pick-lock.
géi-ser *m.* geyser.
ge-la'-da *f.* ice-cold beverage.
ge-la'-do *m.* sherbet; ge-la'-do, =a *adj.* icy, iced, ice-cold.
ge-la-du'-ra *f.* frost, freezing of vegetation.
ge-lar' *tr.v.*, *intr.v.* to freeze, to congeal.
ge-lei'-ra *f.* glacier; ice-house, ice factory.
gê-lo *m.* ice.
ge-la-ti'-na *f.* gelatin.
ge-la-ti-no'-so, =a *adj.* gelatinous.
ge-léi-a *f.* jelly.
ge'-ma *f.* egg yolk; gem.
ge-mar' *tr.v.* to graft (with buds); *intr.v.* to grow buds, to grow shoots.
gê-me-o, =a *m.*, *f.*, *adj.* twin.
ge-mer' *intr.v.*, *tr.v.* to groan, to suffer; to lament.
ge-mi'-do *m.* groan, lamentation.
ge-mí-fe-ro, =a *adj.* gem-producing area or formation; having buds or shoots.
ge-mi-na-ção' *f.* gemination.
ge-mi-nar' *tr.v.* to geminate.
ge-ne-a-lo-gi'-a *f.* genealogy.
ge-ne-ra-la'-do *m.* generalcy.
ge-ne-ra-la'-to *m.* generalcy.
ge-ne-ra-li-da'-de *f.* generality.
ge-ne-ra-lís-si-mo *m.* generalissimo.
ge-ne-ra-li-za-ção' *f.* generalization.
ge-ne-ra-li-zar' *tr.v.* to generalize.
ge-né-ri-co, =a *adj.* generic.
gê-ne-ro *m.* gender; genre, class, kind, order; =s *m.pl.* merchandise, food-stuff, agricultural products.
ge-ne-ro-si-da'-de *f.* generosity.
ge-ne-ro'-so, =a *adj.* generous.
gê-ne-sis *f.* gê-ne-se *f.* genesis.
ge-né-ti-ca *f.* genetics.
ge-né-ti-co, =a *adj.* genetic.
ge-ni-tor' *m.* father.
ge-ne-triz' *f.* mother.
gen-gi'-bre *m.* ginger.
gen-gi'-va *f.* gum (of teeth).
gen-gi-val' *adj.* relative to the gums.
gen-gi-vi'-te *f.* inflammation of the gums.
ge-ni-al' *adj.* genius-like.
ge-ni-a-li-da'-de *f.* geniality.

gê-nio m. genius; temperament, character, make-up; (pop.) temper.
ge-ni-o'-so, =a adj. gifted; temperamental.
ge-ni-tal' adj. genital.
gen'-ro m. son-in-law.
gen'-te f. people, family, humanity; personnel.
gen-til' adj. genteel; nice, kind.
gen-ti-le'-za f. kindness, courtesy, genteelness, gentility.
gen-til'=ho'-mem m. nobleman, gentleman.
gen-ti'-o m. pagan.
ge-nu-fle-xão' f. genuflection, kneeling.
ge-nui-ni-da'-de f. genuineness.
ge-nu-í-no, =a adj. genuine.
ge-o'-do m. geode.
ge-o-dé-sia f. geodesy.
ge-o-gra-fi'-a f. geography.
ge-ó-gra-fo m. geographer.
ge-o-lo-gi'-a f. geology.
ge-ó-lo-go m. geologist.
ge-ô-me-tra m. geometrician.
ge-o-me-tri'-a f. geometry.
ge-ral' adj. general; m. greater or common part; head of religious order.
ge-râ-nio m. geranium.
ge-ra-ção' f. generation, lineage, descendency.
ge-ra-dor' m. creator, producer.
ge-rar' tr.v. to beget; to create; to generate; to cause or produce; intr.v.; —se refl.v. to be born, to develop.
ge-ra-triz' f. creator, producer.
ge-rên-cia f. management, administration.
ge-ren'-te m., f., adj. manager; managing.
ge-rir' tr.v. to manage, to administer.
ger'-me m. germ.
ger-mi-ci'-da m. germicide.
ger-mi-na-ção' f. germination.
ger-mi-nar' intr.v. to germinate.
ges-sar' tr.v. to coat with plaster of Paris.
ges-sei'-ro m. one who works in plaster of Paris.
gês-so m. plaster of Paris; clay.
ges-ta-ção' f. gestation.
ges-tan'-te adj. in gestation.
ges-ti-cu-la-ção' f. gesticulation.
ges-ti-cu-lar' intr.v. to gesticulate.
ges'-to m. gesture.
gi-bão' m. doublet.
gi-gan'-te m. giant.
gi-gan-tis'-mo m. giantism.
gi-ná-sio m. gymnasium; secondary school.
gi-nas'-ta m. gymnast.
gi-nás-ti-ca f. gymnastics.
gi-nás-ti-co, =a adj. gymnastic.
gi-ne-co-lo-gi'-a f. gynecology.
gi-ra'-fa f. giraffe.
gi-ra-ção' f. gyration.
gi-ran'-te adj. gyratory.
gi-rar' intr.v. to gyrate.
gi-ras-sol' m. sunflower.
gi-ra-tó-rio, =a adj. gyratory.
gí-ria f. slang, jargon.
gi-ros-có-pio m. gyroscope.
giz' m. chalk.
gi-zar' tr.v. to chalk, to outline.
gla-be'-la f. glabella.
gla-ci-al' adj. glacial.
gla-ci-ar' m. glacier.
gla-ci-á-rio, =a adj. glacial.
gla-di-a-dor' m. gladiator.
gla-dia-tó-rio, =a adj. gladiatorial.
gla-dí-o-lo m. gladiolus.
glân-du-la f. gland.
gle'-ba f. clod, sod, turf.

gli-ce-ri'-na f. glycerin.
gli-co-gê-nio m. glycogen.
gli'-fo m. glyph, notch, channel, cavity.
glo-bal' adj. global.
glo'-bo m. globe.
glo-bu-lar' adj. globular.
glo-bu-li'-na f. globulin.
gló-bu-lo m. globule, corpuscle.
gló-ria f. glory.
glo-ri-fi-ca-ção' f. glorification.
glo-ri-fi-car' tr.v. to glorify.
glo-rí-o-la f. undeserved glory or praise.
glo-ri-o'-so, =a adj. glorious.
glo'-sa f. interpretation; gloss.
glo-sar' tr.v. to gloss, to interpret.
glos-sá-rio m. glossary.
glo'-te f. glottis.
gló-ti-co, =a adj. glottal.
glo-xí-nia f. gloxinia.
glu-tão' m., adj. glutton.
glú-ten m. gluten.
glu-ti-nar' tr.v. to glue together.
glu-ti-no'-so, =a adj. glutinous.
go-e'-la f. gullet, throat.
go'-la f. collar.
go-la'-da f. navigable channel over a sand-bar.
go'-le m. gulp, swallow.
gôl-fo m. gulf.
gol'-pe m. blow; slash; cut; shock; stroke, accident.
gol-pe-ar' tr.v. to strike, to beat, to wound.
go'-ma f. starch.
go'-mo m. bud, shoot; slice of orange or lemon.
gôn-do-la f. gondola.
gon-do-lei'-ro m. gondolier.
gor'-do, =a adj. fat, fleshy.
gor-du'-ra f. fatness, obesity; fatty substance.
gor-du-ren'-to, =a adj. oily, fatty.
go-ri'-la or **go-ri'-lha** m. gorilla.
gor-je-ar' intr.v. to sing, to trill like a bird.
gor-jei'-o m. happy trilling song of birds; children's chatter.
gor-je'-ta f. tip.
gor'-ra f. hood, beret, stocking cap.
gor'-ro m. beret.
gos-tar' intr.v., tr.v. to like, to be pleased with, to feel friendship for; to experiment, to test; to taste.
gos-tá-vel adj. likeable, tasty.
gôs-to m. taste.
gos-to'-so, =a adj. tasty, appetizing.
go'-ta f. drop; tear.
go-tei'-ra f. gutter, spouting.
go-te-jar' tr.v., intr.v. to drop, to fall in drops, to drip.
gó-ti-co, =a adj. Gothic.
go-ver-na-dor' m. governor.
go-ver-na-men-tal' adj. governmental.
go-ver-nan-ta f. governess; housekeeper.
go-ver-nan'-te adj. governing.
go-ver-nar' tr.v. to govern, to rule, to manage, to direct, to steer.
go-vêr-no m. government; rudder.
go-zar' tr.v. to use, to possess; intr.v. to enjoy.
gô-zo m. use; enjoyment, pleasure.
gra'-ça f. grace; favor; baptismal name.
gra-ce'-jo m. joke, jest.
gra-ci-o'-so, =a adj. gracious, humorous.
gra-ço'-la f. questionable joke.
gra-da-ção' f. gradation.
gra-da-du'-ra f. leveling, grading.
gra-da'-gem f. grading.

gra-dar' *tr.v.* to grade, to level.

gra'-de *f.* grate; grating; trellis; brick mold.

gra-dien'-te *m.* gradient.

gra-de-ar' *tr.v.* to provide with a grating.

gra-dil' *m.* iron fence, iron grating.

gra-du-a-ção *f.* graduation.

gra-du-a'-do, =a *adj.* graduated, classified.

gra-du-al' *adj.* gradual; having steps or grades.

gra-du-ar' *tr.v.* to graduate; —=se *refl.v.* to be graduated.

gra-fi'-a *f.* graph; (way of) spelling.

grá-fi-ca *f.* penmanship; writing.

grá-fi-co *m.* graph; **grá-fi-co,** =a *adj.* graphic.

gra-fi'-la *f.* legend (on coin or medal).

gra-fi'-te *f.* graphite.

gral' *m.* mortar; Holy Grail.

gra'-ma *f.* gross; *m.* gram (weight).

gra-má-ti-ca *f.* grammar.

gra-ma-ti-cal' *adj.* grammatical.

gra-má-ti-co *m.* grammarian; **gra-má-ti-co,** =a *adj.* grammatical.

gra-mi'-nho *m.* scriber, gage.

gra-mo-fo'-ne *m.* gramophone.

gram'-pa *f.* cramp, clamp.

gram'-po *m.* staple; hairpin.

gra-na'-da *f.* grenade; garnet.

gra-na-dei'-ro *m.* grenadier.

gra-na-di'-na *f.* grenadine (fabric).

gran-da-lhão' *adj.* very large.

gran'-de *adj.* large; *m.* wealthy, important person; grandee.

gran-de'-vo, =a *adj.* aged.

gran-de'-za *f.* largeness; grandeur.

gran-di-o'-so, =a *adj.* grandiose.

gran-di-lo-quên-cia *f.* grandiloquence.

gran-dí-lo-quo, =a *adj.* grandiloquent.

gra-nel' *m.* granary; galley proof.

gra-ni'-do *m.* design, engraving (generally on steel).

gra-nir' *tr.v.* to engrave.

gra-ni'-to *m.* granite.

gra-nu-la-ção' *f.* granulation.

gra-nu-la'-do, =a *adj.* granular.

gra-nu-lar' *adj.* granular.

grâ-nu-lo *m.* granule.

grão' *m.* grain, seed; (shortened form of grande).

grão=du-ca'-do *m.* grand duchy.

grão=du'-que *m.* grand duke.

grão=mes'-tre *m.* grand master.

gras-sar' *intr.v.* to rage destructively (of an epidemic or fire); to become widespread.

gras-sen'-to, =a *adj.* oily, greasy.

gras'-so, =a *adj.* oily, greasy.

gra-ti-dão' *f.* gratitude.

gra'-to, =a *adj.* grateful, pleasing.

gra-ti-fi-ca-ção' *f.* tip, bonus; extra allowance.

gra-ti-fi-car' *tr.v.* to tip, to give bonus to.

gra'-tis *adj., adv.* gratis, free.

gra-tui-ti-da'-de *f.* gratuity.

gra-tui'-to, =a *adj.* gratuitous.

grau' *m.* grade; degree; step; title (academic).

gra-ú-do *m.* wealthy, powerful, or influential person; **gra-ú-do,** =a *adj.* important, large.

gra-va-dor' *m.* engraver.

gra-var' *t.v.* to engrave, to sculpture; to stamp, to mark with seal; to fix in memory.

gra-va'-ta *f.* cravat, necktie.

gra'-ve *adj.* grave.

gra-vi-da'-de *f.* gravity; low pitch.

gra-vi-dez' *f.* pregnancy.

grá-vi-do, =a *adj.* pregnant.

gra-vis'-co *m.* serious, doubtful, troublesome.

gra-vi-ta-ção' *f.* gravitation.

gra-vi-tar' *intr.v.* to gravitate.

gra'-xa *f.* grease; saddle or shoe wax.

gra'-xo, =a *adj.* greasy.

gre-de-lém *adj.* flax-flower blue.

gre'-lha *f.* grill, gridiron.

gre-lhar' *tr.v.* to grill, to broil.

gre-mi-al' *m.* gremial.

grê-mio *m.* club; group; association, guild.

gre'-ve *f.* strike.

gre-vis'-ta *m.* striker.

gri-far' *tr.v.* to underline; to slant letters in writing.

gri'-fo, =a *adj.* Italicized; slanted (handwriting); underlined.

gri-lhão' *m.* chain.

gri-lhe'-ta *f.* shackle; fetter; *m.* criminal condemned to be shackled.

gri'-lo *m.* cricket

gri-nal'-da *f.* garland.

gri'-pe *f.* grippe.

gris' *adj.* gray; ash-colored.

gri-sa-lhar' *intr.v.* to turn grey.

gri-sa'-lho *m.* greyish; grey-haired.

gri-zú *m.* firedamp.

gri-tar' *intr.v.* to shout, to speak loudly.

gri-ta-ri'-a *f.* succession of shouts, noisy talk.

gri'-to *m.* cry, outcry, shout.

gro'-sa *f.* gross (twelve dozen); heavy file; kind of dull knife for removing flesh from hides.

gro-sar' *tr.v.* to file, to smooth.

gros-sei-rão' *adj.* rude, impolite.

gros-sei'-ro, =a *adj.* coarse, rough; ill-bred.

gros-se-ri'-a *f.* rudeness; vulgarity.

gros'-so, =a *adj.* gross; big, coarse, thick, swollen.

gros-su'-ra *f.* grossness, thickness, abundance.

gro'-ta *f.* grotto.

gro-tes'-co, =a *adj.* grotesque.

gru-dar' *tr.v.* to glue.

gru'-de *m.* glue.

gru-nhir' *intr.v.* to grunt, to squel like a pig.

gru-par' *tr.v.* to group.

gru'-po *m.* group.

gru'-ta *f.* cave, cavern.

gua-ra-ná *m.* beverage made with powder prepared from seed of guaraná tree.

guar'-da *f.* guard, vigilance, care; =s da fechadura safety catch; *m.* guard, watchman.

guar'-da=chu'-va *m.* umbrella.

guar'-da=co-mi'-da *m.* cupboard, pantry closet.

guar'-da=cos'-tas *m.* coast-guard boat.

guar'-da=fa'-to *m.* wardrobe.

guar'-da=fo'-go *m.* fire-screen.

guar'-da=la'-ma *m.* mudguard.

guar'-da=li'-vros *m.* book-keeper.

guar'-da=lou'-ça *m.* china cupboard; china closet.

guar'-da=ma-ri'-nha *m.* midshipman.

guar-da-na'-po *m.* table napkin.

guar'-da=no-tur'-no *m.* right-watchman.

guar-dar' *tr.v.* to guard, to keep, to keep safe, to put in a safe place; —=se *refl.v.* to avoid, to abstain, to guard against.

guar'-da=rou'-pa *m.* wardrobe.

guar'-da=sol' *m.* parasol.

guar'-da=vis'-ta m. eye-shade.
guar-di-ão' m. custodian.
guar-ne-cer' tr.v. to provide with, to furnish; to adorn.
guar-ni-ção' f. garrison, ship's crew; ornament.
gu'-de m. game of marbles.
gue-de'-lha f. hair, shag, long hair.
guel'-ra f. gills.
guer'-ra f. war.
guer-re-ar' tr.v., intr.v. to fight, to combat, to make war.
guer-rei'-ro m. warrior.
guer-ri'-lha f. guerrilla.
guer-ri-lhei'-ro m. member of a guerrilla band.
gui'-a f. guide; bill of lading; long rein; governor (of an engine); guide post, mile post.
gui-a-dor' m. index (of a book); gui-a-dor', =a adj. guiding.
gui-ão' m. flag, standard; standard-bearer.
gui-ar' tr.v., intr.v. to guide; to navigate; to drive (an automobile).
gui-ché m. peep-hole; ticket window.
gui-dão', gui-don' m. handle bar.
guil'-das f.pl. guilds.

gui-lher'-me m. rabbet-plane.
gui-lho-ti'-na f. guillotine.
guin-das'-te m. crane (machine).
gui-néu m. guinea (coin).
gui-pu'-ra f. guipure.
gui'-sa f. fashion, manner, guise.
gui-sa'-do m. stew.
gui-sar' tr.v. to stew, to sauté; to cook up.
gui-tar'-ra f. guitar; (slang) press for printing counterfeit money.
gui-tar-ris'-ta m. guitar player.
gu'-la f. gluttony; excessive eating and drinking.
gu-lo-di'-ce f. tasty bit, delicacy.
gu-lo'-so, =a m., f. glutton; adj. gluttonous, given to excessive eating.
gu'-me m. cutting edge of knife; (fig.) perspicacity.
gu-mí-fe-ro, =a adj. starch-producing.
gu-rí m. child, youngster.
gus-ta-ção' f. tasting, gustation.
gu'-ta f. gamboge.
gu'-ta=per'-cha f. gutta-percha.
gu-tu-ral' adj. guttural.
gu-tu-ra-li-zar' tr.v. to gutturalize.
guz'-la f. one-stringed guitar, used in Orient.

H

See page 12—GUIDE TO REFORMED SPELLING used in this Dictionary

H, h m. H, h; eighth letter of the alphabet: symbol for hydrogen.
há-bil adj. skilful, clever, able, fit; legally qualified.
ha-bi-li-da'-de f. skill, ability, talent.
ha-bi-li-do'-so, =a adj. skilful, expert; cunning.
ha-bi-li-ta-ção' f. qualification, ability, aptitude.
ha-bi-li-tar' tr.v. to qualify, to enable; —=se refl.v. to petition judicial eligibility.
ha-bi-tan'-te m., f. inhabitant.
ha-bi-tar' tr.v. to live in, to inhabit; intr.v. to reside, to live.
ha-bi-tá-vel adj. habitable.
há-bi-to m. habit.
ha-bi-tu-al' adj. habitual.
ha-bi-tu-ar' tr.v. to accustom.
há-li-to m. breath, odor of the breath.
ha'-lo m. halo.
har-mo-ni'-a f. harmony.
har-mo-ni-o'-so, =a adj. harmonious.
har-mo-ni-zar' tr.v. to harmonize.
har-mô-ni-ca f. harmonica.
har-mô-nio m. harmonium.
har'-pa f. harp.
har-pis'-ta m., f. harpist.
has'-ta f. lance, long spike; auction.
has'-te or hás-te-a f. stem, trunk; standard; flagpole.
has-te-ar' tr.v. to hoist, to raise (a flag); to unfold.
ha-ver' tr.v. to have; impers.v. to be, to happen, to exist; m. credit (in bookkeeping); ha-ve'-res m.pl. property, possessions.
he-brai'-co m. Hebrew.
he-bra-ís-ta m. Hebraist.
he-breu' m. Hebrew.
hec-to-gra'-ma m. hectogram.
hec-to-li'-tro m. hectoliter.

hec-tô-me-tro m. hectometer.
he-di-on'-do, =a adj. fetid, stinking; sordid, repugnant.
he-do-nis'-mo m. hedonism.
he-ge-mo-ni'-a f. hegemony.
hé-li-ce m., f. helix; propeller.
hé-lio m. helium.
he-li-ó-gra-fo m. heliograph.
he-li-o-gra-vu'-ra f. heliogravure.
he-li-ô-me-tro m. heliometer.
he-li-os-có-pio m. helioscope.
he-li-ós-ta-to m. heliostat.
he-li-o-tró-pio m. heliotrope.
he-ma-ti'-na f. hematin.
he-ma-ti'-ta f. hematite.
he-mis-fé-ri-co, =a adj. hemispheric.
he-mis-fé-rio m. hemisphere.
he-mo-fi-li'-a f. hemophilia.
he-mo-glo-bi'-na f. hemoglobin.
he-mor-ra-gi'-a f. hemorrhage.
he-mor-rói-das f.pl. hemorrhoid.
hep-ta-teu'-co m. Heptateuch.
he-rál-di-ca f. heraldry.
he-rál-di-co, =a adj. heraldic.
he-ral'-do m. herald.
he-ran'-ça f. inheritance, heritage.
her-bá-rio m. herbarium.
her-bo-lá-rio m. herbalist.
her-bo-ris'-ta m. herbalist.
her-bo-ri-zar' intr.v. to collect medicinal herbs.
her-cú-le-o, =a adj. Herculean.
her-da'-de f. inheritance, estate, property.
her-dar' tr.v., intr.v. to inherit.
her-dei'-ro m. inheritor.
he-re-di-tá-rio, =a adj. hereditary.
he-re'-ge adj., m., f. heretic.
he-re-si'-a f. heresy.
her-mé-ti-co, =a adj. hermetic.
he-rói m. hero.
he-rói-co, =a adj. heroic.

he-ro-í-na *f.* heroine.
he-ro-ís-mo *m.* heroism.
he-si-ta-ção' *f.* hesitation.
he-si-tan'-te *adj.* hesitating, hesitant.
he-si-tar' *intr.v.* to hesitate.
he-te-ro-do-xi'-a *f.* heterodoxy.
he-te-ro-do'-xo, *a adj.* heterodox.
he-te-ro-ge-ne-i-da'-de *f.* heterogeneity.
he-te-ro-gê-ne-o, *a adj.* heterogeneous.
he-xá-go-no *m.* hexagon.
he-xa-go-nal' *adj.* hexagonal.
hi-a-cin'-to *m.* hyacinth.
hi-a'-to *m.* hiatus.
hi-ber-na-ção' *f.* hibernation.
hi-ber-nar' *intr.v.* to hibernate.
hi-bis'-co *m.* hibiscus.
hi-bri-dis'-mo *m.* hybridism.
hí-bri-do *m.* hybrid.
hi-dráu-li-ca *f.* hydraulics.
hi-dro-a-vi-ão' *m.* sea-plane.
hi-dro-di-nâ-mi-ca *f.* hydrodynamics.
hi-dro-fo-bi'-a *f.* hydrophobia.
hi-dro-gê-nio *m.* hydrogen.
hi-dró-li-se *f.* hydrolysis.
hi-dro-pla'-no *m.* hydroplane.
hi-dro-stá-ti-ca *f.* hydrostatics.
hi-e-rar-qui'-a *f.* hierarchy.
hi-e-ro-gli'-fo *m.* hieroglyph.
hí-fen *m.* hyphen.
hi-la-ri-da'-de *f.* hilarity.
hi-la-rian'-te *adj.* hilarious.
hi-gi-e'-ne *f.* hygiene.
hi-gi-ê-ni-co, *a adj.* hygienic.
hí-men *m.* hymen.
hi-me-neu' *m.* marriage, wedding.
hi-ná-rio *m.* hymnal.
hi'-no *m.* hymn, anthem.
hi-nó-gra-fo *m.* writer of hymn.
hi-no-lo-gi'-a *f.* hymnology.
hi-pe-ra-ci-dez' *f.* hyperacidity.
hi-pér-bo-le *f.* hyperbole.
hi-per-crí-ti-co *m.* hypercritic.
hip-no'-se *f.* hypnosis.
hip-nó-ti-co, *a adj.* hypnotic.
hip-no-tis'-mo *m.* hypnotism.
hi-po-cri-si'-a *f.* hypocrisy.
hi-pó-cri-ta *m., f. adj.* hypocrite.
hi-po-dér-mi-co, *a adj.* hypodermic.
hi-pó-dro-mo *m.* hippodrome.
hi-po-pó-ta-mo *m.* hippopotamus.
hi-po-te'-ca *f.* mortgage.
hi-po-te-car' *tr.v.* to mortgage.
hi-pó-te-se *f.* hypothesis.
hi-po-té-ti-co, *a adj.* hypothetical.
hir-su'-to, *a adj.* nirsute, hairy.
his-pâ-ni-co, *a adj.* Hispanic.
his-pi-dez' *f.* roughness.
hís-pi-do, *a adj.* rough, bristly.
his-so'-pe *m.* sprinkler of holy water.
his-so'-po *m.* hyssop.
his-te-ri'-a *f.* hysteria.
his-té-ri-co, *a adj.* hysterical.
his-tó-ria *f.* history.
his-to-ri-a'-da *f.* complexity, long story.
his-to-ri-a-dor' *m.* historian.
his-tó-ri-co, *a adj.* historic, historical.
his-tri-ão' *m.* buffoon, clown.
ho-di-er'-no, *a adj.* modern, recent, present-day.
ho'-je *adv.* today, at present time, during current period.
ho-lo-caus'-to *m.* holocaust.
hom-bri-da'-de *f.* manliness.
ho'-mem *m.* man; human being.
ho-me-na'-gem *f.* homage.
ho-men-zar-rão' *m.* strapping-big fellow.
ho-men-zi'-nho *m.* little fellow; youth.

ho-me-o-pa-ti'-a *f.* homeopathy.
ho-mi-cí-dio *m.* homicide.
ho-mí-lia *f.* homily.
ho-mo-ge-ne-i-da'-de *f.* homogeneity.
ho-mo-gê-ne-o, *a adj.* homogeneous.
ho-mo-lo-gi'-a *f.* homology.
ho-mos-se-xu-al' *adj.* homosexual.
ho-nes-ti-da'-de *f.* honesty.
ho-nes'-to, *a adj.* honest.
ho-no-ra-bi-li-da'-de *f.* merit, respectability.
ho-no-rá-rio, *a adj.* honorary; ho-no-rá-rios *m.pl.* fee, honorarium.
hon'-ra *f.* honor.
hon-ra'-do, *a adj.* honored, upright.
hon-rar' *tr.v.* to honor.
hon-ra-dez' *f.* honor, integrity.
ho'-ra *f.* hour; time; o'clock.
ho-rá-rio *m.* schedule; dial; regular train.
ho-ri-zon-tal' *adj.* horizontal.
ho-ri-zon'-te *m.* horizon.
hor-mô-nio *m.* hormone.
hor-ren'-do, *a adj.* horrifying; foul.
hor-ren'-te *adj.* horrifying.
hor-rí-vel *adj.* horrible.
hor-ror' *m.* horror.
hor-ro-ro'-so, *a adj.* horrifying.
hor'-ta *f.* vegetable garden.
hor-ta-li'-ça *f.* vegetables.
hor-te-lã' *f.* garden mint.
hor-te-lão' *m.* gardener.
hor-tên-sia *f.* hydrangea.
hor-ti-cul-tu'-ra *f.* horticulture.
hor'-to *m.* small vegetable garden.
hós-pe-da *f.* guest.
hos-pe-da'-gem *f.* hospitality.
hos-pe-dar' *tr.v.* to lodge, to give hospitality to; —se *refl.v.* to put up, to stop.
hos-pe-da-ri'-a *f.* inn, hostelry, boarding-house.
hós-pe-de *m.* guest.
hos-pe-dei'-ro, *a adj.* hospitable, kindly.
hos-pí-cio *m.* hospice.
hos-pi-tal' *m.* hospital.
hos-pi-ta-li-zar' *tr.v.* to hospitalize.
hos-pi-ta-lei'-ro, *a* hospitable, charitable.
hos-pi-ta-li-da'-de *f.* hospitality.
hos'-te *f.* army; throng, host.
hós-tia *f.* host (eccl.).
hos-ti-á-rio *m.* box in which the unconsecrated Eucharistic wafer is kept.
hos-til' *adj.* hostile.
hos-ti-li-da'-de *f.* hostility.
ho-tel' *m.* hotel, hostelry.
ho-te-lei'-ro *m.* hotel owner, hotel manager.
hu'-lha *f.* anthracite coal.
hu-lhei'-ra *f.* coal mine.
hu-lhí-fe-ro, *a adj.* anthracite producing.
hu-ma-ni-da'-de *f.* humanity.
hu-ma-nis'-mo *m.* humanism.
hu-ma-nis'-ta *m.* humanist.
hu-ma-ni-tá-rio, *a adj.* humanitarian.
hu-ma'-no, *a adj.* human.
hu-mil-da'-de *f.* humility.
hu-mil'-de *adj.* humble.
hu-mi-lha-ção' *f.* humiliation.
hu-mi-lhan'-te *adj.* humiliating.
hu-mi-lhar' *tr.v.* to humiliate.
hu-mi-li-a-ção' *f.* humiliation.
hu-mi-li-an'-te *adj.* humiliating.
hu'-mo *m.* humus.
hu-mo'-so, *a adj.* containing humus.
hu-mor'-a-quo'-so *m.* aqueous humor.
hu-mo-ris'-ta *m.* humorist.
hu-mor'-ví-tre-o *m.* vitreous humor.
hu-mo-ro'-so, *a adj.* humorous.

I

I, i *m.* I, i, ninth letter of the alphabet.
i-a'-que *m.* yak.
i-a'-te *m.* yacht.
i-bé-ri-co, =a *adj.* i-be'-ro, =a *adj.* Iberian.
i-çar' *tr.v.* to raise (flag or banner).
í-co-ne *m.* icon.
i-co-nis'-ta *m.* maker of images.
i-co-no-clas'-ta *m.* iconoclast; *adj.* iconoclastic.
i-co-no-lo-gi'-a *f.* iconology.
ic-te-rí-cia *f.* jaundice.
i-da'-de *f.* age.
i-de-al' *m. adj.* ideal.
i-de-a-lis'-mo *m.* idealism.
i-de-a-lis'-ta *m.* idealist.
i-de-a-li-za-ção' *f.* idealization.
i-de-a-li-zar' *tr.v.* to idealize.
i-de-ar' *tr.v.* to conceive, to fancy.
i-déi-a *f.* idea.
i-dên-ti-co, =a *adj.* identic, identical.
i-den-ti-da'-de *f.* identity.
i-den-ti-fi-ca-ção' *f.* identification.
i-den-ti-fi-car' *tr.v.* to identify.
i-de-o-lo-gi'-a *f.* ideology.
i-dí-li-co, =a *adj.* idyllic.
i-dí-lio *m.* idyll.
i-di-o'-ma *m.* idiom.
i-dio-má=ti-co, =a *adj.* idiomatic.
i-di-os-sin-cra-si'-a *f.* idiosyncrasy.
i-di-o'-ta *m.* idiot.
i-di-o-ti'-a *f.* idiocy.
i-di-ó-ti-co, =a *adj.* idiotic.
i-dó-la-tra *m., f.* idolater.
i-do-la-tri'-a *f.* idolatry.
í-do-lo *m.* idol.
i-do-ne-i-da'-de *f.* suitableness.
i-dô-ne-o, =a *adj.* suitable.
i-do'-so, =a *adj.* old, aged.
i-ga-ça'-ba *f.* wide-mouthed pottery jar for water or food stuffs; funeral urn of early inhabitants (Brazil).
ig-na'-ro, =a *adj.* lacking in instruction, ignorant.
íg-ne-o, =a *adj.* igneous.
ig-ni-ção' *f.* ignition.
ig-nó-bil *adj.* ignoble.
ig-no-bi-li-da'-de *f.* ignobleness.
ig-no-mí-nia *f.* ignominy.
ig-no-mi-nio'-so, =a *adj.* ignominious.
ig-no-ra'-do, =a *adj.* obscure, unknwon.
ig-no-rân-cia *f.* ignorance.
ig-no-ran-tão' *m.* ignoramus.
ig-no-ran'-te *adj.* ignorant.
ig-no-rar' *tr.v.* to not know, to be ignorant of.
i-gre'-ja *f.* church.
i-gre-jei'-ro, =a *adj.* pertaining to church; being constantly in church.
i-gre-ji'-nha *f.* little church.
i-gre-jo'-la *f.* tiny church.
i-gre-jó-rio *m.* tiny church.
i-gual' *adj.* equal.
i-gua-lar' *tr.v.* to equal, to make equal.
i-gual-da'-de *f.* equality.
i-gua-ri'-a *f.* delicacy.
i-le-gal' *adj.* illegal.
i-le-ga-li-da'-de *f.* illegality.
i-le-gi-ti-mi-da'-de *f.* illegitimacy.
i-le-gí-ti-mo, =a *adj.* illegitimate.
i-le-gí-vel *adj.* illegible.

i-le-tra'-do, =a *adj.* illiterate.
i'-lha *f.* island.
i'-lha=de=ma'-to *f.* oasis.
i-lhó *m., f.* eyelet; metal ring surrounding eyelet.
i-li-be-ral' *adj.* illiberal.
i-lí-ci-to, =a *adj.* illicit.
il-me-ni'-ta *f.* ilmenite (mineral).
i-ló-gi-co, =a *adj.* illogical.
i-lu-dir' *tr.v.* to illude, to frustrate.
i-lu-mi-na-ção' *f.* illumination.
i-lu-mi-nar' *tr.v.* to illuminate.
i-lu-mi-nu'-ra *f.* illumination of manuscripts and books.
i-lu-são' *f.* illusion.
i-lu-si'-vo, =a *adj.* illusive.
i-lu-só-rio, =a *adj.* illusory.
i-lus-tra-ção' *f.* illustration; distinction, learning.
i-lus-tra-dor' *m.* illustrator.
i-lus-trar' *tr.v.* to illustrate; to make famous; to educate.
i-lus-tra-ti'-vo, =a *adj.* illustrative.
i-lus'-tre *adj.* illustrious.
í-mã *m.* magnet.
i-ma-cu-la'-do, =a *adj.* immaculate.
i-ma'-gem *f.* image, picture.
i-ma-gi-na-ção' *f.* imagination.
i-ma-gi-nar' *tr.v.* to conceive, to think up; —=se *refl.v.* to imagine.
i-ma-gi-ná-rio, =a *adj.* imaginary.
i-ma-gi-na-ti'-vo, =a *adj.* imaginative.
i-ma-gi-ná-vel *adj.* imaginable.
i-ma-gi-no'-so, =a *adj.* imaginative.
i-ma-ni-zar' *tr.v.* to magnetize.
i-ma-te-ri-al' *adj.* immaterial.
i-ma-tu-ri-da'-de *f.* immaturity.
i-ma-tu'-ro, =a *adj.* immature.
im-be-cil' *adj.* imbecile.
im-be-ci-li-da'-de *f.* imbecility.
im-ber'-be *adj.* beardless; very young.
im-bu-ir' *tr.v.* to soak; to imbue.
i-me-mo-ri-al' *adj.* immemorial.
i-me-di-a-ções' *f.pl.* neighborhood, proximity.
i-me-di-a'-to, =a *adj.* immediate; next, following.
i-men-si-da'-de *f.* immensity.
i-men-si-dão' *f.* immenseness.
i-men'-so, =a *adj.* immense.
i-men-su-rá-vel *adj.* immeasurable.
i-mer-gir' *tr.v.* to immerse.
i-mer-são' *f.* immersion.
i-mer'-so, =a *adj.* immersed.
i-mi-gra-ção' *f.* immigration.
i-mi-gran'-te *m., f.* immigrant.
i-mi-grar' *intr.v.* to immigrate.
i-mi-nên-cia *f.* imminence; threat.
i-mi-nen'-te *adj.* imminent.
i-mi-ta-ção' *f.* imitation.
i-mi-tar' *tr.v.* to imitate.
i-mi-ta-ti'-vo, =a *adj.* imitative.
i-mo-bi-li-da'-de *f.* immobility.
i-mo-ral' *adj.* immoral.
i-mo-ra-li-da'-de *f.* immorality.
i-mor-tal' *adj.* immortal.
i-mor-ta-li-da'-de *f.* immortality.
i-mor-ta-li-zar' *tr.v.* to immortalize.
im-pac'-to *m.* impact.
im-pa-gá-vel *adj.* unpayable; humorous, comic.

im-pal-pá-vel *adj.* impalpable.
im-pa-lu-dis'-mo *m.* malaria.
im-par-ci-al' *adj.* impartial.
im-par-cia-li-da'-de *f.* impartiality.
im-par *adj.* odd (of a number not divisible by two).
im-pas-sí-vel *adj.* impassible.
im-pe-cá-vel *adj.* impeccable.
im-pe-di'-do *m.* orderly.
im-pe-di-men'-to *m.* obstruction, impediment.
im-pe-dir' *tr.v.* to prevent, to hinder, to obstruct; to impede.
im-pen-den'-te *adj.* impending.
im-pen-der' *intr.v.* to impend.
im-pe-lir' *tr.v.* to impel.
im-pe-ne-trá-vel *adj.* impenetrable.
im-pe-ni-tên-cia *f.* impenitence.
im-pe-ni-ten'-te *adj.* impenitent.
im-pen-sá-vel *adj.* unthinkable.
im-pe-ra-dor' *m.* emperor.
im-pe-rar' *intr.v.* to rule, to govern; to prevail.
im-pe-ra-ti'-vo, =a *adj.* imperative.
im-pe-ra-triz' *f.* empress.
im-per-cep-tí-vel *adj.* imperceptible.
im-per-do-á-vel *adj.* unpardonable.
im-pe-re-cí-vel *adj.* imperishable.
im-per-fei'-to, =a *adj.* imperfect.
im-pe-ri-al' *adj.* imperial.
im-pe-ri-a-lis'-mo *m.* imperialism.
im-pé-rio *m.* empire.
im-pe-ri-o'-so, =a *adj.* imperious.
im-pe-ri'-to, =a *adj.* not expert, unskilled.
im-per-me-á-vel *adj.* impermeable.
im-per-ti-nên-cia *f.* impertinence.
im-per-ti-nen'-te *adj.* impertinent.
im-per-tur-bá-vel *adj.* imperturbable.
im-pér-vio, =a *adj.* impervious.
im-pes-so-al' *adj.* impersonal.
ím-pe-to *m.* impetus; violence.
im-pe-trar' *tr.v.* to beg; to get by begging.
im-pe-tu-o'-so, =a *adj.* impetuous.
im-pi-e-da'-de *f.* impiety.
im-pi-e-do'-so, =a *adj.* impious, inhuman.
ím-pi-o, =a *adj.* impious.
im-pin-gir' *tr.v.* to impinge.
im-pla-cá-vel *adj.* implacable.
im-plan-tar' *tr.v.* to implant.
im-ple-men'-to *m.* implement.
im-pli-ca-ção' *f.* implication.
im-pli-cân-cia *f.* provocation, ill-will.
im-pli-car' *tr.v.* to implicate.
im-plí-ci-to, =a *adj.* implicit.
im-plo-rar' *tr.v.* to implore.
im-po-li-dez' *f.* impoliteness.
im-po-li'-do, =a *adj.* impolite.
im-pon-de-rá-vel *adj.* imponderable.
im-po-nen'-te *adj.* imposing, magnificent.
im-po-pu-lar' *adj.* unpopular.
im-por' *tr.v.* to impose, to inflict, to impute; —se *refl.v.* to become inevitable; to force oneself on.
im-por-ta-dor' *m.* importer.
im-por-tân-cia *f.* importance, size.
im-por-tan'-te *adj.* important, large.
im-por-tar' *tr.v.* to import; *intr.v.* to matter, to be of importance.
im-por'-te *m.* amount, cost.
im-por-tu-nar' *tr.v.* to importune, to bother.
im-por-tu'-no, =a *adj.* importunate, bothersome.
im-po-si-ção' *f.* imposition.
im-pos-si-bi-li-da'-de *f.* impossibility.

im-pos-sí-vel *adj.* impossible.
im-pos'-to *m.* tribute, impost, =ax; im-pos'-to, =a *adj.* imposed.
im-pos-tor' *m.* impostor.
im-pos-tu'-ra *f.* imposture, hypocrisy.
im-po-tên-cia *f.* impotence.
im-po-ten'-te *adj.* impotent, powerless.
im-pra-ti-cá-vel *adj.* impracticable.
im-pre-cin-dí-vel *adj.* indispensable.
im-preg-na-ção' *f.* impregnation.
im-preg-nar' *tr.v.* to impregnate.
im-pren'-sa *f.* printing press; (fig.) press.
im-pren-sar' *tr.v.* to print, to stamp, to imprint, to impress.
im-pres-são' *f.* impression.
im-pres-sio-nar' *tr.v.* to impress; to move, to stir.
im-pres-sio-ná-vel *adj.* impressionable.
im-pres-si'-vo, =a *adj.* impressive.
im-pres-tá-vel *adj.* useless.
im-pri-mir' *tr.v.* to print, to stamp; to impart, to inculcate.
im-pro-du-ti'-vo, =a *adj.* unproductive.
im-pró-prio, =a *adj.* improper.
im-pro-vi-den'-te *adj.* improvident.
im-pro-vi-sar' *tr.v.*, *intr.v.* to improvise.
im-pru-den'-te *adj.* imprudent.
im-pu-den'-te *adj.* impudent; shameless.
im-pug-nar' *tr.v.* to oppose, to contradict; to impugn.
im-pul-sar' *tr.v.* to impel, to give impulse to; to drive.
im-pul-si'-vo, =a *adj.* impulsive.
im-pul'-so *m.* impulse.
im-pu'-ne *adj.* not punished.
im-pu-ni-da'-de *f.* immunity.
im-pu-re'-za *f.* impurity.
im-pu-ri-da'-de *f.* impurity.
im-pu'-ro, =a *adj.* impure.
im-pu-tar' *tr.v.* to impute.
im-pu-tá-vel *adj.* imputable.
i-mun-dí-cia *f.* lack of cleanliness; rubbish.
i-mun'-do, =a *adj.* filthy; obscene.
i-mu'-ne *adj.* immune.
i-mu-ni-da'-de *f.* immunity.
i-mu-ni-zar' *tr.v.* to immunize.
i-mu-tá-vel *adj.* immutable.
i-na-cei-tá-vel *adj.* unacceptable.
i-na-ces-sí-vel *adj.* inaccessible.
i-na'-ne *adj.* inane; lifeless.
i-na-ni-da'-de *f.* inanity.
i-nap'-to, =a *adj.* inept, inapt, unable.
i-nar-ti-cu-la'-do, =a *adj.* inarticulate.
i-na-ti'-vo, =a *adj.* inactive.
i-na'-to, =a *adj.* innate.
i-nau-di'-to, =a *adj.* extraordinary, unheard of.
i-nau-dí-vel *adj.* inaudible.
i-nau-gu-ra-ção' *f.* inauguration.
i-nau-gu-ral' *adj.* inaugural.
i-nau-gu-rar' *tr.v.* to inaugurate.
in-cal-cu-lá-vel *adj.* incalculable.
in-can-des-cên-cia *f.* incandescence.
in-can-des-cen'-te *adj.* incandescent.
in-can-sá-vel *adj.* tireless; assiduous.
in-car-nar' *tr.v.* to incarnate.
in-cau'-to, =a *adj.* incautious, negligent.
in-cen-di-ar' *tr.v.* to set on fire; to incite.
in-cen-di-á-rio *m.* incendiary.
in-cên-dio *m.* fire.
in-cen-sá-rio *m.* thurible, incensory.
in-cen'-so *m.* incense.
in-cen-ti-var' *tr.v.* to stimulate, to motivate.
in-cen-ti'-vo, =a *adj.* incentive.
in-ces-san'-te *adj.* incessant.

in-ces'-to m. incest.
in-cha-ção' f. swelling; tumor; vanity.
in-cha'-do, -a adj. swollen, enlarged.
in-char' tr.v., intr.v. to swell, to become enlarged.
in-ci-dên-cia f. incidence.
in-ci-den-tal' adj. incidental.
in-ci-den'-te m. incident.
in-ci-ne-rar' tr.v. to incinerate.
in-ci-pi-en'-te adj. incipient.
in-ci-são' f. incision.
in-ci-tar' tr.v. to incite.
in-ci-vi-li-da'-de f. incivility.
in-cle-mên-cia f. inclemency.
in-cle-men'-te adj. inclement.
in-cli-na-ção' f. inclination, bowing.
in-cli-nar' tr.v. to incline, to lower; intr.v. to bow, to bend over.
ín-cli-to, -a adj. distinguished, famous.
in-co-e-rên-cia f. incoherence.
in-co-e-ren'-te adj. incoherent.
in-clu-ir' tr.v. to include.
in-clu-são' f. inclusion.
in-clu-si'-vo, -a adj. inclusive.
in-clu'-so, -a adj. included, enclosed.
in-cóg-ni-ta f. unknown quantity.
in-cóg-ni-to m. incognito; in-cóg-ni-to, -a adj. incognito.
in-com-bus-tí-vel adj. incombustible.
in-co-men-su-rá-vel adj. incommensurable.
in-co-mo-dar' tr.v. to disturb, to inconvenience.
in-cô-mo-do m. inconvenience; slight illness, indisposition; in-cô-mo-do, -a adj. uncomfortable, inconvenient.
in-com-pa-rá-vel adj. incomparable.
in-com-pa-ti-bi-li-da'-de f. incompatibility.
in-com-pa-tí-vel adj. incompatible.
in-com-pe-tên-cia f. incompetence.
in-com-pe-ten'-te adj. incompetent.
in-com-pre-en-sí-vel adj. incomprehensible.
in-co-mu-ni-cá-vel adj. incommunicable.
in-con-ce-bí-vel adj. inconceivable.
in-con-di-ci-o-nal' adj. unconditional.
in-côn-di-to, -a adj. crude, unfinished, unrefined.
in-con-si-de-ra'-do, -a adj. inconsiderate.
in-con-sis-ten'-te adj. inconsistent.
in-con-so-lá-vel adj. inconsolable.
in-cons-tân-cia f. inconstancy.
in-cons-tan'-te adj. inconstant.
in-cons-ti-tu-ci-o-nal' adj. unconstitutional.
in-con-ti-nên-cia f. incontinence.
in-con-ti-nen'-te adj. incontinent.
in-con-ti-nen'-te adv. immediately, without delay or interruption.
in-con-tro-ver-tí-vel adj. incontrovertible.
in-con-ve-ni-ên-cia f. inconvenience; indecency.
in-con-ve-ni-en'-te [adj. inconvenient, unbecoming, improper.
in-con-ver-sí-vel or in-con-ver-tí-vel adj. inconvertible.
in-cor-po-rar' tr.v., intr.v. to incorporate; —-se refl.v. to enter into, to become part of.
in-cor-pó-re-o, -a adj. incorporeal.
in-cor-re'-to, -a adj. incorrect.
in-cor-ri-gí-vel adj. incorrigible.
in-cor-rup-tí-vel adj. incorruptible.
in-cré-du-lo, -a adj. incredulous.
in-cre-men'-to m. increment.

in-cri-mi-nar' tr.v. to accuse, to impute; to incriminate.
in-crí-vel adj. incredible, unbelievable.
in-crus-ta-ção' f. incrustation.
in-crus-tar' tr.v. to incrust.
in-cu-ba-ção' f. incubation.
in-cu-ba-do'-ra f. incubator.
in-cu-bar' tr.v. to incubate.
ín-cu-bo, -a adj. like a nightmare.
in-cul-par' tr.v. to accuse; —-se refl.v. to confess, to compromise oneself.
in-cum-bên-cia f. incumbency.
in-cu-ná-bu-lo m. incunabulum.
in-cu-rá-vel adj. incurable.
in-cú-ria f. carelessness; inertia.
in-cur-são' f. incursion, invasion.
in-cu-tir' tr.v. to infuse, to inspire, to suggest.
in-da-ga-ção' f. investigation, research.
in-da-gar' tr.v. to investigate; to inform, to point out.
in-de-cên-cia f. indecency.
in-de-cen'-te adj. indecent.
in-de-ci-são' f. indecision.
in-de-ci'-so, -a adj. irresolute, vague, uncertain.
in-de-co'-ro m. indecorum.
in-de-co-ro'-so, -a adj. indecorous.
in-de-fe-rir' tr.v. to report negatively, to deny, to refuse (requisition or petition).
in-de-fe-rí-vel adj. that cannot be granted.
in-de-fi-ni'-do, -a adj. undefined, vague, uncertain.
in-de-fi-ni'-to, -a adj. indefinite.
in-de-fi-ní-vel adj. undefinable.
in-de-lé-vel adj. indelible.
in-de-li-ca-de'-za f. indelicacy.
in-de-li-ca'-do, -a adj. indelicate.
in-de-ni-da'-de f. indemnity.
in-de-ni-za-ção' f. indemnification.
in-de-ni-zar' tr.v. to indemnify.
in-de-pen-dên-cia f. independence.
in-de-pen-den'-te adj. independent.
in-des-cri-tí-vel adj. indescribable.
in-des-tru-tí-vel adj. indestructible.
in-de-ter-mi-na'-do, -a adj. indeterminate.
in-de-ter-mi-ná-vel adj. indeterminable.
ín-dex m. index.
in-di-ca-ção' f. indication.
in-di-ca-dor' m. indicator, forefinger; directory, catalogue.
in-di-car' tr.v. to indicate.
in-di-ca-ti'-vo, -a adj. indicative.
ín-di-ce m. index.
in-di-fe-ren'-ça f. indifference.
in-di-fe-ren'-te adj. indifferent.
in-dí-ge-na m. native, original inhabitant.
in-di-gên-cia f. indigence.
in-di-gen'-te adj. indigent.
in-di-ge-rí-vel adj. indigestible.
in-di-ges-tão' f. indigestion.
in-di-ges'-to, -a adj. undigested.
in-dig-na-ção' f. indignation.
in-dig-na'-do, -a adj. indignant.
in-dig-ni-da'-de f. indignity.
ín-di-go m. indigo.
in-di-re'-ta f. belittling side remark; hint; insinuation.
in-di-re'-to, -a adj. indirect.
in-dis-cre'-to, -a adj. indiscreet; in-dis-cre'-to, -a m., f. indiscreet person.
in-dis-pos'-to, -a adj. indisposed, ill.
in-dis-pu-tá-vel adj. indisputable.
in-dis-so-lú-vel adj. indissoluble.
in-dis-tin-guí-vel adj. indistinguishable.

in-dis-tin'-to, =a adj. indistinct.
in-di-vi-dual' adj. individual.
in-di-vi-dua-li-da'-de f. individuality.
in-di-ví-duo m. individual.
in-di-vi-sí-vel adj. indivisible.
ín-do-le f. character, temperament, nature.
in-do-lên-cia f. indolence.
in-do-len'-te adj. indolent.
in-dô-mi-to, =a adj. indomitable.
in-du-bi-tá-vel adj. indubitable.
in-du-ção' f. induction.
in-dul-gên-cia f. indulgence.
in-dul-gen'-te adj. indulgent.
in-dús-tria f. industry.
in-dus-tri-al' adj., m. industrial.
in-dus-tri-o'-so, =a adj. industrious.
in-du-ti'-vo, =a adj. inductive.
in-du-zir' tr.v. to induce, to induct.
i-ne-bri-an'-te adj. intoxicating.
i-né-di-to, =a adj. unpublished.
i-ne-fi-ci-en'-te adj. inefficient.
i-ne-gá-vel adj. undeniable.
i-ne-go-ci-á-vel adj. unnegotiable.
i-nep'-to, =a adj. inept.
i-nér-cia f. inertia.
i-ne-rên-cia f. inherence.
i-ne-ren'-te adj. inherent.
i-ne-rir' intr.v. to inhere.
i-nes-pe-ra'-do, =a adj. unexpected.
i-nes-ti-má-vel adj. inestimable.
i-ne-vi-tá-vel adj. inevitable.
i-ne-xo-rá-vel adj. inexorable.
i-nex-pe-ri-en'-te adj. inexperienced.
i-nex-pi-á-vel adj. inexpiable.
i-nex-pli-cá-vel adj. inexplicable.
i-nex-tri-cá-vel adj. inextricable.
in-fa-li-bi-li-da'-de f. infallibility.
in-fa-lí-vel adj. infallible.
in-fa'-me adj. infamous.
in-fâ-mia f. infamy.
in-fân-cia f. infancy.
in-fan-ta-ri'-a f. infantry.
in-fan-ti-cí-dio m. infanticide.
in-fan-til' adj. infantile, childish, childlike.
in-fa-ti-gá-vel adj. tireless.
in-fe-ção' f. infection.
in-fe-ci-o'-so, =a adj. infectious.
in-fe-tar' tr.v. to infect, to contaminate.
in-fe'-to, =a adj. infected, corrupt.
in-fe-li-ci-da'-de f. infelicity.
in-fe-liz' adj. unhappy.
in-fe-rên-cia f. inference.
in-fe-rir' tr.v. to infer.
in-fe-ri-or' m., adj. inferior; lower.
in-fe-rio-ri-da'-de f. inferiority.
in-fer-nal' adj. infernal.
in-fer-nei'-ra f. tumult, confusion.
in-fer'-no m. hell, inferno.
in-fér-til adj. infertile.
in-fes-tar' tr.v. to infest.
in-fes'-to, =a adj. infested, offensive, hostile.
in-fi-de-li-da'-de f. infidelity.
in-fi-el' adj. unfaithful; m. pagan.
in-fil-tra-ção' f. infiltration.
in-fil-trar' tr.v. to infiltrate.
ín-fi-mo, =a adj. lowest, meanest.
in-fi-ni-da'-de f. infinity.
in-fi-ni-ti'-vo m. infinitive.
in-fi-ni'-to, =a adj. infinite.
in-fi-ni-te-si-mal' adj. infinitesimal.
in-fla-ma-ção' f. inflammation, ignition, kindling, setting on fire.
in-fla-mar' tr.v. to set on fire, to inflame, to incite.
in-fla-ma-tó-rio, =a adj. inflammatory.
in-fla-má-vel adj. inflammable.

in-fla-ção' f. inflation.
in-flar' tr.v. to inflate.
in-fle-tir' tr.v. to curve, to bend; to inflect.
in-fle-xão' f. inflection; bending; bowing.
in-flu-ên-cia f. influence.
in-flu-ir' tr.v., intr.v. to influence.
in-flu-en'-za f. influenza.
in-for-ma-ção' f. information.
in-for-mar' tr.v. to inform.
in-fra-ção' f. infraction.
in-fre-quen'-te adj. infrequent.
in-frin-gir' tr.v. to infringe.
in-fu-são' f. infusion; extract; tea.
in-gen'-te adj. huge, enormous.
in-gê-nua f. ingénue (naïve young girl on stage).
in-ge-nui-da'-de f. ingenuity.
in-gê-nuo, =a adj. ingenuous, simple.
in-ge-rir' tr.v. to swallow; —=se refl.v. to come between, to intervene.
in-glês, =a adj., m., f. English, Englishman, Englishwoman.
in-gle-sar' tr.v. to anglicize.
in-glo-ri-o'-so, =a adj. inglorious.
in-go-ver-ná-vel adj. ungovernable.
in-gra-ti-dão' f. ingratitude.
in-gra'-to, =a adj. ungrateful.
in-gre-di-en'-te m. ingredient.
in-gres'-so m. entrance, admission.
in-ha-la-ção' f. inhalation.
in-ha-lar' tr.v. to inhale.
i-ni-bi-ção' f. inhibition.
i-ni-bir' tr.v. to inhibit.
i-ni-ci-a-ção' f. initiation.
i-ni-ci-a'-do m. initiate, neophyte.
i-ni-ci-al' adj. initial.
i-ni-ci-ar' tr.v. to initiate.
i-ni-ci-a-ti'-va f. initiative.
i-ní-cio m. beginning; inauguration.
i-ni-mi'-go m. enemy; i-ni-mi'-go, =a adj. hostile.
i-ni-qui-da'-de f. iniquity.
i-ní-quo, =a adj. iniquitous.
in-je-ção' f. injection.
in-je-tar' tr.v. to inject.
in-jun-ção' f. injunction.
in-jú-ria f. insult, offense; harm.
in-ju-ri-o'-so, =a adj. insulting.
in-jus-ti'-ça f. injustice.
in-jus'-to, =a adj. unjust.
i-nob-ser-van'-te adj. unobservant.
i-no-cên-cia f. innocence.
i-no-cen'-te adj. innocent.
i-no-cu-la-ção' f. inoculation.
i-no-cu-lar' tr.v. to inoculate.
i-no-fen-si'-vo, =a adj. inoffensive.
i-no-por-tu'-no, =a adj. inopportune.
i-no-va-ção' f. innovation.
i-no-var' tr.v. to innovate.
in-qué-ri-to m. inquiry; inquest.
in-ques-ti-o-ná-vel adj. unquestionable.
in-qui-li-na'-to m. rent, renting.
in-qui-li'-no m. tenant.
in-qui-rir' tr.v. to inquire into, to interrogate.
in-qui-si-ção' f. inquisition.
in-qui-si-to-rial' adj. inquisitorial.
in-sa-ci-á-vel adj. insatiable.
in-sa-ni-da'-de f. insanity.
in-sa'-no, =a adj. insane.
ins-cre-ver' tr.v. to inscribe; to register.
ins-cri-ção' f. inscription.
in-se-gu'-ro, =a adj. insecure.
in-ser-ção' f. insertion.
in-se-rir' tr.v. to insert.
in-ser'-to, =a adj. inserted.
in-se-ti-ci'-da m. insecticide.
in-se'-to m. insect.

in-si-di-o'-so, =a adj. insidious.
in-sig'-ne adj. notable, distinguished, eminent.
in-síg-nia f. insignia.
in-sig-ni-fi-can'-te adj. insignificant.
in-si-nua-ção' f. insinuation.
in-si-nu-ar' tr.v. to insinuate.
in-sí-pi-do, =a adj. insipid.
in-si-pi-ên-cia f. ignorance; imprudence.
in-si-pi-en'-te adj. ignorant, senseless.
in-sis-tên-cia f. insistence.
in-sis-ten'-te adj. insistent.
in-sis-tir' intr.v. to insist.
in-so-la-ção' f. sunning, insolation.
in-so-lên-cia f. insolence.
in-so-len'-te adj. insolent.
in-sol-vên-cia f. insolvency.
in-sol-ven'-te adj. insolvent.
in-sô-nia f. insomnia.
in-sos'-so, =a adj. fresh, lacking salt.
ins-pe-ção' f. inspection.
ins-pe-tar' tr.v. to inspect.
ins-pe-tor' m. inspector.
ins-pi-ra-ção' f. inspiration.
ins-pi-rar' tr.v. to inspire; to inhale.
ins-ta-la-ção' f. installation.
ins-ta-lar' tr.v. to install, to inaugurate.
ins-tân-cia f. request, entreaty, insistence.
ins-tan'-te m. instant; adj. instant, urgent, pressing.
ins-tan-tâ-ne-o, =a adj. instantaneous.
ins-ti-ga-ção' f. instigation.
ins-ti-gar' tr.v. to instigate.
ins-ti-la-ção' f. instillation.
ins-ti-lar' tr.v. to instil.
ins-tin-ti'-vo, =a adj. instinctive.
ins-tin'-to m. instinct.
ins-ti-tu-ir' tr.v. to institute, to found.
ins-ti-tu'-to m. institute.
ins-tru-ção' f. instruction, education.
ins-tru-ir' tr.v. to instruct.
ins-tru-men-ta-ção' f. instrumentation.
ins-tru-men'-to m. instrument.
in-su-bor-di-na-ção' f. insubordination.
in-su-bor-di-na'-do, =a adj. insubordinate.
in-su-li'-na f. insulin.
in-sul-tar' tr.v. to insult.
in-sul'-to m. insult.
in-su-por-tá-vel adj. insupportable, intolerable.
in-sur-gen'-te adj., m. insurgent.
in-sur-rei-ção' f. insurrection.
in-tac'-to, =a adj. intact.
in-tan-gí-vel adj. intangible.
ín-te-gra f. integer; complete text.
in-te-gra-ção' f. integration.
in-te-gral' adj. integral.
in-te-grar' tr.v. to integrate.
in-te-gri-da'-de f. integrity.
ín-te-gro, =a adj. complete, right, perfect, upright, honest.
in-tei-rar' tr.v. to inform; to complete; to certify; —se refl.v. to find out, to become aware.
in-tei'-ro, =a adj. entire, whole.
in-te-lec-tu-al' adj. intellectual.
in-te-lec'-to m. intellect.
in-te-li-gên-cia f. intelligence.
in-te-li-gen'-te adj. intelligent.
in-ten-ção' f. intention.
in-ten-ci-o-nal' adj. intentional.
in-ten-tar' tr.v. to attempt, to try; to intend, to plan.
in-ten'-to m. intent, purpose.
in-ten-den'-te m. administrator, manager, chief.
in-ten-si-da'-de f. intensity.

in-ten-si'-vo, =a adj. intensive.
in-ten'-so, =a adj. intense.
in-ter-ca-lar' tr.v. to intercalate; adj. inserted.
in-ter-câm-bio m. interchange, exchange.
in-ter-ce-der' intr.v. to intercede.
in-ter-cep-ção' f. interception.
in-ter-cep-tar' tr.v. to intercept.
in-ter-ces-são' f. intercession.
in-ter-ces-sor' m. intercessor, mediator.
in-ter-cur'-so m. intercourse, communication.
in-ter-di'-to m. interdict.
in-te-res-san'-te adj. interesting.
in-te-res-sar' tr.v. to interest.
in-te-rês-se m. interest.
in-te-res-sei'-ro, =a adj. selfish, egoistic.
in-ter-fe-rên-cia f. interference.
ín-te-rim m. interim.
in-te-ri'-no, =a adj. temporary, provisional.
in-te-ri-or' m., adj. interior.
in-ter-jei-ção' f. interjection.
in-ter-me-di-á-rio, =a adj., m. intermediary.
in-ter-mé-dio, =a adj., m. intermediate.
in-ter-mi-ná-vel adj. interminable.
in-ter-mis-são' f. intermission.
in-ter-mi-ten'-te adj. intermittent.
in-ter-mu-ral' adj. intermural.
in-ter-na-ci-o-nal' adj. international.
in-ter-nar' tr.v. to intern; to send inland.
in-ter-na'-to m. boarding-school; internship.
in-ter'-no m. boarder, boarding pupil, day pupil, intern; in-ter'-no, =a adj. internal.
in-ter-pre-ta-ção' f. interpretation.
in-ter-pre-tar' tr.v. to interpret.
in-tér-pre-te m. interpreter.
in-ter-ro-ga-ção' f. interrogation, questioning.
in-ter-ro-gar' tr.v. to question, to interrogate.
in-ter-ro-ga-ti'-vo, =a adj. interrogative.
in-ter-ro-ga-tó-rio, =a adj. interrogatory.
in-ter-rom-per' tr.v. to interrupt.
in-ter-rup-ção' f. interruption.
in-ter-rup-tor' m. switch.
in-ter-se-ção' f. intersection.
in-ter-stí-cio m. interstice; interval; pore.
in-ter-ur-ba'-no, =a adj. inter-urban.
in-ter-va'-lo m. interval; intermission.
in-ter-ven-ção' f. intervention.
in-ter-vir' intr.v. to intervene.
in-tes-ta'-do, =a adj. intestate.
in-tes-ti-nal' adj. intestinal.
in-tes-ti'-no m. intestine.
in-ti-ma-ção' f. intimation, hint; summons, citation.
in-ti-mar' tr.v. to intimate; to cite (law), to order with authority; to notify; to challenge; to provoke.
in-ti-mi-dar' tr.v. to intimidate.
ín-ti-mo, =a adj. intimate; m., f. close friend.
in-ti-tu-lar' tr.v. to entitle.
in-to-le-rân-cia f. intolerance.
in-to-le-ran'-te adj. intolerant.
in-to-le-rá-vel adj. intolerable.
in-to-na-ção' f. intonation.
in-to-xi-ca-ção' f. poisoning.
in-to-xi-car' tr.v. to poison.
in-tran-si-gên-cia f. intransigence.
in-tran-si-gen'-te adj. intransigent.

in-tran-si-tá-vel *adj.* impassable, impracticable.
in-tran-si-ti'-vo, =a *adj.* intransitive.
in-tra-tá-vel *adj.* intractable.
in-tra-ve-no'-so, =a *adj.* intravenous.
in-tré-pi-do, =a *adj.* intrepid.
ín-tri-co, =a *adj.* intricate.
in-tri'-ga *f.* intrigue, plot.
in-tri-gan'-te *adj.*, *m.*, *f.* meddling, scheming; schemer.
in-tri-gar' *tr.v.* to intrigue; to scheme, to plot.
in-trín-se-co, =a *adj.* intrinsic.
in-tro-du-ção' *f.* introduction.
in-tro-du-tó-rio *adj.* introductory.
in-tro-du-zir' *tr.v.* to introduce; to put in, to usher in.
in-tro-spec-ção' *f.* introspection.
in-tru-são' *f.* intrusion.
in-tru'-so, =a *adj.* intrusive; *m.* intruder.
in-tu-i-ção' *f.* intuition.
in-tui-ti'-vo, =a *adj.* intuitive.
in-tui'-to *m.* intention, purpose, plan, objective.
i-nu-me-rá-vel *adj.* innumerable.
i-nun-da-ção' *f.* inundation, flood.
i-nun-dar' *tr.v.* to flood, to inundate.
i-nú-til *adj.* useless.
i-nu-ti-li-da'-de *f.* uselessness, inutility.
in-va-dir' *tr.v.* to invade.
in-va-li-da-ção' *f.* invalidation.
in-va-li-dar' *tr.v.* to invalidate.
in-vá-li-do *adj.*, *m.* invalid.
in-va-ri-á-vel *adj.* invariable.
in-va-são' *f.* invasion.
in-vec-ti'-va *f.* invective, abusive language.
in-ve'-ja *f.* envy.
in-ve-jar' *tr.v.* to envy.
in-ve-já-vel *adj.* enviable.
in-ve-jo'-so, =a *adj.* envious.
in-ven-ção' *f.* invention.
in-ven-cí-vel *adj.* invincible.
in-ven-tar' *tr.v.* to invent.
in-ven-ta-riar' *tr.v.* to take an inventory.
in-ven-tá-rio *m.* inventory.
in-ven-ti'-va *f.* inventiveness.
in-ven-ti'-vo, =a *adj.* inventive.
in-ven'-to *m.* invention.
in-ven-tor' *m.* inventor.
in-ver-nal' *adj.* winter, relating to winter.
in-ver'-no *m.* winter.
in-ver'-sa *f.* inverse.
in-ver-ter' *tr.v.* to invert.
in-ver-te-bra'-do *m.*; =a *adj.* invertebrate.
in-ves-ti-ga-ção' *f.* investigation.
in-ves-ti-gar' *tr.v.* to investigate.
in-ves-ti-du'-ra *f.* investiture.
in-ves-tir' *tr.v.* to install in office; to invest (money).
in-ve-te-ra'-do, =a *adj.* inveterate.
in-vi-o-lá-vel *adj.* inviolable.
in-vi-si-bi-li-da'-de *f.* invisibility.
in-vi-sí-vel *adj.* invisible.
in-vo-ca-ção' *f.* invocation.
in-vo-car' *tr.v.* to invoke.

in-vul-ne-rá-vel *adj.* invulnerable.
i-o'-do *m.* iodine.
i-o-do-fór-mio *m.* iodoform.
i-o'-le *f.* yawl; canoe.
í-on *m.* ion.
io-ni-za-ção' *f.* ionization.
ir' *intr.v.* to go.
i'-ra *f.* ire; anger.
i-rar' *tr.v.* to anger, to irritate.
i-ras-ci-bi-li-da'-de *f.* irascibility.
i-ras-cí-vel *adj.* irascible.
i-ri-des-cen'-te *adj.* iridescent.
i-rí-dio *m.* iridium.
i-rí'-te *f.* iritis (inflammation of the iris).
ir-mã' *f.* sister.
ir-man-da'-de *f.* brotherhood, fraternity.
ir-mão' *m.* brother.
i-ro-ni'-a *f.* irony.
i-rô-ni-co, =a *adj.* ironical.
ir-ra-ci-o-nal' *adj.* irrational.
ir-ra-dia-ção' *f.* irradiation.
ir-ra-dian'-te *adj.* irradiant, shining.
ir-ra-di-ar' *tr.v.* to radiate, to shine forth, to irradiate.
ir-re-gu-lar' *adj.* irregular.
ir-re-li-gi-o'-so, =a *adj.* irreligious.
ir-re-me-diá-vel *adj.* irremediable, incurable; inevitable.
ir-re-pa-rá-vel *adj.* irreparable.
ir-re-sis-tí-vel *adj.* irresistible.
ir-re-so-lu'-to, =a *adj.* irresolute.
ir-res-pon-sá-vel *adj.* irresponsible.
ir-re-ve-rên-cia *f.* irreverence.
ir-re-ve-ren'-te *adj.* irreverent.
ir-re-vo-cá-vel *adj.* irrevocable.
ir-re-vo-gá-vel *adj.* irrevocable.
ir-ri-ga-ção' *f.* irrigation.
ir-ri-ga-dor' *m.* syringe, enema bottle.
ir-ri-gar' *tr.v.* to irrigate.
ir-ri-ta-bi-li-da'-de *f.* irritability.
ir-ri-ta-ção' *f.* irritation.
ir-ri-tan'-te *adj.* irritant, irritating.
ir-ri-tar' *tr.v.* to irritate, to annoy.
ir-ri-tá-vel *adj.* irritable.
ir-rom-per' *intr.v.* to break out in eruption, to burst forth.
ir-rup-ti'-vo, =a *adj.* irruptive.
is'-ca *f.* tinder; bait.
is-quei'-ro *m.* cigar lighter.
i-sen-ção' *f.* exemption.
i-sen-tar' *tr.v.* to exempt; to except.
i-sen-'to, =a *adj.* exempt.
i-só-ba-ro, =a *adj.* isobaric.
i-so-la-ção' *f.* isolation; insulation.
i-so-la-dor' *m.* insulator.
i-so-la-men'-to *m.* isolation; insulation.
i-so-lan'-te *adj.* insulating.
i-so-lar' *tr.v.* to isolate; to insulate.
i-sós-ce-les *adj.* isosceles.
ist'-mo *m.* isthmus.
i-tá-li-co, =a *adj.* Italic; italic (type).
i-ta-o'-ca *f.* (Brazil) cave, cavern; (house of stone).
í-tem *adv.* in same manner; *m.* item.
i-te-rar' *tr.v.* to iterate; to repeat.
i-te-ra-ti'-vo, =a *adj.* iterative.
i-ti-ne-ran'-te *adj.* itinerant.
i-ti-ne-rá-rio *m.*, *adj.* itinerary.

J

See page 12—Guide to Reformed Spelling used in this Dictionary

J, j *m.* J, j, tenth letter of the alphabet.

já *adv.* now, at this very moment; already.

ja-bo-ti-ca'-ba *f.* fruit, similar to large black grape, produced on trunk and branches of Brazilian tree.

ja'-ca *f.* durian.

ja-ca-ran-dá *m.* Brazilian rosewood.

ja-ca-ré *m.* crocodile.

jac-tân-cia *f.* boasting, vanity, pride.

jac'-to *m.* impulse; spurt; flash of light.

ja'-de *m.* jade.

ja-gu-ar' *m.* jaguar.

ja-mais' *adv.* never, never at any time.

jam'-ba *f.* jamb, door-jamb.

ja-nei'-ro *m.* January.

ja-ne'-la *f.* window.

ja-ne-lei'-ro, =a *m., f.* person given to watching from window.

jan-ga'-da *f.* fishing raft (common on Brazilian coast).

jan-tar' *m., intr.v.* dinner; to dine.

jan-ta-rão' *m.* banquet.

ja-po-nês *adj.* Japanese.

ja-que'-ta *f.* jacket.

jar'-da *f.* yard (measure equivalent to 91 centimeters).

jar-dim' *m.* garden (usually of flowers only).

jar-di-na'-gem *f.* gardening.

jar-di-nei'-ra *f.* jardiniere.

jar-di-nei'-ro *m.* gardener.

jar-di-nis'-ta *m.* landscape gardener.

jar-gão' *m.* jargon.

jar'-ra *f.* water pitcher, water pot; flower vase.

jar'-ro *m.* large pitcher (with spout and handle).

jar-rê-te *m.* curve back of knee.

jar-re-tei'-ra *f.* garter.

jas-mim' *m.* jasmine.

jas'-pe *m.* jasper.

ja-zer' *intr.v.* to lie, to lie full length; to be dead.

ja-zi'-da *f.* mineral vein, mine; resting-place.

ja-zi'-go *m.* tomb, grave.

je'-ca *adj., m.* (Brazil) crude country man.

je-ca=ta-tú *m.* (Brazil) name and symbol of peasant in interior of Brazil.

jei'-to *m.* mode, manner; talent; leaning.

jei-to'-so, =a *adj.* skilful; making good appearance, good-looking.

je-ju-ar' *intr.v.* to fast.

je-jum' *m.* fast, fasting.

Je-o-vá *m.* Jehovah.

je-re-mi-a'-da *f.* jeremiad.

je-re-mi-ar' *tr.v., intr.v.* to lament, to complain.

je-ri-mú *m.* pumpkin.

je-ri-mu-zei'-ro *m.* pumpkin vine.

jí-ria *f.* slang, jargon.

jo-a-lhei'-ro *m.* jeweler.

jo-a-lhe-ri'-a *f.* jewelry shop.

Jo-ão=Fer-nan'-des *m.* nobody; person of little importance.

jo-ão=nin-guém *m.* nobody, shrimp.

jo-co-si-da'-de *f.* jocosity.

jo-co'-so, =a *adj.* jocose.

jo-ei'-ra *f.* coarse sieve, screen (for separating chaff from wheat).

jo-ei-rar' *tr.v.* to sift or screen grain.

jo-e-lha'-da *f.* blow with the knee.

jo-e-lhei'-ra *f.* knee protector (in football); baggy trousers.

jo-e'-lho *m.* knee.

jo-ga-dor' *m.* player; gambler.

jo-gar' *tr.v.* to play; to risk, to stake; to gamble.

jô-go *m.* game, sport; set; gambling; truck.

jói-a *f.* jewel; entrance fee (in school, club, association).

jó-quei *m.* jockey.

jor-na'-da *f.* journey made or distance traveled in one day; battle.

jor-nal' *m.* day wage; daily newspaper.

jor-na-lei'-ro *m.* day laborer.

jor-na-lis'-mo *m.* journalism.

jor-na-lis'-ta *m.* journalist, newspaper man.

jor-rão' *m.* drag (to level roadways), harrow.

jor-rar' *intr.v.* to spurt; *tr.v.* to cause to rush or spurt out.

jôr-ro *m.* strong jet, spurt.

jo'-vem *m., f., adj.* youth, youthful.

jo-vi-al' *adj.* jovial.

jo-via-li-da'-de *f.* joviality.

ju-bi-leu' *m.* jubilee; fiftieth anniversary.

jú-bi-lo *m.* jubilation.

ju-bi-lo'-so, =a *adj.* jubilant.

ju-deu' *m.* Jew.

ju-di'-a *f.* Jewess.

ju-di-cial' *adj.* judicial.

ju-di-ci-á-rio, =a *adj.* judiciary.

ju-di-ci-o'-so, =a *adj.* judicious.

ju-gal' *adj.* conjugal.

ju'-go *m.* yoke, yoke of oxen; (fig.) oppression.

ju-iz' *m.* judge.

ju-í-zo *m.* judgment; court; opinion; good sense.

ju'-le *m.* joule (unit of work or energy).

jul-ga-men'-to *m.* judgment, sentence, decision.

jul-gar' *tr.v.* to judge; to deem, to think.

ju'-lho *m.* July.

ju-men'-to, =a *m., f.* donkey, ass.

jun-ção' *f.* junction.

jun'-co *m.* wicker, reed, cane; junk (an oriental ship).

jun-gir' *tr.v.* to yoke, to unite; to set in pairs.

ju'-nho *m.* June.

jú-ni-or *adj.* junior.

jun-qui'-lho *m.* jonquil.

jun'-ta *f.* joint; yoke; committee, commission; conference; consultation (of physician).

jun-tar' *tr.v.* to join; to assemble; —=se *refl.v.* to meet together, to assemble.

jun-tei'-ra *f.* carpenter's joining plane.

jun'-to, =a *adj.* together; joined; close, near; *adv.* near, by the side of.

ju-ra'-do *m.* juror; statement made on oath.

ju-ra'-do, =a *adj.* sworn in; sworn.

ju-ra-men'-to *m.* oath; oath-taking.

ju-rar' *tr.v.* to swear; to take oath; to promise solemnly.

ju'-ri m. jury.
ju-rí-di-co, -a adj. juridic.
ju-ris-con-sul'-to m. juris-consult.
ju-ris-di-ção' f. jurisdiction.
ju-ris-di-cio-nal' adj. jurisdictional.
ju-ris-pru-dên-cia f. jurisprudence.
ju-ris'-ta m. jurist; money-lender; owner of public bonds.
ju'-ro m. interest.
Ju-ru-pa-rí m. devil of the Tupis.
jus' m. law, legal right.
ju-san'-te f. out-going tide, low tide.
jus'-ta f. joust.
jus-te'-za f. accuracy, precision.

jus-ti'-ça f. justice.
jus-ti-cei'-ro, -a adj. severe, impartial, rigorous.
jus-ti-fi-ca-ção' f. justification.
jus-ti-fi-car' tr.v. to justify.
jus-ti-fi-cá-vel adj. justifiable.
jus'-to, -a adj. just, fair, upright, correct.
ju'-ta f. jute.
ju-ve-nil' adj. juvenile.
ju-ven-tu'-de f. youth.
jux-ta-li-ne-ar' adj. interlinear.
jux-ta-po-si-ção' f. juxtaposition.
jux-ta-por' tr.v. to juxtapose.
jux-ta-pos'-to, -a adj. contiguous.

K

See page 12—GUIDE TO REFORMED SPELLING used in this Dictionary

K, k m. K, k. This letter does not belong to the Portuguese alphabet. It is used, however, in certain abbreviations accepted internationally and in a few foreign words introduced into the language.

kg abbreviation for kilogram.
kl abbreviation for kiloliter.
km abbreviation for kilometer.

L

See page 12—GUIDE TO REFORMED SPELLING used in this Dictionary

L, 1 m. L, l, eleventh letter of the alphabet.
lá adv. there, in that place.
lã' f. wool.
la-ba-re'-da f. flame, blaze, tongue of flame; (fig.) vivacity.
la-be-la'-do, -a adj. lip-shaped.
la-bi-a'-do, -a adj. lip-shaped.
la-bi-al' adj. labial.
lá-bio m. lip.
la-bi-rin'-to m. labyrinth; maze; handmade lace.
la-bor' m. labor, work.
la-bo-rar' intr.v. to work, to strive; to till; to function.
la-bo-ra-tó-rio m. laboratory.
la-bo-rio'-so, -a adj. laborious, diligent, wearisome.
la-bu'-ta f. labor, toil.
la-bu-tar' intr.v. to strive, to struggle; to toil.
la'-ca f. lacquer.
la-ça'-da f. bow-knot.
la-cai'-o m. footman.
la-çar' tr.v. to tie with bow-knot, to lace up.
la-ça-ri'-a f. ornaments in forms of bows or flourishes.
la-ce-ra-ção' f. laceration.
la-ce-rar' tr.v. to lacerate; to tear, to rend.
la'-ço m. slip knot, loop, snare, lasso.
la-cô-ni-co, -a adj. laconic.
la'-cre m. lacquer.
la-cre-a'-da f. lacquer ornament.
la-cre-ar' tr.v. to ornament with lacquer, to lacquer.
la-cri-mal' adj. lachrymal.
la-cri-mo'-so, -a adj. tearful, doleful; lachrymose.
lac-ta-ção' f. suckling; lactation.

lac-tar' tr.v., intr.v. to suckle, to feed, to nourish; to nurse.
lac-to'-se f. lactose.
lac-ti-cí-nio m. preparation made of milk.
la-cu'-na f. gap; lacuna.
la-cu-no'-so, -a adj. full of gaps.
la-cus'-tre adj. lake, of lakes.
la'-da f. navigable part of stream.
la-dei'-ra f. hill-side, mountain-side.
la-dei-ren'-to, -a adj. steep, inclined.
la-dei'-ro, -a adj. on the side.
la-di'-no, -a adj. astute, cunning, sly; pure.
la'-do m. side, face, surface, facet.
la'-dra f. thief.
la-drão' m. thief.
la-drar' intr.v. to bark; to bawl out; to yelp.
la-dri'-do m. bark, barking.
la-dri-lha-dor' m. tile worker.
la-dri-lhar' tr.v. to cover with tile, to pave with tile or bricks.
la-dri'-lho m. tile, brick, flag-stone.
la-dro-a'-gem f. thievery.
la-dro-ar' tr.v. to steal, to rob.
la-dro-ei'-ra f. robbery; extortion.
la-gar'-ta f. caterpillar.
la-gar-ti'-xa f. small lizard.
la-gar'-to m. lizard.
la'-go m. lake.
la-gô-a f. small lake; swamp.
la-gos'-ta f. lobster.
la-gos-tim' m. small lobster.
lá-gri-ma f. tear; tear-shaped object.
la-gu'-na f. lagoon.
lai-cal' adj. lay.
lai-ci-da'-de f. laity.
la'-ma f. mud; m. Lama priest.
la-ma-çal' m. muddy place.
la-ma-cei'-ra f. muddy place.

la-ma-cen'-to, =a adj. muddy.
lam-ber' tr.v. to lick; to file; to polish.
lam-bi-ção' f. flattery, adulation.
lam-bi-de'-laf.licking;gratuity;flattery.
lam-bi'-do, =a adj. excessively polished.
lam-'bis-car' tr.v. to eat little.
lam-bis'-co m. small portion of food,
  morsel, mouthful.
lam-brís m.pl. wainscoting; veneer.
la-men-tar' tr.v. to lament, to bewail;
  —=se refl.v. to lament, to complain.
la-men-tá-vel adj. lamentable.
la-men'-to m. lament.
la-men-to'-so, =a adj. lamentable, pitiful.
lâ-mi-na f. lamina; blade, sheet of metal.
la-mi-na-dor' m. roller, rolling-machine.
la-mi-no'-so, =a adj. laminated, in
  sheets.
lam'-pa f. lampas (fabric), China silk;
  advantage.
lâm-pa-da f. lamp.
lam-pa-dá-rio m. candelabrum.
lam-pa-ri'-na f. night lamp, night
  candle.
lam-pe-jar' intr.v. to flash like lightning.
lam-pe'-jo m. flash, sudden brilliance.
lam-pi-ão' m. lantern.
lam-pi'-ro m. lightning bug.
lam-prei'-a f. lamprey.
la-mú-ria f. lamentation.
la-mu-riar' intr.v. to wail, to weep, to
  mourn.
lan'-ça f. lance, spear, shaft.
lan-ça=bom'-ba m. bomb discharge.
lan-ça-dei'-ra f. shuttle (in weaving).
lan-ça-du'-ra f. throwing; launching.
lan-ça-men'-to m. entering (of items in
  book-keeping).
lan-çar' tr.v. to throw, to launch; to
  drop, to scatter; to vomit.
lan-cei'-ro m. lancer.
lan'-ço m. throw, rush, spurt; bid (at
  auction); flight of stairs.
lan-cê-ta f. lancet.
lan'-cha f. launch (boat).
lan-char' tr.v., intr.v. to lunch.
lan'-che m. lunch.
lan-gor' m. languor.
lan-go-ro'-so, =a adj. languorous.
lan-gui-dez' f. languidness.
lân-gui-do, =a adj. languid.
la-no-si-da'-de f. woolliness.
la-no'-so, =a adj. woolly.
lan-ter'-na f. lantern; — traseira f. tail
  light.
la-nu'-gem f. down, downiness.
lá-pa-ro m. male hare.
la-pe'-la f. lapel.
la-pi-da-ção' f. stoning; cutting and
  polishing stones.
la-pi-dar' tr.v. to stone; to cut or polish
  stones.
la-pí-de-o, =a adj. hard as stone.
la-pi-do'-so, =a adj. stony.
la-pi-jar' intr.v. to mark with a pencil.
la'-pis m. pencil.
la-pi-sa'-da f. pencil mark.
la-pi-sei'-ra f. pencil box; container for
  pencil leads.
lap'-so m. lapse.
lar' m. fire-place; kitchen fire; (fig.) home;
  household.
la-ra'-da f. live coals; hot ashes, embers.
la-ran'-ja f. orange; — cravo tangerine.
la-ran-ja'-da f. orangeade.
la-ran'-ja=da=Ba-í-a f. navel orange.
la-ran-jal' m. orange grove.
la-ran-jei'-ra f. orange tree.

la-ran-jei'-ro m. orange grower.
la-rá-pio m. petty thief.
lar-de-ar' tr.v. to lard, to stuff with
  bacon.
lar'-do m. sliced bacon; salt pork.
lar'-ga f. abandonment, release; freedom.
lar-gar' tr.v. to free, to let loose; to
  abandon; to let go.
lar'-go m. small public square; lar'-go,
  =a adj. wide; ample, extensive; large
  abundant.
lar-gue'-za f. wideness, width; generosity.
lar-gu'-ra f. width.
la-rin'-ge f. larynx.
la-rin-gi'-te f. laryngitis.
lar'-va f. larva.
las'-ca f. splinter, fragment (of wood,
  metal, stone).
las-cí-via f. lasciviousness.
las-ci'-vo, =a adj. lascivious.
las-si-dão' f. fatigue, lassitude.
las-si-tu'-de f. fatigue, lassitude.
las'-so, =a adj. fatigued, weary, exhausted; slack; dissolute.
lás-ti-ma f. pity; something to be greatly
  regretted.
las-ti-mar' tr.v. to deplore, to lament;
  —=se refl.v. to pity, to lament, to complain.
las-ti-mável adj. regrettable, deplorable.
las-ti-mo'-so, =a adj. pitiful, sad,
  wretched.
las-tra'-gem f. ballasting.
las'-tro m. ballast.
la'-ta f. tin sheet, tin can.
la-tão' m. brass.
la-ten'-te adj. latent.
la-te-ral' adj. lateral.
lá-tex or lá-ti-ce m. latex.
la-ti-fún-dio m. latifundium (large
  landed estate).
la-tim' m. Latin language.
la-ti-ni-da'-de f. Latinity, Latin.
la-ti-nis'-ta m. Latinist.
la-ti'-no, =a adj. Latin.
la-ti-ni-zar' tr.v. to Latinize.
la-ti'-do m. bark.
la-tir' intr.v. to bark, to yelp.
la-ti-tu'-de f. latitude.
la'-to, =a adj. wide; ample; extensive;
  dilated.
la-tri'-na f. latrine.
la-tro-cí-nio m. brigandage.
lau-da-bi-li-da'-de f. laudability.
lau-da-tó-rio, =a adj. laudatory.
lau-dá-vel adj. laudable.
láu-da-no m. laudanum.
láu-re-a f. crown of laurel, laurel-wreath.
lau-re-ar' tr.v. to crown with laurel, to
  honor.
lau-rei'-o m. crowning with laurel.
lau-rel' m. laurel, laurel tree, bay tree.
lau'-to, =a adj. sumptuous, magnificent,
  abundant.
la'-va f. lava.
la-vo'-so, =a adj. like lava.
la-va-dei'-ra f. laundress.
la-va-dou'-ro m. wash-tub; flat stone for
  washing and soaping clothes.
la-va'-gem f. washing; purifying.
la-van-da-ri'-a f. laundry.
la-van-dei'-ra f. laundress.
la-var' to wash; to launder; —=se refl.v.
  to wash; to justify oneself, to clear
  oneself.
la-va-tó-rio m. lavatory; wash-stand.
la-vor' m. manual work; workmanship;
  embroidery; ornament in relief.

la-vou'-ra *f.* agriculture, farming.
la'-vra *f.* cultivation of land; mine; harvest.
la-vra-dei'-ra *f.* farm worker; seamstress.
la-vra-di'-o, *=a adj.* arable.
la-vra'-do *m.* needle work, embroidery.
la-vra'-gem *f.* cultivation, harvest.
la-vran'-te *m.*, *f.* engraver; goldsmith, silversmith.
la-vrar' *tr.v.* to plow, to till; to mine; to carve, to sculpture; to embroider; to take minutes.
la-xa-ti'-vo, *=a adj.* laxative.
la'-xo, *=a adj.* lax.
la-za-ren'-to, *=a adj.* leprous.
la-za-re'-to *m.* lazaretto, hospital, infirmary.
lá-za-ro *m.* leper.
le-al' *adj.* loyal, faithful, sincere.
le-al-da'-de *f.* loyalty, sincerity.
le-ão' *m.* lion.
le-bra'-da *f.* rabbit stew.
le'-bre *f.* hare.
le-cio-nan'-do *m.* pupil.
le-cio-nar' *tr.v.*, *intr.v.* to teach.
le-cio-nis'-ta *m.*, *f.* private teacher.
le-dor' *m.* reader.
le-ga-ção' *f.* legation.
le-ga'-do *m.* legate.
le-gal' *adj.* legal.
le-ga-li-da'-de *f.* legality.
le-ga-li-zar' *tr.v.* to legalize.
le-gar' *tr.v.* to send as legate; to bequeath.
le-gen'-da *f.* legend; inscription.
le-gen-dá-rio, *=a adj.* legendary.
le-gi-ão' *f.* legion.
le-gio-ná-rio *m.* legionnaire.
le-gis-la-ção' *f.* legislation.
le-gis-la-dor' *m.* legislator.
le-gis-la-ti'-vo, *=a adj.* legislative.
le-gis-la-tu'-ra *f.* legislature.
le-gi-ti-mar' *tr.v.* to legalize; to make legitimate.
le-gi-ti-mo, *=a adj.* legitimate.
le-gí-vel *adj.* legible, readable.
lé-gua *f.* league (5000 meters).
le-gu'-me *m.* vegetable.
lei' *f.* law.
lei'-go, *=a adj.* lay, secular.
lei-lão' *m.* auction.
lei-lo-ei'-ro *m.* auctioneer.
lei-tão' *m.* suckling pig.
lei'-te *m.* milk; — **de cal** whitewash; **dentes de** — milk teeth; — **magro** separated milk.
lei-tei'-ra *f.* milk container.
lei-te-ri'-a *f.* dairy.
lei-tô-a *f.* suckling pig.
lei-tor' *m.* reader.
lei-tu'-ra *f.* reading.
lei'-to *m.* bed; bed-stead.
lem-bran'-ça *f.* remembrance; memory, recollection; keepsake; reminder; gift; **=s** *f.pl.* compliments, regards.
lem-brar' *tr.v.* to remind, to bring to mind; to remember; —**se** *refl.v.* to remember.
le'-me *m.* rudder; helm.
len'-ço *m.* handkerchief.
len-çol' *m.* bed sheet; shroud.
len'-da *f.* legend, fable.
le'-nha *f.* fire-wood.
le-nha-dor' *m.* wood-cutter.
le-nhei'-ro *m.* wood-cutter.
le'-nho *m.* trunk, branch; wood.
le-nho'-so, *=a adj.* ligneous; of wood.
le-ni-ên-cia *f.* leniency.
le-nien'-te *adj.* lenient.

le-ni-ti'-vo, *=a adj.* emollient, mitigating, lenitive.
len'-te *m.* professor; lens.
len-tí-cu-la *f.* small lens.
len-ti-dão' *f.* slowness.
len'-to, *=a adj.* slow, prolonged.
len-ti'-lha *f.* lentil.
le-ô-a *f.* lioness.
le-o-par'-do *m.* leopard.
le'-pra *f.* leprosy.
le-pro'-so, *=a adj.* leprous.
ler' *tr.v.* to read.
le'-que *m.* fan.
le-são' *f.* lesion.
le-sar' *tr.v.* to hurt, to damage.
les'-ma *f.* slug, slug snail; good-for-nothing.
le'-so, *=a adj.* hurt; offended; paralytic.
es'-te *m.* east.
le-tal' *adj.* lethal.
le-tar-gi'-a *f.* lethargy.
le'-tra *f.* letter (of alphabet); — **de câmbio** bill of exchange.
le-tra'-do, *=a adj.* lettered, literate, erudite.
le-trei'-ro *m.* label; title; sign; poster.
leu-cor-réi-a *f.* leucorrhea.
le-va'-da *f.* hill, elevation; transporting, conducting.
le-va-di'-ço, *=a adj.* easily moved, movable.
le-van-ta'-da *f.* getting up, arising.
le-van-ta-di'-ço, *=a adj.* careless, restless, insubordinate, hard to discipline.
le-van-ta-men'-to *m.* revolt, insurrection; elevation.
le-van-tar' *tr.v.* to raise; to place upright, to hoist; to increase; to stir up; to awaken; to draw up; —**se** *refl.v.* to rise, to arise, to get up, to stand up.
le-van'-te *m.* Orient.
le-var' *tr.v.* to carry, to take away; to bring, to lead; to wear; to endure; to take (time).
le'-ve *adj.* light in weight; quick; agile; insignificant; indistinct; **de** — lightly.
le-ve-dar' *tr.v.* to leaven, to raise; *intr.v.* to rise, to swell.
lê-ve-do, *=a adj.* light; risen; puffed up, leavened.
le-ve-du'-ra *f.* yeast; leavening.
le-ve'-za *f.* lightness.
le-vian-da'-de *f.* indiscretion, frivolousness, inconsiderate behavior.
le-vi-a'-no, *=a adj.* frivolous, heedless, fickle.
le-vi-da'-de *f.* levity, skill, agility.
lé-xi-co *m.* lexicon, dictionary.
le-xi-có-gra-fo *m.* lexicographer.
lé-xi-con *m.* lexicon, dictionary.
lha'-ma *f.* llama; fabric interwoven with threads of gold and silver.
lha-ne'-za *f.* sincerity; candor.
lha'-no, *=a adj.* honest, unpretentious, frank.
li-ba-ção' *f.* libation.
li-bar' *tr.v.*, *intr.v.* to drink, to enjoy; to make libations.
li-be'-lo *m.* libel; brief.
li-be-ral' *adj.* liberal.
li-be-ra-li-da'-de *f.* liberality.
li-be-ra-ção' *f.* discharge; relief from debt or other obligation.
li-be-rar' *tr.v.* to liberate; to free from obligation.
li-ber-da'-de *f.* liberty, freedom.
li-ber-ta-dor' *m.* liberator.
li-ber-tar' *tr.v.* to free; to liberate.
li-ber-ti'-no, *=a adj.*, *m.* libertine.

li-bi-di-no'-so, =a *adj.* libidinous, lustful.
li'-bra *f.* pound (avoirdupois); pound sterling (English money); old weight called *arratel*, equivalent to 459.5 grams.
li-bré *f.* servant's uniform, livery.
li-ção' *f.* lesson; reading (interpretation of a text).
li-cen'-ça *f.* permit, license; permission.
li-cen-cia'-do *m.* academic degree (somewhat equivalent to the master's degree).
li-cen-ciar' *tr.v.* to grant license; to exempt temporarily from service.
li-cen-cia-tu'-ra *f.* degree of *licenciado;* conferring of *licenciado.*
li-cen-cio-si-da'-de *f.* licentiousness.
li-cen-cio'-so, =a *adj.* licentious.
li-ce-al' *adj.* pertaining to a liceu (secondary school).
li-ceu' *m.* secondary school.
li-ci-tar' *intr.v.* to bid (in public auction).
lí-ci-to, =a *adj.* lawful, licit.
li-cor' *m.* liquor, liqueur.
li'-da *f.* work.
li-dar' *tr.v., intr.v.* to struggle; to struggle for; to strive, to work hard.
li'-ga *f.* league, association; garter.
li-ga-ção' *f.* binding; friendship.
li-ga-du'-ra *f.* ligature.
li-ga-men'-to *m.* ligament.
li-gar' *tr.v., intr.v.* to tie, to bind, to attach, to unite; —se *refl.v.* to join, to become a member.
li-gei-re'-za *f.* lightness, rapidity, agility.
li-gei'-ro, =a *adj.* light; quick; vague; dishonest.
lig-ni'-to *m.* lignite.
li-lás *m.* lilac.
li'-ma *f.* lime (fruit); file.
li-ma'-gem *f.* filing.
li-ma'-lha *f.* filings.
li-mar' *tr.v.* to file; to smooth, to polish.
li-mão' *m.* lemon.
li-miar' *m.* threshold.
li-mi-ta-ção' *f.* limitation.
li-mi-tar' *tr.v., intr.v.* to limit, to restrain; —se *refl.v.* to be circumscribed or restrained.
li-mi'-te *m.* limit.
li-mo-ei'-ro *m.* lemon-tree.
li-mo-na'-da *f.* lemonade.
lim-pa'-do *m.* clearing.
lim'-pa=pés *m.* door-mat; scraper.
lim'-pa=pra'-tos *m.* glutton.
lim-par' *tr.v.* to clear, to cleanse.
lim'-pa=tri'-lhos *m.* cowcatcher (on locomotive).
lim-pe'-za *f.* cleanliness; (fig.) honesty.
lim-pi-dez' *f.* limpidity.
lim-pi-do, =a *adj.* limpid.
lim'-po, =a *adj.* clean; clear, neat; stainless.
lin'-ce *m.* lynx.
lin'-da *f.* boundary, limit.
lin'-de *m.* boundary, limit.
lin-dei'-ra *f.* lintel (of a door or window).
lin-de'-za *f.* beauty; grace.
lin'-do, =a *adj.* pretty, beautiful.
li-ne-a-men'-to *m.* lineament, outline.
lin'-fa *f.* lymph.
lin-go'-te *m.* ingot.
lin-go-tei'-ra *f.* mold in which ingots are cast.
lín-gua *f.* language, tongue.
lin-gua'-do *m.* sole (fish); foolscap, long sheet of paper; sheet of metal.
lin-gua'-gem *f.* language, speech.
lin-gue'-ta *f.* needle (on scales), pointer; latch bolt; ramp.

lin-gui'-ça *f.* sausage.
lin-guís-ti-ca *f.* linguistics.
lin-guís-ti-co, =a *adj.* linguistic.
li'-nha *f.* line; thread; rank; direction; row.
li-nha'-ça *f.* linseed.
li-nha'-gem *f.* lineage.
li-nhal' *m.* flax field.
li'-nho *m.* flax, linen.
li-nho'-so, =a *adj.* like linen, flaxen.
li-ni-men'-to *m.* liniment.
li-nó-le-o *m.* linoleum.
li-no-ti'-po *m.* linotype.
li-qua-ção' *f.* liquation (separation of the metals of an alloy by a heating process).
li-que-fa-ção' *f.* liquefaction.
li-que-fa-zer' *tr.v.* to liquefy, to fuse, to melt.
li-qui-da-ção' *f.* liquidation.
li-qui-dar' *tr.v., intr.v.* to liquidate.
li-qui-dez' *f.* liquidity.
lí-qui-do *m.* liquid.
lí-qui-do, =a *adj.* liquid.
lí'-ra *f.* lyre.
lí-ri-co, =a *adj.* lyric, lyrical.
li-ris'-mo *m.* lyrism.
li-ris'-ta *m., f.* lyrist.
lí-rio *m.* lily.
li'-so, =a *adj.* smooth, soft, even, plain.
li-su'-ra *f.* smoothness, softness; (fig.) sincerity, good faith.
li-son'-ja *f.* flattery, insincere praise.
li-son-je-ar' *tr.v.* to flatter, to fawn on.
li-son-jei'-ro, =a *adj.* flattering.
lis'-ta *f.* list; stripe; directory; menu card.
lis-tão' *m.* wide stripe; long, wide mark; carpenter's rule.
lis'-tra *f.* stripe of different color (from that of rest of cloth).
li-tei'-ra *f.* litter, sedan chair.
li-te-ral' *adj.* literal, according to text.
li-te-rá-rio, =a *adj.* literary.
li-te-ra'-to, =a *m., f.* writer, man of letters.
li-te-ra-tu'-ra *f.* literature.
li-ti-gar' *intr.v., tr.v.* to litigate.
li-tí-gio *m.* litigation.
li-ti-gio'-so, =a *adj.* litigious.
li-to-gra-fi'-a *f.* lithography; lithograph (print).
li-to-ral' *adj.* littoral; *m.* seashore.
li'-tro *m.* liter.
li-tur-gi'-a *f.* liturgy.
li-vi-dez' *f.* lividity.
li-vi-do, =a *adj.* livid.
li-vra-men'-to *m.* delivrance; setting free.
li-vrar' *tr.v.* to free; to release; to defend; —se *refl.v.* to escape from, to be exempted.
li-vra-ri'-a *f.* book shop, book store.
li'-vre *adj.* free, unoccupied, unrestrained.
li-vre=câm-bio *m.* free-trade.
li-vrei'-ro *m.* book seller.
li-vre'-te *m.* small book, booklet.
li'-vro *m.* book.
li-xa-dor' *m.* sanding machine.
li'-xa *f.* sandpaper.
li-xar' *tr.v.* to polish or clean with sandpaper.
li-xei'-ro *m.* rubbish collector.
li'-xo *m.* rubbish, trash.
li-xo'-so, =a *adj.* untidy, dirty, full of rubbish.
li-xí-via *f.* lye.
lo-bal' *adj.* wolfish; sanguinary.
lô-bo, =a *m., f.* wolf.
lo-bri-gar' *tr.v.* to descry, to catch a glimpse of.

lo-ca-ção' f. rental; area or road marked off by stakes.
lo-cal' adj., m., f. local; locale.
lo-ca-li-da'-de f. locality.
lo-ca-li-zar' tr.v. to localize.
lo-ca-tá-rio m. renter, tenant.
lo-ção' f. lotion.
lo-co-mo-ção' f. locomotion.
lo-co-mo-ti'-va f. locomotive.
lo-cu-tó-rio m. grating through which persons may speak with inmates of convent.
lo-da-çal' m. muddy area, mud hole.
lo-dei'-ra f. swamp land.
lô-do m. mud, silt, lode.
lo-do'-so, =a adj. muddy; dirty.
lo-ga-rit'-mo m. logarithm.
ló-gi-ca f. logic.
ló-gi-co, =a adj. logical.
lo'-go adv. immediately, without delay; — que as soon as.
lo-grar' tr.v. to achieve; to obtain; to enjoy.
lo-grei'-ro m. usurer.
lô-gro m. profit, gain.
lo'-ja f. shop, store; lodge; — de miudezas f. shop selling notions.
lo-jis'-ta m., f. shopkeeper.
lom-bi'-nho m. pork rib roast.
lom'-bo m. back; rib roast; sirloin.
lo'-na f. canvas (fabric).
lon'-ge adv. far.
lon-ge'-vo, =a adj. enduring; aged; long-lived.
lon-ge-vi-da'-de f. longevity.
lon-gi-tu'-de f. longitude.
lon-gi-tu-di-nal' adj. longitudinal.
lon'-go, =a adj. long; lengthy.
lo-qua-ci-da'-de f. loquacity.
lo-quaz' adj. loquacious.
los'-na f. wormwood.
lo-ta-ção' f. budget; profit (received from certain area); capacity (ship, truck, theatre).
lo'-te m. lot; batch; capacity.
lo-te-ri'-a f. lottery.
lou'-ça f. table ware (porcelain, pottery, etc.).
lou'-co, =a adj. crazy, insane; playful; m., f. crazy person.
lou-cu'-ra f. insanity.
lou-rar' tr.v., intr.v. to brown slightly; to make color of gold.
lou'-ro, =a adj. golden-haired, blond.
lou'-sa f. slate; school slate; paving stone, flag-stone.
lou'-va=a=deus' m. grass-hopper.
lou-var' tr.v. to praise; to eulogize; to exalt.
lou-vá-vel adj. laudable, praiseworthy.
lou-vor' m. praise, commendation, eulogy.
lu'-a f. moon; — nova new moon; — de mel honeymoon.

lu-ar' m. moonlight.
lu-a-ren'-to, =a adj. moonlit; having moonlight.
lu-bri-car' tr.v. to lubricate; to oil.
lu-bri-fi-can'-te m. lubricant.
lu-ci-dez' f. lucidity.
lú-ci-do, =a adj. lucid.
lu-crar' intr.v. to profit; to take advantage; to take profit.
lu-cra-ti'-vo, =a adj. lucrative.
lu'-cro m. profit, gain.
lu-cro'-so, =a adj. gainful, profitable.
lu-gar' m. place; space; position; spot.
lú-gu-bre adj. lugubrious; gloomy.
lu-gu-bri-da'-de f. lugubriousness, gloom.
lu'-me m. fire; flame; light; (fig.) perspicacity.
lu-mi-nar' m., adj. luminary.
lu-mi-no-si-da'-de f. luminosity.
lu-mi-no'-so, =a adj. luminous.
lu-na-ção' f. lunation (period between two successive new moons).
lu-nar' adj. lunar.
lu-ne'-ta f. spectacles, glasses.
lu'-pa f. magnifying glass.
lú-pu-lo m. hop vine.
lus'-co=fus'-co m. twilight.
lus-tra-ção' f. purging by sacrifice.
lus-trar' tr.v. to gloss, to glaze, to polish; to instruct; intr.v. to shine.
lus'-tre m. gloss, lustre; chandelier.
lus'-tro m. purification; period of five years.
lus-tro'-so, =a adj. glossy, lustrous, shining; illustrious.
lu'-ta f. struggle, combat.
lu-tar' intr.v. to struggle, to fight hard, to exert every effort; to wrestle.
lu'-to m. mourning; mourning clothes.
lu-to'-so, =a adj. sad, funereal; in mourning.
lu'-va f. glove; =s f.pl. bonus.
lu-va-ri'-a f. glove factory, glove shop.
lu-xar' intr.v. to show off, to dress showily; tr.v. to dislocate.
lu'-xo m. luxury, extravagance.
lu-xu-o'-so, =a adj. luxurious, abundant.
lu-xú-ria f. lust, lewdness, lechery; exuberance.
lu-xu-ri-an'-te adj. luxuriant; rich.
lu-xu-ri-ar' intr.v. to yield to lust; to grow luxuriantly.
lu-xu-ri-o'-so, =a adj. luxurious.
luz' f. light; =s f.pl. knowledge, learning.
lu-zei'-ro m. star, luminary; light, brightness; light-house; =s m.pl. eyes.
lu-zen'-te adj. luminous; m. precious stone.
lu-zi-di'-o, =a adj. shining, brilliant.
lu-zi'-do, =a adj. resplendent.
lu-zir' intr.v. to shine; to glisten, to sparkle; to thrive.

M

See page 12—GUIDE TO REFORMED SPELLING used in this Dictionary

M, m m. M, m, twelfth letter of the alphabet.
ma'-ca f. hammock; stretcher.
ma'-ça f. flail, club, bat, mace.
ma-çã' f. apple.
ma-ca'-ca f. female monkey; whip with short, heavy handle; bad luck.

ma-ca-cão' m. jean (coarse fabric); sly fellow.
ma-ca'-co m. male monkey; jack (portable machine for lifting heavy weight).
ma-ça'-da f. blow with a club; grind (tiresome work); boring conversation.
ma-ca-da'-me m. macadam.

ma-ca-da-mi-zar' *tr.v.* to macadamize.
ma-ça-du'-ra *f.* flailing of flax; massage.
ma-ça'-gem *f.* massage; flailing of flax.
ma-çal' *m.* buttermilk.
ma-ça-ne'-ta *f.* knob.
ma-ção' *m.* Freemason; large mace.
ma-ca-que-ar' *tr.v.* to ape, to imitate in ridiculous fashion.
ma-çar' *tr.v.* to club, to tread, to flail; to bore, to weary.
ma-ca-ri'-co *m.* blow-pipe; blow-torch.
ma-car-rão' *m.* macaroni.
ma-ce-ra-ção' *f.* maceration.
ma-ce-rar' *tr.v.* to macerate.
ma-ce'-ta *f.* ma-ce'-te *m.* small hammer, mallet.
ma-cha'-da *f.* hatchet.
ma-cha-da'-da *f.* blow with an axe or hatchet.
ma-cha-do *m.* axe.
ma-char-rão' *m.* adult male panther.
ma'-cho *m.* male (of animal).
ma-chor'-ra *adj.* steril.
ma-chu'-ca *f.* mashing, crushing.
ma-chu-ca-du'-ra *f.* grinding, crushing; bruise, contusion; trituration.
ma-chu-car' *tr.v.* to mash; to tread upon; to pulverize.
ma-ci-ez' *f.* or ma-ci-e'-za *f.* softness, smoothness.
ma-ci'-o, =a *adj.* soft to touch; velvety; pleasing.
ma-cís *m.* mace (spice), mace oil.
ma'-ço *m.* maul, mallet.
ma-ço-na-ri'-a *f.* Freemasonry.
ma-çô-ni-co, =a *adj.* masonic.
má=cri-a-ção' *f.* ill-manners, discourtesy.
má-cu-la *f.* stain, spot, impurity, defect.
ma-cu-lar' *tr.v.* to spot, to stain.
ma-da'-ma *f.* madam, lady.
ma-da-po-lão' *m.* bleached muslin, sheeting.
ma-dei'-ra *f.* wood; *m.* Madeira wine.
ma-dei-ra-men'-to *m.* frame-work.
ma-dei'-ro *m.* large log, beam.
ma-dei'-xa *f.* skein, hank.
ma-dras'-ta *f.* step-mother.
ma'-dre *f.* nun; mother superior; matrix; mother (of vinegar and wine).
ma'-dre=pé-ro-la *f.* mother of pearl.
ma'-dre=sil'-va *f.* honey-suckle.
ma-dri-gal' *m.* madrigal.
ma-dri'-nha *f.* god-mother.
ma-dru-ga'-da *f.* dawn; (fig.) precocity.
ma-dru-ga-dor', =a *adj.* early-rising.
ma-dru-gar' *intr.v.* to arise early, to be the first, to anticipate, to come early.
ma-du-rar' *tr.v.*, *intr.v.* to ripen, to mature.
ma-du-re'-za *f.* maturity, ripeness.
ma-du'-ro, =a *adj.* ripe, mature. matured, mellow.
mãe' *f.* mother; (fig.) origin.
mãe=do=rio *f.* riverbed at flood-times.
ma-es-tri'-na *f.* woman composer, woman conductor.
ma-es'-tro *m.* maestro.
ma-gi'-a *f.* má-gi-ca *f.* magic.
má-gi-co, =a *adj.* magical.
ma-gís-ter *m.* teacher; master; pedant.
ma-gis-té-rio *m.* teaching profession.
ma-gis-tra'-do *m.* judge; magistrate.
ma-gis-tral' *adj.* masterful; pedantic; prepared by prescription.
ma-gis-tran'-do *m.* candidate for teaching position.
ma-gis-tra-tu'-ra *f.* magistrature.
mag-nâ-ni-mo, =a *adj.* magnanimous.
mag-na'-ta *m.* magnate.

mag-né-sia *f.* magnesia.
mag-né-sio *m.* magnesium.
mag-ne'-te *m.* magnet; magnetic iron.
mag-né-ti-co, =a *adj.* magnetic.
mag-ne-tis'-mo *m.* magnetism.
mag-ne-ti-zar' *tr.v.* to magnetize.
mag-ne'-to *m.* magneto.
mag-ne-tô-me-tro *m.* magnetometer.
mag-ni-fi-car' *tr.v.* to magnify.
mag-ni-fi-cên-cia *f.* magnificence.
mag-ni-fi-cen'-te *adj.* magnificent.
mag-ní-fi-co, =a *adj.* magnific.
mag-ni-tu'-de *f.* magnitude.
mag'-no, =a *adj.* (poet.) large, important.
má-go-a *f.* bruise; sadness, sorrow.
ma-go-ar' *tr.v.* to hurt, to bruise, to offend, to embitter.
ma-gre'-za *f.* thinness, leanness.
ma'-gro, =a *adj.* thin, lean; unprofitable.
mai'-o *m.* May.
mai-or' *adj.* greater, larger, older, of age.
mai-o-ri'-a *f.* majority, most.
mai-o-ri-da'-de *f.* majority.
mais' *adv.* more; also; besides; ao — at most; de — too much; — ou menos more or less; *m.* remains, excess.
ma-ís *m.* corn, maize.
mai-se'-na *f.* corn starch.
mai-ús-cu-lo, =a *adj.* capital (letter)
ma-jes-ta'-de *f.* majesty.
ma-jes-to'-so, =a *adj.* majestic.
ma-jor' *m.* major (military officer).
mal' *m.* evil; harm; illness; *adv.* badly, poorly; hardly.
ma'-la *f.* mail pouch; suit-case, trunk.
mal=a-ca-ba'-do, =a *adj.* badly finished.
ma-lan'-dro, =a *m.*, *f.* vagabond, petty thief.
ma-lá-ria *f.* malaria.
mal=as=som=bra'-do, =a *adj.* haunted, visited by ghost.
ma-la-ven-tu-ra'-do, =a *adj.* unfortunate, unhappy.
mal-con-ten'-te *adj.* dissatisfied, malcontent.
mal-cri-a'-do, =a *adj.* rude, ill-mannered.
mal=da'-de *f.* evil, malice, iniquity, mischief.
mal=das=mon-ta'-nhas *m.* sickness from high altitude.
mal-di-ção' *f.* malediction, curse.
mal-di'-to, =a *adj.* cursed, damned.
mal-di-to'-so, =a *adj.* unfortunate, unhappy.
mal-di-zen'-te *adj.* slanderous; *m.*, *f.* slanderer, gossiper.
mal-di-zer' *tr.v.* to slander; to curse.
mal=dos=mer-gu-lha-do'-res *m.* diver's cramp, bends.
mal-do'-so, =a *adj.* malicious, wicked, bad, mischievous.
ma-le-a-bi-li-da'-de *f.* malleability.
ma-le-á-vel *adj.* malleable.
ma-le-fi-cên-cia *f.* maleficence.
ma-le-fi-ciar' *tr.v.* to harm; to bewitch.
ma-le-fí-cio *m.* evil; witchcraft, sortilege.
ma-lé-fi-co, =a *adj.* harmful.
ma-len-ten-di'-do *m.* misunderstanding; =o, =a *adj.* misunderstood.
mal=es-tar' *m.* indisposition; illness.
ma-le-vo-lên-cia *f.* malevolence.
ma-le-vo-len'-te *adj.* malevolent.
ma-lé-vo-lo, =a *adj.* malevolent.
mal-fei'-to, =a *adj.* badly done; misshapen; wicked.
mal-fei-tor' *m.* malefactor.
mal-gra'-do *prep.* in spite of.

ma'-lha *f.* mail (chain armor); knitted fabric; spot or coloration of animals.
ma-lha'-do, *=a adj.* spotted; discolored.
ma-lha-dou'-ro *m.* thrashing-floor.
ma-lhar' *tr.v.* to beat, to thresh; to hammer; to bore, to importune.
ma-lhe'-te *m.* joint, mortise, dove-tail; mallet.
ma'-lho *m.* mallet; sledge hammer.
ma-li-cia *f.* malice.
ma-li-ci-o'-so, *=a adj.* malicious.
ma-lig-nar' *tr.v.* to corrupt, to vitiate.
ma-lig-ni-da'-de *f.* malignity, maliciousness, malignancy.
ma-lig'-no, *=a adj.* malignant, fatal.
ma-lo-gra'-do, *=a adj.* frustrated, unsuccessful.
mal-que-ren'-ça *f.* ill-will, hatred; aversion.
mal-que-ren'-te *adj.* malevolent. *=*
mal-que-rer' *tr.v.* to wish ill, to hate, to have a grudge against.
mal-quis'-to, *=a adj.* hated, disliked.
mal-so-an'-te *adj.* lacking euphony, unpleasing to ear; shocking.
mal'-te *m.* malt.
mal-tra-tar' *tr.v.* to abuse, to treat badly, to damage.
ma-lu'-co *m.* insane person; *=o, =a adj.* lacking in judgment; insane; silly.
ma-lu-qui'-ce *f.* madness, insanity, foolishness.
mal-va-dez' *f.* perversity; cruelty.
mal-va'-do, *=a adj.* cruel, criminal.
mal-ver-sa-ção' *f.* embezzlement, fraudulent conversion.
mal-vis'-to, *=a adj.* questionable; suspect.
ma'-ma *f.* teat, breast.
ma-mad-ei'-ra *f.* nursing bottle.
ma-mar' *tr.v., intr.v.* to suck, to nurse.
ma-má-rio, *=a adj.* mammary
ma-mi'-lo *m.* nipple.
ma-mo'-na *f.* castor oil bean.
ma-mu'-te *m.* mammoth.
ma-na'-da *f.* drove, herd.
man-cal' *m.* bearing (mach.); — **de roda** wheel bearing; — **de eixo** axle bearing.
man-ce'-ba *f.* dissolute woman; concubine.
man-ce-bi'-a *f.* dissolute living; concubinage.
man-ce'-bo *m.* youth.
man'-cha *f.* spot, stain.
man-char' *tr.v.* to stain, to spot; (fig.) to defame.
man'-co, *=a adj., m., f.* maimed; maimed person.
man'-da *f.* reference (sign or number referring reader to footnote or other information).
man-da-chu'-va *m.* magnate, tycoon.
man-da-dei'-ro *m.* messenger.
man-da'-do *m.* command, order, writ, mandate, errand.
man-da-men'-to *m.* commandment.
man-dan'-te *m.* commander, director; instigator.
man-dão' *m.* domineering person; tyrant.
man-dar' *tr.v.* to order, to command; to enjoin; to send, to send forth; to cause, to have; *intr.v.* to rule, to be in command.
man-da-tá-rio *m.* delegate, representative, mandatory.
man-da'-to *m.* mandate; washing feet on Maundy Thursday.
man-dí-bu-la *f.* jaw, lower jaw.
man-di-o'-ca *f.* manioc.

man-do-lim' *m.* or **man-do-li'-na** *f.* mandolin.
man-dril' *m.* mandrel (mach.).
ma-nei'-ra *f.* manner, mode, way, style; placket.
ma-nei-ro'-so, *=a adj.* agreeable, well-mannered.
ma-ne-jar' *tr.v.* to handle, to wield; to manage.
ma-ne'-jo *m.* handling, management; horsemanship; riding ground; drill; trick, cunning.
ma-ne-quim' *m.* manikin, dress form.
man'-ga *f.* sleeve; mango; gas mantle; run-way (for loading cattle).
man-ga-dor' *m.* teaser, joker.
man-ga-nês *m.* manganese.
man-gar' *intr.v.* to play jokes, to jest, to practice teasing.
man'-gra *f.* wheat rust.
man-guei'-ra *f.* rubber hose; mango tree.
ma'-nha *f.* skill; astuteness; bad habit.
ma-nho'-so, *=a adj.* skilful, crafty; unruly, spoiled.
ma-nhã' *f.* morning (time between sunrise and midday) (fig.) beginning.
ma-ni'-a *f.* mania.
ma-ní-a-co *m.* maniac.
ma-ni-a-tar' *tr.v.* to tie the hands of, to manacle.
ma-ni-cô-mio *m.* insane asylum.
ma-ni-cu'-ro *m.* manicure.
ma-ni-fes-ta-ção' *f.* manifestation.
ma-ni-fes-tar' *tr.v.* to manifest.
ma-ni-fes'-to *m.* manifest (document); **ma-ni-fes'-to**, *=a adj.* manifest.
ma-ni-pu-la-ção' *f.* manipulation.
ma-ni-pu-la-dor' *m.* telegraph key; manipulator.
ma-ni-pu-lar' *tr.v.* to manipulate.
ma-ni-ve'-la *f.* crank, handle, lever.
man-jar' *m.* food, dish; — **branco** *m.* blanc-mange.
man-je-dou'-ra *f.* manger; feed-box, crib.
ma-no'-bra *f.* maneuver; rigging; skill, cunning; shifting (of railway cars).
ma-no-brar' *tr.v.* to maneuver, to manage.
ma-no'-pla *f.* iron glove (of armor).
man-são' *f.* mansion, dwelling.
man-sar'-da *f.* mansard roof, garret, attic; delapidated house.
man-sar-rão' *m.* mild person, meek fellow.
man-si-dão' *f.* gentleness, mildness.
man'-so, *=a adj.* gentle, tame, quiet; cultivated (of a vegetable).
man'-ta *f.* blanket, coverlet, scarf; — **de cavalo** horse blanket; — **de sela** saddle blanket.
man-tei'-ga *f.* butter.
man-tei-go'-so, *=a adj.* buttery, like butter.
man-tei-guei'-ra *f.* butter-dish.
man-tel' *m.* altar cloth, table cloth.
man-te-le'-te *m.* short mantle, cloak, hood; mantelet.
man-ter' *tr.v.* to maintain; —*=se refl.v.* to hold out; to persist in.
man-téu *m.* long cloak; petticoat.
man-ti'-lha *f.* mantilla.
man-ti-men'-to *m.* maintenance, subsistence, provision, food.
man'-to *m.* veil; mantle, cloak.
ma-nu-al' *m.* manual, handbook; *adj.* manual, portable.
ma-nu-fa-tor' *m.* manufacturer.

ma-nu-fa-tu-rar' *tr.v.* to manufacture.

ma-nu-mis-são' *f.* liberation, emancipation.

ma-nus-cri'-to *m.* manuscript; **~o, ~a** *adj.* written by hand.

ma-nu-ten-ção' *f.* management, administration, maintenance.

mão' *f.* hand; handwriting; coat (of paint or whitewash); **segunda —** secondhand.

mão'~chei'-a *f.* handful.

mão'~de~o'-bra *f.* labor.

ma'-pa *m.* map; chart; list; catalogue.

ma-po-ão' *m.* poisonous plant, juice of which is used by Indians for poisoned arrows.

ma-po-te'-ca *f.* map collection.

ma-que'-te *f.* wax or clay model (of sculpture).

má-qui-na *f.* machine, engine.

ma-qui-na-ção' *f.* contrivance, machination.

ma-qui-nar' *tr.v.* to plan, to plot, to scheme.

ma-qui-na-ri'-a *f.* machinery.

ma-qui-nis'-ta *m.* machinist, engineer (on ship).

mar' *m.* sea, ocean; **alto —** high seas.

ma-ras'-mo *m.* emaciation, atrophy; stagnation.

ma-ra-vi'-lha *f.* marvel.

ma-ra-vi-lhar' *tr.v.* to surprise.

ma-ra-vi-lho'-so, ~a *adj.* marvelous, wonderful.

mar'-ca *f.* mark; brand, make; trademark; frontier, border; stigma.

mar-ca-ção' *f.* marking, demarkation; branding; coaching (theater).

mar'-ca~de~Ju'-das *m., f.* short person.

mar-ca'-do *m.* sharper, swindler.

mar-ca-dor' *m.* marker, scorer.

mar-car' *tr.v.* to mark; to set, to stigmatize, to brand.

mar-cas-si'-ta *f.* marcasite.

mar-ce-na-ri'-a *f.* cabinet work.

mar-ce-nei'-ro *m.* cabinet-maker.

mar'-cha *f.* march.

mar-char' *intr.v.* to march.

mar-che-ta-ri'-a *f.* marquetry.

mar-che'-te *m.* inlay.

mar-che-tei'-ro *m.* one who makes inlaid work, cabinet-maker.

mar-ci-al' *adj.* martial.

mar'-co *m.* stake, post; landmark; mark (German monetary unit).

mar'-ço *m.* March.

ma-ré *f.* tide.

ma-re-chal' *m.* marshall.

mar-fim' *m.* ivory.

mar-fim'~ve-ge-tal' *m.* ivory nut, vegetable ivory.

mar'-ga *f.* marl.

mar-ga-ri'-na *f.* margarine.

mar'-gem *f.* margin; bank (river); edge; (fig.) facility; **dar —** permit, make possible; **deitar à — to lay aside**, to abandon.

mar-gi-nal' *adj.* marginal.

mar-gi-nar' *tr.v.* to annotate in the margin.

mar-go'-so, ~a *adj.* like marl.

mar-guei'-ra *f.* marl deposit.

ma-ri'-a~ma-cum-bé *f.* game of blindfold.

ma-ri-a'-to *m.* wigwagging.

ma-ri'-do *m.* husband.

ma-ri'-nha *f.* navy, marine; **— mercante** merchant marine.

ma-ri-nhei'-ro *m.* sailor, seaman.

ma-ri'-nho, ~a *adj.* maritime, marine.

ma-rí-ti-mo, ~a *adj.* maritime.

mar-mi'-ta *f.* pot, steamer.

már-mo-re *m.* marble.

mar-mó-re-o, ~a *adj.* of marble, like marble.

mar-mo'-ta *f.* marmot.

mar-quei'-ro *m.* brander.

mar-quês *m.* marquis.

mar-que'-sa *f.* marchioness; marquise, station shed; couch.

mar-que-si'-nha *f.* small parasol, station shed.

mar-rão' *m.* heavy hammer (used in breaking stones).

mar-rom' *adj.* maroon, brown.

mar-ro-quim' *m.* morocco leather.

Mar'-te *m.* Mars.

mar-te-la'-da *f.* hammer blow.

mar-te-lar' *tr.v.* to hammer; to importune.

mar-te'-lo *m.* hammer.

mar-te'-lo~pi-lão' *m.* drop hammer.

mar-ti-ne'-te *m.* pile-driver; piano hammer; style or pointer of a sun dial.

már-tir *m.* martyr.

mar-tí-rio *m.* martyrdom.

mar-ti-ri-zar' *tr.v.* to torture, to afflict.

ma-ru'-jo *m.* sailor, seaman.

mas' *conj.* but; *m.* obstacle, difficulty.

más-ca-ra *f.* mask; face guard (fencing), blind, visor.

mas-ca-ra'-da *f.* masquerade.

mas-ca-rar' *tr.v.* to mask, to disguise, to camouflage.

mas-ca-ri'-lha *f.* half mask.

mas-ca'-te *m.* street peddler.

mas-co'-te *f.* mascot.

mas-cu-li'-no, ~a *adj.* masculine.

mas'-sa *f.* mass; dough, paste; bulk.

mas-sa-crar' *tr.v.* to massacre.

mas-sa'-cre *m.* massacre.

mas-sa'-gem *f.* massage.

mas-sa-gis'-ta *m., f.* masseur, masseuse.

mas-sa-ro'-co *m.* raised dough.

mas-sei'-ra *f.* kneading trough.

mas-so-quis'-mo *m.* masochism.

mas-ti-ga-ção' *f.* mastication.

mas-ti-gar' *tr.v.* to masticate, to chew.

mas-tim' *m.* mastiff (dog).

mas-to-don'-te *m.* mastodon.

mas-to-qui'-no *m.* short razor used by sailors.

mas'-tro *m.* mast, staff, flag pole.

mas-tur-ba-ção' *f.* masturbation.

ma'-ta *f.* thicket, woods.

ma-ta~bi'-cho *m.* drink, snifter.

ma-ta~bor-rão' *m.* blotter, blotting paper.

ma-ta-dor' *m.* murderer; bore.

ma-ta-dou'-ro *m.* slaughterhouse, abattoir.

ma-ta-gal' *m.* large thicket.

ma-ta-go'-so, ~a *adj.* bushy, heavily wooded.

ma-ta'-me *m.* scalloped edge.

ma-tan'-ça *f.* killing, slaughter, butchering.

ma-ta~pi-o'-lhos *m.* thumb.

ma-tar' *tr.v.* to kill, to slay.

ma'-te *m.* decreasing stitch; Paraguay tea.

ma-te-má-ti-ca *f.* mathematics.

ma-te-má-ti-co, ~a *adj.* mathematical.

ma-té-ria *f.* material; matter; **— prima** raw material.

ma-te-ri-al' *m.* material, materiel; *adj.* material.

ma-te-ri-a-li-zar' *tr.v.* to materialize.

ma-ter-nal' adj. maternal.
ma-ter-ni-da'-de f. maternity; maternity-hospital.
ma-ter'-no, =a adj. maternal.
ma-ti-na'-da f. dawn.
ma-ti-nal' adj. morning, early.
ma-ti'-nas f.pl. matins.
ma-tiz' m. shading, gradation of colors.
ma-ti-zar' tr.v. to shade, to variegate; to adorn.
ma'-to m. virgin land with vegetable growth; country as opposed to city.
ma-to'-so, =a adj. shrubby, scrubby.
ma-tra'-ca f. child's rattle; two sticks hinged together at one end and used to attract attention by banging together, generally by street peddlers.
ma-trí-cu-la f. matriculation fee, entrance fee, matriculation; roll; list.
ma-tri-mô-nio m. matrimony.
ma-triz' f. matrix; womb; mother, origin.
ma-tro'-na f. matron.
ma-tro-nal' adj. matronly.
ma-tu-ra-ção' f. ripening.
ma-tu-rar' tr.v. to ripen; intr.v. to ripen, to mature, to mellow.
ma-tu-ri-da'-de f. ripeness, maturity.
ma-tu'-ro, =a adj. ripe, mature.
ma-tu-tar' intr.v. to mull over, to be worried.
ma-tu'-to m. backwoodsman.
mau', **má** adj. bad, evil, perverse; naughty.
mau-so-léu m. mausoleum.
ma-xi'-la f. jaw.
má-xi-ma f. maxim.
má-xi-mo, =a adj. maximum.
me-a-ção' f. dividing in halves.
me-a-da f. skein.
me-a'-do m. half.
me-a-lhei'-ro m. money-box, bank.
me-ar' tr.v. to divide into halves.
me-câ-ni-ca f. mechanics.
me-câ-ni-co m. mechanic; **me-câ-ni-co,** =a adj. mechanical.
me-ca-nis'-mo m. mechanism.
me-ca-ni-za-ção' f. mechanization.
me'-da f. stack, rick (of hay, grain or corn).
me-da'-lha f. medal.
me-da-lhão' m. medallion, locket.
me-da-lhá-rio m. **me-da-lhei'-ro** m. cabinet for medals, collection of medals.
me-dão' m. sand dune.
mé-dia f. median, average; (Brazil) coffee (served with hot milk).
me-di-a-ção' f. mediation.
me-di-a-dor' m. mediator.
me-di-a'-no, =a adj. medium, in the middle; mediocre.
me-di-an'-te prep. by means of, through.
me-di-ar' tr.v. to divide in the middle; to mediate, intr.v. to intervene.
me-di-ca-ção' f. treatment; medication.
me-di-cal' adj. medical.
me-di-ca-men'-to m. medicine.
me-di-car' tr.v. to treat, to prescribe.
me-di-cas'-tro m. quack, charlatan.
me-di-ci'-na f. medicine.
me-di-ci-nal' adj. medicinal.
me-di'-da f. measure.
me-di-e-val' adj. **me-di-e'-vo,** =a adj. medieval.
mé-dio, =a adj. mean, middle, average, intermediate.
me-dí-o-cre adj. mediocre.
me-dir' tr.v. to measure.
me-di-ta-ção' f. meditation.

me-di-ta-bun'-do, =a adj. pensive, melancholy.
me-di-tar' tr.v., intr.v. to ponder, to think about; to reflect, to think.
mê-do m. fear, terror.
me-do'-nho, =a adj. frightening, terrifying.
me-dro'-so, =a adj. timid, fearful; cowardly.
me-du'-la f. marrow, pith, substance.
me-ga-fo'-ne m. megaphone.
me-gas-có-pio m. megascope.
mei'-a f. stocking, sock.
mei'-a-á-gua f. root with only one inclined plane.
mei'-a-ca'-na f. half-round (moulding).
mei'-a-es-qua-dri'-a f. bisector of a right angle.
mei'-a-i-da'-de f. middle age.
mei'-a-lu'-a f. half-moon.
mei'-a-noi'-te f. midnight.
mei'-a-tin'-ta f. half-tone, half shade.
mei'-o-di'-a m. midday, noon.
mei'-o-so-pra'-no m. mezzo-soprano.
mei'-o-tom' m. half tone.
mel' m. honey.
me-la'-ço m. molasses.
me-la'-do m. cane syrup.
me-lan-ci'-a f. watermelon.
me-lan-co-li'-a f. melancholy.
me-lan-có-li-co, =a adj. melancholy, gloomy.
me-lão' f. melon.
me-lar' tr.v. to sweeten with honey, to cover with honey, to make honey-colored.
me-le'-na f. lock of hair.
me-lhor' adj. better, best.
me-lho-ra-men'-to m. improvement.
me-lho-rar' tr.v. to improve, to make better; intr.v. to improve, to get better.
me-lí-fluo, =a adj. mellifluous.
me-li-lo'-to m. sweet clover.
me-lin'-dro m. delicacy, niceness; affected manner, affected preciseness; prudishness; coyness.
me-lin-dro'-so, =a adj. affected, fastidious; delicate; dangerous, risky.
me-lo-di'-a f. melody.
me-ló-di-ca f. melodeon, music-box.
me-ló-di-co, =a adj. melodious.
me-lo-di-o'-so, =a adj. melodious.
me-lo-dra'-ma m. melodrama.
me-lo-dra-má-ti-co, =a adj. melodramatic.
mel'-ro m. **mel-rô-a** f. black bird.
mem-bra'-na f. membrane.
mem'-bro m. member.
me-mo-rá-vel adj. memorable.
me-mó-ria f. memory; memoir.
me-mo-ri-al' m., adj. memorial.
me-na-re'-te m. minaret.
men-ção' f. mention.
men-ci-o-nar' tr.v. to mention.
men-di-can'-te m. beggar; adj. mendicant.
men-di-ci-da'-de f. begging, mendicity.
men-di-gar' tr.v. to beg, to solicit; intr.v. to beg, to go begging.
men-di'-go m. beggar.
me-ne-ar' tr.v. to shake, to wag; to manage.
me-nes-tral' m. minstrel.
me-nin-gi'-te f. meningitis.
me-ni'-na f. child, girl.
me-ni-nei'-ro, =a adj. child-like; fond of children.
me-ni-ni'-ce f. childhood; childishness.
me-ni'-no m. child, boy.

me-nor' *adj.* smaller, less, lesser, smallest, least; *m.*, *f.* minor.

me-no-ri-da'-de *f.* minority.

me'-nos *adv.* less, fewer, least, fewest; *prep.* except.

me-nos-pre-zar' *tr.v.* to depreciate, to disdain; to scorn.

me-nos-prê-zo *m.* disdain, belittling, depreciation.

men-sa-gei'-ro *m.* messenger; runner; courier.

men-sa'-gem *f.* message.

men-sal' *adj.* monthly.

men-sa-li-da'-de *f.* monthly payment.

men-sá-rio *m.* monthly newspaper.

mên-struo *m.* menses.

men-su-ra-ção' *f.* mensuration.

men-su-rá-vel *adj.* mensurable.

men-ta-li-da'-de *f.* psychology.

men'-te *f.* mind, intellect; spirit.

men-tir' *intr.v.* to lie.

men-ti'-ra *f.* lie, falsehood.

men-ti-ro'-so, *=a adj.* lying, false.

men-tol' *m.* menthol.

men-tor' *m.* mentor.

men-tras'-to *m.* wild mint.

mer'-ca *f.* purchase, bartering.

mer-ca'-do *m.* market.

mer-ca-do-ri'-a *f.* merchandise.

mer-can'-te *m.,* *adj.* merchant; *adj.* commercial.

mer-can-til' *adj.* mercantile.

mer-car' *tr.v.* to buy, to purchase, to buy for selling.

mer-cá-vel *adj.* marketable.

mer-ce-ná-rio *m.* =o, =a *adj.* mercenary.

mer-cu-ri-al' *adj.* mercurial.

mer-cú-rio *m.* mercury.

me-re-cer' *tr.v.* to deserve, to merit; *intr.v.* to be worthy.

me-re-ci-men'-to *m.* merit, desert, worth.

me-ren'-da *f.* light lunch; picnic lunch.

me-ren'-gue *m.* **me-ren'-que** *m.* meringue.

mer-gu-lha-dor' *m.* diver.

mer-gu-lhar' *tr.v.,* *intr.v.* to submerge, to sink, to plunge (beneath surface of water), to dive.

me-ri-di-a'-na *f.* meridian line; sun-dial.

me-ri-di-a'-no *m.* meridian; **me-ri-di-a'-no,** *=a adj.* meridian.

me-ri-di-o-nal' *adj.* meridional, southern.

me-ri'-no *m.* merino (kind of sheep).

me-ri-tís-si-mo, *=a adj.* most merited, most deserved.

mé-ri-to *m.* merit.

me-ri-tó-rio, *=a adj.* meritorious.

me'-ro, *=a adj.* mere, simple, pure.

mês' *m.* month; — **lunar** lunar month.

me'-sa *f.* table; board, committee, court.

me-sa'-da *f.* monthly amount, monthly dues.

me-sá-rio *m.* board member.

mes'-cla *f.* mixture.

mes-clar' *tr.v.* to mix.

me-sen-té-rio *m.* mesentery.

mes-mís-si-mo, *=a adj.* very same. .

mes'-mo, *=a adj.* same; self; *adv.* even.

mes-qui'-nho, *=a adj.* niggardly, parsimonious, mean, miserable.

mes-qui'-ta *f.* mosque.

mes-si-â-ni-co, *=a adj.* Messianic.

mes-si'-as *m.* Messiah.

mes-ti-ça'-gem *f.* cross-breeding.

mes-ti'-ço, *=a adj.* mixed, of mixed blood.

mes-tran'-ça *f.* arsenal, ordnance shop.

mes'-tre *m.* teacher; master; foreman; expert.

mes'-tre-es-co'-la *m.* school-teacher.

mes-tri'-a *f.* mastery.

me-ta-bó-li-co, *=a adj.* metabolic.

me-ta-bo-lis'-mo *m.* metabolism.

me-ta'-de *f.* half.

me-ta-fí-si-ca *f.* metaphysics.

me-tá-fo-ra *f.* metaphor.

me-tá-fra-se *f.* metaphrase.

me-tal' *m.* metal.

me-tá-li-co, *=a adj.* metallic.

me-ta-lur-gi'-a *f.* metallurgy.

me-ta-lúr-gi-co, *=a adj.* metallurgic.

me-ta-mór-fi-co, *=a adj.* metamorphic.

me-ta-mor-fo'-se *f.* metamorphosis.

me-te-ó-ri-co, *=a adj.* meteoric.

me-te-o-ri'-to *m.* meteorite.

me-te-o'-ro *m.* meteor.

me-te-o-ro-lo-gi'-a *f.* meteorology.

me-ter' *tr.v.* to place, to put, to put in, to introduce; to cause; — **na cabeça** to memorize, to suggest, to persuade.

me-ti-cu-lo'-so, *=a adj.* meticulous.

mé-to-do *m.* method.

me-to-do-lo-gi'-a *f.* methodology.

me-tra'-lha *f.* shrapnel, cannister.

me-tra-lha-dor' *m.* machine gunner.

me-tra-lha-do'-ra *f.* machine gun.

me-tra-lhar' *tr.v.* to shoot with a machine gun, to attack with a machine gun.

mé-tri-co, *=a adj.* metric.

me'-tro *m.* meter.

me-trô-no-mo *m.* metronome.

me-tró-po-le *f.* metropolis; capital; mother-country.

me-tro-po-li-ta'-no, *=a adj.* metropolitan.

meu', **mi'-nha** *adj., pro.* my, mine.

me-xe-di'-ço, *=a adj.* restless.

me-xer' *tr.v.* to stir, to agitate, to move, to mix up; *intr.v.* to meddle, to move; —*se refl.v.* to be restless, to move about.

me-xi'-da *f.* confusion, disorder, discord.

me-xi'-do, *=a adj.* mixed, stirred around; scrambled.

me-xe-ri-car' *intr.v.* to gossip, to intrigue.

me-xe-ri-quei'-ro *m.* gossiper, troublemaker.

me-zi'-nha *f.* **me-zi-nhi'-ce** *f.* household remedy.

mi-a'-da *f.* miauling.

mi-a'-do *m.* miaow.

mi-ar' *intr.v.* to miaul, to mew.

mi-as'-ma *m.* miasma.

mi'-ca *f.* mica; small portion, bit.

mic-ção' *f.* urinating.

mi-cró-bio *m.* microbe.

mi-cro-fo'-ne *m.* microphone.

mi-cró-fo-no, *=a adj.* microphonic.

mi-crô-me-tro *m.* micrometer.

mí-cron *m.* micron.

mi-cros-có-pi-co, *=a adj.* microscopic.

mi-cros-có-pio *m.* microscope.

mic-tó-rio, *=a adj.* diuretic.

mi-ga'-lha *f.* little bit, small portion, crumb; =s *f.pl.* left-overs.

mi-ga-lhar' *tr.v.* to break into small bits, to crumble.

mi-ga-lhei'-ro *m.* trifler; pedant.

mi-gra-ção' *f.* migration.

mi-gra-tó-rio, *=a adj.* migratory.

mil' *m.* thousand.

mi-la'-gre *m.* miracle.

mi-la-gro'-so, *=a adj.* miraculous.

mi-lê-nio *m.* millennium.

mi'-lha *f.* mile.
mi-lhal' *m.* corn-field.
mi-lhão' *m.* million.
mi-lhar' *m.* thousand.
mi'-lho *m.* corn.
mi-li-cia *f.* militia; warfare.
mi-li-o-ná-rio *m.* millionaire.
mi-lí-pe-de *adj.* having many feet or legs.
mi-li-tan'-te *adj.* militant.
mi-li-tar' *m.* soldier; *adj.* relative to war, army, or troops; *intr.v.* to be member of party or group; to militate; to follow career of arms.
mi-li-ta-ris'-mo *m.* militarism.
mil-reis' *m.* monetary unit of Brazil, written 1$000.
mi-me-o-gra-far' *tr.v.* to mimeograph.
mi-me-ó-gra-fo *m.* mimeograph.
mí-mi-ca *f.* mimicry.
mi-mi-co, -a *adj.* imitating, mimic, sham.
mi-mar' *tr.v.* to mimic.
mi'-mo *m.* present, gift; caress, endearment, delicacy.
mi-mó-lo-go *m.* mimic.
mi-mo'-so, -a *adj.* delicate, dainty, sensitive.
mi'-na *f.* mine.
mi-na-dou'-ro *m.* spring, source.
mi-nar' *tr.v.* to mine.
mi-na-re'-te *m.* minaret.
min-di'-nho *m.* little finger.
mi-nei'-ra *f.* ore deposit, mine.
mi-nei'-ro *m.* miner; mi-nei'-ro, -a *adj.* mining, relative to mines; native of Minas Gerais.
mi-ne-ral' *m.*, *adj.* mineral.
mi-ne-ra-lo-gi'-a *f.* mineralogy.
mi-ne-ra-lo-gis'-ta *m.* mineralogist.
mi-ne-rar' *tr.v.* to mine, to work, to extract; *intr.v.* to mine, to work at mining.
mi-né-rio *m.* ore.
min-gau' *m.* (Brazil) wheat gruel with eggs and sugar.
min-gua'-do, -a *adj.* lacking, needy, poor, unhappy.
min-guan'-te *adj.* decreasing, waning.
min-gu-ar' *intr.v.* to become less, to diminish, to become scarce.
mi-ni-a-tu'-ra *f.* miniature.
mí-ni-ma *f.* minim (music).
mí-ni-mo, -a *adj.* minimum.
mi-nis-té-rio *m.* ministry, department; — da Fazenda Treasury Department; — de Marinha Navy Department; — de Educação e Saúde Department of Education and Health; — de Guerra Department of War; — de Justiça e Negócios Interiores Department of Justice and Internal Affairs; — de Relações Exteriores Department of State (Foreign Affairs); — de Viação e Obras Públicas Department of Transport and Public Works; — do Ar Department of Aviation; — do Trabalho, Indústria e Comércio Department of Labor, Industry and Commerce.
mi-nis-trar' *tr.v.* to aid, to minister to.
mi-nis'-tro *m.* minister; secretary.
mi-no-rar' *tr.v.* to lessen, to soften.
mi-no-ra-ti'-vo *m.* purgative.
mi-no-ri'-a *f.* minority.
mi-nú-cia *f.* minutia.
mi-nu-ci-o'-so, -a *adj.* minute, meticulous, particular.
mi-nús-cu-la *f.* small letter.
mi-nús-cu-lo, -a *adj.* minuscule; tiny.

mi-nu'-to *m.* minute (sixtieth part of hour); mi-nu'-to, -a *adj.* small, minute.
mi-o'-lo *m.* brains; crumb of bread; pith, marrow, essence.
mí-o-pe *adj.* nearsighted.
mi-o-pi'-a *f.* myopia, nearsightedness.
mi'-ra *f.* sight; aim, objective.
mi-ra-dou'-ro *m.* lookout point, turret, belvedere.
mi-ra'-gem *f.* mirage.
mi-rar' *tr.v.* to look at, to view, to desire; *intr.v.* to aim, to plan, to overlook; —-se *refl.v.* to look at oneself, to be reflected.
mi-rí-a-de *f.* myriad.
mi-ro'-ne *m.* spectator, onlooker.
mi-san-tro-pi'-a *f.* misanthropy.
mi-san-tró-pi-co, -a *adj.* misanthropic.
mi-san-tro'-po *m.* misanthrope.
mis-ce-lâ-ne-a *f.* miscellany.
mi-se-rá-vel *adj.* miserable.
mi-sé-ria *f.* misery.
mi-se-ri-cór-dia *f.* compassion.
mi-se-ri-cor-di-o'-so, -a *adj.* compassionate.
mi-se-ro, -a *adj.* miserable; stingy.
mis'-sa *f.* mass; — cantada high mass; — rezada low mass; de réquiem requiem mass.
mis-sal' *m.* missal, mass book.
mis-san'-ga *f.* beads; bead trimming.
mis-são' *f.* mission; doctrinal sermon.
mís-sil *m.*, *adj.* missile.
mis-si-o-ná-rio *m.* missionary.
mis-sí-va *f.* missive.
mis-ter' *m.* urgency, necessity; profession, function.
mis-té-rio *m.* mystery.
mis-te-ri-o'-so, -a *adj.* mysterious.
mis-ti-cis'-mo *m.* mysticism.
mís-ti-co, -a *adj.* mystic.
mis-ti-fi-ca-ção' *f.* mystification.
mis-ti-fi-car' *tr.v.* to mystify.
mis'-to, -a *adj.* mixed.
mis-tu'-ra *f.* mixture.
mis-tu-rar' *tr.v.* to mix, to confuse.
mi-te'-ne *f.* mitten.
mi-ti-ga-ção' *f.* mitigation.
mi-ti-gar' *tr.v.* to mitigate.
mi'-to *m.* myth.
mi-to-lo-gi'-a *f.* mythology.
mi'-tra *f.* miter.
mi-u-de'-za *f.* smallness; precision, care as to details; -s *f.pl.* small change; notions; trifles.
mi-u'-do, -a *adj.* small, little, tiny.
mó *f.* grindstone, whetstone.
mo-a'-gem *f.* grinding.
mó-bil *adj.* mobile.
mo-bi-lá-rio *m.* furniture; mo-bi-lá-rio, -a *adj.* personal; relative to furniture.
mo-bí-lia *f.* furniture, furnishings.
mo-bi-li-da'-de *f.* mobility; inconstancy.
mo-bi-li-za-ção' *f.* mobilization.
mo-bi-li-zar' *tr.v.* to mobilize.
mo'-ca *m.* Mocha (coffee).
mo'-ça *f.* girl, young woman.
mo-ção' *f.* motion.
mo-ce-tão' *m.* robust, good-looking young man.
mo-ce-to'-na *f.* robust, good-looking young girl.
mo-chi'-la *f.* knapsack; duffel bag; haver-sack.
mo'-ço *m.* boy, young man.
mo'-da *f.* custom; manner, fashion; -s

f.pl. articles of feminine apparel; fashions; **casa de =s** woman's apparel shop.

mo-de-la'-gem *f.* modeling.
mo-de-lar' *tr.v.* to model, to reproduce; —**=se** *refl.v.* to take as model.
mo-dê-lo *m.* model.
mo-de-ra-ção' *f.* moderation.
mo-de-ra'-do, =a *adj.* moderate.
mo-de-rar' *tr.v.* to moderate; —**=se** *refl.v.* to avoid excesses.
mo-der-ni-zar' *tr.v.* to modernize.
mo-der'-no, =a *adj.* modern.
mo-dés-tia *f.* modesty.
mo-des'-to, =a *adj.* modest.
mó-di-co, =a *adj.* small, moderate, insignificant.
mo-di-fi-ca-ção' *f.* modification.
mo-di-fi-car' *tr.v.* to modify.
mo-di'-lho *m.* **mo-di'-nha** *f.* popular song.
mo-dis'-ta *f.* modiste, milliner.
mo'-do *m.* mode; manner, way; moderation.
mo-dor'-ra *f.* lethargy, deep sleep.
mo-du-la-ção' *f.* modulation.
mo-du-lar' *tr.v.* to modulate.
mo-e'-da *f.* coin.
mo-e'-da-gem *f.* coining of money minting.
mo-e-du'-ra *f.* grinding.
mo-e'-la *f.* gizzard (of birds).
mo-en'-da *f.* mill-stone; grinding.
mo-er' *tr.v.* to grind, to crush, to reduce to powder; (fig.) to meditate upon, to repeat over and over, to importune.
mo-fen'-to, =a *adj.* musty, moldy.
mô-fo *m.* mold, mustiness.
mo-fo'-so, =a *adj.* musty, moldy.
mo-i'-nho *m.* mill, flour-mill.
mo'-la *f.* spring; (fig.) incentive, motive.
mo-lar' *adj.* molar.
mol-da'-gem *f.* moulding, casting.
mol-dar' *tr.v.* to mould.
mol'-de *m.* mould.
mol-du'-ra *f.* moulding, framing.
mo'-le *f.* bulk, size, volume, mass; *adj.* soft, weak, effeminate, colorless.
mo-le'-za *f.* softness; lack of resolution; laziness.
mo-le'-ca *f.* colored child.
mo-lé-cu-la *f.* molecule.
mo-le-cu-lar' *adj.* molecular.
mo-lei'-ro *m.* miller.
mo-le'-que *m.* colored child.
mo-les-tar' *tr.v.* to molest, to annoy, to disturb, to bother.
mo-lés-tia *f.* illness, disease.
mo-lha'-da *f.* large bundle, bunch.
mo-lha-de'-la *f.* wetting, soaking, bath.
mo-lha'-do, =a *adj.* wet, damp.
mo-lha'-dos *m.pl.* liquid merchandise (wine, beer, oil, etc.).
mo-lhar' *tr.v.* to wet, to moisten, to soak, to dampen.
mo'-lhe *m.* pier, wharf.
mo-lhei'-ra *f.* gravy dish.
mô-lho *m.* gravy, sauce.
mo-lho *m.* bundle; handful.
mo-li-fi-car' *tr.v.* to mollify.
mo-li-ne'-te *m.* windlass, turnstile.
mo-lu'-gem *f.* solder.
mo-lus'-cos *m.pl.* mollusks.
mo-men-tâ-ne-o, =a *adj.* instantaneous, fleeting, rapid.
mo-men'-to *m.* moment; momentum.
mo-men-to'-so, =a *adj.* momentous.
mo-na-cal' *adj.* monastic.
mo-nar'-ca *m.* monarch.

mo-nar-qui'-a *f.* monarchy.
mo-nár-qui-co, =a *adj.* monarchical.
mo-nás-ti-co, =a *adj.* monastic.
mo-na-zi'-ta *f.* monazite.
mon-dar' *tr.v.* to weed, to thin out; (fig.) to correct, to amend.
mo-ne-tá-rio, =a *adj.* monetary.
mon'-ge *m.* friar, monk.
mo-nir' *tr.v.* to admonish.
mo-ni-tor' *m.* monitor, tutor.
mo-ni-tó-ria *f.* notice, warning.
mo-no-cór-dio *m.* monochord.
mo-no-cro'-mo *m.* monochrome.
mo-nó-cu-lo *m.* monocle.
mo-no-fo-bi'-a *f.* monophobia (fear of being alone).
mo-no-ga-mi'-a *f.* monogamy.
mo-no-ge-ni'-a *f.* monogenesis.
mo-no-gra-fi'-a *f.* monograph.
mo-no-gra'-ma *m.* monogram.
mo-nó-li-to *m.* monolith.
mo-nó-lo-go *m.* monologue.
mo-no-pla'-no *m.* monoplane.
mo-no-pó-lio *m.* monopoly.
mo-no-po-li-za-ção' *f.* monopolization.
mo-no-po-li-zar' *tr.v.* to monopolize.
mo-nos-sí-la-bo *m.* monosyllable.
mo-no-te-ís-ta *adj., m., f.* monotheist.
mo-no-ti'-po *m.* monotype.
mo-no-to-ni'-a *f.* monotony.
mo-nó-to-no, =a *adj.* monotonous.
mons'-tro *m.* monster.
mons-tru-o-si-da'-de *f.* monstrosity.
mons-tru-o'-so, =a *adj.* monstrous.
mon'-ta *f.* amount, value, importance, cost.
mon-ta'-da *f.* mount, horse.
mon-ta'-do, =a *adj.* on horse-back.
mon-ta'-gem *f.* mounting; assembling.
mon-ta'-nha *f.* mountain.
mon-ta-nhês *m.* mountaineer.
mon-ta-nho'-so, =a *adj.* mountainous.
mon-tão' *m.* pile, heap.
mon-tar' *tr.v.* to mount; to set; to set up, to assemble; to place on top; to go around; *intr.v.* to go horseback riding; to amount.
mon'-te *m.* hill, mount; total inheritance, share of an inheritance.
mon-te-pi'-o *m.* retirement pension; insurance company; governmental department administering retirement funds.
mon-tês *adj.* mountain, wild.
mo-nu-men-tal' *adj.* monumental.
mo-nu-men'-to *m.* monument.
mo-que-ar' *tr.v.* to barbecue.
mo-quém *m.* grate, grill for barbecue.
mo-quen'-ça *f.* barbecue.
mo'-ra *f.* delay; extension of time.
mo-ra'-da *f.* dwelling, home; stay.
mo-ra'-do, =a *adj.* mulberry-colored.
mo-ra-dor' *m.* resident, inhabitant.
mo-ral' *adj.* moral; *f.* ethics.
mo-ra-li-da'-de *f.* morality, moral, morals.
mo-ra-lis'-ta *m.* moralist, moralizer.
mo-ra-li-zar' *tr.v., intr.v.* to moralize.
mo-ran'-go *m.* strawberry.
mo-rar' *intr.v.* to live, to dwell, to reside.
mo-ra-tó-ria *f.* moratorium.
mor-bi-dez' *f.* **mor-bi-de'-za** *f.* morbidity; delicacy of lines or colors.
mór-bi-do, =a *adj.* morbid; sickly; delicate.
mor-ce'-go *m.* bat.
mor-da'-ça *f.* gag.
mor-da-ci-da'-de *f.* mordacity, corrosiveness; satire.

mor-daz' *adj.* mordant; bitter, sharp, biting.
mor-de-du'-ra *f.* bite, mark of teeth; sarcasm.
mor-der' *tr.v.*, *intr.v.* to bite; to corrode; —**=se** *refl.v.* to become irritated.
mor-do-mi'-a *f.* office of majordomo.
mor-do'-mo *m.* majordomo.
mo-re'-no, **=a** *adj.* brunette; dark, dark-complexioned.
mor-féi-a *f.* leprosy.
mor-fé-ti-co, **=a** *adj.* leprous.
mor-fi'-na *f.* morphine.
mor-fo-lo-gi'-a *f.* morphology.
mor-ga-ná-ti-co, **=a** *adj.* morganatic.
mor'-gue *f.* morgue.
mo-ri-bun'-do, **=a** *adj.* moribund.
mo-rin'-ga *f.* unglazed, porous, pottery water jug.
mor-men'-te *adv.* principally, chiefly.
mor'-mo *m.* glanders.
mor'-no, **=a** *adj.* lukewarm, tepid.
mo-ro-si-da'-de *f.* slowness, delay.
mo-ro'-so, **=a** *adj.* slow; late.
mor-rer' *intr.v.* to die, to become extinct; — **por** to have great affection for.
mor'-ro *m.* hill, low mountain.
mor'-sa *f.* walrus.
mor-se-gão' *f.* bite, pinch, nip.
mor-se-gar' *tr.v.* to bite off, to tear out.
mor-tal' *adj.* mortal.
mor-ta-li-da'-de *f.* mortality.
mor-ta'-lha *f.* shroud.
mor-tan-da'-de *f.* mortality.
mor'-te *f.* death.
mor-tei'-ro *m.* mortar (mil.).
mor-ti-cí-nio *m.* massacre, slaughter.
mor-ti'-ço, **=a** *adj.* dying, failing.
mor-ti-fi-ca-ção' *f.* mortification.
mor-ti-fi-can'-te *adj.* mortifying.
mor-ti-fi-car' *tr.v.* to mortify.
mor'-to, **=a** *adj.* dead, extinct, forgotten, inert.
mor-tó-rio *m.* funeral.
mor-tu-á-rio, **=a** *adj.* mortuary.
mor-tu-ó-rio *m.* burial, funeral.
mó-ru-la *f.* brief delay; morula.
mo-sai'-co *m.* **=o**, **=a** *adj.* mosaic.
môs-ca *f.* house fly; (fig.) beauty spot; insistent person; small tuft of beard.
mos-ca-dei'-ro *m.* flyflap, fly trap; netting.
mos-cão' *m.* large fly.
mos-ca-tel' *m.*, *adj.* muscatel wine or grape.
mos-co-vi'-ta *f.* Muscovite.
mos-que-tão' *m.* musket.
mos-que-tei'-ro *m.* musketeer.
mos-qui-tei'-ro *m.* mosquito-net.
mos-qui'-to *m.* mosquito.
mos-tar'-da *f.* mustard seed.
mos-tei'-ro *m.* monastery.
mos'-to *m.* grape juice.
mos-tra-dor' *m.* face (of clock or watch); counter; show-case.
mos-trar' *tr.v.* to show, to point out.
mo'-te *m.* motto; joke, pun.
mo-te-jar' *intr.v.* to jest, to jeer, to scoff.
mo-tim' *m.* mutiny, insurrection.
mo-ti-va-ção' *f.* motivation.
mo-ti-var' *tr.v.* to motivate.
mo-ti'-vo *m.* motive.
mo-to-ci'-clo *m.* motor-cycle.
mo-tor' *m.* motor; **mo-tor'**, **=triz'** *adj.* motive, driving, moving.
mo-to-ris'-ta *m.* motorist, chauffeur.
mo-tor-nei'-ro *m.* motorman.
mou'-co, **=a** *adj.* deaf, hard of hearing.
mou-qui'-ce *f.* deafness.

mou-qui-dão' *f.* deafness.
mou'-ro, **=a** *m.*, *f.* Moor.
mo-ve-di'-ço, **=a** *adj.* easily moved, movable, moving, quick.
mó-vel *m.* piece of furniture, personal property; motive; *adj.* movable; fickle.
mo-ver' *tr.v.* to move; —**=se** *refl.v.* to move, to stir.
mo-vi-men-tar' *tr.v.* to give movement to.
mo-vi-men'-to *m.* movement.
mo-ví-vel *adj.* movable.
mu' *m.* mule.
mu-ar' *adj.* like a mule, mulish.
mu-ci-la'-gem *f.* mucilage.
mu-ci-la-gi-no'-so, **=a** *adj.* mucilaginous.
mu-ci'-na *f.* mucin.
mu'-co *m.* mucus.
mu-co'-sa *f.* mucous membrane.
mu-co-si-da'-de *f.* mucosity.
mu-co'-so, **=a** *adj.* mucous.
mu-çul-ma'-no *m.* Mussulman.
mu'-da *f.* change, moving; change of voice; moulting, shedding; transplanting.
mu-dan'-ça *f.* change, moving, transfer.
mu-dar' *tr.v.* to change, to transfer, to alter, to substitute; *intr.v.* to change, to move.
mu-dá-vel *adj.* changeable; fickle.
mu-dez' *f.* muteness, dumbness, silence.
mu'-do, **=a** *adj.* dumb, mute.
mu-gi'-do *m.* lowing, bellowing, mooing.
mu-gir' *intr.v.* to low, to bellow, to moo.
mui-ra-qui-tã' *f.* nephrite.
mui'-to *adv.* very; much, a great deal; **mui'-to**, **=a** *adj.* much, many, a great deal of.
mu'-la *f.* female mule.
mu-la-to, **=a** *m.*, *f.* mulatto.
mu-le'-ta *f.* crutch; (fig.) support.
mu-lher' *f.* woman; wife.
mu'-lo *m.* mule.
mul'-ta *f.* fine, penalty.
mul-tar' *tr.v.* to fine.
mul-ti-dão' *f.* multitude.
mul-ti-pli-ca-ção' *f.* multiplication.
mul-ti-pli-ca-dor' *m.* multiplier.
mul-ti-pli-car' *tr.v.*, *intr.v.* to multiply.
mul-tí-pli-ce *adj.* multiple.
múl-ti-plo, **=a** *adj.* multiple.
mú-mia *f.* mummy.
mu-mi-fi-car' *tr.v.*, *intr.v.* to mummify.
mun-da'-no, **=a** *adj.* mundane.
mun-di-al' *adj.* worldly, world-wide.
mun'-do *m.* world.
mu-ni-ção' *f.* munition.
mu-ni-ci-pal' *adj.* municipal.
mu-ni-ci-pa-li-da'-de *f.* municipality.
mu-ní-ci-pe *m.*, *f.* citizen.
mu-ni-ci-pio *m.* municipality.
mu-ni-fi-cên-cia *f.* munificence.
mu-ni-fi-cen'-te *adj.* munificent.
mu-ral' *adj.* mural.
mu-ra-lha *f.* wall, rampart.
mu-ra-men'-to *m.* walling in; rampart, fortification.
mu-rar' *tr.v.* to wall, to surround with wall.
mu'-ro *m.* wall.
mur-char' *intr.v.*, *tr.v.* to wilt, to weaken, to lose freshness.
mur'-cho, **=a** *adj.* wilted, faded, withered; sad, pensive.
mur-mu-rar' *tr.v.*, *intr.v.* to murmur.
mur-mú-rio *m.* murmur, buzzing, humming, buzz.
mur-mu-ro'-so, **=a** *adj.* murmuring.

mur'-ro *m* punch, blow with the fist.
mu'-sa *f.* muse.
mus-cu-lar' *adj.* muscular, having muscles.
mus-cu-la-tu'-ra *f.* musculature, set of muscles.
mús-cu-lo *m.* muscle.
mus-cu-lo'-so, ₌a *adj.* muscular, robust.
mu-seu' *m.* museum.
mus'-go *m.* moss.
mus-go'-so, ₌a *adj.* mossy.
mú-si-ca *f.* music; band, orchestra.
mu-si-cal' *adj.* musical.

mú-si-co, ₌a *adj.* **musical;** *m.,* *f.* musician.
mus-se-li'-na *f.* muslin.
mu-ta-çâo' *f.* mutation; substitution; change of scenes (theatre).
mu-tá-vel *adj.* mutable.
mu-ti-la-çâo' *f.* mutilation, defacement.
mu-ti-lar' *tr.v.* to mutilate, to deface, to mar.
mú-tua *f.* mutual society.
mú-tuo, ₌a *adj.* mutual, reciprocal.
mu-xi-râo' *m.* farm labor of one day given by farmers to each other.

N

See page 12—GUIDE TO REFORMED SPELLING used in this Dictionary

N, n *m.* N, n, thirteenth letter of the alphabet.
na-bal' *m.* turnip patch.
na-bi'-ça *f.* small undeveloped turnip.
na'-bo *m.* turnip.
na-çâo' *f.* nation.
ná-car *m.* nacre, mother of pearl.
na-ci-o-nal' *adj.* national.
na-ci-o-na-li-da'-de *f.* nationality.
na-ci-o-na-lis'-mo *m.* nationalism.
na-ci-o-na-lis'-ta *m.* nationalist.
na-ci-o-na-li-zar' *tr.v.* to nationalize, to naturalize.
na'-da *m.* nothing.
na-da-dor' *m.* swimmer.
na-dan'-te *adj.* swimming, floating.
na-dar' *intr.v.* to swim, to float.
ná-de-ga *f.* buttock, rump.
na-de-guei'-ro, ₌a *adj.* pertaining to buttock or rump.
na-di'-nha *m.* little bit, practically nothing.
naf-ta *f.* naphtha.
naf-ta-li'-na *f.* naphthalene.
naf-tol' *m.* naphthol.
nai'-pe *m.* suit (of cards).
na-mo-ra-dei'-ra *f.* flirt, coquet.
na-mo-ra-dei'-ro *m.* spark, masher.
na-mo-ra'-da *f.* sweetheart.
na-mo-ra'-do *m.* lover.
na-mo-rar' *tr.v.,* *intr.v.* to flirt with, to make love.
na-mô-ro *m.* love-making, flirting.
nan-quim' *m.* nankeen (fabric); India ink; black shoe polish.
nan-zu'-que *m.* nainsook (fabric).
nâo' *adv.* not, no.
na-po-le-âo' *m.* Napoleon (coin).
na-po-le-ô-ni-co, ₌a *adj.* Napoleonic.
nar-ci-sis'-mo *m.* narcissism.
nar-ci'-so *m.* narcissus.
nar-co'-se *f.* narcosis.
nar-có-ti-co, ₌a *adj.* narcotic.
nar-co-tis'-mo *m.* narcotism.
na-ri-gâo' *m.* large nose.
na-ri-gu'-do, ₌a *adj.* having a large nose.
na-ri'-na *f.* nostril.
na-riz' *m.* nose.
nar-ra-çâo' *f.* narration.
nar-rar' *tr.v.* to narrate.
nar-ra-ti'-vo, ₌a *adj.* narrative.
na-sal' *adj.* nasal.
na-sa-li-da'-de *f.* nasality.
nas-cen'-ça *f.* birth, orgin, beginning.
nas-cen'-te *adj.* rising, incipient, new-born; *m.* east; *f.* source, spring.

nas-cer' *intr.v.* to be born, to begin, to arise.
nas-ci'-da *f.* tumor, abscess, boil.
nas-ci-men'-to *m.* birth, origin.
nas-túr-cio *m.* nasturtium.
na'-ta *f.* cream.
na-ta-dei'-ra *f.* cream separator; pan in which cream is exposed for curdling.
na-tal' *adj.* natal; *m.* birthday; Christmas.
na-ta-tó-rio *m.* natatorium.
na-tei'-ro *m.* silt deposited by flood.
na-ten'-to, ₌a *adj.* covered with cream; fertile.
na-ti-vi-da'-de *f.* nativity.
na-ti'-vo, ₌a *adj.* native.
na'-to, ₌a *adj.* hereditary; natural.
na-tu-ral' *adj.* natural.
na-tu-ra-lis'-ta *m.* naturalist.
na-tu-ra-li-zar' *tr.v.* to naturalize.
na-tu-ral'-men-te *adv.* naturally, of course.
na-tu-re'-za *f.* nature.
nau' *m.* sailing vessel, three-master; ship, freighter.
nau-fra-gar' *intr.v.* to shipwreck, to fail.
nau-frá-gio *m.* shipwreck.
náu-se-a *f.* nausea.
nau-se-ar' *tr.v.* to nauseate; *intr.v.* to become nauseated, to get sick.
náu-ti-ca *f.* seamanship.
náu-ti-co, ₌a *adj.* nautical.
na-val' *adj.* naval.
na-va'-lha *f.* razor.
na-va-lha'-da *f.* cut by razor.
na'-ve *f.* nave.
na-ve-ga-çâo' *f.* navigation.
na-ve-ga-dor' *m.* navigator.
na-ve-gar' *tr.v.,* *intr.v.* to navigate.
na-ve-gá-vel *adj.* navigable.
na-ve'-ta *f.* shuttle.
na-vi'-o *m.* ship, vessel.
ne-bli'-na *f.* thick mist, fog.
ne-bu-lo'-sa *f.* nebula.
ne-bu-lo'-so, ₌a *adj.* nebulous.
ne-ces-sá-rio, ₌a *adj.* necessary.
ne-ces-si-da'-de *f.* necessity.
ne-ces-si-ta'-do, ₌a *adj.* needy, poor.
ne-ces-si-tar' *tr.v.* to need, to want, to lack; to make necessary, to necessitate; to require; *intr.v.* to be in need.
ne-cro-lo-gi'-a *f.* necrology.
ne-cro-ló-gio *m.* register of the dead; poem in memoriam.
ne-cro-té-rio *m.* morgue.
néc-tar *m.* nectar.
ne-di-ez' *f.* sleek aspect, smugness.

né-dio, =a *adj.* sleek, well-fed.
ne-fan'-do, =a *adj.* heinous, abominable.
ne-fá-rio, =a *adj.* odious, wicked.
ne'-fas *m.* wrong, injustice; **por fas e por** — right or wrong.
ne-fas'-to, =a *adj.* sad, fatal, ill-omened.
ne-fral-gi'-a *f.* nephralgia.
ne-ga-ção' *f.* negation; inaptitude; want.
ne-gar' *tr.v.* to deny, to refuse; to forbid; to contest; to repudiate; *intr.v.* to say no.
ne-ga-ti'-vo, =a *adj.* negative.
ne-gli-gên-cia *f.* negligence.
ne-gli-gen'-te *adj.* negligent.
ne-go-ci-a-ção' *f.* negotiation.
ne-go-ci-an'-te *m.* merchant, business man; negotiator.
ne-go-ci-ar' *intr.v.* to negotiate, to do business; *tr.v.* to negotiate.
ne-go-ti-á-vel *adj.* negotiable.
ne-gó-cio *m.* business, commerce, enterprise.
ne-gri-dão' *f.* blackness, darkness.
ne'-gro, =a *adj.* black, dark; **ne'-gro** *m.* negro.
ne-gró-fi-lo *m.* negrophile.
ne-gról-de *adj.* negroid.
ne-gror' *m.* blackness, darkness.
ne-gru'-me *m.* blackness, darkness.
ne-gru'-ra *f.* blackness, darkness.
nem *conj.* also not, neither, nor; *adv.* not; **— que** although.
ne-nhum' *pro.* no one, not one, none.
ne-ó-fi-to *m.* neophyte.
ne-ô-nio *m.* neon.
ne-po-tis'-mo *m.* nepotism.
ner'-vo *m.* nerve.
ner-vo-si-da'-de *f.* nervousness.
ner-vo'-so, =a *adj.* nervous.
ner-vu'-do, =a *adj.* strong-nerved; muscular.
nés-cio, =a *adj.* ignorant, stupid, simple.
ne'-ta *f.* granddaughter.
ne'-to *m.* grandson.
neu-ral' *adj.* neural.
neu-ral-gi'-a *f.* neuralgia.
neu-ras-te-ni'-a *f.* neurasthenia.
neu-ras-tê-ni-co, =a neurasthenic.
neu-ri'-te *f.* neuritis.
neu-ro-lo-gi'-a *f.* neurology.
neu-ro-lo-gis'-ta *m.* neurologist.
neu-ro'-se *f.* neurosis.
neu-ró-ti-co, =a *adj.* neurotic.
neu-tral' *adj.* neutral.
neu-tra-li-da'-de *f.* neutrality.
neu-tra-li-zar' *tr.v.* neutralize.
neu'-tro, =a *adj.* neutral.
ne-var' *intr.v.* to snow.
ne'-ve *f.* snow.
ne-vis-car' *intr.v.* to snow a little, to snow in flurries.
ne'-vo *m.* birth-mark.
né-vo-a *f.* dense fog.
ne-vo'-so, =a *adj.* snowy.
ni'-cho *m.* niche.
ni-co-ti'-na *f.* nicotine.
ni-co-ti-nis'-mo *m.* nicotinism.
nic-ta-ção' *f.* winking, blinking.
ní-gua *f.* chigoe (kind of flea).
nim'-bo *m.* nimbus, rain cloud.
nim-bo'-so, =a *adj.* rainy.
nin'-fa *f.* nymph.
ni-nha'-da *f.* nestful.
ni-nha-ri'-a *f.* trifle, bagatelle.
ni'-nho *m.* nest.
ní-quel *m.* nickel.
ni-que-lar' *tr.v.* to nickel-plate.
nir-va'-na *f.* nirvana.

ni-ti-dez' *f.* shine, luster, brightness; cleanliness.
ní-ti-do, =a *adj.* clean, polished, shining.
ni-tra'-to *m.* nitrate.
ni-tri'-do *m.* neighing.
ni-trir' *intr.v.* to neigh (horse).
ni'-tro *m.* niter.
ni'-tro=ben-zi'-na *f.* nitrobenzene.
ni'-tro=ce-lu-lo'-se *f.* gun-cotton.
ni'-tro=gli-ce-ri'-na *f.* nitroglycerine.
ni-vel' *m.* level, spirit-level.
ni-ve-lar' *tr.v.* to make horizontal, to level.
nó *m.* knot, knuckle, tie, bow; **— de Adão** Adam's apple.
no'-bre *adj.* noble.
no-bre'-za *f.* nobleness; nobility.
no-cau'-te *m.* knock-out (boxing).
no-ção' *f.* notion.
no-ci'-vo, =a *adj.* nocuous, harmful.
noc-tam-bu-lis'-mo *m.* noctambulism.
noc-tâm-bu-lo, =a *adj.* noctambulant.
nó-do-a *f.* spot, stain; stigma, shame.
nó-du-lo *m.* nodule.
no-guei'-ra *f.* walnut tree.
noi-ta'-da *f.* night, sleepless night, night of pleasure.
noi-tão' *m.* late night.
noi'-te *f.* night.
noi-ti'-nha *f.* twilight.
noi'-va *f.* bride, fiancée.
noi'-vo *m.* groom, fiancé.
no-jen'-to, =a *adj.* nauseous; repugnant.
no'-jo *m.* nausea; repugnance.
nô-ma-da *adj.* nomadic; =s *m.pl.* nomads.
no'-me *m.* name.
no-me-a-ção' *f.* appointment, naming.
no-me-a'-da *f.* fame, reputation.
no-me-ar' *tr.v.* to name, to appoint, to nominate.
no-men-cla-tu'-ra *f.* nomenclature.
no-mi-nal' *adj.* nominal.
no-na-ge-ná-rio, =a *m.*, *f.*, *adj.* nonagenarian.
nô-nio *m.* vernier scale.
no'-no, =a *adj.* ninth.
no'-ra *f.* daughter-in-law.
nor-des'-te *m.* north-east: (Brazil) region including States of Piauí, Ceará, Rio Grande do Norte, Paraíba, Pernambuco, Alagoas and Sergipe.
nor-des-ti'-no, =a *adj.* relative to the north-eastern States of Brazil.
nor'-te *m.* north.
nos-tal-gi'-a *f.* nostalgia.
nos-tál-gi-co, =a *adj.* nostalgic.
nor'-ma *f.* rule, norm.
nor-mal' *adj.* normal.
nor-ma-li-da'-de *f.* normality, normalcy.
nor-ma-ti'-vo, =a *adj.* normal, standard.
no'-ta *f.* note, memorandum; paper money.
no-ta-ção' *f.* notation.
no-tar' *tr.v.* to note, to note down.
no-tá-rio *m.* notary public.
no-tá-vel *adj.* notable.
no-tí-cia *f.* information, news, notice.
no-ti-ci-á-rio *m.* news section, news bulletin, news broadcast.
no-ti-fi-car' *tr.v.* to notify.
no-to-ri-e-da'-de *f.* notoriety.
no-tó-rio, =a *adj.* notorious.
nó-tu-la *f.* bat.
no-tur-nal' *adj.* nocturnal.
no-tur'-no, =a *adj.* nocturnal.
no'-va *f.* news.
no-va'-to *m.* freshman; novice.
no'-ve *m.* nine.

no-ve-cen'-tos, =as *adj.* nine hundred.
no-ve'-na *f.* nine days; novena.
no-vê-nio *m.* nine-year period.
no-ven'-ta *adj.* ninety.
no-ve'-la *f.* novel.
no-ve-lis'-ta *m.*, *f.* novelist.
no-vê-lo *m.* ball of yarn.
no-vem'-bro *m.* November.
no-vi-ci-a'-do *m.* novitiate.
no-vi-ci-á-ria *f.* section of convent where novices reside.
no-vi'-ço, =a *m.*, *f.* novice.
no-vi-da'-de *f.* newness, novelty; news.
no-vís-si-mo, =a *adj.* latest, last.
no'-vo, =a *adj.* new, recent, modern; young, original.
noz' *f.* nut; walnut; — do Pará Brazil nut; — moscada nutmeg.
nu', nu'-a *adj.* nude, naked.
nu-an'-ça *f.* nuance, shade.
nú-bil *adj.* nubile, marriageable.
nu-bla'-do, =a *adj.* cloudy, overcast.
nu'-ca *f.* nape of the neck.
nu-cle-al' or nu-cle-ar' *adj.* nuclear.
nú-cle-o *m.* nucleus.
nu-dez' *f.* nakedness, nudity.
nu-dis'-ta *m.* nudist.

nu-gá *m.* nougat.
nu-li-fi-car' *tr.v.* to nullify.
nu-lo, =a *adj.* null.
nu-me-ra-ção' *f.* numeration, numbering.
nu-me-ra-dor' *m.* numerator.
nu-me-rar' *tr.v.* to number, to enumerate, to count, to include.
nu-mé-ri-co, =a *adj.* numerical.
nú-me-ro *m.* number.
nu-me-ro'-so, =a *adj.* numerous.
nu-mis'-ma *f.* ancient coin, ancient medal.
nu-mis-ma'-ta *f.* numismatist.
nu-mis-má-ti-ca *f.* numismatics.
nun'-ca *adv.* never.
nun-ci-a-tu'-ra *f.* nunciature.
nún-cio *m.* nuncio.
nup-ci-al' *adj.* nuptial.
núp-cias *f.pl.* wedding, marriage.
nu-tri-ção' *f.* nutrition.
nu-tri-en'-te *adj.* nutritive.
nu-tri-men'-to *m.* food, nutriment.
nu-trir' *tr.v.* to feed, to nourish.
nu-tri-ti'-vo, =a *adj.* nutritive.
nu'-vem *f.* cloud.
nu-vi-o'-so, =a *adj.* cloudy.

O

See page 12—GUIDE TO REFORMED SPELLING used in this Dictionary

O, o *m.* O, o; fourteenth letter of the alphabet; Ó ! *interj.* oh.
o-á'-sis *m.* oasis.
ob-ce-ni-da'-de *f.* obscenity.
ob-ce'-no, =a *adj.* obscene.
ob-du-ra-ção' *f.* obdurateness, obduracy.
o-be-di-ên-cia *f.* obedience.
o-be-di-en'-te *adj.* obedient.
o-be-de-cer' *intr.v.* to obey; to yield.
o-be-lis'-co *m.* obelisk.
o-be-si-da'-de *f.* obesity.
o-be'-so, =a *adj.* obese.
ó-bi-to *m.* death.
o-bi-tu-á-rio *m.* =o, =a *adj.* obituary.
ob-je-ção' *f.* objection.
ob-je-tar' *tr.v.* to object.
ob-je-ti'-va *f.* objective (optics).
ob-je-ti'-vo, =a *adj.* objective.
ob-je'-to *m.* object.
ob-jur-gar' *tr.v.* to objurgate; to censure, to disapprove.
ob-la-ção' *f.* oblation, offering.
ob-li-qui-da'-de *f.* obliquity, obliqueness.
o-blí-quo, =a *adj.* oblique.
ob-li-te-ra-ção' *f.* obliteration.
ob-li-te-rar' *tr.v.* to obliterate.
ob-lí-vio *m.* oblivion.
ob-lon'-go, =a *adj.* oblong.
ob-nó-xio, =a *adj.* obnoxious.
o-bo-é *m.* oboe.
o-bo-ís-ta *m.*, *f.* oboist.
o'-bra *f.* work.
o-bra-dor' *m.* worker, workman.
o'-bra-pri'-ma *f.* master-piece.
o-brar' *intr.v.* to work, to take effect; *tr.v.* to execute, to realize, to make.
o-brei'-ro, =a *m.*, *f.* worker.
o-bri-ga-ção' *f.* obligation.
o-bri-ga'-do, =a *adj.* obliged, grateful; thanks.
o-bri-gar' *tr.v.* to oblige, to compel, to force.

o-bri-ga-tó-rio, =a *adj.* obligatory, compulsory.
ob-scu-re-cer' *tr.v.* to darken, to obscure; to weaken, to sadden; *intr.v.* to turn dark, to become dull.
ob-scu-re-ci-men'-to *m.* darkening, shading, covering.
ob-scu-ri-da'-de *f.* darkness, obscurity.
ob-scu'-ro, =a *adj.* dark, obscure.
ob-se-qui-ar' *tr.v.* to flatter, to wait upon, to favor; to give.
ob-sé-quias *f.pl.* funeral.
ob-sé-quio *m.* favor, kindness.
ob-se-qui-o'-so, =a *adj.* obsequious; kind.
ob-ser-va-ção' *f.* observation.
ob-ser-vân-cia *f.* observance.
ob-ser-van'-te *adj.* observing, practicing.
ob-ser-var' *tr.v.* to observe.
ob-ser-va-tó-rio *m.* observatory.
ob-ser-vá-vel *adj.* observable.
ob-ses-são' *f.* obsession.
ob-ses'-so, =a *adj.* obsessed.
ob-so-le'-to, =a *adj.* obsolete.
ob-stá-cu-lo *m.* obstacle.
ob-sté-tri-ca *f.* obstetrics.
ob-sté-tri-co, =a *adj.* obstetric.
ob-stru-ção' *f.* obstruction.
ob-stru-ir' *tr.v.* to obstruct.
ob-stru-ti'-vo, =a *adj.* obstructive.
ob-ter' *tr.v.* to obtain, to achieve.
ob-tu-ra-dor' *m.* shutter (of a camera).
ob-tu-rar' *tr.v.* to close; to fill (cavity in tooth).
ob-tu'-so, =a *adj.* obtuse.
o-bús *m.* howitzer.
ób-vio, =a *adj.* obvious.
o-car' *tr.v.* to empty, to drain out; to hollow out.
o-ca-si-ão' *f.* occasion.
o-ca-si-o-nal' *adj.* occasional.
o-ca-si-o-nar' *tr.v.* to cause, to occasion.

o-ca'-so *m.* sunset; (fig.) death, end, finish.

o-ce-a'-no *m.* ocean.

o-ce-lo'-te *m.* ocelot.

o-ci-den-tal' *adj.* occidental.

o-ci-den'-te *m.* occident.

ó-cio *m.* spare time; leisure, rest; laziness.

o-ci-o-si-da'-de *f.* idleness, laziness.

o-ci-o'-so, =a *adj.* idle, lazy.

o-clu-são' *f.* occlusion.

ô-co, =a *adj.* hollow, empty; (fig.) futile, vain.

o-cor-rên-cia *f.* occurrence, event, happening, circumstance.

o-cor-rer' *intr.v.* to occur; to happen.

o'-cra *f.* o'-cre *m.* ochre.

oc-to-ge-ná-rio, =a *m.*, *f.*, *adj.* octogenarian.

oc-to-gé-si-mo, =a *adj.* eightieth.

oc-to-go-nal' *adj.* octagonal.

oc-tó-go-no *m.* octagon.

o-cu-la-ção' *f.* grafting.

o-cu-lis'-ta *m.* oculist.

ó-cu-lo *m.* lens, eyeglass; spy-glass; small round window; =s *m.pl.* spectacles, goggles.

o-cul-tar' *tr.v.* to cover up, to hide.

o-cul-tis'-mo *m.* occultism.

o-cul'-to, =a *adj.* occult.

o-cu-pa-ção' *f.* occupation, employment.

o-cu-par' *tr.v.* to occupy, to employ, to busy.

o-di-ar' *tr.v.* to hate, to detest.

ó-dio *m.* hatred, aversion.

o-di-o'-so, =a *adj.* odious, hateful.

o-dô-me-tro *m.* odometer.

o-don-to-lo-gi'-a *f.* odontology.

o-dor' *m.* odor, perfume.

o-do-rí-fe-ro, =a *adj.* odoriferous.

o-do-ro'-so, =a *adj.* odoriferous.

o'-dre *m.* leather bottle; (fig.) very stout person; drunkard.

o-fe-gan'-te *adj.* gasping, panting.

o-fe-gar' *intr.v.* to breathe with difficulty, to gasp for breath; to pant.

o-fê-go *m.* difficult breathing, gasping.

o-fen-der' *tr.v.* to offend; to insult; —se *refl.v.* to be shocked or embittered, to be scandalized.

o-fen'-sa *f.* offense.

o-fen-si'-va *f.* offensive.

o-fen-si'-vo, =a *adj.* offensive.

o-fen-sor' *m.* offender.

o-fe-re-cer' *tr.v.* to offer.

o-fe-re-ci-men'-to *m.* offer, offering.

o-fer'-ta *f.* offering.

o-fer-tó-rio *m.* offertory.

o-fi-ci-al' *m.*, *adj.* official.

o-fi-ci-an'-te *m.*, *adj.* officiant.

o-fi-ci-ar' *intr.v.* to officiate.

o-fi-ci'-na *f.* shop, work-shop.

o-fí-cio *m.* trade, occupation, profession.

o-fi-ci-o'-so, =a *adj.* helpful, useful; disinterested; unofficial.

o-gi'-va *f.* ogive.

o-gi-val' *adj.* ogival.

o'-gro, =a *m.*, *f.* ogre; ogress.

oi-ta'-va *f.* eighth part; eighth (in music); octava.

oi-ta'-vo *m.* eighth.

oi-ten'-ta *adj.* eighty.

oi'-to *m.* eight.

oi-to-cen'-tos, =as *adj.* eight hundred.

o-la-ri'-a *f.* pottery factory.

o-le-a'-do *m.* oilcloth.

o-le-ar' *tr.v.* to oil.

ó-le-o *m.* oil.

o-le-o'-so, =a *adj.* oily, greasy.

ol-fa'-to *m.* sense of smell.

ô-lha *f.* broth.

o-lha'-da *f.* glance, look.

o-lhal'-va *f.* land producing two crops a year.

o-lhar' *tr.v.* to look at; to consider; to overlook; *intr.v.* to look.

o-lhe'-te *m.* eyelet.

o-lhi-man'-co, =a *adj.* cross-eyed, blind in one eye.

ô-lho *m.* eye.

o-lhu'-do, =a *adj.* having large eyes.

o-li-gar-qui'-a *f.* oligarchy.

o-li-gár-qui-co, =a *adj.* oligarchic.

o-li'-va *f.* olive.

o-li-vá-ce-o, =a *adj.* olive-colored.

o-li-var' *adj.* olive-shaped.

o-li-vei'-ra *f.* olive tree.

ol-mei'-ro *m.* ol'-mo *m.* elm tree.

ol-vi-dar' *tr.v.* to forget.

ol-vi'-do *m.* forgetfulness; rest.

om-bre-ar' *intr.v.* to be shoulder to shoulder, to be equal.

om-brei'-ra *f.* shoulder-strap, shoulder piece; jamb, door-jamb.

om'-bro *m.* shoulder, strength, diligence.

ô-me-ga *m.* omega.

o-me-le'-ta *f.* omelet.

o-mi-no'-so, =a *adj.* ominous.

ô-mio *m.* ohm.

o-mis-são' *f.* omission.

o-mis'-so, =a *adj.* negligent, careless; omitted.

o-mi-tir' *tr.v.* to omit, to forget.

o-mo-pla'-ta *f.* shoulder-blade.

on'-ça *f.* ounce (weight); panther.

on'-da *f.* wave.

on'-de *adv.* where, in which.

on-de-a'-do, =a *adj.* wavy, arranged in waves.

on-de-ar' *intr.v.* to wave; to flutter; *tr.v.* to make wavy.

on-dô-me-tro *m.* ondometer.

on-du-la-ção' *f.* undulation.

on-du-lar' *intr.v.* to undulate.

on-du-la-tó-rio, =a *adj.* undulatory.

on-du-lo'-so, =a *adj.* undulatory.

o-ne-rar' *tr.v.* to burden with; to impose (taxes).

o-ne-ro'-so, =a *adj.* heavy; grave; serious; onerous, burdensome.

ô-ni-bus *m.* omnibus, bus.

o-ni-ci-ên-cia *f.* omniscience.

o-ni-ci-en'-te *adj.* omniscient.

o-ni-po-tên-cia *f.* omnipotence.

o-ni-po-ten'-te *adj.* omnipotent.

o-ní-vo-ro, =a *adj.* omnivorous.

ô-nix *m.* onyx.

on'-tem *adv.* yesterday.

on-to-gê-ne-se *f.* ontogeny.

on-to-lo-gi'-a *f.* ontology.

ô-nus *m.* onus, burden, load.

on'-ze *m.* eleven.

on-ze'-na *f.* interest at eleven per cent.

on-ze-nar' *intr.v.* to lend money at a high rate of interest.

on-ze'-no *m.* eleventh.

o-pa-ci-da'-de *f.* opaqueness.

o-pa'-co, =a *adj.* opaque.

o-pa'-la *f.* opal.

o-pa-les-cên-cia *f.* opalescence.

o-pa-les-cen'-te *adj.* opalescent.

op-ção' *f.* option.

ó-pe-ra *f.* opera.

ó-pe-ra=bu'-fa *f.* comic opera.

o-pe-ra-ção' *f.* operation.

ó-pe-ra=cô-mi-ca *f.* comic opera.

o-pe-ra-dor' *m.* operator.

o-pe-rar' *tr.v.* to operate, to operate on,

to carry out; *intr.v.* to operate, to take effect.
o-pe-ra-ri-a'-do *m.* working class.
o-pe-rá-rio *m.* worker, laborer, working-man.
o-pér-cu-lo *m.* operculum; thurible lid.
o-pe-re'-ta *f.* operetta.
o-pi-nar' *tr.v.*, *intr.v.* to think, to opine.
o-pi-ni-ão' *f.* opinion.
o-pi-ni-á-ti-co, *=a adj.* opinionated, proud, haughty.
o-pi-a'-to *m.* opiate.
ó-pio *m.* opium.
o-pi-o-ma-ni'-a *f.* addiction to opium.
o-pi-ô-ma-no, *=a m., f.* opium addict.
o-por' *tr.v.* to oppose; —*se refl.v.* to refuse; to be contrary to.
o-por-tu-ni-da'-de *f.* opportuneness, opportunity.
o-por-tu-nis'-mo *m.* opportunism.
o-por-tu-nis'-ta *m.* opportunist.
o-por-tu'-no, *=a adj.* opportune.
o-po-si-ção' *f.* opposition.
o-pos'-to, *=a adj.* contrary, opposed.
o-pres-são' *f.* oppression.
o-pres-si'-vo, *=a adj.* oppressive.
o-pres-sor' *m.* oppressor.
o-pri-mir' *tr.v.* to oppress.
o-pró-brio *m.* opprobrium.
o-pro-bri-o'-so, *=a adj.* opprobrious.
op-so-ni'-na *f.* opsonin.
op-tar' *intr.v.* to choose.
op-ta-ti'-vo, *=a adj.* optative.
o-pu-lên-cia *f.* opulence.
o-pu-len'-to, *=a adj.* opulent.
o-pús-cu-lo *m.* small work, small study, pamphlet.
o'-ra *conj.* but; now; ... — sometimes ... other times ...; *adv.* now, presently; *interj.* expressing surprise, impatience, doubt.
o-ra-ção' *f.* oration, speech; sentence, prayer.
o-ra-cu-lar' *adj.* oracular.
o-rá-cu-lo *m.* oracle.
o-ra-dor' *m.* speaker, orator, preacher; mediator.
o-ra'-go *m.* patron saint; oracle.
o-ral' *adj.* oral.
o-ran-go-tan'-go *m.* orangutan.
o-rar' *intr.v.* to speak, to make a speech; to pray; *tr.v.* to ask, to beg, to pray for.
o-ra-tó-ria *f.* oratory, eloquence.
o-ra-tó-rio *m.* private chapel; oratorio; **o-ro-tó-rio,** *=a adj.* oratorical.
or'-be *m.* orb, sphere, globe, orbit, world.
ór-bi-ta *f.* orbit.
or-ça-men'-to *m.* estimate, budget, appropriation.
or-çar' *tr.v.*, *intr.v.* to estimate, to compute, to approximate.
or-dei'-ro, *=a adj.* orderly.
or'-dem *f.* order.
or-de-na-ção' *f.* ordinance, decree; arrangement; ordination.
or-de-na'-do *m.* salary, wages.
or-de-nan'-ça *f.* orderly; regulation.
or-de-nar' *tr.v.* to put in order, to arrange; to order; to ordain; *intr.v.* to give orders.
or-de'-nha *f.* milking.
or-de-nhar' *tr.v.* to milk.
or-di-nal' *adj.* ordinal.
or-di-ná-ria *f.* expense; board.
or-di-ná-rio, *=a adj.* ordinary
o-re'-lha *f.* ear; hearing; claw (of hammer); tongue (of shoe); **torcer as** *=s* to be repentant; **ficar de** *=s* **baixas** to be humiliated.

o-re-lha'-do, *=a adj.* having ears.
o-re-lhão' *m.* pull on the ears.
o-re-lhei'-ra *f.* ear of animal, hog's ear.
o-re-lhu'-do, *=a adj.* having large ears.
or-fa-na'-to *m.* orphanage.
or-fan-da'-de *f.* orphanhood; group of orphans; helplessness, privation.
ór-fão *m., adj.* orphan.
or-gan-dí *m.* organdy (fabric).
or-gâ-ni-co, *=a adj.* organic.
or-ga-nis'-mo *m.* organism.
or-ga-nis'-ta *m., f.* organist.
or-ga-ni-za-ção' *f.* organization.
or-ga-ni-za-dor' *m.* organizer.
or-ga-ni-zar' *tr.v.* to organize.
or-gan-sim' *m.* **or-gan-si'-no** *m.* organzine.
ór-gão *m.* organ.
or-gas'-mo *m.* orgasm.
or-gás-ti-co, *=a adj.* orgastic.
or-gi'-a *f.* orgy.
ór-gio, *=a adj.* orgiastic.
or-gu-lhar'-se *refl.v.* to pride oneself, to congratulate oneself.
or-gu'-lho *m.* pride.
or-gu-lho'-so, *=a adj.* proud, arrogant.
o-ri-en-ta-ção' *f.* orientation.
o-ri-en-tal' *adj.* oriental.
o-ri-en-tar' *tr.v.* to orient.
o-ri-en'-te *m.* orient.
o-ri-fí-cio *m.* orifice, opening, hole.
o-ri'-gem *f.* origin.
o-ri-gi-nal' *adj.* original.
o-ri-gi-na-li-da'-de *f.* originality.
o-ri-gin-ar' *tr.v.* to originate.
o-ri-un'-do, *=a adj.* native, proceeding, originating.
or'-la *f.* edge; border; binding on edge of garment; margin; selvage.
or-lar' *tr.v.* to border, to hem, to bind, to finish.
or-na-men-tal' *adj.* ornamental.
or-na-men-tar' *tr.v.* to ornament.
or-na-men'-to *m.* ornament.
or-nar' *tr.v.* to adorn, to beautify, to ornament.
or-na'-to *m.* ornament; adornment.
or-ni-to-lo-gi'-a *f.* ornithology.
or-ni-to-lo-gis'-ta *m.* ornithologist.
or-ques-tra-ção' *f.* orchestration.
or-ques'-tra *f.* orchestra.
or-ques-tral' *adj.* orchestral.
or-ques-trar' *tr.v.* to orchestrate.
ór-qui-de *f.* orchid.
or-to-cro-má-ti-co, *=a adj.* orthochromatic.
or-to-do-xi'-a *f.* orthodoxy.
or-to-do'-xo, *=a adj.* orthodox.
or-to-e-pi'-a *f.* orthoepy.
or-to-gra-fi'-a *f.* orthography.
or-to-pe-di'-a *f.* orthopedics.
or-to-pé-di-co, *=a adj.* orthopedic.
or-va-lha'-da *f.* fall of dew, morning dew.
or-va'-lho *m.* dew; fine, misty rain.
or-va-lho'-so, *=a adj.* dewy, moist with dew.
os-ci-la-ção' *f.* oscillation.
os-ci-lan'-te *adj.* oscillating.
os-ci-lar' *tr.v.* to oscillate.
os-ci-la-tó-rio, *=a adj.* oscillatory.
os-ci-ló-gra-fo *m.* oscillograph.
os-ci-tar' *intr.v.* to yawn, to be drowsy.
os-cu-la-ção' *f.* osculation, kissing.
os-cu-lar' *tr.v.* to osculate, to kiss.
ós-cu-lo *m.* kiss; osculum.
ós-mio *m.* osmium.
os-mo'-se *f.* osmosis.
os-mó-ti-co, *=a adj.* osmotic.

I

os-mô-me-tro *m.* osmometer.
os-sa-men'-ta *f.* skeleton.
os-sa-ri'-a *f.* heap of bones.
os-sá-rio *m.* heap of bones, charnel-house.
ós-se-o, =a *adj.* osseous, bony.
os-sí-cu-lo *m.* small bone; fruit-stone.
os-si-fi-ca-ção' *f.* ossification.
os-si-fi-car' *tr.v., intr.v.* to ossify.
os'-so *m.* bone; (fig.) difficulty.
os-su-á-rio *m.* heap of bones.
os-su'-do, =a *adj.* large-boned.
os-ta'-ga *f.* halyard.
os-ten-si'-vo, =a *adj.* ostensive.
os-ten-só-rio *m.* monstrance, ostensorium.
os-ten-ta-ção' *f.* ostentation.
os-ten-tar' *tr.v.* to show, to display, to show ostentatiously, to show with pride.
os-ten-to'-so, =a *adj.* ostentatious, showy; magnificent.
os'-tra *f.* oyster.
os-tra-cis'-mo *m.* ostracism, banishment.
os-trei'-ra *f.* oyster-bed, oyster garden.
os-tri'-no, =a *adj.* purple.
o-tal-gi'-a *f.* otalgia.
ó-ti-ca *f.* optics.
ó-ti-co, =a *adj.* optic.
o-ti-ma'-tes *m.pl.* important people; magnates; noblemen.
o-ti-mis'-mo *m.* optimism.
o-ti-mis'-ta *m.* optimist.
ó-ti-mo, *adj.* optimum.
o-to-ma'-na *f.* ottoman, couch, divan.
o-to-ma'-no, =a *adj.* Ottoman, Turkish.
ou *conj.* or.
ou-re'-la *f.* selvage; border.
ou-re'-lo *m.* strip of coarse cloth; wide stripe.
ou-ri'-ves *m.* goldsmith.
ou-ri-ve-sa-ri'-a *f.* goldsmith's shop.
ou'-ro *m.* gold.

ou'-ro=fi'-o *adv.* exactly, in equal proportion.
ou-sa-di'-a *f.* daring, bravery, courage, audacity.
ou-sar' *tr.v.* to dare, to have the courage to.
ou-tei'-ro *m.* hill, eminence.
ou-to-na'-da *f.* fall harvest.
ou-to-nal' *adj.* autumnal.
ou-to'-no *m.* autumn.
ou-tor-gar' *tr.v.* to approve; to grant; to declare in public statement; to charter; *intr.v.* to intervene, as interested person, in public statement.
ou'-trem *pron.* others, someone else.
ou'-tro, =a *pro. and adj.* other, another.
ou-tro'-ra *adv.* formerly, in other times.
ou-tros-sim' *adv.* likewise, equally, also.
ou-tro-tan'-to *m.* same thing, equal amount.
ou-tu'-bro *m.* October.
ou-vi'-do *m.* ear, hearing.
ou-vi-dor' *m.* judge; hearer.
ou-vin'-te *m., f.* listener.
ou-vir' *tr.v.* to hear, to listen.
o'-va *f.* roe.
o-va-ção' *f.* ovation.
o-van'-te *adj.* jubilant, triumphant.
o-val' *adj.* oval.
o-va-ri-a'-no, =a *adj.* ovarian.
o-vá-rio *m.* ovary.
o-ve'-lha *f.* sheep, ewe.
o-ve-lhei'-ro *m.* shepherd.
o-ví-pa-ro, =a *adj.* oviparous.
o'-vo *m.* egg.
o-xa-lá *interj.* would that!!
o-xi-da-ção' *f.* oxidation.
o-xi-dar' *tr.v.* to oxidize; — =se *refl.v.* to become rusty, to rust.
o-xi-ge-nar' *tr.v.* to oxygenate.
o-xi-gê-nio *m.* oxygen.
ox-í-to-no *m.* oxytone.
o-zo'-ne *m.* ozone.
o-zo-ni-zar' *tr.v.* to ozonize.
o-zo-te-ri'-ta *f.* ozocerite.

P

See page 12—GUIDE TO REFORMED SPELLING used in this Dictionary

P, p *m.* P, p, fifteenth letter of the alphabet.
pá *f.* spade, shovel; blade; shoulder-blade.
pá-bu-lo *m.* food, pasture; simpleton.
pa-ca'-to, =a *adj.* tranquil, peaceable.
pa-chor'-ra *f.* sluggishness, slowness.
pa-chor-ren'-to, =a *adj.* phlegmatic, sluggish.
pa-ci-ên-cia *f.* patience.
pa-ci-en'-te *adj., m., f.* patient.
pa-ci-fi-ca-ção' *f.* pacification.
pa-ci-fi-car' *tr.v.* to pacify.
pa-cí-fi-co, =a *adj.* pacific.
pa-ci-fis'-mo *m.* pacifism.
pa-ci-fis'-ta *m.* pacifist.
pa'-ço *m.* palace.
pa-co'-te *m.* package, bundle.
pac'-to *m.* pact.
pac-tu-á-rio *m.* signatory (of pact).
pa-da-ri'-a *f.* bakery, pastry shop.
pa-de-cen'-te *adj.* suffering, patient; *m.* person sentenced to death.
pa-de-cer' *tr.v., intr.v.* to suffer, to endure pain.

pa-de-ci-men'-to *m.* pain, affliction, suffering.
pa-dei'-ro *m.* baker.
pa-drão' *m.* model, pattern, standard.
pa-drar'=se *refl.v.* to become a priest, to be ordained.
pa-dras'-to *m.* step-father.
pa'-dre *m.* priest, father.
pa-dre-ar' *intr.v.* to have offspring, to reproduce oneself.
pa-dre'-co *m.* little priest; miserable priest.
pa-dre=nos'-so *m.* Lord's prayer.
pa'-dre=san'-to *m.* Pope.
pa-dri'-nho *m.* god-father.
pa-dro-a'-do *m.* patronage.
pa-dro-ei'-ro *m.* patron.
pa'-ga *f.* pay, salary.
pa-ga-dor' *m.* payer.
pa-ga-do-ri'-a *f.* treasury, paying office.
pa-ga-men'-to *m.* payment.
pa-gan'-te *adj.* paying.
pa-gão' *m.* pagan.
pa-gar' *tr.v.* to pay.
pa-gá-vel *adj.* payable.

pa'-gem *m.* page (youth training for knighthood).
pá-gi-na *f.* page.
pa-gi-na-ção' *f.* pagination.
pa-gi-nar' *tr.v.* to page.
pa'-go, =a *adj.* paid.
pa-go-de *m.* pagoda.
pai' *m.* father.
pai'-na *f.* kapok.
pai-nel' *m.* painting; dashboard.
pa-ís *m.* country, region.
pai-sa'-gem *f.* landscape.
pai-sa-gis'-ta *m., f.* landscape painter.
pai-sa'-no *m.* fellow-countryman; civilian.
pai-xão' *f.* passion.
pa'-la *f.* visor (of cap); metal prongs which secure precious stones in jewelry; cover for chalice (during Mass).
pa-la-ce'-te *m.* small palace.
pa-lá-cio *m.* palace.
pa-la-dar' *m.* palate.
pá-la-mo *m.* web or membrane between toes of certain birds, reptiles and mammals.
pa-lan'-que *m.* out-door terrace or platform; open veranda.
pa-lan-quim' *m.* palanquin.
pa-la-tal' *adj.* palatal.
pa-la-ta-li-zar' *tr.v.* to palatalize.
pa-la-ti-na'-do *m.* palatinate.
pa-la-ti'-no *m.* palace official.
pa-la'-to *m.* palate.
pa-la'-vra *f.* word.
pa-la-vra-ção' *f.* learning to read word by word.
pa-la-vre-a'-do *m.* loquaciousness; jargon, gibberish.
pa-la-vre-ar' *intr.v.* to prattle, to prate.
pa-la-vro'-so, =a *adj.* wordy.
pal'-co *m.* stage (of theatre); portable bed.
pa-le-o-gra-fi'-a *f.* paleography.
pa-le-ó-gra-fo *m.* paleographer.
pa-le-o-lo-gi'-a *f.* paleology.
pa-les'-tra *f.* conversation, discussion.
pa-le'-ta *f.* palette.
pa-le-te-ar' *tr.v.* to spur, to spur on.
pa-le-tó *m.* topcoat.
pa'-lha *f.* straw; cane (of chair seat).
pa-lha'-ço *m.* clown.
pa-lhal' *m.* pa-lhar' *m.* thatched house.
pa-lhe'-ta *f.* reed, pick; paddle; spangle.
pa-lhe-tão' *m.* bit of key.
pa-lhe'-te *adj.* straw-colored.
pa-li-ar' *tr.v., intr.v.* to palliate.
pa-li-a-ti'-vo, =a *adj.* palliative.
pa-li-dez' *f.* paleness, pallidness.
pá-li-do, =a *adj.* pale, pallid.
pa-limp-ses'-to *m.* palimpsest.
pá-lio *m.* portable canopy used in processions.
pa-li-tei'-ro *m.* toothpick-holder.
pa-li'-to *m.* toothpick.
pal'-ma *f.* palm; palm tree; branch of palm tree; horse's hoof.
pal-ma'-da *f.* slap (with palm of hand).
pal-ma-tó-ria *f.* ferule; candlestick.
pal-me-ar' *tr.v., intr.v.* to applaud, to clap.
pal-mei'-ra *f.* palm tree.
pal-me'-ta *f.* wedge.
pal-mi'-lha *f.* insole of shoe; stocking foot.
pal-mi'-to *m.* tender heart of palm shoot.
pal'-mo *m.* span (of hand).
pa-lor' *m.* pallor; paleness.
pál-pe-bra *f.* eyelid.
pal-pi-ta-ção' *f.* palpitation.

pal-pi-tan'-te *adj.* throbbing, palpitating.
pal-pi-tar' *intr.v.* to palpitate; to feel a premonition.
pal-pi'-te *m.* presentiment, premonition, hunch.
pa-lu-dis'-mo *m.* paludism; malaria.
pa-lu-do'-so, =a *adj.* marshy.
pam'-pas *m.pl.* pampas (grassy plains of South America).
pâm-pa-no *m.* shoot, sprig, vine branch.
pam-pa-no'-so, =a *adj.* covered with vine leaves.
pa-na-céi-a *f.* panacea.
pa-na'-do, =a *adj.* breaded, fried in bread crumbs; **água panada** water with toasted bread.
pan-ca'-da *f.* blow; knock; beating; pulsation, sound of clock pendulum.
pân-cre-as *m.* pancreas.
pan-cre-á-ti-co, =a *adj.* pancreatic.
pan-cre-a-ti'-na *f.* pancreatin.
pân-de-ga *f.* jest, joke; noisy laughter and joking.
pân-de-go, =a *adj.* comical, laughing, humorous.
pan-dei'-ro *m.* tambourine.
pan-de-mô-nio *m.* pandemonium.
pan-di'-lha *f.* plot, plan to deceive; *m.* sharper; member of gang.
pa-ne-gí-ri-co *m.* panegyric.
pa-ne'-la *f.* cooking utensil (deep saucepan, pot).
pa-ne-la'-da *f.* potful; stew.
pan-fle'-to *m.* pamphlet.
pâ-ni-co *m.* panic; pâ-ni-co, =a *adj.* panicky.
pa-ni-fi-car' *tr.v.* to convert flour into bread.
pa-ni'-nho *m.* fine cotton fabric.
pa'-no *m.* cloth.
pa-no-ra'-ma *m.* panorama.
pa-no-râ-mi-co, =a *adj.* panoramic.
pan-que'-ca *f.* pancake.
pan-ta'-lha *f.* candle shade, lampshade.
pan-ta-nal' *m.* large marsh; mud hole.
pân-ta-no *m.* morass, bog, mire.
pan-ta-no'-so, =a *adj.* muddy, mirey.
pan-te'-ra *f.* panther.
pan-tó-gra-fo *m.* pantograph.
pan-to-mi'-ma *f.* pantomime.
pan-tu'-fo *m.* bedroom slipper.
pão' *m.* bread, loaf of bread.
pão'=de=ló *m.* sponge cake.
pa'-pa *m.* Pope; gruel, pap, any soft mushy food.
pa-pa'-da *f.* double chin; dewlap (of animals).
pa-pa'-do *m.* papacy.
pa-pa-gai'-o *m.* parrot; kite.
pa-pai'-a *f.* papaya.
pa-pa-í-na *f.* papain.
pa-pal' *adj.* papal.
pa-pei'-ra *f.* goiter.
pa-pel' *m.* paper, document; rôle.
pa-pe-la'-da *f.* large batch of papers; papers in disorder; worthless writings.
pa-pe-lão' *m.* cardboard.
pa-pe-la-ri'-a *f.* stationer's shop.
pa-pe-le'-ta *f.* poster, announcement.
pa-pi'-la *f.* papilla.
pa-pis'-ta *m.* papist.
pa'-po *m.* crop (of a bird).
pa-pou'-la *f.* poppy.
pa-que'-te *m.* steamship.
pa-qui-der'-ma *m.* pachyderm.
par' *m.* couple, pair (male and female); peer; partner; *adj.* equal, even.

pa'-ra *prep.* to, toward, for; for the purpose of.
pa-ra-béns *m.pl.* congratulations, felicitations.
pa-rá-bo-la *f.* parable; parabola.
pá-ra-bri'-sa *m.* windshield (of an auto).
pa-ra-ca'-tas *f.pl.* brogan, brogue (shoe).
pa-ra'-da *f.* stop, delay, pause; parade.
pa-ra-dei'-ro *m.* stopping place; sink, sewer; whereabouts; end, goal.
pa-ra-dig'-ma *m.* paradigm.
pa-ra-do'-xo *m.* paradox.
pa-ra-fi'-na *f.* paraffin.
pá-ra-fo'-go *m.* fire-screen.
pa-rá-fra-se *f.* paraphrase.
pa-ra-frás-ti-co, **=a** *adj.* paraphrastic.
pa-ra-fu-sar' *tr.v.* to screw.
pa-ra-fu'-so *m.* screw.
pa-ra-gão' *m.* paragon.
pa-ra'-gem *f.* stop; car-stop; whereabouts; region, territory.
pa-rá-gra-fo *m.* paragraph.
pa-ra-í-so *m.* paradise.
pá-ra-la'-ma *m.* mud-guard (auto).
pa-ra-le'-la *f.* parallel; parallel line.
pa-ra-le'-lo, **=a** *adj.* parallel.
pa-ra-li-sa-ção' *f.* paralysis.
pa-ra-li-sar' *tr.v.* to paralyse.
pa-ra-li-si'-a *f.* paralysis; — **infantil** infantile paralysis.
pa-ra-lí-ti-co, **=a** *adj.* paralytic.
pá-ra-luz' *m.* lampshade.
pa-ra-mag-ne-tis'-mo *m.* paramagnetism.
pa-ra-nin'-fo *m.* god-father, honor guest of wedding.
pa-ra-nói-a *f.* paranoia.
pa-ra-pei'-to *m.* parapet.
pá-ra-que'-das *m.* parachute.
pá-ra-rai'-os *m.* lightning-rod.
pa-rar' *intr.v.* to stop, to cease; *tr.v.* to stop, to bring to a stop; to parry; to bet.
pa-ra-si-ti-ci'-da *m.* parasiticide.
pa-ra-si'-to *m.* parasite.
pá-ra-sol' *m.* umbrella, parasol.
pá-ra-ven'-to *m.* screen, wind-screen.
par-cei'-ro *m.* partner, associate; **=o**, **=a** *adj.* similar, equal.
par-ce'-la *f.* portion; separate item; fragment.
par-ce-lar' *tr.v.* to divide into parcels, to divide into separate groups.
par-ci-al' *adj.* partial.
par-ci-a-li-da'-de *f.* partiality.
par-ci-mô-nia *f.* parsimony.
par-ci-mo-ni-o'-so, **=a** *adj.* parsimonious.
par'-do, **=a** *adj.* gray; mulatto.
pa-re-cer' *intr.v.* to seem, to look, to be similar; **—=se com** *refl.v.* to look like, to resemble; *m.* opinion.
pa-re-ci'-do, **=a** *adj.* similar, like.
pa-re-dão' *m.* high thick wall.
pa-re'-de *f.* wall.
pa-re-gó-ri-co, **=a** *adj.* paregoric.
pa-re'-lha *f.* pair, team (of animals), brace, couple.
pa-ren-tal' *adj.* parental.
pa-ren'-te *m.* relative, member of same family.
pa-ren-te'-la *f.* relatives; race, family.
pa-ren-tes'-co *m.* relationship, family relationship, consanguinity; similarity.
pa-rên-te-se *m.* parenthesis.
pa-ren-té-ti-co, **=a** *adj.* parenthetical.
pá-re-o *m.* race, on foot or horseback, between two persons.
pa-ri-da'-de *f.* parity.
pa-rir' *tr.v.* to give birth to.

par-la-men-tar', **par-la-men-tá-rio**, **=a** *adj.* parliamentary.
par-la-men'-to *m.* parliament.
par-me-são' *adj.*, *m.* Parmesan.
pá-ro-co *m.* curate, vicar, parish priest.
pa-ró-dia *f.* parody, travesty.
pa-ró-quia *f.* parish.
pa-ro-qui-al' *adj.* parochial.
pa-ró-ti-da *f.* parotid gland.
pa-ro-ti-di'-te *f.* parotitis (mumps).
pa-ro-xis'-mo *m.* paroxysm.
pa-ro-xí-to-no, **=a** *adj.*, *m.* paroxytone.
par'-que *m.* public park; extensive grounds.
par-que'-te *m.* parquet; parquetry, hardwood floor.
par-ri-cí-dio *m.* parricide.
par'-te *f.* part, portion, share.
par-tei'-ra *f.* midwife.
par-tei'-ro *m.* obstetrician.
par-ti-ção' *f.* partition, division.
par-ti-ci-pa-ção' *f.* participation.
par-ti-ci-par' *tr.v.* to inform, to notify, to let know about; *intr.v.* to participate, to share.
par-tí-cipe *adj.* sharing, participating.
par-ti-ci-pi-al' *adj.* participial.
par-ti-cí-pio *m.* participle.
par-tí-cu-la *f.* particle.
par-ti-cu-lar' *m.*, *adj.* particular.
par-ti-cu-la-ri-da'-de *f.* particularity, peculiarity.
par-ti-cu-la-ri-zar' *tr.v.* to specify, to particularize.
par-ti'-da *f.* departure; party; game, match; lot, article, item, entry.
par-ti'-do *m.* party, side; decision.
par-ti-lhar' *tr.v.* to share, to participate in.
par-tir' *intr.v.* to depart, to go away; to go off, to originate; *tr.v.* to divide, to distribute; to break, to break up; **—=se** *refl.v.* to break, to burst; to divide up; to be broken.
par'-to *m.* childbirth.
par-tu-ri-ção' *f.* parturition.
par-vi-da'-de *f.* smallness, silliness, simpleness.
par'-vo, **=a** *adj.* simple, small, absurd, stupid.
pás-co-a *f.* Easter.
pas-co-al' *adj.* paschal.
pas-mar' *tr.v.* to surprise; *intr.v.* to be surprised, to be astounded.
pas'-mo *m.* astonishment, amazement.
pas-mo'-so, **=a** *adj.* surprising, wonderful, amazing.
pas-quim' *m.* pasquinade.
pas'-sa *f.* raisin.
pas-sa-dei'-ra *f.* strainer, sieve, filter; narrow carpet, runner.
pas-sa-di'-ço *m.* corridor, sidewalk, passage.
pas-sa-di'-o *m.* daily food.
pas-sa'-do *m.* past; **pas-sa'-do**, **=a** *adj.* past, gone by.
pas-sa-dor' *m.* strainer.
pas-sa-gei'-ro *m.* passenger; **=o**, **=a** *adj.* fleeting, passing, transitory.
pas-sa'-gem *f.* passage, passing.
pas-sa-ma'-nes *m.pl.* lace, fringes.
pas-sa-men'-to *m.* death.
pas-sa-por'-te *m.* passport.
pas-sar' *tr.v.* to pass, to cross, to hand, to send, to go beyond; *intr.v.* to pass, to pass by; to disappear; to be fair; to happen; to get along.
pas-sa-rei'-ra *f.* aviary.
pás-sa-ro *m.* bird.

pas-sa-tem'-po m. pastime, diversion, recreation.

pas'-se m. pass, permit.

pas-se-ar' tr.v. to walk, to take for a walk, to take for a ride; intr.v. to go walking, to go riding, to take a walk.

pas-sei'-o m. walk; sidewalk; public garden.

pas-sei'-ro, =a adj. pacing, at a pace, slow.

pas-si-lar'-go, =a adj. striding, taking long steps.

pas-si'-va f. (gram.) passive voice.

pas-si-vi-da'-de f. passivity.

pas-si'-vo, =a adj. passive.

pas'-so m. step, pace, gait.

pas'-ta f. paste; batter; brief-case; portfolio.

pas-ta'-gem f. pasture.

pas-tar' tr.v., intr.v. to graze, to pasture.

pas-tel' m. pastry; pastel.

pas-te-la-ri'-a f. pastry shop.

pas-te-lei'-ro m. baker, pastry dealer.

pas-te-lis'-ta m. pastel artist, pastelist.

pas-teu-ri-zar' tr.v. to pasteurize.

pas-ti-çal' m. grazing ground.

pas-ti'-lha f. lozenge, tablet.

pas'-to m. food, grass, grazing.

pas-tor' m. shepherd, pastor.

pas-to-ral' adj. pastoral.

pas-to-rar' tr.v. to tend, to drive to pasture, to watch over.

pa'-ta f. paw foot of animal; fluke of anchor.

pa-ta'-da f. kick; indecorous action.

pa-ta-mal', pa-ta-mar' m. landing (of stairs).

pa-te-ar' intr.v. to stamp the feet to show disapproval; tr.v. to disapprove by stamping the feet.

pa-te'-la f. kneecap.

pá-te-na f. paten; metal plate, metal disk.

pa-ten'-te f. patent; adj. patent, evident.

pa-te'-ra f. peg, hook.

pa-ter-nal' adj. paternal.

pa-ter-ni-da'-de f. paternity.

pa-ter'-no, =a adj. paternal.

pa-té-ti-co, =a adj. pathetic.

pa-tí-bu-lo m. gallows, gibbet.

pa-ti'-fe m., adj. scoundrel, rascal, good-for-nothing.

pa-tim' m. skate.

pa-ti-nar' intr.v. to skate; to skid.

pá-tio m. patio, courtyard.

pa-ti-nhar' intr.v. to skid; to paddle.

pa'-to, =a m., f. duck; pagar o — to pay the price.

pa-to'-la f. large claw of lobster; adj. stupid, silly, foolish, ignorant.

pa-to-lo-gi'-a f. pathology.

pa'-tos m. pathos.

pa-trão' m. master of house, landlord.

pá-tria f. native land, mother country.

pa-tri-ar'-ca m. patriarch.

pa-tri-ar-ca'-do m. patriarchy.

pa-tri-ar-cal' adj. patriarchal.

pa-trí-cio, =a adj. patrician; **pa-trí-cio** m. fellow-countryman.

pa-tri-mo-ni-al' adj. patromonial.

pa-tri-mô-nio m. patrimony.

pá-trio, =a adj. native, hereditary.

pa-tri-o'-ta m., f. patriot.

pa-tri-ó-ti-co, =a adj. patriotic.

pa-tri-o-tis'-mo m. patriotism.

pa-trô-a f. housewife, mistress of the house.

pa-tro-ci-nar' tr.v. to back, to support, to protect, to give aid to.

pa-tro-cí-nio m. protection, aid.

pa-tro'-na f. protectress, patroness; cartridge bag.

pa-tro-na'-gem f. patronage, protection, aid.

pa-tro-na'-to m. patronage, protection, support; employers, management; juvenile poor-house.

pa-tro-ne-ar' tr.v. to administer; to back, to support; to act as patron or patroness.

pa-trô-ni-mi-co, =a adj. patronymic.

pa-tro'-no m. patron, protector.

pa-tru'-lha f. patrol; detachment, detail.

pa-tru-lhar' tr.v., intr.v. to patrol.

pa-tu-á m. straw basket.

pau' m. wood; stick; beam; mast; tree.

pa-úl m. swamp, marsh land.

pau-la-ti'-no, =a adj. gradual, done little by little; slow.

pau-li'-to m. billiard cue.

pau-pe-ris'-mo m. pauperism.

pau'-sa f. pause.

pau-sa'-do, =a adj. deliberate, slow.

pau-sar' intr.v. to pause, to stop.

pau'-ta f. guide lines to be used under paper on which one is writing.

pau-ta'-do, =a adj. ruled with parallel lines; methodical.

pau-tar' tr.v. to rule.

pa-vão' m. peacock.

pá-vi-do, =a adj. terrified.

pa-vi-lhão' m. pavilion; annex; flag; maritime power.

pa-vi-men'-to m. floor.

pa-vi'-o m. wick (of candle), taper.

pa-vô-a f. pea-hen.

pa-vo-na'-da f. spreading of feathers; strutting.

pa-vor' m. fear, consternation.

pa-vo-ro'-so, =a adj. horrible, frightening.

paz' f. peace.

pé m. foot.

pe-ão' m. pedestrian; infantryman; plebian; pawn.

pe'-ça f. piece, part; room of house; piece of furniture.

pé-ca-di'-lho m. pecadillo.

pe-ca'-do m. sin, transgression.

pe-ca-dor' m. sinner.

pe-ca-do'-ra f. sinner, sinful woman.

pe-car' intr.v. to sin.

pe-ço'-nha f. poison, venom.

pec-ti'-na f. pectin.

pe-cu-á-ria f. cattle-raising.

pe-cu-la'-to m. peculation, embezzlement.

pe-cu-li-ar' adj. peculiar.

pe-cu-li-a-ri-da'-de f. peculiarity.

pe-cú-lio m. savings, capital, property.

pe-cu-ni-á-rio, =a adj. pecuniary.

pe-da'-ço m. piece, bit, short space of time.

pe-da-go-gi'-a f. pedagogy.

pe-da-go'-go m. pedagogue.

pe-dan'-te m., f. pedant.

pe-dan-tis'-mo m. pedantry.

pé-de-al-tar' m. priest's fee for performing wedding ceremony or funeral service.

pé-de-ga-li'-nha m. crow's-feet, wrinkles around the eyes.

pé-de-ga'-lo m. hop vine.

pé-de-mo-le'-que m. cake made with mandioca flour.

pe-des-tal' m. pedestal.

pe-des'-tre adj. pedestrian.

pé-de-ven'-to m. tornado.
pe-di-a'-tra m. pediatrician.
pe-di-cu'-ro m. chiropodist.
pe-di'-do m. order, request.
pe-din'-te m., f. beggar, suppliant.
pe-dir' tr.v. to ask, to request; — **emprestado** to borrow.
pé-di-rei'-to m. height of room (distance from floor to ceiling).
pe-dô-me-tro m. pedometer.
pe'-dra f. stone; blackboard.
pe-dra'-da f. stoning, blow with a stone.
pe-dra'-do, *a* adj. paved; spotted, speckled.
pe-dre-go'-so, *a* adj. stony, rocky.
pe-dre-gu'-lho m. large rock; gravel.
pe-drei'-ra f. stone quarry.
pe-drei'-ro m. stone mason.
pe-ga'-da f. footprint, vestige, trace.
pe-ga-di'-ço, *a* adj. infectious.
pe-ga'-do, *a* adj. glued; contiguous; near-by; friendly.
pe-ga-dou'-ro m. handle.
pe-ga-mas'-so m. glue, slime, sticky substance; bore.
pe-gar' tr.v. to glue, to paste, to join; intr.v. to stick, to hold, to take root, to become infected, to seize; — **em** to take hold, to seize; — **com** to quarrel with;
pei-dar' intr.v. to fart, to break wind.
pei'-do m. fart.
pei-tar' tr.v. to bribe.
pei-tei'-ro m. briber, corrupter.
pei-ti'-lho m. breast-cloth; false shirt front, dickey; corset, bodice.
pei'-to m. breast, chest, bosom; heart; lungs.
pei-to-ral' m., adj. pectoral.
pei'-xe m. fish.
pei-xei'-ro m. fish-monger.
pe-jar' tr.v. to hinder, to embarrass, to clog, to overload; intr.v. to become pregnant.
pe'-jo m. timidity, bashfulness, shame.
pe-jo'-so, *a* adj. modest, timid, ashamed.
pe-jo-rar' tr.v. to belittle, to depreciate.
pe-jo-ra-ti'-vo, *a* adj. pejorative.
pe-la'-gem f. hair (of animals).
pe-la'-gra f. pellagra.
pe-la-gro'-so, *a* adj. afflicted with pellagra.
pe-lar' tr.v. to peel, to remove the hair, to remove the skin or bark.
pe'-le f. skin, hide, barrel, peel.
pe-le'-ja f. dispute, struggle, quarrel.
pe-le-jar' intr.v. to fight, to combat, to struggle, to quarrel, to discuss; tr.v. to fight.
pe-li'-ca f. kid glove.
pe-lí-cu-la f. pellicle, film.
pê-lo m. hair.
pe-lu'-do, *a* adj. hairy, shaggy.
pel'-ve, **pel'-vis** f. pelvis.
pél-vi-co, *a* adj. pelvic.
pe'-na f. pain, penalty, punishment; pity, compassion; feather, pen.
pe-na'-cho m. plume.
pe-na'-da f. pen mark, stroke with a pen.
pe-nal' adj. penal.
pe-na-li-da'-de f. pain, punishment; trouble, affliction.
pe-na-li-zar' tr.v. to penalize.
pen-dão' m. flag, standard.
pen-den'-te adj. pendent, hanging.
pen-der' intr.v. to hang down, to be suspended.
pên-du-la f. pendulum clock.
pên-du-lo m. pendulum.
pen-du-rar' tr.v. to hang, to suspend.

pe-nei'-ra f. sieve; screen.
pe-nei-rar' tr.v. to sieve, to screen.
pe-nei'-ro m. large sieve.
pe-ne-tra-bi-li-da'-de f. penetrability.
pe-ne-tra-ção' f. penetration.
pe-ne-trar' tr.v., intr.v. to penetrate.
pe-ne-trá-vel adj. penetrable.
pe'-nha f. rock, cliff.
pe-nhor' m. pledge, pawn, mortgage, token, security, bail; pawned object; **casa de -s** pawnshop.
pe'-ni m. penny (English money).
pe-nín-su-la f. peninsula.
pe-nin-su-lar' adj. peninsular.
pe-ni-tên-cia f. penitence.
pe-ni-ten-ci-al' adj. penitential.
pe-ni-ten-ci-á-ria f. penitentiary.
pe-ni-ten'-te m., f., adj. penitent.
pe-no'-so, *a* adj. grievous, painful; hard.
pen-sa-men'-to m. thought.
pen-são' f. pension; board; boarding-house.
pen-sar' intr.v. to think, to intend; tr.v. to think up, to imagine, to conceive; to dress (a wound).
pen-sa-ti'-vo, *a* adj. pensive, thoughtful.
pen-si-o-nis'-ta m., f. pensioner; boarder.
pen'-so m. dressing, treatment.
pen-tá-go-no m. pentagon.
pen-ta-go-nal' adj. pentagonal.
pen-tâ-me-tro m. pentameter.
pen-ta-teu'-co m. Pentateuch.
pen'-te m. comb; — **fino** fine-toothed comb.
pen-te-a-dei'-ra f. dressing-table.
pen-te-a'-do m. coiffure.
pen-te-a-dor' m. hair-dresser; combing jacket; dressing-gown.
pen-te-ar' tr.v. to comb.
pe-nu'-gem f. down; first soft feathers or hair.
pe-nu-gen'-to, *a* adj. downy.
pe-núl-ti-mo, *a* adj. penultimate.
pe-num'-bra f. penumbra.
pe-nú-ria f. penury.
pe-nu-ri-o'-so, *a* adj. penurious.
pe-ô-nia f. peony.
pe-or' adj. worse; worst.
pe-o-ra-men'-to m. worsening.
pe-o-rar' tr.v. to make worse; intr.v. to get worse.
pe-pi-nei'-ro m. cucumber vine.
pe-pi'-no m. cucumber.
pe-pi'-ta f. nugget (especially of gold).
pep-si'-na f. pepsin.
pép-ti-co, *a* adj. peptic.
pep-to'-na f. peptone.
pe-que-nez' f. smallness.
pe-que-ni'-no, *a* adj. very small, tiny.
pe-que-ni'-to, *a* adj. very small, tiny.
pe-que'-no, *a* adj. small; m., f. boy, girl.
pê-ra f. pear.
pe-ra'-da f. pear jam, pear preserves.
pe-ral' m. pear orchard.
pe-ral'-ta f. dandy, fop.
per-am-bu-lar' intr.v. to perambulate.
pé-ra-pa'-do m. man of low social status.
per-cal' m. percale.
per-ca-li'-no m. percaline.
per-ce-ber' tr.v. to perceive; to understand.
per-ce-bi-men'-to m. perception, understanding.
per-ce-bí-vel adj. perceivable.

per-cep-ti'-vo, =a adj. perceptive.
per-ce-ve'-jo m. bed-bug; thumb tack.
per-cor-rer' tr.v. to look through, to walk through, to peruse; to traverse.
per-cur'-so m. space or time covered in moving from one point to another.
per-cus-são' f. percussion.
per-cus-sor' m. percussion hammer (of a gun).
per-cu-tir' tr.v. to strike, to beat together.
per'-da f. loss, disappearance; death; ruin, destruction.
per-dão' m. pardon, forgiveness.
per-der' tr.v. to lose, to waste; to ruin, to spoil, to corrupt; to miss; intr.v. to lose, to decrease; —se refl.v. to be ruined, to be ship-wrecked; to be lost to sight, to fade away; to be lost, to go astray.
per-di-ção' f. perdition.
per-di-di'-ço, =a adj. easily lost.
per-di'-da f. prostitute.
per-di'-do m. loss; per-di'-do, =a adj. lost.
per-di-gão' m. partridge.
per-di-go'-te m. young partridge.
per-di-guei'-ro m. bird-dog, partridge-hunting dog.
per-dí-vel adj. loseable; hazardous.
per-diz' f. partridge.
per-do-ar' tr.v. to pardon.
per-do-á-vel adj. pardonable.
per-du-rá-vel adj. lasting.
pe-re-ce-dou'-ro, =a adj. perishable, mortal.
pe-re-cer' intr.v. to perish.
pe-re-cí-vel adj. perishable.
pe-re-gri-na-ção' f. peregrination.
pe-re-gri-nar' intr.v. to wander afar; to go on a pilgrimage.
pe-re-gri'-no m. pilgrim, wanderer; pe-re-gri'-no, =a adj. foreign, strange, unusual.
pe-remp-tó-rio, =a adj. peremptory.
pe-re'-ne adj. perennial.
per-fa-zer' tr.v. to finish, to perfect, to complete.
per-fec-ti-bi-li-da'-de f. perfectibility.
per-fec-tí-vel adj. perfectible.
per-fec-ti'-vo, =a adj. perfective.
per-fei-ção' f. perfection.
per-fei'-to, =a adj. perfect.
per-fí-dia f. perfidy.
pér-fi-do, =a adj. perfidious.
per-fil' m. profile.
per-fi-lhar' tr.v. to adopt legally as child.
per-fu-ma'-do, =a adj. fragrant.
per-fu-mar' tr.v. to perfume.
per-fu-ma-ri'-a f. perfumery, perfumer's shop.
per-fu'-me m. perfume, fragrance.
per-fu-mis'-ta m. perfumer.
per-fu-mo'-so, =a adj. fragrant.
per-fun-tó-rio, =a adj. perfunctory.
per-fu-ra-ção' f. perforation.
per-fu-ra-dor' m. perforator.
per-fu-rar' tr.v. to perforate.
per-fu-ra-triz' f. perforator.
per-ga-mi'-nho m. parchment.
per-gun'-ta f. question.
per-gun-ta-dor' m. questioner, one who asks many questions.
per-gun-tar' tr.v. to ask; to question; intr.v. to ask, to inquire.
pe-ri-cár-dio m. pericardium.
pe-ri-do'-to m. peridot.
pe-ri-fe-ri'-a f. periphery.
pe-ri'-go m. peril, danger.
pe-ri-go'-so, =a adj. perilous, dangerous.

pe-rí-me-tro m. perimeter.
pe-ri-ó-di-co, =a adj. periodic.
pe-rí-o-do m. period, era, epoch.
pe-ri-quí'-to m. parakeet.
pe-ris-có-pio m. periscope.
pe-ris-tál-ti-co, =a adj. peristaltic.
pe-rí-cia f. expertness, skill.
pe-ri'-to, =a adj. expert, skillful.
pe-ri-tô-nio m. peritoneum.
pe-ri-to-ni'-te f. peritonitis.
per-ju-rar' tr.v., intr.v. to perjure.
per-jú-rio m. perjury.
per-lon-gar' tr.v. to go along the coast of, to bring alongside; to postpone.
per-lon'-go m. slope of roof (on each side of ridge).
per-ma-nên-cia f. permanence, constancy.
per-ma-nen'-te adj. permanent.
per-ma-ne-cer' intr.v. to stay, to remain.
per-me-ar' tr.v. to permeate; intr.v. to go between.
per-me-á-vel adj. permeable.
per-mis-são' f. permission.
per-mis-sí-vel adj. permissible.
per-mis-sí'-vo, =a adj. permissive.
per-mi-tir' tr.v. to permit, to allow.
per-mu'-ta f. substitution, exchange.
per-mu-ta-ção' f. permutation.
per-mu-tar' tr.v. to exchange, to permute, to share.
per'-na f. leg; stem of letter; dar á — to walk rapidly.
per-na'-da f. large limb of tree; wide step.
per-nal'-to, =a adj. long-legged.
per-nei'-ras f.pl. leggings, puttees.
per-nil' m. pestle, gammon, shin.
per'-no m. bolt, stud pin.
per-noi-tar' intr.v. to pass the night.
pé-ro-la f. pearl.
pe-ro-ra-ção' f. peroration.
pe-ro-rar' intr.v. to perorate.
pe-ró-xi-do m. peroxide.
per-pen-di-cu-lar' adj. perpendicular.
per-pen-dí-cu-lo m. plumb line.
per-pe-tra-ção' f. perpetration.
per-pe-tra-dor' m. perpetrator.
per-pe-trar' tr.v. to perpetrate.
per-pe-tu-ar' tr.v. to perpetuate.
per-pe-tu-i-da'-de f. perpetuity.
per-pé-tuo, =a adj. perpetual.
per-ple-xão' f. perplexity.
per-ple-xi-da'-de f. perplexity.
per-ple'-xo, =a adj. perplexed, uncertain, puzzled.
pers-cru-tar' tr.v. to examine, to investigate; to sound, to scrutinize, to penetrate into.
per-se-gui-ção' f. persecution; pursuing.
per-se-guir' tr.v. to persecute, to pursue.
per-se-ve-ran'-ça f. perseverance.
per-se-ve-rar' intr.v. to persevere.
per-si-a'-na f. shutter.
per-sis-tên-cia f. persistence.
per-sis-ten'-te adj. persistent.
per-sis-tir' intr.v. to persist.
per-so-na'-gem f. personage.
per-so-na-li-da'-de f. personality.
per-so-ni-fi-ca-ção' f. personification.
pers-pec-ti'-va f. perspective.
pers-pi-cá-cia f. perspicacity.
pers-pi-caz' adj. perspicacious.
pers-pi-cu-i-da'-de f. perspicuity.
pers-pí-cuo, =a adj. perspicacious.
per-su-a-dir' tr.v. to persuade; to persuade, to be persuasive; —se refl.v. to believe, to judge.
per-su-a-ção' f. persuasion.

per-su-a-si'-vo, =a *adj.* persuasive.
per-ten-cen'-te *adj.* belonging, relating, pertaining.
per-ten-cer' *intr.v.* to belong, to pertain, to relate, to be characteristic.
per-ti-ná-cia *f.* pertinacity.
per-ti-naz' *adj.* pertinacious.
per-ti-nên-cia *f.* pertinence.
per-ti-nen'-te *adj.* pertinent.
per'-to *adv.* near.
per-tur-ba-ção' *f.* perturbation.
per-tur-bar' *tr.v.* to perturb.
pe-rú *m.* **pe-ru'-a** *f.* turkey.
per-ver-são' *f.* perversion.
per-ver-si-da'-de *f.* perversity.
per-ver'-so, =a *adj.* perverse.
per-ver-ter' *tr.v.* to pervert.
pér-vio, =a *adj.* permeable, open, plain, apparent.
pe-sa-de'-lo *m.* nightmare.
pe-sa'-do, =a *adj.* heavy; slow; hard to digest.
pe-sa'-gem *f.* weighing.
pê-sa-me *m.* condolence, sympathy.
pe-sar' *tr.v.* to weigh; to weigh down upon, to press against; to ponder; *intr.v.* to weigh; to sadden, to grieve.
pes-ca-dor' *m.* fisherman.
pes-car' *tr.v.* to fish.
pes-co'-ço *m.* neck, throat.
pê-so *m.* weight.
pes-pon'-to *m.* backstitch, quilting stitch.
pes-qui'-sa *f.* search, investigation, research.
pes-qui-sar' *tr.v.* to search diligently for, to investigate.
pes-se-ga'-da *f.* peach preserves.
pês-se-go *m.* peach.
pes-se-guei'-ro *m.* peach tree.
pes-si-mis'-mo *m.* pessimism.
pes-si-mis'-ta *m.* pessimist.
pés-si-mo, =a *adj.* worst; very bad.
pes-sô-a *f.* person.
pes-so-al' *adj.* personal; *m.* personnel.
pes-ta'-na *f.* eyelash; **queimar as =s** to study hard.
pes-ta-ne-jar' *intr.v.* to blink.
pes'-te *f.* pest; plague.
pes-tí-fe-ro, =a *adj.* pestiferous.
pes-ti-lên-cia *f.* pestilence.
pes-ti-len-ci-al' *adj.* pestilential.
pé-ta-lo *m.* petal.
pe-ti-ção' *f.* petition.
pe-ti-ci-o-ná-rio *m.* petitioner.
pe-tis'-co *m.* tasty food; steel bar used in striking spark on flint.
pe-tre'-chos *m.pl.* equipment for war; tools, implements, apparatus.
pe-tri-fi-ca-ção' *f.* petrification.
pe-tri-fi-car' *tr.v.* to petrify.
pe-tró-le-o *m.* petroleum.
pe-ú-ga *f.* sock.
pe-tu-lân-cia *f.* petulance.
pe-tu-lan'-te *adj.* petulant.
pe-tú-nia *f.* petunia.
pi'-a *f.* baptismal font.
pi-a-nis'-ta *m.*, *f.* pianist.
pi-a'-no *m.* piano.
pi-ão' *m.* top (toy).
pi-as'-tra *f.* piaster.
pi-ca'-da *f.* insect bite.
pi-ca-dei'-ra *f.* pick, pick-axe.
pi-ca-dei'-ro *m.* riding ground, training ground; beam on which keel of ship is laid.
pi-ca-di'-nho *m.* stew, hash.
pi-ca-dor' *m.* riding-master; picador (in bull-fight); punch.

pi-can'-te *adj.* highly seasoned, sharp.
pi-car' *tr.v.* to pick, to prick, to peck, to sting, to bite; *intr.v.* to bite (of fish).
pi-ca-re'-ta *f.* mattock.
pí-ca-ro, =a *adj.* roguish, knavish, cunning, funny.
pi'-che *m.* pitch.
pi'-co *m.* peak, summit, point.
pi-co-tar' *tr.v.* to punch (tickets), to perforate (stamps).
pi-co'-te *m.* picot.
pic-to-gra-fi'-a *f.* pictography.
pi-e-da'-de *f.* piety.
pi-e-do'-so, =a *adj.* pious, devout, tender-hearted.
pi-e-zo-e-le-tri-ci-da'-de *f.* piezo-electricity.
pig-men'-to *m.* pigment.
pig-meu' *m.*, *adj.* pygmy.
pi-ja'-ma *m.* pyjama.
pi-lão' *m.* pestle; movable weight on scales.
pi-lar' *tr.v.* to pound or beat to remove shell or husk; *m.* pillar, shaft.
pi'-lha *f.* pillaging; pile (Voltaic), battery, electric cell.
pi-lha'-gem *f.* pillage.
pi-lhar' *tr.v.* to pillage, to lay waste.
pi-lhé-ria *f.* witticism, joke.
pi'-lo *m.* javelin, dart.
pi-lo'-ro *m.* pylorus.
pi-lo-ta'-gem *f.* piloting.
pi-lo-te-ar' *tr.v.*, *intr.v.* to pilot.
pi-lô-to *m.* pilot.
pí-lu-la *f.* pill; (fig.) some thing disagreeable.
pi-men'-ta *f.* black pepper.
pi-men-tão' *m.* pimento.
pi-men-tão'-do'-ce *m.* bell pepper.
pi-men-tei'-ra *f.* pepper plant; pepperbox.
pi'-na *f.* felloe, each section of rim of wheel.
pi-ná-cu-lo *m.* pinnacle.
pin'-ça *f.* pincers; clamp; clip.
pin-cel' *m.* paint brush.
pin-ga-dei'-ra *f.* drip pan.
pin-gar' *tr.v.*, *intr.v.* to drip, to drop.
pin-gen'-te *m.* eardrop, pendant.
pin'-go *m.* drop; dripping; stain.
pi-nhei'-ro *m.* pine tree.
pi'-nho *m.* pine lumber.
pi'-no *m.* top; gable; wooden peg.
pin'-ta *f.* newly hatched chicken.
pin-ta'-da *f.* Guinea-hen.
pin-tar' *tr.v.* to paint, to color; *intr.v.* to take on color, to become grey-haired.
pin'-to *m.* frying chicken.
pin-tor' *m.* painter, artist.
pin-tu'-ra *f.* painting.
pi-ar' *intr.v.* to make peeping sounds.
pi'-o *m.* chirping, peeping of young birds.
pi'-o, =a *adj.* pious, devout.
pi-o'-lho *m.* louse.
pi-o-nei'-ro *m.* pioneer.
pi-or-réi-a *f.* pyorrhea.
pi'-pa *f.* hogshead, cask.
pi-pe'-ta *f.* pipette.
pi'-po *m.* small cask, barrel.
pi-po'-ca *f.* pop-corn.
pi-po-que-ar' *intr.v.* to burst, to pop.
pi-que-ni'-que *m.* picnic.
pi-que'-ta *f.* picket, stake, post.
pi-quê-te *m.* picket guard.
pi'-ra *f.* pyre.
pi-râ-mi-de *f.* pyramid.
pi-ra'-ta *m.* pirate.
pi-ra-ta'-gem *f.* piracy.

pi-ra-te-ar' *intr.v.* to live the life of a pirate.

pi'-res *m.* saucer.

pi-rí-fo-ra *f.* lightning bug.

pi-ri-lam'-po *m.* lightning bug.

pi-ro-gra-vu'-ra *f.* pyrography.

pi-rós-ca-fo *m.* steamboat.

pi-ro'-se *f.* pyrosis, heartburn.

pi-ro-tec-ní'-a *f.* pyrotechnics.

pi-ro-xi-li'-na *f.* pyroxylin.

pir-ra'-lho *m.* child, little fellow.

pi-ru-e'-ta *f.* pirouette.

pi-sa'-da *f.* footprint.

pi'-sa=flo'-res *m.* effeminate fellow, man affected in bearing.

pi-sar' *tr.v.* to step on, to trample, to stamp, to bruise, to crush, to overcome, to tread.

pi-são' *m.* fulling-mill.

pis-ca-de'-la *f.* wink, blink, winking.

pis-car' *tr.v.* to wink, to blink.

pis-ci-cul-tu'-ra *f.* fish breeding.

pis-ci'-na *f.* swimming-pool; reservoir for breeding fish.

pis'-co *m.* winking.

pi'-so *m.* step, footstep, ground; nun's fee on entering convent.

pis'-ta *f.* trace, track.

pis-tão' *m.* piston.

pis-to'-la *f.* pistol (gun).

pis-to-lão' *m.* pyrotechnic piece; recommendation.

pi-ta'-da *f.* pinch of snuff.

pi-ta-dor' *m.* snuff user.

pí-ton *m.* python.

pi-to-res'-co, =a *adj.* picturesque.

pí-xi-de *f.* pyx chest, ciborium.

pla'-ca *f.* plaque; sconce; silver coin.

pla-car' *tr.v.* to placate.

pla-cen'-ta *f.* placenta.

pla-ci-dez' *f.* placidity.

plá-ci-do, =a *adj.* placid.

plá-ci-to *m.* promise of chastity (in the consecration of bishops).

pla-gi-ar' *tr.v.* to plagiarize.

pla-gi-á-rio *m.* plagiarist.

plai'-na *f.* carpenter's plane.

pla-na-dor' *m.* glider.

pla-nal'-to *m.* plateau, tableland.

pla-ne-ar' *tr.v.* to plan, to project.

pla-ne-jar' *tr.v.* to plan, to project.

pla-ne'-ta *m.* planet.

pla-ne-tá-rio *m.* planetarium; *adj.* planetary.

pla'-no *m.* plan; plane; **pla'-no,** =a *adj.* smooth, level, even.

plan'-ta *f.* plant; sole; ground-floor; blue-print.

plan-ta-ção' *f.* plantation, planting.

plan-tão' *m.* orderly, work of an orderly.

plan-tar' *tr.v.* to plant, to place, to set.

plas'-ma *m.* plasma.

plás-ti-ca *f.* plastic surgery.

plas-ti-ci'-na *f.* modeling clay.

plás-ti-co, =a *adj.* plastic.

plas-ti-li'-na *f.* modeling clay.

plas-trão' *m.* breastplate; front (of a shirt); plastron.

pla-ta-for'-ma *f.* platform; turn-table (of railway).

pla-téi-a *f.* main floor (of theatre).

pla-ti-ban'-da *f.* hand-railing (around terrace or open porch); edging around flower beds: wide, flat frame.

pla-ti'-na *f.* platinum; shoulder strap (of infantryman).

pla-tô-ni-co, =a *adj.* platonic.

plau-si-bi-li-da'-de *f.* plausibility.

plau-sí-vel *adj.* plausible.

ple'-be *f.* mob, common people.

ple-beu' *adj.* plebeian.

ple-bis-ci'-to *m.* plebiscite.

plei-te-an'-te *m.,* *f.* litigant.

plei-te-ar' *tr.v.* to sue; to contest; *intr.v.* to go to court, to take to law.

plei'-to *m.* litigation, lawsuit.

ple-ná-rio, =a *adj.* plenary.

ple-ni-po-ten-ci-á-rio *m.* plenipotentiary.

ple-ni-tu'-de *f.* fullness, plenitude.

ple'-no, =a *adj.* full, complete, entire, perfect.

ple-to'-ra *f.* plethora.

pleu-rís *m.* or **pleu-ri-si'-a** *f.* pleurisy.

ple'-xo *m.* plexus.

plu'-ma *f.* plume, feather.

plu-ma'-gem *f.* plumage, feathers.

plu-mo'-so, =a *adj.* feathery.

plum-ba-gi'-na *f.* graphite.

plum-ba'-to *m.* diploma with lead seal.

plúm-be-o, =a *adj.* leaden, lead-colored.

plu-ral' *adj.* plural.

plu-ra-li-da'-de *f.* plurality.

plu-to-cra-ci'-a *f.* plutocracy.

plu-vi-al' *adj.* coming from rain.

plu-vi-ô-me-tro *m.* pluviometer.

plu-vi-o'-so, =a *adj.* rainy.

pneu-má-ti-ca *f.* pneumatics.

pneu-ma'-ti-co, =a *adj.* pneumatic; **pneu-má-ti-co** *m.* pneumatic tire.

pneu-mo-co'-co *m.* pneumococcus.

pneu-mo-ni'-a *f.* pneumonia.

pó *m.* dust, powder.

po-a'-lha *f.* fine dust particles suspended in air.

po'-bre *adj.* poor, needy, miserable, worthless.

po-bre-tão' *m.* poverty-stricken person.

po-bre'-za *f.* poverty.

po-ção' *f.* potion.

po-cei'-ro *m.* well-digger.

po'-ço *m.* well, deep pit.

pô-da *f.* pruning.

po-da-dei'-ra *f.* pruning hook, clippers.

po-dão' *m.* pruning hook, clippers.

po-dar' *tr.v.* to prune.

po-der' *tr.v.,* *intr.v.* to be able, can, to have the power, to be able to do; *m.* power, authority, sovereignty, power of attorney.

po-de-ro'-so, =a *adj.* powerful.

po'-dre *adj.* rotten, decayed, fetid.

po-dri-dão' *f.* rottenness; corruption.

po-e-dei'-ra *adj.* that lays many eggs.

po-ei'-ra *f.* dust.

po-ei-ra'-da *f.* cloud of dust, large amount of dust.

po-ei-ren'-to, =a *adj.* dusty.

po-e'-ma *m.* poem.

po-en'-te *m.* west.

po-e-si'-a *f.* poetry.

po-é-ti-ca *f.* poetics.

po-é-ti-co, =a *adj.* poetic.

pois' *adv.* then, why, how, what, therefore.

po-lai'-nas *f.pl.* gaiters, spats.

po-lar' *adj.* polar.

po-la-ri-da'-de *f.* polarity.

po-la-rí-me-tro *m.* polarimeter.

po-la-ri-za-ção' *f.* polarization.

po-la-ri-zar' *tr.v.* to polarize.

pol'-dro *m.* colt.

po-le-ga'-da *f.* inch.

po-le-gar' *m.,* *adj.* thumb, big toe.

po-lei'-ro *m.* roost, perch.

po-lê-mi-ca *f.* polemics.

po-lê-mi-co, =a *adj.* polemical.

po-le-mis'-ta *m.* polemist.

pó-len *m.* pollen.
po-lí-cia *f.* police; policing; *m.* policeman.
po-li-ci-a-men'-to *m.* policing.
po-li-ci-ar' *tr.v.* to police.
po-li-clí-ni-ca *f.* policlinic.
po-li-dez' *f.* politeness.
po-li'-do, ₌a *adj.* polite.
po-li-ga-mi'-a *f.* polygamy.
po-lí-ga-mo *m.* polygamist.
po-li-glo'-ta *m.*, *f.* polyglot.
po-lí-go-no *m.* polygon.
po-lí-gra-fo *m.* polygraph.
po-li-ni-zar' *tr.v.* to pollinate.
po-li-nô-mio *m.* polynomial.
pó-li-po *m.* polyp.
po-lis-sí-la-bo *m.* polysyllable.
po-li-téc-ni-co, ₌a *adj.* polytechnic.
po-lí-ti-ca *f.* politics.
po-li-ti-ca'-gem *f.* politics (in bad sense).
po-lí-ti-co, ₌a *adj.* political.
po-li-ti-quei'-ro *m.* politician.
po'-lo *m.* pole.
pol'-pa *f.* pulp.
pol-po'-so, ₌a *adj.* pulpy, fleshy.
pol-pu'-do, ₌a *adj.* pulpy, fleshy.
pol-tro'-na *f.* upholstered armchair.
po-lu-ção' *f.* pollution.
po-lu-ir' *tr.v.* to pollute.
po-lu'-to, ₌a *adj.* polluted.
pol-vi'-lho *m.* fine powder, dust; tapioca starch.
pól-vo-ra *f.* gun powder.
pol-vo-ri'-nho *m.* powder box, powder horn.
po-ma'-da *f.* pomade.
po-mar' *m.* orchard.
po-ma-rei'-ro, ₌a *adj.* pertaining to an orchard.
pom-bal' *m.* dovecot.
pom'-bo, ₌a *m.*, *f.* dove, pigeon.
po-mi-cul-tu'-ra *f.* raising of fruit trees.
pom'-pa *f.* pomp.
pom-po'-so, ₌a *adj.* pompous.
pô-mu-lo *m.* cheek.
pon'-che *m.* punch (beverage).
pon-chei'-ra *f.* punch bowl.
pon-de-rar' *tr.v.*, *intr.v.* to ponder.
pon-de-ro'-so, ₌a *adj.* ponderous.
pô-nei *m.* pony (horse).
pon-jé *m.* pongee.
pon'-ta *f.* point, tip, peak, stub, bit; cunning.
pon-ta'-da *f.* swift, sharp pain, stitch.
pon-tão' *m.* pontoon; ferry boat; lighter.
pon-ta-pé *m.* kick.
pon'-ta₌sê-ca *f.* engraver's tool; engraving.
pon'-te *f.* bridge.
pon-tei'-ra *f.* tip (of a cane or umbrella).
pon-tei'-ro *m.* hand (of watch or clock); pointer.
pon-tí-fi-ce *m.* pontiff.
pon-ti'-lha *f.* sharp point; gold or silver fringe, lace.
pon-ti-lhão' *m.* small bridge.
pon-ti-lho'-so, ₌a *adj.* punctilious.
pon-ti'-nho *m.* small stitch; subtlety.
pon'-to *m.* dot, point, period; stitch, seam; lace; roll; prompter.
pon-to-ar' *tr.v.* to check; to mark.
pon-to'-so, ₌a *adj.* punctilious, scrupulous.
pon-tu-a-ção' *f.* punctuation.
pon-tu-al' *adj.* punctual.
pon-tu-a-li-da'-de *f.* punctuality.
pon-tu-ar' *tr.v.* to punctuate.
pô-pa *f.* poop, stern.
po-pu-la-ção' *f.* population.

po-pu-lar' *adj.* popular.
po-pu-la-ri-da'-de *f.* popularity.
po-pu-la-ri-zar' *tr.v.* to popularize.
po-pu-lo'-so, ₌a *adj.* populous.
por *prep.* by, for, through, because of.
pôr *tr.v.* to place, to put, to set, to lay; —₌se *refl.v.* to apply oneself, to be converted into, to station oneself; to begin.
po-rão' *m.* hold (of a ship); basement.
por-ção' *f.* portion.
por-ca-ri'-a *f.* piggishness; filth; obscenity; work badly done.
por-ce-la'-na *f.* porcelain.
por-ci'-no, ₌a *adj.* porcine, piggish.
por-ci-o-ná-rio *m.* pensioner, beneficiary.
por-ci-o-nis'-ta *m.* boarding student, paying student.
por'-co, ₌a *m.*, *f.* hog.
po-rém *conj.* but, however.
por-fi-a'-do, ₌a *adj.* obstinate, quarrelsome, insistent.
por-me-nor' *m.* detail, minutia.
por-me-no-ri-zar' *tr.v.* to give details of, to present with minutiae.
por-no-gra-fi'-a *f.* pornography.
po'-ro *m.* pore.
po-ro-si-da'-de *f.* porousness, porosity.
po-ro'-so, ₌a *adj.* porous.
po-ro'-ra *adv.* for the time being, still.
por-quan'-to *conj.* since, seeing that, for the reason that.
por'-que *conj.* because.
por-quê *conj.* why; *m.* cause, reason.
por-quei'-ra *f.* pig-pen.
por-quei'-ro *m.* swineherd.
por'-ta *f.* door, gate.
por'-ta₌ban-dei'-ra *m.* standard-bearer.
por-ta'-da *f.* large door, portal; façade; frontispiece.
por-ta-dor' *m.* bearer, messenger.
por'-ta₌es-tan-dar'-te *m.* standard-bearer.
por-ta'-gem *f.* toll, toll-house, excise; custom.
por'-ta₌jói-as *m.* jewel-case.
por-tal' *m.* portal, entrance.
por'-ta₌la'-pis *m.* pencil-holder.
por-ta-ló *m.* cargo door (on ship).
por-tan'-to *conj.* therefore, consequently.
por-tão' *m.* large door.
por-ta₌pe'-nas *m.* pen-holder.
por-tar' *tr.v.* — **por fé** to legalize, to certify; —₌se *refl.v.* to behave, to comport oneself.
por-ta-ri'-a *f.* main entrance; lodge; patent.
por-tá-til *adj.* portable.
por'-te *m.* postage; transportation; tonnage; freight charges; physical aspect.
por-tei'-ro *m.* porter, door-keeper.
por-ten'-to *m.* portent.
por-ten-to'-so, ₌a *adj.* portentous.
pór-ti-co *m.* portico.
pôr-to *m.* port, harbor.
por-ven-tu'-ra *adv.* perchance, perhaps, maybe.
por-vin-dou'-ro, ₌a *adj.* future.
pos-da-tar' *tr.v.* to postdate.
po'-se *f.* pose.
po-ses-cri'-to *m.* postscript; ₌o, ₌a *adj.* written after.
po-si-ção' *f.* position.
po-si-ti'-vo, ₌a *adj.* positive.
pos-pon'-to *m.* backstitch.
pos-por' *tr.v.* to postpone.
pos-pos'-to, ₌a *adj.* postponed, delayed.
pos'-se *f.* possession; ₌s *f.pl.* property, possessions.

pos-ses-si'-vo, =a adj. possessive.
pos-ses'-so, =a adj. possessed.
pos-ses-sor' m. possessor, owner.
pos-si-bi-li-da'-de f. possibility.
pos-sí-vel adj. possible.
pos-su-i-dor' m. possessor, owner.
pos-su-í-dos m.pl. possessions, property.
pos-su-ir' tr.v. to own, to possess.
pos'-ta f. job, position; post-office.
pos-tal' adj. postal; m. postal card.
pos'-te m. post, stake.
pos-te-ri-da'-de f. posterity.
pos-te-ri-or' adj. posterior.
pos-ti'-ço, =a adj. false, artificial, counterfeit; adopted.
pos-ti'-go m. peep-hole; wicket.
pos-ti-lhão' m. postillion; messenger.
pôs-to m. post; place; office, job; adj. placed, set, put, planted.
pos-tu-la'-do m. postulate.
pos-tu-lar' tr.v. to postulate.
pós-tu-mo, =a adj. posthumous.
pos-tu'-ra f. posture, carriage, deportment; situation; neatness; laying (of eggs); setting (of sun).
po-tás-sio m. potassium.
po-tá-vel adj. potable, drinkable.
po'-te m. large earthen jar for liquids.
po-tên-cia f. power, force, strength, sway, authority.
po-ten-ci-al' m., adj. potential.
po-ten-ta'-do m. potentate.
po'-tro m. colt.
pou'-ca=ver-go'-nha f. knavery, indecency.
pou'-co adv. little; — a — little by little, gradually; pou'-co, =a adj. little; few.
pou-pan'-ça f. saving, economy; stinginess; alimentos de — stimulants.
pou-par' tr.v. to save, to spare, to avoid; intr.v. to economize; —=se refl.v. to save oneself, to avoid.
pou-qui-da'-de f. small portion.
pou-qui-dão' f. small portion.
pou-quí-nho m. small amount.
pou-sa'-da f. inn, lodging.
pou-sar' tr.v., intr.v. to put down, to sit down, to put up (at a hotel), to perch, to roost; to smooth, to rub down.
po'-vo m. people; village; common people; crowd, large number.
po-vo-a'-do m. town, village.
po-vo-a-dor' m. founder, colonizer.
po-vo-a-ção' f. population, town, village.
po-vo-ar' tr.v. to settle, to colonize; to stock, to fill; to suggest, to inspire.
pra'-ça f. square, market, market-place; fortress; office, situation; enlistment; private, enlisted man.
pra'-ga f. plague, curse, bore.
pra-ga'-na f. corn silk; beard on grain.
prag-má-ti-co, =a adj. conventional, usual, according to etiquette.
pra-gue-jar' intr.v. to swear, to curse; tr.v. to swear at, to curse.
prai'-a f. beach, sea-side.
pra-li'-na f. praline.
pran'-cha f. metal plate; plank, board; gang-plank; flat side of sword.
pran'-to m. weeping, lamentation.
pra'-ta f. silver, silver coin, silverware.
pra-ta'-da f. object containing silver.
pra-te-ar' tr.v. to silver, to silverplate.
pra-tei'-ro m. silversmith, silver shop keeper.
pra-te-lei'-ra f. plate-rail, shelf.
prá-ti-ca f. practice, use, experience; routine; sermon, discourse.
pra-ti-can'-te m. practitioner.

pra-ti-car' tr.v. to practice; to make, to cut; to say, to remark; intr.v. to speak, to converse.
pra-ti-cá-vel adj. practicable.
prá-ti-co, =a adj. practical.
pra'-to m. plate, dish; pan of balance; =s m.pl. cymbals.
pra'-xe f. custom, practice, procedure.
pra-zen-tei'-ro, =a adj. pleasing, festive, jovial.
pra-zer' intr.v. to please, to give pleasure; m. pleasure.
pra-zi-men'-to m. satisfaction, delight.
pra'-zo m. term, determined period of time.
pre-âm-bu-lo m. preamble, preface.
pre-ca-ri-e-da'-de f. precariousness.
pre-cá-rio, =a adj. precarious.
pre=ca-ta'-do, =a adj. cautious.
pre-ca-tar' tr.v. to caution; intr.v. to be cautious.
pre-cau-ção' f. precaution.
pre-cau-tó-rio, =a adj. precautionary.
pre'-ce f. prayer; supplication.
pre-ce-dên-cia f. precedence.
pre-ce-den'-te adj. preceding.
pre-ce-der' tr.v. to precede; intr.v. to go in front, to go ahead.
pre-cei'-to m. precept.
pre-cep-tor' m. preceptor, teacher.
pre-ci-ên-cia f. prescience.
pre-ci-en'-te adj. prescient.
pre-cin'-to m. precinct, enclosure.
pre-ci-o-si-da'-de f. preciosity.
pre-ci-o'-so, =a adj. precious.
pre-ci-pi-ta-ção' f. precipitation; haste.
pre-ci-pi-ta'-do, =a adj. impulsive.
pre-ci-pi-tar' tr.v. to precipitate, to accelerate.
pre-cí-pi-te m. precipitous.
pre-ci-pi-to'-so, =a adj. precipitous.
pre-ci-são' f. precision, exactness; need, poverty, necessity.
pre-ci-sar' tr.v. to need; to indicate precisely, to specify; intr.v. to be in need.
pre-ci'-so, =a adj. necessary; precise, exact.
pre-cla'-ro, =a adj. illustrious, brilliant, famous.
pre'-ço m. price, cost, value.
pre-co'-ce adj. precocious.
pre-co-ci-da'-de f. precocity.
pre-con-cei'-to m. preconception, prejudice, superstition.
pre-cur-sor' m. precursor.
pre-da-tó-rio, =a adj. predatory.
pre-de-ces-sor' m. predecessor.
pre-di-ca'-do m. characteristic quality, attribute.
pre-di-ção' f. prediction.
pre-di-le-ção' f. preference, choice.
pre-di-le'-to, =a adj. favorite.
pré-dio m. building.
pre-di'-to, =a adj. predicted.
pre-di-zer' tr.v. to predict.
pre-do-mi-nân-cia f. predominance.
pre-do-mi-nan'-te adj. predominant.
pre-do-mi-nar' intr.v. to predominate.
pre-e-mi-nên-cia f. preeminence.
pre-e-mi-nen'-te adj. preeminent.
pre-emp-ção' f. preemption.
pre-en-são' f. prehension.
pre-ên-sil adj. prehensile.
pre-fa-ci-ar' tr.v. to preface.
pre-fá-cio m. preface.
pre-fei'-to m. town mayor; prefect.
pre-fei-tu'-ra f. prefecture, municipal administration.
pre-fe-rên-cia f. preference.

pre-fe-ren-ci-al' *adj.* preferential.
pre-fe-rir' *tr.v.* to prefer; *intr.v.* to be preferred.
pre-fe-rí-vel *adj.* preferable.
pre-fi'-xo *m.* prefix; **-o, -a** *adj.* prefixed, predetermined.
pre'-ga *f.* tuck, pleat, fold, wrinkle.
prè-ga-ção' *f.* sermon; reprehension.
prè-ga-dor' *m.* preacher.
pre-gão' *m.* proclamation.
pre-gar' *tr.v.* to nail, to fix, to fasten.
prè-gar' *tr.v.* to preach; *intr.v.* to preach, to evangelize.
pre-gue-a-dei'-ra *f.* tucker (on sewing machine).
pre-gue-ar' *tr.v.* to put tucks in.
pre-gui'-ça *f.* laziness, indolence.
pre-gui-ço'-so, -a *adj.* lazy, indolent, serene, calm.
pre-his-tó-ri-co, -a *adj.* prehistoric.
pre-ju-di-car' *tr.v.* to harm, to damage.
pre-ju-í-zo *m.* damage, loss; prejudice, superstition.
pre-la'-do *m.* prelate.
pre-la-tu'-ra *f.* prelateship.
pre-le-ção' *f.* lecture, lesson.
pre-le-ci-o-nar' *tr.v., intr.v.* to lecture, to teach.
pre-li-mi-nar' *adj.* preliminary.
pre'-lo *m.* printing press, press.
pre-lú-dio *m.* prelude.
pre-ma-tu-ra-ção' *f.* prematurity.
pre-ma-tu'-ro, -a *adj.* premature.
pre-me-di-ta-ção' *f.* premeditation.
pre-mi-ar' *tr.v.* to reward, to give a prize to.
prê-mio *m.* premium.
pren'-da *f.* gift, token; talent.
pren-da'-do, -a *adj.* talented, accomplished.
pren-dar' *tr.v.* to present, to give; to endow, to captivate, to win.
pren-der' *tr.v.* to tie, to bind, to make secure; **—se** *refl.v.* to catch, to take hold; to become engaged, to get married.
pren'-sa *f.* press, wine press.
pre-o-cu-pa-ção' *f.* preoccupation.
pre-o-cu-par' *tr.v.* to worry, to preoccupy.
pre-pa-ra-ção' *f.* preparation.
pre-pa-ra'-do *m.* preparation (medicine).
pre-pa-rar' *tr.v.* to prepare.
pre-pa-ra-tó-rio, -a *adj.* preparatory; **pre-pa-ra-tó-rios** *m.pl.* prerequisites.
pre-pa'-ro *m.* preparation.
pre-pon-de-rân-cia *f.* preponderance.
pre-pon-de-ran'-te *adj.* preponderant.
pre-po-si-ção' *f.* preposition.
pre-pó-si-to *m.* plan, intention.
pre-pós-te-ro, -a *adj.* preposterous; inverted, up-side-down; unreasonable.
pre-ro-ga-ti'-va *f.* prerogative.
pres-cre-ver' *tr.v.* to prescribe.
pres-cri-ção' *f.* prescription.
pres-cri'-to, -a *adj.* prescribed.
pre-sen'-ça *f.* presence.
pre-sen'-te *adj., m.* present.
pre-sé-pio *m.* stable, manger; sculpture of the Nativity.
pre-ser-va-ção' *f.* preservation.
pre-ser-va-dor', -a *adj.* preservative.
pre-ser-var' *tr.v.* to preserve.
pre-ser-va-ti'-vo, -a *adj.* preservative.
pre-si-dên-cia *f.* presidency, chairmanship.
pre-si-den-ci-al' *adj.* presidential.
pre-si-den'-te *m.* president, chairman.
pre-sí-dio *m.* presidium, military prison.

pre-si-dir' *tr.v., intr.v.* to preside, to preside over.
pre'-so, -a *adj.* arrested, in prison; held secure.
pres'-sa *f.* haste; urgency.
pres-su-ro'-so, -a *adj.* impatient, in haste.
pres-sá-gio *m.* presage.
pres-são' *f.* pressure.
pres-sen-ti-men'-to *m.* presentiment.
pres-ta-ção' *f.* fulfilment; instalment.
pres-tân-cia *f.* excellence, superiority.
pres-tar' *tr.v.* to give, to lend, to grant, to lend; *intr.v.* to be useful, to be of use; **—se** *refl.v.* to lend oneself, to be ready.
pres-tá-vel *adj.* useful, serviceable.
pres'-tes *adj., adv.* disposed, ready; *adv.* soon; quickly, rapidly.
pres-te'-za *f.* agility, rapidity, promptness.
pres-tí-gio *m.* illusion; prestige, influence; magic, deceit.
pres-ti-gi-o'-so, -a *adj.* magic; influential.
prés-ti-mo *m.* usefulness.
pres-ti-mo'-so, -a *adj.* useful, helpful.
prés-ti-to *m.* procession, train.
pre-su-mir' *tr.v.* to presume; *intr.v.* to be presumptuous, to be vain.
pre-su-mí-vel *adj.* presumable.
pre-sun-ção' *f.* presumption.
pre-sun-ço'-so, -a *adj.* presumptuous.
pre-sun-ti'-vo, -a *adj.* presumptive.
pre-sun'-to *m.* ham.
pre-ten-den'-te *m.* suitor; pretender.
pre-ten-der' *tr.v.* to claim, to seek, to demand, to aspire to, to maintain, to woo; *intr.v.* to strive, to try.
pre-ten-são' *f.* claim, desire, aspiration, pretention.
pre-ten-si-o'-so, -a *adj.* pretentious.
pre-ten'-so, -a *adj.* supposed.
pre-te-rir' *tr.v.* to pass over, to omit, to slight, to supplant.
pre-té-ri-to, -a *adj.* past, elapsed, completed; **pre-té-ri-to** *m.* preterite.
pre-ter-na-tu-ral' *adj.* preternatural.
pre-tês-to *m.* pretext.
pre-ti-dão' *f.* blackness.
pre'-to, -a *adj., m., f.* black; Negro.
pre-va-le-cer' *intr.v.* to prevail.
pre-va-lên-cia *f.* prevalence.
pre-va-ri-car' *intr.v.* to prevaricate.
pre-ven-ção' *f.* foresight, anticipation, prejudice; precaution.
pre-ve-ni'-do, -a *adj.* forewarned, cautious; prejudiced, suspicious.
pre-ve-nir' *tr.v.* to anticipate, to avoid, to prevent, to dispose, to prejudice, to warn; **—se** *refl.v.* to prepare.
pre-ven-tó-rio *m.* preventive infirmary.
pré-vio, -a *adj.* previous.
pre-za'-do, -a *adj.* esteemed, beloved.
pre-zar' *tr.v.* to hold in high esteem; to prize highly.
pre-zá-vel *adj.* estimable, praiseworthy.
pri-ma-do'-na *f.* prima donna.
pri-ma'-gem *f.* primage.
pri-ma'-tas or **pri-ma'-tes** *m.pl.* primates (mammals).
pri-ma-ve'-ra *f.* spring (season).
pri-má-rio, -a *adj.* primary.
pri-maz' *m.* primate (archbishop).
pri-ma-zi'-a *f.* primateship.
pri-mei'-ro, -a *adj.* first.
pri-mí-cias *f.pl.* first fruits, beginning.
pri-mi-gê-nio, -a *adj.* primordial.
pri-mi-ti'-vo, -a *adj.* primitive.

pri'-mo, =a *m., f.* cousin; *adj.* prime, excellent.
pri-mo-gê-ni-to, =a *adj., m., f.* firstborn, oldest child.
pri-mor' *m.* perfection; superior quality.
pri-mor-di-al' *adj.* primordial.
pri-mo-ro'-so, =a *adj.* distinguished, excellent, perfect.
prin-ce'-sa *f.* princess.
prin-ci-pa'-do *m.* principality.
prin-ci-pal' *adj.* principal; *m.* principal; main thing, important factor.
prín-ci-pe *m.* prince.
prin-ci-pi-an'-te *m., f.* beginner.
prin-ci-pi-ar' *tr.v.* to begin, to start.
prin-cí-pio *m.* beginning; principle.
pri-o-ri-da'-de *f.* priority.
pri-são' *f.* prison; imprisonment.
pri-si-o-nei'-ro *m.* prisoner.
pris'-ma *m.* prism.
pris-má-ti-co, =a *adj.* prismatic.
pri-va-ção' *f.* privation.
pri-va'-da *f.* privy, water-closet.
pri-va'-do, =a *adj.* private.
pri-van'-ça *f.* intimacy; rôle of favorite of a king.
pri-var' *tr.v.* to deprive; *intr.v.* to be intimate.
pri-vi-le-gi-a'-do, =a *adj.* privileged, fortunate.
pri-vi-lé-gio *m.* privilege.
pró *adv.* in favor; *m.* advantage, convenience.
prô-a *f.* prow.
pro-ba-bi-li-da'-de *f.* probability.
pro-ban'-te *adj.* authentic, convincing.
pro-bi-da'-de *f.* honesty, uprightness.
pro'-bo, =a *adj.* honest, upright.
pro-ble'-ma *m.* problem.
pro-ble-má-ti-co, =a *adj.* problematic.
pro-ce-dên-cia *f.* source, origin, place of origin.
pro-ce-der' *intr.v.* to proceed.
pro-ce-di-men'-to *m.* procedure; behavior; proceedings.
pró-ce-res *m.pl.* magnates, tycoons, grandees; peers.
pro-ces-sar' *tr.v.* to bring suit against, to try.
pro-ces'-so *m.* process; passage, course; suit; record.
pro-cis-são' *f.* procession.
pro-cla'-ma *m.* bans.
pro-cla-ma-ção' *f.* proclamation.
pro-cla-mar' *tr.v.* to proclaim.
pro-clí-ti-co, =a *adj.* proclitic.
pro-cras-ti-na-ção' *f.* procrastination.
pro-cri-a-ção' *f.* procreation.
pro-cri-ar' *tr.v.* to procreate; *intr.v.* to germinate.
pro-cu'-ra *f.* search, quest, pursuit; effort, endeavor.
pro-cu-ra-ção' *f.* power of attorney.
pro-cu-ra-dor' *m.* attorney, proxy.
pro-cu-rar' *tr.v.* to look for, to seek; to try.
pro-di-ga-li-da'-de *f.* prodigality.
pro-dí-gio *m.* prodigy.
pro-di-gi-o'-so, =a *adj.* prodigious.
pró-di-go *m.* prodigal son; **pró-di-go,** =a *adj.* prodigal.
pro-du-ção' *f.* production.
pro-du-cen'-te *adj.* producing.
pro-du-ti'-vo, =a *adj.* productive.
pro-du'-to *m.* product.
pro-du-tor' *m.* producer; **pro-du-tor',** =a *adj.* productive, producing.
pro-du-zir' *tr.v.* to produce.
pro-fa-na-ção' *f.* profanation.

pro-fa-nar' *tr.v.* to profane.
pro-fa-ni-da'-de *f.* profanity, profanation.
pro-fa'-no, =a *adj.* profane.
pro-fe-ci'-a *f.* prophecy.
pro-fe-rir' *tr.v.* to utter, to pronounce, to declare.
pro-fes-sar' *tr.v.* to teach, to profess, to confess; *intr.v.* to take vows.
pro-fes-sor', =a *m., f.* teacher, professor.
pro-fes-so-ra'-do *m.* professorship, teaching profession, teachers.
pro-fe'-ta *m.* prophet.
pro-fé-ti-co, =a *adj.* prophetic.
pro-fi-ci-ên-cia *f.* proficiency.
pro-fi-ci-en'-te *adj.* proficient.
pro-fí-cuo, =a *adj.* useful, advantageous.
pro-fi-lá-ti-co, =a *adj.* prophylactic.
pro-fi-la-xi'-a *f.* prophylaxis.
pro-fis-são' *f.* profession.
pro-fis-si-o-nal' *adj.* professional.
pro-fli-ga-dor' *m., adj.* profligate.
pro-fun-dar' *tr.v.* to dig, to make deep; to study thoroughly.
pro-fun-dez' *f.* or **pro-fun-de'-za** *f.* profundity.
pro-fun-di-da'-de *f.* depth, profundity, profoundness.
pro-fun'-do, =a *adj.* deep, profound.
pro-fu-são' *f.* profusion.
pro-fu'-so, =a *adj.* profuse.
pro-gê-nie *f.* progeny.
pro-ge-ni-tor' *m.* progenitor.
prog-nós-ti-co *m.* prognostic.
pro-gra'-ma *m.* program.
pro-gre-dir' *intr.v.* to progress, to advance.
pro-gres-são' *f.* progression.
pro-gres-sí'-vo, =a *adj.* progressive.
pro-gres'-so *m.* progress.
pro-i-bi-ção' *f.* prohibition, forbidding.
pro-i-bir' *tr.v.* to forbid, to prohibit.
pro-i-bi-ti'-vo, =a *adj.* prohibitive.
pro-je-ção' *f.* projection.
pro-je-tar' *tr.v.* to project, to throw.
pro-je'-to *m.* project; — **de lei** bill.
pro-jé-til *m.* projectile.
prol' *m.* benefit, advantage.
pro-lap'-so *m.* prolapse.
pro'-le *f.* offspring.
pro-le-ta-ri-a'-do *m.* proletariat.
pro-le-tá-rio, =a *adj.* proletarian.
pro-lí-fe-ro, =a *adj.* proliferous.
pro-lí-fi-co, =a *adj.* prolific.
pro-li'-xo, =a *adj.* prolix.
pró-lo-go *m.* prologue.
pro-lon-ga-men'-to *m.* prolongation, continuation.
pro-lon-gar' *tr.v.* to prolong, to extend; to bring alongside.
pro-mes'-sa *f.* promise.
pro-me-ter' *intr.v.* to promise.
pro-me-ti'-da *f.* fiancée.
pro-mis-cu-i-da'-de *f.* promiscuity, promiscuousness.
pro-mís-cuo, =a *adj.* promiscuous.
pro-mis-só-ria *f.* promissory note.
pro-mis-só-rio, =a *adj.* promissory.
pro-mo-ção' *f.* promotion.
pro-mo-tor' *m.* prime mover, instigator, promotor.
pro-mo-ver' *tr.v.* to promote, to instigate.
pro-mul-ga-ção' *f.* promulgation.
pro-mul-gar' *tr.v.* to promulgate.
pro'-no, =a *adj.* prone.
pro-no'-me *m.* pronoun.
pro-no-mi-nal' *adj.* pronominal.

pron-ti-dão' *f.* promptness, agility, readiness.
pron'-to, =a *adj.* ready, prompt, quick; *adv.* quickly, instantly.
pron-tu-á-rio *m.* police dossier; handbook.
pro-nún-cia *f.* pronunciation.
pro-nun-ci-a-ção' *f.* pronunciation, verdict.
pro-nun-ci-a-men'-to *m.* pronouncement; revolt.
pro-nun-ci-ar' *tr.v.* to pronounce, to utter; —=se *refl.v.* to declare oneself.
pro-nun-ci-á-vel *adj.* pronounceable.
pro-pa-ga-ção' *f.* propagation.
pro-pa-gan'-da *f.* propaganda.
pro-pa-gar' *tr.v.* to propagate.
pro-pe-lir' *tr.v.* to propel.
pro-pen-são' *f.* propension, propensity.
pro-pen'-so, =a *adj.* inclined, disposed.
pro-pi-ci-a-ção' *f.* propitiation.
pro-pí-cio, =a *adj.* propitious.
pro-pi'-na *f.* school fee; membership fee.
pro-pin-qui-da'-de *f.* propinquity.
pro-pín-quo, =a *adj.* close, neighboring.
pro-po-nen'-te *m.*, *f.* proponent.
pro-por' *tr.v.* to propose; to offer; to intend; *intr.v.* to intend; —=se *refl.v.* to offer oneself, to present oneself, to arrange to, to intend to.
pro-por-ção' *f.* proportion.
pro-por-ci-o-nal' *adj.* proportional.
pro-por-ci-o-nar' *tr.v.* to offer, to provide; to proportion.
pro-po-si-ção' *f.* proposition.
pro-pó-si-to *m.* purpose, intent; a — opportunely; in this respect; de — on purpose.
pro-pos'-ta *f.* motion, condition, offer, argument, proposal.
pro-pos'-to *m.* proposition; representative.
pro-pri-e-da'-de *f.* property, characteristic.
pro-pri-e-tá-rio *m.* owner, proprietor.
pró-prio, =a *adj.* own, very, peculiar, same, self, natural, suitable.
pror-ro-ga-ção' *f.* prorogation.
pror-ro-gar' *tr.v.* to prorogue.
pro'-sa *f.* prose.
pro-sa-dor' *m.* prose writer.
pro-sai'-co, =a *adj.* prosaic.
pros-cê-nio *m.* proscenium.
pros-cre-ver' *tr.v.* to proscribe; to banish, to outlaw.
pros-cri-ção' *f.* proscription, banishment.
pros-cri'-to *m.* outlaw, exile.
pros-sé-li-to *m.* proselyte.
pro-só-dia *f.* prosody, pronunciation.
pros-pe-rar' *intr.v.* to prosper.
pros-pe-ri-da'-de *f.* prosperity.
prós-pe-ro, =a *adj.* prosperous.
pros-pe-ti'-vo, =a *adj.* prospective.
pros-pe'-to *m.* prospect; prospectus.
prós-ta-ta *f.* prostate gland.
pros-ti-tu-i-ção' *f.* prostitution.
pros-ti-tu'-ta *f.* prostitute.
pros-tra-ção' *f.* prostration.
pros-trar' *tr.v.* to prostrate; —=se *refl.v.* to fall prone in grief or adoration.
pro-ta-go-nis'-ta *m.*, *f.* protagonist.
pro-te-ção' *f.* protection, support, backing.
pro-te-ger' *tr.v.* to protect, to favor, to back, to guarantee.
pro-te-gi'-do, =a *m.*, *f.* protegée, favorite.
pro-te-í-na *f.* protein.
pro-tes-tan'-te *m.*, *f.* protestant.

pro-tes-tar' *tr.v.*, *intr.v.* to protest.
pro-tes'-to *m.* protest.
pro-te-to-ra'-do *m.* protectorate.
pro-teu' *m.* protean person.
pro-to-co'-lo *m.* protocol.
pró-ton *m.* proton.
pro-to-plas'-ma *m.* protoplasm.
pro-tó-ti-po *m.* prototype.
pro-tu-be-rân-cia *f.* protuberance.
pro'-va *f.* proof; examination; fitting.
pro-va-ção' *f.* test, trial, affliction.
pro-var' *tr.v.* to prove, to test, to suffer; to taste, to sip.
pro-vá-vel *adj.* probable.
pro-ve-dor' *m.* director, manager, superintendent of public or charitable institution.
pro-ve-do-ri'-a *f.* administration, superintendency.
pro-vei'-to *m.* profit, gain, benefit, utility.
pro-vei-to'-so, =a *adj.* profitable, advantageous, useful, advisable.
pro-ve-ni-ên-cia *f.* origin, source.
pro-ve-ni-en'-te *adj.* originating, coming from.
pro-ver' *tr.v.* to provide, to furnish, to endow.
pro-ver-bi-al' *adj.* proverbial.
pro-vér-bio *m.* proverb.
pro-ve'-ta *f.* test tube; measuring cup.
pro-vi-dên-cia *f.* foresight, providence.
pro-vi-den-ci-al' *adj.* providential.
pro-vi-den-ci-ar' *intr.v.* to take measures; *tr.v.* to anticipate.
pro-vi-den'-te *adj.* provident.
pro-vi-men'-to *m.* supplies, stock; appointment, promotion.
pro-vín-ci-a *f.* province.
pro-vin-ci-al' *adj.* provincial.
pro-vin-ci-a-lis'-mo *m.* provincialism.
pro-vir' *intr.v.* to proceed from, to derive from.
pro-vi-são' *f.* provision.
pro-vi-si-o-nal' *adj.* provisional.
pro-vi-só-rio, =a *adj.* provisional, temporary.
pro-vo-ca-ção' *f.* provocation.
pro-vo-car' *tr.v.* to provoke.
pro-vo-ca-ti'-vo, =a *adj.* provocative.
pro-xi-mi-da'-de *f.* proximity, nearness.
pró-xi-mo, =a *adj.* next, near, immediate.
pru-den'-te *adj.* prudent.
pru-mar' *tr.v.* to sound with plumb.
pru'-mo *m.* plumb.
pru-ri-do *m.* itch, itching, temptation.
pru-ri-en'-te *adj.* itching.
pseu-dô-ni-mo *m.* pseudonym.
psi-ca-ná-li-se *f.* psychoanalysis.
psi-co-lo-gi'-a *f.* psychology.
psi-co-ló-gi-co, =a *adj.* psychological.
psi-có-lo-go *m.* psychologist.
psi-co-pa'-ta *adj.*, *m.*, *f.* psychopath.
psi-co-pá-ti-co, =a *adj.* psychopathic.
psi-co'-se *f.* psychosis.
psi-co-te-ra-pi'-a *f.* psychotherapy.
psi'-que *f.* psyche.
psí-qui-co, =a *adj.* psychic.
psi-qui-a-tri'-a *f.* psychiatry.
psi-qui-á-tri-co, =a *adj.* psychiatric.
pto-ma-í-na *f.* ptomaine.
pu-ber-da'-de *f.* puberty.
pu-bli-ca-ção' *f.* publication.
pu-bli-car' *tr.v.* to publish.
pu-bli-ci-da'-de *f.* publicity.
pu-bli-cis'-ta *m.* publicist.
pú-bli-co *m.* public; **pú-bli-co**, =a *adj.* public.

pu-di-cí-cia *f.* modesty, chastity, innocence.

pú-di-co, =a *adj.* modest, chaste.

pu-dim' *m.* pudding; (geol.) conglomerate.

pu-dor' *m.* modesty, timidity, shame, chastity.

pu-e-ril' *adj.* puerile.

pu-e-ri-li-da'-de *f.* puerility.

pu-er-pé-rio *m.* childbirth.

pu-gi-lis'-ta *m., f.* pugilist.

pug-na-ci-da'-de *f.* pugnacity.

pug-nar' *intr.v.* to fight, to battle, to discuss heatedly.

pug-naz' *adj.* pugnacious.

pu-jan'-ça *f.* power, might, strength, force.

pu-jan'-te *adj.* strong, powerful, mighty.

pu-lan'-te *adj.* leaping, jumping, hopping.

pu-lar' *tr.v., intr.v.* to leap, to jump.

pul-cri-tu'-de *f.* pulchritude.

pul'-ga *f.* flea.

pul-gão' *m.* grub, vine-grub.

pu-li-men'-to *m.* polishing; patent leather.

pu-lir' *tr.v.* to polish, to burnish.

pul-mão' *m.* lung.

pul-mo-nar' *adj.* pulmonary.

púl-pi-to *m.* pulpit.

pu'-lo *m.* leap, jump.

pul-sa-ção' *f.* pulsation.

pul-sar' *intr.v.* to pulsate, to throb, to palpitate.

pul-sei'-ra *f.* bracelet.

pul'-so *m.* pulse.

pu-lu-lar' *intr.v.* to bud out rapidly; to grow up, to develop quickly.

pul-ve-ri-zar' *tr.v.* to pulverize.

pul-ve-ro'-so, =a *adj.* powdery.

pu'-ma *m.* puma, cougar.

pun-do-nor' *m.* sense of honor, chivalry.

pun-gen'-te *adj.* pungent.

pun-gir' *tr.v.* to sting, to wound, to afflict, to torture; *intr.v.* to begin to grow.

pu-nha'-do *m.* handful.

pu-nhal' *m.* dagger, poniard.

pu'-nho *m.* fist, closed hand.

pu-ni-ção' *f.* punishment.

pu-nir' *tr.v.* to punish.

pu-ni-ti'-vo, =a *adj.* punitive.

pu-ní-vel *adj.* punishable.

pun-tu'-ra *f.* puncture.

pu-pi'-la *f.* pupil of the eye.

pu-pi-la'-gem *f.* tutelage.

pu-pi'-lo, =a *m., f.* pupil.

pu-ré *m.* or pu-rei'-a *f.* purée.

pu-re'-za *f.* purity.

pur-gan'-te *adj.* purgative.

pur-gar' *tr.v., intr.v.* to purge.

pur-ga-ti'-vo, =a *adj.* purgative.

pur-ga-tó-rio *m.* purgatory.

pu-ri-fi-ca-ção' *f.* purification.

pu-ri-fi-car' *tr.v.* to purify.

pu-ris'-mo *m.* purism.

pu-ris'-ta *m.* purist.

pu'-ro, =a *adj.* pure.

pú-pu-ra *f.* purple.

pur-pu-ra'-do, =a *adj.* cardinal-red, purple; pur-pu-ra'-do *m.* cardinal.

pur-pu-ri'-na *f.* dyestuff prepared from madder.

pu-ru-lên-cia *f.* purulence.

pu-ru-len'-to, =a *adj.* purulent.

pus' *m.* pus.

pús-tu-la *f.* pustule, pimple.

pus-tu-lo'-so, =a *adj.* pimply.

pu-si-lâ-ni-me *adj., m., f.* pusillanimous; cowardly or weak person.

pu-si-la-ni-mi-da'-de *f.* pusillanimity.

pu-ta-ti'-vo, =a *adj.* putative; supposed.

pu-tre-fa-ção' *f.* putrefaction.

pu-tre-fa'-to, =a *adj.* putrefied.

pu-tre-fa-zer' *tr.v.* to rot, to putrefy.

pu-tres-cên-cia *f.* rotting, putrescence.

pú-tri-do, =a *adj.* putrid, rotten.

pu-xa'-da *f.* lead (in cards).

pu-xa-dei'-ra *f.* pull-strap (of shoe or boot).

pu-xa'-do *m.* wing (of a building), annex; pu-xa'-do, =a *adj.* elegant, spruce; tipsy; expensive.

pu-xa-dor' *m.* knob, handle.

pu-xan'-te *adj.* pushing; stimulating.

pu-xão' *m.* push, shove, jerk.

pu-xar' *tr.v.* to pull, to draw, to drag, to pull down, to attract; —-se *refl.v.* to dress elegantly.

Q

See page 12—GUIDE TO REFORMED SPELLING used in this Dictionary

Q, q *m.* Q, q, sixteenth letter of the alphabet.

qua'-dra *f.* square, square room; square bed (in a garden); side of a square; four-spot (at cards); area equal to 132 square meters; age, period, time.

qua-dra'-do *m.* square, second power; gusset (in shirt sleeve); qua-dra'-do, =a *adj.* square, squared.

qua-drân-gu-lo *m.* quadrangle.

qua-dran'-te *m.* quadrant; clock face.

qua-drar' *tr.v.* to square, to raise to the second power; *intr.v.* to please, to suit.

qua-drá-ti-co, =a *adj.* quadratic.

qua-dra-tu'-ra *f.* quadrature, squaring.

qua-dri-co-lor' *adj.* having four different colors.

qua-dri-ê-nio *m.* quadrennium, period of four years.

qua-dril' *m.* hip; rump (cattle).

qua-dri-la-te-ral' *adj.* four-sided, quadrilateral.

qua-dri-lá-te-ro *m.* quadrilateral.

qua-dri'-lha *f.* quadrille; band of robbers; beat (of a policeman); squadron, gang, cavalcade.

qua-dri-lhei'-ro *m.* night-watchman, guard, policeman.

qua-dri-nô-mio *m.* quadrinomial.

quad-ri-va-len'-te *adj.* quadrivalent.

qua'-dro *m.* picture, painting; map, table, list; black-board; scene; staff.

qua-drú-pe-de *adj., m.* quadruped.

quá-dru-plo *m.* =o, =a *adj.* quadruple; fourfold.

qual' *pron.* which, that; as; *interj.* (expressing surprise or horror).

qua-li-da'-de *f.* quality.

qua-li-fi-ca-ção' f. qualification.
qua-li-fi-car' tr.v. to quality.
qua-li-fi-cá-vel adj. qualifiable.
qua-li-ta-ti'-vo, -a adj. qualitative.
qual-quer' adj., pron. any, whoever, whatever.
quan'-do adv., conj. when; — menos at least; de — em — from time to time.
quan-ti'-a f. sum of money; amount.
quan-ti-da'-de f. quantity.
quan-ti-ta-ti'-vo, -a adj. quantitative.
quan'-to adj., pron. how much; how many.
quão' adv. how, as.
qua-ren'-ta m. forty.
qua-ren-tão' m. man about forty years old.
qua-ren-te'-na f. period of forty days.
qua-res'-ma f. Lent.
quar'-ta f. quarter; Wednesday.
quar-ta'-do, -a adj. divided into four parts.
quar-te-ar' tr.v. to divide into four equal parts.
quar-tei-rão' m. row of houses (joined together), block; fourth part of a hundred.
quar-tel' m. barracks.
quar-te-lei'-ro m. orderly.
quar-te'-to m. quartet.
quar-ti'-nha f. earthenware, porous, water bottle.
quar'-to, -a adj. fourth; quar'-to m. quarter; room.
qua'-si adv. almost.
qua-tor'-ze m. fourteen.
qua-ter'-no, -a adj. quaternary.
qua'-tro m. four.
qua-tro-cen'-tos, -as adj. four hundred.
que pron. which, that; conj. that; than.
quê m. something; difficulty, complication.
que'-bra-luz' m. eye-shade, lamp-shade.
que'-bra-mar' m. break-water.
que'-bra-no-zes m. nut-cracker.
que-bran-ta-men'-to m. breaking, infringement, weariness, dejection.
que-bran-tar' tr.v. to break, to break in, to weary, to humble, to dishearten; —se refl.v. to become dejected, to lose courage.
que-bran'-to m. prostration, weakness, grief; evil eye.
que-brar' tr.v. to break, to shatter; to interrupt; to weaken; intr.v. to break, to fail, to become insolvent, to slacken.
que'-da f. fall, falling; ruin, sin; falls.
quê-do, -a adj. quiet, tranquil, motionless, slow.
quar'-ta-fei'-ra f. Wednesday.
que-fa-zer' m. or que-fa-ze'-res m.pl. occupation, business, task.
quei'-jo m. cheese.
quei'-ma f. burning, fire.
quei-ma'-da f. burning of fields.
quei-ma'-do m. burnt odor or taste.
quei-ma-du'-ra f. burn, wound caused by burn.
quei-mar' tr.v. to burn, to scald; intr.v. to burn, to be hot; —se refl.v. to get burned; to get angry, to become impatient.
quei'-xa f. complaint.
quei-xal' m. molar, grinder.
quei-xar'-se refl.v. to complain, to lament, to moan.
quei-xei'-ro m. jaw tooth, molar.
quei'-xo m. jaw, chin.

quei-xo'-so, -a adj. complaining, plaintive.
quem' pron. who, whom; whoever, whomever.
quen'-te adj. hot; biting, animated, bright; enthusiastic.
quen-tu'-ra f. heat, hotness.
que-re'-la f. accusation, charge, suit; complaint, plaintive song.
que-re-lan'-te m., f. complainant.
que-re-lar' intr.v. to go to court, to bring suit.
que-rer' tr.v. to wish, to desire; to like; to demand.
que-ri'-do, -a adj. dear, beloved.
que-ro-se'-ne m. kerosene.
que-ru-bim' m. cherubim.
qué-ru-lo, -a adj. querulous, complaining.
que-si'-to m. query, inquiry.
ques-tão' f. question.
ques-ti-o-ná-rio m. questionnaire.
qui-a'-bo m. okra.
qui-ban'-do m. coarse straw sieve, or screen, used in cleaning coffee, rice, etc.
qui-es-cen'-te adj. quiescent.
qui-e'-to, -a adj. quiet.
qui-e-tu'-de f. quietude.
qui-la'-te m. carat; (fig.) excellence, superiority.
qui'-lo m. chyle; kilogram.
qui-lo'-so, -a adj. chylous.
qui-lô-me-tro m. kilometer.
qui-lo-va'-te m. kilowatt.
qui-me'-ra f. chimera.
qui-mé-ri-co, -a adj. chimerical.
quí-mi-ca f. chemistry.
qui-mi-co m. chemist; quí-mi-co, -a adj. chemical.
quí'-mo m. chyme.
qui-mo'-no m. kimono.
qui'-na f. cinchona, Peruvian bark; corner; five-spot (at cards); each of the five shields which constitute the arms of Portugal.
quin-cun'-ce m. quincunx (arrangement of five objects, particularly trees, with one at each corner and one in the middle).
qui-nhão' m. share, allowance, lot.
qui-nhen-tis'-ta adj. of the sixteenth century.
qui-nhen'-tos, -as adj. five hundred.
qui-ni'-na f. quinine.
quin-qua-gé-si-ma f. period of fifty days.
quin-qua-gé-si-mo, -a adj. fiftieth.
quin'-ta f. farm, ranch; Thursday.
quin-ta-es-sên-cia f. quintessence.
quin'-ta-fei'-ra f. Thursday.
quin-tal' m. vegetable garden, orchard.
quin'-to, -a adj. fifth.
quín-tu-plo, -a adj. quintuple.
quin'-ze m. fifteen.
quin-ze'-na f. fifteen days, fortnight.
qui-os'-que m. kiosk, news-stand.
qui-ro-man-ci'-a f. chiromancy, palmistry.
quis'-to m. cyst.
quis'-to, -a adj. loved, beloved.
qui-tan'-da f. greengrocery.
qui-tan-dei'-ro, -a m., f. greengrocer.
qui'-te adj. free, even, quit, exempt, discharged, released.
qui-xo-tes'-co, -a adj. quixotic.
qui-xo-tis'-mo m. quixotism.
quo-ci-en'-te m. quotient.
quo-ti-di-a'-no, -a adj. daily, day after day.
quo-ti-za-ção' f. fixing quota; share.

quo-ti-zar' *tr.v.* to distribute by quota; to fix the price of.

que'-bra *f.* break, loss, damage, failure, bankruptcy, ruin, defect, breach.

que'-bra=ca-be'-ça *m.* and *f.* worry, puzzle, sorrow.

que'-bra=cos-te'-la *m.* strong embrace.

que-bra-dei'-ra *f.* worry, puzzle, annoyance.

que-bra'-do *m.* fraction.

que-bra-dou'-ro *m.* breakers.

R

See page 12—GUIDE TO REFORMED SPELLING used in this Dictionary

R, r *m.* R, r, seventeenth letter of the alphabet.

rã' *f.* frog.

ra-ba'-do, =a *adj.* provided with a tail, provided with a handle.

ra-ba-na'-da *f.* French toast; stroke with the tail.

ra-ba-ne'-te *m.* radish.

ra-bão' *m.* short tail, stubby tail.

ra-be'-ca *f.* fiddle, violin.

ra-be-cão' *m.* bass violin.

ra-bei'-ra *f.* trail, train of dress.

rá-bia *f.* rabies.

ra-bi-cur'-to, =a *adj.* short-tailed.

rá-bi-do, =a *adj.* rabid.

ra-bi-o'-so, =a *adj.* angry, irritated.

ra-bi-lon'-go, =a *adj.* long-tailed.

ra-bí-ni-co, =a *adj.* rabbinical.

ra-bi'-no *m.* rabbi.

ra-bis'-ca *f.* scrawl, scribbling.

ra-bis-car' *tr.v.*, *intr.v.* to scrawl, to scribble.

ra'-bo *m.* tail, tail feathers; handle; backside.

ra-bo'-so, =a *adj.* having a long tail.

ra-bu'-do, =a *adj.* having a long tail, long-tailed.

ra-bu-gen'-to, =a *adj.* whimpering.

ra'-ça *f.* race, breed; generation.

ra-ção' *f.* ration, allowance.

ra'-cha *f.* gap, slit, chink; chip.

ra-cha-dei'-ra *f.* grafting-knife.

ra-char' *tr.v.* to split.

ra-ci-al' *adj.* racial.

ra-ci'-mo *m.* bunch, bunch of grapes.

ra-ci-mo'-so, =a *adj.* full of bunches, full of grapes.

ra-ci-o-ci-nar' *intr.v.* to reason.

ra-ci-o-cí-nio *m.* reasoning.

ra-ci-o-nal' *adj.* rational.

ra-ci-o-nar' *tr.v.* to ration.

ra-con'-to *m.* narration.

ra-di-a-ção' *f.* radiation.

ra-di-a-dor' *m.* radiator.

ra-di-al' *adj.* radial.

ra-di-an'-te *adj.* radiant, radiating.

ra-di-ar' *intr.v.* to beam, to shine, to sparkle; *tr.v.* to light up, to put a halo on.

ra-di-cal' *adj.*, *m.* radical.

ra-dí-cu-la *f.* radicle.

rá-dio *m.* radium; radius; *f.* radio.

ra-di-o-a-ti-vi-da'-de *f.* radioactivity.

ra-di-o-a-ti'-vo, =a *adj.* radioactive.

ra-di-o-e-le-tri-ci-da'-de *f.* radio-electricity.

ra-di-o-gra'-ma *m.* radiogram.

ra-di-o-lo-gi'-a *f.* radiology.

ra-di-o-ló-gi-co, =a *adj.* radiologic.

ra-di-ô-me-tro *m.* radiometer.

ra-di-os-co-pi'-a *f.* radioscopy.

ra-di-os-có-pi-co, =a *adj.* radioscopic.

ra - di - o - te - le - fo - ni'-a *f.* radio-telephony.

ra-di-o-te-le-gra-fi'-a *f.* radio-telegraphy, wireless.

ra-di-o-te-ra-pi'-a *f.* radio-therapy.

rá-fia *f.* raffia.

ra-gú *m.* ragout.

rai'-a *f.* mark, trace; lines in palm of hand.

rai-ar' *tr.v.* to streak; *intr.v.* to appear on the horizon; to border (on).

ra-í-nha *f.* queen.

rai'-o *m.* beam of light, ray; lightning; =s X X rays.

rai'-va *f.* rabies; anger, fury.

rai-ven'-to, =a *adj.* infuriated, easily angered.

rai-vo'-so, =a *adj.* furious.

ra-iz' *f.* root.

rai-za'-me *m.* mass of roots of a plant.

ra-já *m.* rajah.

ra-ja'-da *f.* blast of wind.

ra'-la *f.* rattling sound in breathing, death rattle.

ra-la-ção' *f.* grating, scraping.

ra-la-dor' *m.* grater.

ra-lar' *tr.v.* to grate, to scrape; to annoy; to irritate.

ra-lhar' *intr.v.* to rail at, to reprehend.

ra'-lho *m.* scolding; heated discussion.

ra'-lo *m.* bottom of sieve, grater.

ra-mi-fi-ca-ção' *f.* ramification.

ra-mi-fi-car' *tr.v.* to divide into branches, to subdivide.

ra'-ma *f.* boughs; branches and leaves; tree-top.

ra-ma'-do, =a *adj.* full of branches.

ra-ma'-gem *f.* branches; flowered work.

ra-ma-lhe'-te *m.* bouquet, corsage.

ra-ma'-lho *m.* large branch (generally cut from tree).

ra'-mo *m.* branch.

ra-mo'-so, =a *adj.* full of branches.

ram'-pa *f.* ramp; inclined plane.

ran'-ço *m.* rancidity.

ran-ço'-so, =a *adj.* rancid.

ran-cor' *m.* rancor.

ran-co-ro'-so, =a *adj.* rancorous.

ran-ger' *intr.v.* to creak, to grind; *tr.v.* to grind, to gnash.

ran-zin'-za *f.* grouchiness, bad humor.

ra-pa'-ce *adj.* rapacious.

ra-pa-ci-da'-de *f.* rapacity.

ra-pa-dei'-ra *f.* scraper, rasp.

ra-pa-du'-ra *f.* shavings; crust of sugar; molded cakes of cane sugar.

ra-pa-pé *m.* drawing back one's foot in making a bow; obsequiousness.

ra-par' *tr.v.* to scrape, to rasp, to wear down, to grate; to cheat; *intr.v.* to scratch, to scratch the ground.

ra-pa-ri'-ga *f.* girl, maiden.

ra-pa-ri-ga'-da *f.* group of girls.

ra-paz' *m.* boy, youth, lad; colored boy.

ra-pa-zi-a'-da *f.* group of boys.

ra-pa-zo'-la *m.* grown-up boy; big boy (i.e., man acting like a boy).
ra-pé *m.* snuff.
ra-pi-dez' *f.* rapidity.
rá-pi-do, =a *adj.* rapid; rá-pi-do *m.* rapids; express train.
ra-pi'-na *f.* rapine, robbery, extorsion, usury.
ra-pi-na'-gem *f.* pillaging.
ra-pi-nar' *tr.v.* to plunder, to pillage.
ra-po-si'-nho *m.* young fox; stink, bad odor.
ra-po'-so, =a *m., f.* fox.
rap-só-dia *f.* rhapsody.
rap-tar' *tr.v.* to kidnap, to abduct.
rap'-to *m.* abduction; rapine; rap'-to, =a *adj.* rapt, enraptured.
ra-que'-ta *f.* racket (for tennis).
ra-quí-ti-co, =a *adj.* afflicted with rickets.
ra-qui-tis'-mo *m.* rickets.
ra-re-ar' *tr.v.* to make rare; *intr.v.* to become rare.
ra-re-fa-ção' *f.* rarefaction.
ra-re-fa'-to, =a *adj.* rarefied.
ra-re-fa-zer' *tr.v.* to rarefy.
ra-re-fei'-to, =a *adj.* rarefied.
ra-re'-za *f.* rareness, rarity.
ra-ri-da'-de *f.* rarity.
ra'-ro, =a *adj.* rare, thin; ra'-ro *adv.* seldom.
ras-ca-dei'-ra *f.* curry comb.
ras-car' *tr.v.* to scratch, to scrape.
ras-cu'-nho *m.* outline, sketch, first plan.
ras-ga'-do, =a *adj.* torn, split, open.
ras-ga-du'-ra *f.* tearing, opening, tear.
ras-gão' *m.* rent, tear; cut (in hill or mountain).
ras-gar' *tr.v.* to tear, to break, to furrow, to trace, to cut.
ras'-go *m.* flourish (in writing); touch of eloquence; flash of wit.
ra'-so, =a *adj.* flat, shallow, smooth.
ras'-pa *f.* scraping, shaving.
ras-pa-dei'-ra *f.* scraper.
ras-pa-dor' *m.* scraper.
ras-pão' *m.* scratch.
ras-par' *tr.v.* to scratch, to scrape, to grate, to erase.
ras-tão' *m.* runner (of vine or plant).
ras-tei'-ro, =a *adj.* crawling, creeping; humble, ordinary, cringing.
ras-te-jar' *tr.v.* to track, to trail, to detect; *intr.v.* to creep, to crawl.
ras-te-lar' *tr.v.* to comb (hemp or flax).
ras-te'-lo *m.* comb; harrow.
ras'-to *m.* trail, vestige, sign.
ra-ta'-da *f.* nest of mice, rat nest.
ra-te-ar' *tr.v.* to rate, to determine according to standard or scale.
ra-tei'-o *m.* rate, ratio.
ra-tei'-ro, =a *adj.* rat-catching.
ra-ti'-ce *f.* extravagance, eccentricity.
ra-ti-fi-ca-ção' *f.* ratification.
ra-ti-fi-car' *tr.v.* to ratify.
ra'-to *m.* rat.
ra-to-ei'-ra *f.* rat-trap.
ra-vi'-na *f.* ravine.
ra-zão' *f.* reason, right.
ra-zo-ar' *intr.v.* to reason.
ra-zo-á-vel *adj.* reasonable.
re-a-ção' *f.* reaction.
re-a-ci-o-ná-rio, =a *adj.* reactionary.
re-a-gir' *intr.v.* to react.
re-al' *adj.* real, true; royal; *m.* real (monetary unit, of which réis is plural).
re-al-çar' *tr.v.* to elevate, to make salient; to enhance.
re-al'-ce *m.* distinction; relievo, luster.
re-a-le'-za *f.* royalty.

re-a-li-da'-de *f.* reality.
re-a-li-za-ção' *f.* realization.
re-al-i-zar' *tr.v.* to realize.
re-a-li-zá-vel *adj.* realizable.
re-a-pa-re-cer' *intr.v.* to reappear.
re-a-ti'-vo, =a *adj.* reactive.
re-bai-xa-men'-to *m.* lowering.
re-bai-xar' *tr.v.* to lower, to tear down; to discredit; —=se *refl.v.* to lower oneself, to humiliate oneself.
re-bai'-xo *m.* lowering.
re-ba'-nho *m.* flock; (fig.) congregation, parishioners.
re-bel'-de *adj., m.* rebellious, rebel.
re-bel-di'-a *f.* rebelliousness.
re-be-li-ão' *f.* rebellion.
re-ben-tar *intr.v., tr.v.* to explode, to arise, to bud out; to break with loud sound.
re-ben'-to *m.* bud, sprout.
re-bi'-te *m.* rivet.
re-bo-an'-te *adj.* echoing.
re-bo-ar' *intr.v.* to echo.
re-bo-ca-dor' *m.* tug-boat; plasterer, white-washer.
re-bo-car' *tr.v.* to plaster; to tow.
re-bô-co *m.* plaster.
re-bo'-que *m.* towing.
re-ca'-do *m.* message; =s *m.pl.* compliments, remembrances.
re-cal-ci-tran'-te *adj.* recalcitrant.
re-cal-ci-trar' *intr.v.* to kick, to resist, to object.
re-can'-to *m.* hiding-place; hidden, quiet spot; recess.
re-ca-pi-tu-la-ção' *f.* recapitulation.
re-ca-pi-tu-lar' *tr.v.* to recapitulate.
re-ce-ar' *tr.v.* to fear; *intr.v.* to be afraid, to be fearful.
re-ce-be-dor' *m.* receiver, tax-collector.
re-ce-be-do-ri'-a *f.* tax-collecting office.
re-ce-ber' *tr.v.* to receive, to entertain, to welcome.
re-cei'-o *m.* fear.
re-cei'-ta *f.* income, receipts; prescription.
re-cei-tar' *tr.v., intr.v.* to prescribe.
re-cém=nas-ci'-do, =a *m., f., adj.* newborn.
re-cen-se-a-men'-to *m.* census.
re-cen'-te *adj.* recent.
re-ce-o'-so, =a *adj.* timid, fearful.
re-cep-ção' *f.* reception.
re-cep-tá-cu-lo *m.* receptacle, retreat, place of refuge, shelter, reservoir.
re-cep-ti-vi-da'-de *f.* receptivity.
re-cep-ti'-vo, =a *adj.* receptive.
re-cep-tor' *m.* receiver.
re-ces-si'-vo, =a *adj.* recessive.
re-ces'-so *m.* recess; retreat.
re-che-ar' *tr.v.* to stuff, to fill with dressing.
re-chei'-o *m.* stuffing, dressing.
re-ci'-bo *m.* receipt.
re-ci'-fe *m.* reef, rocks near surface of water.
re-cin'-to *m.* enclosure, sanctuary.
re-ci-pi-en'-te *adj., m.* recipient; container, receptacle.
re-ci-pro-ca-ção' *f.* reciprocation.
re-ci-pro-car' *tr.v.* to reciprocate.
re-ci-pro-ci-da'-de *f.* reciprocity.
re-cí-pro-co, =a *adj.* reciprocal.
re-ci-tan'-te *m., f.* soloist.
re-ci-tar' *tr.v.* to recite, to declaim.
re-ci-ta-ti'-vo *m.* recitative.
re-cla-ma-ção' *f.* protest.
re-cla-mar' *intr.v.* to protest; *tr.v.* to claim, to demand, to require.

re-cla'-me *m.* advertisement, announcement.

re-cla'-mo *m.* protest; bird call, decoy-whistle; enticement, bait, lure.

re-cli-nar' *tr.v.* to lean; —‍se *refl.v.* to recline, to lie down, to rest.

re-clu-são' *f.* reclusion.

re-clu'-so, ‍a *m., f., adj.* recluse.

re-co-lher' *tr.v.* to gather, to harvest, to receive, to collect, to shelter, to withdraw, to pull in; *intr.v.* to return, to retire; to meditate; —‍se *refl.v.* to return home, to take refuge, to take shelter, to withdraw from the world; to meditate.

re-co-lhi-men'-to *m.* harvesting; refuge, shelter; boarding-school; retreat; meditation, thought.

re-co-men-da-ção' *f.* recommendation.

re-co-men-dar' *tr.v.* to recommend.

re-com-pen'-sa *f.* recompense, reward.

re-com-pen-sar' *tr.v.* to recompense.

re-con-ci-li-a-ção' *f.* reconciliation.

re-con-ci-li-ar' *tr.v.* to reconcile.

re-con-ci-li-á-vel *adj.* reconcilable.

re-côn-di-to, ‍a *adj.* recondite.

re-co-nhe-cer' *tr.v.* to recognize.

re-co-nhe-ci-men'-to *m.* acknowledgment, recognition.

re-co-pi-lar' *tr.v.* to compile.

re-cor-da-ção' *f.* memory; remembrance.

re-cor-dar' *tr.v.* to remember, to bring to mind.

re-cor-tar' *tr.v.* to cut in figures, to cut out; to pink.

re-cor-ti'-lha *f.* pinking scissors, pinking iron.

re-cre-a-ção' *f.* recreation.

re-crei'-o *m.* diversion, recreation.

re-cri-mi-na-ção' *f.* recrimination.

re-cri-mi-nar' *tr.v.* to recriminate.

re-cru'-ta *m.* recruit.

re-cru-ta-men'-to *m.* recruiting.

re-cru-tar' *tr.v.* to recruit.

re-cu-ar' *intr.v.* to withdraw, to move back, to step back, to lose ground, to recoil.

re-cu'-o *m.* withdrawal, recoil, recoiling.

re-cu-pe-ra-ção' *f.* recuperation.

re-cu-pe-rar' *tr.v.* to recuperate.

re-cu-pe-ra-ti'-vo, ‍a *adj.* recuperative.

re-cur'-so *m.* recourse; ‍s *m.pl.* property, resources.

re-cu'-sa *f.* refusal.

re-cu-sar' *tr.v.* to refuse.

re-da-ção' *f.* editing; editorial staff.

re-da-tor' *m.* editor.

re'-de *f.* net, network; netting, hammock.

ré-de-a *f.* rein.

re-den-ção' *f.* redemption.

re-den-tor' *m.* redeemer.

re-do-len'-te *adj.* redolent.

re-do'-ma *f.* glass cylinder (to protect delicate machines or objects from dust).

re-don-de'-za *f.* roundness; surroundings.

re-don'-do, ‍a *adj.* round, circular, spherical; plump.

re-dor' *m.* contour, circuit, neighborhood; ao — around, near by, round about.

re-du-ção' *f.* reduction.

re-dun-dân-cia *f.* redundancy.

re-dun-dan'-te *adj.* redundant, superfluous.

re-dun-dar' *intr.v.* to be superabundant.

re-du'-to *m.* redoubt; enclosure.

re-du-zir' *tr.v.* to reduce, to cut down, to decrease.

re-fei-ção' *f.* meal, repast.

re-fei-tó-rio *m.* refectory.

re-fém *m.* hostage.

re-fe-rên-cia *f.* reference.

re-fe-ri'-do, ‍a *adj.* above-mentioned.

re-fe-rir' *tr.v.* to tell, to narrate; to attribute; —‍se *refl.v.* to allude, to refer.

re-fi-na-ção' *f.* refining, purification.

re-fi-na-men'-to *m.* refining, refinement, subtlety.

re-fi-na-ri'-a *f.* refinery.

re-fle-ti'-do, ‍a *adj.* prudent, thoughtful.

re-fle-tir' *tr.v.* to reflect.

re-fle-tor' *m.* reflector.

re-fle-xão' *f.* reflection.

re-fle-xi'-vo, ‍a *adj.* reflexive.

re-fle'-xo *m.* reflection; re-fle'-xo, ‍a *adj.* reflex.

re-fôl-go *m.* rest period, relief.

re-for-ça'-do, ‍a *adj.* vigorous, robust.

re-for-çar' *tr.v.* to strengthen, to reenforce.

re-fôr-ço *m.* re-inforcement, relief.

re-for'-ma *f.* reform; discharge.

re-for-ma-ção' *f.* reformation, reform.

re-for-ma'-do *m.* discharged soldier.

re-for-mar' *tr.v.* to reform, to modify, to improve; to retire.

re-for-ma-tó-rio *m.* reformatory.

re-fra-ção' *f.* refraction.

re-f.'an-ger' *tr.v.* to refract.

re-fra-tar' *tr.v.* to refract.

re-fra-tá-rio, ‍a *adj.* refractory.

re-fres-can'-te *adj.* refreshing.

re-fres-car' *tr.v.* to refresh, to cool, to alleviate; *intr.v.* to become cool, to cool off; to get supplies.

re-frês-co *m.* refreshment; cooling; relief; fresh provisions.

re-fri-ge-ra-ção' *f.* refrigeration.

re-fri-ge-ra-dor' *m.* refrigerator.

re-fu-gi-a'-do *m.* refugee.

re-fu-gi-ar'-se *refl.v.* to seek refuge.

re-fú-gio *m.* refuge.

re-ful-gên-cia *f.* refulgence.

re-ful-gen'-te *adj.* refulgent.

re-fu-ta-ção' *f.* refutation.

re-fu-tar' *tr.v.* to refute.

re-fu-tá-vel *adj.* refutable.

re'-ga *f.* watering, sprinkling.

re-ga'-ço *m.* lap.

re-ga-di'-o *m.* watering.

re-ga-dor' *m.* watering can.

re-ga-du'-ra *f.* sprinkling, watering.

re-ga-lar' *tr.v.* to treat, to please, to make a gift to.

re-ga-li'-a *f.* royal prerogative.

re-ga'-lo *m.* pleasure, contentment; gift, present; muff.

re-gar' *tr.v.* to water, to sprinkle.

re-ga'-ta *f.* regatta.

re-ga'-to *m.* small stream, creek.

re-ge-ne-ra-dor' *m.* regenerator.

re-ge-ne-rar' *tr.v.* to regenerate.

re-ge-ne-ra-ti'-vo, ‍a *adj.* regenerative

re-gên-cia *f.* regency.

re-gen'-te *m., f.* regent.

re-ger' *tr.v.* to rule, to govern; to direct.

ré-gia *f.* (poet.) royal palace.

re-gi-cí-dio *m.* regicide.

re-gi-ão' *f.* region.

re-gi'-me *m.* regime; regimen; administration; diet; (gram.) object.

re-gi-men-tal' *adj.* regimental.

re-gi-men-tar' *tr.v.* to regiment.

re-gi-men'-to *m.* regiment; discipline; regulation; procedure.

ré-gio, ‍a *adj.* royal.

re-gi-o-nal' *adj.* regional.

re-gi-o-na-lis'-mo *m.* regionalism.

re-gis-tar' *tr.v.* to register; to record.

re-gis'-to *m.* registration, recording; register.

re-gis-trar' *tr.v.* to register, to record.

re-gis'-tro *m.* registration, recording; register.

re-go-zi-jar' *tr.v.* to cheer, to give joy to.

re-go-zi'-jo *m.* rejoicing, deep pleasure, contentment.

re'-gra *f.* rule, principle, model, line, row; religious order; moderation.

re-gra-deí'-ra *f.* ruler.

re-gra'-do, **-a** *adj.* sensible, prudent.

re-grar' *tr.v.* to rule lines on; to regulate, to moderate.

re-gres-são' *f.* return; regression.

re-gres-sar' *intr.v.* to return; to regress.

re-gres-si'-vo, **-a** *adj.* regressive.

re-gres'-so *m.* return; resort.

ré-gua *f.* ruler, yard stick.

ré-gua-tê *f.* T-square.

re-gu-la-dor' *m.* regulator, governor.

re-gu-lar' *adj.* regular; *tr.v.* to regulate, to direct, to guide; to determine; *intr.v.* to be usual, to be the rule; to run well.

re-gu-la-ri-da'-de *f.* regularity.

re-gu-la-ri-zar' *tr.v.* to regularize, to regulate, to put in order, to adapt.

re-gur-gi-tar' *tr.v.* to vomit, to regurgitate; *intr.v.* to overflow, to be full.

re-ha-bi-li-tar'*tr.v.* to rehabilitate; —**-se** *refl.v.* to become rehabilitated.

re-ha-ver' *tr.v.* to recover, to get back, to repossess.

rei' *m.* king.

rei-na'-do *m.* reign, kingdom.

rei-nar' *intr.v.* to reign.

rei'-no *m.* kingdom.

re-in-te-grar' *tr.v.* to restore, to renew.

re-i-te-rar' *tr.v.* to reiterate, to repeat.

rei-tor' *m.* director, president, principal, rector.

rei-to-ra'-do *m.* rectorship.

rei-to-ri'-a *f.* rectorship, rectorate.

re-jei-ção' *f.* rejection.

re-jei-tar' *tr.v.* to reject.

re-ju-bi-lar'-se *refl.v.* to be overjoyed.

re-ju-ve-nes-cer' *tr.v.* to rejuvenate; *intr.v.* to be rejuvenated; —**-se** *refl.v.* to say that one is older than he really is.

re-ju-ve-nes-ci-men'-to *m.* rejuvenescence.

re-la-ção' *f.* relation; notice, description; list, roll.

re-la-ci-o-nar' *tr.v.* to relate, to narrate; to list; —**-se** *refl.v.* to enter into relations.

re-lam-pa-de-jar' *intr.v.* to lighten.

re-lâm-pa-go *m.* lightning; flash of lightning.

re-lam-pa-gue-ar' *intr.v.* to lighten.

re-lam-pe-jar' *intr.v.* to lighten.

re-lan'-ce *m.* glance; de — by chance.

re-lan-ce-ar' *tr.v.* to glance at, to look rapidly at.

re-lap'-so *m.* back-slider; **re-lap'-so**, **-a** *adj.* stubborn; impenitent.

re-la-tar' *tr.v.* to narrate, to relate.

re-la-ti'-vo, **-a** *adj.* relative.

re-la-tor' *m.* reporter; story-teller.

re-la-tó-rio *m.* report.

re-la-xa-ção' *f.* relaxation.

re-la-xa'-do, **-a** *adj.* loose, slack; careless, negligent.

re-la-xar' *tr.v.* to relax, to slacken; to exempt, to forgive, to moderate; —**-se** *refl.v.* to become remiss, to get careless; to get weak.

re'-les *adj.* despicable, ordinary, very weak, mean.

re-le-vân-cia *f.* relevancy.

re-le-van'-te *adj.* relevant.

re-le-var' *tr.v.* to point out, to emphasize; to pardon, forgive, to allow; to mitigate; *intr.v.* to matter, to be important.

re-lê-vo *m.* relief; distinction.

rê-lha *f.* wing of plow.

re-lhei'-ra *f.* furrow opened by plow wing.

re-li-cá-rio *m.* reliquary.

re-li-gi-ão' *f.* religion.

re-li-gi-o'-so, **-a** *m.*, *f.*, *adj.* religious.

re-lí-quia *f.* relic.

re-ló-gio *m.* clock; watch; (Brazil) gas or electric meter; — **de sol** *m.* sun dial.

re-lo-jo-ei'-ro *m.* watchmaker.

re-lu-tân-cia *f.* reluctance.

re-lu-tan'-te *adj.* reluctant.

rel'-va *f.* sod, turf, sward.

rel-va'-do *m.* turfed area.

re-mar' *tr.v.*, *intr.v.* to row.

re-ma-tar' *tr.v.* to end, to conclude, to terminate; *intr.v.*, to end, to come to the end.

re-ma'-te *m.* conclusion, end; fastener; finial.

re-me-di-ar' *tr.v.* to remedy, to treat, to cure.

re-mé-dio *m.* remedy; expedient; aid, help.

re-men'-do *m.* patch.

re-mes'-sa *f.* remittance; shipment.

re-me-ten'-te *m.* remitter; shipper.

re-me-ter' *tr.v.* to send, to ship, to dispatch; to remit.

re-mi-nis-cên-cia *f.* reminiscence.

re-mir' *tr.v.* to save, to redeem, to exonerate.

re-mis-são' *f.* remission.

re-mis'-so, **-a** *adj.* remiss.

re-mi-tir' *tr.v.* to pardon, to restore; *intr.v.* to have intervals of less intensity.

re'-mo *m.* oar.

re-mon'-ta *f.* remount.

re-mon-tar' *tr.v.* to raise, to remount, to mend, to reform.

re-mor'-so *m.* remorse.

re-mo'-to, **-a** *adj.* remote.

re-mo-ver' *tr.v.* to remove, to transfer.

re-mo-ví-vel *adj.* removable.

re-mu-ne-ra-ção' *f.* remuneration.

re-mu-ne-rar' *tr.v.* to remunerate.

re-mu-ne-ra-ti'-vo, **-a** *adj.* remunerative.

re-nas-cen'-ça *f.* renascence; Renaissance.

re-nas-cen'-te *adj.* renascent.

ren'-da *f.* lace; rental, income, receipts.

ren-da'-do, **-a** *adj.* trimmed with lace.

ren-da-ri'-a *f.* lace-making, lace industry.

ren-dei'-ro, **-a** *m.*, *f.* lace-maker, lace merchant; renter.

ren-der' *tr.v.* to conquer, to subject; to yield, to lend; to change, to substitute; *intr.v.* to be productive; to crack open; —**-se** *refl.v.* to surrender, to give in.

ren-di-ção' *f.* surrender; ransom.

ren-di'-lha *f.* narrow, delicate lace.

ren-di-lha'-do, **-a** *adj.* lacy, delicately made.

ren-di-men'-to *m.* surrender; yield; offering; efficiency; hernia.

ren-do'-so, **-a** *adj.* lucrative, profitable.

re-ne-ga'-do *m.* renegade.

re-ne-gar' *tr.v.* to abjure, to renounce, to belie, to disown.

re-no'-me *m.* renown, fame, reputation.

re-no-var' *tr.v.* to renew, to renovate; *intr.v.* to put out shoots or sprouts.
ren'-te *adj.* near, short, close.
re-nún-cia *f.* renunciation, reneging.
re-nun-ci-a-ção' *f.* renunciation.
re-nun-ci-ar' *tr.v.* to renounce, to give up; *intr.v.* to give up; to renege.
re-or-ga-ni-zar' *tr.v.* to reorganize.
re-ós-ta-to *m.* rheostat.
re-pa-ra-ção' *f.* reparation; repairs.
re-pa-rar' *tr.v.* to repair, to mend, to restore, to satisfy; *intr.v.* to observe, to pay attention, to be careful.
re-pa'-ro *m.* repair; entrenchment; observation, notice, attention; restoration.
re-par-ti-ção' *f.* distribution; department, secretariat.
re-par-tir' *tr.v.* to divide, to group, to distribute.
re-pas'-to *m.* repast, feast.
re-pa-tri-a-ção' *f.* repatriation.
re-pa-tri-ar' *tr.v.* to send home, to repatriate; —se *refl.v.* to come home.
re-pe-len'-te *adj.* repellent.
re-pe-lir' *tr.v.* to repel.
re-pê-lo *m.* repulsion, violence.
re-pen'-te *m.* impulse; unreflected action; de — suddenly.
re-pen-ti'-no, -a *adj.* sudden, unforeseen.
re-per-cus-são' *f.* repercussion.
re-per-tó-rio *m.* repertoire.
re'-pes *m.* rep (fabric).
re-pe-ti-ção' *f.* repetition, rehearsal.
re-pe-ti-dor' *m.* repeater; tutor, quizzmaster.
re-pe-tir' *tr.v.*, *intr.v.* to repeat.
re-pi-car' *tr.v.* to ring; *intr.v.* to chime, to ring forth.
re-pi'-que *m.* ringing of bells; chime; alarm, sensation.
re-ple'-to, -a *adj.* replete.
ré-pli-ca *f.* replica.
re-pli-car' *tr.v.* *intr.v.* to refute; to reply to.
re-pô-lho *m.* cabbage.
re-po-lhu'-do, -a *adj.* cabbage shaped; round.
re-por' *tr.v.* to replace, to put back, to restore.
re-por-ta'-gem *f.* reporting, news.
re-pór-ter *m.* reporter, newspaper reporter.
re-po-si-tó-rio *m.* repository.
re-pos'-ta *f.* answer, reply.
re-pos-tei'-ro *m.* curtain, hanging, tapestry.
re-pou-sar *tr.v.*, *intr.v.* to rest, to repose.
re-pou'-so *m.* repose, rest.
re-pre-en-der' *tr.v.* to reprehend.
re-pre-en-são' *f.* reprehension, censure.
re-pre-en-sí-vel *adj.* reprehensible.
re-pre-en-si'-vo, -a *adj.* reprehensive.
re-pre-sá-lia *f.* reprisal.
re-pre-sar' *tr.v.* to curb, to restrain; to dam.
re-pre-sen-ta-ção' *f.* representation, performance.
re-pre-sen-tan'-te *m.* representative, agent.
re-pre-sen-tar' *tr.v.* to represent; *intr.v.* to act, to play, to play a rôle; —se *refl.v.* to imagine.
re-pres-são' *f.* repression.
re-pres-si'-vo, -a *adj.* repressive.
re-pri-men'-da *f.* reprimand.
re-pri-mir' *tr.v.* to repress, to withhold; to prohibit.

ré-pro-bro *m.* -o, -a *adj.* reprobate.
re-pro-du-ção' *f.* reproduction.
re-pro-du-tí-vel *adj.* reproducible.
re-pro-du-ti'-vo, -a *adj.* reproductive.
re-pro-du-zir' *tr.v.* to reproduce.
re-pro-du-zí-vel *adj.* reproducible.
re-pro-va-ção' *f.* reproval, reproof.
re-pro-va'-do, -a *adj.* failed in an examination.
re-pro-var' *tr.v.* to reprove, to fail.
rep-ta-ção' *f.* challenge.
rep-tar' *tr.v.* to provoke, to challenge, to accuse.
rép-til *m.* reptile.
rep'-to *m.* challenge.
re-pú-bli-ca *f.* republic.
re-pu-bli-ca'-no, -a *adj.* republican.
re-pú-bli-co, -a *adj.* republican.
re-pu-di-ar' *tr.v.* to repudiate.
re-pú-dio *m.* repudiation.
re-pug-nân-cia *f.* repugnance.
re-pug-nan'-te *adj.* repugnant.
re-pul-são' *f.* repulse, repulsion.
re-pul-sar' *tr.v.* to repulse.
re-pul-si'-vo, -a *adj.* repulsive.
re-pu-ta-ção' *f.* reputation.
re-pu-tar' *tr.v.* to repute; to make famous.
re-pu-xar' *tr.v.* to repel, to drive back.
re-pu'-xo *m.* buttress, reinforcement of wall or arch; recoil.
re-que-ren'-te *m.* petitioner.
re-que-rer' *tr.v.* to request, to solicit; to address request or petition to.
re-que-ri-men'-to *m.* petition, application.
ré-qui-em *m.* requiem.
re-quin-ta'-do, -a *adj.* highly refined, affected.
re-quin-tar' *tr.v.* to purify, to refine; —se *refl.v.* to be affected.
re-quin'-te *m.* refinement, affectation, excess.
re-qui-si-tar' *tr.v.* to requisition, to require.
re-qui-si'-to *m.* requisite, requirement.
rês *f.* cattle; **má** — good-for-nothing.
rés *adj.* smooth, shallow, low; *adv.* by the foot, by the root.
res-cin-dir' *tr.v.* to rescind.
res-ci-são' *f.* annulment.
rés-do-chão' *m.* ground floor, main floor.
re-ser'-va *f.* reserve.
re-ser-var' *tr.v.* to reserve.
re-ser-vis'-ta *m.* reservist.
res-fri-a-men'-to *m.* cold.
res-fri-ar' *tr.v.* to chill, to cool; *intr.v.* to become cold; —se *refl.v.* to catch cold.
res-ga-tar' *tr.v.* to rescue, to ransom, to redeem.
res-ga'-te *m.* ransom; settlement.
res-guar'-do *m.* care, precaution, diet, preventive measure.
re-si-dên-cia *f.* residence.
re-si-den'-te *m.*, *f.* resident.
re-si-dir' *intr.v.* to reside.
re-si-du-al' *adj.* residual.
re-sí-duo *m.* residue, residuum.
re-sig-na-ção' *f.* resignation.
re-sig-nar' *tr.v.* to resign; —se *refl.v.* to be resigned.
re-sí-na *f.* resin.
re-si-ní-fe-ro, -a *adj.* resiniferous.
re-si-no'-so, -a *adj.* resinous.
re-sis-tên-cia *f.* resistance.
re-sis-ten'-te *adj.* strong, resistant.
re-sis-tir' *intr.v.* to resist.
res'-ma *f.* ream (of paper).
re-so-lu-ção' *f.* resolution.

re-so-lu'-to, =a *adj.* resolute, determined.
re-sol-ver' *tr.v.* to resolve.
res-pec-ti'-vo, =a *adj.* respective.
res-pei-ta-bi-li-da'-de *f.* respectability.
res-pei-tar' *tr.v.* to respect; *intr.v.* to concern.
res-pei-tá-vel *adj.* respectable.
res-pei'-to *m.* respect.
res-pei-to'-so, =a *adj.* respectful.
res-pi-gar' *intr.v.* to glean; (fig.) to compile, to gather up.
res-pi-ra-ção' *f.* respiration.
res-pi-ra-dor' *m.* respirator.
res-pi-ra-dou'-ro *m.* air-vent, ventilation opening.
res-pi-rar' *tr.v.*, *intr.v.* to breathe.
res-pi-ra-tó-rio, =a *adj.* respiratory.
res-plan-de-cen'-te *adj.* resplendent.
res-plan-de-cên-cia *f.* resplendency.
res-plen-den'-te *adj.* resplendent.
res-plen-dor' *m.* resplendency.
res-pon-der' *tr.v.*, *intr.v.* to answer.
res-pon-si'-vo, =a *adj.* responsive.
res-pon'-so *m.* response.
res-pon-sa-bi-li-da'-de *f.* responsibility.
res-pon-sa-bi-li-sar' =se *refl.v.* to become responsible, to assume responsibility.
res-pon-sá-vel *adj.* responsible.
res-pos'-ta *f.* answer, response, reply.
res-sa'-ca *f.* eddy, breakers, billow.
res-sai'-bo *m.* bad taste, bad odor; resentment; touch.
res-sal'-va *f.* certificate exempting individual from military service.
res-sen-ti'-do, =a *adj.* resentful.
res-sen-ti-men'-to *m.* resentment.
res-sen-tir' *tr.v.* to resent; —=se *refl.v.* to resent; to feel the effects of.
res-so-nân-cia *f.* resonance.
res-so-nan'-te *adj.* resonant.
res-sun-ção' *f.* resumption.
res-sur-rei-ção' *f.* resurrection.
res-sus-ci-tar' *tr.v.*, *intr.v.* to resuscitate, to revive.
res-ta-be-le-cer' *tr.v.* to re-establish; —=se *refl.v.* to regain health or strength.
res-tan'-te *adj.* remaining; *m.* remainder, rest.
res-tar' *intr.v.* to remain over, to be left over.
res-tau-ra-ção' *f.* restoration.
res-tau-ran'-te *m.* restaurant; restorative.
res-tau-rar' *tr.v.* to restore.
res-tau-ra-ti'-vo, =a *adj.* restorative.
res-ti-tu-i-ção' *f.* restitution.
res-ti-tu-ir' *tr.v.* to give back, to restore.
res'-to *m.* remainder, left-over; **res'-tos** *m.pl.* ruins; mortal remains.
res-tri-ção' *f.* restriction.
res-trin-gen'-te *m.*, *adj.* restringent.
res-trin-gir' *tr.v.* to restrain, to restrict.
res-tri-ti'-vo, =a *adj.* restrictive.
res-tri'-to, =a *adj.* restricted.
re-sul-ta'-do *m.* result.
re-sul-tan'-te *adj.* resultant.
re-sul-tar' *intr.v.* to result, to follow; to become, to turn out.
re-su-mir' *tr.v.* to summarize, to sum up.
re-su'-mo *m.* resumé.
res-va-lar' *intr.v.* to slide, to slip, to glide.
re'-ta *f.* straight line.
re-tá-bu-lo *m.* retable.
re-ta-guar'-da *f.* rear (of an army).
re-ta-lhar' *tr.v.* to cut into pieces; to divide; to sell at retail.
re-ta-lhei'-ro *m.* retail merchant.

re-ta'-lho *m.* remnant; a — at retail.
re-ta-li-a-ção' *f.* retaliation.
re-ta-li-ar' *tr.v.* to retaliate.
re-tan-gu-lar' *adj.* rectangular.
re-tân-gu-lo *m.* rectangle.
re-tar-da-ção' *f.* retardation, delay.
re-tar-dar' *tr.v.* to retard, to delay; *intr.v.* to move slowly, to be late.
re-tar'-do *m.* delay.
re-ten-ção' *f.* retention.
re-ten-ti'-va *f.* good memory.
re-ten-ti'-vo, =a *adj.* retentive.
re-ter' *tr.v.* to retain; to hold back.
re-ti-cên-cia *f.* reticence.
re-ti-cen'-te *adj.* reticent.
re-tí-cu-lo *m.* small net; reticule; reticulum.
re-ti-dão' *f.* rectitude.
re-ti-fi-ca-ção' *f.* rectification.
re-ti-fi-car' *tr.v.* to rectify.
re-ti'-na *f.* retina.
re-ti-ni'-te *f.* retinitis.
re-ti-ra'-da *f.* retreat.
re-ti-ra'-do, =a *adj.* retiring; solitary.
re-ti-rar' *tr.v.* to pull out, to withdraw, to take back; —=se *refl.v.* to withdraw, to retire, to go home.
re-ti'-ro *m.* retreat; retirement, seclusion, solitude.
re'-to, =a *adj.* straight, direct, upright; **re'-to** *m.* rectum.
re-tó-ri-ca *f.* rhetoric.
re-tó-ri-co, =a *adj.* rhetorical.
re-tor'-ta *f.* retort.
re-tra-ção' *f.* retraction.
re-tra-í-do, =a *adj.* retracted, pushed back; reserved, timid.
re-tra-ir' *tr.v.* to retract, to withdraw, to pull back; to turn aside; —=se *refl.v.* to retire, to retreat.
re-tra'-to *m.* picture, photograph.
re-tre'-ta *f.* tattoo, retreat; privacy; open-air band concert.
re-tre'-te *m.* water-closet.
re-tri-bu-i-ção' *f.* retribution.
re-tro-a-ti'-vo, =a *adj.* retroactive.
re-tró-gra-do, =a *adj.* retrograde.
re-trós *m.* silk thread.
re-tros-pec-ção' *f.* retrospection.
re-tros-pec-ti'-vo, =a *adj.* retrospective.
re-tros-pec'-to *m.* retrospection.
réu *m.* ré *f.* criminal.
reu-má-ti-co, =a *adj.* rheumatic.
reu-ma-tis'-mo *m.* rheumatism.
re-u-ni-ão' *f.* reunion, gathering, meeting.
re-u-nir' *tr.v.* to bring together, to join; —=se *refl.v.* to gather, to meet.
re-ve-la-ção' *f.* revelation.
re-ve-lar' *tr.v.* to reveal.
re-ve-ne-rar' *tr.v.* to revere, to venerate.
re-ver-be-ra-ção' *f.* reverberation.
re-ve-rên-cia *f.* reverence.
re-ve-ren-ci-al' *adj.* reverential.
re-ve-ren-dís-si-mo *adj.* most reverend.
re-ve-ren'-do *m.* reverend.
re-ve-ren'-te *adj.* reverent.
re-ver-são' *f.* reversion.
re-ver-sí-vel *adj.* reversible.
re-ver'-so *m.* reverse; back.
re-ver-ter' *intr.v.* to revert.
re-ve-sar' =se *refl.v.* to take turns.
re-vi-são' *f.* revision.
re-vi-sar' *tr.v.* to revise.
re-vis'-ta *f.* review, magazine, journal.
re-vis-tar' *tr.v.* to review, to examine.
re-vis'-to, =a *adj.* reviewed, examined, corrected.
re-vo-car' *tr.v.* to recall, to revoke.

re-vo-cá-vel *adj.* revocable.
re-vo-gar' *tr.v.* to recall, to revoke.
re-vól'-ta *f.* revolt, insurrection.
re-vol-ta'-do *m.* rebel, revolter; **re-vol-ta'-do,** =a *adj.* indignant.
re-vol-tan'-te *adj.* revolting, repugnant.
re-vol-tar' *tr.v.* to incite to revolt; —=se *refl.v.* to revolt.
re-vol-to'-so, =a *adj.* rebellious.
re-vo-lu-ção' *f.* revolution.
re-vo-lu-ci-o-nar' *tr.v.* to instigate revolt.
re-vo-lu-ci-o-ná-rio, =a *adj.* revolutionary; **re-vo-lu-ci-o-ná-rio** *m.* revolutionist.
re-vol-ver' *tr.v.* to turn around, to turn over in one's mind; to examine over and over.
re-vól'-ver *m.* revolver.
re'-za *f.* prayer.
re-zar' *tr.v.* to say (a prayer); to say, to relate; *intr.v.* to pray; to say prayers; to tell.
ri'-a *f.* mouth of a river.
ri-a-chão' *m.* large stream.
ri-a'-cho *m.* stream.
ri-bal-da-ri'-a *f.* ribaldry, knavery.
ri-bal-di'-a *f.* ribaldry, knavery.
ri-bal'-do *m.* ribald.
ri-bal'-ta *f.* foot-lights (of stage).
ri-bei'-ra *f.* stream; river basin.
ri-bei-ri'-nho, =a *adj.* marginal, river.
ri-bei'-ro *m.* small river.
rí-ci-no *m.* castor oil bean.
ri'-co, =a *adj.* rich.
ri'-co=ho'-mem *m.* grandee, nobleman.
ri-den'-te *adj.* laughing.
ri-di-cu-li-zar' *tr.v.* to ridicule.
ri-dí-cu-lo, =a *adj.* ridiculous.
ri-ei'-ra *f.* rut, track (worn by wheel).
ri'-fa *f.* raffle, lottery.
ri-fão' *m.* proverb, adage.
ri-gi-dez' *f.* rigidity.
rí-gi-do, =a *adj.* rigid.
ri-gor' *m.* rigor.
ri-go-ris'-mo *m.* strict morals.
ri-go-ro'-so, =a *adj.* rigorous.
ri'-jo, =a *adj.* sturdy, hard, strong, vigorous.
rim' *m.* kidney; **rins'** *m.pl.* back, lumbar region.
ri'-ma *f.* rhyme.
ri-mar' *tr.v., intr.v.* to rhyme.
rin-char' *intr.v.* to neigh.
rin'-cho *m.* neigh, neighing.
ri-no-ce-ron'-te *m.* rhinoceros.
ri'-o *m.* river.
ri'-pa *f.* shingle, lath.
ri-pan'-ço *m.* rake, harrow.
ri-par' *tr.v.* to harrow, to rake; to nail (shingles or laths).
ri-que'-za *f.* wealth, richness, abundance.
rir' *intr.v.* to laugh.
ri-sa'-da *f.* laughter.
ri-são' *adj.* laughing, who laughs easily.
ri-sí-vel *adj.* laughable.
ri'-so *m.* laugh, laughter.
ri-so'-nho, =a *adj.* smiling, happy, pleasant.
ris-pi-dez' *f.* harshness, cruelty.
rís-pi-do, =a *adj.* harsh, rough, rude.
rít-mi-co, =a *adj.* rhythmic.
rit'-mo *m.* rhythm.
ri'-to *m.* rite.
ri-tu-al' *adj., m.* ritual.
ri-val' *m., f.* rival.
ri-va-li-da'-de *f.* rivalry.
ri'-xa *f.* quarrel, contention.
ri-xar' *intr.v.* to quarrel, to contend.

ri-xo'-so, =a *adj.* quarrelsome, disorderly.
ro-bus-te-cer' *tr.v.* to strengthen, to make strong; —=se *refl.v.* to become strong.
ro-bus-tez' *f.* robustness, strength.
ro-bus'-to, =a *adj.* strong, robust.
ro'-ca *f.* distaff.
ro'-ça *f.* cleared land; backwoods, country.
ro-ça'-da *f.* clearing.
ro-ça'-do *m.* cleared land, new ground.
ro'-cha *f.* rock.
ro-che'-do *m.* rocky cliff.
ro-cho'-so, =a *adj.* rocky.
ro-ci'-o *m.* dew.
ro-ci-o'-so, =a *adj.* dewy.
ro'-da *f.* wheel; gathering.
ro-da'-gem *f.* wheels; **estrada de —** road for vehicles with wheels.
ro-dan'-te *adj.* moving, rolling.
ro-da-pé *m.* baseboard, washboard.
ro'-da=vi'-va *f.* restlessness, incessant movement.
ro-de-ar' to go around, to put around; to avoid; to surround.
ro-dei'-o *m.* subterfuge, evasion.
ro-dei'-ro *m.* axle (of vehicle); axis; set of two wheels with connecting axle.
ro-do-den'-dro *m.* rhododendron.
ro-e-dor' *m.* rodent.
ro-er' *tr.v., intr.v.* to gnaw.
ro-ga-ções' *f.pl.* public prayers.
ro-gar' *tr.v.* to ask for, to beg for, to pray for; *intr.v.* to ask, to beg.
ro-lan'-te *adj.* rolling.
ro-lar' *tr.v., intr.v.* to roll.
ro-lei'-ro, =a *adj.* rolling.
ro-le'-ta *f.* roulette.
ro-le'-te *m.* small roll; form (for hats).
rô-lha *f.* stopper (of cork or glass), cork.
rô-lo *m.* roller, coil; cylinder.
ro-mã' *f.* pomegranate.
ro-ma'-na *f.* steelyard.
ro-man'-ce *m.* novel.
ro-ma-nes'-co, =a *adj.* romantic, venturesome.
ro-ma-ní *m.* Romany (language of Gipsies of eastern Europe).
ro-mâ-ni-co, =a *adj.* Romance; romanesque.
ro-ma'-no, =a *m., f., adj.* Roman.
ro-mân-ti-co, =a *adj.* romantic.
ro-ma-ri'-a *f.* pilgrimage.
rom'-bo *m.* rhombus.
rom-bói-de *m.* rhomboid.
ro-mei'-ro, =a *m., f.* pilgrim.
rom-per' *tr.v.* to break, to tear; to interrupt; *intr.v.* to break out, to break forth, to begin; to break; —=se *refl.v.* to burst, to tear; to be interrupted.
rom-pi-men'-to *m.* breaking off of relations; cutting through.
ron-ca-du'-ra *f.* growling, rumbling.
ron-car' *intr.v.* to snore; to growl.
ron'-cha *f.* purplish bruise.
ron'-da *f.* round, guard.
ron-dar' *tr.v.* to patrol; *intr.v.* to make the rounds.
ron-quei'-ra *f.* **ron-qui-dão'** *f.* difficult respiration, hoarseness.
ron-rom' *m.* purring.
ro'-sa *f.* rose; **— dos ventos** compass card.
ro-sa'-ça *f.* rosette, rose window.
ro-sá-ce-o, =a *adj.* rosaceous.
ro-sa'-do, =a *adj.* rose-colored.
ro-sá-rio *m.* rosary.
ro-sei'-ra *f.* rose bush.
ro-sei-ral' *m.* rose garden.
ró-se-o, =a *adj.* roseate.

ro-se'-ta f. small rose; rowel.
ros-bi'-fe m. roast beef.
ros-nar' tr.v., intr.v. to murmur words between teeth; to mutter, to grumble; to growl.
ros'-to m. face.
ros'-tro m. beak; bill (of certain insects).
ro'-ta f. defeat, flight (of an army); direction, route.
ro-ta-ção' f. rotation.
ro-tar' intr.v. to rotate.
ro-ta-ti'-va f. rotary printing-press.
ro-ta-ti'-vo, =a adj. rotating, rotative.
ro-ta-tó-rio, =a adj. rotary, rotatory.
ro-tei'-ro m. itinerary.
ro-tim' m. cane, caning (for chair seats).
ro-ti'-na f. routine.
ro-ti-nei'-ro, =a adj. following certain routine.
ró-tu-la f. knee-cap.
ró-tu-lo m. label, lettering, title of book printed on cover.
ro-tun-di-da'-de f. rotundity.
ro-tun'-do, =a adj. rotund; round.
rou-bar' tr.v. to rob, to steal.
rou-bo m. robbery, booty.
rou'-pa f. clothing, linen, suit; — branca underwear; — de cama bed linen.
rou-pão' m. negligee, bath-robe.
rou-pa-ri'-a f. laundry, clothes-press; clothes.
rou'-co, =a adj. hoarse.
rou-que'-nho, =a adj. somewhat hoarse.
rou-qui-dão' f. hoarseness.
rou-xi-nol' m. nightingale.
ro'-xo, =a adj. red, purple-red.
ru'-a f. street.
ru-ben'-te adj. reddish.
rú-be-o, =a adj. red, blood-red.
ru-bí m. ruby.

ru-bi-cun'-do, =a adj. red, ruddy.
ru-bim' m. ruby.
ru-bri'-ca f. rubric.
ru'-de adj. uncultured; stupid; discourteous; coarse.
ru-dez' f. ru-de'-za f. rudeness, coarseness.
ru-di-men-tar' adj. rudimentary.
ru-di-men-to m. rudiment.
ru-e'-la f. narrow street, alley,'lane.
ru'-ga f. wrinkle.
ru-go'-so, =a adj. rough, wrinkled.
ru'-ge=ru'-ge m. sound of swishing skirts.
ru-gi'-do m. roar of lion.
ru-gir' intr.v. to roar.
ru-im adj. bad, useless, perverse, damaged.
ru-í-na f. ruin; destruction.
ru-in-da'-de f. malice, wickedness.
ru-i-no'-so, =a adj. ruinous.
ru-ir' intr.v. to fall, to collapse.
rui'-vo, =a adj. ruddy, reddish, red-haired.
ru-mi-na-ção' f. rumination.
ru-mi-na-dou'-ro m. maw, ruminating stomach.
ru-mi-nan'-te adj. ruminant, ruminating.
ru-mi-nar' tr.v., intr.v. to ruminate.
ru'-mo m. route, direction.
ru-mor' m. gossip, rumor; noise.
rup-tu'-ra f. rupture; hernia.
ru-ral' adj. rural.
ru-ra-lis'-mo m. ruralism.
rus'-ga f. disorder, uproar, quarrel, fight.
rus-ti-ci-da'-de f. rusticity.
rús-ti-co, =a adj. rustic.
ru-ti-lan'-te adj. rú-ti-lo, =a adj. bright, shining, glittering.

S

See page 12—GUIDE TO REFORMED SPELLING used in this Dictionary

S, s m. S, s, eighteenth letter of the alphabet.
sá-ba-do m. Saturday.
sa-bão' m. soap.
sa-bá-ti-co, =a adj. sabbatical.
sa-bá-vel adj. tasty.
sa-be-dor', =a adj. learned, erudite.
sa-be-do-ri'-a f. widsom, knowledge.
sa-ber' tr.v. to know, to know of, to know how, to be able, to understand; intr.v. to have knowledge; to taste; to please; m. knowledge, wisdom.
sa-bi-á m. song bird of Brazil.
sá-bio, =a adj. wise, learned, skilful, prudent; sá-bio m. scholar, scientist.
sa-bo-ne'-te m. toilet soap.
sa-bo-ne-tei'-ra f. soap-dish.
sa-bor' m. taste, savor.
sa-bo-re-ar' tr.v. to taste, to savor.
sa-bo-ro'-so, =a adj. tasty, delicious.
sa-bo-ta'-gem f. sabotage.
sa'-bre m. saber.
sa'-ca=boi' m. cow-catcher.
sa'-ca=bo-ca'-do m. punch.
sa-ca'-da f. exportation; balcony.
sa-ca'-do m. drawee.
sa'-ca=mo'-las m. forceps; wretched dentist.
sa'-ca=na'-bo m. piston rod.
sa-car' tr v. to pull out, to extract; to draw.

sa-ca-ri'-na f. saccharin.
sa-ca-ri'-no, =a adj. saccharine.
sa'-ca=rô-lhas m. corkscrew.
sa-ca-ro'-se f. saccharose.
sa-ca-ro'-so, =a adj. like sugar.
sa-cer-dó-cio m. priesthood.
sa-cer-do-tal' adj. sacerdotal.
sa-cer-do'-te m. priest.
sa-cer-do-ti'-sa f. priestess.
sa-ci-ar' tr.v. to fill, to satiate.
sa-ci-e-da'-de f. satiety.
sa'-co m. sack, bag.
sa-cra-men-tal' adj. sacramental.
sa-cra-men'-to m. sacrament.
sa-crá-rio m. tabernacle, reliquary; heart.
sa-cri-fi-car' tr.v. to sacrifice, to renounce, to abandon; intr.v. to offer sacrifice.
sa-cri-fi-ci-al' adj. sacrificial.
sa-cri-fí-cio m. sacrifice.
sa-cri-lé-gio m. sacrilege.
sa-crí-le-go, =a adj. sacrilegious.
sa-cris-ta-ni'-a f. office of sacristan.
sa-cris-tão' m. sacristan.
sa-cris-ti'-a f. sacristy.
sa'-cro, =a adj. sacred.
sa-cros-san'-to, =a adj. sacrosanct.
sa-cu-dir' tr.v. to shake, to beat (for cleaning), to throw.

sa-di'-o, =a *adj.* healthy, healthful.

sa-dis'-mo *m.* sadism.

sa-dis'-ta *adj., m., f.* sadist.

sa-far' *tr.v.* to use up, to wear out; to take, to rob; —=se *refl.v.* to escape, to run away.

sá-fa-ro, =a *adj.* sterile, uncultivated.

sa-fi'-ra *f.* sapphire.

sa'-fra *f.* harvest; anvil.

sa'-ga *f.* saga.

sa-ga-ci-da'-de *f.* sagacity.

sa-gaz' *adj.* sagacious.

sa-gra'-do, =a *adj.* sacred, holy.

sa-grar' *tr.v.* to consecrate, to dedicate.

sa-gú *m.* sago.

sa-gu-ão' *m.* lobby; vestibule, patio.

sa-guim' *m.* small monkey.

sai'-a *f.* skirt; — de baixa petticoat.

sai'-bro *m.* gravel, coarse sand.

sai-bro'-so, =a *adj.* sandy, full of gravel.

sa-í-da *f.* exit, way out, turn-over.

sa-í-do, =a *adj.* absent, on the outside.

sai-e'-ta *f.* woolen cloth (for linings).

sa-i-men'-to *m.* burial, funeral procession; conclusion.

sa-ir' *intr.v.* to go out, to go away; to come loose, to come from; to deviate; —=se *refl.v.* to escape; to turn out.

sal' *m.* salt.

sa'-la *f.* room; — de espera waiting-room; — de jantar dining-room; — de visitas reception room, parlor.

sa-la'-da *f.* salad.

sa-la-dei'-ra *f.* salad bowl.

sa-la-man'-dra *f.* salamander.

sa-lão *m.* saloon, salon.

sa-lá-ri-o *m.* salary.

sa-laz' *adj.* salacious.

sal-chi'-cha *f.* sausage.

sal-dar' *tr.v.* to liquidate, to settle.

sal'-do *m.* balance; settlement; bargain sale.

sa-lei'-ro *m.* salt-cellar.

sa-le'-ta *f.* small room.

sal-ga'-do, =a *adj.* salty; piquant; expensive.

sal-gar' *tr.v.* to salt.

sa-li-ên-cia *f.* projection, distinction.

sa-li-en-tar' *tr.v.* to emphasize, to make evident; —=se *refl.v.* to become evident.

sa-li-en'-te *adj.* prominent, salient.

sa-li'-na *f.* salt marsh, salt mine.

sa-li-ni-da'-de *f.* saltiness.

sa-li'-no, =a *adj.* saline.

sa-li-nô-me-tro *m.* salinometer.

sa-li'-tre *m.* saltpeter.

sa-li'-va *f.* saliva.

sa-li-var' *tr.v.* to spit, to dribble.

sal-mão' *m.* salmon.

sal-mis'-ta *m., f.* psalmist.

sal'-mo *m.* psalm.

sal-mo-di'-a *f.* psalmody.

sal-mo-ei'-ro *m.* brine-jar, brine-vat.

sal-mo-na'-do, =a *adj.* salmon-colored.

sal-mou'-ra *f.* brine.

sa-lo'-bre or sa-lo'-bro, =a *adj.* brackish.

sa-loi'-o, =a *adj.* of a peasant living in the neighborhood of Lisbon.

sal-pi-ca'-do, =a *adj.* sprinkled with salt; greyish.

sal-pi-car' *tr.v.* to salt, to scatter salt over, to splash, to powder.

sal-ta'-da *f.* leap, jump; assault.

sal-ta'-do, =a *adj.* salient; projecting.

sal-tan'-te *adj.* leaping, jumping; saliant.

sal-tar' *intr.v.* to leap, to jump; *tr.v.* to jump over, to pass over.

sal-te-a-dor' *m.* highwayman.

sal-te-ar' *tr.v.* to assault, to attack, to rob; *intr.v.* to live on plunder; —=se *refl.v.* to be surprised, to start.

sal-tei'-ra *f.* heel-pad.

sal'-to *m.* leap, jump; assault, heel (of shoe).

sa-lu'-bre *adj.* salubrious.

sa-lu-bri-da'-de *f.* salubrity.

sa-lu-tar' *adj.* salutary.

sal'-va *f.* salute, salvo, round, volley; sage; tray.

sal-va-ção' *f.* salvation.

sal-va-dor' *m.* savior, saver.

sal'-va-=guar'-da *f.* safeguard, caution, protection.

sal-var' *tr.v.* to save; to jump over; *intr.v.* to give salvos; —=se *refl.v.* to be saved; to escape a danger.

sal-vá-vel *adj.* saveable.

sal'-va-=vi'-das *m.* life-preserver.

sal'-vo, =a *adj.* safe, saved; omitted, excepted.

sal'-vo-=con-du'-to *m.* safe-conduct.

sam-ber-nar'-do *m.* St. Bernard breed of dogs.

sa-nar' *tr.v.* to cure; to solve.

sa-ná-vel *adj.* curable.

san-ção' *f.* sanction.

san-ci-o-nar' *tr.v.* to sanction.

san-dá-lia *f.* sandal (shoe).

sân-da-lo *m.* sandal-wood (perfume).

sa-ne-ar' *tr.v.* to make sanitary.

sa-ne'-fa *f.* valance.

san-gra-dou'-ro *m.* place on arm where bleeding is made; drain.

san-grar' *tr.v., intr.v.* to bleed.

san-gren'-to, =a *adj.* bleeding, bloody.

san'-gue *m.* blood.

san'-guen-to, =a *adj.* bleeding, bloody.

san-gui'-no, =a *adj.* sanguine.

san-gui-ná-rio, =a *adj.* sanguinary.

san-gui-ni-da'-de *f.* consanguinity.

sa'-nha *f.* ire, fury, rancor.

sa-ni-da'-de *f.* sanity, healthiness.

sa-ni-tá-rio, =a *adj.* sanitary.

san-tei'-ro *m.* devout man; carver of images of saints; dealer in images of saints.

san-ti-da'-de *f.* sanctity, holiness.

san-tís-si-mo, =a *adj.* most holy.

san-to,=a *adj., m., f.* saintly, holy; saint.

são', sã *adj.* well, normal, sane, whole, upright.

sa'-pa *f.* spade.

sa-par' *intr.v.* to work with a spade, to dig with a spade.

sa-pa'-ta *f.* ladies' shoe, low-heeled shoe.

sa-pa-ta-ri'-a *f.* shoe-store.

sa-pa-te-ar' *intr.v.* to flap the soles in dancing; to stamp.

sa-pa-tei'-ro *m.* shoe dealer, shoemaker.

sa-pa-te'-ta *f.* slipper.

sa-pa'-to *m.* shoe.

sa-pi-ên-cia *f.* wisdom, knowledge.

sa-pi-en'-te *adj.* wise, knowing.

sa-pi'-nhos *m.pl.* aphthae, thrush.

sa'-po *m.* toad.

sa'-que *m.* bill of exchange, draft.

sa-que-ar' *tr.v.* to sack, to pillage.

sa-qui'-nho *m.* small sack; cartridge.

sa-ra'-do, =a *adj.* robust, strong; eager; voracious.

sa-ra-go'-ça *f.* brown woollen fabric.

sa-ram'-po *m.* measles.

sa-rar' *tr.v.* to cure; to correct, to mend; *intr.v.* to get well, to heal.

sa-rau' *m.* ball, dance, evening party.

sar-cas'-mo *m.* sarcasm.
sar-cás-ti-co, **=a** *adj.* sarcastic.
sar-có-fa-go *m.* sarcophagus.
sar-di'-nha *f.* sardine.
sar-di-nhei'-ro, **=a** *m.*, *f.* sardine fisherman, sardine dealer.
sár-dio *m.* sard.
sar-dô-ni-co, **=a** *adj.* sardonic.
sar-gen'-to *m.* sergeant.
sar'-na *f.* itch.
sar-nen'-to, **=a** *adj.* itchy.
sar-no'-so, **=a** *adj.* itchy, itching.
sar'-ro *m.* dregs; tartar (on teeth); residue of nicotine deposited on pipestem.
sa-tã' *m.* **sa-ta-naz'** *m.* Satan.
sa-tâ-ni-co, **=a** *adj.* Satanic.
sa-té-li-te *m.* satellite.
sá-ti-ra *f.* satire.
sa-tí-ri-co, **=a** *adj.* satirical.
sa-ti-ri-zar' *tr.v.* to satirize.
sa-tis-fa-ção' *f.* satisfaction.
sa-tis-fa-tó-rio, **=a** *adj.* satisfactory.
sa-tis-fa-zer' *tr.v.*, *intr.v.* to satisfy.
sa-tis-fei'-to, **=a** *adj.* satisfied.
sa-tu-ra-ção' *f.* saturation.
sa-tu-rar' *intr.v.* to saturate.
sa-tur-ni'-no, **=a** *adj.* saturnine.
sa-tur'-no *m.* Saturn; lead (metal).
sa-u-da-ção' *f.* salutation, homage, greeting, compliment.
sa-u-da'-de *f.* longing, yearning; **=s** *f.pl.* regards, greetings.
sa-u-dar' *tr.v.* to greet, to salute; toast.
sa-u-dá-vel *adj.* wholesome, salutary, healthful.
sa-ú-de *f.* health.
sa-xo-fo'-ne *m.* saxophone.
sé *f.* see (eccl.); cathedral.
se-a'-ra *f.* field of grain.
se-a-rei'-ro *m.* small farmer.
se-ben'-to, **=a** *adj.* like tallow; soiled, dirty.
se'-bo *m.* tallow.
se-bo'-so, **=a** *adj.* tallowy.
sê-ca *f.* drought, lack of rain.
se-ca-dou'-ro *m.* dryer, drying place.
se-ca'-gem *f.* drying.
se-can'-te *adj.* drying; importunate, boring; *f.* secant.
se-car' *tr.v.*, *intr.v.* to dry, to wilt, to evaporate.
se-ca-ti'-vo, **=a** *adj.* siccative.
sec-ção' *f.* section, cut, portion.
sec-ci-o-nal' *adj.* sectional.
sec-ci-o-nar' *tr.v.* to section.
se-ces-são' *f.* secession.
se-cre-ção' *f.* secretion.
se-cre-ta-ri'-a *f.* secretariat.
se-cre-tá-ria *f.* desk; secretary.
se-cre-tá-rio *m.* secretary.
se-cre'-to, **=a** *adj.* secret.
sec-tá-rio, **=a** *adj.* sectarian.
se-cu-lar' *adj.* secular, lay.
se-cu-la-ri-da'-de *f.* secularity.
se-cu-la-ri-zar' *tr.v.* to secularize; to relieve from monastic vows; **=se** *refl.v.* to withdraw from a religious order.
sé-cu-lo *m.* century.
se-cun-dar' *tr.v.* to second; to back.
se-cun-dá-rio, **=a** *adj.* secondary.
se-cu'-ra *f.* dryness; thirst.
sê-da *f.* silk.
se-dar' *tr.v.* to calm, to tranquilize.
se-da-ti'-vo, **=a** *adj.* sedative.
sê-de *f.* thirst; dryness; avarice, greediness.
se'-de *f.* seat, headquarters, jurisdictional head.
se-den-tá-rio, **=a** *adj.* sedentary.

se-den'-to, **=a** *adj.* thirsty; very desirous, avaricious.
se-di-ção' *f.* sedition.
se-di-ci-o'-so, **=a** *adj.* seditious.
se-di-men-tar' *adj.* sedimentary.
se-di-men'-to *m.* sediment.
se-di-men-to'-so, **=a** *adj.* containing sediment.
se-do'-so, **=a** *adj.* silky, like silk.
se-du-ção' *f.* seduction.
sé-du-lo, **=a** *adj.* sedulous.
se-du-tor' *m.* seducer; **se-du-tor'**, **=a** *adj.* seductive; attractive.
se-du-zir' *tr.v.* to seduce.
se-du-zí-vel *adj.* seducible.
seg-men-ta-ção' *f.* segmentation.
seg-men'-to *m.* segment.
se-grê-do *m.* secret.
se-gre-ga-ção' *f.* segregation.
se-gre-gar' *tr.v.* to segregate.
se-gui'-do, **=a** *adj.* immediate, continuous.
se-gui-men'-to *m.* following; continuation; result, consequence.
se-guin'-te *adj.* following, next.
se-guir' *tr.v.* to follow; *intr.v.* to come afterward; to continue, to move on.
se-gun'-da *f.* second proof sheet; Monday.
se-gun'-da-fei'-ra *f.* Monday.
se-gun'-do *m.* second; *adv.* according to **se-gun'-do**, **=a** *adj.* second.
se-gu-ran'-ça *f.* assurance, security.
se-gu-rar' *tr.v.* to insure; to secure.
se-gu'-ro, **=a** *adj.* sure, certain, safe, secure.
sei'-o *m.* breast, bosom; gulf, bay.
seis-cen'-tos, **=as** *adj.* six hundred.
sei'-ta *f.* sect.
sei'-va *f.* sap; (fig.) blood.
sei-vo'-so, **=a** *adj.* sappy, succulent.
sei-xal' *m.* pebbly area, pebbly ground
sei'-xo *m.* pebble, flint.
sei-xo'-so, **=a** *adj.* abounding in pebbles.
se'-la *f.* saddle.
se-la-dou'-ro *m.* place for saddle (on animal's back).
se-lar' *tr.v.* to saddle; to seal, to put a stamp on.
se-le-ção' *f.* selection.
se-le-ci-o-nar' *tr.v.* to select.
se-lê-nio *m.* selenium.
se-le'-ta *f.* collection, selection.
se-le-ti'-vo, **=a** *adj.* selective.
se-le'-to, **=a** *adj.* choice, select, special.
se'-lha *f.* tub.
sê-lo *m.* postage-stamp; seal.
sel'-va *f.* forest, woods.
sel-va'-gem *adj.* wild, savage.
sel-vá-ti-co, **=a** *adj.* wild, of the woods.
sel-vo'-so, **=a** *adj.* full of woods.
se-ma'-na *f.* week.
se-ma-nal' *adj.* weekly, relative to week.
sem-blan'-te *m.* face, countenance; semblance.
sem-ce-ri-mô-nia *f.* disregard of social convention; impoliteness.
se-me-a'-da *f.* area sown.
se-me-a-dor' *m.* sower.
se-me-a-du'-ra *f.* sowing.
se-me-ar' *tr.v.* to sow.
se-me-lhan'-ça *f.* similarity.
se-me-lhan'-te *adj.* similar.
sê-men *m.* semen.
se-men'-te *f.* seed
se-mes-tral' *adj.* occurring every six months, for a six months' period.
se-mes'-tre *m.* semester.

sem∘fim' *adj.* endless; *m.* undefined space indeterminate quantity or number.

se-mi-a-nu-al' *adj.* semi-annual.

se-mi-a-nu-lar' *adj.* in form of half-ring.

se-mi-cir-cu-lar' *adj.* semi-circular.

se-mi-cír-cu-lo *m.* semi-circle.

se-mi-na-ção' *f.* semination, seeding.

se∘mi-nal' *adj.* seminal.

se-mi-ná-rio *m.* seminary.

sem∘par' *adj.* without equal; unique.

sem-pi-ter'-no, ∘a *adj.* everlasting, perpetual.

sem'-pre *adv.* always.

sem∘ra-zão' *f.* affront, injustice.

se-na'-do *m.* senate.

se-na-dor' *m.* senator.

se-não' *conj.* save, otherwise, else; *prep.* except; *m.* defect, stain.

se-na-to-ri-al' *adj.* senatorial.

se-nhor' *m.* mister, sir, owner, lord.

se-nho'-ra *f.* mistress, madam, lady, Virgin Mary; miss, young lady.

se-nho-ri-al' *adj.* lordly, seigniorial.

se-nho-ril' *adj.* distinguished, elegant.

se-nho-ri'-o *m.* lordship, power, dominion.

se-nho-ri'-na *f.* girl, young lady.

se-nho-ri'-ta *f.* girl, young lady.

se-nil' *adj.* senile.

se-ni-li-da'-de *f.* senility.

sê-ni-or *adj.* senior.

sen-sa-bor' *adj.* tasteless, insipid.

sen-sa-ção' *f.* sensation.

sen-sa-ci-o-nal' *adj.* sensational.

sen-sa-tez' *f.* good sense, discreetness.

sen-sa'-to, ∘a *adj.* sensible, prudent, circumspect.

sen-si-bi-li-da'-de *f.* sensibility; sensitivity.

sen-si-ti'-vo, ∘a *adj.* sensitive.

sen-sí-vel *adj.* sensitive, appreciable.

sen'-so *m.* sense, clear judgment.

sen-só-rio, ∘a *adj.* sensory.

sen-su-al' *adj.* sensual.

sen-su-a-li-da'-de *f.* sensuality.

sen-su-a-lis'-mo *m.* sensualism.

sen-ten'-ça *f.* sentence.

sen-ten-ci-ar' *tr.v.* to sentence, to pass sentence.

sen-ten-ci-o'-so, ∘a *adj.* sententious.

sen-ti'-do *m.* sense, direction; idea, meaning.

sen-ti-men-tal' *adj.* sentimental.

sen-ti-men-ta-li-da'-de *f.* sentimentality.

sen-ti-men-to *m.* sentiment.

sen-ti-ne'-la *f.* sentry, sentinel.

sen-tir' *tr.v.* to feel, to perceive; to be sorry.

sen-ver-go'-nha *m., f.* shameless person.

sen-za'-la *f.* slave quarters.

sé-pa-lo *m.* sepal.

se-pa-ra-ção' *f.* separation.

se-pa-rar' *tr.v.* to separate.

se-pa-ra'-ta *f.* reprint, off-print.

se-pa-rá-vel *adj.* separable.

sé-pia *f.* sepia.

sep-si'-a *f.* sepsis.

sép-ti-co, ∘a *adj.* septic.

se-pul-cral' *adj.* sepulchral.

se-pul'-cro *m.* sepulcher.

se-pul-tar' *tr.v.* to bury, to inter.

se-quaz' *m.* follower.

se-quên-cia *f.* sequence.

se-quer' *adv.* at least, yet.

se-ques-tra-ção' *f.* sequestration.

se-ques-trar' *tr.v.* to sequester.

ser' *intr.v.* to be; *m.* being, entity.

se-rá-fi-co, ∘a *adj.* seraphic.

se-ra-fim' *m.* seraphim.

se-rão' *m.* night work, evening work; evening party.

se-rei'-a *f.* mermaid.

se-re-na'-ta *f.* serenade.

se-re-ni-da'-de *f.* serenity.

se-re'-no, ∘a *adj.* serene.

se-ri-a-ção' *f.* arranging in series.

se-ri-al' *adj.* serial.

se-ri-ar' *tr.v.* to classify, to arrange in series.

se-ri-ci-cul-tu'-ra *f.* sericulture.

sé-rie *f.* series.

se-rin'-ga *f.* syringe.

se-rin-guei'-ra *f.* Brazilian rubber tree.

se-rin-guei'-ro *m.* rubber gatherer.

se-ri-e-da'-de *f.* seriousness.

sé-rio, ∘a *adj.* serious; *adv.* really.

ser-mão' *m.* sermon.

ser-pen'-te *f.* serpent.

ser-pen-ti'-na *f.* candlestick with three branches.

ser-pen-ti'-no, ∘a *adj.* serpentine.

ser'-ra *f.* saw; mountain range, sierra.

ser-ra-dor' *m.* sawer.

ser-rar' *tr.v.* to saw.

ser-ra-ri'-a *f.* sawbuck, sawhorse; sawmill.

ser-re-ar' *tr.v.* to make like saw, to cut or indent in form of sawteeth.

sér-re-o, ∘a *adj.* saw-like, serrate.

ser-ta-ne'-jo *m.* backwoodsman, inhabitant of interior.

ser-tão' *m.* backwoods, interior area of country.

ser-ven'-te *m., f.* servant.

ser-vi'-ço *m.* service.

ser-vi-di'-ço, ∘a *adj.* used, old, worn out.

ser-vil' *adj.* servile.

ser-vi-lis'-mo *m.* servility.

ser-vir' *tr.v.* to serve; *intr.v.* to be of use; —∘se *refl.v.* to help oneself; to use.

ser'-vo, ∘a *m., f.* servant.

ser-zir' *tr.v.* to darn, to mend.

sês-ma *f.* sixth part.

ses-são' *f.* session.

ses-sen'-ta *m.* sixty.

se'-ta *f.* arrow.

se-ta'-da *f.* wound made by arrow.

se'-te *m.* seven.

se-te-cen'-tos, ∘as *adj.* seven hundred.

se-tei'-ra *f.* loophole.

se-tem'-bro *m.* September.

se-ten'-ta *m.* seventy.

se-ten-tri-o-nal' *adj.* septentrional, northern.

se'-tia *f.* flume, millrace.

se-ti-al' *m.* church pew; settee; terraced area used as seat in natural amphitheatre.

sé-ti-mo, ∘a *adj.* seventh.

se-tor' *m.* sector.

se-ve-ri-da'-de *f.* severity.

se-ve'-ro, ∘a *adj.* severe.

se-xa-ge-ná-rio, ∘a *adj., m., f.* sexagenarian.

se-xa-gé-si-ma *f.* sixtieth part.

se-xa-gé-si-mo, ∘a *adj.* sixtieth.

se'-xo *m.* sex.

sex'-ta∘fei'-ra *f.* Friday.

sex-tan'-te *m.* sextant.

sex-te'-to *m.* sextette.

sex'-to, ∘a *adj.* sixth.

se-xu-al' *adj.* sexual.

se-xu-a-lis'-mo *m.* sexuality.

se-zão' *f.* intermittent fever, malaria.

si-ar' *tr.v.* to close (wings) in order to descend more rapidly.

si-ba-ri'-ta adj., m., f. sybarite.
si-bi-la-çã0' f. hissing, whistling.
si-bi-lan'-te adj. hissing, whistling.
si-bi-lar' intr.v. to hiss, to whistle.
sí-bi-lo m. hissing, whistling.
si-co-fan'-ta m., f. sycophant.
si-co-fan-tis'-mo m. sycophancy.
si-cra'-no m. so-and-so.
si-de-ral' adj. si-dé-re-o, =a adj. sidereal.
si-de-rur-gi'-a f. metallurgy.
si-de-rúr-gi-co, =a adj. metallurgic.
si'-dra f. cider.
si-fã0' m. siphon.
sí-fi-lis f. syphilis.
si-fi-lí-ti-co, =a adj., m., f. syphilitic.
sig-na-tá-rio, =a adj., m., f. signatory.
sig-ni-fi-ca-çã0' f. sig-ni-fi-ca'-do m. meaning, significance.
sig-ni-fi-can'-te adj. sig-ni-fi-ca-ti'-vo, =a adj. significant.
sí-la-ba f. syllable.
si-la-bar' intr.v. to spell, to pronounce in syllables.
si-la-bá-rio m. primer (with words divided into syllables).
si-lá-bi-co, =a adj. syllabic.
si-lên-cio m. silence.
si-len-ci-o'-so, =a adj. silent.
sil-hu-e'-ta f. silhouette.
sí-li-ca f. silica.
si-lo-gis'-mo m. syllogism.
si-lo-gís-ti-co, =a adj. syllogistic.
sil'-va f. bramble, bush.
sil-ves'-tre adj. wild, uncultivated.
sil-vi-cul-tor' m. forester.
sil-vi-cul-tu'-ra f. forestry.
sim' adv. yes.
sim-bó-li-co, =a adj. symbolic.
sim-bo-lis'-mo m. symbolism.
sim-bo-li-zar' tr.v. to symbolize.
sím-bo-lo m. symbol.
si-me-tri'-a f. symmetry.
si-mé-tri-co, =a adj. symmetrical, symmetric.
si-mi-lar' adj. similar.
si-mi-la-ri-da'-de f. similarity.
sí-mi-le m. simile.
sí-mio m. simian.
sim-pa-ti'-a f. sympathy; agreeableness.
sim-pá-ti-co, =a adj. congenial, likeable, sympathetic.
sim-pa-ti-zar' intr.v. to be sympathetic.
sim'-ples adj. simple; m., f. simpleton.
sim-pli-ci-da'-de f. simplicity.
sim-pli-fi-ca-çã0' f. simplification.
sim-pli-fi-car' tr.v. to simplify.
sim-pló-rio, =a adj. naïve, credulous.
si-mu-la-çã0' f. simulation.
si-mu-la'-do, =a adj. feigned, counterfeit.
si-mu-lar' tr.v. to simulate, to imitate.
si-mul-ta-ne-i-da'-de f. simultaneity.
si-mul-tâ-ne-o, =a adj. simultaneous.
si-na-go'-ga f. synagogue.
si-nais' m.pl. birth-marks.
si-nal' m. sign, signal; deposit.
si-na-leí-ro m. signal-man.
sin-ce-ri-da'-de f. sincerity.
sin-ce'-ro, =a adj. sincere.
sín-co-pe f. swoon; syncope.
sin-crô-ni-co, =a adj. synchronous.
sin-cro-nis'-mo m. synchronism.
sin-cro-ni-zar' tr.v. to synchronize.
sin-di-cân-cia f. inquiry, investigation.
sin-di-car' tr.v., intr.v. to inquire, to inquire into.
sin-di-ca'-to m. syndicate; illicit financial speculation; labor union.

si-ne-cu'-ra f. sinecure.
si-nei'-ra f. belfry.
si-nei'-ro m. bell-man, carillonneur.
si-ne'-ta f. small bell.
si-ne'-te m. seal.
sin-fo-ni'-a f. symphony.
sin-fô-ni-co, =a adj. symphonic.
sin-ge-le'-za f. candidness, naïveté, sincerity.
sin-ge'-lo, =a adj. simple, sincere, innocent; single.
sin-grar' intr.v. to sail.
sin-gu-lar' adj. singular.
sin-gu-la-ri-da'-de f. singularity.
si-nis'-tra f. left hand.
si-nis'-tro, =a adj. sinister.
si'-no m. bell.
si-nó-di-co, =a adj. synodic, synodical.
sí-no-do m. synod.
si-nô-ni-mo m. synonym; =o, =a adj. synonymous.
si-nop'-se f. synopsis.
si-nóp-ti-co, =a adj. synoptic, synoptical.
sin-tá-ti-co, =a adj. syntactical.
sin-ta'-xe f. syntax.
sín-te-se f. synthesis.
sin-té-ti-co, =a adj. synthetic.
sin-te-ti-zar' tr.v. to synthesize.
sin-to'-ma m. symptom.
sin-to-má-ti-co, =a adj. symptomatic.
sin-to-ni-zar' tr.v. to tune in.
si-nu-o-si-da'-de f. sinuosity.
si-nu-o'-so, =a adj. sinuous.
si-nu-si'-te f. sinusitis.
si-sal' m. sisal hemp.
sis-mal' adj. concerning earthquakes.
sis'-mo m. earthquake.
sis-mó-gra-fo m. seismograph.
si'-so m. good sense, judgment, prudence.
sis-te'-ma m. system.
sis-te-má-ti-co, =a adj. systematic.
sis-te-ma-ti-zar' tr.v. to systematize.
sis-tál-ti-co, =a adj. systolic.
sis-to-lar' adj. systolic.
sís-to-le f. systole.
sis'-tro m. sistrum, cithern, tabor.
si-su-dez' f. si-su-de'-za f. grave demeanor, seriousness.
si-su'-do, =a adj. grave, serious.
si-ti-ar' tr.v. to besiege, to lay siege to.
sí-tio m. site, locality; rural estate, farm; siege.
si-tu-a-çã0' f. situation.
si-tu-ar' tr.v. to place, to establish, to assign place to.
só adj. alone, solitary; adv. only.
so-a'-da f. sound; rumor, gossip; tone.
so-a-lha'-do m. flooring of room.
so-a'-lho m. floor.
so-ar' intr.v. to make sound, to echo, to be rumored; tr.v. to ring.
sob prep. under.
so-be-jar' intr.v. to be in excess, to be excessive.
so-be'-jo, =a adj. too much, excessive.
so-be-ra-ni'-a f. sovereignty.
so-be-ra'-no, =a m., f. sovereign.
so-ber'-bo, =a adj. proud, arrogant, grandiose.
so'-bra f. rest, remainder, left-over.
so-bra'-do m. second floor.
so-bran-ce'-lha f. eyebrow.
so-brar' intr.v. to be in excess, to be too much.
sô-bre prep. above, beyond, about.
so-bre-car'-ga f. excess load.
so-bre-car-re-gar' tr.v. to overload.
so-bre-ca-sa'-ca f. overcoat, topcoat.
so-bre-di'-to, =a adj. above-mentioned.

so-bre-hu-ma'-no, =a *adj.* superhuman.

so-bre-ma-nei'-ra *adv.* excessively, extraordinarily.

so-bre-me'-sa *f.* dessert.

so-bre-mo'-do *adv.* extraordinarily.

so-bre-na-tu-ral' *adj.* supernatural.

so-bre-no'-me *m.* surname, family name.

so-bres-cri'-to *m.* address on envelope.

so-bres-sa-ir' *intr.v.* to be outstanding, to stand out.

so-bres-sal-tar' *tr.v.* to alarm, to surprise.

so-bres-sal'-to *m.* surprise, unexpected event, shock.

so-bre-tu'-do *m.* heavy overcoat; *adv.* principally.

so-bre-vi-ven'-te *m.* surviver.

so-bre-vi-ver' *intr.v.* to survive.

so-bri-e-da'-de *f.* sobriety.

so-bri'-nho, =a *m.*, *f.* nephew, niece.

só-brio, =a *adj.* sober.

so-car' *tr.v.*, *intr.v.* to strike with fist or hand; to box.

so-ci-a-bi-li-da'-de *f.* sociability.

so-ci-al' *adj.* social.

so-ci-a-li-zar' *tr.v.* to make sociable.

so-ci-á-vel *adj.* sociable.

so-ci-e-da'-de *f.* society; association; company.

só-cio *m.* member, partner.

so-ci-o-lo-gi'-a *f.* sociology.

so-ci-ó-lo-go *m.* sociologist.

so-cor-rer' *tr.v.* to aid, to help, to succor; —=se *refl.v.* to seek help, to ask for aid.

só-dio *m.* sodium.

so-fá *m.* sofa.

so-fis'-ma *m.* sophism.

so-fre-dor' *m.* sufferer.

sô-fre-go, =a *adj.* impatient; greedy.

so-frer' *tr.v.* to suffer, to endure, to tolerate.

so-fri'-do, =a *adj.* patient, long-suffering.

so-fri-men'-to *m.* suffering.

so'-gro, =a *m.*, *f.* father-in-law, mother-in-law.

sol' *m.* sun.

so'-la *f.* sole.

so-lar' *tr.v.* to sole, to put a sole on; *adj.* solar.

so-la-van'-co *m.* jolt, bump (of a vehicle).

sol-da *f.* solder.

sol'da'-do *m.* soldier.

sol-da-du'-ra *f.* soldering.

sol-dar' *tr.v.* to solder.

sol-e-cis'-mo *m.* solecism.

so-le-da'-de *f.* solitude.

so-le'-ne *adj.* solemn.

so-le-ni-da'-de *f.* solemnity.

so-le-ni-zar' *tr.v.* to solemnize.

so-le-tra-ção' *f.* spelling.

so-le-trar' *tr.v.*, *intr.v.* to spell.

sol-fe'-jo *m.* solfeggio.

so-li-ci-ta-ção' *f.* solicitation.

so-li-ci-ta-dor' *m.* solicitor.

so-li-ci-tan'-te *adj.* solicitous; *m.*, *f.* person who solicits.

so-li-ci-tar' *tr.v.* to solicit.

so-li-ci-to, =a *adj.* solicitous.

so-li-ci-tu'-de *f.* solicitude.

so-li-dão' *f.* solitude.

so-li-dez' *f.* solidity.

so-li-dar' *tr.v.* to confirm, to corroborate; to solidify.

so-li-da-ri-e-da'-de *f.* solidarity.

só-li-do, =a *adj.* solid.

so-li-di-fi-ca-ção' *f.* solidification.

so-li-di-fi-car' *tr.v.*, *intr.v.* to solidify.

so-li-ló-quio *m.* soliloquy.

so-lis'-ta *m.*, *f.* soloist.

so-li-tá-ria *f.* tape worm.

so-li-tá-rio, =a *adj.* solitary.

so'-lo *m.* soil, land, earth's surface; solo.

sols-tí-cio *m.* solstice.

sol-tei'-ro, =a *adj.* unmarried, single.

sol-tar' *tr.v.*, *intr.v.* to free, to let go, to loosen, to emit, to unleash.

sôl-to, =a *adj.* free, loose, unbound.

so-lu-ção' *f.* solution, conclusion, decision.

so-lu-çar' *intr.v.* to weep, to sob.

so-lu'-ço *m.* sob.

so-lu-ço'-so, =a *adj.* sobbing.

so-lú-vel *adj.* soluble.

sol-vên-cia *f.* solvency.

sol-ven'-te *adj.* solvent.

sol-ver' *tr.v.* to dissolve; to satisfy, to pay; to solve.

som' *m.* sound.

so'-ma *f.* sum.

so-mar' *tr.v.*, *intr.v.* to add.

so-má-ti-co, =a *adj.* somatic.

som'-bra *f.* shadow, shade.

som-bral' *m.* shady spot, shade.

som-brei'-ro *m.* sombrero.

som-bri'-o, =a *adj.* shady; somber.

som-bro'-so, =a *adj.* shady, producing shadows.

so-me'-nos *adj.* ordinary, inferior.

so-men'-te *adv.* only.

so-nâm-bu-lo, =a *adj.* somnambulant; *m.*, *f.* somnambulist.

so-nân-cia *f.* resonance, melody, music.

so-nan'-te *adj.* sonorous, making a sound.

so-na'-ta *f.* sonata.

so-na-ti'-na *f.* sonatina.

son'-da *f.* plumb bob, plumb.

son-da'-gem *f.* sounding.

son-dar' *tr.v.* to sound, to investigate.

son-da-re'-za *f.* graduated sounding line.

so-ne'-ca *f.* short nap.

so-ne'-to *m.* sonnet.

so-nha-dor' *m.* dreamer.

so-nhar' *intr.v.*, *tr.v.* to dream.

so'-nho *m.* dream.

so'-no *m.* sleep; **doença do —** sleeping sickness.

so-no-lên-cia *f.* somnolence.

so-no-len'-te *adj.* somnolent.

so-no-ri-e-da'-de *f.* sonority.

so-no'-ro, =a *adj.* sonorous.

so-no-ro'-so, =a *adj.* harmonious; noisy.

so'-pa *f.* soup.

so-pei'-ra *f.* soup tureen.

so-por' *m.* drowsiness, sleepiness.

so-po-rí-fe-ro, =a *adj.* soporiferous.

so-po-rí-fi-co, =a *adj.* soporific.

so-po-ro'-so, =a *adj.* drowsy, sleeping.

so-pra'-no *m.* soprano.

so-prar' *intr.v.* to blow; *tr.v.* to blow out, to blow up; to favor; to prompt.

sô-pro *m.*. blowing; breeze, puff, breath.

so-quei'-xo *m.* bandage holding chin and secured at top of head; chin strap.

so-que'-te *m.* ram rod (of a gun).

sor-di-dez' or **sor-di-de'-za** *f.* sordidness.

sór-di-do, =a *adj.* sordid.

sô-ro *m.* whey, serum; buttermilk.

sor-ri-den'-te *adj.* smiling, happy.

sor-rir' *intr.v.* to smile.

sor-ri'-so *m.* smile.

sor'-te *f.* destiny, fate, luck; lot.

sor-te-ar' *tr.v.* to choose by lot; to sort.

sor-tei'-o *m.* choosing by lot; allotment.

sor-ve'-te *m.* fruit ice, sherbet.

sor-ve-tei'-ra *f.* ice-cream freezer.
sos-lai'-o: de — *adv.* askance.
sos-se'-ga *f.* sleeping potion.
sos-se-gar' *tr.v.* to quiet, to calm, to ease.
sos-sê-go *m.* calm, quiet, tranquility.
só-tão *m.* attic.
so-ta'-que *m.* accent (peculiar to certain region or nationality).
so-ta-ven'-to *m.* leeward.
so-tur'-no, =a *adj.* sad, gloomy; sultry.
so-zi'-nho, =a *adj.* all alone.
su-a'-do, =a *adj.* sweaty, perspiring.
su-ar' *intr.v.* to sweat, to perspire.
su-a-ren'-to, =a *adj.* sweaty, full of perspiration.
su-a'-ve *adj.* suave, mellow, delicate, melodious.
su-a-vi-da'-de *f.* suavity.
su-a-vi-zar' *tr.v.* to mitigate, to soften.
su-bal-ter'-no, =a *adj.* subaltern.
su-ben-ten-der' *tr.v.* to understand, to perceive what is not actually expressed or made clear.
su-ben-ten-di'-do, =a *adj.* understood.
su-bi'-da *f.* ascent, rise.
su-bi'-do, =a *adj.* dear; elevated; pompous.
su-bir' *intr.v.* to go up, to come up, to ascend, to rise; *tr.v.* to mount, to ascend; to take up.
sú-bi-to, =a *adj.* sudden, unexpected; *adv.* suddenly.
sub-je-ti-vi-da'-de *f.* subjectivity.
sub-je-ti'-vo, =a *adj.* subjective.
sub-ju-ga-ção' *f.* subjugation.
sub-ju-gar' *tr.v.* to subjugate.
sub-jun-ti'-vo *m.* subjunctive.
su-bli-ma-ção' *f.* sublimation.
su-bli-ma'-do, =a *adj.* sublimate.
su-bli-mar' *tr.v.* to sublimate.
su-bli'-me *adj.* sublime.
su-bli-mi-da'-de *f.* sublimity.
su-bli-nhar' *tr.v.* to underline; to emphasize.
sub-ma-ri'-no *m.* =o, =a *adj.* submarine.
sub-mer-gir' *tr.v.* to submerge.
sub-mer-gí-vel *adj.* submersible.
sub-mer-são' *f.* submersion.
sub-mer-sí-vel *adj.* submersible.
sub-mer'-so, =a *adj.* submersed, submerged.
sub-me-ter' *tr.v.* to subjugate, to make dependent.
sub-mis-são' *f.* submission, subjection.
sub-mis'-so, =a *adj.* submissive, humble.
su-bor-di-na-ção' *f.* subordination.
su-bor-di-na'-do, =a *adj.* subordinate.
su-bor-di-nar' *tr.v.* to subordinate.
sub-scre-ver' *tr.v.*, *intr.v.* to subscribe to, to approve; to sign.
sub-scri-ção' *f.* subscription.
sub-se-quen'-te *adj.* subsequent.
sub-ser-vi-ên-cia *f.* subservience.
sub-ser-vi-en'-te *adj.* subservient.
sub-si-di-á-rio, =a *adj.* subsidiary.
sub-sí-dio *m.* subsidy.
sub-sis-tên-cia *f.* subsistence.
sub-sis-ten'-te *adj.* subsistent.
sub-sis-tir' *intr.v.* to subsist.
sub-so'-lo *m.* subsoil.
sub-stân-cia *f.* substance.
sub-stan-ci-al' *adj.* substantial.
sub-stan-ci-a-li-da'-de *f.* substantiality.
sub-stan-ti'-vo *m.* noun.
sub-sti-tui-ção' *f.* substitution.
sub-sti-tuin'-te *adj.*, *m.*, *f.* substitute.
sub-sti-tu-ir' *tr.v.* to substitute.
sub-sti-tu'-to, =a *adj.*, *m.*, *f.* substitute.

sub-ter-fú-gio *m.* subterfuge.
sub-ter-râ-ne-o *m.* subterrane; =o, =a *adj.* subterranean.
sub-tra-ção' *f.* subtraction.
sub-tra-ir' *tr.v.* to subtract.
su-bur-ba'-no, =a *adj.* suburban.
su-búr-bio *m.* suburb.
sub-ven-ção' *f.* subsidy, subvention.
sub-ver-si'-vo, =a *adj.* subversive.
sub-ver-ter' *tr.v.* to subvert.
su-ção *f.* suction.
su-ca'-ta *f.* junk.
su-ce-der' *intr.v.* to succeed, to follow after.
su-ces-si'-vo, =a *adj.* successive.
su-ces'-so *m.* event, happening, outcome; success.
su-ces-sor' *m.* successor.
su-cin'-to, =a *adj.* succinct.
su'-co *m.* juice, essence.
su-co'-so, =a *adj.* juicy.
su-cu-lên-cia *f.* succulence.
su-cu-len'-to, =a *adj.* succulent.
su-cum-bir' *intr.v.* to succumb.
su-cur-sal' *f.* branch, branch office.
su-fi-ci-ên-cia *f.* sufficiency.
su-fi-ci-en'-te *adj.* sufficient.
su-fi'-xo *m.* suffix.
su-fo-can'-te *adj.* suffocating.
su-fo-car' *tr.v.*, *intr.v.* —=se *refl.v.* to suffocate.
su-frá-gio *m.* suffrage.
su-fra-gis'-ta *f.* suffragist.
su-gar' *tr.v.* to suck.
su-ge-rir' *tr.v.* to suggest.
su-ges-tão' *f.* suggestion.
su-ges-ti'-vo, =a *adj.* suggestive.
su-i-ci-dar'-se *refl.v.* to commit suicide.
su-i-cí-dio *m.* suicide.
su-í-no, =a *adj.* swine.
su-jar' *tr.v.* to dirty, to soil, to spot, to stain.
su-jei-ção' *f.* subjugation.
su-jei'-ra *f.* filth, dirtiness.
su-jei-tar' *tr.v.* to subject; to fasten.
su-jei'-to *m.* subject; individual, fellow; su-jei'-to, =a *adj.* subject; submissive.
su-ji-da'-de *f.* dirtiness.
su'-jo, =a *adj.* dirty, unclean.
sul' *m.* south.
sul-car' *tr.v.* to furrow, to plough.
sul'-co *m.* furrow.
sul-fa'-to *m.* sulphate.
sul-fú-ri-co, =a *adj.* sulphuric.
sul-fu-ri'-no, =a *adj.* sulphur-colored.
sul-fu-ro'-so, =a *adj.* sulphurous.
su'-ma *f.* sum, résumé, epitome.
su-ma-ren'-to, =a *adj.* juicy.
su-má-rio *m.* summary.
su-mi'-ço *m.* disappearance.
su-mi-da'-de *f.* top; notable.
su-mi-di'-ço, =a *adj.* easily lost sight of, disappearing.
su-mi'-do, =a *adj.* seen with difficulty; thin, weak.
su-mir' *tr.v.* to cause to disappear, to sink, to hide, to consume, to waste; —=se *refl.v.* to disappear, to sink, to go out.
su'-mo *m.* juice; highest; most excellent; maximum.
su-mo'-so, =a *adj.* juicy.
sun-tu-á-rio, =a *adj.* sumptuary.
sun-tu-o-si-da'-de *f.* sumptuousness.
sun-tu-o'-so, =a *adj.* sumptuous.
su-or' *m.* sweat, perspiration.
su-per-fi-ci-al' *adj.* superficial.
su-per-fi-ci-a-li-da'-de *f.* superficiality.
su-per-fi'-no, =a *adj.* superfine.

su-pér-fluo, =a *adj.* superfluous.
su-pe-rin-ten-den'-te *adj., m.* superintendent.
su-pe-rin-ten-der' *tr.v., intr.v.* to superintend.
su-pe-ri-or' *adj., m.* superior.
su-pe-ri-o-ri-da'-de *f.* superiority.
su-per-la-ti'-vo, =a *adj.* superlative.
su-per-sti-ção' *f.* superstition.
su-per-sti-ci-o'-so, =a *adj.* superstitious.
su-pi'-no, =a *adj.* supine.
su-ple-men-tá-rio, =a *adj.* supplementary.
sup-le-men'-to *m.* supplement.
sú-pli-ca *f.* supplication.
su-pli-ca-ção' *f.* supplication.
su-pli-can'-te *m., f.* supplicant.
su-pli-car' *tr.v.* to beg, to implore, to supplicate.
su-por' *tr.v.* to suppose.
su-por-tar' *tr.v.* to support; to tolerate.
su-por-tá-vel *adj.* supportable, tolerable.
su-por'-te *m.* support.
su-po-si-ção' *f.* supposition.
su-po-si-tó-rio *m.* suppository.
su-pos'-to, =a *adj.* supposed; false.
su-pre'-mo, =a *adj.* supreme.
su-pres-são' *f.* suppression, elimination, cancellation.
su-pri-men'-to *m.* substitution, supplement, aid.
su-pri-mir' *tr.v.* to suppress, to cancel, to eliminate.
su-prir' *tr.v., intr.v.* to make up for, to supplement, to take the place of, to substitute.

su-prí-vel *adj.* available.
sur-dez' *f.* deafness.
sur-di'-na *f.* mute (in muscial instruments).
sur'-do, =a *adj.* deaf, hard of hearing.
sur'-do=mu'-do, *adj., m.* deaf-mute.
sur-gir' *intr.v.* to arise, to break out, to appear.
sur-pre-en-der' *tr.v.* to surprise.
sur-pre'-sa *f.* surprise.
sur-ri-pi-ar' *tr.v.* to steal.
sus-ce-ti-bi-li-da'-de *f.* susceptibility.
sus-ce-tí-vel *adj.* susceptible.
sus-ci-tar' *tr.v.* to stir up, to rouse, to excite; to suggest.
sus-pei-tar' *tr.v., intr.v.* to suspect.
sus-pei'-to, =a *adj.* suspect.
sus-pen-der' *tr.v.* to suspend.
sus-pen-são' *f.* suspension.
sus-pen'-so, =a *adj.* suspended.
sus-pen-só-rio, =a *adj.* suspensory.
sus-pi-rar' *intr.v.* to sigh; *tr.v.* to sigh for, to long for.
sus-pi'-ro *m.* sigh; deep anxiety.
sus-sur'-ro *m.* murmuring, confused talking in low voice.
sus-tar' *tr.v., intr.v.* to stop, to interrupt.
sus-ten-ta-ção' *f.* sustentation.
sus-ten-tar' *tr.v.* to sustain, to support.
sus-ten'-to *m.* sustenance, food; support.
sus'-to *m.* sudden fright, fear, shock.
su-ta'-che *f.* soutache, braid.
su-til' *adj.* subtle.
su-ti-le'-za *f.* subtleness.
su-tu'-ra *f.* suture.
su-tu-rar' *tr.v.* to unite by suture.

T

See page 12—GUIDE TO REFORMED SPELLING used in this Dictionary

T, t *m.* T, t, nineteenth letter of the alphabet.
ta-ba-ca-ri'-a *f.* cigar-store, tobacco shop.
ta-ba'-co *m.* tobacco.
ta-ba-quei'-ra *f.* tobacco jar or container.
ta-be'-la *f.* list, table, schedule.
ta-be-lar' *adj.* tabular.
ta-be-li-ão' *m.* notary public.
ta-ber'-na *f.* tavern.
ta-ber-nei'-ro *m.* tavern keeper.
ta-bi'-que *m.* thin wall, partition.
tá-bua *f.* board, plank.
ta-bu-a'-da *f.* table (of addition, subtraction, multiplication, division).
ta-bu-lei'-ro *m.* large tray; checker board; low plateau.
ta'-ça *f.* champagne glass.
ta-cão' *m.* shoe heel.
ta-car' *tr.v.* to tap, to brandish.
ta'-cha *f.* tack, small nail; defect, blemish.
tá-ci-to, =a *adj.* tacit.
ta-ci-tur-ni-da'-de *f.* taciturnity.
ta-ci-tur'-no, =a *adj.* taciturn.
ta-ga-re-lar' *intr.v.* to prattle, to be loquacious.
ta-ga-re-li'-ce *f.* indiscretion; talkativeness.
tai'-pa *f.* stucco; mud-wall.
tal' *adj.* such, like, similar, this, that; *m.* goldsmith's anvil.
ta-la-gar'-ça *f.* canvas on which needle-point embroidery is done.

ta-lão' *f.* heel; stub (of check).
ta-lar' *tr.v.* to open, to furrow, to plough.
tal'-co *m.* talcum.
tal-co'-so, =a *adj.* like talcum.
ta-len'-to *m.* talent.
ta-len-to'-so, =a *adj.* talented.
ta'-lha *f.* cut.
ta-lha-men'-to *m.* cutting; engraving.
ta-lhar' *tr.v.* to engrave; to carve; to cut up; *intr.v.* to curdle.
ta'-lhe *m.* size, stature, build.
ta-lher' *m.* silverware for one person at table, cover.
ta'-lho *m.* cut, cutting; pruning.
ta-lis-mã' *m.* talisman.
tal-mu'-de *m.* Talmud.
ta'-lo *m.* stalk, stem.
ta-lo'-so, =a *adj.* having stem or stalk.
ta-lu-dão' *m.* big fellow, giant.
ta-lu'-do, =a *adj.* having a strong stem.
tal-vez' *adv.* perhaps.
ta-man'-co *m.* sandal with wooden sole.
ta-ma'-nho *m.* volume, size; =o, =a *adj.* so large, so distinguished.
ta-ma-rin'-do *m.* tamarind.
tam-bém *adv.* also, too.
tam-bor' *m.* drum, tambour.
tam-bo-ril' *m.* tambourine.
tam'-pa *f.* lid, cover.
tam-pão' *m.* large lid, large cover.
tan-gen'-te *adj., m.* tangent.
tan-ger' *tr.v., intr.v.* to play (instruments).
tan-gí-vel *adj.* tangible.

tâ-ni-co, =a adj. tannic.
ta-ni'-no m. tannin.
ta-ni-no'-so, =a adj. containing tannin.
tan'-que m. tank.
tân-ta-lo m. tantalum.
tan'-to, =a adj. so much, so many; tan'-to adv. so much.
tão' adv. so.
ta-pa'-do, =a adj. stopped up, covered; ignorant, stupid.
ta-pa-men'-to m. closing, covering.
ta-par' tr.v. to cover (with lid), to close.
ta-pê-te m. carpet, rug.
ta-qui-gra-fi'-a f. stenography.
ta-quí-me-tro m. speedometer.
ta'-ra f. tare, deduction, allowance, loss, damage.
tar-dar' tr.v. to delay, to hold up; intr.v. to be long, to be late.
tar'-de adv. late; m. afternoon.
tar-de'-za f. lateness, delay.
tar-di'-nha f. late afternoon.
tar-di'-o, =a adj. late, slow-moving, lazy.
tar'-do, =a adj. slow-moving, lazy.
ta-re'-fa f. task.
ta-re-fei'-ro m. contractor; worker.
ta-ri'-fa f. tariff.
ta-rim'-ba f. bunk; (fig.) soldier's life, life in barracks.
tar-la-ta'-na f. tarlatan, cotton muslin.
tar-ra'-xo m. screw; nail.
tar'-so m. tarsus.
tar-ta-mu'-do, =a adj. stuttering; m., f. stutterer.
tar-tá-ri-co, =a adj. tartaric.
tar-ta-ru'-ga f. turtle.
tas-car' tr.v. to chew; to card, to beat.
tas'-co m. coarse hemp, oakum.
ta-te-ar' tr.v. to feel of, to touch.
tá-til adj. tactile.
ta'-to m. touch; tact.
ta-tu-a'-gem f. tattoo.
ta'-xa f. tax, impost; rate of interest.
ta-xa-ção' f. taxation.
ta-xar' tr.v. to tax.
ta-xí m. taxicab.
ta-xi-der-mi'-a f. taxidermy.
ta-xi-der-mis'-ta m. taxidermist.
tê m. T-square.
te-a'-da f. web, webbing, fine cloth.
te-a'-gem f. texture, webbing.
te-ar' m. loom.
te-a-tral' adj. theatrical.
te-a'-tro m. theatre.
te-ce-dei'-ra f. woman weaver.
te-ce-du'-ra f. weaving.
te-ce-la'-gem f. weaving industry.
te-cer' tr.v. to weave.
te-ci'-do m. cloth.
te'-cla f. key (of piano, typewriter).
te-cla'-da f. key-board.
téc-ni-ca f. technique.
téc-ni-co, =a m., f. technician; adj. technical.
tec-no-lo-gi'-a f. technology.
tec-no-ló-gi-co, =a adj. technological.
tec-nó-lo-go m. technologist.
té-dio m. tedium, ennui, fatigue, weariness.
te-di-o'-so, =a adj. tedious, boring, wearisome.
te-gu-men'-to m. integument.
tei'-a f. webbing, web, cloth, fine cloth.
tei'-ma f. wilfulness, stubbornness, obstinacy.
tei-mar' intr.v. to insist, to be obstinate.
tei-mo'-so, =a adj. obstinate, stubborn.
te-í-na f. active principle in tea.
te'-la f. canvas, painting, picture.

te-lão' m. outer stage curtain (containing advertisements).
te-le-fo-nar' tr.v., intr.v. to telephone.
te-le-fo'-ne m. telephone.
te-le-fo-ne'-ma m. telephone communication.
te-le-gra-far' tr.v., intr.v. to telegraph.
te-le-gra-fi'-a f. telegraphy.
te-le-gra-fis'-ta m. telegrapher.
te-le-gra'-ma m. telegram.
te-lê-me-tro m. telemeter.
te-le-pa-ti'-a f. telepathy.
te-les-có-pi-co, =a adj. telescopic.
te-les-có-pio m. telescope.
te-le-vi-são' f. television.
te'-lha f. tile, tiling.
te-lha'-do m. roof.
te-lha-du'-ra f. roofing, putting on a tile roof.
te-lhal' m. firing oven, kiln.
te-lhar' tr.v. to put a tile roof on, to roof.
te-lhei'-ra f. tile factory.
te-lhei'-ro m. tile manufacturer, tile worker.
te'-lho m. earthenware lid, earthenware cover.
te-lin-tar' intr.v. to ring.
te'-ma m. theme, exercise.
te-men'-te adj. timorous, fearful.
te-mer' tr.v. to fear.
te-me-rá-rio, =a adj. rash.
te-me-ri-da'-de f. rashness, temerity.
te-me-ro'-so, =a adj. fearful, frightful.
te-mí-vel adj. fearful, dreadful.
te-mor' m. reverence, deep respect; fear, fright.
tem-pão' m. long time.
têm-pe-ra f. tempering; tempering bath.
tem-pe-ra-men'-to m. temperament.
tem-pe-ran'-ça f. temperance.
tem-pe-rar' tr.v. to temper, to season, to tune.
tem-pe-ra-tu'-ra f. temperature.
tem-pes-ta'-de f. tempest.
tem-pes-tu-o'-so, =a adj. tempestuous.
tem'-plo m. temple.
tem'-po m. time; weather; a — on time, opportunely.
tem-po-ra'-da f. long period of time, period.
tem-po-ral' adj. temporal; m. heavy storm.
tem-po-râ-nio, =a adj. or tem-po-rá-rio, =a adj. temporary.
tem-po-ri-zar' tr.v. to postpone; intr.v. to delay, to temporize.
te-na-ci-da'-de f. tenacity.
te-naz' adj. tenacious; f. tongs.
ten-ção' f. plan, intention.
ten-ci-o-nar' tr.v. to plan, to intend.
ten'-da f. tent; out-door market stall; small shop.
ten-dão' m. tendon.
ten-dên-cia f. tendency.
ten-den-ci-o'-so, =a adj. prejudiced; tendentious; suspect.
ten-den'-te adj. tending.
ten-der' tr.v. to extend, to offer. to stretch; intr.v. to tend, to be inclined.
tên-der m. tender (of a locomotive).
te-ne-bro'-so, =a adj. dark, gloomy; complex; secret.
te-nên-cia f. lieutenancy.
te-nen'-te m. lieutenant.
te-nor' m. tenor (voice).
ten'-dro, =a adj. tender, soft, delicate, young.
ten-são' f. tension, tenseness.
ten'-so, =a adj. tense, stretched tight.

ten-ta-ção' *f.* temptation.
ten-tá-cu-lo *m.* tentacle.
ten-tar' *tr.v.* to attempt, to try to accomplish; to tempt, to attempt to seduce.
ten-ta-ti'-va *f.* attempt; trial, test.
ten-ta-ti'-vo, ᵃa *adj.* striving; worth trying.
tê-nu-e *adj.* tenuous.
te-nu-i-da'-de *f.* tenuousness; insignificance.
te-o-cra-ci'-a *f.* theocracy.
te-o-crá-ti-co, ᵃa *adj.* theocratic.
te-o-lo-gi'-a *f.* theology.
te-o-ló-gi-co, ᵃa *adj.* theological.
te-ó-lo-go *m.* theologist.
te-or' *m.* tenor, content; text; norm; quality; composition (chemical).
te-o-ré-ti-co, ᵃa *adj.* theoretical.
te-o-ri'-a *f.* theory.
te-ó-ri-co, ᵃa *adj.* theoretical.
te-o-ris'-ta *m.* theorist, visionary.
te-ó-so-fo *m.* theosophist.
te-pi-dez' *f.* tepidity, tepidness.
té-pi-do, ᵃa *adj.* tepid.
ter' *tr.v.* to have, to possess; — de, — que to have to, must; — a palavra to have the floor; — em vista to have in view; ir — com alguem to go to meet someone; — para si to be convinced of; ᵃes *m.pl.* possessions.
te-ra-pêu-ti-ca *f.* therapeutics.
tér-bio *m.* terbium.
ter'-ça *f.* third part; Tuesday.
ter'-ça-fei'-ra *f.* Tuesday.
ter-çar' *tr.v.* to mix three things, to divide into three parts; to cross; *intr.v.* to intercede.
ter-cei'-ro, ᵃa *adj.* third.
ter-ci-á-rio, ᵃa *adj.* tertiary.
ter'-ço, ᵃa *adj.* third.
ter-çol' *m.* stye.
te-re-ben-te'-no *m.* oil or spirits of turpentine.
te-re-bin-ti'-na *f.* turpentine.
ter-gal' *adj.* dorsal.
ter'-go *m.* back.
ter-mal' *adj.* thermal.
ter'-mas *f.pl.* hot springs, thermae.
ter-mi-na-ção' *f.* termination.
ter-mi-nan'-te *adj.* categorical, decisive.
ter-mi-nar' *tr.v.*, *intr.v.* to end, to terminate.
tér-mi-no *m.* term, limit, border, terminal.
ter-mi-no-lo-gi'-a *f.* terminology.
têr-mo *m.* end, limit; term, period; neighborhood.
ter-mô-me-tro *m.* thermometer.
ter-mos-có-pio *m.* thermoscope.
ter'-no *m.* suit of clothes; **ter'-no**, ᵃa *adj.* gentle, sensitive, affectionate.
ter-nu'-ra *f.* tenderness, gentleness, affection, kindness.
ter'-ra *f.* earth, land, soil, ground.
ter-ra'-ço *m.* terrace, veranda.
ter'-ra-no'-va *m.* Newfoundland dog.
ter-rei'-ro *m.* ground; public square.
ter-re-mo'-to *m.* earthquake.
ter-re'-no *m.* land, ground, site, field; **ter-re'-no**, ᵃa *adj.* earthly, worldly.
tér-re-o, ᵃa *adj.* earthy; on the level of the ground.
ter-res'-tre *adj.* terrestrial.
ter-ri-fi-car' *tr.v.* to terrify.
ter-rí-fi-co, ᵃa *adj.* terrific.
ter-ri'-na *f.* soup tureen.
ter-ri-to-ri-al' *adj.* territorial.
ter-ri-tó-rio *m.* territory.

ter-rí-vel *adj.* terrible.
ter-ror' *m.* terror.
ter-ro'-so, ᵃa *adj.* earthy, earth-colored, like earth.
te'-se *f.* thesis.
tê-so, ᵃa *adj.* rigid, stiff, stretched tight.
te-sou'-ra *f.* scissors.
te-sou-ra'-da *f.* cut with scissors.
te-sou-ra-ri'-a *f.* treasury, exchequer.
te-sou-rei'-ro *m.* treasurer.
te-sou-ri'-nha *f.* small scissors.
te-sou'-ro *m.* treasure.
tes'-ta *f.* forehead; head, responsible person.
tes-ta'-da *f.* part of street or road directly in front of a building.
tes-ta-men-tal' *adj.* testamentary.
tes-ta-men'-to *m.* will, testament.
tes-tar' *tr.v.* to leave, to bequeathe.
tes'-te *m.* test.
tes-tei'-ra *f.* head of table, front.
tes-te-mu-nhar' *tr.v.* to witness, to confirm, to show; *intr.v.* to testify.
tes-te-mu'-nho *m.* witness, testimony, deposition.
tes-tí-cu-lo *m.* testicle.
tes-tu'-do, ᵃa *adj.* having large, high forehead.
te-su'-ra *f.* stiffness, rigidity, inflexibility.
tê-ta *f.* teat, nipple.
té-ta-no *m.* tetanus.
te'-to *m.* ceiling; (fig.) roof, protection.
téx-til *adj.* textile.
tex'-to *m.* text.
tex-tu-al' *adj.* textual.
tex-tu'-ra *f.* texture.
tez' *f.* cuticle; epidermis.
tí-bia *f.* tibia.
ti'-co *m.* tiny bit of something.
ti'-fo *m.* typhus.
ti-fói-de *adj.* typhoid.
ti-ge'-la *f.* bowl, porringer.
ti'-gre *m.* tiger.
ti-gri'-no, ᵃa *adj.* tigerish.
ti-jo'-lo *m.* brick.
ti-ju'-co *m.* mud, clay.
til' *m.* tilde, til.
tim-ba'-le *m.* kettledrum.
tim-bó *m.* Brazilian liana.
tim-bo-í-na *f.* alkaloid extracted from bark of a Brazilian liana.
tim'-bre *m.* timbre.
ti-mi-dez' *f.* timidity.
tí-mi-do, ᵃa *adj.* timid.
ti'-mo *m.* thymus.
ti-mol' *m.* thymol.
tím-pa-no *m.* tympanum; ear-drum.
tin-gir' *tr.v.* to dye, to color; to tinge.
ti-ni'-do *m.* tinkling, tinkling sound.
ti-nir' *intr.v.* to tinkle; to shiver with cold or fear.
ti'-no *m.* prudence, tact, good sense, circumspection.
tin'-ta *f.* dye; ink.
tin-tei'-ro *m.* ink bottle, ink stand.
tin-tim'ᵃtin-tim' *adv.* minutely, point by point, with every detail.
tin-tu-a-ri'-a *f.* dyeing establishment.
tin-tu'-ra *f.* dyeing; dye, tincture.
tin-tu-rei'-ro *m.* dyer.
ti'-o, ᵃa *m.*, *f.* uncle, aunt.
ti'-po *m.* type.
ti-po-gra-fi'-a *f.* typography.
ti-po-grá-fi-co, ᵃa *adj.* typographical.
ti'-queᵃta'-que *m.* ticktack.
ti'-ra *f.* strip, strap, narrow piece.
ti-ra-co'-lo *m.* bandoleer.
ti-ra'-gem *f.* pulling; draft; drawing; printing; edition, issue, circulation.

ti'-ra=li'-nhas m. compass.
ti-ra-ni'-a f. tyranny.
ti-râ-ni-co, =a adi. tyrannical.
ti-ra-ni-zar' tr.v. to tyrannize.
ti-ra'-no m. tyrant.
ti'-ra=nó-do-as m. bleach.
ti-ran'-te adj. bordering; m. trace; tie-beam.
ti-rar' tr.v. to pull, to draw, to take out, to take off, to take away, to throw, to remove, to extract; to print; to shoot.
ti'-ro m. shot; firing; gunshot.
ti-ro-cí-nio m. apprenticeship, training.
ti-ro-tei'-o m. firing, rifle fire, fusilade.
tí-si-ca f. pulmonary tuberculosis.
tí-si-co, =a adj. tubercular.
tis'-ne m. soot, color of soot.
ti-tâ-ni-co, =a adj. titanic.
ti-tâ-nio m. titanium.
ti-tu-lar' adj., m. titular.
tí-tu-lo m. title.
tô-a f. tow, tow rope; a — at random, without reflexion.
to-a'-da f. tone, sound, noise, thunder.
to-a'-lha f. towel.
to-a-lhe'-te m. small towel.
to-a-lhi'-nha f. small towel.
to-an'-te adj. in assonance.
to-ar' intr.v. to thunder; to please; to suit.
to'-ca f. hole, burrow; shack.
to'-ca=la'-pis m. leg of compass holding pencil.
to-can'-te adj. relative; touching, moving.
to-car' tr.v. to touch, to play (an instrument), to mention, to touch upon, to approximate.
to'-cha f. torch.
to-chei'-ra f. torch-holder.
tô-co m. tree stump.
to-da-ví'-a conj. but, nevertheless, however.
to'-do m. whole; generality; to'-do, =a adj. whole, all, every; =s m.pl. everybody.
to'-do=po-de-ro'-so, =a adj. all-powerful.
tôl-do m. awning; canvas covering.
to-le-rân-cia f. tolerance.
to-le-ran'-te adj. tolerant.
to-le-rar' tr.v. to tolerate.
to-le-rá-vel adj. tolerable.
to-li'-ce f. foolishness, stupidity.
tô-lo, =a adj. foolish, silly, stupid.
tom' m. tone.
to-ma'-da f. conquest, seizure.
to-mar' tr.v. to take, to get, to catch, to seize, to conquer, to take on.
to-ma'-ra interj. would that!
to-ma'-res: dares e — altercations.
to-ma'-te m. tomato.
to-ma-tei'-ra f. tomato stalk.
tom-ba'-da f. mountain slide.
tom-bar' tr.v. to tear down, to raze; intr.v. to fall down, to tumble to ground with rumbling noise.
tom'-bo m. fall, tumble.
to'-mo m. volume, tome.
to-nal' adj. tonal.
to-na-li-da'-de f. tonality.
to-nel' m. hogshead.
to-ne-la'-da f. ton.
to-ne-la'-gem f. tonnage.
tô-ni-ca f. tonic; tonic vowel.
to-ni-ci-da'-de f. tonicity.
tô-ni-co, =a adj. tonic.
ton-su'-ra f. tonsure.
ton-ti'-ce f. madness, folly; dizziness.

ton'-to, =a adj. dizzy; demented.
ton-tu'-ra f. vertigo, dizziness.
to-pa'-da f. stumble, trip.
to-par' tr.v., intr.v. to encounter, to find; to touch with foot, to strike.
to-pá-zio m. topaz.
to-po-gra-fi'-a f. topography.
to-pó-gra-fo m. topographer.
to'-que m. touch; contact; call (military).
tó-rax m. thorax.
tor-ce-du'-ra f. twisting; sprain.
tor-cer' tr.v., intr.v. to twist, to wind; to cheer.
tor-cí'-da f. wick.
tor-ci-men'-to m. twisting.
tó-rio m. thorium.
tor-men'-ta f. violent storm; disorder, agitation.
tor-men'-to m. torment.
tor-men-to'-so, =a adj. causing anguish; stormy; boisterous; feverish.
tor-nar' intr.v. to return; to reply; to ... again; tr.v. to make, to render; —=se refl.v. to become.
tor=nas-sol' m. sun-flower; litmus.
tor-ne-ar' tr.v. to turn, to make round; intr.v. to participate in tournament or joust.
tor-ne-a-ri'-a f. lathe work, lathe shop.
tor-ne-á-vel adj. capable of being worked on a lathe.
tor-nei'-ra f. faucet, spigot.
tor-ni-que'-te m. turnstile; tourniquet.
tôr-no m. lathe.
tor-no-ze'-lo m. ankle.
tor'-pe adj. dishonest; repugnant; infamous; dull.
tor-pe-cer' intr.v. to weaken, to lose energy.
tor-pen'-te adj. sluggish; numbing.
tor-pe'-za f. vileness, baseness, shamelessness.
tór-pi-do, =a adj. torpid, numb.
tor-pi-tu'-de f. torpidity.
tor-por' m. torpor.
tor-ra'-da f. slice of toast.
tor-rão' m. field; clump, clod; piece, fragment.
tor-rar' tr.v. to toast, to roast; to dry out; to dump on the market.
tôr-re f. tower.
tor-rei'-ra f. excessive heat, heat of the day, hot location.
tor-ren-ci-al' adj. torrential.
tor-ren'-te f. torrent.
tor-ren-to'-so, =a adj. in torrents.
tór-ri-do, =a adj. torrid.
tor'-ta f. pie.
tor-tei'-ra f. pie-pan, pie-plate.
tor'-to, =a adj. not straight, twisted; wrong, disloyal.
tor-tu-o'-so, =a adj. tortuous; winding.
tor-tu'-ra f. torture, torment, punishment.
tor-tu-rar' tr.v. to torture.
tôs-co, =a adj. in natural state, rough, unpolished; uncultured, crude.
tos-qui-ar' tr.v. to shear, to clip.
tos'-se f. cough.
tos-si'-do m. slight cough, fake cough.
tos-sir' intr.v. to cough; tr.v. to cough up.
tos-tão' m. (Portuguese coin).
to-tal' adj., m. total.
to-ta-li-da'-de f. totality.
tou'-ca f. woman's headdress, toque.
tou-ca-dor' m. dressing-table.
tou-car' tr.v. to comb; to dress the hair of.
tou-ci'-nho m. salt pork.

tou-pei′-ra *f.* ground mole.
tou-ra′-da *f.* herd of bulls.
tou-rei′-ro *m.* toreador.
tou′-ro *m.* bull.
to-xe-mi′-a *f.* toxemia.
to-xi-dez′ *f.* toxicity.
to-xi-ci-da′-de *f.* toxicity.
tó-xi-co, =a *adj.* toxic.
to-xi′-na *f.* toxin.
tra-ba-lha-dei′-ra *f.* hard-working woman.
tra-ba-lha-dor′ *m.* hard-working man.
tra-ba-lhar′ *tr.v., intr.v.* to work.
tra-ba′-lho *m.* work.
tra-ba-lho′-so, =a *adj.* difficult; full of work.
tra′-ça *f.* moth.
tra-ça′-do *m.* mark, line, outline.
tra-ção′ *f.* traction.
tra-çar′ *tr.v.* to trace, to outline; to describe, to delineate.
tra-ce-jar′ *tr.v.* to trace a broken line.
tra′-ço *m.* trace, line; vestige; feature.
tra-di-ção′ *f.* tradition.
tra-di-ci-o-nal′ *adj.* traditional.
tra-di-ci-o-na-lis′-mo *m.* traditionalism.
tra-du-ção′ *f.* translation.
tra-du-tor′ *m.* translator.
tra-du-zir′ *tr.v.* to translate.
tra-du-zí-vel *adj.* translatable.
trâ-fe-go *m.* traffic.
tra-fi-can′-te *m.* trader, sharper.
tra-fi-car′ *tr.v., intr.v.* to trade, to deal, to do business, to be dishonest in business.
trá-fi-co *m.* commerce, business.
tra-gé-dia *f.* tragedy.
trá-gi-co, =a *adj.* tragic.
tra-i-ção′ *tf.* reason.
tra-i-ço-ei′-ro, =a *adj.* treacherous, treasonable.
tra-i-dor′ *m.* traitor.
tra-ir′ *tr.v.* to betray, to be disloyal to.
tra-jar′ *tr.v., intr.v.* to wear, to use as clothing, to dress.
tra′-je *m.* suit, clothing, costume.
tram-bo′-lho *m.* clog, encumbrance; pack.
tram-po-lim′ *m.* spring board.
tran′-ca *f.* bar; obstacle.
tran′-ça *f.* braid (of hair).
tran-ça-dei′-ra *f.* hair ribbon.
tran-car′ *tr.v.* to bar, to make fast with bar.
tran-qui-li-da′-de *f.* quiet, tranquillity.
tran-qui-li-zar′ *tr.v.* to quiet, to calm, to tranquillize.
tran-qui′-lo, =a *adj.* tranquil.
tran-sa-ção′ *f.* transaction.
tran-sat-lân-ti-co, =a *adj.* transatlantic.
trans-bor-dar′ *tr.v., intr.v.,* to overflow.
trans-cen-dên-cia *f.* transcendency.
trans-cen-den′-te *adj.* transcendent.
trans-cen-der′ *tr.v., intr.v.* to transcend.
trans-con-ti-nen-tal′ *adj.* transcontinental.
trans-cre-ver *tr.v.* to transcribe.
trans-cri-ção′ *f.* transcription.
tran′-se *m.* fear; trance; crisis, danger; fight.
tran-sep′-to *m.* transept.
trans-fe-rên-cia *f.* transference.
trans-fe-rir′ *tr.v.* to transfer.
trans-fe-rí-vel *adj.* transferable.
trans-for-ma-ção′ *f.* transformation.
trans-for-mar′ *tr.v.* to transform.
trans-fu-são′ *f.* transfusion.

trans-gre-dir′ *tr.v.* to transgress; to violate.
trans-gres-são′ *f.* transgression.
trans-gres-sor′ *m.* transgressor.
tran-si-ção′ *f.* transition.
tran-si-gir′ *intr.v.* to agree, to come to terms; *tr.v.* to conciliate, to settle.
tran-si-tar′ *intr.v.* to go, to journey, to move, to change.
tran-si-tá-vel *adj.* passable, practicable.
trân-si-to *m.* transit, traffic; death.
tran-si-tó-rio, =a *adj.* transitory.
trans-lu-zen′-te *adj.* translucent.
trans-mi-gra-ção′ *f.* transmigration.
trans-mi-grar′ *tr.v.* to transmigrate.
trans-mis-são′ *f.* transmission.
trans-mis-sí-vel *adj.* transmissible.
trans-mis-sor′ *m.* transmitter.
trans-mi-tir′ *tr.v.* to transmit.
trans-mu-dar′ *tr.v.* to transmute.
trans-mu-ta-ção′ *f.* transmutation.
trans-mu-tar′ *tr.v.* to transmute.
trans-mu-tá-vel *adj.* transmutable.
trans-pa-rên-cia *f.* transparency.
trans-pa-ren′-te *adj.* transparent.
trans-pi-rar′ *intr.v.* to transpire, to sweat.
trans-plan-tar′ *tr.v.* to transplant.
trans-por′ *tr.v.* to transpose.
trans-por-ta-ção′ *f.* transportation.
trans-por-tar′ *tr.v.* to transport.
trans-por-tá-vel *adj.* transportable.
trans-por′-te *m.* transportation.
trans-tor-nar′ *tr.v.* to disturb, to upset, to disorganize.
trans-tôr-no *m.* disarrangement.
tran-sub-stan-ci-a-ção′ *f.* transubstantiation.
trans-ver-sal′ *adj.* transverse.
trans-ver′-so, =a *adj.* transverse.
tra-pa′-ça *f.* fraud, chicanery.
tra-pa-ce-ar′ *tr.v., intr.v.* to cheat, to defraud.
tra-pa-cei′-ro *m.* cheat, knave.
tra-pé-zio *m.* trapezium, trapezoid.
tra-pi′-che *m.* warehouse.
tra′-po *m.* rag, scrap; worn-out clothing.
tra-quéi-a *f.* trachea.
trás *prep., adv.* after, behind, over.
tra-san-te-on′-tem *adv.* day before yesterday.
tras-bor-dar′ *tr.v.* to overflow; *intr.v.* to go beyond frontier or border; to be impetuous.
tra-sei′-ra *f.* part behind, tail-end.
tra-sei′-ro, =a *adj.* located behind, rear.
tras-paa-sar′ *tr.v.* to cross; to pierce, to transfix; to copy; to postpone; *intr.v.* to move on, to die, to faint.
tras-pas′-so *m.* delay, postponement; sale; death.
tras-pés *m.pl.* false steps.
tras′-te *m.* piece of furniture; worthless person.
tra-ta-men′-to *m.* treatment; name, title; welcome.
tra-tar′ *tr.v.* to treat; *intr.v.* to endeavor.
tra′-to *m.* treatment; contact, relation; manner; tract, area, terrain; **tra′-tos** *m.pl.* torture, torment, bad treatment.
tra-tor′ *m.* tractor.
trau-ma-tis′-mo *m.* traumatism.
tra-va′-do, =a *adj.* joined, united; intimate.
tra-var′ *tr.v.* to intertwine, to chain together, to secure, to engage.
tra′-ve *f.* wall plate, tie-beam.
tra-ves′-sa *f.* cross-beam; cross-tie, sleeper; street-crossing; platter; side-comb.

tra-ves-sei'-ro *m.* bolster, pillow.
tra-ves-si'-a *f.* crossing.
tra-vês-so, =a *adj.* turbulent, malicious; bothersome.
tra-ves-su'-ra *f.* naughtiness.
tra-zer' *tr.v.* to bring, to conduct, to transport; to wear.
tre'-cho *m.* interval; excerpt; fragment.
tré-gua *f.* truce; rest, respite.
trei-nar' *tr.v.* to train; —=se *refl.v.* to train.
trei'-no *m.* training.
tre-ju-rar' *tr.v.* to affirm, on oath, time after time.
tre'-lho *m.* dasher (of butter churn).
trem' *m.* train; set of utensils; set of furniture; baggage, retinue.
tre'-ma *m.* dieresis.
tre-men'-do, =a *adj.* tremendous, excessive; formidable.
tre-mer' *tr.v.* to fear; *intr.v.* to tremble, to shake.
tre-mo'-nha *f.* hopper.
tre-mor' *m.* tremor; fear; earthquake.
trê-mu-lo *m.* tremolo; =o, =a *adj.* tremulous.
tre-nó *m.* sled, sleigh.
tre-pa-dei'-ra *f.* climbing vine.
tre'-pa=mo-le'-que *m.* high-boy (furniture).
tre-par' *tr.v.*, *intr.v.* to climb up.
tre-pi-da-ção' *f.* trepidation; vibration.
tré-pi-do, =a *adj.* tremulous; fearful.
três *m.* three.
tres-lou-ca'-do, =a *adj.* crazy, demented.
tres-ma-lhar' *tr.v.* to drop stitch in knitting; —=se *refl.v.* to become lost.
tre'-vas *f.pl.* darkness; (fig.) ignorance.
tre'-vo *m.* clover.
tre'-ze *m.* thirteen.
tre-ze'-na *f.* thirteen days.
tre-ze'-no *m.* thirteenth.
tre-zen'-tos, =as *adj.* three hundred.
tri-a'-da *f.* triad.
tri-an-gu-la-ção' *f.* triangulation.
tri-an-gu-lar' *adj.* triangular.
tri-ân-gu-lo *m.* triangle.
tri-bal' *adj.* tribal.
tri'-bu *f.* tribe.
tri-bu'-na *f.* tribune.
tri-bu-nal' *m.* tribunal.
tri-bu-tar' *tr.v.* to impose a tribute; to attribute.
tri-bu-tá-rio *m.* tributary.
tri-bu'-to *m.* tribute.
tri-cen-te-ná-rio, =a *adj.* tercentenary.
tri-ci'-clo *m.* tricycle.
tri-cô *m.* knitting.
tri-côr-nio *m.* three-cornered hat.
tri-den'-te *m.* trident.
tri-e-nal' *adj.* triennial.
tri-ê-nio *m.* triennium.
tri-gal' *m.* wheat field.
tri-gê-me-o *m.* each one of triplets.
tri-gé-si-mo *m.* thirtieth.
tri'-go *m.* wheat.
tri-go-no-me-tri'-a *f.* trigonometry.
tri-guei'-ro, =a *adj.* wheat-colored.
tri-la-te-ral' *adj.* trilateral.
rri'-lho *m.* track.
tri-men-sal' *adj.* every three months.
tri-mes'-tre *m.* period of three months.
trin-ca-fi'-o *m.* shoemaker's thread.
trin'-cha *f.* adze.
trin-char' *tr.v.* to carve.
trin-chei'-ra *f.* trench, ditch.
trin'-co *m.* latch; noise of cracking finger joints.

trin-da'-de *f.* trinity.
tri-nô-mio *m.* trinomial.
trin'-ta *m.* thirty.
trin-te'-na *f.* about thirty.
tri'-o *m.* trio.
tri'-pa *f.* tripe, intestine.
tri-par-tir' *tr.v.* to divide into three parts.
tri-pé *m.* tripod.
tri-pli-car' *tr.v.* to triplicate.
tri'-plo, =a *adj.* triple.
trí-po-de *adj.* three-legged.
trip-si'-na *f.* trypsin.
tríp-ti-co *m.* triptych.
tri-pu-la-ção' *f.* crew (of a ship).
tri-pu-lan'-te *m.* crew member.
tri-qui'-na *f.* trichina.
tris-sí-la-bo *m.* trisyllable.
tris'-te *adj.* sad, depressing.
tris-te'-za *f.* sadness.
tris-to'-nho, =a *adj.* sad, melancholy.
tri-tu'-ra *f.* pulverizing.
tri-tu-rar' *tr.v.* to pulverize.
tri-un-fan'-te *adj.* triumphant.
tri-un-far' *tr.v.*, *intr.v.* to triumph, to win.
tri-un'-fo *m.* triumph.
tri-vi-al' *adj.* trivial.
tri-vi-a-li-da'-de *f.* triviality.
tro'-ca *f.* exchange, barter.
tro-ca-di'-lho *m.* pun, play on words.
tro-car' *tr.v.* to exchange, to substitute.
tro-cá-vel *adj.* exchangeable.
trô-co *m.* change, small change.
tro-féu *m.* trophy.
trom'-ba *f.* trunk (of elephant).
trom-be'-ta *f.* trumpet; *m.* trumpet player.
trom-bo'-ne *m.* trombone.
trom-bo'-se *f.* thrombosis.
trom'-pa *f.* French horn.
tron'-co *m.* trunk (of tree or human body).
tro'-no *m.* throne.
tro'-pa *f.* troop, army.
tro-pe-ça-men'-to *m.* stumbling.
tro-pe-çar' *intr.v.* to stumble.
tro-pe-ço *m.* stumbling-block, obstacle.
trô-pe-go, =a *adj.* lame, crippled.
tro-pi-cal' *adj.* tropical.
tró-pi-co *m.* Tropic.
tro'-po *m.* trope.
tro-quel' *m.* stamp, die.
tró-qui-lo *m.* concave molding.
trou'-xa *f.* bundle of clothing; woman dressed with poor taste or behaving in unseemly manner.
tro-va-dor' *m.* troubador.
tro-vão' *m.* thunder; explosion.
tro-vo-a'-da *f.* thunder storm.
tru-ão' *m.* clown, jester, buffoon.
tru-cu-lên-cia *f.* truculence.
tru-cu-len'-to, =a *adj.* truculent.
tru-ís-mo *m.* truism.
trun-car' *tr.v.* to truncate.
tu'-ba *f.* tuba, trumpet.
tu-ba'-gem *f.* tubing, piping.
tu-ber-cu-li'-na *f.* tuberculin.
tu-bér-cu-lo *m.* tubercle.
tu-ber-cu-lo'-se *f.* tuberculosis.
tu-ber-cu-lo'-so, =a *adj.* tubercular.
tu-be-ro'-sa *f.* tuberose.
tu'-bo *m.* tube; pipe.
tu-ca'-no *m.* toucan (bird).
tu'-do *pron.* everything.
tu'-do=na'-da *m.* inkling, element, trifle.
tu-fão' *m.* hurricane.
tu'-le *m.* tulle.

tú-lio *m.* thulium.
tu-li'-pa *f.* tulip.
tum'-ba *f.* tombstone; *m.* unlucky person.
tu-me-fa'-to, =a *adj.* swollen.
tu-me-fa-zer' *tr.v.* to cause to swell.
tu-mi-dez' *f.* swelling.
tú-mi-do, =a *adj.* swollen, tumid.
tu-mor' *m.* tumor.
tu-mo-ro'-so, =a *adj.* tumorous.
tú-mu-lo *m.* cenotaph; tomb; (fig.) death.
tu-mul'-to *m.* tumult.
tu-mul-tu-á-rio, =a *adj.* rebellious, disorderly.
tu-mul-tu-o'-so, =a *adj.* tumultuous.
tú-nel *m.* tunnel.
tungs-tê-nio *m.* tungsten.
tú-ni-ca *f.* tunic.
tur'-ba *f.* mob, riot.
tur-ban'-te *m.* turban.
tur-bar' *tr.v.* to disturb, to perturb.
túr-bi-do, =a *adj.* turbid.

tur-bi'-na *f.* turbine.
tur-bu-lên-cia *f.* turbulence.
tur-bu-len'-to, =a *adj.* turbulent.
tur'-fa *f.* peat, turf.
tur-gi-dez' *f.* turgidity, turgidness.
túr-gi-do, =a *adj.* turgid.
tu-ri-bu-lá-rio *m.* thurifer.
tu-rí-bu-lo *m.* thurible.
tu-ris'-mo *m.* tourism.
tu-ris'-ta *m.*, *f.* tourist.
tur'-ma *f.* group, section; squad, crew.
tur-ma-li'-na *f.* tourmaline.
tur-var' *tr.v.* to becloud, to darken, to disturb, to dim.
tur'-vo, =a *adj.* clouded, opaque; overcast; muddy.
tus-sor' *m.* tussah (silk fabric).
tu-ta'-no *m.* marrow; gist.
tu-te'-la *f.* tutelage.
tu-te-lar' *tr.v.* to protect, to exercise guardianship over.
tu-tor' *m.* guardian.
tu-to-ri'-a *f.* guardianship.

U

See page 12—GUIDE TO REFORMED SPELLING used in this Dictionary

U, u *m.* U, u, twentieth letter of the alphabet.
u-a-ta-pú *m.* horn which Pará Indians believe attracts fish.
u-ber-da'-de *f.* fecundity, fertility, opulence.
ú-be-re *adj.* fertile, abundant.
u-bi-qui-da'-de *f.* ubiquity.
u-bí-quo, =a *adj.* ubiquitous.
u-fa-nar' *tr.v.* to make proud; —-se *refl.v.* to be proud, to boast, to pride oneself.
u-fa-ni'-a *f.* pride, vanity.
u-fa'-no, =a *adj.* boasting, proud, vain.
ui-var' *intr.v.* to howl.
uí'-vo *m.* howl, mournful cry (of dog and wolf).
úl-ce-ra *f.* ulcer.
ul-ce-ro'-so, =a *adj.* ulcerous.
ul-te-ri-or' *adj.* ulterior.
ul-ti-mar' *tr.v.* to terminate, to conclude.
úl-ti-mo, =a *adj.* last, extreme.
ul-tra-jar' *tr.v.* to insult, to outrage.
ul-tra'-je *m.* insult, outrage.
ul-tra-mar' *m.* land over-seas; ultramarine.
ul-tra-ma-ri'-no, =a *adj.* oversea; ultramarine.
ul-tra-pas-sar' *tr.v.* to pass by, go to ahead, to overtake.
um' *m.* u'-ma *f.* one; a, an.
um-bi'-go *m.* navel.
um-bi-li-cal' *adj.* umbilical.
um-bro'-so, =a *adj.* shaded, shadowy.
u-me-de-cer' *tr.v.* to dampen, to make humid.
ú-me-ro *m.* humerus.
u-mi-da'-de *f.* humidity, dampness.
ú-mi-do, =a *adj.* humid, damp.
u-nâ-ni-me *adj.* unanimous.
u-na-ni-mi-da'-de *f.* unanimity.
un-ção' *f.* anointment; unction.
un-dé-ci-mo, =a *adj.* eleventh.
un-gir' *tr.v.* to anoint.
un-guen'-to *m.* ointment, salve.
u'-nha *f.* nail (of finger or toe); claw; hoof.

u-nha'-da *f.* scratch made by nail or claw.
u-nhar' *tr.v.* to claw, to scratch.
u-ni-ão' *f.* union.
ú-ni-co, =a *adj.* only, alone, unique; superior.
u-ni-cór-nio *m.* unicorn.
u-ni-da'-de *f.* unity; unit.
u-ni-fi-car' *tr.v.* to unify.
u-ni-for'-me *adj.* uniform.
u-ni-for-mi-da'-de *f.* uniformity.
u-ni-gê-ni-to *m.* only child.
u-ni-la-te-ral' *adj.* unilateral.
u-nir' *tr.v.* to unite, to join.
u-nís-so-no *m.* unison.
u-ni-ver-sal' *adj.* universal.
u-ni-ver-sa-li-da'-de *f.* universality.
u-ni-ver-si-da'-de *f.* university.
u-ni-ver-si-tá-rio, =a *adj.* of a university.
u-ni-ver'-so *m.* universe.
un-tar' *tr.v.* to grease, to anoint.
un'-to *m.* lard, fat.
un-tu-o'-so, =a *adj.* greasy, oily, unctuous.
u-râ-nio *m.* uranium.
ur-ba-ni-da'-de *f.* urbanity.
ur-ba-ni-zar' *tr.v.* to urbanize; to civilize.
ur-ba'-no, =a *adj.* urban; urbane.
u-réi-a *f.* urea.
u-re-mi'-a *f.* uraemia.
u-rê-ter *m.* ureter.
u-rê'-tra *f.* urethra.
ur-gên-cia *f.* urgency.
ur-gen'-te *adj.* urgent.
ur-gir' *intr.v.* to be urgent.
u-ri'-na *f.* urine.
u-ri-nar' *intr.v.* to urinate.
u-ri-ná-rio, =a *adj.* urinary.
u-ri-nol' *m.* urinal.
ur'-na *f.* urn.
ur-si'-no, =a *adj.* ursine, bear-like.
ur'-so *m.* bear.
ur-ti-cá-ria *f.* nettle rash, strawberry rash.
ur-ti'-ga *f.* nettle.

u-ru-bú *m.* vulture.
u-sa'-do, *=a adj.* customary; worn out.
u-sar' *tr.v.* to use; to wear; to use up, to wear out; *intr.v.* to make use; to be accustomed; —**se** *refl.v.* to wear out.
u-sá-rio *m.* money-lender.
u-sá-vel *adj.* usable.
u-si'-na *f.* factory, plant, mill.
u-si-nei'-ro *m.* plant manager, owner of a factory.
u'-so *m.* use, practice, custom.
u-su-al' *adj.* usual.
u-su'-ra *f.* usury.
u-su-rá-rio *m.* usurer.
u-sur-pa-ção' *f.* usurpation.

u-sur-par' *tr.v.* to usurp.
u-ten-sí-lio *m.* utensil.
u-te-ri'-no, *=a adj.* uterine.
ú-te-ro *m.* uterus.
ú-til *adj.* utile.
u-ti-li-da'-de *f.* usefulness, utility.
u-ti-li-tá-rio, *=a adj.* utilitarian.
u-ti-li-zar' *tr.v.* to use, to utilize.
u-to-pi'-a *f.* utopia.
u'-va *f.* grape.
u-va'-da *f.* grape jam, grape preserves.
u-val' *adj.* relative to grapes.
ú-vu-la *f.* uvula.
u-vu-lar' *adj.* uvular.
u-xo-ri-cí-dio *m.* wife-killer.

V

See page 12—GUIDE TO REFORMED SPELLING used in this Dictionary

V, v *m.* V, v, twenty-first letter of the alphabet.
va'-ca *f.* cow.
va-cân-cia *f.* vacancy.
va-can'-te *adj.* vacant.
va-car' *intr.v.* to recess; to mind, to devote.
va-ci-la-ção' *f.* vacillation.
va-ci-lan'-te *adj.* vacillating.
va-ci-lar' *intr.v.* to vacillate.
va-ci'-na *f.* vaccine.
va-ci-na-ção' *f.* vaccination.
va-ci-nar' *tr.v.* to vaccinate.
va-cu-i-da'-de *f.* vacuity.
vá-cuo *m.* vacuum.
va-di-a'-gem *f.* vagrancy, idleness.
va-di-ar' *intr.v.* to wander aimlessly; to spend time doing nothing.
va-di'-o *m.* vagrant, vagabond.
va'-ga *f.* open space; vacancy; idleness; opportunity; wave; crowd.
va-ga-bun-da'-gem *f.* vagabondage.
va-ga-bun'-do *m.* vagabond.
va-ga-lu'-me *m.* lightning bug.
va-gão' *m.* railway carriage, railway car; — **restaurante** dining car.
va-gar' *intr.v.* to be vacant; to be idle; to suffice; to wander, to spread; to drift; *m.* leisure; lingering.
va-ga-ro'-so, *=a adj.* slow, inactive, calm, lazy.
va'-gem *f.* husk, shell.
va-gi'-na *f.* vagina.
va-gi-nal' *adj.* vaginal.
va'-go, *=a adj.* vague; unoccupied, free, not taken.
vai'-a *f.* hooting, hissing.
vai-ar' *tr.v.* to hoot, to hiss, to call names.
vai-da'-de *f.* vanity.
vai-do'-so, *=a adj.* vain.
va'-la *f.* irrigation ditch.
va'-le *m.* check, scrip; scrip currency; postal money order.
va-lên-cia *f.* valence.
va-len'-te *adj.* valiant; bold.
va-len-ti'-a *f.* boldness, bravery; prowess; feat of valor; strength, vigor.
va-ler' *intr.v.* to be worth; to deserve; to avail; — **mais** to be better, to be preferable; — **a pena** to be worthwhile.
va-le'-ta *f.* drain, gutter.
va-li'-a *f.* value, merit.
va-li-dar' *tr.v.* to validate.
vá-li-do, *=a adj.* valid; robust.

va-li'-do *m.* favorite.
va-li-men'-to *m.* influence, importance.
va-li-o'-so, *=a adj.* valuable; valid; deserving.
va-li'-se *f.* valise.
va-lor' *m.* value, worth; valor, merit; stock, bond.
va-lo-ri-zar' *tr.v.* to improve the value of.
va-lo-ro'-so, *=a adj.* courageous, energetic.
val'-sa *f.* waltz.
vál-vu-la *f.* valve.
vam-pi'-ro *m.* vampire.
va-ná-dio *m.* vanadium.
van-da-lis'-mo *m.* vandalism.
vân-da-lo *m.* vandal.
van-glo-ri-o'-so, *=a adj.* vainglorious.
van-guar'-da *f.* vanguard.
van-ta'-gem *f.* advantage.
van-ta-jo'-so, *=a adj.* advantageous.
vão', **vã** *adj.* vain, fruitless, futile; frivolous; **vão'** *m.* open space, opening; interval.
va-por' *m.* vapor, steam; steamer, steamship.
va-po-ri-za-dor' *m.* atomizer.
va-po-ri-zar' *tr.v.* to vaporize.
va-po-ro'-so, *=a adj.* vaporous.
va-quei'-ro *m.* cowboy; *=o,* *=a adj.* relative to cattle.
va'-ra *f.* rod, wand; switch, stick; shaft; old measure equivalent to 1.1 meters judgeship.
va-rão' *m.* large stick, iron rod; man, male, distinguished man.
va-rar' *tr.v.* to strike, to beat; to run aground; to pierce; to drive out, to expel.
va-re-jis'-ta *m.* retail merchant.
va-re'-jo *m.* retail; auditing, inventory; firing; censure.
vá-ria *f.* short news item.
va-ri-a-ção' *f.* variation.
va-ri-an'-te *f.* variant.
va-ri-ar' *tr.v., intr.v.* to vary.
va-ri-ce'-la *f.* chicken-pox.
va-ri-co'-so, *=a adj.* varicose.
va-ri-e-da'-de *f.* variety.
va-ri-e-ga-ção' *f.* variegation.
va-ri-e-gar' *tr.v.* to variegate.
vá-rio, *=a adj.* various, varied; **vá-rios,** *=as adj.* different, several.
va-rí-o-la *f.* variola.

va-riz' f. varix.
va-ro-nil' adj. virile.
va-ro-ni-li-da'-de f. virility.
var-re-du'-ra f. sweeping, sweepings.
var-rer' tr.v., intr.v. to sweep.
var-ri'-do, =a adj. crazy, insane.
vár-ze-a f. cultivated field.
va'-sa f. slime, mud, alluvial ooze.
vas-cu-lar' adj. vascular.
va-se-li'-na f. vaseline.
va-si'-lha f. small vessel; keg.
va'-so m. vessel, receptacle, vase.
vas-sa-la'-gem f. vassalage.
vas-sa'-lo m. vassal.
vas-sou'-ra f. broom.
vas-sou-ri'-nha f. small broom.
vas-ti-dão' f. vastness.
vas'-to, =a adj. vast.
vau' m. ford.
va'-za f. hand (at cards).
va-za-dou'-ro m. dumping ground.
va-zão' f. emptying; exportation.
va-zar' tr.v. to empty, to pour out;
    intr.v. to leak, to seep out.
va-zi'-o, =a adj. empty.
ve-a'-do m. deer.
ve-da'-do, =a adj. enclosed, fenced off.
ve-dar' tr.v. to prohibit, to stop; to
    staunch.
vê-do m. fence.
ve-e-mên-cia f. vehemence.
ve-e-men'-te adj. vehement.
ve-ge-ta-ção' f. vegetation.
ve-ge-tal' adj., m. vegetable.
ve-ge-tar' intr.v. to vegetate.
ve-ge-ta-ri-a'-no m. vegetarian.
vei'-a f. vein.
ve-i-cu-lar' adj. vehicular.
ve-í-cu-lo m. vehicle.
vei'-ga f. cultivated plain.
vei'-o m. vein (in wood or in mine).
ve'-la f. candle; sail.
ve-la-dor' m. watchman.
ve-la'-me m. full sail, sails.
ve-lar' tr.v. to watch, to watch over, to
    guard; intr.v. to stay awake, to keep
    burning; to watch, to be awake.
ve-lhi'-ce f. old age.
ve'-lho, =a adj. old, aged.
ve-lho'-te m. old man, old fellow.
ve-lo-ci-da'-de f. velocity.
ve-lo-cí-pe-de m. velocipede.
ve-loz' adj. rapid, quick.
ve-lu'-do m. velvet.
ve-lu-do'-so, =a adj. velvety.
ve-nal' adj. venal.
ve-na-li-da'-de f. venality.
ven-ce-dor' m. victor, winner, con-
    queror.
ven-cer' tr.v. to conquer, to vanquish,
    convince; intr.v. to conquer; —=se
    refl.v. to control oneself; to fall due.
ven-ci-men'-to m. victory; term; salary.
ven-cí-vel adj. conquerable.
ven'-da f. sale; shop; inn; blindfold.
ven-da'-gem f. sale; commission.
ven-dar' tr.v. to blindfold.
ven-da-val' m. storm wind.
ven-dá-vel adj. saleable, marketable.
ven-der' tr.v. to sell.
ven-dí-vel adj. saleable, marketable.
ve-ne'-no m. poison.
ve-ne-no'-so, =a adj. poisonous.
ve-ne-ra-bi-li-da'-de f. venerability.
ve-ne-ra-ção' f. veneration.
ve-ne-rar' tr.v. to venerate, to revere.
ve-ne-rá-vel adj. venerable.
ve-né-re-o, =a adj. venereal.
vê-nia f. leave, permission.

ve-ni-al' adj. venial.
ven'-ta f. nostril; =s f.pl. nose, face.
ven-ta-ni'-a f. strong wind.
ven-tar' intr.v. to blow.
ven-ti-la-dor' m. ventilator; — elétrico
    electric fan.
ven-ti-lar' tr.v. to ventilate.
ven'-to m. wind.
ven-to'-sa f. cupping glass.
ven-to'-so, =a adj. windy.
ven'-tre m. stomach, abdomen.
ven-trí-cu-lo m. ventricle.
ven-trí-lo-quo, =a adj. ventriloquist.
ven-tu'-ra f. luck, good luck, risk,
    danger.
ven-tu'-ro, =a adj. future.
ven-tu-ro'-so, =a adj. lucky, fortunate;
    venturesome.
ver' tr.v. to see.
ve-ra-ci-da'-de f. veracity.
ve-ra-nis'-ta m., f. summer visitor.
ve-rão' m. summer.
ve-raz' adj. veracious.
ver'-ba f. budgetary allowance; clause.
ver-be'-na f. verbena.
ver-be'-te m. index card; note.
ver'-bo m. verb.
ver-bo-si-da'-de f. verbosity.
ver-bo'-so, =a adj. verbose.
ver-da'-de f. truth.
ver-da-dei'-ro, =a adj. true; real.
ver'-de adj. green; — bexiga dark green;
    — claro, =a adj. light green; — cré m.
    green over gold; — mar m. sea-green.
ver-de-cer' intr.v. to become green.
ver-do-en'-go, =a adj. green, not ripe.
ver-dor' m. greenness.
ver-du'-ra f. greenness; green foodstuff,
    greens, vegetables.
ver'-ga f. bar, rod.
ver-go'-nha f. shame, dishonor; blush.
ver-go-nho'-so, =a adj. shameful.
ve-ri-di-ci-da'-de f. truthfulness, verac-
    ity.
ve-rí-di-co, =a adj. truthful.
ve-ri-fi-car' tr.v. to verify; to check;
    —=se refl.v. to take place.
ver'-me m. worm.
ver-me'-lho, =a adj. red, bright red,
    vermilion.
ver-mi-for'-me adj. vermiform.
ver-mí-fu-go m. vermifuge.
ver-mu'-te m. vermouth.
ver-na-ção' f. vernation, foliation.
ver-ná-cu-lo m. =o, =a adj. vernacular.
ver-niz' m. varnish.
ve-ro-sí-mil adj. probable, likely.
ve-ro-si-mi-lan'-ça f. verisimilitude,
    probability, likelihood.
ver-sa'-do, =a adj. versed, expert.
ver-são' f. version, translation.
ver-sar' tr.v. to study, to ponder, to prac-
    tice; intr.v. to treat, to deal.
ver-sá-til' adj. versatile.
ver-sa-ti-li-da'-de f. versatility.
ver-sí-cu-lo m. verse, stave.
ver'-so m. verse.
vér-te-bra f. vertebra.
ver-te-bra'-do m. vertebrate.
ver-te-bral' adj. vertebral.
ver-ten'-te f. slope.
ver-ter' tr.v. to pour, to empty; to trans-
    late; to shed; to suffer; intr.v. to spring,
    to rise, to empty.
ver-ti-cal' adj. vertical.
vér-ti-ce m. vertex.
ver-ti'-gem f. faint, dizziness.
ver-ti-gi-no'-so, =a adj. vertiginous.
ver'-ve f. verve.

ve-sí-cu-la *f.* vesicle.
ve-si-cu-lar' *adj.* vesicular.
vés-pe-ra *f.* evening; eve, day before; **=s** *f.pl.* vespers.
ves-pe-ral' *adj.* of the evening; *m.* book of evening prayers.
ves-per-ti'-no, **=a** *adj.* of the evening.
ves-ti-á-ria *f.* wardrobe; dressing-room.
ves-tí-bu-lo *m.* vestibule.
ves-ti'-do *m.* clothes, dress.
ves-tí-gio *m.* vestige, remains, trace, track.
ves-tir' *tr.v.* to put on, to dress, to wear; *intr.v.* to dress; —**se** *refl.v.* to dress, to get dressed.
ves-tu-á-rio *m.* wearing apparel, suit of clothes.
ve-te-ra'-no *m.* **=o**, **=a** *adj.* veteran.
ve-te-ri-ná-ria *f.* veterinary medicine.
ve-te-ri-ná-rio *m.* veterinary doctor; **ve-te-ri-ná-rio**, **=a** *adj.* veterinary.
ve'-to *m.* veto.
véu *m.* veil; pretext.
ve-xa-ção' *f.* vexation.
ve-xa'-me *m.* vexation, annoyance.
ve-xar' *tr.v.* to vex, to annoy; to maltreat, to humiliate, to molest.
vez' *f.* time, turn.
ví'-a *f.* road, way; track; direction; copy.
vi-a-bi-li-da'-de *f.* viability, ability to live.
vi-a-dor' *m.* traveller.
vi-a-du'-to *m.* viaduct.
vi-a'-gem *f.* voyage, trip, journey.
vi-a-jan'-te *m.* traveller.
vi-a-jar' *intr.v.* to voyage, to travel; *tr.v.* to travel through.
vi-an'-da *f.* viand.
vi-an-dei'-ro *m.* glutton.
vi-á-vel *adj.* passable, traversable; capable of surviving.
ví-bo-ra *f.* viper.
vi-bra-ção' *f.* vibration.
vi-bran'-te *adj.* vibrating, vibrant.
vi-brar' *intr.v.* to vibrate; *tr.v.* to cause to vibrate.
vi-bra-tó-rio, **=a** *adj.* vibratory.
vi-ci-a-men'-to *m.* vitiation.
vi-ci-ar' *tr.v.* to vitiate.
ví-cio *m.* vice, defect.
vi-ci-o'-so, **=a** *adj.* vicious, defective, imperfect.
vi-cis-si-tu'-de *f.* vicissitude.
ví'-da *f.* life, living.
vi-dei'-ro, **=a** *adj.* selfish, self-centered.
vi-den'-te *m.* seer, prophet.
vi-dra'-ça *f.* window pane.
vi-dra-cei'-ro *m.* glazier, manufacturer of window panes, dealer in window panes.
vi-drei'-ro *m.* glass worker.
ví'-dro *m.* glass.
vi-és *m.* bias.
ví'-ga *f.* beam, heavy rafter.
vi-ga-men'-to *m.* framework.
vi-ga-ri-a'-to *m.* vicarship, vicarage.
vi-gá-rio *m.* vicar, priest.
vi-gên-cia *f.* state of being in force.
vi-gen'-te *adj.* in force.
vi-ger' *intr.v.* to be in force.
vi-gé-si-mo, **=a** *adj.* twentieth.
vi-gí-li-a *f.* watching, watchfulness, waking, wakefulness; sentinal, guard, watchman.
vi-gi-ar' *tr.v.* to watch, to spy on, to observe; *intr.v.* to be awake; to be concerned.
vi-gi-lân-cia *f.* vigilance.
vi-gi-lan'-te *adj.* vigilant.

vi-gor' *m.* vigor, strength.
vi-go-ro'-so, **=a** *adj.* vigorous, energetic.
vil' *adj.* vile; base.
ví'-la *f.* town; villa.
vi-la-ni'-a *f.* villainy; miserliness.
vi-lão' *m.* townsman; peasant; knave; miser; *adj.* discourteous; villainous.
vi-le'-za *f.* vileness, baseness.
vi-li-fi-car' *tr.v.* to vilify.
ví'-me *m.* wicker.
vi-na'-gre *m.* vinegar.
vi-na-grei'-ra *f.* cruet.
vin'-co *m.* dent, scratch, rut, bruise.
vin-cu-lar' *tr.v.* to unite, to join, to bind.
vín-cu-lo *m.* tie, bond.
vin'-da *f.* coming, arrival; **boas =s** welcome.
vin-di-ca-ção' *f.* vindication.
vin-di'-ma *f.* grape harvest.
vin'-do, **=a** *adj.* come, arrived.
vin-dou'-ro, **=a** *adj.* future.
vin-ga-dor' *m.* avenger, revenger.
vin-gan'-ça *f.* vengeance.
vin-gar' *tr.v.* to avenge; *intr.v.* to succeed, to thrive.
ví'-nha *f.* vineyard.
vi-nhão' *m.* strong, heavy wine.
vi-nha-ta-ri'-a *f.* wine-making.
vi-nhe'-te *m.* weak wine.
ví'-nho *m.* wine.
vi-no'-so, **=a** *adj.* strong, heady, wine-like.
vin'-te *m.* twenty.
vin-tém *m.* coin worth 20 reis; money.
vin-te'-na *f.* about twenty.
vi-o'-la *f.* viol, viola.
vi-o-la-ção' *f.* violation.
vi-o-lá-ce-as *f.pl.* violets.
vi-o-lão' *m.* viola.
vi-o-lar' *tr.v.* to violate.
vi-o-lá-vel *adj.* violable.
vi-o-lên-cia *f.* violence.
vi-o-len'-to, **=a** *adj.* violent.
vi-o-li'-no *m.* violin.
vi-o-lon-ce'-lo *m.* violoncello.
vir' *intr.v.* to come; to happen.
vi-ra-ção' *f.* gentle, fresh breeze.
ví'-ra=ca-sa'-ca *m.* turn-coat.
vi-ra-men'-to *m.* turning.
vi-rar' *tr.v.* to turn; to develop; *intr.v.* to turn; —**se** *refl.v.* to turn around.
vi-ra-vol'-ta *f.* turning around, about face.
vir'-gem *f.* virgin.
vir-gi-nal' *adj.* virginal.
vir-gin-da'-de *f.* virginity.
vír-gu-la *f.* comma.
vi-ril' *adj.* virile.
vi-ri-li-da'-de *f.* virility.
vir-tu'-de *f.* virtue.
vir-tu-o'-se *f.* virtuoso.
vir-tu-o-si-da'-de *f.* virtuosity.
vir-tu-o'-so, **=a** *adj.* virtuous.
vi-ru-lên-cia *f.* virulence.
vi-ru-len'-to, **=a** *adj.* virulent.
ví'-rus *m.* virus.
vi-são' *f.* vision.
vís-ce-ra *f.* viscera.
vis-con'-de *m.* viscount.
vis-con-des'-sa *f.* viscontess.
vis-co-si-da'-de *f.* viscosity.
vis-co'-so, **=a** *adj.* viscous.
vi-sei'-ra *f.* visor.
vi-si-bi-li-da'-de *f.* visibility.
vi-si-o-ná-rio, **=a** *adj.* visionary.
vi-si'-ta *f.* visit; visitor.
vi-si-ta-ção' *f.* visitation.
vi-si-tar' *tr.v.* to visit; to inspect.
vi-sí-vel *adj.* visible; at home.

vis'-ta *f.* sight; vista.
vis'-to *m.* visa.
vis-to'-so, =a *adj.* showy, elegant, striking.
vi-su-al' *adj.* visual.
vi-tal' *adj.* vital.
vi-ta-li-da'-de *f.* vitality.
vi-ta-mi'-na *f.* vitamin.
vi-te'-la *f.* veal.
ví-ti-ma *f.* victim.
vi-tó-ria *f.* victory.
vi-to-ri-o'-so, =a *adj.* victorious.
ví-tre-o, =a *adj.* vitreous.
vi-tri-fi-car' *tr.v.* to vitrify.
vi-tri'-na *f.* show case, show window.
vi-trí-o-lo *m.* vitriol.
vi-tu-a'-lhas *f.pl.* victuals.
vi-tu-pe-ra-ção' *f.* vituperation.
vi-ú-va *f.* widow.
vi-u-vez' *f.* widowhood.
vi-ú-vo *m.* widower.
vi-va-ci-da'-de *f.* vivacity.
vi-vaz' *adj.* vivacious.
vi-ven'-da *f.* home, residence.
vi-ven'-te *adj.* living.
vi-ver' *intr.v.* to live, to be alive.
vi-ve'-res *m.pl.* provisions.
ví-vi-do, =a *adj.* vivid.
vi-vi-fi-car' *tr.v.* to vivify.
vi'-vo, =a *adj.* alive, living.
vi-zi-nhan'-ça *f.* neighborhood.
vi-zi'-nho, =a *adj.* neighboring; *m.*, *f.* neighbor.
vo-an'-te *adj.* flying.
vo-ar' *intr.v.* to fly.
vo-ca-bu-lá-rio *m.* vocabulary.
vo-cá-bu-lo *m.* word.
vo-ca-ção' *f.* vocation.
vo-cal' *adj.* vocal.
vo-ca-li-zar' *tr.v.* to vocalize.
vo-cê *pron.* you.
vo-ci-fe-ra-ção' *f.* vociferation.
vo-gal' *f.* vowel; *m.* voting delegate.
vo-lan'-te *m.* flywheel, steering wheel, balance wheel; *adj.* flying, winged.
vo-lá-til *adj.* volatile.
vo-li-ção' *f.* volition.
vol'-ta *f.* return, turning around, revolution.

vol-ta'-gem *f.* voltage.
vol-tai'-co, =a *adj.* voltaic.
vol-tâ-me-tro *m.* voltmeter.
vol-tar' *intr.v.* to return; to . . . again; *tr.v.* to turn, to turn around; —=se *refl.v.* to turn, to turn around.
vol-tí-me-tro *m.* voltmeter.
vól-tio *m.* volt.
vo-lu-bi-li-da'-de *f.* volubility.
vo-lu'-me *m.* volume.
vo-lu-mi-no'-so, =a *adj.* voluminous.
vo-lu-mo'-so, =a *adj.* voluminous.
vo-lun-ta-ri-e-da'-de *f.* voluntariness, willfulness, spontaneity, capriciousness.
vo-lun-tá-rio, =a *adj.* voluntary.
vo-lup-tu-o'-so, =a *adj.* voluptuous.
vo-lú-vel *adj.* voluble.
vol-ver' *tr.v.* to turn, to turn over; *intr.v.* to pass, to elapse.
vo-mi-ta'-do *m.* vomit.
vo-mi-tar' *tr.v.* to vomit, to vomit forth.
vô-mi-to *m.* vomit, spew.
von-ta'-de *f.* will, wish, desire, appetite, notion.
vô-o *m.* flight.
vo-ra-ci-da'-de *f.* voracity.
vo-raz' *adj.* voracious.
vór-ti-ce *m.* vortex.
vo-ta-ção' *f.* voting.
vo-tan'-te *m.* voter.
vo-tar' *tr.v.* to vote; *intr.v.* to vote. to cast a vote.
vo-ti'-vo, =a *adj.* votive.
vo'-to *m.* vow; wish; voting.
voz' *f.* voice.
vul-ca-ni'-te *f.* vulcanite.
vul-ca-ni-za-ção' *f.* vulcanization.
vul-ca-ni-zar' *tr.v.* to vulcanize.
vul-cão' *m.* volcano.
vul-gar' *adj.* vulgar; common; well-known; used.
vul-ga-ri-e-da'-de *f.* vulgarity.
vul'-go *m.* mob, rabble, common people.
vul-ne-rá-vel *adj.* vulnerable.
vul'-to *m.* face, aspect; bulk, volume; form; important person; importance.
vul-to'-so, =a *adj.* voluminous.
vul'-va *f.* vulva.
vur'-mo *m.* pus.

X

See page 12—GUIDE TO REFORMER SPELLING used in this Dictionary

X, x *m.* X, x, twenty-second letter of the alphabet.
xa-drez' *m.* chess.
xai-rel' *m.* saddle cloth.
xam-pú *m.* shampoo.
xan-te-í-na *f.* xanthein (yellow coloring matter).
xan-ti'-na *f.* xanthin (yellow coloring matter).
xa-rá *m.*, *f.* person having same baptismal name as another.

xa-ro'-pe *m.* syrup; household remedy.
xe-lim' *m.* shilling (English money).
xe'-que *m.* check (in chess).
xe'-que=ma'-te *m.* check-mate.
xin-gar' *tr.v.* to address insulting words to another, to insult, to offend.
xi'-que=xi'-que *m.* Brazilian cactus.
xis'-to *m.* schist.
xis-to'-so, =a *adj.* schistous.

Z

See page 12—GUIDE TO REFORMED SPELLING used in this Dictionary

Z, z *m.* Z, z, twenty-third letter of the alphabet.

zai'-no, *=a adj.* dark bay (without markings); false, perfidious.

zan'-ga *f.* anger; annoyance; aversion.

zan-ga'-do, *=a adj.* irritated, annoyed; irritable.

zan-gão' *m.* drone; idler, sponger.

zan-gar' *tr.v.* to anger, to annoy, to irritate; —*=se refl.v.* to get angry.

zê-bra *f.* zebra.

ze-bú *m.* zebu.

ze-fir' *m.* zephyr cloth.

zé-fi-ro *m.* zephyr.

ze-la-dor' *m.* zealot, stickler; caretaker.

ze-lar' *tr.v.* to watch over, to guard; *intr.v.* to be zealous.

zê-lo *m.* zeal.

ze-lo'-so, *=a adj.* zealous.

ze-lo'-te *m.* zealot, fanatic.

zê-ni-te *m.* zenith.

ze'-ro *m.* zero.

zi'-gue=za'-gue *m.* zigzag.

zim'-bro *m.* juniper (tree).

zin-car' *tr.v.* to cover with zinc.

zin'-co *m.* zinc.

zin-co-gra-vu'-ra *f.* zincography.

zí-nia *f.* zinnia.

zir-cão' *m.* zircon.

zir-cô-nio *m.* zirconium.

zo-dí-a-co *m.* zodiac.

zom-bar' *intr.v.* to joke, to jest.

zo'-na *f.* zone, belt.

zo-na'-do, *=a adj.* zoned.

zo-o-gra-fi'-a *f.* zoography.

zo-ói-de *adj.* zooid.

zo-o-lo-gi'-a *f.* zoology.

zo-o-ló-gi-co, *=a adj.* zoological.

zo-ó-lo-go *m.* zoologist.

zor-rão' *m.* loafer, lazy fellow.

zor'-ro *m.* fox; bastard; *=o, =a adj.* slow; cunning.

zum-bi'-do *m.* buzz, buzzing noise.

zum-bir' *intr.v.* to buzz.

zu-nir' *intr.v.* to whistle.

zur'-ro *m.* braying.

zur-zi-de'-la *f.* whipping, beating.

zur-zir' *tr.v.* to strike, to whip, to maltreat.

REGULAR VERBS

1st conjugation	2d conjugation	3d conjugation

INFINITIVE

falar *to speak*	vender *to sell*	partir *to leave*

Personal Infinitive

falar	vender	partir
falares	venderes	partires
falar	vender	partir
falarmos	vendermos	partirmos
falardes	venderdes	partirdes
falarem	venderem	partirem

INDICATIVE
Present

falo	vendo	parto
falas	vendes	partes
fala	vende	parte
falamos	vendemos	partimos
falais	vendeis	partís
falam	vendem	partem

Imperfect

falava	vendia	partia
falavas	vendias	partias
falava	vendia	partia
falávamos	vendíamos	partíamos
faláveis	vendíeis	partíeis
falavam	vendiam	partiam

Preterit

falei	vendí	partí
falaste	vendeste	partiste
falou	vendeu	partiu
falámos	vendemos	partimos
falastes	vendestes	partistes
falaram	venderam	partiram

Pluperfect

falara	vendera	partira
falaras	venderas	partiras
falara	vendera	partira
faláramos	vendêramos	partíramos
faláreis	vendêreis	partíreis
falaram	venderam	partiram

Future

falarei	venderei	partirei
falarás	venderás	partirás
falará	venderá	partirá
falaremos	venderemos	partiremos
falareis	vendereis	partireis
falarão	venderão	partirão

Conditional

falaria	venderia	partiria
falarias	venderias	partirias
falaria	venderia	partiria
falaríamos	venderíamos	partiríamos
falaríeis	venderíeis	partiríeis
falariam	venderiam	partiriam

SUBJUNCTIVE

Present

fale	venda	parta
fales	vendas	partas
fale	venda	parta
falemos	vendamos	partamos
faleis	vendais	partais
falem	vendam	partam

Imperfect

falasse	vendeses	partisse
falasses	vendesses	partisses
falasse	vendesse	partisse
falássemos	vendêssemos	partíssemos
falásseis	vendêsseis	partísseis
falassem	vendessem	partissem

Future

falar	vender	partir
falares	venderes	partires
falar	vender	partir
falarmos	vendermos	partirmos
falardes	venderdes	partirdes
falarem	venderem	partirem

IMPERATIVE

fala	vende	parte
falai	vendei	parti

GERUND

falando	vendendo	partindo

PAST PARTICIPLE

falado	vendido	partido

ORTHOGRAPHIC-CHANGING VERBS

Verbs in -car change c to qu before e: ficar, fique, fiquei.
Verbs in -gar change g to gu before e: pagar, pague, paguei.
Verbs in -çar change ç to c before e: começar, comece, comecei.
Verbs in -ger and -gir change g to j before o and a: eleger, elejo; corrigir, corrija.
Verbs in -cer and -cir change c to ç before o and a: vencer, venço, vença.
Verbs in -guer and -guir drop the u before o and a: erguer, ergo; seguir, siga.

IRREGULAR VERBS

The infinitive, gerund, past participle, present indicative, present subjunctive, and preterit indicative of most irregular verbs are listed below in the first four columns. Other irregular tenses are listed in the fifth column with the tense indicated.

inf., gerund, past part.	pres. ind.	pres. subj.	pret. ind.	other irregular tenses
caber *to fit*	caibo	caiba	coube	
	cabes	caibas	coubeste	
cabendo	cabe	caiba	coube	
	cabemos	caibamos	coubemos	
cabido, -a	cabeis	caibais	coubestes	
	cabem	caibam	couberam	
cair *to fall*	caio	caia	caí	
	cais	caias	caíste	
caindo	cai	caia	caíu	
	caímos	caiamos	caímos	
caído, -a	caís	caiais	caístes	
	caem	caiam	caíram	

crer *to believe*	creio	creia	cri
	crês	creias	crêste
crendo	crê	creia	creu
	cremos	creamos	cremos
crido, -a	credes	creais	crêstes
	crêem	creiam	creram

dar *to give*	dou	dê	dei
	dás	dês	deste
dando	dá	dê	deu
	damos	dêmos	demos
dado, -a	dais	deis	destes
	dão	dêem	deram

				fut. ind.
dizer *to say*	digo	diga	disse	direi
	dizes	digas	disseste	dirás
dizendo	diz	diga	disse	dirá
	dizemos	digamos	dissemos	diremos
dito, -a	dizeis	digais	dissestes	direis
	dizem	digam	disseram	dirão

dormir *to sleep*	durmo	durma	dormí
	dormes	durmas	dormiste
dormindo	dorme	durma	dormiu
	dormimos	durmamos	dormimos
dormido, -a	dormís	durmais	dormistes
	dormem	durmam	dormiram

estar *to be*	estou	esteja	estive
	estás	estejas	estiveste
estando	está	esteja	esteve
	estamos	estejamos	estivemos
estado, -a	estais	estejais	estivestes
	estão	estejam	estiveram

				fut. ind.
fazer *to do*	faço	faça	fiz	farei
	fazes	faças	fizeste	farás
fazendo	faz	faça	fêz	fará
	fazemos	façamos	fizemos	faremos
feito, -a	fazeis	façais	fizestes	fareis
	fazem	façam	fizeram	farão

haver *to have*	hei	haja	houve
	hás	hajas	houveste
havendo	há	haja	houve
	havemos	hajamos	houvemos
havido, -a	haveis	hajais	houvestes
	hão	hajam	houveram

ir *to go*	vou	vá	fui
	vais	vás	foste
indo	vai	vá	foi
	vamos	vamos	fomos
ido, -a	ides	vades	fostes
	vão	vão	foram

jazer *to lie*	jaço	jaça	jouve
	jazes	jaças	jouveste
jazendo	jaz	jaça	jouve
	jazemos	jaçamos	jouvemos
jazido, -a	jazeis	jaçais	jouvestes
	jazem	jaçam	jouveram

ler *to read*	leio	leia	li
	lês	leias	lêste
lendo	lê	leia	leu
	lêmos	leamos	lêmos
lido, -a	ledes	leais	lêstes
	lêem	leiam	leram

medir *to measure*	meço	meça	medí
	medes	meças	mediste
medindo	mede	meça	mediu
	medimos	meçamos	medimos
medido, -a	medís	meçais	medistes
	medem	meçam	mediram

ouvir *to hear*	ouço	ouça	ouví
	ouves	ouças	ouviste
ouvindo	ouve	ouça	ouviu
	ouvimos	ouçamos	ouvimos
ouvido, -a	ouvís	ouçais	ouvistes
	ouvem	ouçam	ouviram

pedir *to ask*	peço	peça	pedí
	pedes	peças	pediste
pedindo	pede	peça	pediu
	pedimos	peçamos	pedimos
pedido, -a	pedís	peçais	pedistes
	pedem	peçam	pediram

perder *to lose*	perco	perca	perdí
	perdes	percas	perdeste
perdendo	perde	perca	perdeu
	perdemos	percamos	perdemos
perdido, -a	perdeis	percais	perdestes
	perdem	percam	perderam

poder *to be able*	posso	possa	pude
	podes	possas	pudeste
podendo	pode	possa	pôde
	podemos	possamos	pudèmos
podido	podeis	possais	pudestes
	podem	possam	puderam

				imperf. ind.
pôr *to put*	ponho	ponha	pus	punha
	pões	ponhas	puseste	punhas
pondo	põe	ponha	pôs	punha
	pomos	ponhamos	pusemos	púnhamos
pôsto, posta	pondes	ponhais	pusestes	púnheis
	põem	ponham	puseram	punham

querer *to wish*	quero	queira	quis
	queres	queiras	quiseste
querendo	quer	queira	quis
	queremos	queiramos	quisemos
querido, -a	quereis	queirais	quisestes
	querem	queiram	quiseram

rir *to laugh*	rio	ria	ri
	ris	rias	riste
rindo	ri	ria	riu
	rimos	riamos	rimos
rido	rides	riais	ristes
	riem	riam	riram

saber *to know*	sei	saiba	soube
	sabes	saibas	soubeste
sabendo	sabe	saiba	soube
	sabemos	saibamos	soubemos
sabido, -a	sabeis	saibais	soubestes
	sabem	saibam	souberam

sair *to go out*	saio	saia	saí
	sais	saias	saíste
saindo	sai	saia	saiu
	saímos	saiamos	saímos
saído, -a	saís	saiais	saístes
	saem	saiam	saíram

sentir *to feel*	sinto	sinta	senti	
	sentes	sintas	sentiste	
sentindo	sente	sinta	sentiu	
	sentimos	sintamos	sentimos	
sentido, -a	sentís	sintais	sentistes	
	sentem	sintam	sentiram	

				imperf. ind.
ser *to be*	sou	seja	fui	era
	és	sejas	foste	eras
sendo	é	seja	foi	era
	somos	sejamos	fomos	éramos
sido	sois	sejais	fostes	éreis
	são	sejam	foram	eram

servir *to serve*	sirvo	sirva	serví	
	serves	sirvas	serviste	
servindo	serve	sirva	serviu	
	servimos	sirvamos	servimos	
servido, -a	servís	sirvais	servistes	
	servem	sirvam	serviram	

subir *to go up*	subo	suba	subí	
	sobes	subas	subiste	
subindo	sobe	suba	subiu	
	subimos	subamos	subimos	
subido, -a	subís	subais	subistes	
	sobem	subam	subiram	

				imperf. ind.
ter *to have*	tenho	tenha	tive	tinha
	tens	tenhas	tiveste	tinhas
tendo	tem	tenha	teve	tinha
	temos	tenhamos	tivemos	tínhamos
tido, -a	tendes	tenhais	tivestes	tínheis
	teem or têm	tenham	tiveram	tinham

				fut. ind.
trazer *to bring*	trago	traga	trouxe	trarei
	trazes	tragas	trouxeste	trarás
trazendo	traz	traga	trouxe	trará
	trazemos	tragamos	trouxemos	traremos
trazido, -a	trazeis	tragais	trouxestes	trareis
	trazem	tragam	trouxeram	trarão

valer *to be worth*	valho	valha	valí	
	vales	valhas	valeste	
valendo	vale	valha	valeu	
	valemos	valhamos	valemos	
valido, -a	valeis	valhais	valestes	
	valem	valham	valeram	

ver *to see*	vejo	veja	vi	
	vês	vejas	viste	
vendo	vê	veja	viu	
	vemos	vejamos	vimos	
visto, -a	vêdes	vejais	vistes	
	vêem	vejam	viram	

				imperf. ind.
vir *to come*	venho	venha	vim	vinha
	vens	venhas	vieste	vinhas
vindo	vem	venha	veio	vinha
	vimos	venhamos	viemos	vínhamos
vindo, -a	vindes	venhais	viestes	vínheis
	veem or vêm	venham	vieram	vinham

PART II

ENGLISH-PORTUGUESE

EDITED BY
MARIA de LOURDES SÁ PEREIRA
and
MILTON SÁ PEREIRA

ABBREVIATIONS

abr.	abreviatura	hist. rom.	história romana
adj.	adjetivo	hort.	horticultura
adv.	advérbio	imp.	imprensa
aer.	aeronáutica	ind.	indefinido
agric.	agricultura	Ing.	Inglaterra
anat.	anatomia	int.	interjeição
arq.	arquitetura	ital.	italiano
art.	artigo	j.	jôgo
artilh.	artilharia	lat.	latim, latino
ast.	astronomia	m.	metro
astrol.	astrologia	maq.	maquinaria
aut.	automóvel	mar.	marítimo
av.	aviação	mat.	matemática
biol.	biologia	mec.	mecânica
bot.	botânica	med.	medicina
carp.	carpintaria	met.	metalurgia
cir.	cirurgia	meteor.	meteorologia
com.	comércio	mil.	milita.
conj.	conjunção	min.	mineralogia
const.	construção	mús.	música
cont.	contabilidade	our.	ourivesaria
cost.	costura	parl.	parlamentar
coz.	cozinha	pint.	pintura
des.	desenho	pl.	plural
dir.	direito	poe.	poesia
ecles.	eclesiástico	pol.	política
educ.	educação	pop.	popular
elet.	eletricidade	pref.	prefixo
equiv.	equivalente	prep.	preposição
esg.	esgrima	princ.	principalmente
esp.	esporte	pron.	pronome
E. U.	Estados Unidos	psic.	psicologia
ex.	exemplo	quím.	química
fam.	familiar	rád.	rádio
farm.	farmácia	s.	substantivo
fer.	ferrovia	sid.	siderurgia
fig.	figuradamente	teat.	teatro
fil.	filosofia	tec.	tecido
fin.	finanças	teol.	teologia
fís.	física	tint.	tinturaria
for.	forense	tip.	tipografia
fot.	fotografia	topog.	topografia
geod.	geodésia	V.	veja
geog.	geografia	v.def.	verbo defectivo
geol.	geologia	vet.	veterinária
geom.	geometria	v.i.	verbo intransitivo
ger.	gerúndio	v.t.	verbo transitivo
gram.	gramática	v.t. & i.	verbo transitivo e intransitivo
her.	heráldica		tivo
hidr.	hidráulica	zool.	zoologia

A semi-colon is used to mark off the meaning to which the subjects in italics in parentheses refer.

O ponto e vírgula limita a terminologia específica relativa aos assuntos indicados em itálico, entre parênteses.

PREFACE

This modest work is intended chiefly to help students of the Portuguese language and people who have to use this language for practical purposes.

Although the authors have tried to choose the commonest words of the English language, they have not striven to systematically omit obsolete terms, provided they seemed to be of some possible use. The Portuguese, however, is present-day Portuguese and represents Brazilian usage for the most part.

In order to save space, derivatives and idioms are placed in the majority of cases under the heading of the primary word, which is represented by the mark ⁊ in compounds made by suffixation, by the mark —⁊ in hyphened compounds, and by the mark — in idioms and phrases.

The orthography adopted is that of the Brazilian-Portuguese Agreement, also adopted by the *Pequeno Dicionário Brasileiro da Língua Portuguesa,* second edition.

The authors wish to thank Professor José Famadas for many valuable suggestions which were found useful in the compilation of this dictionary.

M. L. S. P.
M. S. P.

PREFÁCIO

Êste modesto trabalho destina-se principalmente a auxiliar estudantes da língua portuguesa e pessoas que precisem utilizar-se dêsse idioma para fins práticos.

Embora tenham procurado selecionar as palavras mais usadas da língua inglesa, os autores não tiveram a preocupação de omitir sistemàticamente termos arcaicos sempre que êsses lhes pareceram de possível utilidade. A linguagem portuguesa, porém, é a atual e representa sobretudo o uso brasileiro.

Para poupar espaço as palavras derivadas e locuções figuram na maioria das vezes sob a epígrafe da palavra principal, a qual é representada pelo sinal ⊘ nos compostos por aglutinação, pelo sinal — ⊘ nos por justaposição e pelo sinal — nas locuções e frases.

A ortografia seguida é a do Acôrdo Luso-Brasileiro de 1931, também adotada pelo *Pequeno Dicionário Brasileiro da Língua Portuguesa*, 2. edição.

Os autores expressam aquí seus agradecimentos ao Professor José Famadas por muitas sugestões valiosas, que foram utilizadas na elaboração dêste dicionário.

M. L. S. P.
M. S. P.

ENGLISH-PORTUGUESE

A

A, a s. primeira letra do alfabeto; *art.ind.* um, uma; o, a, cada, como em *one dollar a dozen* um dólar a (cada) dúzia; (*mús.*) lá; **A 1** de primeira qualidade.
aback *adv.* atrás, por detrás, às avessas; **to be taken** — ser tomado de surpresa, admirar-se, desconcertar-se.
abacus s. ábaco.
abaft *adv.* (*mar.*) pela pôpa; s. a pôpa de um navio.
abandon *v.t.* abandonar; **-ment** s. abandono.
abase *v.t.* rebaixar, aviltar; **-ment** s. rebaixamento, aviltamento, degradação.
abash *v.* confundir, desconcertar; alguém; **-ment** s. embaraço, perplexidade, humilhação.
abate *v.t.* abater, diminuir.
abatement s. abatimento, extenuação, redução.
abattoir s. matadouro.
abbey s. abadia.
abbess s. abadessa.
abbot s. abade.
abbacy s. dignidade abacial.
abbreviate *v.t.* abreviar, encurtar.
abbreviation s. abreviação, abreviatura.
A B C s. abc, abecedário; rudimentos (de uma matéria); **the ABC powers** as potências do ABC (Argentina, Brasil e Chile).
abdicate *v.t.&i.* abdicar.
abdication s. abdicação.
abdomen s. abdomen, ventre; **lower part of the** — baixo ventre.
abdominal *adj.* abdominal.
abduct *v.t.* sequestrar, raptar; (*anat.*) abduzir; **-ion** s. sequestro, rapto; (*anat.*) abdução.
abed *adv.* na cama.
aberration s. aberração.
abet *v.t.* instigar, induzir; **-tor** s. instigador, cúmplice; **-ment** s. instigação.
abeyance s. suspensão, estado latente; **in** — latente, em suspenso; **estate in** — herança jacente.
abhor *v.t.* detestar; **-rence** s. aversão, repulsão; **-rent** *adj.* abominável, detestável.
abide *v.i.* habitar, morar, residir; permanecer; *v.t.* suportar, sujeitar-se a; **to** — **by** permanecer fiel a, conformar-se com; ater-se a.
ability s. capacidade, habilidade.
abject *adj.* abjeto, desprezível, vil, baixo; **-ion** s. abjeção, baixeza, aviltamento; **-ly** *adv.* abjetamente, vilmente.
abjure *v.t.* abjurar; **-r** s. abjurante.
abjuration s. abjuração.
abjuratory *adj.* abjuratório.
ablation s. ablação.
ablative s. ablativo.
ablaze *adv.&adj.* em chamas, inflamado, ardente.
able *adj.* hábil, capaz, eficiente; —

bodied *adj.* robusto, são; vigoroso; **to be** — **to** ser capaz de, poder.
ably *adv.* habilmente.
ablution s. ablução.
abnegate *v.t.* renegar, negar, renunciar, abjurar; rejeitar.
abnegation s. abnegação, renúncia.
abnormal *adj.* anormal; **-ity** s. anormalidade; **-ly** *adv.* anormalmente.
abnormity s. anormalidade; deformidade; monstruosidade.
aboard *adv.* a bordo.
abode s. domicílio, residência, morada; permanência, estada.
abolish *v.t.* abolir; suprimir; destruir.
abolition s. abolição, supressão.
abominable *adj.* abominável, detestável.
abominate *v.t.* abominar, detestar.
abomination s. abominação; ódio.
aborigene s. indígena, natural do país; **-s** *s.pl.* aborígenes.
aboriginal *adj.* aborígene, primitivo, nativo, indígena; **-ly** *adv.* originàriamente, primitivamente.
abort *v.i.* abortar; **-ion** s. abôrto; **-ive** *adj.* abortivo; **-ively** *adv.* abortivamente.
abound *v.i.* abundar.
about *adv.* ao redor; perto; mais ou menos, aproximadamente, quasi; *prep.* acêrca de, perto de; **to be** — **to** achar-se a ponto de, estar para; **what is it all** —?, de que se trata?
above *adv.* acima, por cima; *prep.* sôbre; acima de; **from** — de cima, do alto; — **all** sobretudo, antes de tudo, em primeiro lugar; **-board** às claras, jôgo franco.
abracadabra s. abracadabra.
abrade *v.t.&i.* usar, desgastar, esfregar demasiadamente.
abrasion s. (*fís.*) abrasão; desgaste.
abreast *adv.&adj.* de frente; lado a lado, par a par; — **of** (*mar.*) na altura de.
abridge *v.t.* abreviar, encurtar.
abridgment s. resumo, compêndio, redução.
abroad *adv.* fóra, no exterior; a larga; **from** — do estrangeiro, do exterior; **there is a rumor** — **that** corre o boato que; **to publish** — divulgar.
abrogate *v.t.* abrogar; anular; cancelar.
abrogation s. abrogação; anulação; cancelamento.
abrupt *adj.* abrupto, brusco, precipitado; alcantilado; **-ness** s. brusquidão, aspereza.
abscess s. abcesso.
abscission s. abcisão, corte.
abscond *v.i.* homiziar-se, esconder-se.
absence s. ausência; distração; — **of mind** distração.
absent *adj.* ausente.
absent *v.i.* ausentar-se.
absent-minded, distraído.
absently *adv.* distraídamente.
absinthe, absinth s. absinto.

absolute *adj.* absoluto; positivo, categórico; *ly adv.* absolutamente, de modo algum.
absolution *s.* absolvição, perdão; remissão.
absolve *v.t.* absolver, perdoar; remir.
absorb *v.t.* absorver; *ent adj.* absorvente.
absorption *s.* absorção.
abstain *v.i.* abster-se; jejuar; privar-se de; *er s.* abstinente; sóbrio.
abstention *s.* abstenção.
abstinence *s.* abstinência; jejum.
abstract *adj.* abstrato; *s.* extrato, resumo; the — o abstrato; *v.t.* abstrair; roubar; desviar; resumir; *ion s.* abstração; distração; desvio.
abstruse *adj.* abstruso, confuso, difícil de compreender; *ly adv.* confusamente.
absurd *adj.* absurdo; disparatado; *ly adv.* absurdamente; *ity s.* absurdo, disparate.
abundance *s.* abundância, fartura.
abundant *adj.* abundante, copioso, farto.
abundantly *adv.* abundantemente, fartamente, copiosamente.
abuse *v.t.* abusar; injuriar; seduzir; exceder-se; maltratar; *s.* excesso, abuso; injúria; sedução.
abusive *adj.* abusivo; injurioso.
abutment *s.* (*arq.*) arcobotante, pegão.
abut *v.i.* confinar, estabelecer linha de contacto.
abutting *adj.* adjacente.
abyss *s.* abismo, precipício; *al adj.* insondável, abismal, abissal.
Abyssinia *s.* Abissínia.
Abyssinian *adj.* abissínio, natural da Abissínia.
acacia *s.* acácia.
academic *adj.* acadêmico; — year ano letivo; *al adj.* acadêmico; *ian s.* acadêmico.
academy *s.* academia.
acanthus *s.* acanto, herva-gigante.
acarpous *adj.* (*bot.*) acárpico.
accede *v.i.* aceder, consentir, assentir, aquiescer; conformar-se.
accedence *s.* aquiescência.
accelerate *v.t.* acelerar, apressar.
acceleration *s.* aceleração.
accelerator *s.* acelerador.
accent *s.* acento, acentuação, tom, inflexão de voz.
accent, accentuate *v.t.* acentuar; pronunciar com clareza, dizer com ênfase; **accentuation** *s.* acentuação.
accept *v.t.* aceitar; receber; admitir; *able adj.* aceitável, plausível; *ance s.* aceitação; *ation s.* acepção; *or s.* aceitante; *ed term* expressão consagrada.
access *s.* acesso, entrada; promoção; admissão, ingresso; ataque febril; *ion s.* acessão; acréscimo; elevação (ao trono).
accessory *adj.* acessório; cúmplice; adicional.
accidence *s.* (*gram.*) morfologia.
accident *s.* acidente; acontecimento; sinistro; — insurance seguro contra acidentes; *al adj.* acidental, fortuito, casual; *ally adv.* acidentalmente, casualmente, por acaso.
acclaim *v.t.* aclamar, aplaudir; *er s.* aclamante.
acclamation *s.* aclamação.
acclimate *v.t.&i.* aclimatar, aclimar.
acclimation *s.* aclimatação, aclimação.
acclimatize *v.t.* aclimatar, aclimar.

acclimatization *s.* aclimatização, aclimatação.
acclivity *s.* subida, encosta, ladeira, aclive.
acclivous *adj.* íngreme.
accolade *s.* abraço; cerimônia ou saudação usada para conferir o grau de cavaleiro, na qual se tocava o ombro do candidato com a lâmina da espada.
accommodate *v.t.* acomodar, arrumar; instalar; adaptar; ajustar; — oneself to ajustar-se a.
accommodating *adj.* acomodatício; amoldável, complacente.
accommodation *s.* acomodação; ajuste; conveniência; alojamento.
accompaniment *s.* acompanhamento.
accompanist *s.* acompanhador.
accompany *v.t.* acompanhar.
accomplice *s.* cúmplice.
accomplish *v.t.* efetuar, realizar, cumprir, executar; *ed adj.* acabado, completo, perfeito; esmerado; consumado; *ment s.* efetuação, realização; aquisição; conseguimento; *able adj.* realizável, praticável, exequível.
accord *v.t.* conceder; adaptar; conciliar; *v.i.* concordar; *s.* acôrdo, convênio, união, concórdia, harmonia; acorde; ajuste; of one's own — de motupróprio; with one — de comum acôrdo; *ance s.* conformidade; *ing as* à medida que, segundo o que; *ing to* segundo, conforme, de conformidade com; *ingly adv.* em consequência, consequentemente.
accordion *s.* acórdeon, harmônica, sanfona.
accost *v.t.* abordar, acostar.
account *s.* conta, computação; estimação; inventário; relato; nota; *v.t.* contar, computar; estimar; of no — nulo, sem valor; on — of por causa de; creditado a; on no — de modo algum, absolutamente; — book livro de contabilidade; current — with interest conta corrente com juros; — day dia de liquidação; — for dar conta de, explicar; *able adj.* responsável; *ancy s.* contabilidade; *ant s.* guarda-livros; *ing s.* contabilidade; — machine máquina de calcular.
accouter, accoutre *v.t.* equipar; vestir; *ment s.* equipamento.
accredit *v.t.* acreditar; sancionar; abonar; *ed adj.* acreditado; sancionado.
accretion *s.* aumento, adição, crescimento, acréscimo.
accrue *v.i.* acrescer; provir; crescer; aumentar; *d interest* juros acrescidos.
accruing interest, juros a vencer.
accumulate *v.t.* acumular, amontoar; *v.i.* aumentar, crescer.
accumulation *s.* acumulação.
accumulator *s.* acumulador.
accuracy *s.* exatidão, precisão.
accurate *adj.* exato, preciso; apurado.
accursed *adj.* execrado, maldito, detestável.
accusation *s.* acusação, denúncia.
accusative (case), acusativo (caso).
accuse *v.t.* acusar, culpar, denunciar; the *ed* o acusado.
accuser *s.* acusador, denunciante.
accustom *v.t.* acostumar, habituar; *v.i.* afazer-se, acostumar-se; *ed adj.* acostumado, habituado; habitual, costumeiro.
ace *s.* ás; within an — of a ponto de, quasi.

acephalous *adj.* acéfalo.
acerate *adj.* acerato.
acerbity *s.* acerbidade, aspereza.
acervate *adj.* amontoado, acumulado.
acervation *s.* acervo, acúmulo, monte.
acetate *s.* acetato.
acetic *adj.* acético.
acetylene *s.* acetilene, ácetileno.
ache *s.* dôr; mal; *v.i.* doer; **head** = — dôr de cabeça.
aching *adj.* dolorido, doído.
achieve *v.t.* executar; completar; realizar; conseguir; consumar, concluir; =**ment** *s.* realização, acabamento; feito, façanha.
achromatic *adj.* acromático, incolor.
acid *s.* ácido *adj.* ácido, acre, azêdo; =**ity** *s.* acidez; =**ulate** *v.t.* acidular.
acidophilus milk, coalhada.
acknowledge *v.t.* reconhecer; confessar, acusar-se de, admitir; — **receipt of** acusar recebimento de.
acknowledgment *s.* reconhecimento, confissão, admissão.
acme *s.* apogeu, cúmulo, cume.
acne *s.* acne, espinha.
acolyte *s.* acólito; sacristão.
aconite *s.* acônito.
acorn *s.* lande, bolota, noz ou fruta do carvalho.
acoustic *adj.* acústico; =**s** *s.* acústica.
acquaint *v.t.* fazer conhecer, informar, dar aviso, comunicar; =**ance** *s.* conhecimento, relação.
acquiesce *v.i.* aquiescer, concordar, anuir, aceder; =**nce** *s.* aquiescência, consentimento tácito, anuência.
acquire *v.t.* adquirir; ganhar; obter; =**ment** *s.* aquisição; =**ments** *s.pl.* saber, conhecimentos.
acquisition *s.* aquisição.
acquisitive *adj.* ávido de adquirir.
acquisitively *adv.* aquisitivamente.
acquit *v.t.* absolver, exonerar de culpa; =**tal** *s.* absolvição.
acre *s.* acre (medida agrária).
acrid *adj.* acre, ácido; picante; =**ity** *s.* acidez, acrimônia.
acrimonious *adj.* acrimonioso, áspero; mordaz, sarcástico.
acrimony *s.* acrimônia.
acrobat *s.* acrobata.
across *adv.* de través, em sentido transversal; *prep.* através de; — **the street** do outro lado da rua.
acrostic *s.* acróstico.
acrotism *s.* (*med.*) acrotismo.
act *s.* ato, ação, feito; *v.t.* representar; produzir, fazer, executar; *v.i.* agir, funcionar; — (**of parliament**) lei (votada); **in the very** — em flagrante delito; =**ing** (*teat.*) representação; =**ing** *adj.* em exercício.
actinic *adj.* actínico.
action *s.* ação; feito; efeito; movimento; gesto; cêna; combate; processo; =**able** *adj.* acionável.
active *adj.* ativo; diligente, eficaz, enérgico; **in** — **service** em atividade; — **voice** voz ativa.
activity *s.* atividade; diligência, prontidão.
activate *v.t.* ativar; reativar.
actor, actress *s.* ator, atriz; agente; comediante.
actual *adj.* real, efetivo, tangível, de fato; =**ity** *s.* realidade; =**ly** *adv.* realmente; =**ize** *v.t.* atualizar, realizar.
actuary *s.* atuário; escrivão; amanuense,

actuate *v.t.* acionar; incitar, estimular; pôr em ação; =**d** *adj.* movido, incitado, provocado.
actuation *s.* realização, operação efetiva.
acuity *s.* perspicácia, acuidade.
acumen *s.* acume, agudeza, sagacidade, perspicácia; discernimento.
acuminate *v.t.* afinar, tornar agudo; *adj.* afilado, pontudo.
acute *adj.* agudo; penetrante, perspicaz; =**ly** *adv.* agudamente, com sutileza; =**ness** *s.* agudeza, finura; argúcia.
A.D. (anno Domini), depois de Cristo.
ad *s.* (*pop.*) anúncio.
adage *s.* adágio, provérbio, rifão.
adamant *adj.* adamantino; inquebrável, inflexível; *s.* diamante; substância muito dura; =**ine** *adj.* adamantino; **to be** — ser inflexível.
Adam's apple (*anat.*) pomo de Adão.
adapt *v.t.* adaptar, acomodar, ajustar; apropriar; =**ation** *s.* adaptação; =**able** *adj.* adaptável.
add *v.t.* acrescentar, somar, adicionar.
addendum, addenda *s.* adenda, suplemento.
adder *s.* víbora, cobra, serpente.
addict *v.t.* devotar; entregar; dedicar; habituar; — **oneself to** dedicar-se, entregar-se a, habituar-se a.
addition *s.* adição; suplemento, apêndice; =**al** *adj.* adicional, suplementar.
addle *adj.* podre, corrompido; — = **headed** *adj.* desmiolado, estouvado, sem juízo.
address *s.* endereço; petição; dedicatória; alocução; discurso; destreza; *v.t.* dirigir-se a; endereçar; =**ee** *s.* destinatário.
adduce *v.t.* alegar; aduzir; fornecer; citar.
adenoids *s.* vegetações adenóides.
adept *s.* perito; *adj.* versado, hábil, experiente.
adequacy *s.* adequação, suficiência; aptidão; proporção.
adequate *adj.* suficiente; eficaz; razoável; adequado, competente, proporcionado.
adequately *adv.* adequadamente; proporcionadamente.
adhere, *v.i.* aderir; unir-se, juntar-se; =**nce** *s.* aderência.
adhesion *s.* adesão.
adhesive *adj.* adesivo; tenaz; pegajoso, viscoso.
ad hoc, ad hoc (*lat.*), específico, especial, (para êste caso).
adieu *int.* adeus; até logo.
ad interim *adv.* temporàriamente, provisòriamente.
adipose *adj.* adiposo, gorduroso.
adiposity *s.* adiposidade, gordura.
adit *s.* (*min.*) passagem, entrada subterrânea.
adjacent *adj.* adjacente, contíguo, juxtaposto; =**ly** *adv.* na proximidade.
adjective *s.* adjetivo; =**ly** *adv.* adjetivamente.
adjoin *v.t.* juntar, unir; acrescentar; =**ing** *adj.* contíguo, adjacente, vizinho.
adjourn *v.t.* adiar, diferir; retardar; transferir; prorrogar; =**ment** *s.* adiamento, prorrogação.
adjudge *v.t.* adjudicar; julgar; decretar, determinar.
adjudicate *v.t.* adjudicar.
adjudication *s.* adjudicação.
adjunct *s.* adjunto, auxiliar; *adj.* adjunto, auxiliar, acessório.
adjure *v.t.* adjurar, pedir com instância.

adjust *v.t.* ajustar; regrar, retificar, harmonizar, coadunar; acomodar, conciliar; coordenar; regular; *ment s.* ajustamento, acomodação; conciliação; ajuste; consêrto; *able adj.* ajustável, conciliável.
adjutant *s.* (*mil.*) ajudante.
adjuvant *adj.* útil; adjuvante.
ad libitum, ad libitum (*lat.*), à vontade, à discrição.
administer *v.t.* administrar; ministrar, dar, fornecer, dirigir, gerir.
administration *s.* administração, gestão.
administrator *s.* administrador, curador.
administrate *v.t.* administrar.
administrative *adj.* administrativo.
admirable *adj.* admirável; maravilhoso.
admirably *adv.* admiràvelmente.
admiral *s.* almirante; — of the fleet comandante da esquadra; rear — contra- almirante; *ty almirantado.
admiration *s.* admiração.
admire *v.t.* admirar.
admirer *s.* admirador.
admiringly *adv.* com admiração.
admissible *adj.* admissível.
admission *s.* admissão; entrada.
admit *v.t.* admitir; reconhecer.
admittance *s.* admissão.
admixture *s.* mistura.
admonish *v.t.* admoestar, repreender; advertir.
admonition *s.* admoestação, repreensão; advertência; *er s.* admoestador.
admonitory *adj.* admonitório.
admonitor *s.* admoestador.
ado *s.* trabalho; tumulto, alarido, barulho; much — about nothing muito alarido por nada.
adolescence *s.* adolescência.
adolescent *adj.&s.* adolescente.
Adonis *s.* Adonis; **adonic** *adj.* adônico; *s.* verso adônico.
adopt *v.t.* adotar; tomar; perfilhar; *ed adj.* adotado, adotivo; *ive adj.* adotivo; *ion s.* adoção; *ively adv.* adotivamente.
adorable *adj.* adorável.
adoration *s.* adoração.
adore *v.t.* adorar.
adorer *s.* adorador.
adorable *adj.* adorável; *ness s.* qualidade de ser adorável.
adorn *v.t.* adornar, ornamentar, ornar, ataviar, enfeitar; *ment s.* ornato, atavio, enfeite, adôrno, ornamento.
adown *prep.* em baixo; *adv.* abaixo.
adrenal *adj.* suprarrenal; — glands glandulas suprarrenais; *in s.* adrenalina.
Adriatic *adj.&s.* Adriático.
adrift *adv.* sem rumo, à mercê do vento ou das ondas.
adroit *adj.* destro, hábil; *ness s.* destreza; *ly adv.* hàbilmente, com destreza.
adulate *v.t.* adular, lisonjear.
adulation *s.* adulação, lisonja.
adulatory *adj.* adulatório, lisonjeador.
adult *s.&adj.* adulto.
adulterate *v.t.* adulterar; falsificar, alterar; corromper.
adulteration *s.* adulteração; falsificação.
adulterer, adulteress *s.* adúltero, adúltera.
adulterous *adj.* adúltero; falso, forjado.
adultery *s.* adultério.
ad valorem, ad valorem, proporcional ao valor.

advance *s.* avanço; adiantamento, progresso; marcha; antecipação; in — adiantado; *v.t.* avançar, adiantar, progredir; marchar; antecipar; *ment s.* adiantamento, progresso; promoção; *d adj.* avançado, adiantado.
advantage *s.* vantagem, benefício, lucro, proveito; *ous adj.* vantajoso, proveitoso, lucrativo; *ously adv.* vantajosamente, proveitosamente.
advent *s.* advento; vinda; aparição; chegada.
adventitious *adj.* adventício.
adventure *s.* aventura; incidente, caso, acaso; *v.t.* aventurar, arriscar; *r s.* aventureiro, especulador; *ss s.* aventureira.
adventurous *adj.* aventuroso, arriscado, incerto, temerário, perigoso.
adverb *s.* advérbio; *ial adj.* adverbial.
adversary *s.* adversário, rival, inimigo, contrário, oponente, antagonista.
adverse *adj.* adverso, contrário, oposto.
adversity *s.* adversidade; infortúnio, desgraça.
advert *v.i.* advertir; observar, fazer alusão; *ence, *ency s.* advertência; observação.
advertise *v.t.* anunciar; publicar, afixar, informar; *v.i.* fazer publicidade, fazer anúncios; — for pôr anúncio para; *ment s.* anúncio, reclame; *r s.* anunciante; noticiador.
advertising *s.* publicidade, reclame.
advice *s.* aviso, conselho; parecer, opinião.
advisable *adj.* digno de consideração; prudente.
advise *v.t.* aconselhar; prevenir, avisar.
advisedly *adv.* deliberadamente, com conhecimento de causa.
adviser *s.* conselheiro; monitor.
advisory *adj.* consultivo.
advised *adj.* aconselhado; ill — imprudente; be — acautele-se, tome cuidado.
advocate *s.* advogado, defensor; partidário; *v.t.* advogar, preconizar.
advocacy *s.* justificação, defesa, advocacia.
advocation *s.* intercessão; apêlo.
advowson *s.* proteção; patronato; padroado.
adze *s.* machadinha de tanoeiro, enxó.
Aegean sea, mar Egeu.
aegis *s.* égide.
Aeolian *adj.* eólio, eólico.
aerate *v.t.* arejar; gaseificar; ventilar; *d drinks bebidas gasosas; *d lemonade, water limonada, agua gasosa.
aeration *s.* aerificação, ventilação.
aerification *s.* aerificação.
aeriform *adj.* aeriforme.
aerify *v.t.* encher de ar.
aerial *adj.* aéreo; *s.* (rádio) antena.
aerie *s.* ninho das aves de rapina; habitação humana situada em lugar muito alto.
aerodrome *s.* aeródromo, campo de aviação.
aerodynamic *adj.* aerodinâmico; *s s.* aerodinâmica
aerolite *s.* aerólito, meteorito.
aerology *s.* aerologia.
aeromechanics *s.* aeromecânica.
aerometer *s.* aerômetro.
aeronaut *s.* aeronauta; *ic adj.* aeronáutico; *ics s.* aeronáutica.
aeroplane *s.* aeroplano, avião.
aeroscope *s.* aeróscopo.

aerostat s. aeronave; =ic adj. aerostático; =ics s. aerostática.
aesthete s. esteta.
aesthetic adj. estético; =al adj. estético; =s s. estética.
afar adv. ao longe, à distancia, longe; from — de longe.
affable adj. afável; cortês, lhano, acccssível.
affability s. afabilidade; cortesia, amabilidade.
affably adv. afàvelmente; amàvelmente.
affair s. negócio; assunto; love — intriga amorosa.
affect v.t. afetar; atingir; impressionar; fingir, aparentar; =ation s. afetação, aparência; =ed adj. afetado, precioso, fóra do natural; =edly adv. afetadamente; =ing adj. comovente; terno.
affection s. afeição; =ate adj. afetuoso, amante, afeiçoado, amoroso, carinhoso.
affective adj. afetivo, emocional.
afferent adj. aferente, que conduz o impulso ao sistema nervoso central.
affiance s. confiança, fé; contrato de casamento; v.t. prometer em casamento; v.i. noivar.
affiant s. depoente.
affidavit s. depoimento de testemunhas juramentadas.
affiliate v.t. perfilhar; adotar; filiar; v.i. filiar-se.
affiliation s. perfilhação, adoção, afiliação, filiação.
affinity s. afinidade; conexão; parentesco por lei.
affirm v.t. afirmar; declarar; assegurar; confirmar; v.i. atestar; depor; =ation s. afirmação; ratificação; declaração; confirmação; =ative adj. affirmativo.
affix s. afixo; adição; v.t. afixar; juntar; fixar; =ture s. afixação.
afflict v.t. afligir; atribular; atormentar; =ion s. aflição, pena; tormento, tribulação, desgôsto; calamidade, infortúnio; =ive adj. aflitivo; =ively adv. aflitivamente.
affluence s. afluência, opulência, fartura, abundância.
affluent adj.&s. afluente, tributário; abundante, opulento, farto, copioso.
affluently adv. opulentamente; fartamente, copiosamente.
afford v.t. dar, fornecer, conceder; can — to ter recursos para, poder.
afforest v.i. plantar bosques ou florestas; =ation s. terra convertida em bosque, reflorestamento.
affray s. assalto; disputa; distúrbio; rixa, refrega; v.t. assustar, alarmar, amedrontar.
affront v.t. afrontar, ofender, insultar, ultrajar; provocar; s. afronta, insulto, ultraje; =ive adj. afrontoso, injurioso.
afield adv. no campo, para o campo; far — muito ao longe.
afire adj. em fogo, ardente, em chamas; inflamado.
afloat adv. à tona d'agua, flutuando; em circulação, passando de uma pessoa para outra; adj. flutuante.
afoot adv. em pé, a pé, em ação ou movimento.
aforesaid adj. supra mencionado.
aforethought adj. premeditado; s. premeditação.
aforetime adv. antigamente, noutro tempo.

a fortiori (lat.) a fortiori, com maior razão.
afoul adv. embaraçado, implicado; em colisão.
afraid adj. temeroso, tímido, receoso, amedrontado, assustado; to be — of ter medo de, temer.
afresh adv. novamente, outra vez.
Africa s. África; =n adj. africano.
aft adv. (mar.) atrás, na parte da pôpa.
after adv. depois, em seguida; conj., depois que; prep. depois, após; conforme, segundo; — all afinal de contas, em resumo; — the event depois do acontecido.
aftermath s. consequências; segunda germinação.
afternoon s. tarde; in the — à tarde.
after-piece s. farça; entremez.
after-taste s. sabor que persiste na bôca; consequências amargas.
afterthought s. reflexão depois de praticado o ato; reflexão tardia.
afterwards adv. depois, depois disso; em seguida, mais tarde.
again adv. ainda outra vez, outra vez, novamente; — and — repetidas vezes; again depois do verbo indica geralmente repetição de ação; em português é frequentemente expresso pelo prefixo re: ex.: to take it — retomar.
against prep. contra; contrário; perto, junto, encostado; — the grain às avessas.
agape adj. boquiaberto.
agate s. ágata.
age, s. idade; século; tempo; época; era; old — velhice; ten years of — dez anos de idade; he is not of — êle não é maior de idade; to come of — ficar maior (de idade); it is =s since há muito tempo que; =d adj. velho, idoso; he has =d considerably envelheceu muito; the =d os velhos.
agency s. ação; diligência; intermédio; agência.
agenda s. notas, memorandum; ordem do dia.
agent s. agente, comissário, representante; mandatário; intermediário; emissário; deputado.
agglomerate v.t. aglomerar; =d adj. aglomerado.
agglomeration s. aglomeração.
agglutinate v.t. aglutinar, colar, ligar.
agglutination s. aglutinação.
agglutinant adj. aglutinante.
aggrandize v.t. engrandecer; elevar, exaltar; ampliar; exagerar; embelezar; =ment s. engrandecimento; exaltação; exagêro; ampliação.
aggravate v.t. agravar; aumentar, intensificar; incomodar, impacientar.
aggravation s. agravação; agravo; provocação.
aggregate adj. agregado, reunido; coligido; de conjunto; v.t. agregar, reunir; s. agregado, agremiação; combinação, agregação, conjunto, total.
aggregation s. agregação.
aggression s. agressão.
aggress v.t. agredir; ofender; atacar.
aggressive adj. agressivo.
aggressively adv. agressivamente.
aggressiveness s. agressividade.
aggressor s. agressor.
aggrieve v.t. agravar; afligir; lesar, molestar; =d adj. ofendido, molestado, lesado; =d party parte ofendida.

aghast adj. espantado, estupefacto, horrorizado, apavorado, perplexo.
agile adj. ágil, vivo, ativo, lépido.
agility s. agilidade, atividade.
agio s. ágio; =**tage** s. agiotagem.
agitate v.t. agitar, revolver; mover; inquietar.
agitation s. agitação.
agitator s. agitador, perturbador.
aglow adj. resplandecente, abrasado, inflamado.
agnail s. unheiro.
agnostic s. agnóstico; =**ism** s. agnosticismo.
ago adv. passado, há tempos atrás, antes; **long** — há muito tempo; **a while** — há algum tempo; **how long** —? há quanto tempo?
agog adj. desejoso; animado; impaciente; adv. com veemência, ardentemente; **to be** — desejar ardentemente.
agonize v.i. agonizar; sofrer angústia; padecer; v.t. agoniar, martirizar, atormentar.
agonizing adj. cruel, atroz, torturante.
agony s. agonia; angústia; **to suffer** — sofrer o martírio.
agrarian adj. agrário.
agree v.t. admitir; fazer concordar; harmonizar; v.i. concordar, convir, entender-se; — to consentir em, comprometer-se a; **quite** — **with** concordar plenamente; =**able** adj. agradável, ameno; aprazível; conveniente; =**d price** preço estipulado; =**ment** s. acôrdo, ajuste, convênio.
agriculture s. agricultura.
agricultural adj. agrícola, agrário.
agricultural implements, instrumentos agrários.
agricultural show, exposição agrícola.
agriculturalist s. agricultor, agrônomo.
agronomist adj. agrônomo.
agronomy s. agronomia.
aground adv. (mar.) encalhado; adj. vencido, fracassado; **to run** — encalhar, dar à costa.
ague s. febre palustre, malária.
ahead adv. avante, para a frente, adiante; **go** — avance, continue; **to get** — adiantar-se.
ahoy int. olá! oh! hei!
aid s. ajuda, auxílio; assistência, socorro; v.t. ajudar, auxiliar; socorrer.
aide-de-camp s. ajudante de campo, ou de ordens.
ail v.t.&i. afligir, sofrer, incomodar, doer; =**ment** mal, incômodo de saúde.
aim s. objetivo; meta; mira, alvo; desígnio; fim; v.t. mirar, apontar; aspirar; pretender, tencionar, visar; — at visar, ajustar, apontar; =**less** adj. sem objetivo, sem desígnio, sem propósito; =**lessly** adv. sem objetivo, sem finalidade.
air s. ar, vento; céu, atmosfera; aspecto do uma pessoa; ária; **to give oneself** =**s** fazer-se de importante; =**craft** aeronave; =**craft carrier** porta-aviões; =**craft exhibition** exposição de aviões; — **current** corrente de ar; — **gun** fuzil de ar comprimido; — **hole** respiradouro; =**line** linha de avião, linha aérea; =**liner** avião de linha regular; =**mail** correio aéreo; **by** =**mail** por avião; =**man** aviador; — **mechanic** mecânico de avião; **Air Ministry** Ministério do Ar; =**pilot** piloto de avião; =**plane** aeroplano, avião; =**race** corrida de avião; =**raid** raid aéreo; =**ship** dirigível; =**station** aeroporto; **tight** impermeável ao ar, hermèticamente fechado; =**way** via aérea; =**woman** aviadora; =**worthy** em bom estado de navegabilidade; v.t. arejar, ventilar; =**ing** s. aerificação, ventilação; =**less** adj. sem ar, abafado; =**y** adj. aéreo, no ar.
aisle s. divisão lateral de uma igreja ou de um palácio.
ajar adj. entre-aberto.
akin adj. aparentado; parente, consanguíneo; análogo.
alabaster s. alabastro.
alabastrine adj. alabastrino.
alacrity s. alacridade; vivacidade, alegria.
alacritous adj. vivo; álacre.
a-la-mode adj. **pie** — torta servida com sorvete em cima.
alarm s. alarme, rebate; tumulto; sobressalto; — **clock** despertador; — **bell** campainha de alarme; =**ing** adj. alarmante; v.t. alarmar, assustar; v.i. tocar o alarme, tocar o rebate.
alas int. ai de mim! infelizmente!
alb s. alva (veste sacerdotal).
albatross s. albatroz.
albino s. albino.
album s. álbum.
albumen s. albumen; clara do ovo.
albumin s. albumina.
albuminous adj. albuminoso.
alchemist s. alquimista.
alchemy s. alquimia.
alcohol s. alcool; aguardente; =**ic** adj. alcoólico; =**ism** s. alcoolismo; =**ize** v.t. alcoolizar.
alcove s. alcova.
alder s. álamo.
alderman s. na Inglaterra, magistrado logo abaixo do prefeito; nos E. Unidos, membro do conselho municipal; vereador.
alert adj. alerta; vigilante, pronto, vivo; =**ness** s. vigilância; vivacidade, agilidade; **on the** — estar alerta, vigilante.
Alexandrine adj.&n. alexandrino (verso).
alfalfa s. alfafa.
algebra s. álgebra.
algebric, algebrical adj. algébrico.
algebrist s. algebrista.
alias adv. aliás; de outro modo; s. outro nome, nome suposto.
alibi s. álibi.
alien adj. estrangeiro, estranho; s. estrangeiro.
alienate vt.. alienar.
alienable adj. alienável.
alienation s. alienação.
alienist s. alienista.
alight adj. aceso; iluminado; v.i. descer, desembarcar; aterrissar, pousar; — **on the water** amerissar.
align v.t. alinhar; =**ment** s. alinhamento, enfileiramento.
alike adj. igual; semelhante; adv. igualmente, do mesmo modo, da mesma maneira; **to be** — parecer-se.
alimentary adj. alimentar, nutritivo, nutriente.
alimentation s. alimentação.
alimentative adj. alimentício; — **canal** tubo digestivo.
alimony s. a limentos (pensão dada pelo marido à mulher em caso de divórcio).
alive adj. vivo, com vida, animado; esperto.
alkali s. álcali.

alkaline *adj.* alcalino.
alkalify, alkalinize *v.t.* alcalinizar.
all *adj.* todo, todos, toda, todas; *adv.* inteiramente, completamente; *s.* o todo, a totalidade; — **the year round** durante todo o ano; — **those who** todos aqueles que; **at** — **hours** a toda hora; **on** — **occasions** em todas as ocasiões; — **right** muito bem; — **the same** assim mesmo; — **of us** todos nós; **that is** — é tudo.
allay *v.t.* acalmar; pacificar; tranquilizar; suavizar, mitigar, aliviar.
allegation *s.* alegação, escusa, pretexto.
allege *v.t.* alegar, pretender; objetar; assegurar, afirmar.
allegiance *s.* fidelidade; obediência; lealdade; **to pay one's** — jurar fidelidade.
allegiant *adj.* leal, fiel.
allegory *s.* alegoria.
allegoric, allegorical *adj.* alegórico.
allegro *adj.* (*mús.*) alegro.
allergy *s.* alergia.
allergic *adj.* alérgico.
alleviate *v.t.* aliviar, mitigar, suavizar, amenizar; moderar, diminuir.
alleviation *s.* alívio, mitigação.
alley *s.* álea; rua estreita; rua de jardim; — **way** passagem entre altos edifícios.
All Fools' Day, primeiro de abril, dia de enganar os tolos.
alliance *s.* aliança; confederação, liga.
alligator *s.* jacaré; — **pear** *s.* abacate.
alliterate *v.t.* aliterar.
alliteration *s.* aliteração.
all-important *adj.* de toda importância.
allocate *v.t.* colocar, distribuir.
allocation *s.* pagamento, distribuição (de verbas).
allocution *s.* alocução.
allot *v.t.* alotar; atribuir; repartir; destinar; **-ment** *s.* distribuição; atribuição; repartição; quinhão; lote, parte, porção de terra.
allow *v.t.* permitir; autorizar; tolerar, consentir; deixar; bonificar; **-ance** *s.* concessão, permissão; pensão; ração; bonificação; indenização.
alloy *s.* liga metálica; *v.t.* ligar metais.
all-powerful *adj.* todo-poderoso.
all-round *adj.* completo.
All Saints' Day, dia de Todos os Santos.
All Souls' Day, dia dos mortos, dia de Finados.
allspice *s.* pimenta da Jamáica.
allude *v.i.* aludir.
allure *v.t.* atrair, engodar, seduzir; **-ment** *s.* engôdo, sedução; isca.
allusion *s.* alusão.
alluvion, alluvium *s.* aluvião.
ally *s.* aliado; confederado; *v.t.* aliar; aparentar; *v.i.* aliar-se, unir-se; aparentar-se.
Alma Mater, (*lat.*) Universidade ou escola a que se pertence.
almanac *s.* almanaque.
almighty *adj.* todo-poderoso; **the Almighty** o Todo-Poderoso.
almond *s.* amêndoa; — **eyes** olhos amendoados, rasgados; — **tree** amendoeira; — **willow** salgueiro branco.
almost *adv.* quasi.
alms *s.* esmola; caridade; — **giving** distribuição de esmolas; — **house** asilo de desamparados; — **box** caixa de esmolas; — **deed** obra de caridade; — **giver** pessoa caritativa; — **man** mendigo.
aloes *s.* aloés.
aloft *adv.* em cima, no alto, por cima de tudo; **to set** — elevar, levantar.

alone *adj.* só, isolado, sem companhia; único; **to let** — deixar em paz; *adv.* sòmente.
along *prep.&adv.* ao longo; adiante; continuadamente; com; em companhia de; **-side of** ao lado de; **to come -side** acostar; **come** — **with me** venha comigo; **all** — todo o tempo.
aloof *adv.* ao longe; à parte, isolado; à distancia, ao largo; *adj.* distante; **-ness** *s.* separação; distância.
aloud *adv.* alto; em voz alta.
alpaca *s.* alpaca.
alpha *s.* alfa (primeira letra do alfabeto grego); **-bet** *s.* alfabeto; **-betical** *adj.* alfabético, **-betize** *v.t.* alfabetizar; **-betization** *s.* alfabetização; — **test** teste de inteligência usado no exército americano em 1917–1918.
Alpine *adj.* alpino, alpestre; **the Alps os** Alpes.
already *adv.* já.
Alsace *s.* Alsácia.
Alsatian *adj.* alsaciano.
also *adv.* também; igualmente; do mesmo modo; além disso.
altar *s.* altar; — **cloth** toalha de altar; — **piece** contra-retábulo; **grand** — altar mór.
alter *v.t.* alterar; modificar; mudar; — **the date** of transferir; **-ation** *s.* alteração; mudança; modificação.
altercation *s.* altercação, disputa.
altercate *v.i.* disputar, altercar.
alternate *adj.* alternado; alternativo; *v.t.* alternar.
alternation *s.* alternação.
alternative *adj.* alternativo.
alternatively *adv.* alternativamente.
although *conj.* ainda que; não obstante; embora; posto que.
altitude *s.* altitude, elevação, altura.
alto *s.* voz masculina mais alta do canto; agora também o contralto é assim chamado.
altogether *adv.* totalmente; inteiramente; ao todo; conjuntamente.
altruist *s.* altruísta; **-ic** *adj.* altruístico.
alum *s.* pedra-ume; alumen.
aluminium, aluminum *s.* alumínio.
always *adv.* sempre.
amalgam *s.* amálgama, mistura; **-ate** *v.t.* amalgamar, misturar; combinar; fundir; *v.i.* fundir-se, misturar-se; **-able** *adj.* combinável, amalgamável; **-ation** *s.* mistura; combinação; amalgamação.
amanuensis *s.* amanuense.
amass *v.t.* amontoar, juntar, acumular; *s.* montão, acúmulo; **-ment** *s.* acúmulo, montão; montante, monte, amontoação.
amateur *s.* amador; diletante; — **status** qualidade de amador.
amatory *adj.* galante; amatório.
amaze *v.t.* espantar; estupefiçar; assombrar; aterrar; **-ment** *s.* espanto, assombro.
Amazon *s.* amazona, guerreira; virago; mulher masculina.
ambassador *s.* embaixador; **ambassadress** *s.* embaixatriz.
amber *s.* âmbar; **-gris** *s.* âmbar cinzento; *v.t.* perfumar com âmbar; **-ed** *adj.* perfumado com âmbar.
ambiguity *s.* ambiguidade; incerteza; dubiedade; equívoco.
ambiguous *adj.* ambíguo, dúbio; incerto, equívoco.
ambition *s.* ambição; cubiça; aspiração.

ambitious adj. ambicioso, fortemente desejoso; (pop.) ativo e empreendedor.

amble v.i. marchar lentamente, sem esfôrço (o cavalo); — **along** ir devagarinho, com calma.

ambrosia s. ambrosia.

ambulance s. ambulância; hospital de campanha.

ambulant adj. ambulante; =ory adj. ambulatório, ambulante.

ambuscade, ambush s. emboscada; cilada; tocaia.

ambush v.i. emboscar-se.

ameliorate v.t. melhorar; aperfeiçoar; v.i. aperfeiçoar-se.

amelioration s. melhoramento, aperfeiçoamento.

amen adv. assim seja, amém.

amenable adj. responsável; sujeito a; tratável; dócil; **every one is — to the laws** todos estão sujeitos à lei.

amend v.t. corrigir; emendar; consertar; melhorar; =s s. indenização; reparação; **make =s for** indenizar, reparar; =**ment** s. correção; emenda (lei ou projeto).

amenity s. amenidade; brandura, docilidade; suavidade.

amenorrhea s. amenorréia.

amentia s. amência, deficiência mental.

America s. América; =**n** s.&adj. americano.

Americana s. coleção de documentos históricos, literários, etnográficos, etc. referentes à América.

Amerindian s. ameríndio, índio americano.

amethyst s. ametista.

amiability s. amabilidade, afabilidade.

amiable adj. amável, afável, agradável.

amiably adv. amàvelmente.

amicable adj. amigável, cordial; =**ness** s. amizade, cordialidade.

amicably adv. amigàvelmente.

amid, amidst prep. entre, no meio de, cercado por.

amidships, no meio do navio.

amiss adv.&adj. erradamentê; inoportuno; impróprio; impròpriamente; vicioso; impuro; com maldade; **do not take it —** não leve isso a mal.

ammonia s. amônia.

ammunition s. munição, provisões; instrumentos de guerra; — **bread** pão de munição.

amnesia s. amnésia, perda da memória.

amnesty s. anistia.

amoeba s. ameba.

among, amongst prep. entre, no meio de, dentro, no numero dos; — **strangers** entre estranhos.

amoral adj. amoral.

amorous adj. amoroso; terno; apaixonado, enamorado; =**ly** adv. amorosamente.

amorphous adj. amorfo.

amortization s. amortização.

amortize v.t. amortizar.

amount s. montante; soma; quantidade; v.i. subir; importar; limitar-se; v.t. somar, calcular.

ampere s. (elet.) ampere, ampério.

amperage s. amperagem.

amphibian s. anfíbio.

amphibious adj. anfíbio.

amphibology s. ambiguidade; anfibologia.

amphitheater s. anfiteatro.

amphitheatrical adj. de anfiteatro.

amphitheatral adj. em fórma de anfiteatro.

amphora s. ânfora, vaso.

ample adj. amplo, espaçoso, grande, largo, extenso; =**ness** s. amplitude, espaço; extensão.

amplifier s. amplificador, ampliador.

amplify v.t. ampliar, amplificar, aumentar, alargar; desenvolver, estender.

amplitude s. amplitude.

amplification s. ampliação; extensão.

amputate v.t. amputar.

amputation s. amputação.

amuck, amok s. loucura homicida.

amulet s. amuleto, talismã.

amuse v.t. divertir, distrair, recrear; =**ment** s. distração, divertimento, recreação, diversão; =**d** adj. divertido.

amusing adj. divertido, engraçado.

amygdala s. amígdala.

amygdaline adj. em forma de amêndoas.

an art. ind. um, uma.

anachronism s. anacronismo.

anachronous adj. anacrônico.

anaemia s. anemia.

anaemic adj. anêmico.

anagram s. anagrama.

analgesia s. analgesia.

analgesic adj. analgésico.

analogous adj. análogo; semelhante.

analogy s. analogia; semelhança.

analyse v.t. analisar.

analysis s. análise.

analyst s. analista.

analytic, analytical adj. analítico.

anarchy s. anarquia; confusão, desordem.

anarchism s. anarquismo.

anarchic adj. anárquico, sem govêrno.

anarchist s. anarquista.

anathema s. anátema; =**tize** v.t. anatematizar.

anatomical adj. anatômico.

anatomy s. anatomia.

anatomist s. anatomista.

ancestor s. ascendente, antepassado.

ancestral adj. ancestral; hereditário.

ancestry s. linhagem, descendência; raça; estirpe.

anchor s. âncora; v.t.&i. ancorar; =**age** s. ancoragem; **sheet —** âncora de salvação; **let us — our hopes in his goodness** depositemos nossas esperanças em sua bondade; **to cast —** lançar âncora.

anchoret, anchorite s. anacoreta, ermitão, solitário.

anchoress s. mulher anacoreta.

anchovy s. anchova, enchova; — **paste** manteiga de anchova; — **pear** fruta das Índias Ocidentais.

ancient s. ancião, velho; adj. antigo, velho; =**s** antepassados; =**ness** s. antiguidade; =**ry** s. antiguidade de linhagem; =**ly** adv. antigamente.

and conj. e; — **so** on assim por diante; — **so forth** assim por diante; **go —** see vá ver; **more —** more cada vez mais; **two — two** dois e dois; **steak —** potatoes bife com batatas; **better —** better cada vez melhor; **worse —** worse de mal a peor; — **yet** no entanto, apesar disso; **now —** then de vez em quando.

andiron s. cão de chaminé.

anecdote s. anedota; historieta.

anemone s. anemona.

aneroid adj. aneróide.

anesthetic adj. anestésico.

anesthesia s. anestesia.
anew adv. de novo, outra vez, ainda, novamente.
angel s. anjo; =ic, =ical adj. angélico; =ica s. angélica (flor); =us s. Angelus, Ave-Maria; =ically adv. angèlicamente.
anger s. cólera, ira, raiva; v.t. irar, enfurecer, meter raiva, encolerizar; irritar.
angina s. angina; — pectoris angina do peito.
angle s. ângulo; v.i. pescar de anzol; =r s. pescador de anzol; — rod cana de pescar.
angling s. pesca de linha.
Anglicism s. anglicismo.
Anglomania s. anglomania.
Anglophile adj.&s. anglófilo.
Anglophobe adj.&s. anglófobo.
Anglo-Saxon adj. anglo-saxão.
angry adj. zangado, irritado, irado, aborrecido; **angrily** adv. com raiva, com ira; **to get** — aborrecer-se, zangar-se, irritar-se; **to be** — with oneself for aborrecer-se consigo mesmo por.
anguish s. angústia; aflição; dôr; =ed adj. angustiado; aflito.
angular adj. angular; =ity s. angularidade; =ly adv. angulosamente, angularmente.
angulous adj. anguloso, tortuoso.
angulation s. angulosidade.
anil s. anil.
aniline s. anilina; — dye tintura de anilina.
animal s.&adj. animal; =ism s. animalidade; sensualidade; =cule s. animálculo; — husbandry criação e cruzamento de animais no campo.
animate v.t. animar, encorajar; adj. animado, dotado de vida.
animation s. animação.
animosity s. animosidade; rancor; aversão, repulsa; ódio.
animus s. disposição; coragem; animosidade.
anise s. anís, herva doce; =ette s. licor de anís.
ankle s. tornozelo; — socks meias curtas.
annals s. anais; crônicas; **annalist** s. analista (o que escreve anais).
anneal v.t. esquentar para dar têmpera; cozinhar outra vez; =ing s. ação de temperar o vidro.
annex v.t. anexar; juntar; incorporar; unir; s. anexo, dependência; =ation s. anexação incorporação.
annihilate v.t. aniquilar; destruir; eliminar; anular.
annihilation s. aniquilação, destruição, extermínio.
anniversary s. aniversário.
anno Domini, era cristã.
annotate v.t. anotar; notar; comentar.
annotation s. anotação; apontamentos; observação.
announce v.t. anunciar; apregoar judicialmente; publicar; proclamar; =ment s. anúncio; aviso; proclamação; declaração; =r s. anunciador de rádio; locutor.
annoy v.t. aborrecer, incomodar, molestar; importunar, contrariar; =ance s. aborrecimento, incômodo, contrariedade; =ing adj. aborrecido, incômodo; importuno; **to be** =ed with estar aborrecido com.
annual adj. anual; s. planta anual; anuário.
annuitant s. que recebe anuidade (pensão).

annuity s. anuidade; renda; pensão.
annul v.t. anular; invalidar; rescindir; abolir, cassar; cancelar; =able adj. anulável; =ment s. anulação; cancelamento; cassação.
annular adj. anular, anelado.
annulate adj. anelado, com aneis.
annulation s. formação de aneis.
annum s. (lat.) ano; per — por ano.
annunciate v.t. anunciar.
Annunciation s. Anunciação.
anode s. anôdio.
anodyne adj. anôdino; calmante.
anoint v.t. ungir, sagrar; untar; consagrar; =ed adj.&s. ungido, untado; sagrado, consagrado.
anomalous adj. anômalo; irregular; anormal; excepcional.
anomaly s. anomalia; irregularidade; anormalidade; =ly adv. anômalamente, irregularmente; anormalmente.
anon adv. logo; em breve, dentro de pouco tempo, daqui a pouco.
anonymous adj. anônimo; =ly adv. anônimamente.
anonymity s. anonimato.
another =adj. outro, outra; ainda um, ainda outro; three days one after — três dias consecutivos; it is just such — é exatamente como o outro.
answer s. resposta; réplica; v.t. responder; replicar; — to the riddle chave do enigma; — for abonar, tornar-se responsável por alguém; to — a fault justificar uma falta; =able adj. responsável.
ant s. formiga; — eater tamanduá, animal comedor de formiga; ='s nest formigueiro.
antagonism s. antagonismo, oposição.
antagonist s. antagonista.
antagonistic adj. antagônico, contrário.
antagonize v.t. hostilizar.
antarctic adj. antártico; the — ocean o oceano glacial Antártico.
ante, prefixo, que traz a idéia de posição anterior.
antecedent s.&adj. antecedente, precedente.
antecede v.t. anteceder, preceder.
antecedency s. antecedência, precedência.
antecessor s. antecessor, predecessor.
antechamber s. antecâmara.
antedate v.t. antedatar; s. antedata.
antediluvian adj. antediluviano.
antelope s. antílope.
ante meridiem (abr. A.M.), antes do meio-dia.
ante mortem, (lat.), antes da morte.
antenna s. antena.
anterior adj. anterior, precedente; =ity s. anterioridade, prioridade, antecedência; =ly adv. anteriormente.
anteroom s. antecâmara, antessala.
anteversion s. anteversão.
anthem s. antífona, canção de louvor, hino.
anther s. (bot.), antera.
anthologize v.t.&i. compilar uma antologia.
anthology s. antologia.
anthracite s. antracite.
anthrax s. antraz; carbúnculo.
anthropoid adj. antropóide, semelhante ao homem.
anthropology s. antropologia.
anti, prefixo, que traz a idéia geral de oposição.

anti-aircraft *adj.* anti-aéreo, contra aviões.
anti-British *adj.* anglófobo.
antibody *s.* (*med.*) anticorpo.
antic *s.* bobo, farsante; **=s** *s.* galhofas, travessuras, macaquice; *adj.* ridículo, grotesco, extravagante, antiquado.
antichrist *s.* anticristo.
anticipate *v.t.* antecipar; prevenir; adiantar; prever.
anticipation *s.* antecipação.
anticipant *adj.* antecipador; expectante.
anti-climax *s.* gradação descendente.
anticyclone *s.* anticiclone.
anti-dazzle lamp or light, farol anti-ofuscante.
antidote *s.* antídoto, contra-veneno.
anti-French *adj.* francófobo.
antimony *s.* antimônio.
antipasto *s.* (*ital.*) antepasto; aperitivo, iguarias servidas antes da refeição para excitar o apetite.
antipathetic *adj.* antipático.
antipathy *s.* antipatia.
antiphony *s.* antífona.
antipodes *s.* antípodas.
antiquarian, antiquary *s.* antiquário.
antiquated *adj.* antiquado, antigo; obsoleto, fora da moda.
antique *adj.* antigo, velho; *s.* antiguidade; obra dos antigos, monumento secular.
antiquity *s.* antiguidade; os antigos; as obras dos antigos.
anti-red *s.* anti-comunista.
antiseptic *adj.* antisséptico.
anti-serum *s.* (*med.*) antisserum.
anti-splash tap nozzle, quebra-jato.
antithesis *s.* antítese.
antithetic, **=al** *adj.* oposto.
antitoxic *s.* antitóxico.
antler *s.* galho, chifre de veado.
antonym *s.* antônimo.
antre *s.* antro, caverna, cavidade.
antrum *s.* antro, caverna, cavidade.
anus *s.* anus.
anvil *s.* bigorna; **the stock of an —** tronco da bigorna; **=ed** *adj.* feito na bigorna.
anxiety *s.* ansiedade; inquietação, angústia.
anxious *adj.* ansio»o, inquieto, angustiado.
anxiously *adv.* ansiosamente.
any *adj.*, *adv.&pron.* algum, alguma, alguns, algumas; quem quer que; qualquer que; nenhum; tudo; mais; alguém; **— farther, — further** mais adiante; **=body** qualquer pessoa; alguém; **=how** como quer que seja, de qualquer maneira; **=wise** de algum modo.
anybody, anyone *s.&pron.* qualquer um; ninguém, nenhum; todo o mundo.
anything *s.&pron.* qualquer coisa; nada; o que quer que seja.
anywhere *adv.* em qualquer lugar, em qualquer parte; em lugar nenhum.
aorta *s.* aorta.
apace *adv.* depressa, prontamente, apressadamente.
apart *adv.* à parte; de parte, separadamente; **— from** com exceção de, abstração feita de.
apartment *s.* apartamento; peça, quarto, sala, aposento.
apathetic *adj.* apático; indolente; passivo; indiferente.
apathy *s.* apatia; indolência; passividade.

ape *s.* macaco, bugio; *v.t.* macaquear, imitar.
aperient *s.* (*med.*) purgativo, laxativo.
aperiodic *adj.* irregular, sem épocas determinadas.
aperitive *s.* aperitivo.
aperture *s.* abertura, orifício, fenda, fresta.
apex *s.* cúmulo, cume, ápice, tôpo, vértice.
aphasia *s.* afasia.
aphonia *s.* afonia.
aphonic *adj.* afônico.
aphorism *s.* aforismo, máxima; sentença breve.
aphrodisiac *adj.* afrodisíaco.
apiary *s.* apiário, colmeal.
apiarian *adj.* apiário.
apiarist *s.* apicultor.
apiece *adv.* por pessoa; por parte; por peça; por cabeça.
apish *adj.* macaqueador, imitador; ridículo.
aplomb *s.* verticalidade; confiança em si; segurança de maneiras.
apogee *s.* apogeu.
apologetic *adj.* apologético.
apologize *v.i.* pedir desculpas.
apology *s.* apologia, desculpas, satisfação, excusa, justificação.
apoplectic *adj.&s.* apoplético; **— fit** ataque de apoplexia.
apoplexy *s.* apoplexia.
apostasy *s.* apostasia.
apostate *s.* apóstata.
a posteriori (*lat.*) a posteriori, raciocínio baseado na observação dos fatos.
apostle *s.* apóstolo; **=s' Creed** o símbolo dos apóstolos, o Credo.
apostolate, apostleship *s.* apostolado.
apostolic, **=al** *adj.* apostólico.
apostrophe *s.* apóstrofe.
apostrophize *v.t.* apostrofar; interpelar.
apothecaries' measures, medidas farmacêuticas.
apothecaries' weight, sistema de pesos usado no aviamento de receitas.
apothecary *s.* farmacêutico, boticário.
apotheosis *s.* apoteose.
appall, appal *v.t.* apavorar, espantar, aterrar, aterrorizar; **=ing** *adj.* horroroso, pavoroso, horrível, apavorante.
appanage, apanage *s.* apanágio; atributo.
apparatus *s.* aparelho; apetrechos; instrumentos.
apparel *v.t.* vestir, ornamentar, enfeitar, ornar, ataviar; *s.* roupa, atavios, vestido, traje.
apparency *s.* aparência.
apparent *adj.* aparente, visível; claro, evidente; **=ly** *adv.* aparentemente; **=ness** *s.* aparência, evidência, clareza.
apparition *s.* aparição; visão.
appeal *s.* apêlo; petição; súplica; apelação; atração; **sex —** atração exercida sôbre o outro sexo; *v.t.* apelar, recorrer; *v.i.* pedir auxílio; clamar.
appear *v.i.* parecer, aparecer; manifestar; comparecer; revelar-se; **=ance** *s.* aparência, aspecto; fisionomia, semblante; aparição.
appease *v.t.* apaziguar, pacificar, conciliar, acalmar, abrandar; mitigar; aplacar; **=ment** *s.* pacificação, conciliação.
appellation *s.* apelação judicial; nome, denominação.
appellee *s.* apelado, réu.
appellor *s.* apelante.

append *v.t.* pendurar; juntar, anexar, acrescentar; ₌age, ₌ix *s.* apêndice; ₌icitis *s.* apendicite.
appertain *v.i.* pertencer.
appetite *s.* apetite.
appetizer *s.* aperitivo.
appetizing *adj.* apetecível, apetitoso.
appetency *s.* desejo, apetência.
applaud *v.t.* aplaudir; louvar; aprovar.
applause *s.* aplauso.
applausive *adj.* laudatório, lisonjeiro.
apple *s.* maçã; — tree macieira; — of the eye menina dos olhos; — of discord pomo de discórdia; — sauce compota de maçã.
appliance *s.* aplicação; esquema; aparelhagem.
applicant *s.* postulante; pleiteante; pretendente.
application *s.* aplicação; solicitação.
apply *v.t.* aplicar; — for solicitar; requerer; pedir; reclamar; subscrever; — to dirigir-se a.
appoint *v.t.* nomear; constituir; designar; indicar; marcar, assinalar; ₌ment *s.* nomeação; indicação; designação; encontro marcado.
apportion *v.t.* repartir; partilhar; distribuir; ₌ment *s.* partilha.
apposite *adj.* apósito; aposto; adequado; pertinente.
apposition *s.* aposição; juxtaposição; ₌ness *s.* propriedade; congruência.
appraise *v.t.* avaliar; estimar, apreciar; ₌ment *s.* avaliação; apreciação, estimação; ₌r *s.* avaliador; taxador.
appreciate *v.t.* avaliar, estimar, apreciar; dar valor a; valorizar.
appreciable *adj.* apreciável; sensível; estimável.
appreciation *s.* apreciação; avaliação; apreço.
apprehend *v.t.* apreender; prender; temer; compreender; conceber, imaginar; *v.i.* pensar.
apprehension *s.* apreensão; cuidado, captura; temor, receio.
apprentice *s.* aprendiz; principiante, noviço; *v.t.* fazer entrar como aprendiz; ₌ship *s.* aprendizado, noviciado.
apprise *v.t.* prevenir; informar, avisar.
approach *s.* aproximação; acesso; chegada; *v.t.* aproximar; abordar; conchegar, juntar; *v.i.* aproximar-se, chegar-se; ₌able *adj.* abordável, aproximável, acessível.
approbation *s.* aprovação, sanção.
approbate *v.t.* aprovar, sancionar.
appropriate *adj.* apropriado; próprio, conveniente, oportuno; *v.t.* apropriar; destinar; adaptar; (*dir.*) usurpar; *v.i.*, (*dir.*) apropriar-se.
approval *s.* aprovação; acôrdo; sanção.
approve *v.t.* aprovar, sancionar; reconhecer.
approximate *v.t.* aproximar; *v.i.* aproximar-se; *adj.* aproximado, próximo; ₌ly *adv.* aproximadamente.
approximation *s.* aproximação.
apricot *s.* damasco.
April *s.* Abril; to make an — fool of passar um primeiro de Abril a.
a priori, (*lat.*) a priori.
apron *s.* avental.
apropos *adv.* a propósito.
apse *s.* abside.
apt *adj.* apto, capaz; próprio; ₌ly *adv.* com aptidão, com capacidade; ₌ness *s.* conveniência; propriedade.

aptitude *s.* aptidão; facilidade; disposição; tendência.
apyretic *adj.* apirético.
aqua fortis, agua forte.
aquamarine *s.* agua marinha.
aqua regia, agua régia.
aquarium *s.* aquário.
aquatic *adj.* aquático.
aqueduct *s.* aqueduto.
aqueous *adj.* aquoso.
aquiline *adj.* aquilino.
Arab *adj.* árabe; *s.* árabe; ₌esque *s.* arabesco.
Arabia *s.* Arábia; ₌ian *adj.* árabe.
Arabian gulf, golfo Arábico.
Arabian nights, as Mil e Uma Noites.
Arabic *s.* o árabe (língua).
arable *adj.* cultivável, arável.
arbiter *s.* árbitro.
arbitrage *s.* arbitragem.
arbitrary *adj.* arbitrário.
arbitration *s.* arbitragem.
arbitrator *s.* árbitro.
arbor *s.* árvore; árvore genealógica; carramanchão; eixo de roda.
Arbor Day, dia da Árvore.
arc *s.* arco.
arcade *s.* arcada, galeria, abóbada arqueada.
arch *s.* arcada; abóbada; *v.t.* arquear, abobadar; *adj.* malicioso; ladino.
archaeological, archaeologic *adj.* arqueológico.
archaeologist *s.* arqueólogo.
archaeology *s.* arqueologia.
archaic *adj.* arcáico, antiquado; fóra da moda.
archaism *s.* arcaismo.
archangel *s.* arcanjo.
archbishop *s.* arcebispo; ₌ric *s.* arcebispado.
archduke *s.* arquiduque; archduchess *s.* arquiduquesa.
archer *s.* arqueiro.
archipelago *s.* arquipélago.
architect *s.* arquiteto; ₌ural *adj.* arquitetural, arquitetônico; ₌ure *s.* arquitetura.
archives *s.* arquivos.
archly *adv.* astutamente; maliciosamente.
archness *s.* astúcia; malícia.
arctic *adj.* ártico; the — ocean oceano Glacial Ártico.
ardent *adj.* ardente, veemente, fogoso; ₌ly *adv.* ardentemente.
ardor *s.* ardor; calor, veemência, zêlo.
arduous *adj.* árduo; penoso, laborioso, duro, difícil; ₌ly *adv.* laboriosamente, árduamente; ₌ness *s.* dificuldade.
are, presente do indicativo do verbo ser (to be), nas três pessoas do plural.
area *s.* área, superfície; zona; extensão; região.
arena *s.* arena.
argentine *adj.* argentino.
argenteous *adj.* argênteo.
argentiferous *adj.* argentífero.
Argentine *s.* Argentina.
argil *s.* argila, barro.
argue *v.t.&i.* argumentar; discutir; arguir; disputar; advogar.
argument *s.* argumento; discussão; tese.
argumentation *s.* argumentação.
argumentative *adj.* argumentativo.
aria *s.* ária.
arid *adj.* árido; esteril; ₌ity *s.* aridez.
aright *adv.* bem; acertadamente; justamente.

arise *v.i.* levantar-se; elevar-se; subir; surgir; originar.
aristocracy *s.* aristocracia.
aristocrat *s.* aristocrata.
aristocratic, aristocratical *adj.* aristocrático.
arithmetic *s.* aritmética; cálculo; *al *adj.* aritmético; *ian *s.* aritmético.
ark *s.* arca; arca de Noé; **the Ark of the Covenant** Arca da Aliança.
arm *s.* braço; arma; brazão; cota de armas; *v.t.* armar; *v.i.* armar-se; — in — de braço dado; **to be up in** *s estar alerta armado; *chair poltrona; *y *s.* exército; *pit *s.* axila.
armadillo *s.* tatú.
armory *s.* arsenal.
arnica *s.* arnica.
aroma *s.* aroma; *tic *adj.* aromático.
around *adv.* em volta, em redor; circularmente; *prep.* em volta de, ao redor de.
arouse *v.t.* despertar; excitar; provocar.
arpeggio *s.* arpejo.
arraign *v.t.* acusar de público; mover processo contra.
arrange *v.t.* arranjar, dispor, ordenar; colocar; organizar; acomodar; *ment *s.* acomodação; disposição; dispositivo; ajuste; combinação.
arrant *adj.* consumado, acabado; péssimo; — **fool** tôlo chapado; **an — lie** uma grande mentira.
arras *s.* tapessaria.
array *s.* ordem; aparelhagem; vestido; ornato; atavios; série; *v.t.* arranjar; ajustar; revestir; dispor em ordem.
arrear *adv.* em atrazo; *s rendas vencidas; **in arrears** atrazado, devedor.
arrest *s.* prisão; arresto; embargo; *v.t.* prender; apreender; embargar; **under** — sob ordem de prisão; *ment prisão, captura, apreensão.
arresting *adj.* espantoso; notável; assombroso.
arris *s.* aresta.
arrival *s.* chegada; **a new** — recémchegado.
arrive *v.i.* chegar; arribar; acontecer; *v.t.* alcançar; conseguir.
arrogance *s.* arrogância; insolência; altivez.
arrogant *adj.* arrogante; insolente; altivo.
arrogantly *adv.* arrogantemente.
arrogate *v.i.* arrogar-se.
arrow *s.* flecha, seta; *head ponta de flecha; — **root** *s.* araruta; *y *adj.* em forma de flecha.
arsenal *s.* arsenal.
arsenic *s.* arsênico; *al *adj.* arsenical.
arson *s.* incêndio voluntário.
art *s.* arte; ofício; artifício, astúcia; — **school** escola de belas artes; **fine** *s belas artes; **black** — magia negra.
arterial *adj.* arterial.
artery *s.* artéria.
arteriosclerosis *s.* arteriosclerose.
Artesian *adj.* artesiano.
artful *adj.* astucioso; engenhoso; artificioso; ardiloso; *ness *s.* artifício; astúcia; ardil; malícia; — **dodger** finório.
arthritis *s.* artrite, gota.
artichoke *s.* alcachofra.
article *s.* artigo; objeto; mercadoria; *s **of association** estatutos; *d **clerk** estagiário, aprendiz.
articulate *v.t.* articular; *v.i.* articular-se.
articulation *s.* articulação.
articular *adj.* articular.

artifice *s.* artifício; ardil, estratagema.
artificer *s.* artífice, artesão, operário.
artificial *adj.* artificial; fictício, postiço.
artillery *s.* artilharia; — **man** artilheiro.
artisan *s.* artesão, artífice.
artist, artiste *s.* artista.
artistic *adj.* artístico.
artistically *adv.* artìsticamente.
artless *adj.* sem arte; natural, simples, ingênuo.
as *adv.&conj.* como; assim como; porque; á medida que; igualmente; assim; — **before** como antes; — **well** — tão bem quanto; assim como, como também; — **far** — até; até onde.
asbestos, asbestus *s.* amianto, asbesto.
ascend *v.t.&i.* ascender, subir, elevar-se; *ancy, *ency *s.* ascendência, influência.
ascension *s.* ascensão.
ascent *s.* ascensão, subida.
ascertain *v.t.* averiguar; verificar.
ascetic *adj.* ascético; *s.* asceta.
ascribe *v.t.* atribuir; imputar.
ash *s.* cinza; *tray cinzeiro.
ashes *s.pl.* cinzas, restos mortais.
Ash Wednesday, quarta-feira de cinzas.
ashamed *adj.* envergonhado; **to be** — envergonhar-se.
ashen, ashy *adj.* cinzento, acinzentado.
ashy pale, lívido, pálido.
ashore *adv.* em terra; **to get** — desembarcar.
Asia *s.* Ásia; — **Minor** Ásia Menor; *tic *adj.* asiático.
aside *adv.* de lado; à parte.
ask *v.t.* perguntar; interrogar; pedir; requerer; convidar; inquirir.
askance *adv.* de soslaio, de esguelha, obliquamente; com desdém.
askew *adv.* obliquamente, de soslaio.
aslant *adv.* obliquamente, atravessado; inclinado.
asleep *adj.* adormecido; **to fall** — adormecer.
asp *s.* áspide, víbora; *ic *s.* áspide; *(bot.)* nardo.
asparagus *s.* aspargo.
aspect *s.* aspecto; semblante; *(astrol.)* fase, aspecto.
aspen *s.* álamo tremente; *adj.* trêmulo.
asperity *s.* aspereza, aspereza.
asperse *v.t.* aspergir; difamar, caluniar.
aspersion *s.* aspersão; difamação, calúnia.
asphalt *s.* asfalto, betume; *v.t.* betumar, asfaltar.
asphyxia *s.* asfixia; *ate *v.t.* asfixiar.
aspirant *s.* aspirante.
aspirate *v.t.* aspirar.
aspiration *s.* aspiração.
aspire *v.i.* aspirar; desejar ardentemente.
aspirin *s.* aspirina.
ass *s.* burro, asno, jumento.
ass's foal, burrico.
ass's milk, leite de jumenta.
assail *v.t.* assaltar; *ant *s.* assaltante.
assassin *s.* assassino; *ate *v.t.* assassinar; *ation *s.* assassinato.
assault *s.* assalto; atentado; *v.t.* assaltar; atacar.
assay *s.* ensaio; prova; verificação; análise; *v.t.* examinar; provar; analisar; — **balance** balança de precisão.
assemblage *s.* reunião; ajuntamento; multidão; montagem.
assemble *v.t.* ajuntar; congregar; reunir; montar (uma máquina, aparelho, etc.); *v.i.* reunir-se; congregar-se.
assembly *s.* assembléia; reunião; *(mil.)* toque de reunir.

assent s. assentimento, consentimento; v.i. consentir, assentir, sancionar.
assert v.t. sustentar; defender; afirmar; fazer valer; =ion s. asserção, afirmação.
assess v.t. taxar; tributar; =ed taxes impostos, direitos; =ment s. cota; contribuição.
asset s. (com.) parcela do ativo; (fig.) vantagem, elemento para um bom êxito; =s s. (com.) ativo; capital; bens; (dir.) bens deixados por morte; monte; **real** =s bens de raiz; **personal** =s bens moveis; =s **and liabilities** ativo e passivo.
assiduity s. assiduidade.
assiduous adj. assíduo.
assiduously adv. assiduamente.
assign v.t. assinar, determinar; designar; consignar; prescrever; =ation s. cessão, trespasse; =ee s. síndico; =ment s. assinação; consignação; prescrição; escritura de cessão de bens, traslado de domínio; tarefa.
assimilate v.t. assimilar.
assist v.t. assistir; ajudar, socorrer; =ance s. assistência, socorro, auxílio; =ant s. assistente, auxiliar.
assize s. **assizes** s.pl. sessão de um tribunal, (usa-se mais no plural).
associate s. sócio; v.t. associar, juntar; v.i. associar-se, juntar-se.
association s. associação.
assort v.t. ordenar, classificar; separar; sortir com variedade; =ment s. sortimento; classificação.
assuage v.t. mitigar, calmar, abrandar, aliviar.
assume v.t. assumir; presumir; usurpar; apropriar.
assuming adj. pretensioso, arrogante.
assumption s. suposição.
assurance s. segurança, certeza, firmeza, convicção, audácia, arrôjo, resolução.
assure v.t. assegurar.
assuredly adv. seguramente, com segurança.
Assyria s. Assíria; =n s.&adj. assírio.
aster s. (bot.) aster, astero.
asterisk s. asterisco; estrela.
astern adv. atrás, detrás, à ré, de pôpa.
asteroid s. asteróide.
asthma s. asma; =tic adj. asmático.
astigmatism s. astigmatismo.
astigmatic adj. astigmático.
astir adv. em movimento; adj. agitado; ativo; levantado.
astonish v.t. espantar; maravilhar; assombrar, pasmar; =ed adj. espantado, assombrado; =ingly adv. espantosamente; =ment s. assombro, espanto.
astound v.t. pasmar; surpreender; =ment s. assombro, espanto.
astray adv.&adj. em mau caminho; desviado, extraviado.
astride, astraddle adv.&adj. escarranchado.
astringent s.&adj. adstringente.
astrologer s. astrólogo.
astrology s. astrologia.
astronomer s. astrônomo.
astronomic, astronomical adj. astronômico.
astute adj. astuto, fino; sagaz.
asunder adv. separadamente, em pedaços.
asylum s. asilo, hospício.
at prep. a, em, de; em casa de; — **all** absolutamente; — **first** primeiramente, antes de tudo; — **hand** à mão; —

home em casa; — **last** enfim, finalmente; — **least** ao menos; — **once** imediatamente; — **war** em guerra.
atheism s. ateismo.
atheist s. ateu.
atheistic adj. ateista.
athirst adv. sedento, ávido.
athlete s. atleta.
athletic adj. atlético.
athletics s. atletismo.
athwart adv. contràriamente, torto; prep. contra, através de, pelo meio de.
Atlantic s.&adj. Atlântico; — **liner** transatlântico.
atlas s. atlas.
atmosphere s. atmosfera.
atmospheric, atmospherical adj. atmosférico.
atom s. átomo; =ic, =ical adj. atômico; =izer s. vaporizador.
atone v.t.&i. expiar; reparar; aplacar; =ment s. expiação; reparação; compensação; sacrifício.
atonic adj. atônico; débil.
atrocious adj. atroz.
atrocity s. atrocidade.
atrophy s. atrofia.
attach v.t. unir; juntar; amarrar; ligar; dar, atribuir (importância, valor, etc.); (dir.) sequestrar; v.i. aderir; =ment s. união; aderência; afeto; fidelidade; (dir.) sequestro.
attack v.t. atacar; s. ataque; criso.
attain v.t. atingir; conseguir; =ment s. obtenção, aquisição.
attar s. essência (principalmente de rosas).
attempt s. tentativa, ensaio; esfôrço; v.t. tentar, intentar; aventurar; atentar.
attend v.t. atender; cuidar; servir; acompanhar; assistir; comparecer; v.i. prestar atenção; dedicar-se; =ance s. serviço; assistência; presença; =ant s. servidor; acompanhante; assistente; criado.
attention s. atenção, cuidado; **to pay** — prestar atenção.
attentive adj. atento; obsequioso, cortês.
attenuate v.t. atenuar.
attest v.t. atestar, declarar, certificar; =ation s. declaração, confirmação; certificado, testemunho.
Attic adj. ático, clássico.
attic s. mansarda, sótão.
attire s. atavio, adôrno; traje; v.t. vestir; ataviar, adornar.
attitude s. atitude; posição, postura.
attorney s. (for.) advogado; procurador legal; **district** — promotor público; =ship s. procuradoria.
attract v.t. atrair; cativar, seduzir; =ion s. atração; atrativo; =ive adj. atraente; interessante; cativante.
attributable adj. atribuível.
attribute s. atributo; v.t. atribuir.
attributively adv. atributivamente; em aposição.
attrition s. atrito, fricção.
attune v.t. harmonizar; afinar.
auburn hair, cabelo castanho avermelhado.
auction s. leilão; =eer s. leiloeiro.
audacious adj. audacioso.
audacity s. audácia.
audaciously adv. audaciosamente, atrevidamente.
audible adj. perceptível ao ouvido, inteligível.

audience s. audiência, assistência, espectadores.
audition s. audição.
auditor s. ouvinte.
auditorium s. auditório.
audit v.t. verificar, examinar; s. verificação, exame ou ajuste de contas; =or s. revisor de contas, contador.
auger s. bróca, trado, pua.
aught s. algo; (mat.) zero, nada; adv. absolutamente.
augment v.t. aumentar.
augur s. augúrio, presságio; v.t. augurar; prognosticar, predizer.
august adj. augusto, majestoso.
August s. Agosto (mês).
auk s. espécie de ave marítima das regiões frias do norte.
aunt s. tia.
aureole s. auréola.
auricle, aurícula do coração; pavilhão auricular.
auricular adj. auricular.
auricula s. (bot.) orelha de urso.
auriferous adj. aurífero.
aurora s. aurora.
auspice s. auspício.
auspicious adj. auspicioso, favorável, de bom augúrio.
austere adj. austero; severo.
austerity s. austeridade; severidade.
austral adj. austral.
Australasia s. Australásia.
Australia s. Austrália.
Australian adj. australiano.
Austria s. Áustria.
Austrian adj. austríaco.
authentic adj. autêntico; =icity s. autenticidade.
author s. autor; =ess s. autora.
authoritative adj. autoritário, acreditado; =ly adv. autoritàriamente.
authority s. autoridade, poder.
authorization s. autorização.
authorize v.t. autorizar.
authorship s. autoria, estado ou profissão de autor.
autobiography s. autobiografia.
autocracy s. autocracia.
autocrat s. autocrata.
autocratic, autocratical adj. autocrático.
autogenous adj. autógeno.
autograph s.&adj. autógrafo.
automatic, automatical adj. automático.
automaton s. autômato.
autonomous adj. autônomo.
autonomy s. autonomia.
autopsy s. autópsia.
autumn s. outono.
auxiliary adj.&s. auxiliar.
avail s. proveito; utilidade; v.t. aprovei-

tar, beneficiar; v.i. ser útil;- able adj. disponível, livre.
avalanche s. avalanche.
avarice s. avareza.
avaricious adj. avaro.
avenge v.t. vingar; punir; =r s. vingador.
avenging adj. vingador.
avenue s. avenida, alameda.
aver v.t. sustentar, afirmar.
average adj. médio, comum; s. média; v.t achar a média de.
aversion s. aversão, repugnância.
aversely adv. com aversão.
averse adj. adverso, contrário.
avert v.t. desviar; afastar.
aviary s. aviário.
aviarist s. avicultor.
aviation s. aviação; — ground campo de aviação, aeródromo.
aviator s. aviador.
avid adj. ávido; =ity s. avidez, cubiça.
avocation s. entretenimento, ocupação das horas de lazer.
avoid v.t. evitar; (jur.) invalidar; =able adj. evitável.
avow v.t. confessar; declarar; =al s. confissão; declaração.
await v.t. esperar.
awake adj. acordado; v.t. acordar; v.i. acordar-se; =ner s. despertador; =ning s. o despertar.
award s. decisão; julgamento; laudo; prêmio; v.t. outorgar; conferir; conceder; (for.) adjudicar.
aware adj. inteirado; sabedor, ciênte; to be — of estar ciênte de; acautelar-se.
away adv. longe, ausente, fóra; to go — ir-se embora; — with you vá-se embora.
awe s. temor reverente, pavor; — struck aterrado, espantado; v.t. infundir terror a, aterrorizar.
awful adj. terrível, tremendo, espantoso, horrível.
awhile adv. um instante, um pouco, um momento.
awkward adj. sem jeito; desastrado, sem graça; the — age a idade ingrata; — incident contratempo.
awl s. sovela, furador.
awn s. aresta; pragana, barba de espiga.
awning s. tenda, toldo, cobertura de pano.
awry adv.&adj. obliquamente, atravessado, oblíquo, torto.
axe s. machado.
axiom s. axioma.
axis s. eixo.
axle s. eixo de roda.
ay int. ai, ah!
azalea s. azaléa.
Azores (the), os Açores.
azure adj. azulado, azul.

B

B, b s. segunda letra do alfabeto; (mús.) si.
baa s. o balido da ovelha ou carneiro.
babble v.t.&i. balbuciar, murmurar confusamente.
babe s. bebê; pessoa ingênua, inexperiente.
Babel s. Tôrre de Babel; plano visionário; babel, confusão.
baboon s. bugio.

baby s. criança de colo; pimpolho; — faced bochechudo; — grand piano de meia cauda; =hood primeira infância; =ish infantil.
Babylonian adj. babilônico.
baccalaureate s. bacharelado.
bachelor s. bacharel; celibatário, solteirão; =s' degree diploma de bacharel.
back s. costas, dorso; adv. atrás, para trás; v.t. montar; secundar, apoiar;

sustentar; apostar; **to come** — voltar; **to give** — devolver.
backbite *v.t.* difamar; falar mal (de alguém) pelas costas.
backbone *s.* espinha dorsal.
back door *s.* porta de trás, porta falsa.
backer *s.* partidário; apostador.
backet *s.* gamela, balde.
backgammon *s.* gamão.
background *s.* fundo de paisagem, segundo plano.
backhand *s.* dorso da mão, reverso.
backing *s.* apôio; garantia, retrocesso.
back number *s.* número atrasado (de um jornal).
back room *s.* quarto dos fundos.
backset *s.* contratempo, revés; infortúnio.
backside *s.* traseira.
backsight *s.* (*geod.*) visada ao ponto de referência.
backslide *v.i.* apostatar, renegar; extraviar-se.
backslider *s.* apóstata; reincidente.
backstairs *s.* escada secreta.
backstitch *s.* posponto.
backward *adj.* atrasado, retrógrado; —, =s *adv.* para trás, de costas; =ness *s.* lentidão, atraso.
backwash *s.* remoinho.
backyard *s.* páteo interior, quintal.
bacon *s.* toucinho.
bacteria *s.* bactéria.
bad *adj.* mau, ruim, nocivo; **from** — **to worse** de mal a peor; =ly *adv.* mal, gravemente.
badge *s.* insígnia, marca, condecoração, distintivo; *v.t.* condecorar, marcar.
badger *s.* texugo; *v.t.* cansar, fatigar, fastidiar.
badness *s.* maldade.
baffle *v.t.* frustar, enganar; desviar.
bag *s.* saco, bolsa; *v.t.* embolsar, ensacar.
baggage *s.* bagagem.
bagpipe *s.* gaita de fole.
bail *s.* caução, fiança; *v.t.* abonar, afiançar.
bailiff *s.* bailio, meirinho.
bait *s.* isca, ceva, engodo; *v.t.* cevar, iscar, engodar.
baize *s.* baeta.
bake *v.t.* cozer ao forno.
baker *s.* padeiro; =y *s.* padaria.
baking *s.* fornada; — **powder** levedura, fermento.
balance *s.* balança, equilíbrio, saldo, resto; — **sheet** balanço, balancete; — **weight** contrapeso; — **wheel** volante; *v.t.* pesar, balancear, equilibrar; *v.i.* hesitar, vacilar; equivaler.
balancing *s.* equilíbrio, balanço.
balcony *s.* sacada, varanda; balcão.
bald *adj.* calvo, pelado; =ness calvície.
balderdash *s.* galimatias, disparate.
bale *s.* fardo, pacote; *v.t.* enfardar, enpacotar; (*mar.*) esvasiar, despejar.
baleful *adj.* sinistro, funesto; triste.
balk *s.* viga; *v.t.* frustrar, impedir.
ball *s.* bola, globo; bala de canhão; baile; **eye=** globo ocular.
ballad *s.* balada, canção.
ballast *s.* lastro, cascalho; *v.t.* lastrar, estabilizar.
ballet *s.* bailado.
ballistics *s.* balística.
balloon *s.* balão.
ballot *s.* cédula para votar; votação; —=**box** urna eleitoral; *v.t.* votar.
balm *s.* bálsamo.
balsam *s.* bálsamo.

baluster *s.* balaústre.
bamboo *s.* bambú.
bamboozle *v.t.* enganar, lograr.
ban *v.t.* proscrever, banir; excomungar; *s.* pregão; interdito.
banana *s.* banana; —=**tree** bananeira.
band *s.* atadura, ligadura; fita; banda de música; — **saw** serra de fita; =**stand** coreto; *v.t.* ligar, unir; *v.i.* associar-se, unir-se.
bandage *s.* atadura, ligadura, faixa; *v.t.* enfaixar.
bandit *s.* bandido.
bandoleer *s.* cartucheira, bandoleira.
bandy *v.t.* reenviar, trocar; *adj.* torto; —=**legged** cambaio.
bane *s.* ruina, calamidade; *v.t.* envenenar; =**ful** *adj.* pernicioso, funesto.
bang *s.* pancada; murro; *v.t.* bater, espancar.
bangle *s.* bracelete; *v.t.* desperdiçar, destruir.
banish *v.t.* banir.
banister *s.* balaústre; =s balaustrada.
bank *s.* margem, ribanceira, borda; banco (assento); (*com.*) banco, casa bancária; *v.t.* represar, aterrar, amontoar; =**er** banqueiro; =**ing** bancário.
bankrupt *s.* falido; *v.i.* falir; =**cy** falência.
banner *s.* bandeira, insígnia.
banns *s.* proclama.
banquet *s.* banquete, festim.
banter *s.* gracejo, chacota, zombaria; *v.t.* escarnecer, zombar; gracejar, troçar.
baptism *s.* batismo; =**al** *adj.* batismal.
baptistery *s.* batistério, pia batismal.
baptize *v.t.* batizar.
bar *s.* barra, tranca; tribunal, fôro, advocacia; balcão, botequim; obstáculo, barreira; (*mús.*) divisão, compasso; *v.t.* trancar, fechar, impedir; excluir; barrar; excetuar.
barb *s.* barba; farpa, aresta (de seta, anzol, etc.); =**ed wire** arame farpado.
barbarian *adj.*&*s.* bárbaro, selvagem; estrangeiro.
barbaric *adj.* inculto; bárbaro.
barbarism *s.* (*gram.*) barbarismo.
barbarity *s.* barbaridade, crueldade.
barbarize *v.t.* barbarizar.
barbarous *adj.* inculto, selvagem; cruel; =ly bàrbaramente.
barbecue *s.* assado de animal inteiro; churrasco; *v.t.* assar um animal inteiro; fazer churrasco.
barber *s.* barbeiro; *v.t.* barbear; pentear.
bard *s.* poeta heroíco entre os celtas e gálios; bardo, trovador, vate.
bare *adj.* nú, descoberto; pelado; simples; só; =**faced** descarado; =**footed** descalço; =ly *adv.* apenas; =**ness** nudez; pobreza; *v.t.* descobrir, despojar; privar.
bargain *s.* ajuste, contrato; compra de ocasião; pechincha; *v.t.* ajustar, contratar; regatear; barganhar; =**er** vendedor; regateador.
barge *s.* barcaça, falúa; =**man** bateleiro; =**master** patrão.
bark *s.* casca (de arvore); bote, barca; *v.t.* descascar, pelar; *v.i.* latir; =**ing** *s.* latido.
barley *s.* cevada.
barm *s.* levedura, fermento.
barn *s.* celeiro, granja; estábulo.
barnacle *s.* marisco.
barometer *s.* barômetro.
baron *s.* barão; =**ess** *s.* baronesa.
barque *s.* barca.
barrack *s.* caserna, quartel; **barraca**; *v.t.* aquartelar.

barrage *s.* barragem.
barratry *s.* barataria; trapaçaria; (*mar.*) ato fraudulento do comandante de um navio prejudicando a carga e interesses dos proprietários.
barrel *s.* barril, barrica; cano de arma de fogo; *v.t.* embarrilar, embarricar.
barren *adj.* estéril, árido; =**ness** *s.* esterilidade, aridez.
barricade *s.* barricada, trincheira; *v.t.&i.* entrincheirar, entrincheirar-se.
barrier *s.* barreira; obstáculo; dique, barragem.
barring *prep.* salvo, afora, exceto.
barrister *s.* advogado.
barrow *s.* carrinho de mão; túmulo; porco castrado.
barter *s.* troca, permuta de mercadoria; *v.t.* negociar permutando mercadoria; trocar, permutar.
barytone *s.* barítono.
basal *adj.* básico, fundamental.
basalt *s.* basalto.
bascule bridge *s.* ponte levadiça.
base *adj.* baixo, abjeto, vil; *s.* base, alicerce; — **coin** moeda falsa; =**ly** *adj.* vilmente, covardemente; =**ment** *s.* porão; =**ness** *s.* baixeza, vileza.
bashful *adj.* tímido, envergonhado; =**ness** *s.* timidez, modéstia.
basic *adj.* básico, fundamental; (*quím.*) básico.
basil *s.* (*bot.*) manjericão.
basilica *s.* basílica.
basilisk *s.* basilesco; iguano.
basin *s.* bacia, vasilha; bacia fluvial; prato de balança.
basis *s.* base, fundamento; pedestal.
bask *v.t.* aquecer (ao sol); *v.i.* aquecer-se (ao sol).
basket *s.* cesto, canastra.
bas-relief *s.* baixo-relêvo.
bass *s.* perca (peixe); (*mús.*) baixo.
bassinet *s.* berço.
bassoon *s.* fagote.
bast *s.* esparto; esteira ou corda feita de esparto.
bastard *s.* bastardo; *adj.* bastardo, ilegítimo; =**y** *s.* bastardia.
baste *v.t.* alinhavar; umedecer (o assado) com a gordura, môlho, etc.; espancar.
bastion *s.* bastião, baluarte.
bat *s.* cajado; clava usada em baseball, cricket, etc.; (*zool.*) morcego; *v.t.* golpear.
batch *s.* fornada de pão; grupo, fornada.
bate *v.t.* diminuir, reduzir; abater (preço); *s.* debate, contenda.
bath *s.* banho; banheiro; banheira; **water** = banho-maria; **knight of the** — ou K.B., cavaleiro da Ordem do Banho; =**e** *v.t.&i.* banhar, banhar-se; =**er** *s.* banhista; =**ing** *s.* banho; =**ing suit** roupa de banho.
bathos *s.* patos (decaída no estilo).
batman *s.* ordenança (militar).
baton *s.* bastão (insígnia de mando); batuta.
battalion *s.* batalhão.
batten *s.* ripa, caibro; sarrafo; *v.t.&i.* cevar, engordar ;adubar; **to — down the hatches** cerrar as escotilhas (do*navio).
batter *v.t.* bater, espancar; desancar; destruir; derribar; *s.* (*arq.*) talude; (*imp.*) pastel; =**ing piece** peça de sítio; =**ing-ram** aríete.
battery *s.* bateria; (*elet.*) pilha, bateria; (*dir.*) agressão.
battle *s.* batalha, combate; *v.i.* lutar, batalhar.

battledore *s.* raqueta.
battlement *s.* ameia, seteira; =**ed** *adj.* ameiado, adentado.
battue *s.* ato de bater o mato para levantar a caça; batida; morticínio, matança.
bauble *s.* ninharia, bagatela.
baulk V. balk.
bawl *v.i.* gritar, vociferar, berrar; *v.t.* apregoar, publicar; *s.* berro, grito.
bay *s.* baía, enseada; (*arq.*) vão, intercolúnio; (*bot.*) loureiro; latido, balido; cavalo baio; *adj.* baio; *v.i.* ladrar; *v.t.* cercar; encurralar.
bayonet *s.* baioneta.
bazaar *s.* bazar; quermesse.
B.C. antes de Cristo (A.C.).
be *v.i.* ser; estar; existir; (com o expletivo *there* equivale a haver: *there is*, há; com alguns adjetivos que indicam sensações equivale a ter: *to be hungry* ter fome; seguido de infinitivo equivale a dever, ter que: *I am to go* devo ir.).
beach *s.* praia, margem; *v.t.&i.* encalhar, dar à praia desembarcar (na praia).
beacon *s.* farol, baliza; *v.t.* assinalar com luz; guiar.
bead *s.* conta; grão; gota; bôlha; espuma; (*arq.*) moldura convexa, astrágalo; =**s** rosário; *v.t.* adornar com contas; *v.i.* fazer espuma; borbulhar.
beadle *s.* bedel, porteiro.
beak *s.* bico; =**er** *s.* vaso de boca larga.
beam *s.* viga mestra; trave; travessão (balança); lança de carro, arado, etc.; largura máxima de uma embarcação; galho (veado); raio (luz); feixe de raios luminosos; *v.i.* radiar; =**y** *adj.* radiante.
bean *s.* fava; feijão.
bear *s.* urso; (*ast.*) ursa; (bolsa) baixista; *v.t.* levar, carregar, ter; trazer; sustentar; suportar; tolerar; dar (testemunho) produzir; apresentar; usar; aguentar; sofrer; impelir; dar à luz; *v.i.* padecer, suportar com paciência; tomar (certa direção); frutificar; =**able** *adj.* suportável.
beard *s.* barba; =**less** *adj.* imberbe.
bearer *s.* portador; árvore ou planta que dá frutos.
bearing *s.* procedimento, conduta; porte, aspecto; relação; produção; colheita; gestação, prenhez; paciência, sofrimento; brasão; (*mar.*) rumo; linha de flutuação; (*mec.*) ponto de apoio; mancal; — **metal** bronze, metal para mancais; **to take a** — determinar um rumo; **take** =**s** orientar-se; (*mar.*) tomar a altura.
beast *s.* animal, bêsta; bruto.
beat *s.* batida, golpe, pancada; toque (de tambor); pulsação; (*mús.*) tempo, compasso; ronda; batida (caça); *v.t.&i.* bater; espancar; vencer; tocar (tambor); marcar (compasso, tempo, etc.); pulsar, palpitar; vibrar; dar uma batida para levantar a caça.
beatify *v.t.* beatificar.
beating *s.* batimento, pulsação; surra; derrota; (caça) batida.
beau *s.* namorado.
beautiful *adj.* belo; magnífico; **beautify** *v.t.* embelezar, aformosear; **beauty** *s.* beleza, formosura; beldade; **beauty parlor** instituto de beleza.
beaver *s.* castor.
becalmed *adj.* (*mar.*) parado por falta de vento.
because *conj.* porque, por causa de.

beck s. aceno; beckon v.i. acenar.
become v.i. fazer-se, tornar-se; — accustomed acostumar-se; v.t. convir, assentar bem; ser próprio; becoming adj. conveniente; apropriado; decente; assentando bem.
bed s. cama, leito; camada; alicerce; canteiro; jazida; — clothes roupa de cama; =room quarto de dormir; =time hora de ir para a cama; v.t. deitar; acamar, assentar, plantar; =ding s. (geol.) estratificação, estratos.
bedeck v.t. adornar, enfeitar.
bedew v.t. regar; umedecer.
bedizen v.t. enfeitar.
bedlam s. hospício (em Londres); maluco; (pop.) casa de loucos.
bedraggle v.t. enlamear; arrastar na lama.
bee s. abelha; =hive colmeia; — keeping apicultura.
beech s. faia; — marten fuinha.
beef s. boi; — steak bife; — tea caldo de carne.
beer s. cerveja.
beet s. beterraba; =root beterraba.
beetle s. escaravelho.
befall v.i. suceder, acontecer, sobrevir.
befit v.t. convir; =ting conveniente, próprio.
before adv. adiante, em frente; antes, anteriormente; prep. antes de; em frente de, perante; conj. antes de, antes que; =hand adv. de antemão, prèviamente.
befriend v.t. favorecer; ajudar, socorrer.
beg v.t.&i. rogar, pedir; mendigar; suplicar.
beget v.t. engendrar; fazer nascer.
beggar s. mendigo; miserável, suplicante; v.t. empobrecer, arruinar; =ly adj. pobre, miserável; =y s. miséria, mendicância.
begin v.t.&i. começar, principiar; encetar; — again recomeçar; =ner s. principiante; aprendiz; autor, inventor; =ning s. princípio, começo; origem.
begone interj. fóra daqui! vai-te!
begonia s. begônia.
begrudge v.t. invejar.
beguile v.t. enganar; seduzir; divertir.
behalf s. patrocínio, favor; in — of, on — of em nome de, em defesa de, a favor de.
behave v.i. comportar-se, conduzir-se, viver; — properly comporte-se bem; behavior s. comportamento, conduta, procedimento.
behead v.t. decapitar; =ing s. decapitação.
b=hest s. ordem, comando.
behind adv. atrás, detrás; prep. por detrás de, atrás de; =hand adv. atrasadamente; adj. atrasado.
behold v.t.&i. ver, olhar; int. vêde! =er s. espectador.
behoof s. proveito.
behoove, behove v.i. convir, ser necessário; incumbir; it =s importa, convém, é preciso.
being s. ser; existência; for the time — atual; atualmente.
belabor, belabour v.t. espancar, sovar.
belated adj. tardio.
belay v.t. (mar.) amarrar.
belch v.i. arrotar; =ing s. arrôto.
beldam s. feiticeira, bruxa.
beleaguer v.t. sitiar.
belfry s. campanário; tôrre.
Belgian adj.&s. belga.
belie v.t. desmentir; trair.

belief s. crença, fé; convicção; believable adj. crível, verossímil.
believe v.t.&i. acreditar, crer; =r s. crente.
belittle v.t. diminuir, fazer pouco, dar pouco valor.
bell s. sino; campainha; guizo; — jar redoma; — clapper badalo.
belladonna s. beladona.
belle s. beldade.
bellicose adj. belicoso; belligerent adj.&s. beligerante.
bellow v.i. bramir, mugir.
bellows s. fole.
belly s. ventre, barriga, pança; bojo; v.i. fazer barriga, inchar.
belong v.i. pertencer, depender, ser; =ing s. pertences; o que é de uso pessoal.
beloved adj.&s. querido, amado.
below adv. em baixo, abaixo, debaixo, por baixo; prep. debaixo, por baixo de, abaixo de.
belt s. cinto, cinturão; (maq.) correia de transmissão; (geog.) faixa, zona; v.t. cingir.
belvedere s. belvedere.
bemoan v.t. deplorar; lamentar.
bench s. banco; assento; tribunal; — mark ponto de referência.
bend s. curva, curvatura, volta; nó; v.t.&i. curvar, curvar-se; dobrar; franzir (as sobrancelhas); entortar; on =ed knees de joelhos.
beneath adv. debaixo, abaixo; prep. debaixo, sob.
benediction s. bênção.
benefaction s. benefício; benefactor s. benfeitor.
benefice s. benefício, favor.
beneficence s. beneficência.
beneficent adj. benéfico.
beneficial adj. vantajoso, útil; beneficiary s. beneficiado; benefit s. benefício; vantagem, proveito; socorro; (teat.) benefício; v.t. beneficiar; v.i. lucrar, beneficiar-se.
benevolence s. benevolência; benevolent adj. benevolente.
Bengal s. Bengala; bengalí; — light fogos de bengala; adj. bengalí.
benighted adj. surpreendido pela noite; na escuridão.
benign, benignant adj. benigno; benignly, benignantly adv. benignamente.
benjamin s. benjoim.
bent adj. curvado, arqueado; s. propensão, tendência; to be — on obstinar-se a, teimar em.
benumb v.t. entorpecer.
benzine s. benzina.
benzoin s. benjoim.
benzol s. benzol.
bequeath v.t. legar; bequest s. legado.
bereave v.t. despojar, privar, tirar; =ment s. lutô.
beret s. boina.
bergamot s. bergamota.
berry s. baga, grão.
berth s. (mar.) ancoradouro; lugar, leito.
beryl s. berilo.
beseech v.t. suplicar, implorar.
beset v.t. cercar, sitiar; =ting adj. habitual, assediante.
beside prep. ao lado de, perto de, fóra de; exceto; =s adv.&prep. além de que, além disso, demais; além de.
besiege v.t. sitiar; =r s. assediador, sitiante
besmear v.t. lambuzar; sujar.
besmirch v.t. sujar.

besom s. vassoura.
besotted adj. embrutecido.
bespangle v.t. lentejoular; espargir.
bespatter v.t. enlamear.
bespeak v.t. encomendar; estipular.
besprinkle v.t. regar, borrifar.
best adj. melhor, o melhor; superior, ótimo; adv. melhor.
bestial adj. bestial.
bestir v.t. mover, pôr em movimento; to — oneself apressar-se, obrar, mover-se.
bestow v.t. dar, conceder; distribuir, conferir; empregar.
bestride v.t. montar, escarranchar.
bet s. aposta; v.t. apostar.
betake v.t. (usado reflexivamente) recorrer; aplicar-se; ir.
bethink v.t. recordar, considerar, refletir; v.i. dar-se conta.
betide v.t.&i. suceder, acontecer.
betimes adv. cedo, a tempo.
betoken v.t. pressagiar; denotar; anunciar.
betray v.t. trair; enganar; atraiçoar; indicar, denunciar; — one's trust abusar da confiança, prevaricar; =al s. traição; =er s. traidor.
betroth v.t. prometer casamento; =al s. noivado; =ed s.&adj. prometido, noivo.
better adj. melhor, preferível; =ment s. melhoramento; so much the — tanto melhor; v.t. melhorar, exceder; =ment s. melhoramento.
better, bettor s. apostador; **betting** s. aposta.
between prep. entre, em; de; — now and then daquí até lá; — you and me entre nós.
bevel s. bisel, chanfradura; v.t. biselar, chanfrar; =ling adj. enviezado.
beverage s. beberagem, bebida.
bevy s. bando, enxame; agrupamento.
bewail v.t. chorar, lamentar, deplorar.
beware v.i. acautelar-se; desconfiar; tomar cuidado; — of pickpockets! cuidado com os batedores de carteira!
bewilder v.t. desencaminhar, desorientar; confundir, deixar perplexo; =ment s. perplexidade, aturdimento.
bewitch v.t. enfeitiçar; encantar; =ing adj. encantador, fascinante; =ingly adv. de modo sedutor.
beyond adv. além, mais longe, do outro lado; prep. além de, acima de, fóra de; the — o além; — doubt fóra de dúvida; — expression inexprimível.
bezel s. engaste; facêta.
bias s. viés; (fig.) propensão, pendor; parcialidade; preconceito; v.t. predispor, induzir; torcer; =sed parcial; to cut on the — cortar enviesado.
bib s. babadouro.
Bible s. Bíblia; **biblical** adj. bíblico.
bibliography s. bibliografia; **bibliophil** s. bibliófilo.
bibulous adj. absorvente; dado a bebida.
biceps s. bíceps.
bicker v.i. altercar; tremular; s. disputa ociosa, altercação.
bicycle s. bicicleta; **bicyclist** s. ciclista.
bid s. lanço (leilão); oferta; v.t.&i. oferecer, licitar; mandar, ordenar; convidar, rogar; to — adieu, farewell, good-by dizer adeus, despedir-se de; to — defiance to desafiar; =der s. licitante.
bide one's time (to) esperar sua hora, reservar-se.
biennial adj. bienal, bisanual.

bier s. ataúde.
bifurcation s. bifurcação.
big adj. grosso, grande; alto; basto; prenho (animal); — traders alto comércio.
bigamist s. bígamo; **bigamous** adj. bígamo; **bigamy** s. bigamia.
bight s. reentrância; enseada, gôlfo.
bigness s. grossura, grandeza.
bigot s. beato, carola; fanático, intolerante; =ry s. fanatismo, intolerância.
bigwig s. (pop.) figurão.
bike s. bicicleta.
bile s. bilis.
bilge s. bojo (de barril, pipa, etc.); (mar.) fundo do porão, sentina.
bilious adj. bilioso.
bilk v.t. frustrar; calotear.
bill s. bico (de ave); cartaz, anúncio, programa; lista, rol, relação; (fin.) nota, letra; (com.) conhecimento, fatura, conta; (parl.) projeto de lei; — of exchange letra de câmbio; — of lading conhecimento de embarque; v.t. fazer rol, relação ou lista de; faturar; afixar, pregar cartaz; v.i. bicotar-se, arrular.
billberry s. amora silvestre.
billet s. ordem de alojamento, boleto; acha de lenha; v.t. aboletar; acantonar.
billiards s. bilhar; **billiard room** salão de bilhares.
billingsgate s. mercado de peixe em Londres; (fig.) calão, linguagem obcena.
billion s. (nos Estados Unidos) bilião; (na Inglaterra) trilhão, mil biliões.
billow s. vaga, onda; v.i. ondear; =y adj. encapelado.
billy goat, bode.
bimonthly adj. bimestral.
bin s. arca, cofre; caixão (para depósito de carvão, cereais, etc.)
bind v.t. atar, amarrar, ligar; obrigar; prender; segurar; debruar; encadernar; (for.) compelir; =er s. encadernador, prendedor, atadura; adstringente; =ing adj. obrigatório, forçado; s. encadernação; debrum; ligação.
bindweed s. trepadeira.
binnacle s. (mar.) bitácula.
binocular s. binóculo; adj. binocular.
biographer s. biógrafo; **biography** s. biografia.
biologist s. biologista, biólogo; **biology** s. biologia.
biped s. bípede; =al adj. bípede.
biplane s. biplano.
birch s. bétula, vidoeiro; vara; v.t. vergastar; =ing s. varada, chibatada.
bird s. pássaro, ave; ='s-eye view vista do alto, por cima; =lime visco; — of prey ave de rapina.
birth s. nascimento; origem, descendência, extração; parto; — certificate certidão de idade; =day aniversário, dia natalício; dia dos anos; =right direito de nascimento, especialmente do filho primogênito.
bis adv. bis.
biscuit s. biscoito; pãozinho.
bisect v.t. dividir em duas partes iguais; =ion s. bisseção.
bishop s. bispo; =ric s. bispado.
bismuth s. bismuto.
bison s. bisão.
bit s. pedaço, migalha, fragmento; pouco; ponta, gume (de ferramenta); freio (de cavalo); palhetão (chave).
bitch s. cadela; — wolf lôba.
bite s. mordedura, dentada; picada;

bocado; *v.t.&i.* morder, picar; **biting** *adj.* mordaz, picante.

bitter *adj.* amargo, acre, azêdo; cruel, encarniçado; — **cold** frio cortante; =**sweet** agridoce; =**ly** *adv.* amargamente; acerbamente; =**ness** *s.* amargor; acerbidade, aspereza; encarniçamento; =**s** *s.* licor amargo.

bittern *s.* butio.

bitumen *s.* betume; **bituminous** *adj.* betuminoso.

bivalve *s.* bivalvo.

bivouac *s.* bivaque; *v.i.* bivacar.

blab *v.t.&i.* divulgar, revelar; dar com a língua nos dentes.

black *adj.* preto, negro; escuro; *v.t.* enegrecer, tisnar; engraxar (sapatos); *s.* preto (côr, pessoa); =**bird** melro; =**board** quadro negro; =**smith** ferreiro; =**mail** *s.* chantagem; *v.t.* fazer chantagem; =**mailer** chantagista.

blackamoor *s.* negro, negra.

blacken *v.t.* tingir de preto, enegrecer; denegrir.

blacking *s.* graxa (para sapatos); engraxadela.

blackish *adj.* escuro; **blackness** *s.* escuridão; negrura.

bladder *s.* bexiga; vesícula.

blade *s.* talo, haste; lâmina, folha (de faca, sabre, etc.); pá (do remo, da hélice, etc.).

blame *s.* reproche, censura; culpa, falta; *v.t.* culpar; reprochar, censurar; acusar; =**less** *adj.* inocente, irrepreensível; =**worthy** *adj.* culpável.

blanch *v.t.&i.* branquear; alvejar; descolorar, empalidecer.

bland *adj.* brando, suave; =**ishment** *s.* lisonja; afago.

blank *adj.* branco, virgem; *s.* lacuna, espaço em branco; bilhete branco (loteria); — **check** cheque em branco; — **verse** verso solto.

blanket *s.* cobertor, coberta; manta.

blare *s.* clangor; *v.t.&i.* retinir, retumbar, trombetear.

blarney *s.* adulação, lisonja.

blaspheme *v.t.&i.* blasfemar; **blasphemer** *s.* blasfemo, blasfemador; **blasphemous** *adj.* blasfematório, blasfemo; **blasphemy** *s.* blasfêmia.

blaze *s.* chama, labareda; fogueira; brilho, fulgor; **in a** — em chamas; *v.i.* chamejar; luzir, brilhar; *v.t.* inflamar; **blazing** *adj.* flamejante, ardente; brilhante.

blatant *adj.* barulhento; bramante.

blast *s.* rajada; corrente de ar; sôpro; estouro, explosão; carga explosiva, mina; — **furnace** alto forno; — **hole** mina; *v.t.* fazer saltar (por explosão); fulminar; destruir, queimar; =**ing** *s.* estouro; *adj.* destruidor; — **powder** pólvora de mina.

blazon *v.t.* blasonar; publicar, proclamar; *s.* brasão; =**ry** *s.* brasão.

bleach *v.t.* branquear, alvejar; =**ing** *s.* alvejamento.

bleak *adj.* triste, sombrio.

blear-eyed *adj.* ramelento.

bleat *v.i.* balar, berrar; —, =**ing** *s.* balido.

bleed *v.t.&i.* sangrar; =**ing** *s.* sangria.

blemish *s.* nódoa, mancha; marca, cicatriz; defeito; *v.t.* manchar, sujar; denegrir.

blend *s.* mistura; *v.t.* misturar; unir, fundir; *v.i.* confundir-se, mesclar-se; combinar (côres); =**ing** *s.* fusão, mistura.

bless *v.t.* benzer; abençoar; =**ed, blest** *adj.* bento; abençoado, bem-aventurado; =**edness** *s.* bem-aventurança, beatitude; =**ing** *s.* bênção; felicidade; graça.

blight *s.* ferrugem (do trigo), murchidão, queima (pelo frio, geada, etc.) *v.t.* murchar, mangrar.

blind *adj.* cego; *s.* estore; veneziana; (*fig.*) véu, máscara; *v.t.* cegar; =**fold** *v.t.* vendar os olhos; =**ly** *adv.* cegamente; =**ness** *s.* cegueira.

blink *s.* piscadela; clarão passageiro; *v.i.* piscar, pestanejar; vacilar; tremeluzir; *v.t.* evitar, encobrir; =**er** *s.* sinal luminoso intermitente, piscapisca; venda, antolhos.

bliss *s.* beatitude, felicidade; =**ful** *adj.* ditoso; bem-aventurado.

blister *s.* empôla, bôlha; vesicatório; *v.t.* empolar.

blithe *adj.* alegre.

blizzard *s.* tempestade de neve.

bloat *v.t.&i.* inchar, entumescer; =**edness** *s.* inflamação.

block *s.* bloco; cepo; partida, lote (de mercadorias, ações, etc.); quarteirão, quadra; (*tip.*) cliché; fôrma; (*maq.*) roldana, polia; — **calendar** folhinha; — **system** sistema de sinalação por secções ou quadras; — **tin** estanho em barra; *v.t.* obstruir, bloquear; — **up** condenar, impedir (porta, entrada, etc.).

blockade *s.* bloqueio; *v.t.* bloquear.

blockhead *s.* imbecil.

blockhouse *s.* fortim.

blond, blonde *adj.* louro, loura.

blood *s.* sangue; raça, parentesco; — **letting** sangria; — **poisoning** envenenamento do sangue; — **pressure** tensão arterial; — **relationship** consanguinidade; =**shed** derramamento de sangue; carnificina; — **sucker** sanguessuga; — **test** exame de sangue; — **thirsty** sanguinário; =**less** *adj.* exangue; sem derramamento de sangue; =**y** *adj.* ensanguentado; sangrento, em sangue; sanguinário.

bloom *s.* flor; frescura; *v.i.* florir; =**ing** *adj.* florescente, florido; *s.* florescência.

blossom *s.* flor; *v.i.* florescer; =**ing** *s.* florescência.

blot *s.* borrão, mancha; rasura; *v.t.* manchar, borrar; sujar; secar (a tinta); — **out** raspar.

blotch *s.* pústula; mancha.

blotting — **case**, — **pad, blotter** *s.* mata-borrão; — **paper** papel mata-borrão.

blouse *s.* blusa.

blow *s.* golpe, pancada; *v.t.* soprar; fazer soar (instrumento); *v.i.* soprar, ventar; tocar (instrumento de sopro); desabrochar; bufar; — **one's nose** assoar-se; — **out** soprar; — **up** *v.t.* fazer saltar, estourar; *v.i.* explodir.

blubber *s.* gordura; *v.i.* chorar, soluçar.

bludgeon *s.* clava, cacete, moca.

blue *adj.* azul; *s.* azul; *v.t.* azular; =**pencil** *v.t.* marcar com lapis azul; riscar, excluir; =**s** *s.* spleen, melancolia.

bluff *adj.* brusco, franco; escarpado; *s.* blefe; ribanceira; *v.t.* blefar.

bluish *adj.* azulado.

blunder *s.* asneira, tolice; êrro crasso; *v.i.* cometer êrro crasso; enganar-se, desatinar.

blunt *adj.* embotado; obtuso; duro, brusco; *v.t.* embotar; **-ly** *adv.* bruscamente; claramente, cruamente; **-ness** *s.* embotamento; rudeza, aspereza.
blur *s.* mancha; borrão; *v.t.* manchar, borrar; velar, nublar; **-red** *adj.* nublado, confuso.
blurt out *v.t.* largar, deixar escapar.
blush *s.* rubor; *v.i.* corar.
bluster *s.* barulho, tumulto; jactância, fanfarronada; *v.i.* soprar com fúria, zunir; bravatear; **-er** *s.* fanfarrão.
boa *s.* boá; — **constrictor** boa.
boar *s.* varrão; **wild** — javali; — **spear** chuço.
board *s.* táboa; taboleiro, taboleta, quadro; mesa; junta, conselho, diretoria; alimento, refeição; pensão; lado, borda; (*mar.*) bordo, bordada; **on** — **a bordo**; — **and lodging** casa e comida; pensão; — **of directors** conselho diretor, diretoria; — **of examiners** banca examinadora; **in -s** cartonado; *v.t.* assoalhar; subir (no trem, bonde, carro, etc.); alimentar, dar pensão; (*mar.*) abordar; *v.i.* hospedar-se, ser pensionista; **-er** *s.* pensionista; interno (aluno); **-ing house** pensão; **-ing school** internato.
boast *s.* jactância; ostentação; *v.t.* alardear; gabar; *v.i.* gabar-se; **-er** *s.* jactancioso; **-ful** *adj.* jactancioso.
boat *s.* bote, canoa, embarcação, barco, navio; — **deck** convés; — **hook croque**; *v.i.* navegar, remar, transportar-se em barco; **-ing** *s.* manejo de um barco; transporte em barco; **-swain** *s.* patrão.
bob *s.* sacudidela; reverência, cumprimento; chumbo, pêso (do fio a prumo, linha de pescar, etc.); disco (do pêndulo); *v.i.* balançar-se, bambalear; **-bed hair** cabelo cortado curto e crespo.
bobbin *s.* bobina, carretel.
bobtail *s.* cauda cortada; **-ed** *adj.* rabão.
bode *v.t.* pressagiar.
bodice *s.* corpinho; **bodily** *adj.* corpóreo, material; *adv.* em conjunto, em peso.
bodkin *s.* agulheta; sovela.
body *s.* corpo; armação, esqueleto; massa, extensão (de água, etc.); — **of a church** nave da igreja; — **of water** extensão de água; **-guard** escolta, capanga.
bog *s.* pântano; *v.t.* atolar, enlamear.
bogey *s.* espetro, espantalho.
boggle *v.i.* recuar, hesitar.
boggy *adj.* pantanoso.
bogus *adj.* falso, espúrio.
boil *s.* furúnculo; espinha.
boil *v.t.&i.* ferver, cozer; — **down** reduzir, condensar; **-ed beef** carne cozida; **-ed egg** ovo quente; **-er** *s.* caldeira; chaleira; tacho; **-er maker** caldeireiro; **-ing** *s.* ebulição, fervura; **-ing point** ponto de ebulição (212° F. ou 100° C.).
boisterous *adj.* barulhento; turbulento.
bold *adj.* intrépido, audaz, temerário; seguro, confiante; **in — type** (*tip.*) em negrita; **-ly** *adv.* intrèpidamente; audaciosamente; francamente; **-ness** *s.* intrepidez, audácia; atrevimento.
bollard *s.* (*mar.*) amarradouro.
Bolivia *s.* Bolívia; **Bolivian** *adj.* boliviano.
bolster *s.* almofada, travesseiro; chumaço; calço, suporte; *v.t.* sustentar; reforçar, apoiar; — **up** *v.t.* escorar.

bolt *s.* dardo, flecha; cavilha, grampo; ferrolho; lingueta (de fechadura); faísca, raio; fuga; *v.t.* aferrolhar; cavilhar, prender; separar, peneirar; tragar; *v.i.* disparar (o cavalo); escapulir, fugir; — **upright** direito como uma seta.
bolus *s.* bolo; pílula grande (para cavalo).
bomb *s.* bomba; *v.t.* arremessar bombas; **-ard** *v.t.* bombardear, canhonear; **-ardment** *s.* bombardeio, bombardeamento.
bombast *s.* ênfase; **-ic** *adj.* bombástico, enfático.
bomber *s.* bombardeador; (*aer.*) avião de bombardeio.
bond *s.* laço, vínculo, ligadura; cadeia, corrente; (*fin.*) vale, obrigação, título; (*dir.*) ato, contrato; caucionamento; fiança; (*quím.*) grau de afinidade; *v.t.* ligar, unir; **-age** *s.* cativeiro, escravidão; obrigação; **-ed** *adj.* garantido; obrigado.
bone *s.* osso; espinha (de peixe); — **of contention** pomo de discórdia; *v.t.* desossar; separar as espinhas (do peixe).
bonfire *s.* fogueira (de festa).
bonnet *s.* bonê; capota.
bonny *adj.* bonito; alegre.
bonus *s.* bonus; prêmio, gratificação; indenização; — **shares** ações de bonificação.
bony *adj.* ossudo.
boo *v.t.* vaiar.
booby *s.* palerma; — **prize** prêmio de consolação.
book *s.* livro; caderno, álbum; **-binder** encadernador; **-binding** encadernação; **-keeper** guarda-livros; **-keeping** escrituração, contabilidade; **-maker** banqueiro (corridas); **-plate** ex-libris; **-seller** livreiro; **-seller & publisher** livraria editora; **-worm** traça, cupim; (pessoa) rato de biblioteca; *v.t.* registrar, lançar; reservar (lugar, acomodação, etc.); *v.i.* registrar-se, inscreverse; **-ing** *s.* inscrição, registro; **-let** *s.* livreto, folheto.
boom *s.* (*maq.*) botalós; (*maq.*) braço de grua; (*fig.*) surto, prosperidade, crescimento repentino; *v.i.* troar, mugir, roncar.
boon *adj.* alegre, jovial; — **companion** bom companheiro; *s.* favor, dádiva.
boor *s.* rústico; campônio; **-ish** *adj.* rústico, grosseiro; **-ishness** *s.* rusticidade, grosseria.
boot *s.* bota, botina, calçado; **-maker** sapateiro; — **tree** fôrma; *v.t.* calçar bota, botina, etc.); **-ee** *s.* sapatinho de malha (de criança).
booth *s.* barraca.
bootless *adj.* inútil.
booty *s.* presa, saque, despôjo; espólio.
booze *v.i.* embebedar-se.
boracic *adj.* bórico; **borax** *s.* bórax.
border *s.* borda, margem; fronteira, limite; orla, debrum; platibanda (jardim); **-land** zona fronteiriça; *v.t.* delimitar; orlar; guarnecer, debruar; *v.i.* limitar, confinar.
bore *s.* perfuração, furo; calibre; alma (de canhão); diâmetro, largura (de poço, cano, cilindro, etc.); (*min.*) sondagem; (*mar.*) macaréu; (*maq.*) broca, trado; (*fig.*) maçada, amolação; — **hole** furo de sonda; *v.t.* perfurar, furar; brocar; (*fig.*) maçar, enfadar; **-dom** *s.* tédio, aborrecimento.

boric adj. bórico.
boring machine (min.) perfuratriz.
born adj. nato; — blind cego de nascença; to be — nascer.
boron s. boro.
borrow v.t. tomar emprestado; =er s. o que toma emprestado; =ing s. empréstimo.
borzoi s. galgo russo.
bosom s. seio, peito; — friend amigo do peito; — sin pecado venial.
boss s. bossa; (pop.) patrão, chefe; — work trabalho em relevo.
botanic, botanical adj. botânico; botanist s. botânico; botanize v.i. herborizar; botany s. botânica.
botch s. remendo; v.t. remendar, atamancar.
both adj.&pron. ambos; um e outro; os dois; conj.&adv. e; tanto como, assim como; ao mesmo tempo.
bother s. confusão; aborrecimento; v.t. incomodar, perturbar.
bottle s. garrafa, frasco, vidro; v.t. engarrafar.
bottom s. fundo; base, assento; pé; fim, motivo; o trazeiro; adj. inferior; o mais baixo; v.t. pôr o fundo; fundamentar; v.i. atingir o fundo; =less adj. sem fundo.
bough s. ramo, galho.
boulder s. rocha; calhau.
bounce s. salto; fanfarronada, bravata; v.i. saltar; bravatear.
bound s. limite, termo; salto; ricochete; to exceed all =s ultrapassar os limites; v.t. restringir, limitar; v.i. saltar, rococheter; — for com destino a; to be — to ter que, ser obrigado a; =ary s. limite, termo; =en duty dever imperioso; =less adj. ilimitado, imenso.
bounteous adj. generoso; bountiful adj. generoso, liberal, beneficente; fecundo; bounty s. generosidade, munificência; prêmio, gratificação; subvenção.
bouquet s. ramalhete; toque (do vinho).
bourn s. arroio.
bourn, bourne s. termo, limite.
bout s. vez, turno; encontro, combate, partida.
bovine adj. bovino.
bow s. laço (de fita, de gravata etc.); arco (arma); arco de violino; cabeçote de sela; argola de chave; arco.
bow s. saudação, cumprimento de chapéu; inclinação, reverência; (mar.) proa; v.t.&i. curvar, inclinar, arquear; — to cumprimentar; inclinar-se.
bowdlerize v.t. expurgar (um escrito).
bowels s. entranhas; intestinos.
bower s. berço; caramanchão.
bowl s. taça, terrina, poncheira, tigela, vaso; fornilho (do cachimbo); concavidade; côncavo (da colher); bola; v.t. fazer rolar (bola); atirar (bola).
bowler (hat) s. chapéu de côco.
bowman s. archeiro.
bowsprit s. (mar.) gurupés.
bow-wow s. latido; totó (cachorrinho).
box s. caixa, cofre, baú; compartimento; camarote (teatro); baia; guarita; boléia; — camera máquina fotográfica (caixão); — office (teat.) bilheteria; — on the ear(s) bofetada; — room depósito, cafarnaum; —=spring mattress enxergão de molas; —=tree & —=wood buxo (árvore); v.t. encaixar; esmurrar; (esp.) boxar; v.t. boxar; =er s. boxista; =ing s. boxe; =ing match luta de boxe.

boy s. menino, rapaz; =hood juventude, puerícia; =ish adj. infantil, pueril.
brace s. braçal; pua; tensão; tira, cinta, atadura; gancho, argola; (imp.) colchete; (plural) suspensórios; v.t. atar, ligar; cercar, rodear; to — the nerves fortificar os nervos.
bracelet s. pulseira, bracelete.
bracing adj. fortificante.
bracken s. (bot.) feto.
bracket s. consolo; estante; parêntese.
brackish adj. salobre.
brad s. ponta; =awl s. furador.
brag s. jactância; v.i. jactar-se.
brahmin s. brâmane.
braid s. trança; cadarço; galão; v.t. entrançar, entrelaçar; guarnecer de sutache.
brain s. cérebro; miolo; =fag fadiga cerebral; — wave idéia luminosa, genial; =less adj. tôlo, insensato.
braise v.t. assar.
brake s. freio, breque; balsa, espinhal; v.t. enfrear; pôr o freio.
bramble s. sarça, espinheiro; =d adj. espinhoso.
bran s. farelo.
branch s. ramo, galho; tronco; linha ou via secundária; sucursal; v.t. ramificar; v.i. ramificar-se.
brand s. tição; espada; raio; estigma; ferrete; v.t. marcar com ferro em brasa; estigmatizar; — new novo em folha; =ish v.t. brandir.
brandy s. aguardente, cachaça.
brass s. latão; descaramento.
brassière s. corpinho, porta-seios.
brassy adj. de latão; descarado, impudente.
brat s. moleque, pirralho, fedelho; rapazinho.
bravado s. bravata.
brave adj. bravo, valente; v.t. arrostar, desafiar; =ry s. bravura.
brawl s. disputa, rixa; v.i. brigar, contender; =er s. brigão, barulhento.
brawn s. polpa; carne de porco; (fig.) força muscular; =y adj. carnudo; musculoso.
bray v.i. zurrar; =ing s. zurro.
braze v.t. soldar; =n adj. de bronze ou latão; (fig.) impudente, descarado.
Brazil s. Brasil; =ian s.&adj. brasileiro; — nut castanha do Pará.
breach s. brecha, infração, rompimento; violação; contravenção; — of promise violação de promessa; — of trust infidelidade, abuso de confiança.
bread s. pão; — winner arrimo de família.
breadth s. largura.
break s. ruptura; fenda; interrupção; vácuo; despontar (do dia); falha; v.t. quebrar, partir; romper, cortar; vencer; violar; infringir, quebrantar; abater (o espírito); v.i. mudar (a voz); despontar (o dia); quebrar, fazer bancarrota; — down abater; — into invadir; — loose descencadear-se; — out rebentar; declarar-se; — through atravessar; — forth brotar.
breakable adj. frágil; frangível.
breakaway s. deslocação, desvio.
breakdown s. prostração; decomposição.
breaker s. quebrador; infrator.
breakfast s. café da manhã; v.i. tomar o café da manhã.
breaking s. ruptura, fratura; transgressão; bancarrota.

breakwater s. quebra-mar.
bream s. brema.
breast s. seio; peito; tetas.
breath s. fôlego, respiração; sôpro; =e v.i.&t. respirar; suspirar; =ing s. respiração; =less adj. sem fôlego; inanimado.
breech s. nádega; trazeira; culatra; =es s. calções.
breed s. raça; v.t.&i. criar, fazer criação; procrear; engendrar; multiplicar, reproduzir-se; =er s. criador; =ing s. criação, reprodução.
breeze s. brisa, viração, aragem; **breezy** adj. ventilado, fresco.
brethren s. irmãos.
breviary s. breviário.
brevity s. brevidade, concisão.
brew v.t. misturar, remexer; pôr de infusão; (fig.) tramar, urdir; v.i. fazer cerveja.
brewer s. cervejeiro; =y s. fábrica de cerveja.
briar s. sarça.
bribe s. subôrno; v.t. corromper; subornar; seduzir; =ry s. subôrno; corrupção.
brick s. tijolo; ladrilho.
bridal adj. nupcial; **bride** s. noiva, recém-casada; **bridesmaid** dama de honra.
bridge s. ponte; bridge (jôgo); v.t. construir pontes.
bridle s. freio; v.t. refrear, conter; enfrear.
brief adj. breve, conciso; fugaz; s. resumo, compêndio; auto jurídico; =less adj. sem causas; =ly adv. brevemente, sumàriamente.
brier s. sarça.
brig s. brigue (embarcação).
brigade s. brigada.
brigand s. salteador; =age s. assalto, roubo.
bright adj. brilhante; claro; vivo; reluzente; alegre; inteligente; =en v.t. clarear, fazer brilhar; lustrar; alegrar; v.i. brilhar; =ly adv. brilhantemente; =ness s. brilho, fulgor; inteligência.
brill s. rodovalho.
brilliancy s. brilhantismo, brilho; **brilliant** adj. brilhante; **brilliantine** s. brilhantina; **brilliantly** adv. brilhantemente.
brim s. borda, extremidade, orla; =ful adj. transbordante; — over transbordar.
brimstone s. enxofre.
brindled adj. malhado.
brine s. salmoura; vagas, ondas; (poe.) lágrimas.
bring v.t. trazer; fazer vir; induzir; persuadir; — about determinar, causar — down abater, diminuir; — forth produzir, dar ocasião a; — forward apresentar (argumento, etc.); (cont.) transportar (uma soma); — home provar de maneira concludente; — in produzir, apresentar; introduzir; — out evidenciar, demonstrar, publicar; — to book chamar às contas; — up criar, educar; =ing up educação.
brink s. bordo, beira.
briny adj. salobre, salgado.
briquet s. briquete.
brisk adj. vivo, animado, alegre, ativo.
briskness s. vivacidade, atividade.
bristle s. cerda; pêlo; v.t. eriçar; v.i. eriçar-se; **bristly** adj. eriçado.
brittle adj. quebradiço; =ness s. fragilidade.

broach s. espêto; sanfona; sovela.
broad adj. largas; lato; amplo; cheio; livre; liberal; =brimmed hat chapéu de abas largas; =cast, =casting rádio difusão; — =minded de idéias largas; =en v.t.&i. alargar, ampliar-se; =ly adv. largamente, abertamente.
brocade s. brocado.
broil s. tumulto, algazarra; v.t. assar, grelhar.
broker s. corretor.
broken adj. quebrado; arrebentado; entrecortado; mal falado (idioma); to be — =hearted ter o coração partido.
bromide s. brometo; **bromine** s. bromo.
bronchia s. brônquios; **bronchitis** s. bronquite.
bronze s. bronze; v.t. bronzear.
brooch s. broche.
brood s. geração; raça; descendência; ninhada; v.i. chocar; (fig.) considerar, pensar, ruminar.
brook s. riacho; v.t. digerir, tolerar; =let s. córrego.
broom s. vassoura; =stick cabo de vassoura.
broth s. caldo; **chicken** — caldo de galinha.
brother s. irmão; — =in =law cunhado; =hood s. fraternidade, confraria; =ly adj. fraternal.
brow s. sobrancelha; fronte; cume; =beat v.t. enrugar a testa, franzir a sobrancelha.
brown adj. pardo, castanho; trigueiro, moreno; v.t. amorenar; tostar; =ish adj. pardacento, amorenado.
browse s. brôto, rebento; v.t.&i. pastar.
bruise s. contusão, mossa, mancha roxa; v.t. magoar, pisar, machucar; =d adj. muchucado, contundido.
brunt s. peso; choque.
brush s. escova; pincel; vassoura; brocha; v.t. escovar; — up desenferrujar, recordar.
brutal adj. brutal; =ity s. brutalidade; =ize v.t. brutalizar; **brute** s. bruto, animal; **brutish** adj. brutal, embrutecido.
bubble s. bôlha; bôlha de ar; bôlha de sabão; bagatela; ninharia; projeto no ar; v.i. borbulhar.
buccaneer s. bucaneiro.
buck s. barrela; gamo; macho de certos animais; rapagão.
bucket s. balde.
buckle s. fivela; v.t. afivelar; anelar; =r s. escudo, broquel.
buckram s. bocaxim.
buckthorn s. espinheiro cambra.
buckwheat s. trigo sarraceno; fagópiro.
bucolic adj. bucólico.
bud s. brôto, renôvo, rebento, botão; (fig.) germe; v.i. brotar, grelar.
Buddhist adj. budista.
budding adj. (fig.) nascente; em germe, em brôto.
budge v.i. mexer.
budget s. orçamento.
buff adj. fulvo; v.t. polir.
buffalo s. búfalo.
buffer s. tampão.
buffet s. aparador; bufete; tapa, sopapo; v.t. sacudir; esmurrar, espancar.
buffoon s. bobo, palhaço; =ery s. palhaçada.
bug s. percevejo.
bugle s. bugula; clarim; — call toque de clarim.

build s. construção; v.t. construir; — up construir, edificar; =er s. construtor; =ing s. construção, edifício; monumento.

bulb s. bulbo; =ous adj. bulboso.

bulge s. bojo; ventre; v.t.&i. bombear; fazer saliência; inflar; fazer água.

bulk s. volume; massa; =y adj. maciço, volumoso.

bull s. touro; bula (papal); disparate; contradição; inconsequência; =dog cão de fila; =fight corrida de touros; =calf novilho; — elephant elefante macho.

bullet s. bala.

bullion s. ouro e prata em barra.

bullock s. boi.

bully s. fanfarrão; capanga; v.t. intimidar.

bulrush s. junco.

bulwark s. buluarte.

bump s. mossa, boça, galo, inchação; v.t.&i. bater, ferir, contundir; encontrar-se de chôfre.

bumper s. copo cheio, copázio.

bumpkin s. grosseiro, vilão.

bunch s. tumor, corcova; molho, feixe; ramo; cacho; =y adj. em cacho.

bundle s. maço, pacote, feixe; v.t. empacotar; entrouxar; fazer feixes.

bung s. tampão, rôlha; v.t. tapar, tamponar.

bungalow s. bangalô.

bungle s. êrro, mau negócio; v.t. estragar; deitar a perder; atamancar.

bunion s. joanete.

bunk s. tarimba.

bunkum s. disparate.

bunting s. estamenha.

buoy s. bóia; — up flutuar, boiar.

buoyant adj. flutuante; elástico; vivo; animado.

burden s. carga; fardo; estribilho; v.t. carregar; embaraçar; oprimir.

burdensome adj. oneroso.

burdock s. bardana.

bureaucracy s. burocracia; **bureaucrat** s. burocrata.

burglar s. ladrão arrombador; =y s. assalto noturno; **burgle** v.t. assaltar, arrombar (casa).

Burgundy s. vinho de Borgonha.

burial s. entêrro.

burlesque adj.&s. burlesco.

burly adj. corpulento.

burn s. queimadura; v.t.&i. queimar; incendiar, calcinar; =ing adj. escaldante, inflamado; s. combustão; ignição.

burnish v.t. brunir, pulir.

burnt adj. queimado.

burr, bur s. pericarpo; meato do ouvido externo; broca (de dentista); pronúncia do r uvular; pronúncia áspera.

burrow s. toca; v.i. meter-se na toca.

burthen s. carga; tonelagem.

bury v.t. enterrar.

bus s. ônibus.

bush s. mouta, mata; arbusto; ramo; pendão; penacho.

bushel s. medida de capacidade (nos EE. UU. equivale a 35,2383 litros; na Inglaterra, a 36,3677 litros).

bushy adj. espesso, cerrado; basto.

busily adv. ativamente.

business s. negócios; comércio; emprêsa; ocupação.

buskin s. coturno, borzeguim.

bust s. busto; seio.

bustard s. abetarda.

bustle s. movimento; animação; turbilhão; v.i. mexer-se, movimentar-se.

busy adj. ocupado, atarefado; movimentado; ativo; diligente.

but conj.,prep.&adv. mas; que; senão; porém; exceto; a menos que.

butcher s. carniceiro, acougueiro; v.t. massacrar; matar.

butchery s. matança.

butler s. despenseiro, chefe dos criados, copeiro.

butt s. alvo; tonel; feixe; beira do bordo; marrada (de carneiro); v.t.&i. marrar; dar com a cabeça contra.

butter s. manteiga; v.t. amanteigar.

butterfly s. borboleta.

buttock s. nádega; anca.

button s. botão; =hole casa (do botão); v.t. abotoar.

buttress s. contraforte; apôio; escora; v.t. apoiar, sustentar.

buxom adj. opulento, rechonchudo; =ness s. opulência.

buy v.t. comprar adquirir; =er s. comprador; =ing s. compra, aquisição.

buzz v.i. zoar, zunir; s. zoada, zunido.

by prep.&adv. por; a, em, perto, pelo, sôbre, conforme, de, com; — the way a propósito.

by-blow s. filho ilegítimo, bastardo.

by-law s. regulamento.

bygone adj. passado, antigo.

by-pass s. passagem lateral, desvio.

bypath s. vereda; atalho.

by-product s. sub-produto.

bystander s. assistente, espectador.

byway s. atalho.

byword s. adágio, rifão.

byzantine adj. bizantino.

C

C terceira letra do alfabeto; (mús.) dó, primeira nota da escala.

cab s. cabriolé, carro de aluguel.

cabal s. cabala; intriga, trama; v.t. maquinar, tramar.

cabaret s. cabaré.

cabbage s. repôlho; couve; — lettuce alface repolhuda.

cabin s. camarote; cabana; guarita; — trunk mala de camarote.

cabinet s. ministério; gabinete; armário; — Council Conselho de Ministros; =maker marceneiro; — minister ministro de Estado.

cable s. cabo, amarra; telégrafo sub-

**marino; cabograma; v.t.&i. telegrafar pelo cabo submarino.

caboose s. (mar.) cozinha (de navio); (fer.) carro para os empregados (em trem de carga).

ca' canny strike (gíria operaria) greve não declarada consistindo na deliberada diminuição do trabalho por parte dos operários.

cacao s. cacau.

cachet s. sêlo; cápsula medicinal; caráter distintivo ou qualidade.

cackle s. cacarejo; loquacidade, verbosidade; v.i. cacarejar, tagarelar; rir-se.

cacoethes s. cacoete.

cactus s. cacto.
cad s. canalha; pessoa de hábitos grosseiros.
caddy s. rapazinho que carrega os paus de golf; mensageiro; caixinha para chá; lata ou caixa pequena.
cadence s. cadência; ritmo.
cadet s. cadete; caçula.
cadge v.t. carregar fardos; mascatear.
cage s. gaiola; jaula, prisão; v.t. engaiolar.
cairn s. monte de pedras (usado em sepulturas nos países setentrionais).
Cairo s. o Cairo.
caisson s. caixa de munições; caixão usado nas construções hidráulicas.
cajole v.t. lisonjear, adular; =ry s. lisonja, adulação; =r s. lisonjeador, adulador.
cake s. bolo, pastel; v.t. amassar; fazer bolo.
calabash s. cabaça.
calamitous adj. calamitoso; **calamity** s. calamidade.
calcareous adj. calcáreo.
calcine v.t. calcinar; v.i. calcinar-se.
calcium s. cálcio.
calculate v.t. calcular; v.i. contar; **calculation, calculus** s. cálculo; **calculating machine** máquina de calcular.
caldron s. caldeirão, caldeira.
calendar s. calendário; — year ano civil.
calender s. calandra; v.t. calandrar, cilindrar.
calf s. bezerro, vitela; barriga da perna; — skin couro de bezerro.
calibrate v.t. calibrar, graduar; regular; **calibre, caliber** s. calibre; espécie, qualidade.
calico s. (tec.) calicó, percal.
California s. Califórnia.
caliph s. califa.
call s. chamada, chamado; convite; visita; comunicação; v.t.&i. chamar, convocar; visitar; convidar; proclamar; fazer visita; fazer vir; — back chamar de volta; — for pedir, reclamar; — off desencomendar, dar contra-ordem; — out chamar, gritar; — upon invocar; implorar; =er s. visitante; =ing s. chamado; convocação.
calliper, caliper s. calibre; compasso; v.t. calibrar.
callosity, callus s. calosidade, calo; **callous** adj. calejado, endurecido.
callow adj. implume; inexperiente, noviço; — youth verde mocidade; rapaz imberbe.
calm adj. calmo; v.t. calmar, acalmar; =ly adv. calmamente, tranquilamente; =ness s. tranquilidade, calma.
calorie s. caloria.
calumniate v.t. caluniar; **calumny** s. calúnia.
Calvary s. Calvário.
calve v.i. parir (a vaca).
calyx s. cálice.
camber s. arqueamento, curvatura; v.t. arquear.
cambric s. cambraia, batiste.
camel s. camelo.
camellia s. camélia.
cameo s. camafeu.
camera s. câmara escura; (pop.) máquina fotográfica.
cami-knickers s. calça-camisa.
camomile s. camomila.
camouflage s. camuflagem; disfarce; v.t. disfarçar, encobrir sob falsas aparências, mascarar.
camp s. campo; — bed leito de campo;

v.t.&i. acampar; **camping out** viver transitòriamente em tendas, acampamento.
can s. lata, lata de conservas; — opener abridor de latas; v.t. enlatar, acondicionar conservas; **canned goods** conservas.
can v.def. poder, saber.
Canada s. o Canadá; **Canadian** s. canadense.
canal s. canal; =ize v.t. canalizar.
canary s. canário.
cancel s. cancelamento; v.t. cancelar, anular.
cancer s. câncer; =ous adj. canceroso.
candelabrum s. candelabro.
candid adj. cândido, alvo; puro; sincero.
candidate s. candidato, postulante, aspirante, pretendente.
candied adj. confeitado; **candy** s. confeito, bala, doce; v.t. cobrir com açucar.
candle s. vela; candeia.
candor, candour s. sinceridade, candura.
cane s. cana; bengala; **sugar** — cana de açúcar; — mill engenho de açúcar; v.t. esbordoar, surrar.
canine adj. canino.
canister s. caixa metálica; caixa para chá, rapé, etc.
canker s. úlcera; enfermidade que ataca as árvores; v.t. gangrenar; corromper; consumir.
cannibal s.&adj. canibal, antropófago.
cannon s. canhão; cano d'arma de fogo; carambola (no bilhar); — shot tiro de canhão; =ade s. canhonada; v.t. canhonear.
canny adj. fino, sagaz, astuto; prudente.
canoe s. canoa, piroga.
canon s. cânon, cânone; — law direito canônico; =ize v.t. canonizar.
canopy s. dossel, sobrecéu; abóbada.
cant s. canto; esquina; declive; afetação, insinceridade no falar; hipocrisia; jíria; uso afetado de linguagem bíblica; v.t.&i. chanfrar; inclinar; falar com hipocrisia; pedir.
cantankerous adj. desagradável; quereloso; rabugento.
cantata s. cantata.
canteen s. cantina; cantil.
canter s. meio galope; hipócrita, tartufo; v.i. andar a cavalo a passo largo ou a meio galope.
canticle s. cântico.
cantilever s. suporte, viga.
canto s. canto; =r s. cantor.
canvas s. lona; tela; velas de navio; quadro a óleo.
canvass v.t. examinar, escrutar; cabalar (votos); solicitar; escrutinar.
canyon, canon s. garganta, desfiladeiro.
cap s. gorro, barrete, boné, quepi, chapéu, carapuça; remate; pináculo; coberta, tampa; v.t. tampar; coroar; rematar; descobrir-se saudando alguém.
capability s. capacidade; **capable** adj. capaz, apto; **capacious** adj. espaçoso; **capacitate** v.t. capacitar, tornar capaz, habilitar; **capacity** s. capacidade; qualidade; habilidade.
caparison s. caparação; equipamento, jaezes; v.t. vestir pomposamente, ajaezar.
cape s. cabo (geográfico); capa curta.
caper s. salto, cabríola, travessura, cambalhota; v.i. cabríolar, dar cambalhotas.
capillary adj. capilar.

capital *adj.* capital, principal; excelente, magnífico; *s.* capital (de país), capital (dinheiro); **-ist** *s.* capitalista; **-ize** *v.t.* capitalizar; — **letter** letra maiúscula.

capitulate *v.i.* capitular.

capon *s.* capão.

caprice *s.* capricho; **capricious** *adj.* caprichoso.

capsicum *s.* pimenta.

capsize *v.t.* fazer sossobrar, fazer virar; *v.i.* sossobrar, virar, capotar.

capstan *s.* cabrestante.

capsule *s.* cápsula.

captain *s.* capitão, comandante de navio.

caption *s.* captura, prisão; (*imp.*) cabeçalho, título de artigo, capítulo, secção, etc.; (*cinema*) subtítulo.

captious *adj.* capcioso, insidioso; **-ly** *adv.* capciosamente, insidiosamente; **-ness** *s.* insídia.

captivate *v.t.* cativar, fascinar; **captive** *s.&adj.* cativo, prisioneiro; **captivating** *adj.* encantador, sedutor, atraente; **captivation** *s.* encanto, fascinação; **capture** *s.* captura, tomada; **capture** *v.t.* capturar.

Capuchin friar frade capuchinho.

car *s.* carro, vagão, automóvel; cabine do elevador.

caracol, caracole *s.* caracol; *v.i.* caracolar.

caramel *s.* caramelo.

carapace *s.* carapaça, casca, cobertura córnea (de animal).

carat *s.* quilate (de ouro, etc.).

caravan *s.* caravana.

caraway *s.* alcaravia, cariz.

carbine *s.* carabina; **-er** *s.* carabineiro.

carbolic acid ácido fênico, ácido carbólico.

carbon *s.* carbono; **-ate** *s.* carbonato; **-ic** *adj.* carbônico; **-iferous** *adj.* carbonífero; **-ize** *v.t.* carbonizar; — **copy** cópia a papel carbono.

carboy *s.* garrafão.

carbuncle *s.* carbúnculo; tumor, inflamação.

carburettor *s.* carburador.

carcass, carcase *s.* carcassa, cadáver; armação, esqueleto.

card *s.* carta (baralho); cartão; ficha.

cardigan *s.* colete tricotado.

cardinal *adj.* cardeal, principal; *s.* cardeal.

care *s.* cuidado, atenção, precaução; preocupação, inquietude; cargo, custódia; — **taker** guardião; — **worn** gasto pela inquietude ou preocupação; — **for** desejar, gostar, interessar-se; *v.i.* preocupar-se, inquietar-se.

careen *v.t.* querenar, reparar; *s.* querena.

career *s.* carreira; curso; corrida; profissão; *v.i.* galopar.

careful *adj.* cuidadoso, atento, cauteloso; diligente; **-ness** *s.* cuidado, atenção; **careless** *adj.* negligente, descuidado; **carelessness** *s.* descuido, negligência, inatenção; relaxamento; **carelessly** *adv.* relaxadamente, descuidadamente, negligentemente.

caress *s.* carícia, afago; *v.t.* acariciar.

caret *s.* (*imp.*) sinal para indicar inclusão de matéria.

cargo *s.* carga, mercadoria, carregamento; — **boat** navio de carga.

caricature *s.* caricatura; *v.t.* caricaturar.

carman *s.* carreteiro, carroceiro; motorneiro.

carmine *s.* carmim.

carnage *s.* carnificina.

carnal *adj.* carnal.

carnation *s.* cravo (flor).

carnelian *s.* cornalina.

carnival *s.* carnaval.

carnivora *s.pl.* carnívoros; **carnivorous** *adj.* carnívoro; **carnivore** *s.* carnívoro.

carob *s.* alfarroba, alfarrobeira.

carol *s.* cantos de alegria, cânticos de Natal; *v.i.* cantar, celebrar.

carousal *s.* orgia, dissipação, pândega; festim; **carouse** *v.i.* embriagar-se, fazer farra.

carp *s.* carpa (peixe); *v.t.* censurar, criticar, vituperar.

Carpathians (the) os Cárpatos (montes).

carpenter *s.* carpinteiro; **carpentry** *s.* carpintaria.

carpet *s.* tapete; *v.t.* atapetar, cobrir de tapete; — **broom** vassoura de tapete; — **knight** herói de salão.

carriage *s.* carruagem, carro, vagão, carroça, veículo; transporte; porte, atitude de uma pessoa, ar de uma pessoa; — **forward** frete a pagar; — **paid** frete pago; — **free** frete livre.

carrier *s.* portador, carregador; mensageiro; — **pigeon** pombo correio.

carrion *s.* carniça, carne corrompida, cadáver de animal.

carrot *s.* cenoura; **-y hair** cabelos vermelhos.

carry *v.t.* alcance (de arma de fogo); ato de carregar; transporte; *v.t.* transportar, transmitir, levar; trazer consigo; comportar-se; produzir; (*cont.*) transportar (somas); — **on** prosseguir, continuar, levar avante; — **about** levar de um lado para o outro, levar daquí para alí; — **into effect** levar a cabo, realizar.

cart *s.* carreta, carro, carroça; *v.t.* guiar ou conduzir carro, carroça, etc.

cartilage *s.* cartilagem.

cartoon *s.* caricatura, desenho humorístico; **-ist** caricaturista, desenhista.

cartouche *s.* cartucho (de pólvora).

cartridge *s.* cápsula, cartucho (de arma).

carve *v.t.* cortar, talhar; esculpir; trinchar; **-r** *s.* entalhador, escultor, gravador; trinchador; **carving** *s.* entalho, escultura; **carving knife** trinchante.

cascade *s.* cascata.

case *s.* caso; estado ou condição; situação; questão; exemplo; negócio; processo; caixa, boceta; estojo; bainha; coberta, envólucro; **pillow** — fronha; *v.t.* encaixar, encerrar.

caseharden *v.t.* endurecer exteriormente; (*met.*) temperar a superfície.

casemate *s.* casamata.

casement *s.* armação; postigo, batente de janela.

cash *s.* dinheiro em espécie; caixa; fundos; — **book** livro caixa; — **box** cofre; — **register** caixa registradora; *v.t.* converter em dinheiro, descontar (um cheque), receber dinheiro; **-ier** *s.* contador, o caixa.

cashmere *s.* casemira.

casing *s.* envelope, cobertura; tampa; encadernação, encaixotamento.

cask *s.* casco; tonel, barril, barrica, pipa; *v.t.* acondicionar em barril, tonel, etc.

casket *s.* escrínio, caixa de joias; esquife

casserole s. caçarola.
cassia s. (bot.) cássia.
cassock s. batina, sotaina.
cast s. tiro; lance; lanço, jato, arremêsso; ar, aparência, porte, modo de apresentar-se; casta; molde; fôrma; tonalidade, matiz; elenco (de teatro); v.t.&i. pensar, imaginar, idealizar; prognosticar: jogar, lançar, arremessar; moldar; adicionar; distribuir; derreter, fundir; — **iron** ferro fundido; — **off** descartado, posto à margem.
castanet s. castanhola.
castaway s. réprobo; perdido; náufrago.
caste s. casta.
castellated adj. acastelado, encastelado, em forma de castelo.
caster s. o que lança, atira ou arroja alguma cousa; fundidor; moldador; **=s** s. galheteiro.
castigate v.t. cástigar; **castigation** s. castigo.
casting s. jato, lance; invenção; fundição; modelagem.
castle s. castelo; fortaleza, cidadela, tôrre; v.i. rocar (jôgo de xadrez); — **builder** visionário, fazedor de castelos no ar.
castor s. castor; **=oil** óleo de rícino.
castrate v.t. castrar; **castration** s. castração.
casual adj. acidental, casual, fortuito; — **laborer** trabalhador por hora; **=ty** s. casualidade, contingência, acidente, desastre, vítima; **=ties** s. (mil.) baixas.
casuistry s. casuística.
cat s. gato; v.t. (mar.) içar (âncora); chicotear; **='s paw** pata de gato; (mar.) brisa, aragem.
cataclysm s. cataclisma.
catacomb s. catacumba.
catafalque s. catafalco.
catalogue s. catálogo; v.t. catalogar.
catapult s. catapulta.
cataract s. catarata.
catarrh s. catarro.
catastrophe s. catástrofe.
catch v.t.&i. apanhar; agarrar; capturar; captar; amarrar; pegar; tomar; surpreender; alcançar; — **cold** resfriar-se; — **fire** pegar fogo; — **hold of** agarrar; — **one's eye** chamar a atenção; — **on** perceber; — **up** pôr em dia, alcançar; s. presa; captura; (esporte) ato de apanhar a bola no ar; (const.) grampo, gato; (mar.) redada; (pop.) bom partido; **=ing** adj. contagioso; atraente.
catechism s. catecismo; **catechize** v.t. catequizar.
categorical adj. categórico; **category** s. categoria.
cater v.i. abastecer, prover, fornecer; **=er** s. provedor, fornecedor.
caterpillar s. lagarta.
caterwaul v.i. miar; **=ing** s. miado, concêrto de gatos.
catgut s. corda de guitarra; corda de tripa.
cathead s. (mar.) serviola.
cathedral s. catedral.
Catherine wheel roda catarina; roda de fogos de artifício.
cathode s. catódio.
catholic adj.&s. católico; **=ism** s. catolicismo.
cattle s. gado; — **market** mercado de gado; — **plague** peste bovina.
Caucasian adj. caucasiano; **the Caucasus** o Cáucaso.

caucus s. reunião de chefes de um partido.
cauldron s. caldeirão.
cauliflower s. couve-flor.
caulk v.t. calafetar.
causative adj. causal, causativo; **cause** s. causa, razão, motivo; **cause** v.t. causar, ocasionar.
causeway s. calçada; caminho elevado por atêrro por causa da umidade.
caustic adj.&s. caústico; **cauterize** v.t. cauterizar; **cautery** s. cautério.
caution s. precaução; atenção, prudência; aviso; v.t. avisar, acautelar; **cautious** adj. prudente, reservado, acautelado, de sobreaviso; **cautiously** adv. prudentemente.
cavalcade s. cavalgada.
cavalier s. cavaleiro; adj. franco; arrogante, desdenhoso.
cavalry s. cavalaria.
cave s. cova, caverna, antro; v.t. escavar, cavar; — **in** v.i. ceder, render-se; — **dweller** homem das cavernas, troglodita.
cavern s. caverna, subterrâneo; **=ous** adj. cavernoso.
caviar s. caviar.
cavil s. chicana; argúcia; v.i. chicanar.
cavity s. cavidade.
caw v.i. grasnar.
cease v.i.&t. cessar; desistir; parar; acabar-se; suspender; impedir; **=less** adj. incessante; **=lessness** s. continuidade.
cedar s. cedro.
cede v.t. ceder.
ceil v.t. pôr o teto (em uma casa); revestir (uma parede).
celebrate v.t.&i. celebrar, solenizar, festejar; **=d** adj. célebre, famoso; **celebrity** s. celebridade.
celery s. aipo.
celestial adj. celestial, celeste.
celibacy s. celibato; **celibate** s. celibatário.
cell s. cela (de religioso ou de prisão), alvéolo, célula.
cellar s. porão, adega; v.t. armazenar no porão ou na adega.
cellist s. violoncelista; **cello** s. violoncelo.
cellular adj. celular.
celluloid s. celulóide; **cellulose** s. celulose.
Celt s. celta; **Celtic** adj.&s. céltico; celta (língua).
cement s. cimento; v.t. cimentar.
censor s. censor; **=ious** adj. crítico; **=ship** s. censura; **censure** v.t. censurar.
census s. censo, recenseamento.
centaur s. centauro.
centenarian s.&adj. centenário; **centenary** s.&adj. centenário.
center s. centro; v.t. centrar, concentrar.
centigrade adj. centígrado.
centipede adj. centopeia.
central adj. central; **=ize** v.t. centralizar; **centre** s. centro, meio, núcleo; **centre** v.t. centrar, concentrar; **centrifugal** adj. centrífugo; **centripetal** adj. centrípeto.
century s. século.
ceramics s. cerâmica.
cereal s. cereal.
ceremonial s. cerimonial; **ceremonious** adj. cerimonioso; **ceremony** s. cerimônia.
certain adj. certo; **=ty** s. certeza; **for a** — seguramente.

certificate s. certificado, diploma, atestado, título; **-d** adj. diplomado, titulado; **certify** v.t. certificar, visar, atestar.

cesspool s. cloaca, fossa.

Ceylon s. Ceilão.

chafe v.t. friccionar; irritar; v.i. desgastarse; irritar-se; s. fricção; irritação.

chaff s. miuçalhas; restos, detritos; picuinhas; frivolidades; v.t. pilheriar.

chaffinch s. tentilhão.

chain s. corrente, cadeia; v.t. acorrentar.

chair s. cadeira, cátedra; v.t. empossar; entronizar; **-man** s. presidente; **-manship** s. presidência.

chalcedony s. calcedônia.

chalice s. cálice, taça.

chalk s. giz; v.t. marcar com giz.

challenge s. desafio, cartel, provocação; recusa; v.t. desafiar, provocar; contestar; recusar; incriminar; objetar.

chalybeate adj. ferruginoso.

chamber s. quarto, gabinete, alcova; dormitório; câmara; tribunal ou sala de justiça; — **maid** criada de quarto; — **of commerce** câmara de comércio; — **music** música de câmara.

chameleon s. camaleão.

chamfer s. chanfro, estria; v.t. estriar, chanfrar.

chamois s. camurça.

champ v.t. mastigar ruidosamente.

champagne s. champanha (bebida).

champion s. campeão; **-ship** s. campeonato.

chance s. acaso, sorte, ocasião; **by** — por acaso; **to take** — aventurar-se, correr risco; adj. casual, acidental, fortuito; adv. casualmente; v.i.&t. acontecer, arriscar.

chancel s. côro de igreja, santuário, presbitério.

chancellery s. chancelaria; **chancellor** s. chanceler.

chancre s. cancro, úlcera; **chancrous** adj. canceroso.

chandelier s. lustre, lampadário.

chandler s. tendeiro, vendeiro.

change s. mudança, alteração; vicissitude; câmbio; trôco, moeda miúda; v.t. trocar, alterar, mudar, substituir; v.i. corrigir-se, transformar-se, alterarse; — **of life** menopausa; **for a** — para variar; **to** — **one's mind** mudar de opinião.

channel s. canal; passagem; riacho; estreito; via; v.t. sulcar; conduzir; estriar; acanalar.

chant s. canto; **-y** s. canção de bordo; v.t. cantar, salmodiar.

chaos s. caos; **chaotic** adj. caótico.

chap s. rapaz, moço, indivíduo, sujeito; mandíbula; racha ou fenda na pele; v.t. fender, rachar; v.i. fender-se, rachar-se.

chapel s. capela.

chaplain s. capelão.

chaperon s. capelo, capuz; pessôa que acompanha moça solteira.

chaplet s. guirlanda, grinalda; terço de rosário.

chapter s. capítulo.

char s. carvão vegetal; carvão animal (para refinação de açúcar); espécie de truta; v.t.&t. carbonizar, carbonizar-se.

character s. caráter, natureza, maneira de proceder; **-istic** adj. caraterístico; **-istic** s. caraterístico, caraterística; **-ize** v.t. caraterizar.

charade s. charada.

charcoal s. carvão de lenha; — **burner** carvoeiro; — **drawing** desenho a carvão.

chare s. tarefa de ocasião, biscate.

charge s. carga; ataque, investida; cargo, emprêgo, encargo, comissão; cuidado; atribuição; acusação, inculpação; preço, imposto, despesa; débito, conta; ordem, mandato; (pl.) honorários; **in** — encarregado; interino; v.t. carregar; confiar, encarregar; imputar, acusar; onerar; (com.) lançar na conta; impor, ordenar; investir sôbre, atacar.

charily adv. prudentemente; econômicamente; cuidadosamente.

chariot s. carro.

charitable adj. caridoso, benfazejo; **charity** s. caridade, assistência, obras pias.

charlatan s. charlatão.

charm s. encanto, sedução, atrativo; berloque; v.t. seduzir, encantar; **-er** s. encantador, sedutor; **-ing** adj. encantador.

charnel house s. ossuário.

chart s. carta, mapa, gráfico, diagrama.

charter s. escritura autêntica; carta patente; título; privilégio; contrato de fretamento de navios; carta constitucional; v.t. estabelecer privilégio; fretar; **-er** s. fretador; **-ed** adj. privilegiado; fretado.

charwoman s. mulher assalariada por hora ou dia para trabalho doméstico.

chary adj. prudente; econômico; sôbrio.

chase v.t. caçar; perseguir, afugentar; (our.) cinzelar; s. caça; caçada; (imp.) rama; (mil.) alma (de canhão); **-r** s. caçador, perseguidor; cinzelador; avião de caça.

chasm s. abismo; vácuo; hiato; rachadura, fenda.

chasse s. caixa, cofre; relicário.

chassé s. um passo de dansa.

chassis s. armação.

chaste adj. casto, pudico; **chastity** s. castidade.

chasten, chastise v.t. castigar; **chastisement** s. castigo.

chasuble s. casula.

chat s. conversa, palestra familiar; v.i. conversar, dar uma prosa.

chattel s. coisa, bens móveis, haveres.

chatter s. garrulice; tagarelice; v.t.&i. tagarelar, conversar; — **box** tagarela, falador.

chauffeur s. chauffeur, motorista.

cheap adj. barato; (fig.) desprezível, sem valor, insignificante; **-ly** adv. a preço baixo; **-er** adj. mais barato; **-ness** s. barateza.

cheat s. trapaceiro, embusteiro; v.t.&i. burlar, fraudar, enganar; **-ing** s. burla, trapaça, embuste, fraude.

check s. obstáculo, impedimento; resistência; controle; freio; repreensão; ficha de jôgo; cheque de banco; cheque no jôgo de xadrez; v.t. freiar; parar, deter; moderar; controlar, verificar; refreiar; registrar; — **book** livro de cheques; **-er** s. verificador, controlador; taboleiro de xadrez.

cheek s. bochecha, maçãs do rosto; (pop.) topete, descaramento, impudência, ousadia, sem cerimônia; — **bone** osso zigomático; **-y** adj. impudente, descarado, ousado.

cheep v.i. piar, pipilar.

cheer s. vivas, aplausos; alegria, regosijo; festim; v.t.&i. alegrar; consolar, animar, alentar; aplaudir, ovacionar; alegrar-se, regosijar-se; =er s. animador, consolador; =ful adj. alegre, animado, jovial; =fully adv. alegremente, animadamente; =fulness s. alegria, animação, jovialidade; =less adj. triste, desanimado; — up cobrar ânimo; ânimo, coragem.

cheese s. queijo; =dairy queijaria; — industry indústria de queijo.

cheetah s. espécie de onça, animal felino da África e da Ásia.

chemical adj. químico; s. produto químico; chemist s. (scientist) químico, (druggist) farmacêutico; chemistry s. química.

cheque s. (usado na Inglaterra) cheque.

cherish v.t. apreciar, estimar; acalentar; acariciar; alimentar.

cherry s. cereja; =pie torta de cerejas; — stone caroço de cereja; — tree cerejeira.

cherub s. querubim.

chervil s. (bot.) cerefólio.

chess s. xadrez; =board taboleiro de xadrez.

chest s. peito, tórax; caixa, baú, arca, cofre; — of drawers, cômoda; — protector peitilho de lã para abrigo.

chesterfield s. sobretudo; sofá.

chestnut s. castanha; =tree castanheiro; adj. castanho (côr).

cheval dressing table penteadeira, psichê.

chevy v.t. caçar.

chew v.t. mascar, mastigar; =ing s. mastigação; chewing-gum goma de mastigar.

chiaroscuro s. claro-escuro.

chicane v.t.&i. chicanar; =ry s. chicana.

chick s. pinto, frangote; =abiddy s. pequenote, rapazinho; =en s. frango, franga; =en heart tímido, covarde; =en pox varicela.

chicory s. chicória.

chickweed s. herva com sementes apreciadas pelos passarinhos.

chide v.t.&i. ralhar, censurar.

chief adj. chefe; primeiro; principal; s. chefe, superior; =ly adv. principalmente, sobretudo; =tain s. chefe, comandante, caudilho; capitão, cabeça.

chiffon s. gaze; enfeite de vestido.

chilblain s. frieiras.

child s. criança; =hood s. infância; =ish adj. infantil; =like adj. como criança, próprio de criança; children s. crianças; =less adj. sem filhos; =birth s. parto; =bed s. parto; with — grávida.

Chile s. Chile; =an s. chileno.

chill adj. frio, gelado; s. frio; arrepio de frio; v.t. gelar, congelar, resfriar; =iness s. frio, frialdade; =y adj. frio.

chime s. carrilhão; v.i. tocar carrilhão; — in with concordar com; chiming clock relógio de carrilhão.

chimera s. quimera, ilusão; chimerical adj. quimérico.

chimney s. chaminé; — sweep limpador de chaminé.

chimpanzee s. chimpanzé.

chin s. queixo; — strap jugular.

china s. porcelana, louça; — cabinet guarda-louça; — shop loja de porcelanas.

China s. China; Chinese adj.&s. chinês;

Chinese lantern lanterna veneziana, lanterna chinesa.

chink s. greta, fenda, rachadura; v.t.&i. fender, rachar; tinir; fender-se.

chintz s. chita da Pérsia, tecido barato de algodão.

chip s. cavacos, aparas, lascas; v.t. picar; cortar em pedaços; lascar; — of the old block tal pai, tal filho.

chiropodist s. pedicura; chiropody s. cuidado dos pés.

chirp s. gorgeio, chilro, trinado, trilo; v.i. trinar, chilrar, gorjear.

chisel s. cinzel, formão; buril, escopro; v.t. cinzelar, burilar.

chit s. criança, meninote, meninota, garoto, fedelho; filhote.

chit-chat s. tagarelice, falatório.

chivalrous adj. cavalheiresco; chivalry s. cavalheirismo.

chive s. cebola; cebolinha.

chivy v.t. caçar.

chlorate s. clorato; chloride s. cloreto; chloride of lime cloreto de cálcio; chlorine s. cloro; chloroform s. clorofórmio; chloroform v.t. cloroformizar.

chocolate s. chocolate, balas de chocolate; — cream creme de chocolate; — pot chocolateira.

choice adj. escolhido, fino, precioso; s. escolha, fina flor, elite; =ness s. excelência.

choir s. côro; — boy menino de côro; — master diretor de um côro.

choke v.t. estrangular; sufocar, abafar; oprimir.

cholera s. cólera (doença).

choose v.t. escolher, eleger.

chop s. talhada, fatia, porção; costeleta; fenda, greta; mandíbula, tenaz; v.t. talhar, cortar; picar carne; rachar; falar com volubilidade; (carp.) desbastar; to — off decepar; v.i. dar cutiladas; virar (o vento); — about girar; =s s. boca, entrada; =py adj. cortado, picado, retalhado; (mar.) agitado.

chopstick s. palito chinês ou japonês para comer (em vez de garfo).

choral adj. (mús.) coral.

chord (mús.) corda, acorde, harmonia; (geom.) corda; (fig.) fibra, corda sensível.

choreography s. coreografia, coregrafia.

chorister s. corista, menino de côro; chorus s. côro; estribilho em côro; concêrto.

Christ s. Cristo; =en v.t. batizar; =endom s. cristandade; =ening s. batismo; =ian adj.&s. cristão; =ianity s. cristandade; =ianize v.t. cristianizar; =ianly adv. cristãmente.

Christmas s. Natal.

chromate s. cromato.

chromatic adj. cromático.

chrome s. cromo; chromium s. cromo; chromium plated cromado.

chronic adj. crônico.

chronicle s. crônica; v.t. registrar, consignar; chronicler s. cronista; chronological adj. cronológico; chronology s. cronologia.

chronometer s. cronômetro.

chrysalis s. crisálida.

chrysanthemum s. crisantemo.

chub s. cabós (peixe).

chubby adj. rechonchudo, gorducho.

chuck s. cacarejo; golpe sêco; peça do tôrno; v.i. cacarejar; v.t. fechar; atirar; golpear; — out pôr para fóra de casa;

— **under the chin** levantar o queixo de.

chuckle *v.i.* rir à socapa; zombar.

chum *s.* camarada, companheiro.

chump *s.* cepo, toro de madeira.

chunk *s.* pedaço; trôço, pedaço de madeira; (*pop.*) pessoa baixa e troncuda.

church *s.* igreja, templo; **the — of England** a Igreja Anglicana; **— service** ofício divino; **— goer** beato, pessôa que vai muito à igreja.

churching *s.* cerimônia religiosa executada em ação de graças a primeira vez que uma mulher, tendo dado à luz, se apresenta na igreja.

churl *s.* saloio; rústico, grosseiro; =**ish** *adj.* grosseiro, brutal.

churn *s.* batedeira de manteiga (máquina); *v.t.* bater manteiga.

cider *s.* cidra (bebida).

cigar *s.* charuto; =**case** porta-charutos.

cigarette *s.* cigarro; **— holder** piteira.

cinder *s.* cinza, cinza de carvão de pedra; brasa.

Cinderella *s.* Gata Borralheira.

cinema, cinematograph *s.* cinema, cinematógrafo; **— star** estrêla de cinema.

cineraria (*bot.*) cinerária.

cinerary *adj.* cinerário.

cinnabar *s.* cinábrio; vermelhão.

cinnamon ꜱ. canela.

cipher *s.* cifr= 'algarismo; zero; nulidade; *v.t.* calcular; cifrar; numerar.

circle *s.* (*geom.*) círculo, circunferência; disco, halo; esfera; (*ast.*) órbita; galerias (teatro); *v.t.* circundar, rodear; *v.i.* rodar, andar em volta; =**t** *s.* círculo pequeno; anel; adôrno circular, diadema, bracelete, etc.; **circuit** *s.* circuito, volta; **circuitous** *adj.* tortuoso; **circular** *adj.* circular; **circulate** *v.t.&i.* circular, fazer circular; **circulating** *adj.* circulante; **circulating decimal** fração periódica; **circulation** *s.* circulação, movimento.

circumcise *v.t.* circuncidar.

circumference *s.* circunferência.

circumflex *adj.* circunflexo.

circumlocution *s.* circunlocução, paráfrase.

circumscribe *v.t.* circunscrever; fixar; limitar.

circumspect *adj.* circunspeto; =**ly** *adv.* com circunspeção.

circumstance *s.* circunstância; **circumstantial** *adj.* circunstancial.

circumvent *v.t.* enganar, iludir.

circus *s.* circo.

cirrhosis *s.* cirrose.

cirrus *s.* (*bot.*) cirro, filamento; (*meteor.*) cirro.

cistern *s.* cisterna.

citadel *s.* cidadela.

cite *v.t.* citar; alegar.

citizen *s.* cidadão; =**ship** *s.* cidadania.

citric *adj.* cítrico; **citron** *s.* cidra.

city *s.* cidade.

civet *s.* almíscar; **— cat** gato de algália.

civic *adj.* cívico.

civil *adj.* cortês, educado; civil; **— commotion** movimento popular; **— engineering** engenharia civil; **— servant** empregado público, funcionário público; **— service** administração pública; =**ian** *s.* paisano; jurisconsulto; jurisperito; =**ity** *s.* civilidade.

civilization *s.* civilização; **civilize** *v.t.* civilizar; **civilizing** *adj.* civilizante.

clack *s.* ruído; estalido; *v.i.* estalar; tagarelar; cacarejar.

claim *s.* reclamação, reivindicação; pretensão; *v.t.* reclamar, reivindicar; pretender; =**able** *adj.* reclamável.

clairvoyance *s.* clarividência; **clairvoyant** *s.* vidente; **clairvoyant** *adj.* clarividente.

clam *s.* ostra pequena americana.

clamber *v.t.&i.* trepar, grimpar.

clamminess *s.* viscosidade, umidade; **clammy** *adj.* viscoso, úmido, pastoso.

clamorous *adj.* clamoroso, barulhento; =**ly** *adv.* clamorosamente, barulhentamente; **clamour, clamor** *s.* clamor; **clamor** *v.i.* clamar, gritar, vociferar; **clamor for** reclamar a altos brados.

clamp *s.* gancho; fixador; encaixe; pinça; *v.t.* prender; agarrar.

clan *s.* clã, tribu.

clandestine *adj.* clandestino.

clang *s.* som, clangor; *v.t.* retinir.

clank *s.* tinido; *v.i.* tinir, retinir.

clap *s.* bulha; estrépito; pancada; estrondo; aplauso; *v.t.&i.* bater palmas, aplaudir.

claret *s.* vinho tinto de Bordéus.

clarify *v.t.* clarificar, esclarecer, aclarar.

clarion *s.* clarim.

clash *s.* choque, conflito, colisão; fragor; disputa; *v.i.&i.* chocar, entrechocar-se; golpear, opor-se, entrar em conflito.

clasp *s.* fivela, gancho; broche; abraço; *v.t.* prender; enganchar; abraçar, cingir.

class *s.* classe; categoria; curso; série; *v.t.* classificar; =**ic, =ical** *adj.* clássico; =**ification** *s.* classificação; =**ify** *v.t.* classificar; =**ing** *s.* classificação; **— consciousness** espírito de casta; **—mate** camarada de classe, camarada de promoção; **— prize** prêmio de honra; **—room** sala de aula.

clatter *s.* bulha, algazarra, alarido, barulho; *v.i.&t.* fazer bulha, algazarra; garrular.

clause *s.* cláusula, artigo; (*gram.*) proposição, oração.

claustral *adj.* claustral.

claw *s.* garra, unha de animal; pata; pinça; *v.t.* arranhar, unhar.

clay *s.* argila, barro; terra; =**ey** *adj.* argiloso; **— pigeon** disco de barro (para tiro ao vôo).

clean *adj.* limpo, asseiado; puro; nítido; *v.t.* limpar; =**er** *s.* limpador, empregada que arruma a casa; =**ing** *s.* limpeza, asseio; =**liness** *s.* asseio, limpeza; nitidez.

cleanse *v.t.* limpar; purificar; purgar; expurgar, depurar.

clear *adj.* claro, límpido, puro; nítido, distinto; **— sighted** clarividente; *v.t.* esclarecer; purgar; desembaraçar; purificar, aclarar; =**ly** *adv.* claramente, nitidamente; =**ness** *s.* clareza, nitidez; pureza.

cleat *s.* (*mar.*) suporte em forma de bigorna, para amarrar o cordame.

cleavage *s.* partição, divisão; (*biol.*) segmentação; **cleave** *v.t.* rachar, partir, dividir; cortar; *v.i.* despedaçar-se; aderir; **cleaver** *s.* cortador; machadinha de açougueiro.

clef *s.* (*mús.*) clave.

cleft *s.* fenda, abertura, racha.

clematis *s.* clematite.

clemency *s.* clemência; **clement** *adj.* clemente.

clench *v.t.* agarrar, segurar, apertar; cerrar (o punho ou os dentes).

clergy *s.* clero; =man eclesiasta, sacerdote; **cleric** *s.* eclesiástico; **clerical** *adj.* clerical; **clerk** *s.* escriturário, amanuense.

clever *adj.* destro, hábil; inteligente; =ness *s.* destreza, habilidade; inteligência.

clew, clue *s.* novêlo; indicação, indício.

click *s.* tique-taque; golpe sêco; gatilho; *v.i.* tinir, tilintar; fazer tique-taque.

client *s.* cliente, parte; =ele *s.* clientela.

cliff *s.* penhasco, despenhadeiro, rocha alcantilada, escarpa.

climacteric *adj.* climatérico, crítico.

climate *s.* clima; **climatic** *adj.* climatérico, climático.

climax *s.* ponto culminante, climax, gradação ascendente.

climb *s.* ascensão, subida; *v.t.&i.* subir, escalar, trepar, ascender; =er *s.* ascensor, trepador; trepadeira (planta).

clime *s.* (*poe.*) região, terra, atmosfera, clima.

clinch *s.* (*box*) luta corpo a corpo; *v.t.* agarrar, empunhar, segurar, pregar.

cling *v.i.* aderir; pegar-se, unir-se, agarrar-se, grudar-se; *v.t.* juntar.

clinic *s.* clínica; =al *adj.* clínico; =ian *s.* clínico.

clink *s.* som, tinido; *v.t.* tinir, tilintar, retinir; rimar.

clinker *s.* escória; ladrilho vidrado.

clip *s.* pinça, prendedor, pegador; *v.t.* pegar, segurar; cortar, tosquear; pinçar, cingir; =pers *s.* tesouras; máquina de cortar cabelos; =ping *s.* cerceadura; recorte (de jornal).

clique *s.* camarilha; compadrio.

cloak *s.* capote, capa; manto; — room vestiário; *v.t.* encapotar; velar, ocultar, encobrir.

clock *s.* relógio; pêndula; — and watch maker relojoeiro; wind up a — dar corda num relógio.

clod *s.* torrão, terra, sólo; massa; — crusher desterroador.

clog *s.* tamanco; galocha; peia; *v.t.* embaraçar; pear; carregar; obstruir, entravar.

cloister *s.* claustro; *v.t.* enclausurar.

close *adj.* fechado; estreito; unido; denso, cerrado; próximo; — shaven barbado de fresco; *adv.* perto, de perto, junto; — up em primeiro plano; *s.* fim, final, encerramento; cercado; prado; recinto fechado; the — of the day o cair do dia; *v.t.* fechar, encerrar; parar, findar; regular, liquidar; trancar, obstruir; terminar; *v.i.* unir-se, encerrar-se; =ly *adv.* de perto, atentamente, estritamente, rigorosamente; =ness *s.* intimidade; proximidade; compacidade; =t *s.* armário embutido, armário, gabinete; latrina; =t *v.t.* esconder, guardar num esconderijo, trancar; **closing** *s.* fechadura, encerramento; **closure** *s.* clausura; cercado; fim, conclusão; oclusão.

clot *s.* coágulo, grumo; *v.i.* coagular.

cloth *s.* pano, tecido, fazenda, toalha, coberta, batina; =e *v.t.* vestir, revestir, trajar; =es *s.* vestido, vestuário, roupa (de toda espécie), roupa de cama; =ier *s.* tecelão; vendedor de tecidos; vendedor de roupas feitas; =ing *s.* vestido, roupa (de toda espécie).

cloud *s.* nuvem, névoa; turba, massa; =burst tromba d'agua; in the =s nas nuvens; *v.t.* obscurecer, nublar, escure-

cer; =less *adj.* sem nuvens; =y *adj.* nublado, nebuloso, sombrio, obscuro.

clout *s.* trapo, esfregão; cueiro, faixa; (*pop.*) tapa; tacha, prego pequeno; *v.t.* enfaixar; remendar; (*pop.*) dar sôco, bater.

clove *s.* cravo-da-Índia.

clover *s.* trevo.

clown *s.* palhaço; vilão; =ery *s.* palhaçada; =ish *adj.* ridículo, cômico.

cloy *v.t.* saciar.

club *s.* clava, maça; clube; círculo; paus (naipe); porrete.

cluck *s.* cacarejo; *v.i.* cacarejar.

clue *s.* indicação, indício; fio (de uma história).

clump *s.* amontoado, massa informe; grupo (árvores); mouta; *v.t.* amontoar.

clumsiness *s.* falta de jeito, inhabilidade, rusticidade; má conformação; **clumsy** *adj.* rústico; mal conformado; desajeitado; **clumsy fellow** pessoa desajeitada, trapalhona, sem jeito.

cluster *s.* cacho; grupo; feixe; *v.t.&i.* agrupar; formar-se em cachos; amontoar.

clutch *s.* garra; apresamento; ninhada de ovos ou de pintos; *v.t.&i.* empunhar; agarrar, agarrar-se.

coach *s.* carruagem, coche; vagão; (*esp.*) treinador, orientador; explicador; *v.i.* conduzir ou andar de carro; (*pop.*) treinar, preparar alguém (para exame ou competição).

coadventurer *s.* co-interessado.

coagulate *v.t.* coagular.

coal *s.* carvão, hulha; =man *s.* carvoeiro; *v.i.* carbonizar; fazer carvão.

coalesce *v.i.* confundir-se; **coalition** *s.* coalisão, liga, bloco, união.

coarse *adj.* grosseiro; rude, brutal; =ness *s.* grosseria, brutalidade.

coast *s.* costa, litoral; — defense ship navio guarda-costas; *v.i.* navegar ao longo da costa, bordejar; =er *s.* navio costeiro.

coat *s.* sobretudo, capote, casaco, casaca, fraque; — of arms escudo de armas, brasão; — of mail cota de malhas; *v.t.* cobrir, revestir; =ee *s.* paletó curto.

coax *v.t.* persuadir por adulação, induzir.

cob *s.* espiga (de milho); antigo peso espanhol (moeda); golpe; aranha; espécie de gaivota; bloco (de pedra, carvão, etc.); *v.t.* bater; dar pancada (nas nádegas).

cobalt *s.* cobalto.

cobble *s.* pedra, paralelepípedo; remendo; *v.t.* remendar grosseiramente, consertar mal.

cobra *s.* cobra; naja.

cobweb *s.* teia de aranha.

cocaine *s.* cocaína.

Cochin-China *s.* Cochinchina.

cochineal *s.* cochonilha.

cock *s.* galo; em palavras compostas indica o macho de qualquer ave; *v.t.* endireitar, levantar, erguer; *v.i.* empertigar-se.

cockade *s.* cocarda, cocar; roseta.

cockatoo *s.* espécie de papagaio comumente encontrado na Austrália.

cockchafer *s.* besouro europeu semelhante ao escaravelho.

cockerel *s.* frango, galo novinho.

cockle *s.* espécie de marisco; (*bot.*) joio; *v.t.&i.* enrugar, enrugar-se; encolher-se.

cockpit *s.* rinhadeira; (*av.*) lugar reservado ao piloto.

cockroach s. barata.
cockscomb s. crista de galo.
cocktail s. (bebida) cocktail.
cocoa s. cacau.
coconut s. côco; — palm, — tree coqueiro.
cocoon s. casulo.
cod, codfish s. bacalhau; cod-liver oil óleo de fígado de bacalhau.
coddle v.t. tratar com carinho, amimar; cozer brandamente em fogo lento.
code s. código; v.t. redigir em código; codicil s. codicilo; codify v.t. codificar.
coefficient s. coeficiente.
coerce v.t. coagir.
coffee s. café; — pot cafeteira.
coffer s. cofre, caixa, burra.
coffin s. caixão, esquife, ataúde.
cog s. dente (de roda); — wheel roda dentada; v.t. dentar (rodas); enganar.
cogency s. fôrça ou poder de convicção; cogent adj. convincente, persuasivo, probante, conclusivo.
cogitate v.i. cogitar, meditar, refletir.
cognate adj. cognato.
cognizance s. conhecimento; cognizant of sabedor de.
cognomen s. cognome; apelido, alcunha.
cohabit v.i. cohabitar.
cohere v.i. aderir; =nce s. coerência; =nt adj. coerente; =ntly adv. coerentemente; cohesion s. coesão; cohesive adj. coesivo.
cohort s. coorte.
coil s. rôlo; serpentina; bobina; v.t. enrolar; v.i. enroscar-se.
coin s. moeda; cunho; v.t. cunhar moedas; fazer, inventar; fabricar; forjar; to — a word inventar uma palavra; =age s. cunhagem; =er s. falsário, fabricador de moedas falsas.
coincide v.i. coincidir; =nce s. coincidência.
coir s. fibra do côco.
coke s. coque (carvão).
colander s. coador.
cold adj. frio; in — blood a sangue frio; — steel arma branca; — storage conservação pelo frio; — store frigorífico; s. frio, resfriado; — in the head resfriado de cabeça; =ness frialdade, frieza, frigidez.
coleopteron s. coleóptero.
colic s. cólica.
collaborate v.i. colaborar; collaborator s. colaborador.
collapse s. colapso, prostração; fracasso; queda; desmoronamento; v.i. desmoronar; cair; fracassar.
collar s. colar, coleira; gola, colarinho; — bone clavícula; v.t. pôr gola ou colarinho; agarrar pelo colarinho (com o mesmo sentido que "abotoar" na jíria carioca).
collate v.t. comparar; cotejar.
collateral adj. colateral; s. caução, garantia.
collation s. cotejo; comparação; colação (refeição).
colleague s. colega.
collect s. coleta; v.t. fazer coleta, recolher; juntar, reunir; cobrar; captar; colecionar; recuperar; perceber; =ed adj. calmo, controlado; =ion s. coleção; ajuntamento, reunião; percepção; compilação; cobrança; =ive adj. coletivo; =or s. coletor, recebedor; colecionador; =orship s. receita; coletoria.
college s. universidade ou uma de suas

escolas, instituição ministrando instrução profissional ou especializada de nível superior; corpo de pessoas tendo interesses ou funções comuns; medical — escola de medicina; — of cardinals colégio dos cardeais; electoral — colégio eleitoral.
collide v.i. colidir.
collier s. operário das minas de carvão; barco carvoeiro; negociante de carvão.
collision s. colisão, encontro, choque.
colloquial adj. familiar, coloquial; =ism s. expressão familiar; colloquy s. colóquio.
collusion s. conluio, conivência; fraude.
colon s. dois pontos (pontuação).
colon s. côlon (parte do intestino grosso).
colonel s. coronel.
colonial adj. colonial; — office ministério das Colônias (Inglaterra); colonist s. colono; colonize v.t. colonizar.
colonnade s. peristilo; colunata.
colony s. colônia.
colophon s. colofão (marca tipográfica).
colossal adj. colossal; colossus s. colosso.
color, colour s. côr, colorido; — blindness incapacidade total ou parcial de distinguir as côres cromáticas; — photography fotografia em côres; v.t. colorir; =ed adj. colorido; de côr; flame — ribbon fita côr de fogo; =ing s. colorido; =less adj. sem côr, incolor; descolorido.
colt s. potro.
Columbia s. Colômbia.
columbine s. (bot.) aquilégia, herva pombinha.
column s. coluna, pilastra.
colza s. colza.
coma s. coma; comatose adj. comatoso.
comb s. pente; crista; favo de mel; v.t. pentear.
combat s. combate; v.t. combater; =ant s. combatente; =ive adj. combativo, batalhador; =iveness s. combatividade.
combination s. combinação; combine v.t. combinar; s. combinação (empregado sobretudo nos E. Unidos para designar uma combinação de pessoas, firmas ou organizações com finalidade política ou comercial).
combings s. cabelos soltos que ficam na escôva.
combustible adj. combustível; combustion s. combustão; combustion chamber (motor) câmara de explosão.
come v.i. vir; chegar; apresentar-se; fazer-se; — on vamos; — across encontrar; — back voltar; — in entrar; — down descer; — for vir buscar; — from proceder de; — off desligar-se; — out sair; aparecer; estrear; — to an agreement entrar em acôrdo; — what may aconteça o que acontecer.
comedian s. comediante, farsista; comedy s. comédia, farsa.
comeliness s. beleza, graça, donaire; comely adj. belo, gracioso, airoso.
comer s. chegado, recém-vindo.
comet s. cometa.
comfort s. conforto, consolação; satisfação; comodidade; v.t. reconfortar, consolar; aliviar; =able adj. confortável, à vontade, cômodo; =er s. consolador, confortador.
comic, comical adj. cômico, humorístico, engraçado, burlesco; — opera ópera cômica; — actor ator cômico.

coming *s.* vinda, chegada; — **out** estréia.

comma *s.* vírgula; — **bacillus** micróbio do cólera.

command *s.* comando, ordem; mandato; *v.t.* comandar, ordenar; controlar; dirigir, dominar; *ant *s.* comandante, chefe.

commandeer *v.t.* requisitar.

commander *s.* comandante, chefe; — **in chief** generalíssimo.

commandment *s.* comando; mandamento.

commemorate *v.t.* comemorar.

commence *v.t.&i.* começar, iniciar; *ment *s.* princípio, começo, estréia; colação de grau, formatura.

commend *v.t.* recomendar; preconizar; encarregar; encomendar; aprovar, elogiar; *able *adj.* recomendável; *ation *s.* elogio, louvor, recomendação.

commensurate *adj.* proporcionado.

comment *s.* comentário; anotações, interpretações; *ary *s.* série de comentários, interpretação; to — on comentar; *ator *s.* comentador.

commerce *s.* comércio, negócio; **commercial** *adj.* comercial, mercantil; **commercial traveler** caixeiro viajante; **commercialism** *s.* comercialismo, mercantilismo; **commercialize** *v.t.* comercializar, mercantilizar; **commercially** *adv.* comercialmente.

commiserate *v.i.* comiserar-se, compadecer-se, condoer-se, apiedar-se, ter pena.

commissariat *s.* comissariado; intendência militar.

commission *s.* comissão, missão, encargo; patente; despacho; **out of** — imprestável, inutilizado; **to put out of** — aposentar, retirar do serviço; *v.t.* nomear, encarregar, pôr em serviço ativo; *aire *s.* servente de hotel, servente de escritório; mensageiro; *er *s.* comissário, emissário.

commit *v.t.* cometer, fazer; confiar; perpetrar; depositar; entregar; encarregar; encomendar; trasladar; to — oneself comprometer-se; declarar-se; to — to memory aprender de memória; to — to writing pôr por escrito.

committee *s.* comitê, comissão.

commode *s.* cômoda; cadeira furada (sôbre um vaso-de-noite).

commodious *adj.* cômodo; *ly *adv.* cômodamente; *ness *s.* comodidade.

commodity *s.* comodidade, conveniência; produto, artigo de comércio ou de consumo (geralmente um de primeira necessidade); bens (excluindo animais e imóveis).

common *adj.* comum, usual, ordinário, vulgar, banal; simples; público; *ly *adv.* comumente, usualmente; *ness *s.* frequência, vulgaridade; *alty *s.* povo, o comum, o vulgo; *er *s.* plebeu; membro da Câmara dos Comuns na Inglaterra; *place banal, comum; *wealth estado, nação; coisa pública; república; comunidade; — law direito comum; — sense senso comum, bom senso; the — weal a coisa pública.

commotion *s.* comoção; perturbação; tumulto, movimento.

communal *adj.* comunal, público; **communism** *s.* comunismo; **communist** *s.* comunista; **communion** *s.* comunhão; **community** *s.* comunidade, sociedade.

commune *v.i.* conversar; comunicar-se; pôr-se em contato.

communicate *v.t.&i.* comunicar, comunicar-se; comungar; **communication** *s.* comunicação; **communicative** *adj.* comunicativo; **communion** *s.* comunhão.

commutator *s.* comutador.

commute *v.t.* comutar, trocar, mudar, permutar.

compact *adj.* compacto, espêsso, cerrado; *s.* pacto, convênio; estojo de bolsa para pó de arroz; *edness *s.* compacidade.

companion *s.* companheiro, camarada; dama de companhia; *able *adj.* sociável; *ship *s.* companhia, sociedade, convívio.

company *s.* companhia, sociedade; acompanhamento; visitas, hóspedes; associação.

comparable *adj.* comparável; **comparative** *adj.* comparativo, comparado; **comparative** *s.* (gram.) comparativo; **compare** *v.t.* comparar; **comparison** *s.* comparação.

compartment *s.* compartimento, divisão.

compass *s.* âmbito, circuito, círculo, recinto; alcance; extensão; limites; (mús.) extensão da voz ou de um instrumento, diapasão; bússola; *v.t.* maquinar, idear; limitar, delimitar, cercar; atingir, conseguir; sitiar.

compassion *s.* compaixão; *ate *adj.* compassivo; *ately *adv.* compassivamente.

compatible *adj.* compatível.

compatriot *s.* compatriota.

compeer *s.* par, igual; camarada, companheiro.

compel *v.t.* compelir, obrigar, forçar.

compendious *adj.* resumido, sumariado; **compendium** *s.* compêndio.

compensate *v.t.* compensar, indenizar; (mec.) compensar; **compensation** *s.* compensação, indenização.

compete *v.i.* competir; — for concorrer para; — with competir com, fazer concorrência a.

competence, competency *s.* competência, aptidão; **competent** *adj.* competente, apto.

competition *s.* competição, concorrência, concurso; **competitor** *s.* competidor, concorrente.

compile *v.t.* compilar.

complacence, complacency *s.* complacência; **complacent** *adj.* complacente; **complacently** *adv.* complacentemente.

complain *v.i.* queixar-se, reclamar; *ant, *er *s.* queixoso, reclamante; **complaint** *s.* queixa, reclamação; lamento, gemido; (med.) doença, enfermidade.

complement *s.* complemento, acessório; *ary *adj.* complementar.

complete *adj.* completo; *v.t.* completar; **completion** *s.* consumação, terminação, acabamento, conclusão.

complex *adj.&s.* complexo.

complexion *s.* tez, cutis; compleição, aspeto físico, aparência.

complexity *s.* complexidade.

compliance *s.* conformidade; docilidade, submissão, condescendência, anuência, consentimento; in — with de acôrdo com; **compliant** *adj.* fácil, complacente, dócil, condescendente.

complicate *v.t.* complicar; **complication** *s.* complicação.

complicity *s.* cumplicidade.

compliment s. elogio; parabens, congratulações; v.t. elogiar; saudar; =s s. cumprimentos, saudações; homenagens, votos; =ary adj. elogioso, lisonjeiro, galante; cortês.

complin, compline s. (ecles). completas.

comply v.i. submeter-se, acquiescer, consentir, ceder; — with conformar-se com, obedecer a, respeitar (regras ou vontades).

component adj. componente; constituinte; s. componente; — part peça constituinte.

compose v.t. compôr; =r s. compositor; **composite** adj. composto, misto; **composition** s. composição, constituição; tema; **compositor** s. tipógrafo.

composure s. compostura; sangue frio, calma.

compound adj. composto; — **interests** juros compostos; s. mistura, combinação, corpo composto; v.t. combinar, unir, compor; v.i. pactuar, transigir.

comprehend v.t. compreender, conceber; conter, encerrar; **comprehension** s. compreensão; **comprehensive** adj. compreensivo, amplo, extensivo, grande, pleno.

compress s. compressa; v.t. comprimir; apertar, condensar; =ion s. compressão; =or s. compressor.

comprise v.t. conter, abarcar, compreender, abranger, incluir.

compromise s. transigência, acôrdo (implicando concessões mútuas) ; v.t.&i. transigir; comprometer.

comptroller s. registador; superintendente; aferidor.

compulsion s. compulsão, fôrça; **compulsorily** adv. compulsòriamente; **compulsory** adj. compulsório.

compunction s. compunção; **compunctious** adj. compungido, contrito.

computation s. computação; **compute** v.t. computar.

comrade s. camarada; =ship s. camaradagem.

con v.t. estudar, decorar; olhar com atenção.

con adv. contra, em oposição; pro and — pró e contra.

concave adj. côncavo; **concavity** s. concavidade.

conceal v.t. esconder, ocultar, encobrir; =ment s. supressão; dissimulação, encobrimento, ocultacão.

concede v.t. conceder.

conceit s. presunção, convencimento, vaidade, suficiência; =ed adj. convencido, presumido, vaidoso, suficiente, cheio de si.

conceivable adj. concebível; **conceive** v.t.&i. conceber; fazer idéia, imaginar; pensar.

concentrate v.t. concentrar; **concentration** s. concentração.

concentric adj. concêntrico.

conception s. concepção.

concern s. preocupação, inquietude; negócio; assunto; ocupação; interêsse; v.t.&i. inquietar; interessar; tocar, pertencer; =ed adj. interessado; preocupado, inquieto; **as far as I am concerned** quanto a mim, no que me diz respeito; =ing prep. concernente, relativo, atinente.

concert s. concêrto, audição; v.t. planejar; fazer acôrdo, ajustar.

concession s. concessão; =aire s. concessionário.

conch s. concha; pavilhão auricular, orelha.

conciliate v.t. conciliar; **conciliation** s. conciliação.

concise adj. conciso; =ness s. concisão.

conclave s. conclave, assembléia.

conclude v.t.&i. concluir; inferir; **conclusion** s. conclusão; **to try conclusions with** medir fôrças com; **conclusive** adj. conclusivo, decisivo.

concoct v.t. confeccionar; maquinar, tramar; =ion s. confecção; trama.

concomitant s. concomitante; **concomitance, concomitancy** s. concomitância, acompanhamento.

concord s. concórdia, acôrdo, concordância; =ance s. concordância.

concourse s. afluência, reunião; junção de várias ruas ou estradas; confluência, campo ou lugar de reunião.

concrete adj.&s. concreto.

concubine s. concubina.

concupiscence s. concupiscência.

concur v.i. convir; conformar-se; entrar em acôrdo; combinar; aquiescer; aprovar; =rence s. cooperação, ajuda; aprovação; assentimento; ponto de interseção; (dir.) direito comum; coincidência de poderes iguais.

concussion s. concussão; abalo, choque violento; — **of the brain** comoção cerebral.

condemn v.t. condenar; =ation s. condenação.

condensation s. condensação; **condense** v.t. condensar, comprimir; **condenser** s. condensador.

condescend v.i. condescender; **condescension** s. condescendência.

condign adj. condigno.

condiment s. condimento, tempêro.

condition s. condição, estado; **on that** — sob esta condição; v.t. condicionar; =al adj. condicional.

condole v.i. condoer-se; lamentar; — **with** dar pêsames a; =nce s. condolência.

condone v.t. passar por cima, fechar os olhos sôbre; **condonation** s. perdão tácito.

conduce v.t. contribuir; conduzir; tender.

conduct s. conduta; manejo; v.t. conduzir; guiar; manejar; =ed tour excursão acompanhada; **conductor** s. condutor; (mús.) maestro; **conductress** s. condutora.

conduit s. conduto, canal, via; cano; (elet.) tubo ou cano que protege o fio.

cone s. cone; (bot.) fruto e semente de algumas espécies de pinheiros; sorvete em casquinha.

confectioner s. confeiteiro, pasteleiro; =y s. doces, balas, confeitos, etc.; ='s shop confeitaria.

confederacy s. confederação; **confederate** s. confederado; **confederation** s. confederação.

confer v.t. conferenciar; conferir; consultar; deferir; gratificar, dar, outorgar; =ence s. conferência.

confess v.t. confessar; v.i. acusar-se, confessar-se; =ion s. confissão; =ional s. confessional; =or s. confessor.

confidant s. confidente; **confide** v.t. confiar, depositar; v.i. confiar, fiar-se; **confidence** s. confidência, confiança; **confident** adj. confiante; **confidential** adj. confidencial.

confine *v.t.* confinar; limitar, restringir, circunscrever; — **oneself to** restringir-se a; **-ment** *s.* prisão, detenção; parto, sobreparto; **to be -d estar de** parto.

confirm *v.t.* confirmar, ratificar, corroborar, sancionar; **-ation** *s.* confirmação, ratificação, aprovação; **-ed** *adj.* inveterado, arraigado; estabelecido; crismado; **-ed invalid** incurável.

confiscate *v.t.* confiscar; **confiscation** *s.* confiscação.

conflagration *s.* conflagração; incêndio.

conflict *s.* conflito; *v.i.* contradizer-se; **-ing** *adj.* contraditório, em conflito.

confluence *s.* confluência; reunião de povo.

conform *v.t.* conformar; *v.i.* conformar-se; **-ably** *adv.* conformemente; **-ation** *s.* conformação; **-ity** *s.* conformidade.

confound *v.t.* confundir; **-ed** *adj.* confuso, perplexo; maldito, odioso.

confraternity *s.* confraria, confraternidade.

confront *v.t.* afrontar; confrontar.

confuse *v.t.* confundir, embaraçar, desconcertar; **-d** *adj.* confuso, embaralhado, obscuro; **-ly** *adv.* confusamente;

confusion *s.* confusão, perplexidade.

confute *v.t.* confutar, refutar; impugnar.

congeal *v.t.* congelar, gelar; *v.i.* congelar-se, tornar-se rígido.

congenial *adj.* congenial; análogo; simpático.

congenital *adj.* congênito.

conger, conger eel *s.* congro (peixe).

congest *v.i.* congestionar; **-ion** *s.* congestão.

conglomerate *s.* conglomerado; aglomerado; *adj.* conglomerado, aglomerado, congregado; *v.t.* conglomerar, aglomerar.

congratulate *v.t.* congratular, felicitar; **congratulation** *s.* congratulação, felicitações, parabéns.

congregate *v.t.* congregar, reunir; *v.i.* reunir-se, juntar-se; **congregation** *s.* assembléia, reunião; agregado; congregação.

congress *s.* congresso; **member of the** — congressista.

congruity *s.* congruência, harmonia; **congruous** *adj.* congruente, harmônico; adequado; consistente.

conic, conical *adj.* cônico.

conifer *s.* (*bot.*) conífera; **coniferous** *adj.* conífero.

conjectural *adj.* conjetural; **conjecture** *s.* conjetura; *v.t.* conjeturar.

conjoin *v.t.* juntar, unir; associar; *v.i.* confederar-se, unir-se, ligar-se; **-t** *adj.* associado, federado, confederado.

conjugal *adj.* conjugal.

conjugate *v.t.* conjugar; **conjugation** *s.* conjugação.

conjunction *s.* conjunção; **conjuncture** *s.* conjuntura.

conjure *v.t.* conjurar; adjurar; encantar; invocar, rogar; enfeitiçar;] **-r, conjuror** *s.* prestidigitador, escamoteador; **conjuring** *s.* prestidigitação; escamoteação.

connect *v.t.* ligar; relacionar; coordenar; reunir; **-ed** *adj.* unido; relacionado; aparentado; **connexion, connection** *s.* conexão, união; relação; parentesco.

connivance *s.* conivência; **connive** *v.i.* estar de conivência, cooperar dissimuladamente; **conniver** *s.* cúmplice.

connoisseur *s.* conhecedor; crítico competente em matéria de arte ou de paladar.

connubial *adj.* conjugal, matrimonial.

conquer *v.t.* conquistar; vencer; **-or** *s.* conquistador; **-ess** *s.* conquistadora; **conquest** *s.* conquista.

consanguinity *s.* consanguinidade.

conscience *s.* consciência; **conscientious** *adj.* concioncioso; **conscientiousness** *s.* consciência.

conscious *adj.* consciente; **-ly** *adv.* cientemente, concientemente; **-ness** *s.* conhecimento, consciência.

conscript *s.* recruta, conscrito; **-ion** *s.* conscrição, recrutamento.

consecrate *v.t.* consagrar, sagrar, benzer; ungir; **-d** *adj.* bento, sagrado, santo; **consecration** *s.* consagração, bênção.

consecutive *adj.* consecutivo.

consensus *s.* consenso, pleno acôrdo, acôrdo geral.

consent *s.* consentimento; acôrdo; permissão, anuência; *v.i.* consentir, anuir, concordar, aquiescer.

consequence *s.* consequência, resultado; importância; **consequent** *adj.* consequente; **consequently** *adv.* consequentemente; por conseguinte.

conservative *adj.* conservador, preservativo; *s.* conservador; **conservator** *s.* conservador; protetor; curador.

conservatory *s.* conservatório; estufa (para plantas).

conserve *v.t.* conservar, preservar; fazer conserva; *s.* conserva.

consider *v.t.* considerar; pensar; examinar; distinguir; tratar com respeito; *v.i.* refletir; **-able** *adj.* considerável; **-ate** *adj.* considerado, ponderado, circunspeto; atencioso; **-ation** *s.* consideração; deliberação; importância; retribuição, remuneração; indenização; **-ing** *prep.* &*conj.* à vista de, visto, levando em conta, visto que, considerando que.

consign *v.t.* confiar; dar; transferir; entregar, encarregar; dispor; consignar; **-ee** *s.* consignatário, destinatário; **-ment** *s.* consignação; expedição; partida; carregamento; **-or** *s.* consignante.

consist *v.i.* consistir, compor-se de, constar de; **-ence** *s.* consistência, firmeza, coerência; **-ency** *s.* consistência; **-ent** *adj.* consequente, coerente, consistente, firme; **-ory** *s.* consistório, junta, assembléia.

consolation *s.* consolação; **console** *v.t.* consolar; *s.* consolo (móvel).

consolidate *v.t.* consolidar; unir; **consolidation** *s.* consolidação; unificação; **-d school** fusão de várias escolas numa.

consonance *s.* consonância; **consonant** *adj.* consoante; *s.* consoante (letra).

consort *s.* consorte, cônjuge, espôso, espôsa; (*mar.*) navio de conserva.

conspicuous *adj.* conspícuo, notável; visível; ilustre, distinto; **-ness, conspicuity** *s.* conspicuidade.

conspiracy *s.* conspiração, conjuração; **conspirator** *s.* conspirador, conjurado; **conspire** *v.i.* &*t.* conspirar, conjurar.

constable *s.* condestável; aguazil, polícia, guarda civil; **constabulary** *s.* polícia (corpo).

constancy *s.* constância; **constant** *adj.* constante; **constantly** *adv.* constantemente.

constellation *s.* constelação.

consternation s. consternação.
constipate v.t. constipar; apertar; constipation s. constipação; apêrto,
obstrução de ventre.
constituency s. circunscrição eleitoral,
colégio eleitoral, eleitores; constituent
adj. constituinte, constitutivo; eleitor;
s. elemento, ingrediente, componente;
eleitor; constitute v.t. constituir; constitution s. constituição; constitu-
tional adj. constitucional.
constrain v.t. constrangir, compelir,
forçar, obrigar; =t s. constrangimento,
coação, compulsão.
construct v.t. construir, fabricar; =ion s.
construção; estrutura; obra, fabricação;
interpretação; explicação; =ional adj.
estrutural; =or s. construtor; =ive adj.
construtivo.
construe v.t. construir; explicar; interpretar.
consul s. cônsul; =ar adj. consular; =ate
s. consulado.
consult v.t. consultar; =ation s. consulta;
=ing, =ative, =atory adj. consultivo.
consume v.t. consumir; =r s. consumidor.
consummate adj. consumado, acabado,
perfeito; v.t. consumir; consumma-
tion s. consumação.
consumption s. consunção, extinção;
(med.) consunção, tuberculose; con-
sumptive adj.&s. consuntivo; tuber-
culoso, tísico.
contact s. contato.
contagion s. contágio; contagious adj.
contagioso; contagiousness s. contágio, contagiosidade.
contain v.t. conter, incluir, encerrar; =er
s. recipiente, caixa, engradado.
contaminate v.t. contaminar, corromper;
contamination s. contaminação.
contango s. (com.) prêmios ou juros
pagos pelo comprador ao vendedor para
adiar o pagamento da compra.
contemplate v.t. contemplar, meditar;
projetar; contemplation s. contem-
plação, meditação; projeto; contem-
plative adj. contemplativo.
contemporaneous, contemporary adj.
contemporâneo; contemporary s. contemporâneo.
contempt s. desprêzo, desdém, menos-
prêzo; — of court contumácia; =ible
adj. desprezível; =uous adj. desdenhoso,
altivo, desprezador.
contend v.t.&i. afirmar, sustentar; discutir; competir; disputar, lutar.
content adj. contente, satisfeito; v.t.
contentar, satisfazer; s. satisfação,
contentamento.
content s. conteúdo; quantidade, porção;
índice das matérias num livro; súmula
de um discurso ou de um livro; volume,
capacidade, área.
contention s. contenda, disputa; altercação, controvérsia; contentious adj.
litigioso, contencioso.
contentment s. contentamento.
contest s. luta; torneio; concurso; v.t.
contestar, disputar.
context s. contexto.
contexture s. contextura.
contiguity s. contiguidade; contiguous
adj. contíguo.
continence s. continência; continent s.
continente; adj. continente, casto;
continental adj. continental.
contingency s. contingência, eventualidade; contingent adj. contingente,

eventual; s. contingência, acidente,
eventualidade; contingente, quota.
continual adj. contínuo; continuance
s. continuação, persistência, permanência; continuation s. continuação,
seguimento; continue v.t.&i. continuar; continuity s. continuidade; continuous adj. contínuo, seguido; con-
tinuously adv. continuamente, segui-
damente.
contort v.t. torcer, retorcer, contorcer;
contortion s. contorsão.
contour s. contôrno; v.t. contornar;
desenhar o contôrno.
contraband s. contrabando.
contrabass s. contrabaixo.
contract s. contrato, escritura; ajuste;
esponsais; adj. contraído; v.t. contrair;
reduzir; apertar; abreviar, condensar;
contratar; =ant s. contratante; =ing
adj. contratante; =ion s. contração;
abreviação; estreitamento; =ual adj.
contratual.
contradict v.t. contradizer, desmentir;
=ion s. contradição, desmentido; =ory
adj. contraditório.
contradistinction s. distinção por
contraste, por qualidades opostas.
contralto s. contralto.
contrariety s. contrariedade; contrarily,
contrary adv. contràriamente; contrary adj. contrário, oposto, inverso; s.
contrário, oposto.
contrast s. contraste, oposição; v.t.&i.
pôr em contraste, contrastar.
contravene v.t. infringir, transgredir;
contravir; contravention s. contravenção; infração.
contribute v.t.&i. contribuir, concorrer;
cooperar, colaborar; contribution s.
contribuição, cooperação; quota; dádiva; contributor s. colaborador, con-
tribuinte.
contrite adj. contrito; contrition s.
contrição.
contrivance s. idéia, plano, invenção;
engenho, artifício, estratagema; con-
trive v.t. idear, inventar; combinar;
tramar, urdir, maquinar.
control s. contrôle, comando, domínio;
v.t. controlar, conter, dominar; =ler s.
registrador; superintendente; inspetor.
contumacy s. contumácia.
contumely s. ultraje, opróbrio, injúria.
contuse v.t. contundir; contusion s.
contusão.
conundrum s. charada, enigma, adivinhação.
convalesce v.i. convalescer, entrar em
convalescência; =nce s. convalescência;
=nt adj.&s. convalescente.
convene v.t. convocar.
convenience s. conveniência, comodidade;
convenient adj. conveniente, cômodo;
conveniently adv. cômodamente.
convent s. convento, mosteiro.
convention s. convenção; =al adj.
convencional, convencionado, estipulado; =alism s. convencionalismo.
converge v.i. convergir; =nt adj. con-
vergente.
conversant adj. versado, experimentado,
conhecedor.
conversation s. conversa, colóquio; =al
adj. da conversação; conversazione s.
reunião social.
converse v.i. conversação, familiaridade,
trato; adj. inverso, contrário, oposto;
v.i. conversar.

conversion s. conversão; transformação, mudança; **convert** s. convertido; v.t. converter, transformar; v.i. converter-se; **convertible** adj. conversível.
convex adj. convexo; •**ity** s. convexidade.
convey v.t. conduzir, veicular, transportar; transmitir, enviar; transferir; •**ance** s. transporte, condução, veículo; cessão, transferência, trasladação de propriedade, escritura do traslado.
convict s. convicto, condenado, presidiário; v.t. provar a culpa ou delito de (alguém); condenar.
convince v.t. convencer; **convincing** adj. convencedor, convincente.
convivial adj. jovial; festivo; sociável.
convocation s. convocação; **convoke** v.t. convocar.
convolvulus s. (bot.) convólvolo.
convoy s. combôio; escolta; v.t. comboiar, escoltar.
convulse v.t. convulsionar, revolucionar; **convulsion** s. convulsão; ⌊**convulsive** adj. convulsivo.
cony, coney s. coelho, pele de coelho.
coo s. arrulho; v.i. arrulhar.
cook s. cozinheiro, cozinheira; v.t. cozinhar; •**ery** s. arte de cozinhar; •**ery book** livro de cozinha; •**y**, •**ie** biscoito.
cool adj. fresco, frio, calmo; **in the —ao fresco**; v.t. esfriar, refrescar; calmar, apaziguar; —•**headed** sereno; s. frescor, frescura; •**er** s. refrigerador; •**ing** adj. refrigerante; •**ness** frescura, frescor, frieza, frio; calma; sangue frio, fleuma.
coomb s. fuligem.
coop s. capoeira, galinheiro; v.t. enjaular, engaiolar, encarcerar.
cooper s. tanoeiro; •**age** s. tanoaria.
cooperate v.i. cooperar; **cooperation** s. cooperação; **cooperative** adj. cooperativo.
coordinate v.t. coordenar.
coot s. espécie de ave aquática, semelhante ao pato.
cop s. cume, cimo; crista; (jíria) polícia (indivíduo).
cope s. capa de asperges; cúpula; qualquer espécie de capa; v.t. cobrir; — **with** fazer frente a, enfrentar.
coping s. cume, alto; (arq.) coroamento; remate.
copious adj. copioso, abundante, rico; nutriente, nutritivo.
copper s. cobre; moeda de cobre; tacho ou caldeira de cobre; v.t. forrar de cobre.
copperas s. caparrosa (designação vulgar dos sulfatos).
coppice, copse s. mata, capoeira.
copulation s. cópula; união.
copy s. cópia; exemplar de uma obra; número de um periódico; modêlo; (imp.) original; material; manuscrito; —•**book** s. caderno; v.t.&i. copiar, imitar; •**ing** s. transcrição; •**ist** s. copista.
copyright s. direito de autor, propriedade literária.
coquet v.t.&i. agir como coquete; namoriscar; •**ry** s. faceirice, coquetismo; •**tish** adj. faceira, coquete.
coral s. coral.
corbel s. modilhão, nicho.
cord s. corda; cordão, cordel, torçal; v.t. encordoar; •**age** (mar.) cordame, cordoalha.
cordial adj. cordial, caloroso; s. cordial; •**ity** s. cordialidade.

corduroy s. veludo de algodão com cordeis em relêvo.
core s. coração, centro; alma; parte central, essência primordial; núcleo; v.t. esvasiar; tirar o centro.
Corea s. Coréa.
corespondent s. cúmplice em adultério numa demanda de divórcio.
cork s. cortiça, rôlha de cortiça; — **screw** saca-rôlhas; v.t. arrolhar; •**y** taste gôsto de rôlha.
cormorant s. corvo marinho; (fig.) glutão; adj. glutão, voraz.
corn s. grão de toda espécie; todo gênero de cereais; milho; calo; — **cob** espiga de milho; — **cure** remédio contra calos.
corned beef carne de vaca salgada.
cornelian s. cornalina.
corner s. canto; ângulo, esquina; esconderijo, recanto; —•**stone** pedra angular; v.t. acuar; (com.) monopolizar, açambarçar.
cornet s. corneta, trombeta; toucado das Irmãs de Caridade.
cornice s. cornija.
cornucopia s. cornucópia.
corolla s. corola.
corollary s. corolário.
corona s. coroa, halo; (elet.) fulguração, descarga luminosa de um condutor; •**tion** s. coroação; **coronet** s. coroa de título nobiliário; grinalda.
coroner s. oficial encarregado de investigar as causas das mortes suspeitas.
corporal, corporeal adj. corporal, corpóreo, material; **corporal** s. cabo de esquadra; **corporate** adj. social, coletivo; incorporado; **corporation** s. corporação; **municipal corporation** municipalidade.
corps s. corpo.
corpse s. cadáver; corpo (morto).
corpulence, corpulency s. corpulência, gordura; **corpulent** adj. corpulento.
Corpus Christi festa do Corpo de Deus.
corpuscle s. corpúsculo.
correct adj. correto; exato, justo; v.t. corrigir; retificar; repreender, castigar; reparar, remediar; •**ed copy** original corrigido; •**ion** s. correção, retificação; castigo, reforma; censura, pena; •**ional** adj. correcional; •**ive** s. corretivo; •**ness** s. correção, exatidão; •**or** s. reformador; revisor.
correlative adj. correlativo.
correspond v.i. corresponder; adaptar-se; manter correspondência; •**ence** s. correspondência, relação; •**ent** adj. correspondente; conforme, conveniente; s. correspondente; •**ing** adj. correspondente; similar.
corridor s. corredor, galeria.
corroborate v.t. corroborar.
corrode v.t. corroer; v.i. corroer-se; **corrosion** s. corrosão; **corrosive** adj. corrosivo.
corrugate v.t. enrugar; franzir.
corrupt v.t. corromper, viciar, perverter; infectar; apodrecer; •**ible** adj. corruptível; •**ion** s. corrupção.
corsair s. corsário.
corset s. colete; — **maker** coleteiro; v.t. vestir colete.
Corsica s. Córsega; **Corsican** adj.&s. corso.
corundum s. coríndon.
coruscate v.i. cintilar.
Cos lettuce alface romana.

cosmetic *adj.&s.* cosmético.
cosmic, cosmical *adj.* cósmico.
cosmopolitan, cosmopolite *adj.&s.* cosmopolita.
cost *s.* custo, preço; despesa; **at all -s a todo preço**; *v.i.* custar.
costermonger *s.* vendedor ambulante de frutas.
costive *adj.* constipado, com prisão de ventre; **-ness** *s.* constipação, prisão de ventre.
costly *adj.* custoso, dispendioso, caro; suntuoso.
costume *s.* costume, traje, vestido, indumentária; **costumier** *s.* alfaite de senhoras.
cosy *adj.* confortável, cômodo, agradável; **— corner** canto íntimo, confortável.
cot *s.* cabana; catre, cama portátil.
coterie *s.* círculo, grupo, reunião.
cottage *s.* cabana, choça; casa de campo, quinta.
cotter *s.* (*mec.*) chave, passador.
cotton *s.* algodão; **— cloth** tecido de algodão; **— industry** indústria de algodão; **— mill** cotonifício, fábrica de tecidos de algodão.
couch *s.* canapé, cadeira de descanso, divã; *v.i.* deitar-se, recostar-se; *v.t.* depositar; indicar; encobrir, dissimular.
cough *s.* tosse; **— mixture** xarope, poção; **— lozenge** pastilha para tosse; *v.i.* tossir; **— up** expectorar.
council *s.* conselho, concílio; **-lor** *s.* conselheiro.
count *s.* conta; conde; *v.t.* contar, numerar, apurar.
countenance *s.* semblante, feição, aspeto, cara, rosto, figura, fisionomia; proteção, patrocínio, apôio; *v.t.* apoiar, animar, aprovar.
counter *s.* contador; calculista, calculador; balcão de estabelecimento comercial; ficha de jôgo; caixa registadora; *adv.* contra, pelo contrário; *v.t.* contradizer; *v.i.* opôr-se.
counteract *v.t.* contrariar; impedir; anular.
counterattack contra-ataque.
counterbalance *s.* contrapêso; *v.t.* contrabalançar, equilibrar.
counterclaim *s.* reconvenção.
counterfeit *adj.* contrafeito, falso; *v.t.* contrafazer; **-er** *s.* contrafator.
counterfoil *s.* talão, canhoto (de cheques ou recibos).
counter instructions contra-ordem.
countermand *v.t.* contramandar; revocar, invalidar, cancelar; (*com.*) desencomendar.
counterpane *s.* cobertura de cama; colcha.
counterpart *s.* contraparte; fac-símile; reprodução, duplicata.
counterpoint *s.* contraponto.
counterpoise *s.* contrapeso; *v.t.* contrabalançar, equilibrar.
countershaft *s.* eixo intermediário; transmissão secundária.
countersign *s.* contra-senha; *v.t.* visar, referendar.
counterstroke *s.* contra-golpe.
countervailing duty direito compensador.
counterweight *s.* contrapêso.
countess *s.* condessa.
counting *s.* conta; recenseamento; **— house** escritório de casa comercial;
countless *adj.* inumerável.

country *s.* país, nação; pátria; campo; aldeia, região rural; **— dance** dansa campestre; **— house** casa de campo; **— life** vida campestre; **—-man** camponês; compatriota.
county *s.* condado, comarca.
couple *s.* par, parelha, casal; *v.t.* emparelhar, juntar, reunir, casar; **-t** *s.* par, casal; versos de rima emparelhada.
coupon *s.* cupom.
courage *s.* coragem; **-ous** *adj.* corajoso.
courier *s.* correio feito por mensageiro especial; estafeta; expresso.
course *s.* curso; carreira; via; direção; canal; trajeto; caminho; conduta, proceder; sistema; serviço de mesa, pratos de que se compõe a refeição; **a five — dinner** jantar com cinco pratos ou serviços; **-s** *s.* menstruação, regras; **in due —** em tempo e lugar; **of —** naturalmente; *v.t.&i.* caçar, correr, perseguir; **coursing** *s.* caça às lebres.
court *s.* côrte; tribunal; conselho; câmara; audiência; séquito; cortejo; (*esp.*) campo; **— martial** conselho de guerra; **-s of justice** Palácio da Justiça; **— yard** pátio; *v.t.* cortejar, fazer a côrte; **— a favor** disputar um favor; **-eous** *adj.* cortês, atencioso; **-esan** *s.* cortesã, mulher pública; **-esy** *s.* cortesia; **-ier** *s.* cortesão, gente da côrte; **-ly** *adj.* cortês; **-eously** *adv.* cortêsmente; **-ship** *s.* côrte.
cousin *s.* primo, prima.
cove *s.* enseada; coberta.
covenant *s.* convenção, pacto; *v.t.* estipular, contratar; prometer; *v.i.* empenhar-se.
cover *v.t.* cobrir; tapar; ocultar; abrigar, proteger; dissimular, revestir; mascarar; percorrer; (*com.*) cobrir, remeter fundos; *s.* cobertura, coberta; tampa; envelope; capa; chapéu; véu; agasalho; abrigo; albergue; máscara; pretexto; tapete; talher (faca, garfo e colher); **— admission** preço de admissão (o que se paga pelo lugar à mesa em restaurantes e salas de baile); **-ing** *s.* cobertura; roupa; **-let** *s.* coberta (de cama); capa (de móveis).
covert *adj.* coberto; encoberto, escondido, dissimulado; *s.* esconderijo; abrigo; asilo; **-ly** *adv.* encobertamente, dissimuladamente.
covet *v.t.* cubiçar, ambicionar; *v.i.* aspirar; **-ous** *adj.* cubiçoso, ambicioso; avarento; **-ousness** *s.* cubiça.
covey *s.* ninhada; bando de pássaros.
cow *s.* vaca; fêmea dos grandes quadrúpedes; **— herd** vaqueiro; *v.t.* intimidar.
coward *adj.* covarde, poltrão; **-ice** *s.* covardia; **-ly** *adv.* covardemente.
cower *v.i.* agachar-se, aninhar-se.
cowl *s.* capuz, capucho de frade.
cowslip *s.* primavera dos campos (flor).
coxcomb *s.* mequetrefe, biltre, tôlo; crista de galo; barrete de bufão em forma de crista de galo.
coxswain *s.* (*mar.*) patrão, timoneiro.
coy *adj.* recatado, tímido, esquivo, reservado; **-ness** reserva, timidez, recato, modéstia.
cozen *v.t.* enganar; fraudar.
crab *s.* caranguejo; (*mec.*) guindaste, cabrestante; (*ast.*) Câncer; **— apple** maçã brava; **-bed** *adj.* áspero, desagradável, azêdo; carrancudo, intratável.

crack *adj.* de elite, de primeira ordem, de qualidade superior; *s.* fenda, grêta; rachadura; abertura; estalido; *v.t.* fender, rachar, rebentar, estalar; **-ed** *adj.* rachado; meio amª lucado.
cracker *s.* petardo; estalo, foguete; biscoito duro; **nut -s** quebra-nozes.
crackle *v.i.* crepitar, estalar; **crackling** *s.* estalido, crepitação.
crackmel *s.* espécie de biscoito duro e quebradiço.
cracksman *s.* salteador; arrombador.
cradle *s.* berço; (*cir.*) arco de proteção para uma ferida; *v.t.* embalar; **to rock the —** embalar o berço.
craft *s.* habilidade; artifício; astúcia; ofício ou arte; perícia; (*mar.*) embarcação; **air- -sman** avião; **-sman** *s.* artífice, artesão; **-y** *adj.* artificioso; cauteloso; astuto, ladino; **-ly** *adv.* astuciosamente.
crag *s.* despenhadeiro, precipício; rochedo, penhasco; **-gy** *adj.* anfractuoso.
cram *v.t.* encher; engordar; fartar; abarrotar; cevar.
cramp *s.* caimbra, espasmo; encolhimento de nervos; gancho; gato de ferro; *v.t.* apertar; sujeitar; constranger; embaraçar; agarrar, enganchar.
cranberry *s.* airela vermelha.
crane *s.* guindaste; grou (ave); *v.t.* suspender, içar, guindar, erguer por meio de guindaste; *v.i.* esticar-se.
cranium *s.* crânio.
crank *s.* manivela; volta, curva, cotovêlo; pessoa excêntrica, original; mania; **— shaft** (*aut.*) árvore da manivela (vilebrequin); *v.t.* dobrar (em forma de cotovêlo); *v.i.* girar, ziguezaguear; manivelar, dar a manivela; *adj.* fora do eixo, sôlto; (*mar.*) mal lastrado, instável (navio).
cranny *s.* fenda, grêta, racha.
crape *s.* crepe.
crash *s.* estrondo, estrépido; esboroamento; quebra, bancarrota, ruína; queda; esmagamento; *v.t.&i.* quebrar, despedaçar; esmagar; cair.
crass *adj.* grosseiro, crasso.
crate *s.* canastra, cesto grande.
crater *s.* cratera.
crave *v.t.* implorar; anelar, desejar ardentemente; **craving** *s.* desejo ardente; sêde; apetência.
craven *adj.* covarde, poltrão.
crawl *s.* rastejo; *v.i.* rastejar, arrastar-se; engatinhar.
crayfish, crawfish *s.* camarão, lagosta.
crayon *s.* esbôço; lápis.
craze *s.* loucura, mania; capricho; *v.t.&i.* enlouquecer.
creak *v.i.* ranger, chiar; cantar (cigarra).
cream *s.* creme; nata; o melhor, a nata; **-y** *adj.* cremoso; **—-colored** côr de creme.
crease *s.* dobra, prega; *v.t.* preguear.
create *v.t.* criar; fazer; produzir; **creation** *s.* criação; **creative** *adj.* criador, criativo; **creator, creatress** *s.* criador, criadora; **creature** *s.* criatura; ser; animal.
creche *s.* asilo diurno para crianças pobres; berçário.
credence *s.* crédito; **credentials** *s.* credenciais; **credibility** *s.* credibilidade, credulidade; **credible** *adj.* crível, acreditável, digno de fé; **credibly** *adv.* de boa fé.
credit *s.* crédito; fé; honra; confiança; influência, autoridade; haver, saldo a

favor; *v.t.* crer, reconhecer; atribuir; honrar; dar crédito; abonar; **-or** *s.* credor; **-able** fidedigno, abonado.
credo *s.* credo.
credulity *s.* credulidade; **credulous** *adj.* crédulo.
creed *s.* credo, crença; profissão de fé, doutrina.
creek *s.* riacho; enseada.
creel *s.* cesta de pescador.
creep *v.i.* rastejar, arrastar-se, deslisar, resvalar; **it makes one's flesh —** faz a gente se arrepiar; **-er** *s.* planta trepadeira; **-ing paralysis** paralisia progressiva.
cremate *v.t.* cremar, incinerar; **cremation** *s.* cremação, incineração; **crematorium** *s.* forno crematório.
crenel *s.* seteira, ameia; **-ate** *v.t.* amelar, guarnecer com ameias.
creole *s.&adj.* crioulo.
creosote *s.* creosoto.
crepitate *v.i.* crepitar.
crescendo *s.* crescendo; *adj.* crescente.
crescent *s.* meia lua, quarto crescente; *adj.* crescente.
cress *s.* agrião.
cresset *s.* farol, lanterna, facho.
crest *s.* crista; topete; cume, cimeira; **—-fallen** de crista caída, **-ed** *adj.* que tem crista; entopetado.
cretonne *s.* cretone.
crevasse *s.* fenda profunda (como a de uma geleira).
crevice *s.* fenda, racha, grêta.
crew *s.* tripulação, equipagem; bando, grupo.
crib *s.* presépio, mangedoura; cabana; caminha de criança; *v.t.* furtar, plagiar.
cribbage *s.* jôgo de cartas.
crick *s.* torcicolo.
cricket *s.* grilo; espécie de jôgo ao ar livre.
crier *s.* pregoeiro; reclamista.
crime *s.* crime.
Crimea *s.* Criméia.
criminal *s.&adj.* criminoso; **— law** direito penal; **criminate** *v.t.* incriminar, culpar.
crimp *v.t.* encrespar, frisar; recrutar; torcer; *adj.* quebradiço, friável; inconsequente.
crimson *adj.* rubro, carmesim, vermelho, encarnado; **— clover** trevo encarnado; *s.* carmesim, vermelho; *v.t.* enrubescer.
cringe *v.i.* ser servil, servir de tapête; *v.t.* bajular; **cringing** *adj.* servil.
crinkle *s.* sinuosidade, ondulação; ruga; *v.i.* serpentear; *v.t.* enrugar, preguear.
cripple *s.* estropiado, aleijado, inválido, coxo; *v.t.* aleijar, mutilar, estropiar; **-d** *adj.* estropiado, aleijado, inválido, coxo; **-d ship** navio avariado.
crisis *s.* crise.
crisp *adj.* quebradiço, frágil; tostado; crespo, frisado; vivificante; vigoroso; refrescante; *v.t.* encrespar, ondular; fazer frágil ou quebradiço.
criss-cross *adj.* cruzado, entrelaçado; *s.* cruz servindo de assinatura ao analfabeto; jôgo de linhas cruzadas; *adv.* em cruz.
criterion *s.* critério.
critic *s.* crítica; crítico, censor; **-al** *adj.* crítico; difícil; decisivo; **-ism** *s.* crítica, juizo crítico, criticismo; **-izable** *adj.* criticável; **-ize** *v.t.* criticar; censurar.
croak *v.i.* grasnar, crocitar.
crochet *s.* crochê (trabalho de agulha); *v.i.* fazer crochê.

crockery s. louça, louça de barro.

crocodile s. crocodilo; — **tears** lágrimas de crocodilo.

crocus s. açafrão.

crone s. velha enrugada; **crony** s. camarada velho, companheiro.

crook s. gancho, garfo; curvatura, curva de caminho; escroque, ladrão; v.t. torcer, retorcer; =ed adj. curvo, encurvado, torto, arqueado; oblíquo; deshonesto, fraudulento; =edly adv. tortuosamente.

crop s. colheita; papo das aves; cabelo cortado rente; v.t. colhêr frutos; pastar; cortar, tosquiar; encurtar; podar; aparar; — up aparecer, surgir.

croquet s. conhecido jôgo, geralmente ao ar livre.

crosier, crozier s. báculo de bispo; Cruzeiro do Sul (constelação).

cross adj. zangado, de mau humor; atravessado, transversal, cruzado; oposto, contrário, adverso; contraditório; —=armed de braços cruzados; — **birth** feto atravessado; — **examination** interrogatório; s. cruz; encruzamento, encruzilhada; v.t. cruzar, atravessar; — oneself persignar-se; — out riscar (alguma cousa, de uma lista por exemplo).

crossing s. cruzamento; travessia, passagem; encruzilhada; — **the line** ducking batismo da linha equatorial.

crotchet s. raridade, excentricidade; (mús.) semínima; — rest, (mús.) pausa; =y adj. excêntrico, maníaco.

crouch v.i. agachar-se, encolher-se; rebaixar-se.

croup s. garupa, anca de cavalo; crupe, angina diftérica.

crow s. corvo; cacarejo do galo; =’s foot pé de galinha (rugas); v.i. cacarejar, cantar de galo, cantar vitória, fazer alarde.

crowd s. multidão, turba, plebe, reunião tumultuosa; — **round** juntar-se em volta de, apertar-se em volta de; =ed adj. cheio, repleto, apinhado, amontoado.

crown s. coroa; diadema; grinalda; v.t. premiar, recompensar; =ing s. coroação; — **land** patrimônio ou terra da coroa.

crucial adj. crucial, decisivo, crítico.

crucible s. cadinho, crisol.

crucifix s. crucifixo; =ion s. crucificação; **crucify** v.t. crucificar.

crude adj. crú, bruto; primitivo; indigesto; =ly adv. cruamente, brutalmente; =ness s. crueza, brutalidade.

cruel s. cruel; =ty s. crueldade.

cruet s. galheta, galheteiro.

cruise s. travessia, cruzeiro, viagem; =r s. cruzador.

crumb s. migalhas em geral, migalhas de pão; v.t. esmigalhar, fazer migalhas; =le v.t. esmigalhar, fazer migalhas; v.i. esmigalhar-se, desmoronar, cair.

crumple v.t. amarrotar, enrugar; v.i. amarrotar-se.

crunch v.t.&i. trincar; moer com os dentes; mastigar barulhentamente.

crupper s. garupa, anca; rabicho (arreio de cavalo).

crusade s. cruzada; =r s. cruzado (guerreiro).

crush s. colisão, choque, compressão violenta; grande apinhamento de gente; v.t. esmagar, comprimir, apertar, espremer; =er s. triturador, compressor.

crust s. crosta, côdea; casca de ferida.

crustacean adj.&s. crustáceo.

crusted adj. com crosta, encrostado; **crusty** adj. encrostado (pão com a casca torrada); (fig.) irritável, rabugento, impertinente.

crutch s. muleta; v.i. andar de muletas.

crux s. enigma, mistério; problema árduo; o nó da questão, o essencial.

cry s. grito, clamor; pregão; promulgação; pranto; v.t.&i. gritar, clamar, exclamar; apregoar; lamentar-se; chorar; bramir.

crypt s. cripta.

crystal s. cristal; adj. de cristal; =line adj. cristalino; =lize v.t. cristalizar.

cub s. filhote de certos animais como: urso, leão, tigre, lôbo, etc.; é tambem empregado às vezes para designar os filhotes da baleia e do tubarão.

Cuban adj.&s. cubano.

cube s. cubo; — **root** raiz cúbica; — **sugar** açucar em tijolos; v.t. elevar à terceira potência; formar cubos.

cubicle s. cubículo, alcova.

cubism s. cubismo; **cubist** s. cubista.

cuckoo s. cuco (ave); — **clock** relógio que imita o canto do cuco quando dá horas.

cucumber s. pepino.

cud s. alimento que se encontra no primeiro estômago dos ruminantes e que deve voltar à boca para ser mastigado uma segunda vez.

cuddle v.t. aconchegar, abraçar, acarinhar; — up abraçar-se, apertar-se contra alguém.

cudgel s. bastão, pau, porrete; v.t. surrar, espancar.

cue s. cauda, ponta, extremo; (teat.) deixa; sugestão; taco de bilhar; trança de cabelo.

cuff s. sôco, golpe, bofetada, sopapo, murro; punho de camisa, canhão de camisa, de casaca, etc.; v.t. esbofetear.

cuirass s. couraça; =ier s. couraceiro.

culinary adj. culinário.

cull v.t. colhêr, recolher.

cullender s. coador.

culm s. (bot.) talo de grama; poeira de carvão.

culminate v.i. culminar, atingir o máximo; **culminating** adj. culminante.

culpability s. culpabilidade; **culpable** adj. culpado; **culprit** s. culpado, acusado.

cultivate v.t. cultivar; **cultivation** s. cultura; **cultivator** s. cultivador; **culture** s. cultura; **cultured** adj. culto.

culvert s. canal; cano subterrâneo.

cumber v.t. embaraçar, estorvar; =some adj. embaraçoso, estorvante, incômodo; **cumbrous** adj. embaraçoso.

cumulative adj. cumulativo.

cumulus s. cúmulo.

cuneiform adj. cuneiforme.

cunning adj. hábil, destro, apto; dissimulado, astuto; s. astúcia, ardil.

cup s. chícara, chávena, taça; (cir.) ventosas; =board guarda-louça; =board love amor interesseiro.

cupel s. copela, cadinho; v.t. copelar.

Cupid s. Cupido.

cupidity s. cupidez.

cupola s. cúpola.

cupping glass s. ventosa.

cur s. cão tinhoso; homem vil.

curable adj. curável.

curacy s. curato; **curate** s. cura, vigário.

curative adj. curativo.

curator, curatrix s. curador, curadora.

curb s. barbela; freio, sujeição; beira da calçada, meio-fio; borda de poço; v.t. refreiar, conter, reprimir, pôr freio.

curd s. coalhada, requeijão; *le v.t. coalhar, coagular.

cure s. cura; restabelecimento; remédio; v.t. curar, sanar; curar a carne, a madeira, etc.; salgar, conservar, defumar; v.i. curar-se, restabelecer-se.

curfew s. toque de recolher.

curiosity, curio s. curiosidade; raridade; bibelô; **curious** adj. curioso.

curl s. cacho, anel de cabelo; v.t. anelar, frisar, encrespar, ondear; v.i. enroscar-se; — **up the lip** franzir o lábio.

curlew s. ave aquática.

curliness s. frisadura, encrespamento; **curly** adj. frisado, anelado.

curmudgeon s. tacanho, avarento, mesquinho.

currant s. groselha.

current adj. corrente, em curso, em voga, circulante; vigente; presente; do dia, da atualidade; s. corrente (de agua, de ar, etc.); — **events** atualidades; — **account** conta corrente; — **money** moeda legal; *ly adv. correntemente, geralmente; **currency** s. circulação, curso; moeda corrente, dinheiro em circulação; uso corrente, valor corrente.

curriculum s. currículo, programa de estudos.

curry s. condimento usado na India; v.t. zurrar; almofaçar; curtir couro; — **favor** disputar favores por meio de adulação; —*comb almofaça.

curse s. maldição, imprecação; flagelo; v.t. maldizer; afligir; blasfemar, jurar; *d adj. maldito.

cursory adj. rápido, apressado, precipitado.

curt adj. breve, sêco; brusco, rude; curto, conciso; *ly adv. bruscamente.

curtail v.t. encurtar, diminuir, abreviar, reduzir; restringir.

curtsy, curtsey s. cortesia, reverência.

curvature s. curvatura; — **of the spine** desvio da coluna vertebral.

curve s. curva; v.t. curvar, encurvar, torcer; v.i. encurvar-se, torcer-se; *t s. curveta, corcôvo; **curvilinear** adj. curvilíneo.

cushion s. almofada, coxim; tablilha (bilhar).

custard s. creme (culinária).

custodian s. guardião, guarda; **custody** s. custódia, guarda; prisão.

custom s. costume, uso, hábito; freguezia, clientela; *s s. taxas alfandegárias; **custom house** alfândega; *ary adj. habitual, usual; *er s. cliente, freguez.

cut s. corte, talho, incisão; redução, corte de despesas, de orçamento, etc.; atalho; forma, estilo, feição; ofensa; golpe; falta, ausência; pedaço, coisa cortada; v.t. cortar, picar, retalhar, recortar; desbastar; reduzir, diminuir, abolir; castrar; golpear; ofender; faltar (a aulas); (pop.) negar o cumprimento a alguém; cortar, talhar roupa; v.i. cortar; romper (os dentes); — **glass** cristal recortado; — **down** abater, pôr abaixo, reduzir; — **off** cortar, amputar, interromper; — **the throat** degolar; — **up** trinchar, cortar em pedaços; — **loose** deixar de lado toda restrição; escapar.

cutaneous adj. cutâneo.

cute adj. lindo, bonito, mimoso; inteligente.

cuticle s. cutícula.

cutlass s. sabre; espadim.

cutler s. cuteleiro; *y s. cutelaria.

cutlet s. costeleta.

cutter s. cortador, talhador, retalhador, trinchador; instrumento de corte; pequena embarcação à vela; bote; **cutting** adj. cortante, incisivo, mordaz; penetrante; amargo, penoso; s. corte, incisão, talho; grêlo, rebento; vala, trincheira; aparas; estaca de plantar.

cuttlefish s. siba.

cutwater s. quebra-mar.

cyanogen s. cianogênio.

cyclamen s. ciclame.

cycle s. ciclo; período; bicicleta.

cyclopedia, cyclopaedia s. enciclopédia.

cygnet s. cisne novo.

cylinder s. cilindro; **cylindric** adj. cilíndrico; **cylindrical** adj. cilíndrico.

cymbals s. címbalo.

cynic s. cínico; *al adj. cínico; **cynicism** s. cinismo.

cynosure s. cinosura, a constelação Ursa Menor; (fig.) centro de atração, ponto de mira.

cypher s. V. **cipher.**

cypress s. cipreste.

cyst s. tumor, quisto.

Czech s. tcheco.

D

D terceira letra do alfabeto; (mús.) ré.

dab s. pancada leve; peixe semelhante ao rodovalho; v.i. esfregar suavemente com alguma cousa macia ou úmida; esponjar.

dabble v.t. salpicar, borrifar, humedecer; v.i. brincar na água; intrometer-se.

dace s. boga.

dachshund s. raça de cachorro de patas curtas e tortas.

dad, daddy s. papai.

dado s. dado (de pedestal de coluna).

daemon s. divindade ou espírito tutelar (religião grega); demônio, diabo (religião cristã).

daffodil s. narciso.

daft s.&adj. tôlo, imbecil, idiota, louco; *ness s. imbecilidade.

dagger s. adaga, punhal.

dahlia s. dália.

daily adj. quotidiano, diário; adv. diàriamente, quotidianamente.

dainties s. gulodices, gulosêimas, manjares, iguarias; **daintily** adv. delicadamente; **daintiness** s. delicadeza; elegância de maneiras; **dainty** adj. delicado, refinado; elegante.

dairy s. leiteria; fábrica de lacticínios; —*maid moça de estábulo; empregada de leiteria; —*man leiteiro.

dais s. plataforma, estrado.

daisy s. margarida.

dale s. vale.

dally v.i. brincar, folgar, entreter-se; demorar-se, atrazar-se.

Dalmatia s. Dalmácia.

dam s. represa; açude, dique; fêmea de animais com cria; v.t. represar.

damage s. dano; prejuizo, estrago, avaria; v.t. avariar; estragar, danificar; =s s. indenização de danos.

damascene v.t. adamascar; adj. adamascado; damasceno, de Damasco.

damask s. damasco (tecido); damasco (côr); adj. adamascado; v.t. adamascar; florear; — **plum** s. damasco (fruta); — **steel** s. aço trabalhado.

dame s. senhora, dama, matrona.

damn v.t. danar; maldizer; =able adj. maldito; =ation s. danação, condenação, maldição; =ed adj. danado, maldito; =ing adj. horrível, terrível.

damp adj. úmido, molhado; s. umidade; dejeção; depressão; gaz deletério; v.t. umedecer, molhar; deprimir; (fis.) amortecer; =er s. amortecedor; registo (de chaminé); apagador; =ness s. umidade.

damsel s. senhorinha, môça solteira.

damson s. espécie de ameixa.

dance s. dansa; baile; — **frock** vestido de baile; — **hall** sala de baile; v.t.&i. dansar, bailar, fazer dansar, fazer saltar; =r s. dansarino; **dancing** s. dansa.

dandelion s. dente de leão (flor).

dandle v.t. ninar; acariciar; fazer saltar sôbre os joelhos.

dandruff s. caspa.

dandy s. janota, almofadinha; (pop.) primor, maravilha.

Dane s. dinamarquês.

danger s. perigo; =ous adj. perigoso.

dangle v.t. suspender; balançar, agitar; brandir; v.i. tremular, estar pendente.

Danish adj.&s.dinamarquês.

dank, =ish adj. úmido.

dapper adj. vivo, veloz, esperto, ligeiro; limpo, asseado, tratado.

dappled adj. malhado.

dare v.i. ousar, atrever-se, arriscar-se; v.t. afrontar, desafiar, arrostar; **daring** adj. ousado, atrevido, audacioso, temerário; s. audácia, bravura, atrevimento; **daringly** adv. ousadamente.

dark adj. escuro; sombrio; negro; obscuro; moreno; enigmático, secreto; triste, desconsolador; s. escuridão, noite, trevas; the — **ages** idade da ignorância, idade média; — **horse** cavalo de corrida de probabilidades desconhecidas; — **girl** moça morena; **in the** — às escuras; =en v.t. obscurecer, escurecer, cegar; confundir, embaralhar; (fig.) entristecer; =ish adj. sombrio, meio escuro; =ly adv. obscuramente, sombriamente; secretamente; =ness s. escuridão, noite, trevas; =some adj. obscuro, sombrio.

darling adj. querido, bem-amado; s. querido, querida, bem amado, bem amada; bem, amor.

darn s. cerzidura; v.t. cerzir.

darnel s. joio.

dart s. dardo, frecha, flecha; movimento rápido; v.t. lançar, atirar; v.i. lançar-se, atirar-se, precipitar-se.

dash s. arremetida, arranco, ataque; incursão; colisão, choque, embate; animação; mistura, condimento, sabor; tinta; travessão (sinal tipográfico); v.t. arrojar, lançar, atirar; quebrar; abater; confundir; misturar, temperar; =ing adj. arrojado, temerário.

dastard s. poltrão, covarde.

data (pl. de **datum**) s. dados, elementos.

date s. data, duração; tâmara; (pop.) encontro marcado; v.t. datar; **out of** — velho, antiquado, fora da moda; — **palm** tamareira.

dative s.&adj. dativo.

datum s. dado, elemento.

daub v.t. borrar, emplastrar; manchar; pintar toscamente; s. borrão; crosta; garatuja.

daughter s. filha; —**in**=**law** nora.

daunt v.t. intimidar; =less adj. intrépido.

davit s. (mar.) viga da âncora; serviola.

dawdle v.i. perder tempo; flanar.

dawn s. aurora, madrugada, alva, amanhecer; v.i. raiar, despontar; amanhecer.

day s. dia; jornada; **the — before a** véspera; **the — after** o dia seguinte; —=**break** a aurora, o despontar do dia; —=**dream** sonho acordado; — **school** externato.

daze v.t. ofuscar; pasmar com excesso de luz, de severidade, de pancada, etc.; s. ofuscamento, deslumbramento.

dazzle s. ofuscamento; v.t. ofuscar, deslumbrar.

deacon s. diácono.

dead adj. morto; inerte; inanimado; (dir.) privado de direitos civís; adv. completamente, inteiramente; — **calm** calma profunda; — **center** ponto morto; — **drunk** completamente bebado; — **tired** morto de cansaço; — **lock** impasse; **the** — os mortos, os finados; — **march** marcha fúnebre; =en v.t. amortecer; retardar, parar; apagar, tirar o brilho; =ly adv. mortalmente; implacàvelmente; adj. mortal, letal, funesto.

deaf adj. surdo; — **and dumb** surdomudo; =en v.t. ensurdecer, atordoar; amortecer; =ness s. surdez.

deal s. parte, porção, quantidade indefinida; negócio; mão (no jôgo de cartas); **a great** — muito, bastante; v.t. distribuir, repartir; dar cartas; v.i. lidar (com pessoas); negociar; =er s. negociante, distribuidor; quem dá cartas no jôgo; =ing s. negócio, negociação; comércio; entendimento; trato.

dean s. deão, reitor de escola universitária.

dear adj. querido, amado, caro; **my** — minha cara, meu caro; =est adj. meu querido, minha querida; =ly adv. carinhosamente, ternamente, com afeição; =ness s. carestia.

dearth s. carestia; fome, falta de víveres; tempos difíceis; esterilidade.

death s. morte, falecimento, óbito, trespasse; — **bed** leito de morte; — **blow** golpe mortal; — **certificate** atestado de óbito; — **duties** direitos de sucessão; — **rate** índice de mortalidade; =less adj. imortal.

debar v.t. excluir, privar.

debase v.t. aviltar; alterar, falsificar.

debatable adj. discutível, contestável; em litígio; **debate** s. debate, discussão; v.t. debater; discutir; agitar.

debauch v.t. corromper, perverter; seduzir; violar; =ee adj. corrompido, pervertido, libertino; =ery s. libertinagem.

debenture s. debênture; título de dívida.

debilitated adj. debilitado; **debility** s. debilidade.

debit s. débito, dívida; v.t. debitar; **debt** s. dívida; **in debt** endividado; **run into debt** endividar-se; **debtor** s. devedor.

decade s. década, dezena de anos.

decadence s. decadência; decadent adj. decadente.

decagon s. decágono.

decamp v.i. decampar; fugir, abandonar o campo.

decant v.t. decantar, transvasar; =er s. frasco; frasco para decantação.

decapitate v.t. decapitar.

decay s. decadência; cárie; declínio; deterioração; v.i. decair, definhar, declinar; deteriorar-se.

decease s. morte, trespasse, falecimento, óbito; v.i. morrer, falecer; =d s. defunto, falecido.

deceit s. engano, fraude, dolo, impostura; =ful¯adj. enganoso, falso; mentiroso; ilusório, enganador; deceive v.t. enganar, fraudar; deceiver s. enganador, impostor.

December s. dezembro

decency s. decência.

decennial adj. decenal.

decent adj. decente; honesto; =ly adv. decentemente; honestamente.

decentralize v.t. descentralizar.

deception s. engano, fraude, dolo, impostura; deceptive adj. enganador, mentiroso.

decibel s. (fis.) decibel.

decide v.t. decidir; determinar, resolver; v.i. decidir-se; =d adj. decidido, determinado; =dly adv. decididamente.

deciduous adj. caduco; sujeito a cair por madureza ou periòdicamente, como as folhas das árvores no outono.

decimal adj. decimal.

decimate v.t. dizimar.

decipher v.t. decifrar.

decision s. decisão, deliberação; decisive adj. decisivo.

deck s. tombadilho, convés; baralho de cartas; v.t. ornamentar, ataviar, engalanar, vestir.

declaim v.i. declamar; declamatory adj. declamatório; bombástico; oratório.

declaration s. declaração; declare v.t. declarar; proclamar; confessar.

declension s. declinação.

decline s. declínio; declinação; decadência; v.i.&t. declinar; recusar; decair; abaixar.

declivity s. declive, rampa, escarpa.

decoction s. decocção, cozimento.

decode v.t. decifrar.

decompose v.t. decompor; v.i. decompor-se.

decorate v.t. decorar, guarnecer, ornamentar; decoration s. decoração; decorative adj. decorativo; decorator s. decorador.

decorous adj. decoroso, decente; conveniente, próprio; decorum s. decoro, decência.

decoy s. armadilha, laço; atrativo, sedução; engôdo; v.t. engodar; atrair por meio de sedução; fazer cair na armadilha.

decrease s. decrescimento, diminuição; v.i. decrescer; v.t. diminuir.

decree s. decreto; édito; v.t. decretar.

decrepit adj. decrépito, caduco; =ude s. decrepitude, caducidade.

decry v.t. desacreditar; rebaixar; vituperar, censurar pùblicamente.

dedicate v.t. dedicar, consagrar; dedication s. dedicação, devotamento; dedicatória.

deduce v.t. deduzir.

deduct v.t. deduzir, subtrair, descontar;

=ion s. dedução, desconto, redução, abatimento.

deed s. ação, ato, feito; proeza, façanha; realidade; (dir.) escritura, contrato; to be taken in the very — ser apanhado em flagrante.

deem v.t. julgar, estimar, avaliar, considerar; =ed adj. considerado, ponderado.

deep adj. fundo, profundo; sagaz, penetrante; solene, grave; absorto; s. profundidade, abismo; — blue azul vivo; — mourning luto fechado; — sea fishing pesca ao largo; =en v.t. aprofundar; cavar; =ly adv. profundamente; sensìvelmente.

deer s. veado, cervo.

deface v.t. desfigurar; mutilar.

de facto adv. de fato.

defalcate v.t. desfalcar, defraudar; defalcation s. desfalque.

defamation s. difamação; defamatory adj. difamatório, difamante, infamante; defame v.t. difamar.

default s. defeito; falha; prevaricação; negligência; v.i. falhar; faltar; delinquir.

defeat s. derrota; v.t. derrotar, vencer; frustrar.

defecate v.t. purgar, clarificar, purificar, depurar; v.i. defecar.

defect s. defeito; deficiência; imperfeição; falta; =ive adj. defeituoso; (gram.) defectivo.

defection s. defecção, deserção, apostasia.

defence s. defesa; =less adj. sem defesa; defend v.t. defender; defendant adj. &s. defensor; (for.) demandado, réu; defencible adj. defensável, defensível.

defer v.t. adiar, aprazar, retardar; deferir; =ence s. deferência, respeito, consideração; =ential adj. deferente.

defiance s. desafio; oposição obstinada.

deficiency s. deficiência, falta, insuficiência; defeito; déficit; deficient adj. deficiente; deficit s. déficit.

defile s. desfiladeiro; desfile; v.i. desfilar; v.t. manchar, profanar, viciar; poluir; deshonrar; =ment s. contaminação; mancha.

definable adj. definível; define v.t. definir; definite adj. definido; determinado; preciso; definitely adv. decididamente; definition s. definição; definitive adj. definitivo.

deflate v.t. esvaziar libertando o gás ou ar; desinchar.

deflect v.t. desviar, apartar; v.i. desviar-se, apartar-se; deflexion, deflection s. desvio, flexão.

defloration s. defloração, defloramento; deflower v.t. deflorar.

deforest v.t. desflorestar.

deform v.t. deformar; =ed adj. deformado, disforme; =ity s. deformidade.

defraud v.t. fraudar; frustrar.

defray v.t. custear, fazer (as despesas).

deft adj. destro, apto, competente; =ness s. destreza.

defunct adj. &s. defunto.

defy v.t. desafiar, afrontar.

degeneracy, degeneration s. degenerescência; degradação; depravação; degenerate v.i. degenerar.

degradation s. degradação, aviltamento; degrade v.t. degradar, aviltar.

degree s. grau.

deify v.t. deificar, divinizar.

deign v.i. dignar-se, condescender.

deity s, divindade, deidade.

deject *v.t.* abater, afligir, desanimar; **-ion** *s.* abatimento, acabrunhamento, desânimo; dejeção.
de jure *adv.* de direito; legalmente, legitimamente.
delay *s.* atraso, demora, retardamento, protelação; *v.t.* atrasar, diferir, retardar; *v.i.* tardar, demorar-se.
dele *v.t.* (*imp.*) suprimir.
delectation *s.* deleite, delícia.
delegate *s.* delegado, deputado; *v.t.* delegar; **delegation** *s.* delegação.
delete *v.t.* apagar, suprimir.
deleterious *adj.* deletério.
deliberate *adj.* deliberado; refletido, lento; pensado; *v.t.* deliberar, refletir, considerar; **-ly** *adv.* deliberadamente; **deliberation** *s.* deliberação.
delicacy *s.* delicadeza; acepipe, manjar; **delicate** *adj.* delicado; fino.
delicious *adj.* delicioso; **delight** *s.* delícia, encantamento; gôzo; deleite; *v.t.* deleitar, encantar, agradar; *v.i.* deleitar-se.
delimitate *v.t.* delimitar.
delineate *v.t.* delinear, traçar; descrever; **delineation** *s.* delineamento; esbôço.
delinquency *s.* delinquência; falta; negligência; **delinquent** *s.* delinquente.
deliquescence *s.* deliquescência.
delirious *adj.* delirante; **to be** — delirar; **delirium** *s.* delírio.
deliver *v.t.* entregar; deixar; passar; franquear; ceder; comunicar; libertar; resignar; distribuir; **to be -d of a boy** dar à luz um menino; **-y** *s.* entrega, remessa, distribuição; parto; **-ance** *s.* entrega; soltura; parto; **-er** *s.* libertador, libertadora.
dell *s.* ravina; pequeno vale.
delphinium *s.* (*bot.*) pé-de-cotovia.
delta *s.* delta.
delude *v.t.* enganar, abusar.
deluge *s.* dilúvio; *v.t.* inundar, alagar.
delusion *s.* ilusão; decepção, engano; **delusive** *adj.* ilusório.
delve *v.t.* cavar; sondar.
demagogue *s.* demagogo; tribuno.
demand *s.* demanda; débito; exigência; **on — a pedido;** *v.t.* exigir, demandar, reclamar, pedir perentòriamente.
demarcate *v.t.* demarcar; **demarcation** *s.* demarcação.
demean *v.i.* portar-se, comportar-se, conduzir-se; **-or, -our** *s.* conduta, comportamento; porte.
demented *adj.* demente; **dementia** *s.* demência.
demerit *s.* desmerecimento.
demesne *s.* domínio.
demigod *s.* semi-deus.
demijohn *s.* garrafão.
demise *s.* morte, falecimento; sucessão ou transmissão da coroa; (*dir.*) cessão de domínio; *v.t.* legar; arrendar; transmitir.
demisemiquaver *s.* (*mús.*) fusa.
demobilize *v.t.* desmobilizar.
democracy *s.* democracia; **democrat** *s.* democrata; **democratic** *adj.* democrático.
demolish *v.t.* demolir; **demolition** *s.* demolição, destruição.
demon *s.* demônio.
demonetize *v.t.* quebrar o padrão da moeda.
demoniac *adj.* demoníaco.
demonstrate *v.t.* demonstrar, manifestar; **demonstration** *s.* demonstração, manfestação; **demonstrative** *adj.* demons-

trativo; **demonstrator** *s.* demonstrador.
demoralize *v.t.* desmoralizar.
demur *s.* pausa, demora; objeção, escrúpulo; *v.i.* demorar, hesitar, vacilar; objetar, pôr dificuldades.
demure *adj.* sério, formal; afetadamente modesto, grave ou sério.
demurrage *s.* demora ou detenção de um navio, carro, etc, além do tempo estipulado; multa paga pela demora.
demurrer *s.* exceção; pessoa hesitante.
demy *s.* formato de papel, de cêrca de 16 x 21 polegadas.
den *s.* antro, caverna, esconderijo, cova, toca, buraco, covil.
denature *v.t.* desnaturar.
denial *s.* desmentido, denegação, negação, negativa; recusa.
denizen *s.* habitante, cidadão, residente; estrangeiro naturalizado.
denominate *v.t.* denominar; **denomination** *s.* denominação; título; designação; seita; religião; **denominational** *adj.* sectário.
denominator *s.* denominador.
denote *v.t.* denotar.
denounce *v.t.* denunciar.
dense *adj.* denso, compacto, espêsso; **density** *s.* densidade, espessura.
dent *s.* depressão, cavidade; saliência; dente (de engrenagem); *v.t.* endentar, dentear.
dental *adj.* dentário, dental; — **surgeon** cirurgião-dentista; **dentate** *adj.* dentado; **dentist** *s.* dentista; **dentistry** *s.* arte dentária; **dentition** *s.* dentição; **denture** *s.* dentadura postiça.
denude *v.t.* desnudar.
denunciation *s.* denúncia.
deny *v.t.* negar; denegar; renegar; recusar.
deodorize *v.t.* desinfetar.
depart *v.i.* partir; afastar-se; **-ed** *s.* defunto, falecido.
department *s.* departamento; divisão; ramo; **-al** *adj.* departamental.
departure *s.* partida, saída; (*mar.*) posição de um navio em latitude e longitude, tomada como ponto de partida no princípio da viagem.
depend *v.i.* depender, apoiar-se, contar com; **-ant, -ent** *s.* dependente; **-ence** *s.* dependência; confiança.
depict *v.t.* pintar; descrever, representar.
deplete *v.t.* esgotar, exhaurir, esvaziar.
deplorable *adj.* deplorável, lamentável; **deplore** *v.t.* deplorar, lamentar.
deploy *v.t.* desdobrar, desenrolar; **-ment** *s.* desdobramento, desfraldamento.
deponent *s.* depoente.
depopulate *v.t.* despovoar; **depopulation** *s.* despovoamento.
deport *v.t.* deportar; **-ation** *s.* deportação.
deportment *s.* proceder; conduta, comportamento; porte.
depose *v.t.* depositar; depor, destronar; *v.i.* depor; prestar declarações.
deposit *s.* depósito; consignação; *v.t.* depositar.
depravation *s.* depravação; **depravity** *s.* depravação; **deprave** *v.t.* depravar; **depraved** *adj.* depravado.
deprecate *v.t.* reprovar.
depreciate *v.t.* depreciar, aviltar; **depreciation** *s.* depreciação; **depreciatory** *adj.* depreciatório, pejorativo.
depredation *s.* depredação.

depress v.t. deprimir; =ing adj. deprimente; =ion s. depressão; abatimento.
deprivation s. privação, carência; de-**prive** v.t. privar, despojar; excluir; destituir.
depth s. profundidade, profundeza, fundo; o mais profundo; abismo; parte interior ou recôndita; vivacidade (da côr); gravidade (do som).
deputation s. deputação, delegação; **depute** v.t. deputar, delegar, incumbir; **deputy** s. deputado; delegado; **deputy chairman** vice-presidente; **deputy professor** professor substituto.
derail v.t. descarrilhar, desencarrilhar; =ment s. descarrilamento.
derange v.t. desarranjar, transtornar, perturbar; tornar louco; =ment s. desarranjo, confusão; loucura.
derelict adj. abandonado; s. navio abandonado; =ion s. abandono.
deride v.t. ridicularizar, zombar; **derision** s. mofa, escárneo; **derisive** adj. irrisório, burlesco.
derivation s. derivação; **derivative** s. derivativo, derivado; **derive** v.t. derivar.
derogate v.t. derrogar; abolir; v.i. subtrair, retirar; **derogatory** adj. derrogatório; depreciativo.
derrick s. grua; tôrre ou armação situada na bôca de um poço artesiano.
dervish s. derviche.
descant v.i. dissertar, discorrer, estender-se; cantar.
descend v.i. descender, proceder; rebaixar-se; v.t. descer, baixar; =ant s. descendente; **descent** s. descida, declive; descendência, linhagem.
describe v.t. descrever, definir, qualificar; **description** s. descrição; **descriptive** adj. descritivo.
descry v.t. descobrir; avistar, divisar.
desecrate v.t. profanar, violar.
desert adj. deserto, êrmo, solitário; s. deserto; mérito, serviço; v.t. desamparar, abandonar, desertar; =ed adj. abandonado, deserto; =er s. desertor; =ion s. deserção, abandono, desleixo.
deserve v.t. merecer; =edly adv. merecidamente, a justo título; **deserving** adj. merecedor, digno de.
desiccate v.t. secar, dessecar, ressecar.
desideratum s. desideratum.
design s. projeto, cálculo (de máquinas, pontes, etc.) modêlo, desenho; plano; intenção; v.t. destinar; projetar, calcular (pontes, etc.); idear, delinear, desenhar; v.i. fazer projetos, planos, etc.
designate v.t. designar; **designation** s. designação; **designative** adj. designativo..
designedly adv. intencionalmente, propositadamente, de propósito.
designer s. desenhista; delineador, maquinador; autor; **designing** adj. maquinador; artificioso, astuto, velhaco; intrigante; s. desenho; arte de desenhar.
desirable adj. desejável; **desire** s. desejo, vontade; v.t. desejar, aspirar; **desirous** adj. desejoso; **desirousness** s. desejo vivo, anelo, ânsia.
desist v.i. desistir, abrir mão.
desk s. carteira, escrivaninha.
desolate adj. desolado, deserto, solitário; v.t. desolar; despovoar; arrasar; devastar, arruinar; **desolation** s. desolação.
despair s. desespêro; v.i. desesperar, perder toda a esperança.
despatch V. dispatch.

desperado s. malfeitor, bandido temerário.
desperate adj. desesperado; arrojado, arriscado, temerário; irremediável; =ly adv. desesperadamente, irremediavelmente, perdidamente; **desperation** s. desespêro, encarniçamento; desesperação.
despicable adj. desprezível, vil.
despise v.t. desprezar, desdenhar, menosprezar.
despite s. despeito; in — of a despeito de, a-pesar de.
despoil v.t. despojar, espoliar, roubar.
despond v.i. desanimar, desalentar-se, perder a coragem, desesperar-se, abandonar-se; =ence, =ency s. desalento, desânimo, abatimento; =ent adj. desanimado, desalentado, abatido.
despot s. déspota; =ic adj. despótico; =ism s. despotismo.
dessert s. sobremesa.
destination s. destino, paradeiro, destinação; **destiny** s. destino; **destine** v.t. destinar.
destitute adj. destituído, desamparado, desprovido; the — os necessitados; **destitution** s. destituição, privação; miséria, indigência.
destroy v.t. destruir; =er s. destruidor; (mar.) navio torpedeiro; **destruction** s. destruição; **destructive** adj. destrutivo; **destructor** s. incinerador (forno).
desultory adj. desconexo, sem ligação; **desultorily** adv. desconexamente, sem método, sem ligação.
detach v.t. separar, desligar, destacar, desprender; =able adj. destacável, separável; =ment s. separação; destacamento; desapêgo.
detail s. pormenor, particularidade; v.t. pormenorizar, particularizar, circunstanciar.
detain v.t. deter, reter; retardar; =er s. detentor.
detect v.t. descobrir, averiguar; surpreender; =ion s. descoberta; =ive s. agente de polícia secreta, investigador, detetive.
detent s. gatilho; =ion s. detenção, retenção; prisão.
deter v.t. dissuadir, desanimar; acovardar.
deteriorate v.i. deteriorar-se.
determinate adj. determinado; **determination** s. determinação, resolução; **determine** v.t. determinar, decidir, resolver; **determined** adj. determinado, resoluto.
detest v.t. detestar, abominar; =able adj. detestável.
dethrone v.t. destronar.
detonate v.i. detonar; v.t. fazer detonar; **detonation** s. detonação; **detonator** s. detonador, explosivo.
detract v.t. tirar, tomar, diminuir; detratar, infamar, difamar, desacreditar; =or s. detrator.
detrain v.i. desembarcar, sair do trem; v.t. (mil.) desembarcar tropas.
detriment s. detrimento, prejuízo; =al adj. prejudicial.
detritus s. detrito.
deuce s. dois (de cartas ou dados); (tenis) igualdade em pontos; (fam.) diabo! peste!
Deuteronomy s. Deuteronômio.
devaluation s. desvalorização.
devastate v.t. devastar, assolar; **devastation** s. devastação, desolação; **devastator** s. devastador.

develop *v.t.* desenvolver; desabrochar; desdobrar; fomentar; produzir; aperfeiçoar; (*fot.*) revelar; **-ment** *s.* desenvolvimento.

deviate *v.i.* desviar-se; *v.t.* desviar.

device *s.* meio, expediente; dispositivo; lema, divisa; esquema, plano, projeto; estratagema, artifício.

devil *s.* diabo, demônio; the —! diabo! **-ish** *adj.* diabólico, satânico; **-ment** *s.* malícia; diabrura.

devious *adj.* desviado, descarrilhado, extraviado; tortuoso; errante.

devise *v.t.* inventar, combinar, imaginar, projetar, idear; *v.i.* formar projetos, planos; maquinar; (*dir.*) legar; **devisor** *s.* testador que lega bens de raiz.

devoid *adj.* falto, baldo, desprovido.

devolve *v.t.* transmitir, entregar; *v.i.* recair, passar a, tocar, incumbir; **devolution** *s.* entrega, devolução, transferência.

devote *v.t.* dedicar, consagrar, devotar; *v.i.* dedicar-se, consagrar-se, devotar-se; **-e** *s.* devoto fervoroso, fanático; **devotion** *s.* devoção, piedade; devotamento, dedicação.

devour *v.t.* devorar.

devout *adj.* devoto; sincero; **-ness** *s.* devoção.

dew *s.* orvalho, sereno, rocio; — **drop** gota de sereno, de orvalho; *v.t.* orvalhar; **-y** *adj.* orvalhado.

dewlap *s.* papada de boi; papo em geral.

dexterity *s.* destreza, habilidade; **dextrous, dexterous** *adj.* destro, hábil, jeitoso.

dextrin *s.* dextrina.

diabetes *s.* diabetes.

diabolic, diabolical *adj.* diabólico.

diacritical *adj.* diacrítico; **diacritic** *adj.* &*s.* diacrítico, sintoma, diagnóstico.

diadem *s.* diadema.

diaeresis *s.* trema.

diagnose *v.t.* diagnosticar; **diagnosis** *s.* diagnose; **diagnostic** *adj.*&*s.* diagnóstico.

diagonal *adj.* diagonal.

diagram *s.* diagrama, gráfico, esbôço, esquema.

dial *s.* quadrante; relógio de sol; mostrador; disco de telefone; *v.t.* discar.

dialect *s.* dialeto.

dialectics *s.* dialética.

dialogue *s.* diálogo.

diameter *s.* diâmetro; **diametric** *adj.* diametral.

diamond *s.* diamante; (*imp.*) tipo de letra de 4 a 4½ pontos; (*geom.*) losango, rombo; naipe de ouros (nas cartas); — **wedding** bodas-de-diamante.

diaper *s.* fazenda de linho adamascado; fralda (de criança); *v.t.* lavrar, adamascar.

diaphanous *adj.* diáfano.

diaphragm *s.* diafragma.

diarrhoea *s.* diarréia, fluxo de ventre.

diary *s.* diário, jornal.

diatonic *adj.* diatônico.

diatribe *s.* diatribe.

dibble *s.* sacho, almocafre.

dibs *s.* nome de um jôgo rural infantil.

dice *s.* dados.

dickens *s.*&*int.* diabo, diacho.

dictate *v.t.* ditar; mandar, ordenar, impor; *s.* ditame, preceito, máxima; **dictation** *s.* ditado; **dictator** *s.* ditador; **dictatorial** *adj.* ditatorial; **dictatorship** *s.* ditadura.

diction *s.* dicção; **-ary** *s.* dicionário.

dictum *s.* sentença, aforismo, máxima.

didactic *adj.* didático; **-s** *s.* didática.

die *s.* dado (jôgo); sorte, azar; cunho de moedas; furador.

die *v.i.* morrer, falecer, sucumbir; — **away, down** or **out** acabar-se, desaparecer gradativamente.

diet *s.* dieta, regime alimentar; *v.t.* pôr em dieta; *v.i.* estar em dieta; **-ary** *s.* regime dietético.

differ *v.i.* diferir, variar, diferençar-se, divergir; **-ence** *s.* diferença, divergência, diversidade; **-ent** *adj.* diferente; **-ential** *adj.* diferencial; **-entiate** *v.t.* diferenciar; **-ently** *adv.* diferentemente.

difficult *adj.* difícil; penoso; **-y** *s.* dificuldade; embaraço; **with -y** dificilmente, com dificuldade; **-ies** *s.* embaraços, apuros.

diffidence *s.* falta de confiança em si mesmo, timidez, humildade, modéstia; **diffident** *adj.* tímido, sem confiança em si próprio.

diffuse *v.t.* difundir, espalhar, propagar; *adj.* difuso, prolixo; **diffusion** *s.* difusão.

dig *v.t.* cavar, escavar; — **up** desenterrar; *s.* (*pop.*) enxadada, cotovelada.

digest *v.t.*&*i.* digerir; **-ible** *adj.* digerível; **-ion** *s.* digestão; **-ive** *adj.* digestivo.

digger *s.* cavador, escavador; **gold** — mineiro de ouro, procurador de ouro.

digit *s.* dedo; dedo (medida); algarismos de 1 a 9 inclusive, e também o 0; **-al** *adj.* digital.

digitalis *s.* digital.

dignified *adj.* digno; **dignify** *v.t.* dignificar, honrar; **dignitary** *adj.*&*s.* dignitário; **dignity** *s.* dignidade.

digress *v.i.* digressionar, divagar, desviar; **-ion** *s.* digressão; **-ive** *adj.* digressivo.

dike *s.* dique, represa; *v.t.* represar; cercar de diques.

dilapidate *v.t.* dilapidar.

dilate *v.t.* dilatar; *v.i.* dilatar-se, expandir-se.

dilatoriness *s.* lentidão, dilação; demora, vagar; **dilatory** *adj.* lento, vagaroso, demorado, dilatório.

dilemma *s.* dilema.

dilettante *s.* diletante.

diligence *s.* diligência, zêlo, assiduidade; **diligent** *adj.* diligente; **diligently** *adv.* diligentemente.

dilly-dally *v.i.* perder tempo.

dilute *v.t.* diluir, dissolver; **dilution** *s.* diluição; **-d** *adj.* diluído.

diluvial *adj.* diluviano.

dim *adj.* obscuro, escuro, sombrio; confuso, indistinto; lerdo; *v.t.* obscurecer, ofuscar; tornar sombrio.

dimension *s.* dimensão.

diminish *v.t.*&*i.* diminuir; **diminution** *s.* diminuição; **diminutive** *adj.* diminutivo; diminuto; pequeno, mesquinho; *s.* (*gram.*) diminutivo.

dimness *s.* obscurecimento; obscuridade; escuridão; ofuscamento.

dimple *s.* covinhas no rosto.

din *s.* ruído, estrépito; *v.t.* atordoar, aturdir, ensurdecer; *v.i.* fazer barulho.

dine *v.i.* jantar; — **out** jantar fora.

dingey *s.* bote pequeno e ligeiro.

dingy *adj.* manchado, sujo; sombrio; sem lustre; moreno.

dining *ger.* de **to dine**; — **car** vagão-restaurante; — **room** salão de jantar, sala de jantar; — **table** mesa de jantar.

dinner s. jantar.
dint s. mossa, amolgadura; pancada, golpe; fôrça, eficácia; **by — of** à força de.
diocesan adj. diocesano; **diocese** s. diocese.
dioptrics s. dióptrica; **dioptrical** adj. dióptrico.
dip s. mergulho, imersão; depressão; inclinação, declive; v.t. mergulhar; imergir; saudar com a bandeira; v.i. mergulhar; inclinar-se.
diphtheria s. difteria.
diphthong s. ditongo.
diploma s. diploma.
diplomacy s. diplomacia; **diplomatic** adj. diplomático; **diplomat** s. diplomata.
dire adj. horrendo, horrível; de mau agouro; deplorável, lamentável; fatal.
direct adj. direto, direito; imediato; claro, inequívoco; em linha reta; — **current** corrente contínua; — **trade** comércio direto; adv. diretamente; v.t. dirigir; administrar, conduzir; endereçar; orientar; **=ion** s. direção; administração; endereço; **=ions** s. instruções, prescrições; **=ly** adv. diretamente; imediatamente, agora mesmo.
director s. diretor, administrador; **=ate** s. junta diretora; diretoria.
directory s. diretório, anuário, almanaque, catálogo.
direful adj. terrível, sinistro, horrível, calamitoso.
dirge s. canto fúnebre, canto de morte.
dirigible adj.&s. dirigível.
dirk s. punhal, adaga.
dirt s. sujeira, imundície, porcaria; lôdo, barro, terra; — **cheap** a vil preço; **=ily** adv. porcamente, sujamente; **=iness** s. sujeira; **=y** adj. sujo, porco, pouco asseado; v.t. sujar, manchar.
disable v.t. inhabilitar, incapacitar; impossibilitar; desmantelar; **=ment** s. incapacidade, invalidez; **disability** s. incapacidade, invalidez.
disabuse v.t. desenganar, tirar de êrro.
disadvantage s. desvantagem; **=ous** adj. desvantajoso.
disaffection s. desafeição, desamor.
disagree v.i. discordar; **=able** adj. desagradável; **=ment** s. desacôrdo, discordância; dissentimento.
disallow v.t. desaprovar, rejeitar.
disappear v.i. desaparecer; **=ance** s. desaparecimento.
disappoint v.t. desapontar; faltar a uma promessa; desiludir, decepcionar; **=ment** s. desapontamento, desilusão, decepção.
disapprobation, disapproval s. desaprovação; **disapprove** v.t. desaprovar, reprovar.
disarm v.t. desarmar; **=ament** s. desarmamento.
disarrange v.t. desarranjar, desajustar.
disarray s. desordem, confusão; v.t. desarranjar, desordenar; desnudar, despir.
disaster s. desastre, sinistro; **disastrous** adj. desastroso.
disavow v.t. repudiar; desaprovar; desautorizar.
disband v.t. (mil.) licenciar as tropas; despedir, expulsar; v.i. dispersar-se, debandar.
disbelief s. incredulidade, descrença.
disbud v.t. espontar (a árvore), aparar os talos.

disburden v.t. descarregar, aliviar.
disburse v.t. desembolsar; **=ment** s. desembôlso.
disc s. disco; pátena.
discard v.t.&i. deixar de lado; despedir; rejeitar; descartar-se.
discern v.t. discernir; **=ible** adj. discernível; **=ing** adj. judicioso, criterioso; **=ment** s. discernimento, critério.
discharge s. descarga; descarregamento; exoneração; absolvição; libertação; quitação; v.t.&i. descarregar; absolver, libertar; disparar; desobrigar; demitir, despedir; exonerar; saldar; desembarcar; licenciar.
disciple s. discípulo; **disciplinarian** s. disciplinário; **disciplinary** adj. disciplinar; **discipline** s. disciplina; v.t. disciplinar.
disclaim v.t. repudiar, desconhecer; **=er** s. repúdio, renúncia, desaprovação.
disclose v.t. revelar; descobrir; divulgar; abrir, destampar; desvendar; **disclosure** s. revelação; divulgação.
discoloration s. descoloração; **discolor** v.t. descolorar, descorar, descolorir.
discomfit v.t. confundir, desconcertar; frustrar; derrotar; **=ure** s. desconcêrto; desbarato, derrota.
discomfort s. desconfôrto, incômodo, mal estar.
discompose v.t. perturbar; desarranjar; transtornar; descompor, desalinhar; agitar; **discomposure** s. perturbação, desordem.
disconcert v.t. desconcertar, perturbar; desorientar.
disconnect v.t. desunir, separar; **=ed** adj. desconexo.
disconsolate adj. desconsolado.
discontented adj. descontente, insatisfeito; **discontentment** s. descontentamento.
discontinuance s. descontinuação, interrupção, suspensão; supressão; **discontinue** v.t. descontinuar; suprimir.
discord s. discórdia; (mús.) dissonância; **=ance** s. discordância; **=ant** adj. discordante, dissonante.
discount s. desconto, redução, abatimento; v.t. descontar, deduzir, reduzir, abater.
discountenance v.t. desaprovar, opor-se a; desconcertar.
discounter s. prestamista; corretor de câmbio.
discourage v.t. desanimar, desencorajar; **=ment** s. desânimo; desencorajamento.
discourse s. discurso; v.i. discorrer.
discourteous adj. descortês, indelicado; **discourtesy** s. descortesia, indelicadeza.
discover v.t. descobrir; **=er** s. inventor, descobridor; **=y** s. descoberta.
discredit s. descrédito; v.t. desacreditar; **=able** adj. deshonroso.
discreet adj. discreto.
discrepancy s. discrepância, contradição.
discrete adj. discreto; separado, diferente.
discretion s. discreção, prudência; **=ary** adj. discricionário.
discriminate v.t. discriminar, discernir, diferenciar; **discrimination** s. discriminação, distinção.
discursive adj. discursivo.
discus s. disco.
discuss v.t. discutir, debater; **=ion** s. discussão.

disdain s. desdém, desprêzo; v.t. desdenhar, desprezar; =ful adj. desdenhoso.
disease s. doença, moléstia, mal; =d adj. doente.
disembark v.t.&i. desembarcar; =ation s. desembarque.
disembody v.t. desencorporar; v.i. desencarnar.
disembowel v.t. estripar, desentranhar.
disenchant v.t. desencantar.
disemcumber v.t. desimpedir, desembaraçar; desentulhar.
disengage v.t. desimpedir, desembaraçar, soltar; =d adj. livre.
disentangle v.t. desembaraçar; desembrulhar; desemaranhar.
disestablish v.t. desoficializar; separar do Estado (a Igreja).
disfavor s. desfavor.
d'sfigure v.t. desfigurar; afeiar, deformar; =ment s. deformação, desfiguramento.
disforest v.t. desflorestar.
disgorge v.t. vomitar; =ment s. vômito.
disgrace s. desfavor; vergonha, deshonra, opróbrio; v.t. desfavorecer; deshonrar, aviltar.
disgruntled adj. enfadado, descontente.
disguise s. disfarce; máscara; v.t. disfarçar, mascarar.
disgust s. repugnância, asco; v.t. inspirar repugnância; fastidiar; enojar; =ing adj. repugnante, asqueroso.
dish s. prato, vasilhame; comida, iguaria; — washer lavador de pratos; v.t. servir (comida).
dishabille s. traje caseiro feminino.
dishearten v.t. desencorajar, desacoroçoar.
disheveled adj. desgrenhado, descabelado, desalinhado.
dishonest adj. deshonesto; infiel, desleal; =y s. deshonestidade; infidelidade, deslealdade.
dishonor, dishonour s. deshonra; v.t. deshonrar; =able adj. deshonroso, indecoroso; =ed check cheque sem fundos.
disillusion s. desilusão; v.t. desiludir, desencantar.
disinclination s. desafeto, desamor; disincline v.t. afastar.
disincorporate v.t. desencorporar; v.i. desencarnar; disincorporation s. desencarnação.
disinfect v.t. desinfetar; =ant s. desinfetante; =ion s. desinfeção.
disingenuous adj. pouco sincero, falso, dissimulado.
disinherit v.t. desherdar.
disintegrate v.t. desintegrar, desagregar, decompor.
disinter v.t. desenterrar, exumar.
disinterested adj. desinteressado; =ness s. desinterêsse.
disinterment s. exumação.
disjoin v.t. desunir, separar, despegar.
disjoint v.t. desarticular, desconjuntar, deslocar; =ed adj. deslocado, desarticulado, desconjuntado.
disk s. disco; pátena.
dislikes. aversão, antipatia, desagrado; v.t. ter em aversão, aborrecer, não gostar de.
dislocate v.t. deslocar, desconjuntar, luxar, desarticular; dislocation s. deslocação, luxação.
dislodge v.t. desalojar, desacomodar; v.i. mudar-se.
disloyal adj. desleal, infiel; =ty s. deslealdade, infedelidade.

dismal adj. lúgubre, triste, funesto.
dismantle v.t. desmantelar; desguarnecer.
dismast v.t. (mar.) desarvorar, desmastrar.
dismay s. consternação, espanto; v.t. consternar; espantar.
dismember v.t. desmembrar.
dismiss v.t. despedir, demitir, destituir, mandar embora; =al s. destituição, despedida, ação de despedir ou demitir.
dismount v.t. desmontar, desarmar; v.i. apear, descer.
disobedience s. desobediência; disobedient adj. desobediente; disobey v.t. desobedecer a; v.i. desobedecer.
disoblige v.t. desagradar, desfeitear, tratar mal; disobliging adj. pouco serviçal, pouco complacente.
disorder s. desordem; irregularidade; doença; v.t. desordenar, perturbar, desarranjar.
disorganize v.t. desorganizar.
disown v.t. repudiar, negar, desconhecer; renegar, renunciar.
disparage v.t. rebaixar, desprezar; desacreditar; depreciar; =ment s. depreciação, rebaixamento; disparaging adj. depreciativo; pejorativo.
disparate adj. desigual, diferente; disparity s. disparidade.
dispassionate adj. desapaixonado, imparcial; =ly adv. desapaixonadamente, imparcialmente.
dispatch s. despacho, expedição; pressa, rapidez; expediente; remessa; v.t. despachar; expedir; remeter; matar.
dispel v.t. dissipar; dispersar.
dispensary s. dispensário; dispensation s. distribuição, repartição; dispensa, isenção; dispense v.t. distribuir, repartir; dispensar; administrar (justiça); isentar; preparar (remédio); dispensatory s. farmacopéia; dispensário.
dispersal, dispersion s. dispersão; separação; difusão; disperse v.t. dispersar; dissipar; propalar; difundir; disseminar.
dispirit v.t. desanimar, deprimir, desalentar, desacoroçoar.
displace v.t. deslocar; remover; desalojar; destituir; =ment s. deslocamento; destituição; remoção.
display s. exibição, ostentação; parada; v.t. exibir, ostentar, expor; desenrolar, estender, mostrar.
displease v.t. descontentar, desgostar; v.i. desagradar; displeasure s. desprazer, descontentamento, aborrecimento.
disposable adj. disponível; disposal s. disposição; manejo; cessão; dispose v.t.&i. dispor; disposition s. disposição; ordem, arranjo; gênio, índole, tendência.
dispossess v.t. desapropriar.
disproof s. refutação.
disproportion s. desproporção; =ate adj. desproporcionado.
disprove v.t. refutar.
dispute s. disputa, contestação, litígio, discussão, altercação; v.t.&i. disputar, discutir, contestar, pleitear.
disqualification s. inabilitação, impedimento, desqualificação; disqualified adj. desqualificado; disqualify v.t. desqualificar; incapacitar.
disquiet v.t. inquietar, desassossegar; =ude s. inquietude, desassossêgo.
disquisition s. dissertação.

disrate _v.t._ desclassificar.
disregard _s._ descuido, negligência; desprêzo; falta de consideração; _v.t._ desdenhar, fazer pouco caso; desatender.
disrelish _s._ repugnância, aversão; desgôsto.
disreputable _adj._ deshonroso, desacreditado, vergonhoso; **disrepute** _s._ descrédito, má fama, má reputação.
disrespect _s._ falta de respeito, irreverência; **=ful** _adj._ desrespeitoso, irreverente.
disrobe _v.t._ despir.
disrupt _v.t._ romper.
dissatisfaction _s._ descontentamento; **dissatisfied** _adj._ descontente.
dissect _v.t._ dissecar; **=ion** _s._ dissecação.
dissemble _v.t.&i._ dissimular; **=r** _s._ dissimulador.
disseminate _v.t._ disseminar, propagar.
dissension _s._ dissenção; **dissent** _s._ dissentimento; dissidência; _v.i._ opor-se; **dissenter** _s._ dissidente.
dissertation _s._ dissertação.
disservice _s._ desserviço, mau serviço.
dissidence _s._ dissidência; **dissident** _s._ dissidente.
dissimilar _adj._ desigual, diferente, dissimilar; **=ity** _s._ dissemelhança, desigualdade.
dissimulate _v.t.&i._ dissimular.
dissipate _v.t._ dissipar; **dissipation** _s._ dissipação.
dissociate _v.t._ dissociar.
dissolute _adj._ dissoluto; **=ness** _s._ dissipação, dissolução; **dissolution** _s._ dissolução.
dissolve _v.t._ dissolver; **=nt** _s._ dissolvente.
dissonance _s._ dissonância; **dissonant** _adj._ dissonante.
dissuade _v.t._ dissuadir, desaconselhar.
dissyllable _s._ dissílabo.
distaff _s._ roca (de fiar).
distance _s._ distância; longitude, afastamento; **keep one's — guardar suas distâncias**; _v.t._ distanciar, afastar; **distant** _adj._ distante; longínquo, afastado.
distaste _s._ aversão, aborrecimento; **=ful** _adj._ insípido, desagradável ao gosto.
distemper _s._ destempêro, arrebatamento de gênio; doença (de cachorro); pintura à tempera; _v.t._ perturbar; tornar mal humorado; pintar à tempera.
distend _v.t._ distender, dilatar, inflar; **distension** _s._ distensão, inflação.
distich _s._ (_poe._) dístico.
distil _v.t._ distilar; **=lation** _s._ distilação; **=ler** _s._ distilador; **=lery** _s._ distilaria.
distinct _adj._ distinto; marcado, preciso; claro; **=ion** _s._ distinção; **=ive** _adj._ distintivo; **=ness** _s._ nitidez; **distinguish** _v.t._ distinguir; **distinguished** _adj._ distinto, com distinção, notável, eminente.
distort _v.t._ deformar; desfigurar, desnaturar; torcer; **=ing mirror** espêlho deformante; **=ion** _s._ distorsão, deformação.
distract _v.t._ distrair, desviar; perturbar; atormentar; tornar louco; **=ed** _adj._ perturbado, perplexo, agitado; louco, demente; **=ion** _s._ distração; perturbação, perplexidade; loucura, demência.
distrain _v.t.&i._ apoderar-se, penhorar; embargar; sequestrar; **=able** _adj._ penhorável, sequestrável; **distraint** _s._ penhora; embargo; execução, tomada de bens.
distress _s._ aflição, angústia, embaraço, apuro; miséria; (_dir._) embargo, seques-

tro; _v.t._ afligir, desolar, angustiar; **=ing** _adj._ angustiante, aflitivo.
distribute _v.t._ distribuir, repartir; **distribution** _s._ distribuição.
district _s._ distrito; região; comarca.
distrust _s._ desconfiança, receio, suspeita; _v.t.&i._ desconfiar, suspeitar, receiar.
disturb _v.t._ perturbar; incomodar; atrapalhar; inquietar; **=ance** _s._ perturbação; incômodo; atrapalhação; barulho, alvorôço, tumulto.
disunion _s._ desunião; **disunite** _v.t._ desunir.
disuse _s._ desuso; **dessuetude**; **=d** _adj._ desacostumado.
ditch _s._ fossa, canal, vala, rêgo; trincheira.
ditto _s._ dito, idem.
ditty _s._ canção, cançoneta.
divan _s._ divã.
dive _s._ mergulho; _v.i._ mergulhar; submergir; aprofundar-se; _v.t._ penetrar.
diverge _v.i._ divergir; **=nce** _s._ divergência; **=nt** _adj._ divergente.
diverse _adj._ diverso, variado; **diversify** _v.t._ diversificar, variar; **diversion** _s._ diversão; divertimento; **diversity** _s._ diversidade, variedade; **divert** _v.t._ desviar, apartar, afastar; divertir.
Dives _s._ rico (o mau rico da parábola).
divest _v.t._ despojar.
divide _v.t._ dividir; separar; cindir; repartir; **=d skirt** saia-calça; **=nd** _s._ dividendo; **=rs** _v.t._ compasso de pontas fixas.
divine _adj._ divino; _s._ sacerdote; teólogo; _v.t._ adivinhar; **divination** _s._ divinação; **=r** _s._ adivinho, adivinhador.
diving _s._ mergulho; **— bell** sino de mergulhador; **=dress** escafandro.
divining rod vara mágica (que faz adivinhar).
divinity _s._ divindade; teologia.
divisible _adj._ divisível; **division** _s._ divisão; **divisor** _s._ divisor.
divorce _s._ divórcio; _v.t._ divorciar; _v.i._ divorciar-se.
divulge _v.t._ divulgar.
dizzy _adj._ vertiginoso; **dizziness** _s._ vertigem.
do _v.t._ fazer; executar; causar; cumprir; render, tributar; cozinhar (**to be done** estar suficientemente cozido); compor; aprender (uma lição); _v.i._ conduzir-se; passar (**the patient is doing fine** o paciente está passando bem); mover-se; obrar, operar, atuar; ser suficiente; **— away with** suprimir; **— one's best** fazer o melhor que pode; **— over** refazer; **over=** exagerar; **— reverence** render homenagem; **— up** compor, arranjar; **— with** tratar com, entender-se com; **that will —** isso serve, isso basta; **— one's hair** pentear-se; **— without** passar sem; **— off** desfazer, tirar.
docile _adj._ dócil; **docility** _s._ docilidade.
dock _s._ doca, dique, estaleiro; (_bot._) bardana; côto (de rabo de cavalo), rabicho de cavalo; _v.t._ cortar, encurtar; pôr um navio no dique.
docket _s._ minuta, sumário, extrato; rótulo; _v.t._ rotular, etiquetar.
doctor _s._ médico, doutor; _v.t._ medicamentar, tratar, receitar; _v.i._ praticar a medicina; **=ate** _s._ doutorado.
doctrinaire _s.&adj._ doutrinário; **doctrine** _s._ doutrina.
document _s._ documento; _v.t._ documentar, provar com documentos.
dodder _s._ (_bot._) cuscuta.

dodge *s.* evasiva; artifício, trapaça; *v.t.* esquivar, evitar; *v.i.* esquivar-se.

doe *s.* fêmea do veado, do antílope, da lebre, do coelho, etc.

doer *s.* fazedor; ator, agente; pessoa ativa.

doff *v.t.* tirar, despojar.

dog *s.* cão, cachorro; macho de certos quadrúpedes; (*ast.*) constelação do Grande Cão e do Pequeno Cão; — **show** exposição canina; — **tired** exhausto; — **days** canícula; **a dead** — pessoa sem importância; *v.t.* seguir os passos de alguém, estar na pista; perseguir; **ged** *adj.* pertinaz, tenaz; **doggedness** *s.* obstinação.

doggerel *s.* verso de pé quebrado.

doggy, doggie *s.* cachorrinho.

dogma *s.* dogma; **tical** *adj.* dogmático; **tize** *v.i.* dogmatizar.

doily *s.* pequenos panos de mesa que se colocam sob os pratos.

doings *s.* feitos e gestos; ações.

doldrums *s.* (*mar.*) calmarias; zona das calmarias equatoriais.

dole *s.* esmolas; distribuição de dinheiro, comida e roupas aos pobres; *v.t.* distribuir em pequenas porções; dar esmolas; **ful** *adj.* triste, melancólico.

doll *s.* boneca; **y** *s.* bonequinha.

dollar *s.* dólar.

dolphin *s.* delfim, golfinho (peixe); dourado (peixe); (*ast.*) constelação do Delfim; (*mar.*) corpo morto.

dolt *s.* basbaque, tôlo e pesadão.

domain *s.* domínio.

dome *s.* cúpula; abóbada; (*poe.*) edifício majestoso, mansão.

domestic *adj.* doméstico, caseiro; nacional, do país; — **trade** comércio interior; *s.* criado, servente; **ate** *v.t.* domesticar; **ated** *adj.* domesticado; **domesticity** *s.* domesticidade.

domicile *s.* domicílio; *v.t.* domiciliar.

dominant *adj.* dominante; **dominate** *v.t.* dominar; **domination** *s.* dominação; **domineer** *v.t.* dominar; **domineering** *adj.* dominante, tirânico.

Dominican *s.* dominicano.

dominion *s.* domínio; território; império; (*dir.*) propriedade, possessão.

domino *s.* dominó; meia mascara.

don *v.t.* vestir, revestir.

donation *s.* doação, dádiva.

done (p.p. do verbo **to do**), feito, bem cozido, bem assado.

donee *s.* donatário.

donkey *s.* asno, burro, burrico; pessoa burra.

donor *s.* doador.

doom *s.* destino, predestinação; sentença, julgamento; *v.t.* julgar, sentenciar; condenar; predestinar à ruina e à destruição; **doomsday** *s.* dia do juizo final.

door *s.* porta; **out of s** ao ar livre; **within s** dentro de casa; **keeper** porteiro.

dormant *adj.* adormecido; latente; inativo; **dormer window** mansarda; **dormitory** *s.* dormitório; — **partner** sócio comanditário.

dormouse *s.* arganaz (rato silvestre).

dory *s.* bote pescador, de fundo plano e bordos salientes.

dose *s.* dose; *v.t.* dosar.

dot *s.* ponto; salpico; *v.t.* pontilhar, marcar um ponto; salpicar; **ted line** linha pontilhada.

dotage *s.* senilidade, segunda infância; carinho excessivo; **dote** *v.i.* caducar; **dotard** *s.* caduco.

double *adj.* duplo; duas vezes; ambíguo; enganoso; — **chin** papada; — **bed** cama de casal; — **dealing** duplicidade; *s.* dôbro; duplo; duplicata; dobra, prega; sósia; *adv.* duplo, dois juntos, em par; *v.t.* dobrar, redobrar; duplicar; **doubly** *adv.* duplamente, aos pares.

doubt *v.t.&i.* duvidar; *s.* dúvida; **ful** *adj.* duvidoso; **less** *adj.* seguro, confiado; *adv.* indubitàvelmente, sem dúvida.

douceur *s.* gratificação, gorjeta; peita, subôrno.

dough *s.* massa de farinha, pasta, massa; (*gíria*) dinheiro.

doughty *adj.* valente, bravo; — **deeds** proezas, altos feitos.

dour *adj.* frio, severo, pouco demonstrativo; inflexível.

douse *v.t.* extinguir, apagar; imergir; mergulhar; (*mar.*) recolher; arriar; (*pop.*) suprimir; afastar.

dove *s.* pombo; — **cot** pombal.

dowager *s.* viúva que goza dos títulos e da fortuna do marido; (*pop.*) senhora de idade e de posição.

dowdy *adj.* desalinhado, mal tratado, mal mal vestido, desleixado, sujo.

dowel *s.* tarugo.

dower *s.* dote; doação; parte que cabe à viúva na distribuição de bens; dom natural, talento.

down *adv.* em baixo, abaixo; baixo; para baixo; no chão, por terra; *adj.* abatido; descendente; *prep.* em baixo, de baixo, abaixo; *v.t.* abater, derrubar; vencer; **fall** queda, ruina; **hearted** desanimado, abatido; **pour** enxurrada, dilúvio; **stairs** em baixo; **stream** rio abaixo.

down *s.* duna; penugem; pêlos; pubescência.

dowry *s.* dote; parte que cabe à viúva na distribuição de bens; dom natural, talento.

doyley *s.* guardanapo de sobremesa; pequeno pano de renda ou bordado que serve como ornamento.

doze *v.i.* cochilar; *s.* sono ligeiro; torpor; **to have a** — tirar uma soneca.

dozen *s.* dúzia.

drab *s.* mulher desleixada, vagabunda, prostituta; côr de um castanho amarelado sem brilho; *adj.* monótono; fôsco.

drachm *s.* dracma (medida).

draff *s.* refugo; desperdício; fezes.

draft, draught *s.* corrente de ar; sucção, aspiração; trago, bebida; projeto, anteprojeto; plano; esbôço, esquema; borrador, minuta; proposta de lei; (*com.*) letra de câmbio, saque; (*mil.*) conscrição, leva, destacamento; (*mar.*) calado, tração; (*plural*) jôgo de damas; *v.t.* fazer um borrador, uma minuta; redigir, escrever; delinear, esboçar; (*mil.*) convocar; **board** taboleiro de damas; comissão de conscrição.

drag *s.* (*mar.*) draga; gancho; charrua de agricultura; carruagem alta e pesada; coisa que retarda o movimento ou a ação; *v.t.* arrastar, puxar; dragar; *v.i.* avançar penosamente ou lentamente, ir se arrastando.

draggle *v t.&i.* arrastar.

dragoman *s.* drogomano (intérprete das legações e consulados no Oriente).

dragon s. dragão; **=fly** libélula.
dragoon s. (mil.) dragão; v.t. acossar, intimidar; submeter por processos violentos.
drain v.t. drenar, escoar, escorrer; esgotar, secar; (fig.) empobrecer; s. dreno, escoadouro; **=age** s. drenagem, escoamento.
drake s. pato.
dram s. dracma; trago; pequena porção.
drama s. drama; **=tic** adj. dramático; **=tize** v.t. dramatizar.
drape v.t. drapejar; **=r** s. fabricante de tecidos; **=ry** s. tapessaria; fabricação de tecidos para ornamento, tais como cortinas, colgaduras, etc.
drastic adj. drástico.
draw s. tração, sucção; atração; loteria; empate; v.t. puxar, arrastar; atrair; sugar, chupar, aspirar; inspirar, respirar; tirar (um prêmio); abrir ou cerrar as cortinas; desenhar; traçar; descrever; esticar; (mar.) calar; v.i. atrair gente, arrastar-se; encolher-se; adeantar-se, mover-se; sacar da espada; (com.) sacar; **— back** recuar; **— down** fazer descer.
drawbridge s. ponte levadiça.
drawer s. gaveta; sacador (de letra de câmbio); extrator; **=s** s. ceroulas.
drawing s. desenho; extração; sorteio; esbôço, esquema.
drawl v.i. arrastar as palavras, pronunciar com dificuldade.
drawn butter môlho de manteiga.
drawn battle batalha indecisa.
dray s. carreta, carrocinha, caminhão pequeno; **— man** carroceiro, carreteiro.
dread adj. terrível, tremendo, espantoso, pavoroso; s. terror, medo; fobia, pavor; v.t.&i. temer, ter medo, recear; **=ful** adj. terrível, medonho, espantoso, tremendo.
dream s. sonho; v.t.&i. sonhar; **=er** s. sonhador.
drear adj. triste, melancólico, pesaroso; **=iness** s. tristeza, pesar, aborrecimento.
dredge s. draga; v.t. dragar, escavar.
dregs s. bôrra, sedimentos, detritos, sujeira, lia.
drench v.t. embeber, ensopar; saturar; dar água ou bebida; s. bebida, trago; purgante; **— rain** enxurrada, dilúvio.
dress s. vestido, roupa, indumentária, traje; v.t. vestir, ataviar, adornar, enfeitar, engalanar; tratar de feridas e ferimentos; pôr a mesa; temperar saladas; pentear o cabelo com apuro; amortalhar; preparar alguma cousa para uso; (mil.) alinhar; **— up** vestir-se com apuro; **— shirt** camisa de smoking; **— rehearsal** ensaio geral; **— clothes** trajes de etiqueta; **=ing** s. traje, roupa, vestuário; têmpero de salada; curativo de chagas e ferimentos com ataduras ou aparelhos; **=er** s. aparador, armário de cozinha; **hair dresser**, cabeleireiro.
dribble s. gota; v.i. gotejar, babar; driblar (futebol).
dried adj. sêco; **drier** s. secativo.
drift s. direção; rumo, tendência; impulso, impulsão; objetos levados pela correnteza, restos de naufrágio; montes formados pelo vento ou pelo mar, como dunas, bancos de areia, etc.; (mar.) desvio de rota causado por correntes; v.t.&i. flutuar, boiar, ser levado pela correnteza; amontoar (o vento).
drill s. perfurador, pua, broca; semeador mecânico; sulcos abertos pelo semeador;

exercício militar; exercício mental ou físico feito com regularidade e disciplina; brim; espécie de mono africano; v.t. perfurar; exercitar; v.i. fazer exercício; **=ing** s. perfuração; exercício.
drily adv. sêcamente, friamente.
drink s. bebida, trago; beberagem; v.t. beber; v.i. beber; embebedar-se; **=ing water** água potável.
drip s. gota, goteira; v.i. gotejar, pingar; **=ping** s. gordura de assado; goteira.
drive s. passeio, avenida, rua larga, estrada; passeio de carro ou automóvel; iniciativa; urgência, pressão; condução (de automóvel); mecanismo de direção ou de transmissão; (com.) saldo, liquidação; v.t.&i. conduzir, dirigir; impelir, dar impulso; compelir, forçar; empurrar, arrastar; (mec.) atuar, mover; **— at** visar (a); **— back** repelir; **— from** expulsar; **— in** ou **into** fazer entrar, arrombar.
driver s. motorista, maquinista, cocheiro, pessoa que conduz; **driving** s. condução; comando, transmissão; adj. motor, motriz; impulsor.
drizzle s. chuvisco, garoa; v.i. chuviscar.
droll adj. cômico, engraçado, estranho, jocoso; **=ery** s. comicidade, jocosidade, palhaçada; **=y** adv. cômicamente, de maneira engraçada.
dromedary s. dromedário.
drone s. zangão; parasita (pessoa); zumbido; sussurro; v.t.&i. sussurrar; falar monòtonamente.
droop v.t.&i. inclinar, inclinar-se; cair; pender; descair; decair; desanimar; consumir-se; baixar; s. inclinação, descaimento; **=ing** adj. pendente; **=ing lashes** pestanas caídas; **=ing forces** fôrças esgotadas.
drop s. gota; queda; baixa; pastilha; pingente; v.t.&i. pingar, gotejar; soltar, deixar cair; abandonar, desprender-se de; renunciar (a); desistir de; baixar; descer; cair; parir (animais); mandar (uma carta); **=per** conta-gotas; **to — a courtesy** fazer uma cortesia; **— a hint** dar uma indireta, dar uma indicação.
dropsical adj. hidrópico; **dropsy** s. hidropisia.
dross s. escória; espuma; bôrra; sedimento; impurezas.
drought s. sêca; aridez; secura.
drove s. manada; rebanho; turba; **=r** s. condutor de gado, tropeiro.
drown v.t. afogar; v.i. afogar-se; **=ing** s. afogamento.
drowsiness s. sonolência, entorpecimento, modorra; **drowsy** adj. sonolento, entorpecido, letárgico; **drowse** v.t.&i. adormecer, estar sonolento; entorpecer.
drub v.t. sovar; bater, açoitar; **=bing** s. pancada, surra, tunda.
drudge v.i. trabalhar demasiadamente, com afã; fatigar-se; s. trabalhador infatigável; **=ry** s. trabalho penoso.
drug s. droga, narcótico; medicamento; v.t. narcotizar.
drugget s. burel; droguete.
druggist s. farmacêutico, droguista.
drum s. tambor; (mec.) cilindro; tímpano do ouvido; v.i. tamborilar, tocar tambor.
drunk adj. bêbado, embriagado; **=ard** s. beberrão, ébrio; **=enness** s. bebedeira, embriaguez.
dry adj. sêco, árido, sequioso; estéril; dessecado; v.t.&i. secar, dessecar.

dryad s. dríade.
dryer s. secativo; **dryness** s. secura, aridez.
dual adj. dual; **-ity** s. dualidade.
dub v.t. armar o cavaleiro; apelidar, alcunhar.
dubious adj. dúbio.
ducal adj. ducal; **duchess** s. duquesa; **duchy** s. ducado.
duck s. pato; marreco; mergulho; reverência; brim; (pop.) esquiva; v.t.&i. mergulhar, dar um mergulho; fazer reverência; evitar um golpe com a cabeça; **-ling** s. patinho, marrequinho.
duct s. canal, via, tubo, conduto.
ductile adj. dúctil, maleável, flexível.
dudgeon s. mau humor; ressentimento.
due adj. devido; próprio, adequado, conveniente, oportuno; (com.) vencido; adv. diretamente; s. dívida; imposto; direitos.
duel s. duelo; **-list** s. duelista.
duenna s. aia, ama, dama de companhia, governante.
duet s. dueto.
duffer s. imbecil, pateta; pexote (em jôgo).
dug s. têta, ubre.
duke s. duque; **-dom** s. ducado.
dulcet adj. doce, suave, harmonioso.
dulcimer s. saltério, marimba.
dull adj. embotado, obtuso; apagado; lerdo; insípido; fastidioso, aborrecido; pesado; opaco, obscuro, fôsco; lento (de percepção); v.t. embotar; entorpecer, obstruir; amortecer; deslustrar; **-ard** s. pesadão; **-ness** s. falta de ponta ou fio; estupidez; falta de brilho; sonolência.
duly adv. devidamente; regularmente; bem.
dumb adj. mudo; (pop.) estúpido, pouco inteligente.
dumbfound v.t. confundir, deixar mudo de espanto.
dumbness s. mutismo, mudez.
dummy adj. suposto, falso, imitado; s. (pop.) testa de ferro; (mil.) simulacro; o morto (no jôgo de bridge).
dump s. tristeza, melancolia; depósito de lixo; v.t. esvasiar, descarregar; (com.) inundar o mercado com artigos a baixo preço; **to be in the -s** estar melancólico.
dun s. credor importuno; côr parda ou castanha escura; v.t. cobrar com insistência, importunar um devedor.
dunce s. ignorante, tolo, lerdo.

dunderhead s. imbecil, estúpido, cabeça dura.
dune s. duna.
dung s. estêrco, estrume, bosta; v.t. estrumar, estercar, adubar.
dunnage s. (mar.) lastro.
duodecimal adj. duodecimal; duodécimo; s. duodécimo.
dupe s. vítima (de engano e lôgro), logrado; **-ry** s. lôgro, tratantada.
duplicate adj. duplo, duplicado; s. dôbro, duplicata; ampliação; v.t. duplicar; copiar, reproduzir.
duplicity s. duplicidade.
durable adj. durável; **duration** s. duração.
duress s. prisão, aprisionamento; compulsão, coação.
during prep. durante.
dusk s. crepúsculo; v.t.&i. escurecer; **-y** adj. obscuro; fôsco; moreno.
dust s. poeira, pó; restos mortais, cinzas; (fig.) abjeção, humilhação; v.t. empoeirar; empoar; espanar, limpar o pó; **-er** s. espanador, aparelho de limpar o pó; **-y** adj. empoeirado.
Dutch adj. holandês, da Holanda; s. holandês.
dutiable adj. sujeito a direitos, passível de direitos alfandegários.
duty s. dever; obrigação; impostos; direitos alfandegários; (agric.) quantidade de água necessária à irrigação de determinada área; **dutiful, duteous** adj. cumpridor dos deveres; obediente, submisso.
dwarf s.&adj. anão; v.t. impedir o desenvolvimento de; definhar, não medrar.
dwell v.i. habitar, morar, residir; permanecer; deter-se, demorar-se; **-er** s. habitante, residente; **-ing** s. habitação, residência, vivenda.
dwindle v.i. definhar; diminuir; minguar; reduzir-se; **dwindling** s. definhamento.
dye s. tintura; v.t. tingir; **-ing** s. tinturaria; tintura; adj. colorante; **-r** s. tintureiro.
dying adj. moribundo, agonisante.
dyke V. dike.
dynamic adj. dinâmico; **-s** s. dinâmica.
dynamite s. dinamite.
dynamo s. dínamo.
dynasty s. dinastia.
dysentery s. disenteria.
dyspepsia s. dispepsia.
dyspnea, dyspnoea s. dispnéia.
dysuria s. disúria.

E

E letra do alfabeto; (mús.) mi.
each adj.&pron. cada, cada um, cada uma; — **other** um ao outro, mùtuamente.
eager adj. ardente, ansioso, desejoso, veemente, impaciente; **to be — for** ambicionar; **-ly** adv. ardentemente, ansiosamente; **-ness** s. ânsia, veemência, impaciência.
eagle s. águia.
ear s. ouvido; orelha; asa (de chícara, vaso, etc); espiga; — **drum** tímpano; **-ring** s. brinco (de orelha); v.i. espigar; v.t. arar.
earl s. conde.
earliness s. precocidade, antecipação; presteza.

early adj. precoce, prematuro; adiantado; primeiro; primitivo; matinal; adv. cedo; — **fruits**, — **flowers** primícias.
earn v.t. ganhar; merecer.
earth s. terra, solo; a Terra; v.t. enterrar, cobrir com terra; **-y** adj. terrento, terroso; terreno; **-ly** adj. terreno, terrestre.
earthquake s. terremoto.
ease s. comodidade; sossêgo; repouso; facilidade; naturalidade; v.t. aliviar, mitigar, suavizar; facilitar; desembaraçar; desafogar.
easel s. cavalete de pintor.
easily adv. fàcilmente, cômodamente; suavemente.

east *s.* este, leste, oriente, levante; *adj.* oriental, do este.

Easter *s.* Páscoa.

easy *adj.* fácil, cômodo, folgado; acomodado;|complacente,condescendente;simples, natural; —going person pessoa de gênio fácil; — labor parto feliz.

eat *v.t.&i.* comer; corroer, consumir; =able *adj.* comível; =ables *s.* comestíveis; =er *s.* comedor; — humble pie humilhar-se; — one's heart sofrer um desgôsto em silêncio.

eaves *s.* aba, beira (de telhado).

ebb *s.* maré vazante, baixamar, refluxo; decadência; *v.i.* baixar (a maré); decair.

ebonite *s.* ebonite.

ebullition *s.* ebulição.

eccentric *adj.* excêntrico; =ity *s.* excentricidade.

Ecclesiastes *s.* Eclesiastes; **ecclesiastic**, **ecclesiastical** *adj.* eclesiástico.

echo *s.* eco; *v.i.* fazer eco, ecoar.

eclectic *adj.* eclético; =ism *s.* ecletismo.

eclipse *s.* eclipse; *v.t.* eclipsar; **ecliptic** *adj.* elíptico.

economic *adj.* econômico; =al *adj.* econômico; =s *s.* economia (ciência); **economist** *s.* economista; **economize** *v.t.&i.* economizar; **economy** *s.* economia.

ecstasy *s.* êxtase; **ecstatic** *adj.* extático.

eczema *s.* eczema.

eddy *s.* remoinho, turbilhão; *v.i.* turbilhonar, remoinhar.

Eden *s.* éden, paraíso.

edge *s.* beira, bordo; gume, fio; borda (das fôlhas de um livro); ponta; aresta; *v.t.* afiar, aguçar; *v.i.* avançar de lado; **edging** *s.* orla, borda; =ed *adj.* afiado, aguçado.

edible *adj.* comível, comestível.

edict *s.* édito.

edifice *s.* edifício; **edify** *v.t.* edificar.

edit *v.t.* editar; redigir; =ion *s.* edição; =or *s.* redator; =orial *adj.* editorial.

educate *v.t.* educar; **education** *s.* educação; **educational** *adj.* educacional, educativo; **educator** *s.* educador.

educe *v.t.* eduzir, fazer sair, tirar, extrair.

eel *s.* enguia.

eerie, **eery** *adj.* fantástico, estranho, sobrenatural.

efface *v.t.* apagar, desmanchar; =able *adj.* desmanchável, delével.

effect *s.* efeito, resultado; repercussão; consequência; *v.t.* efetuar; operar; executar, realizar; =ive *adj.* efetivo, útil; =iveness *s.* eficácia.

effectual *adj.* eficaz.

effeminacy *s.* efeminação; **effeminate** *adj.* efeminado.

effervescence *s.* efervescência; **effervescent** *adj.* efervescente; **effervesce** *v.i.* efervescer.

effete *adj.* esgotado, impotente, estéril, infrutífero, usado, gasto.

efficacious *adj.* eficaz.

efficiency *s.* eficiência; **efficient** *adj.* eficiente, eficaz.

effigy *s.* efígie.

efflorescence *s.* eflorescência; **efflorescent** *adj.* eflorescente.

effluence *s.* emanação, eflúvio; **effluent** *adj.* efluente.

effluvium *s.* eflúvio, efluência.

efflux *s.* efusão, emanação; fluxo, derrame.

effort *s.* esfôrço.

effrontery *s.* desfaçatez, impudência.

effulgence *s.* esplendor, fulgor, resplandescência; **effulgent** *adj.* resplandescente, fulgurante.

effusion *s.* efusão, expansão; **effusive** *adj.* efusivo, expansivo; **effusiveness** *s.* efusão.

eft *s.* lagartixa.

egg *s.* ovo; — shell casca de ovo; — on *v.t.* incitar, provocar; =plant beringela.

eglantine *s.* rosa brava.

ego *s.* ego, eu; =ism *s.* egoismo; =ist *s.* egoista; =istical *adj.* egoista; =tist *s.* egotista.

egregious *adj.* egrégio; que se torna notável por más qualidades; odioso, notòriamente mau.

egress *s.* saída.

egret *s.* pena, penacho, pluma.

eh *int.* hein! que! ah!

eider, **eider duck** *s.* eider, ganso do Norte; **eider down** *s.* edredão.

eight *adj.&s.* oito; =een *adj.&s.* dezoito; =eenth *adj.* décimo oitavo; =h *adj.* oitavo; =y *adj.&s.* oitenta; =ieth *adj.* octogésimo.

either *adj.&pron.* um ou outro; qualquer dos dois; qualquer um; *conj.* ou.

ejaculate *v.t.* ejacular, lançar; **ejaculation** *s.* ejaculação; interjeição, exclamação.

eject *v.t.* lançar, arremessar; expulsar; expelir; =ion *s.* expulsão; evacuação.

eke out *v.t.* suprir; aumentar pouco a pouco.

elaborate *adj.* elaborado, trabalhado; *v.t.* elaborar.

elapse *v.i.* decorrer, transcorrer, passar.

elastic *adj.* elástico; *s.* elástico, borracha; =ity *s.* elasticidade.

elate *v.t.* ensoberbecer, exaltar; =d *adj.* soberbo, desvanecido; **elation** *s.* soberba, exaltação.

elbow *s.* cotovêlo; *v.t.* acotovelar.

elder *adj.* mais velho; *s.* ancião; senhor; antepassado; dignitário; sabugueiro.

elect *v.t.* eleger; escolher; *adj.* eleito; escolhido, predestinado; *s.* eleito, escolhido; =ion *s.* eleição; =ioneer *v.i.* fazer campanha eleitoral; =or *s.* eleitor; =ive *adj.* eletivo.

electric *adj.* elétrico; =al *adj.* elétrico; =ally *adv.* elètricamente; =ian *s.* eletricista; =ity *s.* eletricidade; **electrify** *v.t.* eletrificar; **electrize** *v.t.* eletrizar; **electrocute** *v.t.* eletrocutar; **electrode** *s.* eletródio; **electrolysis** *s.* eletrólise.

elegance *s.* elegância; **elegant** *adj.* elegante; **elegantly** *adv.* elegantemente.

elegy *s.* elegia.

element *s.* elemento; fator; meio ambiente; esfera de ação; célula ou unidade morfológica; (*elet.*) elemento, par; (*quím.*) corpo simples; =s *s.* elementos, noções; agentes naturais; os quatro elementos (fogo, agua, terra e ar); =ary *adj.* elementar, primário.

elephant *s.* elefante.

elevate *v.t.* elevar; alçar; animar, exaltar; **elevation** *s.* elevação; altitude; **elevator** *s.* elevador.

eleven *adj.&s.* onze; =th *adj.* undécimo, décimo primeiro.

elf *s.* elfo, duende, gnomo.

elicit *v.t.* induzir, deduzir; fazer sair.

elide *v.t.* elidir, eliminar.

eligible *adj.* elegível; **elegibility** *s.* elegibilidade.

eliminate *v.t.* eliminar; **elimination** *s.* eliminação.

elision s. elisão.
elixir s. elixir.
elk s. alce (espécie de veado).
ellipse, ellipsis s. elipse; **elliptic, elliptical** adj. elíptico.
elm s. olmo (árvore); — **grove** olmedal, olmedo.
elocution s. elocução; declamação.
elongate v.t. alongar.
elope v.i. fugir com o namorado ou amante; escapar-se, evadir-se; **ment** s. fuga.
eloquence s. eloquência; **eloquent** adj. eloquente; **eloquently** adv. eloquentemente.
else adv. mais, além de; em vez de; de outra forma; de outro modo; pron.& adj. outro; conj. do contrário; **where** adv. em qualquer outra parte; noutra parte; de outra parte; **nothing** — nada mais; **nobody** —, **no one** — nenhum outro, ninguém mais.
elucidate v.t. elucidar, esclarecer, explicar.
elude v.t. eludir, evadir, esquivar; **elusive** adj. evasivo, esquivo.
emaciate v.t.&i. emaciar, emagrecer; extenuar; definhar; **d** adj. emaciado, emagrecido, enfraquecido.
emanate v.i. emanar; **emanation** s. emanação; **emanant** adj. emanante.
emancipate v.t. emancipar, libertar; **emancipation** s. emancipação.
emasculate v.t. emascular, castrar, capar; adj. efeminado; castrado.
embalm v.t. embalsamar.
embank v.t. represar; aterrar; deter; **ment** s. dique, represa, cais; atêrro.
embargo s. embargo.
embark v.t. embarcar; **ation** s. embarcação, embarque.
embarrass v.t. embaraçar; **ment** s. embaraço.
embassy s. embaixada.
embattle v.t. fortificar; dispor para batalha; **d** adj. alinhado, em ordem de batalha.
embed v.t. encaixar, incrustar.
embellish v.t. embelezar.
ember s. brasa; **Ember days** têmporas (dias de jejum); **s** s.pl. cinzas.
embezzle v.t. desfalcar, desviar; v.i. apropriar-se indevidamente; **ment** s. desfalque, peculato; **r** s. peculatário; indivíduo que se apropria indevidamente de bens que lhe foram confiados.
embitter v.t. tornar amargo; envenenar (moralmente).
emblazon v.t. brasonar; ornar com côres brilhantes.
emblem s. emblema; **atic, atical** adj. emblemático.
embodiment s. incorporação; personificação; incarnação; **embody** v.t. incorporar; incarnar; personificar.
embolden v.t. animar, dar coragem.
embolism s. (med.) embolia; (ast.) embolismo, intercalação.
emboss v.t. trabalhar em relêvo, gravar em relêvo; realçar; cravar; estampar.
embrace s. abraço; v.t. abraçar; abarcar, rodear, cingir, compreender; admitir; receber, adotar, aceitar; **ment** s. abraço.
embrasure s. vão (de janela); seteira.
embrocation s. embrocação; **embrocate** v.t. embrocar, fomentar.
embroider v.t. bordar; **er** s. bordador, bordadeira; **y** s. bordado.

embroil v.t. enredar, confundir.
embryo s. embrião; **nic** adj. embrionário.
emend v.t. emendar, corrigir; **ation** s. emenda, correção.
emerald s. esmeralda.
emerge v.i. emergir; brotar; **nce** s. emergência.
emergency s. urgência; ocorrência; emergência; — **brake** freio de emergência; — **exit** saída de emergência.
emeritus adj. emérito.
emery s. esmeril; **wheel** roda de esmeril.
emetic adj.&s. emético.
emigrant s. emigrante; **emigrate** v.i. emigrar; **emigration** s. emigração.
eminence s. eminência; **His Eminence** Sua Eminência; **eminent** adj. eminente; notável; considerável.
emir s. emir.
emissary s, emissário; **emission** s. emissão; **emit** v.t. emitir.
emollient adj.&s. emoliente.
emolument s. emolumento.
emotion s. emoção; **al** adj. emotivo.
empanel V. **impanel.**
emperor s. imperador.
emphasis s. ênfase; **emphasize** v.t. pôr ênfase, acentuar, realçar; **emphatic** adj. enfático.
empire s. império.
empiric, empirical adj. empírico; **empiricism** s. empirismo; **empiricist** s. empírico.
employ v.t. empregar; servir-se de; **ee** s. empregado; **er** s. patrão, empregador; **ment** s. emprêgo; **ment agency** agência de empregos.
emporium s. empório, entreposto.
empower v.t. investir de poder, autorizar.
empress s. imperatriz.
empty adj. vazio, vácuo; vão, inútil; v.t. esvaziar, desocupar, descarregar, evacuar; **emptiness** s. vacuidade, vácuo, vazio; nulidade; — **handed** de mãos vazias; — **headed** cabeça ôca.
empurple v.t. empurpurar, dar a côr de púrpura.
empyrean s.&adj. empíreo.
emulate v.t. emular; rivalizar; competir; **emulation** s. emulação, rivalidade; **emulator** s. êmulo.
emulsion s. emulsão.
enable v.t. habilitar, capacitar, tornar apto.
enact v.t. decretar; **ment** s. decreto.
enamel s. esmalte; v.t. esmaltar, laquear; **ed** adj. esmaltado, laqueado.
enamored, enamoured adj. enamorado.
encage v.t. engaiolar, enjaular.
encamp v.t.&i. acampar; **ment** s. acampamento.
encase v.t. encaixotar, encaixar; revestir, envolver.
encaustic adj. (pint.) encáustico; s. encáustica.
enchain v.t. acorrentar; encadear, algemar; prender.
enchant v.t. encantar; **er** s. encantador, sedutor; **ress** s. encantadora, sedutora; **ing** adj. encantador; **ment** s. encantamento.
encircle v.t. cercar, rodear.
enclave s. território encaixado em terras estrangeiras.
enclose v.t. cercar, cingir, fechar; conter, encerrar, incluir; **d** adj. cercado; incluso; **enclosure** s. cercado; cêrca; recinto; (com.) anexos (de uma carta).

encomium *s.* encômio.
encompass *v.t.* cercar, circundar, rodear, encerrar; abarcar.
encore *s.&int.* bis; *v.t.* bisar.
encounter *s.* encontro; *v.t.* encontrar.
encourage *v.t.* encorajar, animar.
encroach *v.t.* invadir; tomar gradualmente; traspassar; usurpar; passar os limites; *v.i.* imiscuir-se; ＝ment *s.* intrusão, abuso; invasão.
encumber *v.t.* atravancar; amontoar; estorvar; sobrecarregar; **encumbrance** *s.* atravancamento, estôrvo; carga.
encyclic, encyclical *s.* encíclica.
encyclopedia, encyclopaedia *s.* enciclopédia.
end *s.* fim; finalidade; termo; extremidade; cabo; final; *v.t.&i.* finalizar, acabar, findar, terminar, cessar; — to — ponta com ponta; **to make an** — of acabar com; **to make both** ＝s **meet** passar com o que se tem; **at loose** ＝s em desordem; **to the** — that afim de, para que.
end-all conclusão definitiva, ponto final.
endanger *v.t.* pôr em perigo, arriscar, comprometer.
endear *v.t.* tornar caro, fazer amar; ＝ment *s.* carícia, carinho.
endeavor, endeavour *s.* esfôrço, tentativa; *v.i.* esforçar-se por; *v.t.* intentar.
ending *s.* fim, conclusão; terminação, desenlace; (*gram.*) terminação, desinência.
endive *s.* endívia.
endless *adj.* sem fim; infinito; interminável; ＝ly *adv.* infinitamente, perpètuamente, sem fim.
endorse *v.t.* endossar; ＝ment *s.* endôsso; ＝r *s.* endossante.
endow *v.t.* dotar; doar; ＝ment *s.* dote, doação.
endue *v.t.* dotar; revestir, vestir.
endurable *adj.* suportável; **endurance** *s.* resistência, capacidade de sofrimento; **endure** *v.t.* suportar, aguentar, sofrer, resistir.
endwise *adv.* de pé, direito.
enema *s.* lavagem (de intestinos); aparelho irrigador.
enemy *s.&adj.* inimigo.
energetic *adj.* enérgico; ＝s *s.* energética (ciência); **energize** *v.t.* excitar ou dar energia; **energy** *s.* energia, vigor.
enervate *v.t.* enervar; enfraquecer, debilitar.
enfeeble *v.t.* enfraquecer.
enfilade *s.* (*mil.*) fogo de uma tropa ao longo de trincheira, linha, etc.; fogo de enfiada; *v.t.* varrer a tiros.
enfold *v.t.* envolver.
enforce *v.t.* impor, fazer cumprir, observar ou executar uma lei; forçar; ＝ment *s.* execução de uma lei; observância forçada, coação.
enfranchise *v.t.* franquear, libertar; conceder direitos políticos.
engage *v.t.* ajustar, apalavrar; ocupar; comprometer; empregar; (*mil.*) entrar em luta; *v.i.* empenhar-se, obrigar-se, comprometer-se; ocupar-se; travar luta; ＝d *adj.* ocupado, empenhado, comprometido, apalavrado; noivo; ＝ment *s.* compromisso, ajuste, contrato; noivado; (*mil.*) ação, luta, combate, batalha; **engaging** *adj.* atraente, sedutor, insinuante, simpático.
engender *v.t.* engendrar.
eginne *s.* máquina, motor, locomotiva;

— **man** mecânico; ＝er *s.* engenheiro; maquinista; mecânico; *v.t.* manejar; guiar; conduzir; dirigir; ＝ering *s.* engenharia; ＝less *adj.* sem motor.
engrave *v.t.* gravar; burilar; ＝r *s.* gravador; **engraving** *s.* gravura, estampa.
engross *v.t.* copiar caligràficamente; absorver, monopolizar (artigos no mercado); assambarcar; ＝ment *s.* monopólio, assambarcamento.
engulf *v.t.* engolfar, tragar, afundar.
enhance *v.t.* melhorar, acrescentar, aumentar o valor; alçar, realçar.
enigma *s.* enigma; ＝tic, ＝tical *adj.* enigmático.
enjoin *v.t.* prescrever, ordenar, fazer injunções.
enjoy *v.t.* gozar de, fruir; ter prazer em; saborear; — **oneself** divertir-se; ＝able *adj.* agradável; saboroso, divertido; ＝ment *s.* gôzo, prazer.
enlarge *v.t.* aumentar, dilatar, alargar, ampliar; — **upon** estender-se sôbre; ＝ment *s.* aumento, dilatação, ampliação.
enlighten *v.t.* instruir, informar, esclarecer; ＝ed *adj.* culto, ilustrado.
enlist *v.t.* alistar; (*mil.*) recrutar; *v.i.* alistar-se; sentar praça.
enliven *v.t.* animar, estimular, vivificar, alentar; alegrar.
enmity *s.* inimizade.
ennoble *v.t.* enobrecer.
enormity *s.* enormidade; **enormous** *adj.* enorme; **enormously** *adv.* enormemente; **enormousness** *s.* enormidade.
enough *adj.* bastante, suficiente; *adv.* bastante, suficientemente; *s.* o suficiente; *int.* basta!; **strange** — bastante estranho.
enquire V. inquire.
enrage *v.t.* enfurecer, encolerizar.
enrapture *v.t.* encantar, maravilhar, arrebatar, extasiar; **enrapt** *adj.* arrebatado, extasiado.
enrich *v.t.* enriquecer; ＝ment *s.* enriquecimento.
enrol, enroll *v.t.* alistar, matricular; catalogar; envolver, enrolar; *v.i.* alistar-se, matricular-se; (*mil.*) sentar praça; ＝ment *s.* alistamento; matrícula.
enroot *v.t.* arraigar; radicar.
ensconce *v.t.* acomodar, abrigar; ocultar; pôr em lugar seguro.
enshrine *v.t.* guardar como relíquia, cuidadosamente.
enshroud *v.t.* amortalhar; envolver.
ensign *s.* insígnia; bandeira; guarda-marinha.
enslave *v.t.* escravizar, avassalar.
ensnare *v.t.* apanhar no laço; enganar, embair.
ensue *v.i.* seguir-se, seguir, suceder, sobrevir; **ensuing** *adj.* seguinte, subsequente.
ensure *v.t.* assegurar.
entablature *s.* (*arq.*) entablamento.
entail *v.t.* (*dir.*) legar com cláusula a vínculo; vincular, assegurar, perpetuar; acarretar; *s.* vínculo.
entangle *v.t.* embaraçar, enredar; intricar; ＝ment *s.* embaraço, enrêdo, complicação.
enter *v.t.* entrar; penetrar; meter, introduzir; assentar, anotar, registar; ingressar; (*com.*) declarar, aduanar; *v.i.* entrar, introduzir-se, ingressar; entrar em cêna; matricular-se, afiliar-se; — **into** contratar; formar parte de.

enteric *adj.* entérico.

enterprise *s.* emprêsa; atividade, espírito empreendedor; enterprising *adj.* empreendedor.

entertain *v.t.* receber (convidados), hospedar; entreter, divertir; conceber, alimentar (idéia ou projeto); *v.i.* dar recepções e festas; =ment *s.* recebimento, hospitalidade; festa, convite, diversão; =ing *adj.* alegre, divertido; que sabe receber.

enthrall, enthral *v.t.* cativar, escravizar, subjugar; dominar moralmente.

enthrone *v.t.* entronizar; enthronization *s.* entronização.

enthusiasm *s.* entusiasmo; enthusiast *s.* entusiasta; enthusiastic *adj.* entusiástico; enthusiastically *adv.* entusiàsticamente.

entice *v.t.* atrair, seduzir, tentar; =ment *s.* tentação, sedução; enticing *adj.* sedutor, tentador.

entire *adj.* inteiro, integral; =ty *s.* inteireza, integridade.

entitle *v.t.* intitular; dar direito a.

entity *s.* entidade.

entomb *v.t.* enterrar, sepultar.

entomologist *s.* entomologista; entomology *s.* entomologia.

entr'acte *s.* entreato.

entrails *s.* entranhas.

entrain *v.t.&i.* ir ou despachar por trem.

entrance *v.t.* extasiar, fascinar, arrebatar; *s.* entrada; porta, portal; ingresso; declaração (na alfândega).

entrap *v.t.* apanhar, surpreender, apanhar no laço.

entreat *v.t.* suplicar, rogar, implorar.

entrench *v.t.&i.* entrincheirar, entricheirar-se; invadir; traspassar.

entrust *v.t.* confiar; encarregar; depositar.

entry *s.* entrada; vestíbulo, portal, pórtico, saguão; ingresso; apontamento; (*mar.*) registo, declaração de entrada; (*com.*) partida.

entwine *v.t.* entrelaçar; enlaçar, enroscar.

enumerate *v.t.* enumerar.

enunciate *v.t.* enunciar.

envelope *s.* envelope; *v.t.* envolver, cobrir.

envenom *v.t.* envenenar.

enviable *adj.* invejável; envious *adj.* invejoso; envy *v.t.* invejar; *s.* inveja.

environ *v.t.* rodear, cingir; =ment *s.* meio ambiente, ambiência.

environs *s.* arredores, cercanias, imediações.

envisage *v.t.* fazer frente a, encarar; representar-se mentalmente.

envoy *s.* enviado, mensageiro.

epaulette, epaulet *s.* dragonas.

epergne *s.* centro de mesa.

ephemeral *adj.* efêmero.

epic *adj.* épico; *s.* epopéia.

epicure *s.* epicurean *adj.* epicurista.

epidemic *s.* epidemia; =al *adj.* epidêmico.

epidermis *s.* epiderme.

epiglottis *s.* epiglote.

epigram *s.* epigrama.

epigraph *s.* epígrafe.

epilepsy *s.* epilepsia; epileptic *adj.&s.* epilético.

epilogue *s.* epílogo.

episcopal *adj.* episcopal; episcopate, episcopacy *s.* episcopado.

episode *s.* episódio.

epistle *s.* epístola; epistolary *adj.* epistolar.

epitaph *s.* epitáfio.

epithet *s.* epíteto.

epitome *s.* epítome, compêndio, resumo; epitomize *v.t.* resumir.

epoch *s.* época.

epopee *s.* epopéia.

epos *s.* poesia épica; epopéia.

equal *adj.* igual; semelhante; par; *s.* igual, semelhante; *v.t.* igualar; =ity *s.* igualdade; =ize *v.t.* igualar; equable *adj.* igual, uniforme.

equanimity *s.* equanimidade.

equation *s.* equação.

equator *s.* equador; =ial *adj.* equatorial.

equerry *s.* escudeiro.

equestrian *adj.* equestre; *s.* cavaleiro.

equilibrate *v.t.* equilibrar; equilibrium *s.* equilíbrio.

equine *adj.* hípico, equino.

equinoctial *adj.* equinocial; equinox *s.* equinócio.

equip *v.t.* equipar; aprestar; =age *s.* equipagem; =ment *s.* equipamento.

equipoise *s.* equilíbrio.

equitable *adj.* equitativo; equity *s.* equidade.

equivalent *adj.&s.* equivalente.

equivocal *adj.* equívoco; equivocate *v.i.* equivocar-se; equivocation *s.* equívoco.

era *s.* era, época.

eradicate *v.t.* desarraigar, extirpar.

erase *v.t.* raspar, desmanchar; =r *s.* apagador, borracha de raspar, raspador; erasure *s.* raspadura, rasura.

ere *conj.* antes que.

erect *adj.* ereto; direito; têso; erguido; *v.t.* erigir; construir; levantar, instalar; erguer; =ion *s.* ereção; construção, instalação, montagem.

ermine *s.* arminho; pele de arminho; toga, magistratura.

erode *v.t.* corroer, roer; comer; *v.i.* desgastar-se; =nt *s.&adj.* corrosivo, erosivo; erosion *s.* erosão.

erotic *adj.* erótico.

err *v.i.* errar; pecar; transviar-se.

errand *s.* recado, mandado, diligência; — boy menino de recados, de mandados.

errant *adj.* errante, vagabundo; =ry *s.* vida errante.

erratic *adj.* errático; intermitente; irregular.

erratum *s.* errata; erroneous *adj.* errôneo, falso; error *s.* erro.

eructation *s.* eructação.

erudite *adj.* erudito; erudition *s.* erudição.

eruption *s.* erupção.

erysipelas *s.* erisipela.

escalator *s.* escada movente.

escallop *s.* espécie de marisco.

escapade *s.* escapada; aventura; fuga.

escape *s.* fuga, evasão; escapamento (de gás ou líquido); *v.i.* fugir, escapar-se, escapar; *v.t.* escapar de; =ment *s.* fuga; escapamento.

escarpment *s.* escarpa.

escheat *s.* (*dir.*) reversão dos bens à Coroa ou ao Estado por falta de herdeiros; *v.i.* reverter ao Estado (bens); *v.t.* confiscar (bens).

eschew *v.t.* evitar, fugir.

escort *s.* escolta; cavalheiro; *v.t.* escoltar, acompanhar.

escutcheon *s.* escudo de armas; guarnição; espêlho (de fechadura).

espalier *s.* latada (horticultura).

esparto *s.* (*bot.*) esparto.

especial *adj.* especial; **-ly** *adv.* especialmente.
espionage *s.* espionagem.
esplanade *s.* esplanada.
espousal *s.* esponsais; adesão (a uma causa); *v.t.* desposar; abraçar (uma causa).
espy *v.t.* divisar, descobrir, avistar ao longe.
esquire *s.* escudeiro; **Esquire**, **Esq.** título de cortezia que se usa depois do sobrenome de pessoa do sexo masculino sem título nobiliárquico; título correspondente a *Dom*.
essay *s.* ensaio, composição, dissertação; *v.t.* ensaiar, provar, tentar, experimentar.
essence *s.* essência; **essential** *adj.* essencial; primordial; *s.* essencial.
establish *v.t.* estabelecer, fundar; **-ment** *s.* estabelecimento; creação; fundação; estabelecimento.
estate *s.* bens, propriedade, domínio, patrimônio, possessões; — **duty** imposto de sucessão.
esteem *s.* estima; *v.t.* estimar.
estimate *s.* estimação, avaliação, apreciação; opinião; *v.t.* avaliar, estimar, cálcular aproximadamente; **estimation** *s.* cálculo aproximado, avaliação.
estop *v.t.* (*dir.*) excluir.
estrange *v.t.* apartar, afastar, distanciar; alienar.
estuary *s.* estuário.
etch *v.t.* gravar com água forte.
eternal *adj.* eterno; **-ize** *v.t.* eternizar; **eternity** *s.* eternidade.
ether *s.* éter; **-eal** *adj.* etéreo.
ethical *adj.* ético; **ethics** *s.* ética.
ethnography *s.* etnografia; **ethnographical** *adj.* etnográfico.
ethnology *s.* etnologia; **ethnological** *adj.* etnológico; **etnologist** *s.* etnologista.
ethyl *s.* (*quím.*) etilo.
etiolate *v.t.* estiolar, murchar.
etiquette *s.* etiqueta.
etymology *s.* etimologia; **etymological** *adj.* etimológico.
eucalyptus *s.* eucalipto.
Eucharist *s.* Eucaristia.
eugenic *adj.* eugênico; **-s** *s.* eugenia.
eulogistic *adj.* elogioso; **eulogize** *v.t.* elogiar; **eulogy** *s.* elogio.
eunuch *s.* eunuco.
euphemism *s.* eufemismo; **euphemistic** *adj.* eufemístico.
euphonic *adj.* eufônico; **euphonio** *adj.* eufônico; **euphony** *s.* eufonia.
Europe *s.* Europa; **-an** *s.* europeu; *adj.* europeu.
evacuate *v.t.* evacuar.
evade *v.t.* evadir, evitar, esquivar.
evanescent *adj.* evanescente.
evangelic, evangelical *adj.* evangélico; **evangelist** *s.* evangelista.
evaporate *v.t.* evaporar; *v.i.* evaporar-se; **evaporation** *s.* evaporação.
evasion *s.* evasão, evasiva, subterfúgio, escapatória; **evasive** *adj.* evasivo.
eve *s.* vigília, véspera; **on the —** of na véspera de.
even *adj.* plano; igual, regular; uniforme; par (número); exato, preciso; situado no mesmo nível; *adv.* mesmo, até; precisamente; inteiramente; ainda; *v.t.&i.* igualar, aplainar; tornar quites; **of —** **date** da mesma data.
evening *s.* tarde; primeiras horas da noite; vésperas; — **gown** traje de noite.

evenly *adv.* uniformemente, igualmente; **evenness** *s.* uniformidade, igualdade.
event *s.* acontecimento, evento; êxito; **-ful** *adj.* cheio de acontecimentos, movimentado; importante.
eventual *adj.* eventual, fortuito; **-ity** *s.* eventualidade; **eventuate** *v.i.* acontecer, suceder.
ever *adv.* sempre, jamais; **for ever para** sempre; — **since** desde então.
evergreen *s.* árvore sempre verde (em geral pinheiros).
everlasting *adj.* eterno, imortal.
evermore *adv.* sempre, eternamente; **for** — para todo o sempre.
every *adj.* cada; todo, todos; — **day** todos os dias; — **once in a while** de vez em quando; — **one** cada um, cada qual; — **other day** um dia sim e outro não.
everybody *s.* todos; todo o mundo; cada um, cada qual.
everyone *s.* todo o mundo; todos.
everything *s.* tudo.
everywhere *adv.* em toda a parte, em todo lugar.
evict *v.t.* (*dir.*) despejar, expulsar; reentrar em posse legalmente; **-ion** *s.* despejo; evicção.
evidence *s.* evidência, prova, testemunho; deposição, declaração; **to produce** — apresentar prova; *v.t.* evidenciar, patentear, provar; **evident** *adj.* evidente; **evidently** *adv.* evidentemente.
evil *adj.* mau, maligno, perverso; — **days** desgraça; — **disposed person** pessoa mal intencionada; **-doer** malfeitor; — **eye** mau olhado; **the Evil One** o diabo, o demônio; — **speaking** maledicência *adv.* mal, malignamente; *s.* mal, maldade, perversidade.
evince *v.t.* manifestar, testemunhar; revelar.
eviscerate *v.t.* destripar, desentranhar.
evocation *s.* evocação; **evoke** *v.t.* evocar.
evolution *s.* evolução; desenvolvimento; sequência; **evolve** *v.t.* produzir por evolução; desprender (gases); *v.i.* evoluir.
ewe *s.* ovelha.
ewer *s.* jarro.
exacerbate *v.t.* exacerbar.
exact *adj.* exato, preciso; *v.t.* exigir, impor; **-ing** *adj.* exigente; **-ion** *s.* exação; **-ly** *adv.* exatamente, precisamente, **-ness**, **-itude** *s.* exatidão.
exaggerate *v.t.* exagerar.
exalt *v.t.* exaltar.
examination *s.* exame; inspeção; reconhecimento; prova; **examine** *v.t.* examinar; **examinee** *s.* examinando, candidato; **examiner** *s.* examinador; inspetor.
example *s.* exemplo.
exasperate *v.t.* exasperar, enervar.
excavate *v.t.* escavar, cavar; **excavation** *s.* escavação; **excavator** *s.* escavador; máquina escavadora.
exceed *v.t.* exceder, ultrapassar; *v.i.* exceler; **-ingly** *adv.* excessivamente, extremamente.
excel *v.i.* primar, superar, sobrepujar; *v.t.* ser superior a; **-lence** *s.* excelência; **-lent** *adj.* excelente; **-lently** *adv.* maravilhosamente, excelentemente.
except *prep.* exceto, salvo; *conj.* a não ser que; **-ing** *prep.* exceto, com exceção de, salvo; **-ion** *s.* exceção; **-ionable** *adj.* passível de exceção; **-ional** *adj.* excepcional.

excerpt s. excerto, extrato, resumo; v.t. extrair.

excess s. excesso; excedente; **-ive** adj. excessivo, imoderado.

exchange s. câmbio; troca; permuta; v.t. cambiar, trocar, permutar.

exchequer s. tesouro, tesouraria; fundos; Court of Exchequer Ministério da Fazenda.

excise s. imposto (de consumo, vendas, profissões, etc.).

excite v.t. excitar, provocar; irritar; **-ment** s. excitação; exaltação.

exclaim v.i. exclamar, gritar; exclamation s. exclamação.

exclude v.t. excluir; exclusion s. exclusão; exclusive adj. exclusivo.

excommunicate v.t. excomungar.

excrement s. excremento.

excrescence s. excrescência.

excruciating adj. excruciante, pungente.

exculpate v.t. desculpar.

excursion s. excursão.

excuse s. desculpa, escusa; v.t. desculpar; perdoar; isentar, dispensar; — me desculpe-me.

execrable adj. execrável; execrate v.t. execrar.

execute v.t. executar; efetuar; (dir.) legalizar um documento; executar (sentença capital); execution s. execução; legalização de documento; execução (da pena de morte); executioner s. executor; carrasco.

executive s.&adj. executivo.

executor s. executor; testamenteiro; **-y** adj. executório.

exemplary adj. exemplar, modelar; exemplify v.t. ilustrar com exemplos, exemplificar; servir de exemplo.

exempt ad . isento; v.t. isentar; **-ion** s. isenção.

exercise s. exercício; dever; tema; exercício corporal; v.t.&i. exercer; exercitar; fazer exercício ou ginástica; vexar.

exergue s. exergo.

exert v.t. exercer; **-ion** s. esfôrço.

exfoliate v.i. esfoliar-se.

exhalation s. exalação; exhale v.t. exalar.

exhaust v.t. exhaurir, esgotar; s. escapamento; (fís.) vácuo, sucção; **-ion** s. esgotamento; aspiração; **-ive** adj. exhaustivo; profundo, apurado, completo; **-ively** adv. exhaustivamente; a fundo; cabalmente, completamente.

exhibit s. objeto ou instalação de objetos expostos ao público; manifestação; (dir.) documento apresentado como prova; v.t. expor; exibir; **-ion** s. exposição; exibição; bolsa concedida a estudantes na Inglaterra; **-ioner** s. estudante detentor de bolsa na Inglaterra.

exhilarate v.t. alegrar, regozijar.

exhort v.t. exortar.

exhume v.t. exumar.

exigence, exigency s. exigência.

exile s. exílio; exilado; v.t. exilar.

exist v.i. existir; **-ence** s. existência.

exit s. saída; partida.

exodus s. êxodo, saída, emigração; Êxodo (livro bíblico).

exonerate v.t. exonerar.

exorbitance s. exorbitância; exorbitant adj. exorbitante; exorbitantly adv. exorbitantemente.

exorcise v.t. exorcizar.

exotic adj. exótico; s. coisa exótica.

expand v.t. expandir, desenvolver, dilatar; expanse s. extensão, espaço; expansion s. expansão; dilatação; expansive adj. expansivo.

expatiate v.i. estender-se, alargar-se.

expatriate v.t. expatriar; v.i. expatriar-se; s.&adj. exilado.

expect v.t. esperar, aguardar; contar com; (pop.) supor; **-ance**, **-ancy** s. expectativa; **-ant** adj. expectante; **-ation** s. expectativa, esperança.

expectorate v.t. expectorar.

expedience, expediency s. conveniência, utilidade, comodidade; propriedade; expedient adj. expediente, oportuno, conveniente; s. expediente, recurso, meio; expedite v.t. expedir, despachar; acelerar, apressar; expedition s. expedição; expeditionary s. expedicionário; expeditiously adv. expeditamente, prontamente.

expel v.t. expulsar, expelir.

expend v.t. gastar, despender; **-iture** s. despesa; expense s. gasto, custo; desembolso; detrimento; expensive adj. caro, custoso, dispendioso; at any expense a todo custo; at the expenses of à custa de; expenseless adj. pouco ou nada custoso.

experience s. experiência, prática; v.t. experimentar; sentir, sofrer; experiment s. experiência, experimentação; v.i. fazer experiência; **experimental** adj. experimental.

expert s. perito; **-ness** s. perícia.

expiate v.t. expiar.

expiration s. expiração, termo; expire v.t. expirar; v.i. expirar, terminar; vencer-se.

explain v.t. explicar; **-able** adj. explicável; explanation s. explicação; explanatory adj. explicativo, explanatório.

expletive adj. expletivo; s. partícula expletiva; exclamação.

explicit adj. explícito, claro.

explode v.i. explodir; rebentar; v.t. fazer explodir, rebentar ou saltar.

exploit s. proeza, façanha; v.t. explorar; **-ation** s. exploração.

explore v.t. explorar, averiguar, examinar, sondar; **-r** s. explorador.

explosion s. explosão; explosive s. explosivo.

exponent s. intérprete (de música ou teorias); (mat.) expoente.

export v.t. exportar; s. exportação; **-ation** s. exportação; **-er** s. exportador.

expose v.t. expor; mostrar, descobrir; pôr em perigo; publicar, divulgar; comprometer; exposition s. exposição.

expostulate v.i. censurar; fazer observações a; expostulation s. admoestação, censura.

exposure s. exposição ao ar, à água ou à intempérie; exposição (fotografia).

expound v.t. expor, explicar.

express adj. expresso, formal; s. expresso; v.t. exprimir, manifestar, expressar; **-ion** s. expressão; **-ive** adj. expressivo; **-ly** adv. expressamente.

expropriate v.t. desapropriar.

expulsion s. expulsão.

expunge v.t. riscar, desmanchar, apagar, cancelar.

expurgate v.t. expurgar.

exquisite adj. refinado, perfeito, raro; intenso, excessivo, agudo; s. pessoa elegante, bem vestida; — pleasure prazer vivo; — pain dôr aguda.

extempore *adj.* improvisado; *adv.* de improviso, de repente; **extemporize** *v.t.&i.* improvisar.

extend *v.t.* estender; prolongar; **extension** *s.* extensão; prolongamento; **extensive** *adj.* extenso, largo; **extensively** *adv.* extensamente; **extensor** *s.* extensor; **extent** *s.* extensão; alcance; grau, ponto, medida.

extenuate *v.t.* atenuar, minorar.

exterior *adj.* exterior, externo; *s.* exterior.

exterminate *v.t.* exterminar.

external *adj.* externo, exterior; **·ly** *adv.* exteriormente, externamente.

extinct *adj.* extinto; **·ion** *s.* extinção; **extinguish** *v.t.* extinguir; **extinguisher** *s.* extintor.

extirpate *v.t.* extirpar.

extol *v.t.* exaltar, enaltecer.

extort *v.t.* extorquir; **·ion** *s.* extorção; **·ionary** *adj.* extorcionário, extorsivo.

extra *adj.* suplementar; *s.* extra, suplemento; *adv.* extra.

extract *s.* extrato, resumo; *v.t.* extrair; retirar; **·ion** *s.* extração.

extradite *v.t.* extraditar; **extradition** *s.* extradição.

extraneous *adj.* estranho.

extraordinary *adj.&s.* extraordinário.

extravagance *s.* extravagância; **extravagant** *adj.* extravagante; **extravagantly** *adv.* extravagantemente.

extreme *adj.&s.* extremo; **extremist** *s.* extremista; **extremity** *s.* extremidade.

extricate *v.t.* desembaraçar, desenredar, deslindar; tirar de dificuldades.

extrinsic *adj.* extrínseco.

exuberance *s.* exuberância; **exuberant** *adj.* exuberante.

exude *v.i.&t.* exsudar, transpirar.

exult *v.i.* exultar; triunfar.

eye *s.* ôlho; visão; vista; ôlho (da agulha, do queijo, etc.); *v.t.* olhar; observar; **·witness** testemunha de vista; **·sight** vista; **·lash** cílios; **·lid** pálpebra; **·brow** sobrancelha; **·brow tweezers** pinça de arrancar sobrancelhas; **·glasses** óculos; — **doctor** médico oculista.

eyry *s.* ninho de ave de rapina.

F

F letra do alfabeto; (*mús.*) **fá**.

fable *s.* fábula; **·d** *adj.* fabuloso.

fabric *s.* tecido, pano, tela, fabricação, manufatura; estrutura, construção; **·ant** *s.* fabricante; **fabricate** *v.t.* fabricar, manufaturar; **·ation** *s.* fabricação, obra; ficção, fantasmagoria, mentira; **·ator** *s.* fabricador; embusteiro; — **gloves** luvas de tecido.

fabulist *s.* fabulista; **fabulous** *adj.* fabuloso.

façade *s.* fachada.

face *s.* face, rosto, cara; careta; face (de um cristal); superfície; fachada; frente; direito (das roupas); aspecto; superfície ou lado principal das cousas; (*com.*) valor nominal; **·ache** nevralgia facial; — **lifting** circurgia plástica do rosto; **to** — encarar, estar de frente; — **value** valor nominal; *v.t.* encarar; fazer face a; afrontar; encarar uma possibilidade; forrar, cobrir, revestir; **·d with silk** forrado de seda.

facet *s.* facêta; *v.t.* facetar.

facetious *adj.* chistoso, alegre.

facial *adj.* facial; — **angle** ângulo facial.

facile *adj.* fácil; **facilitate** *v.t.* facilitar; **facility** *s.* facilidade.

facing *s.* paramento; revestimento; adôrno; **·s** *s.* paramentos militares.

facsimile *s.* facsímile.

fact *s.* fato; realidade.

faction *s.* fação; bando; dissenção; **factious** *adj.* facioso, sedicioso.

factitious *adj.* fatício, artificial.

factor *s.* fator, elemento; agente comissionado; (*mat.*) fator, coeficiente.

factory *s.* fábrica, usina, manufatura; — **hand** operário de fábrica.

factotum *s.* fac-totum.

faculty *s.* faculdade, aptidão, talento; faculdade (escola); corpo docente (de estabelecimento universitário); conjunto de membros de uma profissão liberal; classe, corporação.

fad *s.* novidade, moda, mania (qualquer cousa que por algum tempo fica exageradamente na moda).

fade *v.i.* murchar, definhar, decair; esvair-se; empalidecer, descolorar-se; — **away** desmaiar; — **out** desaparecer.

fag *v.t.* estafar; *v.i.* estafar-se; *s.* (*pop.*) cigarro.

fagot *s.* feixe de lenha; *v.t.* enfeixar (lenha).

fail *v.t.&i.* falhar, faltar; fracassar; desvanecer, decair; necessitar; declinar; falir; **·ing** *s.* falta, deslise, fraqueza; **·ure** *s.* fracasso, fiasco, insucesso; falência, bancarrota; **without** — sem falta; — **in one's duty** faltar a seu dever; **·ure of issue** inexistência de descendentes.

fain *adj.* disposto, contente; resignado, conformado; *adv.* de bom grado, de preferência.

faint *adj.* fraco, lânguido, abatido, débil, desfalecido; indistinto, tênue; *v.i.* desmaiar, desfalecer; desvanecer-se; **·ing** *s.* desmaio, desfalecimento; **·hearted** medroso, pusilânime; **·ing fit** desmaio, síncope; **·ly** *adv.* desmaiadamente, dèbilmente, indistintamente.

fair *adj.* belo, bonito; claro, louro; leal, justo, reto, imparcial, honrado, franco; regular, médio, passável; distinto, legível; — **copy** cópia nítida, clara; — **weather** bom tempo; — **hair** cabelo louro; — **skin** pele clara; — **play** jôgo leal, honesto; proceder leal; — **sex** belo sexo; — **weather friend** amigo na prosperidade; — **trade** comércio legítimo; — **minded** imparcial, justo; **·ly** *adv.* lealmente; a justo título; suficientemente, medianamente; **·ness** *s.* beleza; tez clara; equidade, lealdade, honestidade.

fairy *s.* fada; — **tales** contos de fada.

faith *s.* fé; confiança; crença; fidelidade, lealdade; **·ful** *adj.* fiel, leal; **·fulness** *s.* fidelidade, lealdade; **·less** *adj.* sem fé, infiel; **·lessness** *s.* infidelidade, deslealdade, perfídia.

fake *s.* fraude; imitação; (*mar.*) volta (de cabo); *v.t.* fraudar, burlar; enrolar (corda em voltas).

fakir *s.* faquir.

falcon s. falcão (ave); falcão (peça de artilh.); =**er** s. falcoeiro; =**ry** s. falcoaria.

fall s. queda, caída, descida; lapso, deslise; degradação; ruína; queda, rendição militar ou naval; queda das folhas; queda de água, catarata, cachoeira; outono; tombo; queda de conduta; queda de temperatura; desembocadura de um rio; baixa ou diminuição (de preços); v.i. cair, descer, baixar; abaixar-se; saltar; abaixar; minguar, decrescer, diminuir; render-se; entregar-se; — **down** cair no chão; — **in love** enamorar-se, apaixonar-se; — **through** fracassar; — **under** cair debaixo, cair sob.

fallacious adj. falaz, enganador, ilusório; **fallacy** s. falácia; sofisma.

fallibility s. falibilidade; **fallible** adj. falível.

falling star estrela cadente.

fallow adj. fulvo; selvagem, silvestre, inculto; s. alqueive; v.t. alqueivar.

false adj. falso; fingido, pérfido; (mús.) desafinado; =**ly** adv. falsamente; pèrfidamente; — **claim** pretensão infundada; — **door** porta simulada; — **faced** hipócrita, falso; — **teeth** dentes postiços.

falsehood s. falsidade.

falsetto s. falsete.

falsify v.t. falsificar, adulterar; **falsity** s. falsidade.

falter v.i. vacilar, tremer; hesitar; balbuciar, tartamudear.

fame s. fama, renome; =**d** adj. afamado, célebre.

familiar adj.&s. familiar; =**ity** s. familiaridade; =**ize** v.t. familiarizar.

family s. família; — **life** vida de família; — **man** pai de família; — **tree** árvore genealógica.

famine s. fome, carestia; **famish** v.t. esfomear.

famous adj. famoso, célebre, afamado.

fan s. leque, ventarola; ventilador; (pop.) aficionado; v.t. abanar; ventilar; soprar.

fanatic s.&adj. fanático; =**al** adj. fanático; **fanaticism** s. fanatismo; **fanaticize** v.t. fanatizar.

fancied adj. imaginário; **fancier** s. grande amador de; **fanciful** adj. de fantasia, fantástico; **fancy** s. fantasia; capricho; idéia; gôsto, inclinação, afeição; v.t. imaginar, figurar; **fancy dress** fantasia (roupa); **fancy dog** cão de luxo.

fang s. presa, dente; raiz de dente; garra, unha.

fantasia s. fantasia; **fantastic** adj. fantástico; **fantasy** s. visão; fantasia.

far adv. longe, ao longe; muito; bem; **from** — de longe; adj. distante, afastado; the — **East** o Extremo Oriente; **as** — **as** the eye can reach até onde a vista pode alcançar.

farce s. farsa, burla; (coz.) recheio; **farcical** adj. burlesco, cômico.

fare s. preço de passagem ou de transporte; passageiro; v.i. viajar, ir; passar (bem ou mal).

farewell s. adeus.

farina s. fécula, amido; **farinaceous** adj. farinhento, farinhoso; **farinose** adj. farináceo.

farm s. fazenda, exploração agrícola, granja; v.t. cultivar; arrendar, alugar; administrar (uma fazenda); =**er** s. fazendeiro.

faro s. campista (jôgo de cartas).

farrago s. mistura, farragem.

farrier s. ferrador.

farrow s. ninhada de porcos; v.i. parir (a porca).

farther adv. mais longe; mais adiante; além, demais; — **on** adv. adiante; mais adiante; mais tarde; **farthest** adj. o mais distante; adv. o mais longe.

farthing s. moeda inglesa equivalente a um quarto de peni.

fasces s. fasces.

fascinate v.t. fascinar; **fascinating** adj. fascinante; **fascination** s. fascinação.

fascine s. faxina (feixe de ramos).

fascism s. fascismo; **fascist** s. fascista.

fashion s. moda, estilo; elegância, bom tom; forma, figura, feitio; v.t. formar, amoldar, dar forma; adaptar, acomodar; idear, inventar; — **book** figurino; =**able** adj. elegante; na moda; =**ably** adv. elegantemente, na moda.

fast adj. ligeiro, rápido; firme, seguro, forte; fixo, estável, imóvel; apertado; indelével, duradouro; veloz; adeantado (relógio); pródigo, dissoluto; adv. depressa, ràpidamente; fortemente, firmemente; estreitamente, apertadamente; profundamente; para sempre; s. jejum; v.i. jejuar; — **asleep** profundamente adormecido; — **color** côr firme; — **friend** amigo seguro; — **knot** nó apertado; **to hold** — segurar firmemente; — **day** dia de jejum.

fasten v.t. fixar, segurar, firmar; pegar; atar, amarrar; unir; v.i. fixar-se; agarrar-se, pegar-se; — **a door** fechar uma porta; — **one's eye** on cravar os olhos em; =**er** s. pregador.

fastidious adj. melindroso; difícil de contentar; dengoso; delicado.

fat adj. gordo; obeso; fértil (terra); s. banha, gordura; toucinho; manteiga; sebo; **to live on the** — **of the land** viver na fartura.

fatal adj. fatal, funesto; =**ism** s. fatalismo; =**ist** s. fatalista; =**ity** s. fatalidade.

fate s. fado, destino, sorte, fatalidade; **to be** =**d** to ser fadado a; =**ful** adj. fatal.

father s. pai; =**hood** s. paternidade; =**less** adj. órfão de pai; =**ly** adv. paternalmente; adj. paternal, de pai; v.t. procrear; ser autor de; tratar como filho; **to father on** ou **upon** imputar a, atribuir a; =**land** pátria; =**in-law** sogro; **step**=— padrasto.

fathom s. toesa (medida); v.t. sondar; aprofundar; penetrar, examinar a fundo; =**less** adj. insondável.

fatigue s. fadiga; (mec.) perda de resistência por esfôrço contínuo; (mil.) faxina (serviço); v.t. fatigar; v.i. fatigar-se.

fatness s. gordura, obesidade; **fatten** v.t. engordar; **fattish** adj. gordo; **fatty** adj. gordo, adiposo; gorduroso.

fatuity s. fatuidade; **fatuous** adj. fátuo.

fauces s. fauce, garganta.

fault s. falta, culpa; defeito; êrro; (geol.) falha; =**less** adj. sem defeitos; sem erros; sem culpa; irrepreensível; =**y** adj. culpado, defeituoso; **to find** — **with** culpar, achar defeito em, censurar.

faun s. fauno.

fauna s. fauna.

favor, favour s. favor, graça, fineza; v.t. favorecer; distinguir, fazer um favor a; parecer-se com; =**able** adj. favorável; =**ite** s. favorito; =**itism** s. favoritismo; **the child** =**s his father** a criança parece-se com o pai.

fawn s. veado novo; fulvo (côr); v.i. bajular, adular; fazer festa.

fear s. medo, temor; v.t.&i. temer, ter medo; **-ful** adj. de meter medo; horrendo; medroso; **-less** adj. sem medo, intrépido; **-lessness** s. intrepidez.

feasibility s. praticabilidade, possibilidade; **feasible** adj. possível, praticável, exequível.

feast s. festa, festim; v.t. festejar, banquetear, regalar.

feat s. feito, proeza; ação; valentia.

feather s. pena; plumagem gênero, espécie; v.t. emplumar, cobrir ou adornar com plumas; v.i. cobrir-se de plumas; **-brained person** pessoa avoada; **weight** pêso pluma (box).

feature s. traços, feições; caraterístico.

February s. fevereiro.

fecund adj. fecundo; **-ate** v.t. fecundar; **-ity** s. fecundidade.

federal adj. federal; **federate** v.t. federar; **federation** s. federação.

fee s. salário, honorário; direitos; retribuição, gratificação, propina; mensalidades de clubes, escolas, etc.

feeble adj. fraco, débil.

feed v.t. alimentar, nutrir; manter; v.i. comer; alimentar-se; s. comida, alimentação; forragem; **pipe, pump, valve** etc., (sid.) tubo, bomba, válvula, etc., de alimentação; **-ing bottle** mamadeira.

feel v.t. sentir; tocar; tomar (o pulso); examinar; v.i. sentir-se, estar, produzir a sensação de; **-er** s. aquele que toca ou apalpa; antena, tentáculo; **-ing** s. tato; sensação; sentimento, emoção; ternura, compaixão; adj. sensível, terno; **-ingly** adv. com emoção; **to — cold** sentir frio; **the room -s warm** o quarto está quente; **to — hungry** estar com fome; **I — like crying** tenho vontade de chorar; **to — sorry for somebody** ter pena de alguém.

feign v.t. fingir, simular; **feint** s. fingimento, dissimulação, artifício; treta; v.i. fazer fita; fingir; fazer um ataque falso.

felicitous adj. feliz, apropriado; oportuno; **felicity** s. felicidade.

feline adj.&s. felino.

fell s. sobrecostura, remate do tecido; pele, couro; adj. cruel, feroz; v.t. derrubar, abater, cortar; sobrecoser.

felloe s. aro (de roda).

fellow s. companheiro, camarada; igual; rapaz, indivíduo, sujeito; **— boarder** comensal; **— citizen** concidadão; **— feeling** compaixão, simpatia, identidade de interesses; **— man** semelhante, próximo; **— member** colega; **— student** colega de colégio; **— traveller** companheiro de viagem; **-ship** s. sociedade, camaradagem, companheirismo; bolsa concedida pelas universidades a certos estudantes.

felo-de-se s. (dir.) suicida.

felon s. criminoso; réu de crime capital; **-ious** adj. criminoso; **-y** s. crime, felonia.

felspar s. feldspato.

felt s. feltro; v.t. cobrir com feltro; fazer fel

female adj. fêmea; s. fêmea; mulher; a **— writer** uma escritora; **— suffrage** sufrágio feminino; a **— dog** uma cachorra.

feminine adj.&s. feminino; **feminism** s. feminismo; **feminist** adj.&s. feminista; **feminize** v.t. feminizar.

femur s. fêmur.

fen s. pântano.

fence s. cêrca, muro; esgrima; (pop.) comprador de artigos roubados; v.t. cercar, murar; v.t.&i. esgrimir; discutir.

fencing s. esgrima; material para construir cêrcas; **fencer** s. esgrimista; cavalo ágil em saltar cêrcas.

fend v.t. aparar, rechassar, resistir; v.i. agir na defensiva; **-er** s. pára-choque (de locomotiva, bonde, etc.); pára-lama (de automóvel).

ferment s. fermento; fermentação, efervescência; v.i. fermentar; **-ation** s. fermentação.

fern s. (bot.) feto.

ferocious adj. feroz; **ferocity** s. ferocidade.

ferret s. furão (animal); v.t. indagar, esquadrinhar.

ferrous adj. ferroso.

ferruginous adj. ferruginoso.

ferrule s. virola; biqueira (de beagala, guarda-chuva, etc.).

ferry s. barca; embarcadouro; v.t.&i. transportar ou atravessar de barca de uma margem a outra; **— boat** barca de passageiros; balsa.

fertile adj. fértil, fecundo; **fertility** s. fertilidade, fecundidade; **fertilize** v.t. fertilizar; **fertilizer** s. adubo.

fervent adj. fervente, ardente; **-ly** adv. ardentemente; **fervor** s. fervor, ardor.

fester v.i. apostemar, supurar, ulcerar-se; s. pústula, fístula, tumor.

festival s. festa, festival; **festive** adj. festivo; **festivity** s. festividade.

festoon s. festão, recorte; v.t. festonar, recortar em festões.

fetch v.t. ir buscar; trazer; alcançar.

fête s. festa, quermesse; v.t. festejar.

fetid adj. fétido; **-ness** s. fetidez.

fetish, fetich s. fetiche, ídolo; **-ism** s. fetichismo.

fetter s. cadeia, corrente; v.t. acorrentar, prender, entravar.

fettle s. estado, forma; **in fine — em boas** condições, em forma.

feud s. guerra, vendeta; feudo; **-al** adj. feudal; **-alism** s. feudalismo.

fever s. febre; **-ish** adj. febril.

few adj.&pron. poucos, poucas; **a —** alguns, algumas; **-er** adj.&pron. menos.

fez s. fêz.

fiasco s. fiasco.

fiat s. decreto, sanção.

fib s. mentira inocente, pêta, lorota; v.i. contar lorotas, mentir sôbre coisas triviais.

fibre s. fibra; **fibril** s. fibrila; **fibrous** adj. fibroso.

fibula s. (anat.) perôneo, peroneu.

fickle adj. volúvel, inconstante; **-ness** s. volubilidade, inconstância.

fiction s. ficção; **fictitious** adj. fictício; **fictive** adj. imaginário.

fiddle s. violino; **— bow** arco de violino; v.i. tocar violino; (pop.) mexer nervosamente com os dedos e as mãos.

fiduciary adj. fiduciário.

fie int. puxa! irra!

fief s. feudo.

field s. campo; campina; campo cultivado; campo de batalha; campo de esportes; **— artillery** artilharia de campanha; **— day** manobras; **— magnet** indutor.

fiend s. demônio; **-ish** adj. diabólico.

fierce adj. feroz, bárbaro, cruel; **-ly** adv. ferozmente; **-ness** s. ferocidade.

fiery adj. de fogo, ardente, fogoso.

fife s. pífano.

fifteen s.&adj. quinze; **fifteenth** adj.&s. décimo quinto; quinze (do mês); **fifth** s.&adj. quinto; cinco (do mês); **fiftieth** s.&adj. quinquagésimo; **fifty** adj.&s. cincoenta; **fifty-fifty** metade e metade.

fig s. figo; — **leaf** folha de figueira; — **tree** figueira.

fight s. luta, combate, batalha; v.i.&t. bater-se, lutar, batalhar, combater; **-er** s. lutador, combatente; **-ing plane** avião de combate.

figment s. ficção, invenção.

figurative adj. figurativo; — **sense** sentido figurado; **-ly** adv. figuradamente; **figure** s. figura; porte, talhe; algarismo; dado numérico; v.t.&i. figurar, delinear, imaginar; calcular, fazer cálculos; **figure of speech** figura de retórica.

filament s. filamento; (bot.) filete.

filbert s. avelã.

filch v.t. escamotar, empalmar; roubar, furtar.

file s. fila; arquivo; classificador; lista para promoção; lima (ferramenta); v.t. arquivar, classificar; registrar, anotar, assentar; limar; v.i. marchar em fila.

filial adj. filial; **filiation** s. filiação.

filibuster s. filibusteiro.

filigrane s. filigrana.

filing s. classificação; arquivamento.

fill s. fartura, abundância; v.t. encher; satisfazer; saciar; suprir; ocupar; terraplenar; obturar; **a king -s a throne** um rei ocupa um trono; **to — a tooth** obturar um dente.

fillet s. filete; tira, **faixa** estreita; filé de carne ou peixe.

filling s. enchimento; recheio; obturação (de dente).

fillip s. piparote; v.i. dar piparotes; v.t. estimular.

filly s. potranca.

film s. película, fita, filme; névoa; v.t. filmar; v.i. enevoar-se, tornar-se obscuro; **-y** adj. enevoado, nublado.

filter s. filtro; v.t.&i. filtrar.

filth s. imundície, sujeira, porcaria; **-ness** s. imundície; **-y** adj. imundo, sujo, porco, asqueroso; **-ily** adv. porcamente.

fin s. barbatana.

final adj. final; **-ity** s. finalidade.

finance s. finança, finanças; tesouraria; v.t. financiar, manejar fundos; dirigir operações financeiras; **financial** adj. financeiro; **financier** s. financista.

finch s. pintassilgo.

find v.t. achar, encontrar; descobrir; ver; procurar; fornecer; s. achado, descoberta; coisa achada; — **out** descobrir, averiguar, verificar; **-er** s. descobridor, inventor; **-ings** s. apetrechos e ferramentas de um ofício; (dir.) laudo, resultado de inquérito; veredito, ou decisão de tribunal.

fine adj. belo, bom, magnífico, excelente, admirável; fino; agradável; s. multa; v.t. multar; refinar (vinho, etc.); **-ly** adv. lindamente, agradàvelmente; **-ness** s. delicadeza; primor; agudeza, sutileza; título (de liga metálica); — **arts** belas artes; — **looking** bonito, bem parecido.

finery s. gala, adôrno, atavios.

finesse s. artifício; astúcia; tato, diplomacia; v.i. valer-se de artifícios e subterfúgios.

finger s. dedo; v.t. tocar, palpar; **-print** impressão digital; **-ing** s. (mús.) dedilhado.

finical adj. melindroso, maneiroso, afetado.

finish v.t.&i. acabar, terminar; polir, aperfeiçoar; acabar-se; acabar com; finalizar; s. fim, terminação; acabamento, polimento; revestimento; **finis** s. fim.

finite adj. finito.

Finland s. Finlândia; **Finnish** s.&adj. finlandês; **Finn** s. finlandês (indivíduo).

fir s. pinho.

fire s. fogo; incêndio; tiro; v.t. incendiar, queimar; disparar; despedir; v.i. incendiar-se, inflamar-se; — **arms** armas de fogo; — **alarm** sinal de incêndio; — **escape** escada de incêndio; — **extinguisher** extintor de incêndio; — **insurance** seguro contra incêndio; **-man** bombeiro; **-proof** à prova de fogo.

firm adj. firme; sólido; consistente; s. firma, sociedade (comercial).

firmament s. firmamento.

firmness s. firmeza.

first adj. primeiro; adv. primeiramente; **-ly** adv. primeiramente, primo; — **of all** antes de tudo; — **rate** de primeira ordem, o melhor; — **-born** primogênito; — **edition** edição original.

firth s. braço de rio, estuário, esteiro.

fiscal adj. fiscal.

fish s. peixe; pescado; (pop.) pessoa pouco firme; lorpa; v.t. pescar; procurar obter por artifício; — **bone** espinha de peixe; **-hook** anzol; **-plate** tala de junção; **-ing** pesca, pescaria; **-ing bait** isca.

fissure s. fissura, fenda; v.t. fender.

fist s. punho; **-icuff** s. sôco.

fistula s. fístula.

fit adj. próprio, apto, conveniente, apropriado, a propósito, adequado; hábil, capaz; disposto, em boa forma; s. ataque, acesso, crise; paixão, capricho; arrebate; arrancos; v.t.&i. ajustar, adaptar, amoldar, encaixar, acomodar, conformar; surtir, prover, equipar, aprestar; dispor, preparar; — **of coughing** acesso de tosse; **to keep** — manter-se em forma; **to see** — julgar conveniente; **to — out** equipar; **out** — equipamento, indumentária; **to — up** ajustar, acomodar; **to — into** encaixar.

fitness s. conveniência, oportunidade, aptidão; **fitter** s. ajustador, montador, provedor; **fitting** adj. próprio, adequado, conveniente; s. ajuste; encaixe; **fittings** guarnições; accessórios.

five adj.&s. cinco; **-year plan** plano quinquenal.

fix s. impasse, apuro, apêrto; v.t. fixar, assegurar, firmar; pôr em ordem, arranjar, endireitar, reparar, compor; (fot.) fixar; (pop.) castigar, desforrar, ajustar contas; **-ing** s. fixação; **-ture** s. coisa fixa ou encravada em algum ponto; adôrno, móveis ou trastes fixos no solo, na parede ou no teto.

fizz v.i. chiar; s. som sibilante; bebida efervescente.

flabbergast v.t. pasmar.

flabbiness s. flacidez; **flabby** adj. flácido.

flaccidity s. flacidez; **flaccid** adj. flácido.

flag s. bandeira, pavilhão, estandarte; laje; penas da parte inferior da perna de certas aves; penas secundárias das asas dos pássaros; v.t.&i. guarnecer de bandeiras; fazer sinais com a bandeira; içar a bandeira; cair, pender; enfraquecer; declinar; desanimar; vacilar; lajear.

flagellate *v.t.* flagelar.
flageolet *s.* flauta pequena.
flagitious *adj.* infame, celerado, facínora.
flagon *s.* frasco.
flagrant *adj.* flagrante.
flail *s.* mangual.
flake *s.* floco; escama, lâmina; faisca; *v.t.&i.* fazer flocos; lascar; **flaky** *adj.* flocoso, escamoso; laminado, folheado.
flame *s.* flama; fogo; chama; *v.i.* chamejar, inflamar; inflamar-se.
flamingo *s.* flamengo, guará (ave).
flank *s.* flanco; *v.t.* atacar de flanco; flanquear.
flannel *s.* flanela.
flap *s.* ponta; fralda, aba, borda, beirada; golpe; *v.t.&i.* golpear ràpidamente; bater (asas); — **ears** orelhas caídas.
flare *s.* chama, flama; fulgor; arrebatamento (de cólera); *v.i.* chamejar, fulgurar; inclinar-se para a parte de fóra (bordos de embarcações).
flash *adj.* barulhento, espalhafatoso; *s.* jato; clarão; relâmpago; resplendor; jato de agua; jíria de ladrões; *v.i.* relampejar; brilhar; resplender; — **in the pan** (*fig.*) fogo de palha.
flask *s.* frasco; garrafa; vidro (de remédio).
flat *adj.* chato, raso; plano; extendido; formal, categórico; liso, unido; insípido; sem graça; monótono; aborrecido; inativo; fôsco; (*mús.*) abemolado; *s.* superfície plana; planície; *v.t.* aplainar, achatar; — **tire** pneumático vazio.
flatter *v.t.* lisonjear, adular; **-er** *s.* lisonjeador; **-ing** *adj.* lisonjeiro; **-y** *s.* lisonja.
flatulence *s.* flatulência; **flatus** *s.* flato, gás.
flaunt *v.t.* ostentar; *v.i.* fazer alarde.
flautist *s.* flautista.
flavor *s.* sabor, gôsto; *v.t.* temperar; **-ing** *s.* tempêro, condimento.
flaw *s.* falha, defeito, imperfeição; falha em papéis legais capaz de torná-los nulos; *v.t.* falhar; *v.i.* tornar-se defeituoso; **-less** *adj.* sem falhas, perfeito.
flax *s.* linho (planta e fibra).
flay *v.t.* esfolar.
flea *s.* pulga; **-bite** mordedura de pulga; dôr insignificante.
fledged *adj.* empenado, cheio de penas.
flee *v.i.* fugir.
fleece *s.* velo, lã de carneiro; *v.t.* tosar, tosquiar; (*fig.*) despojar.
fleet *s.* frota; armada; *adj.* veloz, rápido; *v.i.* flutuar, navegar, nadar; **-ing** *adj.* passageiro, fugaz.
flesh *s.* carne; polpa (da fruta); *v.t.* alimentar (com carne); engordar; saciar; descarnar; — **day** dia gordo; **-ly** *adj.* carnal; sensual; **-y** *adj.* carnudo, gordo.
flexible *adj.* flexível; **flexor** *s.* músculo flexor.
flick *s.* golpe rápido; *v.t.* dar uma vassourada rápida; sacudir, limpar com uma pancada rápida.
flicker *v.i.* adejar, bater as asas; tremer; vacilar (a luz); flutuar; — **mouse** morcego.
flight *s.* vôo; fuga; bando; lanço (de escada); *v.i.* tomar vôo, abalar; emigrar (aves); **-y** *adj.* volátil; inconstante.
flimsy *adj.* sem consistência, frívolo; débil.
flinch *v.i.* recuar, vacilar, acovardar-se; **without -ing** sem vacilação.
fling *s.* arremêsso, tiro; sarcasmo, indireta; salto, brincadeira; coice; farra, folia;

v.t. arremessar, jogar (fora); derrubar; atirar (ao chão); vencer; **to — about** derramar, aspergir; **to — in one's face** lançar em rosto; **to — open** abrir de repente.
flint *s.* sílex; pederneira; **-y** *adj.* silicioso; duro, empedernido.
flippant *adj.* leviano, irreverente, loquaz; **flippancy** *s.* leviandade, irreverência, loquacidade.
flirt *s.* flêrte, namôro; *v.t.* flertar, namorar.
flit *v.i.* voltejar; deslisar; passar rápido; **to — away** desaparecer.
flitch *s.* manta de toucinho; — **beam** (*const.*) viga armada.
float *s.* flutuador, boia de pescador; jangada; salvavidas; *v.i.* flutuar, boiar; deslisar sobre a agua; ser instável; *v.t.* fazer flutuar.
flock *s.* rebanho, manada; grei; multidão (de fiéis); floco de lã; *v.i.* juntar-se, congregar-se; afluir; — **paper** papel aveludado.
floe *s.* massa de gelo flutuante.
flog *v.t.* fustigar, chicotear; **-ing** açoitamento, flagelação.
flood *s.* inundação; dilúvio; transbordamento; enchente; torrente (de lágrimas); menstruação excessiva; (*mar.*) fluxo; *v.t.* inundar.
floor *s.* assoalho, chão, solo; andar, pavimento; recinto (assembléia) *v.t.* assoalhar; pôr no chão; derrubar; vencer, reduzir ao silêncio; **ground** — andar térreo.
flora *s.* flora; *v.i.* floral; **florid** *adj.* florido; **florist** *s.* florista.
floss *s.* bôrra de seda; fio de seda para bordar; (*bot.*) estiletes da flor do milho, cabelo do milho; — **silk** seda frouxa (bordado); **-y** *adj.* leve, sedoso, macio.
flotation *s.* flutuação.
flotilla *s.* flotilha, esquadrilha.
flotsam *s.* destroços de naufrágio (flutuando).
flounce *s.* volante, babado (costura); *v.t.* guarnecer de volantes, de babados.
flounder *s.* sôlha (peixe).
flour *s.* farinha; — **mill** moinho de farinha.
flourish *s.* florescimento; (*mús.*) floreio; (*esg.*) molinete; adôrno; *v.t.* florear, embelezar; brandir; *v.i.* florescer, medrar, crescer; florear.
flout *v.t.&i.* zombar, caçoar, mofar-se; insultar; *s.* mofa, zombaria; insulto.
flow *s.* corrente, torrente; fluxo; (*hidr.*) vazão; *v.i.* escorrer, escoar-se, correr; subir (a maré); *v.t.* inundar; **to — into** desaguar.
flower *s.* flor; *v.i.* florescer; **-ing** *s.* florescência; — **show** exposição de flores.
flowing *adj.* corrente, transbordante; flutuante.
fluctuate *v.i.* flutuar; oscilar; **fluctuation** *s.* flutuação.
flue *s.* tubo de caldeira; chaminé.
fluency *s.* fluência; **fluent** *adj.* fluente; **fluently** *adv.* fluentemente, correntemente.
fluff *s.* penugem; pó.
fluid *s.&adj.* fluido.
fluke *s.* sôlha; unha de âncora; ponta (de flexa, arpão, etc.); (*pop.*) golpe de sorte.
flummery *s.* mingau; espécie de creme; manjar branco.
flunkey *s.* lacaio.
fluorescent *adj.* fluorescente; **fluorine** *s.* flúor.

flurry s. rápida agitação do ar; comoção; chuva brusca ou queda de neve acompanhada de uma rajada de vento; v.t. agitar.

flush adj. à flor de, superficial; igual, ao nível; copioso; rico; robusto; s. rubor, agitação; fluxo rápido, ou copioso; vôo (súbito); abundância; acesso; v.t. animar; nivelar, igualar; limpar (com um jato de agua); v.t. corar; sair (correndo); afluir; ꞏed face rosto congestionado.

fluster v.t. confundir, perturbar; v.i. estar agitado, confundido; s. confusão; perturbação.

flute s. flauta; **flutist** s. flautista.

flutter s. alvoroço, confusão, agitação; v.t. agitar; confundir; sacudir, menear; v.i. agitar-se, alterar-se; adejar.

fluvial adj. fluvial.

fluviatic, fluviatile adj. fluvial.

flux s. fluxo; disenteria; (quím.) fundente.

fly v.i. voar; lançar-se, precipitar-se; correr, passar rapidamente; saltar; rebentar, estalar; desvanecer-se; v.t. fazer voar; fugir de; dirigir um avião; cruzar ou atravessar de avião; — at arrojar-se ou lançar-se sôbre; — away desaparecer, ir-se voando; — in the face of fazer frente a; s. mosca; braguilha; cabriolé, carro de passeio; percurso aéreo de um projétil ou de qualquer outro objeto; comprimento (de bandeira); — weight peso môsca (box).

foal s. potro, potranca; burrico; v.i. parir (a égua).

foam s. espuma; v.i. espumar; ꞏy adj. espumante, espumoso.

focal adj. focal; **focus** s. foco; v.t. focalizar.

fodder s. forragem.

foe s. inimigo, adversário.

foetus s. feto (embrião).

fog s. nevoeiro, bruma, neblina; estado de confusão mental; (fot.) véu; v.t. obscurecer, velar, enublar; ꞏgy adj. enublado, brumoso; velado.

fogy s. pessoa antiquada; ultra-conservador.

foible s. fraco; lado fraco; fraqueza.

foil s. fracasso; derrota; florete; pista, rasto de um animal; folheta, fôlha (de metal); v.t. despistar; frustar; derrotar; burlar.

foist v.t. inserir sub-reptìciamente uma cláusula em algum escrito; passar cousa falsa por verdadeira.

fold s. dobra, prega; envoltório, envólucro; cercado para carneiros; rebanho; (fig.) uma igreja, congregação de fiéis; usado como sufixo indica vezes, ex.: **twofold** duas vezes; v.t. dobrar, preguear; envolver, enlaçar; cingir, incluir, encerrar; — the arms cruzar os braços; ꞏer s. dobrador, dobradeira; pasta; folheto.

foliaceous adj. foliáceo; laminado.

folio s. fólio.

folklore s. folclore.

folks s. gente, pessoas, povo; **my —** minha gente, minha família.

follicle s. folículo.

follow v.t. seguir, ir atrás de; vir depois de; resultar de; v.i. seguir, continuar; seguir-se; ꞏer partidário, adepto, acompanhante; — up levar até o fim; it ꞏs segue-se; — in one's track seguir nas pègadas de alguém.

following adj. seguinte; próximo; subsequente; s. séquito, comitiva, cortejo.

folly s. loucura, desatino.

foment v.t. fomentar, provocar; (med.) fomentar; ꞏation s. provocação, instigação; (med.) fomentação.

fond adj. afeiçoado, amigo; amante, apaixonado; **to be — of** ser afeiçoado a; gostar de.

fondle v.t. acariciar, amimar.

fondness s. afeição, ternura; apêgo; inclinação.

font s. pia de batismo; (tip.) sortimento de tipos de um tamanho e estilo.

food s. alimento, comida, víveres; forragem; **— and drink** o comer e o beber, as comidas e as bebidas; **— for thought** matéria em que pensar, coisa em que pensar.

fool s. tôlo, pateta; nécio; imbecil, idiota; palhaço; v.t. enganar; lograr; v.i. fazer-se de tôlo; **to play the —** fingir-se de tôlo; ꞏhardiness temeridade.

foot s. pé (de homem, animal, mesa, etc.); pata; base; pé (medida); (mil.) infantaria; v.i. correr, andar; mover-se; v.t. pisar, espezinhar; — bath escalda-pés; **by — a** pé; **to put one's — down** tomar uma resolução firme; **to set on —** iniciar, empreender; ꞏbridge ponte para pedestres.

footfall s. ruído de passos ou pisadas.

foothill s. colina ao pé de uma montanha.

fop s. tôlo, fátuo; janota, almofadinha.

for prep. por; para; a; por causa de; quanto a; durante; a-pesar de, a despeito de; afim de; conj. porque; pois; **money — studying** dinheiro para estudar; **eye — an eye** ôlho por ôlho; **you don't convince me — all your clever arguments** você não me convence a-pesar de seus sábios argumentos; ꞏever para sempre; **he fought — years** lutou durante anos; **as — me** quanto a mim; **— and against** o pró e o contra.

forage s. forragem; v.t. forragear.

foray s. incursão súbita; raid.

forbear v.i.&t. abster-se; conter-se; reprimir-se; deixar de; evitar; ꞏance s. indulgência; abstenção; paciência.

forbid v.t. proibir; interdizer; ꞏding adj. proibitivo; repulsivo, repugnante.

force s. fôrça; vigor; energia; (mil.) fôrça, tropa; v.t. forçar; violentar; impelir; ꞏed adj. forçado; compulsório; ꞏful adj. vigoroso; — along fazer avançar; — back rechaçar; — from obrigar a sair; — one's way through abrir seu caminho através.

forceps s. fórceps.

forcible adj. forte; eficaz; potente; enérgico; forçado; **forcibly** adv. enèrgicamente; forçosamente.

ford s. vau; v.t. vadear.

fore adj. anterior, dianteiro; (mar.) de proa; adv. avante, adiante; antes; anteriormente; ꞏarm antebraço.

forebode v.t. prognosticar; pressagiar; **foreboding** s. presságio, pressentimento.

forecast v.t.&i. prever, prognosticar; projetar, traçar; s. prognóstico; plano, projeto.

forecited adj. precitado.

foreclose v.t. impedir; excluir; (for.) tomar posse judicial de bens penhorados ou hipotecados.

foredoom v.t. predestinar.

forefathers s. antepassados, ascendentes.

forefinger s. dedo índice; dedo indicador.

foregoing *adj.* precedente, anterior.
foreground *s.* (*pint.*) primeiro plano, frente.
forehanded *adj.* antecipado; prematuro; previdente.
forehead *s.* testa.
foreign *adj.* estrangeiro; exterior, estranho; — **trade** comércio exterior.
foreknowledge *s.* preciência.
foreland *s.* cabo, promontório.
forelock *s.* topete (cabelo).
foreman *s.* capataz; maioral; chefe; contra-mestre; principal; — **of the jury** presidente do conselho de jurados.
foremast *s.* (*mar.*) mastro do traquete.
foremost *adj.* primeiro; mais avançado.
forenoon *s.* manhã.
forensic *adj.* forense; judicial.
forerunner *s.* precursor.
foresee *v.t.* prever.
foreshadow *v.t.* anunciar, indicar; prefigurar.
foreshorten *v.t.* (*pint.*) diminuir (imagens) para que se mantenha a perspetiva.
foresight *s.* previsão.
forest *s.* floresta.
forestall *v.t.* antecipar; prevenir, impedir.
forester *s.* silvicultor; engenheiro florestal; cangurú gigante.
foretaste *s.* gôsto ou sabor antecipado; *v.t.* prelibar, antegostar, antegozar.
foretell *v.t.* predizer, anunciar.
forethought *s.* previdência; premeditação.
forewarn *v.t.* prevenir, avisar.
foreword *s.* prefácio; advertência; preâmbulo.
forfeit *s.* perda legal de propriedade ou direito por não cumprimento das obrigações ou por crime; multa; penalidade.
forgather *v.i.* reunir-se.
forge *s.* forja; *v.t.* forjar, falsificar; =d *adj.* forjado; =ry *s.* falsificação; =r *s.* falsário.
forget *v.t.* esquecer; — **one's self** exceder-se, passar das medidas; =ful *adj.* esquecido; =fulness *s.* esquecimento.
forgive *v.t.* perdoar; =ness *s.* perdão, remissão.
fork *s.* garfo; forcado; bifurcação; confluência de rios; cruzamento de estradas; *v.i.* bifurcar-se; *v.t.* engarfar; atirar com o forcado (feno, etc.).
forlorn *adj.* abandonado; desconsolado, desolado, desamparado.
form *s.* forma, fórmula; formulário (impresso); figura, feitura; molde; cerimônia; estilo; porte, conduta; aparição, sombra; banco; espécie, variedade; condição mental e física; classe; (*gram.*) forma, inflexão; *v.t.* formar, construir, lavrar, modelar, idear, conceber; fazer, constituir; *v.i.* formar-se; =al *adj.* formal, formalista; cerimonioso; =ality *s.* formalidade; =ation *s.* formação; constituição; **in due** — em devida forma.
former *adj.* precedente, antigo, anterior, passado; =ly *adv.* anteriormente, antigamente, outrora.
formidable *adj.* formidável.
formula *s.* fórmula; =ry *s.* formulário; =te *v.t.* formular; **formulism** *s.* estilo formal; apêgo a fórmulas.
fornication *s.* fornicação; **fornicate** *v.i.* fornicar.
forsake *v.t.* abandonar, desertar; faltar a; renunciar.

forsooth *adv.* (usado quasi sempre ironicamente), na verdade, com efeito, certamente.
forswear *v.t.* abjurar.
fort *s.* forte, fortaleza.
forth *adv.* adiante, avante, para frente; =coming *adj.* prestes a sair; futuro, próximo; =with *adv.* imediatamente.
fortieth *adj.* quadragésimo.
fortification *s.* fortificação; **fortify** *v.t.* fortificar, fortalecer, reforçar; **fortitude** *s.* fôrça; fôrça d'alma; grandeza de ânimo.
fortnight *s.* quinzena, quinze dias; =ly *adv.* de quinze em quinze dias.
fortress *s.* fortaleza.
fortuitous *adj.* fortuito.
fortunate *ad*. afortunado, feliz; =ly *adv.* felizmente; **fortune** *s.* fortuna, sorte.
forty *adj.* quarenta.
forum *s.* fórum.
forward *adj.* avançado; anterior; dianteiro; precoce; extremo, radical; preparado, pronto, disposto; desenvolto, audaz; imodesto; indiscreto; (*com.*) a ser entregue; *adv.* adiante; mais adiante; *v.t.* enviar; transmitir, remeter; apressar, ativar; expedir; =ness *s.* precocidade; pressa; atrevimento.
fossil *s.* fóssil.
foster *v.t.* animar, encorajar; favorecer; alimentar, criar, nutrir; dar asas, alentar, fomentar; — **brother** irmão de leite, irmão adotivo; — **child** filho adotivo.
foul *adj.* sujo, imundo, porco; mau, perverso; infecto; vicioso, viciado; fétido; infame; detestável, vil, injusto; desleal; desfavorável; embaraçado; *s.* falta; golpe desleal, violação das regras estabelecidas (esportes); *v.t.* sugar, emporcalhar; violar as regras estabelecidas; — **breath** hálito fétido; — **dealing** dolo, má fé; — **language** palavras grosseiras, injuriosas.
foulard *s.* fular, seda fina.
found *v.t.* fundar, criar; fundir, derreter.
foundation *s.* fundação, estabelecimento; dotação; fundamento, base, apôio, alicerce; — **stone** pedra fundamental.
foundling *s.* enjeitado, criança enjeitada; — **hospital** casa de expostos.
foundress *s.* fundadora, criadora.
fountain, **fount** *s.* fonte; manancial; mina d'agua, nascente, vertente; repuxo, chafariz; — **pen** caneta-tinteiro; =head *s.* fonte que dá origem à corrente; nascente.
four *adj.&s.* quatro; =fold quatro vezes; —=footed quadrúpede; =teen *adj.&s.* quatorze; =teenth *adj.&s.* décimo quarto; =th *adj.&s.* quarto.
fowl *s.* ave; ave galinácea; *v.i.* caçar aves.
fox *s.* raposa; =y *adj.* esperto, ladino, astuto.
foyer *s.* salão de descanso (de teatro).
fraction *s.* fração.
fractious *adj.* irritável, rebelde; perverso.
fracture *s.* fratura; *v.t.* fraturar.
fraenum V. **frenum.**
fragile *adj.* frágil; **fragility** *s.* fragilidade.
fragment *s.* fragmento, pedaço, estilhaço; =ary *adj.* fragmentário.
fragrance *s.* fragrância, perfume; **fragrant** *adj.* fragrante; perfumado.
frail *adj.* frágil, delicado; *s.* cêsto de junco; =ty *s.* fragilidade.
frame *s.* quadro, armação; estrutura; moldura; esqueleto; molde; bastido

(de bordar); forma; *v.t.* fabricar; armar, formar; construir; ajustar, compor; enquadrar; forjar, idear; to — **up** maquinar; — **of mind** estado de espírito; ▪**er** *s.* autor; armador, construtor; — **saw** serra de volta; — **work** estrutura; **framing** *s.* armação.

franchise *s.* isenção; privilégio; direito de sufrágio.

Franciscan *s.* franciscano.

frank *adj.* franco, sincero; ▪**ness** *s.* franqueza.

frankincense *s.* incenso.

frantic *adj.* frenético.

fraternal *adj.* fraternal; **fraternity** *s.* fraternidade; **fraternize** *v.i.* confraternizar; **fratricide** *s.* fratricida.

fraud *s.* fraude; ▪**ulent** *ad* . fraudulento.

fraught *adj.* carregado, cheio.

fray *s.* luta, rixa, refrega; competição; *v.t.* desgastar, esfregar.

freak *s.* capricho, veleidade; extravagância; monstruosidade; fenômeno; ▪**ish** *adj.* caprichoso; bizarro; monstruoso.

freckle *s.* sarda; *v.t.* manchar de sardas; ▪**d** *adj.* sardento.

free *adj.* livre; franco; desocupado, vago; licencioso, atrevido; liberal, generoso; isento, privilegiado; gratúito; voluntário; *v.t.* libertar, livrar; resgatar; isentar, eximir; — **goods** mercadorias isentas de direitos; — **of charges** gratis; — **port** porto franco; — **will** livre arbítrio; — **trade** câmbio livre; — **thinker** livre pensador; *adv.* gratis; gratuitamente; ▪**ly** *adv.* livremente, sem reservas; expontâneamente.

freedom *s.* liberdade; isenção, imunidade; franquia; licença; — **of speech** liberdade de palavra; — **of the press** liberdade de imprensa.

freeze *v.t.* gelar, congelar, refrigerar; *v.i.* gelar; gelar-se; ▪**r** *s.* refrigerador, congelador; sorveteira; **freezing** *adj.* congelante; glacial; **freezing point** ponto de congelação (temperatura).

freight *s.* frete, carga, carregamento; *v.t.* fretar; carregar.

French *adj.&s.* francês; idioma francês; — **bread** pão francês; ▪**ify** *v.t.* afrancesar; ▪**man** *s.* francês.

frenetic *adj.* frenético.

frenum, fraenum *s.* (*anat.*) freio.

frenzy *s.* frenesí; **frenzied** *adj.* frenético; delirante.

frequent *adj.* frequente; *v.t.* frequentar; ▪**er** *s.* frequentador; ▪**ly** *adv.* frequentemente; **frequency** *s.* frequência.

fresco *s.* fresco (pintura).

fresh *adj.* fresco; recente, novo; refrigerante; puro (ar, água); loução; saudável, robusto; noviço; (*pop.*) descarado, intrometido, petulante; — **from** acabado de chegar, de sair, etc; — **hand** noviço; — **water** água doce; ▪**man** calouro; *s.* manancial, reservatório de água doce; ▪**en** *v.t.&i.* refrescar; ▪**ness** *s.* frescura.

fret *s.* desgaste, atrito, fricção; irritação, aborrecimento, desgôsto; relêvo, realce, cinzeladura; grega; *v.t.* roer, corroer, desgastar; desgostar; aborrecer; bordar em relêvo; *v.i.* aborrecer-se, desgotar-se; agitar-se; ▪**ful** *adj.* irritável, malhumorado.

friable *adj.* friável.

friar *s.* frade, monge; ▪**y** *s.* mosteiro, comunidade (de frades).

friction *s.* fricção.

Friday *s.* sexta-feira.

fried *adj.* frito.

friend *s.* amigo, amiga; ▪**less** *adj.* sem amigos; ▪**liness** *s.* afabilidade, benevolência; ▪**ly** *adj.* amigável, amistoso, servical; *adv.* amigávelmente, amistosamente; ▪**ship** *s.* amizade.

frieze *s.* tecido frisado; (*arq.*) friso.

frigate *s.* fragata.

fright *s.* susto, espanto, medo, terror; ▪**en** *v.t.* assustar, apavorar; ▪**ful** *adj.* terrível, espantoso, de meter medo.

frigid *adj.* glacial, frígido, frio; ▪**ity** *s.* frigidez, frialdade.

frill *s.* casa de abelha (costura); *v.t.* fazer casa de abelha (costura).

fringe *s.* franja, orla; *v.t.* orlar, guarnecer com franjas.

frippery *s.* trapos, roupas velhas; elegância afetada.

frisk *s.* salto, pulo, cambalhota; *v.i.* saltar, pular, brincar, dar cambalhotas.

frit *s.* matéria fundida de que se faz o vidro; *v.t.* fundir, derreter.

fritter *s.* fritura; pedaço, fragmento; *v.t.* cortar, picar; dissipar, gastar, desperdiçar.

frivolity *s.* frivolidade; **frivolous** *adj.* frívolo.

frizz, frizzle *v.t.* frisar, encrespar; *s.* friso, cacho, anel (de cabelo).

frock *s.* roupa de mulher ou de criança; vestido; burel, hábito de frade ou de freira.

frog *s.* rã; inflamação de garganta; alça; porta-espadas na farda do soldado; *v.i.* caçar rãs.

frolic *s.* jôgo, travessura; ▪**some** *adj.* travêsso, alegre.

from *prep.* de; desde; da parte de; por; segundo; — **behind** por detrás, de detrás; — **memory** de memória; **news** — **home** notícias de casa.

frond *s.* fronde.

front *s.* frente, cara, testa; fachada; começo; estrada ou caminho à beira mar; plastrão de camisa ou blusa; (hotéis) primeiro mensageiro na fila; frente, zona avançada das operações militares; *adj.* anterior, dianteiro, fronteiro; da frente; *v.t.* fazer frente a; arrostar; dar para; *v.i.* estar na frente; — **room** quarto da frente, que dá para a rua; — **view** vista da frente.

frontier *s.* fronteira.

frontispiece *s.* frontispício.

frost *s.* geada, frio, gêlo; *v.t.* congelar, gelar; *v.i.* cobrir-se de geada, gelar-se, congelar-se; — **bitten** gelado, congelado; queimado da geada.

froth *s.* espuma, escuma; *v.i.* espumar; ▪**y** *adj.* espumante, escumoso.

frown *s.* franzimento de sobrancelhas; *v.i.* franzir as sobrancelhas; — **down** olhar com maus olhos, desaprovar.

frowzy *adj.* desalinhado, mal tratado, mal penteado, sujo.

frozen *adj.* gelado; congelado; glacial; (*com.*) congelado.

fructify *v.i.* frutificar; *v.t.* fecundar; fertilizar.

frugal *adj.* frugal; ▪**ity** *s.* frugalidade.

fruit *s.* fruto, fruta; ▪**erer** *s.* fruteiro; ▪**ful** *adj.* frutífero. fecundo, frutuoso; ▪**less** *adj.* infrutífero, infrutuoso; vão.

frump *s.* mulher rabugenta e antiquada.

frustrate *v.t.* frustrar; impedir; anular.

frustration *s.* frustração.

frustrum s. (geom.) cone ou pirâmide truncados; tronco de cone ou de pirâmide.
fry s. fritada; peixinho recém-nascido; (pop.) gente miúda, sem importância; v.t. frigir, fritar.
fuchsia s. fúcsia.
fuddle v.t. confundir, embriagar; v.i. embriagar-se.
fudge int. sai daí! ora bolas! s. embuste, conto; coisa sem sentido; bala de chocolate; v.t. inventar.
Fuegian s.&adj. habitante da Terra do Fogo.
fuel s. combustível; -oil óleo combustível.
fugitive adj. fugitivo, passageiro; s. fugitivo.
fugleman s. (mil.) chefe de fila.
fugue s. (mús.) fuga.
fulcrum s. (mec.) fulcro, ponto de apôio.
fulfil v.t. cumprir, realizar; -ment s. cumprimento, desempenho, execução.
full adj. cheio; repleto; completo; ao completo; copioso, abundante; ocupado; largo, amplo; inteiro; adv. inteiramente; completamente; de todo; totalmente; s. máximo; v.i. dar amplitude; tornar grosso ou espesso; — dress traje de cerimônia; — brother irmão por parte de pai e mãe, irmão germano; — powers amplos poderes; — speed a toda velocidade; — moon lua cheia; in — swing em plena operação, em pleno funcionamento; -ly adv. completamente.
fulminate v.t.&i. fulminar.
fullness, fulness plenitude, repleção, enchimento; saciedade; abundância.
fulsome adj. excessivo, exagerado; insincero; repugnante.
fumble v.i. tatear, titubear, manejar sem jeito, andar às tontas.
fume s. fumaça; fumaça aromática; emanação; gás; explosão de cólera; v.i. fumegar; encolerizar-se; v.t. defumar, secar ao fumo; exalar vapores.
fumigate v.t. fumigar; perfumar; fumigation s. fumigação.
fun s. divertimento, diversão; graça, gracejo, chiste; for — por graça; to make — of fazer troça de; to have — divertir-se.
function s. função; cerimônia social; v.i. funcionar; -al adj. funcional; -ary s. funcionário.
fund s. fundos, cabedais, capital; caixa (de caridade, etc.); reservas; v.t. empregar o capital em fundos públicos ou nos de companhias; consolidar (dívidas).
fundament s. fundamento; -al adj. fundamental.

funeral s. funeral, funerais, exéquias; entêrro; adj. funerário; fúnebre.
fungus s. fungo; cogumelo.
funicular adj.&s. funicular.
funnel s. funil; chaminé.
funny adj. cômico, engraçado, divertido.
fur s. pele (abrigo ou adôrno); pêlo de certos animais; v.t. cobrir, forrar ou adornar com peles.
furbelows s. volantes, falbalás, folhos (de saia).
furbish v.t. limpar, pulir, brunir.
furious adj. furioso.
furl v.t. enrolar; (mar.) ferrar (as velas).
furlong s. medida de distância (oitava parte da milha), equivalente a 201,17 metros.
furlough s. (mil.) licença; v.t. licenciar.
furnace s. forno, fornalha; fogareiro.
furnish v.t. fornecer, prover; guarnecer, mobilar; -ed apartments apartamentos mobilados; **furniture** s. móveis, mobília, mobiliário.
furore s. furor.
furred adj. forrado ou coberto de pele; saburrosa (a língua).
furrier s. peleteiro; -y adj. peleteria.
furrow s. sulco, rêgo; v.t. sulcar.
furry adj. feito de peles ou guarnecido de peles; saburrosa (língua).
further adj. mais distante; suplementar, adicional; adv. mais longe, mais adiante; novamente; mais; ademais; além d'isso; ainda; v.t. adiantar, promover, favorecer.
furthermore adv. ademais; além d'isso; outrossim.
furthest adv.&adj. o mais longe, o mais remoto; extremo.
furtive adj. furtivo.
fury s. fúria, furor; frenesí, entusiasmo.
furze s. (bot.) tojo.
fuse v.t.&i. fundir, derreter, fundir-se, derreter-se; s. espoleta; mecha; fusível.
fuselage s. fuselagem.
fusible adj. fusível, fundível.
fusillade s. carga cerrada, fuzilaria.
fusion s. fusão.
fuss s. bulha; alvorôço, estardalhaço; v.i. agitar-se, inquietar-se desnecessàriamente; -y adj. cheio de coisas, difícil vaidoso (indivíduo).
fustian s. fustão; espécie de veludo de algodão; estilo bombástico.
fusty adj. mofado; antiquado.
futile ad. fútil; **futility** s. futilidade.
future adj.&s. futuro.
fuzz s. partículas; pó; penugem; -y adj. coberto de penugem; fôfo.
fy int. que vergonha!
fyke s. bolsa de pescar.

G

G letra; (mús.) sol; — **clef** clave de sol.
gabardine s. gabardine.
gabble v.t. tagarelar, palrar; s. tagarelice.
gable s. (arq.) empena.
gad v.i. errar, vagabundear, andar de um lado para outro; s. ponta, ferrão.
gadfly s. mosca varejeira; tavão.
gaff s. arpão, gancho de ferro; (mar.) vêrga; (jíria) lugar de divertimento barato; v.t. arpoar.
gaffer s. velho camponês; chefe de equipo.
gag s. mordaça; engasgo; (jíria) dito ou

comentário espirituoso; (teat.) interpolação espirituosa do ator; v.t. amordaçar; fazer calar; provocar náuseas.
gage s. caução; desafio.
gaiety s. alegria, jovialidade; **gaily** adv. alegremente.
gain s. lucro, ganho, proveito; v.t. ganhar; alcançar; obter; v.i. to — the clock adiantar o relógio; to — on superar, levar vantagem.
gainsay v.t. contradizer, negar; s. contradição.

gait s. modo de andar; marcha, andadura de cavalo; v.t. treinar um cavalo na marcha.

gaiter s. polaina; botina.

gala s. gala, festa.

galaxy s. galáxia, via láctea; (fig.) reunião de pessoas de importância.

gale s. tormenta, vento forte.

galena s. (min.) galena.

gall s. bilis; fel; amargura, aspereza, amargor; tomadura (ferida que o roçar da sela produz no lombo do cavalo); v.t. esfolar, ferir com a sela; — **bladder** vesícula biliar; — **sickness** doença da vesícula.

gallant adj. galante; valente, bravo; s. galante; **-ly** adv. valentemente; galantemente; **-ry** s. galanteria; valentia, bravura.

galleon s. galeão.

gallery s. galeria; tribuna; varanda; galeria artística, exposição; (teat.) galerias, torrinhas.

galley s. (mar.) galera; cozinha do navio; (imp.) galé; **-tiles** azulejos.

Gallic adj. gaulês; **-an** adj. galicano; **-ism** s. galicismo; **-ize** v.t. afrancesar.

gallinaceous adj. galináceo.

gallipot s. vaso de boticário; (fíria) droguista, farmacêutico.

gallon s. galão (medida).

gallop s. galope; v.i. galopar.

galore adv. muito, em abundância.

galosh s. galocha.

galvanic ad. galvânico; **galvanism** s. galvanismo; **galvanize** v.t. galvanizar; **galvanoplasty** s. galvanoplastia.

gambit s. gambito (jôgo de xadrez).

gamble s. loteria, jôgo de azar; v.i.&t. jogar; **-r** s. jogador; **gambling** s. jôgo.

gamboge s. goma-guta.

gambol s. brinquedo, salto, pulo, travessura, cabriola; v.i. brincar, saltar, pular.

game s. jôgo, brinquedo; caça, presa; competição esportiva; esquema, plano, projeto; v.i. jogar; adj.corajoso, valente.

gammon s. presunto; mentira, pêta.

gamp s. guarda-chuva grande.

gamut s. escala, gama.

gamy adj. bravo, indômito; de caça abundante; (comida) muito condimentada.

gander s. ganso.

gang s. bando; equipo; grupo; quadrilha; **-er** s. chefe de equipo.

ganglion s. gânglio.

gangrene s. gangrena.

gangue s. (min.) ganga.

gangway s. passagem; passagem estreita da Câmara dos Comuns na Inglaterra; (mar.) passadiço; escada do costado.

gannet s. espécie de ave marinha.

gantry s. pórtico; estação de sinais nas linhas férreas.

gaol s. prisão, detenção (casa); **-er** s. carcereiro.

gap s. lacuna, intervalo, brecha, vácuo; (av.) distância mínima entre os planos de um biplano.

gape v.i. bocejar; estar de bôca aberta; abrir ou deixar alguma coisa aberta; — at comer moscas, olhar pasmado.

gaper s. papa-moscas (pessoa).

gar s. sôlho (peixe).

garage s. garage; v.t. guardar (o automóvel) na garage.

garbage s. restos de comida, refugo.

garble v.t. alterar, truncar; expurgar.

garden s. jardim; horta; — **city** cidade-jardim; v.t.&i. cultivar, plantar, ajardinar, tratar de jardins ou hortas; — **bed** canteiro; — **stuff** legumes, hortaliças; — **flower** flor de jardim; — **tools** instrumentos de jardinagem; — **engine** irrigador de plantas; **-er** s. jardineiro.

gardenia s. gardênia.

gardening s. jardinagem; horticultura.

garfish s. sôlho (peixe).

gargle s. gargarejo; v.i. gargarejar.

gargoyle s. gárgula.

garish adj. deslumbrante; vistoso.

garland s. guirlanda; grinalda; antologia.

garlic s. alho.

garment s. roupa, vestuário.

garner s. celeiro; v.t. acumular em celeiro; armazenar.

garnet s. granate, granada (pedra).

garnish s. guarnição, adôrno, aderêço; v.t. guarnecer, ornar, ataviar, adornar.

garret s. mansarda, sótão.

garrison s. (mil.) guarnição; — **artillery** artilharia de praça.

garrulous adj. gárrulo, vivo, loquaz.

garter s. liga.

gas s. gás; (pop.) gasolina; v.t. (quím.) tratar pelo gás; saturar de gás; (mil.) atacar com gases; asfixiar; v.i. desprender gases; — **company** companhia de gás; — **engine** motor a gás; **-holder** gasômetro; — **range** fogão a gás; — **works** fábrica de gás; **-eous** adj. gasoso.

gash s. cutilada; gilvaz; v.t. acutilar; fazer talho grande.

gasify v.t. gaseificar.

gasket s. gacheta.

gasogene s. gasógeno; **gasometer** s. gasômetro.

gasp s. respiração ofegante; dificuldade em respirar; v.i. arfar, respirar com dificuldade.

gassy adj. gasoso; (pop.) contador de vantagens, prosa.

gasteropod V. **gastropod.**

gastralgia s. gastralgia.

gastric adj. gástrico.

gastritis s. gastrite.

gastronomer s. gastrônomo; **gastronomy** s. gastronomia.

gastropod s. gastrópodo; lesma; caracol.

gate s. portão; entrada; portal; pórtico; caminho, passo, garganta; (mec.) válvula de contrôle; **-keeper** porteiro.

gather v.t. reunir, colhêr, recolher; coletar; juntar; (cost.) franzir; s. franzido, prega; **-er** s. coletor; **-ing** s. assembléia, reunião; ajuntamento; acumulação; colheita; coleta; (med.) abcesso.

gaudy adj. pomposo, luxuoso, aparatoso (denotando falta de gôsto).

gauge, gage s. medida, medida padrão; gabarito, bitola; calibre; (mar.) calado; instrumento de medir, manômetro, indicador, calibrador; v.t. medir, aferir, graduar, calibrar; estimar, apreciar, avaliar; (mar.) arquear.

gauger s. arqueador, aferidor.

gaunt adj. sêco, descarnado, magro; abatido, fraco.

gauntlet s. manopla; (fig.) desafio.

gauze s. gaze; tecido vaporoso; **gauzy** adj. vaporoso.

gavotte s. gavota.

gawky adj. desajeitado, rude; bobo, tôlo; s. rústico; tôlo.

gay adj. alegre, festivo; **gayety, gaiety** s. alegria, júbilo.

gaze s. olhar, olhar fixo; to — at contemplar.

gazelle s. gazela.

gazette s. gazeta, jornal; jornal oficial.

gazetteer s. dicionário geográfico.

gear s. (mec.) engrenagem, encaixe; mecanismo de transmissão, de distribuição ou govêrno; jôgo; roda dentada; arreios, jaez; ferramentas; bens móveis; instrumentos; aparelhos; utensílios caseiros; roupas, adornos; (mar.) adriça; v.t. engrenar; aparelhar; equipar; armar; encaixar; — box caixa de engrenagem; — ratio relação de multiplicação; to throw into — engrenar.

gee int. (jíria) caramba! puxa! papagaio!

Gehenna s. geena, inferno.

gelatin, gelatine s. gelatina; -ous adj. gelatinoso.

geld v.t. castrar, capar; -ing s. castração; animal castrado.

gem s. gema, pedra preciosa; joia; v.t. adornar com pedras preciosas.

genealogical adj. genealógico; **genealogy** s. genealogia.

general s. general; adj. geral; in — em geral.

generalissimo s. generalíssimo.

generality s. generalidade; **generally** adv. geralmente.

generalize v.t.&i. generalizar.

generalship s. generalato; tática; estratégia.

generate v.t. gerar, engendrar; produzir, causar; **generation** s. geração; **generative** adj. generativo, fecundo; **generator** s. gerador, procreador.

generic adj. genérico.

generosity s. generosidade.

generous adj. generoso.

genesis s. gênese.

genet s. ginete; gineta (animal).

genetics s. genética.

Geneva s. Genebra.

genial adj. genial; cordial, afável; -ity s. afabilidade; -ly adv. cordialmente.

genital adj. genital.

genitive adj.&s. genitivo.

genius s. gênio.

Genoa s. Gênova.

genteel adj. (atualmente em desuso, êsse vocábulo só é empregado no sentido irônico) urbano, cortês, gentil.

gentian s. (bot.) genciana.

gentile s. gentio (por oposição ao termo "judeu"); pagão; adj. gentílico.

gentility s. nobreza; gentileza, graça, donaire.

gentle ad. suave; dócil, manso; — sex sexo fraco; of — birth bem nascido; -man gentilhomem; cavalheiro; -men of the robe advogados; -ness s. suavidade; **gently** adv. suavemente.

gentry s. gente de boa família e boa educação; na Inglaterra, classe intermediária entre a burguesia e a nobresa.

genuflexion, genuflection s. genuflexão.

genuine adj. genuíno, verdadeiro, autêntico; -ness s. autenticidade.

genus s. gênero (grupo de espécies).

geodesy s. geodésia.

geognosy s. geognosia.

geography s. geografia; **geographer** s. geógrafo; **geographical** adj. geográfico.

geology s. geologia; **geologic, geological** adj. geológico; **geologist** s. geólogo.

geometer s. geômetra; **geometry** s. geometria; **geometrical** adj. geométrico.

Georgia s. Geórgia.

geranium s. gerânio.

germ s. germe.

German adj. alemão; — ocean mar do Norte; s. alemão; — measles quartamoléstia.

germander s. (bot.) maro.

germinate v.i. germinar; **germination** s. germinação.

gerund s. gerúndio.

gestation s. gestação.

gesticulate v.i. gesticular.

gesture s. gesto.

get v.i.&t. obter; ganhar; adquirir; conseguir; arranjar; apanhar; possuir; ter; fazer ter; tomar; buscar; tornar; aprender; ir; passar; ser; estar; introduzir-se, meter-se; — about divulgar-se, tornar-se público; — ahead adiantar-se, ganhar a dianteira; — along estar passando; — back retomar, rehaver; — down descer; — ready preparar-se; — up levantar-se; — better melhorar; — even with ficar quite com; — home chegar em casa; — married casar-se; — in entrar; — on adiantar-se, progredir; — on one's leg arribar, melhorar de condição; — through terminar, ir até o fim; have got to, (pop.) ter que.

getup s. arranjo, disposição; adôrno, traje.

gewgaw s. frivolidade, ninharia; berloque.

geyser s. gêiser.

ghastly adj. macabro; lívido, desfigurado; horrível.

gherkin s. pepino pequeno.

ghetto s. gueto, bairro dos judeus.

ghost s. fantasma; espírito; alma; espectro; (fot. & fís.) imagem falsa ou secundária; mancha; — story história de fantasmas; not a — of a doubt nem uma sombra de dúvida; to give up the — exalar o último suspiro; -ly adj. espectral.

ghoul s. vampiro.

giant s.&adj. gigante; -'s stride passo de gigante.

gibber v.i. farfalhar; -ish s. farfalhada.

gibbet s. fôrca; v.t. enforcar.

gibe s. escárneo, mofa, zombaria; v.t. escarnecer, ridicularizar, mofar, zombar.

giblets s. miúdos (de ave).

giddiness s. vertigem, tonteira; **giddy** adj. vertiginoso.

gift s. presente; dote, dom; doação; talento; -ed adj. talentoso.

gig s. cabriolé, sege; (mar.) escaler.

gigantic adj. gigantesco.

giggle v.i. rir-se sem motivo, rir-se bobamente.

gild s. grêmio; comunidade; corporação; v.t. dourar.

gill s. medida de liquidos; guelra; vale; regato; moça.

gimcrack s. ninharia; brinquedo; berloque.

gimlet s. verruma.

gimp s. (tec.) alamar.

gin s. gim, genebra (bebidas); máquina de descaroçar algodão; laço, armadilha; (mec.) cabra, guindaste; v.t. descaroçar (algodão).

ginger s. gengibre; —-bread pão de gengibre; — hair cabelos ruivos; -ly adv. cuidadosamente.

gingham s. (tec.) guingão.

gipsy s. cigano; boêmio.

giraffe s. girafa.

girandole s. girândola.

girasol, girasole s. girassol.

gird v.t. cingir; cercar, rodear; equipar; preparar; mofar; zombar; — **oneself to a contest** preparar-se para um prélio.

girdle s. cinta; cinto, faixa; v.t. cingir, cercar, rodear; fazer uma incisão circular (numa árvore).

girl s. menina; moça; **-hood** s. mocidade (feminina); **-ish** adj. próprio de menina ou moça.

girth s. cinta; faixa; barrigueira; v.t. cingir.

gist s. substância; busilis; fundamento legal.

give v.t.&i. dar; conceder; outorgar; produzir, causar; fornecer; trazer; fazer; — **back** devolver; — **one's name** dizer seu nome; — **in** ceder; — **out** distribuir; — **up** desistir, abrir mão; — **way** ceder, render-se; — **forth** publicar, divulgar; — **notice** advertir, fazer saber; — **one's self up** entregar-se, render-se; — **rise to** ocasionar, causar; **-n to** dado a, inclinado a; **-r** s. doador.

gizzard s. moela (de ave).

glacial adj. glacial; **glacier** s. geleira.

glad adj. contente, satisfeito; feliz; **-den** v.i. alegrar-se, regosijar-se.

glade s. clareira.

gladiator s. gladiador.

gladiolus s. (bot.) gladíolo.

gladly adv. alegremente, com prazer.

gladness s. alegria.

glamour s. encanto, beleza, elegância, magia, qualidade de brilhar entre os demais.

glance s. resplendor repentino; golpe de vista; olhadela; (min.) sulfeto de brilho metálico; v.i. brilhar, cintilar; lançar uma olhadela; dar um golpe obliquamente; aludir; v.t. relancear; **at the first** — à primeira vista; **— coal** carvão duro e lustroso, antracite.

gland s. glândula.

glanders s. (vet.) mormo.

glare s. deslumbramento; clarão; olhar penetrante; olhar furioso; superfície lisa e brilhante; v.i. brilhar, deslumbrar; lançar olhares de indignação; adj. liso, lustroso; **glaring** adj. deslumbrante; brilhante; evidente; penetrante.

glass s. vidro; cristal; copo; espêlho; lente; ampôla; óculos; binóculo; v.t. espelhar, refletir; **-maker** vidreiro; **-y** adj. vidrado, vítreo.

glaucous adj. glauco.

glaze s. lustre, verniz; v.t. envidraçar; vidrar; envernizar, lustrar; **-d** adj. vidrado; **glazier** s. vidreiro, vidraceiro.

gleam s. fulgor; centelha; v.i. cintilar, fulgurar.

glean v.t. respigar, recolher; **-er** s. respigador, respigadeira.

glebe s. gleba; terra pertencente a igrejas.

glee s. alegria, júbilo; canção alegre para três ou mais vozes.

gleet s. corrimento; blenorragia.

glen s. vale estreito.

glib adj. volúvel; desembaraçado no falar; (pop.) escorregadio.

glide s. deslise; v.i. deslisar; resvalar.

glider s. (av.) planador.

glimmer s. luz trêmula; vislumbre; v.i. lançar uma luz vacilante.

glimpse s. vislumbre; reflexo; centelha; v.i. brilhar fracamente ou intermitentemente; vislumbrar.

glint s. reflexo; v.t. refletir; v.i. luzir, brilhar.

glisten v.i. brilhar, resplandecer; cintilar.

glitter s. brilho, resplendor; v.i. resplandecer, cintilar, rutilar.

gloaming s. crepúsculo, anoitecer; **gloam** v.i. escurecer, anoitecer.

gloat v.i. deleitar-se; contemplar com satisfação maligna.

globe s. globo, esfera; **globular** adj. globular, esférico.

globule s. glóbulo.

gloom v.t. obscurecer, encobrir; sombrear; v.i. obscurecer-se, encobrir-se, entristecer-se; s. obscuridade, trevas; ar sombrio; melancolia, tristeza; **-y** adj. tenebroso, sombrio, escuro; triste; lúgubre.

glorify v.t. glorificar; **glorious** adj. glorioso, resplandescente; **glory** s. glória; resplendor; v.i. vangloriar-se; deleitar-se.

gloss s. lustre, brilho; polimento, verniz; aparência fictícia; glosa, comentário; v.t. lustrar, polir; glosar, comentar; interpretar maliciosamente; **-ary** s. glossário; **-y** adj. lustroso; especioso; plausível.

glottis s. glote.

glove s. luva; — **trade luvaria; -r** s. luveiro.

glow v.i. dar luz ou calor sem chama; luzir suavemente; fosforescer; incandescer; sentir calor, queimar-se; sentir o calor da paixão; animar-se; s. brilho sem chama; incandescência; calor intenso; veemencia.

glower v.i. olhar firmemente; olhar com raiva.

gloze v.i. glosar; brilhar, cintilar; v.t. paliar.

glucose s. glicose.

glue s. cola forte, cola; v.t. colar; **-y** adj. pegajoso.

glum adj. triste, sombrio; aborrecido.

glume s. (bot.) gluma.

glut s. pletora; fartura; abundância; saciedade; excesso; v.t. fartar, saciar; saturar; v.i. comer glutonamente; — **the market** inundar o mercado.

gluten s. glúten.

glutinous adj. glutinoso.

glutton s. glutão, guloso; **-ous** adj. glutão, guloso; **-y** s. gulodice, glutonaria.

glycerin, glycerine s. glicerina.

gnarl s. nó na madeira; v.i. rosnar; **-ed** adj. nodoso.

gnash v.i. ranger os dentes.

gnat s. mosquito.

gnaw v.t. roer; morder, mordicar; corroer; **-ing** s. roedura; crispação.

gneiss s. (min.) gneisse.

gnome s. aforismo, máxima; gnomo.

go v.i.&t. ir, ir-se; andar; passar; partir; tornar-se; assentar, cair bem; aceitar-se; valer; s. moda; energia; voga; giro, marcha, curso; oportunidade, vez, turno; — **about** fazer, empreender; — **abroad** ir ao estrangeiro; — **ahead** prosseguir; — **backward** retroceder; — **by** passar ao lado, passar por alto; — **for** favorecer; ir buscar; — **in for** (pop.) apoiar, gostar de; — **on** continuar; — **over** estudar, examinar; recorrer; passar por cima de; — **through** realizar, levar a cabo; passar, sofrer; — **to the wall** quedar-se; dar-se por vencido; **it is all the** — é à grande moda, é o furor; **it is no** — é inútil, não vai; **on the** — em atividade; — **between** intermediário; alcoviteira.

goad s. aguilhão; v.t. aguilhoar.
goal s. meta, fim objeto.
goat s. cabra; bode; (pop.) bode expiatório.
goatee s. pêra (barba).
gobble v.t. comer glutonamente; v.i.
grugulejar.
goblet s. copo de pé.
goblin s. duende.
God s. Deus; **god** s. deus; — **fearing**
temente a Deus; =**'s house** igreja,
templo.
godchild s. afilhado, afilhada.
goddess s. deusa.
godfather s. padrinho.
godless adj. infiel, ímpio; ateu.
godlike adj. divino.
godly adj. piedoso, religioso.
goer s. transeunte.
goffer v.t. frisar, encrespar; s. frisado;
ferro de frisar.
goggle v.i. revirar os olhos; s. reviramento
de olhos.
goggles s. óculos.
going s. ida; — **and coming** idas e
vindas; =**s on** ocorrências.
goitre s. papo, papeira.
gold s. ouro; — **dust** ouro em pó; — **filled** revestido de
ouro; — **plated** dourado; — **standard**
padrão ouro; =**en** adj. de ouro, dourado;
=**en wedding** bodas de ouro.
golf s. golf, jôgo escossês.
golosh s. galocha.
gondola s. gôndola; **gondolier** s. gondo-
leiro.
gong s. gongo.
good adj. bom; apto, conveniente, vantajoso, útil; legítimo; dócil; competente,
capaz; digno; — **breeding** boas maneiras; — **deal** muito, bastante; —
gracious meu Deus!; — **looking**
bonito; — **natured** de bom genio; —
will boa vontade; int. bem! bom!; s.
bem.
goods s. mercadorias, artigos; bens
móveis; gêneros; — **train** trem de
carga.
goose s. ganso; — **step** passo de ganso.
gooseberry s. groselha.
Gordian adj. intrincado, complicado; —
knot nó górdio.
gore s. coágulo de sangue; v.t. ferir com
os chifres.
gorge s. refeição copiosa; garganta, desfiladeiro; entrave; glutonaria; trago,
bocado; decote de vestido; v.t. engulir,
tragar; fartar, saciar; v.i. saciar-se.
gorgeous adj. magnífico, esplêndido,
suntuoso.
gorilla s. gorila.
gormandize v.i. comer com glutonaria.
gorse s. tojo.
gory adj. ensanguentado; sangrento.
goshawk s. açor.
gosling s. ganso novo.
gospel s. Evangelho; credo; v.t. evangeli-
zar.
gossamer s. fio tênue; filamentos; gaze;
tela finíssima impermeável.
gossip s. mexericos, conversa indiscreta,
comentários sôbre a vida alheia; v.i.
espalhar rumores, comentar indiscreta-
mente a vida alheia.
Goth s. gôdo; =**ic** adj. gótico.
gouache s. guache (pintura).
gouge s. (carp.) goiva.
gourd s. cabaça, calabaça.
gourmand adj.&s. guloso; epicurista.

gourmet s. gastrônomo.
gout s. gota; =**y** adj. gotoso.
govern v.t. governar; guiar, dirigir;
(gram.) reger; =**ment** s. govêrno;
Estado; =**or** s. governador; (mec.)
regulador; =**ess** s. governante.
gown s. vestido; toga; túnica; **house** —
traje caseiro, vestido de interior; v.t.
pôr um vestido, toga, ou túnica.
grab v.t. agarrar, segurar; apoderar-se
indèbitamente; s. presa; (pop.) roubo.
grace s. graça; favor, gentileza; oração
antes ou depois das refeições; concessão
ou privilégio; (teol.) graça; v.t. adornar;
agraciar, favorecer; =**ful** adj. gracioso.
gracious adj. gracioso; =**ness** s. graça,
afabilidade.
gradation s. gradação.
grade s. grau, graduação; classe; qualidade; v.t. graduar, classificar; (eng.)
nivelar; — **up** cruzar raças de animais.
gradient s. rampa, inclinação.
gradual adj. gradual; =**ly** adv. gradualmente.
graduate v.i. formar-se; v.t. conferir um
diploma ou grau; s. formado, graduado
(por universidades); **graduation** s.
formatura; graduação.
graft s. enxêrto; v.t. enxertar.
grain s. grão, semente; veio (madeira,
mármore, etc.); partícula; grão (pêso,
0,0648 gr.); granulação; (tint.) grã,
cochonilha; v.t. granular; granitar;
fingir (pint.).
grained adj. granuloso; áspero.
grammar s. gramática; =**ian** s. gramáti-
co; **grammatical** adj. gramatical.
gramophone s. gramofone.
grampus s. golfinho (cetáceo).
Granada s. Granada.
granary s. celeiro.
grand adj. grande, grandioso; magnífico,
majestoso; — **master** grão mestre; —
piano piano de cauda.
grandchild s. neto, neta.
granddaughter s. neta.
grandeur s. magnificência, grandeza,
fausto.
grandfather s. avô.
grandiloquence s. grandiloquência.
grandiose adj. grandioso; bombástico.
grandma s. (pop.) avó, vovó.
grandmother s. avó.
grandnephew s. sobrinho-neto.
grandness s. grandiosidade.
grandniece s. sobrinha-neta.
grandpa s. (pop.) avô, vovô.
grandsire s. avô; antepassado.
grandson s. neto.
granduncle s. tio-avô.
granite s. granito.
granny s. (pop.) vovó.
grant s. concessão; subvenção; v.t. conceder; outorgar, dispensar; convir em;
dar de barato; **to take for** =**ed** pressu-
por, tomar como certo; =**ee** s. concessionário; =**or** outorgante.
granulate v.t. granular, granitar; =**d**
sugar açucar cristalizado.
granule s. grânulo.
grape s. uva, parreira; — **fruit** s. toronja.
graph s. gráfico, traçado; =**ic** adj. gráfico.
graphite s. grafite.
grapnel s. (mar.) ancoreta; arpéu; fateixa.
grapple v.t. agarrar; amarrar; v.i. agarrar-
se; (mar.) aferrar-se, atracar-se; s. luta,
peleja; arpéu.
grasp s. tomada; ação de agarrar; punho;
mão; garra; presa; alcance; usurpação;

punhado; compreensão; *v.t.* empunhar, agarrar; apoderar-se de; usurpar; tomar; entender; compreender; apanhar o sentido de; *v.i.* agarrar-se fortemente.
grass *s.* grama; erva; pasto; verdura; *v.t.* gramar; pastar; — **widower** marido separado da mulher; — **widow** mulher separada do marido; — **green** verde como a grama.
grate *s.* grade, gelosia; *v.t.* engradar; ralar, raspar.
gratification *s.* gratificação, recompensa; satisfação.
gratify *v.t.* gratificar; satisfazer, contentar.
grating *s.* grelha; rótula.
gratis *adv.* gratis.
gratitude *s.* gratidão.
gratuitous *adj.* gratuito; =**ness** *s.* gratuidade; **gratuity** *s.* graciosidade; gratificação; propina.
gravamen *s.* agravo.
grave *s.* sepultura, túmulo, tumba; =**clothes** mortalha; =**yard** cemitério; *adj.* grave, sério; (*mús.*) grave, baixo, profundo; *v.t.* gravar; esculpir, cinzelar.
gravel *s.* cascalho; (*med.*) cálculo, pedra.
graver *s.* buril, cinzel; gravador.
gravitate *v.i.* gravitar; **gravitation** *s.* gravitação; **gravity** *s.* gravidade.
gravy *s.* môlho; =**boat** molheira.
gray *adj.* cinza; encanecido; *s.* côr cinza; *v.i.* encanecer; — **matter** massa cinzenta.
graze *s.* raspadura, esfoladura; pasto; *v.t.* pastorear, apascentar; passar raspando; *v.i.* pastar.
grease *s.* graxa, gordura, unto; *v.t.* engraxar, untar; lubrificar; **greasy** *adj.* untuoso, gorduroso.
greasiness *s.* untuosidade.
great *adj.* grande; forte; magno; excelente; admirável; =**ly** *adv.* grandemente, muito; =**ness** *s.* grandeza, grandiosidade, magnitude; =**en** *v.t.* engrandecer; *v.i.* crescer, aumentar; — **bellied** barrigudo; grávida; **a** — **while** muito tempo; **a** — **many** muitos.
grebe *s.* ave colimbiforme.
Grecian *adj.* grego; **Greece** *s.* Grécia.
greediness *s.* avidez, voracidade, gula; **greedily** *adv.* vorazmente; **greedy** *adj.* voraz, guloso; ávido.
Greek *adj.*&*s.* grego.
green *adj.* verde; novato, noviço; novo, fresco; recente; *v.t.* pintar ou tingir de verde; esverdear; *s.* côr verde; verdor, verdura; prado, pasto; =**ish** *adj.* esverdeado; — **goods** (E.U.) notas de banco falsificadas; legumes frescos.
Greenland *s.* Groenlândia.
greenness *s.* verdura; verdor; ingenuidade.
greet *v.t.* saudar; acolher; =**ing** *s.* saudação.
gregarious *adj.* gregário.
Gregorian *adj.* gregoriano.
grey V. **gray**.
greyhound *s.* galgo.
grid *s.* grelha, grade.
grief *s.* desgôsto, dor, pena, aflição.
grieve *v.t.* afligir, desgostar; aborrecer; *v.i.* afligir-se, desgostar-se, penar; **grievance** *s.* motivo de queixa; **grievous** *adj.* penoso, cruel, doloroso.
griffin, griffon *s.* grifo (animal fabuloso).
grill *s.* assado na grelha; *v.t.* grelhar; =**ade** *s.* assado na grelha.
grim *adj.* feroz, bárbaro; feio, horrendo.

grimace *s.* careta.
grime *s.* sujidade, porcaria; *v.t.* sujar, emporcalhar; **grimy** *adj.* sujo, imundo; manchado.
grin *s.* rictus ou careta mostrando os dentes; *v.i.* fazer caretas mostrando os dentes; rir-se sarcàsticamente; arreganhar os dentes.
grind *v.t.* triturar, moer; pulverizar; afiar, amolar; ralar; esfregar; pulir, brunir; ranger (os dentes); oprimir; (*pop.*) estudar com afinco; *v.i.* fazer moenda; pulverizar-se; =**er** *s.* pedra de moinho ou de amolar; moinho; amolador; =**ing** *s.* pulverização; moenda; pulimento; =**stone** pedra de afiar; mó.
grip *s.* apêrto de mão; empunhadura; espasmo de dôr; maleta de mão; influenza, gripe; *v.t.* segurar fortemente; dar um forte apêrto de mão a; *v.i.* agarrar-se com fôrça.
gripe *v.t.* segurar, agarrar; afligir; *v.i.* causar cólicas; sofrer dôres de cólicas; =**s** *s.* cólicas.
grisly *adj.* horrível, pavoroso; assustador.
grist *s.* moenda; quantidade de grão a ser moído; (*pop.*) uma quantidade, uma porção.
gristle *s.* cartilagem; **gristly** *adj.* cartilaginoso.
grit *s.* areia, cascalho; firmeza, valor, ânimo.
grizzled *adj.* grisalho, tordilho.
groan *s.* gemido; *v.i.* gemer.
groats *s.* cereal meio moído; milho picado.
grocer *s.* merceeiro; =**y** *s.* mercearia.
grog *s.* beberagem alcoólica, grogue; =**gy** *adj.* tonto, cambaleante.
groin *s.* virilha.
groom *s.* moço de estrebaria; *v.t.* cuidar de cavalos; (*pop.*) vestir com cuidado, preparar, pentear com capricho.
groomsman *s.* padrinho de casamento.
groove *s.* canal, rêgo; fenda; estria; rotina; *v.t.* acanalar; estriar.
grope *v.t.*&*i.* andar às apalpadelas; tatear.
grosbeak *s.* cardeal (pássaro).
gross *adj.* grosseiro, tôsco; descortês; espêsso, denso, grosso; (*com.*) bruto; *s.* grosa; =**ness** *s.* grosseria; grossura.
grotesque *adj.* grotesco.
grotto *s.* gruta.
ground *s.* terra, terreno, solo, território; base, fundamento; razão, motivo, causa; (*pint.*) fundo ou campo; (*elet.*) terra; (*mil.*) campo de batalha; =**s** *s.* sedimentos; jardim, parque, terrenos; *v.t.*&*i.* fundar, apoiar, estabelecer; pôr em terra; ensinar os elementos de alguma ciência; — **water** agua de poço.
groundless *adv.* sem fundamento.
group *s.* grupo; *v.t.* grupar, agrupar.
grouse *s.* galo silvestre.
grout *s.* farinha grossa; sedimento.
grove *s.* alameda; bosque.
grovel *v.i.* rastejar.
grow *v.i.* crescer, aumentar; criar raizes; *v.t.* cultivar; criar; produzir; — **old** envelhecer; — **angry** encolerizar-se; — **late** fazer-se tarde; — **better** melhorar; — **out of** resultar, provir de; **he will** — **out of this whim** êste capricho lhe passará com a idade; — **sad** entristecer-se; — **up** crescer.
growl *s.* rosnadura, grunhido; *v.i.* rosnar, grunhir.
grown-up *s.* adulto.
growth *s.* crescimento; desabrochamento; aumento; produto; produção; acréscimo.

grub *s.* larva, verme; *(jíria)* comida; *v.i.&t.* cavar; roçar, capinar; *(pop.)* comer.

grudge *s.* rancor; ressentimento; *v.t.* dar de má vontade; invejar; *v.i.* resmungar.

gruel *s.* mingau, papa; *(pop.)* castigo.

gruesome *adj.* macabro.

gruff *adj.* rude, brusco, carrancudo.

grumble *v.i.* resmungar, queixar-se, murmurar.

grunt *s.* grunhido; *v.i.* grunhir.

guano *s.* guano.

guarantee, guaranty *s.* garantia; caução; aval; *v.t.* garantir; caucionar.

guard *s.* guarda, sentinela; vigia; condutor de trem; *v.t.&i.* guardar; guardar-se; **-ian** *s.* guardião, guardiã, curador, curadora; tutor; **-ianship** *s.* tutela, patronato; *(for.)* curadoria.

guava *s.* goiaba; — tree goiabeira.

gudgeon *s.* cabós (peixe); isca; otário; *v.t.* trapacear, enganar.

guerrilla *s.* guerrilha.

guess *s.* conjetura, suposição, adivinhação; *v.t.&i.* adivinhar, conjeturar, supor; *(pop.)* pensar, crer.

guest *s.* convidado, conviva; hóspede.

guffaw *s.* gargalhada; *v.i.* dar gargalhadas; rir espetacularmente.

guidance *s.* orientação; direção.

guide *v.t.* guiar; dirigir; conduzir; orientar; *s.* guia; mentor; **-book** guia, manual.

guild, gild *s.* corporação, associação; grêmio, corpo.

guile *s.* dolo, engano; **-less** *adj.* inocente, cândido; ingênuo.

guillotine *s.* guilhotina.

guilt *s.* culpa, delito; pecado, culpabilidade; **-less** *adj.* inocente; **-y** *adj.* culpado, criminoso.

guinea *s.* guinéu.

guise *s.* modo, maneira; aparência.

guitar *s.* guitarra.

gulf *s.* gôlfo; abismo.

gull *s.* gaivota; engano; vítima de engano; *v.t.* enganar.

gullet *s.* esôfago; garganta; gasganete; canal.

gullible *adj.* crédulo.

gully *s.* ravina, barranco; *v.t.* abrir canal; escavar.

gulp *s.* gole, trago; *v.t.* engulir; — up vomitar.

gum *s.* goma; gengiva; — tree seringueira; *v.t.* engomar; **-my** *adj.* gomoso.

gumption *s.* bom senso; sagacidade; iniciativa.

gun *s.* fuzil; canhão; arma de fogo; **-boat** canhoneira; **-ner** *s.* artilheiro; **-nery** *s.* artilharia.

gurgle *s.* gorgolão, borbotão; *v.i.* gorgolejar.

gurnard *s.* peixe cabra.

gush *s.* esguicho, borbotão; efusão; explosão de sentimentos; *v.i.* exprimir sentimentos com efusão; romper em pranto; *v.t.* derramar, verter.

gusset *s.* *(cost.)* refôrço; *v.t.* *(cost.)* reforçar, pôr refôrço.

gust *s.* rajada; arrebatamento, acesso (de gênio); sabor; prazer.

gusto *s.* gôsto, sabor; apreciação artística.

gusty *adj.* ventoso.

gut *s.* intestino, tripa; *(mar.)* estreito; *v.t.* desventrar, estripar, desentranhar; **-s** *s.* *(pop.)* valor, coragem, resistência.

gutta-percha *s.* guta-percha.

gutter *s.* goteira; boeiro; sarjeta; *v.t.* acanalar; *v.i.* jorrar; — language jíria de sarjeta, linguagem baixa.

guttural *adj.* gutural.

guy *s.* *(mar.)* amarra, calabre, ovém; tipo, sujeito; *v.t.* *(mar.)* firmar com amarra; *(pop.)* caçoar.

guzzle *v.t.&i.* beber, tragar, engulir; embebedar-se; **-r** *s.* beberrão.

gymnasium *s.* ginásio.

gymnast *s.* ginasta; **-ic** *adj.* ginástico; **-ics** *s.* ginástica.

gynaecology, gynecology *s.* ginecologia.

gyrate *v.i.* girar, rodar.

gyration *s.* giro, volta.

gyratory *adj.* giratório.

gyroscope *s.* giroscópio.

gyve *v.t.* encadear, algemar; **-s** algemas.

H

H letra do alfabeto.

habeas corpus *s.* habeas-corpus.

haberdasher *s.* comerciante de artigos de pouca monta, agulhas, linhas, etc.; *(E.U.)* comerciante de artigos para homens.

habiliment *s.* roupa, vestido; trajes (usado geralmente no plural).

habit *s.* hábito, costume; hábito (vestimenta); *v.t.* vestir; ataviar; **-ual** *adj.* habitual.

habitable *ad.* habitável; **habitat** *s.* hábitat; **habitation** *s.* habitação.

hack *s.* talho, corte; cavalo de aluguel; cavalo cansado pelo serviço de sela; carro, sege de praça; *v.t.* picar, cortar, despedaçar; alugar (cavalo); *adj.* de aluguel.

haddock *s.* bacalhau pequeno, eglefim.

Hades *s.* o inferno.

haematite *s.* hematita.

haemorrhage *s.* hemorragia.

haft *s.* cabo, punho.

hag *s.* bruxa, feiticeira.

haggard *adj.* feroz, bravio; macilento, descomposto.

haggle *v.i.* regatear; pedir abatimento; *v.t.* talhar, destroçar.

ha-ha *int.* ah-ah-ah! (exprimindo riso, satisfação ou triunfo).

hail *s.* saudação; saraiva, chuva de pedra; *v.i.* saraivar, chover pedras; *v.t.* saudar.

hair *s.* cabelo; cabelos; cabeleira; pêlo; — brush escova de cabelo; — dresser cabeleireiro; — net rede de cabelo; — dressing penteado; **-ed** *adj.* cabeludo, peludo; **-less** *adj.* calvo, pelado; **-y** *adj.* peludo, cabeludo.

hake *s.* espécie de peixe da família do bacalhau.

halberd *s.* alabarda.

halcyon *adj.* quieto, tranquilo; — days dias tranquilos, serenos; *s.* alcíon, alcião.

hale *adj.* são, robusto; forte.

half *s.* metade: meio; *adj.&adv.* meio, quasi; — and — metade e metade, meia a meia; — blood mestiço; — brother meio irmão; —-hearted frio,

indiferente; —=heartedly friamerte, indiferentemente; — mast meio pau (bandeira); — sole meia sola; —=witted bobo, apatetado; —=light penumbra; — year semestre.
halibut s. peixe grande, semelhante ao linguado.
hall s. vestíbulo; saguão; edifício usado para fins públicos ou semi-públicos; edifício universitário; salão.
hallelujah s. Aleluia.
hallo, halloa *int.* olá (saudação habitual).
hallow *v.t.* santificar, consagrar.
hallucination s. alucinação.
halo s. auréola, nimbo.
halt s. alta, parada, paragem; estacionamento; *v.i.* fazer alta; estacionar; mancar, coxear; vacilar; *adj.* coxo.
halter s. corda; cabresto; enforcamento, corda de enforcar; *v.t.* encabrestar; enforcar.
halting *adj.* coxo.
halve *v.t.* partir pelo meio.
halyard s. (*mar.*) dríça, adriça.
ham s. presunto; coxa; jarrete; (*jíria*) mau ator.
hames s. coleira de cavalo de tiro.
hamlet s. aldeia, vila, logarejo.
hammer s. martelo; gatilho de arma de fogo; *v.t.* martelar, bater.
hammock s. rede, maca.
hamper s. canastra; cêsto grande; *v.t.* embaraçar; estorvar.
hand s. mão; mão (no jôgo); execução, mão de obra; lado; ponteiro (de relógio); seta (indicadora); tendência; assinatura; (*com.*) penca de bananas contendo de oito a vinte frutas; — and glove unha e carne; — in de comum acôrdo; on the other — por outro lado; to get the upper — levar vantagem; *v.t.* dar, entregar, passar, pôr em mãos (de alguém); conduzir, dirigir, levar pela mão; *adj.* feito à mão; carregado ou usado na mão; acionado à mão.
handicap s. desvantagem.
handicraft s. mão de obra; ofício, arte mecânica; =sman s. artesão, artífice.
handle s. cabo; punho; *v.t.* tocar, manusear; manipular, manejar; tratar; dirigir; pôr a mão em; negociar em.
handsel s. presente como festas de ano novo; presente de casamento; qualquer presente comemorativo; *v.t.* estrear; presentear.
handsome *ad*. belo, formoso; bem parecido; liberal, generoso; amplo; =ly *adv.* formosamente; generosamente; =ness s. formosura; generosidade.
handy *adj.* à mão; cômodo; manejável; hábil, dextro.
hang *v.t.* pendurar, suspender; enforcar; *v.i.* pender; flutuar; ser enforcado; estar em dúvida, vacilar; — about vaguear, andar em volta de; — back hesitar, vacilar; — in the balance ser ou estar inseguro; — on persistir; ser pesado (a alguém); — together permanecer unidos; s. ladeira; propensão; modo de cair (vestido, etc.); =man s. carrasco.
hangar s. hangar, galpão.
hanger s. carrasco; agomia; talim, boldrié; cabide; hanging *adj.* suspenso; merecedor de fôrca; s. enforcamento; hangings s. cortinas, tapessaria.
hank s. meada, novêlo.
hanker *v.i.* suspirar por; ansiar.
haphazard s. acaso, acidente; =ly *adv.* casualmente, ao acaso.

hapless *adj.* desventurado, miserável, infeliz.
happen *v.i.* acontecer, suceder, sobrevir; — in entrar por casualidade; =ing s. acontecimento.
happiness s. felicidade.
happy *adj.* feliz.
harangue s. arenga; *v.t.&i.* arengar.
harass *v.t.* acossar, cansar, fatigar.
harbinger s. precursor; presságio; *v.t.* pressagiar, anunciar.
harbor, harbour s. porto; refúgio; asilo; albergue; *v.t.* abrigar, amparar; acolher, hospedar; acalentar (uma idéia); *v.i.* refugiar-se, abrigar-se.
hard *adj.* duro, rude; rigoroso; árduo, laborioso; penoso; opressivo; — drink bebida alcoólica; — boiled egg ovo cozido; — to please exigente; *adv.* duramente; com tenacidade; laboriosamente; firmemente.
harden *v.t.* endurecer; enrijecer; calejar; *v.i.* endurecer-se, empedernir-se.
hardihood s. atrevimento, temeridade.
hardness s. dureza, rigor; hardly *adv.* duramente; apenas, escassamente, dificilmente, apenas.
hardy *adj.* forte, robusto, rijo; bravo, intrépido.
hare s. lebre; —=hearted medroso, tímido.
harem s. harém, serralho.
hark *v.t.&i.* escutar; — back voltar ao assunto.
harlequim s. arlequim; harlequinade s. arlequinada.
harm s. mal, dano, prejuizo; *v.t.* danificar, prejudicar; ofender, ferir; =ful *adj.* prejudicial, pernicioso; =less *adj.* inofensivo; =lessness s. inocência, inocuidade.
harmonious *adj.* harmonioso; harmonium s. harmônio; harmonic *adj.* harmônico; harmonize *v.t.* harmonizar; harmony s. harmonia.
harness s. arreios, jaezes; *v.t.* ajaezar, arrear.
harp s. harpa; *v.i.* tocar harpa; =ist s. harpista.
harpoon s. arpão; *v.t.* arpear.
harpsichord s. clavicórdio, cravo.
harpy s. harpia.
harrow s. instrumento com grades usado em agricultura; *v.t.* trabalhar a terra com aparêlho gradeado; atormentar; perturbar; lacerar.
harrowing *adj.* lacerante, lancinante.
harry *v.t.* saquear, pilhar; devastar; molestar, maltratar.
harsh *adj.* duro, rude, áspero; desagradável; =ness s. dureza, aspereza.
hart s. veado.
hartshorn s. amoníaco; corno de veado.
harum-scarum *adj.* negligente; irresponsável.
harvest s. colheita; época da colheita; *v.t.* colher, fazer a colheita; =er s. ceifeiro, segador.
hash s. picadinho; *v.t.* picar, cortar, retalhar.
hasp s. anel de cadeado; *v.t.* fechar com cadeado.
hassock s. genuflexório; coxim.
haste s. pressa; precipitação; =n *v.i.* apressar-se; *v.t.* apressar; hasty *adj.* apressado, precipitado.
hat s. chapéu.
hatch s. ninhada; *v.t.* incubar, chocar ovos; (*fig.*) tramar, maquinar.

hatchet s. machadinha; — **face cara** comprida, rosto de facão.

hatching s. (des.) sombrear com linhas.

hatchment s. brasão e armas do defunto expostos durante os funerais.

hate s. ódio; v.t. odiar, detestar; =**ful** adj. odioso, detestável; =**r** s. inimigo; **hatred** s. ódio.

hatter s. chapeleiro.

haughtily adv. altaneiramente; de modo altivo; **haughtiness** s. arrogância; **haughty** adj. altaneiro, arrogante.

haul s. puxão; redada; transporte por reboque; v.t. arrastar, puxar; — **down the colors** arriar a bandeira.

haunch s. quadril; anca; quarto, perna (de animal).

haunt v.t. assombrar; causar obcessão; frequentar; rondar; v.i. aparecer (fantasma).

hautboy s. charamela, oboé.

have v.t. ter, haver; possuir; gozar de; fazer; — **a mind to** ter vontade de; — **at heart** desejar com veemência; — **one's way** fazer o que quer; —**to** ter que.

haven s. porto; refúgio; asilo.

haversack s. bornal.

havoc s. estrago, estragos; **cry** — **dar** ordem de saque; v.t. pilhar, saquear; assolar.

haw s. fruto e semente do espinheiro branco; int. hum! (exprimindo hesitação no discurso); termo de comando; v.i. gaguejar; falar hesitando.

hawk s. falcão; pigarro; v.i. caçar com falcões; apregoar mercadorias; limpar a garganta; pigarrear.

hawser s. amarra.

hay s. feno; — **fever** febre do feno.

hazard s. acaso; risco, perigo; v.t. aventurar, arriscar; v.i. arriscar-se, aventurarse; =**ous** adj. arriscado.

haze s. bruma, nevoeiro, cerração; ofuscamento mental; v.t. (mar.) fatigar por trabalhos excessivamente pesados.

hazel s. aveleira; =**nut** avelã.

hazy adj. brumoso; vaporoso; nebuloso; confuso, vago.

he pron. êle; **he-man** (pop.) homem de fato, másculo; **he-goat** bode.

head s. cabeça; cérebro; parte superior ou principal; título, cabeçalho; cabeceira; chefe; caudilho; diretor; ponta (de flecha, etc.); cara (de moeda); ponto culminante; nascente (de rio); (mar.) proa; v.t. encabeçar; dirigir; mandar; pôr título; v.i. dirigir-se; adj. principal; de frente; (mar.) de proa; — **of an arrow** ponta da flecha; — **on** de frente; — **or tail** cara ou coroa; — **over heels** precipitadamente, com os pés pelas mãos; **neither** — **nor tail** nem pé nem cabeça; — **cook** cozinheiro chefe; — **sea** mar pela proa.

headache s. dôr de cabeça.

heal v.t. cicatrizar; curar; =**ing** s. cicatrização, cura.

health s. saúde; sanidade; =**y** adj. saudável, sadio.

heap s. monte, montão; v.t. amontoar, acumular.

hear v.t.&i. ouvir, escutar; — **from** ter notícias de (diretamente, como por cartas); — **of** saber de, ouvir dizer; =**ing** s. ouvido; audiência; **within** =**ing** ao alcance do ouvido.

hearken v.i. escutar.

hearse s. coche fúnebre; féretro; v.t. pôr no caixão.

heart s. coração; centro vital; coragem; **copas** (naipe); —=**to**=— franco, sincero; —=**whole** livre; corajoso; **by** — de côr de memória; **have the** — **in the mouth** estar assustadíssimo; **out of** — descoroçoado, desanimado.

hearten v.t. animar, encorajar.

heartless adj. sem coração, sem ânimo.

hearth s. lareira; lar; fogão.

heartily adv. cordialmente, sinceramente.

hearty adj. cordial; disposto; são; sólido; copioso.

heat s. calor; acaloramento, ardor; cio (dos animais); v.t. esquentar; acalorar, excitar; — **lightning** relâmpago; — **unit** unidade térmica; — **stroke** insolação.

heater s. aquecedor.

heath s. urze; matagal; terreno baldio.

heathen s. pagão; idólatra; =**ism** s. paganismo, idolatria.

heather s. variedade de urze.

heating s. calefação.

heave v.t. alçar, levantar, elevar, içar; virar; lançar; forçar para fora; arrojar; exalar; v.i. suspirar, respirar profundamente; levantar-se e baixar-se alternativamente (o peito, o mar); palpitar; s. elevação; alçadura; levantamento.

heaven s. céu, céus; =**ly** adj. celestial.

heavier adj. mais pesado.

heavy adj. pesado; maciço; forte; **grosso**; grande; denso, espesso; carregado; pesaroso, triste; tardo, lento, estúpido; indigesto; — **rain** chuva forte; **heavily** adv. pesadamente; **heaviness** s. peso; entorpecimento; languidez; abatimento; opressão, carga.

Hebraic adj. hebraico.

Hebrew adj. hebreu.

hecatomb s. hecatombe.

heckle v.t. interromper intempestivamente com perguntas irrisórias ou sarcásticas.

hectic adj. consuntiva (febre); héctico; (pop.) excitado, agitado; turbulento; s. héctica, tísica.

hector s. fanfarrão; v.t.&i. contar bravatas, intimidar com bravatas.

hedge s. sebe, cêrca viva; v.t. fechar com sebe; separar com sebe; defender, circundar, rodear; v.i. abrigar-se; cobrir-se.

heed s. atenção; cuidado; v.t. atender, escutar; observar; v.i. prestar atenção, fazer caso.

heedless adj. desatento, descuidado.

heel s. salto; calcanhar; **at the** =**s of ao** encalço de.

hefty adj. sólido, veemente.

hegemony s. hegemonia.

heifer s. vitela.

height s. altura, elevação, altitude; apogeu, cúmulo; **the** — **of folly** o cúmulo da loucura.

heighten v.t. realçar; levantar; elevar.

heinous adj. odioso; atroz, nefando.

heir, heiress s. herdeiro, herdeira; —=**at-law** herdeiro legal; — **apparent** herdeiro forçado; — **presumptive** herdeiro presuntivo.

heirdom s. direito de herança.

helianthus s. helianto, girassol.

helical adj. espiral.

heliotrope s. heliotrópio.

helium s. hélio.

helix s. hélice.

hell s. inferno.

hellenism s. helenismo.

hello int. alô!

helm *s.* (*mar.*) temão, barra do leme; leme; *v.t.* dirigir.
helmet *s.* capacete.
helot *s.* ilota, escravo; =ism *s.* ilotismo.
help *s.* auxílio, ajuda, socorro; remédio; empregado; *v.t.&i.* ajudar, assistir, socorrer; evitar; servir (na mesa); servir-se; — one's self to servir-se de (comida); **he could not — doing this** êle não poude deixar de fazer isso.
helper *s.* ajudante, auxiliar; assistente; **helpful** *adj.* útil, proveitoso; **helpless** *adj.* desvalido, impossibilitado, impotente.
helter-skelter *adv.* a troche e moche, atabalhoadamente.
helve *s.* cabo, punho.
hem *s.* bainha (de roupa); *v.t.* embainhar; *v.i.* pigarrear; hesitar falando.
hematite *s.* hematita.
hemisphere *s.* hemisfério.
hemlock *s.* cicuta.
hemorrhage *s.* hemorragia.
hemorrhoids *s.* hemorróidas.
hemming *s.* (*cost.*) ponto de bainha.
hemp *s.* cânhamo.
hemstitch *s.* (*cost.*) bainha de laçada.
hen *s.* galinha; fêmea de qualquer ave; — **house** galinheiro.
hence *adv.* d'aí, d'ali, d'aquí; desde aquí; *conj.* logo, portanto, em consequência; =forth *adv.* d'aquí por diante, no futuro.
henchman *s.* partidário; apaniguado.
henna *s.* tintura de henê.
her *pron.* ela, lhe, a, la; *adj.* sua, seu, seus, suas.
herald *s.* heraldo, arauto; *v.t.* anunciar.
herb *s.* herva; =aceous *adj.* herbáceo; =al *adj.* herbóreo; =arium *s.* herbário; =ivorous *adj.* herbívoro; =orize *v.i.* herborizar.
Herculean *ad.* hercúleo; **Hercules** *s.* Hercules.
herd *s.* rebanho, grei; multidão; *v.t.* arrebanhar; *v.i.* associar-se; **the — instinct** o instinto gregário; =sman *s.* pastor, vaqueiro.
here *adv.* aquí; cá; neste ponto; — **I am,** aquí estou; =abouts *adv.* por aquí, nestas cercanias; =after *adv.* daquí por diante, para o futuro; =by *adv.* por êste meio, pelo presente, dest'arte.
heredity *s.* hereditariedade.
hereditary *adj.* hereditário; **hereditament** *s.* bens transmissíveis por via de sucessão.
herein *adv.* incluso; =after *adv.* mais abaixo, mais adiante, daquí por diante.
hereof *adv.* acêrca d'isto; d'isto; **hereon** *adv.* sôbre isso, sôbre isto.
heresy *s.* heresia; **heretic** *s.* herético, herege; **heretical** *adj.* herético.
hereupon *adv.* sôbre isso, assim fazendo; **herewith** *adv.* aquí junto.
heritage *s.* herança, patrimônio.
hermaphrodite *s.* hermafrodita.
hermetic *adj.* hermético.
hermit *s.* eremita, solitário.
hernia *s.* hérnia.
hero *s.* herói; =ine *s.* heroina; =ism *s.* heroismo.
heron *s.* garça.
herring *s.* arenque.
hers *pron.* seu, sua, seus e suas, dela; o seu, a sua, o dela, a dela; os seus, as suas, os dela, as dela.
herself *pron.* ela própria; ela; ela mesma.
hesitate *v.i.* hesitar; vacilar; **hesitation** *s.* hesitação.

heterodox *adj.* heterodoxo.
heterogeneous *adj.* heterogêneo.
hew *v.t.* abater (árvores); cortar a machadadas; picar; talhar (pedras).
hexagon *s.* hexágono; =al *adj.* hexagonal.
heyday *s.* cúmulo, apogeu de vitalidade e vigor.
hi *int.* olá.
hiatus *s.* hiato; lacuna.
hibernate *v.i.* hibernar.
hiccup, hiccough *s.* soluço; *v.i.* estar com soluço.
hidden *adj.* escondido, oculto; **hide** *v.t.* esconder, ocultar; *v.i.* esconder-se.
hide *s.* couro, pele.
hideous *adj.* horrível, espantoso, hediondo.
hiding *s.* esconderijo.
hierarchy *s.* hierarquia.
hieroglyph *s.* hieróglifo.
higgle *v.i.* regatear; negociar, revender gêneros de porta em porta.
high *adj.* alto; de altura; eminente; superior; sumo (sacerdote); supremo (tribunal); elevado, digno; vivo, intenso; forte, violento; poderoso; *adv.* altamente; muito, sumamente; a grande altura; arrogantemente; a preço alto; luxuosamente; — **altar** altar-mor; — **and mighty** (*pop.*) arrogante, cheio de si; — **explosive** explosivo de grande potência; — **hat** cartola; — **mass** missa cantada; — **pressure** alta pressão; — **priest** sumo sacerdote; — **spirits** alegria, bom humor; — **words** palavras ofensivas; —=handed despótico, arbitrário; —=minded magnânimo, de idéias largas; — **seasoned** picante, muito temperado.
highball *s.* bebida alcoólica (água, gêlo e whisky).
higher *adj.* mais alto; superior; — **education** educação superior; **highly** *adv.* altamente; fortemente; muito; **highness** *s.* altura, elevação; Alteza (título).
hiker *s.* excursionista a pé, andarilho.
hilarious *adj.* hilariante; **hilarity** *s.* hilaridade.
hill *s.* colina, outeiro, encosta; *v.t.* amontoar; juntar terra em volta.
hillock *s.* montículo; pequena colina.
hilly *ad.* acidentado (terreno).
hilt *s.* cabo, punho, empunhadura (de armas).
him *pron.* lhe, êle, o, lo; =self *pron.* êle próprio, êle mesmo.
hind *s.* corça.
hinder *v.t.* impedir; obstruir; *v.i.* pôr obstáculos; *adj.* posterior.
hindmost *adj.* último, trazeiro.
hindrance *s.* impedimento, empecilho, estôrvo.
Hindi *s.* hindí, idioma moderno do Hindustão.
Hindoo, Hindu *adj.&s.* indú, hindú.
hinge *s.* dobradiça, gonzo, charneira; ponto principal; *v.i.* girar sôbre um gonzo.
hinny *s.* mula, burro.
hint *s.* sugestão, alusão, insinuação; *v.t.* insinuar, indicar, sugerir; *v.i.* dar uma indireta.
hip *s.* (*anat.*) cadeira, quadril; — **bath** banho de assento, semicúpio.
hippodrome *s.* hipódromo.
hippopotamus *s.* hipopótamo.
hire *s.* aluguel; salário; *v.t.* alugar; arrendar; assalariar; — **system** sistema de vendas a prestações; =d *adj.* de aluguel; assalariado; mercenário.

hirsute adj. hirsuto.

his adj.&pron. o seu, a sua, os seus, as suas; seu, sua, seus, suas, d'êle.

hiss v.t.&i. vaiar; s. vaia.

history s. história; **historic, historical** adj. histórico; **historian** s. historiador.

histrionic adj. histriónico; **histrion** s. histrião, palhaço.

hit s. golpe, choque; colisão; sucesso (êxito); v.t. dar, pegar, golpear; atinar, acertar; encontrar, colidir; v.i. colidir; roçar, chocar; acontecer de um modo feliz; sair bem; encontrar por casualidade; acertar; — off improvisar ou representar bem; — the mark atingir o alvo; — against colidir, chocar-se contra; a lucky — golpe de sorte.

hitch v.t. atar, ligar; enganchar; (mar.) amarrar; v.i. mover-se aos saltos; agarrar-se; s. parada; tropêço, dificuldade, obstáculo.

hitch hike v.i. (jíria) viajar obtendo condução de favor em automóveis.

hither adj. citerior; —to adv. até agora, até aquí.

hive s. colmeia.

hoard s. provisão; acumulação; montão; v.t. acumular, juntar, guardar; fazer provisão.

hoarding s. paliçada, tapume.

hoarhound s. marroio.

hoarse adj. rouco; —ness s. rouquidão.

hoary adj. branco; esbranquiçado; branco ou grisalho pela idade.

hoax s. mistificação, engano, burla; v.t. enganar, burlar.

hob s. rústico; palhaço; (pop.) malícia; projeção na parte trazeira ou lateral da lareira.

hobble v.i. coxear, mancar, manquejar; v.t. entravar.

hobby s. mania, passa-tempo predileto.

hobgoblin s. duende.

hobnail s. cravo de ferradura; prego grosso; —ed adj. ferrado, cravado.

hock s. vinho branco do Reno; jarrête (de animais).

hockey s. hockey (jôgo esportivo).

hocus v.t. mistificar, enganar; adulterar.

hod s. pá onde o pedreiro carrega argamassa ou tijolos.

hoe s. enxada, sacho, sachola; v.t. sachar; capinar.

hog s. porco, capado; (pop.) pessoa suja e desagradável.

hogshead s. barrica, pipa, tonel.

hoist s. guindaste, grua; elevador, ascensor; levantamento, ascensão; v.t. levantar, içar; guindar.

hold s. tomada; posse; freio; influência; (mús.) pausa; (mar.) porão; v.t. agarrar; segurar; reter; reservar; suster, apoiar; limitar; prender; ligar; sustentar; considerar; presidir; carregar; manter; possuir; v.i. valer, ser válido; manter-se firme; aguentar; seguir, prosseguir; refreiar-se, abster-se; — back deter, conter; — to aderir; — up parar, deter; levantar, alçar; sustentar; —er s. possuidor, portador (de título); —ing s. detenção, propriedade; posse; arrendamento, inquilinato.

hole s. buraco, orifício; abertura; cavidade; perfuração; poço; cova; v.t. furar, perfurar; a — to crawl out of escapatória, desculpa.

holiday s. feriado; dia de festa; dia santo; férias.

holily adv. santamente; **holiness** s. santidade.

Holland s. Holanda.

hollo v.t. incitar ou perseguir com gritos.

hollow adj. côncavo; ôco; vazio; cavernoso; falso, enganador, insincero; vão, sem valor; s. concavidade; vacuidade; cavidade, buraco; canal, bacia, vale; v.t. cavar; esvaziar; escavar.

holly s. (bot.) azevinho.

hollyhock s. malva hortense, malva rosa.

holocaust s. holocausto.

holster s. coldre.

holy adj. santo; sagrado; bento; — Ghost Espírito Santo; — Land Terra Santa; — water água benta.

homage s. homenagem.

home s. lar; casa paterna; casa, residência; interior; pátria; família; asilo, albergue, refúgio; at — em casa; em seu país; à vontade; adv. para casa; acertadamente; adj. doméstico; interior, de casa, caseiro; nativo, natal; certeiro, que atinge a meta; **Home Department** Ministério do Interior (Inglaterra); **to hit —, to strike —** atingir em cheio.

homeless adj. sem lar.

homeliness s. simplicidade; fealdade.

homely adj. feio, sem graça, sem atrativos; simples.

homeopath s. homeopata.

Homeric adj. homérico.

homespun s. pano tecido em casa; adj. caseiro, feito em casa.

homestead s. herdade; casa de habitação e seus terrenos; propriedade rural.

homeward adj.&adv. de volta para casa; em caminho de casa.

homicide s. homicídio, homicida; **homicidal** adj. homicida.

homily s. homília; sermão.

homing adj. de volta para casa; — pigeon pombo-correio.

homoeopathy s. homeopatia; **homoeopath** s. homeopata.

homogeneous adj. homogêneo.

homonym s. homônimo.

hone s. pedra de afiar.

honest adj. honesto, probo, íntegro; —y s. honestidade, probidade, integridade.

honey s. mel de abelhas; (é usado também com termo de carinho); v.t. tornar doce, cobrir com mel; v.i. falar com carinho.

honor, honour s. honra; v.t. honrar; (com.) aceitar, pagar; —able adj. honrado; honorífico; honroso; **Honorable** título de distinção.

honorarium s. honorários.

honorary adj. honorário; honorífico; sem retribuição.

hood s. capuz; capucho; touca; capelo; v.t. cobrir com capuz.

hoof s. casco (de cavalo).

hook s. colchete, gancho; anzol; v.t. enganchar, prender com colchete.

hook-up s. (rdd.) circuito.

hoop s. arco; anel; aro; argola; v.t. cercar, rodear, pôr arcos ou ligar por meio dêles.

hoot v.i.&t. gritar; vaiar; reclamar aos gritos; s. grito; clamor, vaia.

hop s. salto, brincadeira; baile, dansa; (bot.) lúpulo; (av.) vôo; v.i. saltar, brincar; coxear.

hope s. esperança; v.t.&i. esperar, ter esperanças; — box, — chest canastra onde as moças guardam o enxoval; —ful *adj.* esperançoso; cheio de esperanças; **=less** *adj.* sem esperanças, desesperançado.

hopper *s.* coxo (pessoa que anda saltando por defeito físico); larva de certos insetos; caixa d'água com válvula de descarga; tremonha.

horde *s.* horda.

horizon *s.* horizonte; **=tal** *adj.* horizontal.

horn *s.* chifre; galho (de certos ruminantes); antena (de insetos); corno; (*mús.*) corneta; buzina.

hornet *s.* vespão.

horny *adj.* que tem cornos; chifrudo; caloso.

horology *s.* horologia.

horoscope *s.* horóscopo.

horrible *adj.* horrível; **horrid** *adj.* horrível; hediondo; **horror** *s.* horror.

horse *s.* cavalo; (*mil.*) cavalaria; cavalete de secar roupa; cavalete; (*gíria* de estudantes) cola; *v.t.* prover com cavalos; *v.i.* cavalgar, andar a cavalo; — **boy** menino ou moço de cavalariças; **on =back** a cavalo; — **dealer** negociante de cavalos; — **hair** crina; **=manship** equitação; **=power** cavalovapor; **=shoe** ferradura; **=box** manjedoura; **=gear** arreios; — **play** gracejo grosseiro.

horticultural *adj.* hortícola; **horticulture** *s.* horticultura; **horticulturist** *s.* horticultor.

hosanna *s.* hosana.

hose *s.* meias; mangueira (tubo); *v.t.* puxar água por meio de mangueira; — **the garden** regar o jardim; **hosier** *s.* negociante de meias ou fabricante de meias; **hosiery** *s.* meias em geral; loja de meias.

hospital *s.* hospital; **hospitable** *adj.* hospitaleiro; **=er** *s.* aquele que reside em hospital; **=ity** *s.* hospitalidade.

hospitium *s.* hospício.

host *s.* anfitrião; hóstia; hospedeiro; hoste; multidão; **=ess** *s.* anfitriã; hospedeira.

hostage *s.* refém, penhor.

hostel *s.* pousada, hospedaria; hotel; pensão de estudantes.

hostile *adj.* hostil; **hostility** *s.* hostilidade.

hostler *s.* moço de estrebaria.

hot *adj.* quente; caloroso; ardente; fogoso; picante; violento, furioso; (*pop.*) intolerável; **I gave it him** — disse-lhe boas; **—head** cabeça quente, genioso; **=house** estufa; — **spring** fontes térmicas; **to be in** — **water** estar metido em camisa de onze varas.

hotel *s.* hotel.

hotly *adv.* calorosamente.

hough *s.* jarrête.

hound *s.* cachorro de caça; homem vil; *v.t.* caçar com cachorros; perseguir; açular.

hour *s.* hora; **—=glass** ampulheta; **=ly** *adv.* de hora em hora.

house *s.* casa; mansão; vivenda; habitação; lar; (*com.*) casa de comércio, estabelecimento mercantil; câmara de um corpo legislativo; (*teat.*) sala, público; (*mec.*) caixa, cobertura; *v.t.* albergar; alojar; (*mar.*) cobrir quando há borrasca; (*carp.*) encaixar; (*agric.*) armazenar, pôr a coberto; *v.i.* residir; — **of worship** igreja, templo; — **rent** aluguel de casa; — **of cards** castelo de cartas; — **of Lords** ou **of Peers** Câmara dos Lordes; **=wife** dona de casa.

hovel *s.* cabana, choupana; barraca; telheiro.

hover *v.i.* voltejar; revoltear; ficar suspenso; duvidar, hesitar.

how *adv.* como, de que modo, quanto, quão; — **far até onde?** — **late até que horas?** — **long** quanto tempo? — **soon** quando? **=ever** *adv.* de qualquer modo; por muito; *conj.* não obstante, contudo, posto que; **=ever much** por muito que.

howl *s.* uivo; *v.i.* uivar.

hoyden *s.* menina desenvolta em excesso.

hubbub *s.* grita, alvoroço, bulha; confusão.

huckster *s.* vendedor ambulante de miudezas ou de produtos agrícolas; indivíduo ruim, mercenário.

huddle *v.t.* amontoar desordenadamente; juntar às pressas em confusão.

hue *s.* côr, matiz, tonalidade.

huff *v.t.* tratar com arrogância; ofender; aborrecer; *v.i.* soprar.

hug *s.* abraço; *v.t.* abraçar; apertar; trazer junto a si; acarinhar.

huge *adj.* enorme, imenso; desmedido; **=ly** *adv.* desmedidamente; enormemente.

hulk *s.* batelão; navio velho fora de uso; navio-presídio; carcassa de navio.

hull *s.* casca (de fruta); película; vagem; casco de navio; *v.t.* descascar; lançar um projétil sobre o casco de um navio.

hum *v.i.* zumbir; cantarolar (sem articular); *s.* zumbido.

human *adj.* humano; **=itarian** *adj.* humanitário; **=ity** *s.* humanidade; **=ize** *v.t.* humanizar.

humble *adj.* humilde; *v.t.* humilhar; **=ness** *s.* humildade; humildade de nascimento.

humbug *s.* mistificação, farsa, embuste; *v.t.* fraudar, mistificar.

humdrum *adj.* monótono; banal, fastidioso.

humerus *s.* úmero.

humid *adj.* úmido; **=ity** *s.* umidade.

humiliate *v.t.* humilhar; **humility** *s.* humildade.

humming-bird beija-flor.

hummock *s.* morro, colina; montículo.

humor, humour *s.* humor, gênio, índole; fantasia, capricho; agudeza, chiste, jocosidade, senso do cômico; *v.t.&i.* comprazer, aceder, consentir em; adaptar-se.

humorist *s.* humorista; gracejador.

hump *s.* corcunda; **—=backed** *adj.* corcunda (pessoa).

humph *int.* hum!

hunch *s.* corcova, giba; corcunda; (*pop.*) palpite.

hundred *adj.&s.* cem, cento; **=fold** cêntuplo, centuplicado.

hunger *s.* fome; — **strike** greve da fome; **hungrily** *adv.* àvidamente; **hungry** *adj.* com fome, esfomeado, faminto.

hunk *s.* (*pop.*) um bom pedaço; uma boa porção.

hunt *s.* caçada; associação de caçadores; busca; *v.t.* caçar; seguir, perseguir; buscar; dar busca; (*pop.*) procurar; — **for** procurar; **=er** *s.* caçador; cavalo de caça, cão de caça; **=ing** *s.* caça, caçada; **=ress** *s.* caçadora; **=sman** *s.* caçador.

hurdle *s.* cêrca; barreira; obstáculo (em forma de barreira); obstáculo nas corridas de cavalo; espécie de gaiola engradada onde se levavam os condenados à forca; **=r** cavaleiro que toma parte numa corrida de obstáculos; **=s** *s.* corrida de obstáculos.

hurl *v.t.* lançar, projetar.
hurly-burly *s.* tumulto; alvoroço.
hurrah, hurray *int.* hurral vival
hurricane *s.* furacão.
hurry *s.* pressa, precipitação; *v.t.* apressar, precipitar; *v.i.* apressar-se, precipitar-se.
hurt *s.* lesão, ferimento, contusão; mal, dano, prejuízo; *adj.* magoado, ofendido; ferido; prejudicado; *v.t.&i.* doer; causar mal ou dano; ferir; injuriar, ofender; danificar; **to — one's feelings** ofender os sentimentos de alguém.
husband *s.* marido, esposo.
husbandry *s.* administração dos negócios domésticos; economia rural; produção agrícola; parcimônia.
hush *s.* silence; **—money** preço do silêncio; *v.t.* fazer calar; *int.* psiu! silêncio!
husk *s.* casca, vagem; *v.t.* descascar.
hussy, huzzy *s.* moça desenvolta; estôjo de costura.
hustle *v.t.* empurrar; sacudir; *(pop.)* agir ou mover-se com energia resoluta.
hut *s.* cabana; barraca.
hutch *s.* cabana; canastra, arca; cofre.
hyacinth *s.* jacinto.
hyaena, hyena *s.* hiena.
hybrid *adj.* híbrido.
hydra *s.* hidra.
hydrangea *s.* *(bot.)* hortênsia.

hydrant *s.* máquina hidráulica, registro, válvula.
hydrate *s.* hidrato.
hydraulic *adj.* hidráulico; **—s** *s.* hidráulica.
hydrocarbon *s.* hidrocarboneto; **hydrogen** *s.* hidrogênio.
hydropathy *s.* hidropatia; **hydropathic** *adj.* hidropático.
hydrophobia *s.* hidrofobia.
hydroplane *s.* hidroplano.
hyena *s.* hiena.
hygiene *s.* higiene; **hygienic, hygienical** *adj.* higiênico.
hymen *s.* hímen; himeneu.
hymn *s.* hino.
hyperbola, hyperbole *s.* hipérbole.
hyphen *s.* hífen, traço de união; traço.
hypnotism *s.* hipnotismo.
hipnotize *v.t.* hipnotizar.
hypocondriac *adj.&s.* hipocondríaco.
hypocrisy *s.* hipocrisia; **hypocrite** *s.* hipócrita.
hypodermic *adj.* hipodérmico.
hyposulphite *s.* hipossulfito.
hypothesis *s.* hipótese.
hypothetical *adj.* hipotético.
hyssop *s.* *(bot.)* hissopo; hissope.
hysteria *s.* histeria; **hysterical** *adj.* histérico; **hysterics** *s.* ataques histéricos.
hysterotomy *s.* histerotomia.

I

I letra do alfabeto.
I *pron.* eu.
iambic *adj.* iâmbico; *s.* iambo.
ibex *s.* cabra montês.
ibis *s.* íbis.
ice *s.* gêlo; sorvete; **— cream** sorvete (que leva creme ou leite); **orange — sorvете** de laranja; *v.t.* congelar, gelar.
iceberg *s.* massa de gêlo flutuante.
ichthyology *s.* ictiologia.
icicle *s.* massa pendente de gêlo.
icon *s.* ícone; **—oclast** *s.* iconoclasta.
icy *adj.* gelado; frio; álgido.
idea *s.* idéia; pensamento; **—l** *s.&adj.* ideal; **—ism** *s.* idealismo; **—ist** *s.* idealista; **—listic** *adj.* idealístico.
identical *adj.* idêntico; **identification** *s.* identificação; **identify** *v.t.* identificar; **identity** *s.* identidade.
idiocy *s.* idiotia.
idiom *s.* idioma; *(gram.)* idiotismo; forma e estrutura de uma língua.
idiosyncrasy *s.* idiossincrasia.
idiot *s.* idiota; **—ic** *adj.* idiota.
idle *adj.* ocioso, desocupado; preguiçoso; inútil, vão; *v.i.* folgar, estar ocioso; funcionar (o motor) com o carro parado.
idleness *s.* ociosidade, ócio; **idler** *s.* ocioso, preguiçoso, vagabundo; **idly** *adv.* preguiçosamente, ociosamente.
idol *s.* ídolo; **—ater** *s.* idólatra; **—atrous** *adj.* idólatra; **—atry** *s.* idolatria.
idolize *v.t.* idolatrar.
idyl, idyll *s.* idílio; **—ic** *adj.* idílico.
if *conj.* se.
igneous *adj.* ígneo; **ignition** *s.* ignição, inflamação.
ignoble *adj.* ignóbil.
ignominious *adj.* ignominioso; **ignominy** *s.* ignomínia.
ignoramus *s.* ignorante; **ignorance** *s.* ignorância; **ignorant** *adj.* ignorante.

ignore *v.t.* não fazer caso de; não prestar a mínima atenção a; não tomar conhecimento de.
iguana *s.* iguano.
ill *adj.* doente; enfêrmo; mau; nocivo; daninho; *s.* adversidade; mal; *adv.* mal, maldosamente; **—speak** falar mal; **— fame** má fama; **— temper** mau gênio; **— advised** mal aconselhado; **—fated** malaventurado; **—humored** mal humorado; **—disposed** mal disposto; **—favored** feio, repulsivo; **—sorted** incompatível; **—treat**, **—use** maltratar; **to bear — will** ter rancor; **—timed** intempestivo, inoportuno; **—gotten gains** fortuna mal adquirida.
illegal *adj.* ilegal.
illegible *adj .* ilegível.
illegitimacy *s.* ilegitimidade; **illegitimate** *adj.* ilegítimo.
illicit *adj.* ilícito.
illiterate *adj.&s.* analfabeto.
illness *s.* doença; mal.
illogical *adj.* ilógico.
illuminate *v.t.* iluminar; esclarecer; ilustrar.
illumine *v.t.* iluminar; esclarecer.
illumination *s.* iluminação; esclarecimento; iluminura.
illusion *s.* ilusão; **illusive** *adj.* ilusório.
illustrate *v.t.* ilustrar; **illustration** *s.* ilustração, gravura; **illustrious** *adj.* ilustre.
image *s.* imagem; **—ry** *s.* imagens; **imagination** *s.* imaginação; **imagine** *v.t.&i.* imaginar; **imaginary** *adj.* imaginário.
imbecil *s.&adj.* imbecil.
imbibe *v.t.&i.* embeber; embeber-se; absorver.
imbricate *v.t.* imbricar, sobrepor; *adj.* imbricado.

imbroglio s. imbróglio, mixórdia, confusão.

imbrue v.t. embeber, empapar (referindo-se a sangue).

imbue v.t. embeber, saturar, impregnar.

imitate v.t. imitar; imitation s. imitação; imitator s. imitador.

immaculate adj. imaculado.

immanent adj. imanente, inerente.

immaterial adj. imaterial; sem importância.

immature adj. imaturo.

immeasurable adj. imensurável.

immediate adj. imediato.

immemorial adj. imemorial.

immense adj. imenso; -ly adv. imensamente; immensity s. imensidão, imensidade.

immerse v.t. imergir, mergulhar; immersion s. imersão.

immigrate v.i. imigrar.

imminence s. iminência; imminent adj. iminente.

immoderate adj. imoderado.

immodest adj. imodesto.

immolate v.t. imolar.

immoral adj. imoral; -ity s. imoralidade.

immortal adj. imortal; -ity s. imortalidade; -ize v.t. imortalizar.

immovable adj. inamovível; imutável, firme; imóvel.

immunity s. imunidade.

immure v.t. emparedar, enclausurar, encerrar.

immutable adj. imutável.

imp s. diabinho; criança travêssa.

impact s. choque; percussão.

impair v.t. prejudicar; comprometer; deteriorar; danificar; enfraquecer, reduzir, diminuir.

impale v.t. empalar.

impalpable adj. impalpável.

impanel v.t. formar a lista dos jurados, formar um quadro de pessoal.

impart v.t.&i. dar; conceder; conferir; dar uma parte; dispensar; comunicar; revelar, descobrir, divulgar.

impartial adj. imparcial; -ity s. imparcialidade.

impassable adj. impraticável, intransitável.

impassible adj. impassível.

impassioned adj. apaixonado, ardente.

impaste v.t. (pint.) empastar; guardar numa pasta.

impasto s. (pint.) pasta de tintas; empastamento.

impatience s. impaciência; impatient adj. impaciente; impatiently adv. impacientemente.

impeach v.t. acusar (um funcionário perante um tribunal); denunciar; impugnar.

impecunious adj. pobre, necessitado.

impede v.t. entravar, estorvar; impedir; impediment s. obstrução, obstáculo; impedimento.

impel v.t. impelir, propelir.

impending adj. ameaçador, iminente.

impenetrable adj. impenetrável.

impenitence s. impenitência; impenitent adj. impenitente.

imperative adj. imperativo, imperioso; s. imperativo.

imperceptible adj. imperceptível.

imperfect adj.&s. imperfeito; -ion s. imperfeição.

imperial adj. imperial; -ist s. imperialista.

imperil v.t. pôr em perigo.

imperious adj. imperioso.

imperishable adj. imperecível.

impermeable adj. impermeável.

impersonal adj. impessoal.

impersonate v.t. personificar; impersonation s. personificação; (teat.) papel, caraterização.

impertinence s. impertinência; impertinent adj. impertinente; impertinently adv. impertinentemente.

imperturbable adj. imperturbável.

impervious adj. impenetrável, impermeável.

impetuous adj. impetuoso, arrebatado.

impetus s. ímpeto, impulso.

impiety s. impiedade.

impinge v.i. tropeçar; esbarrar; chocar; topar com; entrar em contato.

impious adj. ímpio.

impish adj. travêsso, ladino.

implacable adj. implacável.

implant v.t. implantar.

implement s. implemento, apetrecho, instrumento; ferramenta; v.t. realizar, tornar efetivo; prover de utensílios.

implicate v.t. implicar; implication s. implicação, subentendido.

implicit adj. implícito, tácito.

implore v.t. implorar, suplicar.

imply v.t. implicar; fazer supor; querer dizer.

impolite adj. descortês, incivil.

impolitic adj. impolítico.

imponderable adj. imponderável.

import v.t.&i. importar; denotar; significar; implicar; interessar; (com.) importar; s. sentido, significação; importância, valor; (com.) mercadoria importada.

importance s. importância; important adj. importante.

importation s. importação; importer s. importador.

importunate adj. importuno; importune v.t. importunar; importunity s. importunidade.

impose v.t. impor; impingir; — upon, — on enganar; imposition s. imposição; taxa; impostura.

impossibility s. impossibilidade; impossible adj. impossível.

impostor s. impostor; imposture s. impostura.

impotence, impotency s. impotência; impotent adj. impotente.

impound v.t. encerrar, aprisionar; recolher (água) num depósito.

impoverish v.t. empobrecer.

impracticable adj. impraticável.

imprecation s. imprecação.

impregnable adj. impregnável.

impregnate v.t. impregnar; fecundar; -d adj. impregnado; fecundada, grávida.

impresario s. empresário.

impress v.t.&i. imprimir; estampar, marcar; impressionar; inculcar; influir; requisitar; s. impressão; sinal, marca; divisa; desapropriação; (mil.) leva de marujos.

impressionism s. impressionismo.

impressive adj. impressivo, impressionante.

imprint s. impressão; marca; sinal; v.t. imprimir; estampar; marcar.

imprison v.t. aprisionar; -ment s. aprisionamento; prisão.

improbability s. improbabilidade; improbable adj. improvável; improbably adv. improvàvelmente.

improper *adj.* impróprio, inconveniente.
impromptu *s.* impromptu, improviso.
impropriety *s.* impropriedade, inconveniência.
improve *v.t.* melhorar, aperfeiçoar; aproveitar; valorizar; *v.i.* melhorar; progredir; valorizar-se; *ment *s.* melhoramento, aperfeiçoamento; progresso; benfeitoria.
improvident *adj.* imprevidente; improvidente; improvidence *s.* imprevidência, improvidência.
improvise *v.t.* improvisar.
imprudence *s.* imprudência; imprudent *adj.* imprudente; imprudently *adv.* imprudentemente.
impudence *s.* impudência, atrevimento; impudent *adj.* impudente; impudently *adv.* impudentemente.
impudicity *s.* impudicícia.
impugn *v.t.* impugnar; refutar.
impulse *s.* impulso, ímpeto.
impulsion *s.* impulsão, impulso; impulsive *adj.* impulsivo.
impunity *s.* impunidade.
impure *adj.* impuro; impurity *s.* impureza.
imputation *s.* imputação; impute *v.t.* imputar.
in *prep.* (denotando situação, estado, modo, disposição, duração, causa, objeto, fim, etc.) de, em, por, com, durante, para, dentro de, a; he is — England está na Inglaterra; the best hotel — Paris o melhor hotel de Paris; — the morning pela manhã; — fun por graça; — ink a tinta; he will come — a week virá d'aquí a uma semana; — his sleep durante o sono; — here aquí dentro; — there alí dentro; *adv.* dentro, em casa, no escritório, etc.; *adj.* interior, interno; que está no poder; que está na vez; *s.* (em geral usado no plural) os de dentro, os de casa.
inability *s.* incapacidade.
inaccessible *adj.* inacessível.
inaccuracy *s.* inexatidão; incorreção; inaccurate *adj.* inexato, errôneo.
inaction *s.* inação.
inactive *adj.* inativo.
inadequate *adj.* inadequado.
inadmissible *adj.* inadmissível.
inadvertently *adv.* inadvertidamente, por inadvertência.
inalienable *adj.* inalienável.
inane *adj.* inane, vazio, oco.
inanimate *adj.* inanimado; inanition *s.* inanição.
inanity *s.* inanidade.
inapplicable *adj.* inaplicável.
inapposite *adj.* fora de própósito.
inappreciable *adj.* inapreciável.
inappropriate *adj.* impróprio.
inapt *adj.* inapto.
inarticulate *adj.* inarticulado.
inasmuch as *conj.* porquanto, visto como.
inattentive *adj.* desatento.
inaudible *adj.* inaudível.
inaugurate *v.t.* inaugurar.
inauspicious *adj.* desfavorável; de mau agouro.
inborn *adj.* inato.
incalculable *adj.* incalculável.
incandescence *s.* incandescência; incandescent *adj.* incandescente.
incantation *s.* encantamento.
incapable *adj.* incapaz; incapacitate *v.t.* incapacitar; incapacity *s.* incapacidade.

incarcerate *v.t.* encarcerar.
incarnate *v.t.* encarnar; incarnation *s.* encarnação.
incautious *adj.* incauto.
incendiarism *s.* incêndio criminoso; incendiary *adj.&s.* incendiário.
incense *s.* incenso; *v.t.* incensar; *v.i.* queimar incenso.
incentive *s.* incentivo.
inception *s.* princípio, começo.
incessant *adj.* incessante; -ly *adv.* incessantemente.
incest *s.* incesto; -uous *adj.* incestuoso.
inch *s.* polegada.
incidence *s.* incidência; incident *s.* incidente; incidental *adj.* incidental.
incinerate *v.t.* incinerar.
incipient *adj.* incipiente.
incise *v.t.* incisar; incision *s.* incisão; incisive *adj.* incisivo.
incite *v.t.* incitar, provocar; -ment *s.* incitamento.
incivility *s.* incivilidade.
inclemency *s.* inclemência; inclement *adj.* inclemente.
inclination *s.* inclinação; incline *v.t.&i.* inclinar; *s.* plano inclinado; inclined *adj.* inclinado.
include *v.t.* incluir; inclusive *adj.* inclusivo.
incognito *adj.,adv.&s.* incógnito.
incoherence *s.* incoerência; incoherent *adj.* incoerente.
incombustible *adj.* incombustível.
income *s.* renda, rendimento; emolumento; — tax imposto sôbre a renda; — tax return declaração de rendas.
incoming *adj.* que está para chegar; montante (maré); *s.* rendimento.
incommensurable *adj.* incomensurável.
incommode *v.t.* incomodar.
incomparable *adj.* incomparável.
incompatibility *s.* incompatibilidade.
incompetence, incompetency *s.* incompetência.
incompetent *adj.* incompetente.
incomplete *adj.* incompleto.
incomprehensible *adj.* incompreensível.
inconceivable *adj.* inconcebível.
inconclusive *adj.* inconcludente.
incongruity *s.* incongruência, incongruidade; incongruous *adj.* incongruente.
inconsequent, inconsequential *adj.* inconsequente.
inconsiderable *adj.* sem importância.
inconsiderate *adj.* considerad..
inconsistency *s.* inconsistência, inconsequência, incoerência; inconsistent *adj.* inconsistente, inconsequente, incoerente.
inconsolable *adj.* inconsolável.
inconspicuous *adj.* pouco evidente, pouco perceptível.
inconstancy *s.* inconstância; inconstant *adj.* inconstante.
incontinent *adj.* incontinente.
incontrovertible *adj.* incontestável.
inconvenience *s.* incomodidade; *v.t.* incomodar; inconvenient *adj.* incômodo.
incorporate *v.t.* incorporar.
incorrect *adj.* incorreto.
incorrigible *adj.* incorrigível.
incorrupt *adj.* incorrupto; -ible *adj.* incorruptível.
increase *v.* aumento, acréscimo; *v.t.&i.* aumentar, acrescer.

incredulity s. incredulidade; **incredible** adj. incrível.

incredulous adj. incrédulo.

increment s. incremento, desenvolvimento, aumento.

incriminate v.t. incriminar.

incrust v.t. incrustar.

incubate v.t.&i. incubar; **incubation** s. incubação; **incubator** s. incubadora.

inculcate v.t. inculcar.

inculpate v.t. inculpar.

incumbent s. beneficiário; titular; adj. obrigatório.

incur v.t. incorrer.

incurable adj. incurável.

incursion s. incursão.

indebted adj. endividado; obrigado; =ness s. dívida; obrigação.

indecency s. indecência; **indecent** adj. indecente, indecoroso.

indecision s. indecisão.

indecorous adj. indecoroso; inconveniente.

indeed adv. verdadeiramente; realmente; deveras; int. realmente! deveras!

indefatigable adj. infatigável.

indefensible adj. indenfensável.

indefinable adj. indefinível; **indefinite** adj. indefinido, vago.

indelible adj. indelével.

indelicacy s. indelicadeza; **indelicate** adj. indelicado.

indemnify v.t. indenizar; **indemnity** s. indenização.

indent s. recorte dentado; (com.) encomenda recebida do estrangeiro; v.t. dentar; lavrar contrato em duplicata; fazer uma requisição; fazer uma encomenda de mercadorias (no estrangeiro); =ure s. ato, contrato, escritura, documento (em duplicata).

independence s. independência; **independent** adj. independent.

indescribable adj. indescritível.

indestructible adj. indestrutível.

indeterminate adj. indeterminado.

index s. índice; índice alfabético; (mat.) expoente.

India s. Índia.

indicate v.t. indicar, designar; **indication** s. indício, indicação; **indicative** adj.&s. indicativo.

indict v.t. acusar; =ment s. acusação, sumário de culpa.

indifference s. indiferença; **indifferent** adj. indiferente; neutro, apático.

indigence s. indigência.

indigenous adj. indígena, nativo.

indigestible adj. indigesto; **indigestion** s. indigestão.

indignant adj. indignado; **indignation** s. indignação; **indignity** s. indignidade.

indigo s. índigo.

indirect adj. indireto.

indiscreet adj. indiscreto; **indiscretion** s. indiscreção.

indiscriminate adj. indiscriminado.

indispensable adj. indispensável.

indisposed adj. indisposto; **indispose** v.t. indispor; **indisposition** s. indisposição.

indisputable adj. indiscutível, indisputável.

indissoluble adj. indissolúvel.

indistinct adj. indistinto.

indite v.t. redigir; compor.

individual adj. individual; s. indivíduo; =ity s. individualidade.

indivisible adj. indivisível.

indolence s. indolência; **indolent** adj. indolente.

indomitable adj. indomável.

indoor adj. interior, interno; de casa; de portas a dentro; =s adv. dentro; em casa.

indubitable adj. indubitável.

induce v.t. induzir, mover, persuadir; =ment s. aliciente; persuasão, induzimento.

induct v.t. instalar; iniciar; =ion s. indução; introdução, preâmbulo.

indulge v.t.&i. condescender; satisfazer; aceder a vontades e caprichos; entregar-se a; gostar de; (com.) prorrogar o prazo; =nce s. indulgência; gratificação; excesso; complacência; favor; (com.) extensão de prazo; =nt adj. indulgente.

indurate v.t. endurecer; v.i. endurecer-se, empedernir-se; adj. endurecido, empedernido.

industrial adj.&s. industrial; =ism s. industrialismo; =ize v.t. industrializar; **industrious** adj. diligente, trabalhador; **industry** s. indústria; operosidade.

inebriate adj. embriagado; v.t. embriagar.

ineffable adj. inefável.

ineffaceable adj. indelével.

ineffective, ineffectual, inefficacious adj. ineficaz.

inefficient adj. ineficiente.

inelastic adj. que não é elástico.

inelegant adj. deselegante.

ineligible adj. inelegível.

inept adj. inepto.

inequality s. desigualdade.

inert adj. inerte.

inestimable adj. inestimável.

inevitable adj. inevitável.

inexact adj. inexato.

inexactitude s. inexatidão.

inexcusable adj. indesculpável.

inexorable adj. inexorável.

inexpensive adj. barato.

inexperience s. inexperiência; =d adj. inexperiente.

inexplicable adj. inexplicável.

inexpressible adj. inexpressivo.

inextinguishable adj. inextinguível.

inextricable adj. intrincado, inextricável.

infallible adj. infalível.

infamous adj. infame; **infamy** s. infâmia.

infancy s. infância; **infant** s. criança, bebê; (dir.) menor; **infanticide** s. infanticídio.

infantile adj. infantil.

infantry s. infantaria.

infatuate v.t. enfatuar; inspirar paixão violenta e fugaz; adj. enfatuado; apaixonado; =d adj. apaixonado; **infatuation** s. enfatuação; paixão.

infect v.t. infetar, infecionar; =ion s. infeção; =ious adj. infetuoso, contagioso.

infer v.t. inferir, concluir, deduzir; =ence s. inferência, conclusão, dedução; =ential adj. dedutivo.

inferior adj. inferior; =ity s. inferioridade; =ity complex complexo de inferioridade.

infernal adj. infernal; **inferno** s. inferno.

infertile adj. estéril.

infest v.t. infestar.

infidel adj.&s. infiel; =ity s. infidelidade.

infiltrate v.i. infiltrar-se; v.t. infiltrar; **infiltration** s. infiltração.

infinite adj. infinito; the — o infinito; =simal adj. infinitesimal; **infinitive** s. infinitivo; **infinity** s. infinidade; imensidão.

infirm *adj.* enfêrmo; **-ary** *s.* enfermaria; **-ity** *s.* enfermidade.
inflame *v.t.* inflamar; **inflammable** *adj.* inflamável; **inflammation** *s.* inflamação.
inflate *v.t.* inflar; inchar; **-d** *adj.* inflado, inchado; afetado, pomposo; **inflation** *s.* inflação; (*fin.*) inflação.
inflect *v.t.* torcer, dobrar; modular, acentuar; (*gram.*) declinar; **-ion, inflexion** *s.* inflexão; (*gram.*) flexão.
inflexible *adj.* inflexível.
inflict *v.t.* infligir; impor; **-ion** *s.* inflição, castigo.
inflow *s.* fluxo, afluência.
influence *s.* influência; crédito; prestígio; *v.t.&i.* influir; influenciar.
influenza *s.* influenza, gripe.
influx *s.* fluxo, afluência; desembocadura (de rio).
inform *v.t.* informar, avisar, comunicar; instruir, ensinar; **— on, — against** denunciar; delatar; **-al** informal, sem cerimônia; **-ality** *s.* informalidade; **-ant** *s.* informante; **-ation** *s.* informação; saber, conhecimentos.
infraction *s.* infração.
infrequent *adj.* raro, infrequente.
infringe *v.t.* infringir; **-ment** *s.* infração.
infuriate *v.t.* enfurecer.
infuse *v.t.* pôr de infusão; infundir, imbuir, insinuar; **infusion** *s.* infusão.
ingathering *s.* colheita.
ingenious *adj.* engenhoso, inventivo; hábil; **ingenuity** engenho.
ingenuous *adj.* ingênuo, cândido.
inglorious *adj.* inglório.
ingoing *adj.* entrante, que entra.
ingot *s.* lingote.
ingrained *adj.* enraizado, arraigado.
ingratitude *s.* ingratidão.
ingredient *s.* ingrediente.
ingress *s.* ingresso.
inhabit *v.t.* habitar; morar, residir; **-able** *adj.* habitável; **-ant** *s.* habitante.
inhale *v.t.* inhalar, aspirar.
inherent *adj.* inerente; próprio.
inherit *v.t.&i.* herdar; suceder como herdeiro; **-ance** *s.* herança; patrimônio.
inhibit *v.t.* inibir.
inhospitable *adj.* inhospitaleiro.
inhumanity *s.* deshumanidade; **inhuman** *adj.* deshumano.
inimical *adj.* inimigo, hostil.
inimitable *adj.* inimitável.
iniquitous *adj.* iníquo; **iniquity** *s.* iniquidade.
initial *adj.&s.* inicial.
initiate *v.t.* iniciar; *adj.* adepto, iniciado.
initiative *s.* iniciativa.
inject *v.t.* injetar; **-ion** *s.* injeção.
injudicious *adj.* imprudente, indiscreto; pouco criterioso.
injunction *s.* injunção.
injure *v.t.* prejudicar; machucar; ferir; fazer mal; ofender; **-d fatally** ferido de morte.
injurious *adj.* prejudicial; pernicioso.
injury *s.* dano, prejuizo; ferimento; mal.
injustice *s.* injustiça.
ink *s.* tinta.
inlaid work trabalho embutido; incrustação.
inland *adj.* interior; nacional, do país; *adv.* no interior do país; *s.* interior (de país).
inlay *v.t.* incrustar; embutir.
inlet *s.* entrada; enseada, angra.

inmate *s.* ocupante; residente (enfêrmo, se se trata de hospital; prisioneiro, se se trata de prisão, etc.); habitante.
inmost *adj.* íntimo, recôndito, profundo.
inn *s.* hospedaria; **—-keeper** hospedeiro.
innate *adj.* inato, congênito.
inner *adj.* interior, interno, oculto.
innermost *adj.* recôndito, profundo.
innings *s.* turno, vez (na política e em alguns esportes).
innocence *s.* inocência; **innocent** *adj.* inocente; **innocently** *adv.* inocentemente.
innocuous *adj.* inócuo.
innovation *s.* inovação, novidade.
innuendo *s.* insinuação, alusão.
innumerable *adj.* inumerável.
inobservance *s.* inobservância; falta de atenção.
inoculate *v.t.* inocular; **inoculation** *s.* inoculação.
inodorous *adj.* inodoro.
inoffensive *adj.* inofensivo.
inoperative *adj.* inoperante.
inopportune *adj.* inoportuno; **-ly** *adv.* inoportunamente.
inordinate *adj.* desmesurado; excessivo; desordenado.
inorganic *adj.* inorgânico.
inpatient *s.* doente hospitalizado.
inquest *s.* pesquisa judicial, investigação; inquérito.
inquire *v.t.&i.* informar-se; inquirir; perguntar; **-r** *s.* investigador, averiguador; **inquiry** *s.* indagação, averiguação, investigação; consulta; informação; **inquiry operator** telefonista de informações.
inquisition *s.* inquisição; **inquisitive** *adj.* perguntador, curioso, inquiridor.
inroad *s.* incursão, irrupção.
insane *adj.* louco; **insanity** *s.* loucura, demência; **— asylum** hospício.
insanitary *adj.* insalubre, malsão.
insatiable *adj.* insaciável.
inscribe *v.t.* inscrever; gravar; dedicar; **inscription** *s.* inscrição; rótulo, letreiro; dedicatória.
inscrutable *adj.* inescrutável, impenetrável.
insect *s.* inseto; **-ivora** *s.* insetívoros; **-ivorous** *adj.* insetívoro.
insecure *adj.* inseguro; **insecurity** *s.* insegurança.
insensate *adj.* insensato.
insensible *adj.* insensível.
inseparable *adj.* inseparável.
insert *s.* inserir, introduzir; **-ion** *s.* inserção.
inset *s.* inserção; (*E.U.*) fôlha extra, metida entre as de um livro, jornal ou revista.
inshore *adj.* ao longo da costa.
inside *s.* o interior, a parte de dentro; conteúdo; (*plural*) entranhas; *adj.* interior, interno; *adv.* dentro; **— out** pelo avêsso.
insidious *adj.* insidioso.
insight *s.* penetração; compreensão; percepção da natureza íntima de uma cousa.
insignia *s.* insígnia.
insignificant *adj.* insignificante.
insincere *adj.* insincero.
insincerity *s.* insinceridade.
insinuate *v.t.* insinuar.
insipid *adj.* insípido.
insist *v.i.* insistir.
insistence *s.* insistência.

insobriety s. intemperança.
insolation s. insolação; tratamento pelo sol.
insolence s. insolência; **insolent** adj. insolente.
insoluble adj. insolúvel.
insolvency s. insolvência.
insomnia s. insônia.
insomuch as, insomuch to até o ponto que; de tal modo que.
inspect v.t. inspecionar; **-ion** s. inspeção; **-or** s. inspetor; **-orship** s. distrito a cargo do inspetor.
inspiration s. inspiração; aspiração; **inspire** v.i.&t. inspirar; aspirar.
inspirit v.t. animar, alentar.
instability s. instabilidade.
install v.t. instalar; **-ation** s. instalação.
instalment s. pagamento parcial, prestação; — **plan** venda a prestação.
instance s. instância, solicitação; exemplo, caso; (for.) instância.
instant s. instante; **-aneous** adj. instantâneo.
instead adv. em lugar, em vez.
instep s. (anat.) tarso, peito do pé.
instigate v.t. instigar, provocar; **instigation** s. instigação.
instil, instill v.t. instilar; inculcar.
instinct s. instinto; adj. animado, impulsionado, movido; **-ive** adj. instintivo.
institute s. instituto; v.t. instituir.
institution s. instituição, instituto, estabelecimento.
instruct v.t. instruir, ensinar; dar instruções; **-ion** s. instrução; instruções, indicações; **-ive** adj. instrutivo; **-or** s. professor, instrutor, monitor.
instrument s. instrumento; (for.) instrumento, documento; **-al** adj. instrumental; **-alist** s. (mús.) instrumentista; **-ality** s. agência, mediação.
insubordinate adj. insubordinado.
insufferable adj. insuportável.
insufficiency s. insuficiência; **insufficient** adj. insuficiente; **insufficiently** adv. insuficientemente.
insular adj. insular.
insulate v.t. isolar; (fís.) isolar; **insulation** s. isolamento; **insulator** s. isolante.
insult s. insulto; v.t. insultar; **-ing** adj. ofensivo, injurioso; insultante.
insuperable adj. insuperável.
insupportable adj. insuportável.
insurance s. seguro; — **company** companhia de seguros; **insure** v.t. segurar; **insurer** s. segurador.
insurgent s.&adj. revoltoso, insurgente.
insurmountable adj. insuperável.
insurrection s. insurreição.
intact adj. intacto.
intake s. admissão; tomada; tomada elétrica.
intangible adj. intangível.
integer s. inteiro; **integral** adj. integral; **integrity** s. integridade.
intellect s. intelecto, inteligência; **-ual** adj.&s. intelectual.
intelligence s. inteligência; notícia; informações secretas; — **department** departamento de informações secretas (principalmente militares ou navais); **-r** s. agente secreto; **intelligent** adj. inteligente; **intelligently** adv. inteligentemente; **intelligible** adj. inteligível.
intemperance s. intemperança; **intemperate** adj. imoderado, excessivo; violento; inclemente (tempo).

intend v.t. tencionar; fazer tenção; **-ed** s. (pop.) noivo, o futuro; adj. almejado, intencional, o que se tem em mira.
intense adj. intenso; **-ly** adv. intensamente; **intensify** v.t. intensificar; **intensity** s. intensidade.
intent adj. atento; — **on** decidido, resolvido a; s. intenção, intento, desígnio, propósito; **-ional** adj. intencional; **-ioned** adj. intencionado; **-ness** s. força de atenção, decisão.
inter v.t. enterrar, sepultar.
intercalate v.t. intercalar.
intercede v.i. interceder.
intercept v.t. interceptar.
intercession s. intercessão; **intercessor** s. intercessor.
interchange s. intercâmbio.
intercourse s. intercâmbio; comércio; correspondência; relações sexuais.
interdict s. veto, proibição; interdito; v.t. interditar; **-ion** s. interdição.
interest s. interêsse; juros; — **on overdue payments** juros de mora; v.t. interessar; **-ing** adj. interessante, atrativo; **in an -ing condition** em estado interessante.
interfere v.i. interferir; meter-se, interpor-se, imiscuir-se; intervir; — **with** embaraçar, impedir, estorvar; **-nce** s. interferência; interposição; obstáculo, impedimento.
interim s. ínterim.
interior s.&adj. interior.
interject v.t. interpor, inserir; v.i. interpor-se, intervir; **-ion** s. interjeição, exclamação; intervenção.
interlace v.t. entrelaçar.
interline v.t. entrelinhar; entretelar; **-ar** adj. interlinear.
interlocutor s. interlocutor.
interloper s. intruso, intrometido.
interlude s. intervalo, entreato.
intermarriage s. casamento entre indivíduos de tribus, nações ou raças diferentes.
intermeddle v.i. misturar-se; intrometer-se.
intermediary s.&adj. intermediário; **intermediate** s. mediador, intermediário.
interment s. entêrro.
intermezzo s. intermezzo.
interminable adj. interminável.
intermission s. intermissão, interrupção, intervalo; **intermittent** adj. intermitente.
intermix v.i. misturar-se.
intern v.t. internar; **-al** adj. interno, interior; intestino; **-ally** adv. interiormente.
international adj. internacional; **-ist** s. internacionalista.
internment s. internamento; — **camp** campo de concentração.
interpolate v.t. interpolar.
interpose v.t. interpor; v.i. interpor-se.
interpret v.t. interpretar; **-ation** s. interpretação; **-er** s. intérprete.
interregnum s. interregno.
interrogate v.t. interrogar; **interrogation** s. interrogação; **interrogative** adj. interrogativo; **interrogatory** s. interrogatório.
interrupt v.t. interromper; **-er** s. interruptor; **-ion** s. interrupção.
intersect v.t. cortar, entrecortar; **-ion** s. interseção.
intersperse v.t. entremear, espalhar.
interstice s. interstício.

intertwine *v.t.* entrelaçar.
interval *s.* intervalo; entreato.
intervene *v.i.* intervir; intervention *s.* intervenção.
interview *s.* entrevista; *v.t.* entrevistar.
interweave *v.t.* entrelaçar, entretecer.
intestate *adj.* intestado.
intestinal *adj.* intestinal; intestine *s.&adj.* intestino.
intimacy *s.* intimidade, familiaridade; intimate *adj.&s.* íntimo; *v.t.* intimar; intimation *s.* intimação.
intimidate *v.t.* intimidar.
into *prep.* dentro, em, entre.
intolerable *adj.* intolerável; intolerance *s.* intolerância; intolerant *adj.* intolerante.
intonation *s.* entoação; intonate *v.t.* entoar; intone *v.t.* entoar.
intoxicate *v.t.* embriagar; (*med.*) intoxicar, envenenar; =d *adj.* embriagado; intoxication *s.* embriaguez; (*med.*) intoxicação, envenenamento.
intractable *adj.* intratável.
intransitive *adj.* intransitivo.
intrench *v.t.* entrincheirar; *v.i.* entrincheirar-se.
intrepid *adj.* intrépido; =ity *s.* intrepidez.
intricacy *s.* complicação, trapalhada; intricate *adj.* complicado, intrincado.
intrigue *s.* intriga, manejo, trama; amor ilícito; enrêdo de peça, de novela, etc.; *v.t.&i.* intrigar, tramar, seduzir; =r *s.* intrigante; intriguing *adj.* intrigante.
intrinsic *adj.* intrínseco.
introduce *v.t.* introduzir; apresentar; dar entrada; pôr em uso; — a bill apresentar um projeto de lei; — into society apresentar na sociedade; =r *s.* introdutor; introduction *s.* apresentação; introdução.
introit *s.* introito.
introspection *s.* introspecção.
intrude *v.i.* introduzir-se (no sentido pejorativo); intrometer-se; =r *s.* intruso, intrometido; intrusion *s.* intrusão.
intuition *s.* intuição; intuitive *adj.* intuitivo.
inundate *v.t.* inundar; inundation *s.* inundação.
inure *v.t.* aguerrir, acostumar, habituar.
invade *v.t.* invadir; =r *s.* invasor.
invalid *adj.* inválido; *s.* inválido, enfêrmo; *v.t.* incapacitar; registar como inválido; =ate *v.t.* invalidar, anular; =ity *s.* invalidez; invalidade, nulidade.
invaluable *adj.* inestimável; inapreciável.
invariable *adj.* invariável.
invasion *s.* invasão.
invective *s.* invectiva; inveigh *v.i.* invectivar.
inveigle *v.t.* seduzir, enganar.
invent *v.t.* inventar, imaginar; =ion *s.* invenção; =ive *adj.* inventivo; =or *s.* inventor.
inventory *s.* inventário; *v.t.* inventariar.
inverse *adj.* inverso; inversion *s.* inversão; invert *v.t.* inverter.
invertebrate *adj.&s.* invertebrado.
invest *v.t.* vestir, revestir; investir, empregar (capital); sitiar, cercar.
investigate *v.t.* investigar; investigation *s.* investigação; investigator *s.* investigador.
investiture *s.* investidura.
investment *s.* (*com.*) aplicação de capital; (*mil.*) sítio, cêrco; investidura, instalação.
inveterate *adj.* inveterado.

invidious *adj.* difamatório; odioso.
invigorate *v.t.* fortificar, estimular.
invincible *adj.* invencível.
inviolable *adj.* inviolável; inviolate *adj.* inviolado.
invisible *adj.* invisível.
invitation *s.* convite; invite *v.t.* convidar; inviting *adj.* convidativo.
invocation *s.* invocação.
invoice *s.* (*com.*) fatura; *v.t.* faturar.
invoke *v.t.* invocar.
involuntary *adj.* involuntário.
involve *v.t.* envolver; enrolar; implicar, comprometer; torcer, emaranhar; =d language língua complicada, difusa.
invulnerable *adj.* invulnerável.
inward *adj.* interior; interno; íntimo; =ly *adv.* internamente; =s *s.* entranhas.
iodine *s.* iodo.
ion *s.* íon.
iota *s.* iota (letra grega).
ipecacuanha *s.* (*bot.*) ipecacuanha.
irascible *adj.* irascível; irate *adj.* irado; ire *s.* ira, cólera.
iridescence *s.* irisação; iridescent *adj.* iridescente.
iridium *s.* irídio.
iris *s.* iris.
irksome *adj.* fastidioso, cansativo.
iron *s.* ferro; *adj.* de ferro, em ferro; férreo; *v.t.* agrilhoar, ferrar; passar (roupa a ferro); =ing *s.* ato de passar roupa.
ironic, ironical *adj.* irônico; irony *s.* ironia.
irradiation *s.* irradiação.
irrational *adj.* irracional.
irreclaimable *adj.* incorrigível; inaproveitável.
irreconcilable *adj.* irreconciliável.
irrecoverable *adj.* irremediável; irreparável.
irredeemable *adj.* irremissível.
irreducible *adj.* irredutível, irreduzível.
irrefutable *adj.* irrefutável.
irregular *adj.* irregular; =ity *s.* irregularidade.
irrelevant *adj.* impertinente; inaplicável.
irreligious *adj.* irreligioso.
irremediable *adj.* irremediável.
irremovable *adj.* inamovível, irremovível.
irreparable *adj.* irreparável.
irrepressible *adj.* irreprimível.
irreproachable *adj.* irreprochável; irrepreensível.
irresistible *adj.* irresistível.
irresolute *adj.* irresoluto.
irrespective of independente de, sem consideração a.
irresponsible *adj.* irresponsável, inconciente.
irretrievable *adj.* irrecuperável, irreparável.
irreverent *adj.* irreverente.
irrevocable *adj.* irrevogável.
irrigate *v.t.* irrigar; irrigation *s.* irrigação; irrigator *s.* irrigador.
irritable *adj.* irritável; irritate *v.t.* irritar; irritation *s.* irritação.
irruption *s.* irrupção.
island *s.* ilha; =er *s.* insular; isle *s.* ilha; islet *s.* ilhota.
isolate *v.t.* isolar; isolation *s.* isolamento; =d *adj.* isolado; solitário.
issue *s.* (*imp.*) edição; tiragem; impressão; número; publicação; prole, sucessão; saída; egresso; evento, consequência, resultado; êxito; decisão; tema

de discussão, problema; (for.) ponto em discussão; — of blood perda de sangue; v.t. lançar, emitir; publicar; distribuir; v.i. sair; correr; emanar; proceder; terminar.
isthmus s. istmo.
it pron.neutro êle, ela; o, a; lhe; isto, isso; — is said that diz-se que; =s pron. seu, sua, seus, suas; o seu, a sua; os seus, as suas; d'êle, d'ela; d'isso, d'aquilo; =self pron. se, sigo, si mesmo; êle próprio, êle mesmo; ela própria; ela mesma.

italic adj. itálico.
itch v.i. coçar, comer, comichar; =ing s. comichão, prurido, coceira; =y adj. sarnoso; comichoso; my arm =es meu braço está comichando.
item s. ítem; artigo, parágrafo; adv. ítem; =ize v.t. especificar, pormenorizar.
itinerary s. itinerário; **itinerant** adj. itinerante.
ivory s. marfim.
ivy s. hera.
izzard s. a letra Z, z; from A to — de cabo a rabo.

J

J letra do alfabeto.
jabber v.i. papaguear, palrar; s. tagarelice.
jacinth s. jacinto.
jack s. espêto; (mec.) macaco; (mar.) bandeira de proa; macho de certos quadrúpedes; valete (figura do baralho); marinheiro; — of all trades pau para toda obra; — up levantar com macaco.
jackal s. chacal.
jackanapes s. mequetrefe; tôlo, convencido.
jacket s. jaqueta; paletó (de homem); colete (de homem); invólucro (de qualquer espécie); cobertura ou capa de livro; (mec.) camisa; — potatoes batatas servidas com casca.
jacobin s. jacobino.
jade s. jade; cavalo ordinário; mulher de má fama; v.t.&i. estafar; =d estafado.
jag s. entalhe, dente; v.t. recortar, dentear.
jaguar s. jaguar.
jail s. prisão, cárcere; — fever tifo.
jam s. geléia; complicação, apuro, apertura; v.t. apertar, comprimir; apinhar; (rád.) interferir, perturbando a transmissão.
Jamaica s. Jamaica.
jamb s. umbral.
jangle s. disputa, altercação; sons discordantes; v.i. altercar, disputar; soar em discordância.
January s. Janeiro.
Japan s. Japão; **japan** s. laca; trabalho laqueado; v.t. laquear; =ese adj. japonês, nipônico; s. japonês.
jar s. jarro, jarra; cântaro; vibração, trepidação; choque; sacudidela; som desagradável; v.t.&i. sacudir, agitar, fazer vibrar; vibrar, trepidar; produzir sons desagradáveis, ranger.
jargon s. dialeto; calão; terminologia técnica pertencente a uma arte, ciência, profissão, etc.
jarring adj. discordante, desentoado.
jasmine, jasmin s. jasmim.
jasper s. jaspe.
jaundice s. icterícia.
jaunt s. excursão, caminhada, passeio; =y adj. vistoso, elegante; despreocupado.
javelin s. dardo, venábulo.
jaw s. mandíbula; queixada; —=bone maxilar.
jay s. gaio (ave).
jealous adj. cioso, zeloso; ciumento; =y s. ciúme.
jeer s. escárneo, mofa; v.t.&i. escarnecer, zombar.
jejune adj. magro, sem substância; insípido.

jelly s. geléia; =fish s. medusa.
jennet s. ginete.
jeopardize v.t. arriscar, expor, comprometer; **jeopardy** s. perigo, risco.
jerboa s. gerbo.
jeremiad s. choradeira, jeremiada.
jerk s. sacudidela; contração (muscular), espasmo; v.t.&i. sacudir; arremessar; =y adj. espasmódico, aos arrancos.
jerry adj. de qualidade inferior; mal feito; —=build v.t. construir mal ou com material inferior; —=builder construtor de casas baratas.
jersey s. jérsei; malha de sêda; — cow vaca de Jersey.
jessamine s. jasmim.
jest s. gracejo, brincadeira, facécia; v.i. gracejar, brincar; =er s. galhofeiro, brincalhão; bobo, palhaço.
Jesuit s. jesuíta; =ical adj. jesuítico.
Jesus s. Jesús; — Christ Jesús-Cristo.
jet s. jato; cano ou tubo de saída; azeviche.
jetsam s. carga atirada ao mar para aliviar o navio.
jetty s. molhe; adj. de azeviche ou côr de azeviche.
Jew s. judeu, israelita.
jib s. (mar.) bujarrona; mover-se para os lados e para trás em desespêro (animal).
jibe V. **gibe.**
jiffy s. (pop.) momento, instante; I will go in a — vou num instante.
jig s. giga (dansa); —=saw puzzle jôgo de paciência.
jilt v.t. abandonar, dar o fora (no namorado).
jingle s. tinido, som metálico; v.t.&i. tinir; fazer tinir.
jingoism s. jacobinismo.
job s. emprêgo; tarefa; trabalho; negócio; — lot mercadorias de ocasião; —=master alugador de cavalos; =ber s. negociante intermediário; negociante de títulos.
jockey s. jóquei.
jocose adj. jocoso.
jocular adj. jocoso; burlesco; =ly adv. jocosamente, por brincadeira.
jocund adj. alegre, festivo.
jog v.t. empurrar, cutucar; tocar alguém para chamar a atenção; v.i. mover-se devagar e sacudindo; — trot trote lento.
joggle s. sacudidela; v.t.&i. sacudir, trepidar, balançar.
John s. João; — Bull Inglaterra, o povo inglês; — Chinaman o povo chinês, qualquer chinês; — Doe Fulano de Tal.

join *v.t.* juntar; unir; reunir; acrescentar; associar; *v.i.* reunir-se; associar-se; unir-se; juntar-se; entrar; **he =ed the army** êle entrou para o exército; — **in** fazer côro; **=er** *s.* marceneiro; **=ery** *s.* marcenaria.

joint *s.* juntura, junta; união; conexão; articulação; quarto (de animal); (*bot.*) nó; *adj.* unido, agrupado, coletivo; associado, misto; *v.t.* juntar, unir, agregar; *v.i.* articular-se; — **author** coautor; — **commission** comissão mista; — **consent** comum acôrdo; — **heir** coherdeiro; — **=stock company** sociedade por ações.

joist *s.* ripa, sarrafo, barrote.

joke *s.* pilhéria, facécia, graça; *v.i.* pilheriar, gracejar.

jollity *s.* jovialidade, alegria, regosijo, bom humor.

jolliness *s.* alegria, regosijo, jovialidade.

jolly *adj.* alegre, divertido, jovial.

jolt *s.* sacudida, solavanco; *v.t.&i.* sacudir; dar solavancos.

jonquil *s.* junquilho.

jostle *v.t.* empurrar; acotovelar; apertar.

jot *s.* iota (letra); — **down** registar, tomar nota.

journal *s.* jornal; diário; periódico; revista (publicação); diário comercial; **=ism** *s.* jornalismo; **=ist** *s.* jornalista.

journey *s.* viagem; jornada; caminhada; trajeto.

joust *s.* justa, peleja, torneio.

jovial *adj.* jovial; **=ity** *s.* jovialidade.

jowl *s.* maxilar inferior; bochecha; papada; cabeça de peixe.

joy *s.* alegria; **=ful, =ous** *adj.* alegre; **=fulness** alegria.

jubilation *s.* júbilo, regozijo; **jubilee** *s.* jubileu.

Judaic *adj.* judaico.

Judas *s.* Judas.

judge *s.* juiz; magistrado; perito; — **advocate** auditor de guerra; *v.t.&i.* julgar; **=ment** *s.* julgamento, sentença; critério, juizo.

judicature *s.* judicatura; justiça; **judi-**

cial *adj.* judicial; **judiciary** *adj.&s.* judiciário; **judicious** *adj.* judicioso.

judo *s.* jiu-jitsu.

jug *s.* cântaro; jarro; bilha, moringa.

juggle *v.i.* escamotear, fazer prestidigitação; **=ry** *s.* prestidigitação; **=r** *s.* prestidigitador.

jugular *s.* jugular (veia).

juice *s.* suco, caldo; **juicy** *adj.* suculento.

jujube *s.* jujuba.

julep *s.* julepe.

July *s.* Julho.

jumble *s.* embrulho, confusão,· trapalhada; *v.t.* embrulhar, atrapalhar.

jump *s.* salto, pulo; estremecimento; *v.t.&i.* saltar, pular; — **over** saltar por cima; — **at** aceitar imediatamente, apressar-se em aproveitar; — **to a conclusion** tirar uma conclusão apressada.

junction *s.* junção; bifurcação; entroncamento; **juncture** *s.* junção; ocorrência, conjuntura.

June *s.* Junho.

jungle *s.* floresta, floresta virgem.

junior *adj.* júnior; *s.* júnior, filho; aluno do penúltimo ano de colégio ou escola.

juniper *s.* junípero.

junk *s.* junco (embarcação); refugo (de ferro, papel, etc.).

junket *v.i.* (*E.U.*) dar banquete à custa dos cofres públicos; *s.* creme gelatinoso, gulodice; (*E.U.*) banquete, festim a custa dos cofres públicos.

juridical *adj.* jurídico; **jurisdiction** *s.* jurisdição; **jurist** *s.* jurista, jurisconsulto.

juror, juryman *s.* jurado; **jury** *s.* juri.

just *adj.* justo; *adv.* exatamente; há pouco; **I have** — **arrived** acabo de chegar; **=ice** *s.* justiça; **=ifiable** *adj.* justificável; **=ification** *s.* justificação; **=ify** *v.t.* justificar; **=ly** *adv.* justamente, equitàvelmente; **=ness** *s.* justiça.

jut *v.i.* projetar-se.

jute *s.* juta.

juvenile *adj.* juvenil, jovem.

juxtapose *v.t.* juxtapor.

juxtaposition *s.* juxtaposição.

K

K letra.

kale *s.* repôlho crespo; (*pop.*) sopa de legumes; (*jíria*) dinheiro.

kaleidoscope *s.* caleidoscópio.

kangaroo *s.* cangurú.

kaolin *s.* caolim.

kedge *s.* ancorote.

keel *s.* quilha; **=son** *s.* sobrequilha.

keen *adj.* acerado; afiado; agudo, penetrante, sutil, vivo; astuto, ladino; veemente, ardente; entusiasta; sensível; acre, mordaz, incisivo; **=ly** *adv.* agudamente; finamente, sutilmente, com vivacidade; **=ness** *s.* agudeza; sutileza; perspicácia; penetração.

keep *v.t.* guardar; ter (criados, secretário, etc.); manter; dirigir, manejar (casa, hotel, etc.); cumprir (a palavra, uma promessa, etc.); deter, demorar; conter; *v.i.* manter-se; conservar-se; ficar; — **a saint's day** guardar um dia santo; — **away** manter-se fora; — **off** afastar-se; — **on** continuar; — **bad hours** deitar-se tarde; — **company** fazer companhia; — **house** manter casa; — **one's**

distance manter-se na reserva, guardar distância; — **one's head** não perder a cabeça; — **pace with** andar ao mesmo passo que; — **track of** seguir, não perder de vista a, acompanhar.

keeper *s.* guardião; guarda; carcereiro.

keepsake *s.* presente, lembrança.

keg *s.* barrilete, barril.

kennel *s.* sarjeta, pequeno canal; canil, casa de cachorro; matilha de cães.

kerb *s.* parapeito; meio fio.

kerchief *s.* coifa; lenço grande; lenço.

kernel *s.* caroço, amêndoa, semente; grão; núcleo, endocarpo; parte central ou essencial das cousas.

kerosene *s.* petróleo; querosene.

kestrel *s.* pequeno falcão, tartaranhão.

ketch *s.* chalupa, galeota.

kettle *s.* chaleira; caldeira; marmita.

key *s.* chave (em todas as suas acepções); tecla (de piano, máquina de escrever, etc.); (*mús.*) pedal, tom, clave; *v.t.* fechar à chave; afinar; **=board** teclado; **=stone** chave (de abóbada); pedra fundamental.

khaki *s.* caqui.
kick *s.* ponta-pé; coice (de arma de fogo); patada; *v.t.&i.* dar ponta-pés; escoucear; recuar (arma de fogo); (*pop.*) fazer oposição violenta.
kid *s.* cabrito, cabrita; (*pop.*) criança, garoto; *v.t.* enganar por gracejo; implicar por gracejo.
kidnap *v.t.* roubar, sequestrar (pessoas).
kidney *s.* rim; temperamento, disposição.
kill *v.t.* matar; assassinar; **-er** *s.* assassino, matador.
kiln *s.* forno.
kilo *s.* quilo.
kilt *v.t.* saiote usado pelos escosseses.
kimono *s.* quimono.
kin *s.* parentes; família; parentesco.
kind *adj.* bom, benévolo, bondoso; **— hearted** bom de coração; *s.* espécie, gênero, classe, sorte, qualidade; **— of** (*pop.*) um tanto, de certo modo; **-liness** *s.* bondade, benevolência; boa índole; **-ness** *s.* bondade; **-ly** *adv.* bondosamente.
kindred *s.* parentela, família; *adj.* aparentado; congênere.
king *s.* rei; rei (figura de baralho); **-'s household** casa real; **-dom** *s.* reinado.
kink *s.* retorcimento; mania; *v.t.* retorcer.
kinship *s.* parentesco, sangue.
kiosk *s.* quiosque.
kipper *s.* salmão ou arenque salgado.
kiss *s.* beijo; *v.t.* beijar.
kit *s.* estojo; indumentária completa; equipamento profissional.
kitchen *s.* cozinha.
kite *s.* milhafre (ave); papagaio (de papel).
kitten *s.* gatinho.
kleptomania *s.* cleptomania; **-c** *s.* cleptomaníaco.
knack *s.* tino; expediente engenhoso; habilidade, arte.
knacker *s.* esfolador de cavalos; comprador de ferros velhos e de material usado.
knapsac *s.* mochila.
knave *s.* velhaco, trapaceiro; valete (figura de baralho).

knead *v.t.* amassar, ligar (pastas ou massas).
knee *s.* joelho; **-l down** *v.i.* ajoelhar-se.
knell *s.* dobre de finados; *v.i.* dobrar a finados.
Knickerbocker *s.* descendente de uma das primeiras famílias holandesas que se estabeleceram em Nova York.
knickerbockers, knickers *s.* calções apertados nos joelhos.
knick-knack *s.* enfeite, ninharia.
knife *s.* faca; *v.t.* esfaquear.
knight *s.* cavaleiro; campeão; cavalo (jôgo de xadrez); **—-errant** cavaleiro errante; *v.t.* armar cavaleiro.
knit *v.t.&i.* tricotar; **-ted** *adj.* tricotado.
knob *s.* protuberância; saliência; nó (na madeira); castão (de bengala); maçaneta.
knock *s.* pancada; golpe; chamada; toque; *v.t.&i.* bater (na porta, etc.); golpear; colidir; **— down** derrubar, vencer, pôr fora de combate; **— under** submeter-se.
knoll *s.* montículo; outeiro.
knot *s.* nó; laço, vínculo; nó de madeira; enrêdo de um drama ou peça; dificuldade, problema; cocarda; grupo, reunião; protuberância; (*mar.*) milha marítima; *v.t.* laçar, amarrar com nós; unir; **-ty** *adj.* nodoso.
know *v.t.&i.* conhecer; saber; **-ingly** *adj.* cientemente; **-ledge** *s.* saber; conhecimento; cultura; ciência; **-n** *adj.* conhecido.
knuckle *s.* junta, articulação; articulação dos dedos; **— down, — under** submeter-se, render-se.
knurl *s.* nó; protuberância; **-y** *adj.* nodoso.
Koran *s.* Corão.
kudos *s.* glória, fama, renome.
kymograph *s.* aparêlho para registrar curvas de pressão; instrumento para registrar os movimentos de um aeroplano no vôo.
kyphosis *s.* curvatura da espinha.

L

L letra do alfabeto.
labial *adj.* labial.
laboratory *s.* laboratório.
laborious *adj.* laborioso; penoso.
labor, labour *s.* trabalho; as classes operárias; tarefa, faina, labor; mão de obra; *v.i.* trabalhar; estar em trabalho de parto; **— party** partido trabalhista; **— troubles** perturbações operárias; **-ed** *adj.* trabalhado; elaborado; laborioso; **-er** *s.* operário; trabalhador.
laburnum *s.* (*bot.*) laburno.
labyrinth *s.* labirinto.
lac *s.* goma laca.
lace *s.* renda; cordão; cadarço, galão; **— insertion** entremeio; *v.t.* atar (com cordões); dar laço; guarnecer com renda ou galão.
lacerate *v.t.* lacerar; dilacerar; **laceration** *s.* dilaceração, laceração.
lack *s.* falta, carência; necessidade; *v.t.* faltar, carecer, necessitar; **-ing in** destituído de; **— of intelligence** falta de inteligência.

lackadaisical *adj.* lânguido; indolente, apático.
lackey *s.* lacaio.
laconic *adj.* lacônico.
lacquer *s.* laca; *v.t.* laquear.
lacrosse *s.* jôgo de bola canadense.
lacteal *adj.* lácteo.
lacuna *s.* lacuna.
lacustrine *adj.* lacustre.
lad *s.* rapaz, moço.
ladder *s.* escada de mão; escada portátil.
lade *v.t.* carregar.
ladle *s.* colherão.
lady *s.* senhora, dama; **— doctor** doutora; **a — friend** uma amiga; **-like** distinta; **— of the manor** castelã; **ladies' man** homem galanteador.
lag *v.i.* atrasar-se; ficar atrás; mover-se lentamente; *s.* atraso; retardamento, retardação.
lager *s.* espécie de cerveja.
lagoon *s.* laguna.
laic *s.* leigo, secular.
laid *pret. e p.p. de* **to lay; — up in bed** acamado.

lain *p.p. do verbo* to lie.
lair *s.* covil; toca; antro.
laity *s.* leigos.
lake *s.* lago; — dwelling habitação lacustre.
lama *s.* lama (sacerdote); lhama (animal).
lamb *s.* cordeiro; =kin *s.* cordeirinho.
lambent *adj.* ligeiro, leve, suave; suavemente luminoso; suavemente radioso.
lame *adj.* coxo, manco, estropiado, aleijado; *v.t.* estropiar; to go — coxear, andar manquejando; — account relação imperfeita; — verses versos de pé quebrado.
lameness *s.* claudicação.
lament *s.* lamentação; canto fúnebre; *v.t.* lamentar; *v.i.* lamentar-se; =able *adj.* lamentável; =ation *s.* lamentação.
lamina *s.* lâmina; =te *v.t.* laminar.
lamp *s.* lâmpada; lanterna; farol; reverbéro.
lampas *s.* inflamação do palato (nos cavalos).
lampoon *s.* pasquim, libelo; *v.t.* satirizar; =er *s.* panfletário.
lamprey *s.* lampreia.
lance *s.* lancêta; lança; lanceiro; *v.t.* lancetar; =rs *s.* lanceiros; =t *s.* lancêta.
land *s.* terra; terreno; solo; *v.t.&i.* desembarcar; — forces fôrças de terra; — measures medidas agrárias; — tax imposto territorial; =scape painter pintor paisagista.
landau *s.* landô; =let *s.* landolé.
landing *s.* desembarque, aterrissagem.
lane *s.* vereda, senda, caminho; álea.
language *s.* língua, idioma, linguagem.
languid *adj.* lânguido; languor *s.* langor; languorous *adj.* langoroso.
lank *adj.* fino, magro; liso (cabelo).
lantern *s.* lanterna.
lanyard *s.* (*mar.*) corda, cabo.
lap *s.* colo, regaço; bainha; aba de casaco ou de paletó; fralda; *v.t.* dobrar; *v.i.* cruzar sôbre; traspassar.
laparotomy *s.* laparotomia.
lapel *s.* lapela.
lapidary *s.* lapidário.
lappet *s.* aba; lóbulo (de orelha); fralda (de camisa).
lapse *s.* lapso; esquecimento; espaço de tempo; *v.i.* decair gradualmente; deslisar; (*for.*) prescrever, caducar.
larceny *s.* furto, roubo.
lard *s.* toucinho; banha de porco; *v.t.* rechear com toucinho; untar banha em.
larder *s.* guarda-comida; despensa.
large *adj.* grande, grosso; largo; forte (pulso); — handwriting letra grande; —=handed liberal, dadivoso; —=hearted magnânimo, generoso; —=sized grande; at — solto, em liberdade; geral, em geral; =ly *adv.* grandemente, em grande parte; =ness *s.* grandeza; liberalidade; grandeza d'alma.
lark *s.* calandra, calhandra (pássaro).
larva *s.* larva.
laryngitis *s.* laringite; larynx *s.* laringe.
lascivious *adj.* lascivo.
lash *s.* chicotada; vergastada; pestana; *v.t.* chicotear, fustigar, açoitar.
lass *s.* moça; rapariga; =ie *s.* mocinha.
lassitude *s.* lassidão.
lasso *s.* laço; *v.t.* laçar.
last *adj.* último; final; *s.* último; fim; fôrma de sapato; medida de pêso (4.000 arráteis, aprox.); *v.i.* durar, perdurar; *adv.* finalmente, por fim; a última vez; — but one penúltimo; — night ontem

à noite; — week a semana passada; — honors últimas honras; at — enfim, por fim; to the — até o fim; =ing *adj.* durável, estável; =ly *adv.* em último lugar, enfim.
latch *s.* ferrôlho, trinco, fechadura; =key chave da porta da frente.
late *adj.* tardio; remoto; tardo, lento; último; falecido; recente, moderno; atrasado; —=comer retardatário; — arrival recém-chegado; *adv.* tarde; há pouco; últimamente; — in the year no fim do ano; to be — estar atrasado.
lately *adv.* últimamente, recentemente; lateness *s.* tardança.
latent *adj.* latente.
later *adj.* posterior, ulterior; — on *adv.* mais tarde, posteriormente.
lateral *adj.* lateral.
latest *adj.* último; novíssimo.
latex *s.* látex.
lath *s.* ripa.
lather *s.* espuma de sabão; *v.i.* fazer espuma; *v.t.* ensaboar.
Latin *s.* latim; *adj.* latino.
latitude *s.* latitude.
latrine *s.* latrina.
latter *adj.* último, mais recente, moderno; êste.
lattice *s.* grade; janela de grade; gelosia.
laud *v.t.* louvar; =atory *adj.* laudatório.
laugh *s.* riso; *v.t.* rir; =able *adj.* risível; =ter *s.* hilaridade; — at rir-se de, caçoar; — in one's sleeve rir-se à socapa; — out rir-se às gargalhadas.
launch *s.* embarcação, lancha, chalupa; *v.t.* lançar ao mar (embarcação); lançar; =ing *s.* lançamento.
launder *v.t.* lavar roupa; laundress *s.* lavadeira; laundry *s.* lavanderia.
laureate *adj.* laureado.
laurel *s.* louro.
lava *s.* lava.
lavatory *s.* lavatório (pia).
lavender *s.* lavanda, alfazema.
lavish *adj.* pródigo; gastador; *v.t.* prodigar; dissipar, malbaratar; =ly *adv.* pródigamente; =ness *s.* prodigalidade.
law *s.* lei; direito; justiça; jurisprudência; — abiding observante da lei; — of multiple proportions lei das proporções múltiplas; — of nations direito internacional; — of nature lei da natureza; =s of war leis de guerra.
lawful *adj.* legal; legítimo; =ness *s.* legitimidade, legalidade; lawless *adj.* sem lei.
lawn *s.* gramado; cambraia fina.
lawyer *s.* advogado; jurista; jurisconsulto.
lax *adj.* solto, frouxo; flácido; relaxado; =ative *s.* laxativo; =ity *s.* frouxidão; flacidez; relaxamento, descuido.
lay *adj.* leigo; secular; profano; *s.* canção; canto; melodia; caída, queda; contôrno; negócio, ocupação; *v.t.* pôr, colocar; pôr (ovos); pôr (a mesa, etc.); enterrar; calmar, aquietar; impor (taxas, cargas, etc.); projetar, traçar; imputar, atribuir; exibir, fazer manifesto; *v.i.* pôr; — brother irmão leigo; — a bill on the table dar entrada a um projeto de lei; — apart reservar, pôr de lado; — about agir vigorosamente; — hold of agarrar, manter seguro; — the blame on fazer cair a culpa sôbre; — open revelar, descobrir; — out gastar; exibir, mostrar; traçar, projetar; amortalhar; — over cobrir, sobrepor; — to heart tomar a peito; — one's self out

esforçar-se; — a wager apostar; — stress on insistir em, fazer atenção a; — down descartar-se, abandonar, desistir; entregar-se; render-se; construir; projetar; prescrever; armazenar.
layer s. galinha poedeira; camada.
lay figure s. manequim.
laying s. postura (de ovos); rebocadura (de argamassa).
layman s. leigo.
layout s. plano, projeto; preparativo; demonstração, disposição, arranjo.
lazaretto, lazaret s. lazareto.
laze v.i. preguiçar; perder tempo.
lazy adj. preguiçoso; laziness s. preguiça; lazily adv. preguiçosamente; —»bones s. preguiçoso, mandrião.
lea s. prado, campo.
leach v.t. lixiviar; s. lixívia, barrela.
lead s. chumbo; plombagina, grafite; (imp.) espaço, entrelinha; (mar.) sonda; — poisoning intoxicação pelo chumbo; v.t. chumbar.
lead s. direção, cor duta; comando; dianteira; primazia; mão (no jôgo); (elet.) linha principal; v.t.&i. conduzir, guiar, dirigir; levar; induzir, mover; mandar, comandar; dominar; — on ir adiante, guiar; — off principiar, dirigir; — up to conduzir a; — along conduzir, acompanhar; — a new life emendar-se, levar vida nova; — astray desencaminhar, extraviar; — by the nose levar pelo nariz.
leaden adj. de chumbo.
leader s. líder, condutor, dirigente; chefe, cabeça; (imp.) artigo de fundo; »ship s. liderança, chefia.
leading adj. principal; primeiro; capital; dominante; — wheels rodas dianteiras de uma locomotiva.
leaf s. fôlha (em todas as suas acepções); — brass ouropel; v.t. folhear.
leaflet s. fascículo.
leafy adj. folhudo.
league s. liga; confederação; sociedade; légua; v.i. aliar-se, confederar-se, associar-se.
leak s. goteira; escapamento (de gás, vapor, etc.); saída, fuga; rombo; v.i. gotejar; fazer água; deixar escapar gás, vapor, etc.; vazar; transpirar (notícia, fato, etc.).
leakage s. V. leak.
lean adj. magro; sêco; v.t. inclinar, reclinar; apoiar; encurvar; v.i. apoiar-se, recostar-se; inclinar-se; — on, — upon encostar-se em; — over inclinar-se; — meat carne magra; »ing s. inclinação, queda; »ing tower tôrre inclinada; »ness s. magreza.
leap s. salto, pulo; sobressalto; v.i. saltar, pular; — year ano bissexto.
learn v.t.&i. aprender; »ed adj. sábio, erudito, instruído; »er s. estudante, aprendiz; »ing s. conhecimento, saber, ciência.
lease s. arrendamento, escritura de arrendamento; aluguel; v.t. alugar, arrendar; — holder locatário.
leash s. trela, ajoujo.
least adj. mínimo; o menor, o mínimo; — common multiple mínimo múltiplo comum; at —, at the — ao menos, pelo menos; not in the — de modo algum; adv. menos.
leather s. couro; adj. de couro; — dresser curtidor; v.t. forrar ou guarnecer de couro; dar uma sova.

leave s. licença; autorização; despedida; v.t. deixar; v.i. partir, sair; ir-se; — of absence licença; — alone deixar quieto; — behind deixar atrás; — off suspender, abandonar (um hábito, etc.)
leaven s. fermento, levedura; v.t. fermentar.
leavings s. restos.
lecherous adj. lascivo.
lectern s. atril.
lecture s. conferência; dissertação; (pop.) pito, sermão, reprimenda; v.i. fazer conferência; (pop.) censurar, admoestar.
lecturer s. conferencista.
ledge s. borda; margem; orla; saliência; recife.
ledger s. (com.) razão, livro mestre; laje de sepulcro.
leech s. sanguessuga.
leek s. alho-porro.
leer s. olhar malicioso; v.i. olhar maliciosamente.
lees s. sedimento, bôrra.
leeward adj. (mar.) sotavento.
left s.&adj. esquerdo; esquerda; adv. à esquerda; —»handed canhoto.
leg s. perna; pata (de animais ou aves); cano (da meia ou da bota); (geom.) cateto; on one's last legs morrendo, agonizante; sem recursos.
legacy s. legado.
legal adj. legal; judiciário; — aid assistência judiciária; — entity pessoa jurídica; »ize v.t. legalizar.
legate s. legado; »e s. legatário.
legation s. legação.
legend s. lenda; inscrição, legenda; »ary adj. lendário.
legerdemain s. prestidigitação.
legible adj. legível.
legion s. legião.
legislate v.i. legislar; legislation s. legislação; legislator s. legislador; legislature s. legislatura; legist s. legista.
legitimacy s. legitimidade; legitimate adj. legítimo; legitimize v.t. legitimar.
legume s. legume; leguminous adj. leguminosa.
leisure s. lazer.
leitmotiv, leitmotif s. leit-motiv.
lemon s. limão; — tree limoeiro; »ade s. limonada.
lend v.t. emprestar; »er s. credor; prestamista; »ing s. empréstimo; prestação.
length s. comprimento; extensão; espaço de tempo; alcance (de um tiro, etc.); at — finalmente, por fim; at full — em toda a extensão; »en v.t. encompridar, esticar; prolongar, dilatar.
lenient adj. leniente; indulgente, clemente; s. lenitivo.
lens s. lente.
Lent s. quaresma.
lenticular adj. lenticular.
lentil s. lentilha.
leonine adj. leonino.
leopard s. leopardo.
leper s. leproso; — hospital leprosário; leprosy s. lepra; leprous adj. leproso.
lesion s. lesão.
less adj. menos; inferior; adv. menos.
lessee s. arrendatário; inquilino.
lesser adj. menor.
lesson s. lição.
lessor s. arrendador; alugador.
lest conj. com medo que; com receio que; para que não.

let *v.t.* deixar, conceder, permitir; arrendar, dar em arrendamento; — **bygones be bygones** esqueçamos o passado; — **down** deixar cair; baixar; — **go** soltar; — **in** deixar entrar, admitir, fazer entrar; — **know** fazer saber, avisar; — **loose** soltar, afrouxar, desatar; — **have** ceder; — **the cat out of the bag** revelar um segredo.

let *s.* estôrvo, obstáculo; **without** — **or hindrance** sem estorvos nem obstáculos.

lethal *adj.* letal.

lethargic *adj.* letárgico; **lethargy** *s.* letargia.

letter *s.* carta; letra; *v.t.* rotular; pôr letras, títulos ou letreiros; **s** *s.* letras, literatura; **s patent** patente (de privilégio); **s of safe conduct** salvo-conduto.

lettuce *s.* alface.

level *adj.* plano, igual; uniforme; direito, reto; nivelado; no nível; *s.* plano; cota; *v.t.* nivelar; aplainar; igualar; **ing**, **ling** *s.* nivelamento.

lever *s.* alavanca; *v.t.* levantar por meio de alavanca.

leviathan *s.* leviatã.

levity *s.* leveza, ligeireza; leviandade.

levy *s.* exação, arrecadação; execução fiscal; imposição; conscrição, recrutamento; leva; *v.t.* impor, arrecadar tributos; executar, penhorar; recrutar; — **war** fazer guerra.

lewd *adj.* impudico, lascivo; **ness** *s.* impudicícia, lascívia.

lexicographer *s.* lexicógrafo.

lexicon *s.* léxico.

liability *s.* obrigação; responsabilidade; (*fin.*) passivo; **liable** *adj.* responsável; obrigado; devedor; solidário; propenso; sujeito, exposto.

liar *s.* mentiroso.

libation *s.* libação.

libel *s.* libelo; difamação; *v.t.* difamar; **lous** *adj.* difamatório.

liberal *adj.&s.* liberal; **ism** *s.* liberalismo; **ity** *s.* liberalidade.

liberate *v.t.* libertar; liberar.

libertine *adj.&s.* libertino.

liberty *s.* liberdade; privilégio; franquia; imunidade.

librarian *s.* bibliotecário; **library** *s.* biblioteca.

librettist *s.* libretista.

license *s.* licença; permissão; libertinagem; licença poética; concessão; *v.t.* licenciar; conceder licença ou permissão; autorizar.

licentiate *adj.&s.* licenciado.

licentious *adj.* licencioso, libertino; **ness** *s.* libertinagem, licenciosidade.

lichen *s.* (*bot.*) líquen.

licit *adj.* lícito.

lick *v.t.* lamber; (*fam.*) derrotar, bater.

lictor *s.* lictor.

lid *s.* cobertura; tampa; **eye** pálpebra.

lie *s.* mentira; *v.i.* mentir.

lie *v.i.* deitar-se, estender-se; jazer; estar situado; estar colocado; estacionar; residir; — **down** deitar-se, estender-se; — **at** importunar; estar exposto; — **by** estar perto, estar à mão; descansar; — **on** depender de; — **in wait** estar de emboscada.

liege *adj.* lígio, feudatário; *s.* vassalo, súdito.

lien *s.* (*dir.*) direito de retenção; penhora.

lieutenant *s.* tenente.

life *s.* vida; existência; *adj.* vitalício; relativo à vida; — **annuity** renda vitalícia; — **insurance** seguro de vida; — **belt** salva-vidas; **less** *adj.* sem vida, inanimado; **like** *adj.* vivo, animado; **long** *adj.* de toda a vida, para toda a vida.

lift *s.* elevador; alçamento; ação de levantar; *v.t.* levantar; alçar; erguer; sublevar; suspender; **to give one a** — ajudar alguém a levantar ou a fazer alguma cousa.

ligament *s.* ligamento; **ligature** *s.* ligadura.

light *adj.* leve; ligeiro; sutil; sôlto, fácil; claro; leviano; frívolo; frágil; delicado; *s.* luz; claridade; iluminação; dia; *v.t.* iluminar; acender; *v.i.* luzir; iluminar-se; brilhar; cair; apear-se; acontecer; **in the** — **of** à luz de; — **complexion** tez clara; — **headedness** delírio; — **horse** cavalaria ligeira; — **literature** literatura leve; — **minded** leviano, irrefletido; — **opera** opereta; — **up** iluminar; **the cat always** **s on its feet** o gato sempre cai em pé.

lighten *v.t.* aliviar; alegrar; iluminar; aclarar; *v.i.* relampejar; diminuir de pêso.

lighter *adj.* mais leve; *s.* acendedor; isqueiro; (*mar.*) gabarra, barcaça.

lightly *adv.* ligeiramente; levemente; **lightness** *s.* leveza, ligeireza; claridade.

lightning *s.* relâmpago, raio; — **conductor**, — **rod** pára-raios.

lights *s.* leves, pulmões (de animais).

ligneous *adj.* lenhoso.

likable *adj.* simpático.

like *adj.* igual, semelhante; parecido; o mesmo que; equivalente; provável; prometedor; *s.* semelhante, igual; gôsto, simpatia; *adv.&prep.* como, semelhante a; provàvelmente; *v.t.&i.* gostar; afeiçoar; querer; achar; comprazer-se em; **s and dislikes** simpatias e antipatias; **to be as** — **as two peas** parecer-se como duas gotas d'agua; — **mad** como louco; **not to have one's like** não ter seu igual; **as you** — como você queira; — **for** — na mesma moeda.

likelihood *s.* probabilidade; aparência; verossimilhança; **likely** *adj.* provável, verossímil; *adv.* provàvelmente.

liken *v.t.* comparar, assemelhar.

likeness *s.* semelhança; parecença; conformidade, igualdade; aparência, ar; retrato.

likewise *adv.* igualmente; também; da mesma forma.

liking *s.* afeição; gôsto; simpatia.

lilac *s.&adj.* lilás.

liliaceous *adj.* liliáceo.

Lilliputian *adj.* liliputiano.

lily *s.* lírio.

limb *s.* membro.

limber *adj.* flexível; frouxo; macio; *s.* (*mil.*) armão.

limbo *s.* limbo.

lime *s.* cal; limão; *v.t.* grudar; cimentar; tratar com cal.

limit *s.* limite; *v.t.* limitar, fixar, restringir.

limousine *s.* limusine.

limp *adj.* flácido; flexível; frouxo; *v.i.* manquejar; andar com dificuldade; executar com dificuldade; **er** *s.* coxo, manco.

limpet *s.* patela (molusco).

limpid *adj.* límpido; **ity** *s.* limpidez.

linden *s.* tília.

line s. linha; fila; fileira; alinhamento; via; traço; contôrno; gênero, especialidade; profissão; departamento; parte; jurisdição; (*poe.*) verso; *v.t.* forrar, revestir; cobrir; reforçar; traçar linhas; esboçar; alinhar.
lineage s. linhagem, descendência.
lineal *adj.* linear; descendente em linha direta.
lineament s. lineamento; traço.
linen s. tela de linho; linho; roupa de baixo branca; — **thread** fio de linho.
liner s. vapor ou avião de uma linha estabelecida.
ling s. espécie de bacalhau.
linger *v.t.* demorar-se; levar tempo; — **out**, — **away** prolongar, dilatar; **-er** s. pessoa que se demora; **-ing death** morte lenta.
lingerie s. roupa branca e fina.
lingo s. dialeto; linguagem estranha ao ouvinte.
lingual *adj.* lingual; **linguist** s. linguista; **linguistics** s. linguística.
liniment s. linimento.
lining s. fôrro; revestimento.
link s. elo; aro, argola, anel de cadeia; *v.t.* unir; enlaçar, encadear; articular.
linnet s. pintarroxo.
linoleum s. linóleo.
linotype s. linotipo.
linseed s. semente de linho, linhaça; — **oil** óleo de linhaça.
lint s. atadura (de fios de linho).
lintel s. vêrga (de porta).
lion s. leão; **lioness** s. leoa.
lip s. lábio; bordo; **-stick** pintura para lábios (baton).
liquefaction s. liquefação; **liquefy** *v.t.* liquefazer.
liqueur s. licor.
liquid *adj.&s.* líquido.
liquidate *v.t.* liquidar; **liquidation** s. liquidação.
liquor s. líquido; bebida alcoólica; licor.
lisp *v.i.* falar ciciando; falar indistintamente.
lissom, lissome *adj.* flexível; ágil.
list s. lista, nomenclatura, quadro, tabela; (*tec.*) ourela; *v.t.* catalogar, inventariar, registar, inscrever; listrar; calafetar; (*com.*) faturar; *v.i.* inclinar-se; (*mar.*) adernar; **-s** s. arena, liça.
listen *v.i.* escutar; **-er** s. ouvinte.
listless *adj.* distraído, desatento; indiferente.
litany s. litania.
literal *adj.* literal.
literary *adj.* literário; **literate** *adj.* alfabetizado; **literature** s. literatura.
litharge s. litargírio.
lithe *adj.* ágil, flexível.
lithia s. litina; **lithium** s. lítio.
litograph s. litografia (estampa); *v.t.* litografar; **-er** s. litógrafo; **-y** s. litografia (arte).
litigant s. litigante; **litigation** s. litígio; **litigious** *adj.* litigioso.
litmus s. (*quím.*) tornassol.
litter s. liteira; maca; barrigada, ninhada (de animais); cama de palha (nas estrebarias); miscelânea; desordem; *v.t.* parir; pôr em desordem.
little *adj.* pequeno; *adv.* pouco; — **by** — pouco a pouco; — **brain** cerebelo; — **girl** meninazinha; **-ness** s. pequenez.
live *adj.* vivo; de vida; vital; ativo; de interêsse atual; ardente; (*elet.*) carre-

gado; — **bait** isca viva; — **coal** carvão ardente, em brasa.
live *v.t.&i.* viver; levar (tal ou qual vida); passar; durar; alimentar-se; morar; residir; habitar; ficar; — **down** sobreviver a; **live on** viver de, alimentar-se de; — **up to** viver de conformidade com; — **up to one's promise** cumprir o prometido; **-lihood** s. vida; subsistência; ganha-pão; **-liness** s. vivacidade, animação; **-ly** *adj.* vivo, animado.
liver s. fígado.
livery s. libré.
livid *adj.* lívido; **-ity** s. lividez.
living *adj.* vivo; com vida; s. vida; subsistência; potencial vital; benefício eclesiástico; — **room** sala de estar; — **being** vivente; — **expenses** despesas de casa e comida; **the** — os vivos.
lizard s. lagarto.
llama s. lama, lhama (animal).
loach s. cadoz (peixe).
load s. carga; fardo; soma de trabalho; (*pop.*) montes, montões, grande quantidade; *v.t.&i.* carregar; embaraçar; suprir com abundância; adulterar; tomar carga; sobrecarregar; — **the wine** adulterar o vinho; **teacher's** — número de alunos e horas de trabalho que cabem a cada professor.
loaded *adj.* carregado; **loading** s. carregamento.
loaf s. pão.
loaf *v.i.* vadiar, passar o tempo na ociosidade.
loam s. barro; argila.
loan s. empréstimo.
loath *adj.* relutante; pouco disposto.
loathe *v.t.* detestar, desprezar; **loathing** s. aversão; **loathful** *adj.* detestável.
lobby s. vestíbulo; corredor; salão de entrada de hotel, teatro, etc.
lobe s. lóbulo.
lobster s. lagosta.
local *adj.* local; regional; s. trem que pára em todas as estações locais; (*pop.*) notícia de intêresse local; **-ity** s. localidade; **-ize** *v.t.* localizar.
locate *v.t.* colocar, situar; localizar; **-d** *adj.* situado.
lock s. fechadura; fêcho; ferrolho; anel (de cabelo); esclusa, comporta; *v.t.* fechar à chave; aferrolhar; fazer passar por comporta; **-s** s. cabelos.
locker s. compartimento com chave; gaveta; escaninho com chave.
locket s. medalhão.
locomotion s. locomoção; **locomotive** s. locomotiva.
locust s. gafanhoto, locusta.
locution s. locução.
lode s. (*min.*) filão, veio.
lodge s. pavilhão; cabana; loja maçônica; *v.t.* alojar, hospedar, albergar; depositar; colocar; plantar, introduzir, fixar; *v.i.* morar, residir; hospedar-se; fixar-se; alojar-se.
lodger s. locatário; **lodging** s. alojamento; vivenda; albergue.
loft s. sobrado, sótão; côro (de igreja); **-iness** s. elevação, altura; **-y** *adj.* alto, elevado; arrogante; sublime, majestoso.
log s. toro; acra, cepo, lenho; barquilha; — **cabin** cabana de madeira; — **book** (*mar.*) diário de derrota.
logarithm s. logaritmo.
logic s. lógica; **-al** *adj.* lógico.
loin s. lombo.
loiter *v.i.* demorar-se, perder tempo.

loll *v.i.* apoiar-se, recostar-se preguiçosamente; espreguiçar-se; pôr a língua para fora (animais).

lonely *adj.* solitário, só; **lonesome** *adj.* só, isolado; **loneliness** *s.* solidão, isolamento.

long *adj.* longo; alongado; grande; comprido; *adv.* muito tempo; muito; a grande distância; *v.i.* anelar, suspirar; — measures medidas de comprimento; — **ago** há muito tempo; — **sighted** présbita; — **for** anelar, suspirar por.

longevity *s.* longevidade.

longing *s.* anelo, desejo veemente.

longish *adj.* um tanto longo.

longitude *s.* longitude.

longitudinal *adj.* longitudinal.

look *s.* olhar; golpe de vista; vista d'olhos; ar; aparência; aspecto, semblante; *v.i.* olhar; parecer; ter aspecto de; — **after** olhar por, cuidar de; — **at** olhar; — **for** procurar; — **into** examinar; — **like** parecer; — **on** olhar; encarar; — **out!** atenção! — **over** percorrer, repassar; **it** *s* **like rain** parece que vai chover; *s* **ing glass** espêlho.

loom *s.* tear; *v.i.&t.* avistar no horizonte; desenhar-se; surgir.

loop *s.* laço, argola, anel, volta; presilha; olhal; curva; *v.t.* fazer presilhas em; pôr argolas; *v.i.* fazer voltas, fazer curvas.

loose *adj.* frouxo; móvel; sôlto, desatado; folgado; indefinido; sôlto (em liberdade); relaxado, dissoluto; descuidado, negligente; *v.t.* afrouxar; soltar; desatar; libertar; aliviar; — **in the bowels** com os intestinos soltos; — **morals** moral relaxada; **to give** — **to dar** rédeas sôltas a; *s* **ly** *adv.* frouxamente; sem coesão; vaga ou indefinidamente; *s* **n** *v.t.* afrouxar, soltar, desatar; relaxar; libertar.

loot *s.* pilhagem, saque; *v.t.&i.* saquear.

lop *v.t.* podar, decotar, desgalhar árvores.

loquacious *adj.* loquaz; **loquacity** *s.* loquacidade.

lord *s.* senhor; — **of creation** senhor da criação; — **of the manor** castelão; **the Lord** o Senhor; *s* **ly** *adj.* senhoril, altivo; *s* **ship** *s.* senhoria.

lore *s.* erudição, saber, ciência.

lorry *s.* autocaminhão, caminhão.

lose *v.t.&i.* perder; — **ground** perder terreno; — **heart** desanimar; — **one's temper** perder a calma, enfurecer-se; — **sight of** perder de vista; *s* **r** *s.* aquele que perde; **loss** *s.* perda; **lost** *adj.* perdido; **lost to** perdido para; insensível a.

lot *s.* lote; quota; parte, porção; partilha; sorte; destino; lote (de terra); (*pop.*) muito, uma quantidade, grande porção; **to draw** *s* **tirar a sorte.**

lotion *s.* loção.

lottery *s.* loteria.

lotto *s.* lôto.

lotus *s.* lotus, loto.

loud *adj.* alto; ruidoso, forte; *adv.* alto, ruidosamente.

lounge *s.* sala de conversa ou repouso; sofá; *v.i.* repousar; folgar; ficar à vontade; *s* **r** *s.* vadio, batedor de calçada.

louse *s.* piolho; **lousy** *adj.* piolhento.

lout *s.* rústico; bruto.

louver *s.* abertura (para ventilação); claraboia.

love *s.* amor; *v.t.&i.* amar; querer, gostar; — **affair** intriga amorosa; **in** — **amando**, enamorado de; **fall in** — apai-

xonar-se; **make** — **to** fazer a côrte a; —*s* **match** casamento de amor; — **all** (*tenis*) zero a zero; *s* **ly** *adj.* belo; adorável; *s* **liness** *s.* beleza, encanto; **lovable** *adj.* amável; apreciável.

lover *s.* amante; namorado; **loving** *adj.* afetuoso, amoroso.

low *adj.* baixo; pequeno; fraco; profundo; vulgar; — **Countries** Países-Baixos; — **relief** baixo-relêvo; —*s* **necked dress** vestido decotado; —*s* **bred** mal educado; — **bow** reverência profunda.

low *v.i.* mugir; berrar; *s.* mugido.

lower *adj.* mais baixo; inferior; baixo; mínimo; *v.t.* abaixar; humilhar; rebaixar, diminuir; — **oneself** rebaixar-se.

lowlands *s.* terras baixas.

lowliness *s.* humildade; baixeza; **lowly** *adj.* humilde; modesto.

loyal *adj.* leal; *s* **ism** *s.* lealdade; *s* **ty** *s.* lealdade.

lozenge *s.* pastilha; (*geom.*) losango.

lubber *s.* lerdo, pesadão; (*mar.*) marinheiro d'água doce.

lubricate *v.t.* lubricar, lubrificar; **lubricator** *s.* lubrificante.

lucerne, lucern *s.* luzerna.

lucid *adj.* lúcido; *s* **ity** *s.* lucidez.

luck *s.* sorte; fortuna; acaso; *s* **less** *adj.* sem sorte, infeliz; *s* **y** *adj.* feliz, afortunado; *s* **y star** boa estrêla.

lucrative *adj.* lucrativo; **lucre** *s.* lucro.

lucubration *s.* elucubração.

ludicrous *adj.* cômico; risível; divertido.

lug *s.* asa (de vasilha, etc.); orelha; *v.t.* puxar, arrastar.

luggage *s.* bagagem.

lugubrious *adj.* lúgubre.

lukewarm *adj.* têpido, morno; *s* **ness** *s.* tepidez.

lull *s.* acalmia; *v.t.&i.* acalmar; moderar; acalmar-se gradativamente.

lull *v.t.* embalar, ninar; adormecer; acalmar; *s* **aby** *s.* canção de berço.

lumbago *s.* lumbago; **lumbar** *adj.* lombar.

lumber *s.* antigalha, antiguidades, velharia; madeira.

luminary *s.* luminária; astro; luz; **luminous** *adj.* luminoso.

lump *s.* pedaço, massa, bloco; protuberância; *v.t.* amontoar; reunir; — **of sugar** torrão de açucar.

lunacy *s.* alienação mental, demência; **lunatic** *adj.&s.* lunático.

lunar *adj.* lunar.

lunch, luncheon *s.* almôço (refeição ligeira ao meio-dia); **lunch** *v.i.* almoçar.

lung *s.* pulmão.

lunge *s.* estocada, investida, arremetida; *v.i.* arremeter; assentar uma estocada.

lupus *s.* lupus.

lurch *s.* guinada; *v.i.* titubear; **leave in the** — deixar em situação difícil; *s* **ing** *s.* cilada.

lure *s.* engôdo, isca; *v.t.* engodar.

lurid *adj.* lúgubre, lívido, pálido; sinistro.

lurk *v.i.* esconder-se, dissimular-se; emboscar-se; *s.* emboscada.

luscious *adj.* saboroso; delicioso; açucarado, meloso.

lush *adj.* viçoso.

lust *s.* luxúria; concupiscência; cobiça; — **after** cobiçar.

luster, lustre *s.* lustre; *v.t.* lustrar; *s* **less** *adj.* fôsco, sem brilho.

lusty *adj.* vigoroso, robusto.

lute s. (mús). alaúde; v.i. tocar alaúde.
luxuriance s. exuberância; **luxuriant** adj. luxuriante, exuberante; **luxurious** adj. luxuoso; voluptuoso; **luxury** s. luxo.
lye s. lixívia, barrela.

lying adj. mentiroso.
lymph s. linfa.
lynch v.t. linchar.
lynx s. lince.
lyre s. lira.
lyric adj. lírico; =ism s. lirismo.

M

m letra do alfabeto.
macaco, macaque s. macaco.
macadam s. macadame.
macaroni s. macarrão.
macaroon s. bolinho de amêndoas.
macaw s. arara (ave).
mace s. maça, clava.
macerate v.t. macerar.
Machiavellian adj. maquiavélico.
machination s. maquinação, intriga.
machine s. máquina; =ry s. maquinismo; **machinist** s. maquinista.
mackerel s. espécie de cavala (peixe).
mackintosh s. capa impermeável.
mad adj. louco; insensato; furioso; encolerizado.
madam s. senhora.
madden v.t. tornar furioso; enfurecer; encolerizar; =ing adj. de dar raiva.
madder s. (bot.) granza.
madly adv. loucamente; **madness** s. loucura; demência.
madonna s. madona.
madrepore s. (zool.) madrépora.
madrigal s. madrigal.
magazine s. revista.
maggot s. larva; fantasia.
magic adj. mágico; s. mágica; encantamento; =al adj. mágico; =ally adv. fantàsticamente; como por encantamento; =ian s. mágico.
magisterial adj. magisterial; magistral; **magistrate** s. magistrado; **magistracy** s. magistratura.
magnanimity s. magnanimidade; **magnanimous** adj. magnânimo.
magnate s. magnata.
magnesia s. magnésia.
magnesium s. magnésio.
magnet s. ímã; =ic adj. magnético; =ics, =ism s. magnetismo; =o s. magneto.
magnificence s. magnificência; **magnificent** adj. magnífico.
magniloquence s. grandiloquência; **magniloquent** adj. grandíloquo.
magnitude s. magnitude.
magnolia s. magnólia.
magpie s. pêga.
mahogany s. acajú, mogno.
maid s. rapariga; moça solteira; criada; — of all work criada para todos os serviços; =’s room quarto da criada; =en s. virgem; donzela; =en name nome de solteira; =enly adj. virginal.
mail s. correio; correspondência; cota de malha.
maim v.t. estropiar, mutilar.
main adj. principal; de maior importância; s. fôrça, poder; a parte principal; o ponto essencial; — line linha ou tronco principal; =ly adv. principalmente.
maintain v.t. manter; sustentar; guardar; conservar; **maintenance** s. manutenção; sustento; apôio; proteção; conservação.
maize s. maís, n.ilho.

majestic adj. majestoso; **majesty** s. majestade.
major adj. maior; grande; principal; s. (dir.) maior; (mil.) major; (educ.) curso principal.
majority s. maioridade.
make v.t. fazer; produzir; ganhar; praticar; fabricar; confeccionar; criar; realizar; formar; tornar; pegar; v.i. dirigir-se; contribuir; — away with desfazer-se de; — it up reconciliar-se, fazer as pazes; — light of fazer pouco caso de; — off fugir, ir-se embora; — a train pegar um trem; — out sair-se (bem ou mal); — up one’s mind resolver, decidir-se; — up fazer; confeccionar; compor; pintar-se, preparar o rosto; — sure assegurar-se; s. fabricação; feitio; forma; figura; estrutura; produção; produto; marca (da fábrica); —=up pintura, arranjo do rosto; =er s. fabricante; construtor; creador; **making** s. fabricação; criação; construção; confecção.
malachite s. malaquita.
maladroit adj. desajeitado.
maladjusted adj. desajustado.
malaise s. indisposição, mal estar.
malaria s. malária.
malcontent adj. descontente.
male adj. másculo; masculino; varonil; viril; macho; s. macho; varão; homem.
malediction s. maldição.
malefactor s. malfeitor.
malevolent adj. malévolo.
malformation s. conformação defeituosa; vício de conformação.
malice s. malícia; malignidade; — aforethought premeditação; **malicious** adj. malicioso; mal intencionado.
malign v.t. difamar; caluniar; adj. maligno; =ant adj. maligno.
malinger v.i. fingir-se de doente.
malleable adj. maleável.
mallet s. malho, maço.
mallow s. (bot.) malva.
malt s. malte.
maltreat v.t. maltratar, brutalizar; =ment s. maus tratos; sevícias.
mama s. mamãe.
mammal s. mamífero; =ia s. mamíferos.
mammillary adj. mamilar.
mammoth s. mamute.
man s. homem; varão; sujeito; criado; peão (jôgo de xadrez); pedra (jôgo de damas); — and wife marido e mulher.
manacle v.t. manietar; =s s. algemas.
manage v.t. treinar (cavalos); gerir, administrar; conduzir; conseguir; v.i. arranjar-se, passar; =ment s. gerência, gestão; direção, administração; conduta, trato; =r s. gerente.
mandarin s. mandarim; tangerina.
mandatary s. mandatário; agente.
mandate s. mandato; encargo; comissão.
mandatory adj. (for.) preceptivo, obrigatório; s. mandatário.

mandible s. mandíbula.
mandolin s. bandolim.
mandrake s. (bot.) mandrágora.
mandrel, mandril s. (mec.) mandril.
mandrill s. (zool.) mandril.
mane s. crina.
manège, manege s. escola de equitação; picadeiro.
manes s. manes.
manfully adv. corajosamente, virilmente.
manganese s. manganês.
mange s. sarna, ronha.
manger s. manjedoura.
mangle s. (tec.) calandra; v.t. mutilar, lacerar; (tec.) calandrar.
mango s. manga; — tree mangueira.
mangrove s. (bot.) mangue-branco, sereíba.
manhood s. virilidade; idade viril.
mania s. mania; loucura; =c adj.&s. maníaco.
manicure s. manicura; **manicurist** s. manicura.
manifest adj. manifesto; v.t. manifestar.
manifesto s. manifesto.
manifold adj. múltiplo.
manikin s. manequim.
manioc s. mandioca.
manipulate v.t. manipular.
mankind s. espécie humana; os homens; **manliness** s. virilidade; **manly** adj. viril, másculo.
manna s. maná.
mannequin s. manequim.
manner s. maneira; ar; modo; jeito; modo de ser; =ism s. maneirismo.
mannish adj. masculino; de homem.
manœuvre, maneuver s. manobra; v.t.&i. fazer manobras, manobrar.
manometer s. manômetro.
mansion s. mansão; castelo; residência.
manslaughter s. homicídio não intencional mas consistindo crime.
mantilla s. mantilha.
mantle s. manto, capa.
manual adj.&s. manual.
manufactory s. fábrica, manufatura, usina; **manufacture** s. manufatura, fabricação, indústria; **manufacturer** s. manufatureiro; industrial; fabricante.
manure s. estêrco; estrume; v.t. estrumar, estercar.
manuscript s.&adj. manuscrito.
many adj.&pron. muitos, muitas; a **great** — muitíssimos, muitíssimas; — a, — an muitos, muitas; as — outros tantos, outras tantas; the — a grande maioria; too — demais; —=colored multicor; —=sided complexo.
map s. mapa; v.t. delinear mapas; — out traçar.
maple s. (bot.) bôrdo.
mar v.t. danificar; inutilizar; deitar a perder; desfigurar; estropiar.
marabou s. marabú.
maraschino s. marasquino.
marasmus s. marasmo.
maraud v.t. saquear; pilhar.
marble s. mármore; bolinha (de gude); =s s. jôgo de gude.
marc s. bagaço (de frutas).
marcasite s. marcassita.
March s. Março.
march s. marcha; desfile; v.i. marchar; — off pôr-se em marcha; — out sair; =ing s. marcha.
marchioness s. marquesa.
mare s. égua.
margarine s. margarina.

margin s. margem; bordo; borda; v.t. margear; marginar; (fin.) depositar fundos como caução para certas transações de bolsa; =al adj. marginal.
marguerite s. margarida (flor).
marigold s. (bot.) calêndula.
marine adj. marítimo; marinho; s. fusileiro naval; marinha; =r s. marinheiro.
marionette s. títere, marionete, fantoche.
marital adj. marital.
maritime adj. marítimo.
marjoram s. (bot.) manjerona.
mark s. marca; sinal; nota; pontos e notas escolares; marco (moeda); v.t. marcar; assinalar; dar notas (escola); anotar; observar; caracterizar; — down anotar, pôr por escrito; — time marcar passo; =ed adj. marcado; pronunciado; acentuado; visado (cheque); =er s. marcador.
market s. mercado; bolsa; praça; venda; preço; consumo; v.t. pôr no mercado; vender; dar saída; comprar ou vender no mercado; =able adj. negociável; =ing s. compra ou venda no mercado.
marking s. marcação; cotação.
marl s. marga.
marly adj. margoso.
marmalade s. geléia espêssa (em geral de laranja).
marmot s. (zool.) marmota.
maroon adj. castanho-avermelhado (côr); s. escravo fugitivo; v.t. abandonar numa ilha deserta; abandonar, deixando sem recursos.
marquetry s. marchetaria.
marquis s. marquês.
marriage s. casamento; núpcias; **married** adj. casado.
marrow s. medula; tutano.
marry v.t. casar; desposar; casar-se com; v.i. casar-se.
marsh s. pântano.
marshal s. (mil.) marechal; v.t. dispor em ordem militar; dirigir; guiar; comandar; =ship s. marechalato.
marshy adj. pantanoso.
marsupial s.&adj. marsupial; **marsupium** s. marsúpio.
mart s. empório; mercado.
marten s. (zool.) marta.
martial adj. marcial; — law lei marcial.
martin s. (zool.) gaivão.
martinet s. militar exageradamente disciplinado.
martingale s. gamarra.
martyr s. mártir; =dom s. martírio; =ize v.t. martirizar.
marvel s. maravilha; v.i. maravilhar-se; =lous adj. maravilhoso.
mascot s. mascote.
masculine adj. masculino; **masculinity** s. masculinidade.
mash s. massa; pirão; v.t. amassar; reduzir a pirão; =ed potatoes pirão de batatas.
mask s. máscara; v.t. mascarar; =ed bali baile de máscaras.
mason s. pedreiro; maçom; =ry s. alvenaria; maçonaria.
masquerade s. mascarada.
mass s. massa; montão; o grosso; missa; — production produção em massa.
massacre s. massacre; v.t. massacrar.
massage s. massagem; v.t. dar massagem; **massagist** s. **masssageuse** s. massagista.
massive adj. maciço.
mast s. mastro; v.t. mastrear.
master s. mestre; professor; diretor;

chefe; patrão; capitão; *v.t.* dominar,
conhecer a fundo; domar; =ful *adj.*
perito; magistral; excelente; imperioso;
arbitrário; =ship *s.* maestria; magisté-
rio; =y *s.* domínio; maestria.
mastic *s.* mastique, almécega; — tree
lentisco.
masticate *v.t.* mastigar; mastication *s.*
mastigação.
mastiff *s.* mastim.
mastodon *s.* mastodonte.
mastoid *adj.* mastóide.
mat *adj.* mate, fôsco; *s.* esteira, capacho;
trançado; tapête; *v.t.* trançar; esteirar,
cobrir com esteira.
match *s.* mecha, pavio, torcida; fósforo;
parelha; competidor; casamento; partido; (*esp. jôgo, etc.*) partida, competição; *v.t.&i.* casar; competir, fazer competir; igualar; emparelhar.
mate *s.* camarada; companheiro; par;
mate (jôgo de xadrez); *v.t.* aparelhar;
cruzar (animais).
material *adj.* material; *s.* matéria; material; fazenda, tecido; ingrediente; =ism
s. materialismo; =ist *s.* materialista; =ize
v.t. materializar; *v.i.* materializar-se.
maternal *adj.* maternal; maternity *s.*
maternidade; maternity doctor médico parteiro.
mathematical *adj.* matemático; math-
ematician *s.* matemático; mathematics *s.* matemática.
matinée *s.* vesperal, matinê.
matriarchy *s.* matriarcado.
matriculate *v.i.* matricular-se; matriculation *s.* matrícula.
matrimonial *adj.* matrimonial; matrimony *s.* matrimônio.
matrix *s.* matriz; molde, fôrma; (*anat.*)
útero.
matron *s.* matrona; =ly *adj.* matronal.
matter *s.* matéria; negócio; questão;
propósito; caso; assunto; artigo; (*med.*)
pus; *v.i.* importar; — of fact feito,
realidade; a — of fact man homem
realista; what is the —? que há? what
is the — with you? que tem você?
mattery *adj.* purulento; importante.
mattock *s.* alvião, picareta.
mattress *s.* colchão.
mature *adj.* maduro; *v.i.* amadurecer.
maturity *s.* maturidade; madureza.
maudlin *adj.* efusivamente sentimental.
maul *v.t.* martelo; malho.
mausoleum *s.* mausoléu.
mawkish *adj.* nauseoso; asqueroso; fastidioso.
maxim *s.* máxima, adágio.
maximum *s.* máximo.
May *s.* Maio; — day primeiro de Maio.
may *v.aux.* poder; ter permissão; it — be
pode ser.
mayonnaise *s.* maionese.
mayor *s.* prefeito; =alty *s.* prefeitura;
=ess *s.* espôsa do prefeito.
maze *s.* labirinto.
me *pron.* me; mim.
meadow *s.* prado; campo; —=sweet
barba de bode (flor).
meager, meagre *adj.* magro; fraco;
pobre; insignificante.
meal *s.* refeição; farinha; — time hora
das refeições; =y *adj.* farinhoso.
mean *v.t.&i.* significar; querer dizer;
pensar; propor-se; pretender; ter a
intenção de; he =s well tem boas inten-
ções; what do you —? que quer você
dizer?

mean *adj.* mau, mesquinho, ruim; vil;
baixo; comum; tacanho, sórdido; médio; *s.* média, meio; =s *s.* meios, meio;
recurso; =while enquanto isso; by all
=s sem falta, por todos os meios; by
fair =s por meios lícitos; she has no
=s ela não tem recursos.
meander *s.* meandro, labirinto; *v.i.*
serpentear.
meaning *s.* significação; sentido; intenção; =less sem sentido.
meanness *s.* baixeza; vileza; maldade.
measles *s.* sarampo.
measurable *adj.* mensurável; apreciável.
measure *s.* medida; unidade de medida;
compasso, cadência; projeto de lei,
(*geol.*) camada; *v.t.* medir; mensurar; —
up to estar à altura de; take — tomar
medidas; out of — além das medidas.
measurement *s.* medida, dimensão.
meat *s.* carne; =y *adj.* carnudo.
mechanic *s.* mecânico; =al *adj.* mecânico;
=ian *s.* mecânico; =s *s.* mecânica;
mechanism *s.* mecanismo; mechanization *s.* mecanização; mechanize *v.t.*
mecanizar.
medal *s.* medalha; =lion *s.* medalhão.
meddle *v.i.* meter-se; imiscuir-se; intrometer-se.
mediaeval *adj.* medieval.
mediate *v.i.* mediar; intervir; interpor-se;
mediation *s.* mediação; mediator *s.*
mediador; mediatrix *s.* mediadora.
median *s.* (*geom.*) mediana.
medical *adj.* médico; — jurisprudence
medicina legal; medicament *s.* medicamento; medicinal *adj.* medicinal;
medicine *s.* medicina; remédio; medi-
cate *v.t.* medicar.
medieval V. mediaeval.
mediocre *adj.* medíocre; mediocrity *s.*
mediocridade.
meditate *v.i.* meditar; meditation *s.*
meditação; meditative *adj.* medita-
tivo.
mediterranean *adj.* mediterrâneo.
medium *adj.* médio, meio; *s.* meio,
agente; veículo; atmosfera; intermediário; médium (espírita).
medley *s.* mistura; macedônia.
medullary *adj.* medular.
meek *adj.* manso, humilde, dócil; =ly *adv.*
mansamente, humildemente; =ness *s.*
mansidão; humildade; docilidade.
meerschaum *s.* (*min.*) espuma do mar;
— pipe cachimbo de espuma.
meet *v.t.* encontrar; achar; fazer face a;
resolver; *v.i.* encontrar-se; reunir-se;
juntar-se; — a charge refutar, responder a uma acusação; — expenses fazer
frente aos gastos; — a situation resolver uma situação.
meeting *s.* encontro; junção; confluência;
entrevista; reunião; concurso; sessão.
megaphone *s.* megafone.
melancholia *s.* melancolia; melancholy
s. melancolia; melancholic *adj.* melancólico.
mellow *adj.* maduro; macio; meloso; doce.
melodious *adj.* melodioso; melody *s.*
melodia.
melon *s.* melão.
melt *v.t.&i.* derreter; fundir; dissolver;
fundir-se, dissolver-se; *s.* substância
derretida; fusão; derretimento; —
away dissipar-se, desvanecer-se; that
=s in the mouth isso derrete-se na
boca; — into tears desmanchar-se em
lágrimas; =er *s.* crisol; fundidor.

member *s.* membro; sócio; associado; representante; **=ship** *s.* qualidade de membro ou sócio.

membrane *s.* membrana.

memento *s.* memento; lembrança.

memoir *s.* memórias; biografia; memorial.

memorable *adj.* memorável; **memorandum** *s.* memorandum; **memorial** *s.* memorial; **memorize** *v.t.* memorizar; **memory** *s.* memória.

menace *s.* ameaça; *v.t.* ameaçar.

menagerie *s.* coleção de animais, especialmente para exibição.

mend *v.t.* remendar; emendar; melhorar; reformar.

mendacious *adj.* mentiroso; **mendacity** *s.* hábito de mentir.

mendicancy *s.* mendicância; **mendicity** *s.* mendicância; **mendicant** *adj.* mendicante.

mending *s.* remendo; reparação; emenda; **mender** *s.* remendador; reparador.

menial *adj.* servil.

meningitis *s.* meningite.

mensuration *s.* mensuração; medida.

mental *adj.* mental; **=ity** *s.* mentalidade; **=ly** *adv.* mentalmente.

menthol *s.* mentol.

mention *s.* menção; *v.t.* mencionar.

menu *s.* cardápio, menu.

mercantile *adj.* mercantil.

mercenary *adj.&s.* mercenário.

mercer *s.* comerciante de sedas; **=ized** *adj.* mercerizado.

merchandise *s.* mercadoria; **merchant** *s.* negociante; comerciante; **the merchant class** o alto comércio.

merciful *adj.* misericordioso, clemente.

merciless *adj.* inclemente.

mercurial *adj.* mercurial; **mercury** *s.* mercúrio.

mercy *s.* misericórdia, clemência, piedade; **at the — of** à mercê de; **— on us!** misericórdia!

mere *adj.* mero.

meretricious *adj.* meretrício.

merge *v.t.* unir, fundir, combinar, absorver; *v.i.* absorver-se, fundir-se.

meridian *s.&adj.* meridiano; **meridional** *adj.* meridional.

meringue *s.* merengue.

merino *s.* merinó, merino.

merit *s.* mérito; *v.t.* merecer; **meritorious** *adj.* meritório.

merlin *s.* esmerilhão (ave).

mermaid *s.* sereia.

merrily *adv.* alegremente; **merriment** *s.* alegria; **merry** *adj.* alegre; **make merry** alegrar-se, divertir-se.

mesh *s.* malha; rede.

mesmeric *adj.* mesmeriano; **mesmerism** *s.* mesmerismo; **mesmerist** *s.* hipnotizador; **mesmerize** *v.t.* hipnotizar.

mess *s.* prato (quantidade de comida); ração; porção; rancho (refeição tomada em conjunto); desordem, confusão, trapalhada; **steward of the — rancheiro**; *v.t.* sujar; fornecer refeições; *v.i.* comer; arranchar-se.

message *s.* mensagem; recado; **messenger** *s.* mensageiro; enviado; embaixador; comissário.

Messiah *s.* Messias.

messuage *s.* casa residencial e suas dependências.

messy *adj.* desarrumado, desordenado; sujo.

metal *s.* metal; **=lic** *adj.* metálico;

=liferous *adj.* metalífero; **=lurgist** *s.* metalúrgico; **=lurgy** *s.* metalurgia.

metamorphose *v.t.* metamorfosear; **metamorphosis** *s.* metamorfose.

metaphor *s.* metáfora; **=ical** *adj.* metafórico.

metaphysical *adj.* metafísico; **metaphysician** *s.* metafísico; **metaphysics** *s.* metafísica.

meteor *s.* meteoro; **=ic** *adj.* meteórico; **=ite** *s.* aerólito; **=ologic, =oligical** *adj.* meteorológico; **=ology** *s.* meteorologia.

meter *s.* metro; medidor.

method *s.* método; **=ical** *adj.* metódico; **=ist** *s.* metodista.

methyl *s.* metilo.

meticulous *adj.* meticuloso.

metonymy *s.* metonímia.

metre V. **meter.**

metric, metrical *adj.* métrico; **metrics** *s.* métrica.

metronome *s.* metrônomo.

metropolis *s.* metrópole; capital; **metropolitan** *adj.* metropolitano.

mettle *s.* têmpera, ardor, brio; **=some** *adj.* brioso, fogoso, valoroso; de têmpera.

mew *s.* miado; jaula; cavalariça; *v.i.* miar; *v.t.* enjaular; engradar; encerrar; **=s** *s.* estábulos do Palácio Real inglês; fileira de estábulos; fileira de garages.

mezzanine *s.* mezanino.

miaow *s.* miado; *v.i.* miar.

miasma *s.* miasma.

mica *s.* mica.

microbe *s.* micróbio.

micrometer *s.* micrômetro.

microphone *s.* microfone.

microscope *s.* microscópio; **microscopic, microscopical** *adj.* microscópico.

mid *adj.* médio; **=night** meia noite; **=shipman** aspirante de Marinha; **=wife** parteira; **— age** meia idade.

middle *adj.* médio; do meio; **—=aged** de meia idade; **— class** classe média; **— finger** dedo máximo; **—=man** intermediário; **—=weight** peso médio; *s.* centro; meio.

middling *adj.* médio; medíocre; *adv.* mais ou menos; sofrivelmente.

midge *s.* espécie de mosca pequena.

midget *s.* pessoa muito pequena.

midnight *s.* meia-noite.

midst *s.* meio; seio, centro.

mien *s.* semblante, ar.

might *s.* poder; força; **=iness** *s.* poder; grandeza; **=y** *adj.* poderoso; **the =y** ones os poderosos.

mignonette *s.* resedá.

migrate *v.i.* emigrar; **migration** *s.* migração; **migratory** *adj.* migratório.

mild *adj.* suave; benigno; leve; ligeiro; manso; moderado.

mildew *s.* môfo; míldio; doença produzida pelo fungo.

mildness *s.* suavidade.

mile *s.* milha.

milfoil *s.* (*bot.*) milefólio.

militant *adj.&s.* militante; **militarize** *v.t.* militarizar; **military** *adj.* militar; **militate** *v.i.* militar; **militia** *s.* milícia.

milk *s.* leite; *v.t.* ordenhar; **=man** leiteiro; **=ing** *s.* ordenha; **=y** *adj.* leitoso; **Milky Way** Via Láctea.

mill *s.* moinho; fábrica; usina; engenho; *v.t.* moer; serrilhar; **steel — fábrica de aço; to go through the — saber uma cousa por experiência.

millepede *s.* centopeia.

miller s. moleiro.
millet s. milhete.
milliard s. bilião.
milliner s. chapeleira; negociante de chapéus para senhoras.
milling s. moenda.
million s. milhão; =aire s. milionário; =th adj.&s. milionésimo.
milt s. glândulas reprodutivas masculinas do peixe; secreção glandular masculina do peixe; v.t. fecundar as ovas dos peixes-fêmeas.
mime s. mímica; farsa; pantomima; bufão; farsante; v.t. imitar; v.i. fazer mímica.
mimosa s. (bot.) sensitiva, mimosa.
mince v.t. cortar muito miúdo; picar; — one's word falar com afetação.
mind s. mente; pensamento; espírito; ânimo; gôsto; propensão; inclinação; intenção; opinião; juízo; parecer; idéia; v.t.&i. fazer atenção a; ocupar-se de; tomar cuidado com; importar-se; fazer caso de; obedecer; atender; never — não importa, não faz mal; to have a — to ter a intenção de; propor-se a; to — one's business tratar da sua vida, dos seus negócios; =ed adj. disposto, inclinado, propenso; =ful adj. atento, cuidadoso; =fully adv. atentamente.
mine pron. o meu, a minha; meu, minha; os meus; as minhas; meus, minhas; a friend of — um dos meus amigos.
mine s. mina; v.t. minar; v.i. minerar; construir mina; explorar mina; =r s. mineiro; =ral s. mineral; =ralogy s. mineralogia; =ralogist s. mineralogista.
mingle v.t. misturar; mesclar; confundir; v.i. misturar-se; confundir-se.
miniature s. miniatura; miniaturist s. miniaturista.
minim s. (mús.) mínima.
minimize v.t. diminuir; atenuar; reduzir ao mínimo; menosprezar; minimum s. mínimo.
mining s. exploração de minas, mineração.
minister s. ministro; pastor; v.t.&i. ministrar; dar; servir; =ial adj. ministerial; ministration s. ministério; ministry s. ministério; sacerdócio; departamento.
mink s. lontra americana; pele de lontra.
minor adj. menor; secundário; inferior; pouco importante; s. menor (de idade); (log.) menor; (mús.) tom menor.
minority s. menoridade.
minster s. basílica; mosteiro.
minstrel s. menestrel; trovador.
mint s. Casa da Moeda; fábrica; (bot.) hortelã, menta; v.t. cunhar; fabricar dinheiro; fabricar, inventar.
minuet s. minueto.
minus prep. menos; s. sinal de subtração.
minute s. minuto; minuta, nota, apontamento; v.t. anotar; tomar apontamentos; =ly adv. minuciosamente.
minutia s. minúcia.
minx s. rapariga desenvolta.
miracle s. milagre; miraculous adj. milagroso.
mirage s. miragem.
mire s. lama; v.t. enlodar; miry adj. lodoso.
misadventure s. revés; acidente; desventura.
misalliance s. matrimônio com pessoa de classe inferior.
misanthrope s. misantropo; misan-

thropical adj. misantrópico; misanthropic adj. misantrópico.
misapply v.t. aplicar mal; fazer mau uso de.
misapprehend v.t. compreender mal; misapprehension s. conceito errôneo; interpretação falsa.
misappropriate v.t. empregar mal; abusar da confiança; dilapidar.
misbehave v.i. comportar-se mal; proceder mal; misbehavior s. mau comportamento.
miscalculate v.i. calcular mal; enganar-se nas contas; miscalculation s. engano de cálculos.
miscarriage s. abôrto; miscarry v.i. abortar.
miscellaneous adj. mesclado; misturado; miscellanea, miscellany s. miscelânea.
mischance s. má sorte; infortúnio; fatalidade.
mischief s. injúria; mal, dano; travessura, diabrura.
misconceive v.i. julgar mal; formar conceito errôneo; misconception s. mal entendido, noção errônea.
misconduct s. má conduta.
misconstruction s. interpretação errônea.
miscreant s. incrédulo; celerado; adj. inescrupuloso.
misdeed s. delito.
misdeliver v.t. entregar errado, extraviar.
misdemeanant s. delinquente; misdemeanor s. delito.
misdirect v.t. dirigir ou endereçar mal.
miser s. avaro; miserável.
miserable s. infeliz, miserável, digno de pena.
miserere s. miserere.
misericord s. misericórdia.
miserly adj. avaro, avarento.
misery s. miséria.
misfire s. falha, fato de não dar fogo; v.i. falhar, negar fogo.
misfortune s. desgraça; infortúnio; adversidade.
misgiving s. pressentimento; premonição.
misgovern v.t. governar mal; =ment s. mau govêrno.
misguide v.t. extraviar; guiar mal; =d adj. extraviado; mal dirigido.
mishap s. contratempo; acidente; infortúnio.
misinform v.t. informar mal.
misinterpretation s. má interpretação.
misjudge v.t. julgar mal.
mislay v.t. perder; extraviar.
mislead v.t. perder; extraviar; induzir em êrro; enganar; seduzir.
mismanage v.t. gerir mal; administrar ou manejar mal; =ment s. má gestão.
misnomer s. engano de nome.
misogynist s. misógino.
misplace v.t. extraviar; colocar mal, fora do lugar.
misprint s. êrro de imprensa; êrro tipográfico; gato.
mispronounce v.t. pronunciar mal; mispronunciation s. vício de pronúncia.
misquotation s. citação truncada; misquote v.t. citar falsa ou errôneamente.
misrepresent v.t. desfigurar, desnaturar, falsificar; =ation s. declaração falsa; relação falsa ou infiel.
misrule s. má administração.
miss s. senhorita, senhorinha; moça solteira.

miss *v.t.&i.* perder (o trem, etc.); errar;
falhar; abster-se de; carecer de; sentir
falta de; escapar de; — one's mark
errar o alvo; — the point não pegar o
sentido; — out passar por alto, omitir.
missal *s.* missal.
missing *adj.* perdido; extraviado; ausente.
mission *s.* missão; *ary *s.* missionário.
missive *s.* missiva.
misspell *v.t.* soletrar mal; *ing *s.* êrro de
ortografia.
misstatement *s.* declaração falsa.
mist *s.* neblina, vapor; *v.t.* empanar; obscurecer; anuviar.
mistake *s.* equívoco; falta; engano;
v.t.&i. enganar-se; equivocar-se; cometer um êrro ou uma falta; *n *adj.* errôneo; **be** *n estar enganado.
mister *s.* senhor.
mistranslation *s.* tradução errônea.
mistress *s.* senhora; patroa; professora;
amante.
mistrust *s.* desconfiança; suspeita; *v.t.*
desconfiar de; suspeitar; *ful *adj.*
desconfiado.
misty *adj.* brumoso; enevoado.
misunderstand *v.t.* compreender mal;
*ing *s.* malentendido; desinteligência;
quiproquó; **misunderstood** *adj.* incompreendido.
misuse *s.* abuso; mau trato; *v.t.* abusar
de; maltratar.
mite *s.* bagatela, um nada; (*zool.*) ácaro.
mitigate *v.t.* mitigar; atenuar.
mitre *s.* mitra; *d *adj.* mitrado.
mitt *s.* mitene.
mix *v.t.* misturar; mesclar; *ed *adj.*
misturado; mesclado; heterogêneo;
*ture *s.* mistura.
mizzle *v.i.* chuviscar; *s.* chuvisco.
mnemonic *adj.* mnemônico.
moan *s.* gemido; *v.i.* gemer.
moat *s.* fosso.
mob *s.* multidão; populaça; turba;
gentalha.
mobile *adj.* móvel; **mobility** *s.* mobilidade.
mock *adj.* falso, não verdadeiro; *v.i.*
zombar, caçoar, mofar; *er *s.* zombador; *ery *s.* zombaria.
mode *s.* moda.
model *s.* modêlo; *v.t.* modelar; *ler *s.*
modelador; *ling *s.* modelagem.
moderate *adj.* moderado; *v.t.* moderar;
moderation *s.* moderação.
modern *adj.&s.* moderno.
modernize *v.t.* modernizar.
modest *adj.* modesto; *y *s.* modéstia.
modicum *s.* pequena quantidade.
modification *s.* modificação; **modify**
v.t. modificar.
modulate *v.t.* modular; **modulation** *s.*
modulação.
modus vivendi modus vivendi.
Mohammedan *s.&adj.* maometano;
*ism *s.* maometismo.
moiety *s.* metade.
moil *v.i.* estafar-se.
moire *s.* (*tec.*) moiré.
moist *adj.* úmido; *en *v.t.* umedecer;
umectar; *ness, *ure *s.* umidade.
molar *adj.&s.* molar.
molasses *s.* melaço.
mold, mould *s.* môfo, bolor; humus;
molde, matriz; modêlo; *v.i.* mofar; *v.t.*
amoldar; dar forma a; modelar; amassar; *er *s.* modelador; *ing *s.* moldura,
modelagem; *y *adj.* mofado.

mole *s.* lunar, verruga; (*zool.*) toupeira;
(*med.*) mola.
molecular *adj.* molecular; **molecule** *s.*
molécula.
molest *v.t.* atormentar, importunar;
*ation *s.* importunidade.
mollify *v.t.* amolecer; abrandar.
mollusk *s.* molusco.
molly-coddle *s.* efeminado; maricas.
molt, moult *v.i.* mudar, mudar de penas;
*ing *s.* muda.
molten *adj.* derretido; fundido.
moment *s.* momento; instante; *ary *adj.*
momentâneo, passageiro.
momentous *adj.* muito importante.
momentum *s.* (*mec.*) momento; ímpeto.
monarch *s.* monarca; *ic, *ical *adj.*
monárquico; *ist *s.* monarquista; *y *s.*
monarquia.
monastery *s.* mosteiro, convento; **monastic** *adj.* monástico, monacal.
Monday *s.* segunda-feira.
monetary *adj.* monetário; **monetize**
v.t. amoedar, transformar em moeda;
money *s.* dinheiro; moeda; sistema
monetário.
monger *s.* traficante, negociante.
mongrel *adj.* mestiço; híbrido.
monk *s.* monge; frade.
monkey *s.* macaco; modo; — **trick**
macaquice.
monochord *s.* monocórdio.
monochrome *s.* monocromo.
monocle *s.* monóculo.
monogamy *s.* monogamia.
monogram *s.* monograma.
monograph *s.* monografia.
monolith *s.* monólito.
monologize *v.i.* monologar; **monologue**
s. monólogo.
monomania *s.* monomania.
monoplane *s.* monoplano.
monopoly *s.* monopólio; **monopolize**
v.t. monopolizar.
monosyllabic *adj.* monosilábico; **monosyllable** *s.* monosílabo.
monotonous *adj.* monótono; **monotony**
s. monotonia.
monotype *s.* monótipo.
monster *s.* monstro.
monstrance *s.* ostensório; custódia.
monstrosity *s.* monstruosidade.
month *s.* mês; *ly *adj.* mensal; *adv.*
mensalmente.
monument *s.* monumento; *al *adj.*
monumental.
moo *v.i.* mugir.
mood *s.* humor; (*gram.*) modo; *y *adj.*
mal humorado.
moon *s.* lua; *beam raio de lua; *light
luar; *stone pedra da lua.
moor *s.* charco; pântano.
Moor *s.* mouro.
moor *v.t.* (*mar.*) amarrar, atracar.
moose *s.* rena da América.
moot *adj.* discutível, contestável; *s.*
discussão; debate; argumento; *v.t.*
discutir; debater.
mop *s.* vassoura de pano; *v.t.* esfregar.
mope *v.i.* ser sem graça e sem espírito; *s.*
pessoa sem graça.
moraine *s.* (*geol.*) morena.
moral *s.* moral; moralidade; *adj.* moral;
*ist *s.* moralista; *ize *v.t.&i.* moralizar,
pregar moral.
morass *s.* pântano.
moratorium *s.* moratória.
morbid *adj.* mórbido.

mordant *adj.* sarcástico, mordaz; *s.* mordente.

more *adj.&adv.* mais; — **and** — cada vez mais; — **or less** mais ou menos; **the** — quanto mais, tanto mais.

morganatic *adj.* morganático.

moribund *adj.* moribundo.

morning *s.* manhã; aurora.

morose *adj.* mal humorado; áspero; triste.

morphine *s.* morfina; **morphinomaniac** *adj.* morfinômano.

morrow *s.* amanhã, dia seguinte.

morsel *s.* um bocado; um pedaço (referindo-se geralmente a um quitute).

mortal *adj.&s.* mortal; **-ity** *s.* mortalidade.

mortar *s.* morteiro, almofariz.

mortgage *s.* hipoteca; *v.t.* hipotecar; **-e** *s.* credor hipotecário.

mortification *s.* mortificação; **mortify** *v.t.* mortificar.

mortuary *adj.* mortuário.

mosaic *s.* mosaico; marchetaria.

mosque *s.* mesquita.

mosquito *s.* mosquito.

moss *s.* musgo.

most *adj.* mais; o mais; a maior parte; *adv.* mais; muito; sumamente; **-ly** *adv.* principalmente; na maior parte.

mote *s.* átomo, argueiro.

moth *s.* traça; **-eaten** roído pela traça.

mother *s.* mãe; — **country** país natal; **—-in-law** sogra; — **of pearl** madrepérola; *v.t.* servir de mãe a; dispensar carinhos maternos a; **-less** *adj.* sem mãe; **-ly** *adj.* maternal.

motif *s.* motivo; tema (em arte e literatura).

motion *s.* movimento; marcha; moção; (*for.*) requerimento; *v.i.* fazer sinal; **-less** *adj.* sem movimento; imóvel.

motive *s.* motivo; móvel; *adj.* motor; motriz.

motley *adj.* mesclado; variado; diverso; *s.* mescla de côres.

motor *s.* motor; *v.i.* ir de automóvel; dirigir um automóvel; **—-car** automóvel; **—-cycle** motocicleta; **-ing** *s.* automobilismo; **-ist** *s.* motorista, automobilista; **-ize** *v.t.* mecanizar.

motto *s.* divisa, lema, mote.

mould V. mold.

moult V. molt.

mound *s.* montículo; monte de terra; trincheira.

mount *s.* monte, montanha; terrapleno; montadura; *v.t.&i.* montar.

mountain *s.* montanha; **-eer** *s.* montanhês; alpinista; **-eering** *s.* alpinismo; **-ous** *adj.* montanhoso.

mountebank *s.* saltimbanco.

mounted *adj.* montado; a cavalo.

mourn *v.t.&i.* lamentar, chorar, sentir; estar de luto; **-ful** *adj.* triste, choroso; **-ing** *s.* luto.

mouse *s.* camondongo; (*jíria*) pessoa medrosa e tímida.

moustache *s.* bigode; **-d** *adj.* bigodudo.

mouth *s.* bôca; embocadura; **—-wash** dentifrício; **-ful** *s.* bocado.

movable *adj.* móvel.

move *s.* movimento; manobra; mudança; jogada (jôgo de xadrez); *v.t.&i.* mover; mover-se; jogar; comover; enternecer; deslocar; mudar-se; — **along** andar, caminhar; — **back** recuar; **-ment** *s.* movimento; marcha; gesto.

mow *s.* molho; *v.t.* segar, fazer colheita, ceifar.

much *adj.* muito; *adv.* muito; mui; excessivamente; **as** — **tanto**; **as** — **as tanto** quanto; **too** — demasiado, demais.

mucilage *s.* mucilagem.

muck *s.* estêrco; porcaria; *v.t.* estrumar.

mucous *adj.* mucoso; — **membrane** mucosa; **mucus** *s.* muco.

mud *s.* lama, lôdo; — **bath** banho de lama.

muddle *s.* confusão; *v.t.* confundir; embriagar; fazer confusão; emaranhar; atrapalhar; **-r** *s.* trapalhão.

muddy *adj.* lamacento, lodoso, barrento; turvo; *v.t.* enlamear; turvar.

muezzin *s.* muezim.

muff *s.* regalo (agasalho); indivíduo desajeitado.

muffle *s.* palha ou cobrir; amortecer (o som); envolver; encobrir; **-d** *adj.* embuçado; abafado (som).

mug *s.* caneca; (*jíria*) cara, bôca; *v.t.* fotografar (criminosos).

muggy *adj.* quente, úmido, pesado (o tempo).

mulatto *s.* mulato.

mulberry *s.* amora; — **tree** amoreira.

mulch *s.* palha ou qualquer outra substância espalhada no chão para cobrir e proteger as raizes das plantas contra o calor ou o frio.

mulct *v.t.* multar; *s.* multa.

mule *s.* mula, mulo; chinelinhas; **-teer** *s.* muleteiro.

mulish *adj.* cabeçudo, teimoso; híbrido, estéril.

muller *s.* pulverizador, pedra para moer grãos ou minérios.

mullet *s.* mugem.

mullion *s.* (*arq.*) coluna que divide o vão da janela.

multicolor *adj.* multicor.

multifarious *adj.* multifário, variado.

multiform *adj.* multiforme.

multimillionaire *s.* multimilionário.

multiple *s.&adj.* múltiplo; **multiplicand** *s.* multiplicando; **multiplication** *s.* multiplicação; **multiplicity** *s.* multiplicidade; **multiplier** *s.* multiplicador; **multiply** *v.t.&i.* multiplicar.

multitude *s.* multidão.

mum, mumm *v.i.* mascarar-se.

mumble *v.i.* murmurar, resmungar, dizer entre os dentes.

mummer *s.* um mascarado.

mummify *v.t.* mumificar.

mummy *s.* múmia.

mumps *s.* cachumba.

munch *v.i.* mastigar (barulhentamente).

mundane *adj.* mundano; terrestre.

municipal *adj.* municipal; **-ity** *s.* municipalidade.

munificence *s.* munificência; **munificent** *adj.* munificente; magnânimo.

muniment *s.* documento; meio de defesa.

munitions *s.* munições.

mural *adj.* mural.

murder *s.* assassinato, homicídio; *v.t.* assassinar, matar; **-er** *s.* assassino; **-ess** *s.* assassina; **-ous** *adj.* homicida, sanguinário.

muriatic *adj.* muriático.

murky *adj.* sombrio, obscuro, tenebroso.

murmur *s.* murmúrio; (*med.*) sôpro no coração; *v.t.&i.* murmurar.

murrain *s.* morrinha; peste dos animais.

muscle *s.* músculo; **-d** *adj.* musculoso; **muscular** *adj.* muscular; musculoso.

Muse *s.* Musa.

muse *v.i.* meditar, concentrar-se.

museum s. museu.
mush s. angú; (pop.) sentimentalidade tôla.
mushroom s. cogumelo.
music s. música; =ian s. músico.
musical adj. músico.
musing s. meditação; adj. contemplativo, pensativo.
musk s. almíscar; — **deer** almiscareiro; =seed ambarina.
musket s. mosquete, =eer s. mosqueteiro.
Muslem s.&adj. maometano.
muslin s. musselina.
musquash s. rato almiscareiro.
mussel, muscle s. mexilhão.
Mussulman s. muçulmano.
must v.aux. dever, ser necessário; you — go now você dêve ir-se agora.
must s. mosto; vinho novo.
mustard s. mostarda.
muster s. chamada; v.t. fazer a chamada, reunir para inspeção.
musty adj. mofado.
mutability s. mutabilidade.
mutation s. mutação.
mute adj. mudo.

mutilate v.t. mutilar; **mutilation** s. mutilação.
mutineer s. amotinador.
mutiny s. motim, revolta; v.i. revoltarse; **mutinous** adj. sedicioso.
mutter v.i. murmurar; dizer alguma cousa entre dentes; resmungar.
mutton s. carne de carneiro.
mutual adj. mútuo; =ity s. mutualidade, reciprocidade.
muzzle s. focinho; açaime, focinheira; boca de canhão; máscara respiratória.
my adj. meu, minha, meus, minhas.
myopia s. miopia; **myopic** adj. míope.
myriad s. miríade.
myriapod s. miriápode.
myrmidon s. esbirro.
myrrh s. mirra.
myrtle s. murta.
myself pron. eu próprio; eu mesmo; mim mesmo; mim.
mysterious adj. misterioso.
mystery s. mistério.
mystic s. místico; =ism s. misticismo.
mystify v.t. mistificar.
myth s. mito; =ology s. mitologia; =ologic, =ological adj. mitológico.

N

N letra do alfabeto.
nabob s. nababo.
nacre s. nácar.
nadir s. (ast.) nadir.
naevus, nevus s. nevo, sinal de nascença.
nag s. piquira (cavalo); v.t.&i. implicar, achar defeito, aborrecer com recriminações.
naiad s. náiade.
nail s. unha; prego; cravo; ponta; v.t. pregar.
naïve adj. ingênuo; =ty, =té s. ingenuidade.
naked adj. nú; — **eye** ôlho nú; =ness s. nudez.
namby-pamby adj. afetado; melindroso.
name s. nome; fama; reputação; v.t. denominar; dar nome a; designar; nomear; **call** =s dizer nomes feios; =less adj. sem nome; =ly adv. a saber.
nankeen, nankin s. nanquim.
nanny s. (pop.) babá; ama; — **goat** cabra.
nap s. sesta; pêlo macio (dos tecidos); v.i. fazer a sesta; **be caught** =ping ser apanhado desprevenido.
naphtha s. nafta.
naphthalene, naphthaline s. naftalina.
napkin s. guardanapo; — **ring** argola de guardanapo.
narcissus s. narciso.
narcotic s.&adj. narcótico.
narrate v.t. narrar, contar.
narration s. narração, relação.
narrative adj. narrativo; s. narrativa.
narrator, narratress s. narrador, narradora.
narrow adj. estreito, apertado; s. passagem estreita; (geog.) estreito; v.t. estreitar, apertar; =ness s. estreiteza.
narwhal s. narval.
nasal adj. nasal.
nascent adj. nascente; **nascency, nascence** s. nascença.
nasturtium s. (bot.) nastúrcio.

nasty adj. sujo; obceno; indecente; nauseoso; (pop.) desagradável, intratável; **nastiness** s. sujeira; maldade.
natal adj. natal.
natation s. natação.
nation s. nação; =al adj. nacional; =ionalism s. nacionalismo; =alist s. nacionalista; =ality s. nacionalidade; =als s. nacionais.
native adj. natural; nativo; originário; s. nativo; indígena.
nativity s. natividade.
natty adj. elegante; bem arranjado.
natural adj. natural; bastardo; =ist s. naturalista; =ization s. naturalização; =ize v.t.&i. naturalizar, naturalizar-se.
nature s. natureza; natural; gênio; good-=d de bom gênio.
naughtiness s. maldade; **naughty** adj. mau, desagradável.
nausea s. náusea; =te v.t. nausear; =ting adj. nauseoso; **nauseous** adj. nauseoso, nauseabundo.
nautical adj. náutico.
nautilus s. náutilo.
naval adj. naval; marítimo.
nave s. cubo (de roda); nave (de igreja).
navel s. umbigo.
navigable adj. navegável.
navigate v.i. navegar.
navigation s. navegação.
navigator s. navegante.
navvy s. trabalhador.
navy s. marinha (de guerra); — **blue** azul marinho.
nay adv. mais ainda; s. resposta negativa; voto negativo; negação.
Neapolitan adj.&s. napolitano.
near adj. próximo; aproximado; íntimo; adv. perto de; ao lado; v.i. aproximar-se de; =ly adv. de perto; quasi; **he** =ly fell êle quasi caiu; **I** =ly missed my train quasi perdi o trem; =ness a. proximidade.
neat adj. limpo, nítido, tratado; =ness s. limpeza.

nebulous adj. nebuloso; **nebula** s. (ast.) nebulosa.
necessarily adv. necessàriamente, forçosamente.
necessary adj. necessário.
necessitate v.t. necessitar; **necessitous** adj. necessitado; **necessity** s. necessidade.
neck s. pescoço; gargalo; (geog.) estreito; (anat.) colo; — **of the uterus** colo do útero.
necklace s. colar.
necktie s. gravata.
neckerchief s. lenço de pescoço.
necrology s. necrologia.
necromancy s. necromancia.
necrosis s. necrose.
nectar s. néctar.
need s. necessidade; v.t.&i. ter necessidade de; querer; precisar; **-ful** adj. necessário.
needle s. agulha; — **-work** trabalho de agulha.
needless adj. desnecessário; **needy** adj. necessitado.
nefarious adj. nefando, iníquo, abominável.
negation s. negação.
negative adj. negativo; s. negativa.
neglect v.t. negligenciar, descuidar; abandonar; s. negligência, descuido; abandono.
negligence s. negligência; **neglectful, negligent** adj. negligente; **negligible** adj. que pode ser negligenciado.
negotiable adj. negociável.
negotiate v.t.&i. negociar; **negotiation** s. negociação; **negotiator** s. negociador.
negress s. negra; **negro** s.&adj. negro.
neigh v.i. rinchar; **-ing** s. relincho, rincho.
neighbor, neighbour s. vizinho; próximo; **-hood** s. vizinhança; arredores; **-ing** adj. próximo, vizinho.
neither pron.&adj. nem um nem outro; nenhum; conj. nem; nem tão pouco; — **will I do it** nem eu tão pouco o farei.
neologism s. neologismo.
neon s. (quím.) neônio.
neophyte s. neófito.
nephew s. sobrinho.
nepotism s. nepotismo.
Nereid s. nereida.
nerve s. nervo; coragem; sangue-frio; **-less** adj. inerte, sem fibra.
nervous adj. nervoso; **-ness** s. nervosidade, nervosismo.
nest s. ninho; v.i. construir ninho.
nestle v.t.&i. abrigar; abrigar-se; agasalhar-se, aconchegar-se.
net s. rede; malha; adj. (com.) líquido.
nether adj. inferior, baixo; — **lip** lábio inferior.
nethermost adj. o mais baixo.
netting s. rede; malha.
nettle s. urtiga; v.t. picar (como a urtiga); irritar.
neuralgia s. nevralgia; **neuralgic** adj. nevrálgico.
neurasthenia s. neurastenia.
neuritis s. (med.) neurite.
neurologist s. neurologista; **neurosis** s. neurose; **neurotic** adj. neurótico.
neuter adj.&s. neutro; **neutral** adj.&s. neutro; **neutrality** s. neutralidade; **neutralize** v.t. neutralizar.
never adv. nunca; — **ending** eterno.

nevertheless adv.&conj. não obstante; no entanto; contudo; mesmo assim.
new adj. novo; recente; fresco; — **-born** recém-nascido; — **-comer** recém-chegado; **-ly** adv. recentemente; **-ness** s. novidade.
newel s. pilastra (da escada).
news s. notícia; novidade; **-paper** jornal; — **agency** agência de informações.
newt s. lagartixa aquática.
next adj. próximo; vizinho; seguinte; adv. depois, em seguida; perto; na próxima vez.
nib s. bico; ponta (pena, etc.); **-bed** adj. bicudo, ponteagudo; v.t. apontar, aguçar; mordicar.
nibble v.t.&i. petiscar; comer aos bocadinhos.
nice adj. bom; agradável; gentil; delicado; **-ly** adv. gentilmente; de modo bonito.
nicety s. delicadeza, amabilidade; esmero; **the niceties of life as** cousas agradáveis da vida.
niche s. nicho.
nick s. entalhe; corte, recorte; talho; ponto crítico; momento oportuno; v.t. fazer cortes ou entalhes; fazer alguma cousa a tempo; tocar no ponto preciso.
nickel s. níquel; v.t. niquelar.
nick-nack s. frioleira, bagatela.
nickname s. apelido; v.t. apelidar.
nicotine s. nicotina.
niece s. sobrinha.
niello s. nigela (liga metálica).
niggard s. tacanho, mesquinho; **-ly** adv. mesquinhamente.
nigger s. negro; negra.
nigh adj. próximo; adv. perto; quasi.
night s. noite; — **club** cabaré; — **dress** camisola de dormir.
nightingale s. rouxinol.
nightly adv. todas as noites; de noite; adj. noturno.
nihilist s. niilista.
nil s. nada.
Nile s. Nilo.
nimble adj. ágil; rápido; ligeiro; **-ness** s. agilidade; presteza.
nimbus s. nimbo.
nine adj.&s. nove.
nineteen s.&adj. dezenove; **-th** adj. décimo-nono.
ninety adj.&s. noventa; **ninetieth** adj. nonagésimo.
ninny s. bobo; pobre de espírito.
nip s. bocado, migalha, fragmento; gole, trago; mordida, beliscadura; (hort.) paralização do crescimento, ou dano devido ao frio; dormência; sarcasmo; v.t. beliscar, morder; picar; queimar (o frio); tornar dormente; machucar; cortar, tosar; **-pers** s. alicate; pinça; torquês.
nipple s. bico do seio, mamilo.
nit s. lêndea.
nitrate s. nitrato; **nitre** s. nitro, azotato de potássio, salitre; **nitric** adj. nítrico.
nitrogen s. nitrogênio, azoto; **nitroglycerin** s. nitro-glicerina.
no adj. não; adj. nenhum, nenhuma; **I have — time** não tenho tempo; **there is — bread** não há pão; **with — money** sem dinheiro; — **smoking** é permitido fumar; — **matter** não importa; — **use** inútil.
nobiliary adj. nobiliário.
nobility s. nobreza.
noble adj. nobre.

nobody *s.* ninguém.
nocturnal *adj.* noturno; **nocturne** *s.*
(*mús.*) noturno.
nod *s.* inclinação (de cabeça); *v.i.* inclinar
a cabeça (consentindo ou cumprimen-
tando); cochilar.
node *s.* nó; protuberância; enrêdo, trama.
nodule *s.* nódulo.
noggin *s.* caneca pequena.
nogging *s.* tabique.
noise *s.* barulho; *=less adj.* silencioso.
noisome *adj.* pernicioso; fétido; repugnante.
noisy *adj.* barulhento.
nolens volens queira ou não queira, por
bem ou por mal.
nomad *adj.* nômade.
nomenclature *s.* nomenclatura.
nominal *adj.* nominal.
nominate *v.t.* nomear, designar; **nomi-
nation** *s.* nomeação, designação; **nom-
inee** *s.* nomeado (pessoa); **nominative**
s. nominativo (caso).
non *pref.* *=combatant* não combatente,
civil; *=stop* sem parada.
nonage *s.* menoridade.
nonagerian *adj.&s.* nonagenário.
nonce *s.* circunstância; **for the** — para
a ocasião; por ora.
nonchalance *s.* falta de interêsse; indiferença, despreocupação.
nonconformist *s.* dissidente (da Igreja
Anglicana).
nondescript *adj.* indefinível.
none *adj.&pron.* nenhum; ninguém;
nada; — **of that** nada disso; **I have** —
não tenho nenhum, não tenho nada.
nonentity *s.* nulidade; pessoa de pouco
valor; (*fil.*) não existência, não ser.
nonplus *s.* perplexidade, estupefação; *v.t.*
estupeficar, deixar perplexo; *=ed adj.*
estupefato; perplexo.
nonsense *s.* absurdo; insanidade; disparate.
nonsuit *v.t.* (*for.*) desistir (da ação).
noodle *s.* talharim; tôlo, pateta.
nook *s.* canto, ângulo; refúgio.
noon *s.* meio-dia; apogeu.
noonday *s.* meio-dia.
noontide *s.* meio-dia; apogeu.
noose *s.* nó corrediço.
nor *conj.* nem.
Nordic *adj.* nórdico.
norm *s.* norma; *=al adj.* normal.
Norman *adj.&s.* normando; **Normandy**
s. Normandia.
north *s.* norte, setentrião; *adv.* ao norte,
para o norte; *=ern adj.* do norte, seten-
trional; *=erner s.* nortista; *=wards adv.*
para o norte, em direção ao norte.
Norway *s.* Noruega; **Norwegian** *adj.&s.*
norueguês.
nose *s.* nariz; **to blow one's** — assoar-se;
v.t.&i. cheirar.
nostalgia *s.* nostalgia; **nostalgic** *adj.*
nostálgico.
nostril *s.* narinas.
nostrum *s.* droga; panacéia.
not *adv.* não; — **at all** de modo algum;
— **guilty** não culpado; — **one** nem
um.
notability *s.* notabilidade.
notable *adj.* notável.
notary *s.* tabelião; notário.
notation *s.* anotação, notação.
notch *s.* entalhe, corte; *v.t.* entalhar,
dentear.
note *s.* nota, memento; marca, sinal;
apontamento; notícia, aviso; (*mús.*)

nota; person of — pessoa de destaque;
=worthy digno de menção; *v.t.* marcar,
distinguir; fazer atenção a; *=d adj.* célebre, de nomeada.
nothing *s.* nada; cousa alguma; — **at all**
nada; *=ness s.* nada, o nada.
notice *s.* observação; atenção; aviso,
notícia, notificação; menção; **at the
shortest** — ao menor sinal; **on short**
— com curto prazo; *v.t.* observar;
prestar atenção; reparar; fazer atenção
a; *=able adj.* digno de atenção.
notify *v.t.* notificar, avisar; intimar.
notion *s.* noção; *=s* (*pop.*) quinquilha-
rias.
notoriety *s.* notoriedade; **notorious** *adj.*
notório; insigne, famoso.
notwithstanding *prep.* a-pesar de; a
despeito de; *adv.* não obstante; *conj.*
ainda que; se bem que.
nought *s.* nada; zero.
noun *s.* nome, substantivo.
nourish *v.t.* alimentar; *=ing adj.* alimentício; *=ment s.* alimento.
nous *s.* mente; razão; intelecto.
novel *adj.* novo, inédito; *s.* romance.
novelette *s.* novela curta.
novelist *s.* romancista.
novelty *s.* novidade; inovação.
November *s.* Novembro.
novice *s.* noviço; aprendiz.
noviciat *s.* noviciado.
now *adv.* agora, atualmente; *conj.* ora,
isto posto; *s.* atualidade, momento
presente; *int.* ora! vejamos! **from** — **on**
de ora em diante.
nowadays *adv.* em nossos dias; hoje em
dia.
nowhere *adv.* em parte alguma.
nowise *adv.* de modo algum, absolutamente.
noxious *adj.* nocivo.
noyade *s.* afogamento.
nozzle *s.* bico, extremidade; esguicho,
bocal de mangueira; (*pop.*) focinho.
nubile *adj.* núbil.
nucleus *s.* núcleo.
nude *adj.&s.* nú; (*arte*) nú.
nudge *s.* cotovelada; acotovelar, dar uma
cotovelada.
nudity *s.* nudez.
nugatory *adj.* fútil; ineficaz; nulo.
nugget *s.* pepita.
nuisance *s.* aborrecimento; estôrvo; incômodo.
null *adj.* nulo.
nullify *v.t.* anular.
nullity *s.* nulidade.
numb *adj.* dormente, entorpecido; *v.t.*
entorpecer.
number *s.* número; algarismo; cifra; *v.t.*
numerar; contar; *=ing s.* numeração;
=less adj. inumerável.
numbness *s.* entorpecimento, dormência.
numeral *adj.* numeral; **numerary** *s.*
numerário.
numerator *s.* numerador.
numerical *adj.* numérico.
numerous *adj.* numeroso.
numismatics *s.* numismática; **numismatist** *s.* numismata.
numskull *s.* lerdo, parvo.
nun *s.* freira, religiosa.
nunciature *s.* nunciatura; **nuncio** *s.*
núncio.
nunnery *s.* convento.
nuptial *adj.* nupcial; *=s s.* casamento,
núpcias.
nurse *s.* enfermeira; ama (de criança);

wet — ama de leite; *v.t.* amamentar; cuidar, tratar (de doente); **·ry** *s.* quarto de crianças; (*agríc.*) viveiro; **nursing** *s.* amamentação, aleitamento; cuidado; **nursing home** casa de saúde; **nursling** *s.* lactente.

nurture *s.* educação; alimentação; *v.t.* educar, criar; alimentar.

nut *s.* noz; porca de parafuso; cravelha; (*gíria*) maníaco.

nutmeg *s.* noz moscada.

nutriment *s.* alimento.

nutrition *s.* nutrição, nutrimento.

nutritious *adj.* alimentício; **nutritive** *adj.* alimentício, nutritivo.

nutting *s.* colheita de nozes; **nutty** *adj.* abundante em nozes; sabendo a nozes; (*pop.*) picante.

nux vomica noz-vômica.

nuzzle *v.i.&t.* focar; aconchegar-se.

nymph *s.* ninfa.

nymphomania *s.* ninfomania.

O

O letra do alfabeto; zero.

O *int.* ai! ó!

oaf *s.* criança retardada; idiota.

oak *s.* carvalho.

oakum *s.* estôpa.

oar *s.* remo; **·sman** *s.* remador.

oasis *s.* oasis.

oast *s.* forno para lúpulo, fumo, etc.

oat *s.* aveia; **·meal** farinha de aveia.

oath *s.* juramento; imprecação.

obbligato *adj.* (*mús.*) obrigatório; *s.* (*mús.*) acompanhamento.

obdurate *adj.* obstinado; duro, inflexível.

obedience *s.* obediência.

obedient *adj.* obediente; **·ly** *adv.* obedientemente.

obeisance *s.* reverência.

obelisk *s.* obelisco.

obese *adj.* obeso; **obesity** *s.* obesidade.

obey *v.t.&i.* obedecer.

obfuscate *v.t.* ofuscar; obscurecer.

obituary *s.* obituário.

object *s.* objeto; propósito; ponto; (*gram.*) objeto, complemento; *v.t.* objetar, opor; reclamar.

objection *s.* objeção; oposição.

objective *s.* objetivo; (*gram.*) objetivo (caso).

objurgation *s.* objurgação.

oblation *s.* oblação, oferenda.

obligate *v.t.* obrigar; **obligation** *s.* obrigação; **obligatory** *adj.* obrigatório; **obliging** *adj.* serviçal, prestável, prestativo.

oblique *adj.* oblíquo; **·ly** *adv.* obliquamente; **obliquity** *s.* obliquidade.

obliterate *v.t.* obliterar.

oblivion *s.* esquecimento, olvido.

oblivious *adj.* esquecido; distraído.

oblong *adj.* oblongo.

obloquy *s.* censura; maledicência.

obnoxious *adj.* ofensivo; odioso; culpado.

oboe *s.* (*mús.*) oboé.

obscene *adj.* obceno; **obscenity** *s.* obcenidade.

obscure *adj.* obscuro; *v.t.* obscurecer.

obscurity *s.* obscuridade; **obscurely** *adv.* obscuramente.

obsequies *s.* obséquias, exéquias.

obsequious *adj.* obsequioso; **·ness** *s.* obsequiosidade, obséquio.

observance *s.* observância; prática ou cerimônia religiosa; observação; **observant** *s.* observante; observador.

observation *s.* observação; escrutínio, exame.

observatory *s.* observatório.

observe *v.t.* observar; notar, reparar; **·r** *s.* observador.

obsess *v.t.* obsedar; **·ion** *s.* obsessão.

obsolete *adj.* obsoleto.

obstacle *s.* obstáculo.

obstetrical *adj.* obstétrico; **obstetrics** *s.* obstetrícia.

obstinacy *s.* obstinação; **obstinate** *adj.* obstinado; **obstinately** *adv.* obstinadamente.

obstreperous *adj.* turbulento, barulhento.

obstruct *v.t.* obstruir; **·ion** *s.* obstrução.

obtain *v.t.* obter; adquirir; alcançar.

obtrude *v.t.* forçar; *v.i.* intrometer-se, impor-se; **·er** *s.* intruso.

obturator *s.* obturador.

obtuse *adj.* obtuso.

obverse *s.* anverso; face principal.

obviate *v.t.* obviar, prevenir.

obvious *adj.* óbvio, evidente, manifesto.

ocarina *s.* (*mús.*) ocarina.

occasion *s.* ocasião; circunstância; *v.t.* ocasionar; dar lugar a; causar; **·al** *adj.* ocasional; **·ally** *adv.* ocasionalmente.

occiput *s.* occipício.

occult *adj.* oculto; **·ism** *s.* ocultismo.

occupant *s.* ocupante; habitante, morador, inquilino.

occupation *s.* ocupação.

occupier *s.* inquilino, locatário.

occupy *v.t.* ocupar; habitar.

occur *v.i.* ocorrer; suceder.

occurrence *s.* ocorrência.

ocean *s.* oceano.

Oceania *s.* Oceania.

ocher, ochre *s.* ocre, oca, ocra.

octagon *s.* octógono; **·al** *adj.* octogonal.

October *s.* Outubro.

octogenarian *s.* octogenário.

octopus *s.* polvo.

octoroon *s.* oitavão.

ocular *adj.* ocular.

oculist *s.* oculista.

odd *adj.* impar; e alguns, e poucos; desirmanado; extraordinário, adicional; singular, estranho, original, engraçado; **forty —** quarenta e poucos; **— job** biscate, trabalho extraordinário; **— or even** par ou impar; **an — glove** luva desirmanada, uma luva só.

oddity *s.* singularidade, raridade; **oddly** *adv.* desigualmente; singularmente, extraordinàriamente.

odds *s.* desigualade; partido, vantagem; diferença; rixa, disputa; (*turfe*) cotação; **tó lay —** of 3 to 1 apostar 3 contra 1; **they are at —** estão de ponta, estão brigados; **— and ends** sobras, remanescentes; miscelânea.

ode *s.* ode.

odious *adj.* odioso; **odium** *s.* ódio.

odoriferous *adj.* odorífero.

odor, odour *s.* odor; **·less** *adj.* inodoro.

Odyssey *s.* odisséia.

oesophagus *s.* esôfago.

oestrus, oestrum *s.* ciclo, cio.

of *prep.* de; **it is five minutes — three** faltam cinco para as tres; **— course** naturalmente; **— late** últimamente.

off *adv.* fora; longe, de longe; d'aquí; de cima; *(mar.)* ao largo; *prep.* fora de; à altura, na altura de; frente a; de; desde; **— New York** em frente, ao largo de Nova York; *adj.* direito, da direita; distante; livre; *(pop.)* errado, incorreto; **two miles — a** duas milhas, distante duas milhas; **— fore foot** pata direita dianteira; **day —** dia livre, dia de folga; **— in his calculations** errado em seus calculos; **— side** lado direito; *(futebol)* fora de jôgo; **-hand** de repente; sem cerimônia; improvisado; brusco; **to be — ir-se** embora; sair; estar fora; *int.* fora!

offal *s.* sobras, sobejos; refugos.

offend *v.t.* ofender, insultar; **-er** *s.* ofensor; culpado, delinquente.

offense, offence *s.* ofensa; culpa, falta; ataque; crime, transgressão; insulto; dano.

offensive *adj.* ofensivo; *s.* ofensiva.

offer *s.* oferecimento; *v.t.* oferecer; propor; **-ing** *s.* oferenda; oblação; **-tory** *s.* ofertório.

office *s.* ofício; escritório; ministério; serviço; exercício, função; agência; **— hours** horas de trabalho.

officer *s.* oficial; funcionário; agente.

official *adj.* oficial; *s.* funcionário.

officialdom *s.* funcionalismo.

officiate *v.i.* oficiar; exercer as funções, fazer as vezes (de alguém).

officious *adj.* oficioso.

offing *s.* alto mar; **in the —** ao largo.

offscourings *s.* refugo; lia; varredura.

offset *s.* projetura, rebento; compensação; equivalência.

offspring *s.* produto, descendência, prole; fruto.

often *adv.* frequentemente; **how —?** quantas vezes?

ogee *s.* *(arq.)* cimácio.

ogive *s.* ogiva.

ogle *s.* olhadela, olhar amoroso; *v.i.* olhar amorosamente, provocantemente.

ogre *s.* ogro; **ogress** *s.* ogra.

oh *int.* ó!; ah!

oil *s.* óleo; petróleo; *v.t.* olear, lubrificar; **-y** *adj.* oleoso.

ointment *s.* unguento.

old *adj.* velho; antigo; **— age** velhice; **— bachelor** solteirão; **— maid** solteirona; **how — are you?** quantos anos tem você?

oleaginous *adj.* oleoso, oleaginoso.

oleander *s.* *(bot.)* loendro.

olfactory *adj.* olfativo.

oligarchy *s.* oligarquia.

olive *s.* azeitona, oliva; **— tree** oliveira.

Olympic games jogos olímpicos.

Olympus *s.* Olimpo.

omega *s.* ômega; fim; têrmo.

omelet, omelette *s.* omelete.

omen *s.* augúrio, presságio, prognóstico.

ominous *adj.* ominoso; nefasto, agourento.

omission *s.* omissão; **omit** *v.t.* omitir.

omnibus *s.* ônibus.

omnipotent *adj.* onipotente; **omnipotence** *s.* onipotência.

omniscience *s.* oniciência.

omnivorous *adj.* onívoro.

on *prep.* sôbre, em cima de; em, no, na; *adv.* em cima; **— credit** fiado; **— duty** em serviço; **— purpose** de propósito;

— the contrary pelo contrário; **— the move** movimentando-se; **— and —** continuamente.

once *adv.* uma vez; uma só vez; em outro tempo; **— more** de novo, ainda uma vez; **— for all** uma vez por todas; **— upon a time** era uma vez.

one *adj.* um; só; único; *s.* um; unidade; *pron.* se, êste, êsse; algum, alguma; aquele, aquela; **-act play** peça em um só ato; **-sided** unilateral; **— and all** todos sem exceção; **— another** um ao outro; **— by —** um por um; **to live according to one's state** viver conforme o que se tem; **no —** ninguém.

oneness *s.* unidade.

onerous *adj.* oneroso.

one's *pron.* seu, sua, seus, suas.

oneself *pron.* se, si, si mesmo, si próprio.

onion *s.* cebola.

onlooker *s.* assistente, espectador.

only *adj.* único; só; *adv.* sòmente; ùnicamente; só; **I have — to say** só tenho a dizer; **— child** filho único.

onomatopoeia *s.* onomatopéia.

onrush *s.* investida; ataque.

onset *s.* ataque, assalto; começo, princípio.

onslaught *s.* investida, ataque, assalto furioso.

onus *s.* carga, pêso; onus.

onward *adj.* progressivo; avançado; *adv.* para a frente.

onwards *adv.* progressivamente; para diante.

onyx *s.* ônix.

ooze *s.* vasa, lôdo; decocção usada no curtimento do couro; *v.i.* exsudar, transpirar, suar; escapar pouco a pouco; **his courage -d away** sua coragem foi-se aos poucos; *v.t.* exsudar.

opacity *s.* opacidade.

opal *s.* opala.

opaque *adj.* opaco.

open *v.t.* abrir; descobrir; destampar; inaugurar; expor, revelar; manifestar; *v.i.* abrir-se; entreabrir-se; desenvolver-se; *adj.* aberto, livre, franco; público; descoberto; **— the ball** abrir o baile; **— air** ar livre; **in the — country** em pleno campo; **in the —** pùblicamente, às claras; **-handed** liberal, generoso, mão aberta; **in the — sea** em alto mar.

opening *s.* abertura; fenda; caminho aberto; princípio; entrada; oportunidade, ocasião; *adj.* inicial; preliminar; de abertura.

openly *adv.* abertamente; pùblicamente.

openness *s.* franqueza, sinceridade.

opera *s.* ópera.

operate *v.t.* operar; explorar; *v.i.* agir; **— on, — upon** *(med.)* operar.

operatic *adj.* lírico, dramático.

operation *s.* operação; exploração; **operating room** sala de operações.

operator *s.* operador; explorador; telefonista; maquinista; telegrafista.

operative *adj.* eficaz, ativo, operatório; *s.* obreiro, operário.

operetta *s.* opereta.

ophthalmia *s.* oftalmia; **ophthalmic** *adj.* oftálmico.

opiate *s.* opiato, narcótico; *adj.* opiáceo, sonífero.

opine *v.i.* opinar.

opinion *s.* opinião; **-ated** *adj.* obstinado.

opium *s.* ópio.

opossum *s.* sarigué, gambá.

opponent s. oponente, adversário; *adj.* oponente, adverso.

opportune *adj.* oportuno; =ly *adv.* oportunamente; **opportunity** s. oportunidade; **opportunism** s. oportunismo; **opportunist** s. oportunista.

oppose *v.t.&i.* opor; opor-se; =d *adj.* oposto, contrário; **opposing** *adj.* oponente, adverso; **opposite** s. contrário, oposto; **opposite to** oposto a, em frente a; **opposition** s. oposição; resistência.

oppress *v.t.* oprimir; =ion s. opressão; =ive *adj.* opressivo; =or s. opressor.

opprobrious *adj.* infamante; **opprobrium** s. opróbrio.

optic *adj.* ótico; =al *adj.* ótico; =s s. ótica; =ian s. oculista.

optimism s. otimismo; **optimist** s. otimista; **optimistic** *adj.* otimista.

option s. opção; escolha; =al *adj.* facultativo.

opulence s. opulência; **opulent** *adj.* opulento.

or *conj.* ou; seja; quer; **2 — 3 times a day** duas ou três vezes por dia.

oracle s. oráculo.

oral *adj.* oral.

orange s. laranja; *adj.* côr de laranja; =ade s. laranjada; =ry s. laranjal.

orang-outang s. orangotango.

oration s. discurso; oração fúnebre; **orator** s. orador; **oratorical** *adj.* oratório; **oratory** s. oratória; oratório (capela).

orb s. globo, esfera, orbe; =it s. órbita.

orc s. orca (peixe).

orchard s. pomar.

orchestra s. orquestra; (*teat.*) platéia; =te *v.t.* orquestrar.

orchid s. orquídea.

orchis s. (*bot.*) órquide.

ordain *v.t.* ordenar; prescrever; decretar.

ordeal s. ordálio; prova; experiência dura.

order s. ordem; regra; estado; classe; classificação; =s ordem sacerdotal; sacramento; (*mil.*) descanso (de arma); *v.t.* ordenar, comandar; estatuir; regular; encomendar; (*mil.*) descansar (armas); =ing s. encomenda; disposição; =ly *adj.* ordenado, regular, arranjado; **on =ly duty** de plantão.

ordinal s.&*adj.* ordinal; número ordinal.

ordinance s. decreto, postura.

ordinary *adj.* ordinário; comum, vulgar; normal; s. refeição (a preço fixo); taverna, casa de pasto.

ordination s. ordenação (eclesiástica).

ordnance s. (*mil.*) intendência; artilharia.

ore s. minério.

organ s. órgão; (*mús.*) órgão.

organdie s. organdí.

organic *adj.* orgânico.

organization s. organização.

organize *v.t.* organizar; *v.i.* organizar-se.

organizer s. organizador.

orient s. oriente; =al *adj.* oriental; =ate *v.t.* orientar.

orifice s. orifício.

oriflamme s. auriflama.

origin s. origem; proveniência; =al *adj.* original; originário; =ality s. originalidade; =ate *v.i.* originar, derivar; *v.t.* dar origem a.

ornament s. ornamento; *v.t.* ornamentar; =al *adj.* decorativo, ornamental; =ation s. ornamentação.

ornate *adj.* ornamentado; decorado.

ornithologist s. ornitologista; **ornithology** s. ornitologia.

orphan s. órfão; =age s. orfanato.

orrery s. planetário.

orthodox *adj.* ortodoxo; =y s. ortodoxia.

orthography s. ortografia.

orthopaedic *adj.* ortopédico; =s, **orthopaedy** s. ortopedia.

orts s. restos; pedaços.

oscillate *v.i.* oscilar; **oscillation** s. oscilação.

osier s. vime.

osmium s. ósmio.

osprey s. águia marinha.

osseous *adj.* ósseo; **ossify** *v.t.* ossificar; **ossuary** s. ossuário.

ostensible *adj.* ostensivo; **ostensibly** *adv,* ostensivamente; **ostensory** s. ostensório.

ostentation s. ostentação; **ostentatious** *adj.* ostensivo.

ostler s. palafreneiro; moço de estrebaria.

ostracism s. ostracismo; **ostracize** *v.t.* pôr no ostracismo.

ostrich s. avestruz.

other *adj.&pron.* outro; **every — day** um dia sim, outro não.

otherwise *adv.* de outro modo, de outra maneira; senão, do contrário.

otter s. lontra.

Ottoman *adj.* otomano.

ought s. alguma cousa; nada; *v.aux.* dever.

ounce s. onça (28,35 gramas).

our *adj.* nosso, nossa, nossos, nossas.

ourselves *pron.* nós mesmos; nós; nos.

ousel s. melro.

oust *v.t.* desapossar, desalojar; despedir; pôr para fora.

out *adv.&prep.* fora; *adj.* ausente, exterior; s. exterior, parte de fora; *int.* fora!; **— of** fora de; **— of breath** sem fôlego; **— of danger** fora de perigo; **— of time** fora do compasso; **to be — of** estar sem; **we are — of coffee** estamos sem café; **— with him** ponha-o lá fora.

outbid *v.t.* oferecer um preço maior, cobrir o preço oferecido; marcar mais (em jôgo de cartas).

outboard *adv.* fora de bordo.

outbreak s. erupção; princípio (de guerra, epidemia, ataque, etc.); tumulto, insurreição.

outbuilding s. dependência (do prédio principal).

outburst s. explosão; acesso; arrancada.

outcast s. desclassificado; pária; proscrito; *adj.* expulso.

outcaste s. pária.

outcome s. consequência, resultado.

outcrop s. (*min.*) afloramento.

outcry s. clamor; grita, gritaria; venda em leilão.

outdistance *v.t.* distanciar, ultrapassar.

outdo *v.t.* exceder, sobrepujar; **— one's self** exceder-se a si próprio.

outdoor *adj.* ao ar livre, fora de casa; **— exercise** exercício ao ar livre; **— relief** socorro a domicílio.

outer *adj.* exterior.

outfall s. saída; embocadura, foz.

outfit s. equipamento; traje; vestuário; *v.t.* equipar.

outflank *v.t.* flanquear.

outflow s. derrame, fluxo; descarga.

outgoing *adj.* de saída, partindo; s. **saída, partida.**

outgrow *v.t.* crescer mais que; passar a idade de; perder com a idade (vícios, costumes, etc.).

outhouse *s.* dependência externa (da casa).

outing *s.* excursão, passeio.

outlandish *adj.* estranho, ridículo.

outlast *v.t.* durar mais que; sobreviver.

outlaw *s.* procrito; *v.t.* proscrever, pôr fora da lei; *ry s.* proscrição.

outlay *s.* desembôlso, gasto.

outlet *s.* saída; orifício de saída; vasão, escoadouro.

outline *s.* esquema, esbôço; plano geral; perfil, contôrno; bosquejo; *v.t.* delinear, esboçar, traçar.

outlive *v.t.* sobreviver.

outlook *s.* vista, perspectiva; panorama.

outlying *adj.* afastado; remoto.

outmanoeuvre *v.t.* manobrar melhor que; frustrar.

outnumber *v.t.* exceder em número.

out-patient *s.* doente externo (mas recebendo tratamento do hospital).

outport *s.* pôrto de mar, pôrto externo.

outpost *s.* (*mil.*) pôsto avançado, guarda avançada.

outpouring *s.* efusão, expansão; emanação; jôrro.

output *s.* produção total; rendimento.

outrage *s.* ultraje, insulto, afronta; *v.t.* ultrajar; *ous adj.* ultrajante, insultante.

outrider *s.* picador, batedor.

outrigger *s.* suporte fora do bordo para a forqueta do remo; barco de regata; (*mar.*) botalós; bimbarra.

outright *adj.* direto; claro, franco; completo, integral.

outset *s.* princípio; estréia, inauguração.

outshine *v.t.* eclipsar.

outside *adj.* exterior, externo; *s.* exterior; parte de fora; *r s.* estranho, forasteiro; leigo, profano.

outsize *s.* tamanho fóra do comum; *d adj.* fora do tamanho comum.

outskirts *s.* imediações, arrabaldes, cercanias.

outspoken *adj.* franco; *ness s.* franqueza; liberdade de expressão oral.

outspread *adj.* divulgado; *v.t.* divulgar, difundir.

outstanding *adj.* notável, proeminente, saliente; pendente; não pago, vencido.

outstretch *v.t.* estender, alargar; **outstretched** *adj.* estendido.

outstrip *v.t.* deixar para trás, passar na frente, sobrepujar.

outturn *s.* produção; (*com.*) artigos produzidos e entregues.

outward *adj.* exterior; externo; (*teol.*) carnal; aparente; *adv.* para fora, para o exterior; *ly adv.* externamente; exteriormente; *for — application* para uso externo; *s adv.* para fora.

outwit *v.t.* frustrar; ser mais esperto que.

outwork *s.* exceder em trabalho; trabalhar mais que.

ouzel *s.* melro.

oval *adj.&s.* oval.

ovary *s.* ovário.

ovation *s.* ovação.

oven *s.* forno.

over *adv.&prep.* encima, por cima, acima; mais de; do outro lado; de ponta a ponta, através; durante; novamente, de novo; *adj.* terminado; *s.* excedente, quebra; *all — em todas as partes; —*

again de novo, outra vez; *— and —* repetidamente.

overact *v.t.* exagerar.

overall *s.* macacão.

overawe *v.t.* intimidar.

overbalance *v.i.* desequilibrar-se, perder o equilíbrio; *v.t.* fazer perder o equilíbrio; *s.* excesso de pêso.

overbearing *adj.* insolente, arrogante.

overboard *adv.* ao mar.

overburden *v.t.* sobrecarregar.

overcast *adj.* obscuro, enuviado; turvo; *v.t.* escurecer, turvar.

overcautious *adj.* excessivamente prudente.

overcharge *s.* carga excessiva; *v.t.* sobrecarregar.

overcoat *s.* sobretudo; capote.

overcome *v.t.* vencer; dominar; subjugar; superar; *— all the difficulties* vencer todas as dificuldades; *— adj.* abatido, prostrado; *— by illness* prostrado pela doença.

overcrowd *v.t.* apinhar; abarrotar, superlotar.

overdo *v.t.* exagerar; *ne adj.* exagerado; cozido ou assado em demasia.

overdose *s.* dose exagerada.

overdraw *v.t.* sacar a descoberto.

overdrive *v.t.* fatigar os animais; (*mec.*) fazer funcionar além da capacidade normal.

overdue *adj.* atrasado; (*com.*) vencido.

overelaborate *v.t.* aperfeiçoar em demasia.

overestimate *v.t.* estimar ou avaliar exagerando o valor.

overexcite *v.t.* sobreexcitar.

overexposure *s.* (*fot.*) exposição demasiada.

overfeed *v.t.* alimentar em demasia; superalimentar.

overflow *s.* transbordamento; *v.i.* transbordar.

overgrow *v.t.* invadir; crescer ou desenvolver-se em excesso; *n adj.* coberto; *th s.* crescimento excessivo; **garden *n* with weeds** jardim coberto de mato.

overhang *v.t.&i.* pendurar-se sôbre; estar pendente; sair do nível; *s.* projeção, saliência, projetura.

overhaul *v.t.* examinar; rever; inspecionar; reparar; alcançar.

overhead *adv.* no alto, ao alto, acima da cabeça; *adj.* médio; (*com.*) geral, indireto; *s.* (*cont.*) despesas gerais.

overhear *v.t.* ouvir (por casualidade).

overheat *v.t.* esquentar, aquecer em excesso.

overindulgence *s.* indulgência excessiva.

overjoyed *adj.* radiante, cheio de alegria.

overladen *adj.* sobrecarregado.

overland *adv.&adj.* por terra; *— route* caminho por terra.

overlap *v.t.* recobrir; transpassar.

overlay *s.* coberta, cobertura; *v.t.* cobrir, sobrepor.

overleaf *adv.* no verso.

overload *v.t.* sobrecarregar.

overlook *v.t.* passar por cima de; ver de um ponto mais alto, dominar (com a vista); vigiar.

overmuch *adv.* demais, em excesso.

overnight *adv.* durante a noite; de noite.

overpay *v.t.* pagar em excesso.

overplus *s.* excedente.

overpolite *adj.* reverencioso, cheio de mesuras.

overpower *v.t.* subjugar, vencer; =**ing** *adj.* poderosíssimo; subjugante.
overproduction *s.* superprodução.
overrate *v.t.* avaliar exagerando o valor; encarecer.
overreach *v.t.* exceder, ir além; enganar.
override *v.t.* estafar (cavalo); ultrapassar; anular.
overripe *adj.* maduro demais.
overrule *v.t.* predominar; governar; afastar; (*for.*), denegar, rejeitar; decidir contra; anular.
overrun *v.t.* invadir; espalhar; infestar.
overseas *adv.* além-mar; *adj.* de além-mar.
overseer *s.* inspetor; superintendente.
overset *v.t.* virar, entornar, derrubar, emborcar; vencer; fazer fracassar.
overshadow *v.t.* obscurecer, eclipsar; sombrear.
overshoe *s.* galocha.
overshoot *v.t.* ir além, ultrapassar.
oversight *s.* inadvertência, esquecimento; vigilância.
oversleep *v.i.* dormir demais, não acordar a tempo.
overspread *v.t.* espalhar; divulgar.
overstate *v.t.* exagerar.
overstep *v.t.* ultrapassar; transgredir.
overstock *v.t.* abarrotar.
overstrain *v.t.* fatigar, cansar.
overtraining *s.* treinamento exagerado.
overt *adj.* manifesto.
overtake *v.t.* alcançar; apanhar em flagrante; surpreender.

overtax *v.t.* taxar em excesso.
overthrow *v.t.* derrubar; vencer; subverter.
overtime *s.* horas suplementares (de trabalho).
overtop *v.t.* ultrapassar, exceder.
overture *s.* abertura, ouverture; proposta.
overturn *v.t.* derrubar, entornar; subverter; *v.i.* emborcar.
overvalue *v.t.* exagerar o valor; majorar.
overweening *adj.* pretensioso, arrogante.
overweight *s.* excesso de pêso; *adj.* acima do pêso.
overwhelm *v.t.* oprimir, esmagar; submergir.
overwork *v.t.* fazer trabalhar em excesso; forçar; *v.i.* trabalhar em excesso.
ovine *adj.* ovino.
oviparous *adj.* ovíparo.
owe *v.t.* dever; **owing to** devido a, por causa de.
owl *s.* coruja.
own *adj.* próprio; individual; verdadeiro; — **cousin** primo-irmão, prima-irmã; **of one's** — **motion** espontâneamente, de motu próprio; *v.t.* possuir; admitir; — **to** confessar.
ownership *s.* propriedade.
ox *s.* boi.
oxide *s.* óxido.
oxidize *v.t.* oxidar.
oxygen *s.* oxigênio.
oyster *s.* ostra.
ozone *s.* ozona.

P

P letra do alfabeto.
pace *s.* passo; passada; modo de andar; *v.i.* andar compassadamente; **to keep** — **with** andar ao mesmo passo que.
pachyderm *s.* paquiderme.
pacific *adj.* pacífico; **pacifist** *s.* pacifista; **pacify** *v.t.* pacificar; **pacifying** *adj.* pacificador.
Pacific Ocean Oceano Pacífico.
pack *s.* fardo; pacote; embrulho; baralho; matilha; súcia; quadrilha (de ladrões); *v.t.* empacotar; enfardar; enfardelar; *v.i.* arrumar as malas; reunir-se; — **away** partir sùbitamente.
package *s.* embrulho, fardo, pacote; **packed** *adj.* embrulhado; apertado; **packed like sardines** apertados como sardinha em lata.
packer *s.* empacotador, enfardador.
packet *s.* embrulho; fardo pequeno; (*mar.*) paquete; *v.t.* embrulhar.
packing *s.* enfardamento; embalagem.
pad *s.* almofada; bloco (de papel); pata de certos animais; *v.t.* forrar, acolchoar; tamponar.
paddle *s.* remo; pá; *v.i.* remar; *v.t.* impelir, propelir; =**r** *s.* remador.
paddock *s.* cercado; parque (para cavalos).
padlock *s.* cadeado; *v.t.* fechar com cadeado.
paean *s.* hino de triunfo.
pagan *s.&adj.* pagão.
paganism *s.* paganismo.
page *s.* página; pagem; *v.t.* paginar; chamar em voz alta (em hotéis, etc.)
pageant *s.* espetáculo; exibição teatral; carro triunfal; parada espetacular; funeral pomposo; =**ry** *s.* pompa.

paginate *v.t.* paginar.
paid *adj.* pago.
pail *s.* balde.
paillasse *s.* esteira.
pain *s.* dor, sofrimento; mal; *v.t.* fazer sofrer; angustiar; entristecer; =**ful** *adj.* doloroso; =**less** *adj.* sem dor; =**taking** cuidadoso.
paint *s.* pintura, côr, tintas; *v.t.* pintar; =**er** *s.* pintor; =**ing** *s.* pintura; =**ress** *s.* pintora.
pair *s.* par; casal; — **of scales** balança; *v.t.* emparelhar.
pal *s.* (*jíria*), companheiro, camarada.
palace *s.* palácio.
paladin *s.* paladino.
palatable *adj.* agradável ao gôsto, saboroso; **palatal** *adj.* palatal.
palate *s.* palato, céu-da-boca.
palatial *adj.* palaciano.
palaver *s.* conferência; debate; palavrório; *v.i.* palrar.
pale *adj.* pálido; lívido; *v.i.* empalidecer; =**ness** *s.* palidez.
paleography *s.* paleografia.
paleontology *s.* paleontologia.
palette *s.* palheta, paleta.
palfrey *s.* palafrém.
palimpsest *s.* palimpsesto; *adj.* palimpséstico.
paling *s.* cêrca, paliçada.
palish *adj.* pálido.
pall *s.* mortalha; pálio.
pallet *s.* palheta; catre.
palliasse *s.* esteira.
palliate *v.t.* paliar; **palliative** *s.* paliativo.
pallid *adj.* pálido; **pallor** *s.* palidez, palor.

T

palm s. palma; — tree palmeira; Palm Sunday Domingo de Ramos; =y days belos dias; — off empalmar, escamotear.

palmistry s. quiromancia; palmist s. quiromante.

palp s. palpo.

palpable adj. palpável.

palpitate v.i. palpitar; palpitation s. palpitação.

palter v.i. usar de rodeios e subterfúgios agir com insinceridade; equivocar.

paltry s. mesquinho; inútil; desprezível.

pampas s. pampas.

pamper v.t. tratar com mimo demasiado.

pamphlet s. panfleto.

pan s. panela; prato da balança.

panacea s. panacéia.

panama s. panamá (chapéu).

pancake s. panqueca.

pancreas s. pâncreas.

pandemonium s. pandemônio.

pander s. alcoviteiro; v.t. alcovitar.

pane s. lado, face, secção; vidro (de janela, porta, etc.).

panegyric s. panegírico.

panel s. painel; almofada (de porta); coxim; lista de jurados, juri.

pang s. apêrto de coração; angústia, ânsia.

Pan-Germanism s. pangermanismo.

panic s. pânico.

pannier s. cêsto; anquinhas.

pannikin s. panela pequena.

panoply s. panóplia.

panorama s. panorama.

pansy s. amor-perfeito (flor).

pant v.i. arquejar; anelar; palpitar; s. arquejo, palpitação.

pantheism s. panteísmo.

pantheon s. panteão.

panther s. pantera.

panting adj. arquejante, ofegante.

pantograph s. pantógrafo.

pantomime s. pantomima.

pantry s. despensa; copa.

pants s. ceroulas; calças.

pap s. papa, mingau.

papa s. papai.

papacy s. papado, pontificado; papal adj. papal.

paper s. papel; jornal; composição (escolar); curl — papelote; waste — papel usado, papel inútil; — kite papagaio de papel; v.t. forrar (de papel).

papist s. papista.

papyrus s. papiro.

par s. par (câmbio); equivalência; his ability is on a — with his rank sua capacidade está à altura de sua posição; at — ao par.

parable, parabola s. parábola.

parachute s. pára-quedas.

parade s. parada; (mil.) parada, desfile.

paradise s. paraíso.

paradox s. paradoxo.

paradoxical adj. paradoxal.

paraffin s. parafina.

paragon s. modêlo; (tip.) parangona; — of beauty modêlo de beleza; v.t. paragonar; ultrapassar.

paragraph s. parágrafo.

parakeet s. periquito.

parallax s. paralaxe.

parallel adj. paralelo; — bars paralelas; s. paralela; paralelo.

parallelepiped s. paralelepípedo.

parallelogram s. paralelogramo.

paralyze v.t. paralisar; paralysis s. paralisia; paralytic s. paralítico.

paramount adj. supremo; superior; eminente.

paramour s. amante.

parapet s. parapeito.

paraphernalia s. adornos, galas; atavios; (for.) bens parafernais.

paraphrase s. paráfrase; v.t.&i. parafrasear.

parasite s. parasita; parasitic, parasitical adj. parasitário.

parasol s. chapéu de sol.

parboil v.t. cozer ligeiramente.

parbuckle s. virador; v.t. levantar ou abaixar por meio de um virador.

parcel s. encomenda postal; embrulho, pacote; parcela; (com.) partida; v.t. dividir por partes.

parch v.t. tostar; torrar; ressecar.

parchment s. pergaminho.

pardon s. perdão; v.t. perdoar; =able adj. perdoável.

pare v.t. descascar; cortar; aparar; — down expenditures reduzir as despesas.

paregoric adj. paregórico.

parent s. pai; mãe; =al adj. paternal, maternal.

parenthesis s. parêntese.

pariah s. pária.

paring s. aparas, recortes.

pari passu adv. pari-passu.

parish s. paróquia, freguezia; adj. paroquial; =ioner s. paroquiano.

Parisian adj.&s. parisiense.

parity s. paridade, igualdade.

park s. parque; bosque; v.t. estacionar (automóvel); =ing s. estacionamento.

parlance s. conversação; debate.

parley s. parlamentação; v.i. parlamentar.

parliament s. parlamento; =ary adj. parlamentar.

parlor, parlour s. salão; locutório; — games jogos de salão.

parochial adj. paroquial.

parody s. paródia; v.t. parodiar.

parole s. palavra de honra, promessa; (dir.) liberdade condicional; v.t. (dir.) dar ou conceder liberdade condicional.

paroxysm s. paroxismo.

parquet s. assoalho; plateía (de teatro).

parricide s. parricídio, parricida.

parrot s. papagaio.

parr v.t. aparar (golpes); evitar.

parse v.t. analisar.

parcimonious adj. parcimonioso; parsimony s. parcimônia.

parsing s. análise gramatical.

parsley s. salsa.

parson s. pároco, vigário; cura, padre; =age s. curato; =age's house presbitério.

part s. parte; porção; lugar, sítio; papel (de teatro); lado, partido; (plural) talentos, dotes naturais; v.t. dividir; separar; repartir; v.i. partir, separar-se; — with separar-se de, desfazer-se de.

partake v.i. participar.

partial adj. parcial; =ity s. parcialidade.

participate v.i. participar.

participle s. particípio.

particle s. partícula.

particular adj. particular; exigente; meticuloso; s. particularidade, singularidade; =s pormenores, indicações, informações; =ity s. particularidade; =ize v.t. particularizar.

parting s. separação, partida, adeus; risca do cabelo.
partisan s. partidário.
partition s. partição; divisão; separação; tabique.
partitive adj. partitivo.
partly adv. em parte; parcialmente.
partner s. associado; sócio; parceiro; par; =**ship** s. sociedade; associação.
partridge s. perdiz.
party s. festa; partido; grupo; bando; recepção; parte.
paschal adj. pascoal.
pass v.t.&i. passar; admitir; ser recebido; pronunciar; aprovar; votar; cruzar; fazer passes; s. passe; passagem; salvo-conduto; — **on** transmitir; prosseguir; =**able** adj. passável; transitável.
passage s. passagem; travessia; trajeto; canal; — **money** dinheiro da passágem.
passenger s. passageiro.
passer-by s. transeunte.
passing s. passagem; **in** — de passagem.
passion s. paixão; flama; ardor; =**ate** adj. apaixonado; ardente; =**ately** adv. apaixonadamente.
passive adj. passivo; **passivity** s. passividade.
passover s. páscoa dos hebreus.
passport s. passaporte.
past s.&adj. passado.
paste s. pasta, massa; v.t. colar.
pastel s. (pint.) pastel; ensaio literário.
pastern s. travadouro; junta da pata (de cavalo).
pasteurize v.t. pasteurizar.
pastille, pastil s. pastilha.
pastime s. passatempo.
pastor s. pastor; =**al** s.&adj. pastoral; =**ale** s. pastoral.
pastry s. massas folhadas, massas, pastelaria.
pasturage s. pastagem; pastos.
pasture s. pasto; v.t.&i. apascentar; pastar.
pasty adj. pastoso.
pat adj.&adv. justo, a propósito; s. pancadinha; v.t.&i. dar pancadinhas; afagar, acariciar.
patch s. remendo; peça embutida em obra de mosaico; mosca (sinal de rosto); v.t. remendar.
pate s. cabeça.
paten s. pátena.
patent adj. patente; patenteado; s. patente; v.t. patentear.
paternal adj. paternal; paterno; **paternity** s. paternidade.
Paternoster s. padre-nosso.
path s. vereda, senda; caminho.
pathetic adj. patético.
pathological adj. patológico; **pathologist** s. patologista; **pathology** s. patologia.
pathos s. patos; sofrimento, aflição; sentimento; **pathetic** adj. patético.
patience s. paciência; **patient** s.&adj. paciente.
patina s. pátina.
patriarch s. patriarca; =**al** adj. patriarcal.
patrician adj.&s. patrício, aristocrático, nobre.
patrimony s. patrimônio.
patriot s. patriota; =**ic** adj. patriótico; =**ism** s. patriotismo.
patrol s. patrulha; v.t.&i. patrulhar.
patron s. patrono, protetor, padroeiro; =**age** s. patrocínio, proteção; patronato;

=**ess** s. padroeira, protetora; =**ize** v.t. patrocinar, proteger.
patronymic adj. patronímico; s. nome patronímico.
patten s. soco, tamanco.
patter s. arenga de saltimbancos, etc.; v.i. recitar orações; falar volùvelmente; v.t. dizer mecânicamente.
pattern s. modêlo; amostra; desenho, padrão; v.t. copiar; servir de modêlo.
patty s. torta ou pastel pequeno.
paunch s. barriga, pança.
pauper s. indigente, pobre, mendigo; =**ism** s. mendicância, pobreza.
pause s. pausa; v.i. fazer pausa.
pave v.t. calçar; preparar (caminho).
pavillion s. pavilhão.
paving s. calçada, ladrilho, pavimento.
paw s. pata.
pawl s. lingueta.
pawn v.t. empenhar, hipotecar; s. penhor, garantia, caução.
pay s. salário; pagamento; ordenado; sôldo; v.t.&i. pagar; prestar, apresentar, fazer; — **attention** prestar atenção; — **my respects** apresentar meus respeitos; — **a visit** fazer uma visita; — **back** restituir, devolver; — **off** despedir; — **day** dia de pagamento.
payable adj. pagável.
payee s. beneficiário.
payer s. pagador, responsável; **payment** s. pagamento.
pea s. ervilha.
peace s. paz; —=**maker** pacificador; =**ful** adj. pacífico; tranqüilo.
peach s. pêssego; — **tree** pessegueiro.
peacock s. pavão; — **blue** azul pavão.
peak s. cume, pico, ponta; viseira; **widow's** — bico de viúva; =**ed** adj. ponteagudo, pontudo; (pop.) magro, abatido.
peal s. repique de sinos; descarga (de artilharia); estrondo.
pear s. pêra.
pearl s. pérola.
peasant s. camponês.
peat s. turfa.
pebble s. seixo.
peccadillo s. pecadilho, pecado venial, pecado leve.
peccary s. pecarí.
peccavi s. minha-culpa, mea-culpa.
peck s. medida de capacidade (nos EE. UU., equivalente a 8,8096 litros; na Grã-Bretanha, a 9,0919 litros); v.t. dar bicadas; picar; (pop.) beliscar (a comida).
pecten s. espécie de molusco.
peculate v.t.&i. apropriar-se indèbitamente de dinheiros confiados à sua guarda; **peculation** s. peculato; **peculator** s. peculatário.
peculiar adj. peculiar, singular; =**ity** s. peculiaridade, singularidade.
pecuniary adj. pecuniário.
pedagogue s. pedagogo.
pedal s. pedal; v.t.&i. pedalar.
pedant s. pedante; =**ic** adj. pedante; =**ry** s. pedantismo.
peddle v.i.&t. mascatear; vender em pequenas quantidades; ser negociante ambulante.
peddler s. bufarinheiro, mascate.
pedestal s. pedestal.
pedestrian s. pedestre.
pedigree s. genealogia.
pediment s. (arq.) frontão.
pedlar V. **peddler**.

pedometer s. pedômetro.
peel s. casca, pele, película; pá de forno; pá de remo; *v.t.&i.* descascar, pelar.
peep s. espiadela, espreita; pio, piado; assomo, aparecimento; mira· — **sight** alça de mira; *v.i.* espiar, espreitar; despontar, assomar; piar; imitar o pio dos pássaros; **at the — of day** ao despontar do dia.
peer s. par; *=age* s. dignidade de par, conjunto de pares; *v.t.* igualar, rivalizar.
peerless *adj.* sem par.
peevish *adj.* impertinente, rabugento.
peg s. cavilha; grampo de segurar roupa; cravelha.
Pegasus s. Pégaso.
pekin s. seda estampada.
pelargonium s. pelargônio.
pelf s. lucro, ganho.
pelican s. pelicano.
pelisse s. peliça.
pellet s. bala; bolinha (de papel); grão de chumbo.
pell-mell *adv.* confusamente, a troche-moche.
pellicle s. película.
pellucid *adj.* límpido, transparente.
pelt s. pele (de animais); *v.t.* lapidar; atirar projéteis; atacar com palavras.
pelvis s. pelvis; **pelvic** *adj.* pélvico.
pen s. pena; cercado pequeno; *v.t.* escrever, compor; pôr no cercado.
penal *adj.* penal; *=ty* s. penalidade; **penance** s. penitência; confissão (sacramento).
penates s. penates (deuses).
pencil s. lápis; pincel; *v.t.* pincelar; fazer um esbôço, contornar; escrever a lapis.
pendant, pendent s. berloque, penduricalho; pendente, pingente.
pendent, pendant *adj.* pendente, suspenso.
pendulum s. pêndulo.
penetrate *v.t.&i.* penetrar.
penguin s. pinguim.
peninsula s. península; *=r adj.* peninsular.
penitence s. penitência; **penitent** *adj. &s.* penitente; **penitentiary** *adj.* penitenciário; s. penitenciário; penitenciária, casa de correção.
pennant s. flâmula, galhardete.
penniless *adj.* sem vintém.
pennon s. bandeira, flâmula.
penny s. peni (moeda).
pension s. pensão, mensalidade; pensão (de hóspedes); *v.t.* pensionar; — **off** aposentar; *=er* s. pensionista.
pensive *adj.* pensativo.
Pentecoste s. Pentecostes.
penthouse s. alpendre; apartamento no terraço.
penultimate *adj.* penúltimo.
penumbra s. penumbra.
penurious *adj.* avarento; **penury** s. penúria.
peony s. (*bot.*) peônia.
people s. povo; gente; pessoas; *v.t.* povoar.
pepper s. pimenta; *v.t.* apimentar; *=y adj.* apimentado; (*fig.*) irascível, colérico.
per *prep.* por; — **annum** por ano; — **cent** por cento.
perambulate *v.t.* perambular; **perambulator** s. carro de criança.
perceive *v.t.* perceber, discernir.
percentage s. percentagem.
perceptible *adj.* perceptível.

perception s. percepção.
perch s. perca (peixe); poleiro; vara; medida de comprimento, de 5½ jardas (5,029 m.); *v.t.* empoleirar; *v.i.* empoleirar-se.
perchance *adv.* por acaso; talvez.
percolate *v.t.&i.* filtrar.
percussion s. percussão.
perdition s. perdição.
peregrination s. peregrinação; **peregrine** s. peregrino, estrangeiro.
peremptory *adj.* peremptório.
perennial *adj.* perene, permanente.
perfect *adj.* perfeito; *v.t.* aperfeiçoar; *=ion* s. perfeição.
perfidious *adj.* pérfido; **perfidy** s. perfídia.
perforate *v.t.* perfurar.
perforce *adv.* a força.
perform *v.t.&i.* fazer; executar; representar; comprir; preencher; *=ance* s. execução; representação; desempenho; *=er* s. executante.
perfume s. perfume; *v.t.* perfumar; *=r* s. perfumista; *=ry* s. perfumaria.
perfunctory *adj.* perfuntório.
pergola s. pérgola.
perhaps *adv.* talvez.
peril s. perigo; *=ous adj.* perigoso.
perimeter s. perímetro.
period s. período; época; têrmo; (*gram.*) ponto; *=ic,* *=ical adj.* periódico; *=ical* s. periódico.
periphery s. periferia.
periphrasis s. perífrase.
periscope s. periscópio.
perish *v.i.* perecer; *=able adj.* perecível.
peristyle s. peristilo.
peritoneal *adj.* peritoneal; **peritoneum** s. peritônio.
perjure *v.t.&i.* perjurar; **perjury** s. perjúrio.
perk *v.t.* adornar, vestir; *v.i.* alçar-se, espigar-se, esticar-se; *=y adj.* aprumado.
permanence s. permanência; **permanent** *adj.* permanente; **permanent wave** ondulação permanente; **permanently** *adv.* permanentemente.
permanganate s. permanganato.
permeable *adj.* permeável.
permeate *v.t.* permear; penetrar.
permissible *adj.* permissível.
permission s. permissão.
permit *v.t.* permitir; s. permissão; licença.
pernicious *adj.* pernicioso.
peroration s. peroração.
peroxide s. peróxido.
perpendicular *adj.&s.* perpendicular.
perpetrate *v.t.* perpetrar; **perpetrator** s. perpetrador, autor.
perpetual *adj.* perpétuo.
perpetuate *v.t.* perpetuar; **perpetuity** s. perpetuidade.
perplex *v.t.* embaraçar; confundir; deixar perplexo; *=ed adj.* perplexo; *=ity s.* perplexidade.
perquisite s. gratificação; gorjeta; lucro eventual.
perry s. bebida fermentada (de pêras).
persecute *v.t.* perseguir; **persecution** s. perseguição; **persecutor** s. perseguidor.
perseverance s. perseverança; **persevere** *v.i.* perseverar.
Persia s. Persia; *=n adj.&s.* persa.
persian blind veneziana.
persist *v.i.* persistir, obstinar-se; *=ence,* *=ency* s. persistência; *=ent adj.* persistente.
person s. pessoa.

personage s. personagem.
personal adj. pessoal; — **effects** bens pessoais.
personality s. personalidade.
personate v.t. representar (alguém); personificar; fazer-se passar por.
personify v.t. personificar.
perspective s. perspectiva.
perspicacious adj. perspicaz; **perspicacity** s. perspicácia.
perspicuous adj. claro, lúcido.
perspiration s. transpiração.
perspire v.i. transpirar.
persuade v.t. persuadir; **persuasion** s, persuasão; **persuasive** adj. persuasivo.
pert adj. vivo, esperto.
pertain v.i. pertencer; ser pertinente.
pertinacious adj. pertinaz, tenaz; **pertinacity** s. tenacidade, pertinácia.
pertness adj. vivacidade.
perturb v.t. perturbar; agitar; =ation s. perturbação.
Peru s. Perú.
perusal s. leitura; **peruse** v.t. ler atentamente.
Peruvian adj. peruviano, peruano.
pervade v.t. penetrar; **pervasive** adj. penetrante, sutil.
perverse adj. pervertido, depravado; **perversity, perversion** s. perversão; **pervert** s. pervertido, depravado; v.t. perverter, corromper.
pervious adj. permeável.
pessimism s. pessimismo; **pessimist** s. pessimista; **pessimistic** adj. pessimista.
pest s. peste.
pester v.t. atormentar, importunar.
pestilence s. pestilência; **pestilencial** adj. pestilento.
pestle s. mão (do almofariz); socador, maça (do pilão); v.t. socar, pulverizar ou misturar (no pilão ou no almofariz).
pet s. animal favorito; favorito; acesso de mau humor; v.t. acarinhar, amimar; v.i. estar de mau humor.
petal s. pétala.
petiole s. pecíolo.
petition s. petição, súplica; requerimento; v.t. fazer uma petição; fazer um requerimento; =er s. peticionário, requerente.
petrel s. petrel.
petrifaction s. petrificação; **petrify** v.t. petrificar.
petroleum s. petróleo.
petticoat s. saia de baixo.
pettifoggery s. rabulice; chicana; **pettifogger** s. rábula.
pettiness s. mesquinharia; pequenez.
pettish adj. rabugento.
petty adj. mesquinho, pequeno.
petulance s. petulância, impertinênc:a.
petunia s. petúnia.
pew s. banco de igreja.
pewit s. ave semelhante à poupa.
pewter s. liga de estanho.
phaeton s. fáeton.
phalanx s. falange.
phantasm s. fantasma; fantasia.
phantasmagoria s. fantasmagoria.
phantasy s. fantasia.
phantom s. fantasma.
Pharaoh s. faraó.
Pharisaical adj. farisáico; **Pharisee** s. fariseu.
pharmaceutical adj. farmacêutico.
pharmacy s. farmácia.
pharyngitis s. faringite; **pharynx** s. faringe.

phase s. fase; aspecto.
pheasant s. faisão.
phenacetin s. fenacetina.
phenomenal adj. fenomenal; **phenomenon** s. fenômeno.
phial s. frasco.
philander v.i. namorar; dirigir galanteios a uma mulher.
philantropic adj. filantrópico; **philantropist** s. filantropo; **philantropy** s. filantropia.
philatelist s. filatelista; **philately** s. filatelia.
philharmonic adj. filarmônico.
philippic s. filípica, invectiva.
Philistine s. filisteu.
philologist s. filólogo; **philology** s. filologia.
philosopher s. filósofo; **philosophical** adj. filosófico; **philosophy** s. filosofia; **philosophize** v.i. filosofar.
philtre, philter s. filtro.
phlebitis s. flebite.
phlegm s. fleuma; mucosidade; =atic adj. fleumático.
phlox s. flox.
phoenix, phenix s. fênix.
phonetic adj. fonético; =s s. fonética.
phonograph s. fonógrafo.
phosphate s. fosfato.
phosphorescence s fosforescência; **phosphorescent** adj. fosforescente.
phosphorus s. fósforo.
photograph s. fotografia (retrato); v.t. fotografar.
photographer s. fotógrafo; **photographic** adj. fotográfico.
photography s. fotografia (arte).
photogravure s. fotogravura.
phrase s. frase; locução; =ology s. fraseologia.
phrenologist s. frenologista; **phrenology** s. frenologia.
phthisis s. tísica.
physic s. medicina; remédio; purgante.
physical adj. físico.
physician s. médico.
physics s. física; **physicist** s. físico.
physiognomy s. fisionomia; **fisiognomonia**.
physiology s. fisiologia.
physique s. físico, constituição.
pianist s. pianista.
piccolo s. (mús.) flautim.
pick v.t. apanhar; colhêr; escolher; palitar (dentes); s. picareta, picão; escolha, elite; — up apanhar; — out escolher, colhêr; — a quarrel comprar uma briga; — at one's food lambiscar; — a fowl depenar uma ave.
pickaback adv. nas costas, nos ombros.
picked adj. escolhido; de elite.
picket s. estaca; (mil.) piquête; grevista (em protesto pacífico em frente do estabelecimento); v.t. cercar de estacas; permanecer em frente do estabelecimento (grevista).
picking s. colheita; escolha; =s s. sobras; despojos.
pickle s. salmoura; conservas no vinagre; v.t. salgar, conservar no vinagre.
picnic s. piquenique, convescote; v.i. fazer um piquenique.
pictorial adj. pictórico, pictorial.
picture s. pintura; quadro; imagem; retrato; fotografia; ilustração; v.t. pintar, desenhar; descrever; — to oneself imaginar.

picturesque *adj.* pitoresco.
pie *s.* torta; pastel.
piebald *adj.* malhado (geralmente de branco e preto).
piece *s.* pedaço; fragmento; peça; parte; *v.t.* remendar; juntar, unir; — **together** coser as partes, juntar; =**meal** *adv.* aos pedaços; gradualmente.
pied *adj.* pintado, de varias côres.
pier *s.* cais, molhe, embarcadouro; pilar, pilastra; — **table** consolo.
pierce *v.t.&i.* furar; penetrar; brocar; **piercing** *adj.* penetrante.
piety *s.* piedade.
pig *s.* porco, leitão; —=**headed** cabeçudo, teimoso; =**gery** *s.* chiqueiro.
pigeon *s.* pombo; =**ry** *s.* pombal.
pigment *s.* pigmento.
pigmy *s.* pigmeu.
pigpen *s.* pocilga.
pike *s.* pico; caminho, estrada; lúcio (peixe).
pilaster *s.* pilastra.
pilchard *s.* sardinha.
pile *s.* pilha; monte; edifício grande e maciço; pilha eletrica; (*tec.*) fêlpa; — **up** juntar, empilhar.
piles *s.* hemorroidas.
pilfer *v.t.* roubar, furtar.
pilgrim *s.* peregrino; =**age** *s.* peregrinação.
piling *s.* estacaria; empilhamento.
pill *s.* pílula.
pillage *s.* pilhagem; *v.t.* pilhar.
pillar *s.* pilar, columna, pilastra.
pillion *s.* selim leve (para mulher); coxim.
pillory *s.* pelourinho.
pillow *s.* travesseiro.
pilot *s.* pilôto.
pimpernel *s.* pimpinela.
pimple *s.* borbulha, espinha.
pin *s.* alfinête; *v.t.* marcar, unir ou pregar com alfinête.
pinafore *s.* avental de criança.
pincers *s.* pinça, tenazes, torquês.
pinch *s.* pitada; beliscão; *v.t.* beliscar, apertar.
pine *s.* pinho; — **tree** pinheiro.
pine *v.i.* languescer, consumir-se.
pineapple *s.* abacaxí, ananas.
ping-pong *s.* pingue-pongue.
pining *s.* nostalgia; tristeza, languidez.
pinion *s.* asa; ponta de asa; carrête; *v.t.* cortar as asas; amarrar, manietar.
pink *adj.* côr de rosa; *s.* cravo (flor).
pinnace *s.* (*mar.*) pinaça.
pinnacle *s.* pináculo.
pint *s.* pinto, medida de capacidade (equiv. a 0,568 litros na Inglaterra e 0,4732 litros nos EE. UU.).
pintle *s.* cavilha, pino; macho (do leme).
pioneer *s.* pioneiro.
pious *adj.* piedoso, religioso.
pip *s.* pevide, gosma (moléstia de galinha); pevide, semente, grão; ponto, marca (nas pedras do dominó, cartas de baralho, etc.); ôlho (de abacaxí).
pipe *s.* tubo, conduto, canal; cano; cachimbo; (*mús.*) charamela, gaita; tubo (de órgão); voz (no canto); *v.i.* tocar órgão; assobiar; =**r** *s.* flautista, gaiteiro.
pipkin *s.* panela de barro.
pippin *s.* espécie de maçã, maçã açucar.
piquancy *s.* gôsto picante; **piquant** *adj.* picante.
pique *s.* irritação, desprazer; *v.t.* irritar, provocar; — **on** ou **upon** gabar-se.
piracy *s.* pirataria; **pirate** *s.* pirata.

pirouette *s.* pirueta; *v.i.* piruetar.
pisciculture *s.* piscicultura.
pistachio *s.* pistache, pistácia.
pistil *s.* pistilo.
pistol *s.* pistola, revólver.
piston *s.* pistão.
pit *s.* buraco, fosso, cova; poço; platéia (teatro); caroço; marca, furo; **arm=sovaco**; **cock**=— rinhadeira; =**fall** trapa, armadilha; *v.t.* marcar (com furos); pôr ou lançar em um buraco; pôr em competição.
pitch *s.* grau de inclinação; declive; ponto, grau; (*mús.*) tom; lance (jôgo); betume, alcatrão; piche; resina; *v.t.* arremessar, atirar (a bola); cravar, fixar (na terra); estabelecer o trunfo (no jôgo de cartas); *v.i.* mergulhar; arfar (o navio).
pitcher *s.* bilha, cântaro; jarro; (*esp.*) o que atira, o que lança a bola, a malha, etc.
piteous *adj.* lastimável.
pith *s.* medula; tutano; miolo; âmago.
pitiable, **pitiful** *adj.* lamentável, de fazer dó.
pitiless *adj.* implacável, sem piedade.
pittance *s.* pequena ração; parcos rendimentos ou salários.
pity *s.* pena, piedade; *v.t.* apiedar-se, ter pena de.
pivot *s.* espigão, gonzo, eixo, veio.
pixy, **pixie** *s.* fada, duende.
placard *s.* cartaz, edital, anúncio; *v.t.* afixar.
place *s.* lugar, sítio, localidade; espaço; praça; *v.t.* colocar, pôr, botar; **to take** — passar-se, acontecer, realizar-se.
placer *s.* colocador; jazida de ouro.
placid *adj.* plácido; =**ity** *s.* placidez.
plagiarism *s.* plágio; **plagiarist** *s.* plagiário; **plagiarize** *v.t.* plagiar.
plague *s.* praga; peste; miséria, calamidade; *v.t.* infestar; atormentar.
plaice *s.* patruça (peixe).
plain *adj.* simples; comum, ordinário; plano, chato, unido, liso; claro, evidente; natural; feio; *s.* planície; **clothes** trajes comuns; — **song** cantochão; — **girl** moça feia; =**ly** *adv.* simplesmente; claramente; distintamente; =**ness** *s.* simplicidade; nitidez; fealdade.
plaintif, =**f** *s.* (*dir.*) querelante.
plait *s.* trança; prega; *v.t.* dobrar em pregas; trançar.
plan *s.* plano, projeto, planta, risco, desenho; *v.t.* planejar, projetar.
plane *adj.* plano; *s.* plano, superfície; avião, aeroplano; plaina; *v.t.* aplainar; *v.i.* pairar.
planet *s.* planeta; =**arium** *s.* planetário; =**ary** *adj.* planetário.
planish *v.t.* aplainar, alisar.
plank *s.* prancha.
plankton *s.* vegetação flutuante.
plant *s.* planta; aparelhagem, instalação; (*pop.*) fábrica; *v.t.* plantar; colocar, fixar, implantar; fundar, estabelecer.
plantain *s.* tanchagem; plátano (espécie de banana).
plantation *s.* plantação, fazenda; **planter** *s.* plantador, fazendeiro.
plaque *s.* placa; medalha, broche; comenda.
plash *s.* charco, lamaçal; aguaceiro (chuva); salpico; *v.t.* entremear, entrelaçar, trançar ramos; *v.i.* salpicar água, lama, etc.; enlamear.

plaster *s.* emplastro; gêsso; cal, rebôco; — **of Paris** estuque; **mustard** — sinapismo; — **stone** gêsso; *v.t.* rebocar, emboçar; pôr um emplastro.

plastic *adj.* plástico; =**ity** *s.* plasticidade.

plat *s.* lote (terreno); planta, plano, mapa; *v.t.* trançar; localizar, fazer a planta, planear (no papel).

plate *s.* chapa; placa; fôlha (de metal); clichê; prato; (*esp.*) taça, copa; *v.t.* dourar, pratear, niquelar; chapear; blindar; =**d** *adj.* blindado, couraçado.

plateau *s.* planalto.

platform *s.* plataforma; estrado, tribuna; plataforma política.

platinum *s.* platina.

platitude *s.* vulgaridade.

Platonic *adj.* platônico.

platoon *s.* pelotão.

plaudit *s.* aplauso, aclamação.

plausible *adj.* plausível.

play *s.* jôgo; recreio; peça teatral; espetaculo; *v.i.* jogar, brincar; *v.t.* representar; tocar; — **cards** jogar cartas; — **the piano** tocar piano; — **upon words** fazer trocadilho; —=**boy** (*pop.*) estróina.

player *s.* jogador; executante; ator; músico.

playful *adj.* brincalhão, folgazão.

plea *s.* alegação, razões, arrazoado; justificação, defesa, desculpa.

pleasant *adj.* agradável, amável; cômodo; =**ness** *s.* amabilidade; confôrto; sensação agradável; =**ry** *s.* brincadeira.

please *v.i.* agradar; aprazer, comprazer; *v.t.* agradar; contentar, satisfazer; **to be** =**d to** ter gôsto em; **to be** =**d with** estar satisfeito com; — **say it again** faça o favor de repetir; **pleasing** *adj.* agradável, amável.

pleasurable *adj.* agradável.

pleasure *s.* prazer; satisfação, agrado.

pleat *s.* prega; *v.t.* preguear.

plebeian *adj.* plebeu.

plebiscite *s.* plebiscito.

pledge *adj.* promessa, voto; penhor, caução, garantia; *v.t.* empenhar, penhorar; beber à saude de.

plenary *adj.* plenário.

plenipotentiary *adj.&s.* plenipotenciário.

plenitude *s.* plenitude.

plentiful *adj.* abundante.

plenteous *adj.* abundante, copioso.

plenty *adj.* abundante, farto; *s.* abundância, fartura; *adv.* bastante, em quantidade suficiente.

plenum *s.* cheio.

pleonasm *s.* pleonasmo.

plethora *s.* pletora.

pleura *s.* pleura; **pleurisy** *s.* pleurís, pleurisia.

plexus *s.* plexo.

pliable, pliant *adj.* flexível; **pliancy** *s.* flexibilidade.

pliers *s.* alicate, tenaz.

plight *s.* condição, estado; *v.t.* empenhar; prometer.

plinth *s.* (*arq.*) plinto.

plod *v.i.* afanar-se, afadigar-se; caminhar pesadamente.

plot *s.* pequeno terreno, lote; conspiração, trama, intriga; enrêdo; planta, plano, diagrama; *v.t.&i.* traçar, delinear; conspirar, maquinar; =**ing paper** papel quadriculado.

plough *s.* charrua, arado; —=**man** la-

vrador; *v.t.&i.* arar; executar laboriosamente.

plover *s.* tarambola (ave).

plow V. **plough.**

pluck *s.* fressura; coragem, resolução; puxão; *v.t.&i.* depenar; arrancar, puxar; reprovar (em exame).

plucky *adj.* corajoso, arrojado.

plug *s.* tampão, rôlha; obturador; vela (de motor); (*elet.*) conector; *v.t.* tamponar, obturar; arrolhar; — **in** *v.t.* (*elet.*) ligar introduzindo o conector na tomada.

plum *s.* ameixa; — **tree** ameixeira.

plumage *s.* plumagem.

plumb *adj.* vertical, a prumo; *adv.* verticalmente, a prumo; *v.t.* sondar; pôr a prumo.

plumbago *s.* plombagina, grafite.

plumber *s.* bombeiro (que conserta encanamentos).

plumbing *s.* solda; ofício de bombeiro.

plume *s.* pluma; penacho; prêmio; *v.t.* adornar com penas; — **oneself on** gabar-se de.

plummet *s.* prumo, fio a prumo; sonda; pêso.

plump *adj.* roliço, gordo, cheio, rechonchudo; =**ness** *s.* gordura.

plunder *s.* saque, pilhagem, roubo; *v.t.* pilhar, saquear.

plunge *s.* mergulho; *v.t.* mergulhar, imergir; =**r** *s.* mergulhador.

pluperfect *s.* mais-que-perfeito.

plural *adj.&s.* plural; =**ity** *s.* pluralidade.

plus *prep.* mais; *adj.* positivo, adicional, extra; *s.* sinal positivo.

plush *s.* (*tec.*), pelúcia.

ply *s.* prega, dobra; inclinação, preconceito; *v.t.* dobrar; trabalhar com afinco; importunar; *v.i.* trabalhar diligentemente; fazer viagens regulares.

pneumatic *adj.* pneumático; — **tire** *s.* pneumático.

pneumonia *s.* pneumonia.

poach *v.t.* escaldar; caçar clandestinamente; =**ed eggs** ovos escaldados.

pocket *s.* bolso; bolsinho; (*min.*) depósito de ouro; *v.t.&i.* embolsar, apropriar-se.

pock-marked *adj.* marcado de bexiga.

pod *s.* vagem.

poem *s.* poema, poesia.

poet *s.* poeta; =**ess** *s.* poetisa; =**ical** *adj.* poético; =**ry** *s.* poesia.

poignant *adj.* acerbo, pungente, lancinante.

point *s.* ponto; ponta; bico; artigo, capítulo, parte; questão; *v.t.* apontar; fazer ponta, aguçar; — **out** indicar; —=**blank** diretamente, a queima-roupa; **to the** — a propósito; =**ed** *adj.* pontudo; =**er** *s.* ponteiro; cão de mostra.

poise *s.* equilíbrio, estabilidade; porte; *v.t.* equilibrar.

poison *s.* veneno; *v.t.* envenenar, intoxicar; =**er** *s.* envenenador; =**ing** *s.* envenenamento; =**ous** *adj.* venenoso.

poke *s.* golpe; empurrão; bolsa, saco; *v.t.&i.* puxar; atiçar (o fogo); andar às tontas; mexer; empurrar; meter; esquadrinhar; — **one's nose into other's affairs** meter o nariz onde não é chamado; =**r** *s.* atiçador.

poky *adj.* apertado, acanhado, estreito; mal-ajambrado.

Poland *s.* Polônia.

polar *adj.* polar; — **bear** urso branco.

pole *s.* polo; poste, mastro; viga, vara, estaca; temão; *v.t.* empar; impelir com vara (a embarcação).
Pole *s.* polonês.
polemical *adj.* polêmico; **polemics** *s.* polêmica.
police *s.* polícia.
policy *s.* política.
Polish *adj.* polonês.
polish *s.* pulimento, lustre; verniz; graxa para sapatos; *v.t.* pulir, brunir; engraxar, lustrar (sapatos); encerar.
polite *adj.* civil, cortês; =ly *adv.* cortêsmente; =ness *s.* cortesia.
politic *adj.* político; **political** *adj.* político; **politician** *s.* político; =s *s.* política.
polka *s.* polca.
poll *s.* escrutínio, voto.
pollard *s.* arvore desramada; animal sem chifre (vaca, carneiro, etc.); mocho; *v.t.* desramar, podar, cortar.
pollen *s.* pólen.
pollute *v.t.* poluir.
polo *s.* polo (jôgo).
polonaise *s.* casaco para senhora, redingote; polonesa (dansa).
poltroon *s.* poltrão.
polyanthus *s.* primavera (flor).
polygamist *s.* polígamo; **polygamous** *adj.&s.* polígamo; **polygamy** *s.* poligamia.
polyglot *adj.&s.* poliglota.
polygon *s.* polígono.
polyp, polypus *s.* pólipo.
polysyllabic *adj.* polissilábico; **polysyllable** *s.* polissílabo.
polytechnic *adj.* politécnico.
polytheism *s.* politeísmo.
pomade, pomatum *s.* pomada.
pomegranate *s.* romã.
pommel *s.* pomo; arção da sela; copo da espada; *v.t.* sovar, surrar.
pomp *s.* pompa, fausto.
pomposity *s.* pomposidade, ênfase; **pompous** *adj.* pomposo, enfático.
pond *s.* laguna; tanque.
ponder *v.i.* refletir, meditar; *v.t.* ponderar, pesar; =able *adj.* ponderável.
pontiff *s.* pontífice; **pontificate** *s.* pontificado; **pontifical** *adj.* pontifical.
pontoon *s.* pontão; chata.
pony *s.* pônei; (*jír.*) burro (tradução juxtalinear).
poodle *s.* podengo (cão).
pooh *int.* basta!
pool *s.* piscina; lago, lagoa; bilhar americano; (*jôgo*) pule, bolo, aposta; (*com.*) cartel; *v.t.* pôr em comum.
poop *s.* (*mar.*) popa.
poor *adj.* pobre; indigente; de pouco mérito; mau; *s.* pobre; indigente; =ly *adv.* pobremente; =ness *s.* pobreza; — health má saude; — little thing coitadinho.
pope *s.* papa; =ry *s.* papismo; =dom *s.* papado.
popgun *s.* espingarda (brinquedo).
popinjay *s.* papagaio; tagarela.
popish *s.* papista.
poplar *s.* álamo.
poplin *s.* tecido de sêda e lã.
poppy *s.* papoula.
populace *s.* populaça, plebe.
popular *adj.* popular; =ity *s.* popularidade; =ize *v.t.* vulgarizar.
population *s.* população; **populate** *v.t.* povoar.
populous *adj.* populoso.
porcelain *s.* porcelana.

porch *s.* pórtico; varanda.
porcupine *s.* porco-espinho.
pore *s.* poro; *v.i.* ter os olhos fitos; olhar com atenção; meditar.
pork *s.* carne de porco.
porosity *s.* porosidade; **porous** *adj.* poroso.
porphyry *s.* pórfiro.
porpoise *s.* marsopa, toninha, porco marinho.
porridge *s.* cozido, sopa, papa.
port *s.* pôrto.
portable *adj.* portátil.
portal *s.* portal.
portcullis *s.* porta de grade levadiça, rastrilho.
portend *v.t.* pressagiar.
portent *s.* portento; mau presságio.
portentous *adj.* portentoso; de mau augúrio.
porter *s.* porteiro; carregador; camareiro de trem.
portfolio *s.* pasta; carteira (títulos).
portico *s.* pórtico.
portion *s.* porção, parte; *v.t.* repartir; dotar.
portliness *s.* corpulência; **portly** *adj.* corpulento.
portmanteau *s.* maleta.
portrait *s.* retrato; **portray** *v.t.* fazer o retrato de; delinear; descrever.
portress *s.* porteira; camareira de trem.
Portugal *s.* Portugal.
Portuguese *s.&adj.* português.
pose *s.* atitude, postura estudada.
position *s.* posição; situação; condição.
positive *adj.* positivo.
posse *s.* brigada; força legal.
possess *v.t.* possuir; =ed *adj.* possuido; possesso; =ion *s.* possessão, posse; =ive *adj.* possessivo; =or *s.* possessor, possuidor.
possibility *s.* possibilidade; **possible** *adj.* possível; **possibly** *adv.* possìvelmente.
post *s.* posta, correio, estafeta, mala; poste, pilar, pilastra; (*mil.*) pôsto, praça, guarnição; *v.t.* anunciar, afixar; postar sentinela; despachar; mandar pelo correio; informar; (*com.*) passar assentamentos do livro diário para o razão; *v.i.* viajar apressadamente.
postage *s.* porte de correio; tarifa.
postal *adj.* postal.
postdate *s.* data posterior, posdata; *v.t.* posdatar.
poster *s.* cartaz.
posterior *adj.* posterior.
posterity *s.* posteridade.
postern *s.* postigo; porta trazeira.
posthumous *adj.* póstumo.
postillion *s.* postilhão.
post meridiem (*abr.* p.m.) depois de meio-dia; da tarde.
post-mortem *s.* autópsia, necrópsia.
postpone *v.t.* pospor, preterir, adiar.
postscript *s.* post-scriptum.
postulant *s.* postulante.
posture *s.* postura, atitude.
post-war *adj.* de após guerra.
posy *s.* flor, ramalhete.
pot *s.* pote; panela; marmita; canjirão; terrina; bolo (no jôgo); *v.t.* meter ou conservar no pote; (*pop.*) juntar; ganhar.
potable *adj.* potável.
potash *s.* potassa; **potassium** *s.* potássio.
potato *s.* batata.

potency s. potência; potent adj. potente, poderoso; potentate s. potentado; potential adj.&s. potencial.
pother s. sufocante nuvem de poeira, vapor ou fumaça; alarido, tumulto.
potion s. poção.
potted adj. em pote; — meats carne conservada em potes.
potter s. oleiro.
pottery s. olaria; cerâmica.
pouch s. sacola, bolsa; v.t. embolsar; v.i. engulir.
pouf s. tufo, pufe.
poultice s. cataplasma.
poultry s. aves domésticas.
pounce s. garra de ave de rapina; pó de lapis ou de carvão; v.i. lançar-se, aferrar-se; v.t. estresir; ornamentar crivando.
pound s. libra (moeda); libra (pêso, 453,59 gramas); tapada, curral; pancada forte; v.t. encurralar; moer; bater.
pour s. dilúvio, chuvarada; v.t.&i. derramar, verter; vasar; it is «ing chove a cântaros.
pout v.i. amuar; arrufar-se, fazer beiço.
poverty s. pobreza.
powder s. pó; «y adj. pulverizado.
power s. poder; fôrça; energia; «ful adj. poderoso; enérgico; «less adj. fraco, impotente.
practicable adj. praticável; practical adj. prático.
practice s. prática; hábito; costume; exercício de uma profissão; clientela; escritório; practise, practice v.t. praticar, exercer (profissão); v.i. proceder; exercer uma profissão, principalmente medicina ou advocacia.
practitioner s. profissional (advogado, médico, etc.) que exerce sua profissão.
prairie s. prado, campina.
praise s. elogio, louvor; v.t. elogiar, louvar.
prance v.i. cabriolar, saltar; empinar-se (o cavalo); (pop.) dansar; v.t. fazer (o cavalo) empinar-se.
prank s. travessura, extravagância.
prate v.i. tagarelar.
pratique s. (mar.) prática, permissão de acesso a um porto, concedida a um navio que satisfez as exigências sanitárias.
prattle s. balbucio; v.t. balbuciar; tagarelar.
prawn s. lagostim.
pray v.t.&i. orar; rogar, suplicar, pedir; «er s. oração; súplica; «er book livro de orações.
preach v.t.&i. pregar; «er s. pregador; «ing s. sermão, prédica.
preamble s. preâmbulo.
prebend s. prebenda.
precarious adj. precário.
precaution s. precaução, previdência; «ary adj. precautório, de precaução.
precede v.t. preceder; «nce s. precedência, prioridade; «nt s. precedente; preceding adj. precedente.
precentor s. chantre.
precept s. preceito; «or s. preceptor.
precinct s. limite, alçada, jurisdição; precinto.
precious adj. precioso.
precipice s. precipício.
precipitation s. precipitação.
precipitate v.t. precipitar; «ly adv. precipitadamente.
precipitous adj. escarpado.

precise adj. preciso; «ly adv. precisamente; precision s. precisão.
preclude v.t. impedir.
precocious adj. precoce; «ness s. precocidade.
preconceived adj. preconcebido.
precursor s. precursor; «y adj. precursor.
predaceous adj. que vive de rapina.
predatory adj. voraz; que vive de rapina; depredatório.
predecease v.t.&i. morrer antes.
predecessor s. predecessor.
predestination s. predestinação.
predicament s. predicamento; condição; situação difícil, dilema.
predicate s. predicado; v.t. afirmar; pregar; implicar como predicado; predication s. predicação, afirmação.
predict v.t. predizer; «ion s. predição.
predilection s. predileção.
predispose v.t. predispor.
predominance s. predominância; predominate v.i. predominar.
pre-eminent adj. proeminente, superior.
pre-eminently adv. por excelência.
pre-emption s. direito de prioridade, direito de opção.
preen v.t.&i. limpar as penas ou o pêlo.
preface s. prefácio; v.t. prefaciar; prefatory adj. a título de prefácio; preliminar.
prefect s. prefeito; «ure s. prefeitura.
prefer v.t. preferir; «able adj. preferível; «ence s. preferência.
preferment s. promoção.
prefix s. prefixo.
pregnancy s. gravidez; pregnant adj. grávida.
prehensile adj. preênsil.
prehistoric adj. prehistórico.
prejudge v.t. prejulgar.
prejudice s. preconceito, prevenção; (dir.) prejuizo; v.t. predispor, prevenir contra; (dir.) prejudicar.
prejudicial adj. prejudicial.
prelacy s. prelatura; prelate s. prelado.
preliminary adj. preliminar; preliminaries s. preliminares.
prelude s. prelúdio.
premature adj. prematuro.
premeditate v.t. premeditar; premeditation s. premeditação.
premier adj. primeiro; s. primeiro ministro; «ship s. presidência do conselho.
premise v.t. estabelecer como premissa; «s s. imóvel, local, lugar.
premise, premiss s. premissa.
premium s. prêmio.
premonition s. premonição; premonitory adj. premonitório.
preoccupation s. preocupação; ocupação prévia; preoccupy v.t. ocupar primeiro; preocupar.
preparation s. preparação; (plural) preparativos; preparatory s. preparatório; prepare v.t. preparar, dispor, aprestar; v.i. preparar-se.
prepay v.t. pagar adiantado.
preponderance s. preponderância.
preposition s. preposição.
prepossess v.t. predispor; «ing adj. atraente.
preposterous adj. absurdo.
prerogative s. prerrogativa.
presage s. presságio.
Presbyterian s.&adj. presbiteriano.
prescience s. presciência.
prescribe v.t. prescrever; (med.) receitar; prescription s. prescrição; (med.) receita.

presence s. presença; **present** adj. presente, atual, corrente; s. presente; **at present** agora, no momento; **for the present** por ora, temporàriamente; **presentable** adj. apresentável; **presentation** s. apresentação.
presentiment s. pressentimento.
presently adv. imediatamente; já; dentro em pouco.
preservation s. preservação, conservação; **preservative** s.&adj. preservativo.
preserve v.t. conservar; s. conserva.
preside v.i. presidir; **presidency** s. presidência; **president** s. presidente.
press s. prensa; pressão; imprensa, jornalismo; prelo; pressa, urgência; apêrto; v.t.&i. imprensar; apertar numa prensa; comprimir, espremer; insistir, apressar; forçar, constranger; — **out** espremer; — **on** passar a ferro; =**ing** adj. urgente, premente; =**ure** s. pressão, compressão; urgência, pressa; opressão, aflição.
prestige s. prestígio.
presume v.t.&i. presumir; **presumption** s. presunção; **presumptuous** adj. presunçoso.
presuppose v.t. presupor.
pretence V. **pretense**.
pretend v.t.&i. fingir; pretender, reclamar.
pretense s. pretensão; pretexto, desculpa; subterfúgio.
pretension s. pretensão.
pretentious adj. pretencioso.
preterite s.&adj. pretérito.
preternatural adj. sobrenatural.
pretext s. pretexto.
prettiness s. boniteza; **pretty** adj. bonito.
prevail v.i. prevalecer; =**ing** adj. predominante, prevalecente; **prevalence** s. prevalência.
prevaricate v.i. prevaricar; **prevarication** s. prevaricação.
prevent v.t. impedir; prevenir; =**ion** s. prevenção, impedimento; =**ive** adj.&s. preventivo.
previous adj. prévio, precedente.
prevision s. previsão.
pre-war adj. de antes da guerra.
prey s. presa; rapina.
price s. preço; prêmio; v.t. estabelecer o preço.
prick s. picada, picadura; golpe; remorso; v.t. picar, espetar, aguçar, avivar; causar remorsos; — **up one's ears** escutar com atenção; =**le** s. aguilhão; =**ly** adj. picante.
pride s. orgulho; amor-próprio; respeito de si mesmo.
priest s. padre, sacerdote; =**ess** s. sacerdotisa; =**hood** s. sacerdócio; =**ly** adj. sacerdotal.
prig s. pedante; =**gish** adj. pedante, presumido.
prim adj. afetado; empertigado.
primacy s. primazia.
prima donna s. primadona, diva.
prima facie prima facie, à primeira vista.
primage s. primagem.
primary adj. primário; primitivo; primeiro; principal, fundamental; elementar.
primate s. primaz; (zool.) primata.
prime s. prima (hora canônica); princípio; flor; primavera; alva, aurora, manhã; nata, elite; (mat.) primo; (mús.) uníssono; adj. primeiro; primitivo; de primeira qualidade; primário; primor-

dial; (mat.) primo; v.t. escorvar; dispor as primeiras côres na tela ou na parede; instruir de antemão; — **of life** a flor da idade, primavera da vida.
primer s. cartilha.
primeval adj. primitivo, primevo.
priming s. escorva; primeira camada de pintura.
primitive adj. primitivo.
primogeniture s. primogenitura.
primordial adj. primordial.
primrose s. primavera (flor).
prince s. príncipe; =**ly** adj. principesco; =**ss** s. princesa.
principal adj. principal; capital; s. diretor (de escola); chefe; (com.) capital; =**ity** s. principado, soberania.
principle s. princípio.
prink v.i. ataviar-se, adornar-se, enfeitar-se; v.t. enfeitar.
print s. impressão, estampa; tipo, caráter de impressão; folheto, periódico, impresso; marca, sinal; v.t. imprimir; estampar; fazer uma tiragem; =**er** s. impressor, estampador; =**er's error** êrro de imprensa; **in** — impresso, publicado; **out of** — edição esgotada; =**ing** s. imprensa, tipografia, impressão; =**ing press** máquina para imprimir ou estampar; =**ing type** tipo de imprensa.
prior adj. anterior, precedente, prévio; — **to antes de**; s. prior;*=**ess** s. priora; =**ity** s. prioridade, anterioridade.
prise V. **prize**.
prism s. prisma; =**atic** adj. prismático.
prison s. prisão; =**er** s. prisioneiro.
pristine adj. primitivo.
privacy s. retiro, solidão, isolamento; segrêdo, reserva; lugar de retiro.
private s. privado, particular; pessoal, íntimo; soldado raso.
privateer s. corsário.
privately adv. em particular.
privation s. privação, carência.
privative adj. privativo.
privet s. (bot.) alfena.
privilege s. privilégio; v.t. privilegiar.
privily adv. em segrêdo; **privy** adj. privado; s. privada.
prize s. presa; captura; prêmio; alavanca; v.t. avaliar; mover por meio de alavanca; — **giving** distribuição de prêmios; — **medal** medalha de honra.
pro adv. a favor, pró; s. voto favorável; **the =s and cons** os prós e os contras.
probability s. probabilidade; **probable** adj. provável.
probate s. verificação de testamento.
probation s. estágio; provação; =**er** s. estagiário, noviço.
probe s. (cir.) tenta; devassa; v.t. (cir.) tentear, sondar; sindicar, fazer uma devassa; penetrar profundamente.
probity s. probidade.
problem s. problema; =**atic**, =**atical** adj. problemático.
proboscis s. tromba, probóscida.
procedure s. marcha a seguir; processo; regulamento parlamentar.
proceed v.i. proceder; provir; prosseguir, continuar; =**s** s. produto, renda, rendimento; =**ing** s. procedimento, processo; =**ings** atos, autos; providências; deliberações; debates.
process s. processo, curso.
procession s. procissão, desfile, marcha, cortejo.

proclaim *v.t.* proclamar; publicar; anunciar; declarar; **proclamation** *s.* proclamação; declaração.
proclivity *s.* inclinação, propensão.
procrastinate *v.i.&t.* adiar, diferir, retardar; procrastinar.
procrastination *s.* procrastinação, adiamento.
procreate *v.t.* procrear.
proctor *s.* procurador; inspetor de alunos.
procuration *s.* procuração, mandato; **procure** *v.t.* conseguir, obter; alcovitar.
prod *v.t.* punçar; agulhar; espetar; (*fig.*) incitar.
prodigal *adj.&s.* pródigo; **-ity** *s.* prodigalidade.
prodigious *adj.* prodigioso; **prodigy** *s.* prodígio.
produce *v.t.* produzir; exibir; mostrar; **-r** *s.* produtor.
product *s.* produto; produção; **-ive** *adj.* produtivo.
profanation *s.* profanação; **profane** *adj.* profano; *v.t.* profanar; **profanity** *s.* irreverência, blasfêmia.
profess *v.t.* professar; **-ion** *s.* profissão; **-ional** *adj.&s.* profissional.
professor *s.* professor; **-ship** *s.* professorado.
proficient *adj.* proficiente, capaz, hábil.
profile *s.* perfil.
profit *s.* lucro, proveito, benefício, ganho; *v.i.&t.* aproveitar, beneficiar; **-able** *adj.* proveitoso, frutuoso; **-ably** *adv.* frutuosamente, proveitosamente; **-eer** *s.* aproveitador.
profligacy *s.* dissolução, libertinagem; **profligate** *adj.* dissoluto, libertino.
profound *adj.* profundo; **-ly** *adv.* profundamente; **profundity** *s.* profundidade, profundeza.
profuse *adj.* profuso, abundante; **-ly** *adv.* profusamente; **profusion** *s.* profusão.
progenitor *s.* progenitor; **progeny** *s.* progenitura, prole.
prognathous *adj.* prognata.
prognosticate *v.t.* prognosticar; **prognostic** *s.* prognóstico; **prognostication** *s.* prognóstico.
programme *s.* programa.
progress *s.* progresso; *v.i.* progredir, fazer progressos; **-ion** *s.* progressão; **-ive** *adj.* progessivo.
prohibit *v.t.* proibir; **-ion** *s.* proibição, interdição; **-ionist** *s.* proibicionista; **-ive** *adj.* proibitivo; **-ory** *adj.* proibitório.
project *s.* projeto; *v.t.* projetar; *v.i.* projetar-se.
projectil *s.* projétil.
projection *s.* projeção; **projector** *s.* projetor.
proletarian *adj.&s.* proletário; **proletariate** *s.* proletariado.
prolific *adj.* prolífico.
prolix *adj.* prolixo; **-ity** *s.* prolixidade.
prologue *s.* prólogo.
prolong *v.t.* prolongar; **-ation** *s.* prolongamento, prolongação.
promenade *s.* passeio.
prominence *s.* proeminência; **prominent** *adj.* proeminente.
promiscuity *s.* promiscuidade; **promiscuous** *adj.* promíscuo.
promise *s.* promessa; esperanças; *v.t.&i.* prometer, **promising** *adj.* prometedor; **promissor** **promissory** *adj.* promissório; **promissory note** letra promissória.

promontory *s.* promontório.
promote *v.t.* promover; favorecer, animar, incrementar.
promoter *s.* promotor, lançador, fundador; **promotion** *s.* promoção; adiantamento.
prompt *adj.* pronto, prestes; *v.t.* incitar, levar, conduzir; sugerir; inspirar; (*teat.*) soprar; **-er** *s.* (*teat.*) ponto; **-itude** *s.* prontidão, presteza.
promulgate *v.t.* promulgar.
prone *adj.* prosternado; propenso; **-ness** *s.* inclinação, propensão.
prong *s.* ponta, dente (do garfo, etc.); forcado.
pronominal *adj.* pronominal; **pronoun** *s.* pronome.
pronounce *v.t.&i.* pronunciar; **pronunciation** *s.* pronunciação, pronúncia; **-ment** declaração formal.
proof *s.* prova; provação; — **against** a prova de; garantido contra; — **reader** (*imp.*) revisor.
prop *v.t.* amparar, escorar; sustentar; *s.* suporte, sustentáculo, escora.
propaganda *s.* propaganda.
propagate *v.t.* propagar.
propel *v.t.* propelir, dar impulso; **-ler** *s.* propulsor; (*mar.*) hélice.
propensity *s.* propensão, inclinação.
proper *adj.* próprio; conveniente.
property *s.* propriedade.
prophecy *s.* profecia; **prophesy** *v.t.`&i.* profetizar; **prophet** *s.* profeta; **prophetess** *s.* profetisa; **prophetical** *adj.* profético.
propinquity *s.* proximidade; propinquidade.
propitiate *v.t.* propiciar; tornar propício; **propitious** *adj* propício.
proportion *s.* proporção; *v.t.* proporcionar; **-al** *adj.* proporcional.
proposal *s.* proposta; **propose** *v.t.&i.* propor; propor casamento.
proposition *s.* proposta; **proposer** *s.* proponente.
propound *v.t.* propor.
proprietary *adj.* de propriedade (direitos); — **medicine** produto farmacêutico (registrado); **proprietor** *s.* proprietário; **propriety** *s.* conveniência, decência, propriedade.
propulsion *s.* propulsão.
prorogue *v.t.* prorrogar; encerrar (a sessão legislativa) por ordem da coroa.
prosaic *adj.* prosáico.
proscenium *s.* proscênio, frente de palco.
proscribe *v.t.* proscrever, interditar.
prose *s.* prosa; — **writer** prosador.
prosecute *v.t.* prosseguir, continuar; (*for.*) processar; **prosecution** *s.* prosseguimento; continuação; (*for.*) processo; acusação; **prosecutor** *s.* **prosecutrix** *s.* (*for.*) acusador, promotor; acusadora, promotora.
proselyte *s.* prosélito.
prosiness *s.* verbosidade; caceteação.
prosody *s.* prosódia.
prospect *s.* vista, perspectiva; futuro; previsão; esperança; *v.t.* explorar, examinar; garimpar; **-ing** *s.* exploração, garimpagem; **-ive** *adj.* em perspectiva; **-or** *s.* explorador, faiscador, garimpeiro.
prospectus *s.* prospecto.
prosper *v.i.* prosperar; **-ity** *s.* prosperidade; **-ous** *adj.* próspero.
prostate *s.* próstata.

prostitute *v.t.* prostituir; *s.* prostituta; *adj.* prostituido, corrupto.
prostrate *adj.* prosternado; abatido, prostrado; *v.t.* prosternar; prostrar, abater.
prostration *s.* prostração.
prosy *adj.* verboso; prosaico; tedioso.
protagonist *s.* protagonista.
protect *v.t.* proteger, guardar, defender; =ion *s.* proteção; =ionist *s.* protecionista; =ive *adj.* protetor; =or *s.* protetor; =ress *s.* protetora; =orate *s.* protetorado.
pro tempore *adv.* a título provisório.
protest *s.* protesto, reclamação; *v.t.&i.* protestar; =ant *s.* protestante.
protocol *s.* protocolo.
prototype *s.* protótipo.
protract *v.t.* prolongar; =or *s.* transferidor.
protrude *v.i.* projetar-se, sobressair; fazer saliência, sair.
protuberance *s.* protuberância.
proud *adj.* orgulhoso; brioso.
prove *v.t.* provar, demonstrar; (*for.*) homologar (testamento).
provender *s.* forragem.
proverb *s.* provérbio; =ial *adj.* proverbial.
provide *v.t.* prover, fornecer; estipular; prever; =r *s.* provedor.
providence *s.* providência; previdência; **provident** *adj.* previdente, prudente, econômico; **providential** *adj.* providencial.
province *s.* província; **provincial** *adj.* provinciano.
provision *s.* provisão; (*plural*) víveres, comestíveis; *v.t.* aprovisionar; =al *adj.* provisório.
proviso *s.* cláusula condicional.
provisory *adj.* provisório.
provocation *s.* provocação.
provoke *v.t.* provocar, incitar; motivar; irritar.
provost *s.* reitor; preboste; superintendente.
prow *s.* proa.
prowess *s.* proeza, valentia.
prowl *v.i.* errar, vaguear; rondar.
proximate *adj.* próximo; imediato.
proximity *s.* proximidade; **próximo** *adv.* do próximo mês.
proxy *s.* mandato, procuração; procurador.
prude *s.* pudica; melindrosa.
prudence *s.* prudência; **prudent** *adj.* prudente.
prudery *s.* pudicícia exagerada; **prudish** *adj.* pudibundo.
prune *s.* ameixa; *v.t.* podar, desbastar.
pruning *s.* poda.
pruriency *s.* comichão; desejo, sensualidade; **prurient** *adj.* pruriente; sensual; **pruritus** *s.* prurido.
Prussia *s.* Prússia; =n *s.&adj.* prussiano.
prussic *adj.* prússico.
pry *v.i.* escrutar, procurar, esquadrinhar; intrometer-se; =ing *adj.* indiscreto, curioso.
psalm *s.* salmo; =ist *s.* salmista; **psalter** *s.* saltério.
pseudonym *s.* pseudônimo.
pshaw *int.* fora!
psychiater, psychiatrist *s.* psiquiatra; **psychiatry** *s.* psiquiatria.
psychic, psychical *adj.* psíquico.
psycho-analysis *s.* psico-análise.
psychology *s.* psicologia; **psychologist** *s.* psicólogo; **psychological** *adj.* psicológico.
ptomaine *s.* ptomaína.
puberty *s.* puberdade.

public *adj.&s.* público.
publication *s.* publicação.
publicist *s.* publicista.
publicity *s.* publicidade.
publish *v.t.* publicar; =er *s.* editor.
publishing *s.* publicação, edição.
puck *s.* duende, gênio.
pucker *s.* prega, ruga; *v.t.* preguear, enrugar.
pudding *s.* pudim.
puddle *s.* poça, lamaçal; cimento hidráulico; *v.t.* (*hidr.*) impermeabilizar, cimentar (o fundo de um canal, poço, etc.).
puerile *adj.* pueril.
puff *s.* baforada, sôpro; esponja de pó de arroz; edredão; (*cost.*) fôfo; (*pastelaria*) folhado; (*imp.*) elogio exagerado; *v.i.* soprar, bafejar; bufar; inchar; *v.t.* soprar, inflar; elogiar exageradamente, incensar.
puffin *s.* mergulhão (ave).
puffy *adj.* inchado, cheio de vento; presumido.
pug *s.* cãozinho chinês; (*pop.*) pugilista; — **nose** nariz chato; *v.t.* argamassar.
pugilism *s.* pugilato, boxe; **pugilist** *s.* pugilista.
pugnacious *adj.* batalhador, belicoso; pugnaz.
pule *v.i.* choramingar.
pull *s.* arranco, puxão; tiragem; esfôrço (de tração); trago (de bebida); cordão de campainha; (*pop.*) influência, favor especial; *v.t.&i.* puxar, arrastar; arrancar, tirar; remar; (*pop.*) prender o cavalo (nas corridas).
pullet *s.* frango.
pulley *s.* roldana; polia.
pullulate *v.i.* pulular.
pulmonary *adj.* pulmonar.
pulp *s.* polpa.
pulpit *s.* púlpito.
pulsate *v.i.* pulsar.
pulsation *s.* pulsação.
pulse *s.* pulso.
pulverize *v.t.* pulverizar.
puma *s.* puma.
pumice (stone) pedra-pomes.
pump *s.* bomba; *v.t.&i.* tirar água com bomba; sondar; — **up the tires** encher os pneumáticos.
pumpkin *s.* abóbora.
pun *s.* trocadilho; *v.i.* fazer trocadilhos.
punch *s.* sôco; ponche (bebida); perfurador, punção; polichinelo; *v.t.* perfurar; puncionar; esmurrar.
puncheon *s.* furador, buril, punção; barril grande.
punctilio *s.* meticulosidade; =ous *adj.* meticuloso.
punctual *adj.* pontual; =ity *s.* pontualidade.
punctuate *v.t.* pontuar.
punctuation *s.* pontuação.
puncture *s.* punção; picada; *v.t.* puncionar; picar.
pungency *s.* pungência; **pungent** *adj.* pungente, acre.
punish *v.t.* castigar; =able *adj.* punível; =ment *s.* castigo, punição.
punster *s.* fazedor de trocadilhos.
punt *s.* bote de fundo chato.
puny *adj.* fraco, débil; inferior.
pup *s.* cachorrinho.
pupa *s.* crisálida, pupa.
pupil *s.* pupila; discípulo, aluno, pupilo.
puppet *s.* fantoche, boneco.
puppy *s.* cachorrinho.
purblind *adj.* quasi cego; obtuso.

purchase s. compra; aquisição; v.t. comprar, adquirir.
purchaser s. comprador.
pure adj. puro; =ness s. pureza.
purgative adj.&s. purgativo.
purgatory s. purgatório.
purge v.t. purgar, clarificar; administrar um purgante.
purge, purging s. purgação; purgante.
purify v.t. purificar; depurar.
purist s. purista.
Puritan s.&adj. puritano.
purity s. pureza.
purl v.i. ondear, serpentear; murmurar; enfeitar com fio metálico.
purlieus s. arredores, arrabaldes.
purloin v.t. roubar.
purple s. púrpura; adj. roxo (côr); **purplish** adj. violáceo.
purport s. significado; substância; teor; v.t. significar, querer dizer, conter.
purpose s. propósito, fim, intenção; =ly adv. de propósito; propositadamente.
purr s. ronrom.
purse s. bolsa.
purser s. comissário (de navio).
purslane s. beldroega, salgadeira (planta).
pursue v.t. perseguir; prosseguir, continuar.
pursuit s. perseguição, caça; pesquisa; carreira, profissão.
purulent adj. purulento.
purvey v.t. prover; =or s. provedor.
purview s. dispositivo (de lei); circunscrição, esfera; escopo, finalidade (de uma lei).
pus s. pus.

push v.t. empurrar; obrigar, constranger; importunar, molestar; avançar, atacar; s. impulso; empurrão; investida, acometida; =ing adj. ativo, diligente, empreendedor.
pusillanimous adj. pusilânime.
puss s. gato; (pop.) menina.
pustule s. pústula.
put v.t. pôr, botar; colocar; fazer (uma pergunta, uma chamada, etc.); aplicar; dirigir; — down reprimir; baixar; — forward avançar; propor; — off diferir, adiar; — on pôr, vestir; tomar; avançar; — out apagar; — out of order desarranjar; — back retroceder; — up with suportar, tolerar.
putrefaction s. putrefação.
putrefy v.t.&i. putrificar; putrefazer.
putrid adj. pútrido.
puttee s. perneira.
putty s. potéia.
puzzle s. quebra-cabeça; problema; enigma; v.t. confundir, tornar perplexo; v.i. ficar perplexo.
puzzled adj. perplexo.
pygmy s. pigmeu.
pyjama s. pijama.
pylon s. pilone; tôrre, poste.
pyorrhoea s. piorréia.
pyramid s. pirâmide.
pyre s. pira, fogueira.
Pyrenees s. Pireneus.
pyrite s. pirita.
pyrotechnics s. pirotécnica.
python s. píton.
pyuria s. piúria.
pyx s. cibório.

Q

Q letra do alfabeto.
qua adv. como; em sua qualidade de.
quack s. charlatão; =ery s. charlatanismo, charlatanice.
quadrangle s. quadrângulo.
quadrant s. quadrante.
quadroon s. quadrarão.
quadruped s.&adj. quadrúpede.
quadruple adj.&s. quádruplo; =ts s. quatro gêmeos.
quaff v.t. beber, tragar.
quagmire s. tremedal, pântano.
quail s. codorniz; v.i. perder a coragem; fraquejar.
quaint adj. estranho, peculiar; pitoresco; =ness s. peculiaridade; curiosidade.
quake v.i. tremer.
qualification s. qualificação; condição; requisito; capacidade; **qualified** adj. qualificado.
qualify v.t. qualificar; v.i. qualificar-se.
quality s. qualidade.
qualms s. náusea súbita; escrúpulo; compunção.
quandary s. perplexidade, dúvida; dilema.
quantity s. quantidade.
quantum s. quantidade, quantum.
quarantine s. quarentena; pôr de quarentena.
quarrel s. briga, rixa, altercação; v.i. brigar.
quarrelsome adj. brigão.
quarry s. pedreira; presa, caça; v.t. explorar (pedreira).
quart s. quarto (medida para líquidos,

equivalente a 0,9463 litros nos EE.UU. e 1,1365 l na Grã-Bretanha).
quarter s. quarto; a quarta parte; moeda (quarta parte do dôlar); trimestre; quarto (de hora); quarteirão; distrito; (plural) residência; (mil.) quartel; clemência; (mar.) alheta; v.t. dividir em quatro partes; abrigar; alojar; acantonar; =age s. pagamento trimestral; alojamento; custo de alojamento.
quarterly adj. trimestral.
quartet, quartette s. quarteto.
quartz s. quarzo.
quash v.t. suprimir; anular, cassar.
quasi adv.&pref. quasi.
quassia s. quássia.
quatrain s. quadra (de versos).
quaver s. garganteio, trinado; (mús.) colcheia; v.i. gargantear, trinar; tremer, tremular.
quay s. cais.
queen s. rainha.
queer adj. estranho, peculiar, singular; original; ecêntrico; =ness s. ecentricidade.
quell v.t. reprimir, abafar; apaziguar.
quench v.t. extinguir; saciar, aplacar (a sêde); esfriar.
querulous adj. queixoso.
query s. questão, pergunta; interrogação; v.t. interrogar.
quest s. pesquisa, indagação, busca; v.i. dar uma busca.
question s. pergunta, interrogação; v.t. perguntar; interrogar, inquirir; =able adj. contestável.

queue s. cauda; — up fazer cauda.
quibble s. chicana; v.i. fazer chicana, chicanar.
quick adj. vivo, rápido, pronto; adv. depressa; =lime s. cal viva; =sand s. areia movediça.
quicken v.t. vivificar, animar; acelerar, ativar.
quickly adv. de-pressa.
quickness s. presteza, rapidez.
quid s. porção (de tabaco) para mascar.
quidnunc s. boateiro.
quid pro quo quiproquó, equívoco.
quiescent adj. quieto; imóvel.
quiet adj. tranquilo; quieto; v.t. aquietar.
quietness s. quietude, tranquilidade, repouso; quietude s. quietude.
quill s. bobina da lançadeira (de tear); espinho (do porco-espinho); pena (de ave); pluma (de escrever).
quilt s. acolchoado (de cama); v.t. acolchoar, estofar.
quince s. marmelo.
quincunx s. quincôncio, quincunce.
quinine s. quinina, quinino.
quinquennial adj. quinquenal.
quinsy s. angina (da garganta).
quint s. (mús.) quinta; sequência de cinco cartas do mesmo naipe.

quintessence s. quintessência.
quintet, quintette s. quinteto.
quintuple adj.&s. quíntuplo.
quintuplets s. cinco gêmeos.
quip s. piada, remoque.
quire s. conjunto de 24 (às vezes 25) fôlhas de papel; mão de papel.
quirk s. subterfúgio; equívoco; piada espirituosa; volta; golpe; viravolta.
quit v.t.&i. deixar, abandonar; largar; despedir-se, deixar o emprêgo.
quite adv. inteiramente, completamente, perfeitamente.
quits adj. quite.
quiver s. tremor; v.i. tremer, estremecer.
quiz v.t. examinar, interrogar, fazer perguntas; ridicularizar; =zical adj. ecêntrico; implicante.
quoin s. canto; pedra angular; cunha.
quoit s. disco, malha, conca; (plural) jôgo de malha; v.t. atirar (concas).
quondam adj. antigo, ex-, que foi.
quorum s. quórum.
quota s. quota.
quotation s. citação; (com.) cotação.
quote v.t. citar; (com.) cotar.
quotidian adj. quotidiano.
quotient s. quociente.

R

R letra do alfabeto.
rabbet s. samblagem; encaixe, juntura.
rabbi s. rabino.
rabbit s. coelho; =ry s. coelheira.
rabble s. canalha, populaça.
rabid adj. furioso, danado; encarniçado.
rabies s. hidrofobia, raiva.
raccoon s. coati.
race s. raça, estirpe, casta; (esp.) corrida, regata; corrente de água; canal estreito; curso, decurso; competição; v.i. competir em velocidade; correr; mover-se ràpidamente; — track pista.
racer s. cavalo de corrida; corredor.
racial adj. racial.
racing s. corrida.
rack s. bastidor; prateleira de bagagem (trem); cabide; grade (da manjedoura); barra dentada, cremalheira; xalmas; ecúleo; suplício, tortura; — railway estrada de ferro de cremalheira; v.t. esticar, retesar; torturar; — rent aluguel de casa elevado ao máximo do valor, extorsivo; — one's brain torturar-se, quebrar a cabeça.
racket s. algazarra, orgia; raqueta; (pop.) extorsão; =eer s. pessoa que obtém dinheiro por extorsão.
racy adj. genuíno, fresco; espirituoso, vivo.
radial adj. radial.
radiance, radiation s. radiação, irradiação, brilho.
radiancy s. brilho, esplendor.
radiant adj. radiante, radioso.
radiate v.i. radiar.
radiator s. radiador.
radical adj.&s. radical.
radioactive adj. radioativo.
radiogram s. radiograma.
radio-gramophone s. radiola.
radiography s. radiografia.
radiotelegraphy s. radiotelegrafia.
radish s. rabanete.
radium s. rádio.

radius s. raio, alcance; (anat.) rádio.
raffle s. rifa, tômbola; v.t. rifar.
raft s. jangada.
rag s. trapo, farrapo; frangalho; — baby boneca de pano.
ragamuffin s. moleque.
rage s. raiva, furor, cólera; mania; frenesí; v.i. enraivecer-se, enfurecer-se; grassar (praga).
ragout s. ragú.
raid s. raid; incursão; ataque; v.t.&i. fazer raides; fazer uma incursão.
rail s. cêrca; corrimão; parapeito; trilho; v.t. cercar com grades, parapeitos, etc.; — at invectivar; =ing s. grade, balaustrada.
raillery s. zombaria.
railway s. trilhos; linha de bonde; caminho de ferro destinado a tráfego leve; na Inglaterra, qualquer estrada de ferro.
railroad s. estrada de ferro, caminho de ferro; companhia de estrada de ferro.
raiment s. roupas, vestuário.
rain s. chuva; =bow s. arco-íris; — water águas pluviais; v.i. chover; =y adj. chuvoso.
raise v.t. levantar, alçar; elevar, erguer; erigir; aumentar; subir; ascender; animar, incitar; causar, ocasionar; inspirar, dar lugar a; arvorar; cultivar; produzir; fazer nascer; criar; =d adj. em relêvo, saliente.
raisin s. passa (uva).
rake s. ancinho, ciscador; inclinação, desvio da vertical; libertino, debochado; v.t. limpar, trabalhar com ancinho; juntar laboriosamente; — up remexer, revolver.
rakish adj. libertino.
rally v.t.&i. reunir, reunir-se; animar, reanimar; refazer-se; (mil.) reunir, reorganizar; s. reunião e reorganização de tropas dispersas; reunião popular, comício.

ram s. carneiro (reprodutor); aríete; (*mar.*) esporão; (*maq.*) martelo, pilão, bate-estaca, etc. (*ast.*) Aries; **steam** — pilão a vapor; **water** — carneiro hidráulico; *v.t.* calcar, socar; bater; encher (batendo, comprimindo); enterrar, fincar (batendo).

ramble s. excursão, passeio; *v.i.* errar, vagar.

rambler s. roseira trepadeira.

rambling *adj.* errante; incoerente, sem nexo, digressivo.

ramification s. ramificação; **ramify** *v.i.* ramificar.

rampant *adj.* desenfreado; exuberante; (*her.*) rampante.

rampart s. muro, muralha, baluarte.

ramrod s. vareta (de espingarda); soquete.

ramshackle *adj.* desmantelado, desorganizado.

ranch s. fazenda de gado.

rancid *adj.* rançoso.

rancorous *adj.* rancoroso; **rancor, rancour** s. rancor.

random *adj.* ao acaso; s. acaso; **at** — ao acaso, a esmo.

range s. extensão, alcance, distância; fila, fileira, linha; classe, ordem; série, gama, escala; cadeia de montanhas; alvo (para tiro); terrenos ou campos de pasto; fogão (de cozinha); *v.t.* alinhar; pôr em fila; dispor em ordem; alcançar; percorrer; *v.i.* variar, oscilar.

ranger s. guarda de florestas.

rank s. linha, fileira; grau, graduação; posição, classe, dignidade; pôsto; (*mil.*) fileiras; (*plural*) exército; *v.t.&i.* dispor em fileiras ou em ordem; classificar; tomar lugar, ser classificado, colocar-se.

rankle *v.i.* inflamar-se, inchar.

ransack *v.t.* pilhar, saquear.

ransom s. resgate; *v.t.* resgatar; redimir.

rant s. declamação; (*pop.*) farra; *v.i.* declamar; censurar com veemência; (*pop.*) farrear.

ranunculus s. ranúnculo.

rap s. piparote; batida (na porta, etc.); vintém; (*fig.*) palha, bagatela; *v.t.&i.* bater; — **at the door** bater à porta; **I don't care a** — não me importa nada.

rapacious *adj.* rapace.

rape s. rapto; estupro; (*bot.*) nabo silvestre, nabiça, colza; — **oil** óleo de colza; *v.t.* raptar; estuprar.

rapid *adj.&s.* rápido; **-ity** s. rapidez.

rapier s. espadim, florete.

rapine s. rapina.

rapt *adj.* arrebatado, extasiado; **-ure** s. arrebatamento, transporte; êxtase; **-urous** *adj.* extático.

rare *adj.* raro; (*coz.*) mal assado.

rarefy *v.t.* rarefazer.

rareness s. raridade.

rascal s. maroto, velhaco; **-ity** s. velhacaria.

rash s. erupção (no corpo); *adj.* temerário; imprudente, precipitado.

rashness s. imprudência, temeridade.

rasher s. fatia fina.

raspberry s. framboesa.

rat s. rato; (*pol.*) trânsfuga; **—-trap** ratoeira; *v.i.* caçar ratos; (*pol.*) desertar, virar casaca.

ratable *adj.* tributável; proporcional.

ratchet s. (*maq.*) roquete.

rate s. taxa; percentagem, razão, relação; ordem, classe; preço; tarifa, imposto; *v.t.* taxar; tarifar; estimar, avaliar;

classificar, cotar; *v.i.* ser classificado; **at any** — custe o que custar; em todo o caso.

rather *adv.* antes, de preferência; especialmente; um tanto.

ratification s. ratificação; **ratify** *v.t.* ratificar.

rating s. classificação.

ratio s. razão, proporção, relação.

ration s. ração; *v.t.* racionar.

rational *adj.* racional.

rationalism s. racionalismo.

rationalization s. racionalização.

rattam, rattan s. junco, rotim.

ratter s. cão rateiro; (*pol.*) desertor de um partido na adversidade.

rattle s. matraca; chocalho; barulho; cirro, estertor; *v.i.* tocar matraca; chocalhar; (*pop.*) palrar, tagarelar; *v.t.* (*pop.*) confundir, agitar, desconcertar.

raucous *adj.* rouco.

ravage *v.t.* devastar, estragar, pilhar; s. devastação, estragos, assolação.

rave *v.i.* divagar, delirar.

ravel *v.t.* embaraçar, complicar; — **out** desembaraçar, desfiar.

raven s. corvo.

ravenous *adj.* voraz; devorante.

ravine s. ravina.

raving s. delírio.

ravish *v.t.* arrebatar; violentar, raptar.

ravishing *adj.* arrebatador, encantador.

ravishingly *adv.* arrebatadoramente.

raw *adj.* crú; bruto; ao natural (matéria prima); **em carne viva**; frio, úmido (tempo); (*fig.*) novato, inexperiente.

rawness s. crueza.

ray s. raio.

raze *v.t.* apagar, riscar; arrasar.

razor s. navalha.

re *pref.* que denota volta (ao estado original) ou repetição.

reach s. alcance; extensão; distância; poder; capacidade; *v.t.* atingir; conseguir; elevar-se a; **beyond one's** — fora do seu alcance.

react *v.i.* reagir; **-ion** s. reação; **-ionary** *adj.&s.* reacionário.

read *v.t.&i.* ler; estudar; **-able** *adj.* legível.

reader s. leitor, leitora; livro de leitura (de texto); (*imp.*) revisor de provas.

readiness s. maturidade; prontidão, presteza; facilidade.

reading s. leitura; lição, estudo; **— room** gabinete de leitura.

ready *adj.* pronto, preparado; disposto, inclinado; **—-made** confeccionado, feito.

reagent s. reativo.

real *adj.* real; positivo; verdadeiro; efetivo; (*dir.*) imóvel; **-ist** s.&*adj.* realista; **-ity** s. realidade; **-ize** *v.t.* realizar; perceber como realidade, compreender.

realm s. reino, reinado; região, domínio.

realty s. bens imóveis.

ream s. resma; *v.t.* escariar.

reamer s. escariador, furador.

reap *v.t.* colhêr, ceifar, segar; **-er** s. ceifeiro, segador; **reaping** s. colheita, sega, ceifa.

reappear *v.i.* reaparecer; **-ance** s. reaparição.

reappoint *v.t.* renomear.

rear s. traseira; cauda; parte posterior; (*mil.*) retaguarda; *adj.* traseiro, de trás; **— admiral** contra-almirante; *v.t.* criar; educar; levantar, elevar; **erigir**.

reason s. razão; causa; motivo; *v.i.* raciocinar, arrazoar, argumentar; — **with** catequizar, procurar convencer; **state the** — **for** motivar, expor a razão; **able** *adj.* razoável; **ing** s. raciocínio.
reassure *v.t.* tranquilizar.
rebate s. dedução, desconto; *v.t.&i.* descontar, deduzir, conceder abatimento.
rebel s.&*adj.* rebelde, revoltoso; *v.i.* revoltar-se, rebelar-se.
rebellious *adj.* rebelde, revoltoso.
rebind *v.t.* reencadernar.
rebirth s. renascimento.
rebound s. repercussão; ressalto; *v.i.* repercutir; ressaltar.
rebuff s. rebate, repulsa; *v.t.* repelir, rebater.
rebuild *v.t.* reconstruir.
rebuke s. reprimenda; *v.t.* repreender, admoestar.
rebut *v.t.* refutar.
recalcitrant *adj.&s.* recalcitrante.
recall s. revocação; chamada (toque, sinal, etc.); *v.t.* revocar, cassar; tornar a chamar; relembrar, recordar.
recant *v.i.* retratar-se; **ation** s. retratação.
recapitulate *v.t.* recapitular.
recapture s. recaptura; recuperação; *v.t.* recapturar, rehaver.
recast *v.t.* refundir.
recede *v.i.* retirar-se; recuar.
receipt s. recibo; receita (culinária); recebimento; **s** (*cont.*) receita, recebimentos.
receive *v.t.* receber; admitir; hospedar, acolher; **r** s. recebedor; receptor; recipiente; (*dir.*) depositário; liquidatário.
recent *adj.* recente.
receptacle s. receptáculo.
reception s. recepção.
recess s. retiro, lugar apartado; nicho; trégua, suspensão; recreio, férias; (*plural*) recônditos.
recipe s. receita; (*farm.*) fórmula.
recipient s. destinatário; recipiente.
reciprocal *adj.* recíproco.
reciprocate *v.t.* retribuir.
reciprocity s. reciprocidade.
recital s. relação, narração; (*mús.*) recital, audição.
recitation s. recitação, declamação; aula.
recitative s. recitativo.
recite *v.t.&i.* recitar, declamar; relatar; dizer a lição.
reckless *adj.* imprudente, descuidado; temerário; **ly** *adv.* temerariamente; **,** negligentemente.
reckon *v.t.&i.* contar, calcular; avaliar, estimar; **ing** s. conta, cálculo; computação; ajuste de contas.
reclaim *v.t.* reclamar, reivindicar; recuperar, aproveitar (material usado); tornar utilizável (terreno); domesticar (o falcão), amansar; reformar, regenerar.
recline *v.i.* reclinar-se, recostar-se.
recluse *adj.* recluso; **reclusion** s. reclusão.
recognition s. reconhecimento; **recognizable** *adj.* reconhecível; **recognizance** s. reconhecimento, obrigação; **recognize** *v.t.* reconhecer.
recoil s. recuo, retrocesso; coice (de arma de fogo, etc.); *v.i.* recuar, retroceder.
recoin *v.t.* recunhar, tornar a cunhar.
recollect *v.t.* recordar; reunir.
recollection s. recordação, memória.
recommence *v.t.&i.* recomeçar.

recommend *v.t.* recomendar; preconizar; **ation** s. recomendação.
recompense s. recompensa; *v.t.* recompensar.
reconcile *v.t.* reconciliar, conciliar.
recondite *adj.* recôndito; abstruso.
reconnoitre *v.t.* (*mil.*) reconhecer.
reconsider *v.t.* reconsiderar.
reconstruct *v.t.* reconstruir; **ion** s. reconstrução.
record s. disco (de vitrola); registo; ata; documento, relação, crônica; história; antecedentes de uma pessoa; (*for.*) memorial, informe; (*plural*) arquivo, protocolo, memórias, dados; *v.t.* registar, consignar; referir; relatar.
recorder s. registador.
re-count *v.t.* recontar; contar pormenorizadamente.
recoup *v.t.* recuperar; reparar, indenizar, ressarcir.
recourse s. recurso; (*for.*) recurso, regresso.
re-cover *v.t.* recobrir.
recover *v.t.* recuperar; *v.i.* restabelecer-se, recuperar a saúde; voltar a si; **y** s. restabelecimento.
recreant *adj.&s.* covarde; desleal, apóstata.
re-create *v.t.* recriar, criar de novo; reanimar.
re-creation s. re-criação, nova criação.
recreation s. recreio, recreação.
recrimination s. recriminação.
recrudescence s. recrudescência.
recruit s. recruta; *v.t.* recrutar; reabastecer.
rectangle s. retângulo; **rectangular** *adj.* retangular.
rectify *v.t.* retificar.
rectilinear *adj.* retilíneo.
rectitude s. retidão.
rector s. reitor; cura; **y** s. reitoria; presbitério.
rectum s. reto.
recumbent *adj.* deitado, inclinado.
recuperate *v.t.* recuperar; *v.i.* restabelecer-se, convalescer.
recur *v.i.* repetir-se, ocorrer outra vez, voltar.
recurrence s. repetição; volta; **recurring decimal** fração periódica.
red *adj.&s.* vermelho; **den** *v.t.&i.* corar, ruborizar-se; tingir de vermelho.
reddish *adj.* avermelhado.
redeem *v.t.* redimir; amortizar; resgatar; **able** *adj.* redimível; resgatável; **er** s. redentor.
Redeemer s. Redentor.
redemption s. redenção; amortização; resgate.
redness s. vermelhidão.
redoubt s. reduto.
redoubtable *adj.* temível; respeitável.
redound *v.i.* ressaltar; ressoar; resultar.
redress s. reparação; correção; desagravo; satisfação; *v.t.* corrigir, reparar; fazer justiça.
reduce *v.t.* reduzir; diminuir; **reduction** s. redução; diminuição.
redundant *adj.* redundante.
re-echo *v.i.* ressoar.
reed s. cana, caniço; charamela, gaita.
reef s. recife; (*mar.*) rizes; *v.t.* (*mar.*) rizar.
reek s. odor fétido; fumo, vapor; *v.i.* fumigar.
reel s. carretel, bobina; *v.t.* enrolar (em carretel); *v.i.* rodar, virar; virar os olhos; cambalear.
re-elect *v.t.* reeleger; **ion** s. reeleição.

re-embark *v.t.* reembarcar.
re-engage *v.t.* contratar de novo; (*mil.*) reencetar, travar de novo (combate); **-ment** *s.* renovação de combate.
re-enlist *v.i.* realistar-se.
re-enter *v.i.* reentrar.
re-establish *v.t.* restaurar, restabelecer.
reeve *v.t.* (*mar.*) passar um cabo, amarrar, gornir.
re-examine *v.t.* rever, reexaminar.
re-export *v.t.* reexportar.
refectory *s.* refeitório.
refer *v.i.* referir, remeter, dirigir; *v.i.* referir-se, aludir; recorrer.
referee *s.* árbitro; *v.t.* arbitrar.
reference *s.* referência; relação; consulta; — **books** livros de consulta.
referendum *s.* referendum.
refine *v.t.* refinar, depurar, purificar; polir; *v.i.* refinar-se; requintar; **-d** *adj.* requintado, distinto; **-ment** *s.* requinte; refinação; **-r** *s.* refinador; **-ry** *s.* refinaria.
reflect *v.t.&i.* refletir, pensar, considerar; (*fis.*) refletir; **-ion** *s.* reflexão; imagem, reflexo; **-ive** *adj.* refletido; **-or** *s.* refletor.
reflexion *s.* reflexão; **reflexive** *adj.* reflexivo.
reflow *v.i.* refluir.
reflux *s.* refluxo.
reform *v.t.* reformar.
reformation *s.* reformação, reforma.
reformatory *s.* reformatório, casa de correção.
reformer *s.* reformador.
refract *v.t.* refratar; **-ory** *adj.* refratário.
refrain *s.* estribilho; *v.i.* refrear-se, abster-se.
refresh *v.t.* refrescar; restaurar; renovar; **-ment** *s.* refresco.
refrigerate *v.t.* refrigerar; **refrigeration** *s.* refrigeração; **refrigerator** *s.* refrigerador, geladeira.
refuge *s.* refúgio; **-e** *s.* refugiado.
refulgent *adj.* refulgente.
refund *v.t.* restituir (dinheiro).
refurnish *v.t.* mobiliar novamente.
refusal *s.* recusa, denegação; direito de opção.
refuse *s.* refugo, escória; sobra, sobejos; *v.t.&i.* recusar, recusar-se.
refute *v.t.* refutar.
regain *v.t.* reganhar; readquirir; reconquistar.
regal *adj.* real, realengo.
regale *v.t.* regalar.
regalia *s.* insígnias reais; regalia.
regard *s.* consideração, respeito; propósito; referência; relação; *v.t.* considerar, respeitar, acatar; **-less** *adj.* sem consideração; indiferente; negligente.
regatta *s.* regata.
regency *s.* regência.
regenerate *v.t.* regenerar; **regeneration** *s.* regeneração.
regent *s.&adj.* regente.
regicide *s.* regicida; regicídio.
regimen *s.* regime; sistema; administração; (*med.*) dieta, regime; (*gram.*) regência.
regiment *s.* regimento; **-al** *adj.* regimental.
region *s.* região; **-al** *adj.* regional.
register *s.* registo, livro de assentamentos; lista, protocolo; registador; indicador, contador; registo (de gás, luz, etc.); *v.t.* registar, inscrever, matricular, protocolar; manifestar, indicar; — **a letter**

registar uma carta; *v.i.* registar-se, inscrever-se, matricular-se.
registered *s.* registado; *adj.* registado, inscrito.
registrar *s.* registador, arquivista.
regress *s.* regresso; retrocesso; *v.i.* regressar; retrogradar.
regret *s.* pena, pesar; *v.t.* sentir, ter pesar, lamentar; **-ful** *adj.* pesaroso; **my -s** minhas desculpas.
regular *adj.* regular; assíduo; **-ity** *s.* regularidade; **-ize** *v.t.* regularizar.
regulate *v.t.* regular; regulamentar.
regulation *s.* regulamentação; regulamento; **regulator** *s.* regulador.
rehabilitate *v.t.* rehabilitar.
rehearsal *s.* ensaio; **rehearse** *v.t.* ensaiar, repetir.
reign *s.* reino; *v.i.* reinar; **-ing** *adj.* reinante.
reimburse *v.t.* reembolsar.
reimport *v.t.* reimportar.
reimpose *v.t.* reimpor.
rein *s.* rédea; govêrno.
reindeer *s.* rena, rangífer.
reinforce *v.t.* reforçar; **-ment** *s.* refôrço.
reinstate *v.t.* reintegrar, restabelecer.
reinsure *v.t.* ressegurar.
reinvest *v.t.* tornar a empregar (o capital).
reinvigorate *v.t.* revigorar.
reissue *s.* reedição.
reiterate *v.t.* reiterar.
reject *v.t.* rejeitar; recusar; **-ion** *s.* rejeição.
rejoice *v.t.* regozijar; *v.i.* regozijar-se; **rejoicing** *s.* regozijo.
rejoin *v.t.&i.* voltar à companhia de, tornar a fazer parte; reunir-se; (*for.*) replicar; treplicar; **-der** *s.* resposta; (*for.*) réplica; tréplica.
rejuvenate *v.t.* rejuvenescer.
rekindle *v.t.* reacender.
relapse *s.* (*med.*) recaída; (*dir.*) recidiva, reincidência; *v.i.* recair, reincidir.
relate *v.t.* relatar, narrar; relacionar; aparentar; *v.i.* dizer respeito, referir-se; concernir; **-d** *adj.* aparentado; concernente, relativo; relatado, dito.
relation *s.* relação, relatório; parente, parentesco; relação, conexão; **-ship** *s.* parentesco.
relative *adj.* relativo; *s.* parente.
relax *v.t.* relaxar, afrouxar, soltar; *v.i.* espairecer; **-ation** *s.* afrouxamento; soltura (de preso); folga, descanso, recreio.
relay *s.* posta; muda (de cavalos, cães, etc.); *v.t.* mudar.
release *s.* soltura, libertação; quitação; cessão (de direito); *v.t.* soltar, libertar, desprender; relevar; pôr em circulação, dar ao público (*dir.*) desistir de.
relegate *v.t.* relegar.
relent *v.i.* abrandar-se; ceder, diminuir; **-less** *adj.* implacável.
relet *v.t.* realugar.
relevant *adj.* pertinente.
reliability *s.* segurança, confiança; **reliable** *adj.* seguro, digno de confiança; **reliance** *s.* confiança, segurança.
relic *s.* relíquia; (*plural*) ruinas; resíduo.
relict *s.* viúva.
relief *s.* relêvo; alívio; socorro; assistência; (*for.*) compensação que o herdeiro de um arrendatário pagava ao senhor feudal para continuar com o arrendamento.
relieve *v.t.* aliviar; socorrer, assistir; realçar; (*mil.*) render; (*for.*) reparar, desagravar.

relight *v.t.* reacender.
religion *s.* religião; **religious** *adj.* religioso; **religiousness** *s.* religiosidade.
relinquish *v.t.* abandonar.
reliquary *s.* relicário.
relish *s.* gôsto, sabor; tempêro; *v.t.* saborear.
reluctance *s.* relutância, repugnância.
reluctantly *adv.* relutantemente, a contra-gôsto.
rely *v.i.* contar (com), fiar-se (em); ter confiança.
remain *v.i.* ficar, permanecer.
remainder *s.* resto, restante; saldo; (*mat.*) resto; *adj.* restante.
remains *s.* restos, vestígios; despojos.
remake *v.t.* refazer.
remand *v.t.* reenviar, fazer voltar; (*for.*) fazer (um preso) voltar para a prisão.
remark *s.* observação; nota; *v.t.&i.* fazer uma observação; advertir; notar.
remarkable *adj.* notável.
remedy *s.* remédio; (*for.*) recurso; *v.t.* remediar.
remember *v.t.* lembrar-se de, recordar-se de; lembrar.
remembrance *s.* lembrança; memória.
remind *v.t.* lembrar, recordar; fazer lembrar; *er *s.* memento.
reminiscence *s.* reminiscência.
remiss *adj.* negligente; *ion *s.* remissão; diminuição.
remit *v.t.* remeter, enviar; remitir; *tance *s.* remessa.
remnant *s.* remanescente; restos.
remodel *v.t.* remodelar, refundir.
remonstrance *s.* protesto, reprovação, impugnação; repreensão, admoestação.
remonstrate *v.i.* protestar, apresentar razões contra; **to** — **with** fazer observações a, repreender.
remorse *s.* remorso; *less *adj.* insensível, sem remorsos.
remote *adj.* remoto, afastado; *ness *s.* afastamento, distância.
remount *s.* (*mil.*) remonta; *v.t.* remontar.
removable *adj.* removível.
removal *s.* afastamento; remoção; mudança; destituição.
remove *v.t.* afastar, remover; suprimir; mudar; destituir; *v.i.* mudar-se.
remunerate *v.t.* remunerar, retribuir; **remuneration** *s.* remuneração.
renaissance *s.* renascimento, renascença.
rename *v.t.* dar outro nome.
rend *v.t.* rasgar, despedaçar; destruir; arrancar.
render *v.t.&i.* dar; render-se; render; prestar; pagar, restituir, devolver; traduzir; recompensar.
rendering *s.* explicação, interpretação; tradução, versão.
renegade *s.* renegado.
renew *v.t.* renovar; *al *s.* renovamento, renovação.
rennet *s.* espécie de maçã; coalheira, coalho.
renounce *v.t.&i.* renunciar; repudiar, abjurar.
renovate *v.t.* renovar.
renown *s.* renome; *ed *adj.* famoso.
rent *s.* aluguel, arrendamento; *v.t.* alugar, arrendar.
rent *s.* rasgão, rotura.; cisão.
rental *s.* aluguel, valor locativo; *adj.* locativo.
renter *s.* locatário.
renunciation *s.* repúdio; renunciação, renúncia.

reopen *v.t.* reabrir.
reopening *s.* reabertura.
reorganize *v.t.* reorganizar.
rep, repp *s.* tecido encordoado de lã ou sêda.
repack *v.t.* refazer as malas; acondicionar de novo.
repair *s.* reparo; *v.t.* reparar, consertar, restaurar; *able *adj.* reparável; **reparation** *s.* reparação.
repartee *s.* réplica, aparte.
repast *s.* refeição, repasto.
repatriate *v.t.* repatriar.
repay *v.t.* restituir, reembolsar; retribuir.
repeal *s.* revogação, abrogação; rescisão; *v.t.* anular, abolir; revogar.
repeat *v.t.* repetir; *edly *adv.* repetidamente.
repel *v.t.* repelir.
repellent *adj.* repelente.
repent *v.i.* arrepender-se; *ance *s.* arrependimento.
repeople *v.t.* repovoar.
repercussion *s.* repercussão.
repertory *s.* repertório.
repetend *s.* (*mat.*) período.
repetition *s.* repetição.
repine *v.i.* amofinar-se.
replace *v.t.* recolocar; substituir; pôr no lugar.
replant *v.t.* replantar.
replay *v.t.* representar outra vez.
replenish *v.t.* encher; **replete** *adj.* cheio; **repletion** *s.* plenitude, repleção.
replica *s.* réplica; reprodução.
reply *s.* resposta; — **paid** com resposta paga; *v.t.&i.* responder.
report *s.* relatório, relato, informação; processo; fama, reputação; rumor, boato; detonação (arma de fogo); *v.t.* relatar, expôr; informar acêrca de; propalar; denunciar, apresentar queixa de; apresentar-se.
reporter *s.* repórter, jornalista, noticiarista.
reporting *s.* reportagem.
repose *s.* repouso; *v.i.* repousar.
repository *s.* repositório; depósito; armazém.
repossess *v.t.* recuperar.
reprehend *v.t.* repreender, censurar; **reprehensible** *adj.* repreensível.
represent *v.t.* representar; *ation *s.* representação; *ative *adj.* representativo; *s.* representante.
repress *v.t.* reprimir; *ion *s.* repressão; (*psic.*) recalque; *ed *adj.* suprimido; (*psic.*) recalcado.
reprieve *s.* (*for.*) suspensão temporária da aplicação de uma pena, *v.t.* suspender temporàriamente a aplicação de uma pena.
reprimand *s.* reprimenda, admoestação, censura; *v.t.* repreender, censurar.
reprint *s.* reimpressão; *v.t.* reimprimir.
reprisal *s.* represália.
reproach *s.* censura, exprobação; *v.t.* censurar, exprobar.
reprobate *s.&adj.* réprobo, malvado; patife; *v.t.* reprovar, condenar.
reprobation *s.* reprovação.
reproduce *v.t.* reproduzir; **reproduction** *s.* reprodução.
reproof *s.* censura, reprimenda.
reprove *v.t.* repreender, censurar; reprovar.
reptile *s.* réptil.
republic *s.* república; *an *adj.&s.* republicano.

republish v.t. republicar.
repudiate v.t. repudiar.
repugnance s. repugnância; repugnant adj. repugnante.
repulse s. repulsa; v.t. repelir, repulsar.
repulsion s. repulsão; repulsive adj. repulsivo.
repurchase v.t. comprar novamente.
reputable adj. honroso; lícito.
reputation s. reputação, renome, fama; reputed adj. suposto, tido por.
request s. pedido; súplica; petição, solicitação; v.t. pedir, rogar, suplicar; requerer.
requiem s. missa de sétimo dia ou de corpo presente, missa de réquiem.
require v.t. requerer; exigir; ter necessidade; =ment s. exigência, requisito.
requisite s. requisito; adj. necessário, indispensável.
requisition s. requisição; v.t. requisitar.
requital s. recompensa, paga, satisfação; compensação; requite v.t. recompensar, pagar.
resale s. venda em segunda mão.
rescind v.t. rescindir; rescission s. rescisão.
rescript s. rescrito.
rescue s. socorro; libertação, resgate; (dir.) ação de tirar das mãos da justiça por violência; v.t. socorrer, salvar, libertar.
research s. pesquisa, busca, investigação.
reseat v.t. sentar novamente; colocar novos assentos (um teatro, etc.).
resemblance s. semelhança, parecença; resemble v.t. parecer-se com, assemelhar-se a.
resent v.t. ressentir-se com; melindrar-se com; ofender-se com; =ment s. ressentimento, mágoa.
reservation s. reservação, reserva; restrição mental; locação.
reserve s. reserva, provisão; cautela; v.t. reservar; =d adj. reservado.
reservist s. reservista.
reservoir s. reservatório.
reset s. nova montagem; nova disposição; v.t. recompor.
reship v.t. reembarcar; =ment s. reembarque.
reside v.i. residir, morar; =nce s. residência; =nt s. residente.
residuary legatee herdeiro universal.
residue s. resíduo; remanescente.
resign v.t. resignar, renunciar; =ation s. renúncia, demissão; resignação.
resilient adj. elástico.
resin s. resina; =ous adj. resinoso.
resist v.t.&i. resistir; =ance s. resistência.
resole v.t. pôr sola nova.
resolute adj. resoluto, determinado; resolution s. resolução, determinação, deliberação; propósito.
resolve v.t. resolver.
resonance s. ressonância; resonant adj. ressonante.
resort s. recurso; refúgio; ponto de reunião; lugar de frequência pública; summer — estação de veraneio.
resound v.i. ressoar, retinir.
resource s. recurso, expediente; (pl.) meios, recursos (pecuniários ou naturais).
respect s. respeito; relação; referência; ponto de vista; aspecto; (plural) cumprimentos, respeitos; v.t. respeitar; =able adj. respeitável; =ful adj. respeitoso; =ing prep. relativamente a; =ive adj. relativo.

respiration s. respiração; respirator s. respirador.
respite s. adiamento, protelação; pausa; suspensão; v.t. adiar; conceder um prazo a; suspender.
resplendent adj. resplendente.
respond v.i. responder; reagir; corresponder; ajustar-se.
response s. resposta; reação.
responsibility s. responsabilidade.
responsible adj. responsável.
responsive adj. sensível, que reage favoràvelmente.
rest s. repouso; (mús.) pausa; v.i. repousar, descansar; apoiar-se.
restate v.t. reafirmar.
restaurant s. restaurante.
restful adj. repousante; resting place lugar de repouso; cemitério; patamar.
restitution s. restituição.
restive adj. obstinado; inquieto, impaciente.
restless adj. inquieto, agitado; turbulento; sem descanso.
restock v.t. reabastecer.
restoration s. restauração; restabelecimento; restituição; restorative adj. restaurador; restore v.t. restaurar; renovar; restituir; restabelecer.
restrain v.t. restringir, limitar; comprimir; restraint s. constrangimento; coerção; sujeição; limitação.
restrict v.t. restringir, limitar; =ion s. restrição.
restring v.t. reencordoar.
result s. resultado; consequência; v.i. resultar.
resume v.t. reassumir; recobrar; reatar (o fio das idéias, de um discurso, etc.); v.i. recomeçar.
resumption s. reassunção; recôbro.
resurrection s. ressurreição.
resurvey s. revisão; novo exame, nova perícia.
resuscitate v.t. ressuscitar.
retail s. varejo (comércio).
retain v.t. reter; guardar, conservar.
retake v.t. retomar.
retaliate v.t. retaliar, revidar.
retaliation s. represália, retaliação.
retard v.t. retardar.
retch v.i. ter náuseas, esforçar-se para vomitar.
retention s. retenção.
retentive adj. tenaz, fiel; retentivo.
reticence s. reticência.
reticle, reticule s. retículo; bolsa de senhora.
retina s. retina.
retinue s. séquito, cortejo.
retire v.t. retirar da circulação; (mil.) reformar; v.i. aposentar-se; retirar-se; recuar; =d adj. reformado, aposentado.
retort s. réplica, aparte; (quím.) retorta; v.t.&i. retorquir, replicar.
retouch v.t. retocar.
retrace v.t. retraçar; voltar pelo mesmo caminho, retroceder.
retract v.i. retratar-se.
retreat s. retiro; refúgio, asilo; (mil.) retirada; v.i. retirar-se, recuar.
retrench v.t. reduzir, diminuir; v.i. cortar despesas, economizar; (mil.) cavar segunda linha de trincheiras.
retribution s. retribuição; castigo merecido.
retrieve v.t. recuperar; restaurar, remediar.
retroactive adj. retroativo.

retrograde *adj.* retrógrado.
retrospect *s.* retrospecto; =ive *adj.* retrospectivo; (*dir.*) retroativo.
return *s.* volta, regresso; restituição; reembôlso; remessa; declaração; estatística; remuneração; relatório; — ticket bilhete de volta; *v.t.&i.* devolver, restituir; voltar, regressar; reembolsar; declarar; eleger; =able *adj.* restituível.
reunion *s.* reunião; reunite *v.t.* reunir; *v.i.* reunir-se.
reveal *v.t.* revelar.
revel *s.* banquete, festança; *v.i.* folgar, divertir-se (desregradamente).
revelation *s.* revelação.
reveller *s.* estróina; revelry *s.* festança.
revenge *s.* vingança; desforra; =ful *adj.* vindicativo, vingativo.
revenue *s.* renda, rendimento; receita; rendas públicas; — stamp sêlo fiscal, estampilha.
reverberate *v.t.* reverberar.
revere *v.t.* reverenciar, venerar; =nce *s.* reverência; =nd *s.* reverendo; reverent *adj.* reverente; reverential *adj.* reverencial.
reverie *s.* sonho, devaneio.
reversal *s.* reversão; inversão; (*for.*) revocação.
reverse *s.* reverso, contrário; inverso; contratempo, revés; *v.t.* inverter; virar pelo avêsso; (*for.*) reformar (uma sentença).
reversion *s.* reversão.
revert *v.i.* reverter.
revet *v.t.* (*eng.&mil.*) revestir; =ment *s.* (*eng.&mil.*) revestimento.
revictual *v.t.*=reabastecer.
review *s.* revista; revisão; crítica literária; *v.t.* rever; (*mil.*) passar revista a; revision *s.* revisão.
revival *s.* renascimento, restauração; restabelecimento; revive *v.t.* reanimar; despertar.
revoke *v.t.* revogar; *v.i.* (*jôgo*) renunciar; *s.* (*jôgo*) renúncia.
revolt *s.* revolta, levante; *v.i.* revoltar-se; =ing *adj.* revoltante.
revolution *s.* revolução; =ary *s.* revolucionário; =ize *v.t.* revolucionar.
revolve *v.t.&i.* rodar, girar, girar; meditar, refletir sôbre.
revolver *s.* revólver.
revue *s.* revista (teatral).
revulsion *s.* revulsão.
reward *s.* recompensa; *v.t.* recompensar.
rewrite *v.t.* reescrever.
rhapsody *s.* rapsódia.
rhetoric *s.* retórica; =al *adj.* oratório, retórico.
rheumatic *s.* reumático; rheumatism *s.* reumatismo.
rhinoceros *s.* rinoceronte.
rhododendron *s.* rododendro.
rhomb *s.* losango, rombo.
rhubarb *s.* ruibarbo.
rhyme *s.* rima; *v.t.&i.* rimar.
rhythm *s.* ritmo, cadência; =ical *adj.* rítmico.
rib *s.* costela; nervura.
ribald *adj.* obceno, licencioso.
ribbon *s.* fita.
rice *s.* arroz.
rich *adj.* rico; =ness *s.* riqueza.
rick *s.* monte, pilha.
rickets *s.* raquitismo; rickety *adj.* raquítico.
ricochet *s.* ricochete.
rid *v.t.* desembaraçar; livrar; to get — of

livrar-se de; =dance *s.* desembaraço, desestôrvo, libertação.
riddle *s.* enigma, charada; joeira, crivo; *v.t.* joeirar, passar por crivo; crivar, furar; resolver, decifrar (charadas).
ride *s.* passeio (a cavalo, de carro, automóvel, etc.); *v.i.* passear (a cavalo, de carro, etc.); — sidesaddle montar à amazona; =r *s.* cavaleiro; o que vai ou passeia de carro, automóvel, etc.; (*parl.*) cauda, aditamento.
ridge *s.* espinhaço; cumiada; leira, margem (feita pelo arado); *v.t.* leirar; formar arestas.
ridicule *s.* ridículo; *v.t.* ridicularizar; ridiculous *adj.* ridículo; ridiculousness *s.* ridículo.
riding *s.* equitação; cavalgada, manejo; passeio (a cavalo, automóvel, carro, etc.); — school escola de equitação; — whip chicote.
rife *adj.* abundante, numeroso; corrente, prevalecente.
rifle *s.* rifle; fuzil; *v.t.* roubar, espoliar; estriar, raiar (arma de fogo).
rift *s.* fenda, greta, brecha; *v.t.* fender, rachar.
rig *v.t.* ataviar, vestir; (*mar.*) aparelhar, equipar; =ging *s.* (*mar.*) cordoalha, escotas.
right *adj.* direito; correto; bom; justo; verdadeiro; *adv.* retamente, justamente; bem; imediatamente; no mesmo instante; *s.* direito; justiça; retidão; direita; razão; *v.t.* endireitar, ajustar; fazer justiça; to be — estar com a razão; —=angled retângulo, retangular; — away imediatamente; — down sem rodeios; on the — à direita; — reverend reverendíssimo.
righteous *adj.* virtuoso; justo; =ly *adv.* virtuosamente, com justiça; =ness *s.* justiça.
rightful *adj.* legítimo; rightly *adv.* justamente; bem.
rigid *adj.* rígido; =ity *s.* rigidez.
rigmarole *s.* série de dizeres confusos.
rigor mortis rigidez cadavérica.
rigor, rigour *s.* rigor; =ous *adj.* rigoroso; =ously *adv.* rigorosamente; =ism *s.* rigorismo.
rill *s.* riacho.
rim *s.* orla, margem, borda; aro; — of the belly peritôneo.
rime *s.* geada.
rind *s.* casca; crosta.
rinderpest *s.* peste bovina.
ring *s.* anel, argola; círculo; arco; aro; circo, arena, liça; toque de campainha; som metálico; disposição circular; olheiras; *v.t.&i.* mover-se em círculo ou em espiral; formar círculo; tocar campainha; repicar (sinos); tinir; soar.
ringlet *s.* cacho (de cabelo); pequeno círculo.
rink *s.* pista.
rinse *v.t.* enxaguar.
riot *s.* tumulto; motim; desordem; excesso; orgia; *v.i.* tomar parte em motins; =er *s.* desordeiro, amotinador; =ous *adj.* tumultuoso.
rip *s.* laceração; rasgão; *v.t.* rasgar, lacerar.
riparian *adj.* ribeirinho.
ripe *adj.* maduro; =n *v.t.&i.* amadurecer; =ness *s.* maturidade; =ning *s.* maturação, amadurecimento.
riposte *s.* resposta rápida; (*esg.*) resposta, bote.

ripple s. ruga; v.t.&i. enrugar.
rise s. elevação; subida; ascenção; rampa;
crescimento; princípio, origem, causa;
nascente; nascimento; aumento; v.i.
levantar-se, ascender, subir, elevar-se;
nascer (plantas); sublevar-se; surgir,
aparecer; encarecer; ressuscitar; **rising**
s. levante; levantar; alvorecer; ascensão; **rising sun** sol levante; **rising
tide** maré montante.
risk s. risco, perigo; v.t. arriscar; **-y** adj.
arriscado.
rite s. rito; **ritual** s. ritual.
rival s. rival, êmulo; v.t.&i. rivalizar,
emular.
rivalry s. rivalidade.
rive v.t. rachar, fender; v.i. fender-se,
rachar-se.
river s. rio; **-side** margem do rio.
rivet s. rebite; v.t. rebitar.
rivulet s. riacho.
road s. caminho; estrada; via; **-ster** s.
automóvel de excursão.
roam v.i. vagar, errar.
roan adj. ruão (cavalo).
roar v.i. rugir, bramir, mugir, berrar.
roast v.t.&i. assar, torrar, tostar.
rob v.t. roubar; **-ber** s. ladrão; **-bery** s.
roubo.
robe s. toga, túnica; vestido.
robin s. pintarroxo.
robust adj. robusto, vigoroso.
rock s. rocha, rochedo, penhasco, penha;
roca; roque (no jôgo de xadrez);
v.t.&i. balançar; embalar; rocar (no
jôgo de xadrez); balançar-se; —
crystal cristal de rocha; **-er** s. embalador; balanço, cadeira de balanço,
berço movediço.
rocket s. foguete.
rocking s. balanço; — **chair** cadeira de
balanço.
rocky adj. rochoso.
rococo s.&adj. rococó.
rod s. vara, vêrga; (maq.) biéla; medida de
comprimento equiv. a 5,029 m; **fishing**
— caniço de pesca.
rodent s. roedor.
roe s. ova de peixe; — **deer** corça.
rogations s. súplicas.
rogue s. vagabundo; velhaco.
roguery s. vagabundagem; velhacaria,
patifaria.
roguish adj. velhaco.
roister v.i. fanfarronar, bravatear.
roll s. rôlo, cilindro; embrulho, pacote;
pãozinho; rol, lista; quadro; matrícula,
registo; — **call** chamada (nominal); —
of the drum rufar do tambor; v.t.&i.
rolar, rodar; enrolar; passar o rôlo;
(met.) laminar; **-ed gold** ouro laminado,
folheado; **-er** s. rôlo, cilindro; rolete; **-er
skates** patins de roda.
rollick v.i. fazer travessuras.
rolling s. rotação, giro; rolamento; (met.)
laminagem; (mar.) balanço, jôgo do
navio; adj. rolante; rodante; ondulante.
Roman adj.&s. romano; —. **nose** nariz
aquilino.
romance s. idílio, romance.
romantic adj. romântico.
romp s. jôgo barulhento; menina com
modos de menino; v.i. brincar barulhentamente.
rood s. cruz, crucifixo.
roof s. telhado; v.t. cobrir.
rook s. espécie de corvo europeu; trapaceiro; tôrre (jôgo de xadrez); v.t.&i.
enganar, fraudar, trapacear.

room s. quarto, sala, salão; lugar, espaço;
-y adj. espaçoso.
roost s. poleiro; v.i. empoleirar-se.
rooster s. galo.
root s. raiz; (mús.) nota fundamental; v.i.
enraizar; lançar raizes; v.t. implantar;
— **out** arrancar, erradicar.
rope s. corda, cordel, cabo, driça; fio (de
contas); v.t. amarrar com corda.
rosary s. rosário; roseiral.
rose s. rosa; **-bud** botão de rosa; **-bush**
roseira.
roseate adj. rosado, róseo.
rosemary s. rosmaninho.
rosery s. roseiral.
rosette s. roseta.
rosin s. colofônia, resina; **-y** adj. resinoso.
rot s. putrefação; cárie; v.i. apodrecer,
cariar.
rota s. rol, lista; rota.
rotate v.t.&i. girar, rodar; rolar; **rotary**
adj. rotativo, giratório; **rotation** s.
rotação, giro; turno, alternação, revezamento.
rote s. rotina.
rotten adj. podre, pútrido; corrupto.
rottenness s. podridão; cárie; putrefação.
rotund adj. redondo, arredondado; pomposo.
rotunda s. rotunda.
rotundity s. rotundidade.
rouge s. vermelho.
rough adj. grosso, áspero; grosseiro,
brusco; bruto; brutal; rugoso; agitado
(mar); v.t. tornar áspero; **-ness** s.
aspereza; rudeza, grosseria.
round adj. redondo; s. círculo; roda;
volta; circuito; partida; prep. ao redór
de, em tôrno de; adv. à roda; circularmente; v.t. arredondar; — **trip** ida e
volta; — **shouldered** curvado; **-about**
adj. indireto, vago; envolvente; **-elay**
s. rondo; dansa de roda; **-ish** adj. arredondado; **-ness** s. redondeza; **-sman**
s. ronda (soldado).
rouse v.t. despertar, excitar.
rout s. derrota, debandada; v.t. derrotar,
desbaratar, destroçar.
route s. caminho, via, rota.
routine s. rotina.
rove v.i. errar, vagar, vagabundar; **-r** s.
vagabundo; pirata.
row v.t.&i. conduzir remando; remar,
vogar; s. fileira; barulho, rixa.
rowdy adj. barulhento, turbulento.
rowel s. roseta (de espora).
rower s. remador; **rowing** s. esporte de
remo.
royal adj. real; **-ist** adj. realista.
royalty s. direitos autorais; realeza,
soberania.
rub v.t.&i. esfregar; friccionar; raspar; s.
fricção; — **out** desmanchar, raspar;
-ber borracha; galocha.
rubbish s. refugo, entulho, lixo, imundície; bobagens, tolices.
rubble s. cascalho; **-work** alvenaria de
pedra bruta.
rubicund adj. rubicundo.
rubric s. rubrica, título.
ruby s. rubí.
ruck s. multidão (indistinta); ruga;
prega; v.t.&i. enrugar, preguear.
rucksack s. saco de alpinista, mochila.
rudder s. leme.
ruddy adj. corado.
rude adj. rude, grosseiro, malcriado; **-ness**
s. grosseria, indelicadeza.

rudiment s. rudimento; **-ary** adj. rudimentar.
rue s. contrariedade; decepção; v.i. arrepender-se, ter remorsos; **-ful** adj. triste, pesaroso.
ruff s. (cost.) golilha; v.t.&i. (j. de cartas) cortar, trunfar.
ruffian s. bandido: adj. brutal.
ruffle s. (cost.) fôfo, franzido; reboliço; v.t. (cost.) fazer tufos em, franzir; afofar (o cabelo); alvoroçar.
rug s. tapête; manta de viagem.
rugged adj. áspero, tôsco; inculto; grosseiro, brutal; **-ness** s. aspereza, brutalidade.
ruin s. ruina, perdição; (pl.) ruinas; v.t.&i. arruinar, perder; destruir; **-ous** adj. ruinoso.
rule s. regra; dominação; govêrno, mando, poder; régua; v.t. regrar; dominar, governar, reinar; reger; **-r** s. governante; régua; **ruling** adj. dominante.
rum s. rum.
rumble v.i. estrondear, roncar, murmurar.
ruminant s.&adj. ruminante; **ruminate** v.i.&t. ruminar.
rummage v.t.&i. revolver; explorar, esquadrinhar.
rumor, rumour s. rumor; boato.
rump s. anca; garupa; cauda.
rumple v.t. amarrotar; enrugar.
run s. corrida; marcha; curso, percurso, trajeto; seguimento, sequência; fileira, fila, série; encosta, ladeira; corrente (de água); v.i. correr; afluir; circular; v.t. fazer correr; dirigir; correr; — **away** fugir; — **into** encontrar-se casualmente com alguém; — **out** of ficar sem; **-about** s. vagabundo; **-away** s. fugitivo.
runner s. corredor; mensageiro; correio; agente de polícia; passadeira (tapête); peça ou parte giratória; tránsfuga; (bot.) rebento.
running s. carreira, corrida, curso; adj. contínuo; sucessivo; corrente; fluente; **two days** — dois dias seguidos.
rupee s. rupia.
rupture s. ruptura; hérnia; v.t. romper, arrebentar.
rural adj. rural.
ruse s. ardil, astúcia.
rush s. correria; investida; acometida; pressa; precipitação; torrente; tropel; junco; v.t.&i. lançar-se, precipitar-se; investir, acometer; empurrar; acelerar; precipitar; adj. urgente.
rusk s. rosca, sequilho; pão torrado; farinha de rosca.
russet adj. pardo, russo; s. variedade de maçã.
rust s. ferrugem; v.t.&i. enferrujar; enferrujar-se.
rustic adj. rústico; **-ity** s. rusticidade.
rustless adj. inoxidável.
rustle v.i. ruflar, sussurrar; fazer um ruído semelhante ao roçar de seda.
rusty adj. enferrujado.
rut s. carril, sulco; (fig.) hábito arraigado, rotina; cio; v.i. estar no cio.
ruth s. compaixão.
ruthless adj. cruel, desapiedado; **-ly** adv. cruelmente, desapiedadamente.
rutilant adj. rutilante.
rye s. centeio.

S

S letra do alfabeto.
sabbath s. dia de descanso (sábado para os judeus e domingo para a maioria dos cristãos).
saber s. sabre; v.t. acutilar; golpear com o sabre.
sable s. zibelina, marta; pele de marta.
sabre s. sabre.
sac s. saco, bolsa.
saccharin, saccharine s. sacarina.
sacerdotal adj. sacerdotal.
sachet s. perfumador (saquinho).
sack s. saco; saque; v.t. ensacar; saquear.
sacrament s. sacramento; **-al** adj. sacramental.
sacred adj. sagrado.
sacrifice s. sacrifício; v.t.&i. sacrificar.
sacrilege s. sacrilégio; **sacrilegious** adj. sacrílego.
sacristy s. sacristia.
sacrosanct adj. sacrossanto.
sad adj. triste, doloroso; **-den** v.t. entristecer, contristar.
saddle s. sela, selim; v.t. selar.
saddler s. seleiro; **-y** s. selaria.
sadly adv. tristemente.
sadness s. tristeza.
safe adj. salvo; seguro; fora de perigo; — **and sound** são e salvo; s. cofre; **-ly** adv. com segurança, a salvo; **-ty** s. segurança.
saffron s. açafrão.
sag v.i. vergar, inclinar; decair; ceder.
sagacious adj. sagaz.
sagacity s. sagacidade.

sage s. sábio, filósofo; (bot.) salva; adj. sábio, prudente.
sago s. sagú.
said p.p. do verbo say; (for.) dito.
sail s. vela, embaração à vela; viagem, excursão marítima; v.i. fazer-se à vela; ir por mar, viajar, navegar; sair, partir; **-er** s. veleiro; **-ing** s. navegação.
sailor s. marinheiro.
sainfoin s. sanfeno.
saint adj. santo; s. santo; v.t. canonizar; **-ed** adj. canonizado; sagrado, santo.
saintliness s. santidade.
sake s. causa, motivo, fim, objetivo, razão; amor, respeito, consideração.
sal s. (quím.&farm.) sal.
salaam s. salamaleque.
salable adj. vendável, vendível.
salacious adj. lúbrico, lascivo.
salad s. salada.
salamander s. salamandra.
salaried adj. assalariado.
salary s. salário, ordenado.
sale s. venda; saldo, liquidação.
salesman s. vendedor; **saleswoman** s. vendedora.
salesmanship s. arte de vender.
Salic law lei sálica.
salient adj. saliente.
saline adj. salino.
saliva s. saliva; **-te** v.i. salivar.
sallow adj. amarelado.
sally s. (mil.) saída, investida; passeio, excursão; dito espirituoso.
salmon s. salmão.

saloon s. salão; bar.
salt s. sal; v.t. salgar; =ing s. salga, salgadura.
saltpetre s. salitre, nitro.
salty adj. salgado, salobre.
salubrious adj. salubre.
salutary adj. salutar.
salutation s. saudação, cumprimento.
salute s. cumprimento, saudação; continência; v.t.&i. cumprimentar, saudar; fazer continência.
salvage s. salvamento; salvados; v.t. salvar.
salvation s. salvação.
salve s. unguento, pomada; v.t. salvar, socorrer, remediar.
salver s. bandeja, salva.
salvo s. salva (de artilharia).
salvor s. salvador.
same adj.&pron. mesmo, igual; =ness s. identidade; monotonia.
sample s. amostra; v.t. provar, experimentar.
sanatorium s. sanatório.
sanctify v.t. santificar.
sanctimonious adj. beato, devoto.
sanction s. sanção; v.t. sancionar; consagrar, ratificar.
sanctity s. santidade.
sanctuary s. santuário.
sanctum s. santuário; gabinete reservado.
sand s. areia; praia; v.t. cobrir de areia, arear.
sandal s. sandália.
sandwich s. sanduíche.
sandy adj. arenoso.
sane adj. são, sadio (de espírito), racional, lúcido.
sanguinary adj. sanguinário.
sanguine adj. sanguíneo; otimista, bem humorado, ardente.
sanitary adj. sanitário; higiênico.
sanitate v.t. sanear.
sanitation s. saneamento; higiene.
sanity s. razão; bom senso.
sap s. seiva; (mil.) sapa; v.i. sapar; v.t. solapar; =per s. sapador.
sapphire s. safira.
sappy adj. cheio de seiva; tôlo.
sarcasm s. sarcasmo.
sarcastic adj. sarcástico.
sarcophagus s. sarcófago.
sardine s. sardinha.
sardonic adj. sardônico.
sargasso s. sargaço.
sarsaparilla s. salsaparrilha.
sarsenet, sarcenet s. (tec.) espécie de tafetá.
sash s. cinto, cinturão; faixa; caixilho de janela.
Satan s. Satanaz; =ic adj. satânico.
satchel s. maleta, sacola; pasta.
sate v.t. fartar, saciar.
sateen s. setineta.
satellite s. satélite.
satiate v.t. saciar, fartar.
satiety s. saciedade.
satin s. setim; =y adj. assetinado.
satire s. sátira; **satiric, satirical** adj. satírico; **satirist** s. autor satírico; **satirize** v.t. satirizar.
satisfaction s. satisfação; reparação, desagravo.
satisfactorily adv. satisfatòriamente.
satisfactory adj. satisfatório; suficiente.
satisfy v.t. satisfazer; contentar; **satisfied** adj. satisfeito.
satrap s. sátrapa.

saturate v.t. saturar.
Saturday s. sábado.
saturnalia s. saturnais.
saturnine adj. saturnino; melancólico.
satyr s. sátiro.
sauce s. môlho; (pop.) impertinência; =r s. pires, molheira; **saucy** adj. impertinente, atrevido.
sauerkraut s. chucrute.
saunter v.i. saracotear; =ing s. saracoteio.
sausage s. salsicha.
savage adj. selvagem, feroz; s. selvagem; =ry s. selvajaria.
savant s. sábio.
save v.t. salvar; guardar, poupar, economizar; v.i. economizar; prep. salvo, exceto.
saving s. economia, reserva; =s bank caixa econômica.
Saviour (the) o Salvador.
savor, savour s. sabor; =y adj. saboroso.
savory s. (bot.) segurelha.
saw s. serra; provérbio, rifão; v.t. serrar.
sawing s. serradura; **sawyer** s. serrador.
saxifrage s. saxífraga.
Saxon adj. saxão.
saxophone s. saxofone.
say s. fala, discurso, locução; v.t.&i. dizer; falar; **you don't** — **so** impossível! será?; =ing s. dito, fala, discurso; provérbio.
scab s. ronha, sarna; crosta (de ferida).
scabbard s. bainha (de espada).
scabby, scabious adj. sarnoso, escabioso.
scaffold s. cadafalso, patíbulo; andaime.
scald s. queimadura; escaldar, queimar.
scale s. escala; (mús.) gama; prato de balança; balança; escama; v.t. escalar; balancear, pesar; raspar, escamar; v.i. descascar; incrustar-se; ascender em escala.
scallop s. vieira, venera (molusco); (cost.) recorte, festão em forma de concha; v.t. festonar.
scalp s. escalpo; v.t. escalpar.
scalpel s. escalpêlo.
scaly adj. escamoso.
scamp s. velhaco, patife; v.t. executar às pressas e imperfeitamente.
scamper v.i. fugir, abalar; s. fuga.
scan v.t. escrutar, esquadrinhar; escandir, medir (verso).
scandal s. escândalo; infâmia, difamação; =ize v.t. escandalizar; =ous adj. escandaloso.
scansion s. escansão.
scanty adj. exíguo; escasso, insuficiente; mesquinho.
scape s. (bot.) pedúnculo; escapada; —=goat bode expiatório.
scar s. cicatriz; v.t. marcar com cicatriz.
scarab s. escaravelho.
scarce adj. raro, escasso; =ly adv. apenas, com dificuldade, escassamente.
scarcity s. escassez, raridade.
scare v.t. espantar, assustar, amedrontar; s. susto, pânico, pavor; =crow s. espantalho.
scarf s. lenço de pescoço; faixa.
scarify v.t. escarificar.
scarlatina s. escarlatina.
scarlet s.&adj. escarlate.
scarp s. escarpa; declive.
scatheless adj. incólume.
scathing adj. que fere; injurioso.
scatter v.t. dispersar, espalhar; semear.
scavenge v.t. varrer, recolher o lixo; =r s. varredor, lixeiro; animal que se nutre de carniça.

scenario s. resumo escrito do desenvolvimento, cena por cena, de uma obra teatral ou cinematógráfica.

scene s. cena; espetáculo; teatro; =ry s. paisagem; (teat.) cenário; **scenic** adj. cênico.

scent s. olfato; perfume, odor; cheiro, rastro; v.t. cheirar, farejar; perfumar; =ed adj. perfumado.

scepter, sceptre s. cetro.

sceptic adj. céptico; =al adj. céptico; **scepticism** s. cepticismo.

schedule s. cédula; horário, plano, programa; lista, catálogo, quadro; v.t. inventariar, catalogar; incluir numa lista; designar, escalar.

scheme s. esquema, projeto, plano; quadro, combinação; v.t. projetar, maquinar; v.i. formar projetos.

schemer s. traçador de esquemas ou planos.

schism s. chisma, cisma.

schist s. (min.) xisto.

scholar s. estudante; pessoa erudita; pessoa com alta especialização em algum campo do domínio intelectual; sábio; =ly adj. sábio, erudito; =ship s. saber, erudição; bolsa de estudos.

scholastic adj. escolástico.

school s. escola, classe; colégio; universidade; conservatório; —=fellow colega de colégio, condiscípulo; =ing s. instrução.

schooner s. escuna, goleta.

sciatic adj. ciático; =a s. ciática.

science s. ciência; **scientific** adj. científico; **scientist** s. cientista.

scimitar s. cimitarra.

scintillate v.i. cintilar.

scion s. rebento, renôvo, esgalho; descendente.

scissors s. tesouras.

sclerosis s. esclerose.

scoff v.i. caçoar, zombar; =ing s. zombaria.

scold s. pessoa rabugenta, megera; v.i.&t. ralhar, repreender severamente.

scollop V. **scallop**.

sconce s. baluarte; lustre; coberta, abrigo; (pop.) bom senso, juízo.

scoop s. colherão; (mar.) bartedouro; (cir.) cureta; alcatruz; buraco, cavidade; v.t. esvasiar com colherão ou bartedouro; — out cavar.

scooter s. patinete (brinquedo).

scope s. escopo, objeto, intento, alvo; alcance, extensão; campo, espaço ou esfera de ação.

scorch v.t. queimar, chamuscar, tostar; criticar ferinamente; abrasar, destruir.

score s. sinal, risco, corte, incisão; contagem, marcação; vinte, vintena; razão, motivo; (mús.) partitura; (pl.) uma porção, quantidade; v.t. contar assinalando com risco, corte, incisão, etc.; lançar na conta de; atribuir; (mús.) orquestrar; =er s. marcador.

scoria s. escória.

scoring s. contagem; orquestração.

scorn s. desprêzo, desdém; v.t. desprezar, desdenhar; =ful adj. desdenhoso.

scorpion s. escorpião.

scotch s. incisão, corte; calço, escora; v.t. calçar, escorar; cortar superficialmente, ferir.

Scotch adj. escossês; =man s. escossês.

scot-free adj. isento de pagamento.

scoundrel s. canalha; adj. velhaco, baixo.

scour s. saída d'agua; diarréia do gado;

v.t.&i. esfregar, tirar as nódoas; purgar; branquear; afugentar; expelir; lavar em agua corrente.

scourge s. açoite; flagelo; v.t. flagelar; castigar.

scout s. explorador, batedor; vedeta; sentinela avançada; escoteiro; v.i. explorar, abrir caminho; (mil.) fazer um reconhecimento; — at desdenhar, rejeitar com desprezo.

scowl v.i. franzir a testa; tomar um ar zangado; s. carranca.

scrag s. pessoa ou animal descarnado.

scraggy adj. descarnado, escanifrado; áspero.

scramble s. entrevero, disputa (para alcançar alguma coisa); =d eggs ovos mexidos.

scrap s. migalhas, sobras; pedaços, fragmentos; restos; — book álbum de recortes; — iron ferro velho; v.t. desembaraçar-se de; jogar fora.

scrape v.t.&i. raspar; esfregar, arranhar; juntar pouco a pouco; tocar mal um instrumento musical; arrastar os pés.

scraper s. raspador, raspadeira; forreta; **scrapings** s. raspas, economias.

scratch s. arranhão, arranhadura, unhada; v.t. arranhar, unhar; coçar; raspar; esgravatar; rabiscar, fazer garatujas; — out riscar, raspar, fazer rasura.

scrawl s. garatujas, rabiscos, garranchos.

scream s. grito; v.i.&t. gritar.

screech v.i. soltar gritos agudos.

screed s. discurso, arenga; (pop.) fragmento, tira, banda.

screen s. biombo, anteparo; cortina; tela (de projeção); veneziana; abrigo; grade; v.t. abrigar; murar; subtrair, ocultar, encobrir; escudar, proteger; projetar (cinema).

screw s. parafuso; hélice; (pop.) usurário; — driver chave de parafuso; v.t. aparafusar.

scribble v.t.&i. escrever mal e às pressas; **scribbler** s. escrevinhador.

scribe s. escriba; escritor; escrevente.

scrimmage s. contenda, luta confusa.

scrip s. certificado; lista; ação (de banco ou companhia); título.

Scripture s. escritura sagrada, bíblia.

scrofula s. escrófula; **scrofulous** adj. escrofuloso.

scroll s. rôlo (de papel ou pergaminho escrito); voluta.

scrub s. coisa usada e velha; pessoa de estatura diminuta ou sem importância; árvore pequena e de qualidade inferior; animal mestiço, sem tipo definido; adj. inferior; v.t. esfregar, lavar; =bing brush escova de esfregar.

scrunch v.t. apertar, espremer.

scrummage V. **scrimmage**.

scruple s. escrúpulo; medida farmacêutica (1,296 gramas); **scrupulous** adj. escrupuloso.

scrutineer s. escrutador; escrutinador; **scrutinize** v.t. escrutar; escrutinar; **scrutiny** s. exame, escrutínio.

scuffle s. rixa, contenda; bulha, tumulto.

scull s. remo; v.t.&i. propelir (um barco) com remo.

scullery s. copa, lavadouro (de cozinha).

scullion s. ajudante de cozinha.

sculptor s. escultor; **sculptress** s. escultora.

sculpture s. escultura; v.t.&i. esculpir.

scum s. espuma; escumalho; lia, escória; refugo.

scumble s. (pint. e des.) fusão das côres; v.t. fundir, unir as côres.

scurf s. caspa.

scurrilous adj. grosseiro, injurioso, pornográfico.

scurvy s. escorbuto; adj. vil, ruim, desprezível.

scutcheon s. escudo d'armas; — grafting enxêrto de borbulha.

scuttle s. balde (de carvão); carreira; (mar.) escotilha; v.t. afundar, pôr a pique (abrindo buracos, as escotilhas, etc.); v.i. escapar, fugir.

scythe s. foice, segadeira.

sea s. mar; — board litoral; — coast costa marítima; —•side resort estação balneária; •weed alga marinha.

seal s. sêlo, sinete; timbre; (zool.) foca; v.t. selar, timbrar, lacrar; confirmar; obturar, tapar.

seam s. costura; (cir.) sutura; (geol.) camada, jazida; v.t. costurar, suturar; •less adj. sem costuras; •stress s. costureira.

séance s. sessão; sessão de espiritismo.

sear adj. sêco, murcho, tostado; v.t. queimar, cauterizar.

search s. procura, pesquisa; (dir.) perquisição; v.t. procurar, escrutar; •er s. pesquisador; •ing adj. penetrante, escrutador.

season s. estação, tempo; v.t. temperar, acondimentar; secar (a madeira); imbuir, persuadir; amadurar; aclimar.

seasonable adj. de estação; oportuno; seasonably adv. [oportunamente; seasoning s. têmpero, condimentação; môlho (de salada).

seat s. assento, banco, lugar (para sentar); fundilhos (das calças); morada; sítio, paragem, situação; v.t. sentar; instalar, empossar.

secede v.i. retirar-se, separar-se.

secluded adj. retirado; seclusion s. retiro, reclusão.

second adj. segundo; — hand de segunda mão; s. segundo; testemunha; v.t. secundar, apoiar; •ary adj. secundário; •ary school escola secundária, ginásio.

secrecy s. segrêdo.

secret s. segrêdo; adj. secreto, escondido.

secretary s. secretária, secretário; secretariat, secretariate s. secretariado.

secretion s. secreção.

secretive adj. dissimulado, reservado.

secretly adv. secretamente.

sect s. seita; •arian s.&adj. sectário.

section s. secção, divisão; corte; parte; artigo; •al adj. seccional, regional, local.

sector s. setor.

secular adj. secular; profano.

secure adj. seguro; v.t. assegurar, garantir; fixar; obter.

security s. segurança, garantia; caução, caucionamento; título, valor.

sedan s. cadeirinha.

sedate adj. sereno; sossegado; sério.

sedative s.&adj. sedativo.

sedentary adj. sedentário.

sedge s. espécie de caniço.

sediment s. sedimento, depósito.

sedition s. sedição.

seditious adj. sedicioso.

seduce v.t. seduzir; •r s. sedutor; seduction s. sedução; seductive adj. sedutor.

sedulous adj. assíduo; •ly adv. assiduamente.

see s. sé, sede pontifical; cátedra, episcopado.

see v.t.&i. ver, olhar; acompanhar; velar, vigiar, tomar sentido; I saw her to the train acompanhei-a ao trem; do you — what I mean? compreende o que quero dizer? — a thing through levar uma coisa até o fim; — to fazer atenção em, cuidar de; — through penetrar, perceber.

seed s. semente; grão; gérmen; v.t. semear.

seedsman s. semeador; vendedor de grãos.

seeing s. visão.

seek v.t.&i. procurar, buscar; explorar; esforçar-se por.

seem v.i. parecer; it •s parece que.

seeming s. aparência, exterior; falsa aparência; adj. aparente; •ly adv. aparentemente.

seemly adj. decente, decoroso.

seer s. profeta, vidente.

seesaw s. gangorra; v.i. balançar-se, balouçar-se.

seethe v.t.&i. ferver, agitar, fervilhar; saturar.

segment s. segmento.

segregate v.t. segregar; separar; segregation s. segregação.

seine s. arrastão (rede).

seismic adj. sísmico; seismograph s. sismógrafo.

seize v.t. agarrar, colhêr, apanhar; apreender, sequestrar; perceber, compreender.

seizure s. apreensão; ataque (de doença).

seldom adv. raramente.

select adj. seleto, escolhido; v.t. escolher, selecionar.

selection s. seleção, escolha.

self s. ego, eu; pessoa (própria); adj. próprio; — acting automático; — communion recolhimento; — control domínio de si mesmo; — denial abnegação, renúncia; — government autonomia; — importance suficiência; — possession sangue frio; — respect dignidade, amor-próprio; — sacrifice dedicação, devotamento; —•willed teimoso, voluntarioso, obstinado.

selfish adj. egoísta; •ness s. egoísmo.

sell v.t. vender; — off liquidar, saldar; •er s. vendedor.

selvage, selvedge s. orla, ourela.

semaphore s. semáforo.

semblance s. aparência, semelhança.

semi pref. semi; •colon ponto e vírgula.

seminary s. seminário.

Semitic adj. semítico.

semolina s. farinha de trigo duro, para massas alimentícias.

sempstress s. costureira.

senate s. senado; senator s. senador.

send v.t.&i. mandar, enviar, remeter, despachar; •er s. remetente.

senile adj. senil; senility s. senilidade.

senior adj. mais velho; mais antigo; s. deão; pai; •ity s. antiguidade.

senna s. (bot.) sene.

sensation s. sensação; impressão; •al adj. sensacional.

sense s. senso, sentido; sentimento; sensação; espírito, razão, bom senso, senso comum; acepção; v.t. perceber (pelos sentidos); sentir, inferir (pela intuição); •less adj. insensato; sem sentido.

sensibility s. sensibilidade.

sensible adj. sensato, razoavel; sensibly adv. sensatamente.

sensitive adj. sensível; sensitivo, impressionável.

sensual *adj.* sensual, carnal; **-ist** *s.* sensualista; **-ity** *s.* sensualidade.

sentence *s.* sentença; máxima; (*gram.*) frase, oração; (*mús.*) frase; *v.t.* sentenciar.

sententious *adj.* sentencioso.

sentiment *s.* sentimento, afeto; **-al** *adj.* sentimental; **-ality** *s.* sentimentalidade.

sentient *adj.* sensível; conciente.

sentinel *s.* sentinela.

sentry *s.* sentinela; — **box** guarita.

separate *adj.* separado; distinto; à parte; *v.t.* separar; **separation** *s.* separação.

sepia *s.* sépia.

sepoy *s.* cipaio.

September *s.* setembro.

septet, septette *s.* septeto, séptuor.

septic *adj.* séptico.

septum *s.* septo.

sepulchral *adj.* sepulcral; **sepulchre** *s.* sepulcro.

sequel *s.* sequela; consequência.

sequence *s.* sequência, seguimento, sucessão.

sequester *v.t.* segregar; (*dir.*) sequestrar; confiscar; **-ed** *adj.* retirado, afastado; **sequestration** *s.* retiro, afastamento; (*dir.*) sequestro.

seraglio *s.* serralho.

seraph *s.* serafim; **-ic** *adj.* seráfico.

Serbia *s.* Sérvia.

sere *adj.* sêco, murcho.

serenade *s.* serenata; *v.i.* fazer serenatas.

serene *adj.* sereno; **serenity** *s.* serenidade.

serf *s.* servo, escravo; **-dom** *s.* servidão.

serge *s.* sarja.

sergeant *s.* sargento.

serial *adj.* em série; **seriatim** *adv.* sucessivamente.

series *s.* série, seguimento.

seringa *s.* seringueira.

serious *adj.* sério; **-ness** *s.* seriedade.

sermon *s.* sermão; **-ize** *v.i.* pregar, fazer sermões; **-izer** *s.* prègador.

serosity *s.* serosidade.

serous *adj.* seroso.

serpent *s.* serpente.

serpentine *adj.* serpentino, sinuoso.

serration *s.* recorte dentado; **serrate** *adj.* dentado, recortado em dentes.

serried *adj.* apertado, comprimido.

serum *s.* sérum, sôro.

servant *s.* empregado; servidor, criado, doméstico; criada, empregada.

serve *v.t.&i.* servir; estar ao serviço de; cumprir (uma sentença); servir (à mesa); tratar; retribuir; (*dir.*) notificar; executar.

service *s.* serviço; servidão; uso; obséquio; aparelho (de mesa); ofício; serviço divino; **-able** *adj.* útil.

serviette *s.* guardanapo.

servile *adj.* servil; **servility** *s.* servilismo; **servitude** *s.* servidão.

sesame *s.* sésamo, gergelim.

session *s.* sessão.

set *s.* série; aderêço; guarnição; adôrno; conjunto (de objetos); bateria; jôgo, coleção; constituição, forma; (*ast.*) movimento, curso, direção, tendência, o pôr (do sol); (*agric.*) pé de árvore; planta nova (para transplante); (*teat.*) decoração; — **of books** coleção de livros; *v.t.&i.* pôr-se (um astro); solidificar-se, endurecer-se; fixar-se; estabelecer-se; pôr; colocar; assentar; fixar, imobilizar; plantar; encastoar, montar;

determinar, aplicar, regular; avaliar; dedicar-se a; *adj.* posto, colocado, fixo; estabelecido; plantado; firme; — **against** indispor; — **aside** pôr de lado; — **milk** coalhar o leite; — **one's mind on** aplicar-se, dedicar-se a; — **off** sair, partir; — **up** estabelecer, fundar, montar, principiar; — **form** formulário; — **of diamonds** aderêço de brilhantes; — **of horses** parelha de cavalos; — **of teeth** dentadura; — **face** rosto imóvel, impassível; — **purpose** firme propósito.

settee *s.* sofá grande.

setter *s.* cão perdigueiro; pessoa que coloca, que monta; compositor.

setting *s.* ocaso, pôr de um astro; decoração, ornamentação (de um ambiente); engaste, cravação; composição; — **of the wind** direção do vento.

settle *s.* banco; *v.t.* regular, regrar; acomodar, arranjar; liquidar, resolver; estabelecer, instalar; constituir; colonizar, povoar; *v.i.* estabelecer-se, fixar-se; tomar estado, casar-se; instalar-se; — **down** instalar-se, tomar juizo, fixar-se; **-d** *adj.* fixo, estabelecido; arraigado; seguro, firme; **-ment** *s.* estabelecimento, instalação; povoado; constituição, termo; liquidação; colonização; **-r** *s.* colono, residente.

seven *adj.&s.* sete; **-th** *adj.&s.* sétimo.

seventeen *adj.&s.* dezessete; **-th** *adj.&s.* décimo sétimo; **-thly** *adv.* em décimo sétimo lugar.

seventy *adj.&s.* setenta; **seventieth** *adj.&s.* setuagésimo.

sever *v.t.* separar, apartar, desunir; cortar, decepar; **-ance** *s.* separação.

several *adj.* diferente, diverso, distinto; vários, alguns.

severe *adj.* severo, rigoroso; grave; **severity** *s.* severidade, rigor.

sew *v.t.* coser, costurar; **-er** *s.* costureiro; esgôto, cano d'agua.

sewing *s.* costura; — **machine** máquina de costura.

sex *s.* sexo.

sextant *s.* sextante.

sextet, sextette *s.* sexteto.

sexton *s.* sacristão.

sexual *adj.* sexual.

shabby *adj.* usado, gasto; mal vestido; mesquinho.

shackle *s.* cadeia, algema; (*fig.*) entrave; *v.t.* algemar, acorrentar; entravar.

shade *s.* sombra; escuridão; trevas; nuança, matiz; espetro, fantasma; ilusão; *v.t.* sombrear, fazer sombra, dar sofmbra; matizar.

shadow *s.* sombra (em todas as suas acepções); *v.t.* sombrear, dar sombra; representar vagamente, indicar; *v.i.* anuviar-se, sombrear-se.

shaft *s.* flecha, dardo, seta; poço; coluna; lança, varal (de carro ou carroça); (*mec.*) árvore, transmissão.

shaggy *adj.* cabeludo; rude.

shagreen *s.* marroquim (couro).

shah *s.* xá, rei da Pérsia.

shake *s.* abalo, estremecimento; concussão; sacudidela; apêrto (de mão); vibração; *v.t.&i.* sacudir; agitar; abalar; tremer; agitar-se; vacilar; mexer; (*mús.*) trinar; **shaky** *adj.* abalado; vacilante; trêmulo.

shale *s.* xisto, rocha folheada.

shall *v.aux.* usado para formar o futuro.

shallot *s.* (*bot.*) chalota.

shallow *adj.* raso; pouco profundo; superficial, frívolo; insípido; =ness *s.* pouca profundidade; trivialidade; superficialidade.

sham *s.* simulação; *adj.* simulado, fingido, fictício; *v.t.&i.* fingir, simular.

shambles *s.* matadouro.

shambling *adj.* pesado, que se arrasta.

shame *s.* vergonha; pudor; escândalo; *v.t.* envergonhar; =ful *adj.* vergonhoso; =less *adj.* sem vergonha, desavergonhado, impudente; =lessly *adv.* descaradamente, impudentemente.

shammy *s.* camurça.

shampoo *s.* massagem e lavagem de cabeça; *v.t.* lavar e friccionar o couro cabeludo.

shamrock *s.* trevo.

shank *s.* perna; haste, cano.

shanty *s.* barraca, cabana.

shape *s.* forma, figura; aspecto; modêlo, molde; condição, estado; *v.t.* formar, dar forma; determinar; moldar, modelar; =less *adj.* sem forma, informe, amorfo; =ly *adj.* bem formado; =r *s.* conformador.

share *s.* parte; quota, quinhão; (*fin.*) ação, valor, título; *v.t.&i.* repartir, participar de.

shark *s.* tubarão.

sharp *adj.* afiado, cortante; agudo, penetrante, sutil; perspicaz, vivo; acre, áspero, mordaz; (*mús.*) sustenido; =en *v.t.* aguçar, afiar; fazer ponta (em lapis, etc.); amolar; (*fig.*) tornar mais esperto; =ener *s.* afiador, amolador; =er *s.* gatuno, velhaco; =ly *adv.* agudamente; sutilmente; severamente, rigorosamente; =ness *s.* agudeza, sutileza, perspicácia; acrimônia, mordacidade.

shatter *v.t.* destroçar, despedaçar, esmigalhar; frustrar (as esperanças); *s.* pedaço, fragmento.

shave *v.t.* fazer a barba; barbear; *v.i.* barbear-se; shaving *s.* ação de barbear ou de raspar; raspas, aparas.

shawl *s.* chale.

she *pron.* ela; *s.* fêmea; —=goat cabra; —=bear ursa; —=wolf lôba.

sheaf *s.* molho, feixe; *v.t.* enfeixar.

shear *v.t.* tosquiar, tosar; =er *s.* tosquiador; =ing *s.* tosquia.

shears *s.* tesouras grandes (para tosquiar).

sheath *s.* bainha, estôjo, fôrro; (*bot.*) espata; (*zool.*) élitro; *v.t.* embainhar; forrar, debruar.

sheave *s.* roldana.

shed *s.* alpendre; telheiro; barraca, abrigo (em geral); *v.t.* derramar, verter; entornar; =ding *s.* derramamento.

sheen *s.* brilho, lustre, resplendor; *adj.* resplandecente.

sheep *s.* carneiro; ovelha; =ish *adj.* acanhado, tímido.

sheer *adj.* puro, sem misturas; cabal, completo; escarpado, abrupto; claro, límpido.

sheet *s.* fôlha; lâmina; lençol; placa; extensão de água; (*mar.*) escota.

sheik, sheikh *s.* xeque (chefe).

shekel *s.* antiga unidade monetária e de pêso da Babilônia.

sheldrake *s.* espécie de ádem.

shelf *s.* prateleira, estante; (*mar.*) escolho; abrôlho.

shell *s.* casca; concha; escama; pele; bainha; vagem; carcassa; bomba; *v.t.* descascar; despolpar; escamar; bombardear, lançar projéteis; *v.i.* descascar-se.

shellac *s.* laca.

shelter *s.* abrigo, cobertura; refúgio; *v.t.* abrigar.

shelve *v.i.* ir em declive; *v.t.* pôr de lado; demitir.

shepherd *s.* pastor; =ess *s.* pastora.

sherry *s.* xerez.

shew V. show.

shield *s.* escudo; amparo, proteção; *v.t.* proteger.

shift *s.* troca, substituição; turno; recurso, expediente; subterfúgio, ardil; turma; *v.t.&i.* trocar, substituir; revezar; transferir; mover-se, mudar-se; mudar; =ing *adj.* movente; instável; =y *adj.* engenhoso, velhaco.

shilling *s.* xelim.

shilly-shally *v.i.* mostrar irresolução.

shimmer *v.i.* brilhar fracamente.

shin *s.* tíbia, canela.

shindy *s.* barulho, rôlo, contenda.

shine *s.* brilho, resplendor; *v.i.* brilhar, luzir, reluzir.

shingle *s.* ripa, sarrafo; burgalhão; *v.t.* ripar; =d hair cabelo curto com o pescoço raspado.

shining, shiny *adj.* brilhante, reluzente.

ship *s.* navio, barco, embarcação, vapor, nau; *v.t.* embarcar; despachar, expedir, remeter; =ment *s.* carregamento, expedição, remessa, embarque; =per expedidor, carregador; =ping *s.* navegação; transporte, expedição.

shire *s.* condado.

shirk *v.t.&i.* esquivar, esquivar-se.

shirt *s.* camisa.

shiver *v.t.&i.* tiritar; tremer, agitar-se; despedaçar, quebrar.

shoal *s.* baixio; multidão, tropel, ajuntamento; cardume.

shock *s.* choque; encontro, colisão; embate; meda; *v.t.* chocar; desgostar; surpreender; escandalizar; *v.i.* colidir; =ing *adj.* escandaloso, ofensivo.

shoddy *adj.* de lã artificial; de falsa aparência.

shoe *s.* sapato, calçado; pneumático; wooden =s tamancos; —=brush escôva de sapatos; *v.t.* calçar; ferrar.

shoot *s.* tiro; rebento, renôvo; caçada; *v.t.* atirar; arremessar, disparar, ferir (com tiro); matar (a tiros); fuzilar; atravessar, varar; *v.i.* caçar; atirar; germinar, medrar; =ing *s.* caçada; tiro ao alvo; =ing pains dôres lancinantes; =ing star estrela cadente.

shop *s.* loja; oficina, fábrica; *v.i.* fazer compras; window =ping olhar as vitrinas.

shore *s.* praia, costa, margem, borda, litoral; escora, pontão; *v.t.* escorar, apoiar.

short *adj.* pequeno; curto; conciso, resumido; breve; —=hand estenografia; —=sighted míope; in — para resumir, enfim; =age *s.* falta, deficiência, crise; =en *v.t.* encurtar, diminuir; =ly *adv.* em breve, brevemente; =ness *s.* brevidade; concisão; curteza.

shot *s.* tiro; golpe, pancada; bala, chumbo; alcance (do tiro); round — bala; grape — metralha.

shot *adj.* de côr variada, com reflexos (tecido).

should *v.aux.* usado para formar o condicional.

shoulder *s.* ombro, espádua; *v.t.&i.* pôr nos ombros; fazer caminho com os ombros; carregar nos ombros.

shout s. grito; barulho; v.t.&i. gritar, vociferar.
shove s. empurrão; v.t.&i. empurrar, impelir.
shovel s. pá; v.t. tirar ou amontoar com a pá.
show s. espetáculo, revista; pompa, ostentação; manifestação; aparência; exposição, concurso; v.t.&i. mostrar, expor, fazer ver, manifestar; anunciar; representar; provar; mostrar-se, aparecer; — in fazer entrar; — out acompanhar, reconduzir; — off mostrar-se.
shower s. bátega, pancada de chuva, carga d'água, aguaceiro; festa na qual se dão presentes a uma noiva; v.i. chover torrencialmente, cair uma carga d'água; v.t. cumular, dar generosamente; molhar.
showy adj. faustoso, pomposo.
shrapnel s. espécie de metralha, que explode no ar.
shred s. retalho, pedaço; v.t. retalhar, cortar em pedaços.
shrew s. megera.
shrewd adj. sagaz, astuto; hábil; =ness s. sagacidade, habilidade, perspicácia.
shriek s. grito; v.i. gritar.
shrill adj. agudo, estridente; =ness s. acuidade.
shrimp s. camarão; (fig.) anão, pigmeu.
shrimping s. pesca de camarão.
shrine s. relicário, sacrário, santuário.
shrink v.t.&i. encolher, encurtar, contrair-se; retirar-se; =age s. encolhimento, contração.
shrivel v.t.&i. enrugar, enrugar-se, encarquilhar, encolher.
shroud s. lençol, mortalha; enxárcia; v.t. amortalhar; abrigar, cobrir.
shrovetide s. entrudo, carnaval.
shrub s. arbusto; =bery s. plantação de arbustos.
shrug s. encolhimento de ombros; v.i. encolher os ombros.
shudder v.i. tremer, estremecer.
shuffle v.t. confundir, misturar, pôr em desordem; baralhar; s. confusão, mistura.
shun v.t. evitar, fugir.
shunt s. desvio; (elet.) derivação; vt. deviar, manobrar; (elet.) derivar.
shut v.t.&i. fechar; v.i. fechar-se; — up! cale a boca!; =ter s. postigo, portinhola.
shuttle s. lançadeira (de tear).
shy adj. tímido, arisco, esquivo; =ness s. timidez.
sick adj. doente; desgostoso; to be — of the stomach ter nauseas; — and tired cansado e abatido; =en v.i. cair doente; v.t. desgostar, enojar.
sickle s. foice.
sickly adj. doentio; fraco.
sickness s. doença.
side s. lado, flanco; costado, margem, borda; partido, facção, campo; — with colocar-se ao lado de, tomar o partido de.
sidereal adj. sideral.
siding s. via lateral, desvio, ramal.
siege s. cêrco, sítio; assento, trono.
siesta s. sesta.
sieve s. peneira, crivo; **sift** v.t. peneirar, passar pelo crivo; esquadrinhar.
sigh s. suspiro; v.i. suspirar.
sight s. vista; visão; aspecto; (topogr.) visada; mira; espetáculo, curiosidade; at — à primeira vista; (com.) à vista; v.t. visar; ver, avistar; reconhecer.

sign s. sinal, marca, indício; taboleta; rubrica; v.t. assinar, rubricar; marcar; v.i. fazer sinais.
signal s. sinal; adj. assinalado; =ize v.t. assinalar.
signer, signatory s. signatário.
signature s. assinatura.
signet s. sêlo, sinete.
significance s. significação, alcance; importância.
significant adj. significante, significativo, importante.
signify v.t.&i. significar, dar a entender; manifestar, declarar; importar.
silence s. silêncio; v.t. fazer calar; estabelecer silêncio.
silent adj. silencioso; — partner comanditário.
silhouette s. silhueta.
silica s. sílica; =te s. silicato.
silk s. sêda; =worm s. bicho da sêda; =y adj. sedoso.
sill s. soleira (da porta); apôio, base.
silliness s. bobagem, tolice; **silly** adj. tôlo, bobo.
silo s. silo.
silt s. lama, lodo.
silver s. prata; v.t. pratear; =y adj. argentino, prateado.
simian adj. símio.
similar adj. similar, igual; =ity s. similaridade; **similitude** s. similitude; =ly adv. similarmente; **simile** s. símile, modêlo; comparação.
simmer v.i.&i. ferver brandamente, a fogo lento.
simony s. simonia.
simoom, simoon s. simum.
simper s. sorriso afetado.
simple adj. simples; =ton s. bobo, tôlo.
simplicity s. simplicidade; **simplify** v.t. simplificar.
simulacrum s. simulacro; **simulate** v.t. simular.
simultaneous adj. simultâneo.
sin s. pecado; v.i. pecar.
since adv.,prep.&conj. desde; já que; pois que; depois; visto que.
sincere adj. sincero; **sincerity** s. sinceridade.
sine s. (mat.) seno.
sinecure s. sinecura.
sine die sine die.
sinew s. tendão; nervo.
sinful adj. culpado; pecador; pecaminoso.
sing v.t.&i. cantar.
singe v.t. chamuscar.
singer s. cantor; cantora; **singing** s. canto.
single adj. solteiro; só; único; — bed cama de solteiro; — out distinguir; **singly** adv. isoladamente.
singsong adj. cantante; s. salmodia. cantarola.
singular adj. singular; s. (gram.) singular.
sinister adj. sinistro.
sink s. pia; cloaca, sentina; v.i.&t. afundar, pôr a pique; submergir, mergulhar; abater; destruir; extinguir; decair; sucumbir, desabar; desmoronar.
sinless adj. sem culpa; inocente.
sinner s. pecador.
sinuous adj. sinuoso.
sinus s. cavidade, abertura; (anat.) sinus.
sip s. sôrvo, pequeno trago; v.t.&i. sorver, beber aos poucos.
siphon s. sifão.
sippet s. pedaço de pão (molhado no leite, sopa, etc.).

sir s. senhor.
sire s. título de respeito que se dá a um soberano; pai; progenitor macho; v.t. procrear.
siren s. sereia; sirena.
sirloin s. filé (carne).
siskin s. verdelhão (pássaro).
sister s. irmã; —-*in-law cunhada.
sit v.i. sentar-se; posar (para modêlo); estar (situado); empoleirar-se; assentar, cair bem (roupa, vestido, etc.); chocar (ovos); — up velar, estar atento.
site s. sítio, terreno, lugar, situação.
sitting s. sessão; audiência; — time época do chôco.
situated adj. situado; colocado.
situation s. situação; lugar.
sitz bath banho de assento.
six adj.&s. seis; *th adj.&s. sexto.
sixteen adj.&s. dezesseis; *th adj.&s. décimosexto.
sixty adj.&s. sessenta; **sixtieth** adj.&s. sexagésimo.
size s. dimensão; tamanho, grossura, medida, número; estatura; calibre; formato, amostra; cola, grude; v.t. classificar, ajustar (segundo o tamanho, grossura, etc.); tomar a medida; aferir (pesos, etc.); cobrir com cola; *able de bom tamanho.
skate s. patim; v.i. patinar; *r s. patinador.
skedaddle v.i. dar ás de Vila Diogo, fugir.
skein s. meada.
skeleton s. esqueleto; carcassa.
sketch s. esquema, esbôço, bosquejo; drama curto; v.t. esboçar, delinear, bosquejar, traçar.
skeptical adj. céptico.
skew adj. oblíquo.
skewer s. espêto pequeno.
ski s. ski; v.i. patinar com ski.
skid s. calço, peia (para rodas); v.t. pear; derrapar.
skiff s. esquife (barco).
skilful adj. hábil, perito.
skill s. habilidade, perícia; ciência, saber; *ed adj. especializado, perito.
skim v.t. escumar; desnatar, desengordurar; folhear (um livro); ler (superficialmente); estudar (por alto); — milk leite desnatado; *mer s. espumadeira; desnatador; *mings s. espuma.
skin s. pele, couro; casca, envólucro; — disease doença de pele; v.t. pelar, tirar a pele, esfolar; — over cicatrizar; *ny adj. magro, descarnado.
skip s. salto, pulo; v.t.&i. saltar, pular; falhar.
skipper s. capitão de navio; patrão.
skirmish s. escaramuça; rixa; v.i. escaramuçar.
skirt s. saia; aba, fralda; borda; v.t. costear, marginar.
skit s. epigrama; peça curta (para teatro ou rádio).
skittish adj. espantadiço, passarinheiro (cavalo); tímido; frívolo.
skittle s. quilha, jôgo inglês no qual se arremessam discos de madeira.
skulk v.i. esconder-se, ficar à espreita.
skull s. crâneo.
skunk s. doninha; tratante (pessoa).
sky s. céu, firmamento; — blue azul celeste; *scraper arranha-céu.
slab s. prancha, tábua; laje.
slack adj. frouxo, lasso, bambo; negligente; fraco; *s s. (pop.) calças; *en v.i.

afrouxar; diminuir; relaxar, soltar; abrandar, moderar.
slag s. escória.
slake v.t. apagar, extinguir; misturar (cal) com agua.
slam s. (j. de bridge) slam; v.t. bater, fechar com violencia.
slander v.t. difamar, caluniar.
slang s. jíria, calão.
slant s. inclinação; v.i.&t. inclinar-se, inclinar.
slap s. tapa, bofetada, palmada; v.t. esbofetear, dar tapas e palmadas; bater em; dar pancada em.
slash v.t. acutilar; cortar, retalhar.
slat s. vareta.
slate s. ardósia; v.t. cobrir com ardósia.
slattern s. mulher desalinhada e maltratada.
slaughter s. matança; carnificina, massacre; v.t. matar; massacrar; abater (gado).
Slav adj. eslavo.
slave s. escravo; *r s. negreiro; v.t.&i. trabalhar como escravo; escravizar.
slaver s. baba; v.i. babar.
slavery s. escravidão; **slavish** adj. servil; **slavishness** s. servilidade.
slay v.t. matar, imolar; *er s. assassino.
sled s. trenó; v.t.&i. andar ou transportar de trenó.
sledge s. trenó.
sleek adj. liso, pulido; suave, brando.
sleep s. sono; *walker sonâmbulo; v.i. dormir; *ness s. sonô, sonolência; *ing adj. adormecido; *less adj. sem sono; *lessness s. insônia; *y adj. sonolento, com sono.
sleet s. pedrisco; v.i. chover pedrisco.
sleeve s. manga; *less adj. sem mangas.
sleigh s. trenó.
sleight-of-hand s. prestidigitação.
slender adj. fino, delgado, esbelto; pequeno; insuficiente; fraco.
slew v.t. virar, fazer virar; torcer.
slide s. escorregadura; resvaladouro, passagem escorregadiça; declive; corrediça; chapa (de projeção); v.t.&i. escorregar, resvalar; deslizar; escoar-se, correr; **sliding** adj. corrediço.
slight adj. leve, ligeiro; pequeno, curto; fraco; s. afronta, tratamento desairoso; v.t. negligenciar, desprezar; desfeitear.
slim adj. esbelto, gracioso; delgado; (pop.) insignificante; astuto.
slime s. limo, lama, lodo; humor viscoso.
sling s. funda (para atirar pedras); atadura, faixa, tiracolo; (mar.) cabo de guindaste; v.t. guindar, suspender.
slip s. resvaladura; escorregão; passo em falso; lapso, engano; pecado venial; deslise; falta; inadvertência; (geol.) deslocamento; fronha; embarcadouro; corda, corrente; fôlha de papel; (pop.) combinação (de mulher); v.t.&i. escorregar, resvalar; deslisar; cair em falta; escapulir, fugir; introduzir-se sutilmente; soltar, desatar; desaparecer; — into introduzir-se; — off descartar-se, tirar de si; to — one's clothes on vestir-se às carreiras, enfiar a roupa; *pery adj. escorregadio, pouco firme.
slipper s. chinelo, chinela.
slit s. fenda; v.t. fender.
slobber s. baba; v.i.&t. babar.
sloe s. abrunho; abrunheiro.
slogan s. grito de guerra; palavra de passe.

slop *v.t.&i.* verter, derramar, sujar, sujar-se; — **pail** vaso de noite.

slope *s.* obliquidade; rampa, declive; *v.i.* inclinar-se, ir em declive.

sloppiness *s.* umidade, lama.

sloppy *adj.* molhado, úmido; (*pop.*) descuidado; confuso, em desordem.

slot *s.* pista, rasto; traço, vestígio; fenda, buraco.

sloth *s.* preguiça, indolência; *ful *adj.* preguiçoso, indolente.

slough *s.* lamaçal; degradação; (*med.*) escara; *v.i.* (*med.*) separar-se (o tecido morto) do são; *v.t.* largar deixar; descartar-se (jôgo de bridge).

sloven *s.* pessoa pouco asseada; *ly *adj.* descuidado.

slow *adj.* lento, tardio, vagaroso; atrasado (relógio); *adv.* vagarosamente; — **down** diminuir a marcha ou velocidade; *ness *s.* lentidão.

slow-worm *s.* cecília, minhocão.

sludge *s.* lôdo.

slug *s.* lesma.

sluggard *s.* preguiçoso; **sluggish** *adj.* preguiçoso; inerte; retardado.

sluice *s.* comporta.

slum *s.* bairro pobre, favela.

slumber *s.* sono; *v.i.* dormitar.

slump *s.* fracasso; queda (de preços); crise; *v.i.* desmoronar-se; cair subitamente.

slur *s.* mancha; exprobação; desdouro; (*mús.*) ligadura, modulação; *v.i.&t.* manchar, sujar; (*mús.*) modular, ligar.

slush *s.* lama de neve derretida.

sluttery *s.* falta de asseio, porcaria.

sly *adj.* astuto, dissimulado.

smack *s.* sabor, gôsto; pequena quantidade; estalo (com a boca ou chicote); beijo estrepitoso; palmada; *v.i.* saber, cheirar; estalar (com a boca); *v.t.* beijar ruidosamente.

small *adj.* pequeno; **fraco**; módico; miúdo, curto; tênue.

smallness *s.* curteza, pequenez.

smart *adj.* vivo, hábil, engenhoso; agudo, picante, pungente; (*Ing.*) elegante; (*E. U.*) inteligente; *v.i.* picar, doer; *ness *s.* agudeza; vivacidade; elegância; talento; **the** — **set** a elite social.

smash *s.* colisão, acidente; bancarrota; *v.t.* quebrar, espatifar; esmagar; *v.i.* espatifar-se.

smattering *s.* tintura, conhecimento superficial.

smear *v.t.* cobrir, untar.

smell *s.* olfato; odor, cheiro, perfume, aroma; *v.t.&i.* cheirar.

smelt *s.* espécie de salmão.

smelt *v.t.* fundir.

smilax *s.* esmilácea.

smile *s.* sorriso; *v.i.* sorrir; **smiling** *adj.* sorridente.

smirch *v.t.* sujar.

smirk *s.* sorriso afetado; *v.i.* sorrir afetadamente.

smite *v.t.* ferir; golpear.

smith *s.* forjador; **black** *s.* ferreiro.

smitten *adj.* profundamente afetado; muito apaixonado.

smock *s.* blusa.

smoke *s.* fumaça, fumo; *v.t.&i.* fumar; fumegar; arder; defumar; *less *adj.* sem fumo; sem fumaça; *r *s.* fumante; **smoky** *adj.* fumegante.

smolder, **smoulder** *v.i.* queimar sem chama; queimar lentamente.

smooth *adj.* liso, unido; igual, plano; suave, brando, macio; *v.t.* alisar, unir;

suavizar, amaciar; *ly *adv.* suavemente; *ness *s.* igualdade; suavidade, doçura.

smother *v.t.* sufocar.

smudge *s.* fumaça sufocante; *v.t.* tisnar, sujar.

smug *adj.* presumido, convencido.

smuggle *v.t.* passar em contrabando; *v.i.* fazer contrabando, contrabandear.

smuggler *s.* contrabandista.

smut *s.* mancha de carvão; obcenidade; *ty *adj.* sujo, tisnado; obceno.

snack *s.* porção pequena; colação.

snag *s.* protuberância; nó na madeira; sobredente; obstáculo ignorado.

snail *s.* (*zool.*) caracol.

snake *s.* cobra.

snap *s.* estalo, golpe sêco; dentada; *v.t.* romper, quebrar; fazer estalar; dar uma dentada em.

slice *s.* fatia, talhada; *v.t.* cortar em fatias.

snapper *s.* ladrão esperto; pessoa que dá um golpe.

snappy *adj.* vivo, enérgico; elegante.

snatch *s.* fragmento; *v.t.* arrebatar, tirar, agarrar, levar precipitadamente.

sneak *s.* matreiro, vilão; gatuno; *v.i.* ir-se às escondidas; *v.t.* surripiar.

sneer *s.* riso de mofa; *v.i.* mofar, zombar.

sneeze *v.i.* espirrar.

sniff *v.i.&t.* fungar, aspirar fortemente pelo nariz.

snigger *v.i.* rir-se à socapa.

snip *s.* tesourada; *v.t.* tesourar.

snipe *s.* narceja; *v.t.&i.* caçar, passarinhar; *r *s.* atirador isolado, franco atirador.

snivel *v.i.* choramingar, fungar; *s.* muco.

snooze *s.* soneca; *v.i.* dormitar.

snore *v.i.* roncar.

snort *v.i.* bufar.

snout *s.* focinho; tromba.

snow *s.* neve; *v.i.* nevar.

snub *s.* desprêzo, falta de atenção; *v.t.* tratar com desprêzo.

snuff *s.* rapé; *v.i.* aspirar; tomar (rapé); farejar.

snuffle *v.i.* fungar, aspirar; falar fanhoso.

snug *adj.* confortável.

snuggle *v.i.* aconchegar-se.

so *adv.&conj.* assim, assim como; portanto; por conseguinte; de modo que; tão, tanto; então; suposto que; — **that** de sorte que; — **to speak** por assim dizer.

soak *v.t.* embeber, empapar, ensopar; *ed *adj.* ensopado, empapado.

soap *s.* sabão.

soar *v.i.* adejar, pairar; tomar o vôo; elevar-se.

sob *s.* soluço; *v.i.* soluçar.

sober *adj.* sóbrio; não embriagado; *v.t.* desembriagar; tornar sóbrio.

soberness *s.* sobriedade.

sociable *adj.* sociável; **social** *adj.* social; **socialism** *s.* socialismo; **socialist** *s.* socialista.

society *s.* sociedade; associação; **sociology** *s.* sociologia.

sock *s.* meia curta.

socket *s.* o ôco de qualquer coisa onde se encaixa outra; — **of a tooth** alvéolo de um dente; — **of the eye** órbita (do ôlho); — **wrench** chave de boca.

sod *s.* céspede, torrão.

soda *s.* soda.

sodden *adj.* molhado, saturado; fervido; mal cozido.

sodium *s.* sódio.

sofa *s.* sofá, divã.

soft *adj.* mole, macio, tenro; brando

suave; flexível; =en v.t. amaciar, amolecer; enternecer; suavizar; =ness s. macieza, doçura; suavidade.
soil s. solo, terra; v.t. sujar, manchar.
sojourn s. temporada; v.i. residir temporàriamente, passar algum tempo.
solace s. consolação; v.t. consolar.
solar adj. solar.
solder, soldering s. solda, soldadura; v.t. soldar.
soldier s. soldado.
sole adj. só; único; exclusivo; s. sola; v.t. pôr solas em (sapato).
solecism s. solecismo.
solemn adj. solene; grave; =ity s. solenidade; =ize v.t. solenizar.
sol-fa v.i. solfejar.
solicit v.t. solicitar; =or s. solicitador, procurador.
solicitous adj. desejoso; inquieto; diligente.
solid adj. sólido; firme, maciço; =ify v.t. solidificar.
soliloquize v.i. monologar; soliloquy s. solilóquio.
solitaire s. solitário; solitary adj. solitário, retirado.
solitude s. solitude, solidão.
solo s. solo; soloist s. solista.
solstice s. solstício.
soluble adj. solúvel; solution s. solução; resolução; saída; solve v.t. resolver; solver.
solvent adj. dissolvente; solvente; solvível; s. dissolvente; solução.
somber, sombre adj. sombrio; escuro.
some adj.&pron. alguns; algum; alguma; algumas; um tanto, um pouco; certo, certos, certa, certas; uns; umas; qualquer; =one alguém, certa pessoa.
somebody pron. alguém, certa pessoa; s. alguém, pessoa de importância.
somehow adv. de certo modo; de alguma forma.
somersault s. salto-mortal; cambalhota.
something s. alguma coisa; qualquer coisa.
sometimes adv. às vezes; por vezes.
somewhat adv. um tanto, um pouco; s. alguma coisa.
somewhere adv. em algum lugar.
somnambulism s. sonambulismo; somnambulist s. sonâmbulo.
somnolent adj. sonolento.
son s. filho.
sonata s. sonata.
song s. canto; canção; cançoneta; cântico; =ster s. cantor; =stress s. cantora.
sonnet s. soneto.
sonorous adj. sonoro.
soon adv. breve; cedo; =er adv. mais cedo; as — as logo que.
soot s. fuligem; =y adj. fuliginoso.
soothe v.t. acalmar; soothing adj. calmante.
soothsayer s. adivinho, profeta.
sop s. pão molhado (no leite, sopa, etc.).
sophism s. sofisma.
sophisticate v.t. sofisticar; desiludir.
sophisticated adj. civilizado, experiente, culto, refinado; sophistry s. sofisticaria.
soporific adj.&s. soporífico.
soprano s. soprano.
sorcerer s. feiticeiro; =ess s. feiticeira; sorcery s. feitiçaria.
sordid adj. sórdido; =ness s. sordidez.
sore adj. doloroso; ferido, ulceroso, em chaga; doente; sensível; s. dôr; chaga, ferida; — throat dôr de garganta.

sorrel s. azedinha, azêda.
sorrow s. tristeza, desgôsto, dôr; v.i. afligir-se, desgostar-se; =ful adj. triste, desgostoso; =fully adv. tristemente, dolorosamente; sorry adj. triste, aborrecido, desconsolado; I am sorry for sinto muito.
sort s. sorte, gênero, espécie, qualidade; maneira, forma, modo; v.t. classificar, separar, dividir por classes; colocar.
sortie s. saída, surtida.
sot s. bêbado contumaz; beberrão.
sough v.i. murmurar; s. murmúrio, sussurro.
soul s. alma; =less adj. sem alma.
sound adj. são, sadio; bom, sólido; profundo; s. som; sonda; canal marítimo; v.t. fazer soar; tocar, tanger; sondar; (med.) auscultar; v.i. soar, ressoar; — sleep sono profundo; =ness s. sanidade, saúde; firmeza, retidão.
soup s. sopa; — plate prato fundo.
sour adj. ácido, azêdo; picante; v.t.&i. azedar; =ly adv. àsperamente, com azedume; =ness s. azedume, acrimônia, aspereza; — milk leite talhado.
source s. fonte; origem, manancial.
souse s. salmoura, escabeche; v.t. pôr de escabeche.
south s. sul; adv. ao sul; adj. do sul, meridional; =ern adj. meridional, do sul; =erner s. sulista; =ward adv. em direção ao sul.
souvenir s. lembrança, recordação.
sovereign adj.&s. soberano; =ty s. soberania.
soviet s. soviet.
sow s. porca; fêmea do javali.
sow v.t.&i. semear; espalhar, disseminar; — one's wild oats fazer as estravagâncias próprias da mocidade.
sower s. semeador.
sowing s. semeadura.
soya bean s. soja-híspida.
spa s. estação de águas.
space s. espaço; intervalo, interstício, entrelinha; v.t. espaçar; spacious adj. espaçoso.
spade s. pá; espadas (naipe); v.t. cavar com a pá.
Spain s. Espanha.
span s. envergadura, dimensão máxima transversal; vão; instante, momento; palmo; parelha (de cavalos, etc.); — new novo em folha; v.t. atravessar, transpor; passar por cima de; medir a palmos.
spandrel s. (arq.) tímpano.
spangle s. lentejoula; =d adj. lentejoulado.
Spaniard s. espanhol; Spanish adj.&s. espanhol.
spaniel s. raça de cão; adulador.
spank v.t. dar palmada, bater; =ing s. surra, palmadas.
spanner s. chave (ferramenta).
spar s. espato; (mar.) vêrga, mastro; luta de box; v.i. treinar boxe, boxar.
spare adj. magro, sêco; disponível, livre; de sobra, sobrecelente; v.t. poupar, economizar; privar-se de; mostrar clemência; sparing adj. econômico, poupado; previdente.
spark s. centelha; faísca, fagulha; lampejo; homem galante e maneiroso; — plug vela de ignição; =le v.i. cintilar, brilhar, faiscar; crepitar; =ling adj. cintilante, brilhante; (vinho) espumante.

sparring s. treinamento (boxe); — **partner** companheiro de treino, treinador.
sparrow s. pardal.
sparse adj. esparso, disseminado; raro; pouco denso.
spasm s. espasmo; **-odic** adj. espasmódico.
spatter v.t. enlamear, respingar, sujar, salpicar.
spatula s. espátula.
spawn s. ova (de peixe); geração; v.t.&i. desovar; gerar ou semear em grandes quantidades.
speak v.i.&t. falar, dizer; **-er** s. orador; **-ing** s. palavra; **we are not on -ing terms** estamos de relações cortadas.
spear s. lança; v.t. lancear, alancear.
special adj. especial; particular; **-ist** s. especialista; **-ity** s. especialidade; **-ize** v.t. especializar-se.
specie s. numerário, moeda.
species s. espécie.
specific adj. específico; determinado, preciso; **-ation** s. especificação; enumeração.
specify v.t. especificar; enumerar, precisar.
specimen s. espécime.
specious adj. especioso.
speck s. sinal, pequena mancha, ponto; partícula; **-le** v.t. mosquear, salpicar.
spectacle s. espetáculo; (plural) óculos.
spectacular adj. espetacular.
spectator s. espectador.
specter, spectre s. espetro; **spectroscope** s. espetroscópio; **spectrum** s. espetro.
spectral adj. espetral.
speculate v.t.&i. especular; agiotar; **speculation** s. especulação; jôgo; **speculative** adj. especulativo; **speculator** s. especulador.
speech s. palavra, linguagem; voz; discurso, alocução; **-less** adj. mudo, sem voz.
speed s. velocidade, rapidez, celeridade; v.t. acelerar, apressar; — **up** ativar; **-ometer** s. velocímetro; **-y** adj. rápido.
spell s. feitiço, encanto; arrebatamento, fascinação; turno, vez; período; ataque, acesso; v.t.&i. soletrar; escrever, ortografar; **-ing** s. soletração; ortografia; **-ing bee** concurso de ortografia; **-ing book** cartilha.
spelter s. zinco.
spend v.t.&i. despender; gastar; passar (tempo).
sperm s. esperma.
spermaceti s. espermacete.
spermatozoon s. espermatozóide.
spew v.t.&i. vomitar.
sphere s. esfera; **spherical** adj. esférico.
sphincter s. esfíncter.
sphinx s. esfinge.
spice s. especiaria.
spick-and-span novo em fôlha.
spicy adj. aromático; apimentado.
spider s. aranha.
spigot s. torneira; espiche.
spike s. espêto; ponta, espigão; cravo, cavilha, prego grande; (bot.) espiga; v.t. (mil.) encravar.
spill s. hastilha; v.t. derramar, entornar.
spin s. giro, volta; v.t. fiar; prolongar, dilatar; adiar; fazer girar; v.i. girar, rodar; fiar.
spinach, spinage s. espinafre.

spinal adj. espinal; — **cord** coluna vertebral.
spindle s. fuso, bilro; eixo; carretel.
spindrift s. salpico (das ondas).
spine s. espinha dorsal; espinho; **-less** adj. sem espinhos; invertebrado.
spinel s. espinela.
spinner s. fiandeiro, fiandeira.
spinster s. solteirona; solteira.
spiny adj. espinhoso.
spiral adj. espiral, em espiral; s. espiral.
spire s. (arq.) agulha; cimo; rôsca, espira, caracol.
spirit s. espirito, alma; gênio; essência; humor, moral, disposição; alcool, bebida espirituosa; — **away** fazer desaparecer; **-ed** adj. ardente, animado, corajoso; **-less** adj. desanimado, sem coragem; **-ual** adj. espiritual; **-ualism** s. espiritualismo; **-ualist** s. espiritualista; **spirituous** adj. alcoólico; **-ism** s. espiritismo.
spirt s. jato; v.i. esguichar.
spit s. espêto (de assar); banco de areia, ponta de terra; v.t. atravessar (com espêto); espetar.
spit s. cuspo, cusparada; v.i. cuspir.
spite s. despeito; rancor, malevolência, ódio; v.t. indignar; irritar; despeitar; **in — of** a despeito de; **-ful** adj. malévolo, maldoso, rancoroso.
spitfire s. ferrabrás.
spittle s. saliva; **spittoon** s. escarradeira.
splash s. salpico, respingo; v.t. salpicar, respingar.
splay v.t. chanfrar, esguelhar; deslocar; espalhar.
spleen s. baço; hipocondria.
splendid adj. esplêndido, magnífico; brilhante; **splendor, splendour** s. esplendor, magnificência.
splice s. junta, entrelaçamento; v.t. entrelaçar (corda); ensamblar, emalhetar; (pop.) casar.
splint s. lasca; (cir.) tala, aparelho (de gêsso, etc.); esquírola; v.t. (cir.) encanar, pôr aparelho, entalar.
splinter s. lasca, estilhaço; farpa; v.t. fazer saltar em estilhaços; despedaçar; v.i. despedaçar-se.
split s. fenda; greta; (fig.) cisão; v.t. fender, rachar; fracionar; cindir; separar, dividir; v.i. separar-se, cindir-se; arrebentar; **-ting headache** dôr de cabeça alucinante; — **ears with noise** arrebentar os tímpanos com o barulho.
splutter s. algazarra, falatório; v.i. falar apressada e confusamente.
spoil s. despôjo, presa; v.t. estragar; corromper.
spoke s. raio (de roda); — **shave** rebote; plaina; v.t. enraiar.
spokesman s. o que fala por outro, porta-voz.
spoliation s. espoliação.
sponge s. esponja.
spongy adj. esponjoso.
sponsor s. responsável, promotor; fiador; padrinho, madrinha (de batismo).
spontaneous adj. espontâneo.
spook s. fantasma, espetro.
spool s. bobina, carretel, rôlo; v.t. enrolar (fio).
spoon s. colher.
spoor s. rasto, pista (de animal selvagem).
sporadic adj. esporádico.
spore s. (bot.&biol.) esporo.

sport s. esporte; (biol.) mutação; =ive adj. esportivo.

spot s. sítio, lugar, paragem, ponto; mancha, borrão; sinal; v.t. manchar, borrar; salpicar; (mil.) assinalar, marcar (no mapa); **on the** — imediatamente; =ted adj. malhado, salpicado; =less adj. sem mancha, imaculado.

spouse s. esposo, esposa.

spout s. esguicho, torneira, repuxo; bico (de bule, chaleira, etc.); v.t.&i. esguichar, jorrar; recitar (pomposamente); declamar; (fir.) empenhar.

sprain s. torcedura.

sprat s. eperlano, sarda (peixe).

sprawl v.i. esparramar-se; estender-se, espichar-se; (agric.) alastrar.

spray s. gotículas (de água); repuxo; chuveiro; borrifo; ramo, apanhado (de flores); vaporizador; v.t. vaporizar, pulverizar; borrifar.

spread s. desenvolvimento; envergadura; propagação, disseminação, expansão; coberta de cama; tapête de mesa; v.t.&i. abrir, estender; desenvolver, esparramar; disseminar, propagar, divulgar, propalar; estender-se; difundir-se; distribuir; cobrir.

spree s. farra, pândega.

sprig s. raminho, renôvo; pimpolho.

sprightly adj. vivo, alegre, esperto.

spring s. primavera; mola; elasticidade; salto, cambalhota; móvel, motivo; fonte, manancial; origem, nascimento; v.t.&i. brotar, rebentar; nascer, proceder, originar-se; saltar, jorrar; fazer saltar (uma mina); saltar por cima; guarnecer de molas; — **mattress** colchão de molas; — **water** agua de mina.

sprinkle v.t. aspergir, regar; salpicar; =r s. regador.

sprint s. corrida de velocidade; =er s. corredor de velocidade.

sprite s. duende; fantasma.

sprout s. renôvo, grêlo; v.i. grelar, brotar.

spruce adj. tratado, asseado; adamado; s. abeto.

spud s. pá estreita.

spur s. espora; esporão (do galo); contraforte (de cordilheira); (arq.) arcobotante; (fig.) aguilhão, estímulo; v.t. esporear; (fig.) aguilhoar, estimular; **on the — of the moment** sob o impulso do momento.

spurious adj. espúrio, falso, falsificado, ilegítimo.

spurn v.t. repelir; repelir com o pé; menosprezar.

spurt v.i. esguichar; s. esguicho, jôrro; esfôrço supremo, arranco.

sputter s. saliva, perdigoto; v.i. falar depressa e indistintamente; falar cuspindo.

spy s. espião; v.t.&i. espionar.

squab s. filhote de pombo; pessoa gorda e baixa; almofada; sofá.

squabble s. briga; v.i. brigar.

squabbish adj. rechonchudo, pesado.

squad s. esquadra (de soldados).

squadron s. esquadrão; esquadra; esquadrilha.

squalid adj. esquálido, sujo.

squall s. ventania com chuva e neve.

squalor s. sordidez, imundície.

squander v.t. prodigar, gastar, esbanjar.

square s. quadrado; praça (quadrada); esquadria, esquadro; nível; adj. quadrado, quadrangular; exatamente correspondente; justo, cabal, perfeito; v.t. quadrar, ajustar; alinhar, compassar; regular; — **meal** refeição farta; — **mile** milha quadrada; — **root** raiz quadrada; — **dealing** boa fé; **to be** — estar com a vida em dia, contas saldadas; =ly adv. em quadrado; diretamente; honestamente.

squash v.t. esmagar, achatar.

squat v.i. agachar-se, acocorar-se; adj. acocorado, agachado.

squeak s. grito; v.i. gritar.

squeal s. grito agudo; v.i. gritar.

squeamish adj. enjoado.

squeegee s. vassoura de borracha, rôdo.

squeeze v.t. espremer, apertar; s. apertão; pressão.

squelch v.i. desconcertar-se.

squib s. busca-pés; foguete; artigo ou discurso satírico.

squid s. calamar, lula.

squint v.i.&t. olhar de esguelha; olhar vesgo; adj. vesgo; s. estrabismo.

squire s. escudeiro; senhor; título de cortezia; v.t.&i. acompanhar, escoltar.

squirrel s. esquilo.

squirt s. seringa; v.t. seringar.

stab s. punhalada; golpe; v.t. apunhalar.

stability s. estabilidade; **stabilize** v.t estabilizar.

stables estrebaria, cavalariça; adj.estável.

stack s. montão de feno, trigo, lenha, etc.; pilha; v.t. empilhar.

stadium s. estádio.

staff s. cajado, bordão; vara, insígnia; bengala; haste, pau da bandeira; pessoal, corpo de assistentes; (mil.) estado-maior; (mús.) pauta.

stag s. veado.

stage s. tablado; estrado; teatro, palco, cena; andaime; estágio; grau, estado, condição; progresso, fase; posta (para cavalos); — **coach** diligência; — **effect** efeito de cêna; v.t. exibir, representar.

stagger v.i. titubear, vacilar; =s s. vertigem (dos cavalos).

stagnant adj. estagnado; **stagnation** s. estagnação, marasmo.

staid adj. grave, sério.

stain s. mancha, mácula; deshonra, deslustre; v.t. manchar, macular; difamar; tingir, colorir; =less adj. imaculado, sem mancha; inoxidável.

stair s. degrau; (plural) escada.

stake s. estaca, poste; pelourinho; bigorna pequena; entrada, parada (de jôgo); risco, perigo; v.t. pôr estacas; apoiar, sustentar; apostar, fazer paradas (no jôgo); **sweep=** loteria, geralmente em combinação com uma corrida de cavalos, na qual o vencedor recebe o total das apostas.

stalactite s. estalactite.

stalagmite s. estalagmite.

stale adj. velho; usado; prescrito (título).

stalk s. haste, talo; pé (de hortaliça).

stall s. baia, estrebaria; quiosque; tenda; (teat.) poltrona; v.t. encurralar.

stallion s. garanhão.

stalwart adj. robusto, vigoroso; bravo.

stamen s. base, fundamento; (bot.) estame; (fig.) força vital.

stammer v.i.&t. gaguejar.

stamp s. cunho, sêlo, estampilha; impressão, marca, sinal; estampa, imagem, medalha; caráter, índole; v.t.&i. sapatear, bater com os pés; calcar (com os pés); estampar, imprimir; estampilhar, selar, cunhar; carimbar.

stampede s. dispersão, fuga; estouro (da boiada); *v.i.* correr em pânico.

stance s. posição; postura.

stanch V. **staunch**.

stanchion s. escora; pontalete.

stand s. lugar, sítio; suporte; pôsto; parada, pausa; estrado, plataforma; pedestal; atitude, opinião; oposição; resistência; estante; *v.t.&i.* estar ou ficar em pé; sustentar-se; estacionar; colocar-se; parar; aguentar; suster-se; permanecer; resistir; deter-se, fazer alto; suportar; defender; — **idle** estar inativo; — **in the way of** fazer obstáculo a; — **up** levantar-se, ficar em pé; — **for** significar; — **by** ser do partido de; — **forth** adiantar-se, avançar; — **in need** necessitar; — **under** sofrer, suportar, aguentar.

standard s. estandarte; padrão, modêlo, norma; critério; tipo, medida; *(mec.)* suporte, pilastra, árvore; *adj.* normal, de regra, de lei; clássico; — **bearer** porta-estandarte; — **price** preço regular; — **scale** escala normal; — **work** obra clássica.

standardize *v.t.* padronizar.

standing s. posição; categoria; lugar; *adj.* em pé; estável, duradouro; estagnado; **of long** — antigo, de longa data; — **water** agua estagnada; — **forces** tropas regulares; — **committee** comitê permanente.

standoffish *adj.* distante; reservado.

stanza s. estrofe, estância.

staple s. empório; escala; produto principal; assunto principal, de maior importância; fibra, filamento; matéria prima, material bruto; chapa de ferro; grampo; *adj.* principal, proeminente; estabelecido, reconhecido; *(com.)* de consumo ou uso corrente.

star s. estrela; astro; *(imp.)* asterisco.

starboard s. *(mar.)* estibordo.

starch s. amido, goma, fécula; *v.t.* engomar; **-y** *adj.* feculento; têso.

stare s. olhar fixo; *v.i.* olhar fixamente; — **at** encarar.

stark *adj.* forte; áspero; têso; —**-mad** louco varrido; —**-naked** nú em pêlo.

starling s. estorninho.

starry *adj.* estrelado.

start s. começo, início, estréia; arrancada, impulso; saída, partida; sobressalto, estremecimento; *v.t.&i.* estremecer; partir, sair; começar, iniciar, estrear; largar (o navio); arrancar (a máquina); sobressaltar-se, assustar-se.

startle *v.t.* assustar, espantar, alarmar; **startling** *adj.* alarmante; impressionante.

starvation s. inanição, fome.

starve *v.t.&i.* passar fome; fazer passar fome; morrer de fome; matar à míngua.

starving *adj.* esfomeado; com muita fome.

state s. estado, disposição, condição; circunstância; pompa, grandeza; estado (corpo político); *v.t.* expressar, declarar, afirmar; expor, manifestar; enunciar, formular.

statement s. enunciado, proposição; declaração, exposição; manifestação; relatório.

statesman s. estadista.

static, statical *adj.* estático; **statics** s. estática.

station s. estação; sítio, situação; pôsto; condição ou posição social; — **house**

pôsto policial; *v.t.* colocar, situar, alojar; destacar.

stationery s. papel, papelaria; artigos de escritório.

statistic, statistical *adj.* estatístico; **statistics** s. estatística; **statistician** s. estatístico.

statuary *adj.* estatuário; s. estatuária; **statue** s. estátua; **statuette** s. estatueta.

stature s. estatura.

status s. estado; título, qualidade; **statutory** *adj.* legal.

staunch *adj.* são, em bom estado; resoluto, determinado; firme, sincero; dedicado; *v.t.* estancar.

stave s. aduela (de pipa); *(mús.)* pauta; *v.t.* quebrar, arrombar, tirar o fundo.

stay s. estadia, residência; espera, parada; impedimento, obstáculo; refôrço; suporte, apôio; estai; *(plural)* colete (de barbatanas); *v.i.&t.* ficar, estar ou continuar na mesma posição ou lugar; parar; demorar-se (em algum lugar); permanecer; apoiar, reforçar; *(dir.)* suspender; — **the stomach** forrar o estômago; — **up** fazer vigília.

stead s. lugar, sítio; **in** — **of** em lugar de.

steadfast *adj.* constante, firme; **-ly** *adv.* com constância; **-ness** s. constância, firmeza.

steady *adj.* firme, constante; estável; seguro, estabelecido; *int.* firme!

steak s. bife.

steal *v.t.&i.* roubar; **-ing** s. roubo; **-thy** *adj.* furtivo; **-thily**, *adv.* furtivamente.

steam s. vapor; exalação; *v.t.* cozinhar a vapor; *v.i.* mover a vapor; emitir vapor.

stearin s. estearina.

steed s. cavalo, corcel.

steel s. aço; isqueiro; fuzil; barbatana; *v.t.* acerar.

steep *adj.* escarpado, alcantilado; excessivo, exorbitante; *v.t.* empapar, impregnar; pôr de infusão.

steeple s. tôrre, campanário; —**-chase** corrida de obstáculos.

steepness s. escarpa, declive, ladeira íngreme.

steer s. novilho; *v.t.&i.* conduzir, dirigir, guiar, governar; **-age** s. proa; **-ing** s. direção; govêrno; volante (de direção).

stellar *adj.* astral.

stem s. haste; cabo, talo, tronco, pedúnculo; *v.t.&i.* ir contra a corrente; opor-se, resistir, deter.

stench s. mau cheiro.

stencil s. chapa ou modêlo (para estresir); *v.t.* estresir.

stenographer s. estenógrafo; **stenography** s. estenografia.

stentorian *adj.* estentóreo.

step s. passo, passada; caminho, progresso, adiantamento; degrau; medida; cadência, compasso; *v.i.* dar um passo; andar; pisar; ir, vir; — **in** entrar; — **aside** pôr-se de lado, afastar-se; — **back** retroceder; — **over** atravessar; — **down** descer; —**on** pisar, andar sôbre; — **forth** avançar; — **after** seguir, ir atrás.

stereoscope s. estereoscópio.

stereotype s. estereótipo.

sterile *adj.* estéril; **sterility** s. esterilidade; **sterilize** *v.t.* esterilizar.

sterling *adj.* esterlino; *(fig.)* puro, verdadeiro; de lei, maciço; s. libra esterlina.

stern *adj.* severo, austero; **-ness** s. severidade, austeridade.

sternum s. esterno.
stethoscope s. estetoscópio.
stevedore s. estivador.
stew s. cozido; v.t. cozer, ferver em fogo brando; guisar.
steward s. despenseiro; intendente, mordomo; comissário; empregado de bordo; ='s **room** despensa; =ess s. empregada de bordo.
stick s. pau, vara, vareta; bengala; batuta; (*plural*) achas de lenha; v.t.&i. cravar, fincar; meter, introduzir; afixar; perseverar, ser constante; aderir; colar; — **by** apoiar, sustentar; — **to** aderir, ficar firme; =iness s. viscosidade.
sticky adj. pegajoso, colante; meloso.
stiff adj. têso, duro; empertigado; — **collar** colarinho duro; =en v.t. endurecer, enrijecer; =ness s. rigidez, dureza; empertigamento.
stile s. escada ou degraus para se transpor um muro.
stiletto s. estilete.
still adj. calmo, tranquilo; silencioso; imóvel, em repouso; adv. ainda, sempre; conj. no entanto, todavia; s. alambique; sossêgo; v.t. acalmar, tranquilizar; =**born** nascido morto; — **water** agua dormente.
stillness s. calma, tranquilidade; silêncio.
stilts s. andas (pernas de pau); estacas; v.t. levantar por meio de andas ou estacas.
stimulant s. estimulante, reconfortante; **stimulate** v.t. estimular; **stimulus** s. estímulo.
sting s. ferrão, aguilhão; picada; (*fig.*) remorso; v.t.&i. picar, dar ferroadas; atormentar; =ing adj. picante.
stingy adj. avaro, mesquinho.
stink s. fedor; v.i. feder.
stint s. limite, restrição; tarefa; v.t. restringir; distribuir tarefa; v.i. ser econômico; desistir.
stipend s. estipêndio.
stipple v.t. gravar com pontos; pintar com pequenas pinceladas.
stipulate v.t. estipular.
stir s. bulha, tumulto; agitação; v.t. mexer, agitar; atiçar (fogo); excitar, instigar; v.i. mexer-se, agitar-se.
stirring adj. vibrante; comovente.
stirrup s. estribo.
stitch s. ponto (de costura); ponto de malha; pontada; v.t. coser; — **up** remendar.
stiver s. sôldo (moeda holandêsa); ninharia.
stoat s. arminho.
stock s. tronco, cepo; estirpe, linhagem; (*for.*) linha direta de uma família; (*com.*) sortimento; capital comercial; provisão; (*fin.*) valores, fundos, ações; (*mec.*) cubo; colmeia; monte de baralho (no jôgo de cartas); v.t. aprovisionar, prover, abastecer; sortir.
stockade s. estacada, paliçada.
stocking s. meia (comprida).
stocky adj. atarracado.
stoical adj. estóico; **stoicism** s. estoicismo.
stoke v.t. atiçar, alimentar (o fogo); =r s. foguista.
stole s. estola.
stolid adj. estólido, fleumático; =ity s. fleuma, impassividade.
stomach s. estômago; v.t. digerir; engulir.
stone s. pedra; caroço; pêso de 6,35 quilos;

v.t. lapidar, apedrejar; tirar os caroços; **stony** adj. pedregoso.
stool s. tamborete, escabêlo; privada; defecação; fêzes.
stoop v.i. inclinar-se, abaixar-se.
stop s. parada, pausa; interrupção, suspensão; oposição; (*mús.*) tecla; registro (de órgão); (*tip.*) ponto; (*fot.*) diafragma; v.t.&i. parar; suspender; interromper; parar, estacionar; ficar; — **press news** informações de última hora; — **up** tapar, obstruir; — **short** parar de repente.
stoppage s. parada; impedimento, obstáculo; obstrução.
storage s. armazenagem.
store s. armazém; loja, depósito, entreposto; bazar; abundância; reserva; v.t. aprovisionar; abastecer; guardar, acumular; ter em reserva; armazenar; =s s. provisões.
stork s. cegonha.
storm s. tempestade, tormenta; borrasca; v.t. atacar, dar assalto; v.i. tempestear; **thunder** — trovoada; =y adj. tempestuoso.
story s. história; conto, narração, fábula; andar, pavimento; — **book** livro de histórias.
stoup s. pia d'agua benta.
stout adj. forte, vigoroso; robusto, corpulento, cheio; bravo, firme; =ness s. corpulência, gordura.
stove s. fogão; estufa.
stow v.t. fechar, guardar, armazenar; arranjar; estivar, arrumar; (*pop.*) economizar; =**away** s. passageiro clandestino.
straddle v.t.&i. escarrapachar, escarrapachar-se; (*pop.*) apoiar dois partidos opostos, jogar com pau de dois bicos.
straggle v.i. extraviar-se, desviar-se; errar, vagar.
straggling adj. esparsas (casas); rala (barba).
straight adj. reto; correto, honesto; direito, em linha reta; franco; liso (cabelo); adv. diretamente; =en v.t. endireitar; arranjar, pôr em ordem; =**forward** adj. direito; franco; =**forwardly** adv. diretamente; =ness s. retidão.
strain s. tensão, cansaço, esfôrço; (*mec.*) esfôrço, deformação; estirpe, raça, descendência; (*mús.*) ária, melodia, acorde; v.t.&i. forçar, fazer esfôrço, submeter a esfôrço; torcer; fatigar; filtrar; =er s. coador, passador.
strait s. estreito; garganta, desfiladeiro; apuro, apêrto; adj. estreito, ajustado, apertado; penoso.
strand s. costa, praia; cordão, cabo (de corda); v.i. encalhar, dar à costa.
strange adj. estranho, singular; desconhecido; =r s. estrangeiro; desconhecido; =ness s. singularidade, estranheza.
strangle v.t. estrangular; **strangulation** s. estrangulamento.
strap s. correia, tira, faixa, banda; v.t. ligar, atar; bater com uma correia; afiar (navalha).
stratagem s. estratagema; **strategical** adj. estratégico; **strategist** s. estrategista.
strategy s. estratégia.
stratified adj. estratificado.
stratum s. leito, camada; (*geol.*) estrato.
straw s. palha; (*fig.*) bagatela, ninharia.

strawberry s. morango; — ice sorvete de morango.

stray v.i. extraviar-se, perder-se; adj. extraviado, desgarrado; s. pessoa ou animal desgarrado.

streak s. traço; veio; lista; v.t. riscar, listrar.

stream s. corrente, curso; torrente; rio, arroio; v.t.&i. correr, manar, derramar com abundância; desfraldar; =lining aerodinamismo; =lined com forma aerodinâmica.

streamer s. flâmula; serpentina.

street s. rua.

strength s. força; poder; resistência, robustez; =en v.t. reforçar; consolidar; fortificar.

strenuous adj. enérgico; intensa (vida); agitado.

stress s. esfôrço, trabalho, carga, fadiga; acento tônico; ênfase; v.t. carregar; acentuar, dar ênfase.

stretch s. alcance, extensão, dilatação; v.t. esticar, desenrolar, desenvolver; forçar; — oneself espreguiçar-se.

stretcher s. esticador, dilatador, estirador; maca.

strew v.t. espargir, derramar, espalhar, semear; salpicar.

stria s. estria.

strickle s. rasoura; pedra de amolar segadeiras.

strict adj. estrito, exato; rigoroso, severo; =ness s. rigor, severidade; =ure s. crítica; (med.) estreitamento.

stride s. tranco; passo largo, passada; v.i. andar a passos largos.

strident adj. estridente.

strife s. luta, conflito; contenda.

strike s. direção; golpe; encontro, choque; greve; v.t.&i. golpear, dar golpes, bater, dar pancada; ferir; atirar, arremessar; atingir; topar, chocar-se, dar de encontro; tocar, soar, retinir; dar badaladas (relógio); acender (fósforo); fazer greve; mover, comover; surpreender, causar impressão; cunhar (moeda); amainar (velas); riscar; arriar; — fire fazer fogo; — down derrubar, abater; — the colors arriar a bandeira; — camp levantar acampamento; — roots lançar raizes; — off riscar, cortar, separar; — through atravessar, varar; it = me ocorre-me, vem-me à idéia; without striking a blow sem desferir um golpe; =r s. grevista; striking adj. surpreendente, notável.

string s. cordão, cordel, fio, barbante; corda (de instrumento de música); fibra, tendão, nervo; série, encadeamento; v.t. encordoar; afinar; enfiar; estirar; amarrar.

stringent adj. rigoroso; convincente.

stringy adj. fibroso; filamentoso.

strip s. tira, faixa, lista; v.t. despojar, despir; estolar; desguarnecer; v.i. despir-se, desnudar-se.

stripe s. lista; tira, barra; (mil.) galão; =d adj. listado.

strive v.i. esforçar-se, fazer por, empenhar-se; lutar por; combater.

stroke s. golpe, pancada; choque; rasgo; badalada (de relógio); braçada (de natação); remada; hemorragia cerebral; v.t. acariciar, afagar; on the — of time ao soar da hora.

stroll s. volta, passeio; v.i. passear, andar.

strolling adj. ambulante.

strong adj. forte; poderoso; vigoroso;

enérgico; resistente; sólido; — box cofre; =hold forte, fortaleza, cidadela; —=minded teimoso; enérgico; =ly adv. fortemente.

strop s. correia, afiador de navalha; v.t. afiar (navalha).

structural adj. estrutural.

structure s. estrutura.

struggle s. luta; v.i. lutar.

strum v.t. tocar mal (um instrumento musical).

strut s. ademanes, pavonada; escora, espeque; v.i. pavonear-se; v.t. escorar.

strychnine s. estricnina.

stub s. tronco, tôco; canhoto (de cheque, recibo, etc.); — book livro-talão; v.t. arrancar; destocar.

stubble s. resteva, restôlho.

stubborn adj. teimoso, obstinado; tenaz.

stubbornness s. teimosia, obstinação; tenacidade.

stucco s. estuque.

stuck-up adj. brioso, orgulhoso.

stud s. tacha, tachão; botão de camisa; barrote, viga; cavalariça; cavalhada; v.t. pregar; pregar tachas; ornar com pregaria; — book registo genealógico de cavalos.

student s. estudante, aluno.

studio s. gabinete, officina, atelier.

studious adj. estudioso.

study s. estudo; gabinete de trabalho; v.i.&t. estudar.

stuff s. matéria, material; tecido; coisa; v.t. rechear; encher, atulhar; entulhar; fartar, saciar; =ing s. recheio; =ed adj. recheado; =y adj. abafado, mal ventilado.

stultify v.t. desacreditar, deshonrar; (for.) alegar ou provar alienação mental.

stumble v.i. tropeçar; dar um passo em falso; s. tropêço.

stump s. tronco; cepo; côto; tôco.

stun v.t. aturdir, atordoar; surpreender, espantar; pasmar; =ning adj. pasmoso; atordoante; maravilhoso.

stunt s. acrobacia; proeza.

stunted adj. esmirrado, raquítico.

stupefy v.t. estupeficar; embasbacar.

stupendous adj. estupendo.

stupid adj. estúpido; =ity s. estupidez.

stupor s. estupor.

sturdy adj. vigoroso, robusto; resoluto.

stutter v.i.&t. gaguejar; =er s. gago.

sty s. pocilga; lupanar; (med.) terçol.

style s. estilo, maneira; gênero, gôsto; elegância; v.t. qualificar, dar título; **stylish** adj. elegante.

stylet s. estilete.

stylograph s. estilógrafo, caneta-tinteiro de ponta cônica.

suave adj. suave.

suavity s. suavidade.

sub-acid adj. agridoce, ligeiramente ácido.

subaltern s. subalterno.

subconscious adj.&s. subconciente.

subcontract s. contrato subordinado aos termos de outro anterior.

subcutaneous adj. subcutâneo.

subdivide v.t. subdividir.

subdue v.t. subjugar, submeter; dominar; suavizar, velar (a luz).

sub-editor s. secretário de redação.

subject s. súdito, vassalo; sujeito, pessoa; assunto, tópico, objeto, matéria; adj. sujeito, submetido, exposto; v.t. sujeitar, submeter; expor.

subjection s. sujeição, dependência.
subjective adv. subjetivo.
subjugate v.t. subjugar.
sublet v.t. sublocar.
sublime adj. sublime; **sublimity** s. sublimidade.
submarine s. submarino.
submerge v.t. submergir; v.i. mergulhar.
submission s. submissão; **submissive** adj. submisso, obediente; **submissiveness** s. submissão, resignação; **submit** v.t. submeter.
subordinate adj. subordinado, subalterno; s. subordinado; v.t. subordinar.
suborn v.t. subornar; **-er** s. subornador.
subpena s. intimação judicial, citação.
subprefect s. sub-prefeito, vice-prefeito.
subrogate v.t. sub-rogar.
subscribe v.t.&i. subscrever; **subscription** s. subscrição.
subsection s. (dir.) alínea.
subsequent adj. subsequente, posterior.
subservience s. subserviência.
subservient adj. subserviente; servil.
subside v.i. baixar; depositar-se; abater-se, calmar-se; **-nce** s. baixa; abatimento, prostração.
subsidiary adj. subsidiário; **subsidy** s. subvenção; subsídio.
subsist v.i. subsistir; viver; **-ence** s. subsistência.
subsoil s. subsolo.
substance s. substância; **substantial** adj. substancial; sólido; **substantially** adv. substancialmente; **substantiate** v.t. substanciar, estabelecer; comprovar.
substantive adj.&s. substantivo.
substitute s. substituto; v.t. substituir.
substratum s. substrato.
substructure s. infra-estrutura.
subtenant s. sublocatário.
subterfuge s. subterfúgio.
subterranean adj. subterrâneo.
subtilize v.t.&i. sutilizar.
subtitle s. subtítulo.
subtle adj. sutil; **-ty** s. sutileza, sutilidade.
subtract v.t. subtrair; **-ion** s. subtração.
suburb s. subúrbio; **-an** adj. suburbano.
subvention s. subvenção.
subversive adj. subversivo; **subvert** v.t. subverter.
subway s. passagem subterrânea; trem subterrâneo.
succeed v.t.&i. suceder, seguir; acontecer; conseguir; ter sucesso.
success s. sucesso, êxito; **-ful** adj. feliz, bem sucedido.
succession s. sucessão.
successive adj. sucessivo.
successor s. sucessor.
succinct adj. sucinto; **-ness** s. concisão.
succulent adj. suculento.
succumb v.i. sucumbir.
such adj. tal, semelhante, igual; — a thing tal coisa.
suck v.t.&i. chupar, mamar; sugar; aspirar; **-le** v.t. dar de mamar, amamentar.
suction s. sucção.
sudden adj. súbito; brusco; **-ness** s. repente, subitaneidade.
suds s. espuma de sabão; agua de sabão.
sue v.t. processar, acionar.
suet s. sebo.
suffer v.t.&i. sofrer, padecer; aguentar, tolerar; permitir; **-able** adj. tolerável, suportável.
sufferance s. sofrimento; tolerância.

sufferer s. vítima: paciente; **suffering** s. sofrimento; adj. sofredor.
suffice v.i. bastar; v.t. satisfazer, prover, suprir.
sufficiency s. suficiência; presunção; **sufficient** adj. suficiente.
suffix s. sufixo.
suffocate v.t. sufocar; asfixiar; **suffocation** s. sufocação; asfixia.
suffragan s. bispo sufragâneo; adj. sufragâneo.
suffrage s. sufrágio; **-tte** s. sufragista (mulher).
suffuse v.t. difundir; derramar, verter; **suffusion** s. derramamento; (med.) sufusão.
sugar s. açucar; v.t. açucarar; **-y** adj. açucarado.
suggest v.t. sugerir; **-ion** s. sugestão; **-ive** adj. sugestivo.
suicide s. suicídio; suicida.
suit s. petição, súplica, solicitação; coleção, série, jôgo; (for.) pleito, litígio; v.t.&i. aparelhar, adaptar, acomodar, adequar; convir; assentar; enquadrar; — of clothes terno de roupa; **-ability** s. conveniência; adaptação; **-able** adj. conveniente, apropriado; próprio.
suite s. apartamento (de hotel); série; acompanhamento; séquito.
suiter, suitor s. pretendente; suplicante; candidato; namorado.
sulk v.i. amuar; **-y** adj. amuado.
sullen adj. rabugento, mal-humorado; **-ness** s. mau gênio; mau humor.
sully v.t. manchar, sujar, macular.
sulphate s. sulfato; **sulphurous** adj. sulfuroso.
sultan s. sultão; **sultana** s. sultana.
sultry adj. abrasador, sufocante, canicular.
sum s. soma, total; suma, substância, essência.
summarize v.t. resumir.
summary adj. sumário; s. sumário, resumo.
summer s. verão; v.i. passar o verão.
summing up resumo (de uma argumentação).
summon v.t. intimar, citar, notificar; convocar; **-s** s. intimação, notificação; v.t. citar, intimar.
sump s. reservatório, caixa (de ralo).
sumptuous adj. suntuoso; **-ness** s. suntuosidade, luxo.
sun s. sol; v.t. insolar, expor ao sol; **-burnt** queimado do sol; **-flower** girasol; **-set** pôr do sol; **-stroke** insolação.
Sunday s. domingo.
sunder v.t. separar.
sundries s. miscelânea; artigos variados de pouca montá.
sunken adj. oco; cavernoso; submerso; encovado.
sunless adj. sem sol; **sunny** adj. insolado.
sup v.i. cear; sorver.
superabundant adj. superabundante.
superb adj. soberbo.
supercilious adj. altivo, arrogante, soberbo.
superficial adj. superficial; **superficies** s. superfície.
superfine adj. superfino.
superfluity s. superfluidade.
superfluous adj. supérfluo.
superheat v.t. superaquecer.
superhuman adj. sobrehumano.
superimpose v.t. sobrepor.

superintend v.t. superintender; **-ence** s. superintendência; **-ent** s. superintendente.

superior adj.&s. superior; **-ity** s. superioridade.

superlative adj.&s. superlativo.

superman s. superhomem.

supernatural adj.&s. sobrenatural.

supernumerary adj.&s. supranumerário.

superscription s. inscrição; título.

supersede v.t. substituir.

superstition s. superstição.

superstitious adj. supersticioso.

supertax s. sobretaxa; imposto adicional.

supervene v.i. sobrevir.

supervise v.t. fiscalizar, controlar, superintender; **supervision** s. fiscalização, inspeção; **supervisor** s. fiscal, inspetor.

supine adj. supino.

supper s. ceia.

supplant v.t. suplantar.

supple adj. flexível, brando; **to make —** tornar flexível.

supplement s. suplemento; v.t. suplementar, completar; **-ary** adj. suplementar.

suppleness s. flexibilidade.

suppliant adj.&s. suplicante; **suplicate** v.t. suplicar; **supplication** s. súplica.

supplier s. fornecedor.

supply s. provisão, fornecimento, abastecimento; suprimento; **supplies** provisões, materiais, artigos, víveres; v.t. fornecer, prover, suprir.

support s. sustento, manutenção; arrimo; v.t. sustentar, manter; apoiar; **in — of** em favor de, em apôio de.

suppose v.t. supor; presumir; **supposition** s. suposição.

suppress v.t. suprimir; **-ion** s. supressão.

suppurate v.i. supurar.

supremacy s. supremacia; **supreme** adj. supremo.

surcharge v.t. sobrecarregar.

sure adj. seguro, certo, assegurado; infalível; **-ness** s. segurança; **-ty** s. segurança; caução; fiador.

surf s. rebentação; ressaca.

surface s. superfície.

surfeit s. saciedade; v.t. saciar; v.i. fartar-se.

surge s. vaga, onda; v.i. encapelar-se, ondear.

surgeon s. cirurgião.

surgery s. cirurgia; **surgical** adj. cirúrgico.

surly adj. brutal, grosseiro.

surmise s. suspeita, desconfiança; v.t. desconfiar, suspeitar.

surmount v.t. sobrepujar, vencer; superar.

surname s. sobrenome.

surpass v.t. exceder; **-ing** adj. superior.

surplice s. sobrepeliz.

surplus s. excedente.

surprise s. surpresa; espanto; v.t. surpreender, espantar; **surprising** adj. surpreendente, espantoso.

surrender s. rendição, capitulação; v.t. entregar; ceder; v.i. render-se, entregar-se; capitular.

surreptitious adj. subreptício.

surrogate s. substituto.

surround v.t. circundar, cercar, rodear.

surrounding adj. circunvizinho; **-s** s. arredores, cercanias.

surtax s. imposto adicional sôbre os rendimentos que excedem certos limites.

survey s. estudo, inspeção crítica (com a finalidade de obter dados); v.t. estudar, examinar (para colher dados); medir (terras); levantar plantas.

survival s. sobrevivência.

survive v.t.&i. sobreviver.

survivor s. sobrevivente.

susceptible adj. suscetível, sensível.

suspect adj. suspeito; s. suspeito; v.t. suspeitar.

suspend v.t. suspender.

suspender s. suspensório; (Ing.) liga (para as meias).

suspense s. suspensão; dúvida, incerteza; **suspension** s. suspensão.

suspicion s. suspeita; **suspicious** adj. suspeitoso; suspeito.

sustain v.t. sustentar; suster; manter; sofrer; suportar.

sustenance s. subsistência, alimento; sustento.

sutler s. vivandeiro.

suture s. sutura.

suzerain s. suzerano; **-ty** s. suzerania.

swab s. esfregão; lambaz.

swagger v.i. fazer de valente; contar bravatas; **-er** s. contador de bravatas; fanfarrão.

swain s. camponês; pastor.

swallow s. andorinha; sorvedouro, abismo; garganta; · trago, bocado; v.t. engulir, tragar.

swamp s. brejo, pântano; v.t. atolar; submergir; **-y** adj. pantanoso.

swan s. cisne.

sward s. relva.

swarm s. enxame; multidão; v.i. pulular, enxamear, abundar; **— up** subir, trepar.

swarthy adj. moreno, trigueiro; tisnado.

swash v.i. marulhar; fanfarronar.

swastika s. suástika, cruz gamada.

swat v.t. bater com força em.

swathe v.t. enfaixar, envolver; s. faixa.

sway s. brandimento; balanço; dominação, poder, mando; v.t.&i. brandir, vibrar, manejar; influenciar; pender, inclinar, oscilar; desviar; governar.

swear v.i.&t. jurar; blasfemar, praguejar; prestar juramento.

sweat s. suor, transpiração; v.i. transpirar, suar.

sweep s. vassourada, varredura; alcance, extensão, curva; movimento; v.t.&i. varrer; vasculhar; assolar, devastar; **-er** s. varredor, limpador de chaminés; **-ing** gesture gesto largo.

sweet adj. doce; açucarado; suave; encantador, belo, gentil; **-heart** namorado, namorada; **— pea** ervilha de cheiro; **— potato** batata doce; **to have a — tooth** gostar de doces; s. doce, bala; **-en** v.t. adoçar, açucarar; **-ness** s. doçura, suavidade, encanto.

swell s. intumescência, inchação, inflamação; modulação sonora; amplidão; vaga, vagalhão, onda; ondulação (de terreno); (pop.) pessoa na moda; v.t.&i. inchar, intumescer, engrossar, inflamar; crescer, aumentar, dilatar; inflar; adj. (pop.) elegante; (jíria) ótimo, de primeira.

swelling s. inchação, inflamação, intumescência; protuberância.

swelter v.t. sufocar de calor; v.i. transpirar profusamente.

swerve s. desvio; v.i. fazer um desvio, apartar-se; desviar-se.

swift adj. rápido; ligeiro, veloz; s. corrente, correnteza (de rio); aspa (de moinho); dobadoura; denominação de vários pássaros semelhantes à andorinha; *ness s. rapidez, ligeireza, velocidade; *ly adv. ràpidamente, velozmente.
swig v.t. beber a grandes tragos.
swill v.t. lavar; beber àvidamente
swim v.i. nadar; s. natação, nado; *ming s. natação, nado; *ming pool piscina de natação.
swindle v.t.&i. extorquir, lograr, enganar, conseguir dinheiro ilìcitamente; *r s. caloteiro, escroque.
swine s. porco, leitão.
swing s. oscilação; balanço; impulso, lance; abalo; v.t.&i. balançar, oscilar; rodar; balançar-se.
swirl s. turbilhão, torvelinho, redemoinho.
switch s. chibata, chibatada; vibração; chave (de caminho de ferro); comutador; v.t. açoitar, dar chibatadas; brandir; comutar, ligar; desviar (trem).
swivel s. torniquete; v.i. rotar.
swoon s. desmaio, desfalecimento; v.i. desmaiar, desfalecer.
sword s. espada; **to fire and** — a ferro e fogo; *fish peixe espada; *smanship s. esgrima.
Sybarite s. sibarita.
sycamore s. sicômoro.
sycophant s. sicofanta.

syllabize v.t. silabar.
syllable s. sílaba.
syllabus s. programa; sílabo.
syllogism s. silogismo.
sylph s. sílfide.
sylvan, silvan adj. silvestre, florestal.
symbol s. símbolo; *ical adj. simbólico; *ize v.t. simbolizar.
symmetrical adj. simétrico; **symmetry** s. simetria.
sympathetic adj. solidário; favorável; —-**strike** greve de solidariedade.
sympathy s. solidariedade, compreensão compaixão, lástima; **sympathize** v.i. compadecer-se, solidarizar-se.
symphony s. sinfonia.
symptom s. sintoma.
synagogue s. sinagoga.
synchronous adj. sincrônico.
syncopate v.t. sincopar; **syncopation,** **syncope** s. síncope.
syndicate s. sindicato; v.i. sindicalizar-se.
synod s. sínodo.
synonym s. sinônimo; *ous adj. sinônimo.
synopsis s. sinopse.
syntax s. sintaxe.
synthesis s. síntese; **synthetic, synthetical** adj. sintético.
syringe s. seringa; v.t. seringar.
syrup s. xarope; *y adj. xaroposo.
system s. sistema; *atic adj. sistemático.

T

T letra do alfabeto.
tab s. alça, aselha.
tabernacle s. tabernáculo.
table s. mesa; — **cloth** toalha de mesa; — **spoon** colher de sopa; — **salt** sal fino; v.t. pôr em cima da mesa.
taboo s. tabú; v.t. declarar tabú, interdizer.
tabular adj. tabular; em quadro.
tabulate v.t. tabular.
tacit adj. tácito.
taciturn adj. taciturno; *ity s. taciturnidade.
tack s. brocha, tacha; (mar.) bordada, guinada; amura; v.t. pregar com tachas, brochas; (fig.) coser; v.i. bordejar; mudar bruscamente.
tackle s. mecanismo, aparelhagem, aviamento; (mar.) talha, cordoalha, enxárcia, poleame; (futebol americano) intercepção; v.t. agarrar; atacar, enfrentar (um problema); (futebol) interceptar, derrubar.
tacky adj. colante, pegajoso, viscoso.
tact s. tato; discernimento; *ful adj. com discernimento e habilidade; *less adj. impolítico, sem tato.
tactics s. tática.
tadpole s. sapinho; rã ainda não adulta.
taffeta s. tafetá.
tag s. agulheta; alça, aselha; lugar-comum, refrão; (jôgo) chicote queimado; — **label** etiqueta (volante); —*rag a canalha; v.t. pôr agulheta; rotular, pôr etiqueta; alcançar, tocar.
tail s. cauda; rabo; cabo, extremidade, ponta; trazeira; reverso (da moeda); *ings s. resíduos.
tailor s. alfaiate.
taint s. infeção; mácula, mancha; v.t.

manchar, macular; corromper; infetar; poluir.
take v.t. tomar, pegar; receber; levar, conduzir; tirar; segurar; supor; — **away** levar; — **hold of** apoderar-se de; — **roots** criar raizes; — **a walk** dar um passeio; — **time** levar tempo; — **up** levantar; adotar; dedicar-se a; **taking** adj. sedutor; (pop.) contagioso.
talc s. talco.
tale s. conto, história, novela.
talent s. talento; *ed adj. talentoso.
talisman s. talismã.
talk s. conversa, palestra, discurso; v.i. falar, conversar, tagarelar; v.t. falar; falar sôbre; *ative adj. loquaz; *er s. palrador, conversador; *ing adj. falante; *ing film fita falada; *ing machine fonógrafo.
tall adj. alto; *ness s. altura.
tallow s. sebo; v.t. ensebar.
tally s. marca; marcação; contagem; v.i. corresponder, estar conforme.
talon s. unha, garra.
tamarind s. tamarindo.
tambour s. bastidor de bordado; tambor.
tambourine s. pandeiro.
tame adj. manso, domesticado; v.t. domesticar, amansar.
tamp v.t. tamponar, socar.
tampion s. tampão; tampa.
tampon s. tampão; v.t., tamponar.
tan v.t. cortir; queimar, tostar.
tangent s.&adj. tangente.
tangerine s. tangerina.
tangible adj. tangível, palpável.
tangle s. nó; emaranhamento; v.t. emaranhar, embaraçar.
tango s. tango.
tank s. reservatório, cisterna, tanque; carro de assalto.

tannery s. cortume; tanner s. cortidor.
tannin s. tanino.
tantalize v.t. tantalizar; supliciar.
tantrums s. nervosismo, mau humor.
tap s. golpe leve; cânula; torneira, válvula (de barril); — dance sapateado; =room s. bar; v.t.&i. bater, tocar; furar (um barril); talhar, fazer incisão (na árvore, para colhêr a seiva); (med.) fazer punção, puncionar.
tape s. fita; banda; faixa.
taper s. vela, círio; v.t. diminuir, afilar; v.i. ir-se afinando, terminar-se em ponta.
tapestry s. tapessaria.
tapioca s. tapioca.
tar s. alcatrão; v.t. alcatroar, brear; provocar.
tardy adj. tardio.
target s. alvo, pontaria.
tariff s. tarifa; v.t. tarifar.
tarnish v.t. empanar, deslustrar.
tarry adj. betuminoso.
tarry v.i. tardar, demorar; habitar; permanecer.
tart adj. acre, ácido; s. torta, pastel.
tartar s. tártaro; =ic adj. tartárico.
tartness s. acidez, azedume.
task s. tarefa; ocupação; v.t. dar tarefa; atarefar; cansar.
taste s. gôsto, sabor; v.t. provar, saborear.
tasteful adj. gostoso; tasteless adj. sem sabor, insípido.
tasting s. degustação; tasty adj. saboroso.
ta-ta int. adeus!, até logo!
tatter s. trapo, farrapo; =ed adj. esfarrapado.
tatting s. espécie de renda de algodão ou linho.
tattle s. garrulice; v.i. tagarelar.
tattoo s. tatuagem.
taunt s. sarcasmo; v.t. censurar com palavras ofensivas.
tavern s. taverna.
tawdriness s. falso brilho; tawdry adj. vistoso mas de mau gosto.
tawny adj. fulvo.
tax s. taxa; imposto; v.t. taxar, lançar impostos.
taxicab s. taxí, automóvel de praça.
taxidermist s. taxidermista.
tea s. chá; =spoon colher de chá.
teach v.t.&i. ensinar; instruir; =er s. professor, professora; =ing s. ensino, instrução.
team s. equipo.
tear s. rasgão; v.t. rasgar.
tear s. lágrima; =ful adj. lacrimoso.
tease v.i.&t. implicar; atormentar, importunar.
teat s. bico de peito; têta, ubre.
technical adj. técnico.
technique s. técnica.
technology s. tecnologia.
tedious adj. tedioso, fastidioso, fatigante; =ness s. tédio, aborrecimento.
teens s. espaço de tempo entre treze e vinte anos de idade.
teethe v.i. romper (dentes); teething s. dentição.
teetotal adj. contra o alcool.
tegument s. tegumento.
telegram s. telegrama.
telegraph s. telégrafo; =ic adj. telegráfico.
telepathy s. telepatia.
telephone s. telefone; v.t.&i. telefonar; telephonic adj. telefônico; telephony s. telefonia.
telescope s. telescópio; telescopic adj. telescópico.

television s. televisão.
tell v.t.&i. dizer, contar, relatar, informar; =er s. relator; pagador (de banco).
temerity s. temeridade.
temper s. gênio; humor, têmpera; temperamento; v.t. temperar; misturar, mesclar; acomodar.
temperament s. temperamento; =al adj. genioso, de temperamento.
temperance s. temperança.
temperate adj. temperado; moderado, sóbrio.
temperature s. temperatura.
tempestuous adj. tempestuoso.
temple s. templo; (anat.) fonte.
temporary adj. temporário.
temporize v.i. contemporizar.
tempt v.t. tentar, induzir; provocar; =ation s. tentação; =er s. sedutor; =ress s. sedutora; =ing adj. tentador.
ten adj.&s. dez.
tenable adj. defensável.
tenancy s. locação; tenant s. locatário.
tend v.t. guardar, vigiar; velar; v.i. tender, ter propensão.
tendency s. tendência; disposição.
tendentious adj. tendencioso.
tender adj. 'tenro; brando; sensível, delicado; =ness s. delicadeza, ternura, suavidade.
tendon s. tendão.
tenement s. habitação, casa, apartamento.
tenet s. dogma, doutrina.
tennis s. tênis (jôgo).
tenor s. tenor; teor.
tense adj. tenso; esticado.
tension s. tensão.
tentacle s. tentáculo.
tenth adj.&s. décimo.
tenuity s. tenuidade; tenuous adj. tênue.
tenure s. posse; gôzo, título de posse.
tepid adj. tépido; =ness s. tepidez.
term s. têrmo; cláusula; duração; sessão; prazo; v.t. nomear, chamar.
terminal adj. terminal, final.
terminate v.t. terminar; termination s. terminação, fim.
terminus s. término, fim; estação final.
termite s. térmita, cupim.
terrace s. terraço.
terrestrial adj. terrestre.
terrific adj. terrífico; terrify v.t. aterrorizar.
territorial adj. territorial.
territory s. território.
terror s. terror; =ize v.t. aterrorizar.
terse adj. terso, conciso; =ness s. concisão.
test s. prova; ensaio; v.t.&i. pôr à prova; dar prova; examinar.
testament s. testamento; =ary adj. testamentário; testator s. testador; testatrix s. testadora.
testicle s. testículo.
testify v.t. atestar, testemunhar; v.i. depor.
testimony s. testemunho.
testy adj. irascível.
tetanus s. tétano.
text s. texto.
textile s. tecido; adj. têxtil.
texture s. tecido, contextura.
than conj. que; do que.
thank v.t. agradecer; bendizer; — Heaven! graças aos céus!; =ful adj. agradecido; =fulness s. agradecimento, reconhecimento, gratidão; =less adj. ingrato; =s s. agradecimentos.

that *adj.&pron.* aquele, aquela, aquilo; êste, esta, isto; êsse, essa, isso; que, quem; o qual, a qual, aquilo que; aquele que; aquela que; *conj.* que; afim de que; para que.

thatch *s.* sapé, palha.

thaw *s.* degêlo; *v.t.&i.* degelar.

the *art.* o, a, os, as.

theatre *s.* teatro; theatrical *adj.* teatral.

thee *pron.* tu, te, ti.

theft *s.* roubo.

their *adj.* seu, sua, seus, suas, deles, delas.

theirs *pron.* o seu, a sua; os seus, as suas; os deles, as delas.

theism *s.* teismo.

them *pron.* os, as, êles, elas; lhes.

theme *s.* tema; assunto; (*mús.*) motivo.

then *adv.&conj.* então, ora, naquele tempo; por conseguinte, logo.

thence *adv.* daí, dalí; desde então; daí por diante; =forth, =forward *adv.* desde então.

theologian *s.* teólogo; theology *s.* teologia.

theorem *s.* teorema.

theory *s.* teoria; theorical, theoretical *adj.* teórico.

theosophy *s.* teosofia.

therapeutic *adj.* teraupêutico; =s *s.* terapêutica.

there *adv.* alí, acolá, lá, naquele lugar; =abouts nas cercanias; =fore em consequência, por conseguinte; =upon em consequência disso; em seguida; =under menos; abaixo; =while entretanto; =with juntamente; sem demora.

thermal *adj.* termal, térmico.

thermometer *s.* termômetro.

these *pron.* êstes, estas, êsses, essas.

thesis *s.* tese.

they *pron.* êles, elas.

thick *adj.* espêsso, denso; grosso; cerrado; =en *v.t.* engrossar, condensar, espessar.

thickness *s.* espessura.

thief *s.* gatuno, ladrão; thieve *v.t.* roubar.

thigh *s.* coxa.

thill *s.* lança, timão, vara.

thimble *s.* dedal.

thin *adj.* fino, tênue, delicado; delgado, franzino; claro, ralo; escasso, ligeiro; *v.t.* adelgaçar, afinar; rarefazer; tornar ralo; atenuar.

thine *pron.* o teu, a tua, os teus, as tuas.

thing *s.* coisa, negócio.

think *v.t.&i.* pensar, imaginar, meditar, considerar, refletir; =er *s.* pensador; =ing *adj.* pensante; *s.* pensamento, opinião.

thinly *adj.* ralo; thinness *s.* finura, tenuidade.

third *adj.* terceiro; *s.* terço.

thirst *s.* sêde; =y *adj.* sedento, sequioso.

thirteen *adj.&s.* treze; =th *adj.* décimo terceiro.

this *adj.&pron.* êste, esta, isto.

thorax *s.* tórax.

thorn *s.* espinho.

thorough *adj.* acabado, completo, inteiro, cabal; =ly *adv.* inteiramente, completamente, a fundo, perfeitamente.

those *pron.* aqueles, aquelas.

thou *pron.* tu.

though *conj.* ainda que, posto que, contudo; as — como se.

thought *s.* pensamento, reflexão, idéia; =ful *adj.* atento, cuidadoso; =less *adj.* desatento, irrefletido.

thousand *adj.&s.* mil; =th *adj.&s.* milésimo.

thraldom *s.* escravidão.

thrash *v.t.* bater, sovar; debulhar.

thread *s.* fio, corda, filamento, linha; *v.t.* enfiar.

threat *s.* ameaça; =en *v.t.* ameaçar.

three *adj.&s.* três.

threshold *s.* soleira, limiar.

thrice *adv.* três vezes.

thrift *s.* economia; =y *adj.* econômico; =less *adj.* pródigo, gastador.

thrill *s.* emoção viva, estremecimento; *v.t.* emocionar, entusiasmar; *v.i.* estremecer, vibrar.

thrive *v.i.* prosperar; thriving *adj.* florescente, próspero.

throat *s.* garganta.

throb *v.i.* bater, palpitar.

throe *s.* dôr; (*plural*) agonias.

throne *s.* trono.

throng *s.* multidão; apêrto, tropel; *v.i.* amontoar-se, vir em tropel.

throttle *s.* garganta, traquéia; *v.t.* estrangular, sufocar.

through *prep.* através; por, pelo meio; de lado a lado; mediante; *adv.* inteiramente, de todo; até o fim; =out *prep.* durante todo; por todo; *adv.* completamente, até o fim; por toda a parte.

throw *s.* tiro, arremêsso; esfôrço; golpe, pancada; *v.t.* arrojar, arremessar, atirar; lançar; — away jogar fora; — down deitar abaixo; — out emitir; rejeitar; confundir, desconcertar.

thrum *v.i.* tamborilar; tocar mal (instrumento).

thrust *s.* golpe, estocada; arremêsso; impulso; investida; *v.t.&i.* empurrar, impelir; apertar, comprimir; arrastar; — aside repelir.

thug *s.* estrangulador; assassino.

thumb *s.* dedo polegar.

thunder *s.* trovão; raio; *v.i.* trovejar.

Thursday *s.* quinta-feira.

thus *adv.* assim, dêsse modo.

thwart *adj.* transversal, atravessado; *s.* banco de remador; *v.t.* cruzar, atravessar; impedir, frustrar.

thy *adj.* teu, tua, teus, tuas.

thyroid *s.* tireóide.

thyself *pron.* ti mesmo; tu mesmo.

tiara *s.* tiara.

tibia *s.* tíbia.

ticket *s.* bilhete; etiqueta, rótulo; (*pol.*) chapa; *v.t.* rotular, pôr etiquetas.

tickle *v.t.&i.* fazer côcegas, sentir côcegas; ticklish *adj.* coceguento; delicado, crítico.

tide *s.* maré; corrente (de agua).

tidiness *s.* limpeza, asseio, ordem.

tidy *adj.* bem arranjado, limpo, asseado; *v.t.* arranjar, arrumar.

tie *s.* laço; gravata; ligação; empate; *v.t.* ligar, unir; *v.i.* empatar.

tiercet *s.* terceto.

tiger *s.* tigre.

tight *adj.* apertado; têso, entesado; estreito, justo, colante; =en *v.t.* apertar, entesar.

tigress *s.* fêmea do tigre.

tile *s.* têlha; *v.t.* cobrir com telhas.

till *s.* gaveta; *prep.* até; *conj.* até que; *v.t.* cultivar, lavrar.

tillage *s.* lavoura; tiller *s.* lavrador.

tilt *s.* tôldo; barraca, tenda; inclinação; torneio; *v.t.&i.* inclinar, virar; inclinar-se, virar-se; justar; cobrir com tôldo.

timber *s.* madeira; madeiramento; viga; *v.t.* madeirar; fornecer madeira.

timbre *s.* timbre.

time s. tempo, momento, época; estação; século, hora; vez; cadência (musical); medida, compasso; at »s às vezes; **just in** — justo a tempo; »**table** indicador; horário; v.t.&i. regular; marcar tempo; dar prazo.
timely adj. oportuno.
timid adj. tímido; »**ity** s. timidez.
timorous adj. medroso.
tin s. estanho; v.t. estanhar; (Inç.) enlatar.
tincture s. tintura; v.t. tingir.
tinge s. tinta, matiz; v.t. tingir.
tingle v.i. formigar, latejar; tinir.
tinsel s. falso brilho, ouropel.
tint s. tinta, matiz, tonalidade; v.t. tingir.
tiny adj. minúsculo, pequeno, ínfimo.
tip s. ponta, bico, extremidade; gorjeta; v.t. virar, entornar; bater de leve; dar gorjeta.
tipple v.i. bebericar.
tipsy adj. bêbado.
tiptoe s. ponta do pé.
tiptop adj. excelente, perfeito.
tirade s. invectiva; trecho de discurso ou de palestra; tirada.
tire s. pneumático; virola; v.t.&i. cansar, fatigar; exceder-se.
tiresome adj. fatigante; **tireless** adj. infatigável, incansável.
tissue s. tecido fino; (biol.) tecido; — **paper** papel-fino.
titbit, tidbit s. gulodice.
tithe s. dízimo; v.t. pagar (o dízimo).
titillate v.t. fazer cócegas; afagar.
title s. título; v.t. intitular, dar título.
titter v.i. rir contidamente; conter parcialmente o riso.
titular adj. titular; honorífico; s. titular.
to prep. a, para; em; para com; diante de; até; segundo; — **and fro** para lá e para cá, para a frente e para trás; — **the end that** afim de que; — **this day** até hoje.
toad s. sapo.
toast s. torrada; brinde, saúde; v.t. torrar, tostar; beber à saúde de.
tobacco s. tabaco, fumo.
today adv. hoje.
toddle v.i. andar com passo curto e incerto.
toe s. dedo do pé; **from top to** — dos pés à cabeça.
toga s. toga.
together adv. juntamente, em companhia; ao mesmo tempo.
toil s. trabalho, labor; v.i. cansar-se, trabalhar muito.
toilet s. toucador; — **paper** papel higiênico.
toilsome adj. penoso, laborioso.
token s. sinal, marca, indício; insígnia; ficha; lembrança.
tolerable adj. tolerável; **tolerance** s. tolerância; **toleration** s. tolerância; **tolerate** v.t. tolerar.
toll s. peagem; v.t.&i. tanger, tocar os sinos, badalar.
tomato s. tomate.
tomb s. túmulo, sepulcro, sepultura.
tome s. tomo, volume.
tomorrow adv. amanhã.
ton s. tonelada.
tone s. tom; som; toada; timbre de voz; tensão; v.t. harmonizar-se.
tongs s. pinças, tenazes.
tongue s. língua; lingueta.
tonic adj.&s. tônico.
tonight adv. esta noite.
tonnage s. tonelagem.

tonsil s. amígdala; »**itis** s. amigdalite.
tonsure s. tonsura, coroa (de padre); v.t. tonsurar.
too adv. demais, em demasia, muito; também; igualmente.
tool s. ferramenta, instrumento; v.t. fazer, dar forma (com ferramenta).
tooth s. dente; »**ache** dôr de dentes; — **paste** pasta dentifrícia; v.t. dentear.
toothsome adj. gostoso.
top s. cume, cimo, alto, tôpo, pico, cúmulo; chefe, cabeça; v.t. coroar; ultrapassar, exceder; dominar.
topaz s. topázio.
toper s. bêbado.
topic s. tópico, assunto, tema.
topography s. topografia; **topographic, topographical** adj. topográfico.
torch s. tocha; archote, facho.
toreador s. toreador.
torment s. tormento, tortura; v.t. atormentar.
tornado s. tornado, furacão.
torpedo s. torpedo; v.t. torpedear.
torpid adj. entorpecido, dormente; inerte.
torpor s. torpor.
torrent s. torrente; »**ial** adj. torrencial.
torrid adj. tórrido.
torsion s. torsão.
torso s. torso.
tortoise s. tartaruga.
tortuous adj. tortuoso.
torture s. tortura, tormento, suplício; »**d** adj. torturado, atormentado.
toss v.t.&i. arremessar; sacudir, agitar; — **up** tirar cara ou coroa; — **off** beber (de um trago só).
tot s. pirralho, pequerrucho.
total s. total; montante; adj. total, global.
totter v.i. cambalear, vacilar.
touch s. tato; toque, contato, comunicação; pancada; traço; pequena quatidade, tintura; v.t.&i. tocar, apalpar; »**ed** adj. meio amalucado; »**iness** s. susceptibilidade; »**ing** adj. tocante, comovedor; »**y** adj. melindroso, susceptível.
tough adj. duro, resistente, tenaz; penoso, difícil; »**en** v.t. endurecer, enrijecer; »**ness** s. dureza, tenacidade.
tour s. volta; viagem; peregrinação; giro; »**ing**, »**ism** s. turismo; »**ist** s. turista.
tournament s. torneio, justa; **tourney** s. torneio.
tourniquet s. (cir.) torniquete.
tousle v.t. (pop.) desordenar, desarrumar.
tow s. estopa; reboque; v.t. rebocar.
toward, »s prep. em direção a, voltado para; para com; cêrca de, perto de.
towel s. toalha.
tower s. tôrre, torreão.
town s. cidade; — **hall** prefeitura; »**sman** s. cidadão; citadino; concidadão.
toxic adj. tóxico; **toxin** s. toxina.
toy s. brinquedo, brincadeira; bagatela; v.i. brincar.
trace s. traço; pista; rasto; vestígio; v.t. traçar, delinear; seguir a pista de; »**ry** s. rendá; rede.
trachea s. traquéia.
track s. rasto, vestígio; pègada; trilho, sulco; pista, caminho; v.t. seguir a pista.
tract s. espaço, extensão; opúsculo; »**able** adj. tratável; **traction** s. tração; »**or** s. trator.
trade s. comércio, negócio; tráfico; ofício, ocupação; indústria; — **union** sindicato operário; v.t.&i. negociar, comerciar, traficar; **trading** s. comércio, tráfico; »**sman** s. comerciante.

tradition s. tradição; **-al** adj. tradicional.
traduce v.t. caluniar; **-r** s. caluniador.
traffic s. tráfico; tráfego; movimento, circulação; **-ker** s. traficante, comerciante.
tragedian s. ator ou autor trágico.
tragedy s. tragédia, drama; **tragic, tragical** adj. trágico; **tragi-comedy** s. tragi-comédia.
trail s. pista, rasto, pègada; v.t. seguir a pista; arrastar; **-er** s. reboque.
train s. trem, combôio; cortejo, comitiva; série, encadeamento; cauda, rabo; cauda (de vestido); v.t. treinar, adestrar, amestrar; **-er** s. treinador; **training** s. treino, ensino; **-ing** ship navio-escola.
trait s. traço.
traitor s. traidor; **traitress** s. traidora; **-ous** adj. traidor, pérfido; **-ously** adv. traiçoeiramente.
trajectory s. trajetória.
trammel s. tresmalho, rede; v.t. entravar, embaraçar.
tramp s. ruído de passos; andarilho; vagabundo; v.t. andar pesadamente; caminhar, marchar.
trance s. transe, êxtase.
tranquil adj. tranquilo; **-lity** s. tranquilidade.
transact v.t.&i. tratar, fazer, dirigir, dispor, negociar; **-ion** s. transação, negócio.
transatlantic adj. transatlântico.
transcend v.t. transcender, passar, exceder; **-ent** adj. transcendente.
transcribe v.t. transcrever.
transfer v.t. transferir; transportar; s. transferência.
transfiguration s. transfiguração.
transfix v.t. atravessar, trespassar.
transform v.t. transformar; **-ation** s. transformação; **-er** s. transformador.
transfuse v.t. transfundir; **transfusion** s. transfusão.
transgress v.t. transgredir; **-or** s. transgressor, violador.
transient adj. transitório, passageiro.
transit s. trânsito, passagem.
transition s. transição.
transitory adj. transitório.
translate v.t. traduzir; **translation** s. tradução; **translator** s. tradutor.
translucent adj. translúcido.
transmission s. transmissão; **transmit** v.t. transmitir; **transmitter** s. transmissor.
transmute v.t. mudar, transmutar.
transparency s. transparência; **transparent** adj. transparente.
transpire v.i. transpirar.
transplant v.t. transplantar.
transport s. transporte; v.t. transportar.
transpose v.t. transpor.
transubstantiation s. transubstanciação.
transverse adj. transversal, transverso.
trap s. armadilha, cilada, laço, rede; v.t. apanhar no laço; fazer cair numa cilada.
trapeze s. trapézio.
trash s. escória; porcaria, imundície; refugo, bagaço.
travel s. viagem; **-er**, **-ler** s. viajante; **-ing**, **-ling** adj. ambulante.
traverse v.t. atravessar.
travesty s. paródia grotesca, disfarce, fantasia, máscara; v.t.&i. disfarçar, fantasiar, mascarar; parodiar, imitar grotescamente.
tray s. bandeja.

treacherous adj. traidor, traiçoeiro;
treachery s. traição.
treacle s. melaço.
tread v.t.&i. andar, caminhar; pisar; andar sôbre; galar; s. passo, andar, pègada; galadura (do ovo).
treason s. traição.
treasure s. tesouro; **-r** s. tesoureiro; **treasury** s. tesouro, tesouraria, repartição arrecadadora do fisco.
treat s. regalo; obséquio, convite; festa; v.t. regalar; tratar; convidar; pagar a despesa de.
treatise s. tratado, discurso.
treatment s. tratamento, trato.
treaty s. tratado.
treble v.t. triplicar.
tree s. árvore; **-less** adj. sem árvores.
trefoil s. trevo.
trellis s. gelosia; rótula; latada; v.t. fazer crescer em latadas.
tremble v.i. tremer; **trembling** s. tremor; adj. trêmulo.
tremendous adj. tremendo, formidável.
tremor s. tremor, trepidação.
tremulous adj. trêmulo.
trench s. fosso, vala, valado, rêgo; trincheira; v.t.&i. cortar, talhar; abrir valas, fossos ou regos; — upon invadir; **-ant** adj. trinchante, cortante; **-er** s. abridor de fossos e valas.
trend s. direção, tendência; v.i. dirigir-se.
trepan s. trépano; v.t. trepanar, fazer trepanação.
trepidation s. trepidação.
trespass s. intrusão; ofensa; **-er** s. intruso.
trial s. processo, julgamento; ensaio, prova.
triangle s. triângulo; **triangular** adj. triangular.
tribe s. tribu; raça.
tribulation s. tribulação.
tribunal s. tribunal.
tribune s. tribuna.
tributary adj. tributário; afluente.
tribute s. tributo; homenagem.
trice s. instante, momento.
triceps s. tricípite.
trick s. fraude, engano, embuste; truque, ardil; v.t. enganar, fraudar; prègar peça; usar de truque; **-ery** s. trapaça, velhacaria.
trickle s. filete, gota, pingo; v.i. escorrer; gotejar.
tricycle s. triciclo.
trident s. tridente.
triennial adj. trienal.
trifle s. bagatela, ninharia, futilidade; v.i. dizer tolices; perder tempo com bagatelas.
trifling adj. insignificante.
trigger s. gatilho; calço.
trigonometry s. trigonometria.
trill s. trinado; vibração; v.i. trinar.
trim adj. bem tratado; ornado; cuidado; belo; s. estado, aparência, apresentação; v.t. preparar, aparelhar; compor, adornar, enfeitar; aparar, cortar, podar; — off podar, aparar.
trinity s. trindade.
trinket s. pingente; joia, bugiaria.
trio s. trio.
trip s. viagem, excursão; passeio, volta; v.i. tropeçar; errar.
tripe s. dobrada, vísceras.
triple adj. triplo; v.t.&i. triplicar.
tripper s. (Ing.) excursionista; tropeçudo.
trite adj. banal, comum, vulgar.

triumph s. triunfo; v.i. triunfar; *al adj. triunfal.
trivial adj. trivial, insignificante.
troat v.i. bramar, berrar.
troglodyte s. troglodita.
troll v.i. girar; pescar arrastando o anzol; rodar; passar de mão em mão.
trolley s. bonde; trole; carro; alavanca de captação da corrente elétrica (de bonde ou trem).
trombone s. trombone.
troop s. tropa; *er s. soldado de cavalaria.
trophy s. troféu.
tropic s. trópico.
tropical adj. tropical.
trot s. trote; v.i. trotar.
troth s. fé; verdade.
troubadour s. trovador.
trouble s. confusão, desordem; embaraço, agitação; incômodo, aflição; transtôrno, inconveniente; v.t. incomodar, perturbar, importunar; transtornar, dar trabalho.
troublesome adj. penoso, difícil; incômodo, importuno.
trough s. gamela, tina.
trounce v.t. espancar, castigar severamente.
troupe s. companhia (teatro).
trousers s. calças.
trousseau s. enxoval.
trout s. truta.
trowel s. trolha, pá ou colher de pedreiro.
truancy s. vadiação, gazeio, falta às aulas; **truant** s. vadio, gazeteiro, estudante que falta às aulas.
truce s. trégua, descanso.
truck s. troca, permuta; **caminhão**; v.t. transportar em caminhões.
truckle v.i. ser servil.
truculent adj. truculento.
trudge v.i. caminhar.
true adj. verdadeiro; justo; seguro, certo; genuíno.
truism s. truísmo.
truly adv. verdadeiramente.
trump s. trombeta, clarim.
trumpery s. fraude, engano; bagatela, ninharia.
trumpet s. trombeta.
truncate v.t. truncar.
trundle s. rodinha; carrinho, zorra.
trunk s. tronco; haste; torso; mala; tromba.
truss s. feixe, molho; trouxa, embrulho; funda (para quebraduras); v.t. enfeixar; atar.
trust s. confiança; fé, crédito; depósito; mandato; v.t.&i. confiar, fiar-se; dar crédito; *ed adj. de confiança; *ee s. depositário, consignatário, síndico; *ful adj. confiante; *worthy adj. digno de confiança.
truth s. verdade; *ful adj. verdadeiro; *fulness s. veracidade.
try s. ensaio, experiência; v.t.&i. ensaiar, experimentar; provar, tentar; (for.) processar, julgar; — on experimentar; *ing adj. difícil.
tub s. tina, cuba, barril; banheira.
tube s. tubo.
tuber, tubercle s. tubérculo; excrescência, nó.
tuberculosis s. tuberculose.
tuberose s. tuberosa.
tubular adj. tubular.
tuck s. estoque; dobra, prega; v.t. dobrar, pregar; — in aconchegar, cobrir, agasalhar.

Tuesday s. terça-feira.
tuft s. tufo, moita; ramalhete; penacho; borla de seda.
tug s. puxão; sacudidela, esfôrço; v.t. puxar; *boat s. (mar.) rebocador.
tuition s. ensino, instrução.
tulip s. tulipa.
tumble s. salto; desarrumação, desordem; v.i. dar saltos, cair, rolar; — down cair, desmoronar-se; v.t. revolver, pôr em desordem, rolar; *r s. acrobata; copo sem pé.
tumour s. tumor.
tumult s. tumulto; *uous adj. tumultuoso.
tun s. tonelada; barril, tonel, pipa.
tune s. ária, tom, toada, som, consonância; v.t. afinar; pôr em harmonia; *r s. afinador.
tunic s. túnica.
tunnel s. túnel; v.t. abrir um túnel em; furar, varar.
tup s. carneiro.
turban s. turbante.
turbid adj. turvo, lodoso.
turbine s. turbina.
turbulence s. turbulência.
turbulent adj. turbulento.
tureen s. terrina, sopeira.
turf s. relva, prado; prado de corridas; v.t. cobrir de relva.
turgid adj. túrgido.
Turk s. turco; *ey s. Turquia; perú (ave); *ish adj. turco; *ish bath banho turco.
turmoil s. ebulição, tormenta, tumulto.
turn s. volta, vez, turno, movimento circular; curva; ângulo; mudança; v.t.&i. virar, revirar, voltar-se; transformar, converter, mudar; — away evitar; demitir; — back voltar; — off fechar; — on abrir.
turncoat s. trânsfuga, renegado; vira-casaca.
turner s. torneiro.
turnip s. nabo.
turnkey s. chaveiro, carcereiro.
turnover s. reviravolta.
turnpike s. barreira.
turpentine s. terebentina.
turpitude s. torpeza.
turquoise s. turquesa.
turret s. tôrre pequena.
turtle s. tartaruga.
tusk s. presa (dos animais).
tussle s. luta.
tutelage s. tutela; **tutelar, tutelary** adj. tutelar.
tutor s. preceptor; (dir.) tutor.
twaddle s. tagarelice.
twang s. som agudo; som fanhoso; v.i. falar fanhoso.
tweak v.t. beliscar.
tweezers s. pinças.
twelve s.&adj. doze; **twelfth** adj.&s. décimo-segundo.
twenty s.&adj. vinte; **twentieth** adj.&s. vigésimo.
twice adv. duas vezes.
twiddle v.t. virar, torcer; brincar, tamborilar.
twig s. rebento, brôto.
twilight s. crepúsculo; penumbra.
twill s. tecido com véios em diagonal; v.t. tecer formando linhas salientes em diagonal (como sarja).
twin adj.&s. gêmeo.
twine s. fio, retroz; v.t. enlaçar; torcer.
twinge s. dôr aguda.

twinkle *v.i.* cintilar; piscar.
twirl *v.i.* girar, voltear.
twist *s.* trança, cordão, fio; contorsão; *v.t.* torcer, retorcer; entrelaçar, trançar; enroscar; -ed *adj.* torcido, retorcido.
twit *v.t.* repreender, lançar em rosto.
twitch *s.* puxão; contração; espasmo; latejo; *v.t.* puxar, arrancar; latejar; *v.i.* ter espasmos.
twitter *v.i.* chilrar, trinar.
two *adj.&s.* dois; -fold *adj.* duplo; *adv.* duplamente.
tympan, tympanum *s.* tímpano.
type *s.* tipo, gênero; (*imp.*) tipo; *v.t.&i.*

escrever à máquina; - writer máquina de escrever.
typhoid *adj.* tifóide; *s.* tifo.
typhoon *s.* furacão.
typical *adj.* típico.
typist *s.* datilógrafa.
typography *s.* tipografia; typographical, typographic *adj.* tipográfico.
tyranny *s.* tirania; tyrant *s.* tirano; tyrannic, tyrannical *adj.* tirânico.
tyro *adj.* novato.
tirocinium, tirociny *s.* tirocínio.
tzar *s.* czar.
tzarina *s.* czarina.

U

U letra do alfabeto.
ubiquity *s.* ubiquidade.
udder *s.* têta, ubre.
ugliness *s.* fealdade; ugly *adj.* feio.
ulcer *s.* úlcera; -ate *v.t.&i.* ulcerar.
ulterior *adj.* ulterior.
ultimate *adj.* último, final.
ultimatum *s.* ultimato.
ultramarine *s.* ultramarino.
ultra-violet *adj.* ultravioleta.
umber *s.* terra de sombra (pintura).
umbrage *s.* sombra; aparência; ressentimento.
umbrella *s.* guarda-chuva.
umpire *s.* árbitro; *v.t.* arbitrar.
unable *adj.* incapaz.
unabridged *adj.* completo.
unacceptable *adj.* inaceitável.
unaccompanied *adj.* desacompanhado.
unaccountable *adj.* inexplicável.
unaccustomed *adj.* não habituado; desacostumado.
unadorned *adj.* sem enfeites, desataviado.
unadulterated *adj.* sem mistura, não falsificado.
unaffected *adj.* natural.
unafraid *adj.* sem mêdo.
unalloyed *adj.* sem liga, sem mistura, puro.
unalterable *adj.* inalterável.
unambiguous *adj.* claro, manifesto.
unambitious *adj.* sem ambição, desambicioso.
unanimous *adj.* unânime; -ly *adv.* unanimemente.
unanswerable *adj.* irrespondível, incontestável.
unappreciated *adj.* não apreciado, incompreendido.
unapproachable *adj.* inabordável.
unarmed *adj.* desarmado.
unassailable *adj.* inatacável.
unassuming *adj.* sem pretensões, modesto.
unattainable *adj.* inatingível.
unattractive *adj.* pouco atraente, sem atrativos.
unavailable *adj.* indisponível.
unavoidable *adj.* inevitável.
unaware *adj.* desprevenido.
unbalanced *adj.* desequilibrado.
unbearable *adj.* intolerável, insuportável.
unbecoming *adj.* impróprio, incoveniente; que não assenta bem.
unbelief *s.* incredulidade; unbeliever *s.* incrédulo.
unbend *v.t.* afrouxar, soltár.

unbiased *adj.* imparcial; sem preconceitos.
unbind *v.t.* desligar, desatar.
unblemished *adj.* sem mácula, imaculado, puro.
unblushing *adj.* desavergonhado.
unbolt *v.t.* abrir; tirar o ferrolho; explicar.
unborn *adj.* por nascer, nascituro.
unbounded *adj.* ilimitado.
unbreakable *adj.* inquebrável.
unbroken *adj.* intacto, inteiro; indômito; contínuo.
unbuilt *adj.* não construido.
unburied *adj.* insepulto.
unbutton *v.t.* desabotoar.
uncanny *adj.* fantástico; descuidado.
unceasing *adj.* incessante; -ly *adv.* incessantemente.
unceremoniously *adv.* sem cerimônia.
uncertain *adj.* incerto; -ty *s.* incerteza.
unchain *v.t.* desencadear.
unchangeable *adj.* imutável.
uncharitable *adj.* pouco caridoso.
unchaste *adj.* impudico.
unchecked *adj.* sem freios, desenfreado.
uncircumcised *adj.* incircunciso.
uncivil *adj.* incivil; -ized *adj.* selvagem.
unclad *adj.* nú.
unclaimed *adj.* não reclamado.
unclassified *adj.* não classificado.
uncle *s.* tio.
unclean *adj.* sujo, impuro; imundo.
unclothed *adj.* despido.
unclouded *adj.* sem nuvens, desanuviado.
uncoil *v.t.* desenrolar, estender.
uncomfortable *adj.* desconfortável, incômodo.
uncommon *adj.* raro, invulgar.
uncommunicative *adj.* taciturno, reservado.
uncompleted *adj.* incompleto.
uncompromising *adj.* intransigente.
unconcern *s.* indiferença, despreocupação.
unconditional *adj.* incondicional; -ly *adv.* incondicionalmente.
unconfirmed *adj.* não confirmado.
unconquerable *adj.* inconquistável.
unconscious *adj.&s.* inconciente; -ness *s.* inconciência.
unconstitutional *adj.* inconstituicional.
unconstraint *s.* desenvoltura, desembaraço.
uncontested *adj.* incontestado.
uncontrollable *adj.* ingovernável.
unconventional *adj.* sem convenções.
unconvincing *adj.* pouco convincente.
uncouth *adj.* grosseiro, rude; estranho

uncover v.t. descobrir; v.i. descobrir-se.
unction s. unção; unctious, unctuous adj. untuoso.
uncultivated adj. inculto.
uncurbed adj. desenfreado.
uncurl v.t. desencrespar.
uncustomary adj. inhabitual.
undated adj. sem data.
undaunted adj. intrépido.
undeceive v.t. desenganar, desiludir.
undecided adj. indeciso.
undecipherable adj. indecifrável.
undefended adj. indefeso.
undefiled adj. sem mancha, incorrupto.
undefined adj. indefinido.
undeniable adj. inegável.
under prep.&adv. debaixo, em baixo; sob; abaixo.
underclothing s. roupa de baixo.
undercurrent s. subcorrente, corrente submarina; tendência oculta.
under-developed adj. pouco desenvolvido.
underdone adj. mal assado, sangrento.
underestimate v.t. subestimar, estimar abaixo do valor verdadeiro.
undergarment s. roupa de baixo.
undergo v.t.&i. sofrer, padecer; passar por.
underground adj. subterrâneo.
underhand adj. clandestino, secreto.
underline v.t. sublinhar.
underling s. empregado subalterno.
undermine v.t. minar, solapar.
undermost adj. o mais baixo, ínfimo.
underneath adv.&prep. por baixo, debaixo de.
underpay v.t. pagar insuficientemente.
underrate v.t. depreciar.
underscore v.t. sublinhar.
under-sea adj. submarino.
understand v.t.&i. compreender; entender; -ing s. inteligência, compreensão.
undertake v.t. empreender; -r s. pessoa encarregada de organizar funerais; undertaking s. empresa; organização de funerais.
undertone s. meia-voz; meia-tinta.
undertow s. ressaca.
undervalue v.t. depreciar; menosprezar; s. preço vil.
underwrite v.t.&i. subscrever; garantir.
undeserved adj. imerecido.
undesirable adj. indesejável.
undetermined adj. indeterminado.
undigested adj. indigesto, não digerido.
undignified adj. sem dignidade.
undisciplined adj. indisciplinado.
undisputed adj. incontestado.
undisturbed adj. tranquilo.
undo v.t. desfazer, desmanchar; -ing s. ruína.
undoubted adj. indubitável.
undress v.t.&i. despir; despir-se.
undue adj. exagerado, excessivo; impróprio; indébito.
undulate v.t. ondular; undulating adj. ondulado; undulation s. ondulação.
unduly adv. indevidamente.
undying adj. imortal.
unearned adj. imerecido; alcançado sem trabalho.
unearth v.t. desenterrar.
uneasiness s. mal-estar, inquietude; uneasy adj. inquieto.
uneducated adj. sem instrução.
unemployed adj. desempregado; unemployment s. falta de trabalho, inatividade.

unending adj. sem fim.
unenterprising adj. sem iniciativa.
unequal adj. desigual.
unequivocal adj. inequívoco.
uneven adj. desigual; ímpar; acidentado.
unexpected adj. inesperado.
unexplained adj. inexplicado.
unexplored adj. inexplorado.
unfailing adj. infalível; incansável.
unfair adj. injusto; desleal; parcial.
unfaithful adj. infiel; -ness s. infidelidade.
unfamiliar adj. estranho.
unfasten v.t. desatar, desapertar.
unfavorable, unfavourable adj. desfavorável.
unfeeling adj. insensível.
unfeigned adj. sincero.
unfinished adj. inacabado.
unfit adj. impróprio; -ness s. impropriedade, incapacidade.
unfold v.t. desdobrar, abrir.
unforeseen adj. imprevisto.
unforgettable adj. inesquecível.
unforgivable adj. imperdoável.
unfortunate adj. infeliz.
unfounded adj. sem fundamento; infundado.
unfriendly adj. hostil.
unfruitful adj. estéril, infrutífero.
ungenerous adj. pouco generoso.
ungodliness s. impiedade; ungodly adj. ímpio.
ungovernable adj. ingovernável.
ungraceful adj. desgracioso.
ungrateful adj. ingrato; -ness s. ingratidão.
unguarded adj. sem defesa; desprotegido; desculdado.
unhappiness s. infelicidade; unhappy adj. infeliz.
unharmed adj. incólume.
unhealthiness s. insalubridade; unhealthy adj. insalubre; doentio.
unheeded adj. desculdado; desprezado.
unhesitatingly adv. sem hesitação.
unhinge v.t. desconjuntar; confundir, perturbar.
unholiness s. impiedade; unholy adj. ímpio.
unhonored adj. desprezado.
unhook v.t. desenganchar.
unicorn adj. unicorne; s. unicórnio.
uniform adj.&s. uniforme; -ity s. uniformidade; -ly adv. uniformemente.
unify v.t. unificar.
unilateral adj. unilateral.
unimaginable adj. inimaginável.
unimpeded adj. sem estorvos, desimpedido.
unimportant adj. insignificante, sem importância.
uninhabitable adj. inhabitável; uninhabited adj. deshabitado.
uninstructed adj. ignorante.
unintelligent adj. pouco inteligente.
unintentional adj. involuntário.
uninterested adj. indiferente; uninteresting adj. sem interêsse, desinteressante.
uninterrupted adj. ininterrupto; -ly adv. ininterruptamente.
union s. união; aliança.
unique adj. único.
unit s. unidade.
unite v.t. unir; reunir; -d adj. unido, junto.
unity s. unidade; união; harmonia.

universal *adj.* universal; **university** *s.* universidade.

unjust *adj.* injusto; **-ifiable** *adj.* injustificável.

unkempt *adj.* despenteado, sem trato; inculto.

unkind *adj.* indelicado, grosseiro; mau; **-ness** *s.* indelicadeza, grosseria; maldade.

unknown *adj.* desconhecido, ignorado.

unlace *v.t.* desapertar; desatar; desenlaçar.

unlawful *adj.* ilegal, ilícito; **-ness** *s.* ilegalidade.

unlearn *v.t.* desaprender.

unless *conj.* a menos que, a não ser que, se não; *prep.* senão, exceto.

unlettered *adj.* iliterato, analfabeto.

unlikelihood *s.* inverossimilhança; **unlike** *adj.* diferente; inverossímil; **unlikely** *adj.* inverossímil; improvável.

unlimited *adj.* ilimitado.

unlined *adj.* sem fôrro.

unload *v.t.* descarregar.

unlock *v.t.* abrir.

unloose *v.t.* desatar, afrouxar; soltar.

unlovely *adj.* desagradável, pouco amável.

unlucky *adj.* infeliz.

unmake *v.t.* desfazer.

unman *v.t.* desanimar; embrutecer; desvirilizar; desguarnecer, desarmar (navio, etc.).

unmanageable *adj.* intratável, indomável.

unmanly *adj.* afeminado; inhumano.

unmannerly *adj.* grosseiro.

unmanufactured *adj.* não manufaturado, bruto.

unmarketable *adj.* invendável.

unmarried *adj.* solteiro.

unmask *v.t.* desmascarar.

unmerciful *adj.* cruel, impiedoso.

unmerited *adj.* imerecido.

unmethodical *adj.* sem método.

unmindful *adj.* descuidado, sem atenção.

unmistakable *adj.* evidente, manifesto; inequívoco.

unmixed *adj.* sem mistura.

unmolested *adj.* em paz, sem ser molestado.

unmoved *adj.* insensível; firme.

unmusical *adj.* dissonante; inharmônico.

unmuzzle *v.t.* tirar o açaimo, desamordaçar.

unnamed *adj.* anônimo, inominado.

unnatural *adj.* afetado; contrário à natureza.

unnavigable *adj.* não navegável, inavegável.

unnecessary *adj.* desnecessário.

unnerve *v.t.* desanimar, tirar a coragem de; debilitar.

unnoticed *adj.* despercebido.

unobtrusive *adj.* discreto; **-ly** *adv.* discretamente.

unoccupied *adj.* desocupado.

unoffending *adj.* inofensivo.

unofficial *adj.* não oficial.

unopened *adj.* fechado, não violado.

unopposed *adj.* sem oposição.

unorganized *adj.* não organizado.

unorthodox *adj.* heterodoxo.

unostentatious *adj.* sem ostentação.

unpack *v.t.* desembrulhar; desarrumar (as malas).

unpaid *adj.* por pagar.

unpalatable *adj.* desagradável ao gôsto.

unparalleled *adj.* sem igual.

unpardonable *adj.* imperdoável.

unparliamentary *adj.* contrário às regras parlamentares.

unpatriotic *adj.* impatriótico.

unpave *v.t.* descalçar, tirar o calçamento; **-d** *adj.* sem calçamento.

unperceived *adj.* despercebido.

unpleasant *adj.* desagradável.

unpleasing *adj.* desagradável.

unpoetical *adj.* sem poesia.

unpolished *adj.* bruto, rude; grosseiro.

unpolluted *adj.* imaculado, impoluto, limpo.

unpopular *adj.* impopular; **-ity** *s.* impopularidade.

unpractical *adj.* pouco prático.

unpractised *adj.* sem prática.

unprecedented *adj.* sem precedente.

unprejudiced *adj.* imparcial.

unpremeditated *adj.* sem premeditação, não premeditado.

unprepared *adj.* desprevenido, não preparado.

unpretentious *adj.* despretensioso.

unprincipled *adj.* sem princípios.

unproductive *adj.* improdutivo.

unprofessional *adj.* contrário à ética profissional.

unprofitable *adj.* infrutuoso; inútil.

unpropitious *adj.* desfavorável, contrário.

unprotected *adj.* desprotegido.

unprovided *adj.* desprovido.

unprovoked *adj.* sem provocação, não provocado.

unpublished *adj.* inédito.

unpunctuality *s.* impontualidade.

unpunished *adj.* impune.

unqualified *adj.* não qualificado; não autorizado; sem restrição.

unquenchable *adj.* inextinguível.

unquestionable *adj.* indiscutível.

unravel *v.t.* desembaraçar, deslindar.

unreadable *adj.* ilegível.

unreal *adj.* irreal, imaginário; **-ity** *s.* irrealidade.

unrealizable *adj.* irrealizável.

unreasonable *adj.* pouco razoável; desarrazoado.

unrecognizable *adj.* irreconhecível.

unredeemable *adj.* irremissível.

unrefined *adj.* bruto, não refinado.

unrefuted *adj.* irrefutado.

unregistered *adj.* não registrado.

unrelenting *adj.* inexorável.

unreliable *adj.* pouco seguro; inexato.

unremitting *adj.* incessante, seguido.

unrepentant *adj.* impenitente.

unreservedly *adv.* sem reserva, abertamente.

unrest *s.* desassossêgo, inquietude; agitação.

unrestrained *adj.* imoderado; desenfreado.

unrestricted *adj.* sem restrição.

unrewarded *adj.* sem recompensa.

unrighteous *adj.* injusto; **-ness** *s.* injustiça.

unripe *adj.* verde; **-ness** *s.* verdor.

unrivaled, unrivalled *adj.* sem rival.

unrivet *v.t.* tirar os rebites de; desfazer.

unroll *v.t.* desenrolar.

unruffled *adj.* imperturbável; calmo, tranquilo.

unruly *adj.* indisciplinado.

unsaddle *v.t.* tirar os arreios; desencilhar.

unsafe *adj.* arriscado, pouco seguro; perigoso.

unsalted *adj.* sem sal.

unsanitary *adj.* insalubre; antihigiênico.
unsatisfactory *adj.* que não satisfaz.
unsavory *adj.* insípido, sem gôsto.
unsay *v.t.* desdizer.
unscathed *adj.* salvo, incólume.
unscientific *adj.* não científico.
unscrew *v.t.* desaparafusar.
unscrupulous *adj.* sem escrúpulos, inescrupuloso.
unseal *v.t.* tirar o sêlo, abrir.
unseasonable *adj.* fora da estação; inoportuno.
unseat *v.t.* invalidar; descolocar.
unsecured *adj.* pouco seguro; arriscado.
unseemly *adj.* inconveniente.
unseen *adj.* despercebido; invisível.
unselfish *adj.* desinteressado; altruísta.
unserviceable *adj.* imprestável.
unsettle *v.t.* deslocar, transtornar; =d *adj.* incerto; indeciso; perturbado; não liquidado.
unshakable *adj.* firme, inabalável.
unshapely *adj.* disforme.
unshaven *adj.* barbado, não barbeado.
unsheltered *adj.* desabrigado; sem teto.
unshoe *v.t.* desferrar (cavalo).
unshrinkable *adj.* que não encolhe.
unsightliness *s.* fealdade; unsightly *adj.* feio.
unsigned *adj.* não assinado.
unsinkable *adj.* insubmersível.
unskilful *adj.* inhábil; =ness *s.* inhabilidade; unskilled *adj.* inexperiente.
unsociable *adj.* insociável.
unsold *adj.* não vendido.
unsolved *adj.* não solucionado, não resolvido.
unsophisticated *adj.* ingênuo, espontâneo; genuíno.
unsound *adj.* vicioso; defeituoso; doentio.
unsparing *adj.* pródigo, generoso.
unspeakable *adj.* indizível.
unspotted *adj.* sem mácula, imaculado.
unstable *adj.* instável.
unsteadiness *s.* instabilidade; vacilação; unsteady *adj.* instável, vacilante.
unstitch *v.t.* descoser.
unstudied *adj.* natural.
unsuitable *adj.* impróprio; inconveniente; =ness inconveniência; impropriedade.
unsupported *adj.* sem apôio, desapoiado.
unsuspected *adj.* não suspeitado; unsuspecting, unsuspicious *adj.* confiante, de boa fé.
unsweetened *adj.* sem açucar.
unsymmetrical *adj.* dissimétrico.
untainted *adj.* incorrupto, puro.
untamable *adj.* indomável.
untaught *adj.* ignorante; inculto.
untenable *adj.* insustentável.
untenanted *adj.* deshabitado.
unthinkable *adj.* inimaginável.
unthread *v.t.* desfiar; desenfiar.
untidiness *s.* desordem.
untie *v.t.* desligar, desatar.
until *prep.* até; *conj.* até que.
untimely *adj.* intempestivo, prematuro; fora de tempo.
untold *adj.* nunca dito, não revelado; indizível, incalculável.
untouchable *s.* que não se pode tocar; pária; untouched *adj.* intacto.
untoward *adj.* desagradável, incômodo; perverso; desajeitado; indecoroso.
untrained *adj.* inexperiente.
untranslatable *adj.* intraduzível.
untraveled, untravelled *adj.* pouco viajado.

untried *adj.* não experimentado; (*for.*) não julgado.
untrimmed *adj.* sem enfeites.
untroubled *adj.* calmo, despreocupado; tranquilo.
untrue *adj.* falso, mentiroso; untruly *adv.* falsamente.
untrustworthy *adj.* indigno de confiança.
untruth *s.* mentira; =ful *adj.* pouco verídico, mentiroso.
untuck *v.t.* desfazer (uma dobra); abrir (a cama).
untwist *v.t.* destorcer.
unused *adj.* desusado; insólito; unusual *adj.* pouco comum, raro; unusually *adv.* extraordinàriamente.
unutterable *adj.* indizível.
unvarying *adj.* uniforme, invariável.
unveil *v.t.* descobrir, desvendar.
unventilated *adj.* mal arejado.
unwarily *adv.* sem precaução, incautamente.
unwarrantable *adj.* indefensável, injustificável.
unwary *adj.* inconsiderado; incauto.
unwavering *adj.* inabalável.
unwearied *adj.* infatigável.
unwell *adj.* indisposto.
unwholesome *adj.* mórbido; malsão; insalubre.
unwieldy *adj.* pesado; incômodo.
unwilling *adj.* pouco disposto; =ly *adv.* de má vontade; =ness *s.* má vontade.
unwind *v.t.* desenrolar.
unwisdom *s.* falta de juízo; unwise *adj.* desajuizado, insensato.
unwonted *adj.* insólito; infrequente.
unworkable *adj.* impraticável.
unworthiness *s.* indignidade; unworthy *adj.* indigno.
unwrap *v.t.* desembrulhar.
unwrinkled *adj.* sem rugas.
unyielding *adj.* inflexível, inabalável; firme.
up *adj.* ascendente; levantado; *adv.* encima, acima, para cima; em pé; *prep.* para cima, acima, encima de; =stairs em cima; — to até; — there lá em cima; —! de pé!, levante-se!
upbraid *v.t.* reprochar, exprobrar.
upheaval *s.* levantamento; convulsão, cataclismo.
uphill *adj.* ascendente; elevado.
uphold *v.t.* sustentar, manter; =er *s.* sustentáculo.
upholster *v.t.*, acolchoar, estofar; =er *s.* estofador.
upkeep *s.* manutenção.
upland *s.* planalto; terras altas.
uplift *v.t.* enobrecer; elevar.
upon *prep.* sôbre, em cima de; em, com; perto de; quasi; a; por.
upper *adj.* superior; alto; de cima; =most *adj.* o mais alto; o mais elevado.
upright *adj.* direito; perpendicular; reto; em pé; justo, íntegro, honesto; em pé, verticalmente; =ness *s.* integridade, retidão.
uprising *s.* sublevação.
uproar *s.* tumulto, barulho.
uproot *v.t.* desarraigar, arrancar.
upset *s.* transtôrno; *v.t.* derrubar, derramar, virar; transtornar, desarranjar.
upshot *s.* desenlace, fim.
upside down *adv.* às avessas; de pernas para o ar.
upstart *s.* novo rico.
upward *adj.* ascendente, para o alto; —, =s *adv.* em cima, para cima; mais, além.

uranium s. urânio.
urban adj. urbano; =e adj. cortês; =ely adv. cortêsmente.
urethra s. uretra.
urge v.t. insistir sôbre; urgir, solicitar; apressar; incitar; fazer pressão moral sôbre; instar.
urgency s. urgência; urgent adj. urgente; urgently adv. urgentemente.
uric adj. úrico; urinal s. urinol; urinate v.i. urinar; urine s. urina.
urn s. urna.
us pron. nós, nos.
usage s. uso, prática, costume, hábito; use s. uso; v.t. usar, empregar, fazer uso de; used adj. usado, servido; useful adj. útil; usefulness s. utilidade; uselessness s. inutilidade.
usher v.t. introduzir, anunciar.

usual adj. usual, habitual, comum.
usufruct s. usufruto.
usurer s. usurário; agiota; usurious adj. usurário.
usurp v.t. usurpar; =ation s. usurpação; =er s. usurpador.
usury s. usura.
utensil s. utensílio; vasilha.
uterine adj. uterino; uterus s. útero.
utilitarian adj. utilitário.
utility s. utilidade.
utmost adj. último, extremo.
utopia s. utopia; utopian adj. utópico; s. utopista.
utter adj. completo; total, extremo; v.t. proferir, pronunciar, dizer; =ance s. articulação; palavra; =most adj. extremo.
uvula s. úvula, campainha (da bôca).
uxorious adj. escravo da mulher.

V

V letra do alfabeto.
vacancy s. vaga, vazio; lacuna; vacância; vacant adj. vago, livre, desocupado; vacate v.i. vagar.
vacation s. férias; vacância.
vaccinate v.t. vacinar; vaccination s. vacinação; vaccine s. vacina.
vacillate v.i. vacilar; vacillation s. vacilação.
vacuity s. vacuidade; vacuous adj. vácuo, vazio; vacuum s. vácuo.
vagabond s.&adj. vagabundo.
vagary s. capricho, veneta.
vagrancy s. vagabundagem; vagrant s.&adj. vagabundo.
vague adj. vago, impreciso; =ness s. vago, imprecisão.
vain adj. vão; vaidoso; =glory s. vanglória.
valance s. sanefa.
vale s. vale.
valediction s. despedida, adeus; valedictory adj. de despedida.
valet s. criado.
valetudinarian adj.&s. valetudinário.
valiant adj. valente.
valid adj. válido; =ate v.t. validar; =ity s. validade.
valise s. maleta.
valley s. vale.
valorous adj. valoroso; valor, valour s. valor.
valuable adj. valioso, de valor, precioso; =s s. valores, objetos de valor; valuation s. avaliação; value s. valor; v.t. avaliar, estimar; valueless adj. sem valor; valuer s. perito, avaliador.
valve s. válvula.
vamp s. pala do sapato; (mús.) acompanhamento; v.t.&i. (mús.) improvisar; acompanhar.
vampire s. vampiro.
van s. carro, vagão; (E. U.) andorinha (veículo).
vanadium s. vanádio.
vandal s. vândalo; =ism s. vandalismo.
vane s. catavento.
vanilla s. baunilha.
vanish v.i. desvanecer-se, desaparecer, eclipsar-se.
vanity s. vaidade; futilidade.
vanquish v.t. vencer; the =ed os vencidos.
vantage s. vantagem.
vapid adj. insípido, desenxabido.

vapor, vapour s. vapor; =ize v.t. vaporizar; =izer s. vaporizador; =ous adj. vaporoso.
variable adj. variável; variant s. variante; variation s. variação.
varicose adj. varicoso; varicosis s. variz.
variegate v.t. variar, variegar; diversificar.
variety s. variedade.
various adj. diferente, diverso.
varnish s. verniz; v.t. envernizar.
vary v.t.&i. variar; diversificar.
vascular adj. vascular.
vase s. vaso.
vaseline s. vaselina.
vassal s. vassalo.
vast adj. vasto, imenso; =ly adv. imensamente, grandemente; =ness s. vastidão.
vat s. tonel, tina.
vault s. abóbada; caverna; adega; subterrâneo; túmulo; salto, pulo; v.t. abobadar, cobrir com abóbada; v.i. saltar, pular; pole =ing salto de vara.
vaunt s. vaidade, ostentação;v.i. jactar-se.
veal s. vitela, carne de vitela.
vector s. vector; (med.) transmissor.
veer v.i. virar, voltar, mudar; s. mudança (de opinião, de rumo, etc.).
vegetable s. legume; vegetal; adj. vegetal; vegetarian s. vegetariano; vegetarianism s. regime vegetariano; vegetate v.i. vegetar; vegetation s. vegetação.
vehemence s. veemência; vehement adj. veemente.
vehicle s. veículo.
veil s. véu; v.t. velar.
vein s. veia; nervura (da fôlha); =ed adj. venoso.
vellum s. pergaminho.
velocipede s. velocípede.
velocity s. velocidade.
velours s. feltro aveludado.
velum s. (anat.) véu, véu do paladar.
velvet s. veludo; =een s. belbutina; =y adj. aveludado.
venal adj. venal; =ity s. venalidade.
vender s. vendedor; vendor s. vendedor; máquina de vender.
veneer s. madeira especial para embutir; v.t. embutir, entalhar; =ing s. trabalho embutido.
venerable adj. venerável; venerate v.t. venerar; veneration s. veneração.

venereal *adj.* venéreo.
vengeance *s.* vingança; **vengeful** *adj.* vingador, vingativo.
venial *adj.* venial.
venison *s.* veação; carne de veado.
venom *s.* veneno; **-ous** *adj.* venenoso.
vent *s.* respiradouro, suspiro; saída, passagem; *v.t.* dar saída; desafogar, desabafar; descobrir; evaporar.
ventilate *v.t.* ventilar; **ventilation** *s.* ventilação; **ventilator** *s.* ventilador.
ventral *adj.* abdominal, ventral.
ventricle *s.* ventrículo.
ventriloquism *s.* ventriloquismo; **ventriloquist** *s.* ventríloquo.
venture *s.* aventura. especulação; sorte; *v.t.* aventurar, arriscar; **-some** *adj.* arriscado; aventureiro.
veracious *adj.* veraz, verídico; **veracity** *s.* veracidade.
veranda, verandah *s.* varanda.
verb *s.* verbo; **-al** *adj.* verbal; **-iage** *s.* verbosidade, loquacidade; **-ose** *adj.* verboso; **-osity** *s.* verbosidade.
verdant *adj.* verdejante.
verdict *s.* veredicto.
verdure *s.* verdura.
verge *s.* vara (insígnia de autoridade); alçada; borda, extremidade; **-r** *s.* bedel, maceiro.
verification *s.* verificação; **verify** *v.t.* verificar.
verisimilitude *s.* verossimilhança, verossimilitude.
veritable *adj.* verdadeiro; **verity** *s.* verdade.
vermicelli *s.* aletria.
vermilion *s.* vermelhão; *adj.* vermelho vivo.
vermin *s.* vermina; **-ous** *adj.* verminoso.
vernacular *adj.* vernacular.
vernal *adj.* primaveril.
veronica *s.* verônica.
versatile *adj.* versátil, mutável, inconstante; **versatility** *s.* versatilidade.
verse *s.* verso, estrofe, poesia; **versicle** *s.* versículo; **versifier** *s.* versificador; **versify** *v.t.&i.* versificar, rimar; **version** *s.* versão.
verso *s.* verso.
versus *prep.* versus, contra.
vertebra *s.* vértebra; **-l** *adj.* vertebral; **-te** *adj.&s.* vertebrado.
vertex *s.* vértice; **vertical** *adj.&s.* vertical; **vertically** *adv.* verticalmente.
vertiginous *adj.* vertiginoso; **vertigo** *s.* vertigem.
verve *s.* espírito, verve.
very *adj.* mesmo; *adv.* muito; bastante; inteiramente; **on that — day** nesse mesmo dia.
vesicle *s.* vesícula.
vespers *s.* vésperas.
vessel *s.* vaso, recipiente; navio, vapor.
vest *s.* colete; camisola de criança; *v.t.* investir; confiar; vestir.
vesta *s.* fósforo pequeno.
vestal *s.* vestal.
vestibule *s.* vestíbulo.
vestige *s.* vestígio.
vestment *s.* vestimenta.
vestry *s.* sacristia.
vetch *s.* ervilhaca.
veteran *s.* veterano.
veterinary *adj.* veterinário.
veto *s.* veto; *v.t.* vetar.
vex *v.t.* contrariar, vexar; **-ation** *s.* contrariedade; vexame; **-atious** *adj.* vexatório; molesto, incômodo.

via *prep.* via, por meio de.
viability *s.* capacidade de viver e crescer; **viable** *adj.* capaz de viver e crescer.
viaduct *s.* viaduto.
vial *s.* frasco.
viand *s.* vianda.
vibrate *v.i.* vibrar; **vibration** *s.* vibração.
vicar *s.* vigário, cura; **-age** *s.* curato, **-ship** *s.* paróquia; vicariato.
vice *s.* vício.
vice versa *adv.* viceversa.
vicinity *s.* vizinhança.
vicious *adj.* vicioso; **-ness** *s.* vício, natureza viciosa.
vicissitude *s.* vicissitude.
victim *s.* vítima; **-ize** *v.t.* vitimar.
victor *s.* vencedor.
victoria *s.* vitória (carruagem).
victorious *adj.* vitorioso.
victory *s.* vitória.
victual *v.t.* abastecer, prover de víveres; **-s** *s.* víveres.
vie *v.i.* rivalizar; competir.
view *s.* vista; perspectiva, aspecto; exame; intento, mira; *v.t.* ver, observar, examinar.
vigil *s.* vigília; **-ance** *s.* vigilância; **-ant** *adj.* vigilante; **-antly** *adv.* vigilantemente.
vignette *s.* vinheta.
vigorous *adj.* vigoroso; **vigor** *s.* vigor.
vile *adj.* vil; abjeto; **-ness** *s.* baixeza, abjeção; **vilify** *v.t.* vilipendiar; aviltar; difamar.
villa *s.* quinta, casa de campo, chácara.
village *s.* aldeia, burgo; **-r** *s.* aldeão.
villain *s.* celerado, bandido, vilão; **-ous** *adj.* vil, infame; celerado; **-y** *s.* vilania.
vindicate *v.t.* vindicar, justificar, defender; **vindication** *s.* vindicação, justificação.
vindictive *adj.* vindicativo.
vine *s.* videira.
vinegar *s.* vinagre; *v.t.* avinagrar.
vinosity *s.* vinosidade.
vinous *adj.* vinoso.
vintage *s.* vindima.
vintager *s.* vindimador.
viola *s.* (*mús.*) alto, violeta.
violaceous *adj.* violáceo.
violate *v.t.* violar; **violation** *s.* violação; **violator** *s.* violador; **violence** *s.* violência; **violent** *adj.* violento.
violet *s.* violeta.
violin *s.* violino; **-ist** *s.* violonista; **violoncello** *s.* violoncelo; **violoncellist** *s.* violoncelista.
viper *s.* víbora.
virago *s.* megera.
virgin *s.&adj.* virgem; **-al** *adj.* virginal; **virginity** *s.* virgindade.
virile *adj.* viril, másculo; **virility** *s.* virilidade.
virtual *adj.* virtual; **virtue** *s.* virtude; **virtuosity** *s.* virtuosidade; **virtuoso** *s.* virtuose; **virtuous** *adj.* virtuoso.
virulence *s.* virulência; **virulent** *adj.* virulento; **virus** *s.* virus.
visa *s.* visto; *v.t.* visar, pôr o visto.
visage *s.* face; aspecto, semblante.
viscera *s.* vísceras, entranhas.
viscous *adj.* viscoso; **viscosity** *s.* viscosidade.
viscount *s.* visconde; **-ess** *s.* viscondessa.
visibility *s.* visibilidade; **visible** *adj.* visível; **visibly** *adv.* visívelmente.
vision *s.* visão; **-ary** *adj.&s.* visionário.
visit *s.* visita; *v.t.* visitar; **-ation** *s.* visitação; **-or** *s.* visitante.

visor s. viseira.
vista s. perspectiva.
visual *adj.* visual.
vital *adj.* vital; **-ity** s. vitalidade; **-ize** *v.t.* vitalizar; **-s** s. partes vitais.
vitamin s. vitamina.
vitiate *v.t.* viciar; **vitiation** s. depravação; invalidação.
viticultural *adj.* vitícola; **viticulture** s. viticultura.
vitreous *adj.* vítreo; **vitrify** *v.t.* vitrificar.
vitriol s. vitríolo.
vituperate *v.t.* vituperar; **vituperation** s. vituperação.
vivacious *adj.* vivo, animado; **-ly** *adv.* vivamente.
vivid *adj.* vívido; **-ness** s. vivacidade; **vivify** *v.t.* vivificar; **viviparous** *adj.* vivíparo; **vivisection** s. vivissecção.
vixen s. raposa.
vizard s. máscara; *v.t.* mascarar.
vocable s. vocábulo.
vocabulary s. vocabulário.
vocal *adj.* vocal; **-ist** s. vocalista; **-ize** *v.t.* vocalizar.
vocation s. vocação; profissão.
vocative s. vocativo.
vociferate *v.i.* vociferar; **vociferous** *adj.* barulhento; **vociferously** *adv.* barulhentamente.
vogue s. voga, moda.
voice s. voz; *v.t.* exprimir; sonorizar.
void *adj.* vasio, nulo; s. vácuo; *v.t.* evacuar; despejar; desocupar; anular.
volatile *adj.* volátil; **volatilize** *v.t.* volatilizar.
volcanic *adj.* vulcânico; **volcano** s. vulcão.
volition s. volição.
volley s. descarga; salva; saraivada; bando.

volplane s. vôo plano; *v.i.* baixar em vôo plano.
volt s. vóltio; **-age** s. voltagem; **-aic** *adj.* voltaico; **-meter** s. voltímetro.
volubility s. volubilidade; **voluble** *adj.* volúvel.
volume s. volume; **voluminous** *adj.* volumoso.
voluntary *adj.* voluntário, livre; **volunteer** s. voluntário.
voluptuary s. voluptuoso; sensualista; **voluptuous** *adj.* voluptuoso; **voluptuousness** s. voluptuosidade.
volute s. voluta.
vomit s. vômito; *v.t.&i.* vomitar.
voracious *adj.* voraz; **-ly** *adv.* vorazmente; **-ness** s. voracidade; **voracity** s. voracidade.
vortex s. turbilhão.
votary s. adorador, partidário, afeiçoado; devoto.
vote s. voto, escrutínio, sufrágio; *v.t.&i.* votar; **-r** s. votante; **voting** s. votação; *adj.* votante.
vouch *v.t.* atestar, comprovar; **-er** s. testemunha; prova, título; documento; recibo; **-safe** *v.t.* conceder; condescender.
vow s. voto; *v.t.&i.* dedicar, consagrar, fazer voto.
vowel s. vogal.
voyage s. viagem; *v.i.* viajar.
vulcanite s. vulcanite; **vulcanize** *v.t.* vulcanizar.
vulgar *adj.* vulgar; trivial, popular; **-ism** s. vulgarismo; **-ity** s. vulgaridade; **-ize** *v.t.* vulgarizar.
vulnerable *adj.* vulnerável.
vulture s. abutre.
vulva s. vulva.

W

W letra do alfabeto.
wad s. molho, feixe; tampão; bucha; *v.t.* acolchoar.
wadding s. entretela; acolchoado.
waddle s. cambaleio; *v.i.* cambalear; remexer-se (andando).
wade *v.i.* vadear, andar (por dentro d'água, lama, areia, etc.); (*fig.*) trabalhar com vigor.
wafer s. hóstia; biscoito de agua e sal.
waffle s. espécie de bolo.
waft s. sinal, bandeira; *v.t.* trazer, levar, conduzir; *v.i.* flutuar, ser levado.
wag s. folgazão, gracejador; *v.t.* agitar; sacudir (a cabeça).
wage s. salário, pagamento; *v.t.* empenhar-se em (guerra, etc.).
wager s. aposta; *v.t.* apostar.
waggish *adj.* pilhérico, malicioso, divertido.
waggle *v.t.&i.* mover-se, agitar-se; mover, abalar, agitar, menear.
wagon, waggon s. vagão; carro; **-er** s. carreteiro.
wagtail s. rabeta, alvéloa.
waif s. coisa perdida; criança abandonada; animal desgarrado.
wail s. lamentação; vagido de criança; *v.i.* lamentar-se; choramingar (a criança).
wain s. carro, carroça, carreta.
wainscot s. forro (de parede); *v.t.* forrar (as paredes).

waist s. cintura; cinta.
wait s. espera; *v.t.&i.* esperar; **-ing** s. espera; **-ress** s. empregada, servente; **-er** s. garçon, servente.
waive *v.t.* renunciar (a); desistir de; dispensar.
wake s. (*mar.*) esteira, águas; **follow in the — of** seguir nas águas de.
wake, waken *v.t.* despertar, acordar; *v.i.* acordar; **-ful** *adj.* privado de sono; vigilante; **-fulness** s. insônia.
walk s. marcha; passeio; volta; avenida; alameda; *v.i.* andar, caminhar; passear; **— in** entrar; **— out** sair; **-er** s. andarilho, pedestre; **-ing** s. marcha, andar; passeio; **-ing tour** excursão a pé.
wall s. muro, muralha; parede; *v.t.* murar, emparedar.
wallet s. carteira (de dinheiro); pasta.
wallow *v.i.* espojar-se.
walnut s. noz.
walrus s. morsa.
waltz s. valsa; *v.i.* valsar.
wan *adj.* pálido, descorado, desmaiado; baço.
wand s. vara, varinha; batuta.
wander *v.i.* vagabundear, errar, vagar; transviar-se; delirar; **-er** s. nômade, vagabundo.
wane s. declínio, queda; diminuição; *v.i.* decrescer, declinar; minguar.

want s. necessidade, falta, carência, deficiência; *v.t.&i.* faltar, fazer falta; necessitar; desejar; querer; precisar.

wanton adj. lascivo, lúbrico, impuro; gratuito, sem motivo; petulante.

war s. guerra; combate; *v.i.&t.* guerrear, combater; **ship** vaso de guerra.

warble *v.i.* gorjear, trinar; **warbling** s. gorjeio, trinado.

ward s. pupilo; tutelado; guarda; defesa; enfermaria; quarteirão; bairro; *v.i.* guardar, fazer ronda; **en** s. guarda, guardião; reitor; **er** s. guarda, zelador.

wardrobe s. guarda-roupa, armário; — **trunk** mala-armário.

warehouse s. armazém; *v.t.* armazenar.

wares s. mercadorias, artigos.

warily adv. prudentemente, com circunspeção; **wariness** s. precaução.

warlike adj. guerreiro, belicoso, marcial.

warm adj. quente; caloroso; *v.t.&i.* aquecer, esquentar; aquecer-se; **ing pan** esquentador; **th** s. calor.

warn *v.t.* prevenir, avisar; **ing** s. aviso, advertência.

warp s. empanamento; prevenção; urdidura; aluvião; *v.t.* empenar; torcer; desviar; *v.i.* empenar, torcer-se; desviar-se; preparar a urdidura no tear.

warrant s. autorização, poder, procuração; mandado; *v.t.* autorizar; justificar; sustentar, manter, assegurar; guarantir; **able** adj. justificável; **y** s. garantia.

warren s. coelheira; parque.

warrior s. guerreiro.

wart s. verruga; cravo; **y** adj. verrugoso.

wary adj. circunspeto, prudente.

wash s. lavagem (de roupa); lixívia; *v.t.&i.* lavar, lavar-se; — **out** lavar; **able** adj. lavável; **er** s. lavador, lavadeira; **ing** s. lavagem, ablução, banho; **to have a** — lavar-se; — **basin** bacia, pia; — **house** lavanderia; —**woman** lavadeira.

wasp s. vespa.

waste adj. inculto; vago; perdido; inútil; não aproveitado; s. estrago, assolação, ruína; perda; refugo, resto; *v.t.* gastar, desperdiçar, estragar, esbanjar; devastar; arruinar; *v.i.* decair, diminuir, gastar-se, definhar; **r** s. gastador; **ful** adj. pródigo, dissipador; **fulness** s. prodigalidade, desperdício; — **paper basket** cesta de papeis.

watch s. relógio; vigilância; vigia, guarda, ronda, sentinela; (*mar.*) quarto; *v.t.&i.* velar, vigiar, guardar, observar, espreitar, espiar; **er** s. vigia, guarda; **ful** adj. vigilante; **fulness** s. vigilância.

water s. água; *v.t.* molhar, banhar, regar; diluir; *v.i.* chorar, lacrimejar; fazer aguada; **ing** s. irrigação; ondulação; **less** adj. sêco, desprovido de água; — **bath** banho-maria; — **color** aquarela; —**course** regato; — **cress** agrião; **fall** queda d'água, cascata; **melon** melancia; — **power** força hidráulica; **proof** capa de chuva; **it makes one's mouth** — faz vir água à boca.

watery adj. aquoso, úmido.

wattle s. pé de árvore; ramo flexível; *v.t.* ligar, cercar, ou cobrir, com ramos de árvores; entrelaçar; **s** s. barbas do galo, barbela de certos animais.

wave s. vaga, onda; ondulação; sinal, gesto com a mão; *v.i.* flutuar, ondular, ondear; tremular; *v.t.* agitar; ondular; **wavy** adj. ondulado, undoso.

waver *v.i.* hesitar, vacilar, flutuar.

wax s. cera; *v.t.* encerar; *v.i.* tornar-se; crescer, aumentar; **y** adj. de cera.

way s. caminho, via, estrada, vereda; rota; modo; meio, expediente; uso, costume, hábito; direção; conduta; **by the** — a propósito; **in the** — no caminho; atrapalhando; — **in** entrada; — **out** saída.

wayward adj. caprichoso, voluntarioso; **ness** s. capricho, teimosia.

we pron. nós.

weak adj. fraco, débil; **en** *v.t.* enfraquecer; atenuar, debilitar; *v.i.* enfraquecer-se; **ly** adj. débil; **ness** s. fraqueza.

weal s. bem, felicidade, ventura; prosperidade; vergão, marca de pancada.

wealth s. riqueza, opulência; **y** adj. rico, opulento.

wean *v.t.* desmamar; **ing** s. desmama.

weapon s. arma; **less** adj. desarmado.

wear s. uso; *v.t.&i.* usar; gastar; consumir; gastar-se; estragar-se; — **out** usar; gastar; **able** adj. usável, em condições de ser usado.

weariness s. fadiga, cansaço.

wearisome adj. fastidioso, incômodo, enfadonho; **ness** s. tédio, cansaço; **weary** adj. fatigado, cansado; *v.t.* fatigar, cansar.

weasel s. doninha.

weather s. tempo; intempérie; *v.t.* resistir, transpor, vencer (dificuldades); arejar, expor ao ar.

weave s. tecedura; *v.t.* tecer; (*fig.*) tramar; **r** s. tecelão; **weaving** s. tecelagem.

web s. tela, teia, tecido; flo, corte; membrana que une os dedos de certos animais.

wed *v.t.&i.* casar; casar-se; **ded** adj. conjugal; **ding** s. casamento, núpcias; **ding ring** aliança.

wedge s. cunha, barra, calço; *v.t.* calçar; rachar com cunhas.

wedlock s. casamento.

Wednesday s. quarta-feira.

wee adj. pequerrucho, pequenino.

weed s. herva daninha, mato, joio; *v.t.* arrancar hervas ou mato, mondar.

week s. semana; **day** dia de semana; **ly** adj. hebdomadário, semanal; s. semanário; adv. semanalmente.

weep *v.i.&t.* chorar; **ing** s. chôro; **er** s. carpideira.

weevil s. gorgulho.

weft s. trama.

weigh *v.t.* pesar; medir, examinar, considerar, ponderar; **ing** s. pesagem; **t** s. pêso; gravidade; **ty** adj. pesado.

weir s. represa, açude.

weird adj. fantástico, estranho, misterioso.

welcome adj. benvindo; s. boas-vindas; *v.t.* acolher, receber.

weld s. soldadura; caldeamento; *v.t.* caldear; soldar.

welfare s. bem-estar, felicidade, prosperidade; ventura, fortuna.

well s. poço; fonte, nascente; *v.i.* manar, nascer; adj. bom, com saúde; conveniente; adv. bem; felizmente; — **behaved** bem comportado; —**being** bem-estar; — **beloved** bem amado; —**bred** bem educado; —**meaning** bem intencionado; —**done** bem cozido; —**known** conhecido; —**to-do** rico, próspero.

welt s. orla, debrum, ribete, cairel.

welter *v.i.* banhar-se; revolver-se n'água; espojar-se, chafurdar.

wen s. tumor; quisto.

wench s. donzela; moça; criada.

wend v.i. prosseguir.

west s. oeste; ocaso, poente; adj. ocidental; *ern adj. ocidental, do oeste.

wet adj. molhado; úmido; chuvoso; v.t. molhar, umedecer; irrigar, regar; *ness s. umidade; — nurse ama de leite.

wether s. carneiro capado.

whack s. pancada, golpe; v.t. espancar, fustigar; bater.

whale s. baleia; *r s. pescador de baleia; baleeiro; baleeira.

wharf s. cais, desembarcadouro; *inger s. proprietário de cais.

what pron.,adj.&adv. que, o que, qual, aquilo que; como; — for? para que?

whatever, whatsoever pron.&adj. qualquer, qual, tudo o que, tudo aquilo que; algum, seja o que fôr; qualquer que seja.

whatnot s. aparador.

wheat s. trigo.

wheedle v.t.&i. seduzir, lisonjear; conseguir alguma coisa por meio de bajulação.

wheel s. roda; v.t.&i. rodar, girar; fazer rodar.

wheeze v.i. ofegar, arquejar.

whelk s. concha, caracol.

when conj.&adv. quando, logo que; depois que; since — ? desde quando? *ce adv. donde; *ever adv. sempre que.

where adv.&conj. onde, em que lugar, em que parte; *abouts adv. perto, nas proximidades, acêrca de; *as conj. enquanto que; como, porquanto; considerando que; *at adv. sôbre o que, à vista do que; *by adv. por onde, pelo qual; *fore adv. para que; pelo que; *in adv. em que; *of adv. de que, de quem, sôbre que; *upon adv. sôbre o que; sôbre que; *ver adv. por todo o lugar, por toda a parte, em qualquer lugar.

wherry s. bote, barco, batel; v.t. transportar em barco.

whet s. estimulante; v.t. estimular; repassar, afiar.

whether conj. se; quer, ou.

whey s. sôro do leite.

which pron.&adj. que, qual, quem, o que, o qual, a qual; *ever pron.&adj. um ou outro; qualquer; qualquer que seja.

whiff s. baforada.

while s. tempo, momento; conj. enquanto; (pop.) até que; whilst conj. enquanto.

whim s. capricho, veneta; extravagância.

whimper v.i. chorar, choramingar, lastimar-se; *er s. chorão.

whimsical adj. caprichoso, exquisito.

whin s. azevinho, azevim.

whine v.i. choramingar; s. chôro afetado, lamúria.

whinny s. rinchar, relinchar.

whip s. chicote; v.t.&i. chicotear, fustigar.

whipping s. açoitamento.

whir v.i. zunir.

whirl s. turbilhão; v.i. girar, turbilhonar.

whirligig s. carapeta, pião.

whisk s. batedor de ovos; espanador, vassourinha; v.t. espanar; bater (ovos).

whiskers s. suíças (barba).

whisky s. whisky.

whisper s. murmúrio, sussurro; v.i.&t. sussurrar, murmurar; *er s. murmurador; *ing s. murmúrio.

whist s. whist (jôgo de cartas); silêncio.

whistle s. assobio, silvo; zunido; v.t.&i. assobiar.

whit s. iota, a mínima parte.

white adj. branco; *ness s. brancura; *n v.t. embranquecer.

whither adv. para onde, aonde.

whiting s. cal; pescada.

whitish adj. esbranquiçado.

whitlow s. panarício.

whittle v.t. cortar, talhar, aparar.

whiz s. zunido, assobio; v.i. zunir, assobiar.

who pron. quem; que.

whoever pron. quem quer que seja.

whole adj. todo; inteiro; integral; intacto; completo; total; cheio; s. todo; totalidade; integralidade; *sale adj. em massa; por atacado; *some adj. são, sadio; salubre, salutar; wholly adv. inteiramente; integralmente; completamente; totalmente.

whom pron. quem; *soever pron. quem quer que seja.

whoop s. grito, vaia, apupo; v.i. gritar, vaiar; *ing cough coqueluche.

whorl s. verticilo; espiral.

whose pron. cujo; cuja; cujos, cujas; de quem; whosoever pron. quem quer que seja; qualquer pessoa que.

why adv.&conj. porque; por que razão; int. mas! como! ué!

wick s. mecha, pavio.

wicked adj. mau, ruim, perverso, malvado; *ness s. maldade, perversidade.

wicker s. vime.

wicket s. postigo, portinhola.

wide adj. largo, amplo, grande, vasto, imenso; to be — awake estar completamente acordado; —*spread muito divulgado; *ly adv. amplamente, largamente; *n v.t. alargar, estender; in a *r sense num sentido mais lato.

widgeon s. marreco.

widow s. viúva; *er s. viúvo; *hood s. viuvez.

width s. largura.

wield v.t. manejar, brandir, empunhar.

wife s. mulher, espôsa.

wig s. peruca, cabeleira.

wight s. pessoa, alguém.

wild adj. selvagem; feroz, bravo, bravio; silvestre; deserto; inculto; *erness s. lugar selvagem; solitude; *ly adv. ferozmente; *ness selvajaria.

wile, wiliness s. astúcia, lôgro, velhacaria.

will s. vontade; intenção; arbítrio; discrição; mandato; testamento; v.t. querer; legar, testar; verbo auxiliar usado para formar o futuro.

willful, wilful adj. voluntário, intencional; *ly adv. voluntàriamente; com premeditação; *ness s. obstinação, maldade.

willing adj. voluntário, espontâneo; pronto, inclinado; *ness s. boa vontade.

willow s. salgueiro.

willy-nilly adv. de bom ou mau grado; queira ou não queira.

wilt v.t.&i. degenerar; murchar; perder a côr.

wily adj. velhaco, fino, astucioso.

wimple s. véu de freira.

win s. vitória; v.t.&i. ganhar, vencer.

wince v.i. recuar; estremecer; mover-se.

winch s. manivela; cabrestante; guincho.

wind s. vento; hálito, respiração; sôpro; ventosidade, flatulência; v.t. soprar; arejar; farejar.

wind *v.t.&i.* enrolar, girar, rodar; serpear; insinuar-se; induzir; dar corda; **-ing** *adj.* sinuoso, tortuoso; *s.* volta, dobra; sinuosidade; (*elet.*) enrolamento.

window *s.* janela; *v.t.* pôr janelas em.

windward *adv.* para o lado do vento; **windy** *adj.* ventoso.

wine *s.* vinho.

wing *s.* asa; ala, flanco; vôo; **-ed** *adj.* alado.

wink *s.* pestanejo, piscadela; *v.i.* piscar, pestanejar; a **-ing light** luz vacilante.

winner *s.* vencedor; **winnings** *s.* ganho, lucros.

winnow *v.t.* joeirar, peneirar; esquadrinhar, investigar.

winsome *adj.* agradável.

winter *s.* inverno; *v.t.&i.* hibernar; passar o inverno.

wipe *s.* limpeza; *v.t.* limpar; enxugar, secar; esfregar.

wire *s.* fio, arame, cabo; telegrama; *v.t.&i.* colocar fios; telegrafar.

wireless *adj.* sem fio.

wisdom *s.* sabedoria, juízo, prudência; **wise** *adj.* sábio, prudente.

wish *s.* desejo, vontade, voto; *v.t.&i.* desejar, querer, anelar; apetecer; ter vontade; **-ful** *adj.* desejoso.

wishy-washy *adj.* desfeito, diluído, desmanchado; fraco.

wisp *s.* punhado; vassourinha; rodilha (para a cabeça).

wistaria *s.* glicínia.

wistful *adj.* pensativo; **-ly** *adv.* fixamente, atentamente.

wit *s.* espírito; graça; finura.

witch *s.* feiticeira, bruxa; **-ery** *s.* bruxaria, feitiço.

with *prep.* com; por, contra, de, a entre; — **that** depois disso.

withdraw *v.t.* retirar; fazer retirar; desistir; **-al** *s.* retirada.

withe *s.* vêrga, vime.

wither *v.t.* secar; *v.i.* murchar, fenecer; **-ing** *adj.* fulminante (olhar); para secagem.

withers *s.* cernelha.

withhold *v.t.* reter, deter, impedir; conter.

within *prep.* em, dentro de; no espaço de; à distância de; *adv.* dentro, por dentro, interiormente; em casa.

without *prep.* sem; fora de; *adv.* fora, por fora, externamente; fora de casa; **to do** — passar sem.

withstand *v.t.* resistir a; opor-se a; impugnar.

withy *s.* vime.

witless *adj.* sem espírito; sem graça.

witness *s.* testemunha; *v.t.* testemunhar; assistir a.

witticism *s.* dito, gracejo, palavra humorística.

wittingly *adv.* premeditadamente; intencionalmente.

witty *adj.* espirituoso; engraçado.

wizard *s.* feiticeiro; **-ry** *s.* feitiçaria.

wizened *adj.* enrugado, sêco.

wo *int.* íh! ué!

woe *s.* dôr, desgraça; infelicidade; miséria; calamidade; **-ful** *adj.* triste, infeliz; lamentável; miserável

wolf *s.* lôbo, lôba.

wolfram *s.* tungstênio.

woman *s.* mulher; **-ish** *adj.* efeminado; **-ly** *adj.* feminino, de mulher.

womb *s.* matriz, ventre; seio; entranhas.

wonder *s.* admiração; assombro, espanto;

prodígio, maravilha; *v.i.* espantar-se, maravilhar-se; **-ful** *adj.* maravilhoso.

wont *s.* costume, hábito, rotina; **-ed** *adj.* habitual.

woo *v.t.* cortejar, fazer a côrte.

wood *s.* bosque, floresta, mato; pau, madeira, lenha; **-en** *adj.* de madeira; **-y** *adj.* lenhoso.

wooer *s.* pretendente, aspirante (à mão).

woof *s.* trama.

wool *s.* lã; **-len** *adj.* de lã; **-y** *adj.* lanoso.

word *s.* palavra; voz; vocábulo, têrmo; *v.t.* enunciar; explicar; **-iness** *s.* verbosidade; **-y** *adj.* verboso.

work *s.* trabalho; obra; labor, ocupação, tarefa, emprêgo, ofício; negócio; *v.t.&i.* trabalhar; manobrar; operar; fazer trabalhar; agir; — **out** executar, elaborar; — **hard** trabalhar firme; **-able** *adj.* exequível; **-er** *s.* operário, trabalhador; **-ing** *s.* trabalho, obra, manobra, funcionamento; **-less** *adj.* desempregado, sem trabalho.

world *s.* mundo; universo; —**-wide** *adj.* universal, mundial; **-liness** *s.* mundanidade; **-ly** *adj.* mundano.

worm *s.* verme; (*maq.*) rôsca sem fim; serpentina (de alambique); — **oneself into** insinuar-se; **-y** *adj.* verminoso, vermicular.

worry *s.* aborrecimento, preocupação, tormento; *v.t.* preocupar, aborrecer, atormentar; *v.i.* preocupar-se.

worse *adj.&adv.* peor; **grow** — peorar.

worship *s.* culto, adoração; afeição profunda; *v.t.&i.* adorar, venerar; **-per** *s.* adorador.

worst *adj.* o peor; *adv.* peor.

worsted *s.* lã fiada.

wort *s.* planta, herva; cerveja ainda não fermentada ou em fermentação.

worth *s.* valor; preço; mérito; *adj.* digno, merecedor; **to be** — valer, merecer; **-less** *adj.* sem valor; **-lessness** *s.* vileza; **-y** *adj.* digno, merecedor.

would *v.aux.* empregado para formar o condicional. Às vezes corresponde a *queria, quisera:* I would I were an artist quisera ser um artista; pode também exprimir hábito: He would go out every morning êle costumava sair todas as manhãs.

would-be *adj.* suposto.

wound *s.* ferida, ferimento, chaga; *v.t.* ferir; the **-ed** os feridos.

wrangle *s.* disputa, rixa, briga, altercação; *v.i.* disputar, altercar, brigar.

wrangling *s.* disputa, rixa.

wrap *s.* agasalho; saída de baile; *v.t.* enrolar, agasalhar; envolver; embrulhar; **-ped** *adj.* agasalhado, envolto; embrulhado; **-per** *s.* envólucro, envelope; vestido frouxo.

wrath *s.* ira, furor, cólera; **-ful** *adj.* enfurecido; colérico.

wreak *v.t.* saciar, desafogar (a raiva, etc.); infligir, exigir (castigo, etc.); *s.* vingança; castigo, punição.

wreath *s.* grinalda, coroa; coroa mortuária; **-e** *v.t.* engrinaldar, coroar, cingir; entrelaçar, entretecer.

wreck *s.* naufrágio; ruína, destruição; *v.t.&i.* naufragar, fazer naufragar; arruinar; **-age** *s.* salvados (do naufrágio ou do incêndio); **to be -ed** naufragar.

wren *s.* carriça.

wrench *s.* (*med.*) luxação, torcedura; arranco, puxão; chave inglesa; *v.t.* arran-

car; tirar, puxar com violência; deslo-car, desconjuntar; torcer.
wrest *v.t.* torcer; arrancar, arreba-tar.
wrestle *v.i.* lutar; **-r** *s.* lutador; **wrestling** *s.* luta.
wretch *s.* infeliz, desgraçado, miserável; **-edness** *s.* infelicidade, miséria.
wrick *s.* esfôrço, torcedura, jeito (nos músculos).
wriggle *v.i.* agitar-se, mexer-se, menear-se; insinuar-se.
wring *v.t.* torcer; arrancar; puxar; extorquir; **-er** *s.* torcedor.
wrinkle *s.* ruga, prega, dobra; *v.t.* enru-gar; dobrar, preguear.
wrist *s.* pulso; **-let** *s.* pulseira.
writ *s.* escritura; ordem; mandado.

write *v.t.&i.* escrever; inscrever; redigir; — **out** traçar, redigir; **-r** *s.* escritor, autor.
writhe *v.i.* torcer-se, contorcer-se.
writing *s.* escrita; escritura; manuscrito; escrito; inscrição; **written** *adj.* por escrito, manuscrito.
wrong *adj.* falso, errado; irregular; *s.* injúria, ofensa, agravo; injustiça; dano, lesão; culpa; êrro; *adv.* mal, sem razão, injustamente; pelo avêsso; erradamen-te; *v.t.* fazer mal a; lesar, prejudicar, ofender; **-ful** *adj.* injusto; **-ly** *adv.* injustamente; mal, erradamente.
wrought *adj.* trabalhado, forjado, la-vrado.
wry *adj.* torcido, torto, disforme.
wryness *s.* torção; obliquidade.

X

X letra do al.abeto.
Xmas abr. de **Christmas** Natal.
xylography *s.* xilografia.

xylonite *s.* celulóide.
xylophone *s.* xilofone.

Y

Y letra do alfabeto.
yacht *s.* hiate.
yam *s.* inhame.
yap *v.i.* latir.
yard *s.* pátio; estaleiro; arsenal; jarda (medida equivalente a 0,9144 m); (*mar.*) vêrga.
yarn *s.* fio; conto, narração, história.
yarrow *s.* (*bot.*) mil-fôlhas.
yaw *s.* guinada.
yawl *s.* iole.
yawn *v.i.* bocejar.
ye *pron.* vós.
yea *adv.* sim; *s.* sim, voto afirmativo.
yean *v.i.* parir (a ovelha).
year *s.* ano; **-book** anuário; **-ly** *adj.* anual; *adv.* annualmente.
yearn *v.i.* compadecer-se, afligir-se; an-siar; **-ful** *adj.* triste, penoso; ansioso.
yeast *s.* fermento, levedura.
yell *s.* uivo; grito de terror; *v.i.* uivar; gritar de terror.
yellow *adj.&s.* amarelo; *v.t.&i.* amarele-cer; **-ish** *adj.* amarelado.
yelp *v.i.* ladrar, latir, ganir; **-ing** *s.* latido; ganido.
yes *adv.* sim.
yesterday *s.* ontem.

yet *conj.* no entanto, contudo; *adv.* ainda.
yew *s.* (*bot.*) teixo.
yield *s.* produção, rendimento; *v.t.* produ-zir, render entregar, ceder; *v.i.* ceder; render-se; sucumbir.
yoke *s.* canga; par, parelha, junta; jugo; *v.t.* atrelar, jungir; emparelhar; unir, casar.
yokel *s.* grosseirão; incivil.
yolk *s.* gema de ovo.
yonder *adj.* longínquo; *adv.* lá longe, acolá.
yore *adv.* outrora.
you *pron.* vós, tu, você; vos, te, o, a; lhe (a você).
young *adj.* jovem; pequeno; *s.* jovens; crias, filhotes; **-er** *adj.* mais jovem; **-ster** *s.* menino, rapazola, mocinho, adolescente.
your *adj.* **yours** *pron.* vosso, vossa; vos-sos, vossas; teu, tua; teus, tuas; seu, sua; seus, suas (de você, de vocês); **-self** *pron.* você mesmo, tu mesmo; **-selves** *pron.* vós mesmos.
youth *s.* mocidade, adolescência; jovem, adolescente; **-ful** *adj.* jovem, juvenil.
yule *s.* Natal; **-tide** *s.* Natal.

Z

Z letra do alfabeto.
zeal *s.* zêlo.
zealot *s.* partidário fanático.
zealous *adj.* zeloso; **-ly** *adv.* zelosamente.
zebra *s.* zebra.
zenith *s.* zênite; apogeu, auge.
zephyr *s.* zéfiro.
zeppelin *s.* zepelim.
zero *s.* zero.
zest *s.* ardor; casca de limão ou laranja; sabor, aroma.

zigzag *s.* zigue-zague.
zinc *s.* zinco.
zip *s.* fêcho (éclair).
zircon *s.* zircônio.
zither *s.* cítara.
zodiac *s.* zodíaco; **-al** *adj.* zodiacal.
zone *s.* zona.
zoological *adj.* zoológico; **zoologist** *s.* zoologista; **zoology** *s.* zoologia.
Zulu *s.&adj.* zulo.
zygomatic *adj.* zigomático.